THE COOKERY YEAR

The Cookery Year

PUBLISHED BY THE READER'S DIGEST ASSOCIATION LIMITED

THE COOKERY YEAR
was edited and designed by
The Reader's Digest Association Limited, London

First Edition Copyright© 1973
First Reprint 1974
The Reader's Digest Association Limited
25 Berkeley Square, London W1X 6AB

Printed in Great Britain

THE COOKERY YEAR

The Publishers wish to express their gratitude for major contributions by the following people:

Editorial Adviser: ELIZABETH POMEROY
Photographer: PHILIP DOWELL
Home Economist: JOY MACHELL

Writers:

Ena Bruinsma
Margaret Coombes
Derek Cooper
Margaret Costa
Denis Curtis
Theodora FitzGibbon
Nina Froud
Jane Grigson
Nesta Hollis
Kenneth H. C. Lo

Elizabeth Pomeroy
Zena Skinner
Katie Stewart
Marika Hanbury Tenison
Silvino S. Trompetto,
  Maître Chef des Cuisines,
  Savoy Hotel
Suzanne Wakelin
Kathie Webber
Harold Wilshaw

Artists:

Colour:
  Roy Coombs
  Pauline Ellison
  Hargrave Hands
  Denys Ovenden
  Charles Pickard
  Josephine Ranken
  Charles Raymond
  Rodney Shackell
  Faith Shannon
  John Wilson

Black and white:
  David Baird
  Brian Delf
  Gary Hincks
  Richard Jacobs
  Rodney Shackell
  Michael Woods
  Sidney Woods

Black and white photography:
  Michael Newton

Many other people and organisations assisted in the preparation of this book. The Publishers particularly wish to acknowledge the help of the following:

Aga Cookers & Boilers; Albrizzi Ltd; Argentine Meat Board; Arts and Crafts of China; Austrian Commercial Delegation; Australian Meat Board;

John Baily & Son (Poulterers) Ltd; G. Bettley; R. A. Bevan (Butcher); Bombay Emporium; Alan Bowen; British Agricultural Export Council; British Field Sports Society; British Safety Council; L. Burkett Ltd (Fishmongers);

Casa Pupo Ltd; Cecil & Co. (Fishmongers); Citrus Marketing Board of Israel; Clare's Hand-made Chocolates; College of Distributive Trades; Commercial Rabbit Association;

Danish Agricultural Producers; Elizabeth David Ltd; Heino Dorner; Jane Dorner; Barbara Dowell; Caroline Dowling; Edwin Ducat; Dutch Counter Ltd; Dutch Dairy Bureau;

Electricity Council; Norma English;

Fawkham Church; Fishmonger's Company; *Fish Trades Gazette*; Floris Bakeries Ltd; Fresh Fruit and Vegetable Information Bureau; Nick Frewing; Doreen Fulleylove; Judith Fulleylove;

Gas Corporation; General Trading Co. (Mayfair) Ltd; Gered, Wedgwood & Spode; German Food Centre Ltd; Good Housekeeping Institute; Stephen Gottlieb; Grants of St James's Ltd; Anthony Guyatt;

Valerie Hall; Doreen Hare; Susan Harris; Harrods Ltd; Harvey Nichols & Co. Ltd; Roy Hay, MBE;

Indiacraft Ltd; Italian Institute for Foreign Trade;

Jacksons of Piccadilly; Delilah Jennis;

Ellen Keeley; Kraft Foods Ltd;

Meg Lake; *Larousse Gastronomique*; Lawleys Ltd; T. & S. Lemkow; Caroline Liddell; Bruno di Lucia;

Mac Fisheries; Paul Manousso, ARIBA; Meat and Livestock Commission; David Mellor, Ironmonger; Ministry of Agriculture, Fisheries & Food; Constance Morley; Mostra Design Ltd;

National Dairy Council; National Federation of Fruit and Potatoes Trades Ltd; New Zealand Meat Producers Board; Osterley House;

William Page & Company Ltd; *Poultry World*; T. J. Poupart Ltd;

Reject China Shop; Cathy Roache; Rosenthal Studio House Ltd; G. Rushbrooke Ltd;

The Scottish Merchant; Strand Palace Hotel; Summit Art Studios Ltd;

Josiah Wedgwood & Sons; White Fish Authority; Wildfowlers' Association of Great Britain and Ireland;

Olena Yenkala

CONTENTS OF THE COOKERY YEAR

Buying for Quality............8–51

by Zena Skinner

A guide to day-by-day marketing. Comprehensive advice on choosing the finest quality home-grown and imported fruit and vegetables, fish and shellfish, poultry and game, meat and offal, as well as British and continental cheeses

Twelve Months of Recipes.........................52–303

More than 500 recipes, all based on fresh food in season. These appear under the headings: soups and starters, fish, meat, poultry and game, rice and pasta, vegetables and salads, sweets and puddings. Each month also contains recipes for savouries and snacks from left-overs; these are contributed by Marika Hanbury Tenison. The monthly recipes finish with menus for special occasions

Recipes by Denis Curtis
New Year Dinners by Silvino S. Trompetto

Recipes by Katie Stewart
Home-made Marmalade by Suzanne Wakelin

Recipes by Katie Stewart
Celebration Dinner Party by Ena Bruinsma

Recipes by Kathie Webber
Easter Customs by Kathie Webber

Recipes by Jane Grigson
Chinese Dinner Party by Kenneth H. C. Lo

Basic Cooking Methods . . . 304–405

by Margaret Coombes and Suzanne Wakelin
    of Good Housekeeping Institute

A step-by-step illustrated guide to basic cooking

Wine with Food 405–406

by Derek Cooper
How to store and serve wine, and using
wine in cookery

The Cook's Workshop 407–413

by Nesta Hollis
Planning and equipping a kitchen;
essential and luxury kitchen tools;
safety precautions

Home Freezing 413–417

by Marika Hanbury Tenison
Choosing a freezer, packaging materials
and containers. Food and prepared dishes
suitable for freezing; storage life and
cooking of frozen food

Glossary 418–420

A dictionary of culinary terms

Index 421–439

Buying

Top Fruit

PAGES 10-11

Soft Fruit

PAGES 12-13

Citrus Fruit

PAGES 14-15

Exotic Fruit

PAGES 16-17

Game

PAGES 32-33

Beef

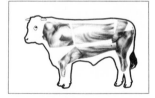

PAGES 34-36

Veal

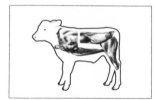

PAGES 36-37

Lamb

PAGES 38-39

for Quality

Vegetables

PAGES 18-23

White Fish

PAGES 24-25

Oily Fish

PAGES 26-27

Shellfish

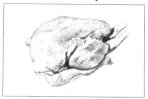

PAGES 28-29

Poultry

PAGES 30-31

Pork

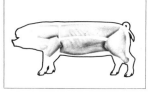

PAGES 40-41

Bacon

PAGES 42-43

Offal

PAGES 44-45

British Cheeses

PAGES 46-47

Imported Cheeses

PAGES 48-51

TO AVOID CONSTANT REPETITION OF BASIC INFORMATION, SOME
TECHNICAL WORDS AND PHRASES USED IN THIS BOOK HAVE BEEN
MARKED WITH AN ASTERISK *. FULL INFORMATION ABOUT TERMS
MARKED IN THIS WAY WILL BE FOUND BY REFERRING TO THE INDEX

Top Fruit

Top fruit, the term used by fruit growers for all tree fruits, includes apples and pears, and also stone fruits such as cherries, nectarines, plums, peaches and nuts. Buy only enough to last a few days, as fruit does not keep for long at room temperature. Apples and pears will store for a couple of weeks if they can be kept in a cool airy cellar or larder, but all stone fruit, with the exception of plums and nuts, are best eaten on the day of purchase.

Egremont Russet

Granny Smith

CRAB APPLE

Cox's Orange Pippin

Worcester Pearmain

Golden Delicious

Bramley's Seedling

Laxton's Superb

Apples These are probably the most popular fruit. Apples are divided into dessert (or eating) and cooking apples. While cooking apples can only be used for culinary purposes, many dessert apples, especially if firm, are also excellent for cooking, particularly in sweets and chutneys.

Dessert apples are available all year round, as many varieties are imported. Cooking apples need not be ripe.

English dessert apples include: *Worcester Pearmain*, thick skin of pale green-yellow, heavily suffused with crimson, and firm, white, sweet flesh (September and October); *Laxton's Superb*, yellow-green to pale lemon skin, marked with dull red, and with firm and juicy flesh (November to April); *Egremont Russet,* reddish-brown skin and crisp firm flesh (October to December); and *Cox's Orange Pippin,* the favourite English dessert apple, with yellow-green to golden-yellow skin, flushed and streaked with orange or red, and firm, crisp, juicy and aromatic flesh (September to May). Other varieties include *George Cave* (mid-July to end August); *James Grieve* (August and September); *Scarlet Pimpernel* (July); *Miller's Seedling* (mid-August to end September); *Laxton's Fortune* (end September to end October); *Ellison's Orange* (October until April); *Lord Lambourne* (October); *Tydeman's Early* (September and October).

Imported apples These come from the Continent, South Africa, Australia, New Zealand, Canada, the United States and South America, and include: *Golden Delicious*, smooth green skin which turns yellow during storage (September to April); and *Granny Smith*, bright green skin, hard and crunchy flesh with sharp flavour (March to August). Other varieties include *Dunn's Seedling*, *Red Delicious* and *Jonathan*.

Cooking apples Almost all cooking apples are home-grown. Varieties include: *Grenadier* (August and September); *Lord Derby* (October onwards); *Bramley's Seedling* (end October to March); *Newton Wonder* (December until March).

Crab apples These small, apple-like fruits are not usually available in the shops. The acid flesh is used for jellies and pickles. Season: September and October.

Apricots Small stone fruits with yellow, juicy and sweet flesh. Buy firm fruits, avoiding any with bruised or squashy skins. Apricots are widely used in pastries, confectionery and liqueurs. Season: May-August and December-February.

Cherries Both sweet and acid cherries are available over a short summer season. Many are imported, but the best white and black cherries are home-grown. Buy firm and dry cherries.

Dessert varieties are either white (or pink) and black. The berries are usually heart-shaped or oval, with juicy flesh which varies from white-yellow to dark red. Among the many home-grown varieties, the following are most often seen: *Napoleon Bigarreau* (mid to late June); *Frogmore Early* (late June); *Merton Heart* (late June to end July); and *White Heart* (late July).

The acid Morello cherry is suitable for jam-making (July to August). Imported cherries are available from April until August.

Nectarines These smooth-skinned stone fruits are a variety of peach, and have a juicy and sweet flesh. They are served as a dessert fruit. Most nectarines are imported, and are in season during autumn and winter. Home-grown nectarines are available June to August. Nectarines are usually expensive, and sold when fully ripe; use on the day of purchase.

Peaches There are two types. Free-stone peaches have juicy soft flesh which comes easily away from the stone. Clingstone peaches have firmer flesh adhering tightly to the stone. Free-stone peaches are considered to have a better flavour but are seldom seen in the shops. Avoid those with bruised skin or brown spots. Imported peaches are available from March until December, and English hothouse peaches from June until October.

Pears Like apples, pears are divided into dessert and cooking varieties. Many are home-grown and, with imported supplies, pears are available from June until April. Pears bruise easily and should be handled with care; they are best bought before fully ripe and left in the airing cupboard for 2–3 days. Ripe pears will yield when gently pressed at the stalk end.

The following are varieties of dessert pears and can also be served poached or lightly stewed: *Conference*, a tapering dark green pear, heavily spotted with russet; pale-yellow, pink-tinged, juicy and sweet flesh (home-grown, end

SWEET CHERRY

Kirke's Blue

Pershore

Victoria

GAGE

APRICOT

HAZEL NUTS

MORELLO CHERRY

Czar

DAMSON

NECTARINE

PEACH, IMPORTED

WALNUTS

Conference

Doyenné du Comice

William's Bon Chrétien

PEACH, ENGLISH

CHESTNUTS

FILBERT NUTS

September to February). *Doyenné du Comice*, large, oval-shaped pear with pale yellow skin, occasionally flushed with red or russet; pale yellow, very juicy, cinnamon-flavoured flesh (home-grown, end October to December; imported, March to June). *William's Bon Chrétien*, large tapering pear with pale green skin faintly dotted with russet; juicy and sweet flesh (home-grown, August and September).

Among the other varieties of dessert pear are: *Emile d'Heyst* (imported, end September to November); *Packham's Triumph* (home-grown, October and November; imported, February to June); and *Winter Nelis* (home-grown, November to January; imported, February to July).

Cooking pears are available from October to December. *Pitmaston Duchesse* is nearly round and with tough yellow to green skin, irregularly spotted with russet. The cream-yellow flesh is soft and juicy. Many firm-fleshed dessert pears are also suitable for culinary purposes.

Plums These include both dessert and culinary varieties. Gages are a type of plum, round and green to yellow in colour. Damsons, too, are plums with dark blue to black skin; they are oval in shape and smaller than gages, and should only be used cooked and for jam-making. Dessert plums should be firm to the touch, with a bloom on the skin; they are often sold

slightly under-ripe and can be kept in a cool larder for 1–3 days before serving.

Czar, large, dark blue, culinary or dessert plum with golden flesh and red juice (early August). *Pershore*, tapering dessert plum, with yellow, faintly red-tinted skin and sometimes mealy flesh (August). *Victoria*, large oval plum, yellow flushed with scarlet, sweet and juicy flesh, suitable for dessert and bottling (late August). *Kirke's Blue*, a large, purple-black plum with a distinct bloom and juicy dark flesh. One of the best plums (September).

Other varieties of plums include: *Warwickshire Drooper* (September); *Cherry Plum* (August); *Monarch* (September); and *Denniston's Superb* (August). Among

the varieties of gages are: *Ouillin's Golden Gage* (August); *Cambridge Gage* (August); and *Jefferson's Gage* (September).

Quinces These are sometimes available in the shops during October and November. They have tough golden skin when ripe, and the firm acid flesh is highly aromatic. Used for jams and jellies, or to flavour pies.

Chestnuts The shiny brown fruits of the sweet chestnut are enclosed in a fleshy outer covering which breaks open when the nuts are ripe. Chestnuts can be roasted, stewed or boiled. The large French chestnuts, known as 'marrons', are sold tinned or as preserved dessert fruits.

Hazel or cob nuts The small, grey-brown nuts are partly covered with leafy husks. Ripe, fresh nuts should have firm, not shrivelled husks. Available throughout the autumn.

Filbert nuts These are a variety of hazel nut, but the fruits are flask-shaped and completely covered by the husks.

Walnuts Most of these nuts are imported for the Christmas trade. The brown shells should have a faint damp sheen. Avoid any which rattle, as they will be dry and shrivelled. Green or under-ripe walnuts are sometimes seen in September and October. They may be eaten fresh, but are more often used for pickling.

11

Soft Fruit

Strawberries, raspberries and currants are all soft fruits which are best used on the day of purchase. They are usually sold in plastic containers, in half or one pound quantities, sometimes in traditional punnets or loose. All soft fruit, with the exception of gooseberries, leave stains on the bottom of the container; avoid any badly stained containers as the fruits are bound to be mushy and often mouldy. As soon as possible after buying, tip berries carefully on to a plate, pick out any mouldy berries and set the remainder well apart on a tray until serving.

Some soft fruits are imported and on sale most of the year. They lack the sweet flavour of home-grown produce. This seasonal guide applies to English fruit only.

Bilberries A small quantity of these berries, also known as whortleberries, find their way into the shops. They are similar to black currants, but smaller and dark blue to purple. They are acid and suitable for pie fillings. Season: July and August.

Blackberries The large cultivated berries are purple to black, juicy and sweet. Being extremely soft, they deteriorate quickly and must be used as fresh dessert berries as soon as possible after purchase. They are also excellent for pie fillings, jams, jellies and wines. Season: August to October.

Black currants These berries are usually sold stripped from their stalks. Look for containers with only a few leaves and no more than 5 per cent of small unripe and red berries. Black currants are always served cooked, as fillings for pies and sponge puddings, and make excellent jams, jellies and fruit syrups. The berries are dark, almost black, with fairly tough skin and juicy, slightly acid, flesh. They are unfortunately no longer readily available, as large crops are bought up commercially. Season: July and August.

Blueberries Originally a wild fruit of heaths and woodlands, blueberries are now grown commercially. They grow in clusters, like red currants, and may be sold ribbed or still on their stalks. The bright blue berries are generally too acid to be served as a dessert fruit, but they are good stewed or made into jelly. Season: July and August.

Gooseberries Both sweet and acid berries are available. The berries may be smooth or hairy. They are used as fillings for pies and tarts, and for jam and jelly-making. Avoid berries with splits and blemishes to the skin.

Culinary varieties include *May Duke*, which has round berries with smooth skin; *Keepsake*, oval, green, slightly hairy berries ripening to whitish-green; *Careless*, large, oval green berries turning milky white, dessert and culinary; *Lancer*, round, pale green gooseberries, with a yellow tinge to the thin skin, dessert and culinary; *Leveller*, oval and yellow-green, almost hairless, berries, excellent flavour as dessert or cooking berries; and *Whinham's Industry*, one of the most popular gooseberries, which ripens to a dark red skin with sweet juicy flesh. Season: end April to end August.

LOGANBERRY

RASPBERRY

BLACKBERRY

Leveller

Whinham's Industry

Royal Sovereign

Cambridge Vigour

Redgauntlet

Grandee

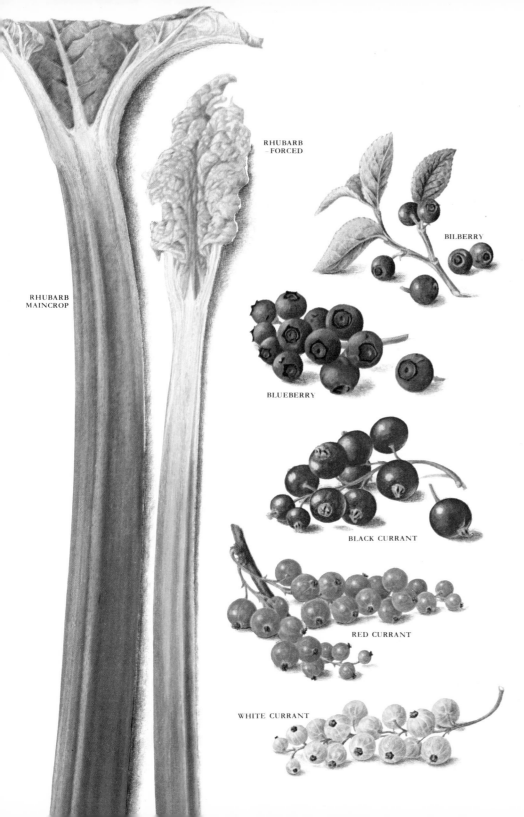

RHUBARB
-FORCED

BILBERRY

RHUBARB
MAINCROP

BLUEBERRY

BLACK CURRANT

RED CURRANT

WHITE CURRANT

Loganberries These are relatively new in commercial fruit-growing, although sweet and juicy. They have the shape of blackberries, but the colour of raspberries. They are up to 2 in. long, tapering, and seedless. Usually sold with the hulls or centres in, loganberries are excellent dessert fruits to serve with cream and sugar. Season: early July to late August.

Raspberries These travel better than most other soft fruit, being less juicy, and are often sold hulled. Raspberries are usually served fresh as a dessert, with cream; they may be used for jams; but the yield is less than with other soft fruits.

There are two types of raspberries, summer crop and autumn berries. Summer fruits, in season during July and August, include *Lloyd George*, which has large, bright red and juicy berries. The *Malling* raspberries, another summer variety, are large, mid to bright red and sweet, particularly recommended for freezing.

Autumn raspberries appear from mid-September onwards. They are generally smaller than summer raspberries, often deeper red and very juicy.

Red currants These bright red, glossy berries are always sold on their stalks, and must be stripped before being served fresh as a dessert, liberally dusted with sugar. They are also suitable for compôtes and fruit salads, and are excellent for jelly-making. Like black currants, and the albino strain, white currants, the supply of these berries is dwindling.

Rhubarb Although strictly a vegetable, rhubarb is used as a fruit. It is extremely acid and must be stewed or poached before eating. The leaves are highly poisonous. Early or forced rhubarb, grown mainly in Yorkshire, has tender, pink and delicately flavoured stalks which do not require peeling. Maincrop rhubarb has a stronger flavour and tough brittle stalks. Season: (forced) mid-December to mid-April; (maincrop) mid-March to end of June.

Strawberries The most popular and eagerly awaited fruit of the berry season. Fresh strawberries are served with cream and sugar, used fresh in cakes and tarts, eaten with ice cream and water ices and used for jams. The sweet and juicy red berries should be used on the day they are bought.

One of the best-known varieties is *Cambridge Vigour*, which has conical light red-scarlet, fairly juicy, moderately sweet berries. *Royal Sovereign*, the favourite English strawberry, is bright pinkish-orange to scarlet, juicy and very sweet-flavoured. *Talisman*, smaller and deeper red than *Royal Sovereign*, is exceptionally juicy and sweet. *Redgauntlet*, with large, scarlet berries turning dark crimson, is grown chiefly in Scotland. *Grandee* is the largest strawberry, almost round in shape and scarlet-crimson in colour. It is a juicy sweet berry. Season: end May to July.

White currants These berries are always served as a dessert fruit, stripped or left on their stalks and served with plenty of sugar. Season: July-August.

Citrus Fruit

All citrus fruits, which include grapefruit, lemon, lime and orange, are imported, chiefly from the Mediterranean countries and South Africa. Although citrus fruits are much used in cooking, they are at their best when served fresh, with the exception of lemon and lime which are too acid. Many types of citrus fruits are also available tinned, some in syrup and some without any sweetening, and the extracted pure juices, particularly of oranges and grapefruit, are also sold tinned or frozen solid, natural or with added sugar.

As all citrus fruits have a fairly thick skin, it is sometimes difficult to tell the state of the fruit. In general, all fruits should have bright, taut and slightly moist skins with a definite aroma. Many greengrocers display fruits cut in half to enable customers to gauge the condition of flesh and juice content and the thickness of the skin. When buying citrus fruit, avoid any that is dry-looking or has soft indentations and blemishes to the skin.

Citrus fruits store fairly well. Lemons and grapefruit can be kept in the vegetable box of the refrigerator for 1–2 weeks, and other types can be stored in a cool larder for about 1 week. They must, however, be used before the skins shrivel. Before cutting or serving the fruits, they should be rolled between the palms or on a flat surface to get an even distribution of juice within the fruit.

All citrus fruits are rich in vitamin C, but there is no scientific evidence to support the theory that this vitamin – or any other, for that matter – builds up the body's resistance to colds. However, vitamin C is still essential to health because it prevents scurvy; and eating citrus fruits or drinking their juice is the pleasantest way of ensuring that the body has enough of this vitamin.

KUMQUAT

LIME

CLEMENTINE

GRAPEFRUIT

LEMON

Clementine This is a cross between orange and tangerine, with a stiff, orange-like skin. It is practically seedless, and the pink-tinged flesh is slightly acid. This popular Christmas fruit, always served fresh, is imported from Cyprus, Israel, Morocco and Spain and is in season from December to February.

Grapefruit The largest of the citrus fruits, it is a squat, round fruit with pale yellow skin which varies in thickness. A spongy soft skin is often an indication of thick peel and a lack of fruit juice and flesh. Grapefruit contain few or no pips, and where they are present they are so large that they can be easily seen and removed. Grapefruit is usually served fresh as a breakfast dish or a starter. It may also be used for making marmalades. It is imported from Brazil, Cyprus, Israel, Jamaica, Morocco, South Africa, Spain and Trinidad. Season: all year round.

Kumquat A small, oval, orange-like fruit with bright yellow skin and juicy, slightly bitter flesh. It may be served fresh, when it is eaten with the skin, or used for marmalades, bottled and preserved in sugar syrup. Originally a Japanese fruit, kumquats are now imported from Morocco. Season: all year round, but in short supply.

Lemon The fruits are large or small with smooth thin or thick knobbly skin. Generally, plump lemons heavy for their size and with smooth oily skins, have less peel and more juice than large, knobbly skinned lemons. Lemons are chiefly imported from France, Spain, Italy, Israel and California in the United States. They are available all year round.

Lime A small fruit, similar to lemon but rounder, and with green-yellow thin skin and tart yellow flesh. It may be substituted for lemon in cooking, and is also used to garnish drinks. It is much used in curry dishes, but is more expensive than lemons. Imported from South Africa and the West Indies. Season: all year round.

Mandarin, mandarine This is another Christmas dessert fruit. It is a type of orange, round but flattened in shape, with loose, oily, bright orange skin and pinkish white flesh, with numerous pips. Imported from Italy, Morocco and Spain. Season: October to March.

Naartje A seedless, small orange-like fruit from South Africa, with loose, bright orange skin. It appears occasionally in the shops, but is more often seen as crystallised whole fruit. Season: November to January.

Orange Both bitter and sweet fruit are available.

The most popular bitter orange is the Seville, a thin-skinned, orange-red fruit with an acid, deep yellow flesh and numerous pips. The flesh is too acid for

BLOOD ORANGE

VALENCIA ORANGE

NAVEL ORANGE

JAFFA ORANGE

ORTANIQUE

SEVILLE ORANGE

UGLI

MANDARIN

SATSUMA

dessert use, but it is excellent and almost exclusively used for making marmalade. Seville oranges are imported from Spain and are only available for a few weeks in January and February.

The shape and flavour of sweet dessert oranges varies according to their origins. Israel exports the world-famous Jaffa oranges. Shamouti oranges, which are a variety of Jaffa orange, are large, oval and thick-skinned. They are almost seedless, with very juicy and sweet flesh.

Navel oranges, from Israel and California in the United States, have thin, smooth skins and are distinguished by the raised embryo growth at one end; they have juicy flesh with few pips.

Blood or Malta oranges are small, with slightly rough skin flushed with red, and have sweet juicy flesh, flecked with red, usually with a number of pips.

Valencias are thin-skinned oranges, rounded, with sweet, very juicy and practically pipless flesh.

Oranges are imported from Brazil, Cyprus, Israel, Italy, Morocco, South Africa, Spain, Tunisia, and from California and Florida. Season: all year round.

Ortanique This cross between an orange and tangerine is similar in size to a Navel orange. It has orange-yellow thin skin and sweet juicy, orange-coloured flesh. Use fresh as a dessert fruit and also good for marmalade. Imported from Spain. Season: October to March.

Satsuma Similar to tangerine, this round and squat orange has smooth, fairly thick skin and pale orange-yellow flesh without pips. Use fresh as a dessert fruit or for marmalades. Imported from Spain and Morocco. Season: October to February.

Tangerine A small type of sweet orange distinguished by its loose, bright-orange to red skin and small, juicy segments. It contains numerous pips, but is a delicious dessert fruit. Also used for

marmalades. Imported from Morocco, Spain and South Africa. Season: October to March.

Ugli, tangelo This cross between a tangerine and a grapefruit is the size of a large grapefruit. It has thick knobbly and greenish-yellow skin; the juicy yellow flesh is sweeter than that of grapefruit and has only a few pips. Imported from Jamaica. Season: October to November, but generally in short supply.

15

Exotic Fruit

This section describes some of the more unfamiliar fruits as well as some of the better known. They are all imported into Britain and reach the shops in prime condition and at higher prices than home-grown fruit. Most of the fruits are served as fresh dessert fruits – for serving and eating suggestions, see pp. 352–4.

Almonds Small, oval, flat nuts in light brown pitted shells. They are available shelled and un-shelled, and are best bought with the thin brown skin on and blanched before use. Ready-blanched almonds tend to be dry. Also available flaked and finely chopped (nibbed), and ground. Available all year round.

Bananas These are normally picked and shipped green, then stored and sold in varying stages of ripeness. The mealy flesh becomes sweeter as it matures. Choose bananas from a bunch rather than buying them loose; they should be golden-yellow, flecked with brown. Avoid any with black spots or patches, and damaged and squashy fruit. For cooking purposes, choose slight-ly under-ripe bananas, as they slice better and can be kept in a cool larder for up to 1 week. Available all year round.

Brazil nuts Hard, dark brown, three-edged shells enclose firm, slightly oily nuts of coconut flavour. They are sold shelled or unshelled. Available December to February.

Cape gooseberries These berries, covered by orange-yellow, shrivelled and papery husks, are the fruits of Chinese lantern (Physalis). The plump, round, golden berries are served as a dessert fruit or made into preserves. Season: February and March.

Chinese gooseberries Egg-shaped or oblong, with brownish-green, hairy skins, these have soft, juicy, sweet, green flesh, pitted with seeds. Available July to February.

Coconuts These large nuts, weighing on average 1–3 lb., have a hard, dark brown outer shell closely covered with tough fibres. At the top of each nut are three small indentations which must be punctured so that the colourless liquid can be shaken out. This is served chilled as a drink. Crack the tough shell by hitting it with a cleaver about one-third of the way down from the top. Prise the shells open, and cut out the tough flesh with a small sharp knife. To test a whole coconut for freshness, shake it to make sure it contains liquid. Available all year round.

Cranberries Small American fruit similar to bilberries. The skins are lustrous, varying in colour from pink to dark red. The hard berries have a sharp, slightly bitter flavour, and are used for preserves and sauces. Available December to February.

Dates Fresh dates are plump and shiny, golden brown in colour and with smooth skins. The pulpy flesh has a sweet sugary flavour. Dried dates should be plump, 1–2 in. long and shiny; avoid any with a shrivelled look or with sugary crystals. Available September to March.

16

WATERMELON

HONEYDEW

OGEN

CHARENTAIS

LYCHEE

POMEGRANATE

BANANA

BRAZIL NUTS

BLACK GRAPES

RED GRAPES

GREEN GRAPES

FRESH FIGS

DRIED FIG

ALMONDS

DRIED DATE

FRESH DATES

PASSION FRUIT

PINEAPPLE

PAWPAW

PERSIMMON

COCONUT

LOQUAT

MANGO

CAPE GOOSEBERRIES

CRANBERRIES

CHINESE GOOSEBERRIES

Figs Fresh or green figs are imported from the Mediterranean countries. The squat, pear-shaped fruits are soft to the touch when ripe, and the skin, which varies in colour from a greenish-yellow to purple or black, has a distinct bloom to it. The juicy pulp is sweet, and usually red and heavily seeded. Fresh figs are available from July to October. Dried figs should come easily out of the box and not be too sticky.

Grapes There is a wide range of black and white dessert grapes, most of them imported but a few grown in Britain under hothouse conditions. The juicy, thin-skinned berries should have a distinct bloom to them. When possible, buy in bunches and avoid any with shrivelled, split or squashed berries, or those which show mould near the stems. The many named varieties include *Muscat*, white or golden berries; *Alicante*, purple black juicy berries; *Almeria*, pale green to golden-yellow skin. Available all year round.

Loquats These stone fruits, also known as Japanese medlars, are imported from Israel. They are similar in shape and size to plums, with smooth, golden-yellow skins. The juicy flesh is sweet and slightly tart. Choose firm fruit. Available June and July.

Lychees, litchis Of Chinese origin, these stone fruits are the size of plums, with hard, scaly skins, turning through pink to brown. The white pulpy flesh is firm, juicy and slippery. Avoid any fruit with shrivelled dry skins. Available December to February.

Mangoes These large stone fruits come in different shapes and sizes; some are round, others long and narrow, kidney or pear-shaped. The largest fruits may weigh up to 5 lb., and the smallest are the size of an average peach. The tough green skins range in colour from green to yellow, orange and red, flushed with pink. The orange-yellow, very juicy flesh has a delicate fragrance and taste. Fresh mangoes are served as dessert fruits; avoid mushy-looking fruits with blemishes. Available January to September.

Melons These refreshing juicy fruits, served as dessert or as a first course, come in different sizes and shapes. When buying melons, always insist on touching them to check for ripeness; a ripe melon will yield to pressure applied gently at the stalk end. Melons are generally available throughout the year, with the exception of watermelons which are available from May to September. The Cantaloup melon has a slightly flattened shape, with green to yellow rough skin. The flesh is heavily scented, succulent and orange-yellow.

Charentais melon is perfectly round and small. The yellow-green, slightly rough skin is marked with downward indentations, and the orange-yellow flesh is faintly scented.

Honeydew melon is the most widely available. It is shaped like a rugby ball and has green, yellow or white wrinkled skin. The sweet flesh is pale green to pink.

Ogen melon has yellow to orange skin marked with faint green stripes. The pale yellow flesh is very sweet and juicy, sometimes with a touch of green.

Watermelon is the largest of all melons. Glossy dark skin surrounds the scarlet and juicy, almost watery, flesh and prominent black seeds.

Passion fruits These tropical fruits are similar in shape and size to large plums. The tough skin is purple and deeply wrinkled when ripe. The aromatic yellow pulp is sweet and juicy, and deeply pitted with small black seeds which are eaten with the flesh. Available all year round.

Pawpaws, papayas Large tropical fruits, pawpaws have smooth skins which ripen through green to yellow or orange. The sweet juicy pulp is orange-pink and the brown-black seeds lie in the centre of the fruit. Excellent as a breakfast or dessert fruit. Available all year round, but scarce.

Persimmons These tropical fruits look like large tomatoes with their leathery skins which turn from yellow to bright red. The orange-yellow juicy flesh has a sharp flavour. Available November and December.

Pineapples Large oval fruits with hard, knobbly top skin, which varies from deep yellow to almost orange-brown. The firm, yellow to cream flesh is sweet and juicy. Look for fruits with stiff leaves. Available all year round.

Pomegranates These are the size of oranges with thin but tough rind. In prime fruits, the rind is pink or bright red, and the juicy flesh crimson. The pulp is packed with seeds, and the flesh is sucked from the seeds. Available in autumn.

Common Vegetables

Ideally, vegetables should come straight from the field or the garden to the kitchen. Though this is seldom possible, there are many clues to the freshness or age of vegetables in the shops. Choose crisp and firm vegetables rather than hard ones, and avoid small vegetables which are probably immature and therefore lacking in flavour. Over-large vegetables, on the other hand, are usually coarse and tough and with a great deal of wastage.

Most fresh vegetables consumed in Britain are home-produced and reach the shops and markets in prime condition. They follow and overlap one another through the year.

Artichokes, Jerusalem These tubers grow in a mass of twisted knobs and are covered with a thin white or purple skin. The crisp sweet flesh is white. Prime tubers are fairly regular in shape, and measure up to 4 in. in length and 2 in. across. Avoid artichokes which are misshapen, small or dirty. Season: October to March.

Asparagus The English season is short, but imported asparagus is available from early in the year. Asparagus is a choice, but expensive, vegetable. It is usually sold in bundles, and graded according to thickness of stem and plumpness of buds. Look for asparagus with tight, well-formed heads and avoid any with thin, wrinkled or woody stems. Season: May and June.

Beetroot Two types are available: long beetroot and globe-shaped. Small globe-shaped beetroot, are sold in bunches from June onwards, but maincrop beetroot is sold by weight either cooked or raw. Buy cooked beetroot with fresh skin which looks slightly moist, and avoid shrivelled beetroot which is usually tough and woody. Uncooked beetroot bleeds easily, and care must be taken not to tear the skin when preparing beetroot for cooking. Season: all year round.

Beans Most beans are eaten in the pod, but some are shelled.

Broad beans These can be long, slender pods, up to 12 in. long with kidney-shaped green-white or dark green seeds, or shorter pods, about 6 in. long, with round seeds. All pods should have a uniform bright green colour, free from black markings. Avoid shrivelled, dry-looking pods in preference for soft and tender pods. These beans are excellent for home-freezing; they must be shelled before cooking, although young broad beans are a delicacy cooked complete with pods. Season: May to August.

French beans These include a number of types, varying from almost flat pods, up to 5 in. long, to shorter and plumper beans; their colour varies from pale to mid-green. Most are stringless when young. Yellow French beans are also available in small quantities. Buy young, crisp beans. Season: year round; scarce and expensive in winter.

Kidney beans These are a type of French bean, usually heavier-podded, with the kidney-shaped beans showing through. The most popular is the purple variety, which turns green when cooked. Choose beans with a distinct bloom. Season: June to mid-November.

JERUSALEM ARTICHOKE

BEETROOTS

SUMMER CABBAGE

SPRING CABBAGE

WINTER CABBAGE

BRUSSELS SPROUTS

WHITE CABBAGE

SAVOY CABBAGE

RED CABBAGE

CHICORY

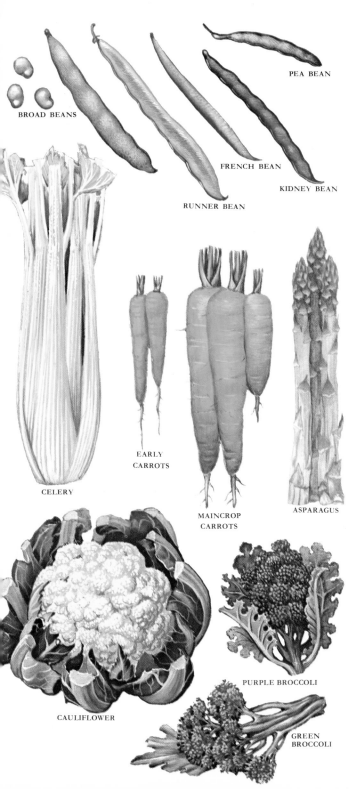

PEA BEAN

BROAD BEANS

FRENCH BEAN

KIDNEY BEAN

RUNNER BEAN

CELERY

EARLY
CARROTS

MAINCROP
CARROTS

ASPARAGUS

CAULIFLOWER

PURPLE BROCCOLI

GREEN
BROCCOLI

Pea beans Not often available in the shops, pea beans have short, bright green pods, about the size of peas, and round seeds. Season: early summer.

Runner beans Larger, coarser and with more flavour than French beans, runner beans at their best have bright green, succulent pods which need stringing before cooking. Avoid tough beans with prominent strings. A runner bean should snap between the fingers. Avoid beans which are limp, misshapen or pitted with brown or black. Season: mid-July to end of October.

Brussels sprouts These are popular in autumn and winter. The flavour is improved by frost. Look for firm, dark green sprouts and avoid those with loose leaves and any which show signs of yellowing and wilting. Season: September to March.

Cabbages There are green, white and red varieties, which may be conical or round, loose-leaved or tightly packed.

Spring cabbages Choose those with bright green and crisp leaves. Season: April and May.

Spring greens Young, mid-green cabbages sold before the hearts have developed. Use on the day of purchase, as they wilt quickly. Season: November to April.

Summer and autumn cabbages These follow spring cabbages, but have larger, more solid heads. Choose only firm, crisp-looking cabbages and check that the base of the stalk is clean. Avoid cabbages with slimy stalk ends and leaves pitted with holes. Season: June to October.

Winter cabbages Popular winter vegetables which usually overlap with autumn cabbages. They may be kept in a cool larder for 2–3 days before use. See that the heads are firm to the touch, and avoid any with wilting outer leaves.

White cabbages Formerly imported, but now widely grown in Britain. They are excellent both for cooking and in salads. Choose firm, compact heads, and avoid any with loose curling leaves or those with brown smudges showing through. Season: October to February.

Savoy cabbages Look for firm green heads with crisp and curling outer leaves. Pale green savoys are almost certainly not fresh. Season: August to May.

Red cabbages These cabbages are used for braising, marinating or for pickling. Fresh red cabbages have a good bloom. Season: August to January.

Carrots These orange-red root vegetables are among the most nourishing and inexpensive vegetables. Young and slender carrots are usually sold in bunches with the foliage intact; they are tender and need only washing before cooking. Maincrop carrots are larger and coarser; they are sold without the leaves and by weight. Available washed and unwashed, but require scraping or peeling. Early carrots showing green in the crown should be avoided, as they are not fully mature; and maincrop carrots should have no woody cores. Avoid pitted and broken carrots. Season: all year.

Celery The stalks of this vegetable are used raw in salads, or braised and used in soups and stews. The common varieties are white or pink, but pale green celery, imported from America and Israel, is also available. Choose thick celery, plump at the base. The condition of the leaves indicates freshness: on prime celery the leaves are pale green and straight. Season: July to March.

Chicory A salad vegetable with a conical white head of crisp leaves packed firmly together. Choose heads that are firmly packed and avoid any which show yellow, curling leaves. Season: January and February.

Cauliflower Both summer and winter varieties are available; on winter cauliflowers the dark green leaves are folded over the white curds, on summer cauliflowers the leaves are opened out. Choose cauliflowers with the creamy-white heads not fully developed and with clean white stalks. Avoid any with limp leaves and loose brown or grey curds. Season: all year round.

Broccoli While cauliflower has one fused head of curds, broccoli develops into numerous shoots, each terminating in a small curd. There are white or green sprouted, as well as purple broccoli. Choose broccoli with small, fresh-looking heads and brittle stalks which snap easily in the fingers. Season: all year round.

Calabrese Type of cauliflower imported from Italy, and now grown commercially in Britain, calabrese has a compact head of white, green or purple firm curds. Season: end July to early November.

Common Vegetables
(*continued*)

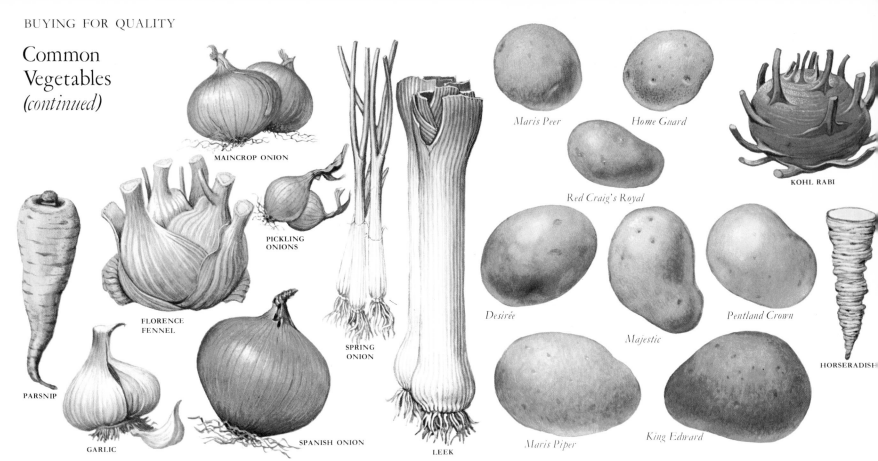

MAINCROP ONION

PICKLING ONIONS

FLORENCE FENNEL

PARSNIP

GARLIC

SPANISH ONION

SPRING ONION

LEEK

Maris Peer

Home Guard

Red Craig's Royal

Desirée

Majestic

Maris Piper

King Edward

Pentland Crown

KOHL RABI

HORSERADISH

Parsnips These vegetables are sold both washed and unwashed. The flavour is improved by a touch of frost. They are best from October onwards before the central cores become woody. Buy parsnips with a crisp clean look and avoid those with long root ends and blemishes, or with soft brown patches on the crown. Season: September to April.

Onions British onions vary in shape and colour from flattish bulbs with brown skins to round bulbs with red-brown or pale straw-coloured skins. There is hardly any difference in the sharp taste. They store well, especially during autumn and winter, if kept in a cool larder. Choose onions which are firm and regular in shape, with papery skins. Onions with shrivelled skins and softness around the neck are almost certainly bad. Season: September to March.

Small pickling onions appear from July to October.

Spanish onions These large onions, often weighing up to 8 oz., are milder in flavour than British onions.

Spring onions, salad onions The term spring onion is a misnomer as this vegetable is in season throughout the year. Spring onions are used to flavour other vegetables, but are essentially salad vegetables. The mild-flavoured bulbs have a thin skin, which peels off easily. Choose spring onions with small bulbs and fresh green foliage, and avoid any with traces of worms or wilting foliage. Season: all year round; scarce in winter. Best, March to May.

Fennel, Florence fennel This vegetable, which looks like a root, is the swollen stem bases with the top leaves removed. It has a distinct aniseed flavour.

Fennel is used fresh in salads, or braised and served with fish dishes. Mainly imported from Italy, fennel is expensive, but always in excellent condition in the shops. Season: all year round. Best in early summer.

Garlic A member of the onion family, which is sold dried only. The white papery skin encloses small, curved segments known as cloves. These are surrounded by a thin layer of skin which must be peeled off. Buy garlic in small quantities only, as one bulb goes a long way. Store in a dry, preferably dark place.

Leeks These thick-stem vegetables are composed of tightly packed skin layers which branch at the top into dark green leaves. The stems are white with a faint onion taste. Look for well-shaped, straight leeks, trimmed at the top. Season: August to May. Best, autumn and winter.

Potatoes More than a dozen different varieties are grown commercially in Britain, and shopkeepers are encouraged to label potatoes as some are better than others for different cooking purposes. Both maincrop and early potatoes are available throughout the year, but home-grown potatoes come into season in May and continue until August.

Early potatoes should be purchased in small quantities as they quickly lose their earthy crisp flavour. Varieties include *Arran Pilot*, *Home Guard*, *Red Craig's Royal*, and *Maris Peer*.

Maincrop potatoes are available from September onwards. They may be bought in larger quantities than early potatoes and stored in a cool airy place. After long storage, the red-skinned varieties tend to lose their colour. Maincrop varieties include *Desirée*, *Kerr's Pink*, *King Edward*, *Red King*, *Golden Wonder*, *Majestic*, *Maris Piper*, and *Pentland Crown*.

Generally, white potatoes are best for boiling and chips, and reds for roasting and frying.

MARROW

BUTTON MUSHROOM

CUP MUSHROOM

FLAT MUSHROOM

CUCUMBER

KALE

LETTUCE

PARSLEY

COS LETTUCE

MUSTARD AND CRESS

CABBAGE LETTUCE

PEAS

MANGETOUT

ENDIVE

Kohl rabi This has a swollen stem, with a turnip-like flavour.

The white or purple-skinned vegetables should be bought young, when they are the size of an orange. Bigger kohl rabi are coarse. Cook the bulbs as celeriac or turnip. Season: July to April.

Horseradish This long, strongly flavoured root is seldom seen fresh in the shops. It is not used as a vegetable, but as an ingredient of cold sauces. Horseradish at its best has straight roots, 1–2 in. thick at the top, and 8–15 in. long. Season: September to end of March.

Marrows Large marrows have coarse, insipid flesh and tough skin. They should be avoided in favour of young marrows, no

more than 12 in. long. The skin should have a dull bloom to it. Season: July to October.

Lettuce Two main types are widely available: cabbage and cos. Cabbage lettuce is further divided into soft-leaved lettuce, the Webb strain being the most popular; this is a crisp cabbage lettuce with crimped leaves. Cos lettuces are oblong with crisp leaves and prominent mid-ribs. They have a sweeter flavour than cabbage lettuce and keep better. Choose lettuce with fresh and bright leaves and avoid any with brown or yellow patches on the hearts. Check the underside for slime. Season: all year round.

Mushrooms These are sold either as buttons, cups or flats

according to age. White and brown types are available with no difference in taste. Large flat mushrooms have more flavour than the young buttons. Choose mushrooms carefully as they turn limp quickly and lose their flavour; use on the day of purchase. Avoid limp, broken mushrooms with a sweaty look to them. Season: all year round.

Cucumbers Hothouse cucumbers are the ones usually seen in the shops, although small amounts of ridge or outdoor cucumbers also appear. Choose straight cucumbers no more than 2 in. wide; the skin should have a clear bloom to it. Season: all year round, best late summer.

Mustard and cress (salad cress)

This is another misnamed vegetable, as boxes of mustard and cress rarely contain any mustard. Buy mustard and cress when it is 3–4 in. long; it should have a bright green colour. Season: all year round.

Peas The earliest are the flat mangetout or sugar peas which are cooked and served in the pods. Early peas (May) have round seeds, while maincrop and late varieties usually have wrinkled seeds. Buy peas with bright crisp pods and avoid any which are so large that they show through the pods. Peas with wet pods are certainly bad. Season: May to October.

Parsley This herb is used mainly for flavouring, in sauces and as

garnish. It is sold loose or in small bundles. Choose parsley with stalks about 8 in. long and fresh green foliage. Avoid any with yellow leaves and tough flowering stems. Season: all year round.

Kale This leaf vegetable is at its best after a touch of frost. The broad leaves vary in colour from dark green to purple. They are heavily crimped and have prominent pale green or white mid-ribs. Avoid kale with yellow or drooping leaves. Season: November to May.

Endive A salad vegetable, similar to lettuce but with pale green, almost yellow and very curly leaves, which have a bitter taste. Season: late autumn and winter.

21

Common Vegetables
(continued)

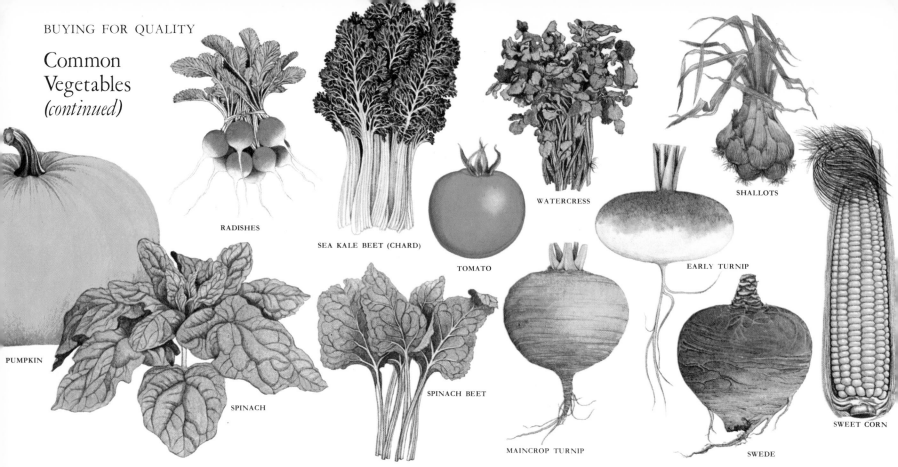

PUMPKIN

RADISHES

SEA KALE BEET (CHARD)

TOMATO

WATERCRESS

SHALLOTS

EARLY TURNIP

SPINACH

SPINACH BEET

MAINCROP TURNIP

SWEDE

SWEET CORN

Pumpkin American pumpkins may weigh up to 100 lb., but those seen occasionally in Britain weigh much less. They are cooked like marrow, but are better for jam or pie fillings. Season: summer and autumn.

Radishes Small, pungent vegetables, used fresh in salads and for garnishing. Radishes may be round and bright red, tapering and pure white, or bright red with white tips. Choose young, not too large radishes with a crisp look. Season: all year round, but scarce in winter.

Spinach There are two types of true spinach, the round-leaved summer variety and the prickly leaved winter spinach. Both have tender dark green leaves which must be handled carefully as they easily bruise. Spinach wilts quickly, and must be used on the day of purchase. New Zealand spinach is similar to other leaf spinach, but with smaller, drier and tougher leaves. Season: all year. Best, March and April.

Sea kale beet, chard or Swiss chard This has spinach-like dark green, crisp and crinkled leaves with prominent white midribs like celery stalks. The stalks as well as the leaves are used as a vegetable. Season: August to March.

Spinach beet Although seldom seen in the shops, this spinach is a favourite vegetable in allotments. It can be sown throughout the year.

Tomatoes Imported tomatoes are available throughout the year, but the best tomatoes are home-grown, in hothouses or in the open under cloches. Season: April to November.

In the autumn green tomatoes for pickles and chutneys are available in many shops. Pick firm and perfect fruit – yellow or soft areas on the skin indicate bad fruit.

The small Canary Island tomatoes are sweet and juicy, and often cheap. They are excellent for soups and purées. Large squat Mediterranean tomatoes are orange and red, with coarse flesh, but excellent for stuffing.

Tomatoes should be firm and regular in shape and bright in colour. The skin should have a matt texture.

Watercress This small-leaved vegetable is mainly used in salads, soups and for garnishing. Avoid any in flower or with a high proportion of yellow or wilting leaves. Season: all year round.

Turnips There are two types of this root vegetable; early and maincrop. Early turnips have tender mustard-flavoured flesh, which may be eaten both raw and cooked. They are usually sold washed, in bunches, and appear in the shops from May until August. Maincrop turnips have a somewhat coarser flesh, but excellent as a boiled vegetable and in soups and stews. Avoid turnips with brown spots and holes, and any with spongy patches. Season: September to March.

Swedes, Swedish turnips These winter vegetables are similar to turnips, but the yellow flesh is milder in flavour. A good vegetable for storing. Avoid roots which are forked. Season: September to May.

Shallots These small onions are chiefly used to flavour delicate sauces. The smooth and firm bulbs have a slight garlic flavour. They may be used in cooking instead of garlic. Season: September to January.

Sweet corn, corn on the cob Best cobs should be plump and full within the bright green stiff leaves. The tassels or 'silks' at the top should be black and withered. Season: July to October; also imported.

Less Common Vegetables

Peppers, pimentoes These tropical vegetable fruits have green, yellow or red skins. They are sold with the stalk ends attached, and before use these must be cut off and the inner white mid-ribs and seeds removed. Excellent for stuffing and for flavouring meat casseroles. Also used fresh in salads and for garnishing. Season: all year.

Aubergine, egg plant Oblong and near-round types of these distinctive vegetables are available. Prime aubergines have a slight bloom to the shiny tough skin; the mealy flesh is yellow-green. Season: all year round.

Salsify This little-known root vegetable has soft white flesh. Look for young salsify roots with fresh grey-green leaves and regular tapered roots. Season: end October to March.

Scorzonera, black salsify This root vegetable, similar to salsify, has purple-brown or nearly black skin. Avoid roots with shrivelled dry skins. Season: October to March.

Globe artichokes These vegetables are imported from Mediterranean countries. The artichoke is the leafy flower head of the plant. The grey-green, stiff leaves overlap each other, and the edible parts of the leaves are the fleshy bases of each leaf. Below the leaves is the fond, which has the finest flavour; the flower filaments, known as the choke, are discarded. Buy artichokes with stiff leaves which have a slight bloom. Season: all year. Best in late summer.

Okra, ladies' fingers Imported mainly from tropical Africa, these vegetables are curved seed pods up to 9 in. long. They are usually eaten green, pod and seeds, when slightly under-ripe, and are served either fresh or cooked in soups and curries.

Sweet potatoes These are not related to ordinary potatoes, the only resemblance being that they are both tubers. Sweet potatoes are globular or elongated and may be white, red or purple. The white to yellow flesh is firm and sweet. Season: winter.

Celeriac This is the edible root of a variety of celery. It is becoming more popular in Britain, although fairly expensive. Celeriac, which may weigh up to 4 lb., has a brown fibrous skin and cream-white flesh with a celery flavour. Look for firm roots showing no signs of mushy flesh. Season: October to March.

Avocado pears These pear-shaped fruits are used as a vegetable rather than a dessert fruit. They have green to purple skins. The oily, pale green, soft flesh surrounds a large stone. As avocado pears are imported they are not always ripe when bought: test for ripeness by pressing the flesh gently at the rounded end – it should yield slightly. Avoid pears with blotched dry skins. Season: all year round.

Courgettes Young marrows harvested at about 6 in. long. In prime courgettes the skins are tender enough to be left on. As they are bitter, they are best blanched before being used fresh in salads. Season: all year round.

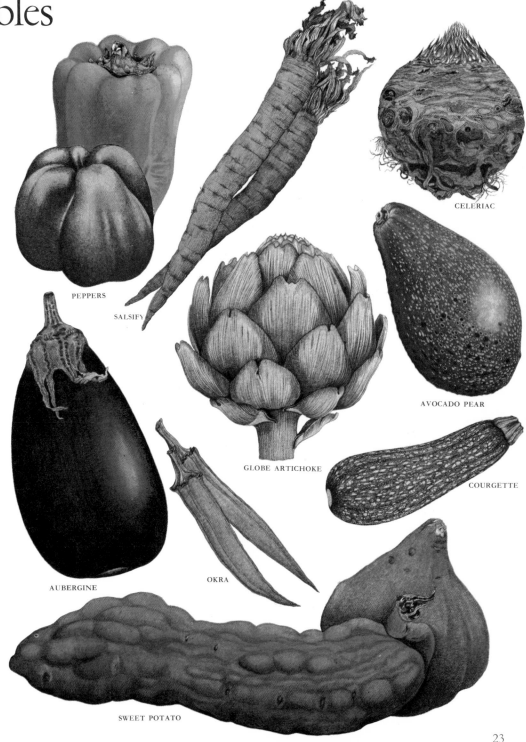

PEPPERS

SALSIFY

CELERIAC

GLOBE ARTICHOKE

AVOCADO PEAR

COURGETTE

AUBERGINE

OKRA

SWEET POTATO

White Fish

Fish can be divided, according to their oil content, into white fish, oily fish and shellfish. All white fish and most oily fish come from the sea. The seas around Britain have for centuries supplied this most basic and nutritious food. The British fleet trawls as far north as Greenland and Newfoundland, and these long-distance trawlers are, in effect, fishing factories; they gut, clean and deep-freeze their catches over several months. There are more than 40 major distribution ports in Britain from which fresh, chilled fish are transported to wholesalers and retailers.

When shopping for fish, always make sure the produce is absolutely fresh – more food poisoning is caused by second-rate fish than by any other food. Fresh fish can be recognised by its firm, even-textured flesh, clear, full and shiny eyes, bright red gills and clean smell. Avoid steaks, cutlets and fillets with a fibrous or watery appearance. Fish whose flesh has a blue or green tinge is almost certainly stale – on flat fish this is most apparent on the dark side.

Small white fish, whether flat or round, are sold whole or filleted. Large fish, such as turbot, halibut, haddock, hake and cod may be purchased whole or as fillets, cutlets and steaks. These basic cuts of fish are shown on the right. The fillet from a large round fish, such as cod (top) is longer and thicker than a fillet from a flat fish such as plaice and sole (below). The steak, also cut from a round fish, is taken from between the middle part of the body and the tail. The cutlet comes from between the head and the middle part of the body.

THE FOUR BASIC CUTS OF FISH

ROUND FISH FILLET

FLAT FISH FILLET

STEAK

CUTLET

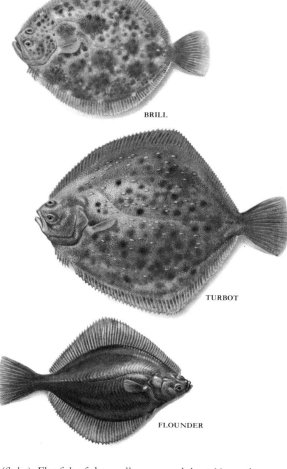

BRILL

TURBOT

FLOUNDER

Bass (sea wolf, sea dace, sea perch, bar). A round silvery fish with greyish-blue back, white underside and pink delicate flesh. Bass may be baked or poached, and small fish can be fried or grilled whole. Available all year; best, May to August.

Bream (sea bream, dorade, chad). A round, bony fish with a deep body, coarse scales and a black spot behind the head. The flesh is pink and delicate. Needs scaling carefully. Fillet, grill or fry small fish, and stuff and bake medium to large-sized bream. Season: June to December.

Brill Flat fish similar to turbot, but smaller. Grey-yellow, with small scales and yellow-white delicate flesh. Stuff and bake large whole fish (up to 6 lb.) and fillet

smaller fish for grilling or frying. Available all year round; best, January to April.

Catfish (rockfish). A round blue-grey fish, with firm flesh tinged with pink. Best used for stews and soups. Season: September to February.

Cod Large round fish with an elongated body which may weigh up to 80 lb. It has an olive-brown back with yellow and brown spots, small, soft grey scales and white underside. The firm white flesh is sold whole, as fillets or steaks, often frozen. Poach or bake small whole cod, grill or fry individual cuts. Best, October to April.

Cod roe The pinkish hard roe and the soft female roe, known as chitterling, are sold smoked,

uncooked, or boiled. Serve smoked roe as an hors-d'oeuvre and boiled roe grilled or fried.

Coley (saithe, coal fish). This round fish has near-black skin and pinkish-grey flesh which goes white when cooked. Usually sold as fillets and suitable for grilling and frying. Available most of the year.

Dab Flat fish related to plaice, but smaller and with rough scaly skin. Sold as fillets, weighing 4–6 oz., suitable for grilling and frying. Season: April to November.

Flounder (fluke). Flat fish of the same family as brill, dab, sole, plaice and turbot. The light brown upper side has orange-red spots while the underside is creamy white. Season: summer and autumn.

Haddock A round fish of the cod family with grey skin. A dark line runs along both flanks and there is a dark smudge behind the gills. The firm white flesh is sold whole or as steaks and fillets, and often smoked. Poach or bake whole fish, and grill, poach or fry steaks and fillets. Available

all year round; best, November to February.

Smoked haddock Large fresh haddock is split, brined, hung tail down by the flaps and smoked for 24 hours. It then becomes pale yellow. Very yellow smoked haddock has probably been artificially coloured. It loses its flavour quickly, and should be used as soon as possible.

Arbroath smokies Small whole haddock smoked to a brown colour. They may be poached or used in mousses, kedgerees, for hors-d'oeuvre or as sandwich fillings.

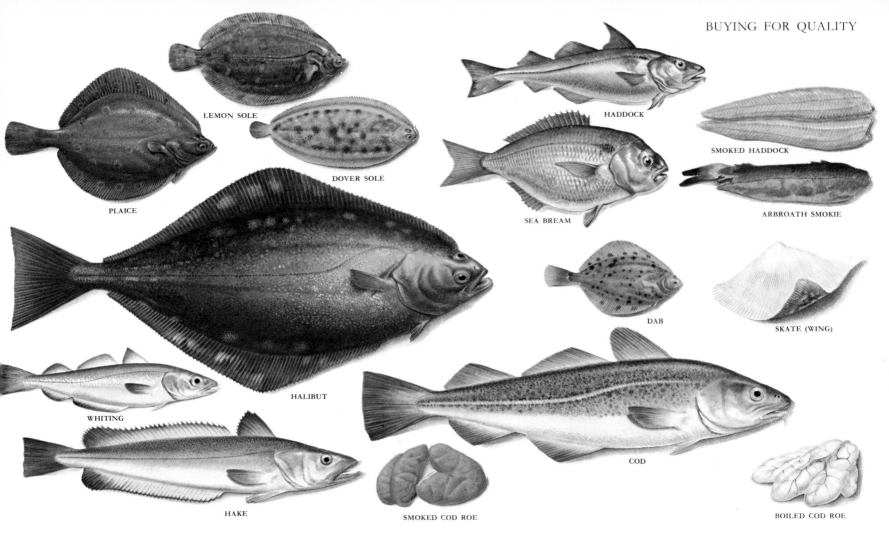

LEMON SOLE

DOVER SOLE

PLAICE

HADDOCK

SMOKED HADDOCK

SEA BREAM

ARBROATH SMOKIE

DAB

HALIBUT

SKATE (WING)

WHITING

HAKE

SMOKED COD ROE

COD

BOILED COD ROE

Hake A round, long and slender fish with scaly grey skin and tender, white, flaky flesh. Sold as cutlets and fillets and suitable for baking. Best, June to January.

Halibut This flat fish may weigh 300–400 lb. It has dark olive skin, marbled with lighter olive. The firm white flesh tends to be dry and is best poached or baked. Sold as fresh and smoked steaks. Best, August to April.

Chicken or Greenland halibut weighs approx. 2–5 lb. May be poached or baked whole. Best, March to October.

Plaice Flat fish, creamy white with red tinge on the underside, grey-brown with orange spots on the upper side. The flesh is soft and white. The best plaice is said to come from the Danish coast; it is sold whole or in fillets, often frozen. Grill, poach or fry. Available all year round; best, January to April.

Icelandic plaice lacks the orange spots on the dark skin.

Skate This flat, ray-shaped fish has slightly moist and slimy skin and pink flesh. Only the skinned wings, with their prominent bones, are sold. Suitable for poaching, grilling and frying. Best, October to April.

Sole (common, Dover or black). Its elongated to oval body is almost completely surrounded by fins and is covered with tiny hard scales, firmly attached to the skin. The colour varies, according to the depth in which the sole is caught, from dark brown to pale grey, but is usually olive-brown with irregular black markings on the upper side. The underside is white. The flesh is finely textured and delicate in flavour. Sold whole or in fillets and can be poached, grilled or fried. Available all year round; best, May to February.

Lemon sole This is wider and more pointed than Dover sole and has light brown skin with darker brown spots on the upper side. The flesh is more stringy and has less flavour. Best, December to March.

Turbot A flat fish with black skin and raised growths on its back. Creamy white on the underside. The white, firm, delicately flavoured flesh is sold whole or as steaks or fillets. Whole turbot may be poached, baked or braised, and fillets and steaks can be grilled or fried. Available all year round, but best and least expensive May to July.

Whiting A round fish belonging to the cod family. Grey olive-green on the back, with pale yellow shading to silvery on the underside. The fine-textured flesh is flaky. Excellent when fresh but deteriorates rapidly. Cook whole, poached, baked or fried. Whiting is at its best, November to February.

Oily Fish

SPRAT

GREY MULLET

SMOKED SPRAT

RED MULLET

CARP

TROUT

PILCHARD

SARDINE

SMOKED TROUT

SALMON TROUT

Oily fish are so called because the oil content is found throughout the flesh, while in white fish the oil is present only in the liver. Oily fish come from the sea and some are also caught in freshwater lakes, rivers and streams or produced in fish farms.

When buying oily fish, look for fresh fish with firm, even-textured flesh, clear, full and shiny eyes, bright red gills and a clean smell.

The herring is the most common oily fish; it is delicious when eaten fresh, but is perhaps more popular salted and smoked. It is probable that more people eat kippers – the most famous smoked variety – than fresh herring, or any other kind of fish.

Generally speaking, there are two methods of smoking fish: hot-smoking, in which the fish are suspended a few feet above the fire and smoked at 150–200°F so that they are partially or wholly cooked; and cold-smoking, in which the fish are hung some distance above a low-smouldering fire and smoked at a temperature of 90°F or below. Hot-smoked fish must be eaten soon after curing; cold-smoked fish will keep longer.

Carp A round freshwater fish with a small mouth, four fleshy appendages called barbules and no teeth. There are several varieties, the best being the mirror or king carp, which is specially reared for eating. Carp caught in lakes, ponds and sluggish rivers often have a muddy smell and taste, and should be soaked for at least 3 hours in salted water before cooking. They are best stuffed and baked or braised. Best, mid-June to March.

Conger eel The most common sea eel, this fish has pale grey to jet-black skin and white, firm flesh of a good flavour, though it may be coarser and more oily than freshwater eel. It is prepared and cooked like common eel. These are ready for eating, and make good hors-d'oeuvre. Best, March to October.

Eel, common A richly flavoured freshwater fish with long, slender body up to 3 ft in length. It has shiny grey-black skin and firm, white flesh. It is always sold alive

and should be cooked as soon as possible after killing. The fishmonger will kill and skin an eel whole. Cut the skinned eel into 3–4 in. long pieces and steam, braise or deep fry them. Best, autumn and early winter.

Herring A small, delicately flavoured and bony saltwater fish, usually weighing about 6 oz. It has silvery-blue scales on the back, silvery flanks and underside, and firm brownish flesh. The skin should have a shiny, bright look, and the flesh should feel firm to the touch. Sold whole or in fillets and suitable for frying and grilling. Herring is also preserved by pickling and smoking. Available all year round. Best, June to March.

Bismarck herring Flat herring fillets marinated in spiced vinegar and onion rings.

Bloater Lightly smoked, salted whole herring. It does not keep well and must be grilled or fried on the day of purchase.

Buckling Whole smoked herring, requiring no cooking. Chiefly used for hors-d'oeuvre.

Herring roes Both hard and soft roes are often in short supply.

Kipper The most common smoked herring. It is split and put in brine before being smoked. Some kippers look dark because artificial colouring is added. These should be eaten as soon as possible after buying. Many kippers are not dyed at all and keep well. All kippers should have a sheen and the flesh should be soft to the touch. Kippers are sold whole, usually in pairs, or as fillets which are also available vacuum-packed and frozen. Best grilled or used for pâtés.

Rollmop Herring fillet marinated in spiced vinegar and rolled round chopped onions, gherkins and peppercorns.

Salt herring Whole or gutted herring preserved in heavy salt brine. It usually needs soaking for 24 hours before filleting.

Mackerel A long, slender, saltwater fish with striped blue and green back, silvery underside and firm flesh. It deteriorates quickly and must be used on the day of purchase. Sold whole or filleted. Suitable for grilling, frying and baking, and may be served hot or cold. Available all year round, best in winter and spring. The roes may be cooked like herring roes, and they are at their best during May and June.

Smoked mackerel Smoked whole and ready for eating. Use and serve like buckling.

Mullet, grey A large estuary fish, 12–15 in. long. It has a grey back, striped on the sides with darker lines, and silvery white underside. The fatty, rather coarse flesh is firm. Suitable for baking, poaching and grilling. Best, July to February.

Mullet, red Red-skinned saltwater fish with firm, white flesh of delicate flavour. It is unrelated to grey mullet. Suitable for grilling or baking. Mainly imported frozen. Best, May to September.

Perch Round freshwater fish with brightly coloured skin and hard scales. As it is difficult to scale, plunge it into boiling water for a few minutes to loosen the

EEL

SMOKED CONGER EEL

SMELT

HERRING

BLOATER

BUCKLING

KIPPER

SALMON

HERRING ROE

MACKEREL

SMOKED SALMON

WHITEBAIT

SMOKED MACKEREL

scales. Wash the fish on both sides before grilling it whole. It is seldom available from fishmongers, catches being landed only by amateur anglers.

Pike A large, lean, freshwater fish with a long body, large flat jaw, the mouth stretching to the eyes, and with numerous strong teeth. It has coarse flesh which needs soaking for 3–4 hours in salted water before being baked or boiled. Not usually on sale – like perch, it is an angler's fish.

Pilchard Small saltwater fish similar to herring. Most pilchards are caught off the coasts of Devon and Cornwall. They deteriorate quickly and are most often sold tinned. Fresh pilchards are grilled or fried whole.

Salmon The king of fish is caught in cool, fast-running rivers. It is a saltwater fish which travels up rivers to spawn, after which it returns to the sea. It has bright silvery scales, red gills and pink-red closely textured flesh of unparalleled flavour. Sold whole or as steaks. Canadian, Norwegian, Alaskan and Japanese salmon is available frozen. Salmon is also sold smoked, tinned and potted. Fresh salmon is at its best, June to July.

Smoked salmon Scotch smoked salmon has strips of fat between the meat and has the best quality. Smoked Canadian and Pacific salmon is less expensive but drier.

Sardine A small, herring-like saltwater fish. It is usually sold tinned and sometimes preserved in brine.

Smelt or sparling Tiny saltwater fish which, like salmon, spawns and is caught in rivers. It has silvery scales and pure white flesh and is fairly rare in Britain. It has a strong aroma which has been compared to that of violets and cucumbers, and a delicate flavour. Clean by pressing the entrails out through a cut just below the gills, and serve smelts shallow or deep-fried. Best, February to March.

Sprat Small, silvery-skinned saltwater fish of the herring family and smaller than the sardine. Clean and cook in the same way as smelts. Best, November to March. Young sprats, known as brislings, are tinned in oil or a sauce, sometimes after being lightly smoked. Whole smoked sprats are also available; they are difficult to skin and bone.

Trout, rainbow The most common trout, reared on fish farms. It is green-gold in colour with whitish flesh. Best grilled or baked in foil. Available all year round, fresh and frozen.

Trout, river or brown This has darker skin than rainbow trout and is spotted. The flesh is superior to that of rainbow trout. Grill or fry. Best, March to September, but in scant supply.

Trout, sea or salmon A freshwater fish, similar to salmon, with silvery scales. The firm flesh has a delicate salmon flavour and is pale pink. Average weight about 4 lb. Cooked as salmon. Best, late spring and summer.

Trout, smoked Rainbow trout smoked to a rich brown colour. Requires no cooking, and is served as hors-d'oeuvre.

Whitebait The fry or young of the herring or sprat; it is about 1½ in. long, silvery in colour and with firm, grey-white flesh. Always deep-fried whole without cleaning. Best, February to July.

27

Shellfish

Shellfish are divided into two groups: crustaceans, such as crabs, lobsters and shrimps, which have jointed shells; and molluscs, such as mussels, oysters and scallops, which have hinged shells. Much confusion exists over the naming of shellfish, particularly when they are imported from the Continent. The British prawn, for example, often has no foreign equivalent, while the larger Dublin Bay prawn is the equivalent of langoustine in France and scampi in Italy. The Dublin Bay prawn is also often known as scampi in Britain, although the true scampi is caught only in the Bay of Naples. The Pacific prawn, imported frozen, has no European equivalent.

The crawfish, also known as spiny lobster or rock lobster (*langouste* in French), should not be confused with the freshwater crayfish (*écrevisse*). This is a common shellfish in France, but not to be found in Britain.

Fresh mussels are not available in shops between April and August, but this rule does not apply on the Continent. Native oysters can be bought only during those months that are spelt with an 'r' – September to April. This has given rise to a widespread belief that oysters and other molluscs should be eaten only when there is an 'r'–in the month. But imported oysters are now available throughout most of the year.

DUBLIN BAY PRAWN

SHRIMPS

COCKLES

WINKLES

CRAB

OYSTER

Clam American mollusc now being cultivated in Britain. It is sold live in its shell. Usually served raw like oyster. It may also be cooked like mussels or used in fish stews and soup. Also available smoked and tinned. In season all year round. Best in autumn.

Cockles Tiny molluscs with white, fluted shells. Usually sold cooked and shelled. Cockles can be used in fish dishes to replace mussels and oysters. Available all year; best, September to April.

Crab This crustacean is grey-brown when alive, brownish-red when cooked. It is sometimes sold alive, but usually freshly boiled by the fishmonger. Also sold 'dressed', that is prepared ready for eating. The average weight of a crab is 2–3 lb.; the claws provide white meat and the shell brown meat. Male crabs (cocks) have larger claws, and the female crabs (hens) often contain edible roes or red coral. Crabs are best when medium-sized and should have both claws attached. When buying crab, shake it lightly; it should feel heavy but with no sound of water inside. Available all year, least expensive May to October.

Crawfish (spiny lobster, rock lobster). A crustacean similar to lobster, but heavier, weighing 5–6 lb. It lacks the large claws, and all the meat is contained in the tail. The flesh is coarser in texture than lobster meat, but should be prepared in the same way. Sold live or cooked, but in scant supply, and most crawfish tails are sold frozen. Season: April to September.

Lobster Crustacean, dark blue when alive and scarlet when boiled. The male lobster is brighter in colour and smaller than the female, with an average weight of 1–2 lb. The female has a broader tail and more tender flesh. The female also contains the coral, spawn or eggs, used for lobster butter and various sauces. Sold live and cooked. When buying lobster, choose a medium-sized one which feels heavy for its size. The tail should spring back when it is straightened out. Avoid lobsters with white shells on their backs as this is a sign of age. Available all year; best, April to August.

Mussels These molluscs with blue-black shells are boiled alive and served in a number of classic sauces. Before cooking, discard any with broken shells and any which do not close when tapped. Mussels are sold by the pint; allow $1\frac{1}{2}$ pints per person. Also available tinned in brine. Season: September to March.

Oysters These highly priced molluscs are usually eaten raw, but may also be cooked. Shells should be closed, or shut when tapped. Some gourmets maintain that a raw oyster should be swallowed whole, others that it should be chewed to release the full flavours. Oysters must be absolutely fresh and should be opened just before serving, and served on ice. Allow six for each person. Season: September to April.

Portuguese oyster A variety of oyster imported from various countries, not just Portugal. It is

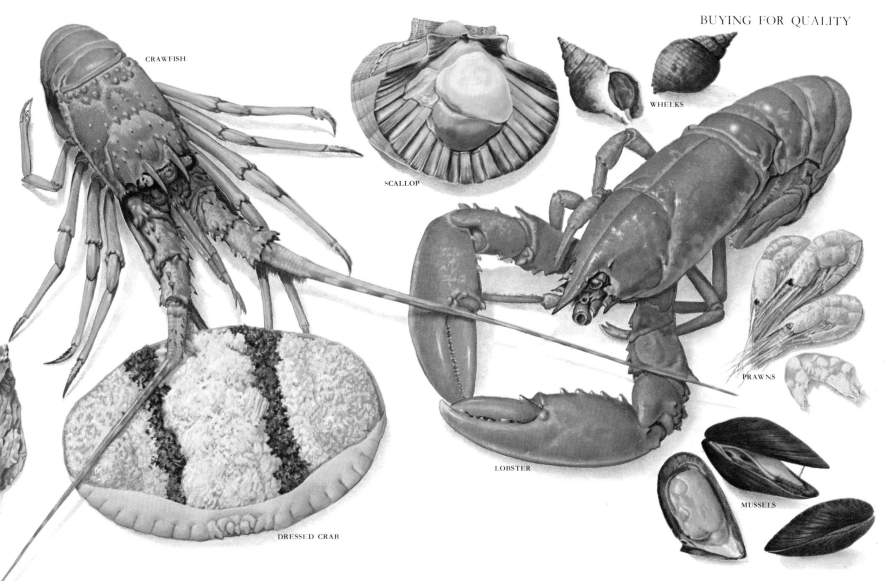

CRAWFISH

SCALLOP

WHELKS

PRAWNS

LOBSTER

MUSSELS

DRESSED CRAB

larger than the native oyster, with a more irregular shell, and has less flavour. Available all year round, but best in the autumn.

Prawns Small, soft-shelled grey crustaceans, the shells of which turn bright red and the flesh pink when boiled. They are usually sold already boiled, with or without their shells. Unshelled they are sold by the pint, and shelled by weight. Available all year round, fresh or frozen.

Dublin Bay prawn (scampi, Norway lobster). The largest British prawn, about 4 in. long. It is pale pink with a hard shell when alive, pink when boiled. Sold alive or cooked, with or without shells. Also sold frozen. Available all year round; best, May to November.

Pacific prawn Even larger than the Dublin Bay prawn, 5–6 in. long, Pacific prawns are imported and available only ready-cooked and frozen in Britain.

Scallops Native molluscs with white flesh and orange roe. They are enclosed in pinkish-brown shells, the rounded halves of which can be thoroughly cleaned and used as hors-d'oeuvre dishes. They are usually sold opened and are poached, baked, grilled or used in stews and soups.

Shrimps, common or brown Small crustaceans with grey-brown soft shells which turn pinkish when boiled. British

shrimps are caught mainly in Morecambe Bay and the Solway Firth and are usually sold cooked in their shells. Available all year round. Frozen, shelled shrimps are imported from Greenland. Shrimps are also available tinned and potted.

Pink shrimps These have a more delicate flavour than brown shrimps, and grey shells which turn rosy-pink when boiled. Usually sold cooked but not peeled or potted.

Whelks These molluscs are nearly always sold cooked and shelled. They are eaten with vinegar and brown bread. Available all year round; best, September to February.

Winkles (periwinkle) Similar to whelks, but smaller. They are sold cooked, shelled or unshelled. A large pin is needed to extract the cooked winkle from its shell. Available all the year; best, October to May.

Poultry

Poultry, which are domestic birds specially bred for the table, include chicken, duck, goose, guinea fowl and turkey. The British eat some 600,000 tons of chicken each year. Nowadays free-range chickens are available only from specialist shops, and the greater proportion of chickens are battery-reared. These, although less tasty, are cheaper.

The flavour of a chicken depends on its age. In a young bird the tip of the breastbone is soft and flexible, and the feet smooth with small scales. When cooked, the flesh is tender and mild in flavour. As the bird ages, the breastbone becomes harder and more rigid, and the scales on the feet coarser. The cooked flesh is also coarser and drier, but the flavour is better developed. The length of time a bird is left after killing and before drawing also influences the flavour – the longer it is left, the stronger the taste.

Duck is one of the more expensive breeds of poultry, all the more so because it yields little meat in comparison to its weight and size. Geese are also expensive because, like ducks, they cannot be reared successfully under factory-farming conditions. It was traditional to serve goose for Christmas dinner, but it was ousted from the festive table by the turkey.

Like all poultry, turkey is now available throughout the year, fresh or frozen, in all sizes. It is also sold in individual portions, many supermarkets offering turkey breast and leg portions.

Poultry giblets are sold either with the bird or separately. They can be used for stocks, stuffings, and pâtés. The most famous pâté is pâté de foie gras, made from goose liver.

Chicken Available throughout the year, fresh or frozen, and usually sold oven-ready – that is plucked, drawn and trussed. Fresh chickens are sometimes sold plucked but not drawn or trussed. A fresh chicken should have a plump, white breast, smooth and pliable legs and a pliable beak and breastbone. Young birds have short, sharp claws. Chickens are usually sold under different names, according to their age and weight, and can be cooked in numerous ways. Whole chickens may be roasted, spit-roasted, pot-roasted and braised. They can be boiled or cooked in a casserole. They can be boned and made into galantines; and jointed they are grilled, fried or stewed.

Poussin A baby chicken, four to six weeks old and weighing up to 1¼ lb. Allow one poussin per person. Suitable for roasting, spit-roasting and grilling.

Double poussin This is six to ten weeks old and weighs about 2 lb. Cook as recommended for poussin. Serves two.

Spring chicken About three months old, with an average weight of 2½ lb. Best roasted to give three portions.

Roasting chicken (or broiler). The most popular size for a family. It is 6–12 months old and weighs 3–4 lb., enough for four people. The larger roasting chicken, weighing 4–6 lb., serves about six people. It is sold divided into individual joints for frying, grilling or baking.

Boiling fowl An older and tougher bird more than 12 months old and weighing up to 7 lb. It is usually meaty but also

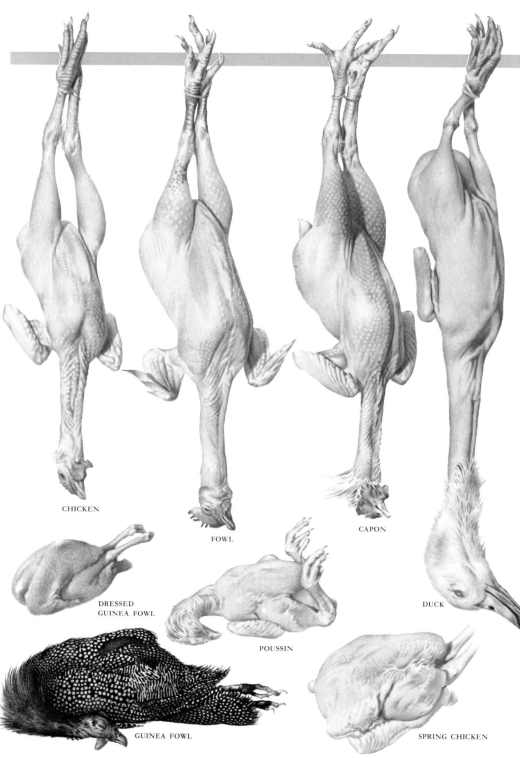

CHICKEN

FOWL

CAPON

DRESSED
GUINEA FOWL

POUSSIN

DUCK

GUINEA FOWL

SPRING CHICKEN

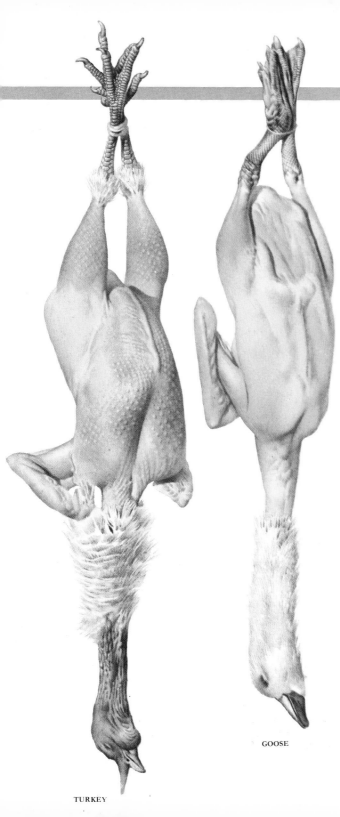

TURKEY

GOOSE

fatty, and is only suitable for boiling, stews or casseroles. Boiling fowl, being in less demand than roasting chicken, generally has to be ordered in advance.

Capon This is young castrated cock, specially bred to give a high proportion of flesh of a good flavour. Usually killed at nine months and weighing 5–8 lb. Excellent as a large roast.

Frozen chickens These are drawn and trussed, ready for roasting, and are sold whole or in joints. They must be completely thawed in the wrapping before being cooked. Never put a frozen chicken in hot water to thaw – the only effect this has is to toughen the flesh. A bird which has to be thawed quickly can be put under cold, slow-running water. The giblets are usually wrapped separately and put inside the chicken – do not forget to take them out before cooking.

Duck The most famous breed is the Aylesbury duck. It is usually sold weighing 4–6 lb., but a duck does not serve as many as a chicken of similar weight. A 4 lb. duck is only enough for four people. Duck is a fatty bird that is best roasted. The breast should be plump, the bird's underbill soft enough to bend and the feet pliable. Available all the year round, fresh or frozen, but fresh birds are at their best from August to December.

Duckling A young duck weighing $3\frac{1}{2}$–4 lb., and at its best from April to July. It is always roasted and will serve no more than three persons.

Goose This is considered by many gourmets to be the best of all poultry. It is a fatty bird with creamy-white flesh which cooks to a light brown, and has a slightly gamy flavour. Average weight is 6–12 lb., but again it serves less per pound than chicken. Allow 12–14 oz. per person. Choose a young bird with soft yellow feet and legs which still have a little down on them. Older birds have stiff, dry webs. Available all the year round fresh or frozen, although supplies are dwindling fast with declining demand. Fresh birds are best from October to February.

Gosling (or green goose). A young goose not more than 6 months old.

Guinea fowl Originally a game bird, but now bred for the table, guinea fowl should be hung for several days. It has grey plumage, tinged with purple and spotted with white. The flesh is firm and creamy-white with a flavour slightly reminiscent of pheasant.

Guinea fowl is sometimes sold as squabs (weight $1\frac{1}{4}$ lb.), chicks (up to $2\frac{1}{4}$ lb.) and fowls (up to $3\frac{3}{4}$ lb.). It is suitable for roasting, braising and casseroles. Available all the year round; best, February to April.

Turkey This is now on sale all the year round, fresh or frozen, whole or in joints, in small as well as large sizes. The weight of a turkey ranges from about 6 lb. to 30–40 lb., the average weight being 10–14 lb. Allow 10–12 oz. per serving. Hen birds are the best buy at seven to nine months old. The legs should be black, the neck short, the breast plump and the flesh pale white, with a faint blue tinge. Turkey is best roasted in foil to eliminate frequent basting.

Eggs Hen eggs come from various chicken varieties, specially bred for laying. The breed of hen affects the colour of the shell and the size of the egg. But the bird's diet makes the real difference to flavour. The best eggs are 'free-range', and the fresher they are the better the flavour. Battery eggs, on the other hand, alter little in taste even when kept for several weeks.

A new egg grading system came into operation when Britain joined the Common Market. The country of origin is now shown by figures only. Boxed eggs of British origin carries the figure 9; this is followed by another number which indicates the region in the country, and the third figure is the packing station. There are three quality classifications – A, B and C. Class A describes fresh, naturally clean eggs, while class B describes eggs less fresh, and usually wet or dry cleaned and often preserved or refrigerated for some weeks. Class C contains eggs suitable only for food manufacture and these are not on sale in shops.

Some boxes of class A may have a red band with the word 'extra' printed on it. This means first quality eggs which have been packed for less than 7 days.

At present there are five egg sizes – large, standard, medium, small and extra small. These are stamped on boxed eggs, but will eventually be replaced by the Common Market grades, of which there are 7. Grade 1 is the largest, at 70 grammes, and the smallest is Grade 7 at 45 grammes. Most recipes are based on the standard egg which roughly corresponds to Grade 4 with an average weight of 57 grammes.

Game

The term game is applied to wild animals and birds which are hunted and eaten. In Britain, there is a close season for most game, when hunting is forbidden. Only rabbits, pigeons and quails are not protected by law and are available throughout the year. Game is usually bought from licensed poulterers or fishmongers, who prepare it for cooking. Although many types of game are commercially frozen and, therefore, are available throughout the year, the flavour of game is only fully appreciated in freshly killed and hung game.

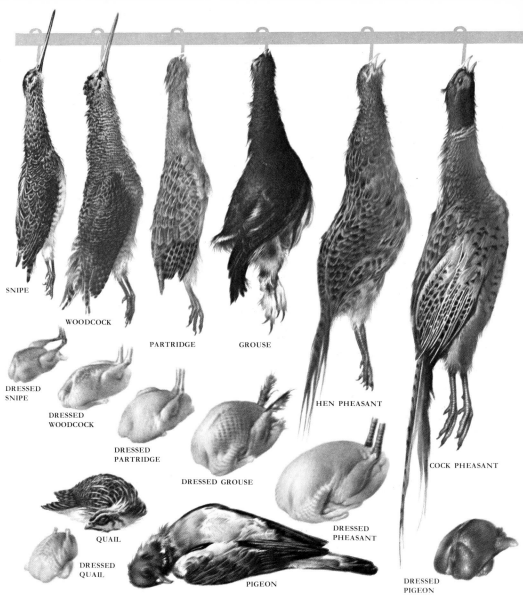

SNIPE

WOODCOCK

PARTRIDGE   GROUSE

DRESSED
SNIPE

DRESSED
WOODCOCK

HEN PHEASANT

DRESSED
PARTRIDGE

COCK PHEASANT

DRESSED GROUSE

QUAIL

DRESSED
PHEASANT

DRESSED
QUAIL

PIGEON

DRESSED
PIGEON

GAME BIRDS

Grouse There are several edible varieties of this small bird in Britain, most of them inhabiting the woodlands, moors and mountains of Scotland. Young birds are suitable for roasting or grilling, older birds are best braised or casseroled. Allow one young bird per person.

Black grouse The cock has glossy black plumage, flecked with purple and blue, and white wing patches. It weighs up to 4 lb. The hen has mottled brown plumage with black bars and weighs about 2 lb. Season: August 20 – December 20 (September 1 – December 20 in Somerset, Devon and New Forest).

Capercaillie The largest grouse, now rare. The cock, weighing up to 10 lb., has dark, metallic-green plumage. The hen is smaller and mottled in colour. Capercaillie are excellent for roasting whole, and a large bird (average weight 7–10 lb.) will serve six persons. Season: October 1 – January 31.

Red or **Scottish grouse** The most common British grouse. The young bird has downy red-brown breast plumes and pointed wings. Serve one bird per person. Season: August 12 – December 10. Best, September.

Ptarmigan or **mountain grouse** Similar to red grouse. The plumage turns white in winter. Cook and serve as for red grouse. Season: August 20 – December 10. Best, September to October.

Partridge There are two varieties, the English or grey partridge and the French, which is slightly larger and has red legs. The young bird has pointed flight feathers. Serve young birds roasted – one per person – and use older birds in casseroles. Season: September 1 – February 1. Best, October to December.

Pheasant The cock and hen are usually sold together as a brace. The cock has long, distinctive tail feathers and neck feathers shot with blue and green. The hen has a shorter tail and less striking plumage. One of the finest game birds for roasting – a hen will serve three and a cock four persons. Season: October 1 – January 31 (England), October 1 – December 10 (Scotland). Best, November to December.

Pigeon (squab) The young bird has fine down under the wings, and pink legs; these become darker in colour as the bird matures. Suitable for pot-roasting or braising and excellent for casseroles. Season: all year round; at their best, August to September.

Quail Rare in Britain, but imported. The young bird has pointed feathers, soft feet and short, rounded spurs. Does not require hanging. Roast and serve one per person. Season: all year round. Best, June to September.

Snipe Small bird with mottled black and brown plumage, reddish at the throat, and white-barred flank. The young bird has soft feet, downy feathers under the wings, and pointed flight feathers. Roast whole, allowing one snipe per person. Season: August 12 – January 31.

Mallard The male has a green head and neck flecked with brown and grey. The female is dark brown or buff-coloured. Excellent for roasting, and the mallard, being the largest of the wild duck, will yield three average portions. Season: September 1 – January 31. Best, October to December.

Teal This small wild duck has grey plumage with a distinctive metallic-green strip round the eye. Excellent for roasting; allow one teal per person. Season: September 1 – January 31. Best, October to January.

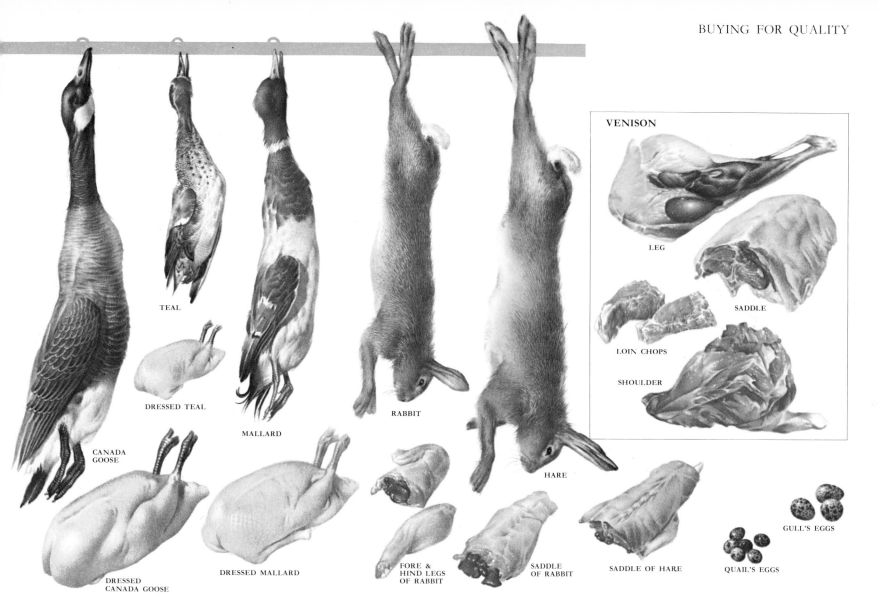

TEAL

DRESSED TEAL

MALLARD

CANADA
GOOSE

RABBIT

VENISON

LEG

SADDLE

LOIN CHOPS

SHOULDER

HARE

DRESSED
CANADA GOOSE

DRESSED MALLARD

FORE &
HIND LEGS
OF RABBIT

SADDLE
OF RABBIT

SADDLE OF HARE

QUAIL'S EGGS

GULL'S EGGS

Wild goose Some wild geese are protected throughout the year, but others, such as the Canada goose, are occasionally available at poulterer's shops. Excellent for roasting. An average bird serves six persons. Season: November to December.

Woodcock This small bird has brown plumage, barred with chestnut and black. The breast should be plump with ample fat. Suitable for roasting or braising; allow one woodcock per person. Season: October 1 – January 31. Best, October to November.

FURRED GAME

Hare There are two types, the English or brown hare and the Scottish or blue hare. A young hare is known as a leveret. A hare may be roasted whole, but usually the saddle is the joint for roasting, while the legs are used for casseroles, stews and pâtés. An older hare is usually jointed and jugged. Season: August 1 to end of February. Best, October to February.

Rabbit The flesh of the wild rabbit often has a gamy flavour. It is prepared and cooked like hare. Rabbits on sale in the shops are domesticated, with a flavour somewhat like that of chicken. Sold whole or jointed, they are used for casseroles, stews and roasting. Season: all year round.

Venison There are three types of venison: the fallow, the red deer and the roe deer. The lean meat should be dark and close-grained, the fat white and firm and the hooves small and smooth. Young males, $1\frac{1}{2}$–2 years old, provide the best meat. Venison is sold in joints, the leg and saddle being the choicest cuts. An average joint serves 8–10 people. The shoulder may be braised or stewed or used as pie fillings. Chops cut from the loin or saddle and the large neck cutlets are excellent for braising or baking. Season: all year.

Beef

For centuries, foreigners have remarked on the Englishman's prodigious appetite for roast beef. This reputation may have been justified in the early 18th century, when men like Robert Bakewell led the way in breeding new, heavier strains of beef cattle. But in modern times, it no longer holds true. Year in and year out, the United Kingdom ranks only sixth in the Western European 'league table' of beef-eating countries – behind France, Belgium, Luxembourg, Italy and West Germany.

Beef comes from castrated bullocks and young heifers which have never calved. The male produces a better proportion of lean meat to fat, but the heifer carries less bone. The best beef comes from young animals, but even so it must, after slaughtering, be matured or 'hung', at low temperatures, to tenderise the meat with the minimum loss of weight and to improve its keeping qualities. Until a few years ago, a hanging period of 12–14 days at a temperature of 2–4°C (35–40°F) was considered ideal, but with the tendency to slaughter younger animals, the hanging period is now a good deal less.

On properly hung beef, the lean meat is red with a brownish tinge, and slightly moist. Very bright red meat shows that the beef has not been hung sufficiently. Dark red, blotchy and dry-looking meat indicates cuts from an older and therefore tough animal. Such cuts are suitable for braising or slow cooking, provided they are well flecked with fat, which will impart tenderness, heighten flavour and prevent the meat becoming too dry during cooking.

The fat around and between the lean should be creamy, even pale yellow in colour, and of a firm texture. The bones should be pink, sometimes with a blue tinge, and shiny.

Quality beef should include little or no gristle. On steaks, for example, a strip of gristle running between the fat and lean layers usually indicates an old animal.

Cheap cuts are as nutritious as expensive ones, the only difference being the time spent on preparing and cooking them. Another point to bear in mind is that price is controlled by supply and demand: because only a given number can be cut from one animal, steaks are always expensive. In summer, stewing and braising beef are not popular, and so are relatively inexpensive. They are ideal for using in dishes that can be stored in the home freezer.

Cuts of beef – and the names by which they are known – vary considerably in different parts of the country. In Scotland and the North of England, for example, leg and shin of beef is known as hough. Avoid unrecognisable cuts, especially nondescript rolled joints which invariably disintegrate during cooking.

The cuts and joints illustrated here may not always be available from supermarkets which specialise in pre-packed meats, but a good butcher will supply a cut of meat at a few days' notice.

Apart from Scottish, English and Irish beef, there is also imported beef from Argentina, New Zealand and Australia. This beef is vacuum-packed and either chilled or blast frozen. The fat on imported beef is nearer white and the meat is pale pink. By law, all butchers must label beef with the country of origin.

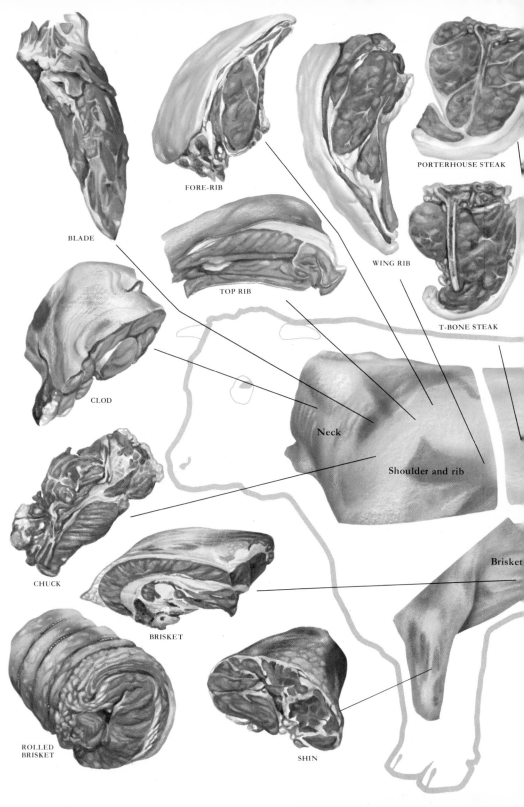

FORE-RIB

PORTERHOUSE STEAK

BLADE

WING RIB

TOP RIB

T-BONE STEAK

CLOD

Neck

Shoulder and rib

CHUCK

Brisket

BRISKET

ROLLED BRISKET

SHIN

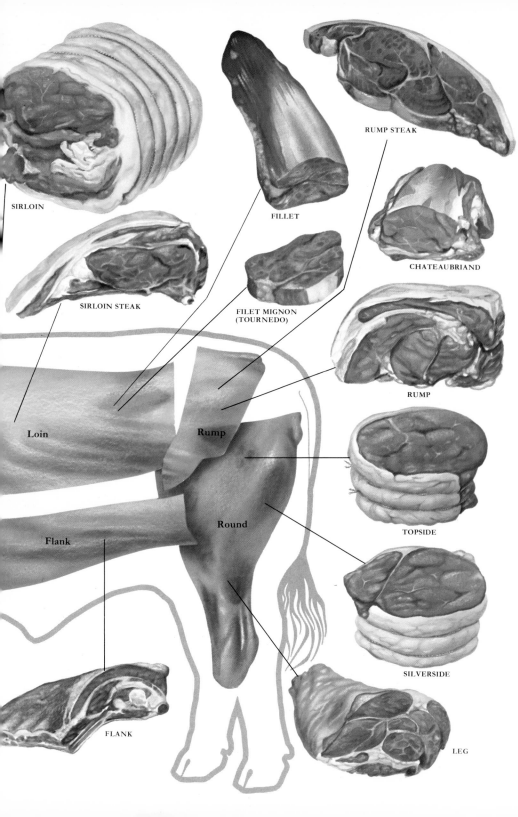

SIRLOIN

SIRLOIN STEAK

FILLET

FILET MIGNON
(TOURNEDO)

RUMP STEAK

CHATEAUBRIAND

RUMP

Loin

Rump

Round

Flank

TOPSIDE

SILVERSIDE

FLANK

LEG

Blade Sold as braising steak and often included with chuck steak which is similar (in Scotland, the blade and chuck together is known as a shoulder). Many butchers dice blade of beef and mix it with chopped kidney; it is marketed as fillings for pies and puddings. Being fairly lean, blade is also excellent for slow-cooked casseroles and stews, and the best mince comes from this cut.

Brisket on the bone One of the least expensive joints, brisket is rather fatty. Choose a joint with as little fat as possible, checking both sides. It is best pot-roasted or braised.

Brisket, rolled Boned and rolled joints are suitable for slow pot-roasting and braising. Boned brisket is often sold salted, ready for boiling. It is then pressed between weights and served cold, cut into thin slices. Brisket is an excellent economical buy, especially when catering for large numbers. Order in advance and ask the butcher to trim the joint of fat.

Chuck The best type of stewing steak, known in the North of England as a chine. It is best braised, stewed or used for pie and pudding fillings. As it is gristly and often tough, do not attempt to fry or grill, in spite of recommendations by the butcher.

Clod Also known as neck or sticking piece. This muscular cut is useful for stewing, for casseroles and pie fillings. It is usually fairly inexpensive, but it includes a high proportion of fat and gristle which must be trimmed off from the meat.

Fillet This lean and boneless piece, which lies below the sirloin, is one of the most expensive. It is usually sliced, at an angle, into individual steaks which, since they shrink in cooking, should be at least $1\frac{1}{4}$ in. thick. Tiny flecks of fat through the lean indicates a fillet that will grill well. It is also sold on order whole, or in large portions, for such dishes as boeuf en croûte. As the fillet is lean meat, it must be larded with thin strips of bacon fat before being roasted whole.

Flank An inexpensive, rather fatty joint, sometimes known as thick flank or buttock steak. It is excellent for pot-roasting, braising or stewing, producing a rich gravy. It may also be fried if cut thinly and flattened.

Leg This always refers to one of the hind legs, which contain a large proportion of tissue and gristle. Although the meat is lean and has a good flavour it is often tough. It is best used for stews, casseroles, puddings and pies, and it is also used for consommé and beef tea for invalids.

Rib (fore) One of the larger roasting joints, which can be cooked either on the bone or boned and rolled.

Rib (top) This large joint contains less bone than fore-rib and is excellent for slow-roasting. Boned and rolled it is better pot-roasted or braised.

Rib (wing) A large joint cut from the loin of beef, close to the sirloin and fillet. It is one of the most expensive beef joints, but produces a perfect roast for a large gathering, such as a dinner party or cold buffet.

35

Beef (continued)

Veal

Rump A large joint from the hind leg, also known as top rump or thick flank. It can be slow-roasted at a low temperature, but it is better pot-roasted or braised. This joint of beef is also good for stews and casseroles.

Shin This comes from the fore-leg and is usually fairly gristly. It is often sold as mince, and is also good for stews, casseroles, puddings or pies and, because of its high gelatine content, for brawns. The shin is a relatively inexpensive joint, but it often contains a great deal of waste.

Silverside A popular, boneless cut which may be slow-roasted or, preferably, pot-roasted. Alternatively, silverside may be salted or spiced before being slowly boiled, and served hot with vegetables. This cut is also excellent when pressed and then cut into thin slices.

Sirloin This is the national joint and traditional roast beef of old England. It is said to have been knighted by a king of England after he had feasted well on a roast loin of beef. It is the ideal – and the most expensive – beef joint for roasting, either on the bone or boned and rolled. It is sold with the fillet attached, and this can be cut off and cooked separately.

Steaks are cut from the upper part of the joint.

Skirt Cut from the lower rump, this is heavy with membranes and gristle which can easily be trimmed away. Skirt may be thinly sliced and fried, but it is better used for mince, or it can be cubed for stews and casseroles.

Steaks These are individual cuts, chiefly from the loin, fillet or rump. They are all very expensive, but tender.

Steak, Chateaubriand A tender, expensive steak, ideally about 1¼ in. thick and cut from the centre of the fillet. Grill or fry. It is large enough to serve two people.

Steak, mignon Also known as filet mignon or tournedos. It is a small cut from the centre of the fillet, but it is not as thick as Chateaubriand steak. Filet mignon is best grilled or sautéed.

Steak, porterhouse A ¾–1 in. thick cut from the sirloin joint. It contains part of the fillet, has no bone, and is suitable for grilling. Avoid any with too much fat, although some fat is necessary to keep the steak moist.

Steak, rump This is considered the best-flavoured steak, excellent for grilling, or frying with onions. This steak should contain a reasonable amount of fat but no gristle.

Steak, sirloin A large steak cut from across the upper part of the sirloin, without the fillet. It is usually cut about 1 in. thick, slightly thinner than Chateaubriand steaks.

Steak, T-bone This is the largest of all steaks and serves two portions. It is a thick cut from across the fillet end of the sirloin and includes both fillet and bone. Grill or fry.

Topside A very lean, boneless joint with a fine grain to the meat. It is best slow-roasted or pot-roasted, but it may also be braised or boiled. If topside is used for roasting, ask the butcher to tie a piece of fat round the joint to keep it moist.

Veal is often in short supply, except in large towns. As it is very dry with little fat, veal requires careful cooking. On its own, veal tends to be bland, and sauces, stuffings and seasonings are often used to provide additional flavour.

When buying veal, look for soft, finely grained and moist flesh, varying in colour from off-white to palest pink. Avoid flabby and wet veal, and also meat which is dry and brown or has a blue tinge or mottling. The lean should have a fine texture with a thin outside layer of firm, creamy-white fat. Bones should be soft and almost translucent. Do not be put off by what may seem an excessive amount of gelatinous tissue around the meat: this is a natural characteristic of the young, immature animal, and the tissues will rapidly soften and shrink during cooking.

In Britain, most calves are slaughtered at the age of three months. They have been reared on a diet of milk and fatty foods, which help to produce white flesh. These calves give high-quality veal, but as it is extremely expensive it is sold almost exclusively to the hotel and restaurant trade. Young calves, known as bobby calves and slaughtered before they are three weeks old, provide veal for the home market. It is less expensive than milk-fed veal, but apart from the top of the leg, this type of veal is more suitable for pie fillings and as stews and casseroles.

Imported veal, mainly from Holland and Denmark, is also available. The flesh is usually paler in colour than home-killed veal, but it compares well in flavour with British quality veal.

Best end of neck This medium-priced cut is seldom sold as a whole joint, but it can be boned, stuffed, rolled and roasted if trimmed of fat and tissue beforehand. It is more often cut into individual cutlets.

Best end cutlets Cut from the best end of the neck, at the top of the loin, these cutlets should be at least 1 in. thick. They should contain a good round eye of meat. Allow two cutlets for grilling or frying per person. Large cutlets may be trimmed away from the bone, and the gelatinous tissue removed. Beat the meat flat and cook it like escalopes.

Breast This is one of the most economical veal joints, and is often sold already boned and stuffed. It is excellent for braising, pot-roasting or slow boiling.

Chump or **loin chops** These come from the rear of the loin and are easily recognisable by the hole in the centre. The kidney is sometimes attached. They are not always an economical buy, as there is a high proportion of bone to meat. They are suitable for grilling or frying.

Escalopes These are cut from the fillet at the top of the hind leg. They contain no fat or tissue, and are considered the finest cuts of veal. Escalopes are cut, with the grain, ¼ in. thick and beaten into very thin slices. As the amount of fillet is very small, slices are sometimes cut from lower on the leg and sold as escalopes; they are less tender.

SCRAG

SHOU[

ROLLED
BREAST

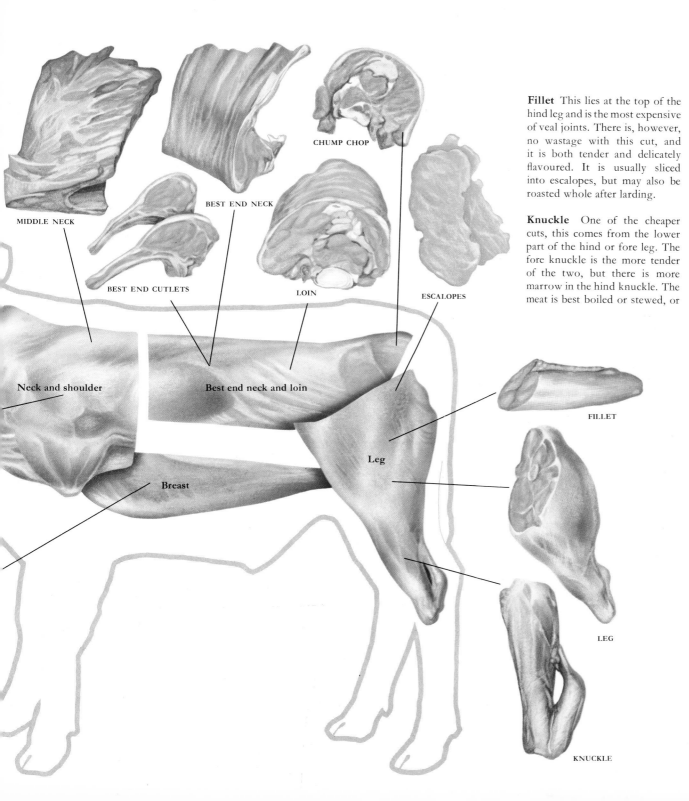

MIDDLE NECK

BEST END NECK

CHUMP CHOP

BEST END CUTLETS

LOIN

ESCALOPES

Neck and shoulder

Best end neck and loin

Breast

Leg

FILLET

LEG

KNUCKLE

Fillet This lies at the top of the hind leg and is the most expensive of veal joints. There is, however, no wastage with this cut, and it is both tender and delicately flavoured. It is usually sliced into escalopes, but may also be roasted whole after larding.

Knuckle One of the cheaper cuts, this comes from the lower part of the hind or fore leg. The fore knuckle is the more tender of the two, but there is more marrow in the hind knuckle. The meat is best boiled or stewed, or it may be trimmed off the bone and used for pie fillings. Boned and stuffed, a knuckle may be pot-roasted or braised.

Leg This is one of the larger and more expensive joints, with plenty of meat to bone. The fillet has been trimmed from the top of the hind leg and the knuckle removed. It is usually roasted on the bone for best flavour, but it may also be boned and stuffed before roasting to make carving easier.

Loin A prime cut, taken from between the best end and hind leg. It is sold as a whole joint on the bone, and is also sold already boned and stuffed. Loin is suitable for roasting. It may also be cut into single bone portions, as chops.

Middle neck An economical cut, but with a high proportion of fat, bone and tissue. It is sold boned or unboned, and can then be pot-roasted or braised. It is, however, better used as pie veal or for stock.

Scrag This is usually sold with middle neck in one piece for pot-roasting or boiling. It is inexpensive, but there is much wastage from bones and tissues. Most butchers chop scrag and offer it as pie veal.

Shoulder Sometimes known as cushion of veal, this is the cheapest roasting joint. It may be cooked on the bone, but is better boned and stuffed. The fore knuckle is sometimes removed and sold separately, leaving the meatiest part which is called the oyster cut.

Lamb

Most sheep are slaughtered when they are between three and fifteen months old and their flesh is sold as lamb. The term 'mutton' is usually applied to the flesh of sheep at least a year old, but there is no rigid dividing line between lamb and yearling mutton. Lamb is delicately flavoured meat, and a rich source of iron and other important minerals; it is rich in vitamins, especially those of the B complex, essential for the release of energy from all foods and for the general health of skin and nerve tissues.

The British eat far more lamb than most other nations, though less than the Australians and New Zealanders. About 40 per cent of the lamb eaten in Britain is home-produced; the remainder comes chiefly from Australia and New Zealand. By law a butcher must label all his meat with the country of origin.

The number of lambs slaughtered in Britain reaches a peak in October and drops to its lowest in the spring. Since the seasons in Australia and New Zealand are the opposite of Britain's, a constant flow of lamb supplies is maintained. Most imported New Zealand lamb is four to six months old.

British lamb varies in colour according to the age and breed of the animal. Meat from a young lamb is usually pale pink; red meat comes from an older animal. But some breeds, hill lambs for example, have a deep colour even when young. The fat should be creamy-white, not oily or yellow – a yellowish tinge shows excessive age.

Most imported and some home-produced lamb is frozen. Frozen meat has a less delicate flavour than fresh and it looks different: the lean is paler and does not have the bloom of fresh meat, while the fat is whiter and crumbles more easily – if the fat looks very brittle it is a sign that the lamb has been frozen too long.

A joint of lamb should have a good depth of lean meat covered by a moderate layer of fat. The skin should be pliable to the touch, not hard or wrinkled. Legs and shoulder joints should have a plump, not flat appearance. A blue tinge in the knuckle bones indicates that the animal is young.

Although the choicest cuts of lamb for roasting, grilling and frying come from the loin, legs and shoulders, do not ignore the cheaper cuts. Best end of neck, scrag and breast may take more time in the kitchen but they can be delicious and are as nourishing as the better-known cuts.

Best end of neck A tasty and versatile cut from between the middle neck and the loin. It may be braised or stewed, and is excellent roasted whole or boned and rolled. For a whole roast, the butcher will saw through the vertebrae – the bone known as the chine bone – without completely removing it. He will also strip off the thin outer skin.

Two best ends of neck are used to shape a crown, from which the skin and excess fat have been removed. The top of the rib bones are trimmed of meat. Most butchers will prepare a crown roast* on request. Fill the hollow of the crown with a stuffing.

Guard of honour is another popular roast, shaped from two best ends in such a way that the

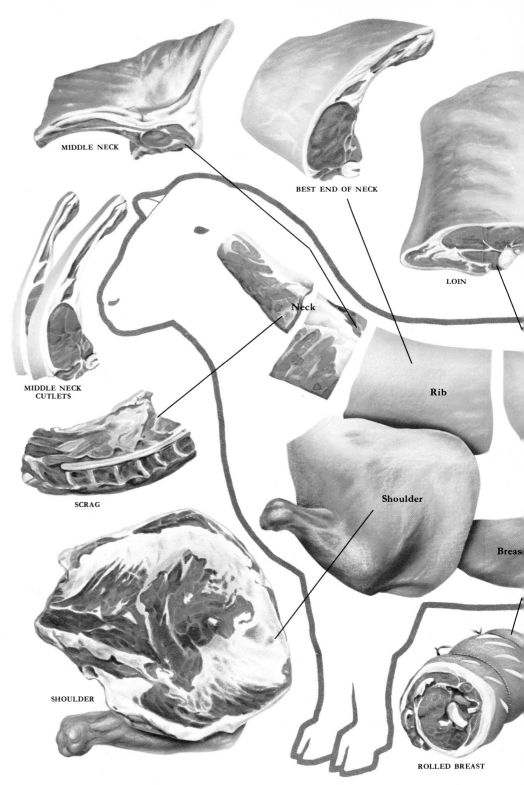

MIDDLE NECK

BEST END OF NECK

LOIN

Neck

MIDDLE NECK CUTLETS

Rib

SCRAG

Shoulder

Breas

SHOULDER

ROLLED BREAST

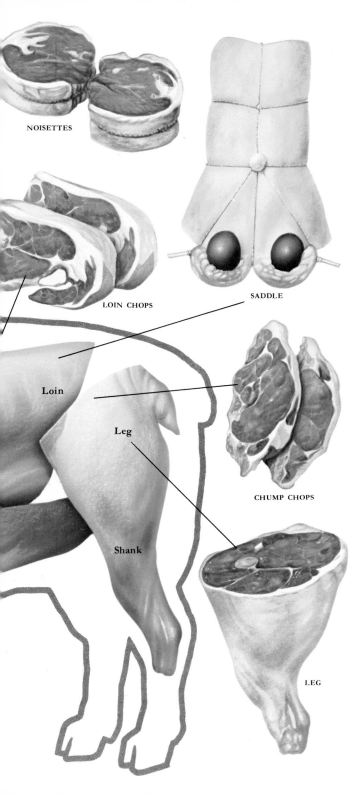

NOISETTES

LOIN CHOPS

SADDLE

Loin

Leg

Shank

CHUMP CHOPS

LEG

trimmed rib bones criss-cross on top. Give the butcher a few days' notice to prepare such a joint.

Breast A very economical cut, which is usually sold boned, stuffed and rolled, for roasting or braising. Lean breast can be chopped into pieces and stewed or boiled.

Chops These individual cuts of lamb come either from the loin or the leg of the animal. They are suitable for grilling, frying or braising.

   Chump chops These chops, $\frac{3}{4}$–1 in. thick, are cut from the top of the leg. They are oval in shape with a small central bone, and are more expensive than loin chops, because each leg of the animal will give only three chops.

   Loin chops Cut from the loin, these chops, about 1 in. thick, have a small T-shaped bone, and a thin, even layer of fat running down the longer edge.

Cutlets These are taken from the neck portion as individual cuts. They have the characteristic long bone, a thin layer of fat and a small round of sweet lean meat, and are suitable for grilling and frying; allow two cutlets per person. French lamb cutlets are from the best end, and 'French' refers to the frilly paper garnish, not the shape of the cutlets. The chine bone is completely removed and about 2 in. of each rib bone is trimmed of meat. After grilling, decorative paper frills are put over the exposed bones.

   Middle neck cutlets These are fattier and more gristly than best end cutlets and are best stewed or braised.

Fillet The upper part of the leg, frequently sold as a separate joint. It has lean meat, little bone and no gristle. It is suitable for roasting whole on the bone. It can also be cut into cubes for kebabs or into thick slices; these are best grilled or fried.

Leg The most popular large roasting joint, weighing 4–5$\frac{1}{2}$ lb. It is sold on the bone and can also be ordered boned and rolled. The leg, being so large, is often divided into two joints: shank and fillet. Whole leg of lamb is suitable for roasting, braising and boiling.

   In Scotland, the leg or 'gigot' includes the chump end of the loin. It is usually divided into three portions, the shank, centre and chump.

Loin This prime joint is usually sold on the bone for roasting whole. A complete loin (saddle) weighs about 6 lb., but it is usually sold in smaller portions. It has a thin even layer of fat just below the skin. Ask the butcher to saw through the chine bone for easier carving. The loin may also be ordered rolled.

Middle neck This cut comes from between the shoulder, the best end of neck and the scrag end. It has a large proportion of bone and fat to meat and is best stewed. It is sold already chopped; remove any bone splinters.

Neck The complete neck is seldom sold whole, but cut into three portions, the scrag and middle for stewing and best end for roasting. Middle neck and scrag end are sometimes sold in one cut.

Noisettes These are small round and thick slices cut from the loin or best end. They are boned, trimmed of fat and shaped into round fillets. The butcher requires notice to prepare noisettes, or they can easily be shaped at home. They are suitable for grilling or frying.

Saddle This large, prime joint comprises both loins and is cut from the best end to the end of the loins and includes the two kidneys. It is usually skinned by the butcher before being dressed. A saddle weighs about 8 lb. and makes an ideal if expensive large roast.

Scrag end of neck This cut nearest the head contains much bone and gristle. It may be cut across into thick slices for slow braising, but is better used for stews and soups.

Shank The lower part of the leg. It has a large proportion of bone and gristle, but the meat is considered to be sweeter than the fillet. Use for roasting, and cut off the lowest part for stews, casseroles or pie fillings.

Shoulder This roasting joint comes from the fore-leg cut and is sold whole or divided into two smaller joints: blade and knuckle. It is the least expensive of the roasting joints, fattier than the leg, but with a sweeter flavour. The shoulder is more difficult to carve than the leg and is therefore often boned and rolled.

   In Scotland, a shoulder is cut as a larger joint, to include part of the neck and the breast. It is then divided into two or three joints and often boned and rolled.

Pork

Most pigs are slaughtered young, mainly because of the growing demand for lean pork. Those kept for breeding are older and fatter, and their carcasses are used in the meat processing and canning industry. Prime pork should be well developed, with small bones and without excessive fat – about $\frac{1}{2}$ in. fat over the lean meat of a loin, for example, is considered ideal.

Fresh pork does not keep as well as lamb or beef, and needs more care in buying, preparation and cooking. It used to be sold mainly during the winter months, owing to a superstition that it should not be sold during warm weather in the months spelt without an 'R'. It is now available all the year round, because of the use of refrigeration and cold storage. Over 90 per cent of fresh pork eaten in Britain is home-produced. It is highly nutritious, because it contains more B_1 vitamins, which prevent fatigue and stimulate the appetite, than any other meat.

The fat should be firm and a clear milky-white colour. Avoid cuts with soft, grey and oily fat which leads to excessive weight loss in cooking and difficulties in carving. The lean should be pale pink, firm and smooth to the touch and with very little gristle. Freshly cut surfaces should look slightly moist and the bones should be pinkish-blue. A good butcher will present pork with clean-cut edges.

The skin, or rind, should be thin, pliable, smooth and free of hairs; in older pigs the skin tends to coarsen and thicken. For crackling, make sure that the butcher scores the rind carefully so that the cuts are close together and penetrate the rind.

All pork joints can be roasted and, with the exception of the loin, salted and boiled. Bear this in mind when buying, since it is often more economical to buy whole joints, such as hand and spring, rather than small portions. The joint can then be separated, by the butcher or at home, into cuts for roasting, boiling or salting, and chops for grilling or frying.

Pork has more flavour if cooked on the bone, but many joints are often sold boned and rolled ready for stuffing. They should be seasoned before cooking and must never be under-cooked.

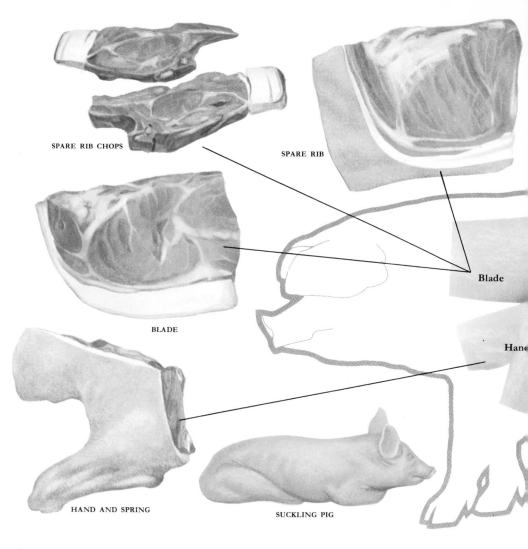

SPARE RIB CHOPS

SPARE RIB

Blade

BLADE

HAND AND SPRING

SUCKLING PIG

Hand

Belly, belly pork This is sometimes known as streaky, draft or flank pork. In London and the Home Counties the flank is the rear end of the belly. It is fairly fatty, and the best cut is a thick belly with a good proportion of lean meat. It is a cheap cut which is sold both fresh and salted. Fresh belly pork is good for roasting and can be boned, stuffed and rolled. It can also be chopped up for stews or sliced for grilling or frying. Salted belly pork should be soaked before boiling.

Blade A small, reasonably priced joint cut from the top part of the fore-leg. It may be roasted on the bone, or boned, stuffed and rolled for roasting or braising.

Chops These large, fairly expensive slices, generally 1 in. thick, come from the loin or the spare rib joints. They are all suitable for grilling, frying or baking. Loin chops weigh on average $\frac{1}{2}$ lb. each and have a thick layer of fat running along the outer edge. Using a pair of scissors,

snip through the fatty layer to its depth, to prevent the chops curling during cooking.

Chump chops These are cut from the hind loin and have a round central bone.

Loin chops Cuts from either the end of the fore loin or from the hind loin. They all have a T-bone, and chops from the hind loin usually come with the kidney left in. Prime loin chops should be cut from 'hogmeats', the trade name for loins of pork which have had the rind and excessive

fat removed. These chops are most suitable for grilling and frying.

Spare rib chops These are cut from the spare rib joint just behind the head. They are not as thick as chump and loin chops, as they are leaner and contain little bone. They are not to be confused with spare ribs, which come from the belly.

Fillet or tenderloin This is the lean and tender muscle which lies underneath the backbone in the

hind loin. It is obtained from bacon pigs when the carcasses are cut up for curing. This choice cut for roasting, braising, grilling and frying is covered in a near-transparent thin skin which must be peeled off. For roasting whole, the fillet is best cut through half its thickness, spread with a filling and rolled up.

Fillet half leg The top end of the hind leg. It is roasted whole on the bone or cut into steaks for grilling or frying.

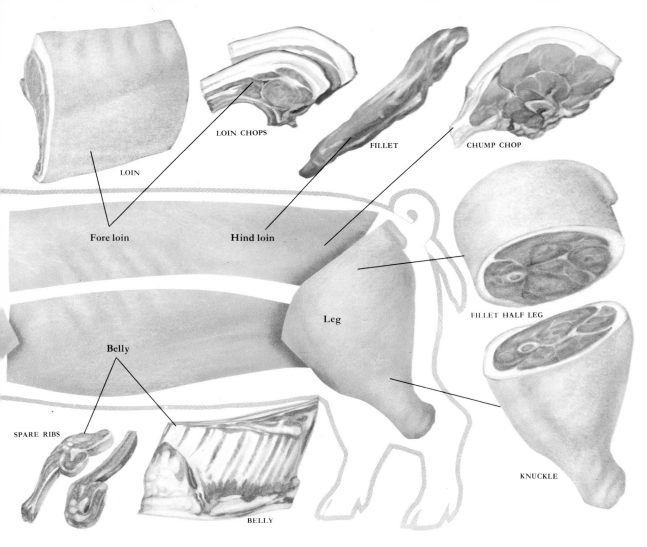

LOIN CHOPS

FILLET

CHUMP CHOP

LOIN

Fore loin

Hind loin

Leg

FILLET HALF LEG

Belly

SPARE RIBS

KNUCKLE

BELLY

Hand The top part of the fore-leg, often sold cut in one with the spring, either fresh or salted. The hand has a large area of rind for crisp crackling, and is ideal, boned, stuffed and rolled, for roasting and braising.

Hand and spring The complete fore-leg, which is known as shoulder in north-east England. Hand and spring is a large, relatively inexpensive joint sold whole or divided into two. When buying this joint, look for one which is compact and well fleshed with fat. It is particularly economical when bought whole. The knuckle end can be cut off and salted for boiling; two or three steaks can be cut from the narrow end and used for grilling or frying, while the centre portion of the joint can be roasted whole.

In Scotland, the hand and spring is known as a runner.

Knuckle In Scotland this large joint is known as hough. It is cut from the lower part of the leg. Knuckle is fairly expensive and can be roasted whole or boned and stuffed. It is also excellent for boiling and stewing. On a prime joint, the knuckle should have a tinge of blue.

Leg Another prime cut for roasting, known as gigot in Scotland. It is a large joint, a whole leg weighing 10–15 lb. It is usually cut into two joints, the upper fillet half leg and the lower knuckle.

Loin Considered by many people to be the choicest cut of pork, the loin is also the most expensive. It is a large joint which may be roasted whole, but it is usually sold as fore loin and hind loin joints, often with the kidney attached. Both loin and chump chops come from this joint.

Fore loin A prime cut for roasting on the bone. The chine bone should be sawn through by the butcher. Like best end of lamb, the joint can also be pre-pared for a crown roast; give the butcher a few days' notice.

Hind loin May be roasted whole or boned and rolled.

Neck end This cut includes the blade bone and the spare rib joint and is known in north-east England as chine. In Scotland it is called shoulder and is cut larger, weighing up to 20 lb. Look for a compact joint, with an even distribution of fat and a large amount of lean. It is usually cut into two joints and roasted off the bone, or braised or stewed.

Spare rib The part of the neck end which remains when the blade has been removed. It is a fairly lean, inexpensive joint with little skin, and a good amount of meat. Spare rib is suitable for roasting, braising or stewing. The meat may also be cut into cubes and used for kebabs, with bacon rolls and pieces of liver.

Spare ribs These are the rib bones from the spare rib joint, cut into single portions. They are delicious roasted, braised or stewed. *Chinese spare ribs*, how-ever, are cut from the lean part of the belly. They are shorter than spare ribs and are trimmed of all fat and have only a thin layer of meat.

Spring The knuckle part of the fore-leg, often sold with the hand, fresh or salted. Use it boned, stuffed and rolled for roasting, pot-roasting or braising.

Sucking (suckling) pig A young pig from three weeks to two months old when slaughtered. It is usually spit-roasted to obtain the golden crisp skin.

41

Bacon, Gammon and Ham

Bacon and ham come from pigs especially reared to produce certain proportions of lean meat to fat. Bacon comes from the body of the pig, and the gammon comes from the hind legs. Bacon and gammon are cured together in brine for 4 days and then stacked in maturing rooms for 7–11 days. At the end of this stage bacon is known as green bacon, the rind is pale, the flesh pink and the flavour is delicate. Green bacon is less expensive than smoked, but does not keep as well.

Gammon is cut from the carcass after brining; it may be smoked separately or left unsmoked.

Further processing by drying and smoking produces smoked bacon, which has dark pink flesh and a golden rind. Smoking considerably increases the keeping quality of gammon and bacon, as well as enhancing the flavour. Bacon, whether green or smoked, should have firm moist flesh and the fat should be white to cream with no yellow or green tinges.

Bacon and gammon are sold in joints, boned and rolled, or in rashers and steaks. Since the introduction of the Landrace pig from Sweden in the 1950's, Britain's farmers have been remarkably successful in meeting the demand for ever leaner bacon. Streaky bacon today means lean bacon streaked with fat, not fat bacon streaked with lean.

Ham, which comes from the hind leg of the pig, is removed from the carcass before salting and is then cured according to local methods. Choose a ham which is short and thick, but not too fatty, with a thin rind. Cooked ham, usually sold sliced, should look fresh with white fat and pink flesh. Both shoulder and collar are cured in the same way as ham. Although they lack its delicate flavour and texture, they can be used instead of ham, particularly cut up or minced. Shoulder and collars are also cheaper than ham.

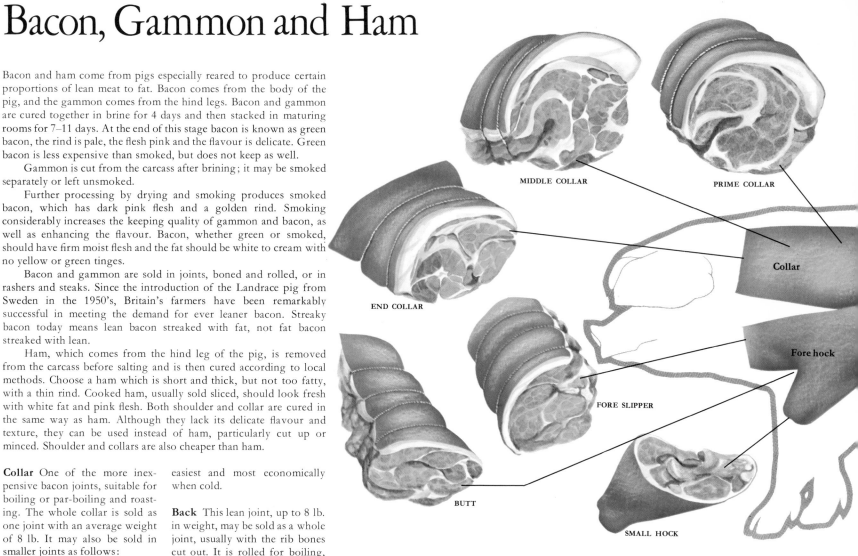

MIDDLE COLLAR

PRIME COLLAR

END COLLAR

Collar

Fore hock

FORE SLIPPER

BUTT

SMALL HOCK

Collar One of the more inexpensive bacon joints, suitable for boiling or par-boiling and roasting. The whole collar is sold as one joint with an average weight of 8 lb. It may also be sold in smaller joints as follows:

End collar A small cut usually weighing up to 2 lb. A good boiling joint, also used as a base for soups.

Middle collar This is a slightly larger and thicker cut than the end collar, and may be cooked in the same way.

Prime collar An excellent small joint for boiling and roasting, equally good cold or for frying and grilling. It may also be cut into rashers, but carves easiest and most economically when cold.

Back This lean joint, up to 8 lb. in weight, may be sold as a whole joint, usually with the rib bones cut out. It is rolled for boiling, braising or baking. It may also be cut into two smaller joints, long back and short. More often, however, back is sold as rashers for grilling or frying.

Top back rashers Taken from the leanest part of the back, these short, perfectly lean rashers are ideal for grilling.

Middle or through cut A good economy buy which contains both back and streaky bacon. The cut may be boned

and rolled, and is ideal for baking. Alternatively, cut the joint into rashers and cut these again into meaty and streaky rashers. The short meaty rashers are good grilled for breakfast, and the streaky for bacon rolls, larding or dicing for stews.

Oyster cut This comes from the rear part of the back and is sold with the bone in. It is sometimes sold as a boned and rolled joint, weighing about 1½

lb., and is suitable for boiling – serve hot or cold. Oyster cut is also sold as small rashers for grilling or frying.

Short back Leaner than top and middle cut, this is nearly always sold as rashers, which are fairly expensive. It may also be cut into ½–¾ in. thick chops, suitable for grilling.

Long back This is the leanest and most choice cut of bacon. It comes from just above the

gammon joint and is equally expensive. Long back rashers are cut thinly and are suitable for grilling and frying.

Gammon A whole gammon, 12–14 lb., is the hind leg of a bacon pig and is cut square at the top, unlike ham. Gammon is more expensive than other bacon joints; it may be par-boiled and baked whole, but is usually cut into four different joints:

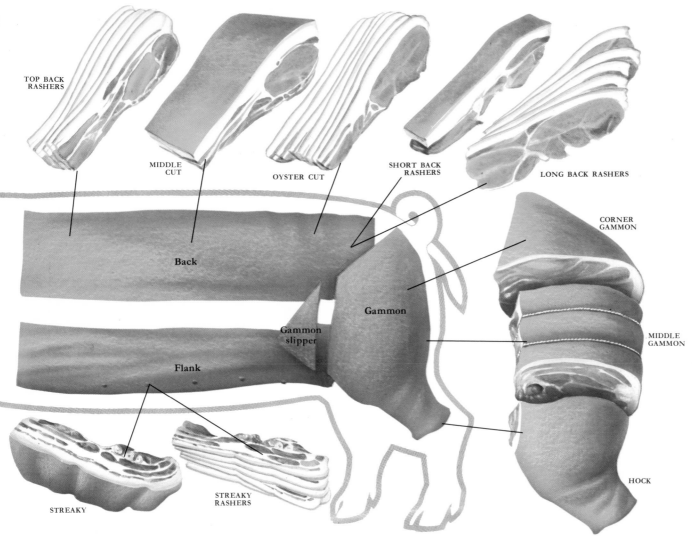

TOP BACK RASHERS

MIDDLE CUT

OYSTER CUT

SHORT BACK RASHERS

LONG BACK RASHERS

CORNER GAMMON

Back

Gammon slipper

Gammon

MIDDLE GAMMON

Flank

HOCK

STREAKY

STREAKY RASHERS

round top. It is removed from the carcass before salting and is then cured according to local recipes. A whole ham weighs approximately 16 lb. and is sold whole or cut into slices. Some butchers will boil whole hams at no extra charge, but as cooking depends on the type of curing, most hams come with instructions. Well-known English hams include Bradenham, Suffolk, Wiltshire and York hams.

Bradenham ham Smaller than most other hams, this is soaked in molasses rather than salt, which turns its skin black. The meat is more red than pink. Bradenham hams are hung for months to develop their distinctive, slightly sweet flavour. This type of ham is not easily obtainable and is expensive.

Suffolk ham Like the Bradenham ham, this is also soaked in molasses. This expensive ham has a full yet delicate flavour.

Wiltshire ham Cured before being removed from the side of the pig, this is, strictly speaking, gammon rather than ham. Therefore, it lacks the flavour of ham cured separately. Mild cured, the Wiltshire ham has a delicate taste, but it does not keep as well as other hams. The cheapest type of English ham.

York ham This ham is cured with dry salt instead of brine and is then lightly smoked. It is firm and tender, and has a delicate pink meat with a mild flavour. York hams weigh about 16–24 lb., and are usually sold at Christmas, although smaller ones, weighing about 12 lb., are available. The name 'York ham' is sometimes loosely used to mean any ham for cooking, to distinguish it from smoked ham, which is eaten raw.

Corner gammon This triangular joint is cut from the top of the leg and weighs about 4 lb. It is a lean joint, suitable for boiling and baking.

Middle gammon A succulent and lean gammon joint from the middle of the leg, of even shape and excellent flavour. It weighs on average 5 lb. and is an ideal joint for boiling and baking. Gammon rashers and steaks for grilling and frying are cut from the joint.

Hock or gammon knuckle The cheapest of the gammon joints, with a high proportion of bone. Usually boned and rolled for boiling.

Gammon slipper This small and lean triangular joint comes from the inside of the hind leg. It is an economical buy and the traditional joint for boiling.

Flank or belly The long belly joint has alternate layers of fat

and lean meat and always contains some gristle. It is sold in small joints for boiling, but it is more often sliced into rashers.

Fore hock This is the whole foreleg of a bacon pig. It is one of the cheapest joints, weighing about 8 lb. Usually cut up and sold in three smaller joints:

Butt The largest of the fore hock joints, weighing up to 4 lb. Suitable for boiling or baking.

Fore slipper A smaller and fattier joint. Like butt it can be boned and rolled; best boiled and served cold.

Small hock The knuckle end, weighing about 3 lb. It is a tough bone joint, and the flesh is best cut from the bone and used in casseroles.

Ham This is the hind leg of the pig and corresponds to the gammon except for its characteristic

Offal

The word 'offal' comes from 'off falls' – those parts of slaughtered pigs, cattle or sheep which are left after the carcass has been cut up. Despite the fact that offal includes some of the most appetising and nourishing food to be bought from the butcher, it has always been given a low status among meats, because of its association with scraps, waste, and parts that are thrown away. It is even spoken of in the homely language of the Anglo-Saxon farmyard, rather than in the polite Norman French which is used for cuts of meat. This is apparent in terms such as calf's liver and pig's liver, rather than veal liver or pork liver. The Americans use the term 'variety meats' to describe offal, but the name has never caught on in Britain.

Many types of offal – liver for example – are excellent sources of the minerals and vitamins necessary for good health. Much offal – brains, sweetbreads and tripe, to mention a few – is also easily digestible and therefore suitable for a building-up diet.

Ironically, certain types of offal, such as brains and calf's liver and sweetbreads, are considered such gourmet's delicacies that they are often priced out of the market for the average housewife. But generally, offal compares favourably with meat in price. It seldom requires lengthy preparation and cooking, and as it contains no bones and little fat or gristle, wastage is cut to the minimum.

Offal does not store well; it should be used on the day of purchase and stored in the refrigerator until prepared for cooking.

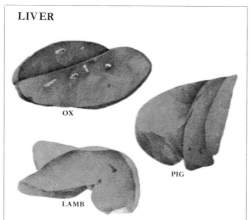

LIVER

OX

PIG

LAMB

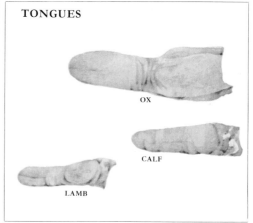

TONGUES

OX

CALF

LAMB

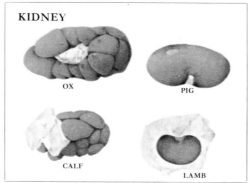

KIDNEY

OX

PIG

CALF

LAMB

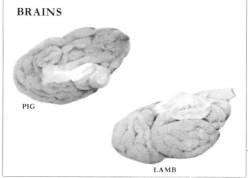

BRAINS

PIG

LAMB

Liver The best and most expensive is calf's liver, the cheapest ox. The latter has the strongest flavour, followed by pig's, lamb's and calf's liver in that order.

Calf's liver The best and most expensive. It is suitable for grilling and frying and should always be cooked slightly underdone, as it quickly becomes hard and dry.

Lamb's liver Less expensive than calf's liver and excellent for frying, grilling and braising. Like calf's liver it should remain pink in the centre after cooking. Also good for pâtés and terrines.

Pig's liver Stronger in flavour and softer in texture than both calf's and lamb's, pig's liver may be grilled or fried. It is, however, better used for pâtés or included in stews and casseroles.

Ox liver A coarse and tough liver, not recommended for grilling or frying. It should be soaked in milk or lightly salted water for a few hours to mellow the strong flavour. It can then be stewed or braised, in $\frac{1}{4}$ in. thick slices, either on its own or in combination with stewing steak.

Kidneys Ox kidney is the largest and coarsest, followed by the similar but smaller and more tender calf's kidney. Lamb's kidney has a different shape, and is usually sold surrounded by a thick, white deposit of suet. Pig's kidney looks similar to lamb's kidney, but is bigger and flatter and lacks the suet.

Calf's kidney In short supply. Prepare and use as for ox kidney. Calf's kidney, being more tender, may also be braised or stewed on its own.

Lamb's kidney The best kidney for grilling or frying. Remove the suet deposit, peel off the skin and snip out the cores before grilling the kidneys.

Pig's kidney May be grilled or fried or chopped up for stews and casseroles. Cut in half and snip out the gristly cores before grilling or frying.

Ox kidney This large kidney, about $1\frac{1}{2}$ lb. in weight, is usually tough and suitable only for slow-cooking stews, pies and meat puddings.

Tongues Ox and lamb's tongues are the most readily available. Calf's tongue is rare, and pig's tongue is always sold with the head.

Lamb's tongue A small tongue weighing only about 8 oz. Should be soaked in slightly salted water before boiling or braising. Skin before serving the tongue hot or cold.

Ox tongue This weighs 4–6 lb. and can be bought fresh or salted. It must be slowly boiled for several hours, and the rough skin removed before serving.

Brains Calf's brains have the most delicate flavour, but are usually in short supply. Lamb's brains are more easily bought and may be used in any recipe for calf's brains. Both types of brains must be soaked in cold water for a couple of hours to remove all blood.

Pig's brains are occasionally available, and should be prepared as calf's or lamb's brains.

Heads Pig's, sheep's and occasionally calf's heads are sold whole or in halves.

Calf's head Bought fresh or salted. A fresh head may be boiled and served hot with a creamy or vinaigrette sauce. Salted calf's head is used for brawns.

Pig's head The best brawn is made from boiled pig's head. The cheeks of the head are sometimes cured and boiled. These are known as Bath Chaps.

Sheep's head Almost as rare as a calf's head. It can be boiled or stewed, used as a base for broths or for pie fillings.

Hearts All hearts make good nutritious eating, but require long slow cooking.

Calf's heart A tender piece of offal, rarely seen. It is suitable for roasting and stewing.

HEADS

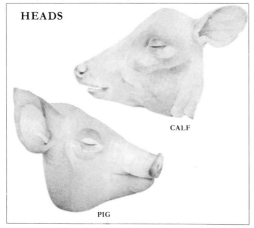

CALF

PIG

SWEETBREADS

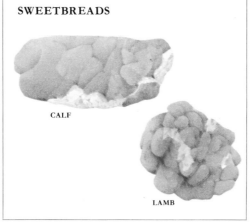

CALF

LAMB

HEARTS

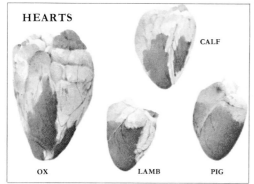

CALF

OX

LAMB

PIG

FEET

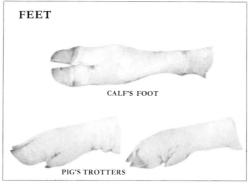

CALF'S FOOT

PIG'S TROTTERS

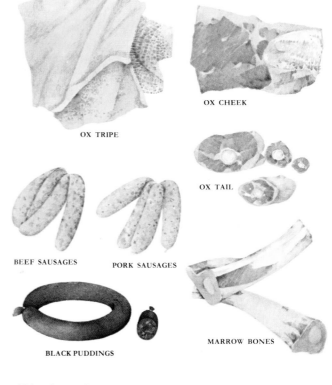

OX TRIPE

OX CHEEK

OX TAIL

BEEF SAUSAGES

PORK SAUSAGES

BLACK PUDDINGS

MARROW BONES

Lamb's heart This is the smallest and most tender heart. It is excellent stuffed and braised, or roasted.

Ox heart A muscular and tough piece of offal weighing up to 4 lb. It is best used chopped in stews and casseroles.

Pig's heart This is larger and less tender than lamb's heart, usually inexpensive and may be stuffed and slowly braised.

Sweetbreads This is the name given to the two portions of the thymus gland, one in the throat and one in the chest cavity (heart bread). Sweetbreads, and especially those from lamb and calf, are sold in pairs and are considered a delicacy. Pig's sweetbreads are not sold.

Calf's sweetbreads These are the least expensive, and more tender than ox, but lack the delicate flavour of lamb's sweetbreads. Suitable, after poaching*, for braising or frying.

Lamb's sweetbreads The finest sweetbreads, and the most expensive. They should be poached, braised or fried.

Ox sweetbreads Large and tough, with a strong flavour that does not compare with that of lamb or calf.

Feet Pig's trotters are the ones most frequently seen, either fresh or brined. Cow heel, once a favourite ingredient for jellied stock, is now rarely seen. Calf's foot, too, is rare and must be ordered well in advance.

Calf's foot This contains a high proportion of gelatine and is ideal for stock to be used with jellied moulds of meat or poultry. It was formerly much used for invalid food.

Pig's trotters These may be used instead of a calf's foot, for making jellied stock, and as a base for lentil soups. They are also suitable, after boiling, for inclusion in braws.

Tripe This comes from the ox and is the lining of the stomach. Tripe from the first stomach is the smoothest and is known as blanket. From the second stomach comes the honeycomb tripe. Both types of tripe should be thick, firm and white; avoid any that looks slimy and grey.

Tripe is usually sold cleaned and partly boiled – ask the butcher how much longer it should be cooked. It can be stewed, boiled in milk, or sliced and deep fried.

Ox cheek Economical cut, used for stews and brawns.

Oxtail This is sold ready skinned and jointed; the fat should be a creamy-white and the lean meat deep red. Excellent braised or in casseroles, and as a basis for soups.

Sausages These are made by blending lean and fat meat with cereal, seasonings and additives. The meat is put into manufactured casings. Sausages should be refrigerated until required.

Beef sausages Also available as chipolatas or small sausages. By law, beef sausages must contain at least 50 per cent meat, of which at least half must be lean. Suitable for grilling and frying.

Pork sausages and chipolatas These must contain at least 65 per cent meat, and at least 50 per cent should be lean.

Marrow bones These thigh and shoulder bones from beef contain delicately flavoured marrow. Poached marrow is used as a spread for hors-d'oeuvre.

Black pudding A Northern favourite, it is a mixture of pig's blood and suet stuffed into pig's intestines and boiled. It is cut into thick slices and fried or grilled.

British Cheeses

There is a vast choice of cheeses available in Britain, either home-produced or imported from the Continent. These include hard, semi-soft and creamy cheeses. This wide choice brings its own problems, however, and since supermarkets have largely replaced the family grocer, who knew each customer's likes and dislikes, the housewife must rely on her own judgment when surrounded by a wide variety of cheeses, some of them unknown to her.

A minority of shops nowadays cut from the whole cheese as and when the customer requires. It is more usual, especially in self-service supermarkets, for the whole cheese to be cut in advance into pieces of varying weight which are then wrapped and put on display.

Since the smaller the piece of cheese the more quickly it will dry out, there is more chance of buying a stale piece when cheese is cut in advance, although the supermarkets argue that with a high turn-over of dairy products and a vigilant staff this should not occur.

However, when buying from either the whole cheese, or a ready-cut pre-packed piece, avoid anything which looks too dry, too hard, too soft and, especially if pre-packed, cheese which looks as if it has 'sweated'.

Suspect any pieces of cheese, particularly the 'hard-pressed' varieties such as English Cheddar, Leicester or Gloucester, which show numerous cracks running in from the edges, or which have a marked difference in colour between the centre and the edge. These are sure signs that it is not fresh and has started to dry out.

Once a cheese has matured it does not improve with keeping, especially when cut, so buy from day to day if possible rather than stocking up with a fortnight's supply.

Ideally, cheese should be kept in a plastic container in a cool larder, but if this is not possible a refrigerator is the next best place.

Never serve either hard-pressed or soft cheeses direct from the refrigerator. Cold temperatures mask the flavour of most foods and cheese is no exception.

Instead, take it from the refrigerator at least one hour before it is to be eaten and serve it at room temperature – like the red wine which accompanies cheese so well.

LANCASTER GLOUCESTER ENGLISH CHEDDAR DUNLOP CANADIAN WINE CHEDDAR CABOC

Ayrshire soft cheese This Scottish cheese is soft and creamy, with a low fat content. It has a nutty, slightly salty flavour, perfect as a table cheese with oatcakes and crispbread.

Caboc A rich, soft, full-cream cheese, Caboc is seldom seen south of Scotland. Pale, almost pure white on the inside, it is rolled in toasted oatmeal, and is best eaten spread on biscuits with no butter.

Caerphilly A moist, white cheese with a mild, slightly salty flavour. Caerphilly is easily digestible and can be eaten in larger quantities than most other cheeses.

Caithness A medium to strong-tasting cheese which spreads and slices well. Caithness has a soft yellow colour and is often tartan-wrapped. It matures early (traditionally in 60 days) and is best when comparatively young.

Cheddar This is probably the most popular of all English cheeses – certainly the best known and most widely sold. English Cheddar has a strong yellow colour and a close, creamy texture. Its full, nutty flavour, varying in strength, makes it a good all-purpose cheese. Scottish Cheddar has a firmer texture than English and often a stronger flavour; a red version is much sought after in Scotland.

Imported Australian and New Zealand Cheddar cheeses are deeper yellow than English Cheddar and have a milder flavour.

Canadian Cheddar is similar in colour, texture and flavour to English. The strongest Canadian Cheddar is Black Diamond.

Canadian Wine Cheddar This moist cheese, matured with red wine, is often sold still wrapped in hessian.

Cheshire The oldest British cheese, Cheshire has a savoury, mellow and slightly salty taste. White Cheshire is really pale yellow in colour. Red Cheshire is coloured with a vegetable dye which makes it look more like Red Leicester. An excellent cheese for grilling.

Blue Cheshire This cheese is a rarity since it has to be kept under special conditions after injections of mould to produce the blue veining inside. It is more expensive than ordinary Cheshire and has a stronger flavour, similar to Stilton.

Cottage cheese Made from skimmed milk curds, cottage cheese is low in calories due to its low fat content. It is almost pure white, with a mild bland flavour.

Crowdie A Scottish type of cottage cheese, made from skimmed milk. The grains are finer than those of ordinary cottage cheese and have a mild, fresh flavour. High in protein.

LEICESTER

CAERPHILLY

DERBY

SAGE DERBY

CHESHIRE

STILTON

CAITHNESS

WENSLEYDALE

MORVEN

BLUE CHESHIRE

RED WINDSOR

Derby Honey-coloured and close-textured, Derby cheese has to mature for at least six months for its mild, distinctive flavour to develop to the full.

Sage Derby This is a variation of Derby with the same characteristics. Chopped fresh sage is incorporated in layers during the cheese-making and complements the mild flavour. In scant supply, Derby cheese is not recommended for cooking.

Dunlop A moist Scottish cheese, rather like English Cheddar but with a softer texture and usually milder in flavour. It has the colour of pale butter. Good for grilling.

Gloucester Properly Double Gloucester, the flavour varies according to maturity. It may be mellow and creamy, or have a distinct 'bite' to it. It should never be pungent. Traditionally, Double Gloucester cheese was the colour of Guernsey milk, but today artificial colouring gives it a rich golden hue. Matured for between three and six months, it has a firm, smooth texture. Serve with crusty bread.

Hramsa Made from double cream, this Scottish soft cheese is flavoured with wild garlic gathered in the Highlands. Serve as a dessert cheese.

Lancashire One of the best cheeses for cooking because of its high fat content, Lancashire has a crumbly texture and an off-white colour. At its best it spreads like butter. Excellent for Welsh Rarebit or grated for topping soups and dishes to be grilled *au gratin*.

Leicester One of the milder cheeses, a true Leicester is characterised by its flaky texture. More compressed varieties, often called Red Leicester because of the orange-red colouring of the rind, are made nowadays. Good for sauces and grillings, and at its best when three months old.

Morven A mild Scottish cheese made in small squares and with a full flavour and texture somewhat similar to that of Dutch Gouda. It is also sometimes available with a flavouring of caraway seeds.

Red Windsor One of the lesser-known English cheeses, Red Windsor has a crumbly texture and a mild flavour similar to that of Caerphilly. It is best eaten with biscuits or salads; not recommended for cooking.

Stilton Between the distinctive patches of blue mould, Stilton when properly ripened should be

a rich creamy colour, not white which is a sign of immaturity. It is at its best between November and April and has a strong, sometimes tangy, lingering taste. Although Stilton dries out very quickly do not be tempted by tradition to soak it in port since this will only mask its true flavour. Best eaten with biscuits, and with a glass of port to accompany it.

Wensleydale Crumbly in texture, Wensleydale varies in colour from white to creamy-yellow, but has a consistently mild taste. In the North it is traditionally served with apple pie. It is also good for cooking.

47

French Cheeses

There are hundreds of different regional cheeses in France, although only a small proportion are imported into Britain. However, these include the best known varieties which have given France its reputation as one of the finest cheese-producing countries.

Camembert and Brie are perhaps the best known of all, but Roquefort, Pont l'Evêque, Port-Salut, various processed and cream cheeses, such as Boursin, Petit Suisse and Crème de Gruyère, are very popular.

Buy Camembert, Brie and similar soft cheeses in small quantities and eat them without delay. This is necessary because soft cheeses do not keep as well as hard varieties, unless they have been processed. They should be soft right through for a perfect flavour. If the cheese is a little under-ripe, allow it to mature for two or three days. Camembert should come from Normandy, and Brie from the Ile de France. Avoid any imitations from other places.

The blue cheeses, such as Roquefort, taste salty because salt is added to them to slow down the growth of mould on the outside while the inside matures. Unlike most other cheeses, these salty cheeses remain good even when they are slightly over-ripe.

French Gruyère and similar cheeses, such as Comté, can be used in the same way as their more famous Swiss counterparts, Gruyère and Emmenthal, to make fondues. In warm weather, store cheese in the refrigerator, covered with polythene or in a plastic container. Take cheese out of the refrigerator some time before it is due to be eaten; Brie and Camembert need about one hour.

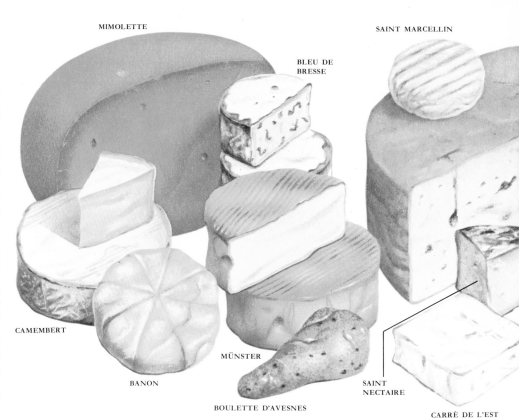

MIMOLETTE

SAINT MARCELLIN

BLEU DE BRESSE

CAMEMBERT

MÜNSTER

BANON

BOULETTE D'AVESNES

SAINT NECTAIRE

CARRÉ DE L'EST

Banon A pungent-tasting cheese, originally made only from goats' milk, Banon is now mixed with cows' milk or made exclusively from cows' milk. If the label does not specify the milk, the cheese will be cows' milk only. Banon is dipped in *eau de vie,* then into rosemary and winter savory leaves, or chestnut leaves which have been soaked in *eau de vie.* Traditionally, Banon is left to ripen and mature in stone jars.

Bleu d'Auvergne, Bleu de Salers A blue cheese, less delicate than Roquefort, made from a mixture of goats', ewes' and cows' milk. This cheese is the same size and shape as Roquefort.

Bleu de Bresse A soft, creamy, dark-veined blue cheese with a

rich taste, sold wrapped in foil and boxed. It is made from unskimmed cows' milk. When over-ripe, it goes salty and dry.

Bleu des Causses, Bleu de l'Aveyron A blue cheese, less piquant than Roquefort, made from cows' milk.

Boulette d'Avesnes, Boulette de Cambrai A spicy buttermilk cheese flavoured with herbs.

Boursin, Boursault Two brand names for the same triple cream cheese, which is soft, thick and flavoured with either herbs, garlic or pepper (*poivre*).

Brie A large, round, soft, pale yellow cheese, about 3 in. thick, with a slightly reddish edible crust and a delicate flavour. One of the

world's great cheeses, Brie is made from cows' milk, and is usually sold in slices.

Brie fermier is made on the farm with modern methods and is considered the best. Brie laitier is factory-made.

Brie is fully ripe when the cheese has a consistent texture. Press the surface and the cheese should bulge but not run. At its best from October to April.

Camembert This world-famous cheese from Normandy is round, soft, creamy, pale yellow in colour, with a thick crust. It has a much stronger taste than Brie. It is made from whole cows' milk. Sold whole in boxes or in individually wrapped portions. The ripeness test is the same as for Brie: do not allow Camembert to become over-ripe,

otherwise it tastes bitter. At its best from October to June.

Cantal, Fourme de Salers This is a hard, strong, pale yellow cheese which is made from cows' milk. It is one of the largest of French cheeses, and comes from the Cantal and Auvergne regions of France. It has a flavour like Cheddar; best between November and May.

Carré de l'Est A square, soft cheese, with a high fat content; it is similar to Camembert but milder in flavour.

Comté A firm, yellowish cheese with holes. Good for cooking.

Coulommiers A soft, yellowish cream cheese which has a white crust tinged with grey. This

cheese has a stronger, less mellow taste than Brie, with a faint almond flavour. Best between November and March.

Demi-sel A small, square, fresh cream cheese, weighing about 4 oz. It has very little salt and tastes almost like cream. Sold wrapped under various brand names. The best and creamiest Demi-sel comes from Normandy.

Epoisses A soft, round cheese with an orange crust, made from curdled milk and sometimes flavoured with black pepper, clove or fennel, then soaked in wine or *eau de vie.* Epoisses comes from Provence.

Fourme d'Ambert A veined sharp blue cheese, shaped like a drum, crumbly in texture and

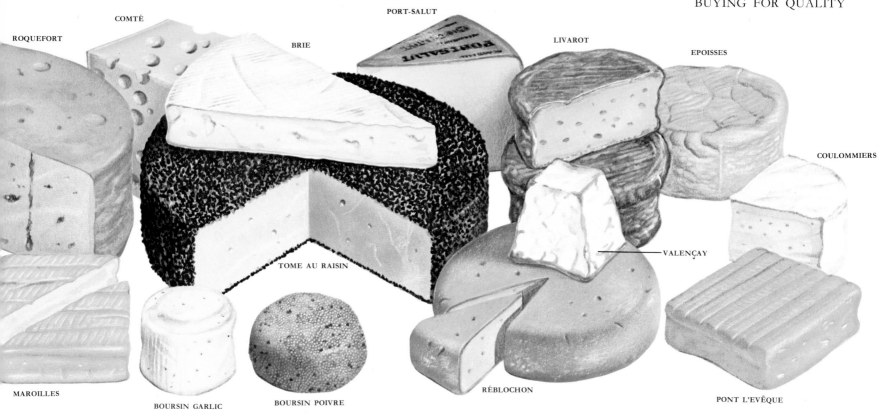

ROQUEFORT   COMTÉ   BRIE   PORT-SALUT   LIVAROT   EPOISSES

COULOMMIERS

TOME AU RAISIN   VALENÇAY

MAROILLES   BOURSIN GARLIC   BOURSIN POIVRE   RÉBLOCHON   PONT L'EVÊQUE

slightly salty. This cheese is from the Auvergne.

Fromage de Monsieur An oval double cream cheese with a high fat content. It can be eaten when it is slightly under-ripe. It is sometimes salty. Made in Normandy.

Gaperon, Gapron A white buttermilk cheese, dry and piquant when ripe.

Gruyère The true Gruyère is only made in the French-speaking area of Switzerland, but essentially the same cheese is made over the border in France. A firm, pale cheese with small holes and a crinkled, slightly greasy, golden-brown rind. Excellent as a dessert cheese, and for cooking, especially *fondues*.

Crème de Gruyère Processed Gruyère cheese, soft with a mild taste, sold in portions.

Langres A semi-hard or creamy cheese, usually sold in slices.

Livarot A soft, yellow cheese with a dark reddish-brown rind; made from skimmed milk. Livarot has a very strong flavour, more pungent than Camembert.

Maroilles A square, semi-hard, slightly salted, yellow cheese with a reddish-brown rind, and a strong flavour and smell.

Mimolette A round orange cheese with grey rind; mild.

Münster A semi-soft, creamy-textured cheese with a reddish

rind and a powerful flavour. Münster, which comes from the Alsace region, is sometimes flavoured with cumin or aniseed. Best, November to April.

Petit Suisse A very creamy un-salted cheese, made from whole milk and extra cream, which has a faintly sour flavour and is often eaten with sugar. It is always sold in small triangles individually wrapped.

Pont l'Evêque A square, semi-soft, pale yellow cheese with a crinkled yellow crust. Pont l'Evêque has a rich, distinctive flavour.

Port-Salut A semi-hard, yellow cheese with a reddish rind and a bland taste which gets stronger when it is fully ripe.

Réblochon A soft cheese, pale cream in colour with an orange to chestnut rind. It has a bland taste which turns bitter when it is over-ripe.

Roquefort A crumbly blue cheese with a delicate but piquant flavour. Roquefort is made from ewes' milk curds sprinkled with breadcrumbs, specially treated with mould to make the characteristic green veins. The cheese is ripened in limestone caves.

Saingorlon A sharp blue cheese, recently introduced, which is the French equivalent of the soft Italian Gorgonzola cheese.

Saint Marcellin A small, round, crumbly cream cheese made from goats' milk. Saint Marcellin has a mild taste with a touch of salt.

Saint Nectaire A semi-hard, pale yellow cheese with a rind blended red, white and yellow and a bland but subtle flavour.

Saint Paulin A semi-hard, yellow cheese with a bland taste indistinguishable from Port-Salut.

Tome de Savoie A semi-hard yellow, strong-flavoured cheese with a reddish rind.

Tome au Raisin A white, slightly chewy cheese covered with a mixture of dried black grape skins and pips.

Valençay or **Levroux** A soft goat cheese, full-flavoured and creamy, with a grey crust made by dusting the cheese with ashes. Best, May to December.

Other Imported Cheeses

Many cheeses are now imported, the majority coming from France. Discounting the New Zealand and Canadian cheddars, Italy, Germany, Denmark, Holland and Switzerland are the biggest cheese exporters.

Several of these foreign cheeses do not differ widely in taste from hard English cheeses, while others, especially pungent cheeses such as Emmenthal, Gruyère, Parmesan and the German Tilsit, have a flavour of their own. All the continental cheeses make ideal table cheeses; for cooking, however, it is best to use foreign cheeses only when they are specified in a recipe – most often the strong-flavoured Emmenthal, Gruyère or Parmesan – since the mild, delicate flavour of many imported cheeses is easily lost during cooking.

When buying continental cheeses look for the same qualities expected in English cheese – moist without being wet or having a 'sweated' look, and firm without appearing to be dried out.

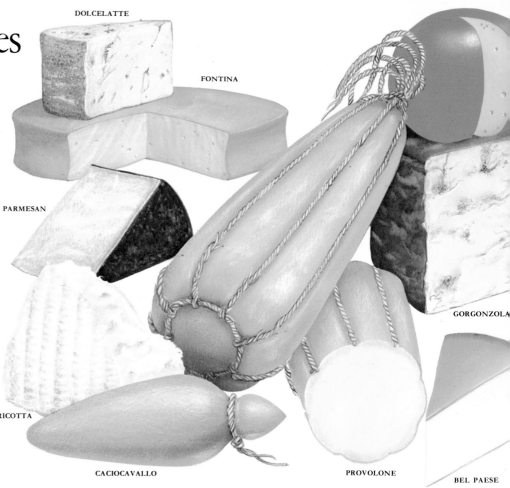

DOLCELATTE

EDAM

FONTINA

PARMESAN

GORGONZOLA

RICOTTA

CACIOCAVALLO

PROVOLONE

BEL PAESE

Bel Paese One of the most famous of Italian cheeses, Bel Paese has an ivory colour and a thin, dark yellow rind. Soft and compact, this cheese has a delicate, slightly salty flavour. It is usually served as a dessert cheese, but it may also be used in cooking as a substitute for Mozzarella.

Bergkäse Dull yellow with a dark brown rind, this hard Austrian cheese has a high fat content and a mild, nutty flavour.

Caciocavallo A hard, Italian curd cheese usually made in a pear shape with a ball at the top. The cheese is white to straw-coloured, sometimes with a few holes, and the rind smooth and thin with thread-like surface marks. It has a mild, semi-sweet flavour.

Danbo Mild flavoured and firm textured, this Danish cheese is easily recognised by its regular, even-sized holes. Sometimes it is given an added – and unusual – taste with caraway seeds.

Danish Blue This cheese is also known as Danablu, and was invented in 1914, at the beginning of the First World War, when the importation of Italian veined cheeses into Denmark was curtailed. The flavour of this white cheese with its close blue veins is strong and rich. Made from homogenised milk with a high cream content, it has a soft, slightly crumbly texture.

Dolcelatte One of the most famous of Italian veined cheeses, Dolcelatte is off-white in colour and has blue-green veins running through it. Full, robust flavour and creamy texture.

Edam This Dutch cheese has a mild flavour and a slightly rubbery consistency. It is always encased in a red wax rind. Edam is not unlike Gouda cheese in flavour. The difference between the two cheeses is due to the fact that Edam is made from partly skimmed milk, while Gouda is made from whole milk.

Edelpilz White around the edges, mottled blue at the centre, this German cheese has a strong flavour and crumbly texture.

Emmenthal Originally from Switzerland, Emmenthal is now also produced in Germany and Denmark, but there is little difference in the flavour. The best kind of Emmenthal is made from milk of the highest quality. The cheese is dull yellow, with holes the size of cherries. It has a distinctly nutty taste. Suitable as a dessert and cooking cheese.

Fontina This cheese is produced in the Valley of Aosta in the mountains of Northern Italy near the Swiss border. It is a soft, fat cheese, slightly straw-coloured and with a few small holes. The orange-coloured rind is often slightly thicker than on other cheeses. Imitations of this cheese are Fontal and Fontinella.

Gorgonzola Probably the best-known Italian cheese, named after the village of Gorgonzola near Milan where the shepherds of Lombardy spent their winters. The cheese is straw-coloured, mottled with green and has a coarse, brown rind. Sharp flavour, sometimes slightly spiced. Ideally, Gorgonzola should be firm and fairly dry.

Gouda A creamy-tasting soft Dutch cheese with a high butter-fat content. Produced in squat moulds, it is golden-yellow in colour. This Dutch cheese, like Edam, is not recommended for cooking.

Gruyère Widely used in cooking because of its full flavour, Gruyère is a hard Swiss cheese, pale yellow in colour, honey-combed with holes and having a brown, wrinkled rind. It is higher in butterfat than Emmenthal and has smaller holes. Gruyère is excellent as an appetiser, cooking or dessert cheese.

Limburger A soft cheese with a very strong smell and a spicy taste. It is made from whole cows' milk. The rind is brown and shiny, and the cheese inside is bright yellow, with few holes. This German cheese was first produced in Belgium.

GOUDA
EMMENTHAL
DANISH BLUE
VACHERIN
TRAPPISTENKÄSE
EDELPILZ
LIMBURGER
MUENSTER
BERGKÄSE
TILSIT
SCHLOSSKÄSE
QUARGEL
MOLBO
DANBO
SAMSOE
GRUYÈRE
MOZZARELLA

Molbo A mild-flavoured Danish cheese which has a slightly acid after-taste. Close-textured with a sprinkling of holes, the cheese is pale yellow and has a red wax rind.

Mozzarella Moulded into a flask, egg or ball shape and tied with raffia, this soft, compact Italian curd cheese has a fairly thick rind and a slightly sour taste. It is mainly used as a staple ingredient for the fillings of pizzas.

Muenster This semi-soft German cheese is less creamy than its French equivalent. It is round,

with a yellow-red rind, and a mild and delicate flavour.

Parmesan Strictly Parmigiano Reggiano, Parmesan is another of the better-known hard Italian cheeses. It is off-white inside its black rind, and strong and fragrant which makes it an excellent cooking cheese. In grated form, Parmesan is one of the staples of the Italian kitchen, being added to soups, polenta (a type of porridge eaten in Italy), vegetable dishes and pasta.

Provolone A hard Italian curd cheese made in many different shapes – truncated cone, pear,

melon or sausage – and tied with strings. The thin, smooth rind varies from yellow to brown, while the cheese itself is creamy-white. Delicate and sweet after an average ripening of two or three months, it becomes spicy and almost sharp if kept longer, or if the curd has been prepared with kids' rennet. A lightly smoked variety is also obtainable.

Quargel An Austrian cheese made in small rounds, yellow at the edges and white in the centre. Piquant flavour.

Ricotta Soft, bland Italian cheese with a distinctly ridged

rind. Made from sheep's milk, it is used for baking in Italy and in various dishes, such as lasagna.

Samsoe A mild-flavoured Danish cheese with a sweet, nutty flavour. Yellow colour with a firm texture and shiny round holes.

Schlosskäse A mild-flavoured soft Austrian cheese, pale yellow in colour with a heavily creased rind.

Tilsit Originally made by Dutch settlers in East Prussia, this German cheese is also produced in Switzerland and Scandinavia.

Tilsit is a savoury, straw-coloured slicing cheese, easily recognisable by its loaf shape and small, irregular holes. It has a sharp, slightly sour taste.

Trappistenkäse Pale yellow cheese with a rich yellow rind, Trappistenkäse is a mild-flavoured, semi-soft German cheese made in loaves or bars. It has a firm consistency with round or slitted holes.

Vacherin Off-white in colour with a rough, mottled rind. This mild-flavoured, semi-soft Swiss cheese is good for spreading or for sandwiches.

Twelve Months

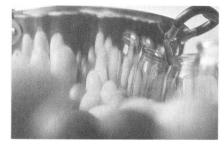

THE QUOTATIONS AT THE HEAD OF EACH MONTH ARE BY THOMAS
TUSSER (*c.* 1524–80) AND ARE TAKEN FROM *FIVE HUNDRETH POINTES
OF GOOD HUSBANDRIE* (1573)

# of Recipes

APRIL

PAGES 116-135

MAY

PAGES 136-155

JUNE

PAGES 156-177

OCTOBER

PAGES 238-259

NOVEMBER

PAGES 260-279

DECEMBER

PAGES 280-303

January

Good husband and huswife, will sometimes alone,
make shift with a morsell and picke of a bone.

This Month's Recipes

*A well-stocked larder or cellar with strings of onions, trays of apples
and parsnips, and sacks of potatoes, which will last through the winter days*

Food in Season

Weather permitting, fish such as coley, mullet, lemon sole, mackerel and scallop are plentiful and good value this month. The game season is nearing its end, and game birds and hares are more suitable for casseroles than for roasting. Turkey is still available and, as demand is low after Christmas, prices are usually well below those of December. Many vegetables, particularly broccoli, Brussels sprouts, cabbages and cauliflowers are at their best, the flavour being improved by a touch of frost. Parsnips are in prime condition.

Christmas fruits are plentiful and less expensive than in December. Forced rhubarb and home-grown pears are in the shops, but most other fruits are imported, including clementines and the first Seville oranges and limes for marmalades.

Fish

Bream, freshwater
Bream, sea
Brill
Carp
Clams
Cod
Coley (or saithe)
Conger eels
Crab
Crawfish (short supply)
Dabs (sporadic)
Dover sole
Dublin Bay prawns
Eels
Flake (also sold as rock salmon)
Flounder (sporadic)
Grey mullet
Haddock
Hake
Halibut
Herring
Lemon sole
Lobster
Mackerel
Mock halibut (or Greenland halibut)
Mussels
Oysters (native)
Oysters, Portuguese
Pike
Prawns
Redfish
Scallops
Shrimps
Skate
Sprats
Trout, rainbow
Turbot
Whiting
Winkles
Witch

Poultry & Game

Chicken
Duck
Guinea fowl
Hare
Mallard
Partridge
Pheasant
Pigeon
Rabbit
Snipe
Teal
Turkey
Venison
Wild goose
Woodcock

Vegetables

Asparagus
Aubergines
Avocado pears
Beetroots
Broccoli, purple
Broccoli, white
Brussels sprouts
Brussels tops
Cabbages
Carrots
Cauliflowers
Celeriac
Celery
Chicory
Courgettes
Cucumbers
Endive
Fennel
French beans
Globe artichokes
Horseradish
Jerusalem artichokes
Kale
Kohl rabi
Leeks
Lettuce
Mushrooms
Onions
Parsley
Parsnips
Peppers
Potatoes, new
Radishes
Salad cress
Salsify
Savoys
Sea kale
Shallots
Spinach
Spring greens
Spring onions
Swedes
Sweet potatoes
Tomatoes
Turnips
Watercress

Fruit

Apples
Apricots
Bananas
Brazil nuts
Chinese gooseberries
Clementines
Cranberries
Dates
Grapefruit
Grapes
Lemons
Lychees
Mandarins
Mangoes
Melons
Nectarines
Oranges
Passion fruit (short supply)
Pawpaws (short supply)
Peaches
Pears
Pineapples
Plums
Pomegranates
Rhubarb (forced)
Satsumas
Strawberries
Tangerines
Walnuts

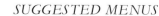

SUGGESTED MENUS

Cream of Brussels Sprouts Soup
Saddle of Venison
Glazed Onions, Bread Croûtons
Iced Tangerines

Smelts with Almonds
Carbonades à la Flamande
Parsnip Croquettes
Rhubarb and Cinnamon Flan

Casserole of Halibut
Fried Rice with Leeks
Fig Pie

Fettucine al Burro
Pigeons with Pâté
Scottish Flummery

Onions à la Grecque
Tenderloin of Pork
Broccoli Spears au Gratin, Sauté Potatoes
Treacle Tart

Terrine of Hare
New Potatoes
Chicory and Orange Salad
Fig Pie

Braised Oxtail
Fried Rice with Leeks or
Rice with Garlic and Walnuts
Fresh Fruit

Savoury Fritters with
Coleslaw in Italian Dressing
Bread Pudding

Soups & Starters

TERRINE OF HARE

Hare, which is among the cheapest of game, is excellent for pâtés and terrines. These freeze well, and the quantities below are sufficient for two terrines. Begin preparations 2 days in advance, and serve the terrine as a first course or main course.

PREPARATION TIME: *45 min.*
COOKING TIME: *1½ hours*

INGREDIENTS *(for 6)* :

MARINADE:
4 bay leaves
8 crushed juniper berries
1 level teaspoon salt
6 peppercorns
½ wine-glass brandy

TERRINE:
1 hare
1 lb. veal and 1 lb. belly pork
¾ lb. rashers streaky bacon
1 level teaspoon each of powdered
* basil, thyme, marjoram, salt*
* and black pepper*

In a large bowl, mix together the marinade* ingredients. Cut 1–1½ lb. of meat, from the saddle and hind legs of the hare, into thin slices and leave for 8–10 hours in the marinade. Turn the meat several times to ensure it is thoroughly impregnated.

The following day mince the veal with the cleaned liver, heart and kidneys from the hare; remove the rind, bones and gristle from the belly pork, and mince it separately.

Line one 2 pint, or two 1 pint, terrine or ovenproof dishes with the streaky bacon, with the rind removed, setting three or four slices aside. (For easier un-moulding, the terrine or dish can be lined with foil before arranging the bacon.) Strain the marinade from the hare. Lay half the minced pork on the bacon, followed by a layer of veal. Sprinkle each layer with the mixed basil, thyme, marjoram, salt and freshly ground pepper. Lay the hare meat over the veal, pour the strained marinade over, and top with the other half of the pork; sprinkle with the remain-

ing seasoning. Cover the top with the reserved bacon and four bay leaves, and protect the terrine with buttered greaseproof paper before putting on the lid. Place in a bain marie* or a roasting pan containing boiling water, reaching just above half-way up the sides of the dish.

Set the bain marie in a pre-heated oven, one shelf up from the bottom; cook at 375°F (mark 5) for 1½ hours or until a skewer pushed gently into the terrine comes away clean and the juices run clear yellow. About 15 minutes before cooking is com-pleted, remove the lid and grease-proof paper to allow the top of the terrine to brown.

Remove from the oven and leave to cool for about 30 minutes; cover the terrine with clean greaseproof paper and weight down with a 2 lb. weight set on a board over the terrine.

Serve the terrine cold, with hot toast for a first course. For a main meal, chicory and orange salad (see December vegetables) and hot new potatoes tossed in butter would be suitable.

ONIONS À LA GRECQUE

PREPARATION TIME: *1 hour*
COOKING TIME: *40 min.*
CHILLING TIME: *2 hours*

INGREDIENTS *(for 6)* :
1½ lb. small onions
SAUCE:
1 pint dry white wine
2 oz. caster sugar
5 tablespoons olive oil
8 juniper berries
Juice of a lemon
Salt and black pepper
1 bay leaf
2¼ oz. tin of tomato paste
6 sprigs parsley
¼ teaspoon basil

GARNISH:
3 tablespoons chopped parsley

This French classic hors-d'oeuvre of baby onions provide an unusual first course. The onions should be served chilled.

Bring a large saucepan, holding at least 3 pints of water, to the boil. Cut the tops and bottoms from the onions and drop them into the boiling water for 1 minute. Drain the onions in a colander; cool slightly before peeling the onions.

Put the wine, water, sugar, oil, juniper berries and lemon juice into a heavy-based pan; season this sauce to taste with salt and freshly ground pepper before adding the peeled onions.

Bring to the boil and simmer over low heat for 20 minutes or until the onions are tender, but not disintegrating. Remove the onions; mark the level of the sauce and boil briskly for about 15 minutes or until it has reduced* to three-quarters. Strain the sauce through a sieve over the onions; leave to cool and chill for a few hours in the refrigerator.

Serve the onions, in the sauce, in soup plates and garnish with the finely chopped parsley.

SCRAMBLED EGG WITH SMOKED SALMON

This is an easily prepared first course for lunch or dinner. It is creamy in texture and has eye-appeal with its garnish of sliced pepper and whole olives.

PREPARATION TIME: *8 min.*
COOKING TIME: *25 min.*

INGREDIENTS *(for 6)*:
8–9 oz. unsalted butter
8 ½ in. thick slices of stale white bread
1 pepper (green or red)
7 eggs
3 tablespoons double cream
Black pepper
¼ level teaspoon salt
¼ lb. shredded smoked salmon
GARNISH:
Red or green pepper
6 parsley sprigs
12 stoned black olives
Watercress

Melt 4–5 oz. of the butter in a sauté pan. With a plain or fluted pastry cutter, 3 in. across, cut six rounds from the bread slices. Cut the other two slices into ½ in. fingers. Soak the bread rounds and slices in the melted butter and then place in an oven pre-heated to 400°F (mark 6) for about 20 minutes or until crisp and golden. Remove and keep warm on a serving dish.

Meanwhile, remove the seeds from the pepper and chop it coarsely. Melt another ounce of butter in a pan and slowly cook the chopped pepper in it for 15 minutes. Drain on absorbent paper and keep hot.

Beat the eggs lightly and stir in the cream, freshly ground black pepper, salt and the salmon.

Melt 3 oz. of butter in a large, heavy-based pan over low heat and pour in the egg and salmon mixture. Stir gently and continuously until the eggs begin to form creamy curds*. Remove the pan from the heat and quickly arrange the soft scramble over the six rounds of bread.

Scatter the drained pepper over the scrambled eggs and garnish with sprigs of parsley. Decorate the serving dish with thin slices of red or green fresh pepper (remove stalk ends and seeds first), small bunches of watercress and stoned black olives. Serve with the fried bread fingers.

CREAM OF BRUSSELS SPROUT SOUP

A generous garnish of toasted almonds gives extra flavour to this soup. It can be served hot or chilled, and it is also suitable for deep-freezing, in which case the clove of garlic should be omitted.

PREPARATION TIME: *40 min.*
COOKING TIME: *2 hours*

INGREDIENTS *(for 6–8)*:

FOR THE STOCK:
4 oz. belly pork
1 carrot
1 small turnip
1 clove garlic
1 onion studded with 2 cloves
6 sprigs parsley
1 bouquet garni
6 peppercorns
1 bay leaf
2 level teaspoons salt

FOR THE SOUP:
2 lb. Brussels sprouts
½ lb. potatoes
1 onion
2 oz. unsalted butter
½ pint milk
½ level teaspoon grated nutmeg
Black pepper
¼ pint single cream
6 oz. flaked almonds

For the stock, put 2 pints of water into a heavy-based saucepan and add the belly pork; cover with a lid and bring to the boil. Peel and slice the carrot and turnip, crush the garlic and add to the stock, along with the clove-studded onion, sprigs of parsley, bouquet garni*, peppercorns, bay leaf and salt. Bring to the boil again and remove any scum after a minute or two. Cover and simmer for 1½ hours, then strain the liquid through muslin into a jug or basin. The stock should yield about 1½ pints; if less, top up with boiling water.

Peel the Brussels sprouts, and thinly slice the potatoes and onion. Melt the butter in a large sauté pan and let the onion and potatoes cook in it slowly for 10 minutes, until they have absorbed the butter, but not taken colour. Toss the Brussels sprouts around with the potatoes and onion, then transfer the contents of the pan to a large saucepan and pour over 1½ pints of stock and ½ pint of milk. Bring this mixture to the boil, cover and simmer for 20 minutes. Add freshly ground pepper and more salt if necessary.

Allow the soup to cool slightly before liquidising in an electric blender or rubbing it through a sieve. (Place in the deep freezer now if the soup is to be stored for any length of time.) Stir the nutmeg and cream into the soup; re-heat carefully without boiling or chill in the refrigerator for a few hours.

Put the flaked almonds on a baking sheet on the middle shelf of the oven pre-heated to 350°F (mark 4); turn the almonds several times until they take on a deep amber colour.

Serve the soup in individual bowls and sprinkle generously with the cold toasted almonds.

Fish

MEDITERRANEAN FISH SOUP

On a cold winter's evening, this thick soup serves almost as a meal in itself. It can be prepared well in advance and re-heated just before serving without losing any of its delicate flavour.

PREPARATION TIME: *35 min.*
COOKING TIME: *45 min.*

INGREDIENTS *(for 6–8)* :
12 oz. each of mullet, whiting and plaice
1 large onion
6 tablespoons olive oil
1 clove garlic
15–16 oz. tin tomatoes
2 level tablespoons tomato paste
1 heaped tablespoon chopped parsley
1½ pints fish stock or water
¼ pint dry white wine
1 bay leaf
Large piece lemon peel
Salt and black pepper
¼ pint double cream
GARNISH:
Prawns
Tomato slices

Clean, fillet and skin the fish*; use the trimmings and bones as a base for the fish stock*. Cut the fish fillets diagonally into 2 in. pieces. Peel and finely chop the onion. Heat the oil in a heavy-based pan and cook the onion in this until soft, but not browned. Crush and add the garlic, fry for a minute or two before adding the tinned tomatoes with their juice, tomato paste and chopped parsley. Mix it all together and simmer slowly for 15 minutes. Add the fish, the stock, wine, bay leaf and lemon peel, bring back to the simmer, cover with a lid and cook slowly for 20 minutes.

Discard the bay leaf and lemon peel. Season with salt and freshly ground pepper and leave the soup to cool slightly.

Remove one piece of fish for each serving and keep warm; liquidise the rest, along with the contents of the pan, until blended to a smooth creamy consistency.

Stir in the cream and re-heat the soup without bringing it to the boil. Place one piece of fish in each individual bowl and pour over the soup. Float slices of skinned tomatoes*, garnished with a few peeled prawns, on top of each bowl.

LEEK PIE

This vegetable pie can be served cold as a substantial first course to an otherwise light evening meal, or hot as a main course for lunch. It freezes well, and can be left in the home freezer for several months.

PREPARATION TIME: *35 min.*
COOKING TIME: *2½ hours*

INGREDIENTS *(for 4–6)* :
1 lb. leeks
3 oz. green bacon or belly pork
Black pepper
⅓–½ pint chicken stock
1 bay leaf
1 egg
2 tablespoons double cream
6 oz. shortcrust pastry (standard recipe)
GLAZING:
1 egg
½ level teaspoon salt

Trim the roots and outer coarse green leaves from the leeks before washing them under running water; prise open the leaf ends to flush away any hidden soil. Cut the leeks diagonally into ½ in.

slices and put them in a 7–8 in. pie dish. Cut off the rind and dice* the bacon; mix with the leeks. Pepper well, just cover with the chicken stock and add the bay leaf. Put the pie on the centre shelf of an oven pre-heated to 300°F (mark 2) and cook for 1½ hours or until the liquid has almost evaporated. Remove the bay leaf.

Let the pie cool slightly, then beat the egg and cream together and stir into the leek mixture. Roll out the pastry*, ⅛ in. thick, on a lightly floured surface, and cut it into a circle to fit the pie dish. Moisten the edge of the pie dish and cover the filling with the pastry. Trim, decorate with pastry leaves, and crimp the edges together to seal.

At this stage, the pie may be stored in the deep freezer. When wanted, the frozen pie can be placed straight in the oven for re-heating. There is no need to thaw it first.

Beat the second egg and salt together, and brush over the pastry to give it a golden glaze while cooking. Make a small slit in the pastry for the steam to escape. Cook the pie, on the centre shelf of the oven set to 400°F (mark 6), until golden brown after about 30 minutes. Leave the pie to cool, and serve cut into wedges, accompanied by a green salad.

HERRINGS IN OATMEAL

For breakfast, herrings make a welcome change from bacon and eggs. They are equally suitable for high tea or supper. In Scotland, where this recipe originates, small trout are often treated in the same way.

PREPARATION TIME: *15 min.*
COOKING TIME: *20 min.*

INGREDIENTS *(for 4)* :
4 small herrings
Salt and black pepper
4 level tablespoons coarse oatmeal
4 oz. unsalted butter
GARNISH:
Lemon wedges

Scale, wash and clean the herrings*; cut off the heads and carefully remove the backbones. Sprinkle a little salt and freshly ground pepper over the inside of each herring. Close the fish to their original shape and coat them evenly and firmly with the oatmeal.

Melt the butter in a heavy-based pan; fry the herrings over gentle heat for 10 minutes on each side. Lift the fish from the pan and arrange on individual serving plates; spoon a little of the butter over each herring and garnish with lemon wedges.

FISH PIE WITH CHEESE CUSTARD

Smoked cod enhances the flavour of this fish pie, topped with a cheese and tomato custard.

PREPARATION TIME: *35 min.*
COOKING TIME: *45 min.*

INGREDIENTS *(for 6)*:
1¼ *lb. cod fillet*
6 *oz. smoked cod fillet*
1½ *pints chicken or fish stock*
1 *onion*
3 *cloves*
1 *clove garlic*
Salt and black pepper
½ *pint white sauce*
1 *lb. tomatoes*
2 *eggs*
½ *pint milk*
2 *oz. Parmesan cheese*
1 *oz. unsalted butter*

Wash and skin the fresh cod, wipe the smoked cod with a cloth and cut both into 1 in. wide slices. Put the fish slices in a deep sauté pan and cover with the chicken stock. Peel and finely slice the onion, add to the fish, together with the cloves and the crushed garlic. Bring slowly to the boil, and season with salt and freshly ground pepper. Simmer for 10 minutes, then remove the cod from the liquid.

Increase the heat and boil the fish liquid rapidly until it has reduced* to ½ pint; strain and use for the white sauce*.

Flake* the fish into a deep 8 in. wide pie dish, pour over the hot white sauce and coat the fish

thoroughly. Skin and slice the tomatoes* in a layer over the fish, and pepper well. Beat the eggs with salt and pepper, beat in the grated cheese and milk. Pour this mixture over the tomatoes and float small knobs of butter on the surface. Bake for 45 minutes or until golden brown, on the centre shelf of an oven heated to 325°F (mark 3).

Sauté potatoes*, cooked in butter, and Brussels sprouts could be served with the pie.

MATELOTE OF EELS

A matelote – not to be confused with matelot (a sailor) – is the French culinary term for a fish stew. In this recipe, eels are used for a wholesome main course for lunch or supper.

PREPARATION TIME: *20 min.*
COOKING TIME: *45 min.*

INGREDIENTS *(for 4–6)*:
1½ *lb. eels*
2 *small onions*
3 *oz. unsalted butter*
13 *fluid oz. dry white wine*
1 *carrot*
1 *clove garlic*
1 *bouquet garni*
½ *level teaspoon ground mace*
Salt and black pepper
1 *egg yolk*
¼ *pint double cream*
GARNISH:
12 *button mushrooms*
12 *button onions*
Fried bread triangles

Ask the fishmonger to skin and clean the eels*. Peel and thinly slice the onions, sauté* half in 2 oz. of the butter for 5 minutes until golden. Wash and dry the eels and cut into 2 in. pieces, add to the onion and continue frying gently, for about 10 minutes, turning the eels until lightly browned. Pour in the wine and bring to a simmer. Peel, slice and chop the carrot, peel and crush the garlic and add these to the pan, together with the remaining onion, bouquet garni*, mace and seasoning. Cover with a lid and simmer for 25 minutes.

Meanwhile, wipe and trim the mushrooms*, peel the button onions and sauté both in the remaining 1 oz. of butter; fry the bread triangles. Remove the

fish and keep warm on a serving dish.

Beat the egg yolk and cream together and add a little of the fish liquid. Blend this into the mixture in the pan and continue gently stirring until the sauce thickens. Pour the sauce over the eels and serve garnished with the mushrooms, onions and bread triangles.

CASSEROLE OF HALIBUT

This is a highly nutritious, easily prepared dish for lunch or dinner. A garnish of puff pastry crescents adds a touch of sophistication.

PREPARATION TIME: *15 min.*
COOKING TIME: *50 min.*

INGREDIENTS *(for 6)*:
2 *lb. piece halibut*
2 *oz. unsalted butter*
1 *heaped tablespoon finely chopped onion*
½ *pint double cream*
Juice of half lemon
2 *heaped teaspoons paprika*
¼ *lb. button mushrooms*
3 *oz. peeled shrimps*
GARNISH:
Puff pastry crescents

Wipe and skin the halibut. Butter an ovenproof casserole dish, place the piece of halibut in this and cook for 15 minutes on the middle shelf of an oven preheated to 325°F (mark 3). Remove from the oven, sprinkle the onion over the fish, pour over the cream mixed with the lemon juice and dust with paprika.

Cover the dish with a lid or foil, return to the oven and cook for a further 20 minutes, basting* twice with the cooking liquid. Trim and slice the mushrooms*,

Meat

and sprinkle them, with the shrimps, over the fish; cook for a further 15 minutes, again basting twice. Transfer the fish to a warm dish and pour over the liquid.

Garnish with puff pastry crescents and serve boiled new potatoes with the fish.

SMELTS WITH ALMONDS

These small salt-water fish are at their best when caught at spawning time in late winter. Their delicate flavour is most apparent when baked or fried. If smelts are not available, young trout can be substituted.

PREPARATION TIME: *10 min.*
COOKING TIME: *10 min.*

INGREDIENTS *(for 6)*:
18 smelts
3 fluid oz. single cream
Seasoned flour
3 oz. unsalted butter
1 tablespoon olive oil
4 oz. flaked almonds

Lightly wash the smelts* in cold water, split and remove the entrails; cut off the heads. Dry the cleaned smelts on a cloth; dip the fish in the cream and roll in seasoned flour*. Melt the butter in a heavy-based frying pan, add the olive oil and gently fry the smelts for 4 minutes on each side.

Remove the smelts from the pan and keep them warm. Increase the heat slightly and fry the flaked almonds in the fat in which the fish has been cooked until they turn light brown. Sprinkle the smelts with the almonds and pour over the butter.

Serve the smelts with thin slices of buttered brown bread.

SUFFOLK STEW

This is one of those hearty, satisfying stews that requires nothing before it, and very little afterwards. Order the best end of lamb chined*, and begin preparations a day in advance.

PREPARATION TIME: *30 min.*
COOKING TIME: *3 hours*

INGREDIENTS *(for 4–6)*:
1 best end of lamb
2 oz. lentils
1 oz. haricot beans
1 oz. pearl barley
2 large potatoes
1 large turnip
4 carrots
4 onions
2 bay leaves
$\frac{1}{2}$ level teaspoon salt
$\frac{1}{2}$ level teaspoon black pepper
1 clove garlic
1 level teaspoon mixed herbs

Soak the lentils, haricot beans and pearl barley in cold water overnight. The following day, peel and roughly chop all the vegetables; put them in a large saucepan. Trim any excess fat from the best end of lamb and cut the meat into single chops. Add these, together with the bay leaves, salt, pepper, crushed garlic and herbs to the vegetables.

Drain the lentils, haricot beans and pearl barley, before adding them to the pan. Pour over 3 pints of water, cover the pan with a lid and bring to the boil. Simmer gently for 3 hours.

Spoon the stew into a warm serving dish. No other vegetables are necessary, but buttered hot muffins would make an unusual accompaniment to the stew.

DURHAM LAMB SQUAB PIE

Originally, this recipe probably contained squabs – or young pigeons – but, in the course of time, meat became the chief constituent of the pie. There are several variations of this English farmhouse dish; the following comes from Durham.

PREPARATION TIME: *30 min.*
COOKING TIME: *1–1$\frac{1}{4}$ hours*

INGREDIENTS *(for 4–6)*:
8 lamb chops
2 lb. potatoes
1 large onion
3 cooking apples
3 oz. unsalted butter
1 heaped teaspoon brown sugar
Salt and black pepper
$\frac{1}{3}$ pint chicken stock

Peel and thinly slice the potatoes and cover with cold water. Trim excess fat from the lamb chops. Peel and finely chop the onion, and peel, core and chop the apples. Melt 2 oz. of the butter in a pan and fry the chops lightly on both sides. Remove them as soon as the blood starts to run. Fry the apples and onion in the fat for about 5 minutes.

Use half the remaining butter to grease the inside of a pie dish. Dry the sliced potatoes and line the base of the dish with half of them. Arrange the chops on the potato bed and spoon the apple and onion mixture over them. Sprinkle over the sugar, a little salt and a couple of twists of pepper from the mill. Cover with the rest of the potatoes and pour over the chicken stock. Melt the remaining $\frac{1}{2}$ oz. butter and brush it over the potato layer. Put the dish on the middle shelf of an oven pre-heated to 350°F (mark 4) and cook for 1 hour or until the potatoes are tender and golden brown.

Serve straight from the casserole. Brussels sprouts tossed in soft brown sugar and allspice could be served with it.

TENDERLOIN OF PORK

The fillet – or tenderloin – of pork is a lean, economical cut of meat. A tenderloin weighs about 12–16 oz. and should be stuffed, marinated* or larded* to prevent the meat drying out.

PREPARATION TIME: *30 min.*
COOKING TIME: *1½ hours*

INGREDIENTS *(for 6):*
1½–2 lb. pork tenderloin
2 oz. unsalted butter
1 clove garlic
STUFFING:
4 oz. fine white breadcrumbs
2 oz. mixed dried fruits
1 level tablespoon finely chopped parsley
1 heaped tablespoon finely chopped onion
1 clove garlic
½ level tablespoon chopped tarragon
2 oz. melted butter
1 orange
1 egg
Salt and black pepper
SAUCE:
1 lb. fresh apricots
1 tablespoon water
1 level tablespoon soft brown sugar
Juice of a lemon
½ level teaspoon curry powder
1 tablespoon Kümmel

Prepare the stuffing first: mix the breadcrumbs, the cut-up fruits, parsley, onion, crushed garlic and tarragon in a bowl. Stir in the melted butter. Add the grated rind of the orange, remove pith and membrane from the flesh, cut this up and mix into the stuffing. Beat the egg lightly and use to bind the mixture. Season with salt and freshly ground pepper.

Trim all the fat off each tenderloin* and remove the transparent skin. Slit the meat lengthways through half its thickness, open it out and flatten with the fist or the edge of a cleaver.

Spread the stuffing over the tenderloins, roll them up tightly from the bottom and tie with string. Melt the butter in a flameproof dish on the stove. Peel and slice the garlic and fry until brown, then remove. Fry the pork for a few minutes in the butter until evenly browned. Cover the pan with the lid and roast for 1 hour 20 minutes (40 minutes to the lb.) on the centre shelf of an oven preheated to 325°F (mark 3). Remove the lid for the last 10 minutes for the meat to brown.

To make the sauce, halve and stone the apricots, tie up the stones in a piece of butter muslin and put them with the apricots in a saucepan. Add the water and stew the apricots until they are tender, stirring constantly. Mix in the sugar, lemon juice and curry powder and cook for 5 minutes or until thick. Remove the stones; beat the apricots to a paste or liquidise in a blender before stirring in the Kümmel.

Before serving, remove the string and carve the meat into slices. Arrange on a serving dish and spoon over a little of the sauce. Offer the remaining sauce separately with, for example, sauté potatoes* and broccoli spears au gratin (see January vegetables).

BRAISED OXTAIL

Oxtail is an inexpensive, nourishing but fatty meat. This stew is best cooked the day before so that the fat can settle and be lifted from the top before the stew is re-heated.

PREPARATION TIME: *40 min.*
COOKING TIME: *4¾ hours*

INGREDIENTS *(for 6):*
2 oxtails
Seasoned flour
1½ oz. beef dripping
2 onions
1 bottle red wine or 1 pint beef stock
1 bouquet garni
Salt and black pepper
2 bay leaves
1 level tablespoon redcurrant jelly
Peel of half lemon and half orange
¾ lb. carrots
2 small turnips
1 tablespoon lemon juice
1 level tablespoon tomato paste
6 oz. mushrooms
GARNISH:
3 level tablespoons chopped parsley
2 level teaspoons grated lemon rind

Chop the oxtails into 2 in. lengths and coat lightly with the seasoned flour*. Peel and slice the onions.

Melt the dripping in a large sauté pan and fry the oxtails in the hot fat for 5 minutes until they glisten, then transfer to a large fireproof cooking pot. Fry the onions in the residue of the fat, and as soon as they begin to take colour add them to the oxtail. Pour the wine or beef stock over the oxtail and onions, put the pot over the heat and bring the wine to the boil. Add the bouquet garni*, salt, pepper, bay leaves,

jelly and peel, and simmer on top of the stove for 2 hours. Strain off the liquid into a wide bowl and leave to cool.

Peel and slice the carrots and turnips and add to the oxtail. Spoon as much fat as possible from the cooled liquid (if it is thoroughly cold, the fat will have settled in a layer on top and can easily be lifted off). Pour the liquid over the oxtail. Add the lemon juice and tomato paste, bring to the boil and immediately place on the lowest shelf of the oven, heated to 275°F (mark 1); cook for 2½ hours. Add the trimmed and sliced mushrooms* to the dish for the last 10 minutes.

Serve sprinkled with parsley mixed with the lemon peel; rice with leeks (see January rice and pasta) would also be suitable.

BOILED BEEF AND CARROTS

This is one of the classic dishes from the English kitchen. Carrots and onions are always cooked with the beef, which should, according to tradition, also be served with dumplings.

PREPARATION TIME: *30 min.*
COOKING TIME: *3¾ hours*

INGREDIENTS *(for 6):*
4 lb. piece salt brisket
1 large onion
4 cloves
1 bouquet garni
6 peppercorns
2 bay leaves
1 rasher streaky bacon
10 small carrots
12 small onions
2 small turnips
¼ pint dry cider
½ level teaspoon dry mustard
½ level teaspoon ground cinnamon

Buy lean brisket; ask the butcher how long the meat has been in brine and soak it in cold water overnight if the meat has been brined for more than three days; otherwise soak for 30 minutes.

Put the brisket in a large saucepan; peel the large onion, stud it with the cloves and add to the beef, together with the bouquet garni*, peppercorns, bay leaves and bacon. Cover with cold water, bring to the boil and after a few minutes remove the scum; keep the meat on the boil and continue skimming for about 10 minutes. Cover the pan with a lid and reduce the heat, then simmer for 1¾ hours. Remove from the heat and lift out the meat; strain the liquid into a basin.

When the liquid has cooled, remove the congealed fat from the surface. Peel the carrots and onions, and peel and coarsely slice the turnips. Arrange the vegetables in a deep pan, with the beef on top. Pour over enough strained liquid and the cider to cover. Sprinkle in the mustard and cinnamon, and cover the pan with a lid. Bring to the boil, then reduce the heat and simmer for 1 hour.

Arrange the piece of beef in the centre of a serving dish and surround with the vegetables; serve the liquid separately in a sauceboat. Winter cabbage, cut into large chunks, or dumplings* may be added to the simmering beef for the last 20 minutes of cooking. Serve with plain boiled potatoes.

CASSOULET

Pork, beans and poultry are the ingredients of this classic farmhouse dish which originates in the Languedoc province of southern France. Goose is the traditional poultry, but other poultry or game can be substituted. Order the meat in advance and begin preparations a day ahead.

PREPARATION TIME: *10 min.*
COOKING TIME: *7¾ hours*

INGREDIENTS *(for 6–8):*
10 oz. haricot beans
1½ lb. piece salt belly pork
3–4 cloves garlic
1 tablespoon golden syrup
4 sticks celery
1 level teaspoon caster sugar
1 large bouquet garni
2 level teaspoons made mustard
Black pepper
6 small joints of poultry or game
  (goose, chicken, duck or rabbit)
8 oz. garlic sausage or pork
  chipolatas

Rinse the haricot beans, cover them with cold water in a basin and leave them to soak for 12 hours. Drain the beans and place them, with the piece of pork on top, in a deep earthenware cooking pot or large casserole. Add all the other ingredients, except the poultry (or game) and sausages. Cover with cold water, put on the lid and cook on the bottom shelf of an oven pre-heated to 400°F (mark 6) for 15 minutes. Lower the heat to 350°F (mark 4) and continue cooking for a further 2 hours, checking after 1 hour that the water just covers the meat. Top up with water if necessary.

Reduce the oven heat to 300°F (mark 2) and continue cooking for a further 3 hours, checking the liquid level frequently and adding a little more water if necessary. Now add the poultry, pushing the joints well down into the beans, and after a further 1½ hours add the cut up garlic sausage or pork chipolatas. Lift the piece of pork to the top of the pot and just above the level of the liquid. Cook for another hour with the lid off, by which time the pork should be brown, and the beans thoroughly cooked without being mushy.

Serve the cassoulet straight from the pot. Crisp, hot French bread is all that is necessary to complement this substantial dish.

SPARE RIBS IN MARSALA

To many people, spare ribs of pork are synonymous with Chinese cooking. This recipe, however, imparts a different flavour to spare ribs.

PREPARATION TIME: *40 min.*
COOKING TIME: *35 min.*

INGREDIENTS *(for 6)*:
6 large spare ribs of pork
3 tablespoons olive oil
2 cloves garlic
2 heaped tablespoons parsley
1 level teaspoon ground fennel
Salt and black pepper
¼ pint fresh orange juice
¼ pint chicken stock
3 tablespoons Marsala wine
GARNISH:
Orange and watercress

Ask the butcher to cut the meat into single rib portions. Trim away as much fat from the ribs as possible, and heat the oil in a heavy-based pan. Peel and crush the cloves of garlic and rub over the ribs; chop the parsley finely and mix with the fennel; rub into the ribs. Put the ribs in the pan, pepper each well, and cook on both sides until pale brown. Pour over the orange juice and stock, add the Marsala, and correct seasoning.

Cook the spare ribs on the middle shelf of an oven pre-heated to 350°F (mark 4) for 35 minutes.

Lift out the ribs and arrange them on a bed of egg noodles*. Skim the fat off the juices and pour these over the meat. Garnish with slices of orange and small bunches of watercress. Broccoli spears au gratin or cauliflower with almonds (see January vegetables) could also be served.

HAMBURGERS WITH PIZZAIOLA SAUCE

One of the classics of the American kitchen – hamburgers – is here combined with a classic Italian tomato sauce.

PREPARATION TIME:
Hamburgers 15 min;
sauce 20 min.
COOKING TIME:
Hamburgers 3–7 min;
sauce 35 min.

INGREDIENTS *(for 4–6)*:
2 lb. lean sirloin or rump steak
1 oz. unsalted butter
Salt and black pepper
SAUCE:
2 onions
2 cloves garlic
2 green peppers
1 dessertspoon olive oil
2 oz. mushroom caps
15–16 oz. tin of tomatoes
2 level teaspoons oregano (or marjoram)
Chilli sauce
Salt and black pepper

Trim any fat from the steak, cut it into pieces and put through the mincer (coarse plate). Shape the mince into six or eight rounds, about 1½ in. thick. Avoid over-handling as this makes them tough. Leave the hamburgers to rest while preparing the sauce.

Peel and mince the onions and garlic. Remove the stalks and seeds from the peppers and cut them crossways into thin slices. Heat the oil in a deep, heavy-based frying pan and, over a gentle heat, cook the onions and garlic until they are pale golden. Add the pepper slices and continue cooking for 15 minutes. Wash or peel the mushrooms*, chop them roughly and add to the pan together with the tomatoes and the oregano or marjoram. Cover and continue cooking for another 10 minutes. Season to taste with chilli sauce, salt and freshly ground pepper. Leave the pan over low heat while cooking the hamburgers.

Melt the butter in a heavy-based frying pan; fry rare hamburgers for 1½ minutes on each side; for pink-rare hamburgers, add another minute each side; for medium, add 2 minutes. Sprinkle with salt and pepper.

Put the hamburgers on a hot serving dish and pour the sauce over them. Serve coleslaw (see January vegetables) as a side dish.

CARBONADES À LA FLAMANDE

This is an adaptation of a Belgian recipe for beef in beer. The ale gives the meat a distinctly nutty flavour, heightened by the garlic crust. The dish is best prepared in advance and later re-heated.

PREPARATION TIME: *55 min.*
COOKING TIME: *2¾ hours*
INGREDIENTS *(for 6)*:

3 lb. lean blade of beef
4 oz. dripping or unsalted butter
1 tablespoon olive oil
3 large onions
4 cloves garlic
Salt and black pepper
2 level tablespoons plain flour
1 level tablespoon soft brown sugar
½ pint strong beef stock
¾ pint brown ale
1 tablespoon wine vinegar
1 bouquet garni
2 bay leaves
GARLIC CRUST:
½ lb. unsalted butter
3 cloves garlic
1 French loaf

Melt the dripping or butter, together with the oil, in a large sauté pan on top of the stove. Cut the beef into ½ in. thick slices, about 3 in. long and 1½ in. wide. Peel and finely slice the onions and crush the four cloves of garlic. Quickly brown the beef slices or carbonades in the fat, drain and put to one side. Lower the heat and in the remaining fat cook the onions until golden, then add the garlic. Layer the onions and beef in a deep casserole, beginning with the onions and finishing with meat; salt and pepper each layer lightly.

Scrape up the juices in the pan in which the beef and onions were cooked, stir in the flour and sugar and increase the heat until the mixture forms a roux*. Stir in a little of the stock until the mixture is smooth; bring to the boil. Add the remainder of the stock, the ale and the vinegar; bring back to the boil and simmer for a few minutes. Put the bouquet garni* and bay leaves in the casserole and pour over the sauce to just cover the meat. Cover the casserole with a lid, and cook on a shelf low in the oven for 2½ hours, at 325°F (mark 3).

The flavour of the carbonades is improved if the casserole is put aside at this stage and re-heated the next day, before making the garlic crust.

For the garlic crust, melt the butter in a frying pan over low heat. Crush the three cloves of garlic and stir into the butter. Cut the French bread into ½ in. thick slices and soak in the garlic butter, until this is completely absorbed. Put the bread on top of the carbonades and cook the casserole in an oven pre-heated to 325°F (mark 3) for 30 minutes. The meat should then be thoroughly heated and the garlic crust should be crisp with a golden tinge.

Serve direct from the casserole. Cauliflower with almonds (see January vegetables) could also be served.

Poultry & Game

PARTRIDGE PUDDING

In this adaptation of an old Saxon pudding, game and steak are combined within a suet crust.

PREPARATION TIME: *30 min.*
COOKING TIME: *3 hours*

INGREDIENTS (*for 4–6*):
1 old partridge
8 oz. suet crust (standard recipe)
4 oz. rump steak
Seasoned flour
2 oz. mushrooms
1 level tablespoon fresh parsley
Pinch of dried mixed herbs
1 wine glass claret
½ pint chicken stock

Prepare the suet crust pastry* and roll it out, ¼ in. thick. Line the inside of a well-greased, 2 pint pudding basin with the pastry, retaining about one-third for the lid. Cut the partridge* into four or six neat joints and the steak into ¾ in. squares; coat lightly with seasoned flour*. Put the meat and game in the basin; clean and coarsely chop the mushrooms* and add them to the meat together with the chopped parsley and herbs. Pour in the claret and enough stock to cover the meat.

Roll out the remainder of the pastry and cover the pudding, pinching the pastry edges well together. Cover the basin with buttered greaseproof paper and tie down tightly with a pudding cloth. Set the pudding in a saucepan of boiling water reaching two-thirds up the sides of the basin; steam for 3 hours, topping up with boiling water if necessary.

Turn the pudding out on to a warm plate and serve with Jerusalem artichokes (see January vegetables) and boiled cabbage.

GUINEA FOWL IN RED WINE

Guinea fowl are now classified as poultry and are raised like free-range chickens; they are also available frozen. The somewhat dry flesh is made tender by cooking the fowl in wine.

PREPARATION TIME: *20 min.*
COOKING TIME: *1 hour*

INGREDIENTS (*for 4–6*):
1 or 2 guinea fowl (jointed)
3 oz. belly pork
2 oz. unsalted butter
Salt and black pepper
16 button onions
3 fluid oz. brandy
1 bottle Beaujolais
¼ pint chicken stock
1 bouquet garni
2 cloves garlic
1 level tablespoon soft brown sugar
4 oz. mushrooms
SAUCE:
1 oz. plain flour
1 oz. unsalted butter
GARNISH:
Parsley sprigs

Cut the belly pork into small cubes and fry in half of the butter in a deep sauté pan. Wipe and season the poultry joints with salt and freshly ground pepper. Remove the pork from the pan and slowly brown the guinea fowl in the butter over gentle heat.

Peel the onions and add to the pan, together with the fried belly pork; turn the onions until they are glazed. Warm the brandy, pour over the guinea fowl and set alight. As soon as the flames have died down, pour over the wine and stock, add the bouquet garni* and the crushed garlic. Stir in the brown sugar; increase the heat to bring the contents of

the pan slowly to boiling point. Check the seasoning, cover with a lid and simmer for 30 minutes.

Meanwhile, trim and clean the mushrooms*, sauté them in 1 oz. of butter, drain and add to the fowl after this has simmered for 30 minutes. Cover and cook for a further 10 minutes or until the guinea fowl is tender. Transfer the contents of the pan to a heated serving dish and keep it warm.

Turn up the heat and boil the liquid in the pan rapidly until it is reduced* to about ¾ pint. Work the flour and butter together to form a paste; remove the pan from the heat and beat in knobs of the paste until the sauce thickens. Return to the heat and bring slowly to the boil. Pour the sauce over the guinea fowl and garnish with parsley.

Boiled new potatoes, tossed in butter and parsley, and young blanched broccoli spears, cooked in butter, could be served as well.

GARDENER'S CHICKEN

A casserole of chicken and vegetables makes a change from roast chicken. Once in the oven, the casserole can be left to cook without supervision.

PREPARATION TIME: *40 min.*
COOKING TIME: *1½ hours*

INGREDIENTS (*for 4–6*):
1 chicken, approx. 3 lb.
2 oz. streaky bacon
2 large onions
2 sticks celery
¼ lb. mushrooms
2–3 oz. unsalted butter
1 lb. new potatoes
½ lb. turnips
15–16 oz. tin of tomatoes
1 bouquet garni
Salt and black pepper
GARNISH:
Fresh parsley and orange rind

Joint the chicken* into four or six pieces, and wipe clean. Dice* the bacon, after first removing the rind. Peel and thinly slice the onions; scrub and coarsely chop the celery; clean and slice the mushrooms*. Melt the butter in a large, heavy-based pan and fry the bacon, onions, mushrooms and celery for 5 minutes. Tip the frying pan to drain the butter to one side, remove the vegetables with a perforated spoon, and spread over the base of a large casserole.

Fry the chicken joints in the butter residue, adding a little more if necessary, until they are golden brown. Remove from the pan and place on the bed of vegetables. Scrape the potatoes, peel and slice the turnips and add these, together with the tomatoes

and bouquet garni*, to the casserole. Season with salt and freshly ground pepper, and cover the casserole with kitchen foil, before securing the lid so that no steam can escape. Cook on the middle shelf of the oven heated to 300°F (mark 2) for about 1½ hours or until tender.

Immediately before serving, sprinkle chopped parsley, mixed with the finely chopped rind of half an orange over the casserole. No additional vegetables are needed.

PIGEONS WITH PÂTÉ

Cooked in this manner and presented on a bed of cabbage brightened with orange wedges, the pigeon achieves dinner-party status. The birds should be prepared a day in advance.

PREPARATION TIME: *40 min.*
COOKING TIME: *2 hours 40 min.*

INGREDIENTS (*for 6*):

	STUFFING:	LONG-COOKED
6 young pigeons	*8 oz. tin of pâté*	CABBAGE:
½ bottle dry white wine	*1 tablespoon port*	*4 oz. belly pork*
2 carrots	*1 egg yolk*	*1 large white cabbage*
1 onion	*½ level teaspoon mixed*	*6 juniper berries*
2 bay leaves	*spice*	*2 oz. unsalted butter*
4 sprigs parsley	*½ teaspoon single cream*	*Black pepper*
2 sprigs thyme	*Salt and black pepper*	*2 level teaspoons salt*
Peel of half orange	GARNISH:	*¼ pint dry white wine*
Peel of half lemon	*Orange wedges*	*or chicken stock*
2 oz. unsalted butter		

Wash the pigeons thoroughly inside and out, and remove the giblets. Put the birds in a basin and pour over the wine; peel and thinly slice the carrots and onion and add to the pigeons, with the bay leaves, parsley, thyme, orange and lemon peel. Marinate* the pigeons for 12 hours.

To make the stuffing, stir the pâté smooth, add the port and stir in the egg yolk. Blend in the spice and cream, and season to taste with salt and freshly ground pepper. Remove the pigeons from the marinade, drain and dry them with a cloth. Spoon the stuffing into the birds–it may be necessary to widen the opening a little–and sew them up; pepper them thoroughly. Melt the butter in a large sauté pan, brown the birds quickly, then transfer them to a flameproof casserole. Pour over the marinade, bring to simmering point on top of the stove; adjust seasoning. Cover with a tight-fitting lid, and cook in the lower half of the oven at 275°F (mark 1) for 2½ hours.

For the cabbage, dice the belly pork into ½ in. pieces and put in a heavy pan in the oven. When the fat is running freely and the pork is crisping, swirl the fat around the sides of the pan before removing the pork. Cut off the outer leaves, stump and core of the cabbage, wash thoroughly and shred it into the pan of fat.

Push the juniper berries and the pieces of belly pork into the cabbage and dot with butter. Pepper well and sprinkle with the salt. Pour over the white wine (or stock) and cover the pan tightly with foil. Cook on the shelf below the pigeons for 2½ hours.

Half-way through check the moisture content of the cabbage, and add water if necessary.

Spread the cooked cabbage and pork over the base of a warm serving dish, place the pigeons on top and pour over the liquid. Garnish the cabbage with wedges of orange.

POACHED PARTRIDGE IN VINE LEAVES

Vine leaves impart an unusual flavour to these succulent game birds. Order the partridge ready for cooking and have the giblets included with the order.

PREPARATION TIME: *25 min.*
COOKING TIME: *1½ hours*

INGREDIENTS *(for 4)*:
2 young partridges
Salt and black pepper
6 lemon slices
2 level dessertspoons quince jelly
13–14 oz. tin of vine leaves
¾ lb. fat green bacon rashers
½ pint dry white wine
1½ pint chicken stock
GARNISH:
Watercress, lemon baskets

Wipe the partridges inside and out and season with salt and black pepper. Put 3 lemon slices and 1 dessertspoon quince jelly inside each bird. Wrap the drained vine leaves round the birds, cover with the bacon rashers and tie firmly with fine string.

Bring the wine and stock to the boil in a large saucepan, together with the giblets. Put the partridge parcels into the boiling water and simmer for 1¼ hours.

Chill the partridges quickly by immersing them in a bowl of iced water until quite cold. Remove from the water, unwrap bacon and vine leaves; dry the partridges thoroughly with absorbent paper.

Serve the partridges whole, on a bed of watercress, garnished with lemon baskets with Cumberland sauce. A lettuce and celery salad (see January vegetables) would be a suitable side dish.

SADDLE OF VENISON

PREPARATION TIME: *25 min.*
COOKING TIME: *2¾ hours*

INGREDIENTS *(for 8–10)*:
1 saddle of venison (6–7 lb.)
2 carrots
1 Spanish onion
2 sticks celery
Salt and black pepper
4 oz. unsalted butter
¼ pint olive oil
2 cloves garlic
2 bay leaves
1 sprig or ½ level teaspoon powdered thyme
½ pint chicken stock
½ bottle port
1 heaped tablespoon plain flour
2 oz. unsalted butter
1 heaped tablespoon redcurrant jelly

For a special dinner occasion, venison in port is an excellent choice. The saddle should have been hung for at least three weeks to ensure a truly succulent roast. A saddle will serve eight people handsomely, and the recipe is also suitable for a smaller joint.

Peel and chop the carrots, onion and celery. Trim any gristle from the venison, wipe well with a cloth and season with salt and pepper. Melt the butter and combine with the olive oil in a large roasting or sauté pan; quickly brown the venison, then remove. Turn up the heat, peel and crush the garlic, and add to the pan together with the bay leaves, thyme and chopped vegetables; cook for 5 minutes without colouring. Return the venison to the pan and cover with foil, making sure it is tightly sealed. Cook for 45 minutes on the bottom shelf of an oven preheated to 375°F (mark 5), then pour in the boiling stock, re-seal and cook for 1 hour.

Remove the pan to the top of the stove; pour the port over the venison and heat until the juices are simmering, then return to the oven. Do not re-seal, but cook for another hour, basting every 15 minutes. If the joint appears to be cooking too quickly, turn the heat down slightly for the last 30 minutes. Transfer the venison to a dish and keep it hot in the oven while making the sauce.

Strain the liquid from the roasting pan into a saucepan and keep at a fast boil until reduced* by half. Meanwhile, combine the flour and butter to make a paste and use knobs of this to thicken the reduced sauce, stirring continuously. Finally mix in the redcurrant jelly, and as soon as this has dissolved, season the sauce with salt and pepper if necessary.

Carve* the joint and arrange the slices on a serving dish. Pour some of the sauce over the meat and surround with glazed onions (see December vegetables), mushroom caps fried in butter, and bread croûtons*. Serve the remainder of the sauce separately.

Rice & Pasta

SPAGHETTI WITH AUBERGINE

In Italy, pasta—and in particular spaghetti—frequently forms the main meal of the day. Often oil and garlic are the only additions, but aubergine gives the pasta an unusual flavour.

PREPARATION TIME: *10 min.*
COOKING TIME: *15 min.*

INGREDIENTS *(for 4–6)*:
$\frac{3}{4}$ *lb. spaghetti*
1 large aubergine
2 level tablespoons salt
6 tablespoons olive oil
Seasoned flour
Black pepper

Remove the stalk end and wipe the aubergine, cut it into thin round slices and place these in layers in a colander. Sprinkle salt over each layer and leave for 1 hour to draw out the excess water. Wipe the slices dry on absorbent kitchen paper, cut them into $\frac{1}{4}$ in. wide strips and coat them lightly with seasoned flour*.

Heat 8 pints of water in a large saucepan and, when boiling, add 1 level tablespoon salt and the spaghetti. Stir continuously until the water returns to the boil. Continue boiling and stirring occasionally for 9 minutes, when the spaghetti should be tender but still slightly undercooked (*al dente*). While the spaghetti is cooking, heat 3–4 tablespoons of olive oil in a frying pan and sauté* the aubergine strips until crisp.

Drain the spaghetti, toss in a colander to remove the last of the water, and pepper well. Warm the remaining olive oil in a saucepan, transfer the spaghetti to a warm serving dish and pour over the oil. Toss well and blend the aubergine strips into the spaghetti.

FRIED RICE WITH LEEKS

This unusual rice dish is especially good with meat courses that contain a lot of sauce, such as casseroles and braised oxtail stews.

PREPARATION TIME: *15 min.*
COOKING TIME: *20 min.*

INGREDIENTS *(for 6)*:
2 lb. leeks
6 oz. Patna rice
2 level tablespoons salt
2 oz. unsalted butter
$\frac{1}{2}$ *level teaspoon curry powder*
Black pepper

Set a pan holding about 6 pints of water to boil for the rice, and a smaller one holding about 1 pint for the leeks. Remove the coarse outer leaves, roots and tops from the leeks, wash well under cold running water, flushing away any dirt trapped in the ends; cut into $\frac{1}{4}$ in. thick slices. Add a tablespoon of salt to each saucepan of boiling water, put the leeks in one and the rice in the other. Stir the rice until it comes back to the boil, cover and boil for 14 minutes. Meanwhile, simmer the leeks for about 5 minutes, then drain them through a colander. Melt the butter in a frying pan, and fry the leeks for about 8 minutes or until just tender.

When it is cooked, turn the rice into a sieve and wash thoroughly under hot running water. Add the drained rice to the leeks in the frying pan, blend with the curry powder; fry for a few minutes, stirring all the time. Season with freshly ground pepper and serve.

FETTUCCINE AL BURRO

This pasta is a speciality of many Roman restaurants and is ideally made from home-made noodles. It may be served as a first course, or as a main course for a light lunch.

PREPARATION TIME: *8 min.*
COOKING TIME: *10–15 min.*

INGREDIENTS *(for 4–6)*:
1 lb. ribbon noodles
1 level tablespoon salt
$\frac{1}{4}$ *lb. unsalted butter*
3 fluid oz. double cream
6 oz. grated Parmesan cheese
Black pepper

Boil 8 pints of water in a large saucepan, and add the salt and the noodles, stirring until the water returns to the boil, to prevent the noodles from sticking together. Cover and continue to boil for 8 minutes until the noodles are tender. Meanwhile beat the softened butter in a bowl until it fluffs; gradually beat in the cream and half the cheese. Drain the noodles and toss them in a colander to remove the last drops of water.

Put the noodles in a hot serving dish, pour over the cheese and cream sauce and toss to coat the noodles thoroughly. Pepper well and serve the remaining cheese in a bowl. A salad of lettuce, sliced fennel root and tomatoes could be served as a side dish.

RICE WITH GARLIC AND WALNUTS

Plain boiled rice is a good substitute for potatoes and vegetables. Here the rice is given additional flavour which makes it a good choice with goulash, curry or braised oxtails.

PREPARATION TIME: *15 min.*
COOKING TIME: *14 min.*

INGREDIENTS *(for 4–6)*:
8 oz. Patna rice
*2 heaped tablespoons finely
    chopped parsley*
2 cloves garlic
1 oz. shelled walnuts
2 oz. grated Parmesan cheese
3 tablespoons olive oil
Salt and black pepper
2 pints chicken stock
1 level tablespoon salt
Juice of half lemon

Pound the parsley in a mortar with the peeled garlic and nuts until a smooth paste is achieved. Beat in the cheese until the mixture is thick, then gradually beat in the oil. Season to taste with salt and freshly ground pepper.

Pour the stock and 6 pints of hot water into a large saucepan and bring to the boil. Add the salt, lemon juice and rice, stirring until the water returns to the boil. Cover and boil for 14 minutes or until the rice is just tender. Drain in a colander and rinse the rice by running hot water through it.

Drain the rice thoroughly and stir with a fork to separate the grains. Spoon it into a hot serving dish; season with a good grating of pepper. Blend the nut mixture into the rice and serve.

Vegetables & Salads

COLESLAW WITH ITALIAN DRESSING

This quickly made winter salad can be served with cold meat or as a side dish with a plain omelette.

PREPARATION TIME: *10 min.*

INGREDIENTS *(for 4–6)*:
1 drumhead cabbage
1 small clove garlic
6 tablespoons olive oil
2 tablespoons white wine vinegar
¼ level teaspoon oregano
¼ level teaspoon crushed fennel
seeds
¼ level teaspoon celery salt
Salt and black pepper

Cut away the coarse outer leaves from the cabbage, remove the core and finely shred the cabbage into a serving bowl. Crush the garlic and put it, with all the other ingredients, in a screw-top jar and shake vigorously. Pour this dressing over the cabbage, toss and serve.

CAULIFLOWER WITH ALMONDS

Cauliflower is an ideal vegetable for fish or meat in rich sauces. Crisp roasted almonds complement its delicate flavour.

PREPARATION TIME: *10 min.*
COOKING TIME: *12 min.*

INGREDIENTS *(for 4)*:
1 large white cauliflower
Salt
2 oz. clarified butter
2 oz. flaked almonds

Dissolve two tablespoons of salt in a large bowl of cold water. Cut away the coarse outer leaves from the cauliflower and break the individual florets from the central stem, leaving a short stalk on each. Drop the florets in the salted water, together with the inner pale green leaves.

Bring a large pan of salted water to the boil; cook the drained cauliflower, covered, over low heat for 5–8 minutes. Drain through a colander.

Meanwhile, fry the almonds in the clarified butter* over low heat until deep brown. Put the cauliflower in a dish and spoon over the almonds and butter.

JERUSALEM ARTICHOKES IN BUTTER

The brown-purple skin of these knobbly tubers hides a white, firm and sweet flesh, reminiscent in taste of globe artichokes.

PREPARATION TIME: *30 min.*
COOKING TIME: *25–40 min.*

INGREDIENTS *(for 6)*:
1½ lb. Jerusalem artichokes
Juice of a lemon
1 level tablespoon salt
2 oz. unsalted butter
Seasoned flour

Strain the lemon juice into a bowl of cold water. Wash and scrape, or thinly peel, the artichokes*, cut them into ¼ in. slices and drop into the water and lemon juice to prevent them going grey. Bring a large pan of water to the boil. Drain the artichokes and drop into the boiling water, with the salt. Boil for 4 minutes, then drain in a colander.

Melt the butter in an ovenproof flat dish in an oven pre-heated to 350°F (mark 4). Coat the artichokes with the seasoned flour*, and roll in the butter. Cook on the middle shelf for about 40 minutes.

PARSNIP CROQUETTES

Parsnip is one of the staple winter vegetables in Britain, and is often served as a mash or purée. These crisp croquettes, which should be prepared in advance, go well with roast or braised meat.

PREPARATION TIME: *30 min.*
COOKING TIME: *5 min.*

INGREDIENTS *(for 4–6)*:
2 lb. parsnips
1 level tablespoon salt
2 oz. unsalted butter
Black pepper
1 level teaspoon nutmeg
Fresh white breadcrumbs
1 beaten egg, strained
Oil for deep-frying

Bring a large pan of water to the boil, and meanwhile peel the parsnips, cutting out the hard centres. Cut the parsnips into thin slices and add, with the salt, to the boiling water. Simmer for 20 minutes, or until the parsnips are tender. Drain thoroughly; rub the parsnips through a coarse sieve and beat in the butter, pepper and nutmeg. Allow to cool slightly then shape into croquettes* about 2½ in. long and 1 in. wide. Roll each croquette in the breadcrumbs, through the strained egg, and through the breadcrumbs again. Leave to rest in the refrigerator for 1 hour.

Fill a deep-fryer a third of the way up with oil and heat until a cube of bread crisps in it*. Dip the frying basket in and out of the oil, place the croquettes in the basket and lower them into the oil. Switch off the heat immediately and in 3 minutes the croquettes should be golden brown.

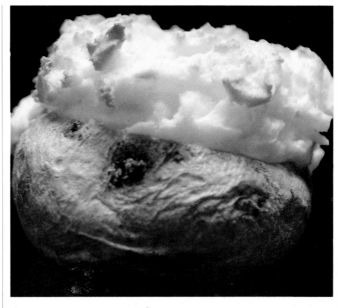

SOUFFLÉ POTATOES

With just a little extra trouble, plain baked potatoes can be transformed into light and fluffy individual soufflés. They are ideal with all meats, particularly so with steak.

PREPARATION TIME: *15 min.*
COOKING TIME: *1¾ hours*

INGREDIENTS *(for 6)*:
6 large potatoes
2 oz. unsalted melted butter
4 fluid oz. double cream
3 eggs
Salt and black pepper

Wash and dry the potatoes, prick them lightly with a fork and bake for 1½ hours or until tender on the middle shelf of an oven pre-heated to 400°F (mark 6). Cut a lid lengthways off the baked potatoes, scoop the flesh out into a bowl and mix in with it the melted butter and cream. Separate the eggs and stir the yolks into the potato mixture. Beat the egg whites with a little salt until stiff and fold into the potato mixture. Season to taste with freshly ground pepper.

Pile this soufflé mixture back into the hollow potato skins, return to the oven and bake at the same temperature for 15 minutes, or until the soufflés are well risen.

Serve immediately, before the soufflés have time to collapse and go flat.

FASOULIA

In Greece, this regional dish of haricot beans is usually served as a vegetable course on its own. It can accompany any kind of meat and is particularly good with lamb. Preparations should begin 12 hours in advance.

PREPARATION TIME: *8 min.*
COOKING TIME: *3¼ hours*

INGREDIENTS *(for 4):*
½ *lb. haricot beans*
1 large onion
¼ *pint olive oil*
2 cloves garlic
1 bay leaf
½ *level teaspoon powdered thyme*
1 tablespoon tomato paste
Juice of a lemon
Salt and black pepper
GARNISH:
Coarsely chopped parsley

Soak the haricot beans in plenty of cold water for 12 hours. The following day, peel and coarsely chop the onion; fry it in the olive oil in a deep sauté pan until it takes colour. Strain the beans and add to the onion, together with the peeled and crushed garlic, the bay leaf, thyme and tomato paste. Cook over a moderate heat for 10 minutes, then add boiling water to cover the beans by about 1 in. Continue cooking at a gentle simmer for about 3 hours or until the beans are quite tender, but not mushy. Add the lemon juice and season to taste. Allow the beans to cool in the liquid which should have the consistency of a thick sauce.

Serve the cold beans in their liquid garnished with parsley.

LETTUCE AND CELERY SALAD

Most rich meat dishes, especially those with sweet stuffings, are better accompanied by a side salad than by a vegetable dish.

PREPARATION TIME: *10 min.*

INGREDIENTS *(for 4–6):*
4 lettuce hearts
4 celery sticks
DRESSING:
1 level teaspoon Dijon mustard
½ *level teaspoon salt*
1 level teaspoon caster sugar
¼ *pint single cream*
¼ *pint olive oil*
3 tablespoons tarragon vinegar
GARNISH:
Celery leaves

Cut each lettuce heart into four; trim off roots and coarse leaves from the celery, scrub and chop the sticks coarsely. Place these ingredients in a serving bowl.

To make the dressing, blend the mustard, salt and sugar in a mixing bowl; stir in the cream. Beat in the olive oil, drop by drop, and when all the oil is absorbed, gradually beat in the vinegar until the dressing has the consistency of thick cream. Pour the dressing over the celery and lettuce, toss and serve garnished with a few celery leaves.

Sweets & Puddings

BROCCOLI SPEARS AU GRATIN

The purple or white sprouting winter broccoli requires undercooking to preserve its flavour. The spears can be served tossed in butter or, as here, in a white sauce.

PREPARATION TIME: *10 min.*
COOKING TIME: *15 min.*

INGREDIENTS *(for 6):*
1½ *lb. broccoli spears*
1 *level tablespoon salt*
½ *pint white sauce*
3 *oz. unsalted butter*
2–3 *heaped tablespoons fresh white breadcrumbs*
Black pepper

Bring a large saucepan of water to the boil. Cut away all coarse leaves from the broccoli and trim the stalks (tough stalks should be pared). Wash well. Salt the water, before adding the broccoli. Bring the water quickly back to the boil and simmer for 5–12 minutes until the broccoli is just tender.

Meanwhile, prepare the white sauce* and set the grill to high.

Drain the broccoli well and place in a shallow gratin* or flameproof dish. Pour over the white sauce to coat the broccoli. Melt 2 oz. of the butter in a small pan, mix in the breadcrumbs and sprinkle them over the broccoli. Dot with the remaining butter, pepper, and place under the grill for a few minutes until the crumbs are golden brown.

FIG PIE

In Lancashire, fig pie was traditionally served on Mothering Sunday in March. This was the only day on which Lenten fasting could be broken.

PREPARATION TIME: *45 min.*
COOKING TIME: *35 min.*

INGREDIENTS *(for 6):*
6 *oz. shortcrust pastry (standard recipe)*
½ *lb. figs (fresh or dried)*
1 *level dessertspoon cornflour*
½ *teaspoon ground mixed spice*
1 *oz. currants*
1 *dessertspoon treacle or golden syrup*

Roll out the pastry*, on a floured surface, to a thickness of ⅛ in. Line a deep 8 in. pie plate with the pastry. Cut the stalks off the figs and place the fruit in a shallow saucepan with enough water to just cover them; cook over low heat until tender. Fresh figs need 5–15 minutes, cooking time depending on their ripeness; dried figs should first be soaked for 12 hours with a squeeze of lemon juice before being stewed for 20 minutes in their soaking liquid.

Drain the figs and retain ½ pint of the liquid; top up with hot water if necessary. Pour a little of the juice into a basin, add the cornflour and mix until it resembles a thin smooth cream. Gradually add the rest of the liquid, stirring well. When well mixed, return it to the saucepan and place over moderate heat. Stir until thickened, then cook for another 2 minutes. Mix in the spice, currants and syrup and remove from the heat.

Arrange the figs over the pastry; pour over the thickened fig liquid, making sure that the currants are evenly distributed. Bake the pie on the middle shelf of the oven heated to 400°F (mark 6) for 30–35 minutes.

Serve hot or cold, with cream or vanilla ice cream*.

SCOTTISH FLUMMERY

Flora MacDonald is reputed to have been half-way through a dish of Scottish Flummery when she was arrested. She had just escorted Bonnie Prince Charlie to his hiding place on the Isle of Skye in 1746.

PREPARATION TIME: *15 min.*

INGREDIENTS *(for 4–6):*
1 *level tablespoon oatmeal*
½ *pint double cream*
3 *tablespoons clear honey*
4 *tablespoons liqueur whisky*
Juice of half lemon

Heat the oatmeal gently in a heavy-based pan until it turns brown, then set aside. Beat the cream until smooth, but not stiff. Melt the honey in a saucepan over a gentle heat until it runs easily, but do not allow it to boil. Fold the honey into the beaten cream and finally stir in the liqueur whisky and lemon juice.

Serve the warm cream and honey mixture in tall individual glasses and sprinkle the brown oatmeal on top.

TREACLE TART

British country cooking is justly famous for its variety of sweet and savoury tarts and pastries. The popularity of this traditional lattice tart has never diminished. It is, in spite of its name, always made with golden syrup.

PREPARATION TIME: *20 min.*
COOKING TIME: *25–30 min.*

INGREDIENTS *(for 6):*
7 *oz. plain flour*
½ *level teaspoon salt*
1 *egg yolk*
5 *oz. unsalted butter*
5 *rounded tablespoons golden syrup*
3 *heaped tablespoons fresh white breadcrumbs*
1 *level teaspoon finely grated lemon rind*
1 *tablespoon lemon juice*

Sieve the flour into a mixing bowl, add the salt and mix in the egg yolk with a fork. Cut the butter into small knobs and rub into the flour until thoroughly absorbed and crumbly. Bind the pastry with cold water, and roll out, ⅛ in. thick, on a lightly floured surface. Line an 8 in. shallow pie plate with the pastry and prick the base lightly with a fork. Mix the other ingredients together and spread over the pastry. Roll out the pastry trimmings, cut them into ½ in. wide strips and lay them in a lattice pattern over the tart; trim the edges neatly. Bake the tart on the middle shelf of an oven preheated to 400°F (mark 6) for 25–30 minutes.

Serve hot or cold with custard*.

ICED TANGERINES

For a special dinner party, this refreshingly tangy and impressive looking ice cream is a fitting ending. Prepare the ice cream a day ahead.

PREPARATION TIME: *30 min.*
COOKING TIME: *25 min.*

INGREDIENTS *(for 6):*
8 medium-sized tangerines
  (preferably the Wilkins
  variety)
6 oz. caster sugar
½ pint water
Juice of half lemon
1 egg yolk
½ pint double cream
GARNISH:
Crystallised violets
Tangerine slices
Camellia leaves
Langues de chat

Wipe the tangerines, cut off the tops and carefully scoop out the flesh from both tops and bottoms. Place six of the empty tangerine skins in a polythene bag in the refrigerator and set the remaining two aside. Squeeze ½ pint of juice from the tangerine pulp. Boil the sugar and water in a saucepan over a high heat for 10 minutes to make a syrup. Remove and allow to cool. Stir into the syrup the tangerine and lemon juices. Beat the egg yolk and stir into the syrup. Return to the heat and cook gently for 5 minutes, stirring continuously. Cool, pour into a freezing container, cover tightly with a lid and place in the freezing compartment of the refrigerator until lightly set, for approximately 1½–2 hours.

Grate the rind of the remaining two tangerines and beat the cream until stiff. Break the frozen syrup

into a bowl and beat vigorously with a fork until it has an even texture. Beat in the cream and tangerine rind until the colour is uniform and the rind evenly distributed. Spoon this ice cream back into the freezing container, cover with a lid and freeze for a further 2½ hours.

Turn out the mixture, break it down as before and beat until the texture is even; return to the freezer. One hour before serving, scoop the ice cream into the empty tangerine skins and fix on the lids at an angle.

Brush the outsides of the tangerines with water and place in the freezer. Ten minutes before serving, remove the tangerines from the freezer in order to let the frost on the skins settle.

Serve on a tray decorated with well-washed camellia (or other glossy evergreen) leaves, crystallised violets and tangerine slices. A dish of langues de chat* could be served separately.

RHUBARB AND CINNAMON FLAN

The first young rhubarb appears in the shops this month. Here, it is combined with cinnamon which counteracts the acidity of the fruit. Serve the flan warm or cold, cut into wedges. It can also be stored in the home freezer.

PREPARATION TIME: *20 min.*
COOKING TIME: *35 min.*

INGREDIENTS *(for 6):*
6 oz. shortcrust pastry (standard
  recipe)
1 lb. rhubarb
2 oz. caster sugar
2 level tablespoons plain flour
½ level teaspoon powdered
  cinnamon
¼ pint double cream

Roll out the pastry* to a thickness of ⅛ in., on a lightly floured surface, and use to line an 8 in. flan ring set on a greased baking sheet. Cut off the roots and any coarse or blemished parts of the rhubarb. Wash, slice them diagonally into ½ in. pieces and arrange over the pastry. Mix the sugar, flour, cinnamon and cream together and spoon over the rhubarb. Put the flan on the middle shelf of an oven pre-heated to 425°F (mark 7) and bake for 30 minutes.

If the flan is to be served warm, let it rest for 10 minutes otherwise it will be difficult to cut.

BREAD PUDDING

The genuine Welsh bread pudding is packed with fruit, spices and peel. It is served warm as a pudding; any left-overs can be served cold at tea-time.

PREPARATION TIME: *35 min.*
COOKING TIME: *2 hours*

INGREDIENTS *(for 4–6):*
8 oz. stale white bread
½ pint milk
2 oz. candied peel
Peel of a small orange
Peel of a lemon
4 oz. currants
2 oz. sultanas
3 oz. shredded beef suet
2 oz. demerara sugar
2 level teaspoons mixed spice
1 large egg
Milk
Butter
Grated nutmeg
Caster sugar

Cut away all the crust from the bread; break the bread into small pieces. Place in a large mixing bowl and pour over the milk; leave to soak for 20 minutes. Finely chop the candied peel, grate the orange and lemon peel, add to the bread and mix in. Add the dried fruit, suet, sugar and mixed spice; blend well. Beat the egg and stir it into the mixture which should have a dropping consistency. If necessary, add a dessertspoon of milk.

Spoon the bread mixture into a well-greased 2 pint pie dish and grate a little nutmeg over it. Bake on the middle shelf of an oven heated to 350°F (mark 4) for 1¾–2 hours or until browned.

Serve hot or cold, liberally sprinkled with caster sugar; serve custard* or cream in a bowl.

Savouries & Snacks

PYTT I PANNA

This classic Swedish leftover dish makes the best use of cooked meat and potatoes.

PREPARATION TIME: *10 min.*
COOKING TIME: *20 min.*

INGREDIENTS *(for 4)*:
1 lb. cooked, diced beef or lamb
5 boiled, chopped potatoes
1½ oz. unsalted butter
1 tablespoon olive oil
8 oz. streaky bacon (diced)
1 large chopped onion
Salt and black pepper
1 tablespoon chopped parsley
1 teaspoon Worcestershire sauce
GARNISH:
4 fried eggs

Fry the potatoes in the butter and oil, over a high heat, until golden brown. Drain on crumpled absorbent paper and keep warm. Fry the meat, bacon and onion over medium heat until the onion softens, and the bacon is cooked. Return the potatoes to the pan, mix the ingredients carefully and season to taste. Cook for another 5 minutes, shaking the pan to prevent sticking. Stir in the parsley and Worcestershire sauce.

Spoon the mixture into a warm serving dish and top with the lightly fried eggs. Serve at once.

SERENA'S MACARONI CHEESE

Ham and fresh tomatoes add colour and flavour to a plain macaroni cheese.

PREPARATION TIME: *20 min.*
COOKING TIME: *20 min.*

INGREDIENTS *(for 4–6)*:
½ lb. macaroni
4 oz. cooked, diced ham
*4 large, skinned and chopped tomatoes**
¾ pint white sauce
6 oz. grated Cheddar or Double Gloucester cheese
Salt and black pepper
2 tablespoons fresh white breadcrumbs
1 oz. unsalted melted butter

Cook the macaroni, uncovered, in plenty of boiling salted water for about 15 minutes. Stir 4 oz. of the cheese into the white sauce*; season to taste.

Fold the drained macaroni, the ham and tomatoes, into the sauce; spoon the mixture into a buttered ovenproof dish. Mix the remaining cheese with the breadcrumbs, sprinkle over the macaroni, and pour the melted butter over. Bake near the top of a pre-heated oven at 400°F (mark 6) for 20 minutes or until the top is crisp and golden.

Serve hot, with a crisp winter salad or a green vegetable.

PIZZA BAPS

These savoury baps make a good hot snack, and can also be served cold in a packed lunch.

PREPARATION TIME: *15 min.*
COOKING TIME: *20–25 min.*

INGREDIENTS *(for 4)*:
4 large baps or soft rolls
4 tablespoons olive oil
1 large, thinly sliced onion
2 oz. sliced button mushrooms
*2 large, skinned and sliced tomatoes**
Salt and black pepper
Basil or marjoram (optional)
6 oz. thinly sliced quick-melting cheese
8 anchovy fillets

Slice the baps in half and brush the surfaces with olive oil (setting 1 tablespoon aside). Cook the onion in the remaining oil until soft; add the mushrooms and cook for another 2 minutes.

Arrange the tomato slices on top of the bap halves, season with salt, pepper and a little basil or marjoram. Spoon the onion and mushroom mixture on top and cover with the cheese. Halve each anchovy fillet and arrange in a cross pattern on top of the cheese.

Bake the baps in the centre of an oven pre-heated to 350°F (mark 4) for 20–25 minutes or until the cheese is golden.

WINTER SALAD

A crisp salad lunch is welcome even on a winter's day. Baked potatoes or crusty bread make it a complete meal.

PREPARATION TIME: *20 min.*
CHILLING TIME: *30 min.*

INGREDIENTS *(for 6)*:
10–12 oz. cooked, diced meat or poultry
½ small white, shredded cabbage
2 large grated carrots
4 sticks finely chopped celery
1 crisp, diced dessert apple
1 tablespoon sultanas
Juice of half lemon
2 tablespoons double cream
½ pint mayonnaise
Salt and black pepper

Mix the meat, all the vegetables, the apple and the sultanas together in a large salad bowl. Whisk the lemon juice and cream into the mayonnaise*; season. Pour this dressing over the salad and blend.

Chill for at least 30 minutes.

SAVOURY FRITTERS

Fritters are cooked meat, fresh fruit or vegetable slices coated in batter and deep fried.

PREPARATION TIME: *15 min.*
COOKING TIME: *10 min.*

INGREDIENTS *(for 6)*:
8 oz. cooked, diced meat
1 large, chopped onion
½ green chopped pepper
2 rashers streaky bacon (diced)
1 tablespoon olive oil
4 oz. plain flour
2 large eggs (separated)
¼ pint milk
Salt and black pepper
Fat for frying

Cook the onion, pepper and bacon in the oil until soft; drain thoroughly on absorbent paper.

Beat the flour, egg yolks and milk until smooth; season to taste. Stir the meat and the onion mixture into this batter, then carefully fold in the stiffly beaten egg whites.

In a deep fryer, heat the fat until smoking hot, then drop dessertspoons of the mixture into the fat, a few at a time; cook until puffed up and golden brown, after 1–2 minutes. Drain on absorbent kitchen paper and keep hot.

Serve the fritters, with a salad, such as coleslaw (see January vegetables).

New Year Dinners

A dinner at home should be planned so that the hostess will have little work once the guests arrive. These two menus can be prepared in advance; keeping the dishes hot is simply a matter of knowing how. About 30 minutes before dinner, heat the oven to 450°F (mark 8), turn off the rings on top and set the hot dishes closely together, covering them with double foil. The heat will rise and keep them warm.

Three-course Dinner

This easy menu, for four, consists of prawn salad, duck with orange, new potatoes and green peas, followed by snow eggs.

La Salade de Crevettes
Le Caneton à l'Orange
Les Pommes Rissolées
Les Petits Pois au Beurre
Les Oeufs à la Neige
WINE: Beaujolais

La Salade de Crevettes

PREPARATION TIME: *20 min.*

1 lb. peeled prawns
3 tablespoons mayonnaise
4 tablespoons double cream
Juice of half lemon
Salt and black pepper
2 large dessert apples, peeled and finely shredded
1 celery heart, shredded
12 shelled walnuts

Serve the ducks garnished with orange segments and strips of orange rind. Pour part of the sauce round the ducks and serve the rest in a sauce boat

Blend the mayonnaise* with the cream, add the lemon juice and season with salt and pepper. Fold in the prawns, apples and celery.

Spoon the salad into a serving bowl and garnish with the walnuts. Leave the salad in a cool place, not the refrigerator, until required.

Le Caneton à l'Orange

PREPARATION TIME: *45 min.*
COOKING TIME: *1¾ hours*

2 ducks (approx. 4–5 lb. each)
4 oranges
1 level tablespoon caster sugar
4 fluid oz. red wine vinegar
10 fluid oz. giblet stock
Juice of half lemon
1 level tablespoon arrowroot
3 tablespoons Curaçao

Peel the oranges over a plate to catch the juice. Remove all pith and divide the oranges into segments. Cut the rind into strips and boil them for 10 minutes in a little water. Drain them and set aside, with the orange segments, for garnishing.

Pre-heat the oven to 400°F (mark 6) and place the trussed ducks* on their sides in a greased roasting tin. Cook for 40 minutes, then turn the ducks on to the other side and cook for 30 minutes. Finally place the ducks on their backs and cook for 30 minutes. Baste* frequently.

Boil the sugar and vinegar until reduced* to a light caramel. Add the stock, reserved orange and the lemon juice and boil for 5 minutes. Thicken the sauce with diluted arrowroot and stir until shiny. Strain the sauce, stir in the Curaçao and pour over the duck.

The table is set with modern tableware, and coloured candles form the centrepiece. On the left, a dish of snow eggs – egg whites set on a custard base

Les Pommes Rissolées

PREPARATION TIME: *15 min.*
COOKING TIME: *20 min.*

1½ lb. small new potatoes
2–3 oz. unsalted butter

Bring the scraped potatoes to the boil in lightly salted water. Remove the pan at once and drain the potatoes.

Melt the butter in a heavy-based pan, and cook the potatoes, covered, until golden.

Les Petits Pois au Beurre

PREPARATION TIME: *5 min.*
COOKING TIME: *8 min.*

1 lb. small peas
1–2 oz. unsalted butter

Cook the peas in lightly salted water until tender. Strain and toss the peas in the butter.

Les Oeufs à la Neige

PREPARATION TIME: *50 min.*

4 eggs, separated
Pinch salt
5 oz. caster sugar
1 pint milk
1 vanilla pod
2 tablespoons brandy

Beat the egg whites stiff with the salt and 2 oz. of the sugar.

Bring ¾ pint of milk to the boil, with the vanilla pod. Spoon the egg whites into four oval shapes and poach* them in the slowly simmering milk for 2–3 minutes. Lift them out and leave to drain.

Make a custard* from the egg yolks, milk, sugar, and the poaching milk. Strain into a dish and stir in the brandy.

Leave the custard to cool, then top with the poached egg whites.

The centrepiece for this formal table is a bowl of roses intertwined with black grapes. On the right, pale green creamed pea soup with tiny bread croûtons

Four-course Dinner

This more elaborate dinner menu for four people can still be prepared in advance. Creamed pea soup is followed by sole fillets, and the main course is chicken with new potatoes and French beans. The chilled dessert is white peaches in chestnut and brandy-flavoured cream. White and red wines, followed by vintage port would suit the menu.

La Crème de Petits Pois
Les Filets de Sole Cubat
WINE: Piesporter Goldtropfchen
Les Suprêmes de Volaille
St Sylvestre
Les Pommes Nouvelles
Les Haricots Verts au Beurre
WINE: Château Talbot 1970
Les Pêches Châtelaine
WINE: Vintage Port

La Crème de Petits Pois
PREPARATION TIME: *10 min.*
COOKING TIME: *20 min.*

10 oz. small, cooked green peas
1 oz. unsalted butter
2 level tablespoons plain flour
2 pints strained stock
2 tablespoons double cream
Salt
Bread croûtons

Rub the cooked peas through a fine sieve or put them in a liquidiser to make a purée*.

Make a smooth roux* from the butter and flour, and blend in the stock. Bring the mixture to the boil, add the pea purée and simmer for 10 minutes.

Strain this soup, add the cream and season with salt. Heat the soup through and serve it garnished with bread croûtons*.

Les Filets de Sole Cubat
PREPARATION TIME: *15 min.*
COOKING TIME: *25 min.*

4 sole fillets
2½ fluid oz. fish stock
2½ fluid oz. white wine
4 oz. chopped button mushrooms
1½–2 oz. unsalted butter
1½ level tablespoons plain flour
7–8 fluid oz. milk
3 oz. grated Parmesan cheese
Salt and black pepper

Lay the folded sole fillets in a buttered fireproof dish and pour over the stock and wine. Cover with buttered greaseproof paper. Poach* the fish in the oven at 350°F (mark 4) for 10 minutes.

Cook the mushrooms in the butter for 3 minutes, sprinkle in the flour and blend thoroughly. Gradually add the milk and bring

the sauce to the boil. Simmer for 5 minutes before blending in half the cheese; season to taste.

Put the drained sole fillets in a flameproof serving dish, spoon over the sauce and sprinkle with the remaining cheese. Put the fillets in the oven or under a hot grill until golden on top.

Les Suprêmes de Volaille St Sylvestre
PREPARATION TIME: *20 min.*
COOKING TIME: *35 min.*

4 boned chicken breasts
5 oz. unsalted butter
1 finely chopped shallot
5 fluid oz. red wine
5 fluid oz. chicken stock
Salt and black pepper

Cook the chicken in 2 oz. of the butter, over gentle heat, for 25 minutes, or until tender.

Arrange the chicken on a serving dish. Add the shallot to the pan, with the wine. Bring to the boil and continue boiling for 1 minute. Add the stock and boil briskly until reduced* by half. Stir in the remaining butter, in small knobs, and season to taste.

Just before serving pour the sauce over the chicken.

Les Pommes Nouvelles
PREPARATION TIME: *15 min.*
COOKING TIME: *20 min.*

1 lb. new potatoes
1½ oz. butter

Boil the unpeeled potatoes until tender, then drain and peel. Keep the potatoes warm, sprinkle with salt and toss in butter.

Les Haricots Verts au Beurre
PREPARATION TIME: *5 min.*
COOKING TIME: *10 min.*

1–1½ lb. prepared French beans
1–1½ oz. unsalted butter

Cook the beans over high heat for about 10 minutes. Drain and toss in butter before serving.

Les Pêches Châtelaine
PREPARATION TIME: *20 min.*
CHILLING TIME: *1–2 hours*

8 tinned white peach halves
2 tablespoons brandy
2 tablespoons chestnut purée
¼ pint double cream

Put the drained peaches in a dish. Blend the brandy, chestnut purée and cream. Spoon over the peaches and chill.

The main course is chicken St Sylvestre. This is named after the 4th-century pope and patron saint of Pisa whose feast day falls on New Year's Eve

February

Ill huswiferie craveth
in secret to borrow.
Good huswiferie saveth
to day for to morrow.

This Month's Recipes

*February is the month when bitter Seville oranges appear. This is the time
to make marmalade, one of the glories of the British breakfast table*

FEBRUARY
Food in Season

The first winter catch of cod should appear in February, with mullet, lemon sole, mackerel, scallops and sprats still in prime condition. Feathered game is in short supply and best used up in warming casseroles. Celeriac, a celery-flavoured root vegetable imported from the Continent, is at its least expensive, together with pale green endive for crisp winter salads. Celery from America and Israel is young and excellent, both for braising and in salads. Provided the ground is not frozen, thus making lifting impossible, leeks are plentiful and economic this month, for soups, casseroles and vegetables dishes. The season for citrus fruit is coming to an end, but home-grown forced rhubarb is at its best and can be served, stewed or poached, on its own or with other fruit.

Fish

Bream, freshwater
Bream, sea
Brill
Carp
Clams
Cod
Coley
Conger eels
Crab
Dabs
Dover sole
Dublin Bay prawns
Flake (also sold as rock salmon)
Flounder
Grey mullet
Haddock
Hake
Halibut
Herring
Lemon sole
Lobster
Mackerel
Mock halibut (or Greenland halibut)
Mussels
Oysters (native)
Oysters, Portuguese
Pike
Prawns
Redfish
Salmon
Scallops
Shrimps
Skate
Sprats
Trout, rainbow
Turbot
Whiting
Witch

Poultry & Game

Chicken
Duck
Guinea fowl
Hare
Partridge
Pheasant
Pigeon
Rabbit
Turkey
Venison
Wild duck
Wild goose

Vegetables

Asparagus
Aubergines
Avocado pears
Beetroots
Broccoli, purple
Broccoli, white
Brussels sprouts
Brussels tops
Cabbages
Carrots
Cauliflowers
Celeriac
Celery
Chicory
Courgettes
Cucumbers
Endive
Fennel
French beans
Globe artichokes
Horseradish
Jerusalem artichokes
Kale
Kohl rabi
Leeks
Lettuce
Mushrooms
Onions
Parsnips
Peppers
Potatoes, new
Radishes
Salad cress
Salsify
Savoys
Seakale
Spinach
Spring greens
Spring onions
Swedes
Sweet potatoes
Tomatoes
Turnips
Watercress

Fruit

Apples
Apricots
Bananas
Cape gooseberries
Chinese gooseberries
Clementines
Cranberries
Dates
Grapefruit
Grapes
Kumquats (short supply)
Lemons
Lychees
Mandarins
Mangoes
Melons
Nectarines
Oranges
Ortaniques (short supply)
Passion fruit (short supply)
Peaches
Pears
Pineapples
Plums
Rhubarb (forced)
Satsumas
Strawberries
Tangerines

SUGGESTED MENUS

Moules Marinière
Pork Tenderloin with Mushrooms
Fried Rice
Candied Oranges Grand Marnier

Steak and Kidney Pudding
Boiled Potatoes and Brussels Sprouts
Compôte of Rhubarb and Bananas

Oeufs en Cocotte
Salmi of Wild Duck
Buttered Broccoli Spears
Crêpes Suzettes

Raie au Beurre Noir
Buttered Potatoes and Green Peas
Steamed Jam Pudding

Leeks Vinaigrette
Chicken Maryland
Chipped Potatoes
Celery and Apple Salad
Citron Fromage

Lancashire Hot Pot
Pickled Red Cabbage
American Cheese Cake

Eggs with Tuna Fish Mayonnaise
Rognons Turbigo
Creamed Potatoes and Buttered Broccoli
Chaussons aux Pommes

Tagliatelle alla Bolognese
Stuffed Green Peppers
Chocolate Cake Mousse

Soups & Starters

MOULES MARINIÈRE

There are several classic versions of this recipe for mussels, cooked in the style of mariners. The following is the most popular and easiest to prepare.

PREPARATION TIME: *30 min.*
COOKING TIME: *10 min.*

INGREDIENTS *(for 4)*:
4 pints mussels
1 small onion
3–4 tablespoons dry white wine
1 oz. butter
1 level teaspoon plain flour
1 level teaspoon chopped parsley

Wash the mussels* in cold water, scrub the shells thoroughly and rinse several times to remove all grit; pull or scrape away the beards. Discard any mussels with broken shells, and any which remain open.

Thoroughly butter the inside of a large saucepan. Peel and finely chop the onion, sprinkle it into the saucepan and add the wine. Place all the mussels in the pan at once, and cover with a lid. Place over high heat and shake the pan for 3–5 minutes until all the mussels have opened. Take the pan from the heat and lift out the mussels, discarding any that have not opened. Remove the empty half shell from each mussel and place the other half with mussel attached in individual soup plates. Keep hot.

Cream the butter and flour together and blend into the liquid remaining in the pan. Stir this sauce over a low heat until it has thickened and is boiling; add the chopped parsley and pour the sauce over the mussels in the plates. Serve at once.

COCK-A-LEEKIE SOUP

Legend has it that this traditional Scottish soup originated in the days when cockfighting was a favourite sport. The loser was then thrown into the stock pot together with leeks; prunes were a later addition for extra flavour.

PREPARATION TIME: *10–15 min.*
COOKING TIME: *2 hours*

INGREDIENTS *(for 6)*:
1 chicken (about 3 lb.)
1 level tablespoon salt
6 peppercorns
6 leeks
6 prunes
GARNISH:
Chopped parsley

Soak the prunes for 6 hours in cold water. Wipe the trussed chicken, rinse the giblets and place both in a deep saucepan. Pour over cold water to cover the chicken (if necessary, split the bird in half so that it remains submerged). Add the salt and peppercorns and bring to the boil. Remove any scum from the surface, cover with a tight-fitting lid and simmer for about 1½ hours.

Meanwhile, trim the coarse leaves off the leeks to within 2 in. of the top of the white stems and cut off the roots. Split the leeks lengthways, wash them well under running cold water, then cut them into 1 in. pieces. Skim the soup again, add the leeks and the soaked prunes, which may be stoned or left whole. Simmer for another 30 minutes.

Lift the chicken and giblets from the soup; remove skin and bones from the chicken flesh. Reserve the best breast pieces for another recipe, and cut the remaining meat into small pieces. Add these to the soup and correct seasoning if necessary.

Just before serving the hot soup, sprinkle finely chopped parsley over it.

EGGS WITH TUNA FISH MAYONNAISE

Tuna – or tunny – is a fish from the warmer parts of the Atlantic, and in Britain is only sold tinned. It is used for hors-d'oeuvre or for light snacks, with salads.

PREPARATION TIME: *20 min.*
COOKING TIME: *6–8 min.*

INGREDIENTS *(for 4)*:
4 eggs
3½ oz. tin of tuna fish
Juice of half lemon
6 anchovy fillets
¼ pint mayonnaise
Black pepper
4 crisp lettuce leaves
GARNISH:
Finely chopped parsley

Put the eggs in a saucepan, cover with cold water and bring to the boil. Simmer for 6–8 minutes to hard-boil. Drain the eggs and cover them with cold water immediately to prevent further cooking. Shell the eggs.

Drain the oil from the tuna fish and mash the fish with the back of a wooden spoon. Blend in the lemon juice, then chop and add two of the anchovy fillets. Rub the mixture through a coarse sieve into a basin and beat until it is a smooth purée*. Add the mayonnaise* and blend in well. Season to taste.

Cut the eggs in half lengthways, with a wet knife blade. Arrange the halves in pairs, rounded sides upwards, on the lettuce leaves, and coat them with the tuna fish mayonnaise. Cut the remaining anchovy fillets in half lengthways and arrange over the eggs; sprinkle with parsley. Serve with thinly sliced brown bread and butter.

Fish

CRÈME DE COQUILLES ST JACQUES

Scallops – known in France as coquilles St Jacques – are the basis for this creamy soup.

PREPARATION TIME: *10 min.*
COOKING TIME: *15–20 min.*

INGREDIENTS *(for 4–6):*
6 fresh scallops
1 lemon
6 parsley stalks
½ pint dry white wine
1 small onion
1½ oz. unsalted butter
1 oz. plain flour
½–¾ pint milk
Salt and black pepper
2 egg yolks
3 tablespoons double cream
GARNISH:
2 heaped tablespoons chopped parsley
Bread croûtons

Slide the scallops* from the flat shells; cut away and discard the beard round each as well as the black threadlike intestines. Cut each scallop into 4–5 pieces and put in a saucepan with the sliced lemon and the parsley stalks. Pour over the wine and bring to a simmer over gentle heat. Cover the pan with a lid, and cook the scallops gently for about 15 minutes or until tender. Take the pan off the heat and remove parsley and lemon.

Peel and finely chop the onion. Melt the butter in a large sauté pan and add the onion; cover and cook gently for about 5 minutes until the onion is soft, but not brown. Take the pan off the heat. Let the onion cool slightly, then stir in the flour and cook for a few minutes over low heat.

Gradually stir in the milk and bring the mixture to the boil, stirring continuously until smooth and thickened. Add the scallops and their liquid; season to taste and re-heat gently.

When ready to serve, blend the egg yolks with the cream; mix in a few spoonfuls of the hot liquid and blend this back into the soup. Serve in individual soup bowls and sprinkle with parsley. Offer a bowl of crisp bread croûtons*.

OEUFS EN COCOTTE

This classic French recipe is a compromise between soft-boiled and poached eggs. Each egg, with a little cream, is baked in a small individual fireproof dish. The cocotte or ramekin dishes are made for this purpose.

PREPARATION TIME: *5 min.*
COOKING TIME: *12 min.*

INGREDIENTS *(for 4):*
8 eggs
1 oz. butter
Salt and black pepper
8 tablespoons double cream

Warm eight ramekin dishes and butter them thoroughly. Crack an egg into each dish, season well with salt and freshly ground pepper and spoon a tablespoon of cream over each egg.

Place the ramekins in a large roasting tin, and fill it with hot water to within ½ in. of the rims of the dishes. Cover the tin with kitchen foil and bake in the centre of a pre-heated oven, at 350°F (mark 4), for 12 minutes.

When cooked, the egg whites should be just set, and the yolks still runny. Serve at once, on their own for a first course, and with crisp toast for a supper dish.

CELERIAC SALAD WITH PARMA HAM

The large celery root – or celeriac – is becoming a popular vegetable in Britain. It can also be served raw in a salad, with Parma ham or thinly sliced salami.

PREPARATION TIME: *10–15 min.*
COOKING TIME: *2–3 min.*

INGREDIENTS *(for 4):*
1 large celeriac
2–3 rounded tablespoons mayonnaise
¼ teaspoon French mustard
8 oz. thinly sliced Prosciutto (Parma) ham

Peel the celeriac. Cut it into narrow slices and then into matchstick-thin pieces. Add to a pan of boiling salted water and blanch* for 2–3 minutes; drain in a colander and allow to cool. Blend together the mayonnaise* and French mustard and toss the celeriac in this dressing.

Arrange the Parma ham on individual plates, allowing three thin slices per person. Divide the salad between the portions.

HOT CRAB SOUFFLÉ

The French invented the soufflé, which is basically a sauce and a savoury or sweet purée* blended with stiffly beaten egg whites. It is always baked in a mould and should emerge from the oven light, fluffy and golden.

PREPARATION TIME: *20 min.*
COOKING TIME: *35–40 min.*

INGREDIENTS *(for 4):*
6 oz. crabmeat, fresh, tinned or frozen
1 oz. butter
1 oz. plain flour
½ pint milk, less 2 tablespoons
Salt and black pepper
Cayenne pepper
2 oz. grated Cheddar cheese
4 eggs

Melt the butter in a saucepan; stir in the flour and cook over low heat for a few minutes. Gradually beat in the milk, stirring continuously until the sauce thickens and comes to the boil. Season to taste with salt, freshly ground pepper and cayenne. Stir in the cheese and leave the sauce to cool for 5 minutes.

Separate the eggs and beat the yolks, one at a time, into the cheese sauce. Flake* the prepared crabmeat finely and blend it into the sauce. Correct seasoning if necessary. Whisk the egg whites until stiff, then add to the crab mixture; fold them in gently with a metal spoon.

Pour the mixture into a buttered 1½ pint soufflé dish and level the top. Bake in the centre of an oven pre-heated to 375°F (mark 5), for 35–40 minutes, until well risen and golden brown. Serve immediately; a tossed green salad could also be served.

HERRINGS WITH MUSTARD SAUCE

The most abundant and inexpensive fish is the herring. Possibly as a legacy from the Second World War when fish was the staple menu, this nourishing fish is still too seldom used. Here, herrings are served with a savoury stuffing for a tasty lunch or supper.

PREPARATION TIME: *25 min.*
COOKING TIME: *35–40 min.*

INGREDIENTS *(for 4)*:

4 large herrings
3 heaped tablespoons fresh white breadcrumbs
1 heaped teaspoon finely chopped parsley
Squeeze of lemon juice
Grated rind of half lemon
Salt and black pepper
Oil
1 oz. butter

SAUCE:
1½ oz. butter
1 oz. plain flour
¾ pint milk
Salt and black pepper
1 level tablespoon dry mustard
1 tablespoon wine vinegar
1 level teaspoon caster sugar
GARNISH:
Lemon wedges and parsley sprigs

Remove the heads from the herrings*, clean, gut and bone them. Wash the herrings and pat them thoroughly dry. Put the breadcrumbs, parsley, lemon juice and lemon rind in a basin; season lightly with salt and freshly ground pepper. Melt the butter and stir into the breadcrumbs to bind the mixture, which should now be moist, but crumbly. Stuff the herrings with the breadcrumb mixture, and if necessary secure them with wooden toothpicks. Slash the skins crossways two or three times on each side; brush the herrings with oil and wrap each in foil. Put the herrings in a well-buttered deep baking dish; cover with lightly buttered greaseproof paper and bake in the centre of a pre-heated oven at 400°F (mark 6) for 35–40 minutes.

For the sauce, melt 1 oz. of the butter in a pan; stir in the flour and cook for 1 minute. Gradually stir in the milk, beating well until the sauce is quite smooth. Bring to the boil and simmer for 2–3 minutes; season with salt and pepper. Blend the mustard powder with the vinegar and stir into the sauce; add the sugar. Check seasoning and stir in the remaining butter.

Transfer the baked herrings to a hot serving dish and garnish with wedges of lemon and sprigs of parsley. Serve the mustard sauce separately. Boiled potatoes or Gallettes Lyonnaise (see November vegetables) go well with the herrings.

SCALLOPS IN THE SHELL

Scallops, with their firm white flesh and coral-red tongues, are still in good supply. In this recipe, they are used for a main course, served in the deep rounded shells which afterwards make useful hors-d'oeuvre dishes.

PREPARATION TIME: *20 min.*
COOKING TIME: *35 min.*

INGREDIENTS *(for 2–4)*:
4 large scallops
4 oz. button mushrooms
¼ pint dry white wine or dry cider
1 slice lemon
1 bay leaf
1 lb. potatoes
1 oz. butter
SAUCE:
1 oz. butter
1 oz. plain flour
Salt and black pepper
1 egg yolk
2 tablespoons double cream
GARNISH:
Chopped parsley

Slide the scallops* off the shells, wash them well under running cold water and remove the black beards and intestines. Cut each scallop into four or six slices. Wipe and thinly slice the mushrooms*. Put the scallops and mushrooms in a pan, with ½ pint of water, the wine (or cider), lemon slice and bay leaf. Bring to the boil, cover with a lid and simmer gently for 15–20 minutes. Strain through a colander and set aside ½ pint of the fish liquid for the sauce. Remove the lemon slice and bay leaf, and keep the scallops and mushrooms hot.

Meanwhile, put the peeled potatoes on to boil and make the sauce. Melt the butter in a saucepan over low heat, stir in the flour and cook gently for a few minutes. Gradually mix in the reserved fish liquid, stirring continuously until the sauce is smooth. Bring to the boil and simmer gently for 2–3 minutes. Add the mushrooms and scallops; season to taste with salt and freshly ground pepper, re-heat gently. Lightly mix the egg yolk and cream, remove the pan from the heat and stir the egg into the fish mixture.

Mash and season the potatoes. Using a large piping bag, fitted with a rosette nozzle, pipe a border of mashed potato around the edges of the deep scallop shells. Brush the potato border with 1 oz. melted butter and place the shells under a hot grill for a few minutes until the potatoes are golden brown.

Spoon the scallops into the centre of each shell and sprinkle them with chopped parsley. Serve with a tossed green salad for a main course, or on their own as a first course for a dinner party.

Meat

RAIE AU BEURRE NOIR

PREPARATION TIME: *10 min.*
COOKING TIME: *30 min.*

INGREDIENTS (*for 4*):
2 lb. wing of skate
Half lemon
1 small onion
1 small bay leaf
2–3 peppercorns
3–4 parsley stalks
½ level teaspoon salt
BEURRE NOIR:
3 oz. unsalted butter
1 tablespoon white vinegar
*1 level tablespoon finely chopped
    parsley*

Skate should never be used absolutely fresh, as a glutinous coating adheres to the skin for up to 10 hours after catching. The flavour is more pronounced when the fish is slightly high.

Rinse the skate, wipe it dry and cut into four portions. Place in a saucepan with ½ pint of water. Slice the lemon; peel and slice the onion and add these to the pan, together with the bay leaf, peppercorns, parsley stalks and salt. Bring slowly to the boil, cover with a lid and simmer gently for 25–30 minutes.

Remove the fish with a perforated spoon and arrange on a hot serving dish. For the sauce, heat the butter in a frying pan over low heat until browned, but not scorched. Remove the pan from the heat; stir the vinegar and chopped parsley into the butter and pour over the skate.

Serve with boiled potatoes coated with butter, and green beans or peas.

FRIED LIVER WITH ONION GRAVY

Liver, whether from lamb, calf or pig, is one of the most nourishing and digestible meats. The flavour is best preserved by steeping the liver in milk before frying.

PREPARATION TIME: *20 min.*
COOKING TIME: *25 min.*

INGREDIENTS (*for 4*):
1 lb. lamb liver
Seasoned flour
1 lb. onions
5 oz. unsalted butter
1 level tablespoon plain flour
¼ pint beef stock
1 teaspoon vinegar
Salt and black pepper

Cut away any skin and gristle from the liver* and cut it into ¼ in. slices. Soak the liver slices in milk for 1 hour. Drain the liver well, pat it dry on absorbent kitchen paper, then coat each slice with seasoned flour*, making sure both sides are evenly coated.

Prepare the gravy before frying the liver: peel and thinly slice the onions. Melt 2 oz. of the butter in a large frying pan, add the onions and fry over low heat for about 20 minutes or until soft and golden brown. Turn frequently to prevent the onion sticking to the bottom of the pan. A pinch of sugar may help the onions to brown more quickly.

Blend 1 oz. of butter with the flour and add in knobs to the hot onions. Stir until melted and blended, then gradually stir in the hot stock. Bring the gravy to the boil, simmer for a moment, then stir in the vinegar and season to taste with salt and ground pepper.

Melt the remaining 2 oz. of butter in a heavy-based pan, add

the liver slices and fry them quickly for about 5 minutes, turning once. Lift them out on to a hot serving dish and pour over the onion gravy. Creamed or boiled potatoes go well with the liver.

STEAK AND KIDNEY PUDDING

The traditional English beefsteak and kidney pudding is always served from the basin in which it was steamed. Have ready a white folded napkin or cloth to tie round the hot pudding basin before serving.

PREPARATION TIME: *30 min.*
COOKING TIME: *3–4 hours*

INGREDIENTS (*for 4*):
1½ lb. lean stewing steak
¼ lb. ox kidney
1 onion
2 level tablespoons seasoned flour
*8 oz. suet crust pastry (standard
    recipe)*
1 oz. butter
Salt and black pepper

Trim away any fat or gristle from the beef, then cut it into ½ in. pieces. Remove the core from the kidney* and cut it into ½ in. pieces. Peel and finely chop the onion. Coat the steak and kidney with seasoned flour* and mix with the onion.

Prepare the suet crust pastry*, and set aside a quarter for the pudding top. Roll out the remainder to a circle, ½ in. thick. Grease a 1½ pint pudding basin well, and fit the pastry to the bottom and sides, allowing it to overhang the edge of the basin by about ½ in. Spoon the meat and onion mixture, with a seasoning of salt and freshly ground pepper, into the basin; pour over enough cold water to come three-quarters up the sides of the basin.

Roll out the remaining pastry to a circle to fit the top of the basin. Damp the edges of the suet crust lining, cover with the pastry top and pinch the edges of the lining and the lid tightly together to seal. Cover the top of the basin with double thickness of buttered greaseproof paper, folding in a wide pleat across the centre, to allow the pudding to rise; secure the paper tightly with string.

Put the basin in a saucepan and pour boiling water around it until it reaches one-third up the sides. Steam briskly for 3–4 hours, topping up with boiling water.

Serve the pudding, usually accompanied by boiled potatoes and Brussels sprouts.

DAUBE DE BOEUF

The French culinary term 'daube' describes a braising method of slowly cooking tougher cuts of meat, usually beef, in red wine stock. This cooking method, in a covered casserole, prevents the meat from shrinking.

PREPARATION TIME: *45 min.*
COOKING TIME: *3 hours*

INGREDIENTS *(for 6)*:
2 lb. lean stewing steak
4 oz. piece green streaky bacon
½ bottle red wine
1 lb. carrots
1 lb. onions
3 oz. butter
1–2 cloves garlic
Bouquet garni
¾ pint beef stock
2 rounded tablespoons tomato purée
1 heaped tablespoon chopped parsley
Salt and black pepper

Trim the fat from the beef and cut the meat into 1 in. pieces. Cut off the rind and dice* the bacon. Put the meat and bacon in a large mixing bowl, pour over the red wine and leave to marinate* for 3–4 hours.

Lift the meat from the marinade (the liquid will be used later). Peel or scrape the carrots and cut them into ¼ in. slices, peel and finely slice the onions. Using half the butter, fry the beef and the bacon in a heavy-based frying pan until they are evenly brown. Lift out the beef and bacon, then fry the prepared vegetables in the remainder of the butter. Peel and chop the garlic and add to the vegetables during frying.

Cover the base of a large casserole dish with half the vegetables, then add the beef and bacon and top with the remaining vegetables. Pour the marinade into the casserole and add the bouquet garni*.

Rinse out the frying pan with the stock. Stir with a wooden spatula to loosen all sediment, and bring the stock to the boil. Stir in the tomato purée and pour this liquid over the contents in the casserole. Add the chopped parsley, cover with a lid and cook for 3 hours in the centre of an oven pre-heated to 300°F (mark 2). Check and if necessary correct the seasoning and remove the bouquet garni. Skim off as much fat as possible from the surface – this is more easily done if the casserole is allowed to cool and then re-heated.

Traditionally, this dish is served with creamed potatoes.

PORK TENDERLOIN WITH MUSHROOMS

The lean fillet or tenderloin of pork usually needs marinating or stuffing to give the meat extra flavour. It can be cooked whole, or cut into thick slices for a quick main course.

PREPARATION TIME: *30 min.*
COOKING TIME: *15 min.*

INGREDIENTS *(for 6)*:
1½ lb. pork tenderloin
2 tablespoons oil
1 tablespoon lemon juice
Black pepper
1 small clove garlic (optional)
SAUCE:
6 oz. button mushrooms
1 onion
2 oz. unsalted butter
2 tablespoons dry sherry
¼ pint double cream

Trim away the thin skin, or sinew, and fat from the pork. Cut the meat crossways into 2 in. thick slices. Lay the slices between two sheets of wet grease-proof paper and beat them flat with a rolling pin. Arrange the slices in a shallow dish. Measure the oil and lemon juice into a basin and season with black pepper. Skin and crush the garlic, and mix it into the oil and lemon juice. Spoon this marinade* over the pork and leave for about 30 minutes.

Meanwhile, trim and thinly slice the mushrooms*. Peel the onion and chop it finely. Melt the butter in a frying pan and gently fry the onion for 5 minutes until it is soft, but not brown. Add the mushrooms and fry for a few minutes. Lift the vegetables from the pan and keep them hot. Drain the pork pieces from the marinade and fry gently in the hot butter for 3–4 minutes, turning once. Transfer the pork to a hot serving dish and keep it warm.

Measure the sherry into the frying pan and heat briskly, stirring until it has reduced* to 1 tablespoon. Return the onion and mushrooms to the pan and season with salt and freshly ground pepper. Stir in the cream. Heat gently, stirring until the sauce is almost boiling. Remove from the heat and pour the sauce over the pork. Serve surrounded by boiled or fried rice*.

LANCASHIRE HOT POT

In Northern England, the 'hot pot' was a tall earthenware pot. Mutton chops were stood upright round the inside and the centre was filled with vegetables. It was usual, too, in the days when they were cheap, to put a layer of oysters beneath the potato crust.

PREPARATION TIME: *30 min.*
COOKING TIME: *2–2½ hours*

INGREDIENTS (*for 4–6*) :

2 lb. middle neck of lamb
Seasoned flour
1 oz. dripping
1½ lb. potatoes
2 onions
6–8 carrots
2 sticks celery
1 leek
Salt and black pepper
¼ level teaspoon mixed herbs
GARNISH:
Chopped parsley

Wipe and bone the neck of lamb*. Put the bones in a saucepan and cover with cold water. Bring to the boil, and after a few minutes remove the scum; cover with a lid and let the bones simmer while the vegetables and meat are being prepared.

Trim away any fat and gristle, and cut the meat into small, even pieces. Roll them in seasoned flour*, before frying in hot dripping until browned and sealed on all sides. Peel the potatoes and cut them into ¼ in. thick slices. Put aside half the slices for the top and place the remainder in the base of a deep buttered casserole dish.

Peel and coarsely chop the onion. Scrape or peel the carrots and slice them thinly. Scrub the celery and chop it finely. Remove the outer coarse leaves and the root of the leek, wash it well and cut it across into thin slices. Mix all the vegetables together in a deep bowl, season with salt and pepper and sprinkle the herbs over them. Arrange layers of seasoned vegetables and meat in the casserole, beginning and ending with a layer of vegetables. Top with the remaining potato slices, arranging them neatly in overlapping circles. Strain the liquid from the bones and pour about ¾ pint of it into the casserole until it just reaches the upper potato layer. Cover with buttered greaseproof paper and a tight-fitting lid. Place in the centre of an oven pre-heated to 350°F (mark 4) and cook for 2–2½ hours.

About 30 minutes before serving, remove the lid and paper from the casserole. Brush the potatoes with a little melted dripping and sprinkle with coarse salt. Raise the oven heat to 400°F (mark 6) and return the uncovered casserole to the oven, placing it above the centre so that the potatoes will crisp and brown slightly.

Sprinkle with finely chopped parsley immediately before serving. The hot pot is a meal on its own, but is traditionally served with pickled red cabbage.

ROGNONS TURBIGO

This French family meal consists of halved fried kidneys, supplemented with button onions and small sausages.

PREPARATION TIME: *25 min.*
COOKING TIME: *20–25 min.*

INGREDIENTS (*for 4*) :
6 lamb kidneys
4 chipolata sausages
2 oz. unsalted butter
8 button onions
1 level tablespoon plain flour
½ pint chicken or beef stock
¼ pint dry white wine
1 rounded teaspoon tomato purée
2 tablespoons dry sherry
Salt and black pepper
1 bay leaf
GARNISH:
Chopped parsley and bread croûtons

Skin the kidneys*, cut them in half and snip out the white core with scissors. Separate the sausages and twist each in opposite directions so that they can be snipped in half.

Melt the butter in a large heavy-based pan. Gently fry the kidneys and sausages until brown, then remove from the pan and keep them hot.

Meanwhile, peel the onions, leaving them whole; put them in a saucepan and cover with cold water. Bring to the boil, simmer for 3–5 minutes, then drain.

Stir the flour into the hot fat remaining in the sauté pan, until well blended; cook gently for a few minutes. Gradually add the stock and wine, stirring well until the sauce is smooth. Bring to the boil, stir in the tomato purée and sherry; season to taste with salt and freshly ground pepper.

Put the kidneys, sausages and onions back into the pan; add the bay leaf, cover with a lid and simmer gently for 20–25 minutes.

Transfer the sausages, kidneys and onions to a hot serving dish. Remove the bay leaf, check seasoning and strain the sauce over the meat. Garnish with crisp bread croûtons* and sprinkle with chopped parsley.

A rice pilaff, or creamed potatoes, and broccoli go well with this dish.

Poultry & Game

MINCE COLLOPS

Collop Monday, the Monday before Lent, was the day on which all meats in the house had to be used up before fasting began. There are numerous recipes for collops. This one, from Scotland, uses beef.

PREPARATION TIME: *5 min.*
COOKING TIME: *45–60 min.*

INGREDIENTS *(for 4):*
1 lb. minced beef
2 onions
1 oz. dripping
Salt and black pepper
½ pint water or beef stock
4 eggs

Peel and finely chop the onions. Melt the dripping in a heavy-based saucepan and fry the onions over low heat for about 5 minutes or until soft. Add the minced beef, cover with a lid and fry until the beef is browned and has separated into grains. Season to taste with salt and freshly ground pepper; pour over the water or stock until the meat is almost covered. Then put the lid on the pan and simmer the contents for 45 minutes. Stir occasionally and take the lid off the pan towards the end of the cooking time. When the meat is cooked, the liquid should have almost evaporated.

Poach the eggs* in simmering salted water until just set. Spoon the meat on to slices of hot toast and top each portion with a poached egg. The mince collops could also be served with creamed potatoes instead of toast.

CIVET DE LIÈVRE

Literally, hare stew, this is a classic recipe from French farmhouse-cooking, reminiscent of traditional English jugged hare.

PREPARATION TIME: *45 min.*
COOKING TIME: *2–3 hours*

INGREDIENTS *(for 6):*
2½–3 lb. hare pieces
2–3 carrots
2 onions
1 clove garlic
1 shallot
3 bay leaves
3 sprigs thyme
6 parsley stalks
Black pepper
3 tablespoons olive oil
1 bottle red wine
2 oz. butter
2 liqueur glasses brandy
1 oz. plain flour
⅓ pint chicken stock
¼ lb. piece green streaky bacon
¼ lb. button mushrooms
1 lb. small onions

GARNISH:
Freshly chopped parsley

The ingredients can be either a whole jointed hare or the legs and rib joints after the saddle has been roasted whole.

Wipe the hare pieces and put them in a large basin. Peel and finely slice the carrots and the onions. Skin and finely chop the garlic and shallot. Add these vegetables, with the bay leaves, thyme, the parsley stalks and freshly ground pepper to the hare. Pour over the oil and wine and marinate* for 24 hours.

Remove the meat from the marinade and pat it dry on absorbent paper. Melt the butter in a large saucepan and fry the meat gently for about 15 minutes, until browned on all sides. Pour the brandy over the meat and, when hot, set it alight. As soon as the flames have died down, sprinkle in the flour, stirring to blend it well with the butter. Add the marinade ingredients and sufficient stock to just cover the meat. Bring to the boil, cover and simmer for 2–3 hours.

Cut the bacon piece into strips, 1 in. long. Place in a saucepan, cover with cold water and bring to the boil. Simmer for 1 minute, then drain. Put the bacon strips in a dry frying pan and sauté* gently until the fat runs. Wipe and trim the mushrooms*, cut each in half and add to the pan. Sauté gently for a few minutes before seasoning, then remove from the pan and set aside. Peel the onions, leaving them whole; put them in a saucepan and cover with cold water. Bring to the boil and simmer gently for 10–15 minutes. Drain and set aside. Lift the hare pieces from the pan and keep them hot. Strain off the liquid and return it to the saucepan. Add more salt and pepper if necessary; if the sauce appears too thin, thicken with a little beurre manié*. Put the hare into the pan, with the bacon, mushrooms and onions. Re-heat gently.

Arrange the meat on a hot serving dish, pour over the sauce and sprinkle with parsley.

Croquette potatoes* and braised celery* could also be served.

SALMI OF WILD DUCK

Salmi a French cookery term – means a rich brown stew or casserole of game. It is a suitable method for making a party dish out of wild duck towards the end of their season.

PREPARATION TIME: *1 hour*
COOKING TIME: *40–50 min.*

INGREDIENTS *(for 6):*
2 wild duck
3 carrots
2 large onions
4 rashers streaky bacon
1 bay leaf
SAUCE:
1 pint duck stock
2 oz. butter
1½ oz. plain flour
1 tablespoon mushroom ketchup (optional)
3–4 tablespoons medium dry sherry or port
Salt and black pepper
Squeeze lemon juice
6–8 stoned green olives

Wipe the ducks inside and out, and rub the skin with coarse salt. Peel and thinly slice a carrot and an onion and put them in a saucepan, together with the duck giblets. Pour over about 1½ pints of cold water, cover with a lid, bring to the boil and simmer for 30 minutes to make the stock.

Meanwhile, cut the rind off the bacon and cover the breast of the ducks with the rashers. Peel and slice the remaining carrots and onions and use them to cover the base of a lightly greased roasting pan. Add the bay leaf, place the birds on the bed of vegetables and roast for 30 minutes only, in the centre of the oven pre-heated to 375°F (mark 5). Remove the birds, discarding the bacon; carve each duck into four portions and place in a casserole dish.

Strain the fat from the roasting pan, but retain the vegetables. Pour 1 pint of strained duck stock into the pan and stir over moderate heat until boiling.

Simmer gently until it has reduced* by about one-third. Meanwhile, melt the butter in a saucepan over low hear. Stir in the flour and cook gently for 5–10 minutes, stirring occasionally until the mixture is nutty brown. Remove from the heat and stir in the hot reduced duck stock. Return the pan to the heat; stir until boiling, then add the mushroom ketchup (if used), sherry or port, a squeeze of lemon and salt and pepper to taste. Strain the sauce over the ducks in the casserole, cover with a lid and place in the centre of the oven pre-heated to 350°F (mark 4). Cook for 40–50 minutes or until the ducks are tender (if the juices that come out, when a meat skewer is gently pushed into the thigh, are clear, the ducks are cooked). Add the olives and allow to heat through for a few moments.

Creamed potatoes and broccoli could be served with the salmi.

CHICKEN MARYLAND

A favourite dish on the American dinner table, chicken Maryland is traditionally accompanied by corn fritters. These batter cakes are, like all the other ingredients in this dish, fried until golden.

PREPARATION TIME: *25 min.*
COOKING TIME: *45 min.*

INGREDIENTS (*for 6*) :

3 lb. chicken, jointed into 8 pieces,
  or 6 chicken joints
Seasoned flour
1 egg
3–4 oz. fresh white breadcrumbs
4–5 oz. unsalted butter
8 lean bacon rashers
3 bananas
1 tablespoon olive or corn oil

CORN FRITTERS:
4 oz. plain flour
1 egg
¼ pint milk
11 oz. tin creamed sweet corn
Salt and black pepper
GARNISH:
Watercress

Remove the skin from the chicken pieces and coat them with seasoned flour*. Lightly beat the egg and dip the chicken portions in this before coating them with breadcrumbs. Shake off any loose crumbs. Melt about 2 oz. of the butter in a large frying pan and fry the chicken pieces for about 10 minutes, until brown on both sides. Turn down the heat, cover the pan with a lid or tight-fitting foil and cook gently, turning the chicken once, for 25–30 minutes – if cooked in the oven, allow 40 minutes at 400°F (mark 6).

Cut the rind from the bacon* and stretch each rasher with the flat blade of a knife. Cut each rasher in half, roll them up and thread them on two skewers. Peel and halve the bananas lengthways; coat them evenly in seasoned flour, ready for frying.

Sift the flour for the corn fritters into a mixing bowl, make a well in the centre and add the egg and milk. Using a wooden spoon, mix from the centre, gradually drawing in the flour from around the sides of the bowl. Beat to make a smooth batter. Stir in the sweet corn and season to taste with salt and freshly ground pepper.

When the chicken pieces are tender, transfer them to a serving dish and keep them warm. Melt 1 oz. of butter in the pan, add the bananas and fry over low heat.

Heat the remaining butter and the oil in a second frying pan. When hot, add tablespoons of the corn fritter batter, cook until golden brown on the underside, then turn each fritter and fry on the other side. Fry the fritters a few at a time – they take 1–2 minutes to cook; keep the fritters warm while frying the next batch. While the last fritters are cooking, put the skewers with bacon rolls under a high grill for about 2 minutes.

Serve the chicken pieces garnished with the corn fritters, bacon rolls and fried bananas and sprigs of watercress. Chipped potatoes* and a tossed green salad go well with this.

Rice & Pasta

TAGLIATELLE ALLA BOLOGNESE

The paper-thin egg noodles or tagliatelle are frequently served in Italy with a substantial sauce of minced beef.

PREPARATION TIME: *25 min.*
COOKING TIME: *45–60 min.*

INGREDIENTS *(for 4–6)*:
8–12 oz. ribbon noodles
1 lb. lean minced beef
1 onion
1 clove garlic
2 tablespoons olive oil
¼ lb. button mushrooms
2 level tablespoons plain flour
15–16 oz. tin of tomatoes
1 level teaspoon salt
Black pepper
1 teaspoon chopped parsley
¼ level teaspoon mixed herbs
2 level teaspoons tomato purée
¼ pint red wine
½ pint beef stock
2–3 oz. Parmesan cheese

Peel and finely chop the onion and the garlic. Wipe and trim the mushrooms*; slice them thinly. Heat the oil in a heavy-based saucepan, and add the onion. Cover with a lid and cook gently for about 5 minutes or until the onion is tender. Add the garlic and minced beef, stirring until the meat is thoroughly browned, then add the mushrooms and fry for a few minutes. Mix in the flour, add the tomatoes and their juice, seasoning, the parsley, mixed herbs and tomato purée. Pour over the red wine and stock and bring to the boil. Lower the heat, cover the pan with a lid and simmer gently for 45–60 minutes.

About 15 minutes before the sauce is ready, put the tagliatelle in a large pan of boiling salted water. Bring back to the boil and cook for 12 minutes. Drain before piling on a hot serving dish. Pour the sauce over the noodles and serve with a bowl of grated cheese.

SPANISH RICE

Rice is often served in place of potatoes and other vegetables. This mixture of rice, onion and tomato is particularly good with grilled or fried chops, steaks or hamburgers.

PREPARATION TIME: *10 min.*
COOKING TIME: *20 min.*

INGREDIENTS *(for 4)*:
6 oz. long grain rice
1 onion
1 green pepper
1 oz. butter
15–16 oz. tin of tomatoes
½ level teaspoon salt
2 level teaspoons caster sugar
1 bay leaf
1–2 oz. Parmesan cheese

Measure the rice into a large pan of boiling salted water. Bring back to the boil and cook the rice for 8–10 minutes, until tender. Drain thoroughly in a colander. Peel and thinly slice the onion. Halve the green pepper, remove the stem, seeds and white midribs and finely shred the flesh.

Melt the butter in a saucepan and add the vegetables. Cover with a lid and cook gently for about 5 minutes or until the onion is soft. Stir in the tomatoes and their juice, the salt, sugar, bay leaf and cooked rice. Simmer, uncovered, for about 15 minutes, stirring to prevent burning.

When ready to serve, remove the bay leaf and arrange the rice mixture on a hot serving dish. Sprinkle with the grated cheese.

NOUILLES FRAÎCHES AU BEURRE

Ribbon egg noodles, also known as tagliatelle, are creamy white. Sometimes spinach is added to the pasta dough to produce green ribbon noodles.

PREPARATION TIME: *5 min.*
COOKING TIME: *12 min.*

INGREDIENTS *(for 4)*:
8 oz. ribbon noodles
1 oz. unsalted butter
Black pepper
1–2 oz. Parmesan cheese

Put the noodles in a large saucepan of boiling salted water, bring back to the boil and cook over moderate heat for about 12 minutes. As soon as the noodles are tender, but still slightly chewy, drain them in a colander.

Melt the butter in a large saucepan; remove it from the heat and tip in the cooked noodles; season with freshly ground pepper.

Using two forks, lift and turn the noodles in the melted butter.

Transfer to a hot serving dish and sprinkle with the grated cheese.

These noodles go well with beef stews, veal scallopine (see March meat), boeuf stroganoff* and similar meat or poultry dishes which are served with plenty of sauce.

Vegetables & Salads

STUFFED GREEN PEPPERS

For this recipe, select squat round peppers that will stand upright. They are quite filling, and one per person is sufficient for a light lunch or supper.

PREPARATION TIME: *20 min.*
COOKING TIME: *50 min.*

INGREDIENTS *(for 4)*:
4 even-sized green peppers
3 oz. long grain rice
1 small onion
2 oz. mushrooms
2 rashers lean bacon
1 oz. unsalted butter
4–6 chicken livers
Salt and black pepper
1 rounded teaspoon chopped parsley
1 small egg
1–2 oz. Parmesan cheese
½ pint tomato sauce

Cut a circle round the base of each green pepper to remove the stem and seeds. Place the peppers in a basin and cover with boiling water. Allow to stand for 5 minutes, then drain thoroughly and set the peppers aside.

For the stuffing, first cook the rice in a large pan of boiling salted water. Simmer for 8–10 minutes or until the rice is tender; drain through a colander. Peel the onion, wash and trim the mushrooms* and chop both finely. Cut the rind from the bacon and dice* the flesh. Melt the butter in a heavy-based pan and sauté* the bacon, onion and mushrooms for a few minutes. Add the chicken livers whole, cook for a few minutes then remove the livers and chop them into tiny pieces; return to the pan. Stir in the cooked rice, salt, pepper and parsley; remove the pan from the heat. Lightly beat the egg and use it to bind the rice and liver mixture.

Arrange the peppers, cut surface uppermost, in a buttered fireproof dish. Spoon the rice mixture into the peppers, and sprinkle them with half the grated cheese.

Spoon 2 tablespoons of cold water into the dish and set it above the centre of an oven preheated to 350°F (mark 4); cook for 35–40 minutes.

Immediately before serving, sprinkle the peppers with the remaining cheese. Serve a bowl of hot tomato sauce* separately.

POTATO GNOCCHI

Served with a tomato sauce, these Italian gnocchi or potato dumplings would make a light supper dish on their own. They can also be served with any kind of grilled or fried meat.

PREPARATION TIME: *30 min.*
COOKING TIME: *12–15 min.*

INGREDIENTS *(for 4)*:
1 lb. potatoes
Salt and black pepper
¼ level teaspoon ground nutmeg
4 oz. plain flour
1 egg
2 oz. butter
2 oz. Parmesan cheese

Peel the potatoes and cut them into 1 in. pieces. Put in a saucepan, cover with cold salted water and bring to the boil. Cook for 15–20 minutes or until tender; drain and return the pan to the heat for a few minutes to dry the potatoes thoroughly.

Rub the potatoes through a coarse sieve into a large bowl. Season to taste with salt and freshly ground pepper, before mixing in the nutmeg and the flour. Beat the egg and stir it into the potatoes, using a wooden spoon; blend thoroughly until smooth. Turn the mixture out on to a floured working surface and knead lightly. Shape the mixture with lightly floured hands, into a roll about 1 in. thick. Cut it into 24 even pieces and shape them into balls – or gnocchi.

Bring a large pan of water to the boil. Drop in the gnocchi, a few at a time, and simmer for 5 minutes. When cooked, the gnocchi will rise to the surface; lift them out carefully with a perforated spoon and put in a warm, buttered serving dish. While the last of the gnocchi are cooking, melt the butter and pour over the gnocchi in the dish. Sprinkle with grated cheese before serving.

LEEKS VINAIGRETTE

In place of the inevitable green salad of lettuce and cucumber, try this cold leek salad as a side dish with any type of meat.

PREPARATION TIME: *15 min.*
COOKING TIME: *30 min.*

INGREDIENTS *(for 4)*:
8 small leeks
1 bay leaf
Salt and black pepper
1 level teaspoon caster sugar
2 tablespoons wine vinegar
¼ level teaspoon made French mustard
3–4 tablespoons olive oil
1 level tablespoon freshly chopped parsley
GARNISH:
2 hardboiled eggs

Remove the coarse outer leaves from the leeks; trim off the roots and cut away the green tops, leaving about 4 in. of white stem on each leek. Slice the leeks in half lengthways, open them carefully and wash well under cold running water to remove all traces of grit.

Tie the halved leeks in four bundles, put them in a pan of boiling salted water and add the bay leaf. Bring back to the boil, then lower the heat to simmering point. Cover the pan with a lid and cook the leeks for 30 minutes or until tender. Lift them carefully from the water and leave to drain and cool.

Arrange the cold leeks in a serving dish and prepare the dressing: put salt and freshly ground pepper in a mixing bowl, add the sugar, vinegar and mustard. Blend thoroughly before adding the oil, mixing well. Taste for sharpness, adding more vinegar if necessary. Stir in the chopped parsley, and spoon the dressing over the leeks. Leave to marinate* until ready to serve.

Garnish the leeks with slices of hardboiled eggs.

CELERY AND APPLE SALAD

This crisp, easily prepared winter salad is excellent with cold ham for a light lunch or supper. It can also be served chilled as a starter to a substantial main course.

PREPARATION TIME: *15 min.*

INGREDIENTS *(for 4)* :
1 head celery
4 red dessert apples
2 tablespoons French dressing
3 rounded tablespoons mayonnaise
2 oz. shelled walnuts
GARNISH:
Watercress

Wash, scrub and finely chop the celery sticks. Wipe the apples, quarter, core and dice* them. Mix the celery and apples at once with French dressing* and then fold in the mayonnaise*. Set aside to chill in the refrigerator.

Just before serving, coarsely chop the walnuts and stir them into the celery and apple. Spoon the salad into a serving dish and garnish with sprigs of watercress.

CREAMED CABBAGE

White cabbage cooked this way goes well with roast beef and lamb, with sausages, chops and hamburgers.

PREPARATION TIME: *15 min.*
COOKING TIME: *25 min.*

INGREDIENTS *(for 4–6)* :
1½ lb. white cabbage
1 small onion
2 oz. unsalted butter
¼ pint hot chicken stock or water
Salt and black pepper
1 level tablespoon plain flour
¼ pint single cream or milk
Pinch grated nutmeg

Remove any damaged outer leaves and quarter the cabbage. Cut out the hard core and shred the cabbage finely. Peel and finely chop the onion. Melt half the butter in a large saucepan, add the onion and cook gently for about 5 minutes, until it is tender and transparent.

Meanwhile, bring ¼ pint of stock or water to the boil. Add the cabbage to the saucepan, and pour over the boiling stock or water; season with salt and freshly ground pepper. Bring to the boil, cover with a lid and cook gently for about 15 minutes, until the cabbage is just tender. If the cabbage dries out before it is completely cooked, top up with boiling water.

Melt the remaining butter in a large pan and stir in the flour. Cook gently for 3 minutes, then gradually stir in the cream. Stir the sauce until thickened and boiling. Season to taste with salt, pepper and nutmeg.

Drain the cooked cabbage thoroughly in a colander and add it to the cream sauce. Toss

well to mix, and check seasoning. Heat the cabbage through and serve at once.

PAN HAGGARTY

A dish which originated in Northumberland, Pan Haggarty can be served on its own for a family supper or as an accompaniment to meat and savoury dishes.

PREPARATION TIME: *15 min.*
COOKING TIME: *30–40 min.*

INGREDIENTS *(for 4–6)* :
2 lb. potatoes
1 lb. onions
4 oz. Cheddar cheese
2 oz. dripping or lard
Salt and black pepper

Peel the potatoes, cut them into ⅛ in. thick slices and pat them dry on a cloth. Peel and thinly slice the onions; grate the cheese. Melt the dripping in a large frying pan and arrange the vegetables and the cheese in layers in the pan, reserving a little cheese for the top. Begin and finish with potato. Season each layer with salt and freshly ground pepper.

Cover the pan with a lid and cook over low heat for 30–40 minutes or until the vegetables are tender. Sprinkle the remaining cheese over the top and brown under a hot grill for a few minutes.

BEETROOT WITH ORANGE

In this recipe, cooked beetroot is combined with orange marmalade, fine-shred or sweet. The two flavours blend surprisingly well and suit any strong game, goose or duck.

PREPARATION TIME: *5 min.*
COOKING TIME: *10 min.*

INGREDIENTS *(for 4)* :
1 lb. cooked beetroot
1 oz. unsalted butter
1 heaped tablespoon marmalade
Juice of half orange
GARNISH:
Slice of orange

Skin and cut the cooked beetroot into dice*. Measure the butter, marmalade and orange juice into a saucepan, heat until the butter melts, then add the beetroot. Simmer gently, stirring occasionally, for about 10 minutes, until the liquid has evaporated and the beetroot is evenly glazed.

Spoon the beetroot into a hot serving dish. Cut towards the centre of a thin orange slice, twist the two halves in opposite directions and place it on the beetroot as a garnish.

Sweets & Puddings

AMERICAN CHEESE CAKE

This transatlantic cheese cake is not baked like the continental version, but set with gelatine. It is chilled and decorated with fruit for an unusual sweet.

PREPARATION TIME: *35 min.*
CHILLING TIME: *3 hours*

INGREDIENTS *(for 6)*:
8 oz. cottage cheese
4 oz. fresh cream cheese
2–3 oz. unsalted butter
3 oz. crushed cornflakes
4 oz. caster sugar
½ oz. powdered gelatine
Rind and juice of a small lemon
2 eggs
Salt
¼ pint double cream
GARNISH:
Black grapes and tinned mandarin oranges

Melt the butter in a small saucepan over low heat. Remove the pan from the heat and with a fork stir in the cornflake crumbs and 1 oz. of sugar. Press this mixture over the base of an 8 in. loose-bottomed flan or cake tin. Put the flan in the refrigerator to chill while preparing the cheese mixture.

Put 3 tablespoons of cold water in a small pan and sprinkle the gelatine evenly on the surface. Set aside to soak for 5 minutes. Meanwhile, rub the cottage cheese through a coarse sieve into a large basin and add the cream cheese. Finely grate the lemon rind and mix in well.

Separate the eggs; add 1½ oz. of sugar and a pinch of salt to the yolks and beat until creamy and light. Gently heat the pan of soaked gelatine, stirring continuously, but do not allow it to boil. Remove from the heat once the gelatine has dissolved, and add the strained lemon juice. Gradually whisk this liquid into the egg yolks, before blending it all into the cheese mixture. Whisk the egg whites until thick, then whisk in the remaining sugar and beat until stiff. Fold the beaten egg whites and the lightly whipped cream into the cheese mixture. Pour into the prepared chilled cake base and level the top. Chill in the refrigerator for 2–3 hours or until firm.

When ready to serve, loosen the sides of the cheese cake with a knife blade. Remove the cake from the tin and decorate the top with halved black grapes and mandarin orange segments.

Serve, cut into wedges, and offer a jug of cream with it.

CHAUSSONS AUX POMMES

These apple turnovers, sold ready-made in most French 'boulangeries', or pastry shops, provide an easily made sweet.

PREPARATION TIME: *25 min.*
COOKING TIME: *30 min.*

INGREDIENTS *(for 4–6)*:
2 large cooking apples
½ oz. unsalted butter
¼ teaspoon grated lemon rind
2 oz. caster sugar
1 level tablespoon sultanas
12 oz. prepared puff pastry
1 egg
Icing sugar

Peel, core and thinly slice the apples. Melt the butter in a saucepan, add the apples and lemon rind. Cover with a lid and cook over low heat until the apples are soft. Beat the apples to a purée*, add sugar and sultanas. Set aside until cold.

Roll out the puff pastry* ¼ in. thick. Using a 3 in. round, fluted pastry cutter, stamp out circles from the pastry; gently roll each circle with a rolling pin to form an oval about ⅛ in. thick. Spoon the apple mixture equally over half of each pastry shape. Brush the edges with beaten egg and fold the pastry over. Press the edges firmly to seal. Slash the top of each pastry with a knife, brush with beaten egg and leave for 15 minutes.

Bake the pastries on wet baking trays, above the centre of an oven, pre-heated to 425°F (mark 7), for 10 minutes. Lower to 375°F (mark 5) and continue baking until golden brown. Dust with sifted icing sugar and serve warm or cold with cream.

CITRON FROMAGE

Shiny, firm lemons are plentiful and good value this month. They can be used for a light mousse to follow a rich main course.

PREPARATION TIME: *30 min.*
CHILLING TIME: *2 hours*

INGREDIENTS *(for 4)*:
Juice and rind of 2 large lemons
1 level tablespoon powdered gelatine
3 eggs
4 oz. caster sugar
¼ pint double cream
GARNISH:
¼ pint whipping cream

Sprinkle the gelatine over 2 tablespoons of water in a small pan and leave to soak for 5 minutes. Separate the eggs, putting the yolks into a large bowl and the whites into another. Finely grate the rind from the lemons, and mix it into the egg yolks, together with the sugar. Squeeze the lemons and strain the juice into the soaked gelatine. Place the saucepan over low heat, stirring continuously. Do not allow to boil, and immediately the gelatine has dissolved remove the pan from the heat.

Whisk the egg yolks and sugar until pale and creamy. Slowly pour in the dissolved gelatine, whisking all the time. Continue to whisk the mixture until it is cool and beginning to thicken. Lightly beat the double cream and fold into the mixture. Beat the egg whites until stiff, then blend them in evenly and lightly.

Pour the mousse into a serving dish or individual dishes and chill until set. Serve a bowl of single cream separately or pipe whipped cream over the mousse.

TARTE TATIN

This is an upside-down apple tart on a pastry base. Fresh or tinned apricots or pineapple can be used in place of apples.

PREPARATION TIME: *30 min.*
COOKING TIME: *35–40 min.*

INGREDIENTS *(for 4)*:
½ *oz. unsalted butter*
2–3 *oz. soft brown sugar*
1 *lb. dessert apples*
PASTRY
4 *oz. plain flour*
2 *oz. unsalted butter*
1 *oz. icing sugar*
1 *egg yolk*

Melt the butter and brush this over the inside of a 7½–8 in. shallow sponge tin. Line the base with greaseproof paper and brush with melted butter. Sprinkle the brown sugar evenly over the paper and press down.

Sift the flour into a basin. Add the butter, cut in knobs, and rub into the flour. Sift in the icing sugar and stir in the egg yolk and 1 tablespoon of water. Mix to a rough dough in the basin, before kneading it on a floured working surface until smooth. Roll the pastry out to a circle the size of the tin and trim neatly. Set aside.

Peel, core and thinly slice the apples. Arrange the slices in circles over the brown sugar. Carefully lift the pastry over the top of the apple slices and press down gently. Bake in the centre of the oven pre-heated to 350°F (mark 4) for 35–40 minutes or until crisp and golden brown.

Cool the tart for about 5 minutes, then turn out, upside-down, on a serving plate. Remove the paper. Serve the tart hot, with a bowl of cream.

STEAMED JAM PUDDING

The well-tried nursery puddings never lose their appeal for children and adults. Fresh bread-crumbs give this suet pudding a particularly light texture.

PREPARATION TIME: *15 min.*
COOKING TIME: *2–2½ hours*

INGREDIENTS *(for 4–6)*:
6 *oz. self-raising flour*
1 *level teaspoon baking powder*
Salt
3 *oz. fresh white breadcrumbs*
4 *oz. shredded beef suet*
4 *oz. caster sugar*
1 *egg*
Milk to mix
1 *tablespoon red jam*
SAUCE:
2 *rounded tablespoons red jam*
2 *oz. caster sugar*

Sift the flour, baking powder and a little salt into a mixing bowl, add the breadcrumbs, suet and sugar, and mix well. Lightly beat the egg and stir into the flour, with sufficient milk to make the dough a soft dropping consistency. Blend thoroughly. Butter a 1½–2 pint pudding basin and place 1 tablespoon red jam in the base. Spoon in the pudding mixture until the basin is two-thirds full. Cover with a double thickness buttered greaseproof paper, fold a pleat in this to allow the pudding to expand as it cooks. Secure the paper with string.

Place the pudding in a steamer over a saucepan half-filled with simmering water, or place the basin on an upturned saucer in a saucepan and fill with boiling water two-thirds up the side of the basin. Cover the pan with a tightly fitting lid and steam for 2

to 2½ hours. Top the pan up with more boiling water if it has evaporated before steaming is finished.

About 10 minutes before the pudding is cooked, prepare the

sauce: put the jam, sugar and 2 tablespoons of water into a pan, stir over low heat to dissolve the sugar, then bring to the boil. Simmer the sauce for 2–3 minutes or until thick and syrupy.

Loosen the sides of the pudding with a knife and turn out on to a hot serving dish. Pour the sauce into a bowl and serve separately.

CRÊPES SUZETTES

Pancakes with lemon are traditionally served on Shrove Tuesday. For a small dinner party, Crêpes Suzettes are more interesting, especially cooked in a chafing dish.

PREPARATION TIME: *30 min.*
COOKING TIME: *2–3 min.*

INGREDIENTS *(for 6)*:
12 pancakes (standard recipe)
1 oz. unsalted butter
2 oz. caster sugar
Juice of 2 oranges
Juice of half lemon
2–4 tablespoons orange liqueur

Cook the pancakes* and keep them hot between two plates over a saucepan of gently boiling water. Melt the butter in a large frying pan, stir in the sugar and cook gently until it is a golden-brown caramel. Add the strained orange and lemon juice and stir until the caramel has dissolved and become a thick sauce. Drop a flat pancake into the pan, fold it in half and then in half again. Push to the side of the pan and add the next pancake. When all the pancakes are in the hot sauce, add the orange liqueur and set it alight when hot. Shake the pan gently to incorporate the flamed liqueur evenly in the sauce.

Transfer the pancakes to a hot serving dish, pour over the sauce from the pan and serve at once.

CANDIED ORANGES GRAND MARNIER

A tangy dinner-party sweet becomes even more attractive to the hostess when it can be prepared the day before. It should be left to chill in the refrigerator.

PREPARATION TIME: *15 min.*
COOKING TIME: *45 min.*
CHILLING TIME: *2–3 hours*

INGREDIENTS *(for 6)*:
6 oranges
6 oz. caster sugar
Juice of half lemon
2 tablespoons Grand Marnier

Cut a slice from the top and bottom of each orange so that it will stand upright. Slice downwards through the orange skin, cutting away the peel and all the white pith, leaving only the orange flesh. Cut the oranges crossways into slices and place them in a serving dish.

Select six of the larger pieces of peel and carefully cut away the pith. Shred the peel finely and put it in a saucepan. Cover with cold water, bring to the boil, then drain – this removes the bitter flavour of the peel. Cover the peel with fresh cold water; bring to the boil and simmer for about 30 minutes or until the orange peel is tender. Drain and set aside.

Put the sugar into a heavy-based saucepan, then stir with a wooden spoon over moderate heat until the sugar has melted and turned to caramel. Remove from the heat and add $\frac{1}{4}$ pint of water – it will boil furiously. When the bubbling stops, return the pan to the heat and stir until the caramel has dissolved and a syrup has formed. Add the shredded peel and bring to the boil. Simmer for 2–3 minutes until the peel is glazed. Draw off the heat, cool for a few moments, then add the lemon juice and the Grand Marnier.

Spoon the syrup and candied peel over the oranges. Set aside until cold, basting the oranges occasionally with the syrup. Chill for several hours before serving, with vanilla ice cream*.

COMPÔTE OF RHUBARB AND BANANAS

Pink tender rhubarb is readily available early in the year. It should be cooked slowly to keep its shape for a compôte.

PREPARATION TIME: *15 min.*
COOKING TIME: *35 min.*
CHILLING TIME: *2 hours*

INGREDIENTS *(for 4)*:
1 lb. rhubarb
6 oz. caster sugar
Juice of an orange
1 lb. bananas

Trim tops and bottoms off the rhubarb, wash the stalks and cut them into 1 in. lengths. Place in a casserole or ovenproof dish and add the sugar and strained orange juice. Stir to blend the ingredients thoroughly, and cover with a lid. Bake for 35 minutes in the centre of the oven pre-heated to 325°F (mark 3). Remove from the oven and leave the casserole to stand, covered, for 5–10 minutes.

Peel and thinly slice the bananas into a serving dish. Pour over the hot rhubarb and the juices. Cool and then chill in the refrigerator. A bowl of cream or vanilla ice cream* could be served with the compôte.

Savouries & Snacks

SHEPHERD'S PIE

As roast beef traditionally graces the Sunday lunch table, so this left-over dish follows for Monday's supper.

PREPARATION TIME: *20 min.*
COOKING TIME: *30 min.*

INGREDIENTS *(for 4–6)*:
2 finely chopped onions
3 oz. unsalted butter
¾ lb. cooked minced beef or lamb
4 fluid oz. beef stock or gravy
1 level tablespoon tomato ketchup
¼ teaspoon Worcestershire sauce
Salt and black pepper
2–3 tablespoons milk
1 lb. mashed potatoes

Cook the onions in 1 oz. of the butter until soft; add the meat and cook until lightly brown. Stir in the stock, ketchup and Worcestershire sauce; season.

Beat the remaining, melted butter and the milk into the potatoes. Put the meat in a greased ovenproof dish, cover with potato and ripple the top with a fork. Bake near the top of an oven heated to 425°F (mark 7) for 30 minutes or until brown.

Serve the pie hot, on its own, or with a green vegetable.

WELSH RAREBIT

The success of this snack – sometimes mistakenly called Welsh rabbit – lies in cooking it over low heat until the cheese has melted.

PREPARATION TIME: *5 min.*
COOKING TIME: *15 min.*

INGREDIENTS *(for 4)*:
8 oz. grated Cheddar cheese
1 oz. unsalted butter
1 level teaspoon prepared English mustard
3 tablespoons beer
Salt and black pepper
4 slices buttered toast

Cook the cheese, butter, mustard and beer in a heavy pan over very low heat; season. Stir occasionally until the mixture is smooth and creamy.

Spoon the cheese on to the toast and put under a hot grill until golden and bubbling.

Serve at once with grilled tomatoes and a green salad.

SOUTHERN SCRAMBLE

This Mediterranean dish of savoury scrambled eggs makes a quick lunch or supper snack.

PREPARATION TIME: *15 min.*
COOKING TIME: *10 min.*

INGREDIENTS *(for 4)*:
1 small finely chopped onion
2 oz. unsalted butter
4 large tomatoes, skinned and roughly chopped
4 oz. diced luncheon meat
3 large eggs
Salt and black pepper
1 tablespoon freshly chopped parsley

Cook the onion in the butter until transparent, add the tomatoes and meat, and cook for a further 2–3 minutes. Stir the lightly beaten eggs into the mixture and season to taste. Continue cooking, stirring occasionally, until the eggs are just set.

Serve the scrambled eggs sprinkled with parsley. Hand crisp toast fingers separately.

COLCANNON

Irish in origin, this dish of left-over potato and cabbage is also known as bubble and squeak.

PREPARATION TIME: *10 min.*
COOKING TIME: *20 min.*

INGREDIENTS *(for 4)*:
1 finely chopped onion
4 rashers lean bacon (diced)
1½ oz. fat or dripping
1 lb. mashed potatoes
8 oz. cooked chopped cabbage
Salt and black pepper

Fry the onion and bacon in the fat until the onion is soft. Lift them out with a perforated spoon.

Mix the potato and cabbage with the bacon and onion; season. Shape the mixture into four flat cakes, about ½ in. thick. Fry in the fat until golden brown.

Serve the cakes topped with a fried egg, or as a vegetable course with cold meat.

CHOCOLATE CAKE MOUSSE

Left-over chocolate cake can be turned into a rich dessert.

PREPARATION TIME: *20–30 min.*
CHILLING TIME: *4 hours*

INGREDIENTS *(for 6)*:
2–4 thick slices stale chocolate cake
3 oz. plain cooking chocolate
3 separated eggs
3 oz. caster sugar
2 tablespoons concentrated frozen orange juice
¼ pint double cream
2 tablespoons grated chocolate

Melt the cooking chocolate in a bowl set over a pan of simmering water. Beat the egg yolks with the sugar until pale and fluffy, and stir in the melted chocolate. Fold in the orange juice and the diced cake.

Whip the egg whites and the cream, separately, until thick. Carefully fold both into the chocolate mixture and turn into a serving bowl or individual small dishes. Chill.

Sprinkle with coarsely grated chocolate before serving.

Home-made Marmalade

Marmalade making is time-consuming but economical, and the result, both in flavour and texture, is well worth the trouble. Marmalades from citrus fruits are basically made in the same way as jams and jellies, but the peel which is an integral part of marmalade is extremely tough and needs long slow cooking. Pectin*, which is essential for a good set, exists in the pith (the yellow-white layer beneath the peel and surrounding the fruit pulp) and in the pips. Both should be tied in muslin and boiled with the chopped peel.

Use an all-purpose thermometer to gauge setting point (220°F), or pour a little marmalade on to a cool saucer – if a wrinkled skin forms within a few minutes, setting point has been reached. Commercial pectin may be used to guarantee a thick set; follow the manufacturer's instructions. After skimming the marmalade, leave it to stand for about 30 minutes, stirring occasionally to distribute the peel evenly. Pour into dry warm jars and seal with paper discs, waxed side down. Cover the jars at once with metal tops and screw rings or with clear cellophane or greaseproof paper; secure these with rubber bands or fine string. Store the marmalade in a cool, dry place.

LEMON   LIME   DUNDEE

Chunky Seville Orange

PREPARATION TIME: 1¼ hours
COOKING TIME: about 2½ hours

INGREDIENTS (yield 10 lb.):
3 lb. Seville oranges
Juice of 2 lemons
6 pints water
6 lb. preserving sugar

Remove any stalk ends from the oranges, scrub and dry them thoroughly. Using a potato peeler or sharp, narrow knife, peel off the rind in thin downward strips, being careful to leave all the white pith behind. Chop or scissor the thin peel into ¼ in. wide strips and set them aside.

Cut the oranges in half and squeeze out all the juice, saving the pips. Cut away the yellow-white pith with a sharp knife, leaving the orange pulp. Chop the pith roughly and tie it in a large piece of muslin, together with the orange pips.

Cut the orange pulp into small chunks and put them in the preserving pan, with the chopped peel and the muslin bag. Strain the orange juice into the pan and add the strained lemon juice and the water.

Bring the fruit mixture to the boil over low heat and simmer, uncovered, for about 2 hours or until the peel is quite soft and the contents of the pan have reduced* by about half.

For chunky or coarse marmalade, first squeeze the juice from the peeled fruit

Remove the muslin bag, and add the sugar, stirring continuously until it has dissolved. Turn up the heat and boil the marmalade rapidly until setting point is reached, after 15–20 minutes. Leave the marmalade to cool for about 20 minutes, then remove any scum.

Dundee

PREPARATION TIME: 35 min.
COOKING TIME: about 2½ hours

INGREDIENTS (yield 10 lb):
3 lb. Seville oranges
3 lemons
3 sweet oranges
6 pints water
6 lb. preserving sugar
1 dessertspoon black treacle

Wash all the fruit thoroughly, put it in a large pan with the water and cover with a lid. Bring to the boil and cook over low heat for about 1½ hours or until the fruit pierces easily.

Lift out the fruit and leave until cool enough to handle. Slice the fruit, scraping out all the pips and adding them to the pan with the cooking liquid. Chop the fruit roughly.

Boil the fruit juices rapidly for 15 minutes or until reduced* by half. Strain the liquid into a preserving pan, add the chopped fruit and bring to the boil. Stir in the sugar and black treacle and boil the marmalade until set.

Clear Seville Orange

PREPARATION TIME: 45 min.
COOKING TIME: 2¼ hours

INGREDIENTS (yield 8 lb.):
3 lb. Seville oranges
6 pints water
Juice of 2 lemons
6 lb. preserving sugar

Prepare the oranges as for chunky orange marmalade. Put the finely shredded peel in a pan with half the water and the strained lemon juice. Bring to the boil and simmer, covered, over low heat for 2 hours, until the peel is tender.

Meanwhile, chop the peeled oranges roughly and put them in another pan with the remaining water. Bring to the boil, cover with a lid, and simmer the fruit for 1½ hours.

Strain the liquid from the orange pulp, through a fine sieve or muslin into the pan with the soft peel. Bring the marmalade mixture to the boil and reduce* slightly before stirring in the sugar. Boil rapidly until set. Pot and cover as before.

| CHUNKY ORANGE | GRAPEFRUIT | THREE-FRUIT | CLEAR ORANGE | TANGERINE |

Grapefruit

PREPARATION TIME: *45 min.*
COOKING TIME: $2\frac{1}{4}$ *hours*

INGREDIENTS *(yield 10 lb.)*:
3 lb. grapefruit
$\frac{1}{2}$ *lb. lemons*
6 pints water
6 lb. preserving sugar

The thick layer of pith beneath the skins of grapefruit ensures a good set of this sweet marmalade.

Grapefruit is more suitable for a jelly-like marmalade – proceed as for clear orange marmalade.

Lemon or Lime

PREPARATION TIME: $1\frac{1}{2}$ *hours*
COOKING TIME: *about 2 hours*

INGREDIENTS *(yield 10 lb.)*:
3 lb. lemons or limes
6 pints water
6 lb. preserving sugar

Choose firm, unblemished fruits with smooth skins.

Proceed as for chunky orange marmalade. For a more jelly-like marmalade, follow the instructions for clear orange marmalade.

Three-Fruit

PREPARATION TIME: *1 hour*
COOKING TIME: *about* $2\frac{1}{4}$ *hours*

INGREDIENTS *(yield 10–12 lb.)*:
3 lb. mixed fruit (approx.
3 grapefruits, 3 sweet oranges
and 3 large lemons)
6 lb. preserving sugar (approx.)

Wash and dry the fruit, cut into quarters, then slice the fruit thinly, setting the pips aside. Measure the fruit and juice and put in a large bowl, with three times the quantity of cold water.

Tie the pips in muslin, add to the fruit and water and leave to stand for 24 hours.

Slice the quartered grapefruits, oranges and lemons on a plate to catch the juices for three-fruit marmalade

Bring the contents of the bowl to the boil and cook over low heat for about 2 hours. Remove the muslin bag, measure the fruit pulp and juice (about 6 lb.). Return to the pan with the same amount of sugar. Stir until the sugar has dissolved, then boil rapidly until set.

The thin tough peel on limes is easiest removed in round, not downward, strips. Use scissors to chop the peel

Tangerine

PREPARATION TIME: $1\frac{1}{4}$ *hours*
COOKING TIME: *about* $1\frac{3}{4}$ *hours*

INGREDIENTS *(yield 5 lb.)*:
3 lb. tangerines
6 lemons
5 pints water
3 lb. preserving sugar

Cut the clean fruit in half and squeeze out the juice, setting the pips aside. Remove the membranes from the tangerines, with a teaspoon, and put them in a bowl, together with the pips and $\frac{1}{2}$ pint of cold water.

Cut the tangerine peel into narrow strips (there is no pith on these fruits). Peel the lemons and add the pith to the pips.

Leave the peel, the fruit juices and the remaining water in a large bowl for about 8 hours.

Bring the contents of the large bowl to the boil, with the fruit membranes, pith and peel tied in muslin. Boil steadily for about 1 hour or until reduced* by half, then remove the muslin bag and add the sugar. Boil until set.

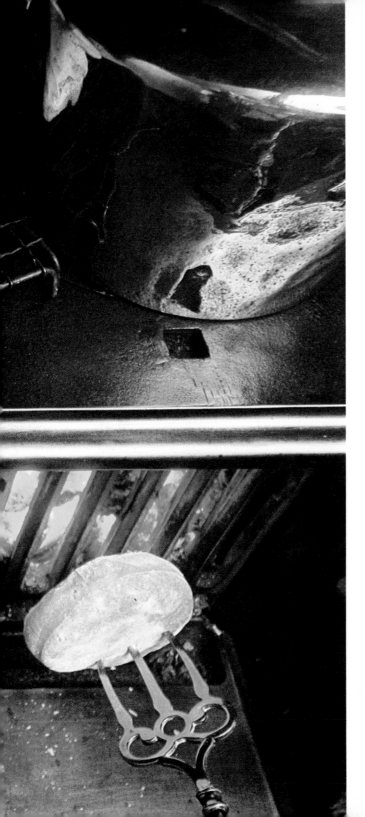

March

Good cooke to dresse dinner, to bake and to brewe,
deserves a rewarde, being honest and trewe.

This Month's Recipes

*The first spring days can be sharp and windy, just right for an afternoon
in front of the fire with toasted muffins and home-made jam*

Food in Season

In early spring, the housewife still has to rely on stored winter vegetables and fruits. Leaf vegetables, apart from broccoli, cabbages and spring greens, are becoming scarce, but towards the end of the month the first young carrots appear. The game season nears its close, with hare being the most economical buy. Scallops and mussels, too, are at the end of their season and are consequently less expensive. Pineapple is widely available and excellent in sweets and with cheese salads.

Fish

Bass
Bream, sea
Brill
Carp
Clams
Cod
Coley
Conger eels
Crab
Dabs
Dover sole
Dublin Bay prawns
Eels
Flake (also sold as rock salmon)
Flounder
Grey mullet
Haddock
Hake
Halibut
Herring
Lemon sole
Lobster
Mackerel
Mock halibut (or Greenland halibut)
Mussels
Oysters (native)
Oysters, Portuguese
Pike
Plaice
Prawns
Redfish
Salmon
Scallops
Shrimps
Skate
Sprats (scarce)
Trout, rainbow
Turbot
Whiting
Winkles
Witch

Poultry & Game

Chicken
Duck
Guinea fowl
Hare
Pigeon
Rabbit
Turkey
Venison

Vegetables

Asparagus
Aubergines
Avocado pears
Beetroots
Broccoli, purple
Broccoli, white
Brussels sprouts
Brussels tops
Cabbages
Carrots (young)
Cauliflowers
Celeriac
Celery
Chicory
Courgettes
Cucumbers
Fennel
French beans
Garlic
Globe artichokes
Horseradish
Jerusalem artichokes
Kale
Kohl rabi
Leeks
Lettuce
Mushrooms
Onions
Parsnips
Peppers
Potatoes, new
Radishes
Salad cress
Savoys
Seakale
Spinach
Spring greens
Spring onions
Swedes
Sweet potatoes
Tomatoes
Turnips
Watercress

Fruit

Apples
Bananas
Cape gooseberries
Grapefruit
Grapes
Kumquats
Lemons
Limes
Lychees
Mandarins
Mangoes
Melons
Oranges
Ortaniques
Passion fruit
Peaches
Pears
Persimmons
Pineapples
Plums
Rhubarb (forced)
Strawberries
Tangerines

SUGGESTED MENUS

Avocado Pears with Prawns
Steak au Poivre
Buttered Broccoli and Potato Croquettes
Orange Soufflés

Navarin of Lamb
Glazed Lemon Tart

French Onion Soup
Goujons of Sole with Tartare Sauce
New Potatoes and Tossed Green Salad
Marquise Alice

Champignons à la Crème
Leek and Chicken Pie
Buttered New Potatoes and Carrots
Velvet Cream

Prawns in Curry Sauce
Boiled Rice
Cheese and Fruit Platter

Danish Liver Pâté
Veal Scaloppine
Almond Rice, Buttered Broccoli
Fruits Rafraichis

Fricadelles
Sugar-browned Potatoes
Aubergine and Tomato Ragoût
Floating Island

Scampi Provençale
Pigeons with Forcemeat Balls
Creamed Potatoes, Buttered Spinach
Charlotte Russe

Soups & Starters

SCAMPI PROVENÇALE

In cooking, the term 'Provençale' implies the use of garlic and tomatoes. This recipe can be used as a first course or as a light lunch or supper dish.

PREPARATION TIME: *15 min.*
COOKING TIME: *15 min.*

INGREDIENTS *(for 4)*:
12–16 oz. shelled scampi
1 onion
1 clove garlic
2 tablespoons oil
15–16 oz. tin of tomatoes
3 tablespoons dry white wine
Salt and black pepper
1 level teaspoon caster sugar
1 rounded teaspoon cornflour
1 rounded tablespoon chopped parsley

Rinse the scampi under cold running water and pat them dry on absorbent paper. Peel and finely chop the onion and garlic. Heat the oil in a large, heavy-based pan, add the onion and fry over low heat for about 5 minutes or until soft, but not browned. Add the garlic and scampi and fry for a further 3 minutes, before blending in the tomatoes and the wine; season to taste with salt, freshly ground pepper and sugar. Bring the mixture to the boil and simmer for about 6 minutes.

Blend the cornflour with 1 tablespoon of water and stir into the scampi. Cook for a few minutes, stirring until the sauce has thickened. Remove from the heat and add the parsley.

As a first course the scampi could be served within a ring of plain boiled rice. For a lunch or supper dish, buttered French beans would also be suitable.

AVOCADO PEARS WITH PRAWNS

These fruits, originally from the Caribbean, are now popular in Europe. They are frequently served plain with vinaigrette dressing, but they can also be served with various fillings, often shellfish.

PREPARATION TIME: *10 min.*
CHILLING TIME: *1 hour*

INGREDIENTS *(for 6)*:
3 avocado pears
2 rounded tablespoons mayonnaise
2 tablespoons double cream
2 rounded tablespoons tomato ketchup
Worcestershire sauce
Juice of half lemon
8 oz. peeled prawns
GARNISH:
Paprika

Place the avocados in the bottom of the refrigerator to chill for about 1 hour before serving.

Measure the mayonnaise*, cream and tomato ketchup into a bowl; add a shake of Worcestershire sauce and the strained lemon juice. Mix thoroughly, then stir in the prawns and leave to chill in the refrigerator.

Just before serving, cut each avocado in half lengthways, with a silver knife, and remove the stone. Carefully rub the cut sides of the avocados with the squeezed lemon to prevent discoloration. Arrange the pears on individual plates and spoon the prawn mixture into the centres. Sprinkle with paprika.

FRENCH ONION SOUP

Although Les Halles in Paris no longer exists, onion soup is permanently associated with that famous market. The porters kept out the cold of a raw winter's morning by drinking vast mugs of this traditional soup.

PREPARATION TIME: *20 min.*
COOKING TIME: *1 hour*

INGREDIENTS *(for 4)*:
1 lb. onions
2–3 oz. unsalted butter
2 pints chicken or beef stock
½ level teaspoon salt
1 oz. plain flour
4 slices French bread, ½ in. thick
4 oz. Gruyère cheese

Peel and thinly slice the onions. Melt 1 oz. of the butter in a large saucepan and add the onions. Cover with a lid and cook over low heat for about 15 minutes, until the onions are soft and transparent. Remove the lid and continue frying the onions, stirring occasionally, until they are golden brown. Stir in the stock and salt. Replace the lid and simmer the soup for 30 minutes. In a small basin, mix the flour with ¼ pint of water until thoroughly blended. Add to the soup and stir until it comes back to the boil. Simmer for 2–3 minutes until the soup has thickened, then draw the pan off the heat.

Meanwhile, butter both sides of each slice of French bread; grate the cheese and sprinkle half over the bread. Bake the bread, on a baking tray, in a preheated oven, at 350°F (mark 4) until the bread is crisp and the cheese has melted. Arrange the bread in individual bowls and pour over the hot onion soup.

Serve the remaining grated cheese in a separate bowl.

GOUGÈRE AU FROMAGE

This choux pastry ring with a cheese filling originated in Burgundy, France. It is often served hot as a first course, but can also be served, thinly sliced, as an appetiser.

PREPARATION TIME: *15 min.*
COOKING TIME: *30 min.*

INGREDIENTS *(for 4–6):*
4 oz. unsalted butter
4 oz. plain flour
1 level teaspoon salt
4 eggs
4 oz. Gruyère cheese
Egg and milk for glazing

Put $\frac{1}{4}$ pint of water in a heavy-based saucepan and add the butter, cut into small knobs. Sift the flour and salt. Place the pan of water and butter over gentle heat; as soon as the butter has melted bring the contents to a brisk boil. Quickly tip in all the flour and, with a wooden spoon, beat for 1 minute over moderate heat until all the ingredients are thoroughly blended. Draw the pan off the heat and continue to beat well for about 5 minutes or until the mixture leaves the sides of the pan clean.

Beat in the eggs, one at a time, blending each thoroughly before adding the next. When ready, the pastry should be smooth and glossy, and stiff enough to hold its shape when piped. Grate the cheese and beat all but 1 oz. into the choux pastry.

Grease and lightly flour a baking tray; trace a circle, about 8 in. across on it. Fit a large nylon piping bag with a 1 in. plain nozzle and fill the bag with the pastry.

Pipe a circle of the choux pastry on to the tray, following the guide line; if necessary, pipe a second layer on top or alongside the first to use up all the pastry. Brush the surface with a lightly beaten egg mixed with a little milk; sprinkle with the remaining cheese. Place in the centre of a pre-heated oven and bake for 30 minutes at 425°F (mark 7). Lift from the baking tray on to a plate, and serve hot, cut in slices.

MINESTRONE

This soup, of Italian origin and with numerous regional variations, is substantial enough to serve as a meal on its own. For the first course of a meal, increase the amount of stock or use less vegetables.

PREPARATION TIME: *15 min.*
COOKING TIME: *30–35 min.*

INGREDIENTS *(for 4):*
1–2 carrots
1–2 sticks celery
1 onion
1 small turnip
1 potato
1 oz. unsalted butter or 2 table-spoons olive oil
1 clove garlic
1½ pints ham or beef stock
2 large tomatoes
1 small leek
1 teacup shredded green cabbage or Brussels sprouts
1 oz. spaghetti or quick-cooking macaroni
Salt and black pepper
GARNISH:
2–3 oz. Parmesan cheese

Peel or scrape the carrot, wash the celery and chop both finely. Peel and finely chop the onion, turnip and potato. Heat the butter or oil in a large, heavy-based pan and add the prepared vegetables, together with the peeled and crushed garlic. Sauté* the vegetables for a few minutes until they begin to soften, then add the hot stock (from a boiled bacon joint or beef stock made up from a stock cube). Cover the pan with a lid and simmer the soup over low heat for 15 minutes or until the vegetables are almost tender.

Skin the tomatoes*; cut them in half, remove all seeds and chop up the tomato flesh. Trim the roots and coarse outer leaves from the leek, wash thoroughly under cold running water, then shred it finely. Add the tomatoes, the leek and washed shredded cabbage or sprouts to the pan; bring the soup back to the boil. Add the spaghetti, breaking it into small pieces, or the macaroni.

Simmer the soup over low heat —without the lid—for a further 10–15 minutes. Season the soup to taste with salt and freshly ground pepper and serve a bowl of grated Parmesan cheese separately.

DANISH LIVER PÂTÉ

The inexpensive pig liver is not much used for grilling or frying, but is ideal for a pâté. This pâté should be left to cool under a heavy weight before being served. It will keep for up to a week in the refrigerator.

PREPARATION TIME: *35 min.*
COOKING TIME: *2 hours*

INGREDIENTS *(for 6–8):*
1 lb. pig liver
½ pint milk
1 onion
1 bay leaf
6 oz. fat green back bacon rashers
6 anchovy fillets
1 level teaspoon salt
Black pepper
¼ level teaspoon each of ground nutmeg, cloves and allspice
1 oz. unsalted butter
1 oz. plain flour
1 egg
½ lb. streaky bacon rashers

Measure the milk into a saucepan. Peel the onion and cut in half; add it, with the bay leaf, to the

Fish

milk and bring to the boil over gentle heat. Remove the saucepan from the heat and allow the milk to infuse* for 15 minutes. Strain through a sieve and set the milk aside.

Trim the rind from the fat bacon rashers and remove any skin and gristle from the liver. Mince the bacon, the liver and anchovy fillets twice through the fine plate. Blend the mixture thoroughly and season to taste with salt, freshly ground pepper and the spices.

Melt the butter in a saucepan, add the flour and cook over low heat for 1 minute; gradually stir in the milk, beating continuously. Bring the mixture to the boil and cook for 2–3 minutes. Draw off the heat and blend in the liver mixture. Bind with the lightly beaten egg.

Line a 1 lb. loaf tin with the streaky bacon rashers, leaving the rashers to hang over the edges. Alternatively, bake the pâté in two ½ lb. loaf tins and store one in the freezer. Spoon the pâté mixture into the tin and fold the bacon rashers over the top.

Cover the tin with a piece of buttered greaseproof paper and place in a large roasting pan holding 1 in. of cold water. Place in the centre of a pre-heated oven and bake for 2 hours at 325°F (mark 3). The pâté is baked when a stainless steel skewer comes away clean.

Remove the pâté from the heat, cover with freshly buttered greaseproof paper and place a heavy weight on top. Leave the pâté until quite cold, preferably overnight, before turning it out. Serve the pâté, cut into thick slices, with hot toast and butter.

PRAWNS IN CURRY SAUCE

Most shellfish are relatively expensive, but combined with a creamy sauce, a small amount will go a long way.

PREPARATION TIME: *20 min.*
COOKING TIME: *5 min.*

INGREDIENTS *(for 4)*:
8 oz. peeled prawns
2 small onions
1 tablespoon olive oil
1 rounded teaspoon curry powder
1 level tablespoon plain flour
¼ pint fish or chicken stock
1 rounded teaspoon tomato purée
1 rounded tablespoon mango
*   chutney or apricot jam*
Juice of half lemon
1 oz. unsalted butter
3 tablespoons double cream

Peel and finely chop one of the onions. Heat the oil in a saucepan and add the onion. Cover with a lid and fry over low heat for 2–3 minutes or until the onion is soft, but not brown. Stir in the curry powder and fry gently for a few minutes; blend in the flour and cook for 2–3 minutes. Gradually add the stock and stir until the sauce thickens and comes to the boil. Add the tomato purée, chutney (or jam) and lemon juice. Simmer for 5 minutes, then strain the sauce through a sieve.

Rinse the prawns in cold water and pat them dry on a cloth. Peel and finely chop the remaining onion. Heat the butter in a frying pan and fry the onion until soft, then add the prawns. Blend in the curry sauce and bring the mixture to the boil. Stir in the cream; remove from the heat.

Arrange the prawns in the sauce within a ring of plain boiled rice.

GOUJONS OF SOLE WITH TARTARE SAUCE

PREPARATION TIME: *20 min.*
COOKING TIME: *2–3 min.*

INGREDIENTS *(for 4)*:
1 large Dover sole
Seasoned flour
1 large egg
1 dessertspoon olive oil
Golden breadcrumbs
Oil for frying
Salt
TARTARE SAUCE:
1 rounded tablespoon mayonnaise
1 tablespoon double cream
1 rounded teaspoon each, chopped
*   parsley, gherkins, capers*
1½ rounded teaspoons chopped
*   onion*
GARNISH:
Lemon wedges

In France, the small, smelt-like goujons or gudgeons are deep-fried and served like whitebait. This recipe is adapted to Dover sole or plaice.

Ask the fishmonger to skin and fillet the sole*; rinse the fillets in cold water and pat them dry on a clean cloth. Making a slanting cut, slice each fillet in half and then cut each half lengthways into three or four narrow strips.

Coat the fish thoroughly with seasoned flour*, shaking off any surplus. Beat the egg lightly and mix in the olive oil; dip the fish pieces in this mixture before rolling them in the breadcrumbs. Set the fish aside in a cool place.

For the sauce mix the mayonnaise*, cream, parsley, gherkins, capers and onions together. Spoon into a serving dish and chill until required.

Heat the oil* in a deep fryer until a small crumb of bread sizzles. Put the fish in the basket and lower it into the hot oil; fry for 2–3 minutes until crisp and golden brown. Remove from the heat and drain the fish on crumpled absorbent paper. Sprinkle with salt and pile the fish on to a hot serving dish. Garnish with wedges of lemon and offer the sauce separately.

A green salad and crusty bread could be served with the fillets.

COULIBIAC

This is a traditional Russian fish pie, totally unlike the British idea of pie. It is usually served hot, with soured cream, but also makes a good buffet choice.

PREPARATION TIME: *2 hours*
COOKING TIME: *30 min.*

INGREDIENTS *(for 8–10)*:
8 oz. tapioca
2 onions
¾ lb. button mushrooms
2 oz. unsalted butter
Salt and black pepper
2 slices middle-cut salmon, each
    1 in. thick
½ pint dry white wine
3 hardboiled eggs
6 thin pancakes
1 lb. prepared puff pastry
1 egg for glazing
½ pint soured cream

Bring a pan of salted water to the boil, sprinkle in the tapioca, stirring all the time. Bring to the boil and simmer gently for 30 minutes, after which the tapioca should be transparent. Drain through a fine sieve and rinse under cold water to remove excess starch. Set the tapioca aside.

Meanwhile, peel and finely chop the onions; wipe, trim and finely chop the mushrooms*. Melt the butter in a large frying pan and add the onions; cover with a lid and cook over low heat for 5 minutes until the onions are soft, but not brown. Increase the heat and add the mushrooms. Season with salt and freshly ground pepper and cook, stirring continuously, for 5 minutes. Remove the pan from the heat, stir in the tapioca; correct seasoning if necessary and leave the mixture to cool.

Wipe the salmon pieces and put them in a saucepan together with the wine and a pinch of salt and pepper. Simmer the salmon gently for about 10 minutes; draw the pan off the heat and let the salmon cool in the liquid. Drain; remove skin and bones from the salmon and flake* the flesh. Hardboil the eggs and bake six small wafer-thin pancakes*.

When ready to assemble the coulibiac, heat the mushroom and tapioca mixture slightly to soften. If necessary warm the pancakes over a pan of boiling water to unstick them. Slice the eggs into rounds. Roll out the puff pastry* to a rectangle no more than ¼ in. thick and approximately 16 in. long by 9 in. wide. Cut the edges straight and reserve the trimmings for decoration. Brush the pastry with the lightly beaten egg to within 1 in. of the edges.

Brush three of the pancakes with egg and lay them in a single line down the pastry. Spoon a quarter of the mushroom mixture in a neat strip, 2–3 in. wide and to within 2 in. of the shorter pastry edges, over the pancakes.

Top with half the flaked salmon and then with another layer of mushroom and all the egg slices. Spoon a further quarter of mushrooms on before the remaining salmon and then the last of the mushrooms. Top finally with the three remaining pancakes, brush with egg and wrap the pancakes round the filling.

Fold the sides of the pastry up and over the top of the filling so that the edges overlap. Brush thoroughly with egg to seal the edges. Fold the pastry ends over the top and seal with egg. Place the coulibiac on a wet baking tray with the sealed edges underneath. Brush the top with egg.

Roll out the pastry trimmings and use for decoration. Cut a small hole in the centre of the pastry and insert a chimney of greaseproof paper.

Place the baking tray on the centre shelf of a pre-heated oven. Bake at 425°F (mark 7) for about 30 minutes or until the pastry is golden brown.

Serve the coulibiac cut in 1½ in. wide slices, with a separate bowl of soured cream.

SMOKED HADDOCK MOUSSE

A mousse, whether savoury or sweet, should be chilled for several hours before serving. This recipe, suitable for a dinner party or a buffet, can be made the day before the occasion.

PREPARATION TIME: *45 min.*
CHILLING TIME: *2–3 hours*

INGREDIENTS *(for 6–8)*:
2 lb. smoked haddock fillet
1 small onion
¾ pint milk
1 bay leaf
1½ oz. unsalted butter
1½ oz. plain flour
Salt and black pepper
Cayenne pepper
½ oz. powdered gelatine
Juice and rind of a lemon
½ pint double cream
ASPIC:
½ level teaspoon powdered gelatine
1 tablespoon lemon juice or vinegar
GARNISH:
½ cucumber

Cut the haddock fillet into 8–10 pieces and put them in a saucepan; peel and slice the onion and add, with the milk and bay leaf, to the fish. Cover the pan with a lid and simmer the fish over low heat for about 10 minutes. Strain the fish through a colander and set the milk aside. Remove all skin and bones, and flake* the haddock flesh finely.

Melt the butter in a saucepan over low heat; stir in the flour and cook for a few minutes until this roux* is light brown. Gradually stir in the milk, beating continuously to get a smooth sauce. Bring this to the boil and cook gently for 2–3 minutes. Season to taste with salt, freshly ground pepper and cayenne, then draw the pan off the heat. Pour the sauce into a large bowl, cover with buttered greaseproof paper and leave to cool. Measure 4 tablespoons of water into a saucepan and sprinkle in the gelatine. Allow to soak for 5 minutes, then stir the mixture over low heat, until the gelatine has dissolved.

Remove the buttered paper and stir the sauce; blend in the fish, melted gelatine and finely grated rind and juice from the lemon. Correct seasoning if necessary. Whip the cream lightly and fold it into the fish mixture; pour this into a 2½–3 pint soufflé dish and leave until set.

For the aspic, measure 2 tablespoons of water into a saucepan and sprinkle over the gelatine. Soak for 5 minutes, then stir over low heat until the gelatine has dissolved. Draw the pan from the heat, add 2 tablespoons of water and the lemon juice. Pour a little aspic on top of the mousse. While this is setting slightly, wash and thinly slice the cucumber. Arrange the slices in a circular pattern on the aspic. Spoon over the remaining aspic, and chill the mousse in the refrigerator until ready to serve.

Serve with thin brown bread and butter or with a green salad tossed in French dressing*.

Meat

SAUERBRATEN

This German farmhouse dish of spiced braised beef is marinated for 4–6 days to flavour and tenderise the meat. It is tradition-ally served with potato dump-lings, but noodles or macaroni are less heavy alternatives and more suited to British taste.

PREPARATION TIME: *15 min.*
COOKING TIME: *1½ hours*

INGREDIENTS *(for 4):*

2 lb. topside of beef	*1 level teaspoon caster sugar*
1 onion	*½ pint wine vinegar*
4 peppercorns	*2 oz. unsalted butter*
1 clove	*1 piece breadcrust*
1 small bay leaf	*2 rounded teaspoons cornflour*
Salt and black pepper	

Wipe the meat with a clean cloth and trim off any fat. Tie the meat with thin string to maintain its round shape and put it in a large earthenware bowl. Peel and slice the onion, and add it to the meat, together with the peppercorns, clove, bay leaf, salt, freshly ground pepper and the sugar. Pour the vinegar mixed with ¾ pint of water over the meat and leave it to stand, covered, in a cold place for 4–6 days, turning it once a day in the marinade*.

Lift the meat from the marinade and pat it thoroughly dry on absorbent paper. Melt the butter in a deep, heavy-based pan, add the meat and brown it quickly all over. Season to taste with salt and pour ½ pint of the strained marinade over the meat. Add the crust of bread (in Germany, a piece of honeycake or ginger-bread is sometimes used as well to give extra flavour). Cover the pan with a lid and simmer over low heat for 1½ hours or until the meat is tender. Add extra marinade if necessary.

Lift out the meat and keep it warm. Strain the gravy through a fine sieve, measure off ½ pint and top up with more marinade if necessary. Blend the cornflour with a little water and stir into the gravy; bring to the boil, stirring until smooth. Check and correct flavour and seasoning— the gravy should taste slightly sweet and sour.

Serve the meat cut into slices, with boiled noodles or macaroni; hand the gravy separately. Glazed carrots (see March vegetables) or a green vegetable would also be suitable.

NAVARIN OF LAMB

Navarin is a French cooking term applied exclusively to a casserole of lamb, or mutton, and young root vegetables. Loin can be used, but best end of neck is also suitable and less expensive.

PREPARATION TIME: *30 min.*
COOKING TIME: *1¾ hours*

INGREDIENTS *(for 4):*
2 lb. best end neck of lamb
Seasoned flour
1½ oz. dripping or vegetable oil
1 lb. young carrots
1 onion
¾ pint chicken or beef stock
1 tablespoon tomato purée
Salt and black pepper
1 bouquet garni
8 small button onions
8 small new potatoes
GARNISH:
Chopped parsley

Ask the butcher to cut the meat into single rib pieces. Trim any fat from the meat and coat the pieces with the seasoned flour*. Melt the fat in a large frying pan and add the meat. Fry as many ribs as possible at one time, turn-ing them to brown evenly on both sides. Remove from the pan and put them in a large casserole. Scrape and thinly slice the carrots, and peel and roughly chop the onion. Add these to the casserole. Drain off most of the fat from the frying pan. Stir in 1 level table-spoon of the seasoned flour; cook over low heat for a few minutes to brown, then gradually stir in the hot stock. Add the tomato purée and bring the sauce to the boil.

Draw the pan off the heat and strain the sauce into the casserole; season with salt and freshly ground pepper. Add the bouquet garni*. Cover the casserole with a lid and place in the centre of a pre-heated oven at 325°F (mark 3); cook for 1¼ hours.

Peel the button onions, leaving them whole. Put them in a sauce-pan and cover with cold water. Bring this to the boil, then drain the onions at once. Scrape the new potatoes and add, with the onions, to the casserole, placing them on top of the meat. Replace the lid and cook the casserole for a further 30 minutes or until the vegetables are tender.

Remove the bouquet garni from the casserole, sprinkle with chopped parsley and serve the navarin straight from the casserole.

MOUSSAKA

The aubergine—or egg plant—is the staple vegetable of the Middle East. It is the basic ingredient in moussaka, meaning aubergine casserole; the dish may also include minced beef or lamb.

PREPARATION TIME: *45 min.*
COOKING TIME: *35–40 min.*

INGREDIENTS (*for 4*):
4 aubergines
1 large onion
4–6 tablespoons olive oil
1 lb. lean minced beef
1 level teaspoon salt
2 rounded teaspoons tomato purée
¼ pint beef stock or water
Black pepper
1 oz. unsalted butter
1 oz. plain flour
½ pint milk
1 egg

Peel and finely chop the onion; heat 1 tablespoon of the oil in a heavy-based pan and gently fry the onions for about 5 minutes, covering the pan with a lid. Add the minced beef and fry until brown and thoroughly sealed. Stir in the salt, tomato purée and stock; season to taste with freshly ground pepper. Bring this mixture to the boil, cover the pan with a lid and simmer gently for 30 minutes or until the meat is tender and the liquid is almost absorbed.

Meanwhile, peel and thinly slice the aubergines, arrange them in a layer on a plate and sprinkle generously with salt; let the aubergines stand for 30 minutes to draw out the bitter juices. Drain, rinse in cold water and pat thoroughly dry on absorbent kitchen paper. Fry the aubergine slices in the remaining oil until golden, then drain on absorbent paper. Arrange a layer of aubergines in the bottom of a large buttered fireproof dish or casserole. Cover with a layer of the meat, another layer of aubergines and so on, until all is used up; finish with a layer of aubergines.

Melt the butter in a saucepan over low heat and stir in the flour. Cook gently for 1 minute, then gradually blend in the milk, stirring continuously. Bring this sauce to the boil, season with salt and freshly ground pepper and simmer for 1–2 minutes. Draw the pan off the heat and beat in the egg. Spoon this sauce over the moussaka; place in the centre of a pre-heated oven and bake at 350°F (mark 4) for 35–40 minutes or until bubbling hot and browned.

This is a rich and substantial meal, best served straight from the casserole. A tomato and onion salad could be served with it.

FRICADELLES

These egg-shaped spicy mince balls appear regularly on the Danish family menu. They are usually served hot, with a sauce, but are also used, cut into thin slices, as toppings for open sandwiches.

PREPARATION TIME: *30 min.*
COOKING TIME: *30 min.*

INGREDIENTS (*for 4*):
1 lb. lean veal
1 small onion
1 heaped teaspoon chopped parsley
¼ level teaspoon dried thyme
1 level teaspoon salt
¼ level teaspoon ground mace or nutmeg
Black pepper
2 thin slices white bread
1–2 tablespoons milk
1 small egg
2 rounded tablespoons seasoned flour
½ pint tomato sauce
2 oz. unsalted butter
GARNISH:
Chopped parsley

Trim fat and gristle from the veal and put the meat through the fine blade of the mincer. Peel and finely chop the onion. Put the minced meat in a bowl and add the onion, parsley, thyme, salt, mace (or nutmeg) and a few twists of pepper.

Trim off the breadcrusts and soak the bread in the milk for a few minutes, then squeeze out the excess liquid. Mash the bread with a fork, and add it to the meat, together with the lightly beaten egg. Blend the ingredients thoroughly, using the fingers, until the mixture is firm. Then, shape the mixture into 10–12 even-sized oblong balls.

Coat the fricadelles with the seasoned flour* and set them aside while preparing the tomato sauce*. Now melt the butter in a heavy-based pan and fry the meat balls over high heat until evenly brown. Turn the fricadelles once only.

Lift the fricadelles from the pan with a perforated spoon and put them in an ovenproof dish. Pour over the hot tomato sauce, cover the dish with a lid and cook for 15–20 minutes on the centre shelf of an oven pre-heated to 350°F (mark 4).

Serve the fricadelles, sprinkled with parsley, from the casserole. Boiled potatoes and/or a green vegetable are usually served with this dish.

VEAL SCALOPPINE

Italian scaloppine are similar to French escalopes, but they are cut against the grain of the meat. Ask the butcher to beat the scaloppine flat and thin.

PREPARATION TIME: *15 min.*
COOKING TIME: *30 min.*

INGREDIENTS (*for 4*):
4 veal escalopes
Seasoned flour
6 oz. unsalted butter
1 tablespoon olive oil
½ lb. button mushrooms
¼ pint Marsala or sweet sherry
½ pint chicken stock

Trim any fat and gristle from the scaloppine and coat them thoroughly with seasoned flour*. Heat 2 oz. of the butter and the oil in a heavy-based pan and fry the meat over low heat for 3–4 minutes on each side, turning once. Lift the meat from the pan and keep it hot.

Poultry & Game

CASSEROLE OF HARE

In March, as the game season is coming to an end, hare is economical to buy. It needs marinating, however, for about 8 hours, to improve the flavour and to draw out the blood.

PREPARATION TIME: *45 min.*
COOKING TIME: *2 hours*

INGREDIENTS *(for 4–6)*:

1 hare
1 large onion
4 peppercorns
4 bay leaves
¼ pint wine vinegar
Seasoned flour
2 oz. unsalted butter
2 onions
1 pint light ale

Juice of a lemon
1 sprig thyme
1 level teaspoon Dijon mustard
1 dessertspoon tarragon vinegar
2–3 level tablespoons caster sugar
Salt and black pepper
8 soaked prunes
2 level teaspoons cornflour

Ask the poulterer to skin the hare* and to joint it into eight portions. Wipe the pieces and put them in a large bowl.

Peel and slice the large onion, and add, with the peppercorns and 2 bay leaves, to the hare. Mix the wine vinegar with 1¼ pints of water and pour over the hare, to cover the pieces completely. Leave the bowl in a cool place to marinate* for about 8 hours, turning the meat occasionally.

Lift the hare from the marinade and dry the pieces thoroughly; coat them with seasoned flour*. Melt the butter in a large frying pan, add the hare and cook until evenly brown all over. Put the pieces of hare in a large saucepan or fireproof casserole. Strain the marinade and pour ¼ pint of it over the meat. Peel and finely chop the onions, and add to the hare, together with the ale, the

lemon juice, two bay leaves, thyme, mustard, vinegar and sugar; season to taste with salt and freshly ground pepper. Bring the mixture to the boil; cover the pan with a lid and leave to simmer gently for 2 hours. About 20 minutes before the end of cooking time add the soaked prunes.

When the hare is cooked, blend the cornflour with a little water to a smooth paste. Add some of the hot liquid from the pan, blend thoroughly before stirring it into the liquid. Bring the mixture back to boiling, stirring gently until the sauce has thickened.

Remove the pan from the heat, lift the pieces of hare and prunes on to a hot serving dish. Correct seasoning if necessary, and pour the sauce over the hare. Serve with creamed potatoes* and a green vegetable.

Pour all but one tablespoon of the hot fat from the pan. Trim and slice the mushrooms* and add to the pan; cook over low heat, tossing the mushrooms until coated in the butter, then stir in the wine and stock. Bring this sauce to the boil and return the scaloppine to the pan. Cover with a lid, lower the heat and simmer gently for 15–20 minutes. Turn the meat once or twice so that it cooks evenly. Arrange the scaloppine and mushrooms on a serving dish and keep it hot. Boil the sauce rapidly until it has reduced by about one-third and has thickened slightly. Whisk in the remaining 4 oz. of butter, draw the pan off the heat and pour the sauce over the veal.

Boiled rice or buttered pasta, and French beans or broccoli, can be served with the scaloppine.

STEAK AU POIVRE

A classic peppered steak is always prepared with whole, crushed peppercorns. It is traditionally served with brandy sauce and is ideal for cooking in a chafing dish at the table.

PREPARATION TIME: *15 min.*
COOKING TIME: *15–20 min.*

INGREDIENTS *(for 4)*:
4 fillet or entrecôte steaks
2 tablespoons whole black peppercorns
2 oz. unsalted butter
1 tablespoon olive oil
2 tablespoons brandy
¼ pint double cream
Salt

Wipe the steaks and trim off any fat and gristle. Crush the peppercorns coarsely in a mortar or on a wooden board with a rolling pin. With the fingers, press the

crushed peppercorns into the surface of the meat on both sides.

Heat the butter and oil in a heavy-based pan; cook the steaks over high heat for 2 minutes, turning them once. This initial hot frying seals the juices and peppercorns in the meat; lower the heat and cook the steaks for 5 minutes for rare steaks, 8–10 minutes for medium-rare and 12 minutes for well-done steaks.

Lift the steaks from the pan on to a hot serving dish; add the brandy to the butter in the pan and set it alight when hot. Draw the pan off the heat and as soon as the flames have died down, gradually stir in the cream. Season the sauce with salt and pour it over the steaks. Freshly cooked broccoli and croquette potatoes*, or a green salad, go well with these steaks.

PIGEONS WITH FORCEMEAT BALLS

These inexpensive little game birds can be ordered cleaned and trussed, ready for cooking. Young, tender pigeons can be roasted or grilled, but at this time of the year they are best used for a casserole.

PREPARATION TIME: *1 hour*
COOKING TIME: *1¼ hours*

INGREDIENTS *(for 6)*:
3 pigeons
¼ lb. streaky bacon
1 oz. unsalted butter
2 level tablespoons plain flour
¾ pint hot chicken stock or water
1 level teaspoon salt
Black pepper
1 bouquet garni
12 button onions
½ lb. button mushrooms
FORCEMEAT BALLS:
¼ lb. fresh white breadcrumbs
2 oz. shredded beef suet
1 rounded tablespoon finely chopped parsley
Finely grated rind of half lemon
Salt and black pepper
1–2 eggs
GARNISH:
Chopped parsley

Dice the bacon, having first removed the rind; heat the butter in a deep, heavy-based pan. Fry the bacon over moderate heat until the fat runs and the bacon pieces are crisp. Remove the bacon from the pan with a perforated spoon and leave to drain on crumpled absorbent paper. Put the pigeons in the pan to brown them, turning several times. Lift out the pigeons and put them in a casserole.

Pour away all but one tablespoon of the hot fat from the pan;

stir in the flour and cook gently for a few minutes until browned. Gradually blend in the hot stock and bring the sauce slowly to the boil. Simmer for a few minutes, then strain the sauce over the pigeons in the casserole. Add the bacon pieces, the salt, a few twists of pepper and the bouquet garni*. Peel the onions and add them whole to the pigeons. Cover the casserole with a lid and place in the centre of a pre-heated oven; cook for 1 hour at 350°F (mark 4).

Meanwhile, trim and finely slice the mushrooms*. For the forcemeat balls, measure the breadcrumbs, shredded suet, chopped parsley and lemon rind into a mixing bowl; season with salt and freshly ground pepper. Beat the eggs lightly and stir them into the mixture with a fork until the forcemeat has a moist, but not too wet, consistency. Using the tips of the fingers, shape the forcemeat into 8–12 round balls and put these, together with the

mushrooms, in the casserole. Replace the lid and continue cooking for 15–20 minutes.

Lift the pigeons from the casserole, cut them in half and arrange them on a hot serving dish. Surround them with the mushrooms, onions and forcemeat balls. Remove the bouquet garni from the sauce before pouring it over the pigeons. Garnish with chopped parsley and serve with sugar-browned potatoes (see March vegetables).

LEEK AND CHICKEN PIE

The leek, the national emblem of Wales, is traditionally served on St David's day, March 1. The chicken for this pie should be boiled well in advance so that it can cool for several hours.

PREPARATION TIME: *35 min.*
COOKING TIME: *1 hour 40 min.*

INGREDIENTS *(for 6)*:
1 chicken (3½–4 lb.)
1 onion
1 bay leaf
½ level teaspoon salt
6 parsley stalks
2–3 leeks
Salt and black pepper
8 oz. shortcrust pastry (standard recipe)
Egg and milk for glazing
¼ pint double cream
GARNISH:
Chopped parsley

Wipe the chicken* inside and out; truss it and put in a large saucepan; cover with cold water. Peel the onion and cut it in half; add the onion, bay leaf, salt and parsley stalks to the chicken. Cover with a lid; bring to the boil over low heat, then simmer gently for 45 minutes. Draw the pan off the heat and let the chicken cool in the liquid.

Lift the fat from the surface of the stock and take out the chicken. Measure ½ pint of stock and set aside (the remainder may be used as the base for a soup). Remove the skin and bones from the cold chicken and cut the flesh into 1 in. pieces.

Trim away the roots from the leeks, and the green tops to within 1 in. of the white stalks. Slit the leeks in half lengthways, and

Rice & Pasta

wash them thoroughly under cold running water; chop the leeks coarsely.

Place a layer of chicken in a buttered 2½ pint pie dish, cover with a layer of leeks and continue with these layers until all the chicken and leeks are used up. Season each layer with salt and freshly ground pepper, and finally add the reserved chicken stock.

On a floured surface, roll out the shortcrust pastry* to a circle large enough to cover the pie dish. Butter the rim of the dish and line with trimmings of pastry. Damp the edges before covering with the pastry lid. Trim and seal the pastry edges together. Make a few slits in the centre of the pastry to allow the steam to escape, and decorate the pie with leaves cut from the pastry trimmings. Brush the pie with lightly beaten egg, mixed with a few tablespoons of milk.

Bake the pie in the centre of a pre-heated oven, for 25 minutes at 375°F (mark 5). Reduce the heat to 325°F (mark 3) and bake for a further 15 minutes. When ready to serve, cut out a portion of the pastry and pour in the warmed cream. Replace the pastry, sprinkle the pie with chopped parsley and serve.

This pie is substantial and requires no extra vegetables. But young carrots, peas, broccoli or new potatoes, tossed in butter, could be served separately.

CHEESE GNOCCHI

Basically, gnocchi is a dough-like mixture, shaped into flat cakes and deep-fried.

PREPARATION TIME: *30 min.*
COOKING TIME: *5 min.*

INGREDIENTS *(for 4)*:
1 pint milk
1 small onion
1 clove
1 bay leaf
6 parsley stalks
4 oz. semolina
4–6 oz. Cheddar cheese
1 rounded tablespoon chopped parsley
Salt and black pepper
Cayenne pepper
1 egg
Golden breadcrumbs
Oil for deep frying
GARNISH:
Parsley sprigs

Measure the milk into a saucepan. Peel the onion, leaving it whole, and stick the clove into it. Put the onion, bay leaf and parsley stalks in the milk. Heat until almost boiling, then draw the pan off the heat, cover with a lid and leave to infuse for 15 minutes.

Strain and re-heat the milk to boiling point. Sprinkle in the semolina, stirring continuously. Cook, stirring frequently, for about 6 minutes until the mixture is quite thick. Draw the pan off the heat and stir in the grated cheese and chopped parsley; season to taste with salt, freshly ground pepper and cayenne pepper. Smooth this gnocchi mixture over a moistened dinner plate, shaping it into a neat circle. Chill for 1½–2 hours.

Cut the gnocchi into eight equal-sized wedge shapes; coat them with the lightly beaten egg and then with the breadcrumbs. Shake off any loose crumbs. Place the gnocchi in a frying basket and fry in hot deep oil* until crisp and golden brown, about 1–2 minutes. Drain thoroughly on crumpled absorbent paper before arranging on a hot serving dish. Garnish with a few sprigs of parsley.

The gnocchi can be served with a crisp green salad.

ALMOND RICE

Many rice dishes make good accompaniments to grilled poultry and gammon in place of potato.

PREPARATION TIME: *5 min.*
COOKING TIME: *25 min.*

INGREDIENTS *(for 4)*:
6 oz. long grain rice
1 onion
1 oz. unsalted butter
1 oz. stoned raisins
¾ pint chicken stock
½ level teaspoon salt
2 oz. roasted flaked almonds
GARNISH:
1 heaped tablespoon chopped parsley

Peel and finely chop the onion. Melt the butter in a saucepan and add the onion; cover the pan with a lid and cook over low heat for about 5 minutes until the onion is soft. Add the rice and toss it with the onion and butter. Stir in the raisins and add the hot stock and the salt. Bring to the boil, lower the heat and cover the pan with a lid. Simmer the rice gently for 15–20 minutes or until it is tender.

When cooked, fluff the rice up with a fork, fold in the almonds and spoon it all into a hot serving dish. Sprinkle with parsley.

CANNELLONI STUFFED WITH SPINACH

Literally 'big pipes', cannelloni are pasta tubes, about 3 in. long and 1 in. in diameter. They are filled with a savoury stuffing and served with tomato sauce.

PREPARATION TIME: *45–60 min.*
COOKING TIME: *20–30 min.*

INGREDIENTS *(for 4)*:
8 cannelloni tubes
1 lb. fresh spinach
½ lb. cooked chicken
1 oz. unsalted butter
1 oz. plain flour
⅓ pint milk
Salt and black pepper
¾–1 pint tomato sauce
3–4 oz. grated Parmesan cheese

Wash the spinach thoroughly and put it in a large saucepan – no water is needed. Cover with a lid and cook over low heat for about 10 minutes. Drain the spinach through a colander, squeezing firmly with a wooden spoon to remove all the moisture. Chop the spinach coarsely and set it aside.

Dice the chicken flesh finely or put it through a mincer.

Melt the butter in a saucepan and stir in the flour; cook gently for 1 minute, then gradually blend in the milk, stirring continuously to get a smooth sauce. Bring to the boil and season to taste with salt and freshly ground pepper; simmer gently for 2–3 minutes or until the sauce has thickened. Take the pan off the heat and stir the spinach and chicken into the sauce; check seasoning.

Put the cannelloni tubes in a pan of boiling salted water and

boil for 15 minutes or until the pasta is just tender. Drain and cool for a few minutes before stuffing the tubes with the spinach and chicken. Using a large piping bag, with a plain nozzle, pipe the stuffing into the tubes.

Arrange the cannelloni in a buttered ovenproof dish, pour the tomato sauce* over them and sprinkle with half the grated cheese. Place the casserole above centre in a pre-heated oven and cook at 350°F (mark 4) for 20–30 minutes or until bubbling hot and brown. Serve at once, with the remaining cheese in a bowl.

Vegetables & Salads

SUGAR-BROWNED POTATOES

The Danes traditionally serve these caramelised potatoes with roast pork, duck and goose and with boiled or baked gammon.

PREPARATION TIME: *20 min.*
COOKING TIME: *10 min.*

INGREDIENTS *(for 4)* :
2 lb. small new potatoes
1 oz. caster sugar
2 oz. unsalted butter

Wash the potatoes thoroughly in cold water; cook them in a pan of boiling salted water for about 10 minutes or until just tender. Drain the potatoes and leave until cool enough to handle, then peel off the skins.

Put the sugar in a frying pan over low heat; stir occasionally until the sugar has melted and is a golden caramel colour. Add the butter and stir until thoroughly blended with the sugar. Rinse the potatoes in cold water—this makes it easier to coat them with the caramel—before adding them to the caramel in the frying pan. Continue cooking over low heat, shaking the pan gently until the potatoes are evenly glazed and golden brown.

Arrange the potatoes at once in a warm serving dish on their own, or use as a garnish with roast meat or whole poultry, or between slices of baked gammon. See picture of Pigeons with Force-meat balls, p. 106.

AUBERGINE AND TOMATO RAGOÛT

This unusual vegetable casserole is particularly good with grilled and fried meats. Select firm, shiny and unblemished aubergines and extract the bitter juices before cooking.

PREPARATION TIME: *40 min.*
COOKING TIME: *30–35 min.*

INGREDIENTS *(for 4)* :
2 large or 3 small aubergines
Salt and black pepper
1 large onion
1 oz. unsalted butter
14–15 oz. tin of tomatoes
1 level teaspoon caster sugar

Peel the aubergines and cut them into $\frac{1}{2}$ in. slices crossways. Arrange the slices on a large plate and sprinkle with salt. Leave them to stand for 30 minutes to draw out the bitter juices. Drain the slices, rinse under cold water and pat them thoroughly dry on absorbent paper.

Peel and thinly slice the onion. Melt the butter in a saucepan, add the onion and cook over low heat for about 5 minutes until soft, but not brown. Add the aubergine slices, mixing them with the onion. Stir in the tomatoes with their juice, and season with freshly ground pepper and the sugar. Cover the pan with a lid and simmer gently for 30 minutes. Correct seasoning if necessary, and serve the casserole at once.

CHEESE AND FRUIT PLATTER

A salad of cheese and fruit makes a light and nourishing lunch on its own. Choose seasonal fruit such as oranges and pineapple, or sliced bananas, first tossed in lemon juice.

PREPARATION TIME: *10 min.*

INGREDIENTS *(for 4)* :
1 small head of lettuce
Bunch watercress
2 oranges
4 pineapple rings
8 oz. plain cottage cheese
French dressing or mayonnaise
GARNISH:
2 oz. shelled walnuts

Separate the leaves of the lettuce and cut off any coarse stems and damaged leaves; wash the leaves and dry them thoroughly on a clean cloth. Remove the lower coarse stems of the watercress, and wash the leaves. Cut a slice from the top and base of each orange before removing peel and all white pith; slice the oranges thinly across.

Arrange the lettuce in the centre of a platter, with the orange slices and pineapple rings around the edge. Arrange the cottage cheese on the fruit and garnish with sprigs of watercress.

Chop the walnuts coarsely and sprinkle them over the cheese. Mayonnaise* or a good French dressing* may be served separately, with crusty bread and/or crispbread and butter.

GLAZED CARROTS

Towards the end of the month, the first young carrots appear. The full flavour of these tender vegetables is retained by cooking them in a buttery glaze. They are suitable for serving with thick meat casseroles, and with roast lamb and pork as well as with grilled chops.

PREPARATION TIME: *10 min.*
COOKING TIME: *20–25 min.*

INGREDIENTS *(for 4)*:
1 lb. young carrots
1 oz. unsalted butter
Salt and black pepper
1 level teaspoon caster sugar
1 heaped teaspoon chopped parsley

Scrub and scrape the carrots and cut them into slices about ¼ in. thick. Melt the butter in a saucepan, add the carrot slices and season with salt, freshly ground pepper and the sugar. Add sufficient cold water to just cover the carrots. Bring to the boil, cover the pan with a lid and simmer gently for 15–20 minutes or until the carrots are tender.

Remove the lid; increase the heat and cook the carrots until the liquid has evaporated and only the butter remains—do not allow the carrots to brown. Draw the pan off the heat; add the parsley and toss with the carrots in the butter glaze. Arrange in a hot serving dish.

SWISS ROSTI

This potato cake should be made from potatoes boiled in their skins the day before. It is usually served with grilled or fried bacon, eggs and sausages.

PREPARATION TIME: *30 min.*
COOKING TIME: *15 min.*

INGREDIENTS *(for 4)*:
2 lb. even-sized potatoes
2–3 oz. unsalted butter
1 level teaspoon salt
Black pepper

Scrub the dirt off the potatoes and put them in a saucepan of cold water; cover with a lid and bring to the boil. Boil for about 7 minutes, until the potatoes are barely tender. Drain and leave until cold, preferably overnight. Skin the potatoes and grate them coarsely.

Melt the butter in a large, heavy-based sauté pan. Add the grated potatoes, sprinkle with the salt and season to taste with freshly ground pepper. Fry over moderate heat for about 15 minutes, and as the potatoes brown underneath turn them with a spatula. Towards the end of the cooking time, press down gently on the potato mixture to form a pancake; allow this to become crisp and brown on the underside.

Just before serving, loosen the cake with the spatula, place a round serving plate over the pan, and invert the potato cake.

PEPERONATA

This spicy casserole of sweet peppers and tomatoes is of Italian origin. It is served hot with grilled meat and fish, or cold as a side salad or a starter.

PREPARATION TIME: *10 min.*
COOKING TIME: *30–35 min.*

INGREDIENTS *(for 4)*:
4 large red or green peppers
1 onion
8 large tomatoes
1 clove garlic
Salt and black pepper
1 oz. unsalted butter
2 tablespoons olive oil
1 level dessertspoon caster sugar (optional)

Peel and finely chop the onion. Remove the stalks and wash the peppers; cut them in half lengthways and remove the inner ribs and the seeds. Cut the peppers into narrow strips. Skin the tomatoes* and chop them coarsely. Peel the garlic and mash it to a paste with a little salt.

Heat the butter and oil in a heavy-based pan; add the onion and peppers. Cover the pan with a lid and fry the vegetables gently until soft, but not brown. Add the tomatoes and garlic and season to taste with freshly ground pepper and sugar. Put the lid back on the pan and continue cooking over very low heat, stirring occasionally, for 25–30 minutes. The mixture should now be soft, and the juices from the tomatoes should have evaporated. Correct seasoning if necessary.

Spoon the mixture into a serving dish and serve hot or cold.

CHAMPIGNONS À LA CRÈME

For mushrooms in cream sauce, choose small firm mushrooms which will not break up during cooking. Serve them with grilled meat or chicken, or on buttered toast as a quick snack.

PREPARATION TIME: *10 min.*
COOKING TIME: *7 min.*

INGREDIENTS *(for 4)*:
1 lb. button mushrooms
2 oz. unsalted butter
Salt and black pepper
Dried mixed herbs
1 level tablespoon plain flour
¼ pint double cream
1 rounded tablespoon chopped parsley
Juice of half lemon

Perfect button mushrooms need only to be rinsed in cold water, drained and patted dry on absorbent kitchen paper. Trim the stalks level with the caps. Melt the butter in a pan and fry the mushrooms for 1–2 minutes, tossing to coat them evenly with the butter. Season to taste with salt, freshly ground pepper and the mixed herbs. Cook for a few more minutes to draw out the juices of the mushrooms.

Sprinkle the flour into the pan and stir thoroughly with a wooden spoon to blend the ingredients. Gradually stir in all the cream; bring the sauce to the boil, stirring continuously until it has thickened. Allow to simmer over low heat for 1–2 minutes then add the parsley and lemon juice and serve immediately.

Sweets & Puddings

FLOATING ISLAND

This popular English dessert is composed of a meringue base or island floating in a sea of rich egg custard.

PREPARATION TIME: *1 hour*
COOKING TIME: *30 min.*

INGREDIENTS *(for 4):*

4 egg whites
½ oz. unsalted butter
8 oz. caster sugar
2 oz. coloured sugar-coated
 almonds

CUSTARD:
4 egg yolks
1 oz. caster sugar
½ pint milk
Vanilla essence

Lightly butter the inside of a 6 in. round, deep cake tin and coat it with a little of the sugar. Separate the eggs, setting the yolks aside for the custard. With a rolling pin, coarsely crush the sugared almonds in a clean cloth. Whisk the egg whites until stiff, then gradually whisk in half the sugar; fold the remaining sugar gently into the stiff egg whites with a metal spoon. Spread a layer of this meringue mixture over the base of the prepared cake tin; follow with a layer of crushed almonds. Repeat until all the meringue and almonds are used up, finishing with a layer of meringue.

Set the filled tin in a shallow baking or roasting tin with boiling water to a depth of 1 in. Place in the centre of the oven and bake for 30 minutes at 350°F (mark 4). Remove the tin from the oven and leave until cool. As the meringue cools it will shrink and should be gently eased away from the sides with the fingers.

To make the custard, beat the egg yolks with the sugar, using a wooden spoon. Heat the milk in a saucepan until almost boiling, then stir it into the egg mixture. Blend thoroughly and strain into a bowl. Set this bowl over a saucepan half-filled with simmering water, and stir the custard gently until cooked and thickened slightly—about 10 minutes. Remove from the heat, add a few drops of vanilla essence and allow the custard to cool, stirring occasionally to prevent a skin forming.

Just before serving, loosen the meringue with the tip of a knife and lift it on to a round deep serving plate. Pour the custard sauce around the meringue, lifting this with a spatula or knife so that the custard runs beneath and round the meringue island.

ORANGE SOUFFLÉS

A light fluffy soufflé is a good choice for rounding off a meal. These individual soufflés are baked in orange shells and should be served straight from the oven before they collapse.

PREPARATION TIME: *30 min.*
COOKING TIME: *20 min.*

INGREDIENTS *(for 4):*

4 large oranges
1 lemon
1 oz. unsalted butter
1 oz. plain flour
1½ oz. caster sugar
3 eggs
GARNISH:
Icing sugar

Wash the oranges and cut them in half crossways. Take out all the orange flesh and remove the white pith; set the shells aside.

Squeeze the orange flesh to extract all the juice and strain it into a bowl together with the strained juice from the lemon. Melt the butter in a saucepan over low heat, stir in the flour and cook for a few minutes until this roux* is lightly coloured. Gradually add the fruit juice, stirring continuously, until the mixture has thickened to a smooth sauce. Bring to the boil, simmer for 1–2 minutes, then take the pan off the heat. Stir in the sugar, and let the sauce cool slightly.

Separate the eggs, and beat one yolk at a time into the sauce, stirring well before adding the next (all these preparations can be made in advance). Whisk the egg whites until stiff, then fold them into the sauce carefully but thoroughly, using a metal spoon.

Fill the orange shells with the soufflé mixture, set them on a baking sheet (or in a tartlet tray to keep them steady). Bake the oranges in a pre-heated oven for 20 minutes at a temperature of 400°F (mark 6).

Serve the oranges immediately, dusted generously with sifted icing sugar.

FRUITS RAFRAICHIS

A fresh-fruit salad is easily prepared from a selection of fruit whose flavours and colours harmonise. Chill the salad for a few hours so that the flavours can develop.

PREPARATION TIME: *30 min.*
CHILLING TIME: *2–3 hours*

INGREDIENTS *(for 6):*

2 oranges
½ lb. black grapes
½ ripe honeydew melon
2–3 ripe pears
2 bananas
4 oz. caster sugar
5 fluid oz. dry white wine
2 tablespoons Kirsch

Choose a deep glass bowl as the serving dish, and place the prepared fruit in layers in the bowl.

With a sharp knife, cut a slice from the top and base of each orange, then cut down each orange in strips to remove the peel and all white pith. Ease out each orange segment and peel off the thin skin. Peel and halve the grapes and remove the seeds. Place in the bowl on top of the oranges and sprinkle with a little of the sugar. Remove the seeds from the melon, cut it in quarters lengthways, cut away the peel and dice the flesh. Add the melon to the bowl with another sprinkling of sugar. Quarter, peel and core the pears, then slice them thinly. Peel the bananas, cut them in half lengthways before dicing them. Put them in the bowl with the remaining sugar.

Mix the fruit carefully, pour over the white wine and the Kirsch. As the fruit soaks in the liquid, press it down so that it is covered with juice and less likely to discolour.

Chill in the refrigerator for 2–3 hours. A jug of cream may be served separately.

ZABAGLIONE

This Italian dish is probably a more popular sweet in countries outside Italy where it is usually chiefly served as a tonic. It is quickly made, but care must be taken to prevent it from curdling while cooking.

PREPARATION TIME: *10 min.*
COOKING TIME: *5 min.*

INGREDIENTS *(for 4):*

4 egg yolks
2 oz. caster sugar
4–6 tablespoons Marsala wine
GARNISH:
Sponge fingers

Put the egg yolks in a mixing bowl, together with the sugar and Marsala wine. Place the bowl over a saucepan half filled with water kept simmering. Whisk the egg mixture continuously over the heat until thick and fluffy (about 5–7 minutes). On no account must the egg mixture reach boiling point.

Remove the bowl from the heat and pour the thickened mixture into warmed serving glasses. Serve at once, garnished with sponge fingers.

MARQUISE ALICE

This French dessert has undergone several changes since its invention by Escoffier, renowned as one of the greatest chefs. The classic decoration of whipped cream and red jam has remained unchanged.

PREPARATION TIME: *1 hour*
CHILLING TIME: *1½–2 hours*

INGREDIENTS *(for 6)* :
½ *oz. powdered gelatine*
4 *egg yolks*
1 *level teaspoon instant coffee*
2 *oz. caster sugar*
¾ *pint milk*
8–10 *sponge fingers*
1–2 *tablespoons rum*
¼ *pint double cream*
TOPPING :
½ *pint double cream*
2–3 *tablespoons sieved red jam*

Put 3 tablespoons of water in a cup, sprinkle the gelatine over the surface. Leave to soak for about 5 minutes. In a mixing bowl, beat the egg yolks, coffee and sugar with a wooden spoon until light and creamy. Heat the milk until almost boiling, then stir it into the eggs. Strain this custard through a coarse sieve into a saucepan, add the soaked gelatine and stir over low heat for about 2 minutes until the gelatine has dissolved. Remove the pan from the heat; pour the custard into a bowl and set it aside until cold and beginning to thicken.

Meanwhile, place the sponge fingers in a shallow plate and pour over the rum. Whisk ¼ pint of cream until thick and fold it into the thickened custard. Pour half this mixture into a moistened 8 in. wide, shallow, round sponge tin. Arrange the sponge fingers like the spokes of a wheel on top, cover with the remaining custard mixture, and leave to chill until firm—about 1 hour in the refrigerator.

When the mixture is firm, loosen the edges inside the sponge tin with the tip of a broad knife. Dip the base of the tin in hot water for a few seconds to loosen, then carefully ease the moulded custard and cream mixture on to the serving plate. Whip the cream for the topping until thick; spoon half of it into a piping bag fitted with a rosette nozzle, and with a palette knife spread the remainder evenly over the top and sides of the custard. Pipe whorls of cream at even intervals round the edge of the dessert.

Spoon the sieved jam into a small piping cornet made of greaseproof paper, snip the end open with scissors, and pipe a small blob of jam into the centre of each whorl of cream.

Chill until ready to serve.

CHARLOTTE RUSSE

Antonin Carême, great master of French cuisine and known as 'the cook of kings and the king of cooks', invented the Charlotte Russe. This was during his brief stay in St Petersburg during the early 19th century.

PREPARATION TIME: *45 min.*
CHILLING TIME: *2 hours*

INGREDIENTS *(for 6)* :
1 *packet lemon or lime jelly*
5 *large bananas*
24–26 *soft sponge fingers*
Juice of half lemon
¾ *pint double cream*

Measure ¼ pint of water into a saucepan, bring to the boil and then remove from the heat. Break the jelly into pieces and add to the hot water, stirring until the jelly has dissolved. Add another ½ pint of cold water. Spoon a little of the jelly into the base of a 7 in. round, deep cake tin. Chill in the refrigerator until set.

Peel one of the bananas and cut it into even thin rounds; arrange them in a neat circle along the edge of the jelly. Spoon over a little more jelly, being careful not to disturb the banana slices. Chill again until the jelly has set. Trim the sides of the sponge fingers so that they will fit closely together; stand them, sugared sides towards the sides of the tin, closely round the inner edge of the tin.

Peel the remaining bananas and mash them with the lemon juice. Whisk the cream until thick, beat in the remaining jelly which by now should be almost set, and then fold the mashed bananas into the cream and jelly mixture. Spoon this into the tin and chill until set firm.

Just before serving, trim the tops of the sponge fingers level with the filling; dip the base of the tin in hot water for 1 minute to loosen it. Place a round serving dish over the tin, invert it and lift the tin away.

Serve the Charlotte Russe with a bowl of fresh cream.

GLAZED LEMON TART

The fresh sharp flavour of this tart is welcome after a rich main course. Preparations for the tart, which can also be served as a pastry with morning coffee, should begin a day in advance.

PREPARATION TIME: *1¾ hours*
COOKING TIME: *25–30 min.*

INGREDIENTS *(for 6)* :

4 oz. shortcrust pastry (standard recipe)
1 level tablespoon plain flour
2 oz. ground almonds
2 oz. unsalted butter
2 oz. caster sugar

1 egg
Rind of a lemon
TOPPING :
2 small lemons
1 vanilla pod
8 oz. caster sugar

Prepare the topping first: scrub the two lemons thoroughly in cold water, then cut them into slices about ⅛ in. thick. Remove the pips carefully and put the slices in a bowl. Cover with boiling water and leave to soak for 8 hours.

Drain the lemon slices, put them in a saucepan and cover with fresh cold water; bring briskly to the boil. Lower the heat, cover the pan with a lid and simmer gently for 1 hour or until the lemon slices are soft. Remove from the heat and let the slices cool in the liquid.

Roll the shortcrust pastry* out on a lightly floured surface, to a circle about 9 in. across. Line a 7–8 in. flan tin with the pastry and prick the base lightly with a fork. Bake the tart blind* for 5 minutes, then set it aside while preparing the filling.

Mix the flour and ground almonds; beat the butter and sugar until soft and light. Beat the egg lightly and blend in the finely grated lemon rind. Gradually stir the egg into the butter mixture, then add the flour and ground almonds. Spread this mixture evenly over the pastry base. Place the tart just above centre of a preheated oven at 375°F (mark 5) and bake for 25–30 minutes or until the tart has risen and is golden brown and firm to the touch. Remove from the oven and leave to cool.

Drain the liquid from the lemon slices, setting aside ½ pint. Add the vanilla pod and the sugar to the lemon liquid and cook in a saucepan over low heat until the sugar has dissolved. Add the lemon slices and simmer gently for about 5 minutes, then carefully lift the soft lemon slices on to a plate. Continue to boil the syrup rapidly until the mixture sets— test by spooning a little on to a saucer. Arrange the lemon slices in a circular pattern over the tart. When the syrup is setting, draw the pan off the heat, remove the vanilla pod, and as soon as the bubbles have subsided, spoon all the syrup over the lemon slices.

Leave the tart to chill in the refrigerator before serving it cold, cut into wedges.

VELVET CREAM

The Elizabethans invented the syllabub—a frothy mixture of sherry, sugar and cream. Velvet cream is adapted from the original recipe and is a compromise between a syllabub and a whipped jelly.

PREPARATION TIME: *30 min.*
CHILLING TIME: *about 3 hours*

INGREDIENTS *(for 6)* :
½ oz. powdered gelatine
2 oz. caster sugar
Rind of a lemon
5 fluid oz. medium dry sherry
½ pint double cream
GARNISH :
Crystallised violets

Put ¼ pint of water in a saucepan and sprinkle the gelatine over the water; add the sugar and finely grated lemon rind. Leave to soak for 5 minutes, then place the saucepan over low heat. Stir until the sugar and gelatine have dissolved, but do not bring to the boil. Draw the pan off the heat and strain the liquid into a small basin. Set aside to cool.

When the gelatine mixture is cold and beginning to thicken, add the sherry and blend thoroughly. Whisk the cream until thick, then gradually blend the gelatine mixture into the cream. Continue whisking until the cream is thick and beginning to set. Pour the cream into serving glasses and chill in the refrigerator for 2–3 hours.

Before serving, garnish each glass with crystallised violets.

Savouries & Snacks

SAVOURY POTATO PANCAKES

This is a substantial vegetable dish on its own. It also goes well served with grills, fried sausages and bacon.

PREPARATION TIME: *20 min.*
COOKING TIME: *15 min.*

INGREDIENTS *(for 4–6)*:
1½ *lb. grated potatoes*
1 *small grated onion*
4 *oz. corned beef (flaked)*
2 *rashers streaky bacon (diced)*
Salt and black pepper
1½ *level tablespoons plain flour*
3 *beaten egg yolks*
Oil for frying

Wring the grated potatoes in a clean cloth to extract excess moisture. Mix together the potatoes, onion, flaked meat and bacon, and season with salt and pepper. Blend the flour into the egg yolks, add to the potato mixture and stir well.

Heat about ¼ in. of oil* in a heavy-based pan until hot. Shape the potato mixture into six 3 in. wide cakes. Turn the cakes once, cooking them over high heat until golden brown. Drain thoroughly on crumpled absorbent paper and keep the first batch warm while frying the remaining potato pancakes.

POTTED HAM OR GAME

Potted meat or game is a 16th-century means of stretching left-overs. The dish will keep in a refrigerator for a few days, provided it is sealed with clarified butter*.

PREPARATION TIME: *10 min.*
COOKING TIME: *5 min.*

INGREDIENTS *(for 4–6)*:
10–12 *oz. cooked ham or game*
Pinch each of dried marjoram,
   thyme and mace
Salt and black pepper
3 *oz. unsalted butter*

Put the chopped meat through the fine blade of a mincer twice. Season the meat to taste with the herbs, salt and pepper. Cook in 2 oz. of the butter for about 5 minutes. Pack the meat into an earthenware jar or pot and set aside to cool.

Heat the remaining butter until foaming, strain through muslin and pour over the meat. Leave the pot in a refrigerator to set. The potted meat can be used for sandwich fillings, or served as a first course with hot toast fingers, or with a salad for a main course.

PADDINGTON PUFFS

Ready-made puff pastry is ideal for making left-over meat into quick savoury snacks.

PREPARATION TIME: *15 min.*
COOKING TIME: *10–15 min.*

INGREDIENTS *(for 4)*:
10 *oz. prepared puff pastry*
8 *oz. cooked meat or liver*
4 *oz. lean bacon*
2 *oz. button mushrooms*
1 *oz. white bread*
2 *sprigs parsley*
1 *small, sliced onion*
1½ *oz. unsalted butter*
1 *tablespoon tomato ketchup*
Salt and black pepper
Oil for deep frying

Finely mince the meat, bacon, mushrooms, bread, parsley and peeled onion. Fry the mince in the butter, for 5 minutes. Stir in the ketchup and season to taste.

Roll out the pastry to a 12 in. square; cut this into 16 squares, and place a heaped dessertspoon of the filling in the centre of half the squares; moisten the edges with water. Cover the filling with the remaining squares and seal the edges firmly together.

Cook the pastry in oil*, heated to smoking point, until they are puffed and golden brown. Drain on crumpled absorbent paper and serve at once.

HERBY SCOTCH EGGS

Scotch eggs, coated with herbs, make a quick light supper or packed lunch.

PREPARATION TIME: *20 min.*
COOKING TIME: *5–10 min.*

INGREDIENTS *(for 4)*:
½ *lb. sausage meat*
4 *hard-boiled eggs*
Plain flour
1 *egg*
½ *packet parsley and thyme*
   stuffing
Fat or oil for deep frying

Divide the sausage meat into four equal pieces and shape them into flat rounds about 4 in. wide. Dust the shelled eggs lightly with flour and wrap each one in the sausage meat, pressing the edges firmly together to make a smooth surface. Coat with beaten egg before rolling the eggs in the herb stuffing.

Cook the eggs in smoking hot fat* until golden brown; drain and leave to cool.

APPLE PURÉE PUDDING

Left-over egg whites can be put to other uses than meringues. Here they are used for a light fluffy apple dessert.

PREPARATION TIME: *5 min.*
CHILLING TIME: *2 hours*

INGREDIENTS *(for 4)*:
1 *pint sweetened apple purée*
1 *level tablespoon powdered*
   gelatine
Juice of a lemon
2 *stiffly beaten egg whites*
¼ *pint double cream (whipped)*
1 *level tablespoon caster sugar*
2 *drops vanilla essence*

Dissolve the gelatine in the lemon juice, placed in a cup over hot water. Stir it into the apple purée, and fold in the egg whites. Pour this mixture into a moist 1½ pint mould, and leave to set in the refrigerator for 2 hours.

Before serving, unmould the pudding and pipe on the cream, sweetened with sugar and vanilla essence.

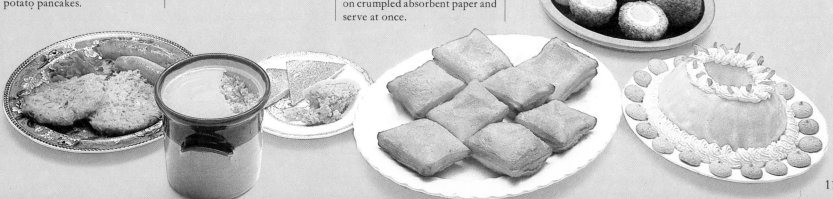

Celebration Dinner Party

The special occasions in life – the celebrations and the triumphs – are usually linked with good food and wine, shared with close friends. There are engagements and weddings, christenings and comings-of-age; exams passed and promotions won, family reunions or some unexpected stroke of good fortune. These are the times for a grand dinner party when cost is a minor consideration. Even if no particular occasion arises, early spring, with Christmas long forgotten and warm summer days still to come, is ideal for a special dinner party.

In the following four-course menu the table is set for 12 for a silver wedding anniversary. The menu is planned so that most of the food can be cooked and prepared early or even the day before.

Menu

Melon and Prawn Basket
Onion and Anchovy Tartlets
Duck Breasts en Croûte,
with Savoury Orange Sauce
Orange Pommes Croquettes
Mushroom Caps with
French Peas
Braised Celery
Crème Brulée
Coffee and Petits Fours
WINES: Chablis, Red Burgundy,
Champagne, Brandy and
Liqueurs

Preparations

The first course, melon basket, can be prepared and assembled during the afternoon and left to chill. Bake the shortcrust tartlets several days in advance and store in an airtight tin. Prepare the filling in the morning and spoon it into the tartlets just before setting them in the oven. The cooked tartlets can be wrapped in foil and kept hot in the warming cupboard for at least 1 hour.

The main course of duck breasts en croûte can also be prepared in advance. Roast the ducklings and prepare the stuffing in the morning. Wrap the breasts in pastry during late afternoon and put them in the oven just before serving the first course.

Prepare the potato croquettes and the sauce early. Fry the croquettes while heating through the sauce.

Prepare the mushroom caps late in the afternoon and cook them while the sauce is heating. Put the prepared celery on to simmer when the duck is put in the oven.

The crème brulée should be made in the morning, or even the night before. The petits fours* will remain fresh for several days if kept in an airtight tin.

For the wines, allow two bottles of white wine, three of red and three of champagne. Serve the white wine and champagne chilled and the red wine decanted and at room temperature.

The table

Give time and thought to setting and decorating the table, as this will form the focal point for several hours. A white cloth is the most suitable, with thin-stemmed glasses and highly polished silver cutlery. The centrepiece, which should be low, may be composed of flowers or fruit, with small china or silver ornaments surrounding it. Light the table with silver candelabra holding white candles, or set the candles in small posies of flowers.

Duck en croûte, garnished with orange slices, arranged round potato croquettes. Celery leaves are used to decorate the mushroom caps filled with peas

The attractively garnished melon

Small tartlets with radish flowers

White gardenias, used in the centrepiece, also decorate the crème brulée

Melon and Prawn Basket
INGREDIENTS:
1 large melon
French dressing
1½ lb. peeled prawns or shrimps
6 heaped tablespoons chopped celery
6 rounded tablespoons mayonnaise
½ pint soured cream
2 level dessertspoons curry powder
Grated coconut

Cut the melon* carefully into the shape of a basket. Remove the pips and scoop the flesh out in balls. Leave them in a French dressing* for 15 minutes.

Set a few prawns aside for garnishing and blend the remainder, with the celery and drained melon balls, into the mayonnaise*, mixed with soured cream and curry powder. Spoon this mixture into the melon basket and sprinkle with grated coconut. Chill in the refrigerator.

Onion and Anchovy Tartlets
INGREDIENTS:
6 oz. shortcrust pastry
2 large grated onions
2 oz. butter
2 hardboiled eggs
2 small tins anchovy fillets
¼ pint double cream

Bake 24 small fluted tartlets from the shortcrust pastry*. Cook the onions in the butter until soft and transparent.

Blend the onions with the finely chopped eggs, the drained and chopped anchovies, and the cream. Spoon the mixture into the tartlets and bake in a pre-heated oven at 350°F (mark 4) for 20–25 minutes.

Duck Breasts en Croûte
INGREDIENTS:
3 ducklings
4 tablespoons lean chopped bacon
2 chopped duck livers
4 tablespoons finely chopped onion
Rind of an orange
1 oz. butter
3 tablespoons chopped green olives
1 tablespoon brandy
1½ lb. prepared puff pastry
1 large beaten egg

Roast the ducklings in the centre of the oven for 45–60 minutes, at 400°F (mark 6). Set aside to cool. Sauté* the bacon, duck livers, onions and orange rind in the butter. Add the olives moistened with the brandy and cook this mixture over moderate heat for about 5 minutes.

Skin the ducklings and carve the breasts off each in two whole slices; cut each breast into two equal portions (set the duck carcasses aside for a pâté to be made the following day). Roll out the puff pastry*, ¼ in. thick, and divide into 12 pieces. Lay a portion of duck breast on each pastry square, spread a little of the bacon and onion mixture over the duck and wrap the pastry round each to form an envelope.

Seal the joins with egg and place the envelopes, seams up, on a moist, floured baking tray. Brush with egg and bake in a pre-heated oven at 400°F (mark 6) for about 25 minutes.

Savoury Orange Sauce
INGREDIENTS:
½ pint Espagnole sauce
Juice of an orange
Juice of half lemon
2 fluid oz. red wine
2 tablespoons red currant jelly
Salt, cayenne pepper, sugar

Rub the Espagnole sauce* through a fine sieve. Add the orange and lemon juices, the wine and jelly; heat the sauce through and season to taste with salt, cayenne and sugar. Pour into a sauce boat and serve with the duck breasts.

Orange Pommes Croquettes
INGREDIENTS:
2 lb. potatoes
2 egg yolks
½ oz. butter
Hot milk
Salt and black pepper
Grated rind of an orange
1 beaten egg
2 oz. dry white breadcrumbs
Oil for frying

Boil and thoroughly drain the potatoes. Put them back over the heat to dry out completely, then rub them through a sieve. Beat in the egg yolks, butter and enough hot milk to make a firm paste. Season to taste and stir in the rind. Set aside until firm.

Shape the potato mixture into croquettes*, about 1 in. wide and 1½ in. long. Coat them with beaten egg and breadcrumbs and deep fry in hot oil*.

Mushroom Caps with French Peas
INGREDIENTS:
24 large mushroom caps
6 oz. unsalted butter
2 lb. small peas (frozen)
4 tablespoons chicken stock
Caster sugar and salt

Wipe and trim the mushrooms*. Sauté* them in 2 oz. of the butter for a few minutes, being careful to retain their shape. Put the peas in a pan of cold water and bring to the boil. Drain the peas thoroughly, and return them to the pan with the remaining butter and the stock; season to taste with sugar and salt.

Cook the peas over low heat until all the liquid has been absorbed, then spoon them on to the hollow mushroom caps.

Braised Celery
INGREDIENTS:
6 heads of celery
1 Spanish onion
6 small carrots
½ pint chicken stock
Salt and black pepper
Beurre manié
Parsley

Trim the roots off the celery and remove any damaged stalks; scrub thoroughly, then cut each celery in half lengthways, and remove the green leafy tops. Blanch* the celery for 10 minutes in boiling water, drain carefully in a colander, and put in a large fireproof dish. Cover with the thinly sliced onion and carrots; pour over the stock and season to taste.

Cover the pan with a lid or foil and simmer the celery over low heat, until tender, after about 40 minutes. About 5 minutes before the end of cooking time, add knobs of beurre manié* to thicken the stock as desired. Serve the celery sprinkled with finely chopped parsley.

Crème Brulée
INGREDIENTS:
2½ pints single cream
12 egg yolks
2 level tablespoons caster sugar
3 tablespoons vanilla essence
4 level tablespoons Demerara sugar

Put the cream in the top half of a large double boiler or in a bowl over a pan of gently simmering water. Carefully stir the egg yolks, beaten with the caster sugar and vanilla essence, into the warm cream. Continue cooking gently until the cream has thickened enough to coat the back of the wooden spoon. Strain the cream through a fine sieve into a large soufflé dish or mould and leave to chill for at least 4 hours.

Sprinkle the sifted Demerara sugar on top of the chilled cream. Set the dish or mould on a bed of ice cubes on the grill pan and place under a hot grill until the sugar has caramelised. Remove the dish and chill in the refrigerator for 2–3 hours.

DUCK PÂTÉ
Cut the meat from the duck carcasses and mince it coarsely, together with the remaining duck liver. Mix with ½ lb. minced veal, 2 oz. white breadcrumbs, 2 tablespoons finely chopped onion, 1 tablespoon chopped chervil and 3 tablespoons chopped parsley. Season to taste. Stir in the grated rind of an orange and 2 tablespoons brandy or dry sherry. Bind the pâté with 2 lightly beaten eggs.

Spoon the pâté into a buttered terrine dish and cover with thin streaky bacon. Bake in a roasting tin half filled with boiling water, in the centre of the oven, at 325°F (mark 3) for 1¼ hours.

April

Good milchcow and pasture, good husbands prouide,
the resdue good huswiues knowes best how to guide.

This Month's Recipes

*Exchanging gifts of gaily decorated Easter eggs
is a custom that originated in pre-Christian times*

117

Food in Season

Fish, such as cod, herring, mackerel, turbot and whitebait, are the best buys this month. English and Welsh spring lamb is available, but is in short supply and more expensive than imported lamb. English cucumbers, lettuce and tomatoes grown in hothouses are now available for picnic salads, and the end of the month brings the first crop of young turnips. Fruit is mainly imported at this time of year, and apart from grapes is of poorer quality than during winter.

Fish	*Poultry & Game*	*Vegetables*	*Fruit*
Bream, sea	Chicken	Asparagus	Apples
Brill	Duck	Avocado pears	Bananas
Clams	Guinea fowl	Beetroot	Grapefruit
Cod	Pigeon	Broad beans	Grapes
Coley	Rabbit	Broccoli, purple	Kumquats
Conger eels	Turkey	Brussels sprouts	Lemons
Crab	Venison	Cabbages	Limes
Dabs		Carrots (young)	Lychees
Dover sole		Cauliflowers	Mangoes
Dublin Bay prawns		Celeriac	Melons (imported)
Eels		Celery	Oranges
Flake (also sold as rock salmon)		Chillies	Ortaniques
Grey mullet		Courgettes	Passion fruit
Halibut		Cucumbers	Pears
Herring		Endive	Pineapples
Lemon sole		Fennel	Pomegranates
Lobster		French beans	Rhubarb
Mackerel		Garlic	Strawberries (imported)
Mock halibut (or Greenland halibut)		Kohl rabi	
Oysters (native, scarce)		Leeks	
Oysters, Portuguese		Lettuces	
Pike		Mushrooms	
Plaice		Onions	
Prawns		Parsnips	
Redfish		Peppers	
Salmon		Potatoes, new (imported)	
Sea trout		Radishes	
Shrimps		Salad cress	
Skate		Salsify	
Trout, rainbow		Spinach	
Turbot		Spring onions	
Whelks		String beans	
Whitebait		Swedes	
Winkles		Tomatoes (English hothouse)	
Witch		Turnips	
		Watercress	

SUGGESTED MENUS

Avocado and Citrus Salad
Lobster Thermidor
Green Salad
Grapefruit in Brandy

Artichokes with Hollandaise Sauce
Veal with Orange
Sauté Potatoes and Glazed Onions
Gâteau St Honoré

Brill Soufflé with Mousseline Sauce
New Potatoes, Cauliflower
Rhubarb Crumble

Whitebait
Steak Diane
New Potatoes, Braised Celery
Banana Fritters

Tomato Ice
Chicken Chaud-froid
Salads, New Potatoes, French Bread
French Apple Flan

Gammon in Puff Pastry
Orange Rice or Apple and Nut Salad
Chocolate Mousse

Blini with Caviar
Lamb with Wine Sauce
Buttered New Potatoes
Fried Leeks
Secret Cake

Soups & Starters

BARBECUED SPARE RIBS

This is a substantial first course, served in the Chinese style, for eating with the fingers. The lean spare ribs are grilled until crisp and served in a spicy sauce.

PREPARATION TIME: *15 min.*
COOKING TIME: *45 min.*

INGREDIENTS *(for 4)*:
12 pork spare ribs
4 level tablespoons clear honey
3 tablespoons soy sauce
3 tablespoons tomato ketchup
Tabasco sauce
1 small clove garlic
Mustard powder
Paprika
Salt and black pepper
Juice of a small orange
4 tablespoons wine vinegar

Ask the butcher for the type of spare ribs used in Chinese cookery: thin ends of the ribs, not the chunky chops.

Wipe the meat and, if not already done, separate it into single rib portions. Grill the ribs for 10–15 minutes under a high grill until they are brown, turning them several times. Arrange them in a single layer in a large roasting tin and pour over the pan juices.

Put the honey, soy sauce, tomato ketchup and a few drops of tabasco sauce into a bowl, peel and crush the garlic and add it. Season to taste with mustard powder, paprika, salt and freshly ground pepper, then add the orange juice and wine vinegar. Mix and pour over the spare ribs.

Cook, uncovered, in the centre of an oven pre-heated to 350°F (mark 4) for 30 minutes. Serve the ribs piping hot in the sauce. Provide finger bowls if possible.

BLINI WITH CAVIAR

In Russia, where this hors-d'oeuvre originates, blini – crisp, light, yeast-raised pancakes – are traditionally served with caviar, soured cream and roughly chopped raw onions.

PREPARATION TIME: *2 hours*
COOKING TIME: *20 min.*

INGREDIENTS *(for 6)*:
2 level teaspoons dried yeast
12 oz. plain flour
2 large onions
½ pint soured cream
7 oz. Danish caviar (lumpfish roe)
1 large lemon
1 oz. unsalted butter
2 large eggs
1 level tablespoon caster sugar
Salt
½ pint milk
Oil for frying

Measure ½ pint and four table-spoons of hand-warm water into a bowl. Sprinkle the dried yeast on the surface and leave the bowl in a warm place for 15 minutes or until the mixture froths. Sift half the flour into a large mixing bowl and gradually add the yeast mixture. Beat to a smooth batter, cover the bowl with a clean cloth and leave the batter to rise in a warm place for about 30 minutes or until it has doubled in volume.

Meanwhile, peel and roughly chop the onions, and put them in a serving bowl. Spoon the soured cream and caviar into two individual serving bowls. Wash the lemon, cut it into six segments and arrange them in another bowl. Chill until serving.

Melt the butter in a small sauce-pan and allow it to cool slightly.

Separate the eggs. Gradually add the remaining flour to the risen batter, then the melted butter, egg yolks, sugar and a pinch of salt. Beat the mixture until smooth. Warm the milk, but do not boil, and gradually add it to the batter, whisking continuously. Cover the batter again and set aside to double as before.

Whisk the egg whites until they stand in soft peaks, and fold them into the risen batter. Cover the batter and leave to rise for the third time.

Heat a little oil in a large heavy frying pan over high heat. Put 2 tablespoons of batter in the pan at a time, to make two pancakes, each about 4 in. wide. If the batter is too thick it can be thinned with a little warm water. Cook the pancakes for about 1 minute on each side or until they are golden brown. Keep them hot on a wire rack in the oven until all the batter is used – it should make 20–24 pancakes.

Serve the blini, two or three to each plate, and offer the bowls of onions, cream, caviar and lemon separately.

SOUSED HERRINGS

In Germany and Scandinavia, fresh, smoked or salted herrings are firm favourites as a first course. They are usually steeped for a few days in a spicy dressing.

PREPARATION TIME: *35 min.*
COOKING TIME: *15–20 min.*

INGREDIENTS *(for 6)*:
6 large herrings
¾ pint cider vinegar
3 juniper berries
6 cloves
1 bay leaf
5 peppercorns
2 large onions
6 level teaspoons Düsseldorf mustard
2 dill-pickled cucumbers

Put the vinegar, ¾ pint of water, juniper berries, cloves, bay leaf and peppercorns in a saucepan and bring to the boil. Simmer this marinade* for 10 minutes, then leave to cool.

Gut and clean the herrings*; remove the heads and backbones but not the tails. Wash the herrings and dry them thoroughly on absorbent kitchen paper. Peel the onions, slice thinly and separate the slices into rings. Open the herrings out flat, and spread 1 teaspoon of mustard over the inside of each. Cut each cucumber into three slices lengthways and place a piece of cucumber crossways at the head end of each herring. Arrange a few of the smaller onion rings down the length of the body and roll each herring from head to tail, securing it with toothpicks.

Arrange the herring rolls in an ovenproof dish and pour over the strained marinade. Sprinkle with the remaining onion rings. Cover the dish with a lid or foil and bake the herrings for 15 minutes in the centre of an oven preheated to 350°F (mark 4). Leave them to cool in the marinade, before setting them to souse in the refrigerator for 2 days.

Remove the toothpicks and serve the herrings on individual plates, with thin slices of buttered wholemeal or coarse rye bread.

ARTICHOKES WITH HOLLANDAISE SAUCE

For this recipe, choose small artichokes which do not break up during cooking, and serve them hot or cold as a first course.

PREPARATION TIME: *30 min.*
COOKING TIME: *about 45 min.*

INGREDIENTS *(for 6)*:
6 globe artichokes
1 level teaspoon salt
½ pint Hollandaise sauce

Wash the artichokes thoroughly under running cold water. Pull off any outer ragged leaves and snip off the sharp points of the remaining leaves with scissors. Trim the stalks of the artichokes so that they stand level. Bring a large pan of water to the boil, add the salt and the artichokes and cover with a lid. Cook for 25–45 minutes, depending on size, or until a leaf pulls off easily. Drain the artichokes upside-down.

Meanwhile, make the Hollandaise sauce* and keep it hot.

Remove the bunch of small centre leaves from each artichoke; stand the artichokes on individual serving plates and serve the Hollandaise sauce in a bowl. Provide finger bowls, and side plates for the nibbled leaves.

TOMATO ICE

The Italians invented the water ice or sorbet, which is an iced and sweetened fruit juice. This adaptation of a sorbet makes a refreshing starter.

PREPARATION TIME: *10 min.*
COOKING TIME: *25 min.*
FREEZING TIME: *4 hours*

INGREDIENTS *(for 6)*:
3 lb. ripe tomatoes
1 small onion
2 level teaspoons marjoram
1 level tablespoon tomato purée
Juice of a lemon
1 level teaspoon caster sugar
GARNISH:
Mint, lemon or cucumber

Wash, wipe and roughly chop the tomatoes. Peel and roughly chop the onion. Put the tomatoes, onion and marjoram in a large saucepan. Bring to the boil, cover with a lid and simmer over low heat for 25 minutes or until the tomatoes are soft. Stir occasionally to prevent the tomatoes sticking to the pan. Rub the mixture through a sieve into a large bowl, and stir in the tomato purée, lemon juice and caster sugar. Leave the mixture to cool. Spoon it into a plastic freezer container, cover with a lid and freeze for at least 4 hours or overnight.

Turn the mixture out when frozen solid, crush it with a rolling pin and pile the tomato crystals into individual serving glasses. Garnish with sprigs of mint, lemon or cucumber slices.

AVOCADO AND CITRUS SALAD

Slightly overripe avocado pears mixed with citrus fruit provide a tangy starter. Alternatively, serve the salad with cold ham, chicken or shellfish.

PREPARATION TIME: *30 min.*

INGREDIENTS *(for 4–6)*:
3 large avocado pears
Juice of a small lemon
1 large grapefruit
1 large orange
Caster sugar
GARNISH:
Orange segments
Mint

Peel the avocados with a silver or stainless-steel knife to prevent discoloration of the flesh. Cut them into quarters, remove the stones; cut the flesh into thin sections and pour the lemon juice over them. Cut a slice from top and bottom of the grapefruit and orange so that they stand flat on a board. Cut downwards, in narrow strips, through peel and pith and remove. With a sharp knife, cut between the flesh and segment skins; put the flesh into a large bowl and squeeze the segment skins over the fruit so that no juice is wasted.

Carefully blend the avocado and lemon juice with the citrus fruits; sweeten to taste if necessary. Spoon the mixture into individual serving dishes and garnish with skinned orange segments and sprigs of mint.

Fish

WHITEBAIT

These tiny, silvery fish – immature herrings and sprats – are caught in vast quantities off the east coast of England. They are eaten whole and have for long been a great tradition in British cookery.

PREPARATION TIME: *10 min.*
COOKING TIME: *6–10 min.*

INGREDIENTS *(for 6)*:
2 lb. whitebait
4 oz. seasoned flour
Oil for deep frying
GARNISH:
Lemon wedges
Parsley

Pick over the whitebait carefully and remove any damaged fish and pieces of weed. Do not wash or overhandle the fish as they bruise easily.

Toss the whitebait gently in the seasoned flour to coat them thoroughly (this is easiest done by shaking them gently, with the flour, in a plastic bag). Heat the oil* in a large fish fryer – when a day-old cube of bread browns in 1 minute, the correct temperature is reached. Place the whitebait in the basket, not too many at a time, and deep-fry each batch for about 2 minutes. Drain on crumpled absorbent paper.

Serve the whitebait hot, garnished with lemon wedges and parsley sprigs. Offer thinly sliced brown bread and butter with it.

LOBSTER THERMIDOR

Lobster is the most expensive of all shellfish, but is also regarded by gourmets as the most delicious. This classic French recipe comes from the famous Café de Paris.

PREPARATION TIME: *50 min.*
COOKING TIME: *1½ hours*

INGREDIENTS *(for 6)*:
3 cooked lobsters (each 1¼–1½ lb.)
½ pint fish stock
¼ pint dry white wine
1 onion
4 peppercorns
1 bay leaf
1 sprig thyme
Salt and black pepper
¾ pint milk
4 oz. unsalted butter
2 oz. plain flour
1 level teaspoon Dijon mustard
2 large egg yolks
¼ pint single cream
1 teaspoon lemon juice
3 oz. Parmesan cheese
2 oz. browned breadcrumbs
GARNISH:
Lettuce

Pour the fish stock* and white wine into a saucepan, bring to the boil and boil briskly until the liquid has reduced* to ¼ pint. Peel the onion, cut it into quarters and put it in another saucepan with the peppercorns, bay leaf, thyme, a pinch of salt and the milk. Bring to the boil, remove the pan from the heat, cover with a lid and leave the milk to infuse for 30 minutes.

Meanwhile, remove the claws from the lobsters*; split each body in half lengthways, through the head and tail and along the centre line of the shell. Set the shells aside, with the feeler claws

intact. Discard the grey sack in the head and the black intestinal tube in the body.

Rub any loose coral (or spawn) through a fine sieve. Remove the meat from the shells and the claws and cut it carefully into ¾ in. cubes. Melt 2 oz. of the butter in a shallow, heavy-based pan and gently fry the lobster meat, turning it frequently, for 3–4 minutes. Remove the pan from the heat and set aside.

Melt the remaining butter in a saucepan, stir in the flour and

cook gently for 2 minutes; remove the pan from the heat. Strain the infused milk through a fine sieve and gradually stir this and the reduced fish stock into the roux*. Bring this sauce to the boil, stirring continuously, and cook gently for 3 minutes, until the sauce thickens. Leave to cool for 2 minutes, then stir in the mustard, egg yolks, sieved coral and the cream. Season with salt, pepper, and stir in the lemon juice.

Coat the inside of the empty lobster shells with a little of the

sauce. Stir half the remaining sauce into the lobster in the pan and carefully spoon the mixture into the shells. Cover with the remaining sauce; grate the Parmesan cheese, mix it with the breadcrumbs and sprinkle over the lobsters. Place the shells under a high grill and cook until the cheese topping is golden brown.

Serve the lobster on a bed of lettuce. Crisp French bread and a tossed green salad are traditional with the lobster.

BRILL SOUFFLÉ

Brill is an ideal inexpensive fish for pies and soufflés, served with a classic Mousseline sauce.

PREPARATION TIME: *30 min.*
COOKING TIME: *45 min.*

INGREDIENTS *(for 4–6)*:
1 lb. brill
Salt and black pepper
1 small bay leaf
1 blade mace
¼ pint milk
3 oz. unsalted butter
3 oz. plain flour
Nutmeg
3 large eggs
MOUSSELINE SAUCE:
Juice of ½ large lemon
2 large egg yolks
4 oz. unsalted butter
Salt and black pepper
4 tablespoons double cream

Wash the brill thoroughly and put it whole into a saucepan; cover with cold water. Add ½ teaspoon of salt, the bay leaf and mace to the fish, and cover the pan with a lid. Bring slowly to simmering point, turn off the heat and leave the pan to stand for 10 minutes. Lift out the fish, set aside ½ pint of the liquid and make it up to ¾ pint with milk.

Remove the skin and bones from the fish and flake* the flesh roughly. Melt 3 oz. of the butter in a large saucepan and stir in the flour. Cook this roux* over low heat for 2 minutes, stirring continuously, then gradually stir in the fish and milk liquid. Bring to the boil, still stirring, and cook for 2 minutes or until the mixture is thick and smooth. Season to taste with salt, freshly ground pepper and nutmeg. Carefully fold the flaked fish into the sauce. Separate the three eggs and beat the yolks into the fish mixture, one by one; whisk the egg whites until stiff then gently fold them in as well.

Spoon the mixture into a prepared 3 pint soufflé dish; cook in the centre of the oven pre-heated to 400°F (mark 6) for 45 minutes or until the soufflé is risen and golden brown on top.

For the sauce, put the lemon juice and 1 teaspoon of cold water in a basin. Beat the egg yolks lightly and stir them into the lemon juice. Stand the basin over a saucepan of gently simmering water, but do not allow the bottom of the basin to touch the water. Stir in ½ oz. of butter and whisk the mixture until thick.

Remove the basin from the heat and gradually whisk in the remaining butter, cut into small knobs. Whisk until the butter is completely absorbed before adding the next knob. Season to taste with salt and pepper. Whip the cream and fold it gently into the sauce. Heat the sauce in the basin over the pan of simmering water, whisking all the time (do not allow the sauce to boil).

Serve the soufflé immediately, and offer the Mousseline sauce in a sauceboat. If wanted, boiled cauliflower or a green salad could be served with the soufflé.

TURBOT AU GRATIN

Turbot is a large flat fish, similar in appearance to halibut, but with creamy-white flesh. The delicate flavour is best retained through simple cooking.

PREPARATION TIME: *30 min.*
COOKING TIME: *1 hour*

INGREDIENTS *(for 6)*:
6 turbot fillets (6 oz. each)
1 small onion
¼ pint dry white wine
1 oz. unsalted butter
1 oz. plain flour
¼ pint milk
Salt and black pepper
1 large egg yolk
2 tablespoons double cream
4 oz. Cheddar cheese

Ask the fishmonger to fillet the turbot and to include the skin and bones with the order. Wipe the fillets and put them in a single layer in a shallow ovenproof dish. Rinse the fish trimmings in cold water and put them in a large saucepan. Peel the onion and add it whole to the pan together with the wine and enough cold water to cover the trimmings. Bring to the boil, cover, and simmer gently for 15 minutes.

Strain this stock through a fine sieve over the fish. Cover the dish with a piece of buttered foil and bake for 20 minutes in the centre of an oven pre-heated to 350°F (mark 4).

Remove the fillets from the oven, drain and arrange them on a hot flameproof serving dish. Strain the liquid from the fish, through muslin. Melt the butter in a saucepan, stir in the flour and cook for 2 minutes.

Gradually stir in the fish liquid and milk, bring the sauce to the boil and cook over low heat, stirring continuously, for 2 minutes. Season to taste with salt and freshly ground pepper; remove from the heat. Lightly beat the egg yolk with the cream, blend in a little of the hot sauce and stir the egg into the sauce; pour it over the fish fillets.

Grate the cheese and sprinkle it over the sauce; put the dish under a hot grill for 5–10 minutes, until the cheese is bubbly brown on top.

Serve the gratin from the dish, with, for example, buttered new potatoes and broccoli spears.

FISH PIE

This dish makes the most of a small amount of cod or haddock. Any white fish combines with the spicy ingredients and pastry.

PREPARATION TIME: *45 min.*
COOKING TIME: *35 min.*

INGREDIENTS *(for 4)*:
1 lb. white fish
Salt and black pepper
1 lb. tomatoes
1 small clove garlic
1 small green pepper
1 large onion
2 tablespoons oil
1 level tablespoon finely chopped parsley
1 bay leaf
4 oz. shortcrust pastry (standard recipe)
1 small egg

Wash the fish, put it in a saucepan with salt, pepper, enough water to cover. Bring to just below boiling point and simmer for 10 minutes. Skin the tomatoes* and chop them roughly. Peel and roughly chop the garlic. Wash the pepper, remove the stalk, inner ribs and all seeds and chop the flesh into small pieces. Peel and roughly chop the onion.

Heat the oil in a frying pan, fry the onion and pepper over low heat for 5–10 minutes. Stir in the tomatoes, garlic, parsley and crumpled bay leaf and cook for a further 5 minutes. Season to taste. Lift the fish from the liquid, remove all skin and bones, and flake* the flesh into the tomato mixture; put it into a deep 8 in. wide pie dish.

On a floured surface, roll out the prepared shortcrust pastry* to a circle to fit the pie dish. Cover the fish with the pastry and make a slit in the centre. Use the pastry trimmings to decorate the pie. Brush with the beaten egg.

Bake the pie in the centre of the oven, pre-heated to 425°F (mark 7) for 30–35 minutes or until golden brown. The hot pie can be served on its own or with a tossed green salad.

Meat

BAKED HAKE

Hake is one of the cheapest and most nourishing fish. It can be cooked in the same way as cod, but flavouring is essential.

PREPARATION TIME: *10 min.*
COOKING TIME: *50 min.*

INGREDIENTS *(for 6)* :
6 hake steaks
Salt and black pepper
Juice of ½ large lemon
3 tablespoons cooking oil
15–16 oz. tin of tomatoes
1 large onion
1 clove garlic
1 small green pepper
Marjoram

Wipe the steaks thoroughly and arrange them in a single layer in a buttered ovenproof dish. Sprinkle them with salt and freshly ground pepper, and pour on the strained lemon juice. Add one tablespoon of cooking oil and cover the dish with buttered foil. Bake in the centre of an oven pre-heated to 350°F (mark 4) for 25 minutes.

Meanwhile, chop the tomatoes; peel and finely chop the onion and the garlic. Wash the pepper, remove the stalk, ribs and seeds; chop the flesh into small pieces. Heat two tablespoons of cooking oil in a large frying pan. Add the onion, garlic and pepper and fry over low heat for 5 minutes. Blend in the tomatoes; season to taste with salt, freshly ground pepper and marjoram. Simmer for a further 10 minutes. Remove the fish from the oven and drain off most of the liquid. Pour the onion and tomato mixture over the fish and return the dish to the oven for 10 minutes.

Serve straight from the dish, with sauté potatoes* and a green vegetable.

VEAL WITH ORANGE

This is reputed to have been Cromwell's favourite meal. It is prepared with a fruity force-meat stuffing and sauce which add extra flavour to the meat.

PREPARATION TIME: *20 min.*
COOKING TIME: *2½ hours*

INGREDIENTS *(for 6)* :
4–5 lb. boned breast of veal
4 oz. fresh white breadcrumbs
2 oz. stoned raisins
2 oz. currants
2 oz. shredded beef suet
Salt and black pepper
Nutmeg
2 large oranges
1 large egg yolk (or 2 small ones)
2 oz. lard
1 oz. cornflour
Caster sugar
6 tablespoons claret

Prepare the forcemeat stuffing first by mixing the breadcrumbs, raisins, currants, suet and a pinch of salt, pepper and nutmeg together in a bowl. Finely grate the rind from the oranges and add to the stuffing, together with the lightly beaten egg yolk. Stir in enough cold water to bind the mixture.

Spread the stuffing over the boned veal, roll it up and tie with thin string at 1 in. intervals. Put the meat in a roasting tin, add the lard and roast the meat for 2½ hours in the centre of an oven, pre-heated to 400°F (mark 6). Baste* occasionally and cover the meat with foil if it browns too quickly.

Put the meat on a serving dish and keep it hot in the oven. Skim all the fat from the juices in the roasting tin and heat them in a small saucepan. Blend the corn-flour with 1 tablespoon of cold water and add to the juices, stirring continuously until the sauce has thickened. Bring to the boil and season to taste with salt, freshly ground pepper, sugar and nutmeg. Stir in the claret and simmer the sauce gently. Remove the pith from the oranges and cut the flesh into small sections. Add these to the sauce and heat it.

Cut the veal into thick slices and arrange them on a warmed serving dish; offer the sauce separately. An orange and green salad, sauté potatoes* and button onions would go well with this joint.

RAISED PORK PIE

The hot-water crust* used for this classic English pie is the earliest known form for a pastry case. It dates back to the 14th century and has found its perpetuity in the famous Melton Mowbray pork pies. The pastry is moulded – or raised – round a floured jar, but tin moulds are now available which make the raising easier.

PREPARATION TIME: *50 min.*
COOKING TIME: *3¾ hours*

INGREDIENTS *(for 4–6)*:
2 veal knuckles
1 bouquet garni
½ level teaspoon salt
6 peppercorns
12 oz. plain flour
¼ level teaspoon salt
4 oz. lard
4 tablespoons milk
1½ lb. lean pork
Salt and black pepper
1 small egg

Ask the butcher to chop the veal knuckles into pieces. Rinse them well in cold water, put them in a large saucepan with the bouquet garni*, salt and peppercorns, and cover with cold water. Bring the water to the boil, and remove the scum. Cover with a lid and simmer for 2 hours. Strain the stock through muslin, leave to cool, then remove the fat from the surface.

Sift the flour and salt into a bowl. Put the lard in a large saucepan with the milk and 4 tablespoons of cold water. Bring this mixture to the boil, remove from the heat and immediately add all the flour and stir quickly until a dough has formed. When cool enough to handle, knead the dough until it is smooth, adding

a few drops of boiling water if it is too stiff. Cut off a third of the dough for the pie lid and keep it warm over boiling water.

Wet the outside of a 2 lb. straight-sided jam jar, flour it well including the bottom. Mould the dough over the bottom of the jar and down the sides, keeping it about ¼ in. thick. Leave the dough to set for 10 minutes, then remove it from the jam jar. If the dough should split and it becomes necessary to remould the pie, place the pastry on a plate over boiling water for a few minutes. If using a tin mould, flour the inside of the mould, and shape the dough, ¼ in. thick, as a lining over the base and up the sides.

While the dough sets, remove all excess fat from the pork and cut the meat into ½ in. cubes.

Season them with salt and freshly ground pepper and stir in 2 tablespoons of cold water. Pack the meat into the pie crust to within ¾ in. of the top.

Roll out the remaining pastry to make a lid for the crust, moisten the pie edge with cold water, put the lid in position and press the edges tightly together to seal. Make a hole in the top of the pie and, unless it is baked in a tin mould, fix a piece of buttered greaseproof paper round the pie to keep it in shape during cooking. Brush the top with the beaten egg. Stand the pie on a lightly greased baking sheet and bake in the centre of an oven pre-heated to 375°F (mark 5) for 1 hour. Reduce the heat to 350°F (mark 4) and cook the pie for another 1–1½ hours.

Remove the pie from the oven, and let it become nearly cold. Strain the veal stock, correct seasoning, and pour the stock through a small funnel into the pie through the hole in the top. Set aside for a couple of hours while the stock sets to a jelly.

Before serving, remove the greaseproof paper or unclip the tin mould. Serve cold, cut into wedges, with a mixed salad.

TRIPE PROVENÇALE

Tripe, which is associated with onions and the near-extinct tripe parlours of the Midlands and the North, has a long history. The Normans introduced it as a food to Britain; the following recipe comes from southern France.

PREPARATION TIME: *20 min.*
COOKING TIME: *2½ hours*

INGREDIENTS *(for 6)*:
2 lb. thick tripe
1 pint chicken stock
Salt and black pepper
1 onion
1 clove garlic
1 oz. unsalted butter
1 lb. tomatoes
Dried thyme
4 tablespoons dry white wine
1 level tablespoon chopped parsley

Wash the tripe thoroughly. Put it in a saucepan and cover with cold water. Bring to the boil. Remove from the heat, drain the tripe and rinse under cold running water. Cut into 2 in. cubes and return them to the saucepan. Pour over the boiling stock and add a pinch of salt. As soon as the stock is boiling again, reduce the heat. Cover the pan with a lid and simmer the tripe for 2 hours.

Meanwhile, peel and roughly chop the onion, and skin and crush the garlic. Melt the butter in a frying pan and gently fry the onion and garlic for about 5 minutes until transparent. Skin the tomatoes* and chop them roughly; add them, with a pinch of dried thyme, the wine and parsley, to the frying pan. Bring this mixture to the boil over gentle heat, cover with a lid and simmer for 30 minutes. Season to taste with salt and freshly ground pepper. If the sauce is still thin, remove the lid and boil the sauce over high heat for 5 minutes until it has reduced* and thickened.

When the tripe has finished cooking, drain it and stir it into the tomato mixture. Cook over low heat for a further 10 minutes. Arrange the tripe on a hot serving dish and surround it with plain boiled rice.

LAMB WITH WINE SAUCE

Traditionally, this Russian dish is served with Kasha – a buckwheat preparation rather like porridge. For the British palate, boiled potatoes might be more acceptable.

PREPARATION TIME: *30 min.*
COOKING TIME: *3¾ hours*

INGREDIENTS *(for 6)*:
2 lb. boned leg of lamb
1 large carrot
1 large onion
Salt
5 peppercorns
1 bay leaf
1 oz. unsalted butter
1 oz. plain flour
1 sugar cube
Juice of ½ lemon
¼ pint dry red wine
1 large egg yolk

Ask the butcher to bone the lamb and to include the bones with the order. Rinse the bones in cold water and put them in a large saucepan. Cut the lamb into 6 even slices, trim away as much fat as possible and add this to the pan. Cover the bones with cold water and bring to the boil. Remove the scum, then cover the pan with a lid and simmer for 2 hours. Strain this stock through a fine sieve or muslin.

Put the lamb slices in a large saucepan and pour over enough of the stock to cover the meat. Bring to the boil, strain the liquid through muslin and pour it back over the lamb slices. Peel the carrot and the onion and add them whole to the pan. Cover with a lid and simmer the lamb for 1½ hours or until it is tender. Add a pinch of salt, the peppercorns and bay leaf and simmer for a further 5 minutes.

For the sauce, melt the butter in a saucepan, stir in the flour and cook for 2 minutes. Gradually add ½ pint strained lamb stock, the sugar, lemon juice and wine. Bring the sauce to the boil, stirring continuously, then simmer for 3 minutes. Let the sauce cool a little, then beat in the egg yolk. Re-heat the sauce gently, but do not allow it to boil. Lift the lamb slices out and arrange them on a hot serving dish; pour the wine sauce into a sauce boat and serve it separately.

GAMMON IN PUFF PASTRY

An inexpensive joint of bacon looks impressive and serves more people when encased in puff pastry which keeps the meat moist. It makes a good lunch or supper dish, but preparations should begin the day before.

PREPARATION TIME: *30 min.*
COOKING TIME: *2¾ hours*

INGREDIENTS *(for 6)*:
4 lb. gammon hock
1 large bay leaf
12 peppercorns
1 blade mace
4–6 parsley stalks
2 sprigs thyme
1 small onion
1 lb. prepared puff pastry
1 egg

Ask the butcher to bone part of the hock, leaving the end bone in to make carving easier.

Soak the gammon for 2 hours in cold water. Drain and place it in a large saucepan. Cover with fresh cold water and add the bay leaf, peppercorns, mace, parsley stalks, thyme and onion. Bring to the boil, turn down the heat, then cover the pan with a lid and simmer for 20 minutes to each 1 lb. Remove the pan from the heat and let the gammon cool overnight in the cooking liquid.

Remove the gammon from the liquid and carefully pull off the skin. Roll out the puff pastry* to an oblong shape, ⅛ in. thick, and place the gammon in the centre. Brush the pastry edges with some of the lightly beaten egg; wrap the pastry over the gammon, and press the edges together to enclose the meat. Seal the edges, pleating the pastry round the bone. Brush with egg.

Cover the bone with a piece of foil to keep it white while cooking. Use the pastry trimmings to decorate the casing, and carefully lift the gammon on to a wet baking tray; brush the pastry with the remaining egg.

Bake the gammon for 20 minutes in the centre of an oven pre-heated to 450°F (mark 8); lower the heat to 350°F (mark 4) and continue cooking for a further 30 minutes. Cover the joint with buttered greaseproof paper as soon as the pastry is golden.

Serve the joint hot or cold. A savoury rice salad*, new potatoes and lettuce with green peas (see June vegetables) are suitable side dishes for the gammon.

LAMB KEBABS

Skewered chunks of meat, or kebabs, are popular in the Middle East. They are usually grilled over a charcoal fire, which imparts a smoked flavour to the meat.

PREPARATION TIME: *20 min.*
COOKING TIME: *10 min.*

INGREDIENTS *(for 4)*:
1½ lb. boned shoulder of lamb
¼ level teaspoon green chilli
1 in. piece root ginger
5 fluid oz. plain yoghourt
¼ level teaspoon ground coriander
¼ level teaspoon ground cumin
1 clove garlic
Juice of ½ lemon
1 level teaspoon salt
GARNISH:
Lemon wedges
Mint

Trim any excess fat from the lamb, wipe with a damp cloth and cut it into 1 in. cubes. Chop the chilli finely; peel the ginger until the green part just shows, and chop it roughly. Put the yoghourt in a large bowl and stir in the coriander, cumin, chilli and ginger. Peel the garlic, and crush it into the yoghourt, before adding the lemon juice and salt. Mix the lamb into the yoghourt and leave to marinate* for at least 30 minutes.

Remove the lamb chunks from the marinade and thread them on to four steel skewers, 8–10 in. long, packing the pieces closely together. Put the skewers under a hot grill and cook, turning from time to time, for 8–10 minutes, or until browned on the outside and pink in the centre.

Arrange the lamb kebabs, on their skewers, on a bed of spiced rice* garnished with lemon wedges and sprigs of mint.

Poultry & Game

SAVOURY KIDNEYS

Grilled or fried kidneys are a favourite dish on the British breakfast or tea table. There is no reason why kidneys should not also be served as a main course for lunch.

PREPARATION TIME: *25 min.*
COOKING TIME: *20 min.*

INGREDIENTS *(for 6)*:
12 lamb kidneys
2 large onions
2 oz. unsalted butter
5 oz. button mushrooms
2 heaped teaspoons cornflour
1 level tablespoon tomato purée
4 tablespoons port or dry sherry
Salt and black pepper
GARNISH:
Parsley

Peel and thinly slice the onions. Melt the butter in a large saucepan and add the onions. Cover the pan with a lid and cook over low heat for 7 minutes. Remove the fat and skin round the kidneys*, and cut them in half, remove the outer skins and snip out the white cores with scissors. Rinse the kidneys, pat them dry on absorbent paper, then cut them into 1 in. chunks. Trim and halve the mushrooms*. Add the kidneys and mushrooms; cook gently for 3 minutes.

Blend the cornflour, tomato purée, port or sherry with 4 tablespoons of cold water in a basin. Pour this mixture into the saucepan and stir gently until the sauce begins to thicken. Season to taste with salt and freshly ground pepper. Reduce the heat and simmer the kidneys for 7–10 minutes, or until they are tender.

Arrange the kidneys on a hot serving dish, pour over the sauce and garnish with sprigs of parsley. Plain boiled rice or pasta goes well with the kidneys.

PORK WITH LEMON

In Portugal, where this recipe comes from, pork is generally of inferior quality to the dairy-fed pigs in Britain. The Portuguese housewife cooks lean pork fillet in a spicy wine sauce.

PREPARATION TIME: *20 min.*
COOKING TIME: *25–30 min.*

INGREDIENTS *(for 4–6)*:
2 lb. pork fillet
1 oz. lard
½ pint dry white wine
4 level teaspoons ground cumin
2 cloves garlic
Salt and black pepper
6 slices lemon
2 level teaspoons ground coriander

Trim away any excess fat and the thin outer skin from the pork fillet, cut the meat into 1 in. cubes and pat them dry on absorbent kitchen paper. Heat the lard in a large sauté pan and brown the meat, turning it continuously to prevent it sticking to the pan. Stir in just over ¼ pint of the wine and add the cumin. Peel the garlic and crush it over the meat; season to taste with salt and freshly ground pepper. Bring the mixture to the boil, lower the heat and simmer for about 25 minutes or until tender. Add the remaining wine, cut the lemon slices into quarters and add them to the pan. Continue cooking, stirring until the sauce thickens slightly. Stir in the coriander.

Spoon the meat and the sauce on to a dish. Plain boiled rice is traditional with the pork.

STEAK DIANE

This famous dish originated in Australia where tender beef fillet is obligatory, but rump steak is equally suitable.

PREPARATION TIME: *20 min.*
COOKING TIME: *10 min.*

INGREDIENTS *(for 6)*:
1½ lb. top rump of beef
1 small onion
1 large lemon
6 oz. unsalted butter
Worcestershire sauce
1 level tablespoon chopped parsley
2 tablespoons brandy

Trim the rump steak and cut it into six even pieces; beat them flat with a rolling pin until they are no more than ¼ in. thick. Peel and finely chop the onion. Grate the lemon rind finely, squeeze out the juice and strain.

Melt 2 oz. of the butter in a large, heavy-based pan and fry the onion for about 5 minutes or until soft and transparent. Lift the onion on to a plate with a perforated spoon and keep warm. Fry two steaks at a time, over high heat for 1 minute only on each side. Lift out and keep hot.

Melt another 2 oz. of butter until foaming and fry two more steaks; repeat with the remaining meat. Return the onions to the pan, stir in the lemon rind and juice, add a few drops of Worcestershire sauce and the parsley. Cook lightly, then put in the steaks. Flame the steaks with warm brandy.

Serve the steaks at once, on a hot serving dish, with the onion and brandy poured over them. New potatoes and braised celery* are suitable vegetables.

CHICKEN PASTIES

These small shortcrust pasties, with a savoury filling, are deep-fried until golden and crisp. They are excellent, hot or cold, for picnics and packed lunches.

PREPARATION TIME: *30 min.*
COOKING TIME: *20 min.*

INGREDIENTS *(for 10–12 pasties)*:
8 oz. shortcrust pastry (standard recipe)
6 oz. cooked chicken
1 level dessertspoon tomato ketchup
1 level tablespoon mayonnaise
Worcestershire sauce
Dry mustard
Salt and black pepper
Oil for deep frying

Roll out the shortcrust pastry*, ¼ in. thick, on a floured surface and cut out 10–12 circles with a 4 in. round cutter. Remove skin and bones from the chicken and dice the meat finely. Mix the chicken with ketchup, mayonnaise* and a few drops of Worcestershire sauce. Season to taste with mustard, salt and freshly ground pepper.

Spoon the chicken mixture on to half of each pastry round and moisten the edges with water. Fold over the pastry and press the edges tightly together, sealing them with the back of a fork.

Heat the oil* in the deep-fryer and fry the pasties, three or more at a time, for 5–10 minutes or until the pastry is golden brown and crisp. Drain the pasties on absorbent kitchen paper.

The pasties can be served while still warm, with buttered new potatoes, beans or peas.

CHICKEN CHAUD-FROID

This is a classic French dish of whole cooked chicken, coated with aspic sauce (chaud-froid sauce) and elaborately garnished. Individual chicken joints are however easier to coat than a whole chicken.

PREPARATION TIME: *1 hour*
COOKING TIME: *1½–1¾ hours*

INGREDIENTS *(for 6)*:
6 chicken portions
1 large onion
1 sprig thyme
1 small bay leaf
1 small carrot
6 parsley stalks
6 peppercorns
¼ level teaspoon salt
½ pint milk
1 oz. unsalted butter
1 oz. plain flour
Salt and black pepper
½ pint aspic jelly
2 level teaspoons powdered gelatine
GARNISH:
Cucumber peel
1 large tomato
1 small green pepper
Peel of a small lemon

Wipe the chicken portions and put them in a large saucepan. Peel the onion, cut off a 1 in. slice and add the larger piece to the pan together with the thyme, bay leaf and enough cold water to cover the chicken. Bring slowly to the boil, remove the scum and cover the pan with a lid. Simmer for 1–1¼ hours or until the meat is tender. Lift out the chicken portions and drain.

Scrape the carrot, leaving it whole, and put it in a saucepan

Rice & Pasta

with the onion slice, parsley stalks, peppercorns, salt and milk. Bring slowly to the boil, then turn off the heat and leave the milk to infuse for 30 minutes.

Melt the butter in a saucepan, stir in the flour and cook for 2 minutes; strain the infused milk and gradually stir it into the butter and flour roux*. Bring the sauce to the boil over low heat, stirring continuously, and cook gently for 2 minutes. Season to taste with salt and freshly ground pepper.

Make up the aspic jelly as directed on the packet, adding the gelatine. Allow the jelly to stand until almost set, then gradually add half to the white sauce, stirring until thick but not set.

Remove the skin carefully from the chicken portions, pat them dry and place on a wire rack. Coat each portion carefully with the aspic sauce, allowing any excess to run off. Leave for 15 minutes to set.

Cut a 1 in. piece of cucumber peel, the tomato, pepper and lemon peel into narrow strips, dip them in the remaining aspic jelly and arrange them in decorative patterns on the chicken pieces. Allow the decorations to set before spooning over the remaining aspic jelly; leave the chicken in a cool place to set completely.

Salads, crusty bread or new potatoes could be served as side dishes with the chicken.

PRAWN RING

A small amount of prawns, crawfish tails or lobster can be stretched to make a family meal by combining the shellfish with rice and vegetables.

PREPARATION TIME: *30 min.*
COOKING TIME: *40 min.*

INGREDIENTS *(for 4)*:
½ *lb. peeled prawns*
2 tablespoons olive oil
1 lb. long grain rice
1½ chicken stock cubes
1½ oz. unsalted butter
1½ oz. plain flour
1 pint milk
5 oz. frozen peas
5 oz. frozen sweetcorn kernels
Salt and pepper
GARNISH:
1 heaped tablespoon chopped parsley
Lemon wedges

Heat the oil in a large, deep sauté pan, add the rice and fry for 5 minutes, stirring continuously. Dissolve the stock cubes in 1½ pints of boiling water and stir into the pan. Simmer the rice for 25 minutes or until it is tender and has absorbed all the liquid.

While the rice is cooking, melt the butter in a saucepan, stir in the flour and cook for 2 minutes. Remove the pan from the heat and gradually stir in the milk until the sauce is smooth. Rinse the prawns and drain in a colander. Boil the peas and sweetcorn together in a little salted water for 5 minutes, then drain.

Return the sauce to the heat and bring to the boil, stirring all the time, until it thickens. Cook gently for 2 minutes, then stir in the prawns, peas and sweetcorn; season to taste with salt and freshly ground pepper. Heat this mixture through over low heat without boiling. Butter a ring mould and pack the rice firmly into it. Allow the rice to settle, then unmould the ring carefully on to a serving plate, fill the centre with the prawn sauce and pour any extra over the rice.

Garnish with parsley and lemon wedges and serve the rice ring on its own or with a green or mixed salad.

FETTUCCINE IN CREAM

The Italians eat huge bowls of egg noodles–fettuccine–for their midday meal. It is usually served simply tossed in butter and cheese or cream. The pasta can be served on its own or with grilled or roast meats.

PREPARATION TIME: *5 min.*
COOKING TIME: *12 min.*

INGREDIENTS *(for 6)*:
1 lb. fettuccine
4 oz. unsalted butter
½ pint double cream
Salt and black pepper

Cook the fettuccine for about 12 minutes in plenty of boiling salted water, preferably in two or three pans as the pasta needs space to swell. The fettuccine is cooked when a single strand is soft (*al dente**) to the bite. Drain the fettuccine in a colander, return it to the saucepan and stir in the butter and cream until every strand is thoroughly coated. Season to taste with salt and freshly ground pepper; turn on to a hot dish and serve at once.

ORANGE RICE

Savoury rice, instead of potatoes, goes well with chicken or veal dishes in cream sauce. The rice can also be used cold as a base for a salad.

PREPARATION TIME: *10 min.*
COOKING TIME: *30 min.*

INGREDIENTS *(for 6)*:
1 lb. long grain rice
1 small onion
3 sticks celery
3 oz. unsalted butter
2 large oranges
Salt and black pepper
2 sprigs thyme

Peel and finely chop the onion; wash the celery and cut into narrow slices. Melt the butter in a large, heavy-based pan and fry the onion and celery over low heat for about 5 minutes, until the onion is soft. Finely grate the rind from the oranges; squeeze the flesh and strain the juice. Add 1½ pints of cold water to the pan, together with the orange rind and juice, a pinch of salt and the thyme. Bring this mixture to the boil.

Wash the rice and pour it into the orange mixture. Bring back to the boil and simmer, stirring occasionally, for about 25 minutes until the rice is tender and the liquid absorbed.

Before serving, remove the thyme and season with freshly ground pepper.

Vegetables & Salads

GNOCCHI ALLA ROMANA

Gnocchi are small dumplings made from a flour, semolina or potato paste. The Roman gnocchi are made from semolina and the paste should be left for several hours to rest. They are served with melted butter and plenty of Parmesan cheese.

PREPARATION TIME: *30 min.*
COOKING TIME: *50 min.*

INGREDIENTS *(for 6):*
1½ pints milk
8 oz. semolina
4 oz. unsalted butter
6 oz. grated Parmesan cheese
Salt and black pepper
Grated nutmeg
3 large eggs

Heat the milk to just below boiling point, then take the pan off the heat and sprinkle the semolina over the milk, stirring continuously. Return the pan to the heat and bring the mixture slowly to the boil, still stirring. Cook for 2 minutes; remove from the heat and stir in 2½ oz. of butter and 4½ oz. of the grated cheese; season to taste with salt, freshly ground pepper and nutmeg.

Lightly beat the eggs and gradually whisk them into the semolina mixture. Pour this paste into a buttered swiss-roll tin and spread it evenly until ½ in. thick.

Set the paste aside for several hours until it is firm and cold.

Cut the paste into 1½ in. wide pieces with a cold, wet knife. Roll the pieces to the size and shape of walnuts (if necessary, roll them in a little semolina to ease shaping). Place them in a buttered oven-proof dish. Sprinkle with salt and pepper. Melt the remaining butter in a saucepan and pour it over the gnocchi; sprinkle with the remaining cheese and cook for 40 minutes or until pale golden, in the centre of the oven pre-heated to 350°F (mark 4). Serve the gnocchi at once.

RATATOUILLE

Casserole or stew of aubergines appears under various names in the Mediterranean countries. It is Moussaka in Greece and the Balkans, Imam Bayildi in Turkey and Ratatouille in Provence, southern France.

PREPARATION TIME: *30 min.*
COOKING TIME: *50 min.*

INGREDIENTS *(for 4):*
2 large courgettes
2 large aubergines
5 large tomatoes
1 large green pepper
1 small red pepper
1 large onion
2 cloves garlic
4 tablespoons olive oil
Salt and black pepper

Cut the stalks off the courgettes and aubergines. Wash well and cut them crossways into ¼ in. thick slices. Put them in a colander, cover with a plate and weight this down; leave for 1 hour to press out excessive moisture. Skin the tomatoes* and chop them roughly. Wash the peppers, remove the white inner ribs and all seeds, and dice the flesh. Peel and coarsely chop the onion and garlic.

Heat the oil in a large frying pan and fry the onion and garlic for 5 minutes over low heat until transparent. Add the peppers, cook for a further 10 minutes, then add the remaining ingredients and season to taste with salt and freshly ground pepper. Cover the pan with a lid and cook the mixture over low heat for 35 minutes, stirring from time to time. Correct seasoning.

Serve ratatouille hot on its own or with grilled or fried meat.

ONION FLAN

The recipe for this rich creamy flan comes from Alsace in France. It can be served hot or cold with a green salad for a main course, or cut into small wedges for a first course.

PREPARATION TIME: *45 min.*
COOKING TIME: *40 min.*

INGREDIENTS *(for 4–6):*
1 lb. onions
2 oz. unsalted butter
1 bay leaf
Salt and pepper
6 oz. shortcrust pastry (standard recipe)
2 large eggs
Grated nutmeg
¼ pint double cream
¼ pint milk

Peel the onions and slice them thinly. Melt the butter in a frying pan and add the onions and bay leaf. Season with salt and pepper and cover the onions closely with a piece of buttered greaseproof paper. Cover the pan with a tight-fitting lid and cook the onions over low heat for 30 minutes or until they are soft and golden. Shake the pan occasionally to prevent the onions sticking.

Prepare the shortcrust pastry* and roll it out, ¼ in. thick, on a lightly floured surface. Line an 8–9 in. wide flan ring, standing on a baking tray, with the pastry. Trim the edge and prick the pastry base with a fork. Beat the eggs lightly in a large bowl and season with salt, pepper and nutmeg. Stir in the cream and milk. Drain the cooked onions in a colander, remove the bay leaf and spread the onions over the pastry case. Strain the egg mixture through a sieve over the onions.

Bake the flan in the centre of an oven pre-heated to 400°F (mark 6) for 40 minutes. When cooked, the pastry should be golden and the filling set; it will sink slightly as the flan cools.

FRIED LEEKS

This dish can be served hot with any lean grilled or roast meat. It can also be served as a side dish or salad with cold ham and chicken.

PREPARATION TIME: *10 min.*
COOKING TIME: *25 min.*

INGREDIENTS *(for 4–6):*
2 lb. leeks
4 tomatoes
6 tablespoons olive oil
2 cloves garlic
1 bay leaf
Salt and black pepper
Juice of ½ lemon

Cut away the roots and any damaged green leaves from the leeks, slice them in half lengthways and wash under cold running water to remove all traces of grit. Cut into 1 in. slices. Skin the tomatoes*. Heat half the oil in a large frying pan and add the leeks. Peel the garlic and crush over the leeks, then add the bay leaf. Season to taste with salt and freshly ground pepper.

Cover the pan with a lid and cook over low heat for 20 minutes. Chop the tomatoes, add them to the pan with the rest of the oil and cook for a further 5 minutes. Remove the bay leaf. Spoon the leeks into a serving dish and sprinkle the lemon juice over.

APPLE AND NUT SALAD

Soured cream is a refreshing, less fatty dressing than mayonnaise. It is here combined with fruits, nuts and vegetables in a crisp salad to serve with cold meat.

PREPARATION TIME: *30 min.*

INGREDIENTS *(for 4–5):*
4 crisp dessert apples
3 teaspoons lemon juice
3 oz. shelled walnuts
¼ pint soured cream
3 oz. red cabbage
3 sticks celery
12 large radishes
2 oz. stoned raisins
Salt and black pepper

Wash and core the apples and chop them into rough chunks. Put them in a bowl and sprinkle the lemon juice over them to prevent the apples going brown. Chop the walnuts roughly and set aside one-third for garnish. Pour the soured cream into a bowl and stir in the apples and walnuts.

Remove any damaged and coarse outer leaves from the cabbage, wash it and cut out the thick centre stalk. Shred it finely, first one way and then the other. Scrub and thinly slice the celery. Remove leaves and roots from the radishes and slice them evenly. Wash the raisins and cut them in half.

Stir all these ingredients into the soured cream and season to taste with salt and freshly ground pepper. Spoon the salad into a serving dish and garnish with the remaining walnuts.

ARTICHOKES WITH MUSHROOMS

Artichoke bottoms with garlic dressing make an unusual side salad for cold meats and poultry. Alternatively, serve the artichokes as a first course.

PREPARATION TIME: *25 min.*
COOKING TIME: *45–60 min.*

INGREDIENTS *(for 6):*
6 large globe artichokes
12 large mushrooms
6 tablespoons olive oil
6 tablespoons white wine vinegar
1 clove garlic
Salt and black pepper

Trim off the stems and rinse the artichokes* thoroughly under cold running water. Put them in a large saucepan of boiling water, cover with a lid and boil until a leaf pulls away easily. Remove the artichokes, drain them upside-down and leave to cool completely.

Wash and trim the mushrooms*; cut them into slices, discarding the stalks. Pour the oil into a small bowl, add the vinegar and peeled and crushed garlic; season to taste with salt and freshly ground pepper.

Pull off and discard all the leaves and the fine filaments round the base of the artichokes. Set the artichoke bottoms on individual serving plates, and arrange the mushroom slices on top; pour over the garlic dressing.

Sweets & Puddings

IMAM BAYILDI

This Turkish dish takes its name from the Imam, or Muslim holy man. He is said to have swooned with pleasure – or from over-eating – after being served this aubergine dish.

PREPARATION TIME: *30 min.*
COOKING TIME: *40 min.*

INGREDIENTS *(for 6)* :
3 large aubergines
Salt and black pepper
Olive oil
3 large onions
12 oz. tomatoes
1 clove garlic
½ level teaspoon ground cinnamon
1 level teaspoon caster sugar
1 level tablespoon chopped parsley
1 heaped tablespoon finely chopped pine kernels (optional)

Cut the leaf bases from the aubergines, wipe them and put them in a large saucepan. Add boiling water and cover with a lid; cook the aubergines for 10 minutes. Drain the aubergines, plunge them into cold water and leave for 5 minutes. Cut them in half lengthways and scoop out most of the flesh, leaving a ½ in. thick shell. Set aside the scooped-out flesh. Arrange the shells in a buttered ovenproof dish and sprinkle them with a little salt and freshly ground pepper. Pour 4 teaspoons of olive oil in each shell and cook the aubergines, un-covered, in the centre of an oven pre-heated to 350°F (mark 4) for 30 minutes.

While the aubergine shells are cooking, peel and finely chop the onions; skin the tomatoes* and chop them. Peel and crush the garlic. Heat two tablespoons of oil in a frying pan, add the onions

and garlic and fry gently for 5 minutes, then add the tomatoes, cinnamon, sugar and parsley; season to taste with salt and pepper. Continue simmering this mixture until the liquid has reduced* by half, after about 20 minutes. Chop the aubergine flesh and add to the frying pan,

with the chopped pine kernels (if used) and cook for a further 10 minutes.

Remove the aubergine shells from the oven, stuff them with the tomato mixture and serve hot or cold, on its own, or with roast and grilled meat.

FRENCH APPLE FLAN

The open flans or tarts with a sweet filling of fruit or jam originate in the Alsace region of France. Remove the metal flan ring which holds the pastry in shape before serving the flan.

PREPARATION TIME: *1 hour*
COOKING TIME: *45 min.*

INGREDIENTS *(for 4–6)* :
2 lb. cooking apples
2 red-skinned dessert apples
6 oz. plain flour
Salt
4 oz. unsalted butter
6 oz. caster sugar
1 large egg yolk
Juice of a lemon
1 level tablespoon apricot jam

Sift the flour and a pinch of salt into a mixing bowl. Cut 3 oz. of the butter into small knobs and rub it into the flour until the mixture resembles breadcrumbs. Mix in ½ oz. caster sugar. Make a well in the centre of the flour, drop in the egg yolk and mix to a stiff dough with a little cold water.

Wrap the pastry in greaseproof paper and leave to rest for 30 minutes. Meanwhile, peel and core the cooking apples and cut them up roughly. Melt the remaining butter in a saucepan and add the apple pieces and 3½ oz. of sugar. Cover with a lid and cook gently for 10 minutes. Strain the apples, saving the juice. Rub the cooked apples through a coarse sieve, then allow this purée* to cool. Wash the dessert apples; core them before cutting them into ¼ in. rings. Sprinkle with a little lemon juice to prevent them going brown.

Roll out the pastry, ¼ in. thick, on a floured surface and use to line a 7 in. flan ring set on a greased baking tray. Trim the pastry edges and prick the base with a fork. Spoon the apple purée over the pastry and smooth the top. Arrange the apple rings in an overlapping pattern on top.

Put the apple juice, 2 table-spoons lemon juice, the jam and remaining sugar in a saucepan. Cook over low heat until the sugar has dissolved, then bring to the boil and boil briskly for 4 minutes. Brush a little of this glaze* over the apple slices.

Bake the flan for 45 minutes in the centre of an oven pre-heated to 400°F (mark 6). If the apple slices brown too quickly, cover the flan with foil. Remove the flan from the oven, brush with the remaining glaze and serve it hot or cold, with a jug of cream.

CHOCOLATE MOUSSE

The featherlight whipped con-coction known as mousse is nearly always served cold. Chocolate mousse is one of the most popular sweets, easy and quick to make.

PREPARATION TIME: *20–30 min.*
CHILLING TIME: *1 hour*

INGREDIENTS *(for 6)* :
12 oz. plain chocolate
½ oz. unsalted butter
1 tablespoon Cointreau
4 large eggs

Break the chocolate into small pieces and put them in a bowl with 4 tablespoons of cold water. Set the bowl over a pan of gently simmering water and leave the chocolate to melt, stirring it occasionally. Let the melted chocolate cook gently for 5 minutes, stirring continuously. Remove the bowl and stir in the butter and Cointreau.

Separate the eggs and whisk the whites until stiff. Beat the yolks into the slightly cooled chocolate mixture, then gently fold in the whites. Spoon the mousse into individual glasses and leave to set in the refrigerator for about 1 hour.

RHUBARB CRUMBLE

In April, rhubarb is larger and slightly tougher than the tender forced rhubarb of early winter. The tart flavour is more pronounced and blends well with a topping of sweet crumble.

PREPARATION TIME: *20 min.*
COOKING TIME: *40 min.*

INGREDIENTS (*for 4–6*):
2 lb. rhubarb
6 oz. caster sugar
6 oz. plain flour
3 oz. unsalted butter
¼ pint double cream
1 piece preserved ginger
1 teaspoon ginger syrup

Wash the rhubarb stalks, top and tail them, discard any damaged pieces and remove tough strings. Chop the stalks into ½ in. sections. Put the rhubarb in a deep baking dish, sprinkle over half the sugar and add 2 tablespoons of cold water. Sift the flour and rub the butter in until it forms a crumbly mixture; blend in the remaining sugar. Cover the rhubarb with this crumble, patting it down well. Bake in the centre of an oven pre-heated to 375°F (mark 5) for about 40

minutes or until crisp and golden on top.

Whip the cream until it stands in soft peaks; flavour with chopped ginger and the syrup.

Serve the crumble warm or cold and offer the cream separately.

SECRET CAKE

The title of this Yorkshire sweet refers to the filling which is hidden within a puff pastry case. It is traditionally served hot, with lashings of cream.

PREPARATION TIME: *30 min.*
COOKING TIME: *35–40 min.*

INGREDIENTS (*for 4*):
2 oz. chopped candied peel
8 oz. currants
2 tablespoons brandy
13 oz. prepared puff pastry
1 oz. caster sugar

Mix the peel and currants together in a bowl, pour over the brandy and leave them to soak for at least 1 hour. Roll the puff pastry* out, ⅛ in. thick, on a floured surface, and cut out two 8 in. rounds.

Place one pastry round on a wet baking tray and top with the brandy-soaked currants and peel. Moisten the edge of the pastry with water and cover with the other pastry round. Press the edges to seal them together, and decorate the top with pastry trimmings. Cut the cake into quarters, but leave the quarters pushed together.

Bake the cake for 15 minutes in the centre of the oven, pre-heated to 450°F (mark 8). Reduce the heat to 425°F (mark 7) and bake for a further 20–25 minutes or until crisp and golden brown.

Sprinkle the cake with caster sugar and serve hot or cold.

GRAPEFRUIT IN BRANDY

PREPARATION TIME: *12 min.*
COOKING TIME: *8 min.*

INGREDIENTS (*for 6*):
4 large grapefruit
4 oz. caster sugar
1 level teaspoon cinnamon
4 tablespoons brandy

The slightly acid flavour of grapefruit is equally refreshing before or after a rich main course. Slices of grapefruit, poached in syrup and doused with brandy, give a clean taste to the palate.

Cut off all the peel and pith from the grapefruit and carefully poke out the pithy core with the little finger. Slice the fruit into 1 in. thick rounds. Put the sugar in a

large saucepan with ¼ pint cold water and the cinnamon. Cook over low heat, stirring frequently, until the sugar has dissolved, then boil this syrup briskly for 2 minutes. Lower the heat, add the grapefruit slices and poach* them gently in the syrup for 6 minutes, turning once.

Arrange the grapefruit slices on a serving dish, pour over the brandy and serve hot or chilled.

GÂTEAU ST HONORÉ

This cake is a Parisian speciality, named after St Honoré, the patron saint of pastrycooks. It is a case of shortcrust and choux pastries, filled with vanilla-flavoured cream.

PREPARATION TIME: *1 hour*
COOKING TIME: *25 min.*

INGREDIENTS *(for 4–6):*
6 oz. plain flour
Salt
2 oz. unsalted butter
1 oz. lard
1 large egg
Vanilla essence
12 sugar cubes
½ pint double cream
½ pint single cream
2 oz. vanilla sugar
GARNISH:
Glacé cherries
Angelica

Sift 4 oz. of the flour and a pinch of salt into a bowl and rub in half the butter and all the lard until the mixture has a crumbly texture. Mix to a stiff dough with cold water. Roll out this shortcrust pastry* on a floured surface, to a 6 in. wide circle, and trim the edge, using a plate as a guide. Place the pastry on a greased baking tray.

Sift the remaining flour and a pinch of salt into a clean bowl. Put the remaining butter and ¼ pint cold water in a saucepan and bring to the boil. Remove the pan from the heat and add the flour all at once; beat the dough until smooth.

Allow this choux pastry* to cool, then beat in the egg and a few drops of vanilla essence. Spoon the pastry into a piping

bag fitted with a large plain nozzle. Pipe small buns, about 1 in. in diameter, closely round the edge of the shortcrust pastry. Pipe the remaining choux pastry into the same sized buns, on a separate greased baking tray. Bake the pastries for 15–20 minutes, or until golden brown, in the centre of an oven preheated to 400°F (mark 6). Remove from the oven and allow the pastries to cool.

Heat the sugar cubes with 2 tablespoons of cold water in a

small pan until the sugar has dissolved. Bring to the boil, but remove from the heat immediately the mixture begins to thicken or turns a pale golden colour. Dip the individual choux buns in this caramel and arrange them on top of the buns on the shortcrust base to form a double layer.

Whip the creams until stiff, stir in the vanilla sugar and spoon into the centre of the gâteau. Garnish with whole glacé cherries and strips of angelica.

CHEESY APPLE PIE

In Yorkshire, housewives by custom serve chunks of cheese with apple pie. This pie is a variation on that theme; the cheesy taste is more prominent if the apples are slightly sour.

PREPARATION TIME: *30 min.*
COOKING TIME: *35–40 min.*

INGREDIENTS *(for 4–6):*
8 oz. plain flour
½ level teaspoon salt
4 oz. unsalted butter
4 oz. Lancashire or Cheddar cheese
2 lb. cooking apples
1 level tablespoon caster sugar
1 egg
1–2 tablespoons milk

Sift the flour and salt into a mixing bowl. Cut the butter into small knobs and rub them into the flour until the pastry mixture is crumbly. Grate the cheese, blend it into the flour and knead the pastry to a stiff dough with a little cold water. Divide the pastry in half, roll out one half on a floured surface and use to line a 7 in. pie plate. Peel, core and slice the apples. Pile them over the pastry and sprinkle with the sugar.

Roll out the remaining pastry; moisten the edge of the plate and cover the pie with the pastry. Press the edges well down to seal, and use the trimmings to decorate the pie. Make an air vent in the centre. Beat the egg lightly with 1–2 tablespoons of milk and brush over the pie to give it a glaze*. Bake for 35–40 minutes in the centre of the oven pre-heated to 425°F (mark 7).

Serve the pie cold.

BANANA FRITTERS

Crisp fruit fritters have been known in Britain since the Middle Ages. They were often sprinkled with rosewater, nutmeg or almond essence. Any of these flavourings can be added to the whipped cream.

PREPARATION TIME: *20 min.*
COOKING TIME: *10 min.*

INGREDIENTS *(for 6):*
6 small bananas
4 oz. plain flour
Pinch of salt
1 large egg
¼ pint milk or milk and water
Oil for deep frying
Caster sugar
½ pint whipped cream

Sift the flour with the salt into a mixing bowl. Make a well in the centre and break in the egg. Add half the liquid and beat the batter* mixture with a wooden spoon until smooth. Gradually add the rest of the liquid and continue beating until the batter is thoroughly blended and has the consistency of pouring cream. If time allows, leave the batter to stand for 1 hour.

Peel the bananas and cut them in half lengthways. Dip them in the batter. Heat a deep-fryer with about 1½ in. of oil* to 375°F. With a perforated spoon, lower three banana halves into the hot oil and fry until crisp and golden, after 2–3 minutes. Drain the fritters on crumpled kitchen paper and keep them warm while frying the next batch.

Serve the fritters on a warmed dish and sprinkle caster sugar over them; serve a bowl of whipped cream separately.

Savouries & Snacks

VICTORIANA DIABLE

Devilled sauces (strong and spicy) were popular in Victorian days. The sauce adds a different taste to left-over meat.

PREPARATION TIME: *5 min.*
COOKING TIME: *35 min.*

INGREDIENTS *(for 4)*:
8–10 slices cooked meat or poultry
1 tablespoon olive oil
2 finely chopped onions
1 crushed clove garlic
1 level tablespoon plain flour
1 level tablespoon Dijon mustard
1 tablespoon white wine vinegar
⅓ pint beef stock
2 level teaspoons soft brown sugar
¼ teaspoon Worcestershire sauce
1 teaspoon chopped capers
1 bay leaf
Salt and black pepper
3–4 level tablespoons browned breadcrumbs
1½ oz. unsalted melted butter

Heat the oil over medium heat, and cook the onions and garlic until golden brown. Blend in the flour. Add mustard and vinegar, and gradually stir in the stock. Bring this sauce to boiling point and stir until thick and smooth. Add the sugar, Worcestershire sauce, capers and bay leaf and season with salt and pepper. Simmer for 5–10 minutes, stirring frequently.

Put the sliced meat in a lightly buttered ovenproof dish. Pour over the sauce (first removing the bay leaf), sprinkle with the breadcrumbs and pour the melted butter over. Bake in the centre of a pre-heated oven at 375°F (mark 5) for about 20 minutes or until golden brown. Serve hot, with buttered rice.

CHICKEN AND CHEESE SAVOURY

A few mushrooms and a little cheese turn scraps of cooked chicken into a tasty meal.

PREPARATION TIME: *10 min.*
COOKING TIME: *15 min.*

INGREDIENTS *(for 4)*:
8 oz. cooked, diced chicken
½ pint thick white sauce
Salt, black pepper and cayenne
1 level teaspoon made English mustard
2 oz. thinly sliced button mushrooms
4 slices buttered toast
2 oz. grated Cheddar cheese

Season the white sauce* with salt, pepper and cayenne to taste, and blend in the mustard. Stir the chicken and mushrooms into the sauce and simmer over low heat until heated through.

Spoon the chicken mixture on to the toast and sprinkle with the cheese. Grill until the cheese is brown and bubbling. A tomato and onion salad, or a green vegetable, goes well with these savouries.

FRIED SAVOURY RICE

A small amount of left-over meat can be used for this version of Chinese fried rice.

PREPARATION TIME: *10 min.*
COOKING TIME: *25 min.*

INGREDIENTS *(for 4–6)*:
10 oz. long grain rice
2 tablespoons olive oil
3 beaten eggs
6 oz. cooked meat
2 shredded lettuce leaves
4 chopped spring onions
2 oz. thinly sliced button mushrooms
1 tablespoon soy sauce

Cook the rice, covered, for about 15 minutes in boiling salted water. Rinse in cold water and drain thoroughly.

Heat the oil in a large, heavy-based pan over medium heat. Pour in the eggs and cook, stirring with a fork, until the eggs are beginning to set. Stir in the rice, the meat cut into matchstick strips, the vegetables and soy sauce. Cook, stirring constantly, until all the ingredients are heated through.

Serve hot, accompanied by boiled peas or beans.

KIDNEY SCRAMBLE

Two breakfast dishes – fried kidneys and scrambled eggs – become a quick snack.

PREPARATION TIME: *10 min.*
COOKING TIME: *10–15 min.*

INGREDIENTS *(for 4)*:
4 finely chopped lamb kidneys
1 oz. unsalted butter
¼ teaspoon Worcestershire sauce
1 level teaspoon tomato ketchup
¼ level teaspoon made English mustard
Salt and black pepper
6 eggs
4 tablespoons single cream
4 slices buttered toast

Fry the kidneys over high heat, in half the butter, until lightly browned. Stir in the sauces and mustard; season with salt and pepper and cook over a moderate heat for a further 2 minutes. Keep the kidneys warm.

Lightly beat the eggs with the cream; season. Melt the remaining butter in a clean pan, and cook the eggs over low heat, stirring occasionally, until just beginning to set. Spoon the eggs on to the toast and top with the kidneys. Serve at once, with a crisp salad.

CLUB SANDWICHES

One of the best inventions of the American kitchen is this triple-decker sandwich.

PREPARATION TIME: *15 min.*
COOKING TIME: *5 min.*

INGREDIENTS *(for 4)*:
12 slices white bread
2 oz. unsalted butter
4 small sliced tomatoes
8 small lettuce leaves
8 rashers streaky bacon
8 thin slices cooked chicken or turkey
4 level dessertspoons mayonnaise

Toast the bread and remove the crusts; butter 8 slices on one side, the remaining 4 slices on both sides. Cover four slices with tomato, top with the bacon, fried without butter until golden and crisp; put those slices buttered on both sides on top, and cover with lettuce and cooked meat. Spoon mayonnaise* over the meat and cover with the last four slices of toast. Press the sandwiches firmly together and quarter them; spear each with a cocktail stick and serve.

Easter Customs

Easter, which falls between March 22 and April 25, is the most holy festival in the Christian year, although many of its customs are pagan in origin. The custom of exchanging eggs goes back to pre-Christian times when eggs, as a token of renewed life, were exchanged at the spring festivals.

Hot cross buns possibly stem from the small wheat cakes eaten at the spring festivals in honour of Astarte, the Phoenician fertility goddess. Her Anglo-Saxon counterpart was Eostre. The cross on the buns, however, is of Christian origin. In orthodox households all over the world, housewives still prepare for the Easter feast: eggs are hardboiled, dyed and decorated, cakes are baked and lamb is prepared for Easter Sunday.

The simnel cake, originally made by servant girls for Mothering Sunday in March, is now baked for Easter in Britain. Most other countries also have their special Easter fare. The Russian housewife bakes a yeast cake, known as *Kulich,* which she wraps in a spotless napkin to take to church for the priest's blessing. In Portugal, the traditional sweet consists of fine strands of egg yolk called Angel's Hair. The Italians bake *Colomba,* which is similar to the Russian *Kulich,* and the Sicilians make *Cassata alla Siciliana* – layers of cake and ice cream covered with chocolate icing. In Poland, the Easter fare is a huge buffet, each item blessed by the priest. Place of honour goes to the Paschal Lamb, made of butter or white sugar.

Good Friday

Possibly as a relic from papal decrees when meat until recently was forbidden on Fridays, Good Friday generally has fish as the main course. Recipes – except for the sole cushions – for this menu, serving eight, will be found on pp. 120, 128 and 130.

Avocado and Citrus Salad
Sole Cushions with
Hollandaise Sauce
Fried Leeks, Sauté Potatoes
Chocolate Mousse

Sole Cushions

INGREDIENTS:
8 large Dover sole fillets
Butter
1 finely chopped onion
4 oz. button mushrooms
1 tablespoon chopped parsley
Salt and black pepper
¼ pint dry white wine
7 oz. prepared puff pastry
1 egg yolk

Butter a shallow ovenproof dish and spread the onion over the base. Cover with the thinly sliced mushrooms and parsley. Fold each sole fillet in three and arrange over the mushrooms. Season with salt and pepper and pour over the wine.

Cover the dish with buttered greaseproof paper and bake in the centre of the oven, at 350°F (mark 4), for 10 minutes. Remove the dish and allow to cool.

Roll out the puff pastry*, ⅛ in. thick, and divide into 16 squares. Spoon the mushroom mixture over half the squares, and top with a sole fillet. Moisten the pastry edges, cover each square with the remaining pastry and seal the edges firmly.

Brush the cushions with the egg yolk and bake them for 15–20 minutes in the centre of the oven at 400°F (mark 6).

Serve the sole cushions hot, with a bowl of Hollandaise sauce*.

Decorating Eggs

Use only white-shelled eggs for decorating. Hardboiled in spinach water, they take on a green colour, and those boiled with raw beetroot turn red. Onion or shallot skins wrapped round the eggs and wound on with brown cotton give an orange-brown mottled effect. Flower petals can be placed on damp eggs, covered with onion skin and kept in place with string or tape. The boiled eggs will then bear the imprint of both petals and onion skins.

Alternatively, add a few drops of vegetable dye or food colouring to the water to dye the eggs carmine, blue, green or yellow. Narrow strips of masking tape can be stuck on to the eggs in geometric patterns. Peeling off the tapes afterwards will reveal white patterns on a coloured background. Polish all boiled eggs with a little olive oil.

The eggs may be boiled before being decorated with wax crayons, vegetable dyes, water colours or oil paints. Complicated designs, for keepsake eggs, should be traced on uncooked eggs, first dipped in vegetable dye.

Easter Sunday

Young spring lamb is traditional at Easter; the lamb symbolises the innocence of Christ.

Stuffed Eggs
Saddle of Lamb with Wine Sauce
Haricots Verts, New Potatoes
Green Salad
Grapefruit in Brandy
(see p. 131)

Stuffed Eggs

INGREDIENTS:
8 hardboiled eggs
1–2 small tins anchovy fillets
1 dessertspoon capers
6 tablespoons olive oil
2 tablespoons lemon juice
French mustard
Black pepper
Lettuce leaves

Halve the eggs lengthways and mash the yolks. Pound them to a paste with the remaining ingredients. Arrange the egg whites on lettuce leaves and pipe the yolk mixture into the cavities.

Saddle of Lamb

INGREDIENTS:
6 lb. saddle of lamb
1½ pints red wine
4 tablespoons medium sherry
4 tablespoons brandy
12 sprigs rosemary
2 oz. dripping
*4 heaped tablespoons red-
   currant jelly*
Arrowroot
MARINADE:
1 finely chopped carrot
2 finely chopped onions
3 parsley sprigs
1 sprig thyme
1 bay leaf
6 peppercorns
2 cloves and 1 blade mace
4 tablespoons malt vinegar

Put all the marinade* ingredients in a pan with ¼ pint of water. Boil for 30 minutes, leave to cool and blend in the wines. Marinate the lamb for 12 hours.

Put the rosemary sprigs into small incisions in the lamb and place it, with the dripping, in a roasting pan. Cook in the centre of the oven, pre-heated to 350°F (mark 4), for 2½ hours.

Boil the marinade briskly until reduced* to 1 pint. Strain, and stir in the jelly. Bring the sauce back to boil and thicken it with diluted arrowroot. Correct seasoning.

The Ukranians are famous for their decorated eggs which resemble miniature mosaics. The complicated designs are traced on uncooked eggs which are dipped, at various stages, in different vegetable dyes. Only a small part of the egg is coloured at a time, the other areas being masked with bees' wax or cotton tape.

Children will delight in a chocolate egg within a chicken egg. Carefully pierce the broad end of a raw egg with a small skewer and shake out the white and yolk. Leave the empty egg to dry out. Pour melted chocolate, through a small funnel, into the egg.

2 oz. caster sugar
2 oz. melted butter
1 beaten egg
1 oz. currants
1–2 oz. chopped mixed peel

Sift 4 oz. of the flour with the sugar. Crumble in the yeast and stir in the milk and water. Leave the mixture in a warm place for 20–30 minutes, until frothy. Meanwhile, sift the remaining flour with the salt and spice. Add the sugar.

Stir the melted butter, together with the egg, into the risen yeast mixture. Gradually fold in the flour, currants and peel.

Knead the dough until perfectly smooth, on a floured surface. Divide into 12 pieces and shape into buns. Set the buns, well apart, on greased and floured baking trays and leave them to rise in a warm place until doubled in size.

Make two slashes on top of each bun to form a cross. Bake just above the centre in an oven pre-heated to 375°F (mark 5) for 15–20 minutes.

Leave the buns to cool on a wire rack; while still warm, brush them with a glaze made from 1½ oz. caster sugar dissolved in 2 tablespoons water.

Easter Cakes

Simnel Cake

INGREDIENTS:
½ lb. unsalted butter
2 large lemons
½ lb. caster sugar
4 large eggs
6 oz. chopped mixed peel
6 oz. sultanas
1¼ lb. currants
14 oz. plain flour
Salt
Baking powder
1 level teaspoon mixed spice
DECORATION:
4 oz. ground almonds
4 oz. icing sugar
4 oz. caster sugar
1 large egg
Lemon essence
Sugar or chocolate eggs

Cream the butter with the grated lemon rind and the sugar until light and fluffy. Beat in the eggs, one at a time, and stir in the peel and fruit. Sift the flour with a little salt, a good pinch of baking powder and the spice. Fold into the creamed mixture. If necessary, add 1–2 tablespoons of milk.

Grease and line a 7 in., round, deep cake tin. Spoon the cake mixture into the tin and level the top. Bake in the centre of the oven, pre-heated to 350°F (mark 4), for 3–3½ hours.

Meanwhile, mix together the ground almonds and all the sugar. Add half the lightly beaten egg, with a few drops of lemon essence and 3 tablespoons strained lemon juice. Knead thoroughly until the almond paste is smooth.

Roll two-thirds of the almond paste out to a 7 in. round and place on top of the cooled cake. Smooth the paste round the sides. The remaining paste is shaped into 11 balls – to represent the Apostles, excluding Judas – and set round the edge of the cake.

The centre of the cake can be decorated with small eggs and golden Easter chicks.

Hot Cross Buns

INGREDIENTS:
1 lb. plain flour
1 level teaspoon caster sugar
1 oz. fresh yeast (or 1 level tablespoon dried yeast)
¼ pint lukewarm milk
2 fluid oz. warm water
1 level teaspoon each salt and mixed spice

May

The land doth will, the sea doth wish,
spare sometime flesh, and feede of fish.

This Month's Recipes

Slim river trout such as these make the finest eating.
Trout living in lakes tend to be larger and coarser in flavour

Food in Season

Fish continues to be in good supply – cod, mackerel and plaice are some of the best buys. River trout and sea or salmon trout, although slightly more expensive, are at their best. The first English asparagus and new potatoes come on to the market, together with young carrots, broad beans, spinach and turnips. Hothouse cucumbers and tomatoes are dropping in price, and gooseberries and apricots are just becoming available in the shops this month.

Fish

Bream, sea
Brill
Clams
Cod
Coley
Conger eels
Dabs
Dover sole
Dublin Bay prawns
Eels
Flake (also sold as rock salmon)
Grey mullet
Haddock
Hake
Herring
Lemon sole
Lobster
Mackerel
Mock halibut (or Greenland halibut)
Oysters, Portuguese
Plaice
Prawns
Redfish
Red mullet
Salmon
Scad (or horse mackerel)
Sea trout
Shrimps
Skate
Trout, river
Turbot
Whitebait
Whiting
Witch

Poultry & Game

Chicken
Duck
Guinea fowl
Pigeon
Rabbit
Turkey
Venison

Vegetables

Asparagus
Avocado pears
Beetroot
Broad beans
Broccoli
Cabbages
Carrots (young)
Cauliflowers
Celery
Chicory
Courgettes
Cucumbers
Endive
Fennel
French beans
Lettuces
Mange-tout peas
Mushrooms
Onions
Parsley
Peas
Peppers
Potatoes, new
Radishes
Salad cress
Salsify
Spanish onions
Spinach
Spring greens
Spring onions
String beans
Sweet potatoes
Tomatoes
Turnips
Watercress

Fruit

Apples
Apricots
Bananas
Cherries
Gooseberries
Grapefruit
Grapes
Kumquats
Lemons
Limes
Lychees
Mangoes
Melons (imported)
Oranges
Pears
Pineapples
Raspberries (imported)
Rhubarb
Strawberries

SUGGESTED MENUS

Pickled Salmon
Beef Paupiettes with Buttered Noodles
Tossed Green Salad
Chilled Almond Soufflé

Cream of Tomato Soup
Lamb Argenteuil
Buttered New Potatoes
Gooseberry Flan

Canapés à la Crème
Trout with Mushrooms,
Buttered New Potatoes and Green Salad
Schwarzwald Kirschtorte

French Turnip Soup
Chicken Livers with Grapes
Croûtes aux Abricots

Fricassée of Eggs
Peking Duck
Chinese Pears

Chicken Liver Pâté
Soles aux Crêpes
Rice Salad with Florence Fennel
Avocado Fool

Asparagus Soup
Beef Stew with Olives
Boiled Potatoes
Napoleon's Bean Salad
Biscuit Tortoni

Soups & Starters

CREAM OF TOMATO SOUP

Imported tomatoes are still cheaper in May than the home-grown product. They are small, but ideal for this soup.

PREPARATION TIME: *15 min.*
COOKING TIME: *20 min.*

INGREDIENTS *(for 4–6):*
1½ *lb. firm tomatoes*
1 onion
1 clove garlic
2 oz. unsalted butter
½–1 *pint beef stock*
Bicarbonate of soda
Salt and black pepper
Caster sugar
¼ *pint double cream*
GARNISH:
2 tablespoons chopped basil or parsley

Skin the tomatoes* and chop them roughly. Peel and finely chop the onion and garlic.

Melt the butter in a heavy-based pan and fry the onion and garlic for 2–3 minutes until soft and transparent. Add ½ pint of stock to the pan, together with the chopped tomatoes and a pinch of bicarbonate of soda. Bring the soup to the boil, then lower the heat and cover the pan with a lid. Simmer for 15 minutes.

Leave the soup to cool slightly before liquidising it. Pour it, through a sieve, back into the pan.

Re-heat the soup, adding more stock until it has the desired consistency. Season to taste with salt, freshly ground pepper and sugar. In a separate pan, bring the cream to near boiling point and add it to the soup. Chop the basil or parsley and sprinkle over the soup just before serving.

PICKLED SALMON

The traditional version of this Scandinavian dish (*gravad lax*) uses fresh dill, but it can also be made with dried dillweed. The pickling adds a subtle flavour to fresh salmon.

PREPARATION TIME: *30 min.*

INGREDIENTS *(for 6):*
1½ *lb. salmon tailpiece*
PICKLE:
1 heaped tablespoon sea salt
1 rounded tablespoon granulated sugar
1 teaspoon crushed black pepper-corns
1 tablespoon brandy (optional)
1 rounded tablespoon fresh dill or 1 level tablespoon dried dillweed
SAUCE:
2 rounded tablespoons made French or German mustard
1 rounded tablespoon granulated sugar
1 large egg yolk
7 tablespoons olive oil
2 tablespoons wine vinegar
1 rounded teaspoon fresh dill or 1 level teaspoon dried dill-weed
Salt and white pepper

Ask the fishmonger to fillet the salmon into two triangles. Mix all the pickling ingredients together and spread a quarter of this mixture over the base of a flat dish. Lay the first piece of salmon, skin down, on top of the mixture and spread half of the remaining pickle over the cut side. Place the other piece of salmon, skin side up, over the first. Spread the top with the remaining mixture, rubbing it well into the skin. Cover the salmon with a piece of foil and a board weighed down with a couple of tins. Leave the salmon to press in a cool place or the refrigerator for anything up to 5 days, but not less than 12 hours, turning the salmon once a day.

Before serving, slice the salmon thinly, either parallel to the skin as with smoked salmon or obliquely to the skin.

For the sauce, beat the mustard with the sugar and egg yolk until smooth. Gradually add the oil and vinegar, mixing thoroughly between each addition. Season to taste with dill, salt and pepper.

Arrange the slices of salmon on individual plates, and serve buttered rye bread and the sauce separately.

CANAPÉS À LA CRÈME

This is a quickly prepared starter, suitable for serving before a substantial main course. The combination of hot crisp bread, salty anchovies and cold clotted cream makes an unusual savoury.

PREPARATION TIME: *8 min.*
COOKING TIME: *10–12 min.*

INGREDIENTS *(for 4)*:
8 slices white bread
12 anchovy fillets
4 oz. clarified butter
4 level tablespoons clotted cream
GARNISH:
Parsley sprigs

Cut a round from each slice of bread with a 3 in. plain or fluted scone cutter. Drain the anchovy fillets and cut each in half lengthways. Melt the clarified butter* in a heavy-based pan and fry the bread until golden brown. Keep the slices warm in the oven on a hot serving dish.

When all the bread has been fried, quickly arrange three anchovy fillets on each slice, spoon over the cream and garnish with a small sprig of parsley.

Serve immediately, before the cream melts into the hot bread.

CHICKEN LIVER PÂTÉ

Pâtés are great favourites as starters, and the following recipe is both economical and quick to prepare. It should be allowed to mature for 2 days, and will store well in the home freezer.

PREPARATION TIME: *30 min.*
COOKING TIME: *45 min.*

INGREDIENTS *(for 6)*:
½ lb. chicken livers
6 oz. sausage meat
1 egg
Salt and black pepper
Ground thyme and marjoram
1 tablespoon brandy
2–3 tablespoons Madeira or brown sherry
¼ lb. pork or bacon fat
1 bay leaf

Remove any stringy bits and discoloured parts from the chicken livers; chop them finely or put them in the liquidiser to make a purée*. Mix the liver purée with the sausage meat, and stir in the egg. Season to taste with salt, pepper, thyme and marjoram and finally stir in the brandy and Madeira (or sherry).

Fry a spoonful of the pâté in a little butter to test seasoning; adjust if necessary. Put the pâté mixture into a 1¼ pint terrine or ovenproof dish. Cut the pork or bacon fat into narrow strips and place them on top of the pâté in a decorative pattern. Set the bay leaf in the centre. Stand the terrine in a roasting pan and pour in enough boiling water to come half way up the dish. Bake in the centre of the oven at 400°F (mark 6) for 45 minutes.

Leave the pâté to cool, then cover with a lid or foil and store in the refrigerator for about 2 days to give the flavours time to develop fully.

Serve the pâté cold, with hot crisp toast or home-baked bread and butter.

ELIZA ACTON'S APPLE SOUP

In 1845, Eliza Acton published her *Modern Cookery*, the first important English cookery book. It included this recipe for a tart apple soup. Miss Acton gives Burgundy as the place of origin, but a similar soup was known in medieval Britain.

PREPARATION TIME: *10 min.*
COOKING TIME: *30 min.*

INGREDIENTS *(for 6)*:
¾ lb. cooking apples
2 pints beef or mutton stock
½ level teaspoon ground ginger
Salt and black pepper
4 rounded tablespoons long grain rice

Remove all fat from the surface of the prepared cool stock*. Wash the apples and chop them roughly, without removing peel or core. Bring the stock to the boil in a large pan, add the apples and cover the pan with a lid. Simmer the soup over low heat until the apples are tender.

Pour the soup through a sieve, rubbing through as much of the fruit pulp as possible. Stir in the ginger and season with salt and ground pepper. Re-heat the soup and remove any scum.

While the soup is cooking, boil the rice in plenty of salted water. Drain thoroughly through a sieve and keep the rice warm.

Spoon the soup into bowls, and serve the rice separately.

FRENCH TURNIP SOUP

The first white turnips of the season appear in May. The French frequently use these tasty, inexpensive root vegetables for a creamy soup.

PREPARATION TIME: *20 min.*
COOKING TIME: *45 min.*

INGREDIENTS *(for 6–8)*:
¾ lb. turnips
½ lb. potatoes
1 leek
1 onion
2 oz. butter
1 oz. plain flour
3–4 pints vegetable stock
Salt and black pepper
2 large egg yolks
3 tablespoons double cream
GARNISH:
Bread croûtons

Peel and dice the turnips and potatoes and rinse them in cold water. Remove the roots and coarse outer leaves from the leek, cut in half and rinse thoroughly under cold running water to remove all traces of dirt. Chop the leek coarsely. Peel and roughly chop the onion.

Melt the butter in a large pan and add the vegetables; cover the pan with a lid and cook the vegetables over low heat for about 10 minutes, without browning them. Add the flour and cook for a few minutes, stirring continuously. Gradually blend in the stock and season to taste with salt and freshly ground pepper. Simmer the soup over low heat for about 30 minutes, or until the vegetables are cooked.

Let the soup cool a little before putting it in the liquidiser or rubbing it through a fine sieve.

Fish

Re-heat the soup over low heat.

Beat the egg yolks with the cream in a small bowl, blend in a little of the hot soup and then stir it all back into the soup. Stir over low heat for a few minutes, without allowing the soup to boil. Correct seasoning if necessary.

Serve the soup at once, with a separate bowl of bread croûtons*.

FRICASSÉE OF EGGS

Nowadays, a fricassée describes poultry prepared in a white sauce though the term originally meant a white stew of meat, fish or vegetables. A fricassée of eggs makes a good first course, served in small dishes or in tartlet moulds of shortcrust pastry.

PREPARATION TIME: *20 min.*
COOKING TIME: *15 min.*

INGREDIENTS *(for 6)*:
6 large eggs
6 parsley sprigs
6 tarragon sprigs (optional)
4 oz. unsalted butter
5–6 fluid oz. double cream
Salt and black pepper
Lemon juice

Hardboil the eggs for about 10 minutes, then plunge them into cold water for a few minutes to prevent further cooking. Shell the eggs, quarter them and set aside. Chop the herbs finely.

Melt the butter in a frying pan, stir in the cream and let the mixture bubble until it has thickened to a sauce. Add the herbs and season to taste with salt, freshly ground pepper and lemon juice.

Re-heat the quartered eggs carefully in the sauce and spoon the mixture into individual serving dishes or tartlets made from shortcrust pastry*.

THE CURÉ'S OMELETTE

A society beauty, engaged in good works, once visited a priest in one of the poorest parts of Paris, to find him dining on an expensive omelette of luxurious fresh tunny fish and carp roes. Today, this omelette is made with tinned tuna fish and fresh herring roes, but the result is still superb.

PREPARATION TIME: *20 min.*
COOKING TIME: *10 min.*

INGREDIENTS *(for 4)*:
8 oz. soft herring roes
3–3½ oz. tin tuna fish
1 shallot
3 oz. unsalted butter
8 eggs
Salt and black pepper
2 oz. maître d'hotel butter

Pour boiling water over the roes and leave them to stand for 30 seconds to blanch*. Drain the roes and chop them roughly, discarding any discoloured parts. Drain the oil from the tuna and flake* the fish with a fork. Peel and finely chop the shallot and cook over low heat in 2 oz. of the butter, until soft and transparent.

Add the roes and the tuna to the shallot, crushing the mixture down with a fork. Cook for a few minutes, then remove the pan from the heat and leave the mixture to cool slightly. Beat the eggs in a bowl and stir the fish mixture into them. Season to taste with salt and pepper.

Melt the remaining butter in an omelette pan and cook one large or four small omelettes*. Spread the maître d'hotel butter* on a warm serving dish, place the omelette on top and serve immediately.

TROUT WITH MUSHROOMS

This recipe from the Pyrenees combines fresh river trout with button mushrooms, served in a Pernod sauce.

PREPARATION TIME: *10 min.*
COOKING TIME: *15 min.*

INGREDIENTS *(for 4)*:
4 trout (each weighing 6–8 oz.)
Seasoned flour
3–4 oz. clarified butter
8 oz. button mushrooms
1 clove garlic
2–3 tablespoons Pernod or Pastis
¼ pint double cream
Salt and black pepper

Wipe the trout lightly with a damp cloth, but do not remove the blue-grey outer coating. Slit the trout along the belly and remove the entrails. Coat each trout with seasoned flour*, shaking off any excess. Melt the clarified butter* in a large, heavy-based pan and fry the trout over moderate heat for 5 minutes on each side, or until golden brown and crisp.

Meanwhile, trim the mushrooms* and slice them thinly. Peel and crush the garlic. Lift the trout on to a serving dish and keep them warm. Fry the mushrooms and garlic in the trout juices, over low heat, for 3–4 minutes. Stir in the Pernod and let the liquid bubble rapidly for a few minutes. Add the cream, stirring continuously until the sauce has reduced* to the consistency of thick cream. Season to taste with salt, freshly ground pepper, and a little more Pernod if necessary. Pour the sauce over the trout.

Serve immediately, with boiled buttered potatoes and a crisp green salad.

Meat

WHITING WITH ORANGE SAUCE

Fish with orange was as popular in the 18th century as fish with lemon is today. Originally, sharp Seville oranges were used, but the mixture of orange and lemon in this French recipe is equally good.

PREPARATION TIME: *10 min.*
COOKING TIME: *40 min.*

INGREDIENTS *(for 6)* :
6 whiting
Salt and black pepper
1 lemon
1 orange
4 tablespoons double cream
¼ pint dry white wine
3 large egg yolks
Cayenne pepper
4 oz. unsalted butter
Seasoned flour
GARNISH:
1 orange
Chopped parsley

Clean and wash the whiting, and fillet each into two. Dry the fillets thoroughly on absorbent kitchen paper and season with salt and pepper; sprinkle over the juice of half a lemon. Set aside. Grate the rind from the orange and set aside; squeeze the juice of the orange and remaining lemon into a bowl.

For the sauce, stir the cream, wine and egg yolks into the fruit juices and set the bowl over a pan of simmering water. Whisk the sauce mixture continuously until it has the consistency of thin cream. Season to taste with salt, pepper and cayenne, and blend in the orange rind. Cut half the butter into knobs and beat them one by one into the sauce. Keep the sauce hot, but do not allow it to boil.

Coat the whiting fillets with seasoned flour*. Melt the remaining butter in a large, heavy-based pan and fry the fillets until golden brown on both sides.

Garnish the fillets with orange wedges and chopped parsley. The sauce can be served separately or poured over the fish. Offer crusty French bread with which to mop up the sauce.

SOLES AUX CRÈPES

The combination of buttered fillets of sole with featherlight strips of pancake is a speciality from Bayeaux in northern France.

PREPARATION TIME: *15 min.*
COOKING TIME: *25 min.*

INGREDIENTS *(for 6)* :
12 fillets of sole
Seasoned flour
4 oz. clarified butter
3 oz. unsalted butter
1 heaped tablespoon chopped parsley
BATTER:
2 oz. plain flour
¼ level teaspoon salt
1 egg
2½ fluid oz. milk
GARNISH:
Lemon wedges

Begin by making the batter so that it can rest while the fillets are being fried. Sift the flour and salt into a bowl, make a well in the centre and add the lightly beaten egg. Mix thoroughly and add 4 tablespoons water and milk gradually, beating well, until the batter is free from lumps and has the consistency of single cream. Add more water to the batter if necessary.

Wipe the sole fillets on a damp cloth, coat them with seasoned flour* and shake off any surplus. Melt the clarified butter* in a large pan and fry the fillets until golden brown on both sides, turning once. Arrange the fillets on a serving dish and keep them warm.

Butter a clean frying pan and fry three or four pancakes from the batter. Roll the pancakes up and cut them, crossways, into ½ in. strips. Melt the remaining butter and re-heat the pancake ribbons, turning them until they are hot and golden. Blend in the chopped parsley and pile the pancake strips over and among the sole fillets. Garnish with wedges of lemon.

A rice salad with Florentine fennel (see May rice and pasta) would be a tasty side dish.

SALMON STEAKS WITH CREAM

Fresh salmon is the king of fish, and its delicate flavour should never be smothered by a rich sauce or mayonnaise. This recipe is a simple but successful way of cooking salmon steaks so as to retain their flavour.

PREPARATION TIME: *5 min.*
COOKING TIME: *20–25 min.*

INGREDIENTS *(for 6)* :
6 salmon steaks, each 1 in. thick
Salt and black pepper
2 oz. butter
¾–1 pint single cream
Small bay leaf
GARNISH:
Lemon wedges

Wipe the steaks with a damp cloth and season them with salt and freshly ground pepper. Butter an ovenproof dish, large enough to take the salmon steaks in a single layer. Pour over enough cream to cover the fish. Lay the bay leaf on top and cover the dish with foil.

Bake the steaks in the centre of a pre-heated oven, at 375°F (mark 5) for 20–25 minutes, basting with a little extra cream if necessary.

Serve the salmon in the cooking dish and garnish with wedges of lemon. Buttered new potatoes with parsley, and a crisp salad of lettuce and cucumber, are traditional with salmon.

BEEF STEW WITH OLIVES

Shin or leg of beef is an inexpensive cut and excellent for stewing. The gelatinous part holding the nuggets of meat together adds a good texture to the sauce and prevents the meat becoming stringy during cooking.

PREPARATION TIME: *20 min.*
COOKING TIME: *3¼ hours*

INGREDIENTS *(for 4–6)* :
2½–3 lb. shin of beef
Seasoned flour
1 large onion
1 large carrot
2 cloves garlic
Cooking oil
¼ pint red wine
1 pint beef stock
Bouquet garni
1 teaspoon anchovy essence
Salt and black pepper
4–6 oz. black or green olives
GARNISH:
Chopped parsley

Remove skin and any large lumps of fat from the beef. Cut the meat into 1–1½ in. chunks and coat with seasoned flour*. Peel and finely slice the onion, carrot and garlic. Pour a thin layer of oil into a large frying pan; when hot, fry the meat and vegetables until brown. Transfer the contents of the pan to a casserole dish.

Pour the wine and a little stock into the frying pan. Boil these juices rapidly, scraping in all the residue. Pour into the casserole, adding enough stock to cover the meat. Tuck in the bouquet garni*, stir in the anchovy essence and plenty of freshly ground pepper. Cover with a lid or foil. Simmer the casserole in the centre of an oven, pre-heated to 300°F (mark

2), for 2–3 hours or until the meat is tender.

Remove the cooked meat and vegetables to a shallow warm serving dish and sprinkle with a little salt. Boil the liquid in the casserole rapidly until it has reduced* and thickened to a rich sauce. Remove the bouquet garni. Add the olives and simmer for 5 minutes. Correct seasoning if necessary. Pour some of the sauce over the meat and serve the remainder in a sauce boat.

Garnish the meat with parsley and surround with triangles of toast or boiled potatoes.

SWEETBREADS À LA CASTILLANE

Calf sweetbreads are the classic basis of this recipe from Tours in France. These are both rare and expensive and lamb sweetbreads make a good alternative.

PREPARATION TIME: *25 min.*
COOKING TIME: *30 min.*

INGREDIENTS *(for 6)*:
1½–2 lb. lamb sweetbreads
¾–1 pint chicken stock
*1 dessertspoon lemon juice or
   white wine vinegar*
4 dessert apples
4 oz. butter
4 ripe bananas
Caster sugar
Seasoned flour
2½ fluid oz. brandy
¼ pint double cream
Salt and black pepper

Put the sweetbreads* in a basin with 1 teaspoon of salt and enough tepid water to cover. Leave to soak for 1 hour, then drain.

Put the sweetbreads in a saucepan and cover with chicken stock; add the lemon juice or vinegar.

Bring to the boil over low heat, then simmer calf sweetbreads for 10 minutes and lamb sweetbreads for a few minutes only, until they loose their pink raw look. Drain the sweetbreads through muslin and set the liquid aside.

When the sweetbreads have cooled, cut off any fibres, pieces of tube or discoloured parts, but leave the thin skin round the sweetbreads intact.

Wash the apples, but do not peel or core them. Cut them into large pieces and put them in a pan with 2 oz. of butter. Cover with a lid and cook over low heat until quite soft. Rub the apples through a sieve to make a fine purée*. Peel and mash the bananas and blend into the apple purée. Add sugar and lemon juice to taste. Spoon the purée over the base of a serving dish and keep it warm.

Cut the sweetbreads into ½ in. thick slices and toss them in seasoned flour*. Brown them lightly in the remaining butter in a heavy-based pan over moderate heat. Add ¼ pint of the reserved liquid and continue cooking the sweetbreads until the liquid has reduced* to a syrupy coating consistency. Turn the sweetbreads over from time to time. If the liquid reduces too quickly before the sweetbreads are cooked, after about 25 minutes, add a little more stock. Lift the sweetbreads from the pan and arrange them on top of the purée.

Add the brandy to the pan juices, stirring well, before blending in the cream. Cook the sauce over low heat for a few minutes until thick and creamy.

Pour the sauce over the sweetbreads or serve it in a sauce boat. Boiled and buttered rice goes well with this meal.

PORK WITH PISTACHIO NUTS

A loin of pork is particularly suitable as a main dish for a cold buffet. Leave it to season for two or three days in saltpetre, which gives a pink glow to cold pork. If saltpetre is unobtainable, green uncooked bacon rashers placed down the middle of the joint can be used to impart a similar flavour and colour.

PREPARATION TIME: *20 min.*
COOKING TIME: *2½ hours*

INGREDIENTS *(for 8–10)*:
4–5 lb. loin of pork
¼ teaspoon saltpetre
1 rounded tablespoon salt
1 level tablespoon brown sugar
1 oz. pistachio nuts
Black pepper
¼ pint dry white wine

Buy the pork two or three days before it is wanted and ask the butcher to bone and skin the joint, and to include the bones and the skin with the order. Mix together the saltpetre, salt and

brown sugar; rub it into the pork, particularly on the boned side. Place the pork, boned side down, in a deep dish and leave in a refrigerator for two days.

Before cooking, pat the meat dry with a clean cloth. Make small incisions with a sharp knife in the fat and press in the shelled pistachio nuts. Sprinkle the meat with plenty of freshly ground black pepper; roll it neatly and tie securely with string.

For the cooking, use a deep, ovenproof pot into which the meat fits snugly with the bones and skin tucked round the sides. Pour the wine and ¾ pint of water over it. Add a little more water if the meat does not fit tightly into the dish. Cook, uncovered, in an oven pre-heated to 350°F (mark 4) for 30 minutes until the fat has coloured. Then cover with a double layer of foil; reduce the temperature to 300°F (mark 2) and continue cooking in the oven for a further 2 hours.

When the pork is cooked, remove the bones and skin and leave the meat to cool in the juice, which will set to a jelly. Remove the jelly when set and chop it up finely. Scrape the fat from the top of the meat and put into a serving jar. Carve the cold pork into ¼ in. thick slices and arrange them on a dish garnished with the chopped jelly.

Serve with wholemeal bread and the jar of pork fat. The pistachio nuts give the pork a distinctive flavour and an attractive appearance – green and purple against the pink and white of the pork. A green salad, tossed in a French dressing*, would go well with the cold pork.

LAMB ARGENTEUIL

In its classic form, this recipe uses asparagus from the district of Argenteuil in France. Tender English asparagus gives an equally delicate flavour.

PREPARATION TIME: *30 min.*
COOKING TIME: *1 hour*

INGREDIENTS (*for 6*):
2 lb. asparagus
2 lb. boned shoulder of lamb
4 small onions
2 oz. butter
1 heaped tablespoon seasoned flour
¼ pint double cream
Salt and black pepper
Lemon juice

Wash and scrape the asparagus*, but do not trim; tie in three or four bundles with soft tape and cook in a large pan of lightly salted water. When the asparagus is tender, after 15–20 minutes, drain well and set the cooking liquid aside. Cut off the asparagus tips about 3 in. down the stems. Put the tips aside and first liquidise, then sieve the stems to make a purée*, discarding any tough or stringy parts.

Trim as much fat as possible off the lamb and cut the meat into 2 in. pieces. Toss them in the seasoned flour* to coat evenly. Peel and roughly chop the onions. Melt the butter in a deep frying or sauté pan, and cook the meat and onions until brown. Gradually blend in about ½ pint of the asparagus liquid, stirring continuously until the sauce is smooth and creamy. Simmer until the meat is tender (about 50 minutes), stirring occasionally and removing any fat which rises to the surface of the sauce. If the liquid evaporates too quickly, cover the pan with a lid.

When the meat is cooked, stir the asparagus purée and cream into the sauce. Season to taste with salt, freshly ground pepper and lemon juice. The sauce should be fairly thick.

Arrange the asparagus tips round the edge of a warm serving dish and spoon the meat and sauce into the centre. Boiled new potatoes are all that is needed with the meat.

GRATIN OF HAM

The Morvan district of Burgundy is famous for its cured hams. These are often served with a cream sauce, as in the following recipe. York ham is more readily available in Britain and makes a delicious substitute.

PREPARATION TIME: *15 min.*
COOKING TIME: *45 min.*

INGREDIENTS (*for 6*):
12 slices quality cooked ham
   (approx. 1½ lb.)
¼ lb. button mushrooms
1 oz. butter
1 onion
3 shallots
4 fluid oz. dry white wine
8–10 oz. tinned tomatoes
½ pint double cream
Salt and black pepper
1 oz. grated Parmesan cheese

Arrange the slices of ham, overlapping each other, in a large, shallow flameproof dish.

Trim the mushrooms* and slice them thinly. Melt the butter in a small frying pan and cook the mushrooms for about 8 minutes over low heat. Spoon them, with the butter, over the ham. Peel and finely chop the onion and shallots and put them in a small pan with the wine. Bring to the boil and continue boiling over high heat until the wine has reduced* to about 1½ tablespoons. Chop the tomatoes roughly and add to the onions. Cover the pan with a lid and simmer over low heat for 10 minutes. Rub the onion and tomato mixture through a fine sieve, and put the resulting purée* in a clean pan.

Blend the cream into the purée and bring this sauce to the boil. Season to taste with salt and

freshly ground pepper. Pour the sauce over the ham and mushrooms and sprinkle the cheese on top. Bake the ham gratin near the top of the oven, pre-heated to 450°F (mark 8) for 10 minutes or until bubbling and brown on top.

Serve the gratin while still bubbling, with boiled and buttered rice and a green salad.

BEEF PAUPIETTES

Paupiettes are thin slices of meat, usually beef, which are stuffed with forcemeat and rolled into cork shapes which the French call *alouettes sans têtes* (larks without heads). The meat should be cut very thinly: ask the butcher to cut it on the bacon slicer.

PREPARATION TIME: *45 min.*
COOKING TIME: *1½ hours*

INGREDIENTS (*for 4*):
1½ lb. topside of beef, cut in
   thin slices
2 rounded teaspoons French
   mustard
Salt and black pepper
STUFFING:
3 oz. green lean bacon
4 oz. cooked chicken or pork
1 shallot
1 large clove garlic
1½ oz. butter
2 oz. fine white breadcrumbs
1 egg
1 level tablespoon chopped parsley
½ level teaspoon chopped thyme
2½ fluid oz. brandy
SAUCE:
1 lb. mixed vegetables (onions,
   carrots, turnips, peas, green
   beans, parsnips)
1½ oz. beef dripping or lard
½ pint beef stock
¼ pint red wine
Beurre manié (1 oz. flour, 1 oz.
   butter)

Beat the beef slices wafer-thin between two pieces of waxed paper; each slice should measure about 4 sq. in. Spread a little mustard over each slice; season with salt and ground pepper.

Remove the rind and chop the bacon finely, together with the chicken or pork. Peel and finely chop the shallot and garlic. Melt the butter in a small frying pan over moderate heat and cook the shallot and garlic until soft and transparent.

In a mixing bowl, blend together the bacon, chicken, shallot and garlic. Add the breadcrumbs and the lightly beaten egg. Stir in the thyme and parsley, and season the stuffing with salt and pepper; add the brandy.

Spoon the stuffing equally on the beef slices; roll up each slice and tuck the ends over to keep the stuffing in place. Tie each paupiette securely with fine string. Set the meat aside.

To make the sauce, peel and finely chop the onion, then brown it lightly over moderate heat in the lard or dripping. Wash and prepare the vegetables used, then chop them finely. Add these to the onion and cook for a few minutes to brown slightly. Spoon the vegetables into a large shallow casserole and put the paupiettes on top in a single layer. Pour the stock and wine into the pan in which the vegetables were fried, scraping up all the residue.

Pour the pan juices over the meat, cover the casserole with a lid and cook in the centre of the oven, pre-heated to 325°F (mark 3) for 1½ hours. Remove the lid after 20 minutes. Turn the meat once during cooking.

Lift the paupiettes from the casserole, remove the string and arrange the meat on a warm serving dish. Surround them with the vegetables. Pour the cooking liquid into a small saucepan and boil rapidly to reduce* the sauce by a third. Thicken the sauce with beurre manié*, and heat it through. Spoon a little of the sauce over the meat and serve the rest in a sauce boat.

Serve with buttered noodles or creamed potatoes.

PORK NOISETTES WITH PRUNES

This is a speciality from Tours in the Loire district where some of the finest French pork and wine are produced. It is an easily prepared dish, but the prunes – large Californian ones – should be soaked overnight.

PREPARATION TIME: *15 min.*
COOKING TIME: *1 hour*

INGREDIENTS *(for 6)*:
6 slices pork fillet, each 1 in. thick, or 6 boned loin chops
1 lb. large prunes
½ bottle dry white wine
Seasoned flour
2 oz. unsalted butter
1 heaped tablespoon red currant jelly
¾ pint double cream
Salt and black pepper
Lemon juice

Leave the prunes in a bowl to soak in the wine overnight. Put the prunes and the wine in a pan and simmer, covered, for 20–30 minutes or until tender.

Trim any excess fat off the pork fillets or chops. Coat them with seasoned flour*, shaking off any surplus. Melt the butter in a heavy-based pan and brown the meat lightly over gentle heat,

turning it once only. Cover the pan with a lid and simmer the pork for 30 minutes.

When the meat is nearly done, pour the prune liquid into the pan. Increase the heat and boil rapidly for a few minutes until the liquid has reduced* slightly. Lift the meat on to a warm serving dish and arrange the prunes round it. Keep the meat and prunes warm in the oven while making the sauce.

Stir the redcurrant jelly into the juices in the pan, and boil this sauce over high heat until it has the consistency of syrup. Gradually blend in the cream, stirring continuously until the sauce is smooth and thick. Season with salt, pepper and lemon juice.

Pour the sauce over the meat and serve at once. Traditionally, the noisettes are served with boiled potatoes only.

TRIPE FRITTERS

Tripe is always sold blanched and par-boiled, but make sure to ask the butcher how much longer it should be cooked. The additional cooking time can vary from 30 minutes to 2 hours.

PREPARATION TIME: *20 min.*
COOKING TIME: *1–2½ hours*

INGREDIENTS *(for 6)*:
2 lb. tripe
Bouquet garni
2 onions
2 carrots
2 leeks
1 stick celery
12 black peppercorns
1–2 level teaspoons salt
½ pint fritter batter
Oil for deep frying
GARNISH:
6 lemon wedges

Put the tripe in a large pan, cover with water and add the bouquet garni*. Cover the pan with a lid and bring the tripe slowly to the boil. Meanwhile, peel and thinly slice the onions and carrots, wash the leeks and the celery thoroughly and cut them into thin slices. Add the vegetables, peppercorns and 1 teaspoon of salt to the pan; reduce the heat and simmer the tripe until tender.

While the tripe is cooking, make up the fritter batter*. Leave it to rest for 1 hour, adding the egg white just before coating the fritters.

Drain the cooked tripe thoroughly in a colander; the stock can be used as base for a soup or casserole. Leave the tripe to cool slightly, then cut it into strips about 1 in. by 1½ in. Fold the beaten egg white into the fritter batter and coat the tripe strips thoroughly, a few at a time. Heat the oil* in the deep-fryer and fry the fritters until golden brown and crisp. As the fritters are ready, lift them out with a perforated spoon on to a baking tray covered with crumpled absorbent paper. Keep the fritters warm in the oven while frying the next batches.

Serve the crisp fritters garnished with lemon wedges. A tossed green salad or tomatoes and onions in a French dressing* would be suitable side dishes.

BRAINS IN CURRY SAUCE

Brains, like any other offal, require careful cleaning, and soaking for at least 1 hour. But they are so tasty, nourishing and inexpensive that they are worth a little trouble.

PREPARATION TIME: *15 min.*
COOKING TIME: *30–35 min.*

INGREDIENTS *(for 4–6)*:
2 lb. calf brains
1 pint milk
1 onion
1 clove garlic
2 oz. butter
1 heaped tablespoon plain flour
1 rounded teaspoon curry powder
½ pint chicken stock
½–¾ lb. white or black grapes
¼ pint double cream (optional)
Salt and black pepper

Cover the brains with cold water, add 2 level tablespoons of salt and leave to soak for 1 hour. Rinse them thoroughly under cold running water and remove the fine skin that covers the brains. Cut away any fibres and discoloured parts and remove any bone splinters. Put the brains in

a pan with enough milk to cover. Bring to the boil and simmer for 10 minutes or until the brains are firm. Drain and set the milk aside. Cut the brains into ½ in. thick slices and arrange them on a serving dish; cover with foil and keep warm.

Peel and finely chop the onion and garlic. Melt the butter in a saucepan and cook the onion and garlic over gentle heat for 5 minutes. Stir in the flour and curry powder, mixing well. Gradually add the chicken stock and ¼ pint of the milk in which the brains were cooked; blend thoroughly. Simmer this sauce until it has reduced* to the consistency of thick cream.

While the sauce is cooking, peel the grapes* and remove the pips. Add the grapes to the sauce and simmer for a further 5 minutes. Stir in the cream and season to taste with salt and freshly ground pepper.

Pour the sauce over the brains and serve with plain boiled rice and with triangles of toast.

Poultry & Game

CHICKEN LIVERS WITH GRAPES

Chicken livers are readily available, either fresh or frozen, and usually at bargain prices. They make a good lunch or supper dish, served in a wine sauce delicately flavoured with grapes.

PREPARATION TIME: *25 min.*
COOKING TIME: *10–12 min.*

INGREDIENTS *(for 6)*:
1½ lb. chicken livers
Salt and black pepper
¾ lb. large green grapes
6 slices white bread
6 oz. butter
2 tablespoons cooking oil
3–4 fluid oz. Madeira, port or sweet sherry

Rinse the chicken livers in cold water and pat them dry. Cut away the white, stringy pieces and any discoloured parts which may have been in contact with the gall bladder – they add a bitter flavour if left in. Season the livers with salt and freshly ground pepper and set aside.

Peel and pip the grapes*. Remove the crusts from the bread slices. Melt 4 oz. of the butter in a pan, together with the oil; when hot, fry the bread golden brown on both sides. Stand the fried bread upright on a baking tray and keep warm in the oven.

Melt the remaining butter and cook the livers for 3–5 minutes on each side; they should be slightly pink in the centre. Remove from the pan and keep warm. Stir the wine into the pan juices and reduce* by rapid boiling until the sauce has thickened to a syrupy consistency. Add the grapes to the sauce and let them heat through.

To serve, arrange the hot bread on a serving dish, top with chicken livers and spoon the grapes on top. Serve immediately, before the sauce soaks into the fried bread.

CHICKEN BREASTS WITH SAGE

In Italy, where this dish originated, chicken breasts (*petto di pollo*) are usually cooked with a strong flavouring of herbs.

PREPARATION TIME: *10 min.*
COOKING TIME: *45 min.*

INGREDIENTS *(for 6)*:
3 chicken breast portions
Seasoned flour
1 tablespoon olive oil
1 tablespoon butter
2 oz. thin gammon rashers
¼ pint dry white wine
¼ pint chicken stock
12 sage leaves
Salt and black pepper

Remove the skin from the chicken portions and cut off the wings and bones. Fillet the breast off the bones and cut each portion into halves, lengthways. Coat the chicken with seasoned flour*. Heat the oil and butter in a sauté pan over moderate heat and lightly brown the chicken.

Cut the gammon into narrow strips and add to the chicken. When the chicken is golden brown, pour in the wine and enough stock to come about two-thirds up the chicken breasts. Add the roughly chopped sage.

Cover the pan with a lid and simmer the chicken over moderate heat for 15–20 minutes. Remove to a serving dish and keep it warm. Increase the heat and rapidly boil the liquid until it has reduced* to a thin coating consistency. Season to taste with salt and pepper.

Pour the sauce over the chicken fillets and serve at once with fresh white bread.

PEKING DUCK

Several local variations are combined in this version of the classic Chinese recipe. It did not, in fact, originate in Peking, but in Inner Mongolia, and became famous in Peking restaurants only in the last century. Serving and eating Peking duck is a matter for some ceremony; the crackling skin is sliced off and served with sliced duck meat, to be wrapped in pancakes, with spring onions and a spicy sauce.

PREPARATION TIME: *2 hours*
COOKING TIME: *1½ hours*

INGREDIENTS *(for 4–6)*:
1 large duck (approx. 5–6 lbs.)
2 tablespoons brandy, vodka or gin (optional)
18 spring onions
PANCAKES:
1 lb. plain flour
2 tablespoons sesame seed oil
TABLE SAUCE:
4 rounded tablespoons Hoisin (or plum) sauce
1 level dessertspoon sugar
1 dessertspoon sesame seed oil
BASTING SAUCE:
3 tablespoons soy sauce
1 heaped tablespoon caster sugar

The essence of Peking duck is its crisp skin which is stripped off the cooked duck and served separately. To obtain this, the skin of the uncooked duck should be thoroughly dried. Wipe and dry the duck and pass a length of string under the wings so that it can be suspended from a rod or broom handle, placed across the seats of two chairs. Set a plate under the duck to catch any drips. Rubbing the skin with alcohol aids the drying process. Direct a blast of cold air on to the duck

from an electric fan or fan heater and leave it for at least 3–4 hours. Alternatively, hang the duck overnight in a draughty place.

Remove any bits of roots and blemished leaves from the onions – trimming them to a length of 3–4 in. Wash them thoroughly. Use a sharp knife to make two cuts, ½–¾ in. long, at the bulb end of each spring onion, then make two similar cuts at right angles to the first cuts. Put the onions in a large bowl of iced water and leave in the refrigerator until required. The cut end will fan out to resemble a brush.

To make the pancakes, sift the flour into a bowl and, mixing all the time, add about 1 pint of boiling water, to make a soft dough that leaves the sides of the bowl clean. The amount of water needed depends on the type of flour. Knead the dough for 10 minutes on a lightly floured surface, until it becomes rubbery. Cover with a cloth and leave for 20 minutes. Roll the dough out, ¼ in. thick, and cut it into rounds with a plain 2 in. scone cutter. Brush the top of half the rounds with sesame seed oil and place an unbrushed round on top. Roll out each pair of pancakes (about 14) as thinly as possible, to a diameter of about 6 in.

Heat an ungreased griddle or heavy frying pan for 30 seconds, then lower the heat. Put in the first pancake, turning it when bubbles appear on the surface and the underside is flecked with brown and looks floury. Cook all the pancakes in this way (they may puff up into balloons), and allow them to cool. Wrap the cooked pancakes in several foil parcels and store them in the refrigerator until needed.

Rice & Pasta

Mix the table sauce ingredients together in a small pan, add 1 tablespoon of cold water and bring the sauce to the boil; stir over low heat for 2–3 minutes. Pour the sauce into a serving bowl and leave to cool.

Mix the ingredients for the basting sauce with $\frac{1}{4}$ pint of cold water, and brush the sauce all over the duck. Place the duck, breast upwards, on an open grid or wire rack in a roasting pan. Pour in enough boiling water to reach $\frac{1}{4}$ in. up the sides of the pan. Roast the duck in the lower part of a pre-heated oven at 400°F (mark 6) for $1\frac{1}{4}$ hours. Brush with the basting sauce every 15 or 20 minutes. After 45 minutes turn up the heat to 450°F (mark 8). Put the parcels of prepared pancakes into the oven to re-heat for the last 20 minutes.

To assemble the final dish, cut off the duck skin with scissors or a sharp knife, in 1–2 in. squares; place on a serving dish and keep warm. Carve the meat into long thin slivers and arrange on another dish to keep warm. Pile the pancakes on a hot dish and cover with a napkin or folded cloth to keep them warm. Put the onion brushes in a bowl or dish and arrange all these dishes, with the table sauce, in the centre of the table.

To eat the dish, carefully pull the two halves of a pancake apart, starting where the join can be seen quite clearly. Dip an onion brush in the sauce and brush it liberally on to the soft moist side of the open pancake. Top with pieces of duck skin and slivers of meat; fold and roll up the pancake.

The Chinese use chopsticks to eat the pancakes, but fingers and a fork are just as effective. Finger-bowls with tepid, lemon-scented water are useful.

PASTA WITH ANCHOVY SAUCE

Anchovies are netted daily off the coasts of Italy and are part of the national diet. From Calabria, in southern Italy, comes this recipe for thick pasta – spaghetti or noodles – in anchovy sauce. The sauce is also popular for flavouring rice and vegetable salads.

PREPARATION TIME: *5 min.*
COOKING TIME: *15 min.*

INGREDIENTS (*for 6*):
$1\frac{1}{4}$ lb. noodles
Small tin of anchovy fillets
$\frac{1}{2}$ pint olive oil
5 oz. fresh white breadcrumbs
Chilli powder

Bring a large pan of lightly salted water to the boil. Cook the noodles for about 12 minutes, or until *al dente**.

While the noodles are cooking, drain the anchovies, chop and mash them finely with a fork. Cook the anchovies in a small pan, with half the olive oil, over moderate heat until they have dissolved into a smooth paste. Heat the remaining oil in a separate pan and fry the breadcrumbs until brown. Season the breadcrumbs with chilli powder to taste.

Drain the cooked noodles thoroughly in a colander. Put them in a hot serving dish and mix in the anchovy paste. Serve the seasoned breadcrumbs in a separate bowl.

RICE SALAD WITH FLORENCE FENNEL

The sweet aniseed flavour of bulbous Florence fennel blends well with rice and pernod-flavoured mayonnaise. The salad is usually served with cold meat or fish.

PREPARATION TIME: *30 min.*
COOKING TIME: *20 min.*
CHILLING TIME: *30 min.*

INGREDIENTS (*for 4–6*):
6 oz. long grain rice
2 Florence fennel roots
7–8 oz. tin of tuna fish
4 oz. stoned black olives
$\frac{1}{4}$ pint mayonnaise
1 tablespoon Pernod
GARNISH:
3 hardboiled eggs
6 spring onions

Bring a large pan of lightly salted water to the boil and cook the rice for 20 minutes. Rinse and drain the rice thoroughly in a sieve and set it aside to cool.

Trim the fennel*, wash the roots in cold running water, then cut them into thin slices. Drain the oil from the tuna fish and break the flesh up with a fork. Mix the rice, fennel, tuna and olives together in a salad bowl. Stir the Pernod into the mayonnaise* and fold this dressing into the salad.

Trim the spring onions and cut them in half lengthways. Shell and quarter the eggs. Garnish the salad with the onions and eggs and leave it to chill in the refrigerator for 30 minutes.

SPAGHETTI ALL'UOVA

Known as poor man's spaghetti, this pasta dish has no meat sauce, but is served just with eggs and Pecorino cheese. This cheese, made from sheep's milk, is a speciality from the Sabine district.

PREPARATION TIME: *10 min.*
COOKING TIME: *10–15 min.*

INGREDIENTS (*for 6*):
$1\frac{1}{4}$ lb. spaghetti
Salt
2–3 oz. Pecorino or Parmesan cheese
6 eggs
8 oz. butter

Bring a large pan of lightly salted water to the boil, add the spaghetti and cook, uncovered, for 10–12 minutes or until *al dente**.

Meanwhile, grate the cheese into a serving bowl. Break the eggs into a large basin and beat them lightly. Put half the butter on a serving dish, and cut the remainder into knobs.

Drain the cooked spaghetti through a colander and put it into a large hot serving bowl. Stir in the eggs quickly, tossing the spaghetti and eggs thoroughly with two spoons until the eggs have set.

Dot the spaghetti and egg mixture with the knobs of butter and serve at once.

Vegetables & Salads

RICE CAKES

In central and northern Italy, these small sweet cakes are often fried and sold piping hot on street corners. This recipe is for a slightly more elaborate version which could be served as a snack or as a sweet.

PREPARATION TIME: *10 min.*
COOKING TIME: *30 min.*

INGREDIENTS *(for 6)*:
5 oz. Italian or long grain rice
½ pint milk
Salt
4 oz. caster sugar
1½ oz. butter
1 lemon
2½ oz. plain flour
3 eggs
1 liqueur glass rum
Cooking oil
2 heaped teaspoons powdered
  cinnamon

Bring a large pan of water to the boil, add the rice and boil steadily for 7 minutes. Drain the rice through a sieve, rinse under cold running water and return to the pan with the milk. Cook over moderate heat for about 10 minutes, or until the milk is almost completely absorbed.

Remove the pan from the heat and stir in a good pinch of salt, a dessertspoon of sugar and the butter. Grate the rind from the lemon into the rice and then cut the lemon into wedges. Allow the rice to cool until tepid; stir in the flour. Separate the eggs and beat the yolks into the rice together with the rum.

Whip the egg whites until stiff and dry, then fold them carefully into the rice mixture. Heat sufficient oil to half-fill the basket in the deep fryer; when hot, drop dessertspoons of rice mixture into the oil, a few at a time. Cook until the rice cakes are delicately golden brown, then remove and drain on crumpled absorbent paper. Do not overcook, as this hardens the outer layer of rice.

Serve the rice cakes with the wedges of lemon and a bowl of sugar mixed with the cinnamon.

ASPARAGUS WITH NEW POTATOES

English asparagus appears in the shops this month, at a fairly high price. Imported asparagus, although not of the same quality, is cheaper. This recipe, for a light lunch or supper, also includes a soup so as to make maximum use of the asparagus.

PREPARATION TIME: *45 min.*
COOKING TIME: *30 min.*

INGREDIENTS *(for 6)*:
2 lb. asparagus
2 lb. new potatoes
½ level teaspoon salt
6 thin slices Parma or finely
  cured ham
8 oz. unsalted butter
Lemon juice
GARNISH:
1 rounded tablespoon fresh
  chopped parsley

Wash the asparagus* carefully and lightly scrape the spears, away from the tips. Cut off the lower 2 or 3 in. of each spear where the wood begins and set these pieces aside. Tie the asparagus in bundles with soft tape.

Wash and scrape the potatoes, put them in a large saucepan with the reserved pieces of asparagus. Cover with plenty of cold water, then add the salt and bring the water to the boil. Stand the bundles of asparagus upright in the pan and cover with lid (if the pan is not deep enough, cover with foil). Cook over moderate heat for about 15 minutes or until the asparagus tips are tender to the touch.

Remove the asparagus bundles from the pan, but leave the potatoes to cook until tender. Untie the asparagus and divide into six equal portions. Wrap a slice of ham round each portion and arrange them round the edge of a serving dish.

Lift the cooked potatoes from the pan and drain them (setting aside the liquid and asparagus pieces for the soup). Put the potatoes in the centre of the serving dish. Melt the butter over low heat, pour a little over the potatoes and serve the remainder, seasoned with a little lemon juice, in a sauce boat.

Sprinkle the parsley over the potatoes and serve the dish warm rather than hot.

ASPARAGUS SOUP

Use the asparagus water and stem sections from the previous recipe, together with:

1 large onion
1 small clove garlic
2 oz. butter
1 heaped tablespoon plain flour
Milk
Salt and black pepper
¼ pint single or double cream
GARNISH:
Chopped chervil or parsley

Peel and finely chop the onion and garlic. Melt the butter in a large saucepan and cook the onion and garlic in this until soft and transparent. Stir in the flour and cook for a few minutes, before gradually blending in the asparagus water. Add the stem sections and cook the soup for 10 minutes.

Take the pan off the heat, leave the soup to cool slightly, then put it first through the blender and then through a sieve to make a purée*. Add milk to the desired soup consistency and season to taste with salt and freshly ground pepper. Re-heat the soup and blend in the cream, without letting it boil.

Serve the soup in individual bowls and sprinkle the chopped chervil or parsley on top.

PISSALADIÈRE

This strongly flavoured tart is a speciality of the region round Nice. It is somewhat similar to the Italian pizza, but the pastry base is of lighter texture. It makes a substantial lunch or supper dish on its own.

PREPARATION TIME: *20 min.*
COOKING TIME: *1¼ hours*

INGREDIENTS *(for 6–8)*:
6 oz. plain flour
1 level teaspoon cinnamon
3 oz. unsalted butter
1 egg
2 lb. onions
3 cloves garlic
6 tablespoons olive oil
15–16 oz. tin of tomatoes
1 level tablespoon tomato paste
2 lumps sugar
Bouquet garni
Salt and black pepper
4 oz. black olives
2 small tins anchovy fillets

Sift together the flour and cinnamon into a mixing bowl; cut up the butter and rub it into the flour until the mixture resembles breadcrumbs. Add the lightly beaten egg and enough cold water to make the pastry come cleanly away from the sides of the bowl.

Knead the pastry lightly on a floured board and then roll out, ¼ in. thick. Line a 10–11 in. wide flan or tart tin with the pastry; prick the base lightly with the prongs of a fork. Bake the tart blind* in the centre of an oven pre-heated to 400°F (mark 6) for about 15 minutes or until set, but not brown.

Peel the onions and slice them thinly; peel and finely chop the garlic. Heat the oil in a large, heavy-based pan and cook the onions and garlic over low heat until soft and transparent (after about 40 minutes).

Chop the tomatoes roughly and put them in a clean pan with the tomato paste, sugar and bouquet garni*; boil rapidly to reduce* the mixture to about six tablespoons. Remove the bouquet garni and stir the tomatoes into the cooked onions. Season to taste with pepper and a little salt, bearing in mind the saltiness of the anchovies and olives. Spoon the onion and tomato mixture into the tart case and arrange the anchovy fillets in a criss-cross pattern on top; decorate with the olives. Bake the tart in the centre of an oven, pre-heated to 400°F (mark 6) for 20 minutes; brush the top with a little olive oil after 10 minutes.

Pissaladière is best served hot as soon as baked.

JEWISH EGGS AND PEAS

Fresh or even frozen green peas are excellent for this adaptation of an 18th-century German recipe. It can be served as a first course or as a supper dish on its own.

PREPARATION TIME: *20 min.*
COOKING TIME: *15–20 min.*

INGREDIENTS *(for 6)*:
2½ lb. peas
5 tablespoons olive oil
¼ level teaspoon nutmeg
¼ level teaspoon mace
Cayenne pepper
Salt and black pepper
Caster sugar
7 eggs
3–4 fluid oz. single cream

This dish should be cooked in a shallow, flameproof casserole which can be brought straight to the table. Shell the peas (they should now measure 1½ pints) and put them in the casserole with 2 fluid oz. of water, the oil, spices, a few twists of freshly ground pepper and about ¼ teaspoon salt. Cover the pan with a lid and simmer until the peas are half cooked, after about 8 minutes. Correct seasoning if necessary.

Remove the casserole from the heat and make six depressions in the peas with a large spoon. Break the eggs, one at a time, into a saucer and slip an egg into each depression. Return the casserole to the heat, cover with a lid and cook for a further 8–10 minutes, or until the whites have set.

Beat the remaining egg with the cream. Pour this mixture over the cooked eggs and place the dish under a hot grill for 2–3 minutes to set. Serve with crusty bread and butter.

NAPOLEON'S BEAN SALAD

In exile on St Helena, Napoleon was still emperor at his own table. This salad of haricot beans is said to have been a favourite of his and was served every day at lunchtime. The beans should be soaked for at least 8 hours before cooking.

PREPARATION TIME: *10 min.*
COOKING TIME: *2–3 hours*
CHILLING TIME: *1 hour*

INGREDIENTS *(for 6)*:
½ lb. dried haricot beans
1 onion
1 carrot
Bouquet garni
Salt and black pepper
½ cup of finely chopped parsley, chervil, tarragon, chives or spring onions
5 tablespoons olive oil
1 tablespoon tarragon vinegar
1 rounded teaspoon prepared French mustard
½ level teaspoon caster sugar

Soak the beans in a bowl of water for 8 hours or overnight. Drain the beans and put them in a large pan or casserole. Peel and quarter the onion and carrot, and add them, with the bouquet garni* and plenty of black pepper, to the beans. Pour over sufficient water to cover the beans by ½ in. Put a lid on the pan and cook in the centre of a pre-heated oven, at 275°–300°F (mark 1–2) for 3 hours, or on top of the stove at simmering point, for 2 hours. If necessary, top up with water during cooking so that the beans do not dry out.

Season the cooked beans to taste with salt and cook for another 5 minutes. Drain the beans through a colander, remove the onion, carrot and bouquet garni, and put the beans in a large serving bowl. Add the chopped herbs, oil, vinegar, mustard and sugar to the beans. Stir to blend the ingredients thoroughly and leave to chill in the refrigerator for about 1 hour.

LIMOGES POTATO PIE

In spring the country round Limoges in France can be as wet and cold as in England. Consequently, the regional food tends to be warm and filling. This potato pie can be served as a supper dish on its own or as a first course.

PREPARATION TIME: *35 min.*
COOKING TIME: *35 min.*

INGREDIENTS *(for 6)*:
1 lb. prepared puff pastry
1½ lb. new potatoes
3 oz. onion
3–4 cloves garlic
Salt and black pepper
Nutmeg
2 oz. butter
3 fluid oz. single cream
3 fluid oz. double cream
1 egg
Bunch of fresh parsley, chives and chervil

Roll out half the puff pastry* on a lightly floured board and use to line a 10 in. flan ring or shallow cake tin. Wash and scrape the potatoes. Slice them thinly, using a mandoline* or the cucumber blade on a grater, into a bowl of cold water to prevent them turning brown.

Bring a pan of lightly salted water to the boil, put in the sliced potatoes and cook for 2 minutes only, after the water has returned to the boil. Drain the potatoes thoroughly through a colander. Peel and finely chop the onion and garlic.

Put a layer of potato slices on top of the pastry base, sprinkle with the onion and garlic and season with a little salt, nutmeg and freshly ground pepper. Repeat these layers, seasoning each, until all the vegetables are used up, finishing with a layer of potato. Dot the vegetables with the butter, cut into small knobs. Mix the creams together and pour about half over the potatoes.

Roll out the remaining pastry and cover the pie, sealing the edges firmly. Make a small hole in the centre of the pastry lid for the steam to escape. Beat the egg into the remaining cream and brush a little of this mixture over the pastry to glaze it while cooking. Score the pastry lightly into sections with a sharp knife – this makes it easier to cut the finished pie into portions.

Bake the pie near the top of a pre-heated oven at 450°F (mark 8) for 30 minutes. Protect the pastry with a piece of buttered paper if the pastry browns too quickly.

Chop the fresh herbs finely and blend them into the remaining egg and cream mixture. When the pie is cooked, pour the cream and egg mixture into the centre hole using a small kitchen funnel. Do this slowly in case there is not room for all the cream. Return the pie to the oven for 5 minutes, then serve at once.

Sweets & Puddings

SAVOURY CUCUMBER

Cucumber is most often used raw in salads or for garnishing, and rarely appears as a cooked main course. In this French recipe, stuffed cucumbers are served hot as a savoury snack.

PREPARATION TIME: *10 min.*
COOKING TIME: *50 min.*

INGREDIENTS *(for 6)*:
3 cucumbers
6 oz. long grain rice
1 large onion
4½ oz. butter
8 oz. mushrooms
4 rashers lean smoked bacon
Salt and black pepper
3 eggs
GARNISH:
Chopped parsley

Wash, but do not peel, the cucumbers. Cut each in half crossways, then cut each half in two lengthways. Scrape out the seeds with the point of a teaspoon and discard. Cook the cucumbers for 10 minutes in boiling, lightly salted water; drain through a colander and keep warm.

Cook the rice in a large pan of boiling salted water for 25–30 minutes. While the rice is cooking, peel and chop the onion, and cook over gentle heat in 2 oz. of the butter until translucent, but not brown.

Trim and thinly slice the mushrooms*; add to the onions. Remove the rind and cut the bacon into narrow strips; add to the mixture in the pan and season with salt and freshly ground pepper. When the rice is cooked, drain in a sieve and rinse under cold running water. Stir it into the onion mixture, adding 2 oz. of butter. Cook over low heat, stirring occasionally, for 5–10 minutes.

Lightly beat the eggs and season with salt and pepper. Cook two or three small omelettes* in the remaining butter. Roll the omelettes up and cut them into strips about ½ in. wide. Add these to the rice mixture.

To serve, arrange the cucumber 'boats' on a hot dish and spoon the rice mixture over them. Sprinkle with chopped parsley.

SCHWARZWALD KIRSCHTORTE

This is a rich chocolate cake with a filling of whole black cherry jam. It is a speciality from the Bavarian area of southern Germany, famous for its cakes.

PREPARATION TIME: *40 min.*
COOKING TIME: *20–30 min.*

INGREDIENTS *(for 6–8)*:
7 oz. plain chocolate
2 tablespoons milk
7 oz. unsalted butter
7 oz. caster sugar
Salt
4 rounded tablespoons plain flour
3 large or 4 small eggs
2–3 tablespoons Kirsch
8 fluid oz. double cream
2 level tablespoons vanilla sugar
8 oz. black cherry jam
GARNISH:
1 dessertspoon icing sugar

The cake is best made 4 or 5 days in advance and stored in an airtight tin or wrapped in foil. It should not, however, be assembled until just before serving.

Butter three 9½ in. or four 7–8 in. sandwich tins, preferably with loose bottoms (if these are not available, line the tins with buttered greaseproof paper).

Put the chocolate and milk in a bowl and stand it over a pan of simmering water. Stir thoroughly until the chocolate has melted and the mixture is liquid. Remove the bowl from the heat and beat in first the butter, cut into knobs, and then the caster sugar and a pinch of salt. Beat for 3 or 4 minutes by hand or with an electric beater. Separate the eggs. Fold in the flour and add the egg yolks, one at a time. Whip the egg whites until stiff and fold them into the cake mixture. Divide the mixture equally between the sandwich tins.

Bake the cakes in the centre of the oven pre-heated to 400°F (mark 6) for 20–30 minutes or until firm to the touch. The cakes will not have risen much – the outside will be crisp and the centre moist and slightly sticky. Turn the cakes out and leave to cool on a wire rack. Store when completely cold.

Assemble the cake just before serving. Sprinkle each chocolate layer with Kirsch; whip the cream until thick, flavour with the vanilla sugar* and spread over all but one of the chocolate layers. Spread the jam equally over the creamed layers, sandwich the cake together, topping with the last chocolate cake layer.

Sprinkle the top of the cake with sifted icing sugar and serve.

GÂTEAU DE PITHIVIERS FEUILLETÉ

This puff pastry cake is a speciality of Pithiviers, a small town just south of Paris. The recipe and the petal pattern were invented by the chef Antonin Carême, in the 19th century.

PREPARATION TIME: *20 min.*
COOKING TIME: *50 min.*

INGREDIENTS *(for 6)*:
1 lb. prepared puff pastry
4 oz. ground almonds
4 oz. caster sugar
1½ oz. unsalted melted butter
2 egg yolks
2 tablespoons double cream
2 tablespoons rum (optional)
1 egg for glazing
2 level dessertspoons icing sugar

Divide the prepared puff pastry* in half. Roll the pastry out, on a floured surface, and use one piece to line a 9½ in. wide buttered pie plate. Set the other pastry round aside.

Blend together the almonds, sugar and melted butter in a large bowl. Beat in the egg yolks, one at a time, then beat in the cream and lastly the rum, if used. Spoon this filling over the pastry, spreading it level, but leaving 1 in. clear round the edge. Brush the pastry rim with water and place the other pastry round over the filling. Press the edges firmly together with the fingers to seal.

Make 12 evenly spaced nicks, with a sharp knife, round the edge of the pastry. Push up the pastry at each nick, with both thumbs, so that the edge is scalloped into 12 curves or petals. Beat the egg lightly and brush it over the pastry to glaze it. Leave to stand for 5 minutes.

Make a ½ in. wide hole in the centre of the pastry top. Mark, with a knife, scallop lines inside the curved edge and trace curving lines from the centre hole to the curves to represent flower petals.

Bake the cake near the top of a pre-heated oven, at 450°F (mark 8) for 10–15 minutes or until the pastry is well risen. Lower the heat to 400°F (mark 6) and bake for a further 20–30 minutes when the top should be lightly browned.

Remove the cake from the oven and set aside; turn the oven heat up to 450°F (mark 8). Sift the icing sugar evenly over the cake and return it to the oven for a few minutes until the sugar has melted to a golden brown glaze.

Serve the gâteau lukewarm with a jug of single cream.

CHINESE PEARS

Despite its name this unusual and aromatic dessert is French in origin. It is sweet and rich, suitable for a dinner party. Williams or other squat dessert pears are excellent for this recipe.

PREPARATION TIME: *35 min.*
COOKING TIME: *35 min.*

INGREDIENTS *(for 6)*:
6 large ripe pears
3 oz. sultanas
3 oz. pine kernels
3 level dessertspoons honey
1 oz. unsalted butter
¼–⅓ pint dry white wine
3 dessertspoons ginger syrup
5 oz. redcurrant jelly

Peel the pears thinly and cut a small slice from the base of each, so that it will stand upright. Remove a ¾–1 in. lid from the top of each pear and scoop out the core and pips. Roughly chop the sultanas and pine kernels, mix with the honey and spoon the mixture into the pear cavities. Replace the lids.

Grease an ovenproof dish with the butter and stand the pears in the dish together with any remaining sultana mixture. Pour over the white wine and cover the dish with foil. Bake the pears in the centre of an oven pre-heated to 350–375°F (mark 4–5) for about 30 minutes or until tender – the time varies according to the type and ripeness of the pears.

When cooked, place the pears in individual serving bowls and keep them warm in the oven. Pour the cooking juices into a small saucepan and add the ginger syrup and redcurrant jelly. Boil over moderate heat until the jelly has dissolved. Pour this sauce over the pears and serve at once.

GOOSEBERRY FLAN

Towards the end of May the first gooseberries appear. This sweet is based on an English recipe from the 18th century when puréed, wine-flavoured fruits were popular.

PREPARATION TIME: *1 hour*
COOKING TIME: *15 min.*

INGREDIENTS *(for 6)*:
1½ lb. gooseberries
4 oz. plain flour
1 rounded tablespoon icing sugar
5½ oz. unsalted butter
1 large egg yolk
3 large eggs
Caster sugar
3 teaspoons orange-flower water or 2 tablespoons muscat-flavoured white wine

Sift together the flour and icing sugar into a large bowl. Cut up 2½ oz. of the butter and rub into the flour until the mixture resembles fine breadcrumbs. Add one egg yolk and sufficient water to bind the pastry.

Roll the pastry out, on a lightly floured surface, to ¼ in. thickness and use to line a buttered 8–9 in. wide, loose-bottomed flan tin. Prick the pastry with a fork and bake it blind* in the centre of a pre-heated oven, at 350°F (mark 4) for 15 minutes.

Wash and drain the gooseberries, but do not top and tail the fruit. Put them in a large saucepan with 2½ fluid oz. of water. Cover the pan with a lid and cook over low heat for 10 minutes, then increase the heat and cook until the gooseberries have burst and are soft.

Rub the gooseberries through a sieve and sweeten this purée* with caster sugar to taste. Put the purée in a clean pan. Stir over low heat, adding the remaining 3 oz. of butter in small pieces. Beat the three eggs.

Remove the pan from the heat and stir in the eggs. Return the pan to the heat and cook, stirring continuously, until the purée thickens. It should not be allowed to boil. Cool slightly, then add orange-flower water or wine to taste.

If necessary, re-heat the flan case. Spoon the gooseberry purée into the pastry case and serve it warm, with cream.

CHILLED ALMOND SOUFFLÉ

This rich soufflé with a crunchy topping makes an excellent sweet for a dinner party. It should be prepared several hours in advance and left to chill.

PREPARATION TIME: *25–30 min.*
COOKING TIME: *5–10 min.*
CHILLING TIME: *3–4 hours*

INGREDIENTS *(for 6)*:
4 oz. whole shelled almonds
7 oz. caster sugar
½ pint milk
1½ vanilla pod
3 large egg yolks
½ oz. gelatine
½ pint double cream
1 level tablespoon icing sugar
GARNISH:
2 oz. blanched almonds
2 oz. digestive biscuits

Split the unblanched almonds in half. Put 4 oz. of sugar and 2 tablespoons of cold water into a small pan and cook over low heat, stirring until the sugar dissolves. Bring this syrup to the boil and continue cooking, without stirring, until the syrup turns golden brown. Stir in the almonds. Remove the pan from the heat and spread the mixture to cool on non-stick or buttered greaseproof paper. As soon as the mixture is cool and set, crush it to a fine powder in a moulinette or electric grinder, or with a rolling pin.

To make the soufflé, bring the milk, vanilla pod and remaining sugar to the boil over low heat. Put the egg yolks in a large bowl and gradually pour in the hot milk, beating all the time to prevent curdling. Set the bowl over a pan of barely simmering water and beat until the custard thickens slightly. Take the bowl from the heat and remove the vanilla pod. Dissolve the gelatine in 4 tablespoons of hot water, allow it to cool a little, then add to the custard, stirring well. Strain the mixture into a bowl.

When the mixture is cool but not set, whip the cream with the icing sugar until thick, and fold into the custard. Whisk the egg whites until stiff, but still moist, and fold them in as well. Finally blend in, to taste, the crushed almond mixture.

Tie a piece of foil round a straight-sided 1 pint soufflé dish, so that the foil extends by about 1 in. round the top. Pour in the soufflé mixture and leave to set in the refrigerator for 3–4 hours.

For the garnish, roast the almonds under a hot grill until lightly browned, then grind them finely. Crush the digestive biscuits with a rolling pin and blend with the almonds. Before serving, remove the foil collar from the soufflé and press the almond mixture into the exposed sides and over the top.

151

A portion of croûte aux abricots, topped with whipped cream and garnished with chopped angelica. A perfect light dessert after a rich main course

Biscuit Tortoni is an impressive sweet. Victor Hugo, who often dined at the Tortoni restaurant, is said to have been extremely fond of this ice cream

CROÛTES AUX ABRICOTS

A croûte is a classic French garnish of bread. For a dessert, the croûtes should be sweet bread, and brioches are the most suitable. Slices of currant bread or milk loaf can also be used.

PREPARATION TIME: *10 min.*
COOKING TIME: *20 min.*

INGREDIENTS *(for 6)*:
12 ripe apricots
6 oz. caster sugar
3 brioches
6–8 oz. clarified butter
¼ pint double cream
1 liqueur glass Kirsch (optional)
GARNISH:
Angelica

Cut the apricots in half and remove the stones. Bring the sugar and 2 tablespoons of cold water to the boil in a saucepan, then add the apricots and poach them gently for 6–8 minutes; they should be tender and retain their shape. Carefully lift out the apricots and keep them warm. Turn up the heat and boil the syrup rapidly until it has reduced* to a thick syrup. Do not allow it to caramelise. Let the syrup cool.

Trim the crusts from the brioches or bread and cut into six slices, ½ in. thick; fry them in clarified butter* on both sides until golden brown. Keep warm. Whip the cream lightly and flavour it to taste with the apricot syrup and Kirsch (if used).

To serve, arrange the fried bread on a dish and put four apricot halves on each slice. Top with a swirl of cream and garnish with finely chopped angelica.

BISCUIT TORTONI

During the 19th century, Tortoni's restaurant in Paris was famous for its buffet table, patronised by many great writers.

PREPARATION TIME: *15 min.*
FREEZING TIME: *3 hours*

INGREDIENTS *(for 6–8)*:
¾ pint double cream
¼ pint single cream
2 oz. icing sugar
Salt
12 macaroons
3 fluid oz. brown sherry
GARNISH:
Wafers or ratafia biscuits

About 1 hour before beginning preparations, turn the refrigerator to its coldest setting.

Whip the creams together with the sugar and a pinch of salt, until the mixture is firm but not stiff. Spoon into a 9 in. loaf tin or plastic box, cover with a lid or a double layer of foil and freeze the cream until nearly solid.

Put the macaroons into a plastic or greaseproof paper bag and crush them to fine crumbs with a rolling pin. Set aside a third of the crumbs for decoration.

Break up the frozen cream mixture into a basin and blend in the sherry and remaining macaroon crumbs with a hand whisk. The mixture should stay light and bulky; add a little more sugar and sherry if necessary. Spoon the cream mixture into the washed and dried container, cover and return to the freezing compartment of the refrigerator.

When the cream has frozen quite firm again, remove it from the refrigerator and invert the container on to a serving plate. Rub the container with a cloth wrung out in very hot water until the ice cream drops out. Press the macaroon crumbs lightly into the top and sides of the ice with a broad-bladed knife.

AVOCADO FOOL

The origin of the word 'fool' to describe a purée of pressed fruit mixed with cream or custard goes back to the 16th century. It was then a synonym for a trifling thing – of small consequence. This avocado fool is an unusual, refreshing sweet, best flavoured with lime.

PREPARATION TIME: *20 min.*
CHILLING TIME: *2 hours*

INGREDIENTS *(for 6)*:
3 large avocado pears
2 limes or 1 large lemon
1 rounded tablespoon icing sugar
4 fluid oz. double cream

Peel the avocado pears* and remove the stones. Dice the avocado flesh finely. Cut a thin slice from the middle of one lime or the lemon and divide the slice into six small wedges; set aside. Squeeze the juice from the fruit and put it into a liquidiser, together with the icing sugar.

After 30 seconds add the diced avocado and liquidise until the mixture has become a smooth purée*. Whip the cream and fold it into the purée, adding more sugar and fruit juice to taste.

Spoon the avocado fool into six individual glasses and chill in the refrigerator for at least 2 hours. Garnish with the reserved lime or lemon wedges, and serve with sponge fingers.

Savouries & Snacks

CORNISH PASTIES

For centuries the pasty was the midday meal of Cornish miners. The pastry envelope contains a filling of vegetables, meat or poultry.

PREPARATION TIME: *20–30 min.*
COOKING TIME: *40 min.*

INGREDIENTS *(for 4)*:
8 oz. shortcrust pastry
   (standard recipe)
6 oz. stewing beef
2 coarsely grated potatoes
1 small turnip, coarsely grated
1 finely chopped onion
Salt and black pepper
½ oz. unsalted butter
1 egg

Trim any excess fat from the beef and cut or scrape the meat into paper-thin slices with a sharp knife. Mix the meat with the vegetables.

Roll out the pastry*, about ¼ in. thick, on a lightly floured board and, using a large saucer as a guide, cut out four circles. Pile the filling in the centre of each pastry circle. Season with salt and pepper and top with a knob of butter. Dampen the pastry edges with cold water and carefully draw up two edges to meet on top of the filling. Pinch and twist the pastry firmly together to form a neat fluted and curved pattern. Cut a small air vent in the side of each pasty.

Brush the pasties with the lightly beaten egg and place them on a greased baking tray. Bake in the centre of a pre-heated oven at 425°F (mark 7) for 10 minutes. Reduce the heat to 350°F (mark 4) for 30 minutes.

BARBECUED SAUSAGES

A spicy basting sauce, more often used with outdoor grills, adds tang to grilled sausages.

PREPARATION TIME: *10 min.*
COOKING TIME: *20 min.*

INGREDIENTS *(for 4)*:
1 lb. pork sausages
2 tablespoons olive oil
2 level tablespoons tomato
   ketchup
2 level teaspoons mustard
½ teaspoon Worcestershire sauce
Salt and black pepper

Pierce the skin of the sausages with the prongs of a fork. Arrange them in one layer in a roasting tin or ovenproof dish. Mix together the oil, ketchup, mustard and Worcestershire sauce. Season with salt and pepper and pour this marinade over the sausages; leave for at least an hour, turning them occasionally.

Bake in the centre of a hot oven, pre-heated to 400°F (mark 6), for 20 minutes, basting frequently, until the sausages are well browned.

Serve hot with creamed potatoes and grilled tomatoes or cold in buttered rolls.

SALMON DREAMS

Golden fried salmon sandwiches provide a quick snack. For a light lunch or supper dish, a crisp salad or a green vegetable may be served with them.

PREPARATION TIME: *15 min.*
COOKING TIME: *8–10 min.*

INGREDIENTS *(for 4)*:
16 slices white bread
2 oz. unsalted butter
7½ oz. tin red salmon
2 oz. cream cheese
1 level tablespoon grated
   Cheddar cheese
Salt and black pepper
1 egg
1 tablespoon milk
Paprika
Fat or oil for frying

Using a 2–3 in. scone cutter, cut 16 circles from the bread, and butter each circle.

Drain the salmon and remove any skin and bone. Mash the flesh with a fork, stir in the cream cheese and grated cheese. Season with pepper and a little salt. Spread the mixture thickly on half the bread circles, top with remaining slices and sandwich firmly together.

Beat together the egg and milk. Season with salt, pepper and paprika. Dip the sandwiches in the beaten egg and fry them in hot fat until crisp and golden. Drain on crumpled kitchen paper and serve at once.

LAMPLE PIE

The name is an 18th-century corruption of lamb and apple pie. The herbs add a fresh taste to left-over meat.

PREPARATION TIME: *20 min.*
COOKING TIME: *35 min.*

INGREDIENTS *(for 4–6)*:
6–8 oz. cooked lamb
4–6 oz. cooked ham or bacon
½ lb. cooking apples (peeled and
   sliced)
1 large thinly sliced onion
Salt and black pepper
¼ level teaspoon each, rosemary
   and sage
½–¾ pint chicken stock
1 tablespoon tomato paste
6 oz. shortcrust pastry
   (standard recipe)
1 beaten egg

Mince the cut-up lamb and ham, and arrange in layers with the apple and onion in a 7–8 in. buttered pie dish. Sprinkle each layer with a little salt, pepper and herbs. Mix the stock with the tomato paste and pour it over the pie. Cover the pie with rolled out shortcrust pastry*, sealing the edges firmly; cut an air vent in the centre of the pastry for the steam to escape. Brush the pastry with egg.

Bake in the centre of the oven, pre-heated to 450°F (mark 8), for 10 minutes, then lower the heat to 350°F (mark 4) and cook for a further 25 minutes. Serve hot with potatoes and a green vegetable or cold with a salad.

SPANISH CAKE DESSERT

Stale sponge or fruit cake and a little left-over fruit salad are here transformed into a delicious warm pudding.

PREPARATION TIME: *10 min.*
COOKING TIME: *15 min.*

INGREDIENTS *(for 4–6)*:
4 large slices stale sponge or
   fruit cake
6 oz. fruit, fresh or tinned
¼ pint fresh or frozen orange
   juice
1 tablespoon rum
1 level teaspoon cornflour
½ pint single cream
2 egg yolks
2 oz. caster sugar
Salt
Vanilla essence

Arrange the cake in a lightly buttered ovenproof dish and top with fruit. Pour over the orange juice and rum, and bake in the centre of a pre-heated oven at 375°F (mark 5) for 10–15 minutes.

Mix the cornflour with a little cream. Beat the egg yolks with the remaining cream and stir in the cornflour mixture, sugar and a pinch of salt. Cook this custard over a low heat, stirring continuously, until smooth. Whisk for a further 3 minutes until the custard is thick and glossy. Add vanilla essence to taste, pour the custard over the warm cake and fruit and serve at once.

以食為天

To eat is heaven!—Confucius

To the Chinese, cooking is part of their cultural heritage, it is their daily—and often only—entertainment and pleasure. Through the centuries, the Chinese culinary art has involved infinite patience and a perfect composition of ingredients. The foremost object is to preserve the individual crisp or soft textures and the natural flavours.

In China, a meal served at home consists of four or five dishes which are arranged on the table like a buffet. The table is laid with rice bowls, chopsticks and china spoons, and savoury soup or green tea is drunk throughout the meal.

At parties and banquets, the food is served dish after dish, in Western fashion, but the menu comprises a great many more dishes. A traditional Manchu banquet includes 300 dishes, and even in modern China, official state banquets rarely have less than a dozen. Wine is served at such occasions, usually yellow wine, the best known of which is Shao Shing (rice wine). For Western tastes, however, dry, light white wines are recommended.

This menu, for six persons, has been composed for a Chinese meal at home, with all the dishes served at the same time. Sweet and sour pork, and red-cooked chicken can be served with plain boiled or quick-fried rice and washed down with a savoury cucumber soup. Toasted fish and spare ribs are served first, on their own, with wine. The meal concludes, in Chinese fashion, with a pure dish – in this case, quick-fried spinach. Desserts are rarely served in China, except at banquets, but a Peking fruit salad has been included here.

Stir-frying is a classic Chinese cooking method: finely shredded or thinly sliced ingredients are fried for a few minutes in very hot oil. They are continuously turned over and over with a spoon or spatula, rather like scrambling eggs, to ensure even cooking.

Red-cooking is another classic cooking method; a red-cooked dish cooked in soy sauce – is included in almost every Chinese meal.

The correct way to use Chinese chopsticks : Place one chopstick where the thumb and forefinger meet. Rest it between the third and little finger. Hold the second chopstick between the thumb and forefinger. Use the middle finger to move the second chopstick.

  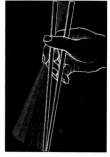

Red-cooked Chicken with Chestnuts

PREPARATION TIME: *8–10 min.*
COOKING TIME: *1½ hours*

INGREDIENTS:
1 chicken (approx. 3 lb.)
1 thinly sliced onion
3 tablespoons vegetable oil
6 tablespoons soy sauce
6 tablespoons medium sherry
½ level tablespoon caster sugar
¾ lb. tinned chestnuts

Using a sharp cleaver, chop the chicken, through the bones, into 12–18 pieces.

Heat the oil in a flameproof casserole and stir-fry the onion and chicken pieces for 6–7 minutes over high heat. Add ¼ pint of cold water and the soy sauce, cover the casserole with a lid and cook in the centre of a pre-heated oven, at 350°F (mark 4) for 40 minutes. Add the sherry and sugar to the casserole, turn the contents over a few times, then replace the lid and cook in the oven for a further 25 minutes.

Remove the casserole, turn the contents over once more, stir in the drained chestnuts and return to the oven for another 15 minutes. Serve the chicken straight from the casserole, or on a warmed serving dish.

Spare Ribs and Cucumber Soup

PREPARATION TIME: *5–10 min.*
COOKING TIME: *1¼–1½ hours*

INGREDIENTS:
1 lb. lean Chinese spare ribs
2 cucumbers
1½ pints chicken stock
   (flavoured with 2 slices of fresh root ginger)
1 level teaspoon salt
Black pepper
1 chicken stock cube

Cut the spare ribs* into single portions if the butcher has not done so already, and trim off as much fat as possible. Wash, but do not peel, the cucumber, and cut it, crossways, into 3 in. wide chunks. Divide each cucumber piece into six or eight long strips. Put 1 pint of cold water in a flameproof casserole, add the spare ribs and bring to the boil. Continue boiling for 5 minutes and remove any scum. Pour off two-thirds of the water, and add the stock and salt. Season to taste with freshly ground pepper.

Cook the casserole, covered with a lid, in the centre of a pre-heated oven, at 350°F (mark 4) for 55 minutes. Add the cucumber strips and the crushed stock cube and cook at the same temperature for a further 15–20 minutes.

Pour the soup into individual bowls, and serve the spare ribs separately or with the soup.

Spare Ribs

Arrange the hot spare ribs on a serving dish. Set small bowls or saucers containing soy sauce, white wine vinegar and mustard on the table. The spare ribs are dipped into any or all of these sauces.

Toasted Fish

PREPARATION TIME: *10–12 mins.*
COOKING TIME: *10–12 mins.*

INGREDIENTS:
1 lb. sole or plaice fillets
5 large slices white bread, each ⅓ in. thick
2 eggs
1 level teaspoon salt
⅔ lb. fresh white breadcrumbs
Oil for deep frying
GARNISH:
2 tablespoons chopped parsley

Cut the crusts from the bread, and divide each slice into 6 equal squares. Cut the skinned fish fillets into pieces to fit the bread squares. Beat the eggs lightly with the salt.

Spread half the breadcrumbs over a large plate. Coat the bread and fish squares in the egg, then place the bread squares on the crumbs and top each piece with a square of fish. Sprinkle the remaining breadcrumbs over the bread and fish squares until they are completely covered.

Heat the oil* in a deep fryer fitted with a basket. Fry four or five cubes at a time, for 2½–3 minutes. Drain the toasted fish on crumpled absorbent paper, and keep them hot while frying the next batch.

Serve the fish on a warmed dish, and sprinkle with parsley.

Fried Rice with Bacon and Eggs

PREPARATION TIME: *5 min.*
COOKING TIME: *5–6 min.*

INGREDIENTS:
¾ lb. cooked long grain rice
2 onions
4 rashers green streaky bacon
4 eggs
1 level teaspoon salt
3 tablespoons vegetable oil
3–4 oz. green peas
2 oz. unsalted butter

Peel and thinly slice the onions. Remove rind and gristle and cut the bacon into narrow strips, crossways. Beat the eggs lightly with the salt. Cook the peas in butter for 3 minutes over low heat.

Heat the oil in a large frying pan and stir-fry the onions and bacon over high heat for 2 minutes. Add the eggs and reduce the heat. Tilt the pan until the eggs cover the base; allow them to set, then scramble them immediately, being careful not to break the scrambled eggs into too small pieces. Add the rice, mix it in with the onion, bacon and egg, and finally blend in the peas.

Fried rice should be light and dry, with the eggs, bacon and peas showing distinctly.

Reading left to right, top row:
Toasted fish, fried rice, sweet and
sour pork, red-cooked chicken
with chestnuts, spare ribs, quick-fried
spinach, vinegar, mustard, cucumber
soup, chilli sauce and soy sauce

Sweet and Sour Pork

PREPARATION TIME: *5–6 min.*
COOKING TIME: *8 min.*

INGREDIENTS:
2 lb. lean pork (boned)
2 level tablespoons cornflour
8 tablespoons vegetable oil
2½ tablespoons soy sauce
1 green pepper
SAUCE:
1 level tablespoon cornflour
2 level tablespoons caster sugar
2 tablespoons white wine vinegar
2 tablespoons fresh orange juice
1½ tablespoons soy sauce
1½ level tablespoons tomato purée
1½ tablespoons pale sherry

Mix all the sauce ingredients, with 6 tablespoons of water, in a bowl, blending thoroughly until smooth. Cut the pork into $\frac{1}{2}-\frac{3}{4}$ in. cubes and toss them in cornflour.

Heat 6 tablespoons of oil in a frying pan, and fry the pork cubes over high heat for 4–5 minutes, turning them often until nearly brown. Pour off all the oil, add the soy sauce and mix with the pork, over low heat, for 1 minute. Draw the pan off the heat.

Heat the remaining oil in a separate pan, and add the green pepper, cut into strips, 1 in. long by ½ in. wide. Stir-fry in the oil for 1½ minutes, over moderate heat. Reduce the heat, stir the sauce and pour it over the pepper. Stir continuously until the sauce thickens and becomes translucent.

Add the pork cubes and turn them in the sauce for 1 minute.

Quick-fried Spinach

PREPARATION TIME: *3–4 min.*
COOKING TIME: *4–5 min.*

INGREDIENTS:
1½ lb. fresh spinach
2 cloves garlic
3 tablespoons vegetable oil
3 level tablespoons soy sauce
1 level teaspoon caster sugar
1½–2 oz. unsalted butter

Wash the spinach thoroughly in several changes of clean water; drain thoroughly. Remove the tough midribs and any bruised leaves. Peel and crush the garlic.

Heat the oil in a large saucepan; add the garlic and salt and stir-fry over high heat for 30 seconds. Add all the spinach, stirring it constantly in the hot oil for 3 minutes. Stir in the soy sauce, sugar and butter and continue cooking, turning all the time for another 2 minutes. Serve immediately.

Ice-mountain Fruit Salad

PREPARATION TIME: *20 min.*

INGREDIENTS:
Chipped ice
Fresh and tinned fruit: lichees,
  guavas, ginger in syrup, straw-
  berries, oranges, mangoes,
  pineapple, black grapes
Preserving sugar

Drain or clean the various fruits thoroughly, and cut them into small chunks or slices. Arrange the fruit in an attractive colour pattern on a bed of chipped ice. For a special occasion, build the chipped ice up into a miniature ragged mountain and set the fruit on the mountain ledges.

Place saucers of sugar on the table and dip the fruit in this.

June

At Dinner, at Supper, at morning, at night, give thanks unto God, for his gifts so in sight.

This Month's Recipes

Tea on the lawn with cucumber sandwiches and strawberries and cream captures the nostalgia of an Edwardian summer

Food in Season

This month abounds with fresh summer produce, ideal for a heatwave. Fresh lobsters and salmon, asparagus and home-grown strawberries are at the expensive end of the scale, with haddock and mackerel, fresh green peas and cool home-made ice creams at the other.

Salad vegetables are plentiful—watercress, cabbage and cos lettuces, English tomatoes, cucumbers, spring onions and radishes. Tender broad beans and fresh garden peas are also good buys. Raspberries, red and black currants and apricots appear at the same time as strawberries.

Fish

Bass
Bream, sea
Brill
Clams
Cockles
Cod
Coley
Conger eels
Crab
Dabs
Dover sole
Dublin Bay prawns
Eels
Grey mullet
Haddock
Hake
Herring
Lemon sole
Lobster
Mackerel
Mock halibut (or
    Greenland halibut)
Oysters, Portuguese
Plaice
Redfish
Red mullet
Salmon
Scad
Scallops
Sea trout
Shrimps
Skate
Trout, rainbow
Turbot
Whiting
Witch

Poultry & Game

Chicken
Duck
Guinea fowl
Pigeon
Quail
Rabbit
Turkey
Venison

Vegetables

Asparagus
Aubergines
Avocado pears
Beetroot
Broad beans
Cabbages
Carrots
Cauliflowers
Celery
Courgettes
Cucumbers
Endive
French beans
Globe artichokes
Horseradish
Lettuces
Mange-tout peas
Mushrooms
Okra
Onions
Parsley
Peas
Peppers
Potatoes
Radishes
Salad cress
Spinach
Spring onions
Sweet potatoes
Tomatoes
Turnips
Vegetable marrow
Watercress

Fruit

Apples
Apricots
Bananas
Blackberries
Black currants
Cherries
Figs
Gooseberries
Grapefruit
Grapes
Lemons
Limes
Loganberries
Lychees
Mangoes
Melons
Oranges
Peaches (imported)
Pears (imported)
Pineapples
Plums (imported)
Raspberries
Red currants
Rhubarb
Strawberries

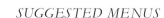

SUGGESTED MENUS

Fresh Asparagus
Salmon en Croûte
Buttered New Potatoes
Cucumber Salad
Strawberry Ice Cream

Cold Crab Tart
Lamb in Red Wine
Roast Potatoes and Buttered Carrots
Black Currant and Mint Pie

Pork Chops with Apple
Buttered Potatoes and Braised Chicory
French Toast with Fruit Sauce

Stuffed Anchovy Eggs
Gammon with Apricot Stuffing
Buttered Potatoes and Creamed Spinach
or Tomato Salad and Courgette and Chives Salad
Strawberry Water Ice

Curries: Hot Chilli Fish and
Madras Beef Curry, Vindaloo of Eggs
with Boiled Rice
Peach Melba

Asparagus in Mornay Sauce
Poulet Sauté Marengo
Buttered Noodles
Green Salad with Sauce Vinaigrette
Soft Fruit Gâteau

Soups & Starters

CHILLED WATERCRESS SOUP

Watercress is most often used as a garnish or in salads. It also makes a good basis for a smooth-textured chilled soup. (See picture on p. 174.)

PREPARATION TIME: *20 min.*
COOKING TIME: *45 min.*
CHILLING TIME: *2 hours*

INGREDIENTS *(for 6–8)* :
2 bunches watercress
¾ lb. potatoes
1 onion
2 pints brown stock or bouillon
1½ oz. butter
1 bay leaf
1 clove garlic (optional)
Salt and black pepper
3 tablespoons double cream
GARNISH:
Grated nutmeg (optional)

Wash the watercress thoroughly in cold water and discard any tough stalks and yellow leaves. Peel and thickly slice the potatoes and the onion. Put the potatoes, onion, watercress, stock, butter, bay leaf and peeled garlic (if used) in a large saucepan. Season with salt and pepper.

Bring the soup to the boil, cover the pan with a lid and simmer until the potatoes and onion are quite soft. Remove the bay leaf and rub the soup through a coarse sieve. Alternatively, let the soup cool a little before liquidising it.

Return the smooth soup to the pan, stir in the cream and heat the soup through without boiling. Pour into individual bowls and leave to cool before chilling.

Just before serving, sprinkle a little freshly grated nutmeg over the soup. Serve with Melba toast*.

FRESH ASPARAGUS

In June, home-grown asparagus appears on the market. The season lasts for only a few weeks, and while imported asparagus is available for a longer period, it lacks the flavour of fresh English asparagus.

PREPARATION TIME: *10 min.*
COOKING TIME: *15 min.*

INGREDIENTS *(for 4)* :
2 lb. asparagus
6–8 oz. butter
* or 6 tablespoons olive oil*
2 tablespoons white wine vinegar
Salt and black pepper

Wash the asparagus carefully and lightly scrape the lower parts of the stems, away from the delicate tips. Young fresh asparagus needs no further preparation, but if the stems are woody towards the base, trim off the wood, keeping the stems at a uniform length.

Tie the asparagus in bundles of 10–12, using soft tape so as not to damage the stems. Bring a large pan of lightly salted water to the boil. Place the bundles of asparagus upright in it, with the tips above the water. Time of cooking varies according to the age, size and length of the asparagus, but as a general rule asparagus is cooked when the tips are soft to the touch.

Untie the asparagus and drain carefully without breaking the tips. Serve the asparagus on individual plates, either warm with melted butter or cold with a French dressing*, served separately. Asparagus is tradition-ally eaten with the fingers. Dip the tips in the butter or dressing and leave any woody parts of the stems. Finger bowls, with luke-warm water and a slice of lemon are required.

ASPARAGUS IN MORNAY SAUCE

Cook the asparagus as already described and make the sauce from the following ingredients:

1 oz. butter
1 oz. plain flour
½ pint milk
2 tablespoons asparagus water
2 tablespoons double cream
4 oz. Cheddar cheese
Salt and black pepper

Melt the butter in a saucepan, add the flour and cook this roux* for a few minutes until thoroughly blended. Gradually stir in the milk, until the sauce is smooth and has thickened. Blend in the asparagus water and cream. Grate the cheese and add 3 oz. to the sauce. Season to taste with salt and freshly ground pepper.

Put the drained asparagus in a buttered flameproof serving dish, and pour over the sauce. Sprinkle with the remaining cheese and put the dish under a hot grill until bubbly and brown on top. Serve immediately.

Fish

AVOCADO PEAR BRISTOL FASHION

Scarlet lobster and green avocados make an attractive starter for a special occasion. Avocado pears should always be prepared at the last minute, otherwise the delicate green flesh turns brown.

PREPARATION TIME: *25 min.*

INGREDIENTS *(for 4)* :
2 large avocado pears
1 medium-sized lobster
3 fluid oz. double cream
1 dessertspoon lemon juice
Cayenne pepper
Salt
Paprika

Ask the fishmonger to split the cooked lobster* in two halves. Remove the grey sac in each half of the head and the black intestinal tubes. Prise out all the lobster meat from the body, tail and claws, and set the thin scarlet crawler claws aside for garnish.

Chop the lobster meat finely, put it in a basin and stir in the cream and lemon juice. Season to taste with cayenne pepper.

Cut the pears in half lengthways and remove the stones. Using a silver teaspoon, scoop out some of the avocado flesh, leaving about ½ in. lining to hold the shape of each half shell. Dice the flesh finely and fold it into the lobster mixture. Season with salt if necessary.

Pile the lobster mixture into the avocado shells and sprinkle with a little paprika. Arrange the claws on top in a decorative pattern.

FRIED COD ROES

Fresh cod roe is a highly nutritious, easily digested food. Ideally, it should be bought uncooked or at least freshly boiled, as it dries up quickly. Serve it for a light lunch or a hearty Sunday breakfast.

PREPARATION TIME: *5 min.*
COOKING TIME: *25–30 min.*

INGREDIENTS *(for 4–6)* :
1–1½ lb. fresh cod roe
1 bay leaf
Seasoned flour
1 egg
2–3 tablespoons fresh white bread-crumbs
3 oz. lard
Salt and black pepper
GARNISH :
Lemon wedges

Wash the fresh roe carefully in cold running water. Put it in a saucepan with the bay leaf, and cover with cold, lightly salted water. Bring slowly to the boil and cook the roe, covered, over very low heat, for about 15 minutes. Drain the roe carefully. Place it on a wooden board, cover with a lightly weighted plate, and leave to press until quite cold.

Cut the cold roe into 1 in. thick slices, and coat with seasoned flour*. Beat the egg lightly and dip the slices in the egg, before coating them evenly with the breadcrumbs.

Melt the lard in a heavy-based pan and fry the slices over moderate heat until golden brown on both sides. Cover the pan with a lid to prevent the hot lard splashing.

Serve the fried roe immediately, garnished with lemon wedges, and with buttered toast.

BRAINS IN BLACK BUTTER

Calf brains are traditionally used in this classic French recipe. But they are often difficult to obtain, and lamb brains are equally good.

PREPARATION TIME: *30 min.*
COOKING TIME: *35 min.*

INGREDIENTS *(for 4)* :
2 sets lamb or calf brains
1 bay leaf
Salt and black pepper
6 oz. unsalted butter
½ tablespoon caper vinegar
1 tablespoon capers

Soak the brains in a bowl of cold, lightly salted water for at least 30 minutes to remove all blood. Drain the brains, remove any bone fragments and peel off the outer transparent skin. Rinse the brains again in cold water and divide each set into two (if using the larger calf brains, each set should be cut into thick slices).

Put the brains in a saucepan and cover with cold, lightly salted water. Bring to the boil over moderate heat, and carefully remove any scum. Lower the heat, add the bay leaf, and cover the pan with a lid; cook the brains gently for 20 minutes. Drain well and transfer the brains to a warm serving dish. Sprinkle with salt and freshly ground pepper.

Melt the butter in a small pan over moderate heat and let the butter brown without burning it. Stir in the vinegar and capers, and pour this sauce over the brains immediately.

Serve the brains with crusty bread to mop up the butter.

HADDOCK BARRIE

Fresh haddock and prawns are here combined in a cheese sauce and finished off as a gratin.

PREPARATION TIME: *15 min.*
COOKING TIME: *30 min.*

INGREDIENTS *(for 4)* :
4 fresh haddock fillets, each approx. 6 oz.
12 peeled prawns
Seasoned flour
2 oz. butter
1 oz. plain flour
½ pint milk
2 oz. Cheddar cheese
1 small onion
Salt and cayenne pepper
3 fluid oz. double cream

Wash the fillets thoroughly and pat them dry on absorbent paper. Coat each fillet lightly with seasoned flour*. Use half the butter to grease a shallow flameproof dish and arrange the fillets in a single layer in this.

Melt the remaining butter in a small pan, stir in the flour, cook for a few minutes, then gradually add the milk to make a white sauce*. Grate the cheese and blend it into the sauce, together with the peeled and finely chopped onion. Chop the prawns roughly and stir them into the sauce. Season with salt and cayenne pepper, and stir in the cream.

Pour the sauce over the fish and bake in the centre of an oven pre-heated to 400°F (mark 6) for 30 minutes. If by that time the top has not browned, put the dish under a hot grill for a few minutes.

Serve the fillets at once; plain boiled rice or new potatoes and a green vegetable, such as spinach, go well with this dish.

SALMON EN CROÛTE

June is the height of the salmon and asparagus season. This recipe is a superb blend of these two ingredients, which are wrapped in featherlight puff pastry. The dish makes a perfect main course for a dinner party and can be served hot or cold.

PREPARATION TIME: *45 min.*
COOKING TIME: *40 min.*

INGREDIENTS *(for 4–6)*:

1 small grilse or piece of salmon
   (approx. weight 1½ lb.)
¾–1 lb. asparagus
2 tablespoons double cream
½ level teaspoon chopped dill
Salt and black pepper
3 thin gammon rashers
7½–8 oz. prepared puff pastry
1 egg yolk
1 tablespoon milk
GARNISH:
Lemon wedges

Ask the fishmonger to skin and fillet the fish. Otherwise cut the head off the salmon* and wash the fish thoroughly to remove all traces of blood. Carefully peel off the skin with a sharp knife before removing the backbone. Leave the fish in two long fillets.

Wash and trim the asparagus*, tie in a bundle and cook upright in a pan of lightly salted water for 20–30 minutes or until the tips are soft to the touch. Drain the asparagus thoroughly, and cut off the soft tips (the stems can be used in an omelette), and rub them through a coarse sieve or liquidise. Blend the cream and dill into this asparagus purée* and season to taste with freshly ground pepper.

Spread the asparagus purée over one half of the salmon, and put the fish together (any remaining purée can be spread on the top). Wrap the gammon slices round the salmon and set it aside.

Roll out the puff pastry*, on a floured surface, to a rectangle, about 12 in. by 10 in. Place the salmon in the centre of the pastry and wrap the pastry over the fish. Beat the egg yolk lightly with the milk and brush the edges of the pastry. Seal the long joint firmly with more egg. Tuck in the short ends of the pastry neatly and seal with egg.

Place the salmon on a wet baking tray, with the seam beneath. Cut one or two holes in the pastry for the steam to escape, and decorate the top with leaves made from the pastry trimmings. Brush with the remaining egg and milk. Bake in the centre of an oven pre-heated to 425°F (mark 7) for 20 minutes, then lower the heat to 375°F (mark 5) and bake for a further 20–25 minutes or until the pastry is golden brown.

Serve the salmon, hot or cold, cut in slices, and garnished with lemon wedges. New potatoes tossed in butter and dill, and a cucumber salad, are traditional side dishes.

MACKEREL WITH CUCUMBER

The cool, pale green look of young cucumber heralds summer. Its clean taste suits oily fish, such as mackerel and trout. The dish can be served hot or cold.

PREPARATION TIME: *25 min.*
COOKING TIME: *35 min.*

INGREDIENTS *(for 4)*:
4 mackerel (about ½ lb. each)
3 oz. butter
1 small cucumber
Salt and black pepper
2 tablespoons white wine vinegar
   or dry white wine

Gut and clean the mackerel* and cut off the heads. Wash the fish and pat them dry on absorbent paper. Grease a large, shallow, ovenproof dish with 1 oz. of the butter. Wash and dry the cucumber and slice it thinly; put a layer of cucumber slices over the base of the dish. Place the mackerel on top and cover with the remaining cucumber slices. Season to taste with salt and freshly ground pepper.

Sprinkle the vinegar or wine over the fish and cucumber, and dot with 1 oz. of butter cut into small knobs. Cover the dish with a lid or foil and bake on the centre shelf of an oven pre-heated to 400°F (mark 6) for 30 minutes.

Remove the dish from the oven and transfer the fish and cucumber to a serving dish. Keep it warm if the mackerel is to be served hot. Strain the juices from the fish through a fine sieve into a saucepan. Bring to the boil and continue boiling briskly, adding the remaining butter in bits and stirring occasionally. When the liquid has reduced* by about half and resembles a glaze*, pour it over the mackerel and serve at once or leave to cool.

For a hot main course, serve with potatoes tossed in butter and chopped parsley, and with young peas. Served cold, a green salad and garlic potatoes (see December vegetables) could complement the dish.

COD GOURMET

Cod is the most popular fish in Britain and can be cooked in a number of ways. This recipe for poaching it in white wine, mushrooms and shallots is ideal for a light summer meal.

PREPARATION TIME: *15 min.*
COOKING TIME: *25 min.*

INGREDIENTS *(for 4)*:
4 cod fillets (approx. 5 oz. each)
1–2 tablespoons plain flour
3 oz. unsalted butter
3 shallots
¼ lb. mushrooms
Salt and black pepper
2 tablespoons dry white wine
1 dessertspoon lemon juice
GARNISH:
1 tablespoon chopped parsley

Wash and skin the cod fillets. Pat them dry on absorbent paper and coat with a little flour. Grease a large, shallow, ovenproof dish with 1 oz. of the butter and arrange the fillets in this. Peel and finely chop the shallots. Melt the remaining butter in a pan and fry the shallots over low heat for 2–3 minutes, until transparent. Wipe and trim the mushrooms*, slice them thinly and add to the shallots. Cook for a further 2 minutes, then season to taste with salt and freshly ground pepper.

Spoon the shallot and mushroom mixture over the cod fillets and pour over the wine. Cover the dish with a lid or foil and bake for 25 minutes in the centre of an oven pre-heated to 400°F (mark 6).

Serve the fish straight from the dish. Sprinkle with lemon juice and garnish with parsley. Tiny buttered potatoes and young peas go well with this dish.

Meat

MONTE CARLO HADDOCK

Win or lose, a night at the Casino can take its toll in exhaustion. The little restaurants along the coast of Monte Carlo used to specialise in breakfasts that would leave a gambler refreshed. Such a meal was this.

PREPARATION TIME: *10 min.*
COOKING TIME: *20–30 min.*

INGREDIENTS *(for 4)*:
1 lb. smoked haddock fillet
1 pint milk
1 bay leaf
2 oz. butter
2 oz. plain flour
Salt and cayenne pepper
3 oz. Cheddar cheese
4 eggs

Wash and dry the haddock fillet before putting it in a large pan with the milk and bay leaf. Poach* the fillet, uncovered, over moderate heat for about 10 minutes. Carefully lift out the fish with a perforated spoon, remove the skin and divide the fillet into four portions. Arrange these in a warm flameproof dish and keep hot in the oven.

Strain the milk and use it, with the butter and flour, to make a white sauce*. Season to taste with salt and cayenne pepper. Stir in the grated cheese.

Poach the eggs* in a pan of lightly salted, simmering water until they are just set. Lift the eggs out with a perforated spoon and place one egg on each haddock portion. Pour over the sauce and place the dish under a hot grill for 2–3 minutes, until lightly browned.

Serve with creamed spinach (see June vegetables).

CRAB TART

Most savoury tarts or flans are baked blind – that is the pastry is partly cooked before the filling is added. They are ideal for summer fare, since they are quick to make and equally tasty served hot or cold.

PREPARATION TIME: *20–30 min.*
COOKING TIME: *30 min.*

INGREDIENTS *(for 4–6)*:
PASTRY:
8 oz. plain flour
¼ level teaspoon salt
¼ level teaspoon cayenne pepper
2 oz. butter
2 oz. lard
1 oz. Cheddar cheese
1 egg yolk
FILLING:
½–¾ lb. crab meat
3 eggs
2 teaspoons lemon juice
1 coffeespoon Worcestershire sauce
4 fluid oz. double cream
Salt

For the pastry, sift the flour, salt and cayenne pepper into a mixing bowl. Rub in the butter and lard, cut into knobs, until the mixture is crumbly. Grate in the cheese; bind the pastry with the egg yolk and a little cold water. Leave the pastry to rest for 30 minutes.

Roll this shortcrust pastry* out on a lightly floured surface, and use to line a 9 in. wide flan ring. Prick the base of the pastry and bake it blind* in the pre-heated oven at 400°F (mark 6) for 10 minutes or until golden.

Extract the meat from the crab* and flake* it finely into a bowl. Beat the eggs lightly with the lemon juice and Worcestershire sauce and stir it into the crab meat before blending in the cream. Add salt to taste.

Spoon the crab mixture into the pastry case and bake in a pre-heated oven at 375°F (mark 5) for 25–30 minutes.

Serve the tart, hot or cold, cut into wedges, and with crusty bread and a mixed salad.

BEEF WITH GREEN PEAS

Topside of beef is rather tough and is usually stewed or braised. It can, however, be made into a succulent joint by pot-roasting it slowly in a close-fitting casserole.

PREPARATION TIME: *10 min.*
COOKING TIME: *2–2½ hours*

INGREDIENTS *(for 6)*:
2½–3 lb. lean topside of beef
Salt and black pepper
2 oz. unsalted butter
1½ lb. fresh green peas

Wipe the meat with a damp cloth and season with freshly ground pepper. Melt the butter in a heavy-based frying pan over high heat and brown the beef in it on all sides to seal in the juices.

Put the meat in an ovenproof casserole into which it will fit fairly closely. Shell the peas and put them round the sides of the beef, and pour the butter from the pan over the meat. Cover the casserole with a lid and cook in the centre of a pre-heated oven at 325°F (mark 3) for 2 hours. At this stage the meat will be rare – allow another 30 minutes for well-done meat.

Lift out the beef, carve into thin slices and arrange them on a warmed serving dish, surrounded by the peas. Boiled new potatoes with a little chopped mint are ideal for this dish.

VEAL IN TOMATOES

The fillet of veal used in this recipe was formerly known as a cushion of veal. The joint, which is cut from the top of the hind leg and boned, is best cooked in a casserole.

PREPARATION TIME: *20 min.*
COOKING TIME: *1½–2 hours*

INGREDIENTS *(for 6)*:
2½ lb. fillet of veal
Salt
2 oz. unsalted butter
1½ lb. tomatoes
2 onions
6–8 black peppercorns
Sprig tarragon (fresh or dried)

Wipe the meat with a damp cloth and tie it neatly with string to keep its shape during cooking. Season lightly with salt. Melt half the butter in a flameproof casserole over moderate heat, and brown the meat on all sides to seal in the juices.

Skin and roughly chop the tomatoes*. Peel and finely chop the onions. Melt the remaining butter in a pan and fry the tomatoes and onions over moderate heat for 3–4 minutes. Grind the pepper into the tomato mixture, add the tarragon and pour it all over the meat in the casserole. Cover with a lid or foil and bake in the centre of a pre-heated oven at 300°F (mark 2) for 1½–2 hours.

Remove the string and serve the veal hot, cut into thick slices, with the tomato sauce spooned over. Plain boiled spaghetti, tossed in butter, would make this a substantial meal.

PORK CHOPS WITH APPLE

Tart cooking apples are traditionally served with pork to counteract the fattiness of the meat. They appear as stuffings and sauces with roasts, and can also, as here, be used with oven-cooked chops.

PREPARATION TIME: *15 min.*
COOKING TIME: *1 hour 10 min.*

INGREDIENTS *(for 4)* :
4 thick pork chops
1–2 oz. unsalted butter
Salt and black pepper
3–4 large cooking apples
Juice of a lemon

Trim any excess fat from the chops, wipe them dry with a damp cloth, and put them in a buttered ovenproof dish. Season to taste with salt and freshly ground pepper. Peel, core and thinly slice the apples and arrange over the chops to cover them completely. Melt the remaining butter and brush some of it over the apple slices. Sprinkle with lemon juice and cover the dish closely with a lid or foil.

Cook the chops in the centre of a pre-heated oven, at 325°F (mark 3) for 1 hour. Remove the foil, brush the apples with the remaining butter and cook for a further 10 minutes, or until the apples are lightly browned but not dry, and the chops are tender.

Serve the chops from the cooking dish or on a warmed serving plate. Small new potatoes and braised chicory (see June vegetables), go well with the sharp apple taste.

TERRINE DE CAMPAGNE

The French word 'terrine' originally meant an earthenware dish, but by extension it now also refers to the contents of the dish, whether fish, meat or poultry. This farmhouse-style terrine of calf liver and veal is a good choice for a picnic, lunch or supper. It should, like all other terrines, be served cold.

PREPARATION TIME: *20 min.*
COOKING TIME: *2 hours*

INGREDIENTS *(for 4–6)* :
12 oz. thin rashers streaky
  bacon
$\frac{3}{4}$ lb. calf liver
1$\frac{1}{2}$ lb. minced veal
1 large onion
2 cloves garlic
1 heaped tablespoon tomato
  purée
$\frac{1}{4}$ level teaspoon summer savory
  or sage
$\frac{1}{4}$ level teaspoon oregano
4 oz. butter
$\frac{1}{4}$ pint dry red wine
Salt and black pepper
4 bay leaves

Remove the rind and any gristle from the bacon and stretch the rashers with the flat blade of a knife. Line a 2 pint terrine* or soufflé dish with the bacon, allowing the rashers to hang over the edges.

Clean the liver, removing any gristle, and put the meat through the coarse plate of a mincer. Peel the onion and chop it finely. Mix together the liver, onion and veal in a large bowl. Peel the garlic and crush it over the meat mixture. Stir in the tomato purée, savory and oregano. Melt the butter and stir into the terrine

mixture together with enough wine to give a moist but not wet consistency. Season to taste with salt and freshly ground pepper.

Spoon the mixture into the dish, over the bacon rashers. Arrange the bay leaves on top and fold over the bacon rashers.

Cover the dish with a lid or tight-fitting foil. Cook the terrine for 2 hours on the middle shelf of an oven pre-heated to 350°F (mark 4).

When cooked, remove the lid from the dish, cover with fresh foil and a flat board. Place a

heavy weight on the board and leave overnight.

Serve straight from the terrine or turn out on to a serving dish and cut into wedges. Crusty bread and a tossed green salad make this terrine a substantial main course.

LAMB IN RED WINE

A leg of lamb makes a good choice for a large gathering. Spices and wine give a fresh summer taste to succulent English or Welsh lamb, now in season.

PREPARATION TIME: *15 min.*
COOKING TIME: *1¾–2 hours*

INGREDIENTS *(for 6–8)*:
4–5 lb. leg of lamb
2 cloves garlic
¼ oz. lard
Salt and black pepper
Ground ginger
2 onions
2 carrots
2 oz. unsalted butter
3–4 sprigs of thyme
½ pint dry red wine

Wipe the lamb thoroughly with a damp cloth. Peel the garlic and cut each clove into three or four slivers. With the point of a sharp knife, make small incisions in the meat and press the garlic into these. Rub the skin with the lard, a little salt, freshly ground pepper and dust with ginger. Peel the onions and carrots and chop them roughly.

Melt the butter in a roasting pan, and quickly brown the meat over moderate heat to seal in the juices. Remove the meat from the pan and cook the onions and carrots for a few minutes in the butter until golden. Spoon the pan mixture into a large oven-proof dish, add the thyme and place the meat on top; cover with a lid or foil.

Roast the meat in the centre of an oven pre-heated to 425°F (mark 7) for 25 minutes, then pour over the wine and reduce the heat to 350°F (mark 4) for a further 1–1¼ hours. Baste* two or three times with the wine.

Remove the joint and keep it warm on a serving dish in the oven. Strain the cooking juices and boil them briskly until they have reduced* by about one-third. Remove any fat by drawing absorbent kitchen paper over the surface of this gravy. Heat through and correct seasoning.

Serve roast potatoes and young carrots, tossed in parsley, with the lamb. Pour the gravy into a sauceboat and serve it separately.

CURRIES

It is a popular misconception in the Western world that a curry consists of pieces of meat or poultry in a curry-flavoured sauce. A curry proper, as served daily in India, Pakistan and Malaysia, is an array of fish, meat, poultry and vegetable dishes, each flavoured with a compound of spices, usually sold in Europe as curry powder.

The following selection (for 6–8) has been adapted to Western eating habits. The dishes are all fairly hot, and it is advisable to experiment with the amount of curry powder, adding too little at first rather than too much. Meat curries benefit from being made a day in advance, to allow the flavours to develop and blend.

HOT CHILLI FISH CURRY

PREPARATION TIME: *15 min.*
COOKING TIME: *1 hour 10 min.*

INGREDIENTS:
6 oz. shelled prawns or 1 lb. cooked diced fish fillets
2 onions
1 clove garlic
1 oz. unsalted butter
1 level tablespoon curry powder
1 level coffeespoon chilli powder
1 pint chicken stock
2 tablespoons tomato purée
Juice of a lemon
1 dessertspoon golden syrup
1 star aniseed (optional)
Salt and black pepper

Peel and coarsely chop the onions, and peel and crush the garlic. Melt the butter in a heavy-based pan and fry the curry and chilli powders over low heat for about 1 minute. Add the onions and garlic and cook for a further 2–3 minutes. Gradually stir in the stock and add the tomato purée, lemon juice and syrup. Add the star aniseed if used and simmer this sauce, covered with a lid, for about 1 hour. The sauce will now be quite thick.

Remove the aniseed, stir in the prawns or fish and cook for about 10 minutes. Season to taste with salt and freshly ground pepper.

MADRAS BEEF CURRY

PREPARATION TIME: *20 min.*
COOKING TIME: *about 2½ hours*

INGREDIENTS:
1½ lb. chuck steak
1 large onion
2 cloves garlic
3 oz. lard or dripping
1½ heaped tablespoons curry powder
2 pints beef stock
Juice of half lemon
2 bay leaves
Salt and black pepper
1 tablespoon brown sugar
2 tablespoons tomato purée

Peel and finely chop the onion and garlic. Melt half the lard in a heavy-based pan, stir in 1 heaped tablespoon of curry powder and fry over low heat, stirring continuously, for 1 minute. Add the onion and garlic, and fry for a further 2 minutes. Pour in the stock and lemon juice, and add the bay leaves. Bring this to the boil, cover and simmer over low heat for 45 minutes.

Meanwhile, trim any fat and gristle from the meat and cut it into 1 in. pieces. Season the meat with salt and freshly ground pepper and dust with the remaining curry powder. Melt the rest of the lard in a heavy-based pan and fry the meat for 2–3 minutes over high heat, until it is brown on all sides.

Strain the curry stock through a coarse sieve over the meat; stir in the sugar and tomato purée. Cover the pan with a lid and simmer the meat for about 1½ hours or until tender. By this time the stock will have reduced* and become a thick sauce. At this stage, more curry powder may be added; it should be lightly fried in a little fat before being added to the sauce.

Set the curry aside to cool. Skim off any fat which has settled on the surface before re-heating the curry.

VINDALOO OF EGGS

PREPARATION TIME: *15 min.*
COOKING TIME: *1½ hours*

INGREDIENTS:
8 eggs
2 onions
1 oz. unsalted butter
1 level dessertspoon curry powder
1 level coffeespoon chilli powder
1 heaped tablespoon plain flour
¼ pint white wine vinegar
¾ pint chicken, beef or veal stock
1 bay leaf
1 sprig thyme
Salt and black pepper

Hard-boil the eggs for 8 minutes, then plunge them into cold water, remove the shells and set the eggs aside to cool. Peel and finely chop the onions. Melt the butter in a heavy-based pan, and fry the curry and chilli powders for 1–2 minutes over low heat. Blend in the flour to make a thick paste. Add the onions and cook for about 2 minutes, stirring all the time. Gradually stir in the vinegar and stock until the sauce is quite smooth. Add the bay leaf and thyme, and season to taste with salt and freshly ground pepper.

Simmer the sauce, covered, for about 1 hour, stirring occasionally. Cut the eggs in half lengthways and arrange them in an ovenproof serving dish; strain the curry sauce through a coarse sieve over the eggs.

Leave the eggs to steep in the sauce for 2–3 hours. Cover the dish with a lid or foil and heat it through in the oven, at a temperature of 400°F (mark 6) for about 30 minutes. Serve hot from the dish.

Serve the three hot curry dishes together, with a bowl of plain boiled rice. Provide small dishes of spicy pickles and chutneys, such as lime and mango, sweet pepper and tomato chutneys.

Grated coconut, thin onion rings, sliced bananas in a little lemon juice and diced cucumber in sweet wine vinegar also make refreshing side dishes. A bowl of plain yoghourt is cooling and also helps in digesting spicy curries.

Chapatis – small griddle pancakes of unleavened bread – are served with curries in India. Popadams, which are more popular in Malaysia, are wafer-thin pancakes, fried until crisp and golden.

GAMMON WITH APRICOT STUFFING

Baked stuffed hams and gammons are often credited to American cookery, but the recipe originated in the Cotswolds centuries ago. The American glazed crust is a great improvement on the English flour and water crust.

PREPARATION TIME: *15–20 min.*

COOKING TIME: $2\frac{1}{4}$ *hours*

INGREDIENTS *(for 8–10):*
6 lb. piece of gammon (boned)
$\frac{1}{3}$ pint red wine
2 bay leaves
$\frac{1}{2}$ lb. apricots
$\frac{1}{2}$ level teaspoon arrowroot (optional)
Cloves
2–3 heaped tablespoons Demerara sugar

Ask the butcher to bone and roll the gammon, leaving plenty of room for the stuffing. Put the meat in a large basin, add the wine and bay leaves and leave to marinate* for at least 6 hours; turn the meat frequently.

Wash and dry the apricots, cut them in half and remove the stones. Lift the meat from the marinade, and put the wine and bay leaves in a saucepan. Add the apricots and bring to the boil over low heat. Simmer for about 10 minutes or until the apricots are soft and the wine has been absorbed. Remove the bay leaves, and let the apricots cool slightly.

Pat the gammon thoroughly dry. Stuff as much of the apricot purée as possible into the gammon joint (any surplus can be made into a purée* boiled up with extra wine and thickened with a little arrowroot to make a

sauce). Wrap the stuffed joint tightly in a double layer of foil, and make a slit in the centre of the foil for the steam to escape. Place on a baking tray and cook the gammon in the centre of the oven pre-heated to 350°F (mark 4) for 2 hours.

Remove the gammon from the oven, unwrap the foil and let the joint cool slightly. With a sharp knife, slit the skin lengthways and remove it entirely, leaving a layer of fat no more than $\frac{1}{8}$ in. thick over the meat. Make shallow diagonal cuts, $\frac{3}{4}$ in. apart, through the fat to form a pattern of diamond shapes, and insert a whole clove at each intersection. Pat the Demerara sugar firmly over the gammon and transfer it to a roasting tin.

Glaze* the joint in the oven, pre-heated to 425°F (mark 7), for about 15 minutes or until the sugar has melted and set to golden brown.

Serve the gammon hot or cold, cut into thin slices. Creamed spinach (see June vegetables) and buttered potatoes would be suitable for a hot joint, and salads ideal with the cold meat.

Poultry & Game

DUCK PAPRIKA

The Hungarians traditionally flavour many of their poultry and meat dishes with paprika. This recipe makes a change from plain roast duck and is a good main course for a dinner party.

PREPARATION TIME: *15 min.*
COOKING TIME: *1¼–1½ hours*

INGREDIENTS *(for 4–6)*:
1 duck (5–6 lb.)
2 onions
1 clove garlic
1½ oz. unsalted butter
1 oz. plain flour
1 level dessertspoon paprika
⅓ pint red wine
Salt and black pepper
4–5 tomatoes
Chicken or duck stock
1 rounded teaspoon arrowroot

Wipe the duck inside and out with a damp cloth, pat it thoroughly dry and truss it neatly. Peel and finely chop the onions and garlic. Melt the butter in a large flameproof casserole or sauté dish, and cook the onions and garlic for a few minutes until transparent. Add the duck, and brown on all sides. Lift the duck from the pan, sprinkle in the flour and paprika and cook for a few minutes. Pour in the wine and stir until this is a smooth sauce. Season to taste with salt and freshly ground pepper. Return the duck to the pan.

Skin and roughly chop the tomatoes* and add them to the duck, thinning with a little stock if necessary.

Cover the dish with a lid and simmer over low heat for about 1¼ hours or until the duck is tender. It may be necessary to add more stock.

When cooked, remove the duck and carve it into six to eight portions; arrange these on a serving dish and keep hot. Skim any fat off the sauce; if necessary, blend a little arrowroot with cold water and stir into the sauce to thicken it. Spoon the sauce over the duck and serve with savoury rice*.

POULET SAUTÉ MARENGO

According to legend, this now-classic dish was invented by Napoleon's chef after the Battle of Marengo in 1800. The ingredients, which then included freshwater crayfish, were apparently at hand in the devastated countryside.

PREPARATION TIME: *45 min.*
COOKING TIME: *1 hour*

INGREDIENTS *(for 6)*:
1 chicken (approx. 4½ lb.) or 8 chicken portions
2 onions
1 clove garlic
2 oz. unsalted butter
3 tablespoons olive oil
1 oz. plain flour
¼ pint chicken stock
½ pint Marsala
6 tomatoes
12 button mushrooms
1 white truffle (optional)
Salt and black pepper
1 liqueur glass brandy

Wipe the chicken or the portions thoroughly with a clean damp cloth (cut a whole chicken* into eight neat portions). Peel the onions and garlic, roughly chop the onions, and crush the garlic. Heat the butter and oil in a large sauté pan over moderate heat, and fry the onions, garlic and chicken pieces until light golden. Sprinkle over the flour and cook, stirring, until all the fat is absorbed and the flour is slightly browned. Gradually stir in the stock and Marsala and bring the mixture to the boil. Lower the heat and let the chicken simmer in the sauce.

Skin and roughly chop the tomatoes*, trim the mushrooms* and slice them finely. Chop the truffle finely, if used. Add the tomatoes, mushrooms and truffle to the pan. Season to taste with salt and freshly ground pepper. Cover the pan with a lid or foil and simmer over low heat for about 1 hour, or until the chicken is tender. Stir occasionally to prevent the sauce sticking. About 10 minutes before the end of cooking time, stir the brandy into the sauce.

Serve hot, with boiled new potatoes or with plain buttered noodles. For the traditional garnish, place six whole cooked crayfish round the chicken.

CHICKEN IN MUSHROOM SAUCE

This method of cooking chicken produces a light, easily digestible meal, particularly suitable for invalids. Any remains of the chicken and mushroom sauce can be made into a creamed soup.

PREPARATION TIME: *25 min.*
COOKING TIME: *1½ hours*

INGREDIENTS *(for 6)*:
1 chicken (approx. 3½ lb.)
2 onions
2 sticks celery
1½ oz. unsalted butter
Salt and black pepper
1 bay leaf
12–16 button mushrooms
Worcestershire sauce
1 level tablespoon plain flour
2½ fluid oz. double cream
GARNISH:
1 tablespoon finely chopped parsley

Peel and finely chop the onions; scrub the celery and chop finely. Melt 1 oz. of the butter in a large heavy-based pan over low heat; cook the onion and celery until soft and just beginning to colour.

Meanwhile, wash and wipe the trussed chicken*, inside and out; clean the giblets and liver. Put the chicken, giblets and liver in the pan with the onion and celery, with enough water to cover the chicken. Bring to the boil, remove any scum and add salt, freshly ground pepper and the bay leaf. Cover the pan with a lid and simmer gently for about 1½ hours, or until the chicken is tender. Lift the chicken on to a warm dish and keep it hot. Strain the cooking liquid and set aside.

Trim and thinly slice the mushrooms*. Melt the remaining butter in a small pan and cook the mushrooms over low heat for 2–3 minutes. Add a few drops of Worcestershire sauce and sprinkle the flour over the mushrooms. Cook, stirring continuously, until all the fat has been absorbed into the flour. Gradually blend in about ¼ pint of the strained chicken liquid, to make a smooth sauce. Correct seasoning if necessary. Stir in the cream and heat the sauce through.

Carve the chicken* and arrange the slices and joints in a deep serving dish. Pour the mushroom sauce over it and garnish with chopped parsley. Serve with broccoli spears and plain potatoes, or buttered rice.

Rice & Pasta

CHICKEN PILAF

A pilaf is basically an Eastern method of cooking rice with various spices. It can be served plain to replace potatoes, but is more often mixed with cooked meat, chicken or fish.

PREPARATION TIME: *20 min.*
COOKING TIME: *1 hour*

INGREDIENTS *(for 6)*:
¾ lb. cooked chicken
2 onions
1 clove garlic
4 oz. unsalted butter
10 oz. long grain rice
1½ pint chicken stock
16 button mushrooms
Saffron
Salt and black pepper
3 tomatoes

Peel and finely chop the onions and garlic. Melt the butter in a large fireproof casserole dish and fry the onion and garlic until soft. Add the rice and continue frying, stirring continuously, until the rice is transparent. Pour the stock over the rice.

Trim the mushrooms* and chop them roughly. Add them to the rice with a pinch of saffron and season with salt and freshly ground pepper. Bring the mixture to the boil, and stir it thoroughly before covering the casserole.

Cook the rice in the centre of the oven, pre-heated to 350°F (mark 4), for 40 minutes. Meanwhile, skin the cooked chicken and chop it roughly; skin and chop the tomatoes*. Blend these ingredients thoroughly into the rice and return it to the oven. Continue cooking at the same temperature for about 20 minutes, or until the rice has absorbed all the liquid. If the rice dries up too quickly, add a little more stock – the pilaf should be slightly moist.

Serve the pilaf at once. A green salad could be served, but it is quite substantial on its own.

SPAGHETTI ALLE VONGOLE

Spaghetti with clams (vongole) is a regular dish on the dinner menu in southern Italy. Surprisingly, cheese is never served with this spaghetti dish.

PREPARATION TIME: *15 min.*
COOKING TIME: *30 min.*

INGREDIENTS *(for 4–6)*:
1 lb. spaghetti
Salt
1½ oz. butter
4 cloves garlic
1 tablespoon olive oil
3 fluid oz. white wine
1 large tin clams

Cook the spaghetti, uncovered, for 10–15 minutes in plenty of boiling salted water. Drain the spaghetti thoroughly in a colander, and put in a warmed serving dish. Add the butter and toss the spaghetti in this.

While the spaghetti is cooking, peel and finely chop the garlic. Heat the oil in a small pan and fry the garlic for 2–3 minutes over moderate heat. Pour the wine over the garlic and increase the heat to boiling point to reduce* the wine a little. Add the clams with 2–3 tablespoons of their liquid and heat the mixture through over low heat.

Just before serving, pour the clams in the sauce over the spaghetti. Serve with crusty bread and a tomato salad.

LOBSTER RAVIOLI

Ravioli – little egg pasta cushions – are usually bought ready made and then filled with a savoury stuffing. They bear little resemblance to fresh pasta, but here, for a special occasion, is a recipe for home-made ravioli, with a luxury filling. To reduce the cost, crab meat can be substituted for the lobster.

PREPARATION TIME: *1½ hours*
COOKING TIME: *10 min.*

INGREDIENTS *(for 4)*:
RAVIOLI:
8 oz. plain flour
¼ level teaspoon salt
2 large eggs
1½ oz. butter
1 small egg
FILLING:
½–¾ lb. lobster or crab meat
1 tablespoon double cream
Squeeze of lemon
Cayenne pepper
SAUCE:
½ pint white sauce
3 tablespoons double cream
1 heaped teaspoon tomato purée
Juice of half lemon
Cayenne pepper
GARNISH:
Parmesan cheese

Sift the flour and the salt into a mixing bowl and make a well in the centre. Lightly beat the 2 eggs and pour into the flour; mix thoroughly. Melt the butter in a small saucepan and add to the flour. Knead the mixture to a stiff paste with a little cold water.

Turn the paste on to a floured surface and knead for 10 minutes until shiny. Set the paste aside to rest for at least 1 hour.

Meanwhile, make the filling for the ravioli: chop the lobster or

crab meat finely into a mixing bowl, add the cream and season to taste with lemon juice and cayenne pepper.

Roll out the paste, on a floured surface, to a paper-thin 24 in. square. With a teaspoon, drop the filling over one half of the paste, at intervals of 1½ in. Brush between the fillings with lightly beaten egg. Turn over the other half of the paste and press down firmly with the fingers between the fillings. Cut through the filled squares with a pastry wheel. Dust the ravioli squares with a little flour and set them aside for at least 1 hour before cooking.

When ready for cooking, bring a large pan of lightly salted water to the boil. Drop the ravioli into the water and cook for about 7 minutes. Drain on absorbent paper and keep them hot on a serving dish.

Serve the ravioli with a white sauce*, enriched with cream and tomato purée. Season to taste with lemon and cayenne pepper and add any leftovers from the filling. Heat the sauce through without boiling and serve in a sauce boat. Finally, grate Parmesan cheese into a separate bowl, and pass it round with the hot ravioli and sauce.

Vegetables & Salads

CANNELLONI WITH CREAMED HADDOCK

The pasta tubes known as cannelloni are usually served with a creamed stuffing of meat or chicken. For a summer meal, fish makes a lighter filling, excellent for lunch or supper.

PREPARATION TIME: *30 min.*
COOKING TIME: *45 min.*

INGREDIENTS *(for 4–6)*:

1 lb. smoked haddock fillet
1 pint milk
2 bay leaves
12 cannelloni tubes
3 fluid oz. double cream

Salt and black pepper
2 oz. unsalted butter
1 oz. plain flour
4 oz. Cheddar cheese

Wash and dry the haddock; put it in a wide pan with the milk and the bay leaves. Bring the milk slowly to the boil and poach* the haddock over low heat for about 10 minutes. Remove the pan from the heat, lift out the haddock with a perforated spoon and leave to cool. Strain the milk through a sieve and set it aside.

Bring a large pan of water to the boil, add 2 teaspoons salt and put in the cannelloni. Boil, uncovered, for about 15 minutes or until the pasta is just tender. Drain the cannelloni in a colander and rinse under cold water. Leave it to drain completely on crumpled kitchen paper.

While the cannelloni is cooking, remove the skin and bones from the haddock and flake* the flesh into a bowl. Pound with a pestle or mash with a fork until smooth, and gradually work in the cream. Season to taste with salt and freshly ground pepper.

Fit a forcing bag with a plain nozzle, fill it with the haddock mixture and pipe it into the cannelloni tubes. Arrange them in one layer in an ovenproof dish greased with ½ oz. of butter.

Make a thick white sauce* from the remaining butter, the flour and strained milk. Grate the cheese coarsely and stir 3 oz. into the sauce. Cook for a few minutes over low heat, then pour it over the cannelloni.

Sprinkle the remaining cheese over the sauce and put the dish in a pre-heated oven, at 375°F (mark 5) for 25 minutes or until the cheese is bubbly and golden brown on top.

Serve the cannelloni in the sauce while still hot. Crusty bread and a salad of cucumber and celery in a vinaigrette* sauce could be served with the pasta.

CREAMED SPINACH

Young crisp spinach leaves should be cooked as soon as possible after buying or gathering them. This dish goes well with most roast meats, particularly with ham and gammon.

PREPARATION TIME: *10 min.*
COOKING TIME: *10–15 min.*

INGREDIENTS *(for 4)*:

2 lb. spinach
½ level teaspoon salt
1 oz. butter
¼ level teaspoon grated nutmeg
3 fluid oz. double cream

Remove the stalks and coarse midribs from the spinach and throw away any bruised leaves. Wash the spinach thoroughly in several lots of cold water to get rid of all sand and grit. Put the spinach in a large saucepan with only the water clinging to the leaves. Cook over low heat, shaking the pan, until the spinach has reduced in volume and made its own liquid. Add the salt and cover the pan with a lid.

Cook gently for 5–8 minutes, then drain the spinach thoroughly through a fine sieve, squeezing out as much liquid as possible with a potato masher.

Chop the spinach roughly on a board. Melt the butter in the saucepan, add the spinach and nutmeg and heat through before stirring in the cream. Spoon into a hot serving dish.

TOMATO SALAD

The first home-grown tomatoes should be in the shops now. They make a refreshing starter to a meal, or they can be served as a side dish with cold meats.

PREPARATION TIME: *20 min.*
CHILLING TIME: *1 hour*

INGREDIENTS *(for 6)*:

12 tomatoes
1 level dessertspoon caster sugar
Salt and black pepper
4 tablespoons olive or corn oil
2 dessertspoons white wine vinegar
1 level tablespoon chopped chives or tarragon

Skin and thinly slice the tomatoes* and place them in a shallow serving dish. Sprinkle over the sugar, and season to taste with salt and freshly ground pepper. Mix the oil and vinegar together, and sprinkle over the tomatoes. Add chopped chives or tarragon and leave the salad to chill in the refrigerator for at least 1 hour before serving. Turn the tomato slices once or twice to absorb the dressing.

MUSHROOM SALAD

Mushrooms should be used as soon as possible after gathering. They tend to go limp when exposed to the air and should on no account be stored in the refrigerator.

PREPARATION TIME: *15 min.*

INGREDIENTS *(for 4–6)*:

1 lb. large mushrooms
Salt and black pepper
1 dessertspoon Worcestershire sauce
1 tablespoon soy sauce

Wash and trim the mushrooms*, and slice them as thinly as possible into a deep serving dish. Season to taste with salt and freshly ground pepper, and sprinkle over the Worcestershire and soy sauces. Mix the salad well and set aside for about 1 hour, turning the mushroom slices from time to time in the dressing.

The mushrooms will have made quite a lot of juice by the time they are ready for serving; this is an essential part of the dressing and should not be drained off.

COURGETTE AND CHIVES SALAD

Baby marrows, known as courgettes or zucchini, are becoming increasingly popular as a vegetable. They are also suitable for a fresh chilled salad to serve with cold meat and poultry.

PREPARATION TIME: *10 min.*
COOKING TIME: *5 min.*
CHILLING TIME: *1 hour*

INGREDIENTS *(for 4)* :
¾ lb. courgettes
1 tablespoon olive or corn oil
Juice of half lemon
Salt and black pepper
1 heaped tablespoon chopped
*   chives*

Wash the courgettes thoroughly and top and tail them. Bring a large pan of lightly salted water to the boil, drop in the courgettes and boil for 5 minutes to soften them slightly and reduce the bitterness of the skin. Drain the courgettes immediately in a colander and rinse in cold water.

Cut the drained courgettes crossways into ½ in. thick slices and put them in a shallow serving

dish. Make a dressing from the oil and lemon juice, season with salt and freshly ground pepper and pour over the courgettes. Add the chopped chives and blend thoroughly before chilling the salad.

SALAD ELONA

This unusual salad of cucumber and strawberries is an ideal side dish to serve with cold chicken and turkey, or with delicately flavoured fish such as salmon and turbot.

PREPARATION TIME: *15 min.*
CHILLING TIME: *1 hour*

INGREDIENTS *(for 4–6)* :
1 small cucumber
12 large strawberries
Salt and black pepper
1–2 tablespoons dry white wine
*   or white wine vinegar*

Peel the cucumber and slice it thinly. Wash and hull* the strawberries, drain them in a colander and then cut them into thin, even slices. Arrange the slices in a decorative pattern in a shallow serving dish—an outer circle of cucumber, slightly overlapped by a circle of strawberry, then more cucumber, finishing with a centre of strawberry slices. Season lightly with salt and freshly ground pepper. Sprinkle the wine or vinegar over the salad and chill in the refrigerator before serving.

This selection of summer salads shows, from left to right, Courgettes with Chives, Mushroom Salad, Tomato Salad and Salad Elona

Sweets & Puddings

PEAS AND SPRING ONIONS

It is a happy coincidence that spring onions and young garden peas both appear in June. They make an excellent combination to serve with roast lamb or chicken.

PREPARATION TIME: *15–20 min.*
COOKING TIME: *20–30 min.*

INGREDIENTS *(for 4–6)*:
2½ lbs. fresh green peas
10–12 spring onions
½ pint chicken stock
Beurre manié (½ oz. flour, ½ oz. butter)
Salt and black pepper

Shell the peas. Trim the roots and outer leaves from the onions; wash them and cut the stems off the onions, leaving about 1 in. of green on each bulb. Put the onions in a pan with the stock and bring slowly to simmering point. Cook gently until they begin to soften, then add the peas and continue to cook over low heat until the peas are tender, after about 20 minutes.

When the peas are just cooked, crumble in the beurre manié* and stir carefully, so that the peas do not break up, until the stock has thickened to a sauce. Season to taste with salt and freshly ground pepper. Serve hot.

BRAISED CHICORY

The sharp, clean taste of chicory – or Belgian endive – goes particularly well with roast pork, goose or duck.

PREPARATION TIME: *15 min.*
COOKING TIME: *35 min.*

INGREDIENTS *(for 4)*:
4 heads of chicory
1 small onion
1 oz. unsalted butter
Salt and black pepper
¼ pint chicken or beef stock
GARNISH:
Chopped parsley

Wash the chicory, trim off the root ends and cut each head in half lengthways. Scoop out the small piece of tough core at the base of each heart.

Peel and finely chop the onion. Melt the butter in a flameproof casserole over low heat and fry the onion in the butter until soft and transparent, but not browned. Add the chicory, fry until golden on both sides, then season to taste with salt and freshly ground pepper.

Remove the dish from the heat. Pour the stock over the chicory, cover the dish closely with a lid or foil and cook in the centre of an oven pre-heated to 350°F (mark 4) for 35 minutes.

Serve the braised chicory straight from the dish, sprinkled with finely chopped parsley.

LETTUCE AND GREEN PEAS

Young peas are traditionally cooked with fresh mint. Here, additional flavour is given by adding lettuce leaves to provide an unusual vegetable combination for spring lamb or duckling.

PREPARATION TIME: *15 min.*
COOKING TIME: *25 min.*

INGREDIENTS *(for 4–6)*:
10 outer cos lettuce leaves
2 lb. fresh green peas
1 teaspoon chopped mint
1 oz. butter
1 level teaspoon caster sugar
Salt and black pepper

Wash the lettuce leaves thoroughly, but do not dry them. Use half to line the base of a heavy saucepan. Shell the peas and put them, with the mint, on top of the lettuce. Add the butter, cut into knobs, and the sugar. Sprinkle with salt and freshly ground pepper, and lay the remaining lettuce leaves on top of the peas.

Cover the pan with a lid and cook over gentle heat for about 25 minutes or until the peas are tender, shaking the pan occasionally to prevent sticking.

Carefully spoon the lettuce and peas, with the cooking liquid, into a deep warm dish and serve immediately.

PEACH MELBA

During the 1892–3 opera season Escoffier, then chef at the Savoy Hotel, London, created this now classic sweet for Dame Nellie Melba, the famous Australian opera singer. It originally consisted of peaches and vanilla ice cream, the raspberry purée being a later addition.

PREPARATION TIME: *12 min.*

INGREDIENTS *(for 4)*:
2 large peaches
8 oz. fresh raspberries
2 oz. caster sugar
¾ pint vanilla ice cream

Put the peaches in a bowl and cover with boiling water. Leave for no more than 1 minute, then drain and peel them. Cut the peaches in half, carefully remove the stones and set the fruit aside. Rub the raspberries through a fine sieve into a mixing bowl; sweeten the resulting purée* with the sugar.

Assemble the sweet by placing two scoops of vanilla ice cream* in each individual serving glass; place one peach half on top, rounded side up and spoon over part of the raspberry purée. Serve at once.

SOFT FRUIT GÂTEAU

This dessert cake consists of a sponge case filled with fresh fruit and cream. It can be assembled to look like a jewellery box by setting the sponge lid at an angle and letting strawberries, raspberries or stalks of red currants appear over the edge.

PREPARATION TIME: *50–60 min.*
COOKING TIME: *15 min.*

INGREDIENTS *(for 6–8)*:

4 eggs
4 oz. caster sugar
4 oz. self-raising flour
¼ level teaspoon salt
½–¾ lb. mixed soft fruit (strawberries, raspberries, red currants)
½ pint double cream
3 oz. icing sugar

Lightly grease and flour a rectangular sponge tin, approximately 14 in. by 8 in. Put the eggs and sugar into a deep mixing bowl, and whisk until the eggs are pale and thick enough for the whisk to leave a trail. Sift the flour and salt together, and fold gently into the creamed egg mixture.

Spoon this sponge mixture into the prepared tin, spreading it evenly and making sure the corners are filled. Bake just above the centre of a pre-heated oven at 375°F (mark 5) for 15 minutes, or until the sponge is golden and firm to the touch.

Turn the sponge out on to a wire rack and leave to cool completely, preferably overnight. Meanwhile, clean the fruit, wash and drain it thoroughly on absorbent kitchen paper. Whip the double cream until it is thick and fluffy.

Carefully cut the sponge across into two halves, with a sharp knife. Spread just over half of the whipped cream over one half. Cut an oblong out of the other half, leaving an outer, unbroken edge, 1 in. wide, all round.

Carefully lift this frame on to the cream-covered base and fill the box, or cavity, with the fruit, reserving a few pieces for decoration. Sprinkle the sieved icing sugar over the fruit, and cover the box with the lid set at a slight angle. Pipe the remaining cream on to the lid and decorate with the reserved fruit.

The cake will keep for 2–3 hours in a refrigerator, but it should not be assembled too far in advance, or the fruit will become mushy and stain the cream.

BLACK CURRANT AND MINT PIE

The first black currants appear during the second half of the month, but at any time of year whole frozen black currants can be used for this sharp, refreshing sweet.

PREPARATION TIME: *30 min.*
COOKING TIME: *35–40 min.*

INGREDIENTS *(for 6)*:
1 lb. black currants
1 heaped dessertspoon chopped mint
4 oz. caster sugar
8 oz. shortcrust pastry (standard recipe)

Top and tail the black currants and wash them in a colander, dipping it into several lots of cold water. Drain the black currants thoroughly and put them in a shallow, 7 in. wide pie dish. Mix the finely chopped mint with the sugar and sprinkle it evenly over the black currants.

Roll out the prepared shortcrust pastry* on a floured surface, to a thickness of about ¼ in. Cover the pie dish with the pastry and decorate with pastry leaves or flowers from the trimmings. Make a slit in the centre of the pastry for the steam to escape. Brush the surface with water and sprinkle over a little extra caster sugar.

Bake the pie on the middle shelf of an oven pre-heated to 400°F (mark 6) for 35–40 minutes or until golden.

Serve the pie cold, with a jug of fresh cream.

STRAWBERRY ICE CREAM

PREPARATION TIME: *15–20 min.*
FREEZING TIME: *12 hours*

INGREDIENTS *(for 6)* :
½ *lb. strawberries*
3 *oz. icing sugar*
Squeeze lemon juice
¼ *pint double cream*
¼ *pint single cream*
GARNISH :
6–8 large strawberries

This sweet, perfect for a warm summer's evening, makes a little fruit go a long way. It is best if prepared the day before.

Hull* and wash the strawberries in a colander, drain them thoroughly and cut them into small pieces. Put them in the liquidiser, with the sieved sugar and lemon juice (alternatively, rub the strawberries through a fine sieve and add the sugar and lemon juice to the purée*).

Whisk the two creams until thick, but not stiff; blend this well into the strawberry purée.

Spoon the strawberry mixture into a plastic freezing container, cover with a lid and leave to freeze for 12 hours. One or two hours before serving, remove the ice cream from the freezing compartment and thaw slightly in the refrigerator.

Scoop the ice cream into individual glasses and decorate with slices of fresh strawberries.

STRAWBERRY WATER ICE

Water ices are both easy and economical to make. They are refreshing at any time of day and make a perfect summer sweet after a rich main course. Turn the refrigerator to its coldest setting before freezing them.

PREPARATION TIME: *10 min.*
FREEZING TIME: *minimum 3 hours*

INGREDIENTS *(for 4–6)* :
½ *lb. strawberries*
1 *oz. icing sugar*
¾ *pint lemonade*
2 *egg whites*

Wash and hull* the strawberries, drain them thoroughly in a colander, then cut them into small pieces. Rub the strawberries through a sieve and stir the sugar into the purée*. (Alternatively, put the fruit and sugar in a liquidiser to purée.) Add enough lemonade to the strawberry purée to make ¾ pint liquid. Spoon the mixture into an ice cube tray or a plastic freezing container, cover with foil or a lid and put in the freezing compartment of the refrigerator.

When the mixture is beginning to freeze round the sides of the container, remove from the freezer. Scrape the frozen bits into the centre of the container with a fork to break up any ice crystals. Whip the egg whites until stiff, but not dry, and fold them into the strawberry mixture. Return to the freezer, either in the original container or spooned into small moulds. Cover and freeze the ice until set.

Serve the water ice spooned into glasses or in their moulds.

BRANDY APRICOT TRIFLE

Fresh apricots, imported from Spain, are usually plentiful at this time of year. They form the basis of this rich dessert, suitable for a dinner party.

PREPARATION TIME: *20 min.*
COOKING TIME: *30 min.*
CHILLING TIME: *2 hours*

INGREDIENTS *(for 4–6)* :
1 *lb. fresh apricots*
1 *pint custard*
¼ *pint white wine*
2 *oz. caster sugar*
3 *fluid oz. brandy*
8 *oz. Ratafia biscuits*
¼ *pint double cream*

Prepare the custard* and set aside to cool. Wash and dry the apricots, cut them in halves and remove the stones. Put the wine and sugar in a pan and bring slowly to the boil. When the sugar has dissolved, add the apricot halves and cook them in this syrup, over low heat, until softened; set aside to cool.

Put the apricots in a trifle or serving dish and pour over the syrup and brandy. Set aside 6–8 Ratafia biscuits for decoration and crush the remainder with a rolling pin. Sprinkle them over the apricots and brandy, stirring carefully to let the biscuits absorb the liquid. Spoon the custard, which should now be almost at setting point, over the apricots and chill the trifle in the refrigerator for about 2 hours.

Just before serving, whip the cream until stiff and pipe it in swirls over the trifle. Decorate the top with the remaining Ratafias.

Savouries & Snacks

OMELET ALFONSE

The owner-chefs of small French bistros are experts at turning left-over meat and vegetables into savoury omelettes.

PREPARATION TIME: *10 min.*
COOKING TIME: *10 min.*

INGREDIENTS *(for 3–4)*:
6 eggs
4 tablespoons double cream
2 oz. cooked diced ham
2 oz. cooked peas
2 oz. cooked chopped carrots
Salt and black pepper
1 oz. unsalted butter
2 oz. grated Cheddar cheese

Beat the eggs lightly and stir in half the cream. Fold in the ham, peas and carrots; season with salt and pepper.

Melt the butter in a large omelette pan, and cook the egg mixture over moderate heat for about 6 minutes, poking through the mixture once or twice with a knife to release air. When the omelette is just set, fold it neatly in half and slide on to a fireproof serving dish. Mix the cheese with the remaining cream and spread over the omelette. Place under a hot grill until browned. Serve immediately, with a tomato or mushroom salad.

QUICK CHICKEN PÂTÉ

Pâté is a popular start to a meal, but it usually takes a long time to produce. This recipe quickly transforms a little left-over chicken into a well-flavoured pâté.

PREPARATION TIME: *10 min.*
COOKING TIME: *5 min.*
CHILLING TIME: *30 min.*

INGREDIENTS *(for 4)*:
2 oz. fat bacon (diced)
4½ oz. liver paste
4 oz. cooked, finely chopped chicken
1 crushed clove garlic
1 teaspoon finely chopped parsley
1 teaspoon finely chopped chives
Salt and black pepper

Fry the bacon, without extra fat, for about 5 minutes over medium heat. Pour off the fat and blend it with the liver paste; mix in the bacon, chicken, garlic, parsley and chives. Season with salt and pepper.

Pack the pâté in a small earthenware dish, cover and chill for at least 30 minutes in the refrigerator.

Serve with hot toast.

MIDSUMMER SALAD

Left-over cold meat and salad vegetables can be combined into an eye-catching, refreshing salad.

PREPARATION TIME: *20 min.*
CHILLING TIME: *30 min.*

INGREDIENTS *(for 4)*:
12 oz. thinly sliced cold meat or poultry
8 fluid oz. double cream
1 teaspoon lemon juice
2 oz. sliced button mushrooms
2 large or 4 small grated carrots
Salt and black pepper
Nutmeg
1 bunch watercress
½ peeled cucumber, thinly sliced
1 shredded lettuce

Mix the cream with lemon juice, and fold in the mushrooms and carrots; season with salt, pepper and nutmeg. Pile the mushroom mixture in the centre of a shallow serving dish and surround it with rings of watercress, cucumber and meat. Finish with a circle of shredded lettuce.

Chill the salad in the refrigerator before serving.

STUFFED ANCHOVY EGGS

Savoury eggs are often served as an appetiser with drinks. They can also be served as a hot savoury, with creamed spinach (see June vegetables).

PREPARATION TIME: *20 min.*
COOKING TIME: *15 min.*

INGREDIENTS *(for 4)*:
8 hardboiled eggs
2 oz. tin anchovy fillets
2 level tablespoons tomato ketchup
2 tablespoons double cream
Salt and black pepper
2 oz. grated Cheddar cheese
½ pint white sauce
½ level teaspoon paprika

Cut the shelled eggs in half lengthways and take out the yolks. Mash the drained anchovy fillets with a fork, and stir in the egg yolks. Pound to a smooth paste with a pestle or wooden spoon. Blend in the ketchup and cream, and season to taste.

Fill the egg whites with the yolk mixture and arrange them, cut side down, in a buttered fireproof dish. Stir half the cheese into the white sauce* and pour over the eggs. Sprinkle with the remaining cheese and dust lightly with paprika. Brown the dish under a hot grill.

FRENCH TOAST WITH FRUIT SAUCE

Fried fritters of stale bread – a version of French toast – can make a delicious family pudding.

PREPARATION TIME: *10 min.*
COOKING TIME: *10 min.*

INGREDIENTS *(for 6)*:
8 thick slices stale white bread
¼ pint milk
2 eggs
2 oz. caster sugar
¼ teaspoon vanilla essence
8 oz. tin of apricots
Juice of half lemon
1–2 oz. unsalted butter

Remove the crusts from the bread and cut each slice into 3 fingers. Whisk the milk and eggs, and stir in the sugar and vanilla essence.

Make a purée* from the apricots and their syrup, by rubbing them through a coarse sieve or blending in a liquidiser. Stir in the lemon juice and heat the purée over moderate heat. Keep warm.

Dip the bread fingers in the milk and egg mixture, and fry them in the butter until golden brown. Drain on crumpled kitchen paper and arrange on a warm serving dish. When all the fingers are cooked, pour the purée over them before serving. A jug of cream may be offered as well.

Summer Wedding Receptions

Holding a wedding reception at home may appear to be a formidable undertaking for the housewife, but it has several advantages which make the idea well worth considering. The main advantage, of course, is that it saves a great deal of money and, in addition, the food can be better, or at least more original, than that supplied by most catering companies and hotels for these functions. With careful planning, a reception held in familiar surroundings, imaginatively transformed for the occasion, will make a wedding day to remember.

The following menus offer a choice between a full-scale wedding breakfast for 12 people and a buffet for 50. The breakfast will give few problems on the day itself, since all the food can be made 24 hours earlier. The buffet, however, requires more careful planning. First measure the room where the reception is to be held – it is necessary to allow at least 4 sq. ft per person. Remember, too, that some furniture, such as tables for food and drinks and chairs for elderly guests, is essential. Three reception rooms, approximately 10 ft by 12 ft, or the equivalent, would be ideal; arrange the food in one room and drinks in another so that the guests will circulate. A very pleasant alternative, if the lawn is big enough, is to hire a marquee and arrange the buffet on tables inside it. The marquee should measure at least 25 ft by 30 ft.

Tableware can be a problem, and is best borrowed from friends. It can be hired from catering firms, but this is usually expensive. Cardboard plates with coated surfaces are far cheaper and eliminate washing up. Cutlery can be borrowed or hired, or inexpensive plastic sets purchased. The wine merchant from whom the wine is ordered will also supply glasses on a pay-for-breakage basis.

Wedding Breakfast for Twelve

Chilled Watercress Soup
Cold Poached Salmon
Potato Salad with Chives
Salad Elona
Green Salad with French Dressing
Raspberries with Cream
Cheese and Biscuits
Fruit
Coffee
Bavarian Cup – Champagne

Chilled Watercress Soup
Double the quantities for the recipe shown on p. 159. Cook the soup the night before and leave to chill in the refrigerator until just before serving.

Poached Salmon A 6–7 lb. salmon will be sufficient. Poach* it the day before in a court bouillon* and leave it to cool before skinning it. Bone the salmon*, leaving it whole, and keep it overnight in a cool place. Garnish the salmon next morning. Lay alternate thin slices of cucumber and hardboiled eggs down the centre and secure them with a little aspic. Decorate the dish with watercress, prawns in their shells and radish flowers*. Wrap the dish in plastic film and leave in a cool place until needed.

Set the table for the wedding breakfast round a low flower arrangement. On the table (top) are bowls of watercress soup, garnished with tiny leaves, and Italian bread sticks (grissini) in a tall glass. To garnish the poached salmon, arrange a collar of thick cucumber slices below the head to hide the gills

Salads For the potato salad, allow 4 lb. small new potatoes, $\frac{1}{2}$ pint mayonnaise* mixed with $\frac{1}{4}$ pint double cream, and a small bunch of chives. Boil the potatoes the night before, and peel them. In the morning, dress the potatoes with the mayonnaise and sprinkle with the chopped chives. Set the salad aside.

For Salad Elona, double the quantities given on p. 169.

The green salad requires 2 large cos lettuces, 2 bunches of watercress and 1 large head of celery.

Prepare the salad in the morning, mix the French dressing* and store both in the refrigerator. Dress the salad before serving it.

Raspberries with Cream These must be prepared on the morning of the wedding. Allow 4 lb. raspberries, a serving bowl of caster or sifted icing sugar, and $1\frac{1}{4}$ pints double cream. Wash the raspberries carefully, drain and put in a serving dish. Chill until required, together with the lightly whipped cream.

Cheeseboard This might include a soft cream cheese, a Camembert, wine-matured Cheddar and Blue Stilton. Offer a selection of biscuits and serve with fresh fruit, such as peaches, grapes and bananas.

Drinks Welcome the guests with dry sherry – 2 bottles will be ample. During the meal serve cool refreshing Bavarian cup, and toast the bride and groom in well-chilled champagne. Allow 3 bottles of champagne – each of

which will provide 8 glasses – for the toast.

Bavarian Cup Four jugs of this barely alcoholic drink will be required. In each jug, slice 10–12 large strawberries and pour over a miniature bottle of Grand Marnier (or other orange-based liqueur). Leave to infuse for 30 minutes, then add a tray of ice cubes. Pour 1 bottle of Riesling wine over the strawberries soaking in Grand Marnier, and top up with half as much soda water.

Serve the Bavarian cup from wide-necked jugs or from bowls and ladle a few strawberry slices into each glass

175

Buffet Menu for 50 Guests

Chicken and Mushroom
Vol-au-vents
Prawn and Scampi Vol-au-vents
Roast Stuffed Turkey
Whole Baked Glazed Ham
Mixed Green salad, Tomato,
Mushroom and Potato salads
CHEESES: Blue Stilton, Cheddar,
Double Gloucester, Brie,
Camembert, Dolce Latte,
French Bread and Butter,
Radishes, Celery
Trifles
Fruit Salads and Cream
Coffee

Preparations As these are somewhat more time-consuming for a large-scale buffet, the wise hostess will ask a couple of friends to help her both with the advance preparations and on the day itself. The hard work can be finished the day before: the vol-au-vents stuffed, the turkey roasted and the ham glazed. The trifles and the

fruit salads can be made and left to refrigerate until the next day.

On the wedding day itself, arrange the food, tableware, cutlery and glasses and cake on the buffet. Decorate the trifles and fruit salads, assemble the cheeseboards and set the wine to chill in a bath of ice cubes. Fix paper frills round the turkey legs and ham bone. Leave the carving to the host or a competent guest; this can be done during the buffet as required.

Vol-au-vents Order 10 dozen vol-au-vent cases from the baker, giving him at least 1 week's notice. For the fillings, simmer a chicken (approx. 5 lb.) in water,

with 2 onions, 2 sticks celery, 1 bay leaf, a sprig of tarragon, salt and pepper. Leave the cooked chicken to get cold, and meanwhile reduce* the stock to 2 pints. Strain the stock and use it for a thick white sauce*. Blend $\frac{1}{4}$ pint double cream into the sauce. Skin

the chicken, chop the meat finely and mix with half the sauce. Blend in $\frac{1}{2}$ lb. lightly sautéed mushrooms and spoon the filling into half the vol-au-vent cases.

Blend enough tomato purée into the remaining sauce to colour it delicately. Sharpen with the juice of half a lemon. Stir in $\frac{3}{4}$ lb. finely chopped prawns and scampi and fill the remaining cases.

Heat the vol-au-vents on baking trays in a moderate oven for 15 minutes before serving.
Roast Stuffed Turkey Order a dressed turkey, weighing 22 lb. and use a forcemeat stuffing* for the body and a chestnut purée*

for the breast. Cook the turkey, wrapped in foil, at a temperature of 350°F (mark 4) for 6 hours, and for the last 30 minutes at 400°F (mark 6) without foil to brown the turkey.

Glazed Ham Most butchers will supply the ham cooked at no extra charge. Score the top of the ham into a diamond pattern and brush it with a glaze* of honey and light brown sugar. Set the ham for 30 minutes in the centre of a pre-heated oven at 450°F (mark 8). Garnish with halved glacé cherries, spiked with whole cloves.

Salads For the green salads, allow 8 cabbage and 8 cos lettuces, with 6 bunches of watercress. Make the tomato salad from 7 lb. tomatoes, and for the mushroom salad (see recipe on p. 168) use 3 lb. mushrooms: for the potato salad, use 6 lb. small new potatoes,

1 pint mayonnaise* blended with ½ pint double cream, and a small bunch of chives.

Cheeseboards Make up at least two cheeseboards from 7 lb. assorted cheeses, 6 bunches of

radishes and 6 large heads of celery. Allow 8 long French loaves and 2½ lb. of butter.

Trifles and Fruit Salads Make 5 large sherry trifles* and decorate them on the day with piped whirls of cream. Mix the fruit salads from equal amounts of fresh and tinned drained fruit. Choose 6 large tins of different fruits and mix with 1½ lb. dessert apples, 1 large fresh pineapple, 2 lb. strawberries, 1 lb. seedless grapes, 8 large oranges and 8 large pears. Heat, but do not boil, ½ bottle medium dry Sauterne with 3–4 tablespoons caster sugar. Pour this syrup over the bowls of fruit salad and set aside to cool.

Generous shakes of Angostura bitters give a refreshing flavour.

Drinks The toast to the happy couple should traditionally be drunk in a sparkling wine – champagne for preference – but German Hock or Moselle wines, Italian Spumanti, French Vouvray and white Burgundy and Spanish dry white wines are all cheaper and make good substitutes. Each bottle provides 8 glasses.

A glass of sherry on arrival, and a choice of inexpensive red or white wines are perfectly adequate. Alternatively, serve jugs of Bavarian cup (see wedding breakfast), and make one or two jugs of fruit juice for the children.

July

Not rent off, but cut off, ripe beane with a knife,
   for hindering stalke of hir vegetive life.
So gather the lowest, and leaving the top,
   shall teach thee a trick, for to double thy crop.

This Month's Recipes

*High summer brings an abundance of fruit and vegetables; and
fresh from the garden they are so much tastier*

Food in Season

Salad vegetables are plentiful this month, and are coming down in price. Asparagus too, though somewhat woody, is cheaper now than at the height of the season. At the same time, fresh shellfish, particularly crab, lobster, prawns and shrimps, are at their best, and though fresh salmon is never cheap, it is generally at its most reasonable during July.

The first imported peaches appear in the shops and are usually good value. Black and red currants, home-grown cherries and dessert gooseberries are even better buys. During July, there is often a surplus of these fruits which are ideal for making jams; so too are the strawberries, now past their prime as dessert fruits, and the raspberries, at the height of their season.

Fish

Angler tail
Bream, sea
Brill
Clams
Cod
Coley
Conger eels
Crab
Dabs
Dover sole
Dublin Bay prawns
Eels
Flounders
Grey mullet
Haddock
Hake
Halibut
Herring
Lemon sole
Lobster
Mackerel
Mock halibut (or
   Greenland halibut)
Oysters, Portuguese
Pike
Plaice
Prawns
Redfish
Red mullet
Salmon
Scad
Scallops
Sea trout
Shrimps
Skate
Trout, rainbow
Turbot
Witch

Poultry & Game

Chicken
Duck
Guinea fowl
Pigeon
Quail
Rabbit
Turkey
Venison

Vegetables

Asparagus
Avocado pears
Aubergines
Beetroots
Broad beans
Cabbages
Carrots
Cauliflowers
Celery
Chillies
Corn on the cob
Courgettes
Cucumbers
Endive
Fennel
French beans
Garlic
Globe artichokes
Horseradish
Lettuces
Mushrooms
Okra
Onions
Parsley
Peas
Peppers
Potatoes
Radishes
Runner beans
Salad cress
Shallots
Spinach
Spring onions
Sugar peas
Tomatoes
Turnips
Vegetable marrows
Watercress

Fruit

Apples
Apricots
Bananas
Blackberries
Black currants
Cherries
Figs
Grapefruit
Grapes
Gooseberries
Lemons
Limes
Loganberries
Lychees
Mangoes
Melons
Nectarines
Oranges
Passion fruit
Peaches
Pears
Persimmons
Pineapples
Plums
Raspberries
Red currants
Rhubarb
Strawberries

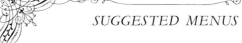

SUGGESTED MENUS

Lettuce Soup
Spiced Brisket of Beef
Tomatoes with Horseradish Mayonnaise
Clafouti Limousin

Stuffed Eggs Provençal
Truites Jurassienne
Mushroom and Prawn Salad
Raspberry Yoghourt Sorbet

Shrimp and Mushroom Flambé
Pigeons with Olives
Brown Tom
Coeur à la Crème

Crab Quiche
Turkey Escalopes Cordon Bleu
French Beans Mimosa
Cold Caramel Soufflé

Russian Herring Roes
Sesame Chicken with Spiced Rice
Cucumber au Gratin
Summer Pudding

Cucumber Cups with Prawns
Osso Buco
Risotto Bianco
Baked Stuffed Peaches

Lebanese Cucumber Soup
Luxury Pizza
Crisp Salad with French Dressing
Fresh Fruit

Soups & Starters

SHRIMPS AND MUSHROOMS FLAMBÉ

This is a light and easily made starter for a dinner party. Fresh shrimps can be used, but the creamy taste of potted shrimps blends better with mushrooms and brandy.

PREPARATION TIME: *10 min.*
COOKING TIME: *10 min.*

INGREDIENTS *(for 4)*:
6 oz. potted shrimps
8 oz. button mushrooms
1½ oz. unsalted butter
Pinch nutmeg
Black pepper
4 slices brown bread
2 tablespoons brandy

Trim and wipe the mushrooms*; slice them thinly. Melt the butter in a small frying pan and cook the mushrooms for 2–3 minutes until slightly softened. Add the shrimps to the pan and stir over moderate heat until they are heated through. Season to taste with a little nutmeg and a few twists of freshly ground pepper.

Toast the bread and arrange it on individual warmed serving plates; keep warm.

Warm the brandy in a small pan, pour over the shrimps and set alight. As soon as the flames have died down, spoon the shrimp and mushroom mixture on to the hot toast and serve immediately.

LEBANESE CUCUMBER SOUP

There are many variations of this popular Middle Eastern soup. It can only be served cold, but is refreshing in hot weather and looks tempting with a few pink shrimps floating on top.

PREPARATION TIME: *15 min.*
CHILLING TIME: *about 1 hour*

INGREDIENTS *(for 4–6)*:
1 large or 2 small cucumbers
½ pint single cream
5 fluid oz. natural yoghourt
1 clove garlic
2 tablespoons tarragon vinegar
Salt and black pepper
2 level tablespoons finely chopped mint

GARNISH:
1 tablespoon finely chopped cocktail gherkins
Sprigs of mint
18 shrimps (optional)

Wash and dry the cucumber. Do not peel it, but grate it coarsely into a bowl. Stir in the cream and the yoghourt. Peel and crush the garlic, and add to the cucumber, together with the vinegar. Season to taste with salt and freshly ground pepper. Stir in the chopped mint. Chill the soup in a refrigerator for at least 1 hour.

Serve the pale green soup in individual bowls.

For a summery look, garnish each bowl with chopped gherkins or a sprig of fresh mint. On special occasions, float a few shelled prawns on top of the soup instead of the green garnish.

RUSSIAN HERRING ROES

A dinner party in Russia always begins with Zakuski – an hors-d'oeuvre tray with more numerous delicacies than in Europe. This makes an inexpensive chilled first course.

PREPARATION TIME: *25 min.*
CHILLING TIME: *1 hour*

INGREDIENTS *(for 4–6)*:
8–12 oz. soft herring roes
4 bay leaves
3 tablespoons white wine vinegar
8 peppercorns
1 cucumber
2–3 level dessertspoons capers
2–3 tablespoons olive oil
Salt and black pepper
GARNISH:
Chopped fresh parsley

Remove all blood and discoloured parts from the roes and put them, with the bay leaves, in an ovenproof dish. In a small pan, boil ½ pint of water, the vinegar and peppercorns for 3–4 minutes, then pour this marinade* over the roes. Cover the dish with a lid or foil and bake in the centre of a pre-heated oven at 375°F (mark 5) for 10 minutes. Remove from the oven and let the roes cool in the marinade.

Peel the cucumber, slice it in half lengthways and remove the seeds with a pointed teaspoon. Chop the cucumber finely into a bowl, mix in capers and olive oil, and season to taste with salt and freshly ground pepper.

Drain the roes. Put the cucumber mixture in a shallow serving dish, pile the roes on top and chill for about 1 hour in the refrigerator.

Before serving, sprinkle the roes with parsley. Offer thinly sliced brown bread and butter with the roes.

SMOKED TROUT MOUSSE

This mousse, which has a creamy texture and smoky flavour, makes an attractive starter to a meal. It can be prepared a day in advance and kept in the refrigerator until required.

PREPARATION TIME: *15 min.*
CHILLING TIME: *1 hour*

INGREDIENTS *(for 4–6)*:
¾ *lb. smoked trout*
4 oz. cottage cheese
5 fluid oz. soured cream
Juice of half lemon
Salt and black pepper
GARNISH:
Finely chopped parsley

Remove the skin and bones from the flesh of the trout, and flake* the meat into a liquidiser. Sieve the cottage cheese and add, with the soured cream, to the flaked fish. Blend the mixture until smooth. Alternatively, pound the flaked fish to a smooth paste with a mortar and pestle, before mixing in the sieved cottage cheese and the soured cream. Season to taste with the lemon juice, salt and pepper. Spoon the mousse into individual ramekin dishes and leave to chill in the refrigerator.

Sprinkle finely chopped parsley in a neat border round the edge of each dish. Serve with fingers or triangles of hot brown toast and butter.

STUFFED EGGS PROVENÇALE

Stuffed eggs are always popular – as a first course, with drinks or at picnics and buffets. This is one of the many versions of the classic French recipe.

PREPARATION TIME: *40 min.*
COOKING TIME: *15 min.*

INGREDIENTS *(for 4–6)*:
6 eggs
1 oz. stoned black olives
1 oz. tinned tuna fish
1 oz. anchovy fillets
1 oz. capers
1 level teaspoon French mustard
4–6 tablespoons olive oil
2 teaspoons brandy
Black pepper
Lemon juice
GARNISH:
Lettuce or watercress

Hardboil the eggs and plunge them into cold water. When cold, shell the eggs, halve them lengthways with a sharp knife and carefully remove the yolks. Set aside. Using a mortar and pestle, pound the olives to a smooth paste. Add the drained tuna, anchovy fillets and capers, and continue pounding until the mixture is perfectly smooth. Blend in the mustard, and gradually work in the olive oil and brandy, until the mixture is creamy and thick.

Season to taste with freshly ground pepper and a little lemon juice. Press the egg yolks through a coarse sieve and blend them into the fish mixture.

Pile the stuffing into the hollow egg whites or pipe it through a bag fitted with a rosette nozzle. Arrange the stuffed eggs on a bed of lettuce or watercress, and serve with crusty bread and butter.

LETTUCE SOUP

A surplus of home-grown lettuce, or those not quite crisp enough for a salad, can be used for an economical soup. The pale green, light-textured soup is ideal on a chilly summer day.

PREPARATION TIME: *10 min.*
COOKING TIME: *15 min.*

INGREDIENTS *(for 4–6)*:
8 oz. lettuce leaves
Salt
1 small onion
1½ oz. butter
¾ *pint chicken stock*
Black pepper, caster sugar, grated nutmeg
¾ *pint milk*
1–2 egg yolks
2 tablespoons single cream
GARNISH:
Bread croûtons

Wash the lettuce leaves thoroughly and blanch* them for 5 minutes in boiling salted water. Drain and rinse under cold running water. Chop the leaves; peel and finely chop the onion.

Melt the butter in a saucepan and fry the onion in it for 5 minutes, until soft. Add the lettuce shreds, setting a few aside. Pour the stock over the onions and lettuce and bring the soup to the boil. Season to taste with salt, freshly ground pepper, sugar and nutmeg.

Allow the soup to cool slightly before liquidising it or rubbing it through a sieve. Add the milk to the soup and reheat gently; simmer for 5 minutes.

Lightly beat together the egg yolks and cream. Spoon a little of the hot, but not boiling, soup into this and blend thoroughly. Pour the egg mixture into the soup and simmer gently until the soup thickens. On no account should it reach boiling point, or the eggs will curdle.

Just before serving, add the rest of the lettuce shreds. Ladle the soup into plates and serve with a bowl of crisp bread croûtons*.

TARAMASALATA

A Greek hors-d'oeuvre (*mézé*) nearly always includes a dish of creamy pâté made from the dried, salted and pressed roe of the grey mullet. Smoked cod roe is an excellent substitute for mullet.

PREPARATION TIME: *30 min.*
CHILLING TIME: *45 min.*

INGREDIENTS *(for 4–6)*:
8 oz. smoked cod roe
1 onion
1–2 cloves garlic (optional)
4 slices white bread, each ¾ *in. thick*
5 tablespoons milk or water
6–8 tablespoons olive oil
Juice of a large lemon
Black pepper

Choose a soft and plump piece of smoked roe (or use paste from a jar). Scoop the roe out of its skin and into a mixing bowl. Peel and grate the onion and squeeze to remove the water. Peel and crush the garlic if used. Remove the crusts and set the bread to soak in the milk.

Add the onion (and garlic) to the roe and beat thoroughly with a wooden spoon until quite smooth. Squeeze the bread dry and beat it into the roe mixture. Add the oil, alternately with the lemon juice, little by little as for a mayonnaise*. Beat vigorously after each addition until the mixture is a creamy purée.

Season to taste with freshly ground pepper and pack into a pot or individual ramekin dishes. Cover and chill lightly.

Serve with hot crisp toast, unsalted butter, and black olives and lemon wedges.

Fish

SMOKED HADDOCK SOUFFLÉ

Warm sunny days call for light delicate meals. This soufflé is easy to prepare. It can constitute the main course, or it can be made in small individual soufflé dishes and served as a first course.

PREPARATION TIME: *30 min.*
COOKING TIME: *30 min.*

INGREDIENTS *(for 4–6)*:
¾ *lb. smoked haddock fillet*
½ *pint milk*
2½ *oz. unsalted butter*
1 *oz. plain flour*
Grated rind of half lemon
2 *level tablespoons grated*
  Parmesan cheese
Cayenne pepper
4 *eggs*
1 *level tablespoon finely chopped*
  parsley

Wash the haddock fillet and pat it dry with absorbent paper. Put it in a large shallow pan and pour over the milk with 1 tablespoon of water. Bring slowly to the boil, then remove the pan from the heat. Lift out the fish and allow to cool slightly; set the cooking liquid aside. Remove skin and bones from the haddock and flake* the flesh into a mixing bowl. Mash it finely with a fork.

Melt 2 oz. of the butter in a small pan and blend in the flour; remove from the heat and gradually add the haddock liquid, stirring continuously. Return the pan to the heat and simmer until the sauce thickens to a creamy consistency. Flavour the sauce with the lemon rind, cheese and cayenne; stir in the haddock.

Separate the eggs and beat the yolks into the sauce, one at a time. Whisk the egg whites until stiff, but not dry, and fold them carefully into the fish mixture. Butter a 1½–2 pint prepared soufflé dish* or 6 small soufflé dishes; sprinkle over the parsley.

Spoon the haddock mixture into the dish and bake in the centre of the oven, pre-heated to 400°F (mark 6), for 30 minutes or until well risen and golden.

Plain buttered potatoes and a green vegetable could accompany the soufflé for a main course.

FILLETS OF SOLE DUGLÉRÉ

A French chef, Dugléré, invented this now-classic dish in the 19th century. It can be served hot, but is traditionally presented cold as a main course.

PREPARATION TIME: *20–30 min.*
COOKING TIME: *25 min.*

INGREDIENTS *(for 4)*:
2 *Dover soles, about 1 lb. 4 oz.*
  each
2–3 *shallots*
4 *large tomatoes*
2 *oz. unsalted butter*
½ *small clove garlic*
Salt and black pepper
¼ *pint fish stock*
¼ *pint dry white wine*
⅓–½ *pint double cream*
Beurre manié
1 *teaspoon chopped fresh tarragon*
  (optional)
1 *egg yolk*
Lemon juice
Tabasco
GARNISH:
Chopped parsley

Ask the fishmonger to fillet the soles* and to include the bones and skin with the order. Use these for making the fish stock*. Peel and finely chop the shallots. Skin the tomatoes*, remove the seeds and chop the flesh finely. Use ½ oz. of butter to thoroughly grease a shallow, flameproof dish. Peel and cut the garlic and rub it lightly round the dish. Wash the sole fillets and pat them dry with a clean cloth. Arrange them in a single layer in the dish, and season with salt and freshly ground pepper.

Sprinkle the shallots over the fish and top with the tomatoes. Pour over the strained stock and the wine, and cover the dish with buttered greaseproof paper. Bring the contents of the dish to simmering point on top of the stove, then lower the heat. Poach* the sole gently for about 7 minutes, or until cooked but still firm. Alternatively, bake the fish in the centre of an oven pre-heated to 350°F (mark 4) for about 15 minutes.

When cooked, carefully lift the fillets out. Drain them and cool. Bring the cooking liquid, with the shallots and tomatoes, to the boil and reduce* by at least a quarter. Take the pan from the heat and stir in the cream; add knobs of the beurre manié* and whisk until completely absorbed. Blend in the tarragon if used. Melt the remaining butter and beat with the egg yolk; blend this into the cream sauce. Correct seasoning and leave to cool.

Just before serving, arrange the sole fillets on a large flat dish and sprinkle them with a little lemon juice. Stir a few drops of Tabasco into the sauce. Coat the fillets with the sauce and sprinkle with parsley.

This rich dish needs no more than a plain green salad and perhaps a few boiled potatoes to complement it.

MACKEREL WITH TOMATOES

Mackerel is sometimes known as the poor man's trout – unjustly so, for although both are oily fish, their flavours are quite distinct. Mackerel is at its best and most plentiful in summer, and makes an excellent main course.

PREPARATION TIME: *30 min.*
COOKING TIME: *20 min.*

INGREDIENTS *(for 4–6)*:
6 *medium mackerel*
Seasoned flour
3 *tablespoons cooking or olive oil*
1 *onion*
2 *oz. mushrooms*
1 *clove garlic*
¾ *lb. firm tomatoes*
1 *oz. butter*
Salt and black pepper
1 *rounded teaspoon chopped*
  parsley
2 *teaspoons wine vinegar*

Clean and fillet the mackerel*. Wash the fillets, wipe them dry on a clean cloth and coat them with seasoned flour*, shaking off any surplus. Heat 2 tablespoons of the oil in a heavy-based frying pan and, when hot, fry the fillets for about 10 minutes, or until golden brown, turning once.

While the mackerel is frying, peel the onion and garlic, and wipe and trim the mushrooms*. Finely chop the onion and mushrooms, and crush the garlic. Skin the tomatoes* and slice them thinly. Heat the remaining oil in a clean pan and fry the onion for a few minutes over moderate heat. Add the mushrooms and garlic, and cook very slowly for a further 5 minutes. Season to taste with salt and freshly ground pepper, and stir in the parsley and vinegar. Fry the tomato slices for 3 minutes in the butter, using a separate pan over gentle heat.

To serve, arrange the warm mackerel fillets on a serving dish, put the tomatoes between them and spoon a little of the onion mixture on to each fillet. Serve with new potatoes and a salad.

Meat

SALMON KEDGEREE

In the 19th century, kedgeree – of Indian origin – was an established country house breakfast dish. Nowadays it more frequently makes its appearance as a light lunch or supper dish.

PREPARATION TIME: *5 min.*
COOKING TIME: *30 min.*

INGREDIENTS *(for 4–6)*:
8 oz. cooked salmon
Salt, black pepper and cayenne
6 oz. long grain rice
1 onion
2 oz. butter
2 hardboiled eggs
GARNISH:
Chopped parsley

Remove any skin and bones from the salmon, and flake* it carefully. Bring 1 pint of water to the boil in a large saucepan, adding a pinch each of salt, pepper and cayenne. Add the rice, cover tightly with a lid or foil, and cook over low heat for about 25 minutes, or until all the water is absorbed and the rice is fluffy.

While the rice is cooking, peel and finely chop the onion. Melt a little of the butter in a pan and fry the onion until soft and transparent. Set aside. Roughly chop the whites of the hardboiled eggs, and press the yolks through a sieve.

Cut the remaining butter into small knobs and stir into the cooked rice, with the flaked salmon, onion and egg whites. Season to taste and heat the mixture through gently.

To serve, pile the kedgeree up on a warmed flat dish and decorate with the sieved egg yolks, arranged in a star or cross pattern. Sprinkle generously with chopped parsley, and offer hot buttered toast fingers.

TRUITES JURASSIENNE

River trout are at their best and least expensive in July. The sauce comes from the Jura region in France.

PREPARATION TIME: *15 min.*
COOKING TIME: *35–45 min.*

INGREDIENTS *(for 6)*:
6 medium trout
2 oz. unsalted butter
2 shallots or 1 small onion
½ pint rosé wine
¼ pint Hollandaise sauce
1 rounded tablespoon double cream
Salt and black pepper
GARNISH:
Bread croûtons, chopped parsley

Clean the trout, leaving on the heads and tails. Lay them side by side in a buttered fireproof dish. Peel and finely chop the shallots and sprinkle over the fish. Pour over the wine and cover the dish with buttered greaseproof paper or foil. Cook in the centre of a pre-heated oven at 300°F (mark 2) for 25 minutes.

Meanwhile, prepare the Hollandaise sauce* and heat without boiling. When the trout are cooked, lift them carefully on to a cloth and remove the skins. Keep warm on a serving dish.

Strain the cooking liquid and reduce* it by fast boiling until there are only 2–3 tablespoons left. Let this cool slightly, then stir it into the warm Hollandaise sauce; finally stir in the cream. Adjust the seasoning.

To serve, pour the sauce over the fish. Garnish with fried bread croûtons* and a sprinkling of chopped parsley. Boiled potatoes and mushrooms cooked in a little butter go well with the trout.

LAMB KIDNEYS EPICURE

Grilled or devilled kidneys belong to the English breakfast table. The nutritious, inexpensive kidneys can also be served as a main course.

PREPARATION TIME: *15 min.*
COOKING TIME: *15 min.*

INGREDIENTS *(for 4)*:
8 lamb kidneys
   (approximately 1¼ lb.)
1 oz. butter
1 small shallot
1 rounded tablespoon plain flour
½ pint beef stock
Salt and black pepper
1 level tablespoon Dijon mustard
1 level dessertspoon redcurrant
   jelly
2 tablespoons double cream
1 tablespoon port

Remove any fat from the kidneys* and slice them in half lengthways. Put them in a basin and cover with boiling water; leave for 2 minutes. Drain and dry the kidneys; remove the skin and snip out the cores with scissors. Cut each half into 3–4 slices. Melt the butter in a frying pan and cook the kidneys over moderate heat for 3–4 minutes, until lightly browned.

Remove the kidneys from the pan and keep them warm. Peel and finely chop the shallot and cook in the pan juices until softened. Blend in the flour and gradually add the stock. Simmer the sauce, stirring frequently, until smooth and creamy. Season to taste with salt and freshly ground pepper. Blend in the mustard, redcurrant jelly, cream and port. Re-heat the kidneys in the sauce over low heat, but do not let the sauce reach boiling point or it will separate.

Pile the kidneys and the sauce over a bed of fluffy boiled rice. Grilled mushrooms could be an extra vegetable.

SWEETBREADS WITH BEURRE NOISETTE

Ideally, this lunch or supper dish should be made with calf sweetbreads. These are often difficult to come by, and lamb sweetbreads make a good and inexpensive alternative. Both types of sweetbreads should be soaked for several hours before cooking.

PREPARATION TIME: *30 min.*
COOKING TIME: *40 min.*

INGREDIENTS *(for 4–6)*:
1¼ lb. calf or lamb sweetbreads
4 tablespoons white wine vinegar
1 carrot
1 stick celery
¾ pint chicken or veal stock
½ bay leaf
1 sprig thyme
6 peppercorns
6 oz. clarified butter
Salt and black pepper
Seasoned flour
1½ oz. unsalted butter
1 tablespoon olive oil
GARNISH:
Chopped fresh parsley
Lemon wedges

Soak the sweetbreads for at least 3 hours in several changes of cold water to remove all traces of blood. For the last 1½ hours, soak the sweetbreads in fresh cold water with 1 tablespoon of vinegar. Put them in a pan with fresh cold water and bring slowly to the boil. Take the pan off the heat, drain the sweetbreads and cool under running water. Remove the black veins and pull off as much as possible of the thin skin around them, without tearing the sweetbreads. Wrap them in a clean cloth and let them cool between two weighted plates or wooden boards to flatten them. Meanwhile, scrape, wash and slice the carrot and celery.

Put the sweetbreads in a pan, cover with the stock by about 1 in. and add the carrot, celery, bay leaf, thyme and peppercorns. Put the pan over low heat and bring slowly to simmering point; cook for 10 minutes, uncovered. Remove the sweetbreads, strain the stock through a fine sieve and leave the sweetbreads in the stock until they are cool enough to handle.

Remove the sweetbreads from the stock and dry them on a clean cloth. Heat the remaining vinegar in a small pan and boil until it has reduced* by two-thirds. In a separate pan, heat the clarified butter* gently and, when light brown, stir in the vinegar. Season to taste with salt and freshly ground pepper.

Cut the sweetbreads into thick slices and coat lightly with seasoned flour*. Melt the unsalted butter and oil together over moderate heat and cook the sweetbreads in it for about 3 minutes on each side, or until lightly browned. Remove the sweetbread slices to a heated serving dish and pour the brown butter over them.

Sprinkle with chopped parsley and serve at once garnished with wedges of lemon. They go well with boiled rice and cucumber au gratin (see July vegetables).

SPICED BRISKET OF BEEF

INGREDIENTS *(for 8–10) :*
4 lb. lean boned brisket of beef
10 oz. kitchen salt
2 shallots
3 bay leaves
1 level teaspoon potassium nitrate (saltpetre)
1 level teaspoon allspice
4 rounded tablespoons brown sugar
1 level teaspoon powdered cloves
1 level teaspoon powdered mace
½ level teaspoon crushed black peppercorns
½ level teaspoon chopped thyme

PREPARATION TIME: *20 min.*
COOKING TIME: *4–5 hours*

This Irish dish is part of the traditional cold Christmas buffet. It also makes a perfect dish for summer, ideal for a buffet or a large dinner party. The beef should be left to steep in spices for 8 days before being cooked and pressed.

Wipe the boned, but not rolled, meat with a clean damp cloth and put it in a large bowl. Rub the meat well on all sides with 8 oz. of the salt. Cover the bowl with muslin and leave for 24 hours in the lower part of the refrigerator or in a cool place.

Peel and finely chop the shallots and the bay leaves. Put these in a bowl with the remainder of the salt and the rest of the ingredients and mix together. Each day, rub this mixture well into the salted meat, pouring off any liquid that may have formed. All the spicing mixture should have been absorbed after 7 days.

Roll the spiced meat neatly and tie it securely with fine string. Put it in a heavy-based pan and cover with warm water. Simmer, covered, over low heat for 4–5 hours. Let the meat cool in the liquid, then lift it out. Place it between two plates with a heavy weight on top and leave it to press for 8 hours.

Serve the spiced brisket cold, sliced and accompanied by baked potatoes, a selection of salads and pickled beetroot and gherkins.

low heat for 1½ hours, or until the meat is tender.

While the veal is cooking, mix the ingredients for the garnish.

Pour the sauce over the meat and sprinkle with the garnish. The marrow is usually left in the bones, but it can also be extracted and spread on the toast. In Italy, osso buco is served with Risotto alla Milanese (see December rice and pasta), but buttered egg noodles are more suitable for a summer meal.

VITELLO TONNATO

In Italy, this cold terrine of veal in tuna fish sauce is a stand-by for hot summer days. The classic version uses boiled veal, but in some regions the meat is roasted instead. It should be made the day before and left to chill overnight.

PREPARATION TIME: *30 min.*
COOKING TIME: *1¾ hours*

INGREDIENTS *(for 6)*:
2½ lb. leg or loin of veal
1 carrot
1 onion
1 stick celery
4 peppercorns
1 level teaspoon salt
3–3½ oz. tin of tuna fish
4 anchovy fillets
¼ pint olive oil
2 egg yolks
Black pepper
1½ tablespoons lemon juice
GARNISH:
Capers
Gherkins
Fresh tarragon (if available)

Ask the butcher to bone the meat, tie it in a neat roll and include the bones with the order.

Scrape and wash the carrot and peel the onion; quarter both.

Scrub and chop the celery. Put the meat into a large saucepan together with the bones. Add the vegetables, peppercorns, salt and enough water to cover the meat. Bring the water quickly to the boil, turn down the heat, cover the pan with a lid and simmer for about 1¾ hours, or until the meat is tender. Lift the meat carefully out of the pan and set aside to cool. Reduce* the cooking liquid by fast boiling, strain through muslin and set aside.

To make the sauce, drain the tuna and anchovy and put in a bowl with 1 tablespoon of the oil. Mash with a fork until thoroughly mixed. Blend in the egg yolks and season with pepper. Rub this paste through a sieve into a small bowl. Stir in half the lemon juice, then add the remaining oil, little by little, beating well after each addition. When the sauce has become thick and shiny, add more lemon juice to taste. Stir in about 2 tablespoons of the veal liquid to give the sauce the consistency of thin cream.

Cut the cold meat into thin slices and arrange them in a terrine. Cover the meat completely with the sauce, then wrap the dish closely in foil and leave overnight to marinate*.

Before serving, garnish the dish with capers, a few sliced gherkins or with a sprig of tarragon. Cold savoury rice* or a tossed green salad could complement the meat.

NOISETTES OF LAMB SHREWSBURY

These little round fillets—or noisettes—are cut from the loin or best end of lamb. They are excellent as the main course for a dinner party, especially as the time-consuming sauce can be made well in advance.

PREPARATION TIME: *15–25 min.*
COOKING TIME: *2 hours for sauce*
30 min. for the noisettes

INGREDIENTS *(for 4–6)*:
8–12 noisettes of lamb
2½ oz. unsalted butter
1 tablespoon olive oil
SAUCE:
1 small carrot
1 small onion
2 sticks celery
1 oz. lean bacon
1½ oz. butter
Lamb trimmings
1 oz. plain flour
1 pint brown stock
½ pint dry white or red wine
1 rounded dessertspoon tomato purée
Bouquet garni
1 sprig or ½ teaspoon dried rosemary
Salt and black pepper
2–3 tablespoons redcurrant jelly

The noisettes* (2–3 oz. each) can be cut from cutlets from the loin or from best end of neck; the latter are smaller, but have a more delicate flavour. Most butchers will prepare the noisettes on request, but ask for the trimmings to be included with the order. Alternatively, cut the piece of meat into single cutlets, remove the bone from each, and shape the meat into a neat round, about 2 in. across. Tie firmly with string.

OSSO BUCO

PREPARATION TIME: *30 min.*
COOKING TIME: *1¾–2 hours*

INGREDIENTS *(for 6)*:
2½ lb. shin of veal
Seasoned flour
3 carrots
2 sticks celery
1 onion
2 cloves garlic
2 oz. butter
8 fluid oz. dry white wine
8 fluid oz. chicken or veal stock
15–16 oz. tin of tomatoes
Salt and black pepper
Caster sugar
1 sprig or ½ teaspoon dried rosemary
GARNISH:
4 tablespoons finely chopped parsley
Finely grated rind of 2 large lemons
2–3 cloves finely chopped garlic

Italy is the homeland of this appetising, inexpensive stew of veal with marrow. The traditional Milanese garnish – known as *gremolata* – adds a colourful look to the finished dish.

Ask the butcher to saw the veal into pieces, about 1½ in. thick. Wash and dry the meat and remove any chips of bone. Coat the veal pieces with seasoned flour*. Clean the vegetables and chop them finely.

Melt the butter in a heavy-based pan, large enough to take all the meat in one layer. Brown the meat and the vegetables. When the meat has taken colour, stand each piece upright to prevent the marrow falling out during cooking. Pour over the wine and stock and add the tomatoes with their juice. Season to taste with salt, freshly ground pepper and sugar. Then add the rosemary. Simmer, covered, over

Poultry & Game

Prepare the sauce first: scrape the carrot, peel the onion and scrub the celery; dice these vegetables. Cut the rind from the bacon and chop the flesh into small dice; blanch* for a few minutes. Melt the butter in a heavy pan over moderate heat. Fry the diced vegetables, chopped lamb trimmings and bacon in this for 10 minutes. Remove the pan from the heat and stir in the flour; return the pan to a low heat and cook for a further 10 minutes, stirring continuously, until the mixture is light brown. Take the pan off the heat.

Bring the stock and wine to the boil in a separate pan; whisk this into the vegetable mixture. Stir in the tomato purée and add the bouquet garni* (with fresh rosemary if used). Simmer the sauce, partly covered, over gentle heat for at least 2 hours, stirring occasionally to prevent sticking.

Remove any scum from time to time. When the sauce is thick enough to coat the back of a spoon, remove it from the heat. Strain the sauce through a coarse sieve and remove any fat which rises to the top.

About 30 minutes before serving, re-heat the sauce gently, stir in the redcurrant jelly and powdered rosemary (if used); simmer until the jelly has melted. Season to taste and keep warm.

Heat the butter and oil in a heavy-based pan and cook the prepared noisettes over moderate heat for 4–6 minutes on each side, depending on the size. They should be well browned, and slightly pink inside.

Serve the noisettes with the thick, dark brown sauce poured over them. Boiled new potatoes and courgettes or green beans are suitable vegetables.

SESAME CHICKEN WITH SPICED RICE

Sesame seed and oil is used throughout the Far East, and particularly in Japan, to impart a mildly spicy flavour to their cooking. This chicken dish is served on a bed of spiced rice which also goes well, hot or cold, with other chicken or meat dishes.

PREPARATION TIME: *50 min.*
COOKING TIME: *25 min.*

INGREDIENTS *(for 4)*:
2 chickens (each about 3 lb.)
6 oz. long grain rice
3 oz. plain flour
Salt and black pepper
½ oz. powdered sesame seed or
  1 level tablespoon sesame seeds
3 oz. butter
1 teaspoon olive oil
½ pint chicken stock
3 tablespoons dry white wine
½ level teaspoon ground coriander
¼ level teaspoon ground ginger
Chilli powder
½ pint double cream

For this dish, use only the chicken breasts, and set the leg joints aside for another recipe or store them in the home freezer.

Skin the chickens, and with a sharp knife carefully carve each breast away from the bone in one piece. Remove the legs. Use the skin, the wings and the carcasses to make a strong white stock*. Strain the stock through muslin and reduce* it by fast boiling to ½ pint.

Before cooking the chicken, put the rice in a large pan of boiling salted water. Season the flour with salt, freshly ground pepper and the sesame powder or seed, and coat the chicken breasts evenly. Melt 2 oz. of the butter in

a heavy-based pan, add the oil and fry the chicken, over moderate heat, for 3 minutes on each side or until lightly golden. Drain off the butter and pour the stock and wine over the chicken. Cover the pan with a lid, and simmer over low heat for 10–15 minutes or until the chicken is tender.

Stir the remaining butter into the cooked rice. Season to taste with salt and pepper, and blend in the coriander, ginger and a pinch of chilli powder. Pile the spiced rice on to a warm serving dish and keep it hot.

Lift the chicken breasts from the pan and arrange them on the rice. Stir the cream into the liquid in the pan and simmer, stirring continuously, until the mixture is a thick and creamy sauce. Pour over the chicken and serve.

PIGEONS WITH OLIVES

Small woodpigeons can be roasted or grilled like other game birds. But since the meat is rather dry, they are more suitable for braising or a casserole.

PREPARATION TIME: *1 hour*
COOKING TIME: *2 hours*

INGREDIENTS *(for 4)*:
4 pigeons
3 onions
1 carrot
4 oz. salted belly pork or green
  streaky bacon
2 cloves garlic
Seasoned flour
2–3 tablespoons brandy
¼ pint dry white wine or vermouth
¼ pint pigeon stock
4 oz. green stuffed olives
1 bouquet garni
4 large slices white bread
1 tablespoon olive oil

Skin the pigeons carefully. Cut along and down each side of the breastbone on each pigeon so that each breast, leg and wing comes away in one piece.

Wash the pigeon halves thoroughly in cold water and dry them on a clean cloth. Clean the carcasses and giblets thoroughly.

Peel and finely slice one onion, scrape and roughly chop the carrot. Put the carcasses, giblets, onion and carrot in a saucepan and cover with cold water. Bring to the boil and simmer, covered with a lid, until all the meat has come off the bones. Strain the stock and set aside.

Meanwhile, remove the rind from the pork or bacon and cut the meat into ½ in. wide strips, crossways. Put the strips in a large flameproof casserole over a moderate heat and cook until the fat runs. Peel and finely chop the remaining onions, and peel and crush the garlic. Add these to the pork and cook until soft.

Coat the pigeons thickly with the seasoned flour*. Add them to the onion mixture and brown them well on both sides. Warm the brandy, set it alight and pour over the pigeons, shaking the casserole until the flames die down. Add the wine and ¼ pint of the stock. Put in the olives and bouquet garni* and bring to the boil. Remove the casserole from the heat and cover closely with foil and a lid. Cook the pigeons in the centre of a pre-heated oven at 300°F (mark 2), for 1½–2 hours or until tender.

Fry the bread golden in the oil and arrange two pigeon halves on each slice. Top with the pork and olives and pour over the strained gravy. Serve with mashed potatoes or spiced rice*.

TURKEY ESCALOPES CORDON BLEU

Fresh turkey is often less expensive in summer than at Christmas. It makes a good main choice for a dinner party, especially as escalopes can now be bought ready-cut.

PREPARATION TIME: *20 min.*
COOKING TIME: *25 min.*

INGREDIENTS (*for 4*) :
4 turkey escalopes
4 slices lean cooked ham
4 thin slices Fontina, Bel Paese,
  or Gruyère cheese
4–6 oz. button mushrooms
3 oz. unsalted butter
Seasoned flour
1 tablespoon olive oil
Black pepper
1–2 tablespoons chopped parsley
4–6 tablespoons stock
GARNISH (OPTIONAL) :
Watercress

Buy the turkey escalopes ready-cut, or cut them from a large uncooked bird which is intended for a casserole, risotto or for deep-freezing in portions. The white breast meat should give 5 slices, about 1½ in. thick, from each side. Before slicing the breast, cut down slantwise behind the wishbone and remove this to give another escalope. Store the surplus escalopes in the home freezer.

Cut the ham and cheese slices to fit the escalopes. Trim the mushrooms* and slice them thinly; cook until soft in ½ oz. of the butter and set them aside. Coat the turkey escalopes evenly, but not too thickly, with the seasoned flour*.

Melt the remaining butter and the oil in a large frying pan over moderate heat. Fry the escalopes for about 5 minutes on each side. Place a slice of ham on each escalope, spoon over a thin layer of mushrooms and season lightly with freshly ground pepper. Sprinkle a little of the parsley over the mushrooms and cover with a slice of cheese. Pour the hot stock over the escalopes. Cover the pan closely with a lid or foil and cook over low heat for about 10 minutes or until the cheese has melted.

Lift out the escalopes and arrange on a hot serving dish; sprinkle over the remaining parsley or garnish with sprigs of watercress. The richness of the escalopes is best offset by a dish of buttered ribbon noodles and a tossed green salad.

POULET À LA CRÈME

This recipe for a casserole of chicken in a rich cream and calvados sauce comes from Normandy. It loses nothing of its flavour if any leftovers are re-heated later.

PREPARATION TIME: *10 min.*
COOKING TIME: *1¼–1½ hours*

INGREDIENTS (*for 4–6*) :

1 chicken (3–4 lb.)
1 Spanish onion
2 oz. cooked ham or lean bacon
Salt and black pepper
2½ oz. butter
4 tablespoons calvados or brandy
1 dessertspoon finely chopped
  celery leaves
½ pint dry still cider or
  unsweetened apple juice
2 large egg yolks
¼ pint double cream
GARNISH :
2 dessert apples
1 oz. unsalted butter

Peel and finely chop the onion, and dice the ham or bacon after removing the rind. Wipe the trussed chicken inside and out with a clean damp cloth and set the giblets aside. Season the chicken with salt and pepper.

Melt the butter in a pan over moderate heat and cook the onion until soft and transparent. Stir in the ham or bacon and cook for another 2–3 minutes. Brown the chicken lightly all over in the butter. Warm the calvados or brandy in a small pan and set alight (calvados will produce a fair amount of flame). While the spirit is still flaming, pour it over the chicken. Shake the pan gently until the flames die out.

Add the chicken neck, gizzard and heart to the pan, but omit the liver. Sprinkle in the chopped celery leaves and pour over the cider or apple juice; let it come to the boil, then simmer for a few minutes. Turn the chicken on its side and cover the pan closely with foil and then a lid. Cook over low heat. (If necessary, put the contents in a casserole and cook at 325°F (mark 3) in the centre of the oven.)

After 20–25 minutes cooking, turn the chicken over on the other side and cook for a similar period, still covered. Finally, turn the chicken breast upwards, cover and cook for a further 10 minutes.

While the chicken is cooking, peel and core the apples for the garnish. Cut them, without breaking, into ¼ in. thick rings. Melt the butter in a small pan and fry the apple rings until golden brown, turning once.

Lift the chicken on to a warm serving dish and keep hot. Strain the liquid, and reduce* slightly by fast boiling. Remove the pan from the heat. Beat together the egg yolks and the cream; mix in a few spoonfuls of the warm liquid, and whisk into the pan juices. Stir over low heat until the sauce has thickened.

Just before serving, pour the hot sauce over the chicken and garnish with the apple slices. Little more than a green salad is needed, but boiled potatoes could also be served.

Rice & Pasta

LUXURY PIZZA

The classic Italian pizza comes from Naples, and consists of a light yeast dough with a savoury filling. The cheese should by tradition be Mozzarella (buffalo cheese), but any quick-melting cheese, such as Bel Paese, Fontina or Gruyère, is suitable.

PREPARATION TIME: *1¾ hours*
COOKING TIME: *20–25 min.*

INGREDIENTS *(for 6)*:

8 oz. plain flour
1 level teaspoon salt
2½ fluid oz. milk
¾ oz. fresh or ⅓ oz. dried yeast
1 level teaspoon caster sugar
1½ oz. unsalted butter
1 large egg
FILLING:
2 large onions
2 small cloves garlic

1 lb. tomatoes
2 tablespoons olive oil
1 level tablespoon chopped fresh
*   marjoram or ½ teaspoon dried*
*   oregano*
Salt and black pepper
6 oz. quick-melting cheese
GARNISH:
1 tin anchovy fillets
2–3 oz. black olives

Sift the flour and salt into a warm bowl and make a well in the centre. Heat the milk until tepid and use a few drops to cream together the yeast and sugar. (If using dried yeast, follow the manufacturer's instructions.) Pour the yeast mixture and the rest of the milk into the flour, together with the melted butter and beaten egg. Work the dough with the hand until it is smooth and leaves the sides of the bowl clean. Shape the dough into a ball and put it into an oiled polythene bag. Leave it in a warm place until it has doubled in size.

Meanwhile, prepare the filling: peel and roughly chop the onions and garlic. Skin the tomatoes* and chop them roughly. Heat the olive oil in a heavy-based pan and cook the onion and garlic over moderate heat until soft and transparent. Add the tomatoes to the pan. Cook for about 10 minutes, then stir in the marjoram or oregano. Season to taste. Set the

filling aside. Cut the cheese into thin wedge-shaped slices, and drain the anchovy fillets.

When the dough has risen, knead it lightly with the fingertips for 1–2 minutes. Shape it into a circle 12 in. across. Put it on a greased and floured baking tray. Cover the dough with the onion and tomato mixture to within 1 in. of the outer edge. Arrange the cheese on top in a fan-like pattern, slightly overlapping the slices. Decorate the cheese with the anchovies and dot with olives.

Bake the pizza near the top of an oven pre-heated to 425°F (mark 7) for 20–25 minutes or until the cheese has melted and browned slightly, and the dough is well risen.

Pizza is best served straight from the oven, but it can also be served cold, or re-heated in the oven, at low heat. A crisp salad tossed in a well-seasoned dressing* would be ideal with the pizza for a main course.

GNOCCHI VERDI

The Italians take infinite trouble over their pasta dishes, and these small spinach dumplings require both patience and practice. They are, however, so light and tasty that they are worth mastering. The quantities are sufficient for a light main course for four or for a first course for six.

PREPARATION TIME: *20 min.*
CHILLING TIME: *2 hours*
COOKING TIME: *15–20 min.*

INGREDIENTS *(for 4–6)*:
1 lb. fresh spinach
4 oz. butter
6 oz. cottage or cream cheese
2 eggs
2 tablespoons double cream
3 level tablespoons plain flour
3 oz. grated Parmesan cheese
Salt and black pepper
Nutmeg

Wash the spinach thoroughly in several lots of cold water. Put the spinach in a large pan with a closely fitting lid. Cook, without extra water, over moderate heat for about 5 minutes or until the spinach is just soft. Drain thoroughly in a sieve, pressing out all moisture. Chop the spinach finely.

Melt 2 oz. of the butter in a pan, add the spinach and cook, stirring constantly, for about 2 minutes or until all moisture has evaporated; if necessary squeeze the spinach in a sieve again. Rub the cottage cheese through a sieve, add to the spinach and cook for a further 3–4 minutes, stirring all the time. Remove the pan from the heat. Fold the lightly beaten eggs into the spinach. Stir in the cream, flour and 1 oz. of

Parmesan cheese. Season to taste with salt, freshly ground pepper and grated nutmeg. Turn the gnocchi into a flat dish and chill for 2 hours or until firm.

Bring a large pan of lightly salted water to simmering point. Shape the gnocchi into small balls, no more than ¾ in. wide, between floured hands. Drop the balls into the simmering water, a few at a time. As soon as they puff up and rise to the surface, remove them carefully with a perforated spoon.

Arrange the gnocchi in a buttered flameproof dish, melt the remaining butter and pour over them. Sprinkle with the remaining cheese and put the dish under a hot grill until the cheese has melted and browned.

Serve at once.

Vegetables & Salads

RISOTTO BIANCO

Rice is the staple food in northern Italy, as pasta is in the south. An Italian risotto is always served as a meal on its own – usually plain, with just butter and cheese.

PREPARATION TIME: *10 min.*
COOKING TIME: *20–25 min.*

INGREDIENTS *(for 4–6):*
8 oz. Italian rice
1 small onion
1 small clove garlic
3 oz. butter
2 teaspoons olive oil
1½ pints white stock
Salt and black pepper
4 oz. grated Parmesan cheese

Peel and finely chop the onion and garlic. Heat 2 oz. of the butter with the oil in a deep sauté pan and cook the onion and garlic until soft and just beginning to colour. Add the cleaned rice to the pan. Cook over low heat, stirring continuously, until the rice is yellow and shiny.

Add a third of the hot stock to the rice; bring to the boil, stir, then cover the pan with a lid. Cook over moderate heat until all the liquid is absorbed, then gradually stir in the remaining stock. Cover the pan again, and simmer the rice, stirring occasionally, until all the stock has been absorbed, after about 15 minutes. The rice should then be creamy and firm. Watch the risotto carefully while cooking to see that it does not dry out.

Season the risotto to taste with salt and freshly ground pepper. Stir in the remaining butter and half the cheese. Spoon the risotto into a warm shallow dish, stir lightly with a fork, and sprinkle with the rest of the cheese.

FRENCH BEANS MIMOSA

A green salad need not be composed of the ubiquitous lettuce and cucumber – crisp cooked beans make a refreshing change.

PREPARATION TIME: *10 min.*
COOKING TIME: *3–4 min.*

INGREDIENTS *(for 4–6):*
1 lb. young French beans
Salt
6 tablespoons olive oil
2 tablespoons lemon juice
GARNISH:
1 large hardboiled egg

Top, tail and wash the beans, leaving them whole. Cook them in salted water for 3–4 minutes – they should stay crisp. Drain the beans and arrange them in a round shallow serving dish, radiating from the centre.

Pour the olive oil, mixed with the lemon juice over the still warm beans. Add more salt if necessary, and set the beans aside to cool.

Separate the white and yolk of the hardboiled egg. Chop the white finely and rub the yolk through a coarse sieve.

Before serving, decorate the beans. Arrange the egg white in the centre of the dish and scatter the yolk among the beans to resemble mimosa.

SPINACH WITH MUSHROOMS

This dish of spinach purée and mushrooms in a cheese sauce is best served on its own. It makes a light lunch or supper dish.

PREPARATION TIME: *20 min.*
COOKING TIME: *20 min.*

INGREDIENTS *(for 4–6):*
2 lb. fresh spinach
3 oz. butter
Salt and black pepper
Grated nutmeg
8 oz. button mushrooms
1½ oz. plain flour
¾ pint milk
4 oz. Cheddar cheese

Remove any stalks and coarse midribs from the spinach, and wash the leaves thoroughly in several lots of cold water. Put the spinach into a large pan, salt lightly and cook, covered with a lid, over moderate heat for 5–7 minutes or until the spinach has softened. Drain thoroughly in a colander, squeezing out all moisture. Rub the spinach through a coarse sieve or put it in a liquidiser to make a purée*.

Melt 1 oz. of the butter in a pan and re-heat the purée gently. Season to taste with salt, freshly ground pepper and nutmeg. Spread the purée over the base of a buttered flameproof dish. Trim the mushrooms*, removing the stalks. Arrange the mushrooms on top of the spinach, rounded side up, and place the dish under a low grill.

Use the remaining butter, the flour and milk to make a smooth white sauce*. Season to taste and continue cooking until the sauce thickens. Add the grated cheese and simmer for a few minutes.

Pour the hot sauce over the spinach and mushrooms and return to the grill. Turn up the heat and grill until the sauce is bubbly and brown. Serve immediately.

AUBERGINES WITH HAM

The increasing popularity of aubergines has occasioned a number of new recipes, apart from the well-tried classics, like Moussaka* and Ratatouille*. For this hot lunch or supper dish, the aubergines are filled with a ham and cheese stuffing.

PREPARATION TIME: *25 min.*
COOKING TIME: *20 min.*

INGREDIENTS *(for 4):*
4 aubergines
6 oz. ham, in ¼ in. thick slices
¼ pint olive oil
2 oz. unsalted butter
1 level tablespoon plain flour
½ pint milk
Salt and black pepper
Juice of half lemon
3–4 oz. dry white breadcrumbs

Remove the stalk ends from the aubergines and wipe them with a damp cloth. Cut each fruit in half lengthways with a sharp knife, and carefully scoop out the flesh without breaking the skin. Finely dice the aubergine flesh and the ham.

Heat the oil in a heavy-based pan over moderate heat and fry the aubergine shells until brown, turning them over with a fish slice. Remove and drain on crumpled kitchen paper. Cook the diced aubergine flesh in the oil in the pan and, when softened and lightly browned, remove from the pan and drain. Melt half the butter in another pan and cook the ham until brown.

Sprinkle the flour into the pan in which the aubergine was cooked and blend until the oil is absorbed. Gradually add enough milk to make a thick white sauce*, stirring all the time. Mix in the cooked ham and aubergine; add lemon juice and season to taste.

Spoon this mixture into the aubergine shells and set them in a buttered baking dish. Sprinkle breadcrumbs over the stuffing and dot with the remaining butter. Bake near the top of the oven, pre-heated to 400°F (mark 6) until brown. Serve at once.

CUCUMBER AU GRATIN

Firm cucumber with a crisp finish of cheese makes a good side dish with grilled fish or chicken.

PREPARATION TIME: *15–20 min.*
COOKING TIME: *30 min.*

INGREDIENTS *(for 4–6):*
2 cucumbers
Salt and black pepper
1½–2 oz. butter
6 oz. grated Gruyère cheese

Peel the cucumbers and cut them into 3 in. pieces. Slice each piece in half, lengthways, and remove the seeds. Cook the cucumber in boiling salted water for 10 minutes, then drain and dry.

Arrange a layer of cucumber in the base of a buttered fireproof dish. Sprinkle with a third of the cheese and season with salt and freshly ground pepper. Repeat these layers, finishing with cheese. Dot the top with butter.

Bake the gratin in the centre of a pre-heated oven at 400°F (mark 6) for 30 minutes.

MUSHROOMS AND PRAWNS

This is a refreshing salad for a hot day. It can be served as a light lunch with thin brown bread and butter, as a side salad or as a starter.

PREPARATION TIME: *15 min.*
STANDING TIME: *1 hour*

INGREDIENTS *(for 4):*
8 oz. large mushrooms
8 tablespoons olive oil
2 tablespoons lemon juice
1–2 cloves garlic
Sea salt and black pepper
4 oz. shelled prawns
GARNISH:
3 level tablespoons chopped parsley

Wipe and trim the mushrooms*; slice them thinly into a shallow salad dish. Mix together the oil and lemon juice in a small bowl. Season with the peeled, crushed garlic and freshly ground pepper (do not add salt yet). Pour this dressing over the mushrooms and turn the slices carefully so that they are well coated. Leave the mushrooms for about 1 hour in a cool place.

The mushrooms absorb a lot of oil while standing, and if necessary add a little more oil just before serving. Add the prawns and sprinkle lightly with sea salt. Garnish with the chopped parsley.

TOMATOES WITH HORSERADISH MAYONNAISE

For this dish choose large firm tomatoes of even size. Serve them chilled as a side dish with cold meat or with grilled steaks and chops.

PREPARATION TIME: *20 min.*
CHILLING TIME: *2 hours*

INGREDIENTS *(for 4–6):*
8 firm tomatoes
¼ pint mayonnaise
Salt
¼ pint double cream
Lemon juice
2 rounded tablespoons fresh grated horseradish
GARNISH:
Chopped chives, chervil, basil or parsley

First prepare the mayonnaise* and set it aside. Skin the tomatoes*, and slice off the tops with a serrated knife. Carefully scoop out the seeds and juice with a teaspoon, without breaking the flesh. Sprinkle the inside of the tomato cups with salt, stand them upside down on a plate to drain, and chill them in the coldest part of the refrigerator for 2 hours.

Lightly whip the cream and mix it into the mayonnaise; add lemon juice to taste and stir in the grated horseradish (the tomato caps may also be chopped and stirred into the mayonnaise). Chill on the bottom shelf of the refrigerator for about 1 hour.

Just before serving, spoon the horseradish mayonnaise evenly into tomato cups and sprinkle with chopped herbs.

BEANS IN SOURED CREAM

The first home-grown runner beans appear towards the end of the month. Preserve their crispness and flavour by cooking them for a few minutes only and finish them off in an unusual cream dressing. Serve with roast or grilled meat and poultry.

PREPARATION TIME: *15 min.*
COOKING TIME: *15–20 min.*

INGREDIENTS *(for 4–6):*
1 lb. runner beans
5 fluid oz. soured cream
Salt and black pepper
Grated nutmeg
½ level teaspoon caraway or dill seeds (optional)
2 oz. butter
1½ oz. coarse, fresh white breadcrumbs

Top, tail and string the runner beans, slice them crossways into 1 in. pieces. Cook the beans in a pan of boiling salted water for 5 minutes, then drain thoroughly. Season the soured cream to taste with salt, freshly ground pepper and nutmeg, and add the caraway or dill seeds if used. Toss the beans in this dressing to coat them thoroughly.

Use ½ oz. of the butter to grease an ovenproof dish. Melt the remaining butter and toss the breadcrumbs in it. Put the beans in the dish and top with the breadcrumbs. Bake in the centre of an oven pre-heated to 350°F (mark 4) for 15–20 minutes, or until the topping is crisp and brown.

Serve the beans at once.

Sweets & Puddings

BROWN TOM

The name of this dish describes a casserole of fresh tomatoes with a crumble of bacon and brown breadcrumbs. Serve it on its own, or with grilled sausages for lunch or supper.

PREPARATION TIME: *20 min.*
COOKING TIME: *30–35 min.*

INGREDIENTS *(for 4)*:
1 *lb. tomatoes*
1 *large onion*
2 *rashers lean bacon*
4 *large slices wholemeal bread*
1 *level tablespoon chopped parsley*
1½ *level teaspoons chopped fresh basil*
1½ *oz. butter*
Salt and black pepper
Caster sugar

Peel and roughly chop the onion; cut the rind off the bacon and chop the rashers into pieces. Put the onion and bacon through the fine blade of the mincer. Remove the crust and crumble the bread into the bacon and onion mince. Now add the herbs. Skin and thinly slice the tomatoes*.

Put a layer of the bacon and crumb mixture in the bottom of a buttered, shallow fireproof dish. Cover this with a layer of tomatoes and season with salt, freshly ground pepper and a little sugar. Repeat these layers until all the ingredients are used up, finishing with a layer of bacon crumbs.

Dot with the remaining butter and bake near the top of the oven at 400°F (mark 6) for 30–35 minutes or until brown and bubbling. Serve at once.

PEPPER, ANCHOVY AND TOMATO SALAD

This unusual and tasty salad goes perfectly with grilled veal chops and with most chicken dishes. It can also be served on its own as a light beginning to a substantial meal.

PREPARATION TIME: *35 min.*
CHILLING TIME: *30 min.*

INGREDIENTS *(for 4)*:
2 *large sweet red peppers*
3 *large tomatoes*
2 *small tins anchovy fillets*
1 *small clove garlic*
3–4 *tablespoons olive oil*
Juice of half lemon
Salt and black pepper

Put the peppers under a hot grill, turning them frequently until the skins are charred and black all over. The black outer skin then rubs off easily under cold running water. Remove the stalk ends and seeds from the peppers and cut out any white pith. Cut the flesh into wide strips with scissors. Skin the tomatoes*, cut them into slices and remove the seeds. Drain the anchovy fillets and rinse them in cold water to remove excess oil and salt; ease them carefully apart.

Arrange the pepper strips on a flat serving dish with the sliced tomatoes, and lay the anchovy fillets on top in a lattice pattern.

Peel and crush the garlic and mix with the oil. Pour this dressing over the salad and sprinkle with lemon juice, salt and very little freshly ground pepper. Chill for at least 30 minutes before serving.

CLAFOUTI LIMOUSIN

A clafouti is a sweet pancake batter baked with fresh fruit. In the Limousin province of France, where the pudding originates, it is traditionally made with black cherries.

PREPARATION TIME: *15 min.*
COOKING TIME: *30 min.*

INGREDIENTS *(for 6)*:
1½ *lb. black cherries*
3 eggs
3 level tablespoons plain flour
Salt
5 level tablespoons caster sugar
¾ *pint milk*
1 tablespoon dark rum (optional)
2–3 level tablespoons unsalted butter

Remove the stalks from the cherries, wash and dry the fruit thoroughly. Beat the eggs lightly together in a bowl; blend in the sifted flour and a pinch of salt before adding 3 tablespoons of sugar. Heat the milk until lukewarm and gradually pour it into the egg mixture, stirring continuously. Add the rum if used.

Butter a wide, shallow, fireproof dish thoroughly. Put in the cherries, pour the batter over them and dot with the remaining butter. Bake in the centre of an oven, pre-heated to 425°F (mark 7) for 25–30 minutes. When the dish is cooked, the cherries will have risen to the top and the batter will have set like a baked custard.

Sprinkle the pudding with the remaining caster sugar and serve lukewarm.

RASPBERRY YOGHOURT SORBET

A sorbet will be welcome on a hot summer's evening. One of the most delicious is made from raspberries, which are in plentiful supply. Adding yoghourt to this sorbet enhances its flavour.

PREPARATION TIME: *15 min.*
CHILLING TIME: *2–3 hours*

INGREDIENTS *(for 6)*:
8 oz. raspberries
2–3 oz. caster sugar
½ *pint natural yoghourt*
Juice of half lemon
½ *oz. powdered gelatine*
2 egg whites

Make a thick purée from the raspberries by rubbing them through a sieve and into a bowl. Sweeten to taste with the sugar. Stir the yoghourt and the lemon juice into the sweetened purée.

Place 4 tablespoons of cold water in a small bowl and sprinkle the powdered gelatine over it. Leave the gelatine to stand for 5 minutes and then set the bowl over a pan of hot water. Stir until the gelatine has dissolved and the liquid is clear.

Add the liquid gelatine to the raspberry purée. In a separate bowl, beat the egg whites until stiff but not dry, and then fold them into the purée.

Spoon the mixture into a container, cover with a lid and set in the freezing compartment of the refrigerator. When almost frozen, beat up the purée with a rotary whisk. Then allow the mixture to freeze firmly.

COEUR À LA CRÈME

This is a classic French summer sweet, made from cheese and cream. Traditionally, it is set in little heart-shaped moulds (which are now available in Britain) and served with cream and soft summer fruit.

PREPARATION TIME: *20 min.*
CHILLING TIME: *12 hours*

INGREDIENTS *(for 4–6)*:
8 oz. unsalted cream cheese or cottage cheese
½ *pint double cream*
2 level dessertspoons caster sugar
2 egg whites
8 oz. soft fruit
¼ *pint single cream*

Rub or press the cheese through a fine sieve and mix with the double cream before stirring in the sugar. (Cream cheese makes a richer, denser mixture than cottage cheese.) Beat the egg whites until stiff, but not dry, and fold them into the cheese and cream mixture.

Line the heart-shaped moulds with fine muslin (to make unmoulding easier). Alternatively, use a 6 in. wide, shallow cake tin as a mould. Pierce a few holes in the base for draining, and line the tin with muslin.

Spoon the cheese and cream mixture into the prepared moulds and place them on a wide plate or in a sieve. Leave in the refrigerator overnight to drain and chill.

Just before serving, unmould the cream cheese on to a serving plate. Pour over the single cream, and serve with fresh raspberries or other soft fruit, or with a sweetened fruit sauce.

BAKED STUFFED PEACHES

Traditionally this Italian sweet is made with amaretti – tiny macaroons made from apricot kernels or small almonds. If these are unobtainable, ratafia biscuits make a good substitute.

PREPARATION TIME: *20 min.*
COOKING TIME: *20–30 min.*

INGREDIENTS *(for 4–6)*:
4 large peaches
2 level dessertspoons caster sugar
1 level tablespoon unsalted butter
1 egg yolk
2 oz. amaretti or ratafia biscuits

Cream together the sugar, butter and egg yolk in a small bowl. Crush the biscuits with a rolling pin and add these to the creamed mixture.

Pour boiling water over the peaches and leave for 2–3 minutes.

Peel off the skin, halve the peaches and remove the stones. Enlarge the cavities slightly by scooping out some of the flesh with a pointed teaspoon. Add this pulp to the egg mixture and blend well.

Pile the stuffing into the peach halves and arrange them in a buttered fireproof dish. Bake on the centre shelf of a pre-heated oven, at 350°F (mark 4), for 20–30 minutes or until the peaches are soft, but still shapely.

Serve the peaches warm, with a bowl of cream.

COLD CARAMEL SOUFFLÉS

The bitter-sweet taste of caramel makes a refreshing end to a summer meal.

PREPARATION TIME: *35 min.*
SETTING TIME: *2½ hours*

INGREDIENTS *(for 4)*:
4 oz. caster sugar
½ oz. powdered gelatine
Juice of a lemon
2 eggs plus 1 egg yolk
2 tablespoons caster sugar
6 tablespoons double cream

To make the caramel, put 4 oz. of sugar with ½ pint of water in a small, heavy-based pan over low heat. Cook without stirring until the sugar has dissolved. Increase the heat and boil the syrup rapidly until it is pale golden brown. Remove the pan from the heat and stand it on a cold surface. Add 4 tablespoons of hot water, and pour the caramel into a warm bowl.

Dissolve the gelatine in 3 tablespoons of warm water to which the lemon juice has been added. Separate the eggs and beat the 3 egg yolks with 2 tablespoons of caster sugar in a bowl. Place the bowl over a pan of hot water and beat the egg mixture until it thickens. Remove the bowl and let the egg mixture cool.

Blend the caramel and the dissolved gelatine thoroughly into the egg mixture. Leave to cool.

Whisk the 2 egg whites until stiff, and lightly whisk the cream. When the soufflé mixture is cold, but not completely set, fold in the cream and the egg whites.

Spoon the mixture into individual soufflé dishes to set. Chill for about 30 minutes.

SUMMER PUDDING

The origin of this classic English pudding is unknown, but as early as the 18th century it was served to patients who were not allowed rich pastry sweets. This does not in the least make it invalid food – it is a delicious composition of fresh summer fruits.

PREPARATION TIME: *30–40 min.*
CHILLING TIME: *8 hours*

INGREDIENTS *(for 6)*:
6–8 slices stale, crustless white bread, ½ in. thick
1½ lb. mixed soft fruits
4 oz. caster sugar

Strawberries, raspberries, red and black currants, as well as black cherries, are all suitable for this dish, and can be mixed according to taste and availability. The more varied the fruits, the tastier the result, but avoid using too many black currants as their flavour and colour will tend to dominate the summer pudding.

Line the bottom of a 1½-pint soufflé dish or pudding basin with one or two slices of bread to cover the base completely. Line the sides of the dish with more bread, if necessary cut to shape, so that the bread fits closely together.

Hull* and carefully wash the fruit, and remove the stones from the cherries. Put the fruit in a wide heavy-based pan and sprinkle the sugar over it. Bring to the boil over very low heat, and cook for 2–3 minutes only, until the sugar melts and the juices begin to run. Remove the pan from the heat and set aside 1–2 tablespoons of the fruit juices. Spoon the fruit and remaining juice into the prepared dish and cover the surface closely with the rest of the bread.

Put a plate that fits the inside of the dish on top of the pudding and weight it down with heavy tin or jar. Leave the pudding in the refrigerator to chill for 8 hours.

Before serving, remove the weight and plate. Cover the dish with the serving plate and turn upside-down to unmould the pudding. Use the reserved fruit juice to pour over any parts of the bread which have not been soaked through and coloured by the fruit juices.

Serve with a bowl of cream.

Savouries & Snacks

CREAM CHEESE AND BACON TART

This is a quick and delicious variation of a French quiche, suitable for a supper or a picnic.

PREPARATION TIME: *25 min.*
COOKING TIME: *30 min.*

INGREDIENTS *(for 4–6):*
6 oz. shortcrust pastry (standard recipe)
4 rashers smoked streaky bacon
1 egg
3 egg yolks
½ lb. cream cheese
¼ pint double cream
Salt and black pepper
3 skinned, sliced tomatoes
GARNISH:
Chopped chives

Line an 8 in. flan ring or tart tin with the rolled-out pastry*. Cut the bacon rashers crossways into ¼ in. strips; fry, without extra fat, over moderate heat for 3 minutes, without browning. Drain on crumpled kitchen paper, then arrange in the bottom of the pastry case.

Beat the egg and egg yolks, add the softened cream cheese and continue beating until the mixture is smooth. Gradually beat in the cream. Season with salt and pepper, and pour the mixture over the bacon. Arrange the tomatoes on top.

Bake the tart in the centre of the oven, pre-heated to 400°F (mark 6), for 20 minutes, then lower the heat to 350°F (mark 4), and bake for a further 10 minutes or until set.

Serve the tart garnished with chopped chives. Cut it into wedge shapes and serve it hot with a green vegetable, or cold with a green salad.

CHICKEN AND HAM LOAF

This dish makes good use of left-over chicken. It is excellent for picnics and packed lunches and also stores well in the home freezer.

PREPARATION TIME: *1¼ hours*
COOKING TIME: *1 hour*

INGREDIENTS *(for 6–8):*
8 oz. cooked skinned and diced chicken
1 crusty sandwich loaf
3 oz. butter
2 finely chopped onions
½ lb. thinly sliced mushrooms
1 tablespoon chopped parsley
Salt and black pepper
½ lb. sausage meat
6 oz. lean bacon (diced)
8 oz. cooked diced ham
2 tablespoons dry sherry (optional)
¼ teaspoon each sage and thyme

Cut a ½ in. slice off the top of the loaf and carefully pull out the soft bread inside (use for making breadcrumbs). Leave ½ in. inner lining of bread to preserve the shape. Melt 2 oz. of the butter and brush this on to the loaf, inside and out.

Replace the lid and put the loaf on a baking tray in the centre of a pre-heated oven, at 400°F (mark 6). Bake for 10 minutes or until crisp and golden. Leave to cool.

Cook the onions in the remaining butter until soft, add the mushrooms and cook for a further 2 minutes. Stir in the parsley and season with salt and pepper.

Mix together the sausage meat, bacon, ham and 3 heaped tablespoons of breadcrumbs, stir in the sherry and herbs and season to taste. Press half the sausage mixture well down into the loaf case; cover with half the onion and mushroom mixture. Arrange the chicken on top and cover with the onion and a final layer of sausage meat. Replace the lid and wrap the loaf in foil. Bake in the centre of the oven, 375°F (mark 5) for 1 hour.

Serve the loaf hot or cold, cut into thick slices.

GUACAMOLE

This is a Mexican hors-d'oeuvre or dip of avocado pears. Very ripe avocado pears, suitable for mashing, are often sold cheaply.

PREPARATION TIME: *10 min.*
CHILLING TIME: *30 min.*

INGREDIENTS *(for 6):*
3 ripe avocado pears
½ small grated onion
2 crushed cloves garlic
1 tablespoon lemon juice
1 tablespoon olive oil
Salt and black pepper
Cayenne pepper
¼ teaspoon Worcestershire sauce
Tabasco sauce

Cut the avocado pears* in half with a sharp silver or stainless steel knife. Remove the stones. Mash the avocado flesh with the onion and garlic until smooth. Blend in the lemon juice and oil; season to taste with salt, freshly ground pepper, cayenne and the sauces. Chill for 30 minutes.

Serve on individual plates on lettuce leaves, or in serving glasses. Mixed raw vegetables, such as celery sticks, or slices of carrot, green pepper and radish, could be used for the dip.

CUCUMBER CUPS WITH PRAWNS

For a quick cool starter, few ingredients combine so well for flavour and eye-appeal as cucumber and shellfish.

PREPARATION TIME: *15 min.*
CHILLING TIME: *30 min.*

INGREDIENTS *(for 6–8):*
1 large plump cucumber
2 finely chopped mint leaves
2 tinned pimentoes (chopped)
5 fluid oz. natural yoghourt
½ lb. small peeled prawns
Salt and pepper
Paprika

Chop the stalk end off the cucumber and cut the remainder into eight equal pieces. Stand the cucumber sections upright on a serving dish and, with a pointed spoon, hollow out the centres to form cup shapes. Leave about ¼ in. around the sides and base.

Add the mint and pimento to the yoghourt, and fold in the prawns. Season with salt and pepper. Spoon the mixture into the cucumber cups and sprinkle with a little paprika. Chill for 30 minutes and serve with thin slices of buttered brown bread.

A Birthday Party for Young Children

Most mothers would probably agree that the most exhausting of all parties are those for children's birthdays. But proper planning and advance preparations can take much of the strain out of coping with a handful of boisterous children. Issue proper invitations to the young guests and state the times when the party will start and finish. A birthday party for the 6–8 year olds should generally not last longer than 2–2½ hours.

Most young children are fussy with their food and shy away from unfamiliar and elaborate concoctions. They are fond of savoury food, such as potato crisps, sausage rolls and mild cheese, and prefer sweets such as jellies and ice cream. The climax of the party is, of course, the birthday cake.

For drinks, serve fresh or frozen orange juice, lemonade or fruit-flavoured milk shakes with plenty of coloured drinking straws.

Serve the food towards the end of the party when the children have come to know each other. Keep the various food portions small enough to be eaten with the fingers or small plastic spoons and arrange all the food on the table at the same time, so that the children can choose for themselves.

Protect the dining table against the inevitable overturned drinks and spilt food. A paper tablecloth or heavy-duty coloured paper provide a gay background for the food and can simply be thrown out afterwards. As an extra precaution, cover the table with oilcloth, if available, before putting on the paper cloth. Plastic or heavy-duty paper plates and cups avoid breakages and save on the washing-up.

Provide dainty or amusing paper hats for the young guests, and decorate the table with coloured balloons, crackers and paper streamers. Children usually expect a small leaving present, such as a bag of sweets, an orange or apple, or an inexpensive toy – small plastic cars, coloured pencils or crayons, drawing books and paper dolls need not strain the budget.

On the right is a section of a birthday table showing food popular with young children. Reading from left to right and from top: potato crisps and a 'hedgehog' of grilled cocktail sausages. Below these is a soft bridge roll with cheese and pineapple filling, small sausage rolls and a checker-board of white and red cheese squares. Other bridge rolls contain a tuna fish and tomato ketchup filling, followed by savoury biscuits and twiglets. Sandwiches are cut into fancy shapes after being spread with red jam.

Sandwiches & Savouries

Cut small sandwiches of white bread in round, oval or other fancy shapes, or as letters of the alphabet. Butter the sandwiches lightly and spread them with a variety of fillings, such as soft cream cheese mixed with finely grated cucumber, or mashed hard-boiled eggs bound with a little cream and flavoured with cress. Non-runny jam and bananas sweetened with brown sugar make a good filling, or Marmite with grated cheese.

Split small bridge rolls in half, spread them with butter and top with, for example, mashed salmon or tuna fish mixed with a little tomato ketchup, or with softened cream cheese blended with finely chopped pineapple.

Grill chipolatas or cocktail sausages; leave them to cool before skewering them on wooden cocktail sticks. Small lukewarm sausage rolls, potato crisps and savoury biscuits are all favourites with children.

Sweets & Jellies

Make these in small individual portions and provide small plastic spoons with which to eat them.

Orange baskets Cut firm oranges in half and scoop out the flesh carefully without breaking the skins. Press the flesh through a strainer and use the juice as the base for orange drinks. Fill the empty orange halves with fresh or tinned fruit salad, and before serving top with vanilla ice cream.

Bunnies on the lawn Dissolve a packet of lime jelly as directed on the packet. Pour the jelly over the base of a large shallow dish and leave to set. Place thoroughly drained, halved pears, rounded sides up, on the jelly. Pipe fluffy tails from thick cream at one end of each pear and use toasted almonds to represent the ears. Small chocolate buttons become the eyes, and pieces of glacé cherries the tongues.

Strawberry boats These are always popular with children and are easy for them to handle. Bake the pastry boats in advance and keep in a tin until required.

Sift 6 oz. plain flour with a pinch of salt and rub in 2½ oz. butter and ¾ oz. lard. Mix to a dough with a little cold water. Leave the dough in a cool place for 30 minutes, then roll it out thinly and use it to line small well-greased boat moulds. Prick the pastry with a fork before baking the boats blind* for 10 minutes, in the centre of a pre-heated oven, at 400°F (mark 6).

Spread a thin layer of custard* or red currant jelly over the base of the cooled boats and top with halved strawberries or any other seasonal fruit.

Biscuits & Cakes

Small iced cup cakes and biscuits are more appealing to children than large sponge cakes, the birthday cake apart. Cup cakes are easily made from a Genoese sponge* mixture; bake the cakes in small paper cases and when cold cover them with soft, coloured icing*. Before the icing has quite set, decorate the cakes with chocolate buttons, jelly babies or Smarties.

Clock cake is a different kind of birthday cake. It can be made in advance and decorated on the day.

Cream 6 oz. unsalted butter with 6 oz. caster sugar and the grated rind and juice of a lemon. Add 3 egg yolks, one at a time, beating thoroughly, then fold in 6 oz. self-raising flour and a pinch of salt. Whisk the three egg whites until stiff and carefully fold them into the sponge mixture. Spoon this into a buttered and floured round sandwich tin, 9 in. across. Bake in the centre of a pre-heated oven, at 375°F (mark 5), for 40–50 minutes. Cool on a wire rack and remove from the tin.

Cover the cooled cake with apricot glaze* and leave to set.

For the decoration, sift 1 lb. icing sugar into a bowl and set it over a pan of simmering water. Add 4 tablespoons warm water and a squeeze of lemon juice to the sugar. Beat thoroughly for 1 minute, then add food colouring (green, red, orange or yellow) and continue beating until the sugar has dissolved. Spread the warm icing evenly over the top and sides of the cake.

Place 12 chocolate buttons round the edge of the cake. Colour the remaining icing a different shade and spoon it into a forcing bag fitted with a fine writing nozzle. Pipe two circles on top of the cake to represent the clock rim, then pipe numerals, 1–12, on to the buttons and pipe on the clock hands. The minute hand should point to 12 and the hour hand to the age of the birthday child.

Some children may be disappointed if there are no candles to blow out on the cake. The candles can be set inside the clock rim against the appropriate numbers.

August

Dry August and warme,
Doth harvest no harm.

This Month's Recipes

*Picnic fare for a warm day in August: tarte Basquaise is served with
rice salad and stuffed tomatoes; in the background, melons with raspberries*

Food in Season

Fish is plentiful and relatively inexpensive this month. Trout is nearing the end of its season and is, therefore, cheaper than in spring and early summer; sole and the less expensive plaice are also available. Crabs are at their best at this time of year. The glorious 12th of the month marks the beginning of the game season, and by the end of the month grouse are available in many poulterers' shops.

Home-grown corn on the cob, French beans and runner beans make their appearance and the first vegetable marrows are in the shops, together with maincrop peas. Cultivated blackberries and home-grown plums are other good buys.

Fish

Angler tail
Bass
Bream, sea
Brill
Clams
Cod
Coley
Conger eels
Crab
Dabs
Dover sole
Dublin Bay prawns
Eels
Flounders
Grey mullet
Haddock
Hake
Halibut
Herring
Lemon sole
Lobster
Mackerel
Mock halibut (or
   Greenland halibut)
Oysters, Portuguese
Plaice
Prawns
Redfish
Red mullet
Salmon
Scad
Sea trout
Shrimps
Skate
Trout, rainbow
Turbot
Whiting
Witch

Poultry & Game

Chicken
Duck
Grouse
Guinea fowl
Hare
Pigeon
Quail
Rabbit
Snipe
Turkey
Venison

Vegetables

Asparagus
Aubergines
Avocado pears
Beetroots
Broad beans
Cabbage
Calabrese
Carrots
Cauliflower
Celery
Corn on the cob
Courgettes
Cucumbers
Endive
Fennel
French beans
Garlic
Globe artichokes
Leeks
Lettuces
Mushrooms
Okra
Onions
Parsnips
Peas
Radishes
Runner beans
Salad cress
Shallots
Spring onions
Swedes
Tomatoes
Vegetable marrows
Watercress

Fruit

Apples
Apricots
Bananas
Blackberries
Black currants
Cherries
Damsons
Figs
Gooseberries
Grapefruit
Grapes
Greengages
Lemons
Loganberries
Lychees
Melons
Mulberries
Nectarines
Oranges
Peaches
Pears
Persimmons
Pineapples
Plums
Raspberries
Red currants
Strawberries
Walnuts
Watermelons
White currants

SUGGESTED MENUS

Cucumber, Prawns and Mushrooms
Veal Escalopes in Ginger Wine
Ragoût of Lettuce and Peas
Granita al Caffe

Gazpacho Andaluz
Plaice with Oranges
Tossed Green Salad
Buttered New Potatoes
Victoria Plums in Wine

Chilled Carrot Soup
Salmi of Grouse
Fried Breadcrumbs or Bread Sauce
Peaches with Soured Cream

Chicken Yoghourt Soup
Boeuf à la Mode en Gelée
Cucumber in Soured Cream
Melon Ice Cream

Eggs Baked in Tomatoes
Baked Forehock of Bacon
Carrots Paysanne
Raspberry and Banana Trifle

Kipper Pâté and Toast
Pork cooked in Milk
Corn on the Cob
Baked Tomatoes
Danish Layer Cake

Salade Niçoise
Spaghetti with Tuna Sauce
Lemon Syllabub

Soups & Starters

CHILLED MULLIGATAWNY SOUP

Mulligatawny soup – a favourite among the British in India, and brought home by them – is a rich meat stock strongly flavoured with curry. This version transforms the traditional soup into a cool summer starter.

PREPARATION TIME: *20 min.*
COOKING TIME: *30 min.*
CHILLING TIME: *1½–2 hours*

INGREDIENTS *(for 6)*:
1 onion
1 carrot
2 oz. unsalted butter
3 level tablespoons plain flour
1 level dessertspoon curry powder
2½ pints beef stock
2 tablespoons mango liquid
GARNISH:
Cauliflower florets

Peel and finely chop the onion and carrot. Melt the butter in a large pan over moderate heat and cook the vegetables until the onion is transparent. Sift the flour and curry powder together and stir into the vegetables. Continue cooking over moderate heat, stirring constantly, until the mixture is a deep brown colour. Gradually stir in the hot stock and bring the soup to the boil. Simmer over low heat for 30 minutes, then set aside to cool slightly.

Put the soup through a coarse sieve, or liquidise it for 1–2 minutes, then stir in the mango liquid. Chill for at least 1½ hours.

Before serving, remove any fat from the surface of the soup. Pour into bowls and garnish with tiny florets of raw cauliflower.

SALADE NIÇOISE

There are numerous versions of this Provençal hors-d'oeuvre, but all have in common the basic ingredients of lettuce, eggs, anchovy fillets, black olives and tomatoes.

PREPARATION TIME: *25 min.*

INGREDIENTS *(for 6)*:
2 eggs
½ lb. French beans
¾ lb. firm tomatoes
½ onion
1 lettuce heart
½ green pepper
¼ pint garlic-flavoured French dressing
4 oz. tin of tuna fish
Small tin anchovy fillets
2 oz. small black olives

Hardboil the eggs for 8–10 minutes, then plunge them into cold water. Shell and quarter them, and set aside to cool. Top and tail the French beans, wash them and cook in boiling salted water for 5–8 minutes; drain and set aside to cool.

Skin the tomatoes* and cut into quarters. Peel and thinly slice the onion, break it into individual rings. Wash and dry the lettuce. Clean the pepper, cut out the core and seeds, and slice it thinly.

Put half the French dressing* in a shallow bowl and toss the shredded lettuce and beans in it. Drain and flake* the tuna fish and arrange it, with the drained anchovy fillets, olives, green pepper and onion rings, on top of the lettuce and beans. Surround with the quartered tomatoes and hardboiled eggs. Sprinkle over the remaining dressing and serve the salad immediately.

GAZPACHO ANDALUZ

On a hot summer day, a chilled soup is particularly welcome. This Andalusian salad soup is also decorative, served with several crisp, colourful garnishes. In Spain, ice cubes are added to each soup bowl before serving.

PREPARATION TIME: *35 min.*
CHILLING TIME: *1–2 hours*

INGREDIENTS *(for 6)*:
1½ lb. tomatoes
4 large, ½ in. thick slices stale white bread
2 large cloves garlic
2 dessertspoons herb or red wine vinegar
3–4 tablespoons olive oil
¾ pint tinned tomato juice
2 tinned sweet red peppers
1 large Spanish onion
1 small cucumber
Salt and black pepper
2 tablespoons mayonnaise (optional)
¾ pint iced water
GARNISH:
1 small cucumber
2 small peppers
4 large tomatoes
Bread croûtons
Black olives
Raw onion rings, hardboiled eggs (optional)

Skin the tomatoes*, remove the seeds and chop the flesh finely. Cut the crusts off the bread and crumble it finely into a large bowl. Peel and crush the garlic into the bowl. Stir in the vinegar and gradually add as much olive oil as the crumbs will absorb. Stir in the tomato flesh and juice and mix thoroughly. Chop the red peppers finely; peel and grate the onion and cucumber and stir all three into the tomato mixture. Season to taste with salt and freshly ground pepper. Put the mixture into a liquidiser until smooth, or rub it through a fine sieve.

The soup should be perfectly smooth – it can be made more creamy by the addition of mayonnaise*. Dilute the soup with iced water until it has the consistency of thin cream. Adjust seasoning.

Chill the soup in the refrigerator.

The garnishes are traditionally served in separate small bowls, and the contents stirred into the soup until it is nearly solid. Peel and dice the cucumber, chop the prepared peppers and the skinned tomatoes. Fry the bread croûtons*, and peel and thinly slice the onion. Small stoned black olives and sliced hard-boiled eggs can also be served.

EGGS BAKED IN TOMATOES

This light and colourful starter can also be served as a snack. Ideally, the tomatoes should be the large, squat and slightly mis-shapen tomatoes from the Provence region of France.

PREPARATION TIME: *40 min.*
COOKING TIME: *20 min.*

INGREDIENTS (*for 4*):
4 large firm tomatoes
Salt and black pepper
1 clove garlic
4 eggs
2 level teaspoons tomato purée
4 teaspoons double cream
1 tablespoon grated Parmesan cheese
4 slices bread
1 oz. unsalted butter
2 teaspoons olive oil

Wash the tomatoes, wipe them dry and slice off the tops with a sharp knife. Carefully scoop out the pulp with a spoon and sprinkle the inside of the shells with salt and the peeled and finely chopped garlic. Turn the tomato shells upside down to drain for 30 minutes.

Break an egg carefully into each tomato shell, keeping back as much as possible of the white. Season with salt and freshly ground pepper. Blend the tomato purée with the cream and spoon gently over the eggs. Sprinkle each with a little grated Parmesan cheese. Put the tomatoes in a fireproof dish and bake near the top of a pre-heated oven at 350°F (mark 4) for 15–20 minutes, or until the eggs have just set.

Meanwhile, cut the bread into rounds with a fluted scone cutter. Heat the butter and oil in a pan and fry the bread until crisp and golden brown on both sides.

As soon as the eggs are set, arrange one tomato on each round of bread and serve at once.

CHICKEN YOGHOURT SOUP

In the Middle East, yoghourt is used in many dishes instead of cream. It gives a refreshing tang to a soup.

PREPARATION TIME: *15 min.*
COOKING TIME: *20 min.*

INGREDIENTS (*for 6*):
15–16 fluid oz. natural yoghourt
1½ level teaspoons cornflour
1½ pints chicken stock
5 egg yolks
3 level tablespoons ground almonds
Salt and black pepper
2 level tablespoons chopped mint
½ oz. unsalted butter

Stabilise the yoghourt before cooking, by blending the corn-flour with a little water, and gradually beating it into the yoghourt. Pour the mixture into a saucepan and bring it slowly to the boil over moderate heat, stirring continuously. Simmer the yoghourt gently, for 10 minutes or until thickened.

Meanwhile, bring the chicken stock to the boil in another pan. Remove from the heat, let it cool slightly, while lightly beating the egg yolks. Spoon a little of the stock into the eggs and blend thoroughly, before stirring this mixture into the stock. Heat over low heat until just simmering – if brought to boiling point, the eggs will curdle – stirring all the time until the stock thickens. Gradually, stir the yoghourt into the stock.

Blend the ground almonds into the soup, and correct seasoning if necessary. Sauté* the chopped mint for 1–2 minutes in a little butter and blend into the soup just before serving.

CUCUMBER WITH PRAWNS AND MUSHROOMS

Cucumber is usually served raw in salads or sandwiches, but it loses nothing of its flavour or freshness by being cooked. This quick little hors-d'oeuvre has something of the delicate taste of Chinese food.

PREPARATION TIME: *15 min.*
COOKING TIME: *15 min.*

INGREDIENTS (*for 4*):
1 large or 2 small cucumbers
Salt and black pepper
4 oz. button mushrooms
1½ oz. butter
1 rounded teaspoon plain flour
2½ fluid oz. chicken stock
2½ fluid oz. single cream
Soy sauce (optional)
4 oz. shelled prawns
GARNISH:
Finely chopped chives, basil or dill
Cucumber twists

Wash the cucumber, but do not peel it. Cut it into ½ in. dice and cook for 3–4 minutes in boiling, lightly salted water. Rinse the cucumber in cold water and drain thoroughly in a colander. Trim the mushrooms* and cut them into ¼ in. thick slices.

Melt the butter in a small pan and cook the mushrooms for 2–3 minutes or until lightly browned. Add the diced cucumber and simmer, covered with a lid, for 2–3 minutes over low heat. Sprinkle in the flour and blend thoroughly; gradually add the stock and cream, stirring the mixture until smooth. Bring gently to the boil and season to taste with salt, freshly ground pepper and a few drops of soy sauce. Simmer for another 2–3 minutes, then stir in the prawns and heat through.

Spoon into a warmed serving dish or individual deep scallop shells. Sprinkle with the herbs and decorate with thin twists of cucumber. Serve the cucumber mixture immediately, with thinly sliced brown bread and butter, or crisp toast fingers.

CHILLED CARROT SOUP

As young home-produced carrots become more plentiful, it is well worth trying this soup of Mexican origin. It can be served hot, but the subtle creamy flavour is more pronounced if the soup is chilled.

PREPARATION TIME: *20 min.*
COOKING TIME: *45 min.*
CHILLING TIME: *1 hour*

INGREDIENTS (*for 6*):
1¼ lb. carrots
1 onion
3–4 cloves garlic
1 oz. butter
2 pints beef stock
8 fluid oz. double cream
Salt and black pepper
GARNISH:
Finely chopped parsley

Fish

Peel and thinly slice the onion; peel and crush the garlic. Melt the butter in a heavy-based pan, and cook the onion and garlic gently over low heat. Keep the pan covered with a lid until the onion is soft and transparent but not coloured. Meanwhile, top, tail and scrape the carrots, and then chop them roughly. Add these to the onion and continue cooking, covered, for about 8 minutes. Bring the beef stock to the boil and pour it over the vegetables. Bring the contents of the pan to simmering point and maintain this over lowest possible heat for about 30 minutes.

Remove the soup from the heat and allow to cool slightly before liquidising it until smooth. Alternatively, rub the soup through a fine sieve into a bowl.

In a separate bowl, lightly whisk half the quantity of cream until it holds its shape. Stir the whisked cream into the soup and season to taste with salt and freshly ground pepper. Chill the soup in the refrigerator for at least 1 hour.

Serve the soup in individual bowls, trickling into each a good dessertspoon of the remaining cream. Sprinkle with the finely chopped parsley.

PLAICE WITH ORANGES

Cold poached plaice fillets coated in mayonnaise make a quick and simple meal on a hot day. The richness of the sauce is balanced by an orange garnish in a sharp French dressing.

PREPARATION TIME: *20 min.*
COOKING TIME: *20 min.*

INGREDIENTS *(for 4–6):*
3 good-sized plaice or lemon soles
Juice of half lemon
3 oranges
Salt and black pepper
1½ oz. butter
¼ pint mayonnaise
Paprika
Small tin anchovy fillets
2 tablespoons French dressing

Ask the fishmonger to skin the fish on both sides and to fillet each plaice* into two. Wash the fillets and dry them thoroughly on a clean cloth. Sprinkle them with the lemon juice and the juice of half an orange, then season with salt and freshly ground pepper. Finely grate the rind from one orange over the fish. Roll up the fillets, beginning at the head, and secure with wooden cocktail sticks or toothpicks. Lay the rolled fillets in a buttered ovenproof dish.

Squeeze the juice of half an orange over the fish. Dot with small pieces of butter and cover the dish with buttered grease-proof paper or foil. Bake in the centre of a pre-heated oven at 350°F (mark 4) for about 20 minutes, or until the fillets are tender, but still firm. Remove from the oven and leave to cool.

Lift the cold fillets carefully on to a shallow serving dish, and remove the toothpicks. Add the juice and grated rind of half an orange, drop by drop, to the mayonnaise* and coat the fillets with it. Sprinkle with paprika and arrange two halved anchovies over each fillet.

Peel the remaining oranges, removing all pith, and cut them into thin round slices with a sharp serrated knife. Dip the orange slices in the French dressing* and serve separately or as a garnish to the fillets.

Serve with a salad of blanched, sliced courgettes, strips of red and green pepper and onion rings.

SALMON TROUT IN JELLY

This makes an excellent and attractive centrepiece for a special dinner occasion or a cold buffet. It also has the advantage of being prepared well in advance.

PREPARATION TIME: *30 min.*
COOKING TIME: *1–1½ hours*

INGREDIENTS *(for 8):*
1 salmon trout, approx. 2½–3 lb.
½ oz. gelatine
1 tablespoon white wine vinegar
3 fluid oz. dry sherry
2 egg whites
STOCK:
1 carrot
1 onion
Bouquet garni
4 peppercorns
1½ tablespoons wine vinegar
½ level teaspoon salt
GARNISH:
4 oz. peeled prawns
Watercress

Begin by making the stock, putting all the ingredients, with 1 pint of water, in a pan. Bring to the boil, cover the pan with a lid and simmer for 20 minutes. Strain the stock through muslin.

Remove the fins and gills from the salmon trout, if not already done by the fishmonger, and cut a 1 in. deep inverted V out of the tail to make it resemble a mermaid's tail. Wash the fish thoroughly to remove all traces of blood, and put it in a fish kettle, or a large flameproof dish. Pour over the warm stock and cover with a lid or foil. Cook the fish for 25–30 minutes on top of the stove, or for 50 minutes in the oven, pre-heated to 350°F (mark 4), basting with the stock.

Leave the fish to cool in the liquid. When quite cold, snip the skin near the head with a pair of scissors and peel it carefully off, leaving the head and tail intact. Split the fish along the backbone with a sharp knife and snip the bone below the head and above the tail. Ease the backbone out carefully without breaking the salmon trout.

Strain the fish liquid, through muslin, into a saucepan. Dissolve the gelatine in a small cupful of the liquid, and heat the remainder over moderate heat, whisking steadily until the liquid is hot. Stir in the dissolved gelatine, the vinegar, sherry and the egg whites; whisk steadily until the mixture comes to the boil. Draw the pan off the heat at once and leave the liquid to settle for 5 minutes. Bring to the boil again, draw it off the heat and leave it to settle once more. The liquid should now look clear; otherwise repeat the boiling process again. Strain the liquid through a clean cloth and set aside to cool.

Spoon a little of the cool jelly over the base of a serving dish and leave it to set. Lift the salmon trout carefully on top of the jelly. Garnish the fish with the prawns and spoon over a little of the jelly. When the prawns have set, spoon jelly over the whole salmon and leave to set.

Serve the salmon trout garnished with sprigs of watercress and the remaining chopped jelly.

SWEET-SOUR SALMON

In German cookery, a sweet-sour sauce is frequently served with fish and with braised meat. It is often served hot, but the sweet-tangy flavour is more pronounced when chilled.

PREPARATION TIME: *10 min.*
COOKING TIME: *35–40 min.*
CHILLING TIME: *2–3 hours*

INGREDIENTS *(for 4):*
4 salmon steaks
Salt and black pepper
2 large onions
2 tablespoons white wine vinegar
2 rounded tablespoons soft light-brown sugar
Juice of 2 lemons
2 egg yolks
GARNISH:
Cucumber slices

Wash and dry the salmon steaks. Season with salt and freshly ground pepper and arrange in a shallow ovenproof dish. Cover with peeled and sliced onions.

Pour boiling, lightly salted water over the fish to barely cover it. Seal the dish with foil and bake in the centre of a pre-heated oven at 325°F (mark 3) for 20–25 minutes, or until cooked. Lift the salmon steaks carefully out of the dish with a perforated spoon, and arrange them on a serving dish.

Strain the cooking liquid through muslin and measure ½ pint into a saucepan; add the vinegar, brown sugar and lemon juice. Simmer over low heat until the liquid has reduced* slightly. Beat the egg yolks in a small bowl and stir in a tablespoonful of the reduced liquid; blend thoroughly and gradually add all the liquid. Set the bowl over a pan of simmering water, and stir the sauce continuously until it thickens to a coating consistency.

Pour the sauce over the salmon and cool before chilling for at least 2 hours in the refrigerator.

Garnish the salmon steaks with thin slices of unpeeled cucumber and serve with boiled potatoes and a crisp green salad.

TROUT WITH BRETON SAUCE

Breton sauce is reminiscent of mayonnaise, but is easier to make and less oily. The sharp flavour of the sauce makes it a perfect foil for cold trout, mackerel or herring.

PREPARATION TIME: *25 min.*
COOKING TIME: *25–30 min.*

INGREDIENTS *(for 4–6):*
4 large trout
1 tablespoon olive oil
SAUCE:
2 level tablespoons Dijon mustard
2 egg yolks
1 dessertspoon wine, cider or tarragon vinegar
Salt and black pepper
3 oz. unsalted butter
2 tablespoons chopped fresh parsley and chives
GARNISH:
½ cucumber

Wash and clean the trout thoroughly; cut off the heads and dry the fish on a clean cloth. Wrap each trout in a piece of oiled aluminium foil and put them in a fireproof dish. Bake in the centre of a pre-heated oven at 325°F (mark 3) for 25–30 minutes.

Remove the dish from the oven and open the foil packets to allow the trout to cool slightly. Split each fish along the belly and, with a pointed knife, carefully loosen the backbone; ease it out gently so that most of the small bones come away with it. Set the trout aside to cool.

To make the sauce, beat the mustard, egg yolks and vinegar together until well blended; season to taste with salt and freshly ground pepper. Put the butter in a bowl over a pan of hot water and stir until it has softened, but not melted. Gradually add the butter to the egg mixture, beating all the time, until the sauce has the consistency of thick cream. Stir in the finely chopped herbs.

Before serving, gently peel the skin from the cold trout, cut each into two fillets and arrange on a serving dish. Pour the sauce over. Peel the cucumber, cut it in half lengthways and scrape out the seeds with a pointed teaspoon. Dice the flesh and sprinkle it over the trout.

Serve with crusty bread and butter as a main course or, in small quantities, as a starter for a dinner party.

SOLE VÉRONIQUE

The French culinary term 'véronique' describes a dish, usually fish, served in a sauce made from white wine and cream. The traditional garnish is muscat grapes, but any other type of large white grapes may be used.

PREPARATION TIME: *20 min.*
COOKING TIME: *25 min.*

INGREDIENTS *(for 4–6):*
8 fillets of sole
2 shallots
3 button mushrooms
1 sprig parsley
1 bay leaf
Salt and black pepper
3 teaspoons lemon juice
¼ pint medium dry white wine
6 oz. white muscat grapes
¾ oz. unsalted butter
2 level tablespoons plain flour
¼ pint milk
¼ pint double cream

Wash the fillets, pat them dry on a clean cloth and arrange them in a lightly buttered ovenproof dish. Peel and finely chop the shallots; trim the mushrooms* and slice them thinly. Sprinkle both over the fish and add the parsley and bay leaf. Season with salt, freshly ground pepper and 2 teaspoons of lemon juice.

Pour the wine over the fish, adding sufficient water to barely cover the fillets. Seal the dish closely with foil, and bake in the centre of a pre-heated oven at 350°F (mark 4) for 15–20 minutes, or until tender. Meanwhile, peel the grapes*, cut them in half and remove the pips.

Remove the dish from the oven, carefully lift the fillets out and keep them warm. Strain the liquid into a small saucepan. Boil rapidly over high heat until it has reduced* by about half. Melt the butter in a separate pan and stir in the flour; blend well and cook over moderate heat for 2 minutes.

Make the reduced liquid up to ½ pint with the milk and gradually add it to the roux*, stirring continuously. Simmer over low heat until the sauce has the consistency of thick cream. Stir in the cream and the remaining lemon juice and bring the sauce back to boiling point. Remove from the heat, correct seasoning and fold in two-thirds of the grapes.

Fold the fillets in half and arrange them on a flameproof serving dish. Pour the sauce over the fish and brown under a hot grill. Arrange the remaining grapes at either end of the dish and serve at once. Green beans mimosa (see July vegetables) and buttered potatoes would go well with the fish.

Meat

CRAB MOUSSE

On a hot day, a light and fluffy cold mousse is the perfect meal. The mousse can be made well in advance.

PREPARATION TIME: *45 min.*
CHILLING TIME: *3 hours*

INGREDIENTS *(for 6)*:
1 large crab (1–1¼ lb.)
1 level tablespoon grated
  Parmesan cheese
Salt and black pepper
Cayenne pepper
Juice of half lemon
6 fluid oz. aspic jelly
2½ fluid oz. double cream
2 egg whites
GARNISH:
Cucumber slices

This dish needs at least 8 oz. of crabmeat; extract the meat from the body and claws and finely flake* both the brown and white meat into a bowl. Add the grated Parmesan cheese and pound thoroughly. Alternatively, put the meat in a liquidiser, with the cream, for 1–2 minutes. Season with salt, freshly ground black pepper, cayenne and lemon juice.

Make up the aspic jelly and allow it to cool but not set; stir it into the crab mixture and add the cream (if not already used). Leave the mixture until cold and thick. Beat the egg whites until frothy but not dry, then fold them into the crab mixture. Turn the mousse into a soufflé dish and leave to set in a refrigerator for at least 3 hours.

Garnish the mousse with thin cucumber slices. A potato and chive salad and a tossed green salad would be suitable.

BOEUF À LA MODE EN GELÉE

Most classic recipes for cold jellied beef use the expensive fillet, but topside, poached slowly to a near-jelly consistency, makes an excellent alternative. The dish, ideal for buffet entertaining, should be prepared a day in advance.

PREPARATION TIME: *30 min.*
COOKING TIME: *4½–5 hours*

INGREDIENTS *(for 6–8)*:
3 lb. topside or top rump of beef
¼ lb. pork fat
1 calf's foot
½ pint dry red wine
2 cloves garlic
Salt and black pepper
1–2 tablespoons beef dripping
2 tablespoons brandy
2 shallots
2 bay leaves
½ pint beef stock or water
15 small onions
10 young carrots

Order the meat in advance and preferably larded with the pork fat. Have the calf's foot chopped into pieces. If the meat is not larded, cut the pork fat into strips, narrow enough to go through the eye of a larding needle, and long enough to be threaded through the meat. Pull the fat strips through the meat and trim them off at each end.

Put the meat in a deep bowl, pour over the wine and marinate* for about 4 hours, turning the meat frequently.

Peel the garlic, cut it into small strips and push them into the meat with the point of a knife. Season with salt and pepper.

Bring a large pan of salted water to the boil and blanch* the

calf's foot pieces for 10 minutes. Drain and set aside.

Melt half the dripping in a heavy-based deep pan or flame-proof dish over high heat, and brown the meat all over to seal in the juices. Reduce the heat. Pour the brandy over the meat, let it warm through slightly, then set it alight. When the flames have died down, add the calf's foot pieces.

Peel and finely chop the shallots and add them, with the bay leaves, to the pan. Heat the stock or water in a separate pan, blend in the wine and pour it over the meat. Bring this liquid to boiling point, cover the pan

tightly with foil and the lid. Cook in the centre of a pre-heated oven, at 300°F (mark 2), for 3 hours.

Meanwhile, peel the onions, leaving them whole. Wash and scrape the carrots and split them in half lengthways. Heat the remaining dripping in a small pan and lightly brown the vegetables. Add them to the meat after 3 hours' cooking and simmer for a further 1–1½ hours.

Lift the meat on to a dish and remove the vegetables with a perforated spoon. Let the liquid cool, then strain it through muslin into a bowl. Leave the liquid in the refrigerator overnight to set to a jelly.

The next day, carefully scrape the surface fat from the jelly with a spoon dipped in hot water. Cut the meat into neat thin slices and arrange them in a deep serving dish together with the carrots and onions. Melt the jelly in a saucepan over low heat, then pour it carefully over the meat and vegetables. Leave the dish in a cool place to allow the jelly to re-set.

Serve the jellied beef with a selection of salads, such as a crisp green salad tossed in a sharp French dressing*, a tomato salad and a cold potato salad.

VEAL ESCALOPES WITH GINGER WINE

These thin cuts from the veal fillet are usually served with a creamy sauce. This is frequently made from white wine or Marsala – the ginger wine in this recipe adds an unusual, slightly spicy flavour.

PREPARATION TIME: *10 min.*
COOKING TIME: *15 min.*

INGREDIENTS *(for 4)*:
4 veal escalopes, each ¼ in. thick and weighing about 3 oz.
Seasoned flour
2 oz. unsalted butter
1 teaspoon olive oil
6 tablespoons ginger wine
1 dessertspoon lemon juice
3 tablespoons double cream
Salt and black pepper
GARNISH:
4 lemon twists
1 dessertspoon chopped parsley

Cut off any fat from the escalopes and trim them into neat shapes. Dust them lightly with the seasoned flour*. Heat the butter and oil in a heavy-based pan over moderate heat and fry the veal until golden brown on both sides. Lift the slices on to a serving dish and keep them warm.

Add the ginger wine to the pan and bring it gently to the boil, scraping up the pan juices with a rubber spatula. Reduce the heat and simmer slowly for 5 minutes, or until the wine is syrupy. Stir in the lemon juice and the cream, and simmer for a further 2–3 minutes, or until the sauce has a pale coffee colour. Season to taste with salt and freshly ground pepper. Pour the sauce over the meat and garnish each escalope with a lemon twist sprinkled with chopped parsley.

Serve the escalopes with plain boiled potatoes and French beans.

BAKED FOREHOCK OF BACON

Forehock is one of the most economical bacon joints, ideal for a family meal and providing plenty of left-over meat to serve cold or in sandwiches. The joint is here served with peaches; for a dinner party, middle cut of gammon could replace the bacon.

PREPARATION TIME: *20 min.*
COOKING TIME: *2–2¼ hours*

INGREDIENTS *(for 8)*:
4 lb. boned, rolled forehock of bacon
8 peppercorns
3 cloves
Bouquet garni
2–3 oz. demerara sugar
¼ pint medium dry cider or unsweetened apple juice
4 peaches
3 oz. unsalted butter
1½ oz. honey or dark brown sugar
Cinnamon

Soak the bacon in cold water overnight. The next day, put the joint in a large pan with sufficient cold water to cover it completely. Add the peppercorns, cloves and bouquet garni*. Bring to the boil over moderate heat, remove any scum from the surface, and cover the pan with a lid. Reduce the heat, and simmer the bacon for 1¼ hours.

Lift the meat from the pan, leave it to cool and set, then remove all the string. Cut away the rind with a sharp knife, score the fat in a diamond pattern, at ½ in. intervals, and press the demerara sugar firmly all over the fat. Put the joint in a roasting tin, heat the cider or apple juice and pour it over the meat, basting* it without disturbing the sugar.

Skin the peaches*, cut them in half and remove the stones, and enlarge the cavities slightly with a pointed teaspoon. Blend the butter, honey (or sugar) and a pinch of cinnamon until creamy. Spoon this mixture into the peach halves.

Bake the joint in the centre of a pre-heated oven, set at 350°F (mark 4), for ½ hour, basting frequently with the juice. Place the peaches round the joint and raise the temperature to 400°F (mark 6) and bake for a further 15 minutes, or until the top of the joint is golden and shiny.

Serve the joint whole or sliced, garnished with the peaches. Plain boiled potatoes and a tossed green salad, or carrots paysanne (see August vegetables) would make good vegetable dishes for the bacon.

PORK COOKED IN MILK

The Italians frequently pot-roast meat and chicken in milk. For this recipe, choose boned leg of pork or, more economically, blade or the fore-end of a hand. It can be served hot or cold.

PREPARATION TIME: *10 min.*
COOKING TIME: *2 hours*

INGREDIENTS *(for 6)*:
2½ lb. boned rolled pork
Salt and black pepper
1 clove garlic
12 coriander seeds
2 onions
2 slices cooked ham
1 tablespoon olive oil
1½ pints milk

Ask the butcher to bone the meat and to take the skin and part of the fat off the pork before rolling it. Wipe the meat with a clean damp cloth and rub it all over with salt and freshly ground pepper. Peel the garlic and cut it lengthways into small strips. Make small incisions in the meat with the point of a knife and push in the garlic strips and coriander seeds.

Peel and finely chop the onions; dice the ham. Heat the oil in a heavy-based pan or flameproof dish into which the meat will fit closely. Fry the onions and ham in the oil for a few minutes until they begin to colour. Put in the meat and brown it lightly all over. In a separate pan, bring the milk to boiling point, then pour it over the pork so that it reaches ½ in. over the meat.

Cook the pork, uncovered, over low heat (set the pan on an asbestos sheet), for about 1 hour. The milk should be kept barely at simmering point during cooking and will form a cobwebby skin which gradually turns pale golden brown. After 1 hour break the milk skin and turn the meat over, scraping all the skin from the sides into the bottom of the pan.

Continue cooking the meat slowly for a further 45 minutes, or until the milk has reduced to a cupful of thick sauce.

Lift the meat on to a serving dish and pour the sauce with the bits of onion and ham over it.

Serve the pork hot or cold, with boiled potatoes and a crisp green side salad.

LIVER WITH DUBONNET AND ORANGE

Lamb – or the more expensive calf – liver is most suitable for this recipe. The fruity, sweet-wine sauce blends surprisingly well with juicy, slightly under-cooked liver.

PREPARATION TIME: *15 min.*
COOKING TIME: *10–15 min.*

INGREDIENTS (for 6) :
1 lb. lamb liver
2 small onions
1 clove garlic
1 tablespoon olive oil
1½ oz. butter
Seasoned flour
SAUCE:
1 tablespoon orange juice
8 tablespoons red Dubonnet
2 rounded tablespoons fresh
   chopped parsley
Rind of an orange, coarsely grated
1 teaspoon finely grated lemon
   rind

Wash the liver, trim off any tough and discoloured parts and dry it thoroughly. Cut the liver into slices, ½ in. thick and coat them with seasoned flour*.

Peel and finely chop the onions and garlic. Heat the oil and butter in a large, heavy-based pan over moderate heat and cook the onion and garlic, covered, until soft and beginning to colour.

Add the liver slices to the onions, in a single layer, and cook over low heat. As soon as the blood begins to run, turn the liver over and cook the other side for a slightly shorter time.

When cooked, arrange the liver on a warm serving dish. Cover with the onion, lifted from the pan with a perforated spoon. Keep the dish hot.

To make the sauce, stir the orange juice and Dubonnet into the pan juices. Boil rapidly until the liquid has reduced* by half. Remove the pan from the heat and stir in most of the chopped parsley, grated orange and lemon rind, reserving a little for garnish.

Pour the sauce over the liver, sprinkle with the parsley and orange and lemon rind. Serve at once, with creamed potatoes and a green vegetable.

BRAISED SHOULDER OF LAMB

This recipe comes from New Zealand and is ideal for imported lamb. The boned shoulder is rolled round a savoury apricot stuffing.

PREPARATION TIME: *30 min.*
COOKING TIME: *2½ hours*

INGREDIENTS: *(for 6) :*
4 lb. boned shoulder of lamb
Salt and black pepper
1 pint stock
6 carrots
6 celery sticks
6 turnips
2 large onions
STUFFING:
3 oz. dried apricots
1 oz. butter
1 tablespoon chopped onion
4 tablespoons fine white bread-
   crumbs
1 teaspoon chopped parsley
1–2 tablespoons milk

Put the dried apricots in cold water and soak overnight. Drain and chop them finely.

To make the stuffing, melt the butter in a frying pan over moderate heat and cook the onions until soft and transparent. Remove from the heat and add the breadcrumbs and the parsley; season to taste. Stir in enough milk to give a soft consistency, and add the apricots.

Sprinkle the cut surface of the lamb with salt and pepper. Spread the stuffing over the meat, roll it up and tie with string. Place the joint in an ovenproof casserole.

Put the casserole in a pre-heated oven, set at 450°F (mark 8), and cook for 15 minutes, uncovered. Pour in half the stock and reduce the heat to 350°F (mark 4). Cover and cook for 45 minutes. Meanwhile, prepare and roughly chop the carrots, celery, turnips and onions.

Arrange the vegetables round the joint and add the remaining stock. Cover and cook for another 1¼ hours.

Remove the casserole from the oven, and lift the meat and the vegetables on to a serving dish.

Skim the fat from the pan juices, and reduce* them by half. Pour this gravy into a sauce boat and serve separately.

JAMBON À LA CRÈME

The classic French recipe for a whole York ham, cooked and then dressed in a cream sauce, can easily be adapted for a small family meal

PREPARATION TIME: *20 min.*
COOKING TIME: *20 min.*

INGREDIENTS *(for 4–6) :*
8 thick slices cooked ham
6 oz. button mushrooms
7 fluid oz. dry white wine
3–4 shallots
1 lb. tomatoes
2½ oz. butter
1½ level tablespoons plain flour
8 fluid oz. double cream
Salt and white pepper
2 oz. Parmesan cheese

Trim the mushrooms* and slice them thickly. Cook them in a shallow pan, with the wine, until the wine has reduced to about 3 tablespoons. Lift the mushrooms out with a perforated spoon and set them aside.

Peel and finely chop the shallots, add them to the wine in the pan and cook until virtually all the wine has evaporated. Skin the tomatoes*, remove the seeds and chop the flesh roughly.

In a separate pan, melt 2 oz. of the butter, stir in the flour and cook for 2 minutes. Gradually add the cream to make a smooth sauce. Season to taste with salt and pepper. Stir in the cooked shallots and the chopped tomatoes. Bring the sauce to the boil, then lower the heat and simmer for 5–6 minutes, stirring occasionally to prevent sticking.

Arrange the ham in a lightly buttered flameproof dish, sprinkle with the mushroom and pour over the cream sauce. Grate the cheese evenly over the sauce and dot with the remaining butter. Put the dish under a medium grill until the ham is heated through and the cheese is lightly browned and bubbly. Alternatively, cook the dish in the centre of a pre-heated oven, at 400°F (mark 6), until the cheese is browned.

Buttered noodles and a tossed green salad, or boiled potatoes and creamed spinach (see June vegetables) would be suitable.

Poultry & Game

KIDNEYS IN SHERRY

Lamb and sheep kidneys are economical and suitable for this Spanish family dish. For a special occasion, calf kidneys transform the dish into a luxury meal, when other fortified wines, such as port or Madeira, might be substituted for the sherry.

PREPARATION TIME: *20 min.*
COOKING TIME: *15 min.*

INGREDIENTS *(for 4)*:

10–12 lamb kidneys
1 onion
1 small clove garlic
3 tablespoons olive oil
1 small bay leaf
1 level tablespoon plain flour
4 tablespoons beef stock
1½ tablespoons chopped parsley
Salt and black pepper
5 tablespoons dry sherry
GARNISH:
Chopped parsley

Remove the fat deposits and the outer membranes from the kidneys*, cut them in half lengthways and snip out the cores with scissors. Cut each half into three or four slices.

Peel and finely chop the onion and garlic. Heat half the oil in a small frying pan, over moderate heat, and add the onion, garlic and bay leaf. Cook, stirring frequently, for about 5 minutes, or until the onion is soft and transparent. Stir in the flour and blend thoroughly. Gradually add the stock and cook over high heat, stirring all the time, until the mixture thickens and comes to the boil. Blend in the parsley, reduce the heat and simmer the mixture over low heat for 3 minutes, then remove the bay leaf. Set the mixture aside.

Heat the remaining oil in a large frying pan. Season the kidneys with salt and a little pepper and fry in the oil, over moderate heat, for about 5 minutes, turning them frequently to brown quickly on all sides without burning. Lift the kidneys on to a plate, and pour the oil from the pan before adding the sherry. Bring the sherry to the boil, scraping in the brown sediment at the bottom of the pan. Blend the onion mixture into the sherry, and add the kidneys. Bring to boiling point, and simmer for 2–3 minutes. Adjust seasoning.

Serve the kidneys in the sauce, on a bed of fluffy saffron-flavoured rice, garnished with parsley. Grilled mushroom caps or halved tomatoes would also be suitable.

MUSTARD RABBIT

Wild rabbit went into this French farmhouse stew, perfect for a chilly late summer day when autumn seems near. Today, all rabbits sold in Britain are bred for the table.

PREPARATION TIME: *15 min.*
COOKING TIME: *1½–2 hours*

INGREDIENTS *(for 4–6)*:

2½–3 lb. rabbit or 6 rabbit
   joints
4 rounded tablespoons Dijon
   mustard
Seasoned flour
2 oz. unsalted butter
2 oz. green streaky bacon
1 onion
1 clove garlic
½ pint double cream
GARNISH:
Chopped chervil or parsley
Bread croûtons

Wash and dry the rabbit* thoroughly. Cut it into six or eight neat joints and put them in a large bowl. Cover with cold salted water and leave to soak for 1–2 hours. Drain and dry thoroughly. Coat the rabbit joints evenly with mustard and leave them in a cool place overnight, covered with muslin.

The following day dust the rabbit lightly with seasoned flour*, shaking off any surplus. Melt the butter in a flameproof casserole and lightly brown the joints on both sides; lift them out and set aside. Remove the rind, and roughly chop the bacon. Peel and finely chop the onion and garlic. Fry the bacon for 2–3 minutes in the butter, then add the onion and garlic and continue cooking over low heat until the onion is soft.

Return the rabbit joints to the casserole, cover closely with a lid or foil and simmer over low heat for 30 minutes. Remove the casserole from the heat and stir in the cream. Cover again and cook over low heat on top of the stove, or in an oven pre-heated to 325°F (mark 3) for about 45 minutes, or until the rabbit is tender. Stir once or twice.

Serve the rabbit straight from the casserole, sprinkled with the fresh herbs and garnished with bread croûtons*. Buttered rice or boiled potatoes can be served with the rabbit, together with a green vegetable.

DUCK WITH APRICOTS

Bitter-sweet oranges are a classic flavouring and garnish with duck. This recipe provides the sharper tang of fresh apricots; tinned apricots may be used instead.

PREPARATION TIME: *10 min.*
COOKING TIME: *2½ hours*

INGREDIENTS *(for 4)*:

1 duck, approx. 5 lb.
Salt and black pepper
3 oz. butter
1 tablespoon olive oil
½ pint veal or chicken stock
¼ pint medium dry white wine
1 lb. fresh apricots
Juice of half orange
1 tablespoon apricot brandy
2 tablespoons brandy

Wipe the prepared duck* thoroughly, inside and out; rub the skin with salt and freshly ground pepper. Heat the butter and oil in a large pan or roasting tin, and brown the duck on all sides. Lift the duck into a large flameproof casserole.

Add the stock and wine to the roasting tin, heat until the liquid reaches boiling point, then pour it over the duck. Cover the casserole with a lid or foil and cook the duck in the centre of the oven pre-heated to 325°F (mark 3) for 1½–2 hours.

Rice & Pasta

Wash and dry the apricots, cut them in half and remove the stones. Put half the apricots round the duck after 45 minutes.

Lift the cooked duck on to a serving dish and keep it warm. Strain the cooking liquid and skim off as much fat as possible. Rub the cooked apricots through a sieve and reserve the purée*. Pour the strained liquid back into the casserole and boil it briskly until it has reduced* by a third. Add the orange juice and thicken this sauce with the apricot purée.

Arrange the remaining fresh apricot halves round the duck. Warm the brandies, pour them over the duck and set alight. Serve at once, with boiled potatoes and a green salad. Offer the sauce separately.

SALMI OF GROUSE

The glorious twelfth of August marks the beginning of the grouse season. The young birds are usually roasted whole and served, one per person, on a slice of bread. Unless quite young and tender, the birds are better used in a salmi – a cooking method of partly roasting the birds before finishing them off in game stock and serving them in a wine sauce.

PREPARATION TIME: *10 min.*
COOKING TIME: *1½ hours*

INGREDIENTS *(for 2–4):*
2 grouse
1 onion
Salt and black pepper
4 oz. mushrooms
8 fluid oz. red wine
12 juniper berries
1 tablespoon unsalted butter
1 level tablespoon plain flour
GARNISH:
Chopped parsley

Order the grouse trussed and barded*, and ask the poulterer to include the giblets with the order. Put the grouse, breast side down, in a roasting tin and cook them for 15 minutes in the centre of a pre-heated oven, at 375°F (mark 5). Remove the grouse from the oven, cut off the barding fat round each bird and carve the breasts off neatly. Slice each breast piece in half and set aside.

Put the grouse carcasses in a pan, cover with cold water and simmer, with the peeled and chopped onion, for about 30 minutes. Strain this stock through muslin and season with salt and freshly ground pepper.

Trim the mushrooms* and slice them thickly.

Put the grouse breasts in a wide shallow pan, add the mushrooms and sufficient stock to cover the contents. Put a lid on the pan and simmer over low heat for about 30 minutes.

Meanwhile, blend the wine into the remaining stock, add the grouse giblets and the mashed livers. Crush the juniper berries lightly and add to the wine stock. Bring to the boil and simmer for 10–15 minutes.

Lift the cooked grouse from the pan and arrange the pieces on a serving dish. Keep it warm in the oven and pour the liquid into the wine stock. Blend the butter and flour together, and add, in knobs, to the stock. Stir continuously, over low heat, until it thickens to a sauce. Simmer for a few minutes; adjust seasoning.

Pour the sauce over the grouse and sprinkle with finely chopped parsley. Traditionally, grouse is served with game chips*, fried breadcrumbs and/or bread sauce* and sprigs of watercress.

ARANCINI SICILIANI

'Sicilian oranges' is the literal translation of this lunch or supper dish. The 'oranges' are crisp rice balls with a savoury filling of cheese and ham.

PREPARATION TIME: *45 min.*
COOKING TIME: *30 min.*

INGREDIENTS *(for 6):*
8 oz. Italian or short grain rice
2 oz. grated Parmesan cheese
2 small eggs
½ pint thick tomato sauce
Salt and black pepper
2 oz. Bel Paese cheese
2 oz. cooked ham, chicken or salami
1–2 oz. fine fresh breadcrumbs
Oil for deep frying
2–3 tablespoons single cream (optional)
GARNISH:
Fresh mint or basil leaves

Bring a large pan of salted water to the boil, add the rice and cook rapidly until just tender, after 15–20 minutes. Rinse and drain the rice thoroughly.

Put the rice in a bowl, stir in the Parmesan cheese, the lightly beaten eggs, 1 tablespoon of tomato sauce* and a little salt.

Blend the ingredients thoroughly, then set aside until cold.

Dice the Bel Paese cheese and the meat finely and put them in a bowl. Stir in 2 tablespoons of the tomato sauce and season to taste with salt and pepper.

Take 1 dessertspoon of the cold rice and mould it in the well-floured palm of the hand; put a teaspoon of the cheese and meat mixture into the hollow, top with a little more rice and shape it all into a ball about 1½ in. wide. When all the balls (about 12) have been shaped, coat them thickly with breadcrumbs.

In a deep frier, heat the oil* until hot, and fry the rice balls, two or three at a time, until golden brown. Drain on crumpled absorbent paper and keep the rice balls hot.

Just before serving, garnish each 'orange' with a herb leaf. The remaining tomato sauce can be thinned with a little single cream, heated through without boiling, and served separately.

ANCHOVY EGGS WITH NOODLES

Savoury stuffed eggs are often served as an hors-d'oeuvre, but they can also form the basis for an economical and quick lunch or supper dish.

PREPARATION TIME: *20 min.*
COOKING TIME: *15 min.*

INGREDIENTS *(for 6):*
1 lb. ribbon noodles
¾ pint white sauce
3–4 oz. grated Parmesan cheese
12 eggs
3 tablespoons anchovy essence
3 oz. unsalted butter
¼ pint double cream
Salt and white pepper

Prepare the white sauce* first, then stir the grated cheese into it and keep it warm. Put the eggs in a large pan of cold water and hardboil them over gentle heat for 10–12 minutes.

Shell the eggs under cold running water. Cut them in half lengthways and carefully remove the yolks. Keep the whites warm in a bowl of hot water. Rub the egg yolks through a sieve into a bowl and blend in 2 oz. of softened butter, the anchovy essence and the cream. Season to taste with freshly ground white pepper.

Spoon the yolk mixture into a forcing bag fitted with a rosette nozzle and pipe it into the egg whites. Arrange the filled eggs, rounded side down, in a lightly buttered flameproof dish. Cover with foil and heat the eggs through in the centre of a pre-heated oven at 300°F (mark 2) for about 8 minutes.

Meanwhile, cook the noodles in a large pan of boiling salted water until just tender, after 8–10 minutes. Drain thoroughly and keep warm.

Remove the eggs from the oven, pour the hot cheese sauce carefully over them and put the dish under a hot grill for 2 minutes until the sauce is brown and bubbly.

Toss the noodles in the remaining butter, season with salt and pepper and turn into a warm serving dish.

Serve the anchovy eggs separately, and offer a side salad of tomatoes or crisp cos lettuce.

Vegetables & Salads

SPAGHETTI WITH TUNA SAUCE

Lighter and more summery than spaghetti with a tomato or meat sauce, this dish makes a good family meal. Serve it with crusty bread and a green salad, tossed in French dressing*.

PREPARATION TIME: *10 min.*
COOKING TIME: *15 min.*

INGREDIENTS *(for 4–6)*:
1 lb. spaghetti
1 clove garlic (optional)
2 tablespoons olive oil
2 oz. butter
8 fluid oz. chicken stock
3 tablespoons dry white wine or vermouth
6 oz. tin of tuna fish
Salt and black pepper
GARNISH:
2 tablespoons finely chopped parsley

Bring a large pan of salted water to the boil, add the spaghetti and bring back to the boil. Cook for 7–12 minutes or until the spaghetti is just resistant to the bite (*al dente**). Stir occasionally with a wooden spoon.

Peel and finely chop the garlic. Heat the oil and half the butter, and fry the garlic for 1–2 minutes, then stir in the stock and wine. Boil briskly over high heat until the liquid has reduced* to about ¼ pint. Drain the oil from the tuna fish, flake* the meat and add it to the stock. Season with salt and freshly ground pepper.

When the spaghetti is cooked, drain it thoroughly in a colander and toss it in the remaining butter. Put the spaghetti in a serving dish, pour over the tuna sauce and sprinkle with the chopped parsley. Serve at once.

SPINACH ROLL

Late summer spinach or even the frozen variety is ideal for this Yugoslavian puff pastry dish. It will serve as a light meal on its own, or it can be part of a packed lunch or picnic.

PREPARATION TIME: *45 min.*
COOKING TIME: *30 min.*

INGREDIENTS *(for 4)*:
2 lb. fresh spinach
12 oz. prepared puff pastry
3 oz. cottage cheese
3 eggs
1 oz. grated Parmesan cheese
Salt and black pepper
1 egg yolk

Roll the prepared puff pastry* out on a floured surface to a rectangle 12 in. long by 8 in. wide, and ¼ in. thick. Lightly grease and flour a baking tray.

Wash the spinach thoroughly, discarding any stalks and tough midribs. Put it, still wet, in a large saucepan. Cover with a lid and cook over low heat for 5–7 minutes, or until just tender. Drain the spinach thoroughly in a colander. Chop it finely, and drain again (do not squeeze it completely dry).

Rub the cottage cheese through a sieve to remove any lumps. Separate the eggs. Lightly beat the yolks and add them to the spinach in a mixing bowl. Blend in the cottage and the Parmesan cheese, season with salt and freshly ground pepper. Beat the egg whites until stiff and fold into the mixture.

Moisten the edges of the pastry with cold water and spoon the spinach mixture down the centre of the rectangle and to within 1 in. of the shorter edges. Quickly fold

the pastry over the spinach, close the edges tightly, and seal all three sides firmly with the lightly beaten egg yolk. Roll out the pastry trimmings and use to decorate the top of the roll, brush with the remaining egg yolk to glaze the pastry.

Make two or three slits in the top of the pastry for the steam to escape. Carefully lift the pastry roll on to the baking tray.

Bake in the centre of a pre-heated oven, at 450°F (mark 8) for 20 minutes, then reduce the temperature to 350°F (mark 4) for another 10 minutes, or until the pastry is well risen and golden brown. Serve the roll, hot or cold, cut into thick slices.

LEEKS IN YOGHOURT SAUCE

The first young leeks come on the market towards the end of the month. They are served cold with chicken or fish.

PREPARATION TIME: *15 min.*
COOKING TIME: *30 min.*

INGREDIENTS *(for 4–6)*:
8 slender leeks
Juice of a large lemon
1 level coffeespoon salt
12 black peppercorns
12 fennel seeds
6 coriander seeds
6 sprigs parsley
2 shallots
SAUCE:
8 fluid oz. natural yoghourt
3 egg yolks
2 teaspoons lemon juice
Salt and black pepper
Dijon mustard
GARNISH:
Fresh chopped parsley

Prepare a broth from ¾ pint of water, the lemon juice, spices, herbs and peeled and sliced shallots. Bring the broth to the boil and cook for 10 minutes.

Meanwhile, trim the leeks, slit them halfway down from the top and wash them thoroughly under cold running water.

Put the leeks in a frying pan, wide enough to take them in one layer; pour the strained broth over them. Cover the pan with a lid and simmer the leeks gently for 10–15 minutes, until soft. Leave them to cool in the liquid.

For the sauce, beat the yoghourt, egg yolks and lemon juice together in a bowl, and place it over a pan of gently simmering water. Cook the sauce, stirring frequently, until it has thickened, after about 15 minutes. Season with salt, pepper and mustard, and set aside.

Before serving, drain the leeks thoroughly and cut each into two or three diagonal pieces. Arrange them in a serving dish, spoon the yoghourt sauce over the leeks and sprinkle with parsley.

RAGOÛT OF LETTUCE AND PEAS

Peas that are no longer quite young are the main components of this French vegetable stew. It makes a filling dish on its own, but can also be served with roast meat and poultry.

PREPARATION TIME: *25 min.*
COOKING TIME: *45 min.*

INGREDIENTS *(for 4)*:
2 large cabbage lettuce
2 lb. fresh peas
12–16 large spring onions
6 oz. lean cooked ham or boiled bacon
3 oz. butter
Salt and black pepper
1–2 sugar cubes
GARNISH:
Fried bread triangles

Shell the peas, setting aside about a dozen of the smaller pods. Remove the coarse outer leaves from the lettuce, and cut the heads into quarters lengthways; wash and drain thoroughly. Trim the roots and stems from the spring onions. Cut the ham or bacon into ½ in. cubes.

Melt 2½ oz. of the butter in a large, heavy-based pan over moderate heat. Put the lettuce, peas, pea pods and spring onions into the pan and coat them carefully in the butter. Season to taste with salt and freshly ground pepper. Add the ham or bacon and 3 tablespoons of hot water; cover the pan with a tight lid.

Cook over very low heat for 35–45 minutes depending on the age of the peas; they should be tender but not mushy when cooked. Shake the pan from time to time to prevent sticking.

Before serving, remove the pea pods and stir in the sugar lumps and remaining butter.

Serve the ragoût hot, garnished with triangles of fried bread.

CORN ON THE COB

Sweet corn is a favourite vegetable in America and is gaining popularity in Europe. Corn on the cob should be milky-white in colour and with soft tender kernels. Serve the cobs as a separate vegetable course.

PREPARATION TIME: *10 min.*
COOKING TIME: *5 min.*

INGREDIENTS *(for 4)*:
4 corn cobs
4–6 oz. butter
Salt and black pepper
2 level teaspoons caster sugar

Pepper butter, to be served with the cobs, should be made well in advance so that it can be chilled. Stir the butter until smooth and season highly with freshly ground pepper and extra salt to taste. Shape the butter into an oblong roll and wrap it in foil or greaseproof paper. Chill in the refrigerator.

Remove the leaves and silky tassels from the cobs and put them, with the sugar, in a shallow pan holding just enough boiling water to cover them. Keep the water on the boil and cook the cobs for no more than 5 minutes. Drain.

Serve the cobs at once, with the butter cut into ¼ in. thick slices on a separate plate. Insert special cob holders, small skewers or strong toothpicks at either end of each cob by which to hold it, and provide finger bowls.

COURGETTES IN HOLLANDAISE SAUCE

The delicate flavour of young marrows – or courgettes – is best preserved when served with melted butter or a simple sauce.

PREPARATION TIME: *30 min.*
COOKING TIME: *30 min.*

INGREDIENTS *(for 6)*:
½ lb. courgettes
1 oz. unsalted butter
Salt and black pepper
Juice of half lemon
SAUCE:
7 oz. unsalted butter
3 egg yolks
1–2 tablespoons lemon juice
1 tablespoon water or dry white wine
Salt and black pepper
3 tablespoons grated Parmesan cheese

Wash the courgettes and trim off the stalks; blanch* in boiling water for 1–2 minutes. Drain, wipe dry and cut the courgettes in half lengthways. With a pointed teaspoon, take out a shallow groove in each half.

Arrange the courgettes, cut side up, in a large, shallow, lightly buttered flameproof dish. Sprinkle with salt, freshly ground pepper and the lemon juice. Cut the remaining butter into small pieces over the courgettes and cover the dish tightly. Bake in the centre of a pre-heated oven at 350°F (mark 4) for 25 minutes.

Meanwhile, cut 6 oz. of the butter into small pieces and let it melt slowly in a small, heavy-based pan over low heat. As soon as the butter has melted, remove the pan from the heat, and pour the butter into a jug.

Put the 3 egg yolks into the same pan and beat thoroughly with a wire whisk. Add 1 tablespoon of lemon juice and 1 of water (or wine), with a good pinch of salt; beat again. Add ½ oz. of cold butter to the egg yolk mixture and put the pan over low heat on an asbestos sheet. Cook, whisking steadily, until the egg yolks are creamy and beginning to thicken enough to coat the wires of the whisk. Remove the pan from the heat and beat in the remaining butter.

Add the melted butter to the egg mixture, drop by drop, whisking continuously. As the mixture thickens, the butter may be added more rapidly. When the sauce has the consistency of thick cream, season to taste with salt, pepper and lemon juice. If the sauce is too thick, it can be thinned with 1–2 dessertspoons of water or single cream. Finally, stir in 2 tablespoons of cheese.

Spoon the sauce into the grooves of the cooked courgettes, and sprinkle with the remaining cheese. Put the dish under a hot grill until the cheese is lightly browned. Serve at once, with roast chicken or lean roast meat.

Sweets & Puddings

CARROTS PAYSANNE

In cookery, paysanne refers to vegetables cooked in butter and used to garnish meat and poultry. Young carrots make a good accompaniment to grilled meat.

PREPARATION TIME: *15 min.*
COOKING TIME: *30 min.*

INGREDIENTS *(for 4–6)*:
1 lb. small carrots
1 large onion
2 rashers lean bacon
2½ oz. unsalted butter
¼–½ pint chicken stock or water
1 teaspoon caster sugar
4 tablespoons double cream
Salt
GARNISH:
Finely chopped parsley

Trim the tops and roots from the carrots, scrape them and wash thoroughly. Blanch* the carrots for 5 minutes in boiling salted water, then drain in a colander.

Peel and thinly slice the onion. Cut off the rinds and dice the bacon. Melt the butter in a wide shallow pan over low heat, and cook the onion and bacon until just soft and beginning to colour.

Add the carrots to the bacon and onion, and pour over enough stock or water to barely cover the vegetables. Cover the pan with a lid and cook over moderate heat until the carrots are tender. Lift out the carrots and keep them hot.

Boil the liquid over high heat until it has reduced* to a few tablespoons. Add the sugar and cream, and season to taste with salt. Simmer the liquid, uncovered, until the sauce has thickened slightly.

Pour the cream sauce over the carrots and sprinkle with parsley.

GREEN BEANS WITH MUSCATEL SABAYON SAUCE

In Tuscany, where this recipe originates, the sauce is traditionally made with muscatel grape juice. Sabayon is a French corruption of the Italian Zabaglione*, and the sauce should have the same fluffy consistency.

PREPARATION TIME: *15 min.*
COOKING TIME: *15–20 min.*

INGREDIENTS *(for 6)*:
1½ lb. French or runner beans
Salt
SAUCE:
2 egg yolks
2 tablespoons muscatel grape juice, or 2 tablespoons dry white wine sweetened with 1 level tablespoon caster sugar
1 tablespoon white wine vinegar

Top and tail the French beans before washing them. Runner beans should be trimmed in the same manner and the strings removed before slicing them into 1 in. long pieces. Bring a pan of salted water to the boil and cook the beans for 4–6 minutes; do not overcook. Drain the beans through a colander and put them in a shallow serving dish to keep them warm.

Meanwhile, put all the sauce ingredients in a bowl, mix lightly with a fork and place over a pan of simmering water. Whisk the sauce until it is thick and frothy, and rises in the bowl.

Pour the sauce over the beans and serve at once, with grilled fish or meat.

CUCUMBER IN SOURED CREAM

This unusual salad, in a refreshing summery dressing, goes well with both hot and cold meats. It is especially suitable with roast beef, veal or chicken.

PREPARATION TIME: *15–20 min.*
CHILLING TIME: *2 hours*

INGREDIENTS *(for 4–6)*:
1 large or 2 small cucumbers
1½ level tablespoons plain flour
½ level teaspoon each of salt, caster sugar and dry mustard
2 tablespoons tarragon or white wine vinegar
2 egg yolks
4 tablespoons olive oil
5 fluid oz. soured cream
2 tablespoons finely chopped chives

Put the flour, salt, sugar and mustard in a small, heavy-based pan with 1 tablespoon of water. Cook over low heat, stirring until the ingredients are thoroughly blended. Gradually add the vinegar and 2 tablespoons of water. Continue cooking until the mixture has thickened to a smooth sauce. Bring this quickly to the boil, then simmer for 2–3 minutes.

Remove the pan from the heat and beat the egg yolks into the sauce, one at a time. Add the oil, a few drops at a time. Chill in the refrigerator.

About an hour before serving, stir the soured cream and the chopped chives into the sauce. Return it to the refrigerator.

Wash and peel the cucumber (remove the seeds if necessary) and cut it into ½ in. cubes. Just before serving, stir the cucumber into the soured cream.

VICTORIA PLUMS IN WINE

The slightly acid flavour of these home-grown plums makes them suitable for sweet compôtes and puddings. Their flavour is brought out to the full by poaching them in a syrupy wine and serving them while still warm.

PREPARATION TIME: *5 min.*
COOKING TIME: *30 min.*

INGREDIENTS *(for 6)*:
1½–2 lb. firm Victoria plums
3 oz. caster sugar
½ pint tawny port, medium dry sherry or Madeira wine
2 tablespoons flaked almonds

Dissolve the sugar in ½ pint of water and simmer for 10 minutes. Stir in the wine and bring the syrup to simmering point again.

Remove the stalks from the plums, wash and dry them. Add the plums, one at a time, to the simmering syrup. Cover the pan with a lid and remove from the heat. Leave the plums in the syrup for 10 minutes.

Lift out the plums with a perforated spoon and put them in a serving dish. Cover the dish with a plate or foil, and leave in a warm place. Boil the syrup over high heat until it has reduced* by about one-third and thickened slightly. Pour it over the plums.

Meanwhile, toast the flaked almonds for about 5 minutes in the oven until golden. Scatter these over the plums and serve at once, with a jug of single cream.

GRANITA AL CAFFÉ

Strong, bitter black coffee, preferably a continental roast, should be used for this Italian water ice. It is sometimes served with whipped cream.

PREPARATION TIME: *10 min.*
CHILLING TIME: *3–4 hours*

INGREDIENTS *(for 4):*
$\frac{3}{4}$ *pint strong black coffee*
$4\frac{1}{2}$ *level tablespoons caster sugar*
$\frac{1}{4}$ *pint whipping cream*

Turn the refrigerator to its coldest setting 1 hour before beginning preparations. Melt 4 tablespoons of sugar in $\frac{1}{4}$ pint of water over moderate heat, stirring until the sugar has completely dissolved. Bring this syrup to the boil and boil steadily for 5 minutes. Remove from the heat and leave the syrup to cool.

Stir the strained coffee into the cold syrup, and pour the mixture into ice cube trays. For the best texture, the dividers should be left in the trays so that the ice will set in cubes. Put the trays into the freezing compartment for at least 3 hours. Stir the ice occasionally with a fork to scrape the frozen crystals round the edges into the centre.

Turn the frozen cubes into a bowl and crush them lightly with a pestle or break them up with a fork. Spoon the ice into individual glasses and serve at once with a separate bowl of whipped cream, sweetened with the remaining sugar.

PEACHES WITH SOURED CREAM

Golden firm peaches from Italy are at their best and least expensive this month. They make refreshing summer sweets – on their own, poached in white wine or cooked in a pastry case. Here, poached peaches are served chilled with a soured cream topping.

PREPARATION TIME: *35 min.*
CHILLING TIME: *30 min.*

INGREDIENTS *(for 6):*
6 large peaches
8 oz. vanilla sugar
Caster sugar
10 fluid oz. soured cream
GARNISH:
1 oz. Demerara sugar or 1 oz. toasted flaked almonds

Dissolve the vanilla sugar* in $\frac{1}{2}$ pint of water in a small pan and cook over moderate heat. Simmer this syrup for 5 minutes.

Wash and dry the peaches thoroughly, then poach* them lightly in the syrup for 5–10 minutes, depending on the ripeness of the fruit.

Lift the peaches from the syrup, leave to cool slightly, then peel off the skins and cut the peaches in half. Remove the stones, and slice the peaches into a serving bowl, one layer at a time, sprinkling each layer with a little caster sugar. Strain the syrup and set aside for another use.

Cover the top of the peaches with a thick layer of soured cream and chill for 30 minutes. Just before serving, sprinkle the top with Demerara sugar or toasted flaked almonds.

DANISH LAYER CAKE

There are numerous versions of the Danish layer cake, from a simple jam sandwich to a huge eight-layer concoction of wafer-thin sponge cakes in alternating layers of thick cream and fruit. It is served with morning coffee and afternoon tea, as an after-dinner sweet or with evening coffee.

PREPARATION TIME: *45 min.*
COOKING TIME: *25 min.*
CHILLING TIME: *1 hour*

INGREDIENTS *(for 6):*
4 eggs
Rind and juice of half lemon
5 oz. icing sugar
3 oz. plain flour
1 oz. cornflour
$\frac{1}{2}$ *level teaspoon baking powder*
FILLING:
$\frac{1}{2}$ *oz. gelatine*
1 pint double cream
2 level dessertspoons vanilla sugar
4 slices fresh or tinned pineapple
3 oz. dark bitter chocolate

Separate the eggs and put the yolks in a large bowl, together with the lemon rind and juice. Sift the icing sugar into the yolks and beat until fluffy and pale cream in colour. Whisk the egg whites in a separate bowl until they stand in soft peaks, then fold them carefully into the yolk mixture. Sift the two flours and baking powder together and blend into the sponge mixture.

Grease a loose-bottomed round cake tin, 8 in. wide, and line with buttered greaseproof paper. Spoon the sponge mixture into the tin, smoothing it level round the sides. Bake in the centre of a pre-heated oven at 350°F (mark 4) for 25 minutes or until the sponge is golden and well risen.

Loosen the edges of the sponge with a sharp knife and turn the cake out on a wire rack to cool. When completely cold, cut the cake into three thin rounds and sandwich with the filling.

Dissolve the gelatine in a few spoonfuls of warm water and leave to cool slightly. Whip the cream, setting one-third aside for the topping. Fold the cooled gelatine into the remaining cream and sweeten with the vanilla sugar*. Peel and trim the pineapple slices (or drain thoroughly if using tinned pineapple); set one slice aside and chop the other three finely. Grate the chocolate and blend into the cream with the chopped pineapple. Leave the filling to set.

Assemble the layer cake about 2 hours before serving. Divide the filling equally over two sponge layers and spread it evenly; put the layers together and top with the last plain sponge. Spread a thin layer of the whipped cream on top and pipe the remainder, through a narrow rosette nozzle, round the edge and down the sides of the cake. Garnish the top with the reserved pineapple, cut into small chunks.

Chill the layer cake in the refrigerator for about 1 hour and serve it cut into wedges.

MELON ICE CREAM

The Italians introduced water ices or sorbets to Britain during the reign of Charles I, at least two centuries before cream ices became known. Today, virtually any sweetened fruit juice can be made into ice cream with egg custard and cream.

PREPARATION TIME: *30–40 min.*
CHILLING TIME: *3 hours*

INGREDIENTS *(for 4)*:
1 large Ogen melon
4 oz. caster sugar
4 egg yolks
5 tablespoons ginger wine
2 tablespoons lemon juice
¾ pint double cream

A few hours before preparing the ice cream, set the refrigerator to its coldest setting.

Slice about 1½ in. off the top of the melon; remove the seeds and fibres with a small spoon. Scoop all the melon pulp into a small saucepan, taking care not to pierce the shell. Add the sugar and place the pan over low heat until the sugar has melted into the melon, and the mixture is a soft pulp. Mash with a fork.

Beat the egg yolks until light and creamy, and add them to the melon pulp, stirring well. Continue cooking and whisking over low heat, so that the eggs will not curdle, until the mixture has the consistency of thin cream.

Pour the melon mixture into a bowl and leave it to cool completely. Stir in the ginger wine and lemon juice, mix thoroughly, then fold in the lightly whipped cream. Cover the bowl with foil and chill in the refrigerator for 30 minutes.

Spoon the melon cream into a freezing tray or container, cover with foil or the lid, and freeze for 2–3 hours. Stir the ice cream several times during freezing to prevent crystals forming.

Pile the ice cream into glasses or the chilled melon shell and serve at once. Any surplus ice cream can be stored for several months in the home freezer.

GREENGAGES WITH APRICOT PURÉE

The small, round, golden-yellow greengages make their brief appearance in the latter half of August. They are excellent as dessert fruits, and for puddings.

PREPARATION TIME: *25 min.*
COOKING TIME: *30 min.*

INGREDIENTS *(for 4)*:
1 lb. greengages
½ lb. fresh or 4 oz. dried apricots
1 oz. caster sugar
½ teaspoon grated lemon rind
4 slices white bread
1½–2 oz. unsalted butter
1–2 oz. vanilla sugar

Make the apricot purée first: wash and dry the apricots, cut them in half and remove the stones. Leave dried apricots to soak overnight in cold water.

Put the apricots in a pan, cover with fresh cold water and cook, uncovered, over moderate heat until tender. Drain thoroughly and rub the apricots through a coarse sieve; flavour this purée with sugar and lemon rind.

Wash and dry the greengages, and cut them in half. Remove the stones. Cut the crusts from the bread and spread the slices with half the butter. Lay the slices, buttered side up, in a greased ovenproof dish. Arrange the greengages on top with a tiny knob of butter in each half; sprinkle with the vanilla sugar*.

Bake in the centre of the oven, pre-heated to 350°F (mark 4), for about 30 minutes, or until the greengages are tender.

Serve the greengage pudding warm, and offer the warmed apricot purée separately.

LEMON SYLLABUB

In Elizabethan times, one of the favourite wines in Britain was a still dry wine produced around Sillery in the Champagne district of France. Bub was a slang term for a bubbly drink, and by association syllabub came to describe a drink or sweet made by mixing frothy cream with still wine.

PREPARATION TIME: *20 min.*
STANDING TIME: *6 hours*
CHILLING TIME: *3 hours*

INGREDIENTS *(for 6)*:
1 lemon
1½–2 fluid oz. brandy
3 oz. caster sugar
½ pint double cream
¼ pint sweet white wine
GARNISH:
Rind of a lemon

Peel the lemon thinly with a potato peeler. Squeeze out the juice and add enough brandy to make the liquid up to 2½ fluid oz. Pour the liquid into a small bowl, add the peeled lemon rind and leave to stand for at least 6 hours.

Strain the liquid through a fine sieve and stir in the sugar until it has dissolved completely. Whip the cream until it holds its shape. Mix the wine into the lemon and brandy, then add this liquid to the cream, a little at a time, whisking continuously. The cream should absorb all the liquid and still stand in soft peaks. Pile the mixture into individual glasses and chill for several hours.

For the garnish, thinly peel the lemon rind and cut into narrow strips; blanch* for 2–3 minutes in boiling water.

Serve the syllabub with a cluster of drained lemon strips.

Savouries & Snacks

SUNDANCER EGGS

Baked eggs are one of the classic quick snacks, equally welcome at breakfast or at midnight.

PREPARATION TIME: *10 min.*
COOKING TIME: *8–10 min.*

INGREDIENTS *(for 4)*:
8 eggs
8 thin rashers lean bacon (diced)
2 oz. butter
*4 oz. finely chopped button mush-
    rooms*
Salt and black pepper
4 tablespoons double cream
Chervil
4 slices white bread
Oil or lard for frying

Fry the bacon in the butter, over moderate heat, for 3 minutes. Add the mushrooms and cook for a further 2 minutes. Season with salt and pepper. Spoon this mixture into eight small ramekin dishes, and break an egg into each dish. Top with cream and sprinkle with a little freshly chopped chervil.

Bake in the centre of a pre-heated oven at 350°F (mark 4) for 8–10 minutes or until the egg whites are just set.

Meanwhile, cut the crust off the bread and slice it into narrow fingers. Deep-fry in hot oil or lard until crisp and golden. Serve two ramekins per person and offer the bread separately.

NORTH COAST KIPPER PÂTÉ

This rich smoky fish pâté keeps well in the refrigerator. It is excellent as a sandwich filling, or as a first course with toast.

PREPARATION TIME: *20 min.*

INGREDIENTS *(for 4)*:
2 boned kippers
1 tablespoon double cream
3–4 oz. softened butter
1 tablespoon lemon juice
Cayenne pepper
¼ teaspoon ground mace

Place the kippers, head down, in a jug, pour over enough boiling water to cover all but the tails and leave to stand for 5 minutes. Pour off the water and remove all skin and any small bones from the kippers. Set aside to cool.

Pound the kippers until smooth, then blend in the cream and butter, add the lemon juice and season with cayenne and mace. Store the pâté in an earthenware jar, in the refrigerator.

RARE ROAST BEEF SALAD

Cold roast beef, marinated in a piquant dressing, is here transformed into a complete main course for a hot summer day.

PREPARATION TIME: *15 min.*
CHILLING TIME: *1¼ hours*

INGREDIENTS *(for 4)*:
½–¾ lb. roast beef
4 tablespoons olive oil
1 tablespoon wine vinegar
*1½ level teaspoons dry English
    mustard*
4 finely chopped anchovy fillets
2 teaspoons finely chopped capers
1 level tablespoon chopped chives
*1 level tablespoon finely chopped
    parsley*
Black pepper
8 cooked, thinly sliced potatoes
2 hardboiled eggs

Cut the beef into matchstick strips. Blend the oil, vinegar and mustard thoroughly and add the anchovy fillets, capers, chives and parsley; season with pepper. Marinate* the meat in this dressing for at least 1 hour.

Arrange the potato slices round the edge of a serving dish. Pile the meat salad in the centre and garnish with chopped hard-boiled eggs. Chill, and serve with a green salad.

BAKED TOMATOES

A little left-over meat and rice can be made into a savoury filling for tomatoes. Serve them with boiled potatoes and green beans.

PREPARATION TIME: *20 min.*
COOKING TIME: *35 min.*

INGREDIENTS *(for 6)*:
12 large firm tomatoes
1 finely chopped onion
6 oz. cooked minced meat
4 oz. cooked rice
1½–2 oz. butter
2–3 tablespoons stock
1 tablespoon single cream
*2 teaspoons Worcestershire
    sauce*
2 tablespoons chopped parsley
Pepper
2 oz. grated cheese
1 tablespoon breadcrumbs

Cut a thin slice from the top of each tomato and scoop out the pulp. Cook the onion in the butter until soft. Add the meat, rice, stock, cream, Worcestershire sauce and parsley. Season with pepper and cook for 3 minutes.

Fill the tomato cases with the meat mixture and put in a lightly buttered ovenproof dish. Sprinkle with the grated cheese and breadcrumbs, and bake in the centre of a pre-heated oven at 375°F (mark 5) for 15–20 minutes.

RASPBERRY AND BANANA TRIFLE

Always a favourite with children, trifle can be quickly made from stale sponge cake and the remains of yesterday's custard.

PREPARATION TIME: *20 min.*
CHILLING TIME: *30 min.*

INGREDIENTS *(for 6)*:
4 slices plain sponge cake
*3 heaped tablespoons raspberry
    jam*
4 thinly sliced bananas
½ pint custard sauce
¼ teaspoon vanilla essence

Cut the cake into ½ in. cubes and put in a serving dish or individual glasses. Spoon the jam over the cake and top with banana.

Warm the custard* through and flavour it with vanilla essence. Let the custard cool slightly before pouring it over the bananas. Chill the trifle in the refrigerator before serving.

Eating out of Doors

There is something irresistibly festive about eating out of doors and, because of the instability of the weather, a picnic in Britain becomes an occasion to be treated with as much reverence as a well-planned party.

Forget about flasks of tea and packets of soggy sandwiches and choose instead picnic fare to suit both the occasion and the company. Few people have the opportunity for the grand picnic banquets at Glyndebourne or Ascot, but with a little planning and imagination, a family picnic can become a feast to remember.

Containers for the food are important. Picnic boxes, bowls and flasks of polythene and plastic are available everywhere, and although insulated boxes, bags and wide-necked thermos jars are more expensive, they do ensure crisp salads and chilled – or hot – drinks and soups.

Pack chilled or hot soups in thermos jars, and take along a carton of cream to trickle into the soup, and a garnish of chopped lettuce, chervil or watercress packed separately in a small plastic box. A mousse or pâté can be packed in the dishes in which they were prepared or cooked. A whole joint, such as tongue, ham, spiced brisket of beef or cold stuffed loin of pork, is easiest carried whole, wrapped in foil, and carved at the picnic. Small chicken joints, lamb cutlets, grilled sausages and hardboiled stuffed eggs can be packed in individual polythene bags.

Pour sauces and salad dressings into screw-top jars. Pack salad ingredients separately in individual plastic bags so that guests can make their own salads. Rice salads and potatoes, both dressed while still hot with mayonnaise* and a sprinkling of chopped herbs, are best packed in rigid containers.

Thirst-quenching drinks are the most suitable for a picnic; well-chilled white or rosé wines, beer and cider are preferable to heavy red wines. Take fresh apple juice, lemonade or milk for the children – and plenty of iced coffee for everyone.

Family Picnics

For a simple family picnic, pastry dishes which are easy to eat with the fingers cannot be excelled.

A strongly flavoured soup such as mulligatawny* makes an excellent starter and can be served hot or cold, according to the weather.

For the main course, choose from veal terrine de campagne*, pizza*, bacon and cream cheese tart*, Cornish pasties* or savoury cold pies. Fried hamburgers in soft baps, topped with cream cheese and raw onion rings, are good alternatives, and should be individually wrapped. Salads might include lettuce, watercress and tomatoes, with a separate French dressing* or mayonnaise.

Ice creams make ideal picnic sweets, but need careful packing. Spoon crunchy brown-bread ice cream straight into a wide-necked vacuum jar, and pack any spaces with sliced peaches or pears.

Brown-bread Ice Cream

PREPARATION TIME: *20 min.*
FREEZING TIME: *2–3 hours*

INGREDIENTS *(for 6):*
½ *pint double cream*
1 oz. vanilla sugar
3 oz. stale, crustless brown bread
3 oz. soft dark brown sugar

An hour before preparing the ice cream turn the refrigerator to its coldest setting. Blend the cream and vanilla sugar* in a bowl and whisk until fluffy. Spoon the mixture into shallow ice trays or a polythene container, cover with foil or the lid, and put into the freezing compartment of the refrigerator. When the mixture has begun to set round the edges, take it out of the freezer and stir the sides into the middle to prevent ice crystals forming. Repeat this twice during freezing.

Reduce the bread to fine crumbs and mix with the brown sugar. Spread the crumbs on a lightly oiled baking tray and put this into the centre of an oven, pre-heated to 400°F (mark 6). Leave until the sugar caramelises and the crumbs are golden brown; stir them occasionally. Leave to cool, then break up into crumbs again with a fork.

When the ice cream is nearly set, turn it into a chilled bowl, beat with an egg whisk and stir in the crumbs. Spoon the mixture into the ice trays and return them, covered, to the refrigerator. Freeze until firm.

Children's Picnic Boxes

Young children prefer simple food and often need to be catered for separately. Surprise boxes are a good idea to encourage finicky eaters to join in the fun.

Pack an individual lunch or refrigerator box for each child, labelling it with the owner's name. Fill it with a choice of savoury and sweet items, all separately wrapped. These could include a small Cornish pasty, a hollowed-out soft roll filled with creamy scrambled egg or chopped hard-boiled egg and tomato. Pack a hardboiled egg in greaseproof paper with an individual twist of salt. Fill a 3 in. piece of celery stick with cream cheese, or make a plain cheese sandwich interesting by cutting it out as the child's initial.

Jelly, trifle or rice pudding can be set in individual moulds and wrapped in plastic film. A gingerbread figure decorated with coloured icing, or an iced cup cake or biscuit, make attractive sweets. Include an apple, a plastic cup and a spoon and drinking straws wrapped in a paper napkin.

A Romantic Picnic for Two

A picnic can be a very romantic occasion deserving a careful choice of menu (see picture on p. 198). Chilled carrot soup* is a perfect starter followed by Tarte Basquaise. Serve the flan with lettuce, spring onions and tomato cups filled with horse-radish mayonnaise*.

Tarte Basquaise
PREPARATION TIME: *30 min.*
COOKING TIME: *40 min.*

INGREDIENTS *(for 2)*:
4 oz. shortcrust pastry (standard recipe)
1 small, finely chopped onion
1 finely chopped clove garlic
1 tablespoon butter
1 egg
1 egg yolk
¼ pint double cream
1 oz. fresh white breadcrumbs
4 skinned, chopped tomatoes
1 diced red pepper
Salt and black pepper
Grated Parmesan cheese

Roll the prepared shortcrust pastry* out, ¼ in. thick. Use it to line a 6 in. flan ring set on a greased baking tray. Cook the onion and garlic in the butter until soft, then set aside.

Beat the egg and the egg yolk with the cream and pour over the breadcrumbs in a bowl. Stir in the tomatoes and red pepper, and season to taste with salt, pepper and cheese.

Spoon the onion mixture over the pastry base and top with the egg and cream. Bake the flan in the centre of the oven, at 375°F (mark 5), for 40 minutes.

For dessert, cut a small melon in half, and pile fresh raspberries into the two hollows. Wrap each half in plastic film and chill thoroughly before packing.

A Formal Picnic Party

This menu, composed for outdoor entertaining, features elegant but simple food. For a first course serve crab mousse*, made in individual soufflé dishes which can be wrapped in foil and stacked in the hamper. Veal stuffed with kidneys, which is easily carved, makes an excellent and substantial main course dish for a formal picnic party.

Veal Stuffed with Kidneys
PREPARATION TIME: *25 min.*
COOKING TIME: *3 hours*

INGREDIENTS *(for 8)*:
5 lb. loin of veal
½ lb. calf kidneys
Salt and black pepper
2 cloves garlic
2–3 sprigs marjoram or thyme
1 small onion
2 carrots
¼ pint dry white wine
GARNISH:
Watercress

Ask the butcher to bone the loin and to include the bones with the order. Trim the fat off the kidneys* and remove the outer skin; snip out the cores with scissors. Lay the boned meat flat on a board and spread the kidneys over the cut side. Season with salt and freshly ground pepper. Peel and finely chop the garlic and herbs; sprinkle them over the kidneys. Carefully roll up the meat and tie it securely with string at 1–2 in. intervals.

Rub the outside of the meat thoroughly with salt and pepper, place it in a roasting tin, and surround with the veal bones. Peel and roughly chop the onion; scrape and finely chop the carrots. Arrange the vegetables round the meat. Heat the wine, with ¼ pint of water, in a small pan and pour over the meat. Cover the tin with foil or a lid and cook in the centre of the oven, pre-heated to 350°F (mark 4) for 2¼ hours. Turn the meat over half-way through cooking, and add more wine and water if necessary. Remove the covering for the last 30 minutes to brown the meat.

Lift the meat from the pan and set it aside to cool. Pour the pan juices, bones and vegetables into a pan and simmer over low heat for 45 minutes. Strain the liquid into a bowl and leave until cool. Let the liquid set to a jelly in the refrigerator before removing any fat which settles on the top.

Serve the stuffed veal with cold chopped jelly, cos lettuce, sliced tomatoes, cucumber in soured cream*, and new potatoes dressed in mayonnaise.

For dessert, there is soft fruit, chilled and packed in a wide-necked thermos flask, to be served with Coeur à la crème*. A selection of cheeses, with biscuits and butter, completes the meal.

217

September

September blowe soft,
Till fruite be in loft.

This Month's Recipes

All is safely gathered in: at harvest festival, churches throughout the land are decorated with autumn's fruits and crops

SEPTEMBER
Food in Season

This month the shops are full of fresh, home-grown fruit and vegetables. Plums, damsons and greengages are at their best and juiciest, both for eating and preserving. The first English apples and dessert pears also appear, and peaches reach the lowest price of the season. Now that fresh vegetables such as peas, cauliflowers, onions, courgettes and tomatoes are both cheap and plentiful, this is the best of all months for making pickles and chutneys.

The season for native oysters from Whitstable and Colchester begins this month. The blue-black mussels are also available now, at a lower price than oysters. Game is excellent for taste and value.

Fish

Angler tail
Bass
Bream, sea
Brill
Clams
Cod
Coley
Conger eels
Crab
Dabs
Dover sole
Dublin Bay prawns
Eels
Flake (also sold as rock salmon)
Grey mullet
Haddock
Hake
Halibut
Herrings
Lemon sole
Lobster
Mackerel
Mock halibut (or Greenland halibut)
Mussels
Oysters (native)
Oysters, Portuguese
Pike
Plaice
Prawns
Redfish
Red mullet
Salmon
Scad
Shrimps
Skate
Sprats
Trout, rainbow
Turbot
Whiting
Witch

Poultry & Game

Chicken
Duck
Goose
Grouse
Guinea fowl
Hare
Mallard
Partridge
Pigeon
Quail
Rabbit
Snipe
Teal
Turkey
Venison
Wild duck
Wild goose

Vegetables

Aubergines
Avocado pears
Beetroots
Brussels sprouts
Cabbages
Calabrese
Carrots
Cauliflowers
Celeriac
Celery
Chicory
Corn on the cob
Courgettes
Cucumbers
Endive
Fennel
French beans
Garlic
Globe artichokes
Horseradish
Leeks
Lettuce
Mushrooms
Okra
Onions
Parsnips
Peas
Peppers
Potatoes
Pumpkin
Radishes
Salad cress
Spring onions
Swedes
Sweet potatoes
Tomatoes
Turnips
Watercress

Fruit

Apples
Bananas
Bilberries
Blackberries
Blueberries
Chinese gooseberries
Cranberries
Damsons
Figs
Grapefruit
Grapes
Greengages
Lemons
Loquats
Lychees
Mangoes
Melons
Mulberries
Oranges
Peaches
Pears
Pineapples
Plums
Pomegranates
Raspberries
Strawberries
Watermelons

SUGGESTED MENUS

Spinach Ramekins
Baked Stuffed Shoulder of Veal
Courgettes Gratiné
Poires Flambées

⊛

Tarte Ricotto
Pescada à la Marina
Peppers with Risotto Stuffing
Crisp Green Salad
Berry Lemon Pudding

⊛

Melon and Ham Gondolas
Grouse à la Grandmère
Cauliflower Polonaise
Creamed Potatoes
Quiche Reine-Claude

⊛

Borshch
Wild Duck with Bigarade Sauce
Tomatoes with Green Peas
Hazelnut Gantois

⊛

Egg Cocktail
Beef Jardinière
Buttered Cabbage
Fruity Rice Pudding

⊛

Potage Paysanne
Épigrammes d'Agneau
French Fried Cabbage
Apple and Almond Paradise Pudding

⊛

Paella Valencia
Green Salad with Sauce Vinaigrette
Blackberry Swiss Charlotte

Soups & Starters

LAMB AND LEMON SOUP

This Greek soup is a thick and meaty broth, and almost a meal in itself.

PREPARATION TIME: *15 min.*
COOKING TIME: *3¼ hours*

INGREDIENTS *(for 6)*:
2 lb. scrag of lamb, chopped
2 carrots
1–2 turnips
2 onions
2 leeks
1 stick celery
1 sprig parsley
2 bay leaves
½ teaspoon dried oregano or thyme
½ teaspoon dried marjoram
2 oz. pearl barley or long grain
*   rice*
Salt and black pepper
Juice of a lemon
2 egg yolks
GARNISH:
1 lettuce heart

Trim as much fat as possible off the lamb, put the meat into a large saucepan with 2 pints of water and bring to the boil. Meanwhile, wash and scrape the carrots and turnips and chop them roughly; peel and roughly chop the onions. Trim the leeks and wash them under cold running water. Scrub the celery and chop this and the leeks roughly.

Remove any scum from the broth. Add the vegetables to the lamb, together with the herbs and barley (if using rice, add this 1 hour later). Season to taste with salt and freshly ground pepper. Cover the pan and simmer the broth for 2–2½ hours, or until the meat comes away from the bones.

Remove the bay leaves and parsley and lift out the meat. Leave the soup to simmer while picking the meat off the bones. Chop up the lamb and return it to the pan.

Remove the broth from the heat and allow it to get cold (if possible leave overnight). Lift off the fat which has solidified in a layer on top of the broth. Bring the soup back to the boil and, just before serving, beat the lemon juice and the egg yolks together in a small bowl. Mix in 3 or 4 tablespoons of the hot broth and add this mixture to the pan; heat the broth through without boiling.

Serve the soup sprinkled with finely shredded lettuce heart.

BORSHCH

There are numerous variations of this famous Russian soup, but beetroot and soured cream are traditional in every borshch, whether it is served hot or cold.

PREPARATION TIME: *25 min.*
COOKING TIME: *1 hour 20 min.*

INGREDIENTS *(for 6)*:
1 lb. uncooked beetroot
1 onion
1 leek
1 carrot
1 turnip
1 large potato
1 stick celery
2 pints strong beef, chicken or
*   duck stock*
1 bay leaf
1 tablespoon chopped parsley
Salt and black pepper
1 level tablespoon tomato purée
1 level teaspoon caster sugar
1 tablespoon lemon juice
5 fluid oz. soured cream
GARNISH:
3 level tablespoons chopped mint
*   or chives*

Peel the beetroot, set aside 4 oz. and dice the remainder finely. Peel and thinly slice the onion; trim the roots and coarse outer leaves from the leek, wash it thoroughly under cold running water and chop it finely. Wash and peel the carrot and turnip, and shred into very thin strips. Wash, peel and dice the potato. Scrub the celery and chop it finely.

Put the prepared vegetables in a large pan with the stock, bay leaf, parsley, and a good seasoning of salt and freshly ground pepper. Cover the pan with a lid and simmer the soup for 30 minutes. Mix together the tomato purée, sugar and lemon juice in a small bowl and add to the soup. Continue cooking the soup over low heat for a further 30 minutes or until the root vegetables are tender.

Ten minutes before serving, grate the reserved beetroot and add it to the soup. Thin with a little more stock if necessary. Stir 4 or 5 tablespoons of the soup into the soured cream and gradually stir this mixture back into the soup. Heat the soup through without boiling and serve at once, sprinkled with chopped mint or chives.

To serve the borshch cold – borshch givrée – chill the soup (it can be puréed* if preferred) thoroughly before adding the soured cream. Before serving, add a little more lemon juice. Pour the soup into individual bowls, each containing an ice cube, and top with a swirl of soured cream. Finely chopped spring onion, hardboiled egg and grated cucumber can also be sprinkled on the top as a garnish.

MELON AND HAM GONDOLAS

Sweet ripe melon combines perfectly with Italian raw smoked ham, known as Prosciutto, or with the Westphalian variety from Germany.

PREPARATION TIME: *12 min.*

INGREDIENTS *(for 6)*:
½ large ripe honeydew melon
6 wafer-thin slices smoked ham
Juice of a lemon
Black pepper
GARNISH:
Lemon wedges

Chill the melon thoroughly. Cut it into six long slices, scoop out the seeds and cut the skin away. Place one piece of melon on each slice of ham and wrap the ham neatly over the melon. Sprinkle with lemon juice and freshly ground pepper.

Serve the melon gondolas garnished with wedges of lemon.

SPINACH RAMEKINS

This unusual appetiser is a creamy pâté of spinach, sardines and eggs. Serve it with plenty of Grissini (Italian bread sticks) or Melba toast*.

PREPARATION TIME: *10–15 min.*

CHILLING TIME: $\frac{1}{2}$–*1 hour*

INGREDIENTS *(for 4)* :
1 lb. spinach
1 onion
$\frac{1}{2}$ *level teaspoon dried tarragon*
2 level dessertspoons finely chopped parsley
1 hardboiled egg
4 sardines
2 tablespoons double cream
Salt and black pepper
GARNISH:
1 hardboiled egg
4 anchovy fillets

Pull the spinach leaves off the stalks and wash in several lots of cold water to remove all traces of soil. Peel and finely chop the onion. Put the wet spinach in a large saucepan with the onion, tarragon and parsley; cover with a lid. Cook over low heat for 7–10 minutes, or until softened, then drain thoroughly.

Chop one hardboiled egg and the boned sardines and blend with the spinach. Rub the mixture through a coarse sieve, or liquidise it to a purée*. Stir in the cream and season to taste with salt and freshly ground pepper. Spoon the creamed spinach into individual ramekins or small serving dishes and chill in a refrigerator until set.

For the garnish, separate the white and yolk of the hardboiled egg; chop the white finely and sieve the yolk. Decorate each ramekin with alternate rows of white and yolk. Split the anchovy fillets in half and lay them on top in a criss-cross pattern.

TARTE RICOTTO

Quick and easy to prepare, this savoury pastry can be made as one large flan and served cut into wedges. It is more attractive made in small tartlet moulds and is equally suitable served with drinks, as a starter or as a dinner savoury.

PREPARATION TIME: *15 min.*
COOKING TIME: *15–20 min.*

INGREDIENTS *(for 6)* :
6 oz. plain or rich shortcrust pastry (standard recipe)
8 oz. cream cheese
Salt and black pepper
2 eggs
2 oz. smoked salmon or ham
2 level teaspoons grated lemon rind or chopped parsley
1$\frac{1}{2}$–2 oz. Gruyère cheese
GARNISH:
Watercress
Black olives

Roll out the prepared shortcrust pastry*, $\frac{1}{4}$ in. thick, on a lightly floured surface. Line a greased 7–8 in. flan ring or individual tartlet moulds with the pastry.

Stir the cream cheese smooth in a bowl, and season to taste with salt and freshly ground pepper. Beat the eggs lightly and gradually stir them into the cream cheese. Shred the smoked salmon or ham and add to the cheese, together with the grated lemon rind and/or parsley. Spoon the cream mixture into the flan or individual tart cases and smooth level with the edge. Using a cheese slicer or a very sharp knife, cut the Gruyère cheese into thin slivers; lay them on top of the cream filling.

Bake the flan or tartlets in the centre of a pre-heated oven, at 400°F (mark 6) for 15–20 minutes or until the filling is well risen and golden brown.

Serve hot, garnished with sprigs of watercress and whole black olives.

POTAGE PAYSANNE

This farmhouse vegetable soup makes a substantial meal on its own. Select vegetables according to availability and choice – the quantities in the recipe are merely a guide. Peas, green beans and watercress may be added when the soup comes to the boil.

PREPARATION TIME: *30 min.*
COOKING TIME: *1 hour*

INGREDIENTS *(for 6)* :
2–3 carrots
1–2 turnips
2–3 parsnips
1–2 leeks
$\frac{1}{2}$ *small head of celery*
1 large onion
2 oz. mushrooms
2 rashers streaky bacon
$\frac{1}{2}$ *lb. tomatoes*
2 oz. butter
2–3 dessertspoons plain flour
$\frac{1}{4}$ *pint milk*
Salt and black pepper
Lemon juice
Mixed herbs
GARNISH:
1 level dessertspoon chopped mint or parsley
Bread croûtons

Wash and peel the carrots, turnips and parsnips; dice them finely. Remove the roots and outer coarse leaves from the leeks, wash them thoroughly under cold running water and chop roughly. Scrub the celery and slice the sticks finely; peel and roughly chop the onion. Trim and slice the mushrooms* finely. Remove the rind from the bacon and dice the rashers. Skin and roughly chop the tomatoes*.

Melt the butter in a large heavy-based pan and fry the bacon, onion, celery and mushrooms over moderate heat until soft, but not browned. Add the prepared carrots, turnips, parsnips and leeks and fry them lightly. Remove the pan from the heat and stir in enough flour to absorb the remaining fat. Gradually blend in the milk. Return the pan to the heat and bring the soup to the boil, stirring continuously. Add the tomatoes, stir well and bring the soup to simmering point.

If necessary, thin the soup with water or more milk. Season to taste with salt, freshly ground pepper, lemon juice and a pinch of mixed herbs. Cover the pan with a lid and simmer the soup over very low heat, until the root vegetables are tender, after about 45 minutes.

Serve the soup hot, garnished with mint or parsley and crisp bread croûtons*. Garlic bread or a separate bowl of grated cheese would make the soup even more substantial.

Any left-over soup can be sieved or liquidised and thinned to taste with milk or tomato juice. Before serving, stir a little cream into each bowl and garnish as before.

Fish

CRAB PUFFS

These little pastry puffs may be served hot or cold as a main course or buffet dish, allowing two per person. For a first course, one per person is sufficient. The filling can be made with all white crabmeat, or with mixed white and brown, which gives a richer filling.

PREPARATION TIME: *40 min.*
COOKING TIME: *15 min.*

INGREDIENTS *(for 4)*:
4 oz. crabmeat
2 oz. button mushrooms
1 oz. unsalted butter
2 level tablespoons chopped
 watercress
2–3 level teaspoons plain flour
2–3 fluid oz. single cream
1 tablespoon dry sherry
Salt and black pepper
1–2 teaspoons lemon juice
8 oz. prepared puff pastry
1 egg
GARNISH:
Lemon wedges
Watercress sprigs

Trim and thinly slice the mushrooms*. Melt the butter in a pan over low heat, and fry the mushrooms and flaked crabmeat for a few minutes. Mix in the chopped watercress. Remove the pan from the heat and stir in sufficient flour to absorb all the fat. Stir in the cream and return the pan to the heat, cooking gently for 4–5 minutes. Remove from the heat, add the sherry and season to taste with salt, freshly ground pepper and lemon juice. Set aside to cool.

Roll out the puff pastry*, on a lightly floured surface, to a rectangle, 16 in. by 8 in. Cut the pastry into eight 4 in. squares with a sharp knife. Put a dessertspoon of the crab mixture into the centre of each square. Brush the pastry edges with a little beaten egg, and fold each square into a triangle. Press the edges firmly together, completely sealing in the filling. Crimp the edges with a fork and brush the top of each puff with beaten egg. Make two or three slits in the top of each puff to allow the steam to escape.

Place the puffs on a damp baking tray. Bake just above the centre of a pre-heated oven, at 450°F (mark 8) for 10–15 minutes or until the puffs have risen and are golden brown.

Serve the crab puffs hot or cold, garnished with lemon wedges and sprigs of watercress. A tossed green salad would be a suitable side dish for a main course.

MACKEREL IN CIDER

Mackerel are the only fish allowed to be sold on the streets of London on Sundays. This is because it is essential to cook these fish as soon as possible after catching. The recipe given here comes from Somerset.

PREPARATION TIME: *20 min.*
COOKING TIME: *35 min.*

INGREDIENTS *(for 4)*:
4 mackerel
Salt and black pepper
2 dessert apples
1 small onion
7 oz. Cheddar cheese
2–3 oz. butter
2 oz. fresh white breadcrumbs
3–4 tablespoons dry cider
GARNISH:
Lemon wedges
Freshly chopped parsley

Cut off the heads and slit the fish down the belly; gut the mackerel* and clean thoroughly in cold water. The backbones may be removed from the mackerel, but this is not essential. Dry the mackerel thoroughly on absorbent kitchen paper and season them with salt and pepper.

Peel and coarsely grate the apples, onion and 3 oz. of the cheese. Melt the butter in a small pan over low heat. Mix the grated apple, onion, cheese and the breadcrumbs together in a bowl and bind with 1 tablespoon of the melted butter. Stuff the mackerel with this mixture and secure the opening of each with two or three wooden skewers.

Grate the remaining cheese finely. Place the mackerel side by side in a fireproof dish and sprinkle 1 tablespoon of grated cheese over each. Pour over the remaining melted butter and sufficient cider to cover the base of the dish. Lay a piece of buttered kitchen foil or greaseproof paper loosely over the dish and place in the centre of a pre-heated oven, at 350°F (mark 4). Bake for 25–35 minutes, or until the mackerel are cooked through and golden brown.

Serve the mackerel straight from the dish, garnished with lemon wedges and parsley.

Potatoes in their jackets make a perfect addition to this dish.

PESCADA À LA MARINA

The South Americans, even more than the French, are great believers in marinating meat and fish before cooking them. The marinade, which imparts an unusual flavour to fish fillets, is used for the sauce.

PREPARATION TIME: *1 hour*
 20 min.
COOKING TIME: *15 min.*

INGREDIENTS *(for 4)*:
1½ lb. haddock or cod fillet
1 egg
3–4 oz. fresh white breadcrumbs
Oil for frying
MARINADE:
4 tablespoons olive oil
2 tablespoons lemon juice
1 small onion
1 clove garlic
1–2 bay leaves
1 level teaspoon salt
Black pepper and ground nutmeg
MARINA SAUCE:
4 fluid oz. dry white wine
2 egg yolks
GARNISH:
2 dessertspoons finely chopped
 parsley

Make the marinade* first, by blending together the olive oil and lemon juice; peel and finely chop the onion and garlic. Add to the oil, together with the bay leaves, salt, freshly ground pepper and a pinch of nutmeg.

Wash the fish fillet and divide into four or six portions. Place them in a shallow dish and pour over the prepared marinade. Leave for about 1 hour, turning the fish from time to time.

Lift out the fish, setting the marinade aside. Dry the fillets thoroughly on absorbent kitchen paper. Lightly beat the egg and brush it over the fish before coating with breadcrumbs. Press the crumbs well in, and shake off any surplus. Leave the coating to harden while making the sauce.

Bring the marinade to the boil, then strain it through a fine sieve into a bowl. Add the wine. Beat the egg yolks together in a separate bowl and gradually stir in the wine and marinade. Place the bowl over a saucepan of gently simmering water and stir continuously with a wooden spoon until the sauce thickens sufficiently to coat the back of the spoon. If the sauce shows signs of curdling, add a tablespoon of cold water and remove the bowl from the heat.

Heat the oil in a heavy-based pan and fry the fish until golden brown on both sides, turning once. Drain on absorbent paper.

Serve the fish hot, sprinkled with parsley. Serve the Marina sauce separately and offer creamed potatoes and buttered beans. The fillets may also be served cold with a sauce tartare* and a crisp green salad.

MOULES À LA POULETTE

In France, the mussels in this classic dish are served in their half shells and eaten with the fingers. The sauce is mopped up with bread. Alternatively, remove the mussels entirely from the shells and serve them in the sauce as a soup.

PREPARATION TIME: *30 min.*
COOKING TIME: *10 min.*

INGREDIENTS *(for 4–6)*:
8 pints mussels
1 bay leaf
1 parsley sprig
1 shallot
6 black peppercorns
¾ pint dry white wine
¼ pint double cream
2 egg yolks
2 tablespoons chopped parsley
Black pepper
Lemon juice

Clean the mussels* thoroughly, discarding any with broken or open shells. Scrape away all grit and remove the beards. Put the mussels in a large, heavy-based saucepan with the bay leaf, parsley, peeled and finely chopped shallot and the peppercorns. Pour over the wine, cover the pan with a lid and cook the mussels over high heat until the shells open.

As the shells open, remove the mussels from the pan, throw away the empty top halves and place the mussels in their half shells in a warmed casserole. Cover them with a clean cloth to prevent them drying out, and to keep them warm. Strain the cooking liquid through muslin.

Mix the cream and egg yolks together in a bowl and blend in a few tablespoons of the mussel liquid. Add to the remaining liquid, together with the chopped parsley. Season to taste with freshly ground pepper and lemon juice. Re-heat the liquid, without boiling, until it has thickened slightly.

Serve the mussels in individual deep soup plates, with the sauce poured over them. Set a finger bowl with a slice of lemon by each plate. Offer plenty of crusty bread and provide a spare bowl or plates for the empty mussel shells.

Meat

BAKED STUFFED SHOULDER OF VEAL

This is one of the less expensive cuts of veal. It is braised rather than roasted, to preserve the juices. Make the stock the day before if possible, since it takes 3–4 hours to cook.

PREPARATION TIME: *35 min.*
COOKING TIME: *1¾ hours*

INGREDIENTS *(for 6)*:

3 lb. boned shoulder of veal
2 oz. butter
¼ pint dry white wine
1¼–½ pint stock
STOCK:
1 large onion
2 carrots
1 stick celery
Bouquet garni
STUFFING:
¾ pint stock

4 oz. long grain rice
Pinch saffron
4 oz. streaky bacon
1 bunch watercress
2 oz. shelled walnuts
1 lemon
*Salt and freshly ground black
    pepper*
1 egg
GARNISH:
Watercress

Ask the butcher to bone out the shoulder of veal and to include the chopped bones with the order. Put the bones, together with the cleaned and chopped stock vegetables, in a saucepan and cover with cold water. Add the bouquet garni* and a good seasoning of salt and black pepper. Cook this stock for about 3 hours, strain and set aside.

With a sharp knife, open the cavities in the meat to make pockets for the stuffing. Cook the rice, with the saffron, in ¾ pint of the reserved stock for 12–14 minutes or until tender.

Meanwhile, cut the rind and gristle from the bacon rashers. Wash and chop the watercress, chop the walnuts finely and grate the rind from the lemon. Fry the bacon rashers in a little of the butter, over low heat, until crisp. Remove the bacon from the pan, drain and chop it.

Put the drained rice in a mixing bowl, and add the bacon fat from the pan, the bacon, watercress, walnuts and lemon rind. Season to taste. Bind the stuffing with the lightly beaten egg.

Spread the stuffing evenly into the pockets of the veal, roll up the joint and tie with string.

Brown the veal briskly in the remaining butter in a roasting tin. Pour over the wine and roast the veal in the centre of a pre-heated oven at 350°F (mark 4), for about 1½ hours. Baste* frequently with the wine, adding a little stock if necessary.

Put the joint on a warm serving dish and remove the string. Add ¼ pint of stock to the roasting tin. Boil over high heat until the liquid is light brown and has reduced* by about half. Pour the gravy into a warm sauce boat.

Serve the sliced veal garnished with sprigs of watercress. Roast potatoes go well with the meat; so do courgettes gratiné (see September vegetables).

MEAT ROLL EN CROÛTE

Golden crisp puff pastry is often used to make a covering for such expensive dishes as fillet of beef, boned poultry, or salmon. The same delicious crust can be used to encase minced savoury meat.

PREPARATION TIME: *25 min.*
COOKING TIME: *1¾ hours*

INGREDIENTS (*for 6*):

2 lb. lean minced pork
1 onion
1 clove garlic
2 level tablespoons chopped parsley
Salt and black pepper
1 dessertspoon Worcestershire
    sauce
3 eggs
4 oz. Bel Paese or Gouda cheese
6 oz. button mushrooms
8 oz. prepared puff pastry
¼ pint stock or bouillon
GARNISH:
Watercress

Peel and finely chop the onion and crush the garlic. Mix together the pork, onion, garlic and parsley in a large bowl; season to taste with salt and freshly ground pepper. Beat the Worcestershire sauce with two of the eggs and stir into the meat mixture. Butter a 2 lb. loaf tin thoroughly and press in half the meat mixture in an even layer. Dice the cheese finely, trim and chop the mushrooms* and put both on top of the meat, then cover with the remaining pork, levelling off the surface smoothly. Cover the tin with buttered foil or greaseproof paper.

Place the tin in a roasting pan containing about ½ in. of water, and bake in the centre of a pre-heated oven, at 375°F (mark 5), for 1¼ hours. Remove the pan from the oven. Carefully pour off the liquid round the meat in the tin and set it aside for gravy. Leave the meat in the tin to cool and shrink slightly.

Raise the oven heat to 450°F (mark 8). Roll out the puff pastry*, on a lightly floured surface, to a thin rectangle measuring roughly 12 in. by 8 in. Turn the meat out of the tin and place it in the centre of the pastry; wrap the pastry over and round the meat, sealing the edges with lightly beaten egg.

Put the pastry-wrapped meat loaf, join underneath, on a damp baking tray and brush the top with egg. Decorate the loaf with the pastry trimmings, and cut two or three slits in the pastry for the steam to escape. Bake in the oven for 20–25 minutes or until the pastry is well risen and golden brown.

Skim the fat from the reserved gravy and put it, with the stock, in a small saucepan. Boil rapidly until it has reduced* slightly. Season to taste and pour into a warm sauce boat.

Serve the crusty meat roll hot, garnished with sprigs of watercress and surrounded with halved grilled tomatoes, grilled mushroom caps and boiled buttered potatoes.

ROAST PORK WITH APPLE AND NUT STUFFING

Blade or shoulder of pork is a good joint for roasting, as the meat is tender and has plenty of rind for crisp crackling. When boned and stuffed it is easily carved even by the unskilled.

PREPARATION TIME: *20 min.*
COOKING TIME: *2 hours*

INGREDIENTS (*for 6*):
3½ lb. blade of pork, boned
1 small onion
2 oz. cashew nuts or peanuts
2 oz. white crustless bread
1 cooking apple
1 stick celery
1 dessertspoon chopped parsley
1 oz. butter
Salt and black pepper
½ teaspoon dried summer savory
Lemon juice
2–3 tablespoons vegetable oil
¼ pint dry cider

Peel and finely chop the onion and roughly chop the nuts. Dice the bread; peel, core and dice the apple. Wash and finely chop the celery and parsley.

Melt the butter in a small pan over moderate heat and fry the onion and nuts until they are just turning colour. Add the bread, apple, celery and parsley to the onion and nuts and continue cooking until the apple has softened. Season to taste with salt, pepper, summer savory and lemon juice.

Make sure that the rind of the joint is deeply scored*. Open up the pocket and spread the stuffing evenly. Roll up the joint and tie securely with string at regular intervals.

Place the joint in an oiled roasting tin; brush the rind with oil and sprinkle generously with salt. Roast above the centre of an oven pre-heated to 400°F (mark 6) for 20–30 minutes, until the crackling is crisp and golden. Move the tin to a shelf just below the centre and reduce the temperature to 350°F (mark 4). Cook for a further 1½ hours or until the juice comes out amber-coloured when a skewer is pushed into the meat.

Put the joint on a serving plate and keep it warm. Leave the residue in the roasting tin to settle, then carefully skim or pour off the fat. Add the cider to the pan juices and bring to the boil over moderate heat, scraping in all the residue. When the gravy has coloured, season to taste and pour it into a warm sauce boat.

Roast potatoes and buttered cabbage or runner beans are ideal with this tasty joint.

ÉPIGRAMMES D'AGNEAU

This classic French recipe is an unusual and highly successful way of cooking breast of lamb. It is also an economical dish, for the stock can be used as the basis for lamb and lemon soup (see September soups). The intriguing title is credited to an 18th-century marquise. Unaware of the meaning of the word *épigramme,* overheard in a conversation, she ordered her chef to produce a dish of épigrammes!

PREPARATION TIME: *30 min.*
COOKING TIME: *2 hours*
STANDING TIME: *3 hours*

INGREDIENTS *(for 4–6)*:
2 breasts of lamb (unboned and weighing about 3 lb.)
1 onion
2 leeks
1–2 sticks celery
3–4 carrots
Bouquet garni
2 level teaspoons salt
6 peppercorns
1 large egg
2–3 oz. dry white breadcrumbs
2 oz. unsalted butter
2 tablespoons corn oil
GARNISH:
Watercress sprigs
Lemon wedges

Peel and slice the onion. Cut the roots and coarse outer leaves from the leeks, wash them thoroughly under cold running water and chop them roughly. Scrub the celery and scrape or peel the carrots; chop both roughly.

Trim as much fat as possible from the breasts of lamb, and put them in a large pan, with the prepared vegetables, the bouquet garni*, salt and peppercorns. Cover with cold water and bring to the boil. Remove any scum from the surface, then cover the pan with a lid and simmer gently for 1½ hours. Remove the meat from the pan, leave to cool slightly, then carefully pull out all the bones. Strain the cooking liquid through a fine sieve and use it as the basis for a soup.

Lay the meat flat between two boards and place a heavy weight on top. Leave until quite cold, then trim off any remaining fat and cut the meat into 2 in. squares. Dip the meat in the lightly beaten egg and coat evenly with the breadcrumbs. Set aside until the coating has hardened.

Heat the butter and oil in a heavy-based pan and fry the meat squares until crisp and golden on both sides, after about 20 minutes. Drain on crumpled absorbent kitchen paper.

Serve the épigrammes on a warmed dish and garnish with sprigs of watercress and lemon wedges. Sauté potatoes*, broccoli spears and a sauce Bernaise* or tartare* would go well with the épigrammes.

CHATEAUBRIAND STEAK

This famous dish is named after the 18th-century French writer, Chateaubriand. It cannot be served for less than two persons, as it is a double fillet steak cut from the thick end of the fillet. In Britain, it is sometimes called a Porterhouse steak.

PREPARATION TIME: *5 min.*
COOKING TIME: *8–10 min.*

INGREDIENTS *(for 2)*:
12–14 oz. thick fillet steak
½ oz. melted butter
Salt and black pepper
GARNISH:
Watercress
Maître d'hôtel butter

Trim the fillet and if necessary flatten it slightly – it should be 1½–2 in. thick. Brush one side with melted butter and season with freshly ground pepper. Do not add salt as this will extract the juices.

Put the steak, buttered and seasoned side up, under a hot grill and cook under high heat to brown the surface and seal in the juices. Turn the steak over, brush with the remaining melted butter and season with pepper. Turn the heat down and grill the steak for a further 4–5 minutes, turning it once only. The steak should be cooked through, but remain rosy-pink inside.

Lift the steak on to a board and carve it, at a slight angle, into six even slices. Remove the sliced steak, in one movement, on to a warm serving dish and garnish with sprigs of watercress and slices of maître d'hôtel butter*.

Traditionally, a chateaubriand steak is served with château potatoes and a sauce Bearnaise*. A tossed green salad makes an excellent side dish.

GAMMON STEAKS IN MADEIRA SAUCE

English or sweet-cured gammon is ideal for this easily made appetising dish. Danish gammon can also be used, but it should first be soaked for 1 hour in cold water to reduce the salt content.

PREPARATION TIME: *20 min.*
COOKING TIME: *20–25 min.*

INGREDIENTS *(for 4)*:
4 gammon steaks, each ½–¾ in. thick
4–6 oz. mushrooms
1 large onion
4 large tomatoes
2 oz. butter or lard
¼ level teaspoon dried basil
¼ level teaspoon dried marjoram
2 fluid oz. Madeira or sweet sherry
4 fluid oz. ham stock or bouillon
Salt and black pepper
1 teaspoon caster sugar
Lemon juice

Cut the rind off the steaks and trim the fat. Wipe the mushrooms, remove the stalks and chop them roughly, leaving the caps whole. Peel and thinly slice the onion; skin the tomatoes* and chop them roughly.

Heat the butter or lard in a heavy-based pan over moderate heat until it stops bubbling. Fry the gammon steaks until golden on both sides, after about 8 minutes, turning once only. Remove the gammon from the pan and keep hot in the oven.

Fry the onion, mushroom caps and stalks lightly in the pan juices until softened; add the tomatoes, the basil and marjoram. Cover the pan with a lid or kitchen foil and simmer for about 5 minutes, shaking the pan from time to time.

Return the gammon steaks to the pan and add the Madeira or sherry, with enough stock to almost cover the meat. Season to taste with salt, freshly ground pepper, sugar and lemon juice. Cover the pan again and continue cooking over low heat for 10 minutes or until the gammon is tender.

Arrange the steaks on a hot serving dish with the sauce poured over them. Baby sprouts, tossed in butter, and creamed potatoes or fluffy boiled rice, to mop up the sauce, would be suitable with the gammon.

CHINESE PANCAKES

Deep-fried pancake rolls with a savoury filling figure on almost every Chinese menu. There are a wide variety of fillings – this one contains pork and prawns – but bean sprouts are an essential ingredient.

PREPARATION TIME: *45 min.*
COOKING TIME: *15 min.*

INGREDIENTS (*for 4*):
8 thin pancakes
1 spring onion
1 stick celery
2 oz. button mushrooms
2 oz. cooked lean pork
2 oz. peeled prawns
6–8 tinned water chestnuts
2 oz. fresh or tinned bean sprouts
1 tablespoon vegetable oil
2 teaspoons soy sauce
1 tablespoon dry sherry
2 level teaspoons cornflour
2 tablespoons chestnut liquid
1 egg
Oil for deep frying

Trim the root and top from the spring onion, leaving on it most of the green, and chop it finely. Wash and scrub the celery, trim the mushrooms* and chop both finely. Chop the pork and peeled prawns roughly and thinly slice the water chestnuts. Trim any damaged ends from fresh bean sprouts and blanch* in boiling water for 5 minutes. Drain and chop the sprouts roughly.

Make eight very thin pancakes* and pile them on top of each other, between sheets of greaseproof paper, to keep them soft and pliable while preparing the filling.

Heat the vegetable oil in a frying pan over low heat and fry the spring onion, celery and mushrooms until soft. Add the pork and prawns and fry lightly. Stir in the water chestnuts, bean sprouts, soy sauce and sherry.

Blend the cornflour to a smooth paste with the chestnut liquid in a small bowl and stir this mixture into the pan. Continue cooking, stirring thoroughly, for 3–5 minutes, until the cornflour is cooked and all the ingredients are well glazed.

Spoon equal portions of the filling in the centre of each pancake. Brush the edges with lightly beaten egg and fold two sides of each pancake over the filling. Fold the opposite sides over to make a small neat parcel and seal the edges with beaten egg. Turn the parcels upside down to firm the joins and set them aside for 10–15 minutes.

Heat the frying oil*, with the frying basket in the pan, to 375°F and fry the pancake parcels, two or three at a time, until crisp and golden. As each batch is finished, lift it carefully on to crumpled absorbent paper to drain.

Keep the pancakes hot while frying the next batch. Serve at once, with boiled rice and a crisp lettuce and celery salad (see January vegetables).

BEEF JARDINIÈRE

Joints of beef, such as topside, silverside and brisket, are not tender enough to oven-roast successfully. They do, however, make excellent pot roasts, cooked with fresh vegetables (*jardinière*). Topside and silverside are lean joints, but brisket usually needs some of the fat trimmed off before being rolled and tied.

PREPARATION TIME: *25 min.*
COOKING TIME: *2½–3 hours*

INGREDIENTS (*for 6*):
3 lb. rolled topside, silverside or brisket of beef
8 small onions
½ lb. small carrots
2 young turnips
2 oz. beef dripping
4 fluid oz. dry red wine
2 bay leaves
½ level teaspoon mixed herbs
6 peppercorns
1 level teaspoon salt
½ lb. young runner or French beans or fresh peas
1 lb. potatoes (optional)

Peel the onions, leaving them whole. Scrape or peel the carrots, and peel and quarter the turnips. Melt the dripping over high heat in a large heavy-based pan or flameproof casserole. Brown the meat quickly on all sides in the fat to seal in the juices. Add the onions and fry until golden. Put the carrots, turnips and wine into the pan, together with the bay leaves, mixed herbs, peppercorns and salt.

Cover the pan with a close-fitting lid or foil and simmer over low heat on top of the stove or in the centre of an oven pre-heated to 300°F (mark 2), for 2½–3 hours or until the meat is tender. If the liquid evaporates during cooking, add a little beef stock or water.

Top, tail and string the beans and cut them into 1 in. pieces. Alternatively, shell the peas. Cook them in lightly salted boiling water for 10 minutes or until just tender.

Remove the meat from the pan, carve it and arrange the slices on a hot serving dish. Surround the meat with the vegetables and garnish with the beans. Remove the bay leaves from the pan juices; skim off the fat or soak it off the surface with absorbent kitchen paper. Season the gravy to taste with salt and freshly ground pepper and pour it into a warm sauce boat.

Potatoes may be added to the meat for the last hour of cooking, or served separately.

Poultry & Game

WILD DUCK WITH BIGARADE SAUCE

Wild duck (mallard or teal) have less fat than the domestic variety, but a stuffing of fresh oranges imparts both moisture and flavour. The rich sauce is traditionally made with bitter oranges (bigarade oranges), but a good variation is achieved by using sweet oranges sharpened with lemon juice.

PREPARATION TIME: *25 min.*
COOKING TIME: *45–55 min.*

INGREDIENTS *(for 4)* :
1 large or 2 small wild duck
1–2 oranges
Poultry dripping or cooking fat
Bouquet garni
Salt and black pepper
BIGARADE SAUCE:
1 large onion
1 stick celery
2 oz. mushrooms
2 rashers streaky bacon
4 oz. carrots
2 small or 1 large orange
1 small or ½ large lemon
2 oz. dripping
3–4 dessertspoons plain flour
4 fluid oz. red wine
4 fluid oz. tomato juice
¼ pint giblet stock
½ teaspoon dried mixed herbs
Salt and black pepper
2 level dessertspoons redcurrant jelly
2 fluid oz. port

Ask the poulterer to include the neck and giblets with the order. Wipe the duck inside and out with a clean damp cloth. Peel and quarter the orange and put it inside the duck. Spread the duck breast with dripping or fat and place the bird in a greased roasting tin. Cover the tin with foil and roast just above centre of an oven pre-heated to 400°F (mark 6) for 45 minutes or longer, according to size. The duck is cooked when a skewer inserted in the thigh lets out colourless juices. Remove the foil after 30 minutes' roasting.

While the duck is cooking, roughly chop the liver and set it aside. Put the neck and giblets in a pan with ½ pint of water, the bouquet garni* and a seasoning of salt and freshly ground pepper. Cover the pan with a lid and simmer the stock for 15–20 minutes.

For the sauce, peel and finely chop the onion, scrub and chop the celery and trim the mushrooms* before slicing them. Remove the rind and gristle and chop the bacon finely.

Scrape or peel the carrots and chop them finely. Grate the rind from the orange and lemon, squeeze the juices and set both aside. Melt the dripping in a heavy-based pan and fry the onion, celery, mushrooms and bacon until soft. Add the carrots to the pan and continue cooking over medium heat until the onion begins to colour.

Stir in enough flour to absorb all the fat and cook, stirring continuously, until the mixture is a pale caramel colour. Remove the pan from the heat and gradually blend in the wine, tomato juice, duck livers and ¼ pint of strained giblet stock. Stir until smooth, then return the pan to the heat and bring the sauce slowly to the boil, stirring all the time. Add the mixed herbs and salt and pepper to taste; blend in the orange and lemon rind, and juices.

Cover the pan with a lid and simmer the sauce over low heat for about 30 minutes or until the vegetables are tender. If necessary, thin the sauce with more giblet stock.

When the duck is cooked, lift it carefully from the roasting tin, tail downwards so that the orange juice runs back into the pan. Put the duck on a serving dish and keep it warm. Pour the fat slowly from the pan, and add sufficient giblet stock to cover the base of the tin. Boil rapidly on top of the stove, scraping in all the brown residue from the bottom and sides of the pan. Cook until the liquid is lightly coloured, then stir it into the bigarade sauce. Stir in the redcurrant jelly and port, and continue cooking over low heat until the jelly has dissolved. Adjust seasoning.

Carve the duck and arrange the slices on a warm serving dish; spoon over a little of the sauce and serve the remainder in a sauce boat. A border of duchesse potatoes* can be piped round the duck, and fresh young sprouts would also be suitable.

GROUSE À LA GRANDMÈRE

Mature grouse which have escaped the guns for some years are not tender enough for plain roasting. They can, however, be made into a tasty casserole, flavoured with herbs and brandy.

PREPARATION TIME: *30 min.*
COOKING TIME: *1½ hours*

INGREDIENTS *(for 4)* :
4 mature grouse
8–12 button onions
1 stick celery
8 oz. mushrooms
4 oz. butter
2–3 level dessertspoons plain flour
1 pint stock or bouillon
Fresh thyme, marjoram and rosemary
Salt and black pepper
3–4 tablespoons double cream
2 tablespoons brandy
Lemon juice
4 small slices crustless white bread
GARNISH:
1 dessertspoon chopped parsley

Peel the onions, leaving them whole. Scrub the celery, trim the mushrooms* and chop both roughly. Melt half the butter in a flameproof casserole and, when hot, brown the neatly trussed grouse all over, together with the onions.

Lift out the grouse and onions, and fry the celery and mushrooms in the butter until soft. Remove the pan from the heat, stir in sufficient flour to absorb all the fat, and return the pan to the heat. Cook the roux* until brown, then gradually blend in the stock or bouillon. Bring the mixture to simmering point and season to taste with the herbs, salt and freshly ground pepper.

Return the grouse and onions to the casserole, cover with a lid and cook over low heat on top of the stove for about 1½ hours or until the grouse are tender. Mix the cream and brandy together, blend in 2 or 3 tablespoons of the

Rice & Pasta

sauce from the grouse, and stir it back into the casserole. Sharpen to taste with lemon juice and adjust seasoning.

In a clean pan, fry the bread in the remaining butter until crisp and golden. Drain the bread on crumpled absorbent paper, then arrange it on a hot serving dish. Place one grouse on each bread slice, pour over a little sauce and sprinkle with parsley. Pour the remaining sauce into a sauce boat. Serve with fluffy creamed potatoes and cauliflower polonaise (see September vegetables).

ROAST SADDLE OF HARE

A whole hare may be too large for a small household, but the saddle can be roasted in one piece, and the legs can be used for a pâté which can be stored. The age of a hare can be tested by splitting the ear of the furred animal – on a young hare it will tear easily. Tough ears and blunt claws indicate an older animal which is best jugged or made into a pie or pudding.

PREPARATION TIME: *25 min.*
COOKING TIME: *1 hour*

INGREDIENTS *(for 4)* :
Saddle of a young hare
8 rashers streaky bacon
1½ oz. butter
8 oz. egg noodles
Salt and black pepper
2 tablespoons brandy or brown stock
7½ fluid oz. soured cream
Dried rosemary
GARNISH:
Fresh rosemary

Order the hare* skinned and have it cut into the complete saddle and four leg joints.

Insert the point of a sharp knife under the skin or thin membrane which covers the saddle and carefully peel it off. Place the saddle in a greased roasting tin.

Remove the rind and gristle from the bacon and put the rashers over the saddle. Spread the butter, which has been softened, over the bacon. Roast the hare in the centre of an oven pre-heated to 375°F (mark 5) for about 50 minutes or until tender.

About 15 minutes before the hare is ready, bring a large pan of water to the boil and add 4 teaspoons of salt and the noodles. Cook for about 10 minutes, until the pasta is just tender, then drain in a colander. Remove the crisp bacon from the hare, chop it finely and mix it into the noodles with a tablespoon of fat from the roasting tin. Season with freshly ground pepper.

Lift the saddle from the tin and keep it warm while making the sauce: carefully pour off the fat, leaving the pan juices in the tin. Add the brandy (or stock) and the soured cream to the pan juices, together with a little dried crushed rosemary. Put the pan over low heat on top of the stove and stir the gravy, scraping up all the residue from the pan. Season to taste with salt and pepper.

Carve the saddle of hare* lengthways along the backbone and arrange the slices on a warmed serving dish; surround with the noodles. Pour the sauce over the hare and garnish with sprigs of fresh rosemary. Green beans tossed in butter would be a suitable side dish.

PAELLA VALENCIA

Probably the most famous of all Spanish dishes, paella has many local variations. All, however, contain the basic ingredients of chicken, onion and saffron-flavoured rice. In Spain, paella is cooked in and served straight from a two-handled iron pan (*paella*) from which the dish takes its name.

PREPARATION TIME: *1 hour*
COOKING TIME: *1 hour*

INGREDIENTS *(for 6)* :
1 chicken (about 2½ lb.)
3 parsley sprigs
1 bay leaf
1 sprig marjoram
Salt and black pepper
½ lb. ripe tomatoes
1–2 red or green peppers
8 oz. peas or green beans
1 tin artichoke hearts (optional)
1 pint mussels
1 onion
2 fluid oz. olive oil
12 oz. long grain rice
6 oz. large peeled prawns
4 oz. chorizo (paprika) or garlic sausage
Powdered saffron
GARNISH:
6 large unpeeled prawns
6 lemon wedges

Cut the leg and wing portions off the chicken, before severing the whole breast section from the lower carcass. Divide the breast section, lengthways, in two along the breastbone. Leave the flesh on the bone to prevent shrinkage during cooking.

Put the remaining carcass and the giblets in a large pan, add the parsley, bay leaf and marjoram and enough cold water to cover. Season thoroughly with salt and freshly ground pepper. Bring the stock to the boil, then cover with a lid and simmer for about 30 minutes. Strain the stock through a fine sieve and set aside.

While the stock is cooking, prepare the vegetables and shellfish: skin the tomatoes* and chop them roughly. Wash the peppers, cut off the stalk bases, remove the seeds and cut the flesh into narrow slices or strips. Shell the peas or remove the strings from the green beans and cut into 2 in. lengths. Drain and halve the tinned artichokes if used. Clean the mussels* thoroughly. Peel and finely slice the onion.

Heat the oil in a paella dish or a large, heavy-based pan over moderate heat. Fry the chicken joints until golden on both sides; remove from the pan and divide each into smaller pieces. Fry the onion in the oil, stirring constantly, until transparent, then add the rice and fry until it is a pale biscuit colour. Return the chicken pieces to the pan, together with the prepared vegetables, the mussels and the peeled prawns.

Pour over enough chicken stock to cover all the ingredients. Cover with foil or a lid and simmer slowly until the stock is absorbed and the rice is just tender. Stir occasionally while cooking, and add more stock if necessary until the rice is cooked, without being mushy.

Lift the mussels from the pan and keep them warm. Slice the sausage thinly and add to the mixture in the pan together with the artichokes and a pinch of saffron, just enough to give the rice a golden colour. Stir thoroughly and season to taste with salt and freshly ground pepper.

Remove the top shells from the mussels and arrange the bottom shells with the mussels on top of the rice.

Serve the paella in the pan, garnished with the unpeeled prawns and wedges of lemon. A bowl of green salad, dressed with a sauce vinaigrette*, can be served as a side dish, but the paella is a vast, substantial meal in itself.

Vegetables & Salads

LUMACHINE CON COZZE

This is an Italian dish of egg pasta shells (lumachine) and mussels. Young, fresh mussels are available now, but at other times of the year, bottled mussels, without their brine, may be used.

PREPARATION TIME: *30 min.*
COOKING TIME: *25 min.*

INGREDIENTS *(for 4):*
2 pints fresh mussels
1 lb. ripe tomatoes
1 clove garlic
2 dessertspoons olive oil
1 level tablespoon chopped
*   parsley*
½ level teaspoon each, dried
*   marjoram and basil*
8 oz. lumachine
Salt and black pepper
Lemon juice

Scrub and clean the mussels* thoroughly. Remove the beards, and discard any mussels with broken or open shells.

Skin the tomatoes* and chop them roughly. Peel and finely chop the garlic. Heat the oil in a frying pan and lightly fry the garlic. Add the tomatoes, parsley and herbs and bring this mixture to simmering point.

Put the cleaned mussels in a large saucepan and cover with a lid. Cook over moderate heat, shaking the pan occasionally, until the mussels open. Remove the mussels from the shells and set them aside. Strain the cooking liquid through muslin to remove any sandy sediment, and stir it into the tomato mixture. Simmer over low heat for 20 minutes.

While the tomatoes are cooking, bring a large pan of water to the boil, add 2–3 teaspoons of salt and cook the pasta shells for 12 minutes or until tender, but not soft. Drain in a colander and cover with a clean cloth to keep the pasta warm.

Add the mussels to the tomato sauce and heat through. Season to taste with freshly ground pepper, adding salt only if necessary, and sharpen with lemon juice. Put the pasta shells in a warmed deep serving dish and pour the mussels and sauce over them. Serve at once, with crusty bread.

GREEK RICE RING

Particularly attractive when moulded in a ring, this spicy rice dish, served hot or cold, makes a light meal on its own. Kebabs, shellfish or chicken make it even more substantial.

PREPARATION TIME: *20 min.*
COOKING TIME: *20–40 min.*
SETTING TIME: *1 hour*

INGREDIENTS *(for 6):*
8 oz. long grain rice
Salt and black pepper
Lemon juice
2 large ripe tomatoes
2 level dessertspoons finely
*   chopped chives*
2 level dessertspoons finely
*   chopped parsley*
8 green olives
½ level teaspoon each, dried
*   basil and marjoram*
1 red pepper
4 tablespoons olive oil
2 tablespoons tarragon vinegar
GARNISH:
Black olives

Cook the rice in a large pan of boiling salted water, with a teaspoon of lemon juice, for about 15 minutes or until the rice is just tender. Drain the rice in a colander and cover with a dry cloth to absorb the steam and keep the rice dry and fluffy.

While the rice is cooking, skin the tomatoes*. Chop them finely and put them in a large bowl together with the chives, parsley and finely chopped green olives. Blend in the dried herbs. Scald the pepper in boiling water for 5 minutes, cut off the stalk end and remove the seeds. Cut the pepper into narrow strips; set eight strips aside and chop the remainder finely. Add them to the tomato mixture.

Mix the still-warm rice into the tomato mixture. Blend the oil and vinegar together in a small bowl and season to taste with salt and freshly ground pepper. Add enough of this dressing to moisten the rice thoroughly; adjust seasoning and sharpen to taste with lemon juice. Press the rice firmly into a ring mould and leave to set in a cool place for at least 1 hour.

To serve hot, cover the rice mould with buttered foil or greaseproof paper and place it in a roasting tin containing about ½ in. of boiling water. Heat on top of the stove for 15–20 minutes, then remove the covering and place the serving dish over the mould. Turn it upside-down, and give a sharp shake to ease out the rice. Garnish with black olives and strips of red pepper.

Invert half a grapefruit in the centre and skewer grilled lamb kebabs* in a fan arrangement in the grapefruit.

For a cold lunch, unmould the rice ring, as already described, without re-heating it. For a more substantial meal, fill the centre with cooked chicken, scampi or lobster in Mousseline sauce*.

CAULIFLOWER POLONAISE

Plainly cooked cauliflower is an excellent accompaniment to meat or poultry served in a rich sauce. The attractive garnish makes the dish particularly appetising.

PREPARATION TIME: *15 min.*
COOKING TIME: *20 min.*

INGREDIENTS *(for 4–6):*
1 cauliflower
2 oz. butter
2 hardboiled eggs
2 oz. dried breadcrumbs
2 level tablespoons chopped
*   parsley*
Salt and black pepper
Lemon juice

Cut off the tough outer leaves and thick stalk base of the cauliflower.

Wash thoroughly. Cook the cauliflower whole in boiling salted water for 10–15 minutes or until just tender. Drain in a colander and cover with a dry cloth to keep warm.

Meanwhile, shell the eggs, remove the yolks and rub them through a sieve; chop the whites finely with a stainless steel knife. Melt the butter in a small pan and fry the breadcrumbs until crisp. Remove the pan from the heat, stir in the parsley and season with salt, freshly ground pepper and lemon juice.

Place the cauliflower in a warm serving dish, sprinkle with the roasted breadcrumbs, and garnish with the egg yolks and whites in an attractive pattern.

TOMATOES WITH GREEN PEAS

Large firm tomatoes are ideal for stuffing, and may be served with grilled or roast meats. They can also be served as a hot first course, allowing one tomato per person. The stuffing used in this month's recipes for marrow and peppers can also be used – in fact all three stuffings are interchangeable.

PREPARATION TIME: *20 min.*
COOKING TIME: *15 min.*

INGREDIENTS *(for 6)*:
6 large firm tomatoes
1 small onion
1½ oz. butter
½ pint cooked peas
1 level dessertspoon chopped fresh mint
Salt and black pepper
1 egg yolk
GARNISH:
Black olives

Remove the leaf bases, and wash and dry the tomatoes thoroughly. Slice off the top of each with a sharp, serrated knife, and carefully take out the core and seeds with a pointed teaspoon. Turn the tomatoes upside-down to drain thoroughly while making the stuffing.

Peel and finely chop the onion. Melt 1 oz. of the butter in a small, heavy-based pan and cook the onion over moderate heat until soft, but not coloured. Add the cooked peas and chopped mint to the onion. Cook the mixture for 3 minutes, stirring all the time. Allow the mixture to cool slightly, then rub it through a coarse sieve or liquidise it to a purée*.

Return the purée to the pan and season to taste with salt and freshly ground pepper. Beat the egg yolk lightly, then add it to the peas and onions. Stir over low heat until the mixture thickens. Remove from the heat and set the stuffing aside to cool and stiffen.

Season the inside of the drained tomatoes with salt and pepper and spoon in the prepared stuffing. Replace the tomato lids and secure each with a wooden cocktail stick.

Arrange the tomatoes in a well-buttered ovenproof dish and cover tightly with foil. Bake in an oven pre-heated to 375°F (mark 5) for 15 minutes or until the tomatoes are just tender, but still retaining their shape.

Serve the tomatoes hot, garnished with an olive on top of each cocktail stick.

PEPPERS WITH RISOTTO STUFFING

Large, squat peppers filled with a savoury rice stuffing make a light lunch or supper dish on their own. They also go well with grilled sausages, kidneys or bacon.

PREPARATION TIME: *15 min.*
COOKING TIME: *40–50 min.*

INGREDIENTS *(for 4)*:
4 even-sized peppers
1 onion
1½ tablespoons olive oil
4 oz. long grain rice
15–16 oz. tin of tomatoes or tomato juice
2 oz. grated Cheddar cheese
Salt and paprika

Peel and finely chop the onion, and cook it until transparent, in 1 tablespoon of the oil in a heavy-based pan. Add the rice and fry, stirring continuously, until the rice is a pale biscuit colour. Add sufficient tomatoes or juice to float the rice off the bottom of the pan. Cover with a lid or foil and cook slowly over low heat. Stir frequently to prevent the rice sticking, adding more tomato juice as the rice absorbs the liquid. After about 20 minutes, when the rice is tender, remove the pan from the heat and stir in the grated cheese. Season to taste with salt and paprika.

Wash and dry the peppers. Use a sharp knife to cut off the stalk ends with a small circle of pepper attached to each. Set the stalks aside and remove the seeds and ribs carefully from the peppers without breaking the skins. Scald the peppers for 5 minutes in a pan of boiling, lightly salted water. Lift out the peppers and drain them, upside-down.

Brush the base of an ovenproof dish with oil. Spoon the rice and tomato stuffing into the peppers and place them upright in the dish. Brush the skins lightly with oil and put 2 or 3 tablespoons of water in the bottom of the dish. Cover it tightly with foil and bake in a pre-heated oven, at 375°F (mark 5) for about 20 minutes or until tender.

Arrange the peppers on a warmed serving dish and replace the stalk 'caps' at an angle so that a little of the stuffing shows.

FRENCH FRIED CABBAGE

Use firm white cabbage for this recipe. The deep-fried, crisp, but feather-light shreds make an excellent accompaniment to grilled fish or meat.

PREPARATION TIME: *5 min.*
COOKING TIME: *10 min.*

INGREDIENTS *(for 4)*:
½ medium-sized white cabbage
¼ pint milk
2 oz. plain flour
Oil for deep frying
Salt

Discard any dark or damaged outer leaves, wash the cabbage and cut out the hard central stalk. Shred the cabbage finely.

Dip a few cabbage shreds at a time in the milk, then toss them in the flour on a sheet of grease-proof paper.

Heat the oil* to 375°F in a deep-fryer; put a few shreds of coated cabbage into the frying basket and fry for 1–2 minutes until crisp and golden. Drain on crumpled kitchen paper and keep hot until all the shreds have been fried.

Sprinkle the cabbage with salt and serve at once, before the crispness is lost.

231

Sweets & Puddings

STUFFED MARROW RINGS

Young, home-grown marrows appear on the vegetable market this month, and usually at a reasonable price. Stuffed and baked, marrow makes a good lunch or supper dish on its own.

PREPARATION TIME: *25 min.*
COOKING TIME: *45 min.*

INGREDIENTS *(for 2–4):*
1 short thick marrow (about 2 lb.)
3 oz. butter
2 oz. mushrooms
4 oz. lean cooked ham
1 level dessertspoon chopped parsley
¼ level teaspoon dried summer savory
Salt and black pepper
2–3 dessertspoons fresh white breadcrumbs

Wash the marrow and wipe it dry; cut it into rings 1½–2 in. thick. Remove the peel unless the marrow is very young and tender. Spoon out the seeds. Butter a large ovenproof dish thoroughly and arrange the marrow rings in this in a single layer.

Trim the mushrooms* and chop them roughly. Dice the ham. Heat 1 oz. of the butter in a pan and lightly fry the mushrooms and ham for 2–3 minutes. Add the parsley and savory, and season to taste with salt and freshly ground pepper. Stir in enough breadcrumbs to bind the stuffing.

Lightly sprinkle the marrow rings with salt and pepper before filling them with the stuffing. Dot with the remaining butter and cover the dish tightly with foil so that the marrow will cook in its own steam. Bake in the centre of a pre-heated oven at 375°F (mark 5) for 45 minutes or until the rings are tender.

Serve the marrow rings straight from the dish, with a hot cheese or tomato sauce*.

COURGETTES GRATINÉ

The subtle flavour and light consistency of courgettes make them an excellent accompaniment to delicately flavoured fish, chicken or veal dishes.

PREPARATION TIME: *5 min.*
COOKING TIME: *25–30 min.*

INGREDIENTS *(for 4):*
6 courgettes
2 oz. butter
Salt and black pepper
1½ oz. Cheddar or Lancashire cheese
4 tablespoons double cream (optional)

Wipe the courgettes with a clean damp cloth; do not peel them, but cut off the stalk ends. Slice each courgette in half lengthways with a sharp knife.

Melt the butter in a shallow, flameproof dish and fry the courgettes, cut side downwards, until light golden. Turn the courgettes over, season them with salt and freshly ground pepper and sprinkle the grated cheese over them.

Cover the dish with a lid or foil and bake in the centre of a preheated oven at 375°F (mark 5), for 20 minutes.

Heat the cream in a small pan over moderate heat. Do not let it reach boiling point, and pour it over the courgettes just before serving.

BERRY LEMON PUDDING

The large cultivated blackberries now in season go well with the lemon flavour of this pudding, which can be eaten hot or cold.

PREPARATION TIME: *25 min.*
COOKING TIME: *45 min.*

INGREDIENTS *(for 4):*
½ lb. blackberries
1 oz. unsalted butter
4 oz. caster sugar
1 lemon
2 eggs
¼ pint milk
1 oz. plain flour
¼ pint whipping cream

Cream together the butter and 2 tablespoons of the sugar in a mixing bowl. Wash the lemon and finely grate the rind into this mixture; squeeze the juice from the lemon and strain it in as well. Beat thoroughly.

Separate the eggs and beat the milk into the yolks. Add this little by little to the creamed mixture, alternately with the sifted flour and remaining sugar, beating until the mixture is thoroughly blended. Whisk the egg whites until stiff, but still moist, and fold them into the lemon mixture.

Hull* the blackberries, setting a few large ones aside for decoration. Put the remaining berries in the base of a 1 pint soufflé dish. Pour the creamed mixture over the berries and set the dish in a roasting tin containing 1 in. of hot water. Bake the pudding in an oven pre-heated to 375°F (mark 5) for 40–45 minutes or until the top is golden brown and set. Test by pressing the top with a finger – the pudding is cooked if it leaves no imprint.

The top of the pudding will have set to a sponge-like mixture over a creamy lemon sauce covering the berries. If the pudding is served hot, sprinkle it generously with caster sugar and decorate with the remaining berries. Offer a bowl of whipped cream separately. For a cold dessert, pipe swirls of whipped cream over the top and garnish with the blackberries.

BLACKBERRY SWISS CHARLOTTE

The classic Charlotte, which probably originated in France, is a cold dessert of cooked fruit, set in a mould of sponge fingers. In this version, cultivated blackberries are used, but autumn raspberries or loganberries are equally suitable. The Swiss meringue topping is crisp on top with a soft marshmallow texture underneath.

PREPARATION TIME: *40 min.*
COOKING TIME: *25 min.*

INGREDIENTS *(for 4–6):*
1 lb. cultivated blackberries
4 oz. caster sugar
2 level dessertspoons cornflour
2 small egg yolks
2½ fluid oz. double cream
Lemon juice
4 oz. sponge fingers
MERINGUE TOPPING:
2 small egg whites
4 oz. icing sugar
2½ fluid oz. blackberry syrup

Hull* the blackberries and set aside a dozen large berries for decoration. Put the caster sugar and ½ pint of water in a pan over low heat until the sugar has dissolved to a syrup. Add the blackberries to the syrup and cook over very low heat for 10 minutes, or until tender but still whole. Drain the syrup into a measuring jug, and set the blackberries aside.

Put the cornflour into a small pan and gradually blend in ½ pint of the blackberry syrup; cook over low heat for 3–4 minutes, stirring constantly, until the mixture is clear and beginning to thicken. Remove from the heat.

Separate the eggs, setting the whites aside for the meringue. Beat together the yolks and cream and gradually stir this into the thick syrup mixture. Sharpen and sweeten to taste with lemon juice and caster sugar.

Cut one rounded end off each of the sponge fingers. Put a ½ in. layer of the blackberry cream in the base of a 1 pint soufflé dish. Stand the sponge fingers, cut edge downwards, closely round the inside of the dish to make a casing. Put a single layer of blackberries over the cream, followed by another layer of cream and so on, finishing with a layer of blackberry cream.

For the meringue topping, put the egg whites in a mixing bowl with the icing sugar and 2½ fluid oz. of blackberry syrup. Place the bowl over a pan of boiling water and whisk the mixture steadily until it stands in soft peaks. Remove the bowl from the pan and continue whisking until the meringue is cool. Swirl or pipe it over the blackberry cream.

Bake the Charlotte in the centre of a pre-heated oven at 300°F (mark 2) for 20 minutes or until the meringue topping is delicately coloured. Serve the dessert cold, decorated with the reserved fresh blackberries.

POIRES FLAMBÉES

This French recipe for pears in brandy is an ideal sweet to cook in a chafing dish at the table. Fresh firm peaches and apricots are also excellent cooked in this way.

PREPARATION TIME: *15 min.*
COOKING TIME: *10 min.*

INGREDIENTS *(for 4)*:
4 ripe firm dessert pears
4 pieces stem ginger
1 oz. unsalted butter
2 tablespoons brandy
1–2 tablespoons ginger syrup
2 tablespoons double cream

Peel the pears thinly, cut them in half and carefully scoop out the cores with a pointed teaspoon. Quarter each piece of stem ginger and set aside.

Heat the butter in a chafing dish, a shallow flameproof dish, or a frying pan over moderate heat. Fry the pears, cut side down, until golden brown. Turn the pears over and fry the other side. Fill a warmed tablespoon with brandy, set it alight and pour it over the pears. Repeat with the remaining brandy.

Arrange the pears on individual plates, placing two ginger pieces in each cavity. Add the ginger syrup and cream to the pan juices and stir over gentle heat until well blended and heated through. Spoon a little sauce over each portion and serve immediately.

APPLE AND ALMOND PARADISE PUDDING

The combination of creamed rice, fruit and crisp topping makes this pudding a great favourite with children. Pears or other autumn fruit can be used instead of apples.

PREPARATION TIME: *30 min.*
COOKING TIME: *35 min.*

INGREDIENTS *(for 4)*:
2 oz. long grain or pudding rice
¾ pint milk
¼ teaspoon vanilla essence
4–5 oz. caster sugar
1½ lb. cooking apples
3 fluid oz. double cream
3–4 rounded tablespoons apricot jam
TOPPING:
1 large egg white
2 level tablespoons ground almonds
2 level tablespoons caster sugar
2 tablespoons flaked almonds

Put the rice and milk in a heavy-based saucepan and bring slowly to simmering point. Cover with a lid, and cook over low heat for about 25 minutes or until the rice is cooked, but still slightly nutty in texture (pudding rice needs only about 15 minutes). Stir frequently during cooking to prevent sticking. Sweeten the rice to taste with vanilla essence and a little sugar. Leave to cool.

Peel, core and slice the apples. Put 4 oz. of sugar with ½ pint of water in a saucepan over low heat and stir until all the sugar has dissolved. Bring this syrup to simmering point, then add the apple slices. Cook gently for 5 minutes or until just tender and retaining their shape. Lift the slices carefully into a colander to drain and cool.

Whip the cream lightly and fold it into the cooled rice. Spread the apricot jam over the base of a shallow, 7 in. wide ovenproof dish or pie plate. Cover the jam with apple slices and spoon over creamed rice.

Beat the egg white for the topping until stiff. Mix together the ground almonds and caster sugar and fold in the egg white. Spoon this mixture over the rice and scatter the flaked almonds on top. Put the dish under a hot grill for a few minutes until the almonds are crisp and golden. Serve at once.

HAZEL NUT GANTOIS

A gantois, or Flemish pastry, consists of crunchy biscuits layered with fresh fruit and whipped cream. The pudding is topped with crisp golden caramel.

PREPARATION TIME: *1 hour*
CHILLING TIME: *30 min.*
COOKING TIME: *25–30 min.*

INGREDIENTS *(for 4–6)*:
4 oz. shelled hazel nuts
4½ oz. plain flour
2 oz. plus 1 level teaspoon caster sugar
3 oz. unsalted butter
1 lb. raspberries or 6–8 peaches
½ pint whipping cream
CARAMEL TOPPING:
3 oz. caster sugar

Put the hazel nuts in the grill pan and grill under medium heat, shaking the pan frequently, until the nuts are toasted. Rub them in a colander with a dry cloth to remove the skins. Weigh off 1 oz. of the nuts, chop them coarsely and set aside. Grind the remainder in a coffee mill or chop them very finely.

Sieve the flour into a mixing bowl and add the ground nuts and the sugar. Rub in the butter until the mixture resembles fine breadcrumbs, then knead lightly for a few minutes. Chill the dough in a refrigerator for at least 30 minutes, or until quite firm.

Meanwhile, pick over the raspberries and hull* them, or peel the peaches* and cut them into thin slices.

Shape the firm dough into a thick sausage, on a lightly floured board. Divide the dough into four equal pieces and roll each piece out to a 7 in. circle, about

⅛ in. thick. Lift the circles carefully on to greased baking trays. Bake in the centre of a pre-heated oven, at 350°F (mark 4) for 15 minutes or until the biscuits are golden brown and firm. Remove to a wire tray and leave to cool.

For the caramel topping, put 3 oz. sugar and 3 dessertspoons of water in a small pan over low heat. Stir until the sugar has completely dissolved. Turn up the heat and boil the syrup briskly, without stirring, until it is caramel-coloured.

Pour enough of the caramel over one biscuit circle to cover it, spreading it evenly with an oiled knife. Sprinkle the coarsely chopped nuts round the edge of the caramel-covered biscuit, and arrange a quarter of the raspberries or peach slices in the centre. Trickle over the remaining caramel or pull this into thin threads to make a spun sugar* veil on top of the biscuit.

Whip the cream and sweeten to taste with a little sugar. Assemble the cake by spreading the cream in equal layers over the remaining three biscuits; arrange the fruit evenly on each layer. Put the biscuits on top of each other, finishing with the caramel-topped biscuit. Serve at once.

QUICHE REINE-CLAUDE

Lorraine is the land of quiches and Alsace of guiches. Both are names for an open flan with a cream filling combined with sweet or savoury ingredients. This flan is filled with greengages (Reine-Claudes) and served with pâtisserie cream.

PREPARATION TIME: *40 min.*
COOKING TIME: *30 min.*

INGREDIENTS *(for 6)*:

1 flan case
½ lb. greengages
4 level tablespoons greengage jam
1 tablespoon lemon juice
¼ pint double cream

PÂTISSERIE CREAM:
2 eggs
2 oz. caster sugar
1 oz. plain flour
½ pint milk
½ teaspoon vanilla essence or 2 dessertspoons lemon juice

Bake or buy a 7 in. flan case, made from sweet shortcrust* or pâté sucré* pastry. Leave the baked flan to cool completely before assembling the sweet.

Make the pâtisserie cream next as this too should not be used until quite cold: put 1 whole egg and 1 egg yolk in a mixing bowl (set aside the remaining egg white). Whisk the sugar with the eggs until creamy and near white, then whisk the sifted flour into the eggs, and gradually add the milk. Pour the mixture into a small saucepan and bring to the boil, whisking continuously.

Simmer this custard-cream over very low heat for 2–3 minutes to cook the flour. Flavour to taste with vanilla essence or lemon juice and pour the cream into a shallow dish to cool. Stir from time to time to prevent a skin forming.

Spread the cold pâtisserie cream over the base of the flan case. Cut the greengages in half, remove the stones and arrange the fruit over the cream.

Put the greengage jam in a small, heavy-based pan, with 3 tablespoons of water and the lemon juice. Cook over low heat, stirring until the jam has dissolved and the mixture is clear. Increase the heat and boil rapidly to form a glaze*. Do not over-boil – the glaze is ready when it will coat the back of the spoon and falls off in heavy drops. Rub the glaze through a coarse sieve.

Spoon the glaze over the greengages, covering them completely; brush the top edge of the flan with the remaining glaze to give a smooth finish. Set the flan in a cool place until the glaze has set.

Just before serving, whip the remaining egg white until stiff, but still moist. Whip the cream into soft peaks and fold in the white; sweeten to taste with a little sugar and serve in a separate bowl to accompany the quiche.

Savouries & Snacks

CRUSTADES WITH CREAM SAUCE FILLING

Crisp bread cases are quick to prepare and make good substitutes for pastry cases and vol-au-vents.

PREPARATION TIME: *20 min.*
COOKING TIME: *15 min.*

INGREDIENTS *(for 4)*:
16 thin slices white bread
3–4 tablespoons olive oil
6 oz. cooked ham or poultry (minced)
1 small, finely chopped onion
½ oz. butter
2 oz. cooked, diced vegetables
¼ pint white sauce
Salt and black pepper

Cut circles from the bread slices with a 3 in. pastry cutter; brush them on both sides with olive oil and press them into deep patty or castle-pudding tins. Bake in the centre of the oven pre-heated to 400°F (mark 6) for 8–10 minutes or until crisp and golden brown. Remove from the tins and set aside to cool.

Fry the onion in the butter until soft, then add the meat and vegetables.

Season the white sauce* with salt and pepper. Stir in the vegetables and meat, and spoon the mixture into the crustades. Bake in a pre-heated oven at 375°F (mark 5) for 5 minutes.

Serve the hot crustades on their own as a starter, or with vegetables as a main course.

CHICKEN SALAD

Left-over chicken and potato form the basis for this substantial lunch or supper.

PREPARATION TIME: *25 min.*
CHILLING TIME: *30 min.*

INGREDIENTS *(for 4)*:
4–6 oz. cooked, diced chicken
2 cooked, diced potatoes
½ small, peeled and diced cucumber
2 thinly sliced spring onions
2 sticks chopped celery
¼ pint French dressing
1 crushed clove garlic
1 level teaspoon paprika
1 small lettuce
4 hardboiled eggs
2 tablespoons mayonnaise
2 tablespoons tomato ketchup

Put the chicken, potatoes, cucumber, onions and celery in a bowl. Pour over the French dressing*, to which has been added the garlic and paprika. Toss the salad ingredients well.

Arrange the cleaned lettuce leaves on a large flat serving dish and pile the salad in the centre. Halve the eggs lengthways and arrange them around the chicken. Mix the tomato ketchup and mayonnaise* together and pipe or spoon over the eggs. Chill the salad for at least 30 minutes.

EGG COCKTAIL

This quickly made starter is also excellent as a sandwich filling.

PREPARATION TIME: *20 min.*
COOKING TIME: *8 min.*

INGREDIENTS *(for 4–6)*:
5 hardboiled eggs
½ pint mayonnaise
1 teaspoon grated onion
1 tablespoon chopped green pepper
1 tablespoon tomato ketchup
1 tablespoon double cream
Salt and black pepper
2 chopped spring onions
6 black olives, stoned and chopped
3 shredded lettuce leaves
GARNISH:
Lemon slices

Mix the mayonnaise*, onion, green pepper, tomato ketchup and cream together; season with salt and pepper. Fold in the roughly chopped eggs, spring onions and olives.

Arrange the lettuce shreds in individual serving glasses and pile the egg mixture on top. Garnish each with a thin lemon slice and serve with brown bread and butter or hot buttered toast.

For a sandwich filling, the shredded lettuce can be mixed into the egg cocktail and spread thickly on bread.

VEGETABLE AND CHEESE SOUFFLÉ

Cooked vegetables are incorporated into a cheese soufflé to make this light supper dish.

PREPARATION TIME: *20 min.*
COOKING TIME: *25–30 min.*

INGREDIENTS *(for 4)*:
4 oz. cooked, diced vegetables
1½ oz. unsalted butter
1 level tablespoon plain flour
¼ pint milk
3 eggs
2 oz. grated Cheddar cheese
Salt and cayenne pepper

Melt 1 oz. of the butter over moderate heat. Blend in the flour, and cook the roux* over low heat for 1 minute. Gradually add the milk, stirring continuously until the sauce thickens.

Separate the eggs, and beat the yolks, one at a time, into the sauce. Stir in the vegetables and cheese, and season with salt and cayenne. Whip the egg whites until stiff, but not dry, and fold them carefully into the sauce.

Turn the mixture into a buttered 1½–2 pint soufflé dish and bake in the centre of a pre-heated oven, at 375°F (mark 5) for 25–30 minutes, or until well risen.

Stuffed peppers or marrow rings (see September vegetables) go well with this soufflé.

FRUITY RICE PUDDING

Creamed rice mixed with fruit and with a toffee-like topping is the kind of nursery pudding that is an instant success with the family.

PREPARATION TIME: *5 min.*
COOKING TIME: *10 min.*

INGREDIENTS *(for 4)*:
15–16 oz. tin creamed rice
15–16 oz. tin fruit cocktail
5 level dessertspoons soft brown sugar
¼ pint single cream (optional)

Heat the creamed rice in a saucepan and mix in the drained fruit cocktail. Spoon the mixture into a warmed flameproof serving dish and top with the sugar.

Place the pudding under a hot grill until the sugar has melted and is bubbling. Leave to cool a little before serving with a jug of cream.

Summer Barbecues

Barbecues – or as the Americans more aptly call them 'cook-outs' – are becoming more popular in Britain. Barbecue units range from an inexpensive, do-it-yourself brickbuilt feature with a simple grill welded over a metal brazier tray, to more elaborate affairs with electrically operated rotating spits. The latter often come equipped with warming ovens, attached working surfaces and usually with detachable hoods.

Free-standing barbecue units are adjustable and either circular or rectangular. The necessary fuel is charcoal, which is available in lumps or briquettes. Pile the charcoal in a 1 in. deep layer over crumpled paper in the centre of the fire basket, pour over an eggcup full of methylated spirit, and set it alight. Leave the fire to burn steadily for about 20 minutes. Rake out the coals in an even layer over the basket, cover with more charcoal and let it burn for 20–35 minutes, depending on the strength of the wind. A steady-burning charcoal fire is essential for barbecue cooking; it is ready when it looks ash-grey by daylight and glows red in the dark; do not allow it to burn fiercely enough to burst into flame.

Although the temperature of the fire cannot be adjusted, most barbecue units have grills and/or fire baskets that can be lowered or raised according to the amount of heat needed for cooking. Keep extra coals round the edge of the fire basket to push into the centre when needed. Always keep a bottle of water handy to sprinkle over flare-ups – enough to douse any flames, but not to extinguish the fire.

Fire-tongs to move coal to or from the centre of the fire bed are necessary; so too is a rake to clear the dead ashes, and bellows to encourage a dying fire.

Before planning a barbecue party, master the art of cook-outs: how to build up a fire, and how to maintain and control the heat. Learn, by experience, the approximate time for cooking various foods and the amount of food that can be cooked in reasonable time.

Prepare the food in advance and set it out on a table next to the barbecue with several pairs of tongs for turning and lifting out the grilled food. Kebabs are probably the most popular recipe for out-door cooking: small pieces of meat, vegetables and fruit threaded on 6 in. to 12 in. long metal skewers.

Meats and poultry should be marinated* before grilling. Trim off all fat before grilling, or the fat will drip on to the coals and cause flare-ups. Have ready a devil or marinating sauce, with brushes, and for extra aroma throw sprigs of thyme and/or rosemary on the coals.

Grilled corn cobs

Insert short skewers at both ends of the cleaned cobs, brush with melted butter or oil and grill for about 10 minutes, turning once or twice and basting often.

Danish scampi

Wrap large peeled prawns in stretched rashers of lean back bacon; thread three or four on each skewer. Baste with barbecue sauce and grill for about 10 minutes, turning the skewers from time to time.

Small chickens, corn cobs and kebabs can all be grilled at the same time. Skewered duck, whole trout and hamburgers are ready for grilling

Fish

It is not always easy to cook fish outdoors as the flesh quickly disintegrates over heat. But firm fish, such as flounder, cut into steaks or fillets, are excellent grilled. Marinate the fish for about 1 hour in white wine, with the juice of a lemon, 1 finely chopped onion and a little powdered cloves and cinnamon. Cook straight on the grill for 10–15 minutes, turning once. Sprats or sardines can also be marinated, threaded on skewers and grilled for about 10 minutes.

Small trout and mackerel, thoroughly cleaned and dried, may be grilled whole. They should be marinated for 1 hour in a dressing consisting of 4 fluid oz. dry white wine, 4 tablespoons olive oil, 2 peeled and crushed garlic cloves, 2 level teaspoons crushed rosemary, thyme or marjoram, 2 level tablespoons chopped parsley, $\frac{1}{4}$ level teaspoon ground black pepper.

Make three or four slits in the skin of each marinated fish, sprinkle them with fresh dill, fennel or thyme, and wrap them in individual foil parcels. Cook at the edge of the grill for about 30 minutes.

Meat

Any lean, not-too-thick cuts of meat will grill well on a barbecue. Beefburgers, pork sausages rolled in lean back rashers of bacon, trimmed lamb and pork cutlets, and steaks should all be marinated for at least 1 hour. Brush the meat with oil and turn it once only during grilling.

Allow 10 minutes for well-done steaks and burgers, and 15 minutes for sausages and cutlets. Baste with barbecue sauce.

Meat marinade

Put the following ingredients into a screw-top jar: 2 tablespoons olive oil, 2 tablespoons lemon juice, 2 tablespoons tomato juice, 2 tablespoons dry white wine, 2 teaspoons Worcestershire sauce, 2 teaspoons soy sauce. Shake the ingredients thoroughly and pour over the meat.

Barbecue sauce

In a large bowl, blend together 1 level teaspoon chilli powder, 1 level teaspoon celery salt, 2 tablespoons soft brown sugar, 2 tablespoons wine or tarragon vinegar, 2 tablespoons Worcestershire sauce, 3 level tablespoons tomato ketchup, $\frac{1}{4}$ pint beef stock or water, Tabasco sauce to taste.

Kebabs

These can be any combination of meat and vegetables, interspersed with firm fruit. Cut all ingredients into 1 in. cubes and thread on long skewers, allowing two per person. Slices of lean leg of lamb, lean rump steak, lamb kidneys, cocktail sausages or chipolatas, button mushrooms and onions, squares of red or green pepper, fresh bay leaves, sprigs of rosemary and slices of blanched courgettes are all suitable. Tiny firm tomatoes can be threaded at the end of the skewers where they will receive least heat. Cubes of fresh or tinned pineapple, fresh firm apricots, peaches and crisp apples also grill well. Prepare the kebabs in advance and marinate for at least 1 hour.

Grill the kebabs for 15–20 minutes, turning them once and brushing with barbecue sauce.

Poultry

If the barbecue has a rotating spit, small chickens can be threaded on to the spit, thoroughly brushed with oil and left to cook for about 2 hours. Baste frequently with devil sauce. Marinate poultry portions in meat marinade and grill for 25 minutes.

Devil sauce

Mix together 1 level teaspoon dry mustard with 1 level teaspoon ground ginger and 2 level tablespoons caster sugar. Rub this over the poultry and leave for 30 minutes. For basting, blend 2 tablespoons oil with 2 tablespoons soy sauce, 2 tablespoons fruit sauce, 1 tablespoon Worcestershire sauce, 2 level tablespoons tomato ketchup, juice of a small orange and a dash of Tabasco.

Duck sangrila

Joint one duck into eight portions and steep in a meat marinade. Thread one duck joint on a large skewer with thick slices of orange and onion, interspersed with button mushrooms. Cubes of pineapple may also be added to the skewers. Brush with olive oil and sprinkle with salt and ground pepper. Grill for 35–40 minutes over hot coals or on the spit.

Vegetables

As most vegetables have a high water content, they do not grill well. Potatoes, however, are an exception. Clean large potatoes, rub them with salt and wrap them tightly in foil parcels. Cook at the edges of the grill for about 50 minutes, turning once, or for 20 minutes in the fire basket among the charcoal. Serve with butter or soured cream.

Sweets

A fresh fruit salad, thoroughly chilled, with a bowl of chilled soured cream, makes a refreshing finish to a grilled meal. But if guests and hosts have not tired of barbecue cooking, try grilled bananas. Slice slightly under-ripe bananas in half (retaining the skins), spread a little honey on each half, sprinkle with lemon juice and soft brown sugar. Sandwich the bananas together again and put them back in the skins. Grill for 5–8 minutes and serve with vanilla ice cream.

Firm peaches, peeled and halved, can be grilled for a few minutes at the edges of the grill. Sprinkle with soft brown sugar and serve them with sweetened cream or ice cream.

Grapefruit halves can be sprinkled with soft brown sugar and a few drops of Cointreau. Pipe stiffly beaten egg whites on top and grill over hot coals.

With outdoor grills, serve salads such as tomatoes with onion rings, chicory or cos lettuce with watercress and avocado pear, and diced apple and celery

October

By noone see your dinner, be readie and neate,
let meate tarrie servant, not servant his meate.

This Month's Recipes

*A feast of pheasants, served with game chips, roasted chestnuts and bread
sauce, makes a sumptuous main course for a special October occasion*

Food in Season

Despite the onset of the first frosts, fresh fruit and vegetables are still abundant. English apples and pears are at their best and though plums are at the end of their season, their passing is compensated by the arrival of the first fresh figs from the Mediterranean. Imported grapes are a good buy at this time, and cob and hazel nuts are making their first appearances in the shops.

The first scallops, too, are arriving at the fishmongers, but the most economical fish of the month is probably the plump autumn herring. October 1 sees the opening of pheasant shooting, but the early birds are extremely expensive. Partridge, which have been in season for a month, and grouse, are both cheaper, though if there is any doubt about the ages of these birds, they should be stewed or casseroled; only younger game is suitable for roasting. Furred game, such as hare, is sold at reasonable prices, and makes a change for Sunday lunch.

Fish

Angler tail
Bass
Bream, sea
Brill
Carp
Clams
Cockles
Cod
Coley
Conger eels
Crab
Dabs
Dover sole
Dublin Bay prawns
Eels
Flake (also sold as
   rock salmon)
Freshwater bream
Grey mullet
Haddock
Hake
Halibut
Herrings
Lemon sole
Lobster
Mackerel
Mock halibut (or
   Greenland halibut)
Mussels
Oysters (native)
Oysters, Portuguese
Pike
Plaice
Prawns
Redfish
Scad
Scallops
Shrimps
Skate
Sprats
Trout, rainbow
Turbot
Whiting
Winkles
Witch

Poultry & Game

Chicken
Duck
Goose
Grouse
Guinea fowl
Hare
Mallard
Partridge
Pheasant
Pigeon
Quail
Rabbit
Snipe
Teal
Turkey
Venison
Wild duck
Wild goose
Woodcock

Vegetables

Asparagus
Aubergines
Avocado pears
Beetroots
Broccoli
Brussels sprouts
Brussels tops
Cabbages
Carrots
Cauliflowers
Celeriac
Celery
Chicory
Corn on the cob
Courgettes
Cucumbers
Endive
French beans
Fennel
Garlic
Globe artichokes
Horseradish
Jerusalem artichokes
Leeks
Lettuce
Mushrooms
Onions
Parsley
Parsnips
Peas
Peppers
Potatoes
Pumpkins
Radishes
Runner beans
Salad cress
Salsify
Shallots
Spinach
Spring onions
Swedes
Sweet potatoes
Tomatoes
Turnips
Vegetable marrows
Watercress

Fruit

Apples
Bananas
Blackberries
Blueberries
Chestnuts
Chinese gooseberries
Cranberries
Coconuts
Damsons
Dates
Figs
Filberts
Grapefruit
Grapes
Lemons
Loquats
Medlars
Melons
Nectarines
Oranges
Pawpaws
Pears
Plums
Pineapples
Pomegranates
Quinces
Satsumas
Strawberries
Walnuts

SUGGESTED MENUS

Avocado Pear and Nut Salad
Hock with Cider and Raisins
Chick Pea Patties
Baked Cabbage
Delices de Poires au Chocolat

Mexican Hot Pot Soup
Finnan Filled Pancakes
Calabrese with Poulette Sauce
Fresh Fruit

Honeydew Cups
Faisan au Verger
Scalloped Potatoes
Shoo Fly Pie

Coquilles en Brochette
Veal Rolls with Frittata Filling
Baked Marrow
Duchesse Potatoes
Hungarian Hazelnut Torte

Spare Ribs of Pork in Cider
Westphalian Beans and Pears
Queen of Puddings

Rillettes of Pork
Carré D'Agneau Dordonnaise
Turkish Fried Carrots
Damson and Apple Tansy

Rigatoni with Hare Sauce
Tossed Green Salad
Fresh Figs and Yoghourt

Soups & Starters

AVOCADO PEAR AND NUT SALAD

Avocado and dessert pears discolour quickly when peeled. For this salad it is essential to mix the dressing first and sprinkle the diced pears generously with lemon juice before blending them quickly into the dressing.

PREPARATION TIME: *15 min.*
CHILLING TIME: *1 hour*

INGREDIENTS *(for 6)* :
3 avocado pears
7½ fluid oz. soured cream
2 teaspoons tarragon vinegar
Salt and black pepper
French mustard or Worcestershire sauce
Caster sugar
Juice of a lemon
1 large or 2 small dessert pears
3 tablespoons salted almonds or peanuts
GARNISH:
Chopped chives

Put the soured cream in a mixing bowl and stir in the vinegar. Season to taste with salt, freshly ground pepper, mustard or Worcestershire sauce and a little sugar. Mix thoroughly.

Cut the avocado pears in half, remove the stones and carefully scoop out the flesh with a small silver teaspoon. Leave a narrow inner lining of flesh on the avocado shells and set them aside. Cut the flesh into dice and put them in a bowl. Sprinkle with lemon juice. Peel, core and dice the dessert pear, add to the avocado and sprinkle with the remaining lemon juice.

Chop the salted almonds roughly and set a little aside for garnishing. Mix the remainder with the avocado and pears. Pour over the dressing and blend thoroughly. Pile the salad into the avocado shells and wrap each half in foil. Chill for 1 hour.

Just before serving, unwrap the avocado shells, arrange them on small plates and garnish with the chopped almonds and chives.

GAME SOUP WITH PORT WINE

This is a rich, sustaining soup for cold autumn days. It can be made from neck of venison or from any game bird, such as pheasant, partridge or grouse, that is too tough for roasting or grilling.

PREPARATION TIME: *55 min.*
COOKING TIME: *2½–3 hours*

INGREDIENTS *(for 6)* :
1 lb. venison or a 2 lb. game bird
1 large onion
1 parsnip or turnip
1 carrot
1 leek
3 sticks celery
½ lb. mushrooms
4 oz. butter
1 bay leaf
Thyme, marjoram and basil
Salt and black pepper
1–2 cloves garlic
2 oz. plain flour
5 fluid oz. port or burgundy
GARNISH:
Bread croûtons

Cut the venison into 2–3 in. chunks, trimming off any gristle. If a game bird is being used, chop it, through the bone, into small portions; clean thoroughly. Peel and roughly chop the onion, parsnip and carrot. Wash all dirt off the leek and celery under cold running water and chop them roughly as well. Trim and thinly slice the mushrooms*.

Melt half the butter in a large pan over moderate heat and fry the meat, turning it frequently, until it begins to colour. Add the onion, leek and celery to the pan and brown it evenly. Put the parsnip, carrot and bay leaf, together with a pinch of thyme, marjoram and basil into the pan. Season with salt, freshly ground pepper and the crushed garlic. Pour in about 3 pints of water, or sufficient to cover the contents in the pan; bring to the boil over high heat.

Remove any scum which rises on the surface, then add the mushrooms. Cover the pan with a lid and simmer over low heat for about 2 hours or until the meat is perfectly tender.

Strain the stock through a fine sieve and leave to cool slightly. Remove the bay leaf and all bones, then put the meat and vegetables in the liquidiser with a little of the soup, to make a thick purée*.

Melt the remaining butter in a large, clean pan over moderate heat; blend in the flour and cook, stirring continuously, until the roux* is caramel coloured. Take the pan off the heat and gradually blend in the port and about ½ pint of stock. Return the pan to the heat, bring to simmering point, stirring all the time, then blend in the meat and vegetable purée and about 1½ pints of stock to make a thick soup. Heat the soup through over low heat for about 15 minutes and correct seasoning if necessary.

Serve the soup in individual bowls, garnished with small bread croûtons*.

MEXICAN HOT POT SOUP

This is the kind of winter soup which is a meal in itself. The ingredients include red kidney beans and chick peas which can be bought tinned or dried. Dried beans should be soaked overnight.

PREPARATION TIME: *10 min.*
COOKING TIME: *45 min.*

INGREDIENTS *(for 4)* :
1 large onion
1 green or red pepper
2 oz. bacon fat or butter
½ lb. minced beef
15–16 oz. tinned tomatoes
14 oz. tinned or dried red kidney beans
8 oz. tinned or dried chick peas
¾ pint stock or bouillon
½ level teaspoon chilli powder
Salt
GARNISH:
Lettuce

Peel and finely chop the onion; cut off the stalk base of the pepper, remove the seeds and chop the pepper finely. Melt the fat in a large heavy-based pan, and fry the onion until it begins to colour. Add the meat and continue frying over medium heat until it is well browned.

Add the tomatoes with their juice, the drained or soaked beans, chick peas and chopped pepper. Stir in the stock or bouillon, mixing thoroughly. Season to taste with chilli powder and a little salt. Cover the pan, and simmer the soup for 30 minutes. Allow to cool, then put through a liquidiser or rub it through a coarse sieve.

Reheat the thick soup before serving. Garnish with finely shredded lettuce and serve with hot garlic bread: cut a white crusty loaf into thick slices and spread each with garlic butter*. Put the slices back to the original loaf form, wrap it in foil and heat in the oven for about 10 minutes, at 350°F (mark 4).

RILLETTES OF PORK

In France, most country towns have their own versions of rillettes – a coarse-textured terrine of pork and pork fat. It makes a pleasant change from smooth pâtés and is inexpensive to make.

PREPARATION TIME: *30 min.*
COOKING TIME: *4 hours*

INGREDIENTS *(for 6)*:
2 lb. belly pork
¾ lb. pork fat
Salt and black pepper
1 clove garlic
1 bay leaf
1 sprig parsley
1 sprig thyme or rosemary

Order the belly pork boned and with the rind taken off. Wipe the meat with a damp cloth and cut it into narrow strips. Dice the pork fat finely and season the meat and fat with salt, freshly ground pepper and the peeled crushed garlic. Pack the meat and fat into a casserole or terrine. Push the herbs down into the centre of the meat and pour about ¼ pint of water over it. Cover the casserole with a lid or foil.

Bake for 4 hours in the centre of the oven pre-heated to 275°F (mark 1). Stir the contents of the casserole occasionally to prevent a crusty top forming. When the meat is tender, turn the contents

of the casserole into a sieve placed over a mixing bowl; leave until the fat has dripped through the sieve and into the bowl. Remove the herbs and shred the meat with two forks or put it in a liquidiser for a few moments to make a coarse purée*. Adjust seasoning if necessary.

Pack the meat into one large earthenware pot, or several small ones. Pour enough liquid fat over the jar to cover the meat by ¼ in. Leave in a refrigerator until the fat on the surface has set solid.

Serve the terrine with crusty French bread for a first course and with a watercress salad for a cold snack.

HONEYDEW CUPS

A well-chilled melon salad is a good choice before a rich main course. Honeydew or cantaloupe melons are the least expensive, but for a special occasion, choose three small Ogen or Charantais melons.

PREPARATION TIME: *40 min.*
CHILLING TIME: *1 hour*

INGREDIENTS *(for 6)*:
1 honeydew or cantaloupe melon
1 cucumber
Salt and black pepper
6 tomatoes
DRESSING:
1–2 level tablespoons caster sugar
3 tablespoons lemon juice or
tarragon vinegar
6 tablespoons salad oil
GARNISH:
1 dessertspoon each, chopped mint,
chives, and chervil or parsley

Peel the cucumber and cut it into ½ in. dice; sprinkle with salt and leave to stand for 30 minutes. Cut the melon in half, crossways, and remove the seeds. Carefully scoop out the flesh in small balls, or cut it into small wedges. Skin the tomatoes*, cut them in half and remove cores and seeds. Chop the tomato flesh roughly.

Mix the ingredients for the dressing, adding the oil last of all. Rinse the cucumber in cold water and pat dry on absorbent kitchen paper.

Put the melon, tomato and cucumber in a large bowl, pour over the dressing and mix well. Chill the salad in the refrigerator for at least 1 hour, stirring occasionally.

Serve the salad in individual glass bowls and sprinkle with the mixed chopped herbs.

FISH MOUSSE WITH BERCY SAUCE

This mousse is prepared like a soufflé, but as it is steamed in the oven instead of being baked, it can be kept waiting for tardy guests without collapsing. It is here served as a main course with a classic Bercy Sauce, but can also be served in small individual moulds as a first course.

PREPARATION TIME: *30 min.*
COOKING TIME: *1½ hours*

INGREDIENTS *(for 4–6)*:
1 lb. haddock or cod fillets
1½ pints court bouillon
1 oz. butter
1 oz. plain flour
2½ fluid oz. milk
2 eggs
2½ fluid oz. double cream
2 rounded dessertspoons chopped
parsley
1–2 teaspoons anchovy essence
Lemon juice
Salt and black pepper
3–4 tablespoons
breadcrumbs
BERCY SAUCE:
1 small onion
2 oz. unsalted butter
¼ pint dry white wine or cider
½ pint fish stock
2 level dessertspoons plain flour
2½ fluid oz. double cream
Salt and black pepper
GARNISH:
Lemon slices
Parsley sprigs

Wash the fish carefully and bring the court bouillon* to the boil. Simmer the fish, uncovered, over low heat in the bouillon for 8–10 minutes or until tender. Lift the fish out with a perforated spoon and set the liquid aside. Remove skin and any bones from the fish and flake* it finely into a bowl. Mash it with a fork or make it into a coarse purée* in the liquidiser.

Melt the butter in a saucepan over moderate heat, stir in the flour and cook this roux* for 2 minutes, without colouring. Make the milk up to $\frac{1}{4}$ pint with the fish liquid, and gradually blend this into the roux to make a thick white sauce*. Cook the sauce for 3–5 minutes, stirring continuously and adding a little more fish liquid if the sauce gets too thick. Mix in the fish purée. Separate the eggs, and beat the yolks with the cream; add them to the fish mixture, together with the parsley. Season to taste with anchovy essence, lemon juice, salt and freshly ground pepper.

Whisk the egg whites in a bowl until stiff, but still moist. Fold them into the fish mixture. Toast the breadcrumbs on a baking tray in a warm oven and meanwhile brush a 1 pint Charlotte mould or cake tin with oil and line it evenly with the toasted crumbs.

Spoon the fish mixture into the mould – it should three-quarters fill it. Cover the top with a piece of buttered kitchen foil and place the mould in a roasting tin with $\frac{1}{2}$ in. of water in the bottom. Bake in the centre of a pre-heated oven at 325°F (mark 3), for 1–1$\frac{1}{4}$ hours or until the mousse is well risen and set.

About 30 minutes before the mousse is ready, prepare the sauce. Peel the onion and chop it finely. Fry it over low heat in half the butter until soft, then add the wine and fish stock. Increase the heat and rapidly boil the liquid, uncovered, until it has reduced* by half. Knead the flour with the remaining butter to a

beurre manié*, shape it into small knobs and drop them, one at a time, into the liquid. Stir this sauce over gentle heat until it thickens, then stir in the cream. Do not let the sauce reach boiling point or it will curdle and separate. Season to taste with salt and freshly ground pepper.

Unmould the mousse on to a warm serving dish and garnish with lemon slices and sprigs of parsley. The sauce can be poured over the mousse or into a separate sauce boat. Buttered spinach or broccoli spears au gratin (see January vegetables) would be suitable vegetables with the mousse.

DEVILLED CRAB

Devilled dishes first appeared on English menus early in the 19th century. The main ingredient, which may be meat, poultry or fish, is cooked in a sharp hot sauce, topped with breadcrumbs and finished off under the grill or in the oven.

PREPARATION TIME: *20 min.*
COOKING TIME: *5–10 min.*

INGREDIENTS *(for 4)*:
2 medium-sized crabs
5 fluid oz. double cream
1 level teaspoon French mustard
1–2 teaspoons anchovy essence
1 teaspoon Worcestershire sauce
1–2 dessertspoons lemon juice
Pinch cayenne pepper
Salt and black pepper
1 tablespoon oil
2 rounded tablespoons toasted
    breadcrumbs
2 level tablespoons grated
    Cheddar cheese
GARNISH:
Watercress
Lemon wedges

Twist the large claws and the legs off the crabs* and extract all the meat. Remove any white meat and all the brown meat from the shells; flake* all the white meat into a bowl and stir in the soft brown crabmeat.

Mix the cream, mustard, anchovy essence and Worcestershire sauce together in a saucepan. Season to taste with lemon juice, cayenne, salt and freshly ground pepper. Stir all the crabmeat into the cream and heat the mixture through over moderate heat without boiling.

With a knife handle, tap sharply round the line on the thin undershell of each crab. Remove the loose pieces. Scrub the shells thoroughly in cold water, dry them and brush, inside and out, with a little oil. Spoon the crab mixture into the shells, and cover with a topping of breadcrumbs and grated cheese. Put the shells on a baking tray, in the centre of a pre-heated oven at 400°F (mark 6), or under a hot grill, until the cheese is brown and bubbly on top.

Arrange the crabs in their shells on a bed of watercress, and garnish with lemon wedges. Thin, buttered brown bread is traditional with crab and is sufficient for a first course.

For a main course, put halved and skinned tomatoes* under a hot grill for a few minutes, together with trimmed mushroom caps. Serve the tomatoes and mushrooms as a side dish with the hot crab.

FINNAN FILLED PANCAKES

Cured haddock from Findon in Kincardineshire, known as Finnan Haddie, is cleaned and split before being smoked. This dish can be served as a main course, allowing two pancakes per person, or as a first course when one will be enough.

PREPARATION TIME: *20 min.*
COOKING TIME: *30 min.*

INGREDIENTS *(for 4)*:
$\frac{1}{2}$ lb. cooked smoked finnan
    haddock fillet
$\frac{1}{2}$ pint pancake batter
1 small onion
2 tablespoons chopped celery
4 oz. mushrooms
3$\frac{1}{2}$ oz. unsalted butter
15–16 oz. tinned tomatoes
Caster sugar, salt and black
    pepper
Lemon juice
3–4 tablespoons grated Cheddar
    or Gruyère cheese
GARNISH:
Lemon wedges
Parsley sprigs

Make eight small thin pancakes* from the batter and set them aside. Peel and finely chop the onion, and prepare the celery. Trim and thinly slice the mushrooms*.

Melt 1$\frac{1}{2}$ oz. of the butter and fry the onion, celery and mushrooms until soft. Add the tomatoes, and season with sugar, salt and freshly ground pepper. Simmer the contents of the pan, uncovered, until it has reduced* to a thick purée*.

Meanwhile, remove the skin from the haddock, and flake* the flesh. Add the haddock to the onion and tomato mixture, sharpen to taste with lemon juice and adjust seasoning.

Spoon 2 tablespoons of the filling down the centre of each pancake and fold the sides over to form an envelope. Arrange the stuffed pancakes side by side in a shallow flameproof dish. Melt the remaining butter and pour it over the pancakes. Sprinkle generously with grated cheese and set the dish under a hot, pre-heated grill or in the oven until the cheese is bubbly brown.

Garnish the pancakes with lemon wedges and parsley sprigs and serve with buttered peas.

Meat

COQUILLES EN BROCHETTE

The season for fresh scallops begins this month. They are often served in a cream sauce, but in this French recipe they are skewered and grilled with bacon and peppers. Allow three or four scallops per skewer, and two skewers per person for a main course, one for a first course.

PREPARATION TIME: *25 min.*
COOKING TIME: *15–20 min.*

INGREDIENTS (*for 2–4*):
12 scallops
2 shallots
¼ pint dry white wine
1 parsley sprig
Salt and black pepper
1 egg
2 tablespoons fresh white bread-crumbs
½ lb. thin rashers green streaky bacon
2 green peppers
16 mushroom caps
2 tablespoons oil
GARNISH:
Fresh bay leaves

Slide the scallops* from the flat shells and remove the gills and black threads. Peel the shallots and cut them in half. Put the scallops in a saucepan with the shallots and parsley, a little salt and freshly ground pepper; add sufficient wine to cover. Poach* the scallops over gentle heat for about 7 minutes or until tender.

Lift out the scallops, cut out the orange-coloured roes and coat them in the lightly beaten egg and the breadcrumbs. Set aside. Cut each white scallop part in half horizontally. Remove the rind from the bacon, stretch the rashers with the blade of a knife

and cut each into three. Wrap a piece of bacon around each white scallop portion.

Remove the stalk ends and seeds from the peppers, wash and dry them, then cut them into 1 in. wedges. Wash or trim the mushrooms*, leaving them whole. Thread the scallops (the coated roes and the bacon-wrapped white pieces) on to skewers, alternating with the pepper squares and the mushroom caps.

Brush the skewers with oil and put them under a hot, pre-heated grill. Cook for 8–10 minutes, turning the skewers several times to grill evenly.

Arrange the skewers on a bed of plain or saffron-coloured rice garnished with fresh bay leaves. A bowl of remoulade* or tartare sauce* would go well with the scallops.

KIDNEYS IN SAUCE CREOLE

Sauce Creole, the classic sauce of the West Indies, is composed mainly of sweet peppers, tomatoes and fiery Tabasco sauce – which is hotter than sweet chilli sauce. It is usually served as a garnish with rice.

PREPARATION TIME: *15 min.*
COOKING TIME: *15–20 min.*

INGREDIENTS (*for 4–6*):
1¼ lb. calf or pig kidneys
1 small onion
15–16 oz. tinned tomatoes
1 clove garlic
1 small green pepper
1 dessertspoon capers
2 oz. unsalted butter or 2 tablespoons olive oil
1 level teaspoon soft brown sugar
1 level tablespoon tomato chutney
Salt
Tabasco or chilli sauce
Lemon juice
6–8 black olives

Skin the kidneys* and cut them into thin slices. Snip out the white cores with scissors. Peel and thinly slice the onion. Peel the garlic. Wash the pepper, remove the stalk and the seeds and chop the flesh. Chop the capers.

Heat the butter, or oil, in a heavy-based pan and cook the onion over moderate heat until soft and transparent. Turn up the heat, add the sliced kidneys and fry them for 3–4 minutes or until browned, stirring frequently.

Crush the garlic into the pan and add the chopped tomatoes with their juices, the pepper and capers. Stir in the sugar and tomato chutney, and season to taste with salt, Tabasco or chilli sauce and lemon juice.

Cover the pan with a lid or foil and simmer over low heat for 10–15 minutes. Meanwhile, halve and stone the olives and add them to the kidneys.

Spoon the kidneys and the sauce over ribbon noodles tossed in butter. A crisp green salad could be served as a side dish.

SPARE RIBS OF PORK IN CIDER

With the onset of cool autumn weather, casseroles give a warm and welcoming glow to the evening meal. Lean spare ribs or shoulder chops of pork are ideal for this easily prepared dish; veal chops may also be cooked in the same way.

PREPARATION TIME: *30 min.*
COOKING TIME: *45 min.*

INGREDIENTS *(for 6)* :
6 spare rib chops
½ lb. mushrooms
1 large onion
3 oz. butter
1 level teaspoon dried savory
Salt and black pepper
¼–⅓ pint dry cider
4–6 oz. Cheddar cheese
6 tablespoons toasted breadcrumbs

GARNISH:
Parsley sprigs

Wipe and trim the mushrooms*, set six or seven caps aside and slice the remainder thinly. Peel the onion and chop it finely. Grease a shallow ovenproof dish with a little of the butter and arrange the sliced mushrooms over the base. Scatter the onion and savory over the mushrooms, and season with salt and pepper.

Trim most of the fat off the chops and lay them on top of the vegetables. Pour over enough cider to come just level with the meat, and push the mushroom caps, dark side uppermost, between the chops.

Grate the cheese and mix it with the breadcrumbs. Spread this mixture evenly over the chops and the mushroom caps, and dot with the remaining butter. Bake in the centre of a pre-heated oven at 400°F (mark 6) for 45 minutes, or until the chops are tender and the topping crisp and brown.

Serve the spare ribs straight from the dish, and garnish each mushroom cap with a small sprig of parsley. Runner beans and jacket potatoes dressed with soured cream and chopped chives go well with this dish.

CARRÉ D'AGNEAU DORDONNAISE

Walnuts and liver pâté are an integral part of many dishes from the Dordogne region of France. They are both used in this recipe, which transforms best end of lamb into a party dish.

PREPARATION TIME: *30 min.*
COOKING TIME: *1¼ hours*

INGREDIENTS *(for 4–6)* :
2 best end necks of lamb
2–3 oz. shelled walnuts
½ small onion
4 oz. pâté de foie truffé
4 tablespoons fresh white bread-crumbs
2 tablespoons finely chopped parsley
Salt and black pepper
Lemon juice
2 tablespoons cooking oil
4 fluid oz. dry white wine
1 level teaspoon powdered rose-mary

Order the best ends skinned and boned and ask the butcher to include the bones with the order. Trim any excess fat off the meat before wiping it with a damp cloth. Chop the walnuts finely or put them through an electric grinder. Peel and grate the onion. Stir the pâté smooth, and beat in the walnuts and onion. Mix the breadcrumbs and parsley into the stuffing, and season with salt, pepper and lemon juice.

Spread the underside of each best end with the stuffing. Roll the meat neatly and tie with string at 2 in. intervals. Put the two meat rolls in an oiled roasting tin and brush them with oil. Cook in the centre of the oven pre-heated to 400°F (mark 6) for about 20 minutes, or until golden brown. Reduce the heat to 375°F (mark 5) and cook for a further 40–50 minutes, or until tender.

Meanwhile, put the lamb bones in a saucepan with salt and pepper. Cover with cold water, bring to the boil and simmer the stock for 30–40 minutes.

Remove the meat from the roasting tin, leave to cool and set slightly before removing the string. Put the meat back in the oven to keep warm. Carefully pour off the fat in the roasting tin and add the wine to the meat juices. Bring to the boil on top of the stove, add about ½ pint of strained stock and the rosemary. Cook this gravy over high heat until it has reduced* slightly. Correct seasoning and strain the gravy into a warm sauce boat.

Serve the lamb, cut into thick slices, on a warm serving dish. Rissolé potatoes (see January vegetables), Brussels sprouts and halved grilled tomatoes could be arranged round the meat.

STEAK TARTARE

This dish of raw steak, garnished with raw onions and egg yolk is becoming increasingly popular. It is served with a number of finely chopped vegetables to which guests help themselves.

PREPARATION TIME: *15–20 min.*

INGREDIENTS *(for 4)* :
1 lb. fillet or rump steak
2 onions
1 cooked beetroot
4 tablespoons capers
1 large green or red pepper
2 tablespoons finely chopped parsley
¼ pint tartare sauce or mayonnaise
1–2 level teaspoons made French mustard
Salt and black pepper
Tabasco sauce
4 egg yolks

GARNISH:
Grated horseradish

Peel and thinly slice the onion. Set four onion rings aside and chop the remainder finely. Peel and finely dice the beetroot. Chop the capers. Remove the stalk end and the seeds from the pepper and dice the flesh.

Make the tartare sauce* or the mayonnaise* (flavour the latter with mustard and a few drops of Tabasco sauce). Chill the sauce while assembling the dish.

Scrape the steak into fine thin shreds with a sharp knife or put it through the fine blade of a mincer. Season to taste with salt and freshly ground pepper, and shape the mixture into four flat rounds. Arrange them in the centre of a serving dish. Make a shallow hollow in the centre of each steak, put an onion ring round the depression and slip an egg yolk inside (the egg yolk may also be set in a half shell within the onion ring).

Arrange the chopped vegetables in small mounds round the steaks, and sprinkle the steaks and vegetables with finely grated horseradish. Serve the chilled sauce separately, with a tossed green salad and slices of buttered rye bread.

Dolmas is a Turkish dish of vine leaves with a lamb and rice stuffing

Boiled hock in a cider and raisin sauce surrounded by cooked split peas

DOLMAS

In Turkey, one of the most popular main course dishes is fresh vine leaves stuffed with rice and minced lamb. Only tinned vine leaves are available in Britain but young cabbage leaves make excellent substitutes.

PREPARATION TIME: *40 min.*
COOKING TIME: *1 hour*

INGREDIENTS *(for 4–6):*
12 fresh vine or cabbage leaves or
    6½ oz. tin of vine leaves
1 onion
4 oz. long grain rice
3 oz. butter
1½ pints white stock
1 lb. lean minced lamb
1 level dessertspoon chopped fresh
    mint or parsley
1 level teaspoon powdered rose-
    mary
Salt and black pepper
Juice of half lemon
5 fluid oz. natural yoghourt

Peel the onion and chop it finely. Melt 1 oz. of the butter in a large heavy-based pan and fry the onion and rice until lightly coloured. Add enough stock to cover the rice and cook over low heat until tender. Stir frequently and add more stock if necessary.

Leave the rice and onion to cool and set. Stir in the minced lamb, the mint or parsley and rosemary and mix thoroughly. Season to taste with salt and freshly ground pepper. Blanch* the fresh vine or cabbage leaves for a few minutes in boiling water, then remove the coarse stalks. If using tinned vine leaves, unravel them carefully without breaking them.

Spread out the leaves and put a spoonful of the lamb and rice filling on each; fold the leaves over to make small, neat parcels. Pack them closely in layers in a flameproof casserole or sauté pan. Add enough stock to cover, and sprinkle with the lemon juice; dot with the remaining butter. Put a plate on top of the stuffed vine parcels to keep them under the liquid.

Cover the dish with a lid or foil and simmer over low heat for about 1 hour. Lift out the vine parcels with a perforated spoon and arrange them on a warm serving dish. Serve the yoghourt in a separate bowl.

HOCK WITH CIDER AND RAISINS

Bacon, cooked with dried peas or beans, is one of the oldest known English dishes, dating back to the 14th century. It later developed into another classic dish – salt pork or bacon with pease pudding. In the 18th century, small hot pease puddings were sold from barrows as hot chestnuts are today. The following is a 20th-century version of the medieval recipe.

PREPARATION TIME: *20 min.*
COOKING TIME: *2½ hours*

INGREDIENTS *(for 6):*
2–2½ lb. hock or shoulder of
    gammon
½ lb. split peas, lentils or chick
    peas
1 small onion
2 tablespoons chopped celery
1½ oz. butter
1½ oz. plain flour
½ pint dry cider
2 oz. stoneless raisins
¼ pint gammon stock
2 teaspoons Demerara sugar
2 tablespoons chopped parsley

Wash the hock and place it in a large bowl, together with the peas or lentils. Cover with cold water and leave to soak for 8 hours or overnight. Drain the meat and peas, put them in a large heavy-based pan and cover with fresh cold water. Bring to the boil, then lower the heat and cover the pan with a lid. Simmer for 1½ hours or until the hock is tender.

Lift the meat from the pan and set it aside to cool slightly. Leave the peas to cook for a further 30–40 minutes or until quite tender. Skin the hock carefully while still warm, and cut the meat into 1 in. cubes, discarding the fat.

Peel and finely chop the onion, and prepare the celery. Melt the butter in a heavy-based pan over moderate heat, and fry the onion and celery for a few minutes until soft. Remove the pan from the heat and stir in the flour until it has absorbed all the butter. Gradually stir in the cider to make a smooth sauce. Return the pan to the heat and bring the sauce to simmering point, stirring continuously. Mix in the raisins, and add sufficient gammon stock to make a creamy sauce. Blend in the sugar and continue cooking and stirring over low heat for a further 10 minutes.

Add the cubed hock to the cider sauce, heating it through thoroughly and stirring occasionally. Drain the peas or lentils thoroughly and toss them in a little butter and parsley. Spoon the meat and sauce into the centre of a warmed serving dish and surround with a border of the peas. Alternatively, make the peas into chick pea patties (see October vegetables).

VEAL ROLLS WITH FRITTATA FILLING

A frittata is an Italian cross between an omelette and a pancake. It is a traditional filling for rolled veal and is first fried like thin pancakes and then spread over the meat. The frittatas can also be served as a garnish with veal escalopes.

PREPARATION TIME: *30 min.*
COOKING TIME: *1½ hours*

INGREDIENTS *(for 4)*:

8 veal escalopes (about 3 oz. each)
2 eggs
2 oz. chopped mortadella sausage or lean ham
2 level dessertspoons chopped fresh parsley
2–3 level dessertspoons grated Parmesan cheese
3 oz. butter
4–6 oz. button mushrooms
1 onion
2–3 level dessertspoons plain flour
¼ pint milk
¼–½ pint stock or bouillon
Salt and black pepper
Lemon juice
Dried mixed herbs

Beat the escalopes thin between sheets of greaseproof paper. Trim them neatly and set aside. Beat the eggs lightly and stir in the chopped sausage, the parsley and grated cheese.

Melt a little butter in a small omelette pan and, when hot, spoon in enough of the egg mixture to thinly cover the base of the pan. Cook the frittata until golden brown, then turn it and cook the other side. Cook the remaining mixture, to make eight frittatas in all.

Cover each escalope with a frittata, trimming these to the shape of the meat. Roll up each escalope and tie at intervals with fine string.

Trim the mushrooms* and cut them in half if large. Peel the onion and slice it thinly. Melt the remaining butter in a heavy-based pan and fry the veal rolls over high heat until golden brown. Lift the rolls from the pan. Fry the mushrooms and onion in the remaining butter in the pan until soft, then draw the pan off the heat. Blend in enough flour to absorb all the fat, and gradually stir in the milk and ¼ pint of stock. Lower the heat and bring the sauce to simmering point, stirring continuously. Cook for about 5 minutes, then season with salt, pepper, lemon juice and dried herbs.

Add the veal rolls to the sauce, thinning it with a little more stock if necessary – the sauce should cover the rolls completely. Put a lid on the pan and simmer over low heat for about 1 hour or until the meat is tender.

Lift out the veal rolls, remove the string, and arrange them on a hot serving dish. Spoon a little of the sauce over the meat and serve the remainder in a sauce boat. Duchess potatoes* and buttered broccoli or beans would be good vegetable dishes.

TOURNEDOS EN CROÛTE

The small, thick round slices – or tournedos – cut from the fillet of beef are among the most expensive cuts of meat. But for a special occasion, tournedos can be encased in puff pastry, and a 4 oz. portion of meat will then be sufficient for each person.

PREPARATION TIME: *30 min.*
COOKING TIME: *40 min.*

INGREDIENTS *(for 6)*:
6 tournedos
2 oz. unsalted butter
12–13 oz. prepared puff pastry
4 oz. pâté with mushrooms or truffles
1 egg
1 onion
4 fluid oz. red wine
½ pint beef stock
Salt and black pepper
GARNISH:
Watercress

Trim any excess fat off the tournedos and wipe them with a damp cloth. Heat the butter in a heavy-based pan and brown the meat quickly on both sides to seal in the juices. Set aside to cool.

Roll out the puff pastry* on a floured surface, to a rectangle, ⅛ in. thick (the thickness of a 10p coin). Divide the pastry into six equal squares, each large enough to wrap round a tournedo. Spread one side of each tournedo with pâté and place it, pâté side down, on a pastry square. Brush the edges of the pastry with cold water and draw them together over the meat to form a neat parcel. Seal the edges carefully.

Place the pastry parcels, with the seams underneath, on a wet baking tray. Lightly beat the egg and brush over the pastry. Make two or three slits in each parcel for the steam to escape, and decorate with leaves cut from the pastry trimmings. Brush with beaten egg.

Bake the tournedos in the centre of a pre-heated oven at 425°F (mark 7) for 15–20 minutes. At this point, the pastry should be well risen and golden brown and the meat will be rosy-pink in the middle. For well-done steaks, lower the heat to 350°F (mark 4) and cook for a further 10 minutes.

Make the sauce while the tournedos are cooking. Peel and finely chop the onion and fry until just coloured in the butter left in the pan. Add the wine and let it bubble over moderate heat for 2–3 minutes, stirring up the residue from the pan. Blend in the stock and simmer for a further 5 minutes. Season with salt and pepper.

Arrange the tournedos on a warm serving dish garnished with sprigs of watercress. Pour the sauce into a sauce boat and serve with scalloped potatoes and Turkish fried carrots (see October vegetables).

Poultry & Game

FAISAN AU VERGER

This is an excellent Normandy method of cooking older or slightly tough cock pheasants with apples. Whole or jointed pheasants and guinea fowl which have been stored in the home freezer are also suitable.

PREPARATION TIME: *40 min.*
COOKING TIME: *45 min.*

INGREDIENTS (*for 4*):
1 pheasant
1 bay leaf
1 sprig parsley
Salt and black pepper
1 onion
2 sticks celery
2 cooking apples
2–3 level tablespoons plain flour
1½ oz. butter
¼ pint cider
2½ fluid oz. double cream
GARNISH:
2 dessert apples
Celery leaves

Joint the pheasant by first removing the legs, then cut away the two breast sections down and along the backbone. Leave the flesh on the bone, so that it will not shrink during cooking, and cut off the wing pinions.

Put the pheasant carcass, the neck and the cleaned giblets into a pan, together with the bay leaf, parsley, and a seasoning of salt and freshly ground pepper. Cover with cold water, put the lid on the pan and simmer this stock over low heat for about 20 minutes.

Peel and thinly slice the onion. Cut the leafy tops off the celery and set aside for garnish. Scrub the celery sticks and chop them finely. Peel, core and roughly chop the cooking apples.

Coat the pheasant joints lightly with a little flour, and heat the butter in a flameproof casserole or heavy-based pan. Fry the pheasant over high heat until golden brown all over, then remove from the casserole. Lower the heat and fry the onion and celery for 5 minutes. Add the apples and fry for a further 5 minutes. Draw the casserole from the heat and stir in sufficient of the remaining flour to absorb all the fat. Gradually blend in the cider and ½ pint of strained pheasant stock. Bring this sauce to simmering point over low heat, stirring continuously.

Put the pheasant back into the casserole, and if necessary add more stock to the sauce until it almost covers the joints.

Season to taste with salt and freshly ground pepper, and cover the casserole with a lid.

Cook the casserole in the centre of a pre-heated oven, at 325°F (mark 3), for 45 minutes or until tender. Remove the pheasant and keep warm in the oven. Boil the sauce briskly on top of the stove, stir into the cream and pour this mixture back into the pan; adjust seasoning.

Return the pheasant joints to the sauce and serve straight from the casserole. Alternatively, arrange the joints on a warm deep serving dish and spoon the sauce over them. Surround with the cored, but unpeeled apples, cut into thick slices and fried in a little butter until golden. Push a small tuft of celery leaves through the centre of each apple slice.

Scalloped potatoes (see October vegetables) could also be served.

PINTADE VIGNERON

In this French recipe, guinea fowl is cooked with white grapes. This domesticated game bird has a flavour reminiscent of pheasant, which may be cooked in the same way. A guinea chick will provide two servings and a fully grown bird three. They are usually sold ready trussed and barded with pork fat.

PREPARATION TIME: *30 min.*
COOKING TIME: *55 min.*

INGREDIENTS (*for 3*):
1 guinea fowl
1 onion
Bouquet garni
Salt and black pepper
½ lb. white grapes
Juice of a lemon
1 oz. butter
4 rashers fat bacon (optional)
4 fluid oz. dry white wine
2 egg yolks
2½ fluid oz. cream
GARNISH:
Lemon wedges and vine leaves or
*   6 oz. white grapes*

Clean the giblets thoroughly and put them in a saucepan with 1 pint of cold water. Peel and quarter the onion, add it to the giblets with the bouquet garni* and a good seasoning of salt and freshly ground pepper. Bring to the boil, remove any scum and simmer the stock, covered, for 20 minutes. Strain and set aside.

Meanwhile, peel the grapes* if they are thick-skinned, and remove the pips. Sprinkle them with a little lemon juice and salt before stuffing them into the guinea fowl. Sew up the vent. Melt the butter and brush it all over the bird. Remove the rind and gristle from the bacon and tie the rashers over the breast of the guinea fowl if not already barded*.

Roast the guinea fowl in the centre of a pre-heated oven, at 400°F (mark 6), for 30 minutes. Remove the bacon or fat and continue cooking the guinea fowl for a further 15 minutes or until golden brown and tender. Place on a serving dish and keep it warm in the oven.

Pour the wine into the roasting tin and bring to the boil on top of the stove, scraping up all the residue. Pour it into a measuring jug, making it up to $\frac{1}{4}$ pint with the giblet stock. Beat the egg yolks with the cream in a bowl and gradually stir in the wine and stock mixture. Place the bowl over a saucepan containing $\frac{1}{2}$ in. of gently simmering water. Stir this sauce continuously until it has thickened enough to coat thinly the back of a wooden spoon. Do not let the sauce reach boiling point or it will curdle. Correct seasoning and sharpen to taste with lemon juice.

Garnish the guinea fowl with lemon wedges arranged on fresh vine leaves, or with small bunches of unpeeled white grapes. Pour the sauce into a warm sauce boat and serve with, for example, rissolé potatoes (see January vegetables) and cauliflower polonaise (see September vegetables) over which the crisp bacon has been crumbled.

SPATCH-COCKED GROUSE WITH ROWAN JELLY

Spatch-cocking is a distortion of an 18th-century Irish term for providing unexpected guests with a quick meal. A farmyard chicken was dispatched (killed), split and fried or grilled. The term has since come to define the cooking method and is especially suitable for small game birds which do not require hanging.

PREPARATION TIME: *35 min.*
COOKING TIME: *30 min.*

INGREDIENTS *(for 2)*:

2 young grouse
2–3 tablespoons olive oil
1–2 tablespoons lemon juice
Salt and black pepper
2 oz. butter
4 rashers green streaky bacon
2 large slices white bread
2 fluid oz. dry vermouth
1 rounded dessertspoon rowan or quince jelly
GARNISH:
2 level tablespoons chopped parsley

For spatch-cocking, split each grouse along the backbone without separating the two halves. Open it out and beat it flat. Cut off the feet and push up the flesh on the legs so as to expose about 1 in. on each drumstick. Make a slit with a sharp knife below each thigh joint, just above the vent. Push up the leg and insert the bare bone in the slit. Fold the pinions underneath the wings so that they lie flat. Hold each grouse in position by inserting skewers in a crossways pattern from each wing to leg joint.

Brush the grouse with 2 tablespoons of olive oil mixed with 1 tablespoon of lemon juice. Sprinkle the birds with salt and pepper and set aside for 20 minutes for the oil to soak in.

Melt the butter in a large, heavy-based pan and fry the grouse over high heat for 5 minutes on each side. Lower the heat and continue cooking the grouse for another 5–7 minutes on each side. Lift the grouse on to a warm serving plate.

Trim the rind and gristle from the bacon. Remove the crusts from the bread and cut each slice into two triangles. Fry the bacon and the bread in the pan until quite crisp (adding the remaining oil if necessary). Lift out and keep warm. Pour the fat from the pan, leaving about 1 tablespoon. Add the vermouth and boil over high heat, scraping up the residue in the bottom of the pan. Stir in the rowan or quince jelly and cook until it has melted. Sharpen the gravy to taste with lemon juice.

Remove the skewers from the grouse, and pour the gravy over the birds. Arrange the crisp bacon and fried bread around the grouse and sprinkle with parsley. Serve with game chips* and green beans Tuscany style (see November vegetables).

CHICKEN KIEV

This classic recipe of deep fried chicken fillets stuffed with savoury butter comes from Russia. Only two fillets can be cut from each chicken, but individual breast portions may be used provided they are large. The initial preparation should be done well in advance to allow time for chilling.

PREPARATION TIME: *40 min.*
CHILLING TIME: *2 hours*
COOKING TIME: *15 min.*

INGREDIENTS *(for 4)*:

2 roasting chickens (2½–3 lb. each)
4 oz. unsalted butter
Grated rind and juice of a small lemon
2 tablespoons fresh chopped tarragon or parsley
Ground nutmeg (optional)
Salt and black pepper
1 large egg
4 oz. fresh white breadcrumbs
Fat or oil for deep frying
GARNISH:
Watercress

Cream the butter in a bowl with the lemon rind, tarragon (or parsley) and a pinch of nutmeg. Season to taste with salt, freshly ground pepper and a little lemon juice. Shape the butter into a rectangular block, wrap it in foil and leave in the refrigerator until it has set solid.

Meanwhile, carefully fillet the breast and wing in one piece from each side of the breastbone of the chicken. Remove the wing pinions and carefully peel away all the skin. Lay the breast fillets between sheets of greaseproof paper and beat them flat. Joint the remaining chicken, and store in the home freezer or use in another recipe.

Cut the hard butter into four finger-length pieces and place one in the centre of each chicken fillet. Fold the edges over neatly and roll the fillet up tightly. Secure with fine string. Beat the egg lightly and brush over the chicken rolls before coating them evenly with breadcrumbs; press them in thoroughly. The chicken rolls may be coated a second time for a crisper finish, patting the egg with a brush so as not to disturb the first coating. Roll again in crumbs. Leave the rolls in the refrigerator until the coating has set, after 1 hour.

Heat the fat or oil* to 375°F in a deep-frier. Fry the chicken rolls in two batches, until golden brown, after about 6 minutes. Do not allow the fat to get too hot or the chicken will brown before it is cooked. Drain the rolls on crumpled absorbent paper.

Arrange the chicken rolls on a warmed serving dish and garnish with small bunches of watercress. New potatoes and sliced courgettes cooked in butter make good side dishes with the chicken.

Rice & Pasta

RIGATONI WITH HARE SAUCE

This rich pasta dish of rigatoni or short ribbed macaroni comes from the Tuscany region of Italy. It is served with a thick sauce of wine and hare, and is an ideal way of using up the remains of a hare.

PREPARATION TIME: 25 min.
COOKING TIME: 1¼ hours

INGREDIENTS (for 4):
12 oz. rigatoni or broad noodles
4 hare legs
4 oz. green streaky bacon
1 clove garlic
1 onion
1 stick celery
4 oz. mushrooms
1 tablespoon lard or bacon fat
2–3 dessertspoons flour
4 fluid oz. red wine or 2 fluid oz.
    Marsala or brown sherry
Salt and black pepper
Powdered thyme and marjoram
Rind and juice of half lemon
3–4 oz. grated Parmesan cheese

Slice the meat off the legs of the hare and remove the tough tendons. Chop the meat into ½ in. pieces and set aside. Remove the rind from the rashers and chop the bacon roughly. Peel and finely chop the garlic, and finely slice the onion. Scrub and chop the celery, and trim and slice the mushrooms*.

Heat the lard or fat in a deep, heavy-based pan over moderate heat and fry the bacon, garlic, onion and celery for about 5 minutes, or until just taking colour. Add the hare meat and mushrooms and cook for a few minutes until lightly browned.

Remove the pan from the heat and stir in enough flour to absorb all the fat. Return the pan to the heat and fry the mixture until brown, stirring continuously. Add the wine and gradually blend in ¾ pint of water to make a thick sauce. Season to taste with salt, freshly ground pepper and a pinch of thyme and marjoram. Cover the pan with a lid and simmer over low heat for 1 hour. Add the grated lemon rind and sharpen with lemon juice.

Meanwhile, cook the rigatoni or noodles in a large pan of salted water for 12–15 minutes. Drain thoroughly in a colander. Arrange the rigatoni round the edge of a serving dish and spoon the hare sauce into the centre. Sprinkle a little cheese over the sauce and serve the remainder in a separate bowl. Serve a tossed green salad with the pasta.

SCHINKEN-FLECKERL

Most pasta dishes are of Italian origin, but this recipe for noodles with ham is traditional both in Austria and Switzerland.

PREPARATION TIME: 15 min.
COOKING TIME: 40–45 min.

INGREDIENTS (for 4):
8 oz. pasta squares or short cut
    noodles
1 dessertspoon olive oil
2 tablespoons toasted
    breadcrumbs
Salt and black pepper
8 oz. lean ham
2 shallots or 1 small onion
2 oz. butter
7½ fluid oz. soured cream
2 eggs
2 oz. grated Gruyère or Cheddar
    cheese
GARNISH:
1 small green pepper

Grease a timbale mould* or a round, 6 in. wide cake tin with the oil and coat it evenly with the breadcrumbs.

Bring a large pan of salted water to the boil and add the pasta or noodles. Bring back to the boil and cook over high heat for 10–15 minutes or until al dente*. Drain thoroughly in a colander and put the pasta in a large bowl.

While the pasta is cooking, dice the ham, and peel and finely chop the shallots or the onion. Melt the butter in a small frying pan and cook the shallots over moderate heat for 5 minutes or until soft and transparent. Blend the contents of the pan into the pasta.

Blend the soured cream and eggs in a small bowl, stir in the ham and grated cheese, and add this mixture to the pasta. Blend thoroughly, and season to taste with salt and freshly ground pepper.

Spoon the pasta mixture into the prepared mould or tin and place it in a roasting tin with enough cold water to reach 1 in. up the sides of the mould. Bake in the centre of an oven pre-heated to 400°F (mark 6) for 30 minutes, or until the mixture has set and is light brown on top.

Remove the mould from the oven and allow the mixture to cool and shrink slightly before unmoulding it on to a warmed serving dish. Garnish with wedges or small squares of lightly grilled green pepper. Halved tomatoes and trimmed mushroom caps, put under a hot grill for a few minutes, would also be suitable.

ITALIAN SUPPLÌ

Rice balls – or supplì – are popular in Italy, both as a light lunch or as a first course. The risotto may be flavoured with saffron instead of tomato as in this recipe, and chopped ham or salami may be substituted for the prawns. The cheese must be soft so that it will pull into threads when the rice balls are broken open. The Italians call it supplì al telefono.

PREPARATION TIME: 30 min.
CHILLING TIME: 45 min.
COOKING TIME: 15 min.

INGREDIENTS (for 6):
8 oz. rice, Italian or short grain
1 onion
2 oz. butter
14 oz. tin of tomato juice
¼ pint chicken stock or water
1–2 tablespoons grated Parmesan
    cheese
Salt and black pepper
Paprika
2 large eggs
8 oz. Mozzarella or Bel Paese
    cheese
4 oz. peeled prawns
3 oz. fresh white breadcrumbs
Oil for deep frying

Peel and finely chop the onion. Melt the butter in a large heavy-based pan and cook the onion until transparent. Add the rice and fry it in the butter, stirring continuously until it is just turning colour. Pour in the tomato juice, cover the pan with a lid and cook over low heat until the liquid is absorbed and the rice is just tender. Stir frequently, and add a little chicken stock or water if the tomato juice is absorbed before the rice is cooked.

Take the pan off the heat and stir in the grated Parmesan cheese; season to taste with salt, freshly ground pepper and a little paprika. Beat the eggs lightly and blend into the risotto mixture. Turn it into a bowl and leave in the refrigerator to cool and stiffen.

Cut the Mozzarella or Bel Paese cheese into ½ in. cubes. Put a level tablespoon of the cold risotto in the palm of the hand. Press a prawn and a cube of cheese into the centre, cover with another spoonful of risotto and shape the mixture into a ball. Continue until all the risotto, prawns and cheese are used up – the mixture will make 12–14 balls.

Roll the rice balls in the breadcrumbs. Heat the cooking oil* in a deep frier to 375°F and fry the rice balls in batches until crisp and golden, about 4 minutes to each batch. Drain the rice balls on crumpled absorbent paper while frying the next batch.

Serve the supplì hot on its own, or with a crisp celery salad, or a green salad tossed in French dressing*.

Vegetables & Salads

CALABRESE WITH POULETTE SAUCE

Green broccoli, or calabrese, is also known as Cape Broccoli. In this recipe, it is served with a classic French vegetable sauce whose creamy-white colour contrasts well with the curds.

PREPARATION TIME: *10 min.*
COOKING TIME: *30 min.*

INGREDIENTS *(for 4–6)*:
2 lb. Calabrese (green broccoli)
Salt and black pepper
2 oz. butter
1 rounded dessertspoon plain flour
1 egg yolk
Juice of half lemon
2 tablespoons double cream

Trim the tough stalk and any leaves off the broccoli head or heads. Wash thoroughly in cold water. Put the broccoli in a large pan of boiling salted water. Cover the pan with a lid and simmer over low heat for about 15 minutes or until just tender. Lift the broccoli carefully into a colander to drain; set the liquid aside and cover it with a dry cloth to keep it warm.

Melt the butter in a small saucepan, then take the pan off the heat. Stir in the flour to make a roux*, and gradually blend in ½ pint of the broccoli liquid. Bring this sauce to the boil over low heat and simmer for about 10 minutes. Beat the egg yolk with 1 dessertspoon of lemon juice and 2 tablespoons of the hot sauce. Remove the sauce from the heat and blend in the egg mixture.

Stir in the cream. Keep the sauce warm, but do not allow it to boil or the egg and cream will curdle. Season to taste with salt, freshly ground pepper and more lemon juice. Put the broccoli in a warm deep serving dish and pour over the sauce.

WESTPHALIAN BEANS AND PEARS

A blending of sweet and sharp flavours is characteristic of German cookery. This recipe for French or runner beans makes a good vegetable dish with grilled or roast pork and ham.

PREPARATION TIME: *15 min.*
COOKING TIME: *30 min.*

INGREDIENTS *(for 4–6)*:
1 lb. French or runner beans
4 large cooking pears
¾ pint stock or bouillon
Lemon rind
4 rashers green streaky bacon
2 level tablespoons soft brown sugar
1 tablespoon tarragon vinegar

Peel the pears and cut them in half lengthways. Remove the cores and cut each half across into three or four pieces. Bring the stock to the boil, and drop in a thin piece of lemon rind, together with the pears. Simmer, uncovered, over low heat for 10 minutes.

Meanwhile, top and tail the beans (remove the strings as well from runner beans). Wash the beans and add them to the pears. Continue cooking over low heat.

Remove the rind and any gristle from the bacon and cut the rashers, crossways, into ½ in. wide strips. Fry the bacon strips, with no additional fat, in a pan over low heat, until the fat runs and the bacon becomes crisp. Remove the bacon from the pan with a perforated spoon and keep it warm. Stir the sugar into the fat in the frying pan, blend in the vinegar and 2 tablespoons pear and bean liquid. Mix thoroughly, then add to the pan with the pears and beans. Simmer, uncovered, until the liquid has reduced* to a syrupy sauce and the beans are tender. Remove the lemon.

Spoon the beans, pears and liquid into a hot serving dish and sprinkle with the bacon.

CHICK PEA PATTIES

These pea patties can also be made from split peas or lentils. Serve the patties with boiled or baked ham, or with grilled bacon.

PREPARATION TIME: *50 min.*
COOKING TIME: *2¼ hours.*

INGREDIENTS *(for 4)*:
½ lb. chick peas
1 onion
1 pint ham or bacon stock
1 oz. butter
2 level tablespoons chopped parsley
Salt and black pepper
1 large egg
2 oz. bacon fat or dripping

Leave the dried peas to soak in a bowl of water for 8 hours or overnight. Drain the peas and put them in a saucepan with the stock. Bring to the boil, cover the pan with a lid and simmer over low heat for about 2 hours.

Drain the peas and make them into a coarse purée* in a liquidiser or a mouli*. Peel and finely chop the onion. Fry the onion in the butter over low heat for 5 minutes or until just colouring.

Blend the cooked onion into the pea purée, together with the finely chopped parsley. Season to taste with salt and pepper; bind the purée with beaten egg. Spread the mixture on a flat plate and divide it into eight equal portions. Roll each portion into a ball between floured hands, then flatten it into a round patty shape. Chill the patties for about 30 minutes or until set.

Heat the fat in a heavy-based pan over moderate heat, and fry the patties until golden brown on both sides, turning once.

Drain the patties on crumpled absorbent paper before serving.

MARROW EN CASSEROLE

Marrow has such a high water content that it loses most of its flavour if steamed or cooked in water. But firmness and taste is preserved by cooking marrow in butter in a casserole. It goes well with grilled meat and fish.

PREPARATION TIME: *10 min.*
COOKING TIME: *30 min.*

INGREDIENTS *(for 4–6)*:
1 young marrow (approx. 2 lb.)
1½ oz. butter
2 level tablespoons mixed fresh herbs – tarragon, mint, parsley and chives
Salt and black pepper

Cut the marrow into 1 in. thick slices; peel and cut them into rough chunks, discarding the seeds. Butter an ovenproof dish thoroughly. Add the marrow with the remaining butter cut into small knobs and sprinkle with the fresh, finely chopped herbs. Season with salt and freshly ground pepper.

Cover the dish with a lid or foil and bake in the centre of a pre-heated oven at 350°F (mark 4) until just tender, after about 30 minutes. Be careful not to overcook. Serve the marrow at once, straight from the dish.

TURKISH FRIED CARROTS

In Turkey, cold or warm yoghourt is often used to dress vegetables and salads. Young or maincrop carrots are equally suitable for this dish, which goes well with grilled and roast lamb.

PREPARATION TIME: *15 min.*
COOKING TIME: *20 min.*

INGREDIENTS *(for 4):*
1 lb. carrots
Salt and black pepper
1 level tablespoon seasoned flour
2 tablespoons olive oil
½ pint natural yoghourt
GARNISH:
1 level tablespoon chopped mint or 1 level teaspoon caraway seeds

Peel or scrape the carrots and wash them. Cut them, crossways, into ¼ in. thick slices. Bring a pan of salted water to the boil and cook the carrots for about 10 minutes or until nearly tender. Drain in a colander, then spread the carrots on absorbent paper to dry thoroughly.

Toss the carrots in seasoned flour*, shaking off any surplus. Heat the oil in a heavy-based pan and fry the carrots over moderate heat until golden brown. Season to taste with salt and freshly ground pepper. Put the yoghourt in a separate pan over low heat, and let it warm through. Do not let it reach boiling point or it will curdle.

Spoon the carrots into a hot serving dish, pour over the yoghourt, and sprinkle with mint or caraway seeds.

CHESTNUT AND POTATO PURÉE

Chestnuts are traditionally served as stuffing or as garnishes with game birds. This purée of potato and chestnuts is an excellent vegetable to serve with game, turkey or roast ham.

PREPARATION TIME: *20 min.*
COOKING TIME: *30 min.*

INGREDIENTS *(for 6–8):*
¾ lb. fresh chestnuts or 8 oz. tin chestnut purée
1 pint stock or bouillon
¾ lb. mashed potatoes
Salt
2 oz. butter
4–5 tablespoons single cream
Ground nutmeg or black pepper
4 rounded tablespoons chopped celery heart

Make a small cut on the flat side of each chestnut and roast them on top of the stove in a chestnut pan or on a baking tray near the top of a hot oven. After 5–10 minutes, the skins will crack. Peel the two layers of skin from the chestnuts while still warm.

Put the stock in a saucepan, add the peeled chestnuts and cover the pan with a lid. Bring to the boil, then simmer the chestnuts for 20 minutes or until tender. Drain the chestnuts and rub them through a coarse sieve.

Blend the chestnut purée with the mashed potato, stir in the butter and heat the mixture through over low heat. Blend in enough cream to give the purée a fluffy texture, and season with salt and ground nutmeg or pepper.

Blend in the chopped celery just before serving.

SCALLOPED POTATOES

For this recipe, choose firm, maincrop potatoes which will not break up during long, slow cooking. The potato gratin can be served with any type of grilled or roast meat, or it can be made into a main dish by adding minced ham or flaked cooked fish between the potato layers.

PREPARATION TIME: *15–20 min.*
COOKING TIME: *1½ hours*

INGREDIENTS *(for 6):*
1½ lb. potatoes
1 onion
4 oz. Cheddar cheese
2 oz. butter
Salt and black pepper
1 egg
½ pint milk

Peel and wash the potatoes, and cut them into thin slices. Peel and finely chop the onion, and grate the cheese. Use a little of the butter to grease a shallow, ovenproof dish. Arrange the potato slices in layers in the dish, sprinkling each layer with onion, cheese, salt and freshly ground pepper. Finish with a thick layer of cheese and dot with the remaining butter.

Beat the egg and milk together and pour this mixture carefully over the potatoes. Cover the dish with buttered greaseproof paper or foil. Bake in the centre of an oven pre-heated to 350°F (mark 4) for 1½ hours, or until the potatoes are tender, and the topping is golden. If cooked too quickly, the egg and milk will curdle.

BAKED CABBAGE

Firm white winter cabbage is one of the least expensive vegetables. Baked in a cheese sauce, it goes well with sausages and bacon.

PREPARATION TIME: *30 min.*
COOKING TIME: *15 min.*

INGREDIENTS *(for 6):*
1½ lb. white cabbage
2 oz. butter
2 oz. plain flour
¼ pint milk
Salt and black pepper
Ground mace or nutmeg
2 oz. salted chopped peanuts
2–4 oz. grated Cheddar cheese

Discard any damaged outer leaves and cut the cabbage into quarters. Cut out the centre stalk and shred the cabbage finely.

Heat ½ in. of water in a large heavy-based saucepan and add 1 teaspoon of salt. Put in the washed cabbage, a handful at a time, seasoning each layer with freshly ground black pepper.

Cover the pan with a lid and cook over low heat for about 10 minutes, or until the cabbage is cooked, but still crisp.

Meanwhile, make a thick white sauce* from the butter, flour and milk. Season to taste with salt, pepper and mace (or nutmeg).

Butter an ovenproof dish lightly and arrange a layer of cabbage over the base. Cover with some of the sauce and sprinkle with nuts and cheese. Fill the dish with layers of cabbage, sauce, nuts and cheese, finishing with cheese. Bake in the centre of an oven pre-heated to 425°F (mark 7) for 15 minutes, or until the cheese is golden brown.

Serve the cabbage at once.

Sweets & Puddings

SHOO FLY PIE

This pie, a favourite in the deep south of the United States, takes its name from its extreme sweetness. Flies and bees are so attracted to the pie that it is necessary to shoo them away while the pie is cooling.

PREPARATION TIME: *30 min.*
COOKING TIME: *35 min.*

INGREDIENTS *(for 6)*:
4 oz. shortcrust pastry (standard recipe)
4 oz. stoneless raisins
2 oz. soft brown sugar
¼ level teaspoon bicarbonate of soda
TOPPING:
4 oz. plain flour
½ level teaspoon cinnamon
¼ level teaspoon ground nutmeg
¼ level teaspoon ground ginger
2 oz. unsalted butter
2 oz. soft brown sugar

Prepare the shortcrust pastry* and roll it out thinly on a lightly floured board. Line a 7 in. flan tin or shallow pie plate with the pastry. Crimp* the edges between finger and thumb for a decorative finish. Prick the base of the pastry all over with a fork and cover with the raisins. Mix 2 oz. of brown sugar with 4 dessertspoons of hot water and the bicarbonate of soda; pour over the raisins.

For the topping, sift together the flour and spices. Cut the butter into small knobs and rub them into the flour until the mixture resembles fine breadcrumbs. Stir in the brown sugar and sprinkle over the filling.

Bake the pie on the shelf above the centre of a pre-heated oven, at 425°F (mark 7), until the pie begins to brown. Reduce the heat to 325°F (mark 3) and bake for a further 20 minutes, or until the topping has set.

Cut the pie into wedges and serve it warm or cold. A jug of cream may be offered although it is not traditional.

DAMSON AND APPLE TANSY

This English pudding recipe dates back to the 15th century. It takes its name from tansy, a bitter-tasting herb which was once popular for flavouring sweets – it now describes a buttered fruit purée with eggs and breadcrumbs.

PREPARATION TIME: *15 min.*
COOKING TIME: *40 min.*
CHILLING TIME: *1 hour*

INGREDIENTS *(for 4)*:
½ lb. damsons
½ lb. cooking apples
2 oz. unsalted butter
4 oz. caster sugar
2 egg yolks
4 level dessertspoons fresh white breadcrumbs
¼ pint double cream
1 dessertspoon lemon juice

Wash the damsons. Peel, core and thinly slice the apples. Melt the butter in a saucepan with 2½ fluid oz. of cold water. Cover with a lid and boil the fruit over low heat until soft, stirring from time to time.

Remove the pan from the heat and rub the fruit through a coarse sieve. Return the purée* to the pan and stir in sugar to taste. If the purée is thin, cook it over low heat until it has reduced* slightly and thickened to a dropping consistency. Take the pan off the heat and blend in the beaten egg yolks and the breadcrumbs. Stir the mixture over low heat until quite thick, then leave to cool.

Whisk the cream lightly and fold it into the cooled purée. Sharpen to taste with lemon juice. Spoon the mixture into serving glasses and chill in the refrigerator for 1 hour.

Before serving, whipped cream may be piped over the tansy.

FRESH FIGS AND YOGHOURT

French or Italian purple-skinned figs with sweet red centres are available in Britain for a short season during the autumn. This refreshing sweet may evoke memories of the Mediterranean – especially if fresh fig or vine leaves are arranged beneath the dessert glasses.

PREPARATION TIME: *15 min.*
CHILLING TIME: *2 hours*

INGREDIENTS *(for 4)*:
8 fresh figs
¼ pint double cream
¼ pint natural yoghourt
3–4 level tablespoons soft brown sugar

Put the figs in a large bowl of hot water for 1 minute. Drain them thoroughly, peel off the skins and quarter each fig. Whisk the cream lightly and blend it into the yoghourt.

Spoon a little of the cream mixture into four small serving glasses. Top with a layer of figs, followed by more cream and figs, and finish with a layer of cream mixture. Sprinkle each layer with brown sugar.

Chill in the refrigerator for at least 2 hours to allow the sugar to melt into the cream.

Shoo fly pie is an ideal dessert for people who like their puddings sweet

Mediterranean fresh figs in sweetened yoghourt make a refreshing sweet

DELICES DE POIRES AU CHOCOLAT

Large ripe winter pears, such as 'Comice', are ideal for this attractive dessert of chocolate-covered pears. It makes a good choice for a dinner party as it can be prepared a day in advance and left in the refrigerator.

PREPARATION TIME: *20 min.*
COOKING TIME: *20 min.*
CHILLING TIME: *2–3 hours*

INGREDIENTS *(for 4)*:
4 ripe dessert pears
½ oz. shelled walnuts
½ oz. glacé cherries
4 oz. dark plain chocolate
4 dessertspoons cold black coffee
1 oz. unsalted butter
1–2 dessertspoons rum
2 eggs
GARNISH:
Angelica, or whipped cream and chopped pistachio nuts

Peel the pears thinly and cut out the cores from the base of the fruit, leaving the stem and top intact. Cut a small sliver from the base of each pear so that it will stand upright. Roughly chop and mix together the walnuts and cherries and press a little of this mixture into the core cavities of the pears. Stand the pears upright in one large or four small shallow serving dishes.

Break up the chocolate and put it in a bowl with the coffee. Stand the bowl over a saucepan of boiling water and stir occasionally until the chocolate has melted. Remove the bowl from the heat and stir in first the butter and then the rum. Separate the eggs and beat the yolks, one at a time, into the chocolate mixture. Whisk the egg whites until stiff, but still moist, and fold them carefully into the chocolate. The consistency should be similar to that of a mousse.

Spoon the chocolate mixture over the pears until they are evenly coated. Soften the angelica strips in hot water, cut into ½ in. lengths and slice them crossways into eight diamond shapes. Make a small slit on either side of each pear stalk and insert an angelica diamond, twisting them to resemble small leaves.

Chill the chocolate pears in the refrigerator for 2–3 hours or overnight.

Piped whipped cream and chopped pistachio nuts are also attractive garnishes.

HUNGARIAN HAZEL NUT TORTE

Hungarian dessert cakes – or torte – are internationally famous, and several of them were perfected by Dobos, a 19th-century Hungarian confectioner. This classic hazel nut torte has a chocolate cream filling and a caramel topping. It improves in flavour if kept for a day or two in a completely airtight tin.

PREPARATION TIME: *30 min.*
COOKING TIME: *30–40 min.*

INGREDIENTS *(for 6)*:
4 oz. unblanched hazel nuts
4 eggs
5 oz. caster sugar
FILLING:
2 oz. unsalted butter
2 oz. icing sugar
1 rounded dessertspoon chocolate powder
1 rounded teaspoon instant coffee
TOPPING:
3 oz. caster sugar
12 hazel nuts

Lightly grease two round 7 in. sandwich tins. Grind the unblanched hazel nuts finely in a liquidiser or coffee grinder. Separate the eggs and whisk the whites until stiff, but still moist. Whisk the egg yolks with 5 oz. of caster sugar until pale lemon in colour and the mixture trails off the whisk in ribbons.

Fold the ground nuts and whisked egg whites alternately into the egg yolks. Divide the mixture equally between the two sandwich tins and bake in the centre of an oven pre-heated to 350°F (mark 4) for 30 minutes, or until set. Test by pressing the top of the cakes with a finger – it should leave no impression. Remove the cakes from the oven, and allow them to shrink slightly before turning them out to cool on a wire rack.

Meanwhile, prepare the filling: cream the butter until fluffy and sift the icing sugar, chocolate and coffee together; beat it gradually into the butter. When the cakes are cool, sandwich them together with the filling. Set the torte aside while preparing the caramel topping.

Put 3 dessertspoons of water and 3 oz. of caster sugar in a small, heavy-based saucepan. Stir the contents over low heat until dissolved into a clear syrup. Increase the heat and boil the syrup rapidly, without stirring, until it is a rich golden colour.

Remove the pan from the heat immediately and pour most of the caramel over the top of the cake. Spread it evenly with an oiled knife and mark the topping into portions with an oiled knife. Garnish the top quickly with the whole nuts before the caramel hardens. As the remaining caramel cools it can be trickled over the nuts or pulled into a spun sugar veil* and arranged on top of the cake.

Savouries & Snacks

ALPINE FONDUE

Ideally, this cheese fondue should be cooked in an earthenware fireproof dish, but a heavy-based saucepan may be used instead.

PREPARATION TIME: *5 min.*
COOKING TIME: *15–20 min.*

INGREDIENTS *(for 4–6):*
2 peeled cloves garlic
¾ lb. diced Gruyère cheese
¼ pint milk
¾ pint dry white wine
1 tablespoon Kirsch
Salt and white pepper
1 French loaf

Rub the sliced garlic round the sides and base of the cooking receptacle. Cook the cheese and milk over very low heat, stirring continuously with a wooden spoon, until the cheese melts and the mixture becomes smooth and creamy. Gradually blend in the wine and Kirsch; season with salt and pepper and heat the fondue through without boiling.

Heat the French loaf in the oven until crisp. Cut it into 1 in. cubes and serve with the fondue. Use forks or skewers for dipping the bread into the cheese.

SAVOURY EGG BÉNÉDICT

This unusual version of egg and bacon makes a quick snack. For a lunch or supper dish, a salad or green vegetable would make it a complete meal.

PREPARATION TIME: *5 min.*
COOKING TIME: *15–25 min.*

INGREDIENTS *(for 4):*
¼ pint Hollandaise sauce
½ level teaspoon dry mustard
Cayenne pepper
Mixed herbs
4 slices cooked ham or 4 rashers back bacon
2 oz. unsalted butter
4 eggs
4 slices thick white bread

Make the Hollandaise sauce* and season it with the mustard, a little cayenne and mixed herbs. Keep it warm. Trim the ham to fit the bread or fry the bacon rashers in a little butter until crisp. Meanwhile, poach the eggs* lightly in simmering salted water and toast the bread.

Butter the toast, cover each slice with ham or bacon, and top with an egg. Pour over the warm sauce and serve at once.

MUSHROOMS WITH BACON

Bacon and mushrooms are inexpensive ingredients for savoury snacks or meals in a hurry.

PREPARATION TIME: *10 min.*
COOKING TIME: *20 min.*

INGREDIENTS *(for 4):*
¼ lb. sliced button mushrooms
½ oz. butter
8 thin rashers streaky bacon
½ pint white sauce
¼ level teaspoon mixed herbs
Cayenne, salt, black pepper
4 slices buttered white toast

Cook the mushrooms in the butter over low heat for 3 minutes. In a clean pan, fry the bacon until crisp – do not use any fat – then drain on kitchen paper and crumble the bacon into small pieces.

Make the white sauce*, add the mixed herbs and season with salt, freshly ground pepper and cayenne. Gently fold the mushrooms and bacon into the sauce; heat through. Pile the mixture on to the buttered toast and serve at once.

FRIDAY NIGHT SPECIAL

Ready-made fish cakes provide a speedy if uninspired meal. But served with cheese, tomato sauce and scalloped potatoes*, they become a family treat.

PREPARATION TIME: *5 min.*
COOKING TIME: *15 min.*

INGREDIENTS *(for 4–6):*
12 fish cakes
1 tablespoon olive oil
1 finely chopped clove garlic
1 small, finely chopped onion
15–16 oz. tinned tomatoes
1 level tablespoon tomato purée
½ level teaspoon caster sugar
¼ level teaspoon sage
Salt and black pepper
Fat or oil for frying
12 thin slices Cheddar cheese

Heat the oil in a pan and cook the garlic and onion over medium heat until the onion is transparent. Add the tomatoes with their juice, the tomato purée, sugar and sage; season with salt and freshly ground pepper. Bring this sauce to the boil, then simmer for 5 minutes.

Heat the fat in a heavy-based pan and fry the fish cakes until crisp and golden on both sides. Top the drained fish cakes with cheese, and grill until the cheese has melted; arrange on a serving dish, and pour over the sauce.

QUEEN OF PUDDINGS

Although this is usually thought of as a nursery sweet, both children and fathers come back for a second and third helping.

PREPARATION TIME: *15 min.*
COOKING TIME: *30–35 min.*

INGREDIENTS *(for 4–6):*
4 oz. white bread, crusts removed
1 pint Jersey milk or single cream
2 oz. unsalted butter
3 eggs, separated
Grated rind of a lemon
5 oz. caster sugar
4 rounded tablespoons apricot or strawberry jam

Cut the bread into ½ in. cubes and put them in a lightly buttered baking dish. Heat the milk and butter until just warm, then add the beaten egg yolks, the lemon rind and 3 oz. of the sugar. Pour this custard over the bread. Bake the pudding in the centre of a pre-heated oven, at 350°F (mark 4), for about 20 minutes or until set. Remove from the oven and spread the jam over the pudding.

Whisk the egg whites until stiff, and fold in the remaining sugar. Pile this meringue over the jam, and return the pudding to the oven for another 10 minutes or until the top is crisp.

Indian/Malay Curry Lunch

Basically, a curry is a stew or casserole of fish, shellfish, meat, poultry or vegetables, cooked in a spicy sauce. The art of blending herbs and spices, which forms the basis of Indian and Malay cooking, can be traced back for 6000 years.

Just as ancient are the stringent rules for preparing and eating curry – rules which vary according to climate, the type of local produce, religious background and racial origins.

In general, the hotter the climate, the hotter the curry. The mildest curries are Kashmiri, from the mountains in the north of the Indian sub-continent, whereas the much hotter Vindaloo curries come from the baking plains of the south. Curries from the north also tend to be based on meat, while rice and vegetable curries predominate in the south. The type of meat depends on religion: Hindus never eat beef; and while some eat fish, chicken or lamb, others are entirely vegetarian. Moslems will not touch pork, but most eat beef.

Most Indian and Malay dishes are cooked in vegetable oil or *ghee* – the equivalent of clarified butter. In Britain, *ghee*, and other ingredients used in the following recipes, can be bought from shops specialising in Oriental produce. Ready-made curry powder is not used in genuine Indian cookery: the cook daily makes up his own *garam masala*, or blend of spices.

Main dishes are all served at the same time, with side dishes of sambals, yoghurt, salads, chappatis or poppadoms, coconut, rice and chutneys. Guests help themselves, first to rice then to the other dishes. Before the main curry courses, serve a starter such as a Malayan satay or Indian samosas. A soup can be served either before or with the curry courses. The main course should include one chicken or meat curry with plenty of gravy and one dry curry, one fish or prawn dish, one or two vegetable dishes and several side dishes.

The 'correct' thing to drink with curry is nothing at all. Indians do not even sip water but wait until after the meal. Western taste buds usually find a curry on its own rather fierce, so serve water, cool lager or light ale.

To conclude the meal, serve chilled fresh fruit salad or ice cream; or, for a change, crisp, sweet jalebis.

Coconut cream and milk

Fresh or desiccated coconut yields both cream and milk which are used in many soups and sauces.

Drill two or three holes at the top of the coconut and shake out the colourless liquid. Saw the coconut in half and scrape out the flesh. Shred it finely, pour over $\frac{1}{4}$ pint boiling water and leave for 20 minutes. Squeeze through a muslin bag to produce cream.

For coconut milk, put the squeezed coconut and $\frac{1}{4}$ pint cold water in a pan, and bring to the boil. Remove from the heat, leave for 20 minutes, then squeeze through muslin again. Coconut cream and milk can also be made in a liquidiser.

Curry ingredients

Fresh and dried herbs and spices are widely used in Eastern cooking. A typical selection might include:

1. *Rice flour* 2. *Dried shrimps*
3. *Coriander seeds* 4. *Mustard seeds*
5. *Cardamom seeds* 6. *Rose essence*
7. *Ground nuts* 8. *Almonds*
9. *Pistachio nuts* 10. *Long grain rice* 11. *Soy sauce* 12. *Pomegranate seeds* 13. *Dried chillies*
14. *Cinnamon sticks* 15. *Ground cumin* 16. *Fresh chillis*
17. *Coconut* 18. *Ground turmeric*
19. *Root ginger* 20. *Bay leaves*
21. *Mango* 22. *Parsley*
23. *Lemon* 24. *Dried tamarind*
25. *Mint*

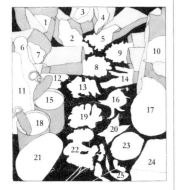

Garam Masala

This mixture of spices is an essential ingredient of curry dishes. The Indian cook blends spices each day according to his own choice, but the following recipe is suitable for all curries.

INGREDIENTS: *2 oz. coriander seeds; 2 oz. black peppercorns; 1½ oz. cumin seeds; 4 teaspoons whole cloves; 20 peeled cardamom seeds; 2 level tablespoons ground cinnamon*

Grind the whole seeds in a coffee grinder. Blend the ground mixture with the cinnamon and use as required. Any surplus can be stored in an airtight jar and will keep for up to a month.

Soups & Starters

Kashmiri Yoghourt Soup

PREPARATION TIME: *30 min.*
CHILLING TIME: *30 min.*

INGREDIENTS: *1 peeled diced cucumber; salt; 1 peeled clove garlic; 1 tablespoon white wine vinegar; 1½ pints natural yoghourt; 1 tablespoon olive oil; 1 tablespoon chopped mint*

Put the cucumber in a dish, sprinkle with salt and leave for 30 minutes. Rub the inside of a large serving bowl with the sliced garlic. Rinse the bowl with the vinegar, and shake it out. Spoon the yoghourt into the bowl, stirring until it has thinned down, adding a little water if necessary.

Drain the cucumber, mix into the yoghourt and chill for 30 minutes. Just before serving, blend in the olive oil, a few drops at a time, and sprinkle with mint.

Malayan Beef and Prawn Soup

PREPARATION TIME: *30 min.*
COOKING TIME: *2 hours*

INGREDIENTS: *1 lb. lean beef; 3 onions; 2 cloves garlic; knob fresh ginger; ¾ level teaspoon ground turmeric; 1 level teaspoon ground coriander; 8 oz. shelled prawns; 3 level tablespoons butter; salt; 1 tablespoon fresh lime or lemon juice*

Put the beef in a pan with 2½ pints cold water, 1 peeled and quartered onion, and 1 flattened clove of garlic. Bring to the boil, cover and simmer for 1 hour.

Peel and mince the onion and pound it with the remaining garlic, ginger, turmeric and coriander. Chop the prawns roughly and fry them in 2 tablespoons butter for 2 minutes. Add the pounded onion mixture and fry for 3–4 minutes.

Using a perforated spoon, lift out the onion and garlic from the soup. Add the prawn and onion mixture and continue simmering the soup until the beef is quite tender. Take out the beef, slice it thinly and return it to the soup. Season to taste with salt. Cut the remaining onion into thin rings and fry until crisp.

Stir the lime juice into the soup, and sprinkle with onion rings.

Samosas

PREPARATION TIME: *50 min.*
COOKING TIME: *15 min.*

INGREDIENTS: *6 oz. plain flour; salt; 4 tablespoons ghee; 4 fluid oz. curds or yoghourt; 1 onion; 1½ teaspoons fresh ginger; 1 level tablespoon coriander seeds; 1 level teaspoon chilli powder; ¾ lb. mashed potatoes; 1–1½ teaspoons garam masala; 1½ tablespoons sieved mango; 1–2 tablespoons milk; fat for frying*

Sift the flour and a pinch of salt into a bowl, stir in 3 tablespoons ghee and the curds (or yoghourt); knead gently into a soft dough. Shape the dough into a ball, and cover with a large bowl. Rest the dough for 25–30 minutes while preparing the stuffing: peel and finely chop the onion and ginger, and pound the coriander seeds. Heat the remaining ghee and fry the onion until just soft. Blend in the coriander, ginger and chilli powder, and simmer for 2–3 minutes. Add the mashed potato; season to taste with salt, and blend in the garam masala and the mango pulp. Simmer until all moisture has evaporated. Remove from the heat and allow to cool.

Roll out the dough thinly and cut into 2½ in. squares. Brush the edges with milk or water, fold each square corner to corner, to make a triangle, and seal.

Heat the fat and deep fry a few samosas at a time until golden brown on both sides. Drain on crumpled paper and serve hot.

Beef Satay

PREPARATION TIME: *20 min.*
STANDING TIME: *2 hours*
COOKING TIME: *20 min.*

INGREDIENTS: *1½ lb. lean beef; 1 tablespoon blanched almonds; 1 tablespoon sliced root ginger; 1 level teaspoon ground coriander; 1 level teaspoon ground turmeric; ½ pint coconut milk; salt and black pepper; 1 level teaspoon brown sugar*

Pound the almonds, ginger, coriander and turmeric to a paste in a mortar and gradually dilute it with coconut milk. Cut the meat into bite-size cubes, sprinkle them with salt and ground pepper. Marinate* the meat in the spiced coconut milk for 2 hours.

Remove the meat from the marinade and thread the cubes on to bamboo skewers; sprinkle them with sugar and grill, turning and basting* frequently with the marinade. Allow two skewers per person and serve with satay sauce.

Satay Sauce

PREPARATION TIME: *15 min.*
COOKING TIME: *15 min.*

INGREDIENTS: *2 onions; 1–2 tablespoons peanut oil; 3 oz. roasted peanuts; ½ level teaspoon chilli powder; 1 level teaspoon light brown sugar; salt; 1 tablespoon soy sauce; juice of half lime*

Peel and thinly slice one onion and fry in the hot peanut oil. Peel and finely chop the second onion and pound it with the peanuts and chilli powder in a mortar or liquidiser. Add this paste to the pan and fry for a further 3 minutes, stirring continuously. Gradually dilute the mixture with ¼ pint warm water and stir in the sugar. Cook for a few minutes until the sauce has the consistency of single cream. Season to taste with salt, soy sauce and lime juice. Serve the sauce hot.

Fish

Curried Fish, Bombay Style

PREPARATION TIME: *20 min.*
COOKING TIME: *35 min.*

INGREDIENTS: *2 oz. ghee; 2 lb. fish fillets (cod, hake, halibut or turbot); 1 chopped onion; 2 chopped cloves garlic; 1–2 dried, chopped chillis; 1 level teaspoon ground coriander; ½ level teaspoon ground turmeric; ½ level teaspoon ground mustard seeds; 1 level teaspoon rice flour; ½ pint coconut milk; juice of half lemon; salt*

Cut the fish fillets in 2 in. pieces. Heat the butter over moderate heat and fry the onion until soft and transparent. Add the garlic, chillis and the ground spices, stir and reduce the heat.

Dilute the rice flour with coconut milk, pour it over the contents in the pan and blend well. Add lemon juice and season to taste with salt. Simmer the sauce gently, until it thickens, add the fish, and simmer for 20 minutes or until tender.

Prawns in Coconut, Malay style

PREPARATION TIME: *10 min.*
COOKING TIME: *20 min.*

INGREDIENTS: *2 large, finely chopped onions; 2–3 tablespoons ghee; 1 rounded teaspoon garam masala; 1 sliced green pepper; 12 cooked, unshelled prawns; salt; ½ pint coconut cream*

Fry the onions over low heat in the ghee, until soft and pale golden. Add the garam masala and cook for a further 2–3 minutes. Blend in the pepper. Cover and simmer for 10 minutes. Add the prawns, season with salt, and cook for 1 minute.

Keep the heat as low as possible; stir in the coconut cream and simmer until the prawns and the sauce are heated through. Do not let the sauce boil.

257

Satays – diced meat on skewers – are popular in the East. They are served as hors-d'oeuvre with drinks and sold from stalls on street corners

Indian sweets are sweetmeats rather than desserts, and jalebis are typical of these. Jalebi powder is a yellow colouring compound

Poultry & Meat

Elachi Murghi

PREPARATION TIME: *30 min.*
COOKING TIME: *45 min.*

INGREDIENTS: *2 spring chickens; salt; 2 finely chopped onions; 4 oz. ghee; 1 rounded teaspoon ground cardamom; 1 level teaspoon black peppercorns; 4 oz. chicken livers; 1½ oz. fresh white bread-crumbs; vegetable oil*

Wipe the cleaned chickens thoroughly and rub them inside with salt. Fry the onions gently in 3 tablespoons ghee until soft. Add the cardamom and ground peppercorns; reduce the heat and continue cooking the onions for 6–7 minutes. Add the chopped chicken livers and cook until brown. Season.

Simmer the mixture for 7–8 minutes, then remove from the heat and stir in the breadcrumbs. Stuff the chickens with this spicy filling. Brush them with oil and set the chicken on the spit or on a trivet in the roasting pan. Roast the chickens in the centre of a pre-heated oven at 400°F (mark 6), for 35–40 minutes, basting* with the remaining ghee.

Roghan Josh (Kashmir)

PREPARATION TIME: *25 min.*
COOKING TIME: *1¼ hours*

INGREDIENTS: *2 lb. boned leg of lamb; knob fresh ginger; 3 oz. ghee; 1 level dessertspoon ground coriander; 1½ level teaspoons garam masala; salt; chilli powder; 2 oz. blanched almonds; 1 oz. blanched pistachio nuts; 4 tablespoons double cream*

Cut the meat into 1 in. pieces. Peel and chop the ginger and sprinkle over the meat. Heat the ghee in a large sauté pan and fry the lamb and ginger over high heat until evenly brown. Add the coriander and garam masala; season to taste with salt and chilli powder

and gradually blend in 1 pint cold water. Bring to the boil, lower the heat and simmer, covered, until the lamb is tender and the liquid evaporated.

Pound half the almonds in a mortar, adding a teaspoon of iced water from time to time, until a smooth paste is obtained. Mix the cream into the almond paste, then stir this mixture into the lamb. Cook for another 5 minutes over lowest possible heat. Serve the lamb and sauce sprinkled with the chopped almonds and nuts.

Beef Kofta

PREPARATION TIME: *20 min.*
COOKING TIME: *55 min.*

INGREDIENTS: *1 lb. lean minced beef; 2–4 fresh, finely chopped chillies; 1 tablespoon finely chopped onion; 1 clove garlic, crushed; salt and black pepper; pinch ground cinnamon; 1 large egg; plain flour; 4–5 tablespoons ghee; 2 thinly sliced onions; 1–2 rounded tablespoons garam masala; 1 pint fresh coconut milk; lime or lemon juice*

Blend the beef with the chopped chillies, onion and garlic. Season with salt, pepper and cinnamon and bind with the beaten egg. Roll the mince, between floured hands, into walnut-size balls.

Heat 2–3 tablespoons ghee and fry a few meat balls at a time, turning them carefully, until evenly browned all over. Remove the fried balls and drain.

Fry the sliced onion over low heat in the ghee left in the pan, until soft and transparent. Blend in the garam masala and cook for a further 5 minutes, stirring all the time. Gradually blend in the coconut milk, simmer for 2 minutes, correct seasoning, and sharpen with a dash of lime juice.

Heat the kofta balls in the sauce for 25–30 minutes. Shake the pan gently from time to time.

Nasi Goreng

This Malay rice dish with omelette is an excellent way of using up left-over cooked meat, poultry, fish, shellfish and vegetables.

PREPARATION TIME: *30 min.*
COOKING TIME: *35 min.*

INGREDIENTS: *8 oz. long grain rice; 2 oz. dried shrimps; 6 oz. peanut oil; 2 finely chopped onions; 1 finely chopped clove garlic; 1 finely shredded, fresh chilli or ½ level teaspoon chilli powder; 8 oz. cooked diced meat; salt and black pepper*
OMELETTE: *1–2 tablespoons butter or vegetable oil; 3–4 chopped spring onions; 1 skinned, chopped tomato; salt and chilli powder; 3–4 tablespoons soy sauce; 4 eggs; cucumber slices*

Boil and drain the rice. Spread it on a dish to cool and meanwhile soak the shrimps in cold water.

Heat the oil in a large pan and fry the onions until transparent. Add the garlic and chilli and fry for 3 more minutes. Stir in the meat and cook for 2 minutes, before adding the rice and the drained shrimps. Continue frying stirring frequently, until the rice turns pale golden. Season to taste. Put the rice mixture on a warm serving dish.

For the omelette, fry the spring onions in the oil until soft. Add the tomato and cook for a further 2–3 minutes. Season with salt, chilli powder and half the soy sauce. Cook for 3 minutes. Beat the eggs lightly and stir them into the pan, cover and cook the omelette, over low heat, until set. Remove from the pan, and shred the omelette finely.

Arrange the omelette over the rice, sprinkle with the remaining soy sauce and garnish with cucumber slices. Serve a bean sambal and a dish of crispy bananas separately.

Vegetables & Side Dishes

Aubergines with Yoghourt

PREPARATION TIME: *40 min.*
COOKING TIME: *10 min.*

INGREDIENTS: *2–3 aubergines; salt; olive oil; ½ pint natural yoghourt; 1–2 crushed cloves garlic*

Cut the washed and dried aubergines crossways into thin slices; sprinkle them with salt and leave to stand for 30 minutes. Rinse in cold water, dry and sprinkle lightly with salt.

Heat ¼ in. olive oil in a pan and fry the aubergines, in single layers, until golden on both sides. Drain on crumpled paper and arrange the aubergines on a serving dish. Serve cold.

Stir the garlic into the yoghourt and serve this dressing separately.

Mixed Vegetable Curry

PREPARATION TIME: *15 min.*
COOKING TIME: *30 min.*

INGREDIENTS: *2–3 cloves garlic; 3 tablespoons ghee; 2 level tablespoons garam masala; juice of half lime or lemon; 1 chopped onion; 3 or 4 skinned and roughly chopped tomatoes; 8 oz. peeled and quartered potatoes; 8 oz. sliced green beans; 8 oz. shelled peas; caster sugar; salt*

Crush and pound the garlic, and mix it into a smooth paste with the garam masala and lime juice. Heat the ghee and fry the paste over low heat for 5 minutes, stirring constantly. Add the onion and cook for 2 more minutes, then stir in the tomatoes, 2–3 tablespoons water and a pinch of sugar. Cook for 5 minutes.

Add the potatoes, beans and peas; season with salt and pour over enough water to barely cover the vegetables. Simmer, covered, until the potatoes are cooked, after 15–20 minutes.

Bean Sambal

PREPARATION TIME: *15 min.*
COOKING TIME: *15 min.*

INGREDIENTS: *1 small onion; 1–2 cloves garlic; 2 fresh red chillies (seeded); small piece (½ teaspoon) tamarind; 2–3 tablespoons peanut oil; 1 lb. French beans; 1 small bay leaf; 1 dried lemon leaf; 1 teaspoon brown sugar; salt; ½ pint coconut milk*

Pound the peeled and chopped onion and garlic, the chopped chillies, and the tamarind until they are reduced to a smooth paste. Fry the paste in the oil for 5 minutes.

Top, tail and wash the beans, cut them into 2 in. pieces and stir into the spiced paste. Add the bay and lemon leaves, together with sugar and salt to taste. Gradually blend in the coconut milk. Bring the mixture to the boil, then simmer for 10–12 minutes. Remove the bay and lemon leaves.

Mint Chutney

INGREDIENTS: *2 oz. fresh mint leaves; 8 spring onions; 2 small fresh green chillies; salt; 1 level teaspoon sugar; 1 level teaspoon garam masala; 1 tablespoon pomegranate seeds; 1 tablespoon sieved mango pulp or lime juice*

Wash, drain and finely chop the mint leaves. Chop the spring onions and the chillies. Pound the ingredients with salt, sugar and garam masala. Add the crushed pomegranate seeds, and pound until smooth. Mix in the mango and spoon into a bowl.

Crispy Bananas

Peel six small bananas and cut them in half lengthways. Dip them in lemon juice and coat with brown sugar. Deep fry the bananas in peanut oil in a large shallow pan, until crisp and golden. Drain on crumpled paper and serve at once.

A selection of dishes for a curry party, arranged on an Indian *thali*, a deep metal tray. Reading from left to right are:
1. Crisp poppadoms
2. Boiled rice 3. Mango chutney 4. Onion salad
5. Lime pickle 6. Roghan Josh
7. Benyaal chutney
8. Yoghourt with diced cucumber
9. Elachi Murghi 10. Prawns in coconut. In the foreground, bean sambal, plain yoghurt and fried aubergines, crispy bananas

Jalebis

PREPARATION TIME: *30 min.*
RESTING TIME: *8 hours*
COOKING TIME: *15 min.*

INGREDIENTS: *6 oz. plain flour; salt; ¾ level tablespoon baking powder; 3 tablespoons curds or natural yoghourt; 1 lb. caster sugar; 1 teaspoon jalebi powder or powdered saffron or turmeric; rose or jasmine water; ghee or oil for deep frying; chopped pistachio nuts for garnish*

Sift the flour, with a pinch of salt and the baking powder into a bowl; gradually stir in ½ pint warm water, and then the curds,

beating until the batter is smooth. Cover the bowl with a cloth and leave in a warm place to ferment for 8 hours.

Dissolve the sugar in 1 pint of water, add the jalebi powder and a few drops of flower water. Boil over high heat until the syrup thickens; remove from the heat and keep the syrup warm over a pan of hot water. Heat the ghee or oil in a large, shallow pan until bubbling. Heat the batter in a separate pan, stirring continuously; if necessary, beat in more flour and water until the batter has the consistency of thick cream. Pipe the batter into the

hot ghee through a piping bag fitted with a fine plain nozzle. Move the nozzle so as to form rings within rings. As soon as one circle is done, close the nozzle with the tip of a finger, and repeat the pouring.

Fry a few jalebis at a time, until golden brown on both sides. Remove with a perforated spoon, drain on crumpled paper, then plunge the jalebis into the warm syrup and leave for at least 15 minutes.

Lift out the jalebis with a perforated spoon and sprinkle them with pistachio nuts. Serve jalebis hot or cold.

November

The chimney all sootie would not be made cleane,
   for feare of mischances, too oftentimes seene:
Old chimney and sootie, if fier once take,
   by burning and breaking, soone mischeefe may make.

This Month's Recipes

*Piping hot soup, sizzling fried sausages, roasted chestnuts and baked
apples help to keep November's cold at bay on Guy Fawkes' Night*

Food in Season

Root vegetables such as maincrop carrots, parsnips and turnips are plentiful this month. They make a meat casserole stretch further as well as adding extra flavour. Winter cabbages, cauliflower, broccoli and Brussels sprouts have replaced fresh salad vegetables and are usually cheaper and in larger supplies.

Eels, plaice and herrings are economical, and scallops are less expensive than in October. The first tiny sprats appear, and skate is also at its best.

The game season is at its height, with snipe and teal to be seen in high-class poulterers' shops; wild goose and pheasant are also available. The first clementines, tangerines and satsumas make their appearance, together with Brazil nuts and walnuts. Imported cranberries, from America and Canada, should now be made into jams and jellies ready for the turkey in December.

Fish

Angler tail
Bass
Bream, freshwater
Bream, sea
Brill
Carp
Clams
Cod
Coley
Conger eels
Crab
Dabs
Dover sole
Dublin Bay prawns
Eels
Flake (also sold as
  rock salmon)
Flounder
Grey mullet
Haddock
Hake
Halibut
Herrings
Lemon sole
Lobster
Mackerel
Mock halibut (or
  Greenland halibut)
Mussels
Oysters (native)
Oysters, Portuguese
Pike
Plaice
Prawns
Redfish
Scad
Scallops
Shrimps
Skate
Sprats
Trout, rainbow
Turbot
Whitebait
Whiting
Winkles
Witch

Poultry & Game

Chicken
Duck
Goose
Guinea fowl
Grouse
Hare
Mallard
Partridge
Pheasant
Pigeon
Quail
Rabbit
Snipe
Teal
Turkey
Venison
Wild duck
Wild goose
Woodcock

Vegetables

Asparagus
Aubergines
Avocado pears
Beetroots
Broccoli
Brussels sprouts
Brussels tops
Cabbages
Carrots
Cauliflowers
Celeriac
Celery
Chicory
Chillies
Courgettes
Cucumbers
Fennel
Garlic
Horseradish
Jerusalem artichokes
Kale
Kohl rabi
Leeks
Lettuce
Mushrooms
Onions
Parsley
Parsnips
Pumpkin
Radishes
Salad cress
Salad onions
Salsify
Savoys
Spinach
Spring greens
Swedes
Sweet potatoes
Tomatoes
Turnips
Watercress

Fruit

Almonds
Apples
Bananas
Brazil nuts
Chestnuts
Chinese gooseberries
Clementines
Cranberries
Coconuts
Dates
Grapefruit
Grapes
Figs
Filberts
Mandarins
Medlars
Melons
Oranges
Pawpaws
Peaches
Pears
Pineapples
Pomegranates
Tangerines
Satsumas
Uglis
Walnuts

SUGGESTED MENUS

Buckling with Horseradish Cream
Coeur Coriandre
Creamed Potatoes
Crêpes Georgette

Petits Royales au Parmesan
Bream Plaki
Galette Lyonnaise
Meringue Mont Blanc

Smoked Eel Smetana
Savoury Game Pie
Celeriac and Potatoe Purée
Linzertorte

Chicken and Almond Soup
Crown of Pork
Green Beans, Tuscany Style
Apple and Nut Strudel

Haricot Lamb Casserole
Roasted Onions
Bread and Butter Pudding

Prawn Cocktail
Orange-Glazed Lamb Roast
Austrian Cabbage with Soured Cream
Tutti-Frutti Pudding with Orange Foam Sauce

Leeks Niçoise
Lasagne Verde al Forno
Green Salad with Sauce Vinaigrette
Crème Caramel à l'Orange

Soups & Starters

NEW ENGLAND FISH CHOWDER

The traditional chowder or fish soup cum stew is a perfect cold-weather dish which takes less than an hour to prepare and cook. Any type of white fish fillet may be used, and prawns can be substituted for the crabmeat.

PREPARATION TIME: *20 min.*
COOKING TIME: *20–25 min.*

INGREDIENTS *(for 4–6)*:
1 lb. cod fillet
1 large onion
½ lb. potatoes
2 oz. mushrooms
3 oz. pickled belly pork
1 oz. butter
2 level dessertspoons flour
½ pint milk
2 oz. chopped white crabmeat
Salt and black pepper
Lemon juice
2 level tablespoons chopped parsley
GARNISH:
Bread croûtons

Wash the fish and cut it into three or four pieces. Peel and roughly chop the onion. Peel the potatoes and cut them into ½ in. cubes, trim the mushrooms* and slice them. Bring 1 pint of water to the boil, add 1 level teaspoon salt and the fish and simmer over low heat for 10 minutes. Drain the fish and set the liquid aside. Remove the rind and gristle and dice the pork. Fry the pork in a sauté pan over low heat until the fat runs. Add the butter and continue frying until the pork crisps. Add the potatoes, onion and mushrooms to the pork and fry for a further 5 minutes.

Remove the pan from the heat and stir in the flour, then gradually add the milk. Bring the mixture to simmering point, then stir in ¾ pint of the reserved fish stock. Add the fish, which will break up naturally, and the crabmeat. Simmer for 10 minutes, season to taste with salt, freshly ground pepper and lemon juice; stir in the parsley.

Serve the chowder with a bowl of crisp bread croûtons*.

SMOKED EEL SMETANA

This quick starter is reputed to have been a favourite of Smetana, the Czech composer. For a special occasion it makes a change from smoked trout or salmon.

PREPARATION TIME: *15 min.*

INGREDIENTS *(for 4)*:
8 oz. smoked eel fillets
2 hardboiled eggs
1 level teaspoon made French mustard
3 tablespoons olive oil
1 tablespoon tarragon vinegar
3 tablespoons soured cream
Salt and black pepper
Caster sugar
2 rounded tablespoons chopped beetroot

Peel off any skin and arrange the fillets on four individual serving plates. Cut the eggs in half and rub the yolks through a coarse sieve; chop the whites finely. Mix together the yolks, mustard, oil, vinegar and cream. Season to taste with salt, freshly ground pepper and sugar. Add the beetroot to the dressing.

Arrange the dressing along one side of the eel fillets and sprinkle with the chopped egg white. Serve with thin slices of brown bread and butter.

PRAWN COCKTAIL

The Americans invented the colourful prawn cocktail, now a popular international starter. The prawns can be replaced with lobster or white crabmeat, or mixed shellfish can be used to make a seafood cocktail.

PREPARATION TIME: *15 min.*
CHILLING TIME: *1 hour*

INGREDIENTS *(for 4)*:
8 oz. shelled prawns
8 level tablespoons tomato ketchup or chutney
¼ pint double cream or mayonnaise
1 level dessertspoon creamed horseradish
1 teaspoon Worcestershire sauce or a few drops Tabasco
Lemon juice
4 rounded tablespoons finely shredded lettuce heart
GARNISH:
4 thin lemon slices

Remove the grey veins from the prawns and select four of the largest; set them aside for garnish.

Blend together the tomato ketchup and cream (or mayonnaise*), add the creamed horseradish and flavour to taste with Worcestershire sauce or Tabasco. Sharpen with lemon juice.

Divide the shredded lettuce into four equal portions and place in the bottom of serving glasses. Arrange the prawns over the lettuce and cover with the sauce. Chill the cocktails in the refrigerator for about 1 hour.

Just before serving, hang one of the reserved prawns from the rim of each glass. Opposite the prawn, fix a thin lemon slice; slit to the centre and press over the edge of the glass.

CHICKEN AND ALMOND SOUP

Feather Fowlie is the true name of this traditional Scottish soup. By adding cream to the soup, it was given a French touch to please Mary, Queen of Scots.

PREPARATION TIME: *30 min.*
COOKING TIME: *about 3½ hours*

INGREDIENTS *(for 6)*:
1 boiling fowl (4–5 lb.)
1 lb. mixed root vegetables (onions, carrots and turnips)
3 sticks celery
10 black peppercorns
½ level teaspoon salt
Bouquet garni
2 oz. ground almonds
3 rounded tablespoons fresh white breadcrumbs
¼ pint double cream
GARNISH:
Chopped parsley or chives
Bread croûtons

Peel and roughly chop the vegetables. Put the cleaned chicken in a large saucepan, together with the vegetables, peppercorns, salt and bouquet garni*. Cover with cold water and bring to the boil over high heat. Remove any scum from the surface, lower the heat and cover the pan with a lid. Simmer for 2–3 hours or until the fowl is tender.

Lift the chicken from the stock; let it cool slightly before removing the skin and cutting all the flesh off the carcass. Put the meat in the liquidiser, with the vegetables.

Put the purée in a large clean pan, mix in the almonds and breadcrumbs and stir in about 2 pints of the chicken stock, strained through a sieve. Bring the soup to the boil and simmer over low heat for 30 minutes, stirring frequently.

Before serving, blend half a cup of hot soup with the cream and stir this mixture back into the soup. Correct seasoning and serve the soup garnished with finely chopped parsley or chives and with bread croûtons*.

Soups & Starters

Fish

PETITS ROYALES AU PARMESAN

Edwardian hostesses frequently served this dish as a first course. It is a moulded custard, delicately flavoured – in this case with Parmesan cheese. In the good old days, the cook would prepare the consommé from bone stock – however, a good tinned consommé works equally well.

PREPARATION TIME: *20 min.*
COOKING TIME: *35 min.*
CHILLING TIME: *3 hours*

INGREDIENTS *(for 4)*:
2 eggs plus 3 egg yolks
½ pint consommé
1 level dessertspoon chopped parsley or chervil
1 level teaspoon powdered thyme or oregano
¼ pint double cream
1 oz. grated Parmesan cheese
1–2 oz. grated Gruyère or Emmenthal cheese
GARNISH:
Watercress sandwiches

Beat the eggs and egg yolks together. Bring the consommé to the boil over low heat, together with the parsley (or chervil), chives and thyme (or oregano). Simmer, uncovered, for 5 minutes. Gradually strain the consommé into the eggs, stirring all the time. Blend in 2 tablespoons of cream.

Butter four dariole moulds* and pour the consommé mixture into them. Set them in a roasting tin, containing ½ in. of water; cover the moulds with a piece of buttered greaseproof paper. Bake in the centre of an oven, pre-heated to 350°F (mark 4) for about 15 minutes or until set. Remove the moulds from the

oven and leave to cool, before chilling in the refrigerator for a few hours.

About 20 minutes before serving, pre-heat the oven to 400°F (mark 6). Unmould the darioles on to a buttered oven-proof dish. Pour over the remaining cream, cover with grated Parmesan and sprinkle generously with Gruyère cheese. Place the dish near the top of the oven and bake until the cheese melts and turns golden.

Serve at once, with a separate plate of thin sandwiches of brown buttered bread and finely chopped watercress.

BUCKLING WITH HORSERADISH CREAM

Whole smoked herrings, known as buckling, are inexpensive appetisers. They look particularly attractive served in deep scallop shells, and can be prepared well in advance.

PREPARATION TIME: *15 min.*
COOKING TIME: *30 min.*

INGREDIENTS *(for 4)*:
2 large buckling
4 tablespoons double cream
2–3 teaspoons lemon juice
2 rounded teaspoons grated horse-radish
1 teaspoon tarragon vinegar
Salt and black pepper
Caster sugar
½ cucumber
GARNISH:
Lemon slices

Fillet each buckling into two halves, carefully removing the roe, skin and all bones. Break the fillets up into bite-sized pieces.

Blend the cream with the lemon juice, horseradish and vinegar, and season to taste with salt, freshly ground pepper and sugar.

Cut the unpeeled cucumber into thin slices and use to line four deep scallop shells or individual shallow serving dishes. Mix the buckling carefully into the dressing and pile the mixture into the centre of the shells.

Top each portion with a lemon slice and serve with thin brown bread and butter.

FRITTO MISTO MARE

The Mediterranean abounds with small fish which the locals mix happily together and deep fry *(fritto misto)* until crisp and golden. They can be fried in a light, almost transparent batter or simply dusted with flour before frying – in that case prawns should be fried in their shells, and the heads need not be removed from the small fish.

PREPARATION TIME: *30 min.*
COOKING TIME: *35 min.*

INGREDIENTS *(for 6)*:
½ lb. smelts
½ lb. sprats
½ lb. prawns
Olive or corn oil for deep frying
BATTER:
2 dessertspoons vegetable oil
4 oz. plain flour
Salt
1 egg white
GARNISH:
Parsley sprigs, lemon wedges

Make the batter* first so that it has time to rest while the fish is being prepared. Blend the oil with ½ pint of tepid water and gradually stir it into the flour sifted with a pinch of salt. Beat the batter until quite smooth. Just before using it, fold the stiffly beaten, but still moist egg white into the batter.

Cut the heads off the smelts and sprats and shell the prawns. Heat the oil* to 375°F (a cube of bread will crisp in 1 minute when the oil is hot enough). Dip the fish and the prawns, one at a time, in the batter, using either tongs or a small perforated spoon. Hold them over the bowl for a moment to allow the surplus batter to drip off, then put them into the basket in the hot oil and fry for 5–6 minutes, until crisp and golden. Fry the fish in small batches and drain on crumpled absorbent paper.

Serve the fish on a heated dish, garnished with parsley sprigs, lightly fried in the oil, and lemon wedges. A sauce tartare* and crusty bread are also suitable.

TURBOT DUGLÉRÉ

This classic French dish can also be made with halibut steaks or thick fillets of Dover sole, which should be folded over in two. For a first course, half quantities only are necessary. The fish should be flaked, mixed with dugléré sauce (tomato, cream and parsley), and served in small dishes.

PREPARATION TIME: *15 min.*
COOKING TIME: *35 min.*

INGREDIENTS *(for 4)*:
4 turbot steaks
Fish trimmings
1 oz. butter
Juice of a lemon
Salt and black pepper
4 fluid oz. dry white wine
SAUCE:
2–3 tomatoes
1 oz. butter
2–3 level dessertspoons plain flour
*2 level dessertspoons fresh
    chopped parsley*
2½ fluid oz. double cream
GARNISH:
Lemon twists and parsley sprigs

Wash and trim the turbot steaks and put the trimmings in a pan of cold water to make a court bouillon*.

Butter a shallow ovenproof dish thoroughly. Rub the steaks with lemon juice, place them in the dish and season with salt and freshly ground pepper. Add the wine and sufficient court bouillon to come to the top of the fish without covering it. Place a piece of buttered foil or greaseproof paper over the turbot and cook in the centre of a pre-heated oven, at 375°F (mark 5), for 25 minutes, or until a white curd appears on the fish to show that it is cooked.

Lift the turbot steaks on to a warm serving dish, and strain the cooking liquid.

While the fish is cooking, skin the tomatoes*. Remove the pulp in the centre of the tomatoes with a teaspoon and rub it through a sieve to remove the seeds. Set the tomato liquid aside and cut the flesh into thin strips.

Melt the butter for the sauce in a small pan, remove from the heat and stir in sufficient flour to absorb all the butter. Blend in the tomato liquid and about ½ pint of the reserved fish liquid. Return the pan to the heat and bring the sauce to simmering point, stirring continuously. Cook over low heat for 3–5 minutes. Add the tomato strips and the parsley, and then stir in the cream; do not let the sauce boil again. Adjust seasoning with salt, pepper and lemon juice and pour the sauce over the fish.

Garnish the turbot steaks with lemon twists* and sprigs of parsley. Serve with Duchess potatoes* or with small moulds (timbales*) of boiled and buttered rice.

FILETS DE SOLE WALEWSKA

This classic dish is named after the beautiful Polish Countess Maria Walewska, who was so devoted to Napoleon that she begged in vain to be allowed to accompany him into exile in Elba. It is composed of sole and craw-fish (or langouste), garnished with slices of truffle. If truffles are too expensive, use small mushrooms.

PREPARATION TIME: *40 min.*
COOKING TIME: *1¼ hours*

INGREDIENTS *(for 4)*:
2 Dover sole (1¼ lb. each)
1 bay leaf
1 large parsley sprig
1 small onion
6 peppercorns
Salt
Juice of a large lemon
4 fluid oz. dry white wine
*4 cooked crawfish tails (each
    weighing 6 oz.)*
4 oz. unsalted butter
1½ oz. plain flour
¼ pint milk
*3–4 oz. grated Cheddar or
    Gruyère cheese*
2½ fluid oz. double cream
Salt and black pepper
GARNISH:
*8 thin slices of truffle or 8 small
    flat mushrooms*
Lemon slices
Parsley sprigs

Ask the fishmonger to skin and fillet each sole* and cut it into four. Put the bones and skin into a pan with the bay leaf, parsley, peeled onion and whole pepper-corns; cover with lightly salted water. Simmer the fish trimmings over low heat for 20–30 minutes then strain this court bouillon* and set it aside.

Wash and trim the fillets. Rub them with lemon juice to whiten them, then arrange them in a buttered shallow ovenproof dish. Pour over the wine and sufficient court bouillon to nearly cover the fillets. Cover the dish with lightly buttered greaseproof paper, and cook in the centre of a pre-heated oven, at 375°F (mark 5), for 20–25 minutes.

Meanwhile, remove the shells from the crawfish tails and take out the flesh in one piece. Cut each crawfish in half lengthways.

When the sole fillets are cooked, lift them out carefully with a perforated slice and keep them warm. Pour the liquid into a pan, boil over high heat for 5 minutes to reduce* it, and strain off 8 fluid oz.

Make a roux* with half the butter and all the flour. Gradually stir in the milk and bring this sauce to simmering point. Blend in the reserved fish liquid and cook for a further 5 minutes. Stir in the grated cheese until it has melted. Gradually add the cream. Season to taste with salt and freshly ground pepper. Cover the pan with a lid and keep the sauce warm without further cooking.

Heat the remaining butter and sauté the crawfish tails over high heat for about 3 minutes until they are just turning colour.

Arrange the sole fillets in a circle on a round, warm serving dish, with the tail ends towards the centre, and set the crawfish round the edge of the dish. Stir the sauce, which should now just coat a wooden spoon; otherwise thin it with a little fish liquid.

Coat the fillets carefully with the sauce and put the dish under a hot grill for 1 minute to glaze the sauce.

Garnish each fillet with a slice of truffle – if mushrooms are used, sauté them lightly in a little butter and place them, dark side uppermost, on the fillets. Decorate the dish with lemon twists* and tiny sprigs of parsley. Serve with Duchess potatoes* and mange-tout peas.

Meat

BREAM PLAKI

Large fish such as bream, brill and John Dory are well suited to being cooked by this Greek method. The fish is baked whole in the oven, and tomatoes and lemon are obligatory in a plaki.

PREPARATION TIME: *15 min.*
COOKING TIME: *45 min.*

INGREDIENTS *(for 4–6)*:
2–3 lb. bream
1 large onion
1 large clove garlic
1 level teaspoon fennel or coriander seeds
3 tablespoons olive oil
Salt and black pepper
1 large lemon
1–2 level tablespoons chopped parsley
15–16 oz. tin of tomatoes
4 fluid oz. dry white wine

Peel and thinly slice the onion and peel the garlic. Crush the fennel or coriander seeds in a mortar or with a broad-bladed knife. Scale and clean the fish* and place it whole in an oiled baking dish; sprinkle generously with salt, freshly ground pepper and the juice from half the lemon.

Heat the remaining oil in a pan and fry the onion and crushed garlic over medium heat, until soft and transparent. Stir in the tomatoes, with their juice; add the parsley, crushed seeds and wine. Cook this sauce for a few minutes until well blended, then season with salt and pepper.

Pour the sauce over the bream, topping up with a little water, if the baking dish is large. Cut the remaining lemon into thin slices and lay them on top of the fish. Cover the dish with foil or a lid, and bake in the centre of a pre-heated oven, at 375°F (mark 5), for about 45 minutes.

When cooked, arrange the bream on a heated serving dish, and pour the sauce over it. Serve with jacket or floury boiled potatoes.

SKATE WITH CAPERS AND BEURRE NOIR

Capers and beurre noir (black butter) are classic French garnishes with skate and cod. In Britain, skate is usually sold skinned on one side, but in France it is left unskinned.

PREPARATION TIME: *20 min.*
COOKING TIME: *30–35 min.*

INGREDIENTS *(for 4–6)*:
2 lb. wing of skate
1 pint court bouillon
2 oz. unsalted butter
2–3 tablespoons wine vinegar
Salt and black pepper
1 tablespoon capers
GARNISH:
1 level tablespoon chopped parsley

Skate is usually sold already prepared by the fishmonger; otherwise rinse it thoroughly and trim off the gristly bones round the edges. Cut the skate into strips about 4 in. long and 2 in. wide. Poach* them over low heat in a pan of court bouillon* for 25–30 minutes. Lift the fish out with a perforated spoon and leave to drain on a cloth. Carefully scrape the skin off the fish. Place on a warm serving dish.

Heat the butter in a frying pan until nut-brown then immediately pour it over the skate. Put the vinegar in the pan, add a little salt and a few twists of pepper and cook over high heat until reduced* to 1 tablespoon. Mix in the capers and pour over the fish.

Sprinkle chopped parsley over the skate and serve with boiled or creamed potatoes.

VEAL CHOPS MAGYAR

Paprika is the most usual spicing in Hungarian dishes. It varies considerably in strength according to its origin, and the sauce should be tasted after being cooked for a while.

PREPARATION TIME: *20 min.*
COOKING TIME: *1¼ hours*

INGREDIENTS *(for 4)*:

4 large veal chops
Seasoned flour
½ lb. mushrooms
1 onion
1 oz. butter
1 tablespoon oil
3–4 level dessertspoons plain flour
½ pint milk
½ pint veal stock or chicken bouillon
Salt
Juice of a small lemon
1 small tin (2¼ oz.) tomato concentrate
3–4 level teaspoons paprika
2 level teaspoons caster sugar
¼ pint single cream
GARNISH:
6–8 mushroom caps
Paprika
1 level tablespoon chopped parsley

Trim the fat off the chops and coat them with seasoned flour*. Trim the mushrooms* and, if large, cut them into quarters or halves. Peel and thinly slice the onion. Heat the butter and oil in a flameproof casserole, pat the loose flour off the chops and fry them over high heat until golden brown, turning once. Remove the chops from the pan and fry the mushrooms and onion for a few minutes, until soft.

Remove the casserole from the heat and stir in sufficient flour to absorb the fat. Gradually blend in the milk and then the stock, stirring continuously. Bring to simmering point and cook for 3 minutes until the sauce has thickened. Season to taste with salt and lemon juice. Mix the tomato concentrate, paprika, sugar and cream together in a small bowl. Blend in 3 or 4 dessert-spoons of the hot sauce and pour the mixture back into the sauce, stirring thoroughly.

Return the veal chops to the casserole. They should be completely covered by the sauce, so add a little more stock if necessary. Cover the casserole with a lid and cook over low heat for 45 minutes or until the veal is tender, stirring from time to time to prevent sticking. Do not allow to reach boiling point or the sauce will separate.

Adjust seasoning and arrange the chops in the centre of a serving dish with the sauce spooned over them. Surround with a border of fluffy rice, garnished with the whole mushroom caps fried in a little butter. Set the mushrooms, dark side uppermost, on the rice and fill the centre of each with paprika. Sprinkle chopped parsley between the mushrooms.

CROWN OF PORK

This is an impressive and colourful main course for a large dinner party. The crown, which should be ordered in advance, is cut from the loin of pork and cannot be constructed from less than 12 cutlets. The crown should have the fat carefully trimmed off by the butcher, as it cannot crisp when filled with a stuffing.

PREPARATION TIME: *35 min.*
COOKING TIME: $2\frac{1}{2}$ *hours*

INGREDIENTS *(for 10–12)*:

1 crown of pork (12 cutlets)
Lard
1 bouillon cube
STUFFING:
1 large onion
3 oz. celery
6 oz. carrots
6 tinned pineapple rings
2 tablespoons corn oil
3 oz. cooked rice

4 level dessertspoons chopped
   fresh parsley
1 level teaspoon dried savory
1–2 level teaspoons paprika
3 oz. sultanas
Salt and black pepper
Lemon juice
GARNISH:
6 tinned pineapple rings
Watercress

Prepare the stuffing first. Peel and finely chop the onion, celery and carrots. Finely chop six pineapple rings and set the juice aside.

Heat the oil in a pan over moderate heat and fry the onion and celery until just turning colour. Add the rice, carrots and parsley, together with the savory, paprika, pineapple and sultanas. Mix all the ingredients thoroughly and heat through. Season to taste with salt, freshly ground pepper and lemon juice. Set the stuffing aside to cool.

Stand the crown of pork in a greased roasting tin and cover the meat thoroughly with melted lard. Spoon the stuffing into the centre of the crown and cover it with a piece of foil. Wrap foil round each cutlet bone to prevent it charring. Roast the crown in the centre of a pre-heated oven, at 375°F (mark 5) for $2\frac{1}{4}$ hours or until amber-coloured juice runs out when a skewer is inserted in the meat. Lift out the crown and keep it warm on a serving dish in the oven.

Fry the pineapple rings for garnishing in the hot fat in the roasting tin for about 4 minutes or until golden brown on both sides. Slit through one side of each ring and arrange in a curling twist round the crown of pork.

Pour the fat carefully from the roasting tin and add the pineapple juice to the residue in the pan. Crumble the bouillon cube into the juices and bring the gravy to boiling point. Cook over high heat until the gravy is brown and has reduced* slightly. Pour into a warm sauce boat.

Remove the foil from the tips of the cutlets and replace with paper frills. Garnish with small sprigs of watercress between the pineapple twists. Serve the crown with roast or rissolé potatoes* and with green beans.

CHILLI CON CARNE

The Mexican national dish of beef and bean stew is ideal on a cold winter's night. It is strongly flavoured with chilli powder, and for an even spicier dish, a few crushed cumin seeds may also be added. The beans should be soaked overnight in cold water, or use the tinned variety.

PREPARATION TIME: *30 min.*
COOKING TIME: $1\frac{3}{4}$–2 *hours*

INGREDIENTS *(for 6)*:
1 lb. lean minced beef
12 oz. dried or 2 large tins red
   kidney beans
2 onions
2 tablespoons olive oil
15–16 oz. tin of tomatoes
2 level teaspoons chilli powder
   or 1 finely chopped chilli pepper
Salt
Cumin seeds (optional)

Soak the dried kidney beans in cold water overnight. The following day drain the beans thoroughly. Peel and thinly slice the onions.

Heat the oil in a flameproof dish over low heat and fry the onions until soft. Stir in the meat and continue frying, stirring occasionally, until the meat has browned. Blend in the drained kidney beans, add the tomatoes with their juice, and season to taste with chilli, salt and crushed cumin seeds.

Cover the pan with a lid and cook on top of the stove or in the centre of a pre-heated oven, at 300°F (mark 2) for 1 hour if tinned beans are used. Allow 2 hours for dried soaked beans.

Serve the stew straight from the dish, with crusty bread and a tossed green salad.

COEUR CORIANDRE

Hearts are usually stuffed and braised slowly for several hours as they tend to be dry. In this French farmhouse recipe they are marinated in lemon juice before being braised in an apple and cider sauce, with an unusual spicing of coriander.

PREPARATION TIME: *20 min.*
COOKING TIME: *1–1½ hours*

INGREDIENTS *(for 4)*:
4 lamb or 2 calf hearts
Juice of a lemon
½ lb. onions
2 medium cooking apples
2–3 rounded tablespoons plain flour
1½ oz. butter
Salt and black pepper
2 bay leaves
¼ pint cider
1 level teaspoon crushed coriander seeds
1 level teaspoon caster sugar
2 thin slices unpeeled lemon

Cut the hearts in slices, about ½ in. thick, and remove all fat, gristle and blood vessels. Put the slices in a basin with the lemon juice and leave to marinate* for 30 minutes. Meanwhile, peel and slice the onions and the cored apples.

Drain the heart slices and coat them with flour, then fry them in the butter in a flameproof casserole over high heat. Add the onion and continue frying until pale golden. Season well with salt and freshly ground pepper. Add the bay leaves and the cider. Cover the heart slices with the apple and sprinkle them with coriander seed and sugar. Lay the lemon slices on top of the apples.

Put the lid on the casserole and simmer over low heat on top of the stove or in a pre-heated oven, at 300°F (mark 2), for about 1 hour or until tender. When cooked, remove the lemon slices and bay leaves and stir the apple slices into the sauce.

Serve the casseroled hearts with creamed potatoes.

TOURNEDOS ROSSINI

The Italian composer Rossini (1792–1868) enjoyed a great reputation not only as a musician, but also as a creator of gourmet dishes. The following is one of his best-known culinary masterpieces, traditionally garnished with truffles or flat mushrooms.

PREPARATION TIME: *15 min.*
COOKING TIME: *20 min.*

INGREDIENTS *(for 6)*:
6 tournedos of beef
6 slices white bread
4–5 oz. unsalted butter
1 tablespoon vegetable oil
2 fluid oz. Madeira, Marsala or brown sherry
¼ pint Espagnole sauce
¼ pint brown stock
Salt and black pepper
GARNISH:
6 slices pâté de foie gras
6 slices truffle or 6 flat mushrooms

Ask the butcher to trim the tournedos and tie them neatly. Cut six circles from the bread slices to fit the tournedos exactly.

Heat 2 oz. of butter and the oil in a large frying pan over medium heat and fry the bread until crisp and golden. Drain on crumpled paper and keep hot.

Heat 1½ oz. butter in a sauté pan and fry the tournedos over high heat, turning once, for 1½-2 minutes on each side. They should be rich brown on the outside and rosy-pink inside. Lift out and keep warm. Add the wine to the sauté pan, stirring to scrape up all the residue in the pan. Cook until the juices have reduced*, after about 2 minutes. Blend in the prepared Espagnole sauce* and the stock and leave the sauce to cook, uncovered, until it has thickened.

Meanwhile, heat the remaining butter in a clean sauté pan and fry the slices of foie gras over high heat, until golden. Lift out and keep warm. Lightly sauté the truffles or mushrooms in the remaining butter.

To serve, arrange the bread circles on a warmed dish, set a tournedo on each and top with a slice of foie gras and truffle or mushroom, dark side uppermost. Correct the seasoning of the sauce. Pour sufficient round the bread to cover the base of the dish and spoon the remainder into a warm sauce boat. Serve with matchstick potatoes* and buttered spinach or baby sprouts.

HARICOT LAMB CASSEROLE

This French country-style casserole is made from one of the least expensive cuts of meat, but has great appeal to both eye and palate. Ask the butcher to joint the lamb into single ribs.

PREPARATION TIME: *35 min.*
COOKING TIME: *1¾ hours*

INGREDIENTS *(for 4–6)*:
3 lb. middle neck of lamb
3 leeks
6 fresh or 15–16 oz. tinned tomatoes
½ lb. carrots
2 cloves garlic
2 tablespoons oil
1 tablespoon caster sugar
Salt and black pepper
2 dessertspoons plain flour
¾ pint stock or bouillon
1 bay leaf
½ level teaspoon powdered thyme
½ lb. French or runner beans

Pre-heat the oven to 450°F (mark 8). Trim the roots and coarse outer leaves off the leeks, wash them thoroughly and chop them roughly. Skin the tomatoes*. Peel or scrape the carrots, but leave them whole, and peel the garlic cloves.

Heat the oil in a flameproof casserole on top of the stove and quickly brown the lamb joints on both sides. Sprinkle with sugar, lower the heat and toss the contents until the sugar caramelises slightly. Season with salt and pepper, and sprinkle in half the flour.

Place the casserole, uncovered, in the hot oven for 5 minutes. Turn the meat over, season again and sprinkle with the remaining flour. Bake for a further 5 minutes. Reduce the oven heat to 325°F (mark 3). Remove the casserole, lift out the meat, and lightly fry the leeks in the casserole on top of the stove. Add the stock and bring to the boil, scraping up any residue on the bottom of the casserole. Put in the meat, add the tomatoes, carrots, bay leaf, thyme and crushed garlic. Cover the casserole with a lid and bring to simmering point. The sauce should almost cover the meat; add a little more stock if necessary.

Return the casserole to the centre of the oven and cook for 1½ hours or until the meat is tender. Top and tail the beans, and string them if necessary. Cut them into ½ in. pieces and cook in boiling salted water for 10 minutes, or until just tender. Drain, and add to the casserole and cook them in the sauce for a further 5 minutes.

Serve the lamb straight from the casserole, with potatoes baked in their jackets.

SCALLOPINI WITH ARTICHOKES AND LEMON SAUCE

For this easily prepared dish, choose small veal escalopes (scallopini), ¼ in. thick. Veal cutlets may be used instead but will require longer cooking. Be sure to buy *fonds* (bottoms) of artichokes, not the hearts.

PREPARATION TIME: *15 min.*
COOKING TIME: *25 min.*

INGREDIENTS *(for 4)*:
8 veal escalopes (each about
  2–3 oz.)
Seasoned flour
2 oz. butter
1 rounded dessertspoon finely
  chopped shallot or onion
12 oz. tin artichoke bottoms
4 fluid oz. dry white wine
½ pint chicken stock or bouillon
2 small lemons
¼ pint double cream
Salt and black pepper

Trim any fat from the escalopes and coat them in seasoned flour*. Heat the butter in a heavy-based pan over medium heat and fry the escalopes for a few minutes, until golden brown, turning once. Add the shallots and artichoke bottoms, and pour over the wine. Bring the mixture to simmering point, and reduce the heat. Add sufficient stock or bouillon to cover the veal completely. Grate the rind from the lemons and set aside, and add the squeezed lemon juice to the sauce. Cover the pan with a lid and cook over low heat for 20 minutes or until the veal is tender.

Stir in the cream and simmer the sauce for a further 5–6 minutes, uncovered, until the sauce has a creamy texture.

Adjust seasoning with salt and freshly ground pepper.

Arrange the escalopes in the centre of a warmed serving dish and surround with a border of buttered noodles or fluffy rice. Pour the sauce over the meat and top with a scattering of grated lemon rind.

ORANGE-GLAZED LAMB ROAST

A fruit-flavoured glaze and stuffing transform a leg of lamb into a dish fit for a special occasion. Ask the butcher to bone the lamb, but not to roll it.

PREPARATION TIME: *20 min.*
COOKING TIME: *2¼ hours*

INGREDIENTS *(for 6–8)*:
4–4½ lb. leg of lamb (boned)
1 large onion
Grated rind of 2 oranges
1 oz. butter
3 oz. fresh white breadcrumbs
2 oz. sultanas
2 oz. raisins
2 oz. currants
½ level teaspoon dried rosemary
½ level teaspoon dried thyme
Salt and black pepper
Juice of an orange
GLAZE:
2 oz. soft brown sugar
Juice of half lemon
Juice of an orange
2 tablespoons Worcestershire
  sauce
SAUCE:
4 fluid oz. red wine
½ pint beef bouillon
GARNISH:
Orange slices and watercress

Prepare the stuffing for the lamb first. Peel and finely chop the onion and grate the rind from two oranges. Melt the butter in a pan over medium heat and fry the onion for 3 minutes. Mix together in a bowl the breadcrumbs, sultanas, raisins, currants and the fried onion. Blend in the orange rind, rosemary and thyme and season to taste with salt and freshly ground pepper. Bind the stuffing with squeezed juice of one orange.

Wipe the meat with a damp cloth, and pack the stuffing into the lamb. Tie the joint into a neat shape, securing it with string. Put it in a greased baking tin.

Place the glaze ingredients in a small pan and cook over low heat for 1 minute, then spoon the glaze over the meat. Roast in the centre of a pre-heated oven, at 375°F (mark 5), for 2 hours, basting* frequently.

Remove the joint to a warm serving dish and keep it hot. Stir into the pan the wine and bouillon for the sauce, and boil over high heat, scraping up all the residue from the glaze. Continue boiling briskly until the sauce has reduced* and thickened slightly. Correct seasoning if necessary.

Serve the joint, having first removed the string, and garnish with thin orange twists* and with sprigs of watercress. Pour the sauce in a warm sauce boat. Galette Lyonnaise (see November vegetables) and buttered baby sprouts or salsify would go well with the joint.

Veal escalopes and artichoke fonds are arranged on a bed of buttered noodles

Glazed leg of lamb garnished with thin orange twists and sprigs of watercress

Poultry & Game

FLAMED PORK FILLET WITH APRICOTS

This quick and easy dish is suitable for cooking in a chafing dish at the table, once all the ingredients have been prepared. Prunes may be used instead of apricots; they should be soaked in water for 3–4 hours.

PREPARATION TIME: *25 min.*
COOKING TIME: *15 min.*

INGREDIENTS *(for 4)*:
1¼ *lb. pork fillet*
Seasoned flour
2 tablespoons dry sherry
4 oz. dried apricots
1 oz. unsalted butter
2 tablespoons brandy
2½ fluid oz. soured cream
Salt and black pepper
Lemon juice

Put the apricots and the water in which they were soaking into a saucepan, add the sherry and cook over low heat for 15 minutes. Trim any fat off the pork fillet and remove the outer skin. Cut it into 1½ in. thick slices or round medallions and toss them in the seasoned flour*.

Heat the butter in a frying pan or chafing dish over medium heat and fry the pork on both sides until golden and tender, turning once only. Pour off any surplus fat. Heat the brandy, set it alight and pour it over the pork. Add the strained apricots and stir until the brandy flames have burnt out.

Mix the soured cream with the apricot liquid and pour it into the pan. Simmer for a few minutes, then season to taste with salt, freshly ground pepper and lemon juice. Serve with fluffy boiled rice.

WILD DUCK WITH MANDARINS

The largest wild duck is the mallard, which usually provides three or four servings; teal and widgeon are even smaller. As the meat is tough, wild duck are best roasted continental style with liquid in the roasting pan, and should be served with a fruit-flavoured sauce. The recipe is also successful for domestic duck.

PREPARATION TIME: *35–40 min.*
COOKING TIME: *1 hour*

INGREDIENTS *(for 3–4)*:
1 large mallard
Bouquet garni
4 oz. cooked noodles
1 onion
1 level dessertspoon fresh chopped parsley
½ level teaspoon dried thyme
Pinch nutmeg
4 dessertspoons honey
2 dessertspoons beer
2 egg yolks
2½ fluid oz. double cream
3 mandarin oranges
2 fluid oz. port
Lemon juice
Salt and black pepper
GARNISH:
Mandarin slices and watercress

Clean the duck giblets and put them in a saucepan with water to cover; add salt, freshly ground pepper and the bouquet garni*. Cover the pan with a lid and cook for about 25 minutes or until the giblets are tender. Strain and set the cooking liquid aside. Skin the gizzard and chop this, the heart and the liver finely.

Chop the drained noodles roughly and mix in the giblets, chopped onion, herbs and nutmeg. Mix half the honey and half the beer with the egg yolks and cream and stir this into the noodle mixture. Open the vent and remove any knobs of fat from the duck, spoon in the stuffing and close the opening.

Put the duck in a roasting pan, breast downwards and pour water into the pan to a depth of ½ inch. Roast in the centre of a pre-heated oven, at 375°F (mark 5), for 20 minutes, basting* occasionally. Remove the duck from the roasting pan, put in a wire rack and replace the duck, breast upwards. Pour the remaining honey and beer over the duck and continue roasting for a further 30 minutes, or until the duck is crisp and golden and the legs are tender when tested with a skewer.

Meanwhile grate the rind from the mandarin oranges and set aside. Having first removed the pith and pips, put the fruit in the liquidiser.

When the duck is ready, lift it on to a warm serving dish. Add the mandarin pulp and rind to the pan, together with the port and ½ pint of the reserved giblet stock. Boil on top of the stove over high heat until the gravy has reduced* and thickened slightly. Sharpen with lemon juice and adjust seasoning. Strain the gravy into a warm sauce boat.

Garnish the duck with watercress sprigs and thin slices of unpeeled mandarin. Serve with roast or Duchess potatoes* and buttered green beans.

SAVOURY GAME PIE

The traditional English game pie is usually cooked under a covering of puff or suet crust pastry. The continental pastry crust for this pie is less trouble than a puff pastry and richer and lighter than suet crust. The pie filling may be venison, hare or game bird, all of which should be marinated.

PREPARATION TIME: *45 min.*
COOKING TIME: *about 3 hours*

INGREDIENTS *(for 6)*:
1½ *lb. haunch or shoulder of venison*
2 oz. pickled belly pork
½ *lb. mushrooms*
2–3 level dessertspoons plain flour
Salt and black pepper
MARINADE:
1 onion
1 stick celery
7 coriander seeds
7 allspice or juniper berries
2 bay leaves
2 sprigs parsley
Pinch marjoram
8 fluid oz. red wine
2½ fluid oz. olive oil
PASTRY:
½ *lb. plain flour*
½ *level teaspoon salt*
4 oz. butter
1½ *oz. lard*
2 egg yolks
1 egg

Cut the venison into 1 in. cubes, removing all gristle. Prepare the vegetables and spices for the marinade*: peel and finely chop the onion, scrub the celery and chop it finely, and crush the coriander seeds and allspice or juniper berries.

Put the venison in a large bowl, in layers with the prepared vegetables and crushed spices. Add the bay leaves, parsley sprigs and marjoram and pour over the wine mixed with the oil. Cover the bowl and leave the venison to marinate for at least 8 hours.

Pre-cook the pie filling to avoid over-baking the pastry. Dice the pickled pork and fry it over low heat to extract all the fat. Add the butter to the pan, together with the trimmed and sliced mushrooms*. Blend in sufficient flour to absorb all the fat and cook this roux* for about 3 minutes.

Lift the venison from the marinade and strain this through a sieve. Gradually blend the marinade liquid into the roux, add the venison, and bring the sauce to boiling point. Thin with a little water if necessary, and season to taste with salt and freshly ground pepper. Cover the pan with a lid and simmer over low heat for 1½ hours. Adjust seasoning if necessary and leave the venison to cool while making the pastry.

Sift the flour and salt into a mixing bowl. Rub in the butter and lard until the mixture has a breadcrumb consistency. Beat the egg yolks with 2 tablespoons of cold water and blend into the flour. Knead the pastry dough until it leaves the sides of the bowl clean, adding more water if necessary. Leave the kneaded dough to rest in a cool place for at least 1 hour.

Spoon the cold venison and sauce into a deep pie dish, setting a pastry funnel in the centre. Roll out the pastry on a floured surface, to a thickness of ¼ in. Cut off ½ in. wide pastry strips and place them on the moistened rim of the pie dish. Brush with water before covering the filling with the remaining pastry. Seal the pastry edges, trim them with a knife and knock up*. Scallop the edges and brush the pastry with lightly beaten egg; decorate with leaves cut from the pastry trimmings and brush with more egg. Make a few slits in the pastry for the steam to escape.

Bake the pie in the centre of a pre-heated oven, at 425°F (mark 7), for 20 minutes, then reduce the heat to 375°F (mark 5) and bake for a further 30 minutes or until the pie is golden brown.

Serve the game pie hot, with creamed celeriac and potato purée (see November vegetables).

PERDRIX AUX CHOUX

Partridge with cabbage is a classic French farmhouse method of cooking older game birds. Gourmets maintain that the casserole should be cooked with older partridge, which are then replaced with young, oven-roasted partridge just before serving. Grouse and plump wood pigeon may also be cooked in this way.

PREPARATION TIME: *30 min.*
COOKING TIME: *2 hours*

INGREDIENTS *(for 4):*
2 plump partridge
4 rashers green streaky bacon
2 level tablespoons plain flour
1 oz. lard or bacon fat
4 pork chipolata sausages
4 oz. pickled belly pork
1 large onion
1 small white cabbage
Salt and black pepper
5 fluid oz. red wine

If not already done by the poulterer, truss the partridge neatly, bard* the breasts with the bacon rashers and secure with string. Peel and thinly slice the onion. Roll the birds in the flour and pat off the surplus.

Heat the lard or fat in a flame-proof casserole or large pan and brown the birds and the sausages all over, then remove from the pan. Remove the rind and gristle and cut the pickled pork into ½ in. chunks, then put into the casserole together with the sliced onion; fry until both are just turning colour. Pour off any remaining fat. Remove any coarse outer leaves from the cabbage, wash it and blanch* for 5 minutes in boiling salted water. Cut into quarters, remove the tough centre stalk and shred the cabbage coarsely.

Put half the shredded cabbage in the pan and mix with the pork and onion. Add a few twists of pepper – the pork is already salty – put in the partridge and cover with the remaining cabbage.

Pour over the wine, cover the casserole tightly and cook over low heat on top of the stove, or in the centre of a pre-heated oven at 325°F (mark 3), for about 2 hours or until tender, depending on the age of the birds. If the liquid evaporates during cooking add more wine or a little chicken stock.

To serve, lift out the partridge, remove the string and cut each bird in half. Arrange the partridge and sausages on the cabbage. Serve with potatoes in their jackets.

VENISON CUTLETS

For this dish, cutlets from a young, well-hung deer are preferable, otherwise they will take a long time to cook and would require marinating for 24 hours. The whisky sauce lends a distinctive flavour to the game.

PREPARATION TIME: *20 min.*
COOKING TIME: *1¾–2 hours*

INGREDIENTS *(for 6):*
6 venison neck cutlets
2 oz. green streaky bacon
1 onion
2 carrots
2 sticks celery
Juice of a lemon
12 juniper berries
1 level teaspoon dried marjoram or thyme
Salt and black pepper
1½ oz. butter
1 oz. plain flour
1¼–½ pint stock or water
2 tablespoons whisky
2 level dessertspoons cranberry sauce
Juice of a small orange
GARNISH:
Bread croûtons
Whole cranberries or orange wedges

Trim the venison cutlets and beat them lightly to flatten them. Remove the rind and gristle from the bacon and chop the rashers roughly. Peel and finely chop the onion, carrots and celery.

Rub the cutlets with lemon juice and crush the juniper berries in a mortar or with the blade of a knife. Mix with the marjoram or thyme, and add a few twists of ground pepper; rub this mixture into both sides of each cutlet.

Heat the butter in a flameproof casserole dish and fry the bacon

over low heat until the fat runs. Turn up the heat and brown the cutlets briskly on both sides, then remove from the casserole. Fry the onion, carrots and celery until lightly coloured; season with salt. Sprinkle the flour over the vegetables and cook over low heat until the mixture is light brown. Blend in the stock and the whisky, bring the sauce to simmering point. Put the cutlets back in the sauce, making sure that it just covers the top of the meat – if necessary add a little more stock.

Cover the dish with a lid and cook in the centre of a pre-heated oven at 325°F (mark 3) for

about 1½ hours or until the meat is tender. Remove the cutlets from the dish and keep them warm. Add the cranberry sauce and orange juice to the sauce, adjust seasoning and sharpen to taste with lemon juice.

Arrange the cutlets upright round a mound of celeriac or chestnut and potato purée (see November and October vegetables); intersperse the cutlets with fried bread croûtons* and garnish with whole cranberries or peeled orange wedges. Paper frills may be fixed to the cutlets. Pour the sauce into a warmed sauce boat and serve separately.

271

Rice & Pasta

BANGKOK CHICKEN AND RICE

In spite of its name, this is one of the great dishes from the famous Indonesian Rijstafel. It makes an attractive centrepiece for a buffet, surrounded by small dishes of colourful fresh vegetables and fruit to which guests help themselves.

PREPARATION TIME: *35 min.*
COOKING TIME: *2¾ hours*

INGREDIENTS *(for 6–8)*:
1 small boiling chicken (approx. 3½ lb.)
1 lb. onions
1 bay leaf
1 sprig parsley
Salt and black pepper
1 lb. long grain rice
3 tablespoons olive or vegetable oil
2 level tablespoons peanut butter
½ level teaspoon chilli powder
4 oz. peeled prawns
4 oz. diced cooked ham
1 level teaspoon cumin seeds
1½ level teaspoons coriander seeds
1 clove garlic
Pinch ground mace
GARNISH:
Half a cucumber
2 hardboiled eggs
8–12 unpeeled prawns

Put the chicken in a large pan, with one whole peeled onion, the bay leaf and parsley sprig. Add a seasoning of salt and freshly ground pepper and enough cold water to cover the chicken. Bring to the boil, remove any scum from the surface, then cover the pan with a lid and simmer over gentle heat for about 2 hours or until the chicken is tender.

Lift out the chicken and leave to cool slightly. Strain the stock through a fine sieve and use it to

cook the rice until just tender. Drain the rice through a colander and cover it with a dry cloth.

Remove the skin from the chicken and cut the meat into small pieces. Peel and thinly slice the remaining onions. Heat the oil in a large pan, and fry the onions over low heat until they begin to colour. Stir in the peanut butter and chilli powder. Add the peeled prawns, diced ham and the chicken and finally the rice, which should now be dry and fluffy. Continue frying over low heat, stirring frequently until the rice is slightly brown. Crush the cumin and coriander seeds and the peeled garlic, and stir them, with the mace, into the rice. Season to taste with salt.

Pile the rice and chicken mixture on to a hot serving dish and garnish with thin slices of unpeeled cucumber, wedges of hardboiled egg and large prawns.

Arrange a number of small side dishes or bowls round the chicken. A suitable selection might include apricot and mango chutney; sliced tomatoes, dressed with sugar and lemon juice; peeled, sliced oranges; and sliced green and red pepper with raw onion rings, both in a vinaigrette sauce*. Other bowls could contain small wedges of fresh pineapple, sweetened with icing sugar; fried sliced bananas with lemon juice; and fresh shredded and toasted coconut. Shelled almonds or cashew nuts fried in a little butter are also frequently served with a Rijstafel.

LASAGNE VERDE AL FORNO

The district round Bologna in Italy is famous for its lasagne – pasta squares often coloured with spinach (*verde*). The pasta is usually baked in the oven with a Bolognese *ragù* or meat and vegetable stew with alternating layers of thick Béchamel sauce. This dish is an ideal main course for a small party as all the preparations can be done well in advance of cooking.

PREPARATION TIME: *1 hour*
COOKING TIME: *20 min.*

INGREDIENTS *(for 6)*:
½ lb. green lasagne
2 oz. fat ham or bacon
1 small onion
1 carrot
2 oz. button mushrooms
1 oz. butter
6 oz. minced beef
2–3 oz. chicken livers (optional)
1 rounded tablespoon tomato concentrate
5 fluid oz. dry white wine
½ pint beef stock or bouillon
1 level teaspoon caster sugar
Salt
¾ pint Béchamel sauce
2 oz. grated Parmesan cheese

Chop the ham or bacon, having first removed rind and gristle. Peel and finely chop the onion and carrot and trim the mushrooms* before slicing them thinly.

Melt half the butter in a large, heavy-based pan over low heat and fry the ham (or bacon) until the fat runs, then add the vegetables and fry them lightly. Crumble in the minced beef, and add the cleaned and chopped chicken livers if used. Blend in the tomato concentrate. Continue frying, and stir continuously until the meat has browned. Add the wine and let the mixture bubble for a few minutes before adding the stock. Season to taste with sugar, and add salt if stock is used. Cover the pan with a lid and simmer over low heat for 30–40 minutes. Meanwhile make a thick Béchamel sauce*.

Cook the lasagne in a large pan of boiling salted water for 10–15 minutes or until just tender, stirring occasionally. Drain the pasta through a colander and drop it into a large basin of cold water to prevent it sticking together.

Thoroughly butter a shallow ovenproof dish, about 10 in. by 8 in. Cover the base with a thin layer of the meat mixture, then Béchamel sauce and lastly the drained lasagne. Repeat these layers until all the ingredients are used up, finishing with Béchamel sauce. Sprinkle the top with the Parmesan cheese.

Bake in the centre of the oven, pre-heated to 400°F (mark 6), for about 15–20 minutes or until the top is crisp and bubbly. Serve straight from the dish accompanied by a tossed green salad.

Vegetables & Salads

TAGLIATELLI ALLA CARBONARA

Many pastas, such as tagliatelli (flat egg noodles), spaghetti and macaroni were formerly cooked over a charcoal burner (*alla carbonara*). By extension the term now covers a pasta dish cooked with bacon, eggs and cheese.

PREPARATION TIME: *10 min.*
COOKING TIME: *15 min.*

INGREDIENTS *(for 6)*:
8 oz. tagliatelli
2 oz. streaky green bacon
2 oz. cooked ham
1 oz. butter
1 tablespoon olive oil
4 eggs
2 oz. grated Cheddar cheese
1 oz. grated Parmesan cheese
Salt and black pepper

Remove the rind and gristle from the bacon and chop the rashers roughly; dice the ham. Cook the tagliatelli in plenty of well-salted boiling water for 10–15 minutes or until just tender. Drain thoroughly in a colander.

While the tagliatelli is cooking, heat the butter and oil in a pan over moderate heat and fry the bacon and ham until they are crisp. Beat the eggs and cheeses together in a bowl.

Add the drained pasta to the bacon and ham and stir carefully until evenly coated with fat. Pour in the beaten eggs and cheese and continue stirring over gentle heat until the eggs thicken. Be sure to remove the pan from the heat before the eggs scramble.

Spoon the mixture into a warm dish and serve at once, with a bowl of grated Parmesan cheese and with crisp green salad.

LEEKS À LA NIÇOISE

French vegetable dishes or salads prepared *à la niçoise* imply the addition of tomatoes and usually a garlic flavouring. This dish can be served hot with grilled fish, meat or chicken or cold as an hors-d'oeuvre.

PREPARATION TIME: *15 min.*
COOKING TIME: *20 min.*

INGREDIENTS *(for 4)*:
2 lb. young leeks
½ lb. tomatoes
3–4 tablespoons olive oil
Salt and black pepper
1 large clove garlic
1 tablespoon fresh chopped parsley
Lemon juice

Cut the roots and most of the green tops off the leeks, so they are of even length. Rinse them thoroughly under cold running water and dry them on absorbent paper.

Skin the tomatoes* and chop them roughly.

Heat the oil in a flameproof casserole over medium heat and put in the leeks side by side. Fry until lightly coloured underneath, then turn them over and season with salt and freshly ground pepper. Cover the casserole with a lid, and cook the leeks over gentle heat for 10 minutes or until the thick white part is tender. Lift out the leeks and keep them warm.

Add the tomatoes, crushed garlic and parsley to the casserole and cook briskly for 2 or 3 minutes, stirring continuously. Adjust seasoning and sharpen to taste with lemon juice. Put the leeks back into the sauce and serve hot or cold.

GALETTE LYONNAISE

This savoury potato dish with its classic Lyonnaise flavouring of onion and cheese is excellent with both fish and meat. Extra cheese may be mixed with the potato in addition to the topping.

PREPARATION TIME: *35 min.*
COOKING TIME: *25 min.*

INGREDIENTS *(for 4)*:
1 lb. potatoes
½ lb. onions
2½ oz. butter
1 egg
Salt and black pepper
Pinch nutmeg
2 tablespoons grated Cheddar or Parmesan cheese
GARNISH:
Parsley sprigs

Peel the potatoes, cut them into even pieces and boil them in lightly salted water. Rub the potatoes through a coarse sieve. Peel and finely chop the onions. Heat 2 oz. of butter and cook the onions over low heat until they are soft and golden. Stir the contents of the pan into the potatoes. Add the beaten egg and season to taste with salt, freshly ground pepper and nutmeg.

Spoon the potato mixture into a greased, shallow ovenproof dish; smooth the top, sprinkle over the grated cheese and dot with the remaining butter. Bake the potatoes in the centre of a preheated oven, at 400°F (mark 6), for about 20 minutes or until golden brown on top.

Serve the potatoes straight from the dish, garnished with sprigs of parsley.

CELERIAC AND POTATO PURÉE

Celeriac, or celery root, is a turnip-shaped, knobbly root vegetable, more popular on the Continent than in Britain. It has a strong celery flavour, and the leaves can be used for flavouring soups and stews. As a purée, it is particularly good with game.

PREPARATION TIME: *10 min.*
COOKING TIME: *45 min.*

INGREDIENTS *(for 4–6)*:
1 lb. celeriac
¾ lb. cooked mashed potatoes
1½ oz. butter
3 tablespoons double cream
Salt and black pepper

Scrub the celeriac thoroughly in cold water to remove all traces of dirt. Put it in a pan of boiling

salted water and cook, unpeeled, for 35–40 minutes or until quite tender. Leave to cool slightly, then peel the celeriac and chop it finely. Purée* it through a sieve, or in a mouli*.

Blend the celeriac purée with the mashed potatoes, add butter and cream, and season to taste with salt and freshly ground pepper. Heat the purée through over low heat before serving.

ROASTED ONIONS

The sweet flavour of large Spanish onions is particularly enhanced by roasting them whole.

PREPARATION TIME: *5 min.*
COOKING TIME: *2½–3 hours*

INGREDIENTS *(for 6)*:
6 large Spanish onions
2–3 oz. butter
Coarse salt
GARNISH:
Parsley sprigs

Line a deep roasting tin with foil to prevent the sugar contained in the onions from sticking to the tin. Cut the roots from the unpeeled onions, and stand them upright in the roasting tin. Bake in the centre of the oven, preheated to 350°F (mark 4), for 2½

hours or until the onions are tender when tested with a skewer.

Remove the tin from the oven, carefully peel off the onion skins, and set the onions on a hot serving dish. Open the tops slightly with a pointed knife blade and push a knob of butter into each. Sprinkle the onions with salt, and top each with a small sprig of parsley.

Sweets & Puddings

AUSTRIAN CABBAGE WITH SOURED CREAM

Most classic Austrian cooking belongs to the period of the Austro-Hungarian Empire and includes Hungarian, Yugoslavian and Czech dishes. Soured cream and paprika are characteristic of both Hungarian and Austrian recipes. They are combined in this vegetable dish which goes well with roast veal and pork.

PREPARATION TIME: *20 min.*
COOKING TIME: *30 min.*

INGREDIENTS *(for 4)*:
1 small white cabbage
1 small onion
1–2 oz. butter or bacon fat
¼ pint soured cream or ¼ pint
  double cream soured with lemon
  juice
Salt and black pepper
½ level teaspoon paprika

Remove any discoloured or coarse outer leaves and cut the cabbage into quarters. Cut out the stalk and shred the cabbage. Wash and drain it thoroughly. Peel and finely chop the onion.

Heat the butter or fat in a flameproof casserole over moderate heat and cook the onion lightly until softened. Add the cabbage and sauté until it is thoroughly coated with the fat. Stir in the soured cream and season to taste with salt, freshly ground pepper and paprika.

Cover the dish with a lid and bake below centre in an oven, pre-heated to 325°F (mark 3), for about 30 minutes. It is essential to bake the cabbage at low heat or the cream will separate.

Serve the cabbage at once, straight from the casserole.

GREEN BEANS, TUSCANY STYLE

This spicy Italian method of cooking beans is a useful way of ringing the changes on runner beans towards the end of their season. French beans may also be cooked by this means, and both go well with roast or grilled meat and poultry.

PREPARATION TIME: *10 min.*
COOKING TIME: *15 min.*

INGREDIENTS *(for 4)*:
1 lb. runner beans
2 oz. butter
1 tablespoon olive oil
1 level dessertspoon chopped fresh
  sage or 1 tablespoon chopped
  fresh parsley
1 large clove garlic
Salt and black pepper
1 level tablespoon grated
  Parmesan cheese

Wash, top, tail and string the runner beans. Cut them into 2 in. chunks, not finely sliced as in the English style. Cook the beans in boiling salted water over low heat until just tender. Drain the beans thoroughly and cover them with a cloth to keep warm.

Heat the butter and oil over moderate heat; stir in half the sage or parsley and the peeled and crushed garlic. Fry for 1 minute, then add the beans. Season to taste with salt and freshly ground pepper and stir over low heat for 5 minutes.

Mix in the Parmesan cheese, and serve the beans at once, sprinkled with herbs.

TUTTI-FRUTTI PUDDING WITH ORANGE FOAM SAUCE

A steamed pudding is an ideal winter sweet especially when it is composed of a light-textured sponge and colourful fruit. It is served with a feather-light orange-flavoured sauce.

PREPARATION TIME: *40 min.*
COOKING TIME: *2 hours*

INGREDIENTS *(for 6)*:
2 oz. prunes
2 oz. dried apricots
2 oz. glacé cherries
1 oz. angelica
4 oz. unsalted butter
4 oz. caster sugar
Grated rind and juice of an orange
2 eggs
3 oz. self-raising flour
2 oz. fresh white breadcrumbs
3 dessertspoons golden syrup
6 tinned apricot halves or 6
  stoned prunes
ORANGE FOAM SAUCE:
1 oz. unsalted butter
Grated rind and juice of an orange
1 level dessertspoon plain flour
2 oz. caster sugar
1 egg
Lemon juice

Finely chop the dried prunes, apricots, glacé cherries and angelica. Thoroughly grease a 1½-pint pudding basin. Cream together the butter and sugar until light and fluffy, then add the grated orange rind. Whisk the eggs lightly and gradually beat them into the butter. Mix the sifted flour and the breadcrumbs together and lightly fold them into the pudding mixture. Add the orange juice and fold in the chopped fruit.

Coat the bottom of the pudding basin with golden syrup and arrange the six apricot halves or soaked stoned prunes in a circle over the syrup. Spoon over the pudding mixture and cover the bowl with buttered foil or a double layer of greaseproof paper. Tie securely with string. Place the pudding basin in a steamer or in a pan with boiling water reaching two thirds up the sides of the basin. Steam for 1¾–2 hours or until the pudding has risen and is set.

While the pudding is steaming, prepare the sauce: cream the butter with the grated orange rind and gradually beat in the flour mixed with the sugar. Separate the egg and beat the yolk into the butter and flour mixture, add the orange juice – made up with water to 5 fluid oz. Do not worry if the mixture curdles at this stage, it will become smooth again as it cooks.

Cook the sauce in a small heavy-based saucepan over low heat, stirring constantly, until the sauce thickens and the flour is cooked through. Add a little extra water if necessary to keep the sauce to a pouring consistency. Remove the pan from the heat and cover with a lid to keep warm.

Just before serving, fold the stiffly beaten egg white into the sauce and sharpen with a little lemon juice.

Unmould the cooked pudding on to a hot serving dish, and serve the orange foam sauce separately.

CRÈME CARAMEL À L'ORANGE

Caramel custard is a favourite international dessert, especially after a rich or spicy main course. In this Spanish recipe, the caramel custard is given additional flavour by fresh or frozen orange juice.

PREPARATION TIME: *30–35 min.*
COOKING TIME: *25 min.*
CHILLING TIME: *2 hours*

INGREDIENTS *(for 4)*:
Rind of an orange
½ pint orange juice
3 eggs plus 3 egg yolks
3 level dessertspoons caster sugar
CARAMEL:
4 oz. caster sugar

Finely grate the rind from the orange and leave it to steep in the orange juice.

Meanwhile, warm but do not grease four dariole moulds* and make the caramel. Put the sugar and 4 dessertspoons of cold water in a small, heavy-based pan over low heat; stir gently until the syrup is clear. Turn up the heat and boil briskly, without stirring, until the syrup turns a golden caramel colour. Pour a little caramel into each dariole mould. Twist the moulds quickly until they are evenly coated with the caramel (use thick oven gloves to handle the moulds as they will be very hot).

Heat the orange juice and rind in a pan over low heat. Whisk the whole eggs, egg yolks and sugar until creamy and when the orange juice is on the point of boiling, strain it into the eggs, stirring briskly. Pour the orange cream into the prepared dariole moulds and set them in a roasting pan with 1 in. of hot water.

Cover the moulds with buttered greaseproof paper and bake in the centre of a pre-heated oven at 350°F (mark 4) for about 30 minutes or until completely set.

Remove the moulds from the oven, leave them to cool and then chill in the refrigerator for at least 2 hours. Just before serving, unmould the cream caramels on to individual plates and serve with a jug of cream.

CRÊPES GEORGETTE

These pancakes with a rum-flavoured pineapple filling are said to have been created for Georgette Leblanc, close friend of the Belgian poet Maeterlinck.

PREPARATION TIME: *30 min.*
COOKING TIME: *30 min.*

INGREDIENTS *(for 6)*:
½ pint pancake batter
6 pineapple rings
½ pint vanilla-flavoured pâtisserie cream
3–4 tablespoons rum
2 oz. melted butter
Icing sugar

Prepare the pancake batter* and use it to make 12 very thin pancakes. Drain and finely chop the pineapple rings. Make the pâtisserie cream next (see September sweets and puddings), and flavour it with 1–2 dessertspoons rum. Mix the chopped pineapple into the cream. Put 2 dessertspoons of the warm cream mixture in the centre of each pancake and fold the two sides over it.

Place the stuffed pancakes side by side in a well-buttered, warmed, flameproof dish. Brush them with the melted butter, and

dredge generously with sifted icing sugar. Heat a metal skewer and press it in a criss-cross pattern on to the sugar.

Set the dish under a hot grill for about 5 minutes to glaze the sugar topping. Just before serving, warm the remaining rum, set it alight and pour it over the pancakes.

MERINGUE MONT BLANC

The original recipe, by Escoffier, was named Mont Blanc aux Marrons, the cooked chestnuts being rubbed through a sieve into a peak shape capped with whipped cream. In this version, the flan case is made of meringue and is filled with sherry-flavoured chestnut purée and whipped cream. The meringue and the filling can both be prepared in advance, but the sweet should not be assembled until just before serving.

PREPARATION TIME: *35 min.*
COOKING TIME: *1 hour*

INGREDIENTS *(for 6)*:
2 egg whites
1 dessertspoon corn oil
4 oz. caster sugar
FILLING:
2 oz. unsalted butter
1 oz. caster sugar
8 oz. tin sweetened chestnut purée
2–3 dessertspoons dry sherry
Lemon juice
½ pint whipped cream
GARNISH:
1 oz. pistachio nuts

Line a large baking tray with greaseproof paper and on it draw two 7 in. pencil circles. Brush the paper lightly with oil.

Whisk the egg whites until stiff and dry, add 2 dessertspoons of the sugar and whisk again until stiff. Lightly fold in the remaining sifted sugar. Put this meringue mixture into a forcing bag fitted with a large rose nozzle. Pipe a ring of meringue inside one of the marked circles, and spread the other circle completely with meringue, about $\frac{1}{4}$ in. thick. Pipe the remaining meringue into eight small rosettes.

Bake the meringue in the centre of an oven pre-heated to 275°F (mark 1), for about 1 hour or until the meringues are crisp, dry and coffee-coloured. Lift the rosettes off the paper, turn this upside-down and carefully peel it off the meringue ring and flat base. Leave on a wire rack to cool.

For the filling, cream together the butter and sugar; stir the

chestnut purée until smooth and beat it into the creamed butter and sugar, little by little or it will curdle. Flavour to taste with sherry and lemon juice.

To assemble the sweet, place the meringue base on a flat serving dish. Fit a forcing bag with a plain nozzle and pipe a little of the whipped cream round the edge of the meringue base; set the ring on top. Fill the centre of the case with the chestnut mixture, piling it up into a mound. Pipe a little of the whipped cream on the base of each rosette and arrange them on top of the meringue ring. Pipe the remaining cream over the chestnut mound to resemble snow and scatter the blanched, chopped pistachio nuts over the purée.

APPLE AND NUT STRUDEL

Austria, and particularly Vienna, is renowned for its rich pastries and cakes. Among them all, the strudel recipe is probably the most popular, in spite of the fact that a true strudel dough needs practice to get it really thin. This famous pastry should be almost transparent, or as the Austrians say, 'thin enough to read your love letters through'.

PREPARATION TIME: *1 hour*
COOKING TIME: *40 min.*

INGREDIENTS *(for 6)*:
4 oz. plain flour
4 dessertspoons vegetable oil
2–3 dessertspoons corn oil
Flour for rolling out
2 oz. unsalted butter
FILLING:
2 oz. unsalted butter
3 oz. fresh white breadcrumbs
2 oz. hazel nuts or walnuts
1 lb. cooking apples
1 level teaspoon ground cinnamon
2 oz. caster sugar
2 oz. sultanas
Grated rind of half lemon

Sift the flour into a warmed bowl; make a well in the centre and stir in the vegetable oil mixed with 4 dessertspoons warm water. Work the mixture into a soft dough, adding more warm water as required. Knead the dough thoroughly on a lightly floured surface, then roll it into a long sausage shape. Pick up the strudel dough by one end and hit it against the pastry board. Repeat this lifting and hitting process, picking it up by alternate ends, for about 10 minutes or until bubbles appear under the surface of the dough.

Knead the elastic strudel dough into a ball and leave it to rest on a plate for 30 minutes under an inverted, warm bowl.

Meanwhile, heat the butter for the filling, and gently fry the breadcrumbs until golden. Chop the nuts roughly. Peel, core and roughly chop the apples.

Spread a large, clean tea towel over the table top and sprinkle it evenly with flour. Roll out the strudel dough on the cloth, as thinly as possible, and brush it with a little warm oil to keep it pliable. Place the hands under dough and stretch it over the backs of the hands by pulling them away from each other until the dough is paper-thin. Work on one area at a time, until all the dough is nearly transparent.

When the dough is thin enough, trim off the uneven edges with a sharp knife or scissors. Melt the 2 oz. of butter and brush it

over all the dough; spread the fried breadcrumbs on top. Cover these with the chopped apples to within 2 in. of the edges. Mix the cinnamon and sugar, and sprinkle over the apples, together with the chopped nuts, sultanas and grated lemon rind. Fold the lower edge of the dough over the filling, then lift the edge of the cloth and roll the strudel up like a Swiss roll. Seal the join with water, and tuck under the ends.

Lift the strudel and roll it off the cloth on to a greased baking tray, join underneath. Curve the strudel into a horseshoe shape and brush the top with the remaining melted butter. Bake in the centre of a pre-heated oven, at 425°F (mark 7), for 10 minutes, then lower the heat to 400°F (mark 6) for about 30 minutes or until golden brown.

Serve the strudel hot or cold, dredged with sifted icing sugar.

LINZERTORTE

This classic Austrian torte, named after the town of Linz, is popular both as a dessert and as an accompaniment to morning or afternoon coffee. It is traditionally served with *Schlagsahne*. This consists of ¼ pint of sweetened whipped cream into which stiffly beaten egg white is folded just before serving.

PREPARATION TIME: *30 min.*
CHILLING TIME: *1½ hours*
COOKING TIME: *1 hour*

INGREDIENTS *(for 6)*:
3 oz. plain flour
½ level teaspoon ground cinnamon
3 oz. caster sugar
3 oz. unblanched ground almonds or hazel nuts
Grated rind of half lemon
4 oz. unsalted butter
2 egg yolks
¼ teaspoon vanilla
¾ lb. thick raspberry jam
GLAZE:
1 egg yolk
1 tablespoon double cream

Sift the flour, cinnamon and sugar into a mixing bowl. Add the ground almonds and finely grated lemon peel; blend thoroughly before rubbing in the butter until the mixture resembles breadcrumbs.

Beat the egg yolks with the vanilla essence and stir into the flour and almond mixture. Using a wooden spoon, work it into a soft dough. Wrap in greaseproof paper or foil, and chill for 1 hour in the refrigerator.

Grease a loose-bottomed flan tin 8 in. wide by 1½ in. deep. Knead the dough to soften it slightly, then press it with the fingers over the base of the tin and up the sides. The lining should be not more than ¼ in. thick, and the surplus dough should be pushed up over the top edge and trimmed off neatly with a knife. Spread the jam evenly over the base of the flan.

Knead the pastry trimmings together and roll them out on a well-floured board to a rectangle 8 in. by 3 in. Cut this into six

strips, each ½ in. wide. Lift the strips, one at a time, with a palette knife, and lay them across the raspberry filling in a lattice pattern. Press the ends of the strips into the pastry lining. Run a sharp knife round the top of the tin to loosen the pastry which extends above the lattice pattern, then fold it inwards and down on to the strips to make a ½ in. wide border.

For the glaze, beat the egg yolk and cream together and brush it over the lattice and border. Chill the torte for 30 minutes in the refrigerator, then bake it in the centre of a pre-heated oven at 350°F (mark 4) for about 1 hour or until crisp and lightly browned.

Leave the torte to cool and shrink slightly, then loosen the edge with a knife. Place the tin on a jar and gently push down the flan rim. Slide the torte on to a serving plate, and serve it warm or cold with a bowl of *Schlagsahne*.

Savouries & Snacks

STUFFED CABBAGE LEAVES

The outer leaves of white cabbage are used to encase left-over meat. Jacket potatoes and a tomato sauce make this into a good main course.

PREPARATION TIME: *15 min.*
COOKING TIME: *30 min.*

INGREDIENTS *(for 4)*:
8 large cabbage leaves
2 tablespoons olive oil
2 finely chopped onions
½ lb. cooked chicken or ham (minced)
2 level teaspoons chopped parsley
2 level tablespoons sage and onion stuffing
½ level tablespoon tomato purée
½ oz. butter
7–8 oz. tinned tomatoes
Salt, black pepper and cumin

Trim the cabbage leaves into squares or rectangles; blanch* them in boiling salted water for 3 minutes. Drain thoroughly and leave to cool.

Heat the oil in a heavy-based pan; add the onions and cook over low heat until transparent. Stir in the meat, parsley and stuffing, the tomato purée, 3 tablespoons of boiling water, the butter and tomatoes. Season with salt, pepper and cumin. Bring to the boil and simmer for 5 minutes.

Spread out the cabbage leaves; divide the filling equally over each and roll the leaves into parcels. Put them in a lightly buttered baking dish (joins downwards); cover the dish with foil or a lid and bake for 25 minutes in the oven at 350°F (mark 4).

Serve the cabbage leaves with a thick tomato sauce*.

CHEESE AND CHUTNEY DIP

This savoury dip for a first course or to serve with drinks can be created very quickly.

PREPARATION TIME: *10 min.*
CHILLING TIME: *30 min.*

INGREDIENTS *(for 6)*:
½ lb. cream cheese
2 tablespoons double cream
2 level teaspoons curry powder
1 rounded tablespoon tomato ketchup
2 teaspoons lemon juice
4 tablespoons finely chopped chutney or sweet pickle
GARNISH:
Celery leaves

Blend the softened cream cheese and cream until smooth. Stir the curry powder into the tomato ketchup, with the lemon juice, and add to the cheese, together with the chutney or pickle. Mix well before piling into a serving dish. Chill for about 30 minutes.

Serve the dip with crisp crackers, cheese biscuits or potato crisps. Alternatively, offer strips of fresh carrots, celery, green pepper and cauliflower florets and garnish the cheese dip with celery leaves.

COUNTRYSIDE POTATOES

Day-old jacket potatoes are here transformed into a light main course, served with a tomato or green salad.

PREPARATION TIME: *10 min.*
COOKING TIME: *20 min.*

INGREDIENTS *(for 4)*:
4 large baked potatoes
2 rashers back bacon
4 oz. cream cheese
1–2 tablespoons top of milk
2 teaspoons chopped parsley
Salt and black pepper
2 oz. grated Cheddar cheese

Cut the potatoes in half, scoop out the flesh and mash it finely. Quickly fry the bacon, without any fat, until crisp; drain on kitchen paper and crumble the bacon into the mashed potato. Blend in the softened cream cheese, the milk and parsley. Mix thoroughly and season with salt and freshly ground pepper.

Pile the mixture back into the potato skins and sprinkle with cheese. Bake in the centre of a pre-heated oven, at 400°F (mark 6) for about 20 minutes.

FISHERMAN'S PIE

Left-over cooked fish forms the basis for this savoury dish which is covered with a mustard-flavoured cheese pastry.

PREPARATION TIME: *25 min.*
COOKING TIME: *25–30 min.*

INGREDIENTS *(for 4–6)*:
½ lb. cooked white fish
½ lb. cooked smoked haddock
Juice of a lemon
2 tablespoons chopped parsley
Half a small chopped green pepper
2 hardboiled, chopped eggs
¾ pint white sauce
Salt and black pepper
6 oz. self-raising flour
1½ oz. butter
1 level dessertspoon dry mustard
2–3 oz. grated Cheddar cheese
¼ pint milk

Fold the skinned and flaked* fish, the lemon juice, parsley, green pepper and eggs into the white sauce*. Season with salt and pepper. Spoon the mixture into a 2 pint fireproof dish.

Sift the flour into a bowl and rub in the butter. Add the mustard and cheese and sufficient milk to make a soft pliable pastry dough. Knead this lightly on a floured surface, and roll out to a circle, ¾ in. thick, large enough to cover the dish. Cut the pastry into eight triangles and place over the fish so that the points meet in the centre. Brush with milk and bake for 25 minutes, at 425°F (mark 7), or until golden.

BREAD AND BUTTER PUDDING

Slightly stale buttered bread is the basis for this traditional English nursery pudding which appeals equally to children and husbands.

PREPARATION TIME: *15 min.*
COOKING TIME: *30 min.*

INGREDIENTS *(for 4)*:
8 slices buttered white bread
2 oz. sultanas
Grated rind of a lemon
2 eggs
3 level tablespoons caster sugar
1 pint vanilla-flavoured milk

Remove the crusts and cut the bread into 1 in. squares. Place them in a lightly buttered fireproof dish, with alternate layers of sultanas mixed with grated lemon rind.

Beat the eggs lightly with 2 tablespoons of the sugar and all the milk. Pour this custard over the bread. Sprinkle the remaining sugar over the top, and bake the pudding in a pre-heated oven, at 350°F (mark 4) for about 30 minutes.

Breakfasts and High Teas

The British Isles are outstanding for their excellent breakfast dishes, and no other country can offer anything like the number of regional breakfasts still common in many households.

Many of these dishes are also eaten for 'high tea', a meal which is common in Scotland, the north of England and the Midlands, as well as in Cornwall, Wales, the Isle of Man and Ireland. High tea is a direct survival of the 17th-century eating habit of having dinner at 5 p.m.; later in the evening a small supper, known as 'rear supper' was served. This established eating pattern suited equally the hard-working labourer who, hungry after a long day's work, wanted his meal as soon as he came home, and the 'gentleman about town' who, after his dinner, would play cards or frequent taverns or theatres.

Breakfasts

The first meal of the day should be substantial enough to provide energy for the day's work, for children and adults alike. This is particularly important today when many people make do with a snack or sandwich lunch.

Porridge or corn flakes may be followed by fried bacon and eggs, with sausages, tomatoes and mushrooms. Kippers are universal favourites, so are herrings in oatmeal (see January fish), kedgeree (see also July fish) and smoked haddock poached* in milk and butter. Grilled kidneys or cod roe with Irish potato cakes are also delicious. Boiled, poached or scrambled eggs are popular, and no breakfast table is complete without toast, butter and marmalade.

Porridge is the traditional Scottish breakfast, described by Robert Burns as 'Chief o' Scotia's food'. It takes little time to prepare and cook: for four generous portions allow 5 oz. medium rolled oatmeal to 2 pints of water.

Bring the water to the boil over medium heat and, as soon as it is bubbling, pour in the oatmeal, in a steady but slow stream, with one hand, stirring constantly with the other. As soon as the mixture comes back to the boil, pull the pan to the side of the heat, cover with a lid and simmer gently for 10 minutes. Stir in $\frac{1}{4}$ level teaspoon salt, re-cover the pan and continue simmering for about 10 minutes.

In Scotland, porridge was eaten with horn spoons from birch bowls. It is traditionally served with cream and salt.

Kedgeree is an English breakfast or high tea dish, of Indian origin. *Khicharhi* (or kedgeree) originally consisted of rice, onion, lentils, spices, fresh limes, butter and fish.

For four persons, take 2 hard-boiled eggs, 1 lb. cooked smoked haddock, $\frac{1}{2}$ lb. boiled rice, nutmeg, lemon juice, salt and cayenne pepper; also $\frac{1}{4}$ pint single cream and 2 oz. butter.

Cut the eggs into small wedges and blend them with the flaked fish and the rice. Season to taste with grated nutmeg, lemon juice, salt and cayenne. Stir in the cream. Butter a deep, ovenproof dish and spoon in the kedgeree mixture. Dot with the remaining butter, cover the dish with a lid and bake in the centre of a pre-heated oven, at 350°F (mark 4), for about 30 minutes. Garnish kedgeree with chopped parsley.

Kippers are a highly popular breakfast dish throughout Britain. The finest, pale oak-smoked kippers come from the Isle of Man, but are, unfortunately, seldom exported. For grilled kippers with scrambled eggs, allow 1 pair of kippers and 1 egg per person.

Scissor the heads and tails off the kippers, place them on a layer of foil, skin upwards, on the grill pan and grill them under high heat until the skin begins to curl. Turn the kippers over and grill the other side, allowing 2–3 minutes on each side.

Meanwhile, beat the eggs lightly and season with pepper only. Melt a knob of butter in a small pan and scramble the eggs for about 2 minutes, until creamy and moist. Serve at the side of the grilled kippers.

Devilled kidneys have been popular in Britain since the 18th century, when the thrifty housewife invented a spicy sauce to add sparkle to jaded palates.

For four portions, clean and halve 8 lamb kidneys*. Prepare a devil sauce by mixing 2 teaspoons Worcestershire sauce, 2 teaspoons mushroom ketchup and 1 level tablespoon dry mustard with 2 oz. melted butter. Season with salt, white pepper and cayenne.

Heat 2 tablespoons oil or butter in a pan and fry the kidneys for 3 minutes on each side. Arrange them in a flameproof serving dish, spread the devil sauce evenly on top of the kidneys and put under a hot grill for 1 minute.

Cod roe and bacon is a favourite breakfast dish in Cornwall, the north of England and Ireland.

Peel the skin off 1 lb. cooked cod roe and cut the roe into $\frac{1}{2}$ in. thick slices. Coat these in lightly seasoned flour* and fry in a little lard or dripping until golden brown. Fry bacon rashers in the pan with the cod roe, and serve with potato cakes (see High Teas).

Alternatively, mash the peeled roe with an equal amount of cooked mashed potatoes; season with salt and pepper and bind with 2 lightly beaten eggs. Shape the mixture into round cakes, about 2 in. wide and $\frac{3}{4}$ in. thick. Fry for about 10 minutes or until golden brown on both sides.

Traditional breakfast dishes: cod roe and bacon, kedgeree, devilled kidneys and grilled kippers with scrambled eggs

High Teas

The frying pan has been the death of many traditional high tea dishes, most of which have been superseded by fried chops and chips, sausages and chips, or fish and chips. There are, however, many savoury, more easily digested dishes still served for high tea throughout the country.

Ham and haddie comes from the Moray Firth area in Scotland. It is an unusual combination of smoked ham and haddock.

For four servings, poach* $\frac{1}{2}$–$\frac{3}{4}$ lb. smoked haddock in water for 5 minutes. Remove all skin and bones, and cut the fish into four equal portions. Melt $1\frac{1}{2}$ oz. butter until foaming, and lightly fry 4 small slices cooked, smoked ham. Put the haddock on top of the ham, and season with freshly ground black pepper. Cover with a lid and cook gently for 5 minutes. Pour 3 tablespoons single cream over the haddock and brown the dish under a hot grill for 2 minutes.

Anglesey eggs is a happy mixture of two favourite Welsh foods: leeks and cheese. It makes four generous servings.

Chop 6 cleaned leeks into $\frac{1}{2}$ in. slices and cook them in boiling salted water for 10 minutes. Drain thoroughly and add them to 1 lb. hot mashed potatoes, together with 1 oz. butter, salt and pepper to taste. Beat the leek and potato mixture thoroughly until pale green and fluffy.

Slice 8 hardboiled eggs and arrange them in the centre of a large shallow fireproof dish; spoon the potato mixture round them. Keep the dish warm while making $\frac{1}{2}$ pint white sauce*; stir in 2 oz. grated Cheddar cheese. Pour the cheese sauce over the eggs and sprinkle with 2 tablespoons of grated Cheddar cheese. Bake in the centre of a pre-heated oven, at 400°F (mark 6), for 20 minutes or until the cheese is golden brown on top.

Shrimp paste served with toast is a familiar sight on the tea table in Yorkshire. It vies in popularity with Pan Haggerty (see February meat).

For the shrimp paste, take $1\frac{1}{2}$ pints of cooked shrimps. Peel the shrimps and boil the washed shells in water for 30 minutes. Put $\frac{1}{3}$ lb. cod or fresh haddock fillets in a pan and strain over them enough shrimp liquid to just cover the fish. Simmer for 10 minutes, then lift out the fish and reduce* the stock to 1 tablespoon.

Pound or liquidise the fish, with a few drops of anchovy essence and one anchovy fillet; season with ground mace and cayenne pepper. Set aside to cool. Weigh the mixture and add an equal amount of butter, beating until the paste is smooth. Blend in the shrimps and cook the paste in a pan, without boiling, for 3 minutes. Press the paste into a deep glass or china dish and leave it to cool. Pour clarified butter* over the shrimp paste and serve it chilled.

Dublin coddle is said to have been a favourite of Dean Swift, the 17th-century Irish satirist. It is a substantial cold-weather dish which will easily serve six.

Cut 8 thick slices of uncooked ham or bacon into 2 in. chunks; put them, with 16 pork chipolatas, into a pan of boiling water. Boil for 5 minutes, then drain and set the liquid aside. Put the ham and sausages in a large, fireproof dish, layered with 4 large chopped onions and 2 lb. peeled and sliced potatoes. Sprinkle 4 tablespoons chopped parsley over the layers

Traditional Irish potato cakes, and barm brack glazed with melted honey

Typical high tea dishes. Left to right, top row: Ham and haddie, Dublin coddle, shrimp paste, grilled mackerel with gooseberry sauce, and Anglesey eggs

and season with salt and pepper. Pour over sufficient liquid to barely reach the top of the contents, then cover with greaseproof paper or a lid.

Cook the coddle in the centre of a pre-heated oven, at 350°F (mark 4), for $1\frac{1}{2}$–2 hours or until the liquid has reduced* by half. Remove the greaseproof paper halfway through cooking. Traditionally, fresh soda bread* is served with this dish.

Mackerel with gooseberry sauce is a true Cornish dish. In the West Country, rhubarb may substitute for gooseberries.

Clean and bone 4 mackerel* and fill them with a stuffing made

from the following: 4 heaped tablespoons white breadcrumbs, 1 level tablespoon chopped parsley and grated peel from a lemon. Bind the stuffing with a lightly beaten egg and season with nutmeg, salt and black pepper. Secure the stuffed mackerel with wooden cocktail sticks.

Brush the mackerel with melted butter and grill them under moderate heat for about 8 minutes on each side.

For the sauce, cook $\frac{1}{2}$ lb. gooseberries in 3 fluid oz. water, with 2 level tablespoons caster sugar, 1 oz. butter and 1 tablespoon fresh chopped fennel (or 1 teaspoon ground). Cook until the gooseberries pop open.

Tea breads. No high tea is complete without a selection of fresh, home-baked bread, and most regions have their own favourites. Scotland and the north of England have produced the most original recipes. Shortbread, drop and griddle scones are well known, so are Singing Hinny, Yorkshire teacakes, parkins, soda bread and Welsh cakes (recipes for all these will be found in the bread, cake and biscuit sections).

Potato cakes originated in Ireland, but are also known in Scotland and parts of the north.

Sift 8 oz. self-raising flour with 1 teaspoon salt and rub in 3 oz. butter or margarine. Mix in 6 oz. warm mashed potatoes and add about $2\frac{1}{2}$ fluid oz. milk to make a soft dough. Roll out, $\frac{1}{2}$–$\frac{1}{3}$ in. thick, and cut the dough into 10–12 rounds, 3 in. across (caraway seeds may be sprinkled on top). Bake the cakes on lightly floured baking trays in a preheated oven, at 450°F (mark 8), for 20–30 minutes. Serve the cakes split, spread with butter.

Barm brack is an Irish tea bread, similar to the Welsh Bara Brith and the Manx Bonnag.

Soak 1 lb. sultanas, 1 lb. stoned raisins and 1 lb. soft brown sugar in $1\frac{1}{2}$ pints black tea (or 1 pint tea and $\frac{1}{2}$ pint Irish whiskey) overnight. The next day add, gradually, 1 lb. plain flour and 3 lightly beaten eggs to the fruit and sugar mixture. Blend in 3 level teaspoons baking powder, and (optional) 3 teaspoons mixed spice.

Spoon the mixture into three greased loaf tins, 8 in. long by 4 in. wide and 3 in. deep. Bake in the centre of a pre-heated oven, at 300°F (mark 2), for $1\frac{3}{4}$ hours.

Leave the loaves to cool on a wire rack. Glaze the tops lightly with melted honey.

December

Cheese, apples and nuts, joly Carols to heare,
as then in the countrie is counted good cheare.

This Month's Recipes

*A Wassail bowl filled with warm ale, wine and spice, and with fruit
floating on top, brings a touch of Merrie England to the Christmas table*

Food in Season

At no other time of year do the shops provide such a choice of home-grown and imported foods. Fruiterers display Cox's apples, fresh oranges, shiny tangerines and other citrus fruit, nuts, dried figs and dates. Butchers' windows exhibit succulent roasts of pork, plump turkeys, fat geese and ducks. For plainer eating while preparing for the Christmas feast, try halibut, herrings, mackerel, plaice and scallops, which are now cheap enough to use in chowders.

Winter vegetables at their best include cabbages, mild-flavoured leeks, maincrop parsnips and Brussels sprouts, their taste being improved by a touch of frost. Also available are the less well-known but delicious Florence fennel, Jerusalem artichokes and sweet potatoes.

Fish

Angler tail
Bass
Bream, freshwater
Bream, sea
Brill
Carp
Clams
Cockles
Cod
Coley
Crab
Dabs
Dover sole
Dublin Bay prawns
Eels
Flake (also sold as rock salmon)
Flounder
Grey mullet
Haddock
Hake
Halibut
Herrings
Lemon sole
Lobsters
Mackerel
Mock halibut (or Greenland halibut)
Mussels
Oysters (native)
Oysters, Portuguese
Pike
Plaice
Redfish
Scad
Scallops
Shrimps
Skate
Sprats
Trout, rainbow
Turbot
Whiting
Winkles
Witch

Poultry & Game

Chicken
Duck
Goose
Grouse
Guinea fowl
Hare
Mallard
Partridge
Pheasant
Pigeon
Quail
Rabbit
Snipe
Teal
Turkey
Venison
Wild duck
Wild goose
Woodcock

Vegetables

Aubergines
Avocado pears
Beetroots
Broccoli
Brussels sprouts
Brussels tops
Cabbages
Carrots
Cauliflowers
Celeriac
Celery
Chicory
Chillies
Courgettes
Cucumbers
Endive
Fennel
French beans
Garlic
Horseradish
Jerusalem artichokes
Kale
Leeks
Lettuces
Mushrooms
Onions
Parsley
Parsnips
Peppers
Potatoes
Salad cress
Salsify
Savoys
Sea kale
Spinach
Spring greens
Spring onions
Swedes
Sweet potatoes
Tomatoes
Turnips
Watercress

Fruit

Almonds
Apples
Apricots
Bananas
Brazil nuts
Cherries
Chestnuts
Clementines
Coconuts
Cranberries
Dates
Figs
Grapefruit
Grapes
Lemons
Mandarins
Mangoes
Melons
Oranges
Pawpaws
Peaches
Pears
Pineapples
Pomegranates
Rhubarb
Satsumas
Strawberries
Tangerines
Walnuts

SUGGESTED MENUS

Cream of Jerusalem Artichoke Soup
Pork Chops with Almonds and Sherry
Brussels Sprouts with Soured Cream
Garlic Potatoes
Fresh Fruit

Crème Vichyssoise
Turbot with Sweet Corn
Broccoli Spears au Gratin
Paris-Brest

Pears in Tarragon Cream
Wild Goose in Cider
Red Cabbage
Meringue à la Reine

Quail Eggs in Pâté
Filet de Boeuf en Croûte
Baked Cauliflower Cheese
Glazed Onions
Champagne Charlie

Eggs in Provençal Sauce
Mackerel in White Wine Sauce
Buttered Spinach
Sauté Potatoes
Soured Cream Flan

Shrimps Baked in Soured Cream
Lamb à la Greque
Chicory and Orange Salad
Apple Rum Meringue

Waldorf Salad
Spaghettini with Mussel Sauce
Orange Chiffon Cream

Soups & Starters

SHRIMPS BAKED IN SOUR CREAM

This easily made starter can be prepared well in advance and then baked just before serving. If soured cream is not available, it can be made quite easily by adding the strained juice of half a large lemon to ¼ pint single or double cream.

PREPARATION TIME: *10 min.*
COOKING TIME: *10 min.*

INGREDIENTS *(for 4):*
8 oz. peeled shrimps
Black pepper
5 fluid oz. soured cream
Fresh white breadcrumbs
2 oz. unsalted butter
GARNISH:
Parsley sprigs

Butter four small flameproof dishes, and spoon about 2 tablespoons of shrimps into each. Season thoroughly with freshly ground pepper, and cover with soured cream.

Sprinkle a thin layer of fine breadcrumbs over the cream and dot with knobs of butter. Bake in the centre of an oven preheated to 375°F (mark 5) for 10 minutes. Finish the shrimps under a hot grill for a minute or two or until the breadcrumbs are golden brown on top.

Garnish each dish with a sprig of parsley, and serve with chunks of warm wholemeal bread and butter.

CREAM OF JERUSALEM ARTICHOKE SOUP

Sweet-flavoured home-grown Jerusalem artichokes, which appear on the market in late autumn and early winter, are the basis for this chilled cream soup. It freezes well.

PREPARATION TIME: *30 min.*
COOKING TIME: *45 min.*
CHILLING TIME: *3 hours*

INGREDIENTS *(for 8):*
1½ lb. Jerusalem artichokes
Juice of a lemon
1 onion
¼ cucumber
2 oz. butter
1½ pints chicken stock
½ pint dry white wine (optional)
6 parsley stalks
Salt and black pepper
½ pint double cream
GARNISH:
¼ pint plain yoghourt
3 level tablespoons fresh chopped parsley

Peel the artichokes, cut them into ½ in. chunks and leave them in a bowl of cold water to which the strained lemon juice has been added. Peel and thinly slice the onion; wipe and slice the cucumber.

Drain the artichokes and dry them on a cloth. Melt the butter in a large sauté pan and add the artichokes, the onion and cucumber. Cook the vegetables in the butter for 5 minutes over low heat – do not allow them to colour. Pour over the stock and wine. Bring the soup to the boil and add the parsley stalks. Season with salt and freshly ground pepper. Cover the pan with a lid and reduce the heat.

Simmer the soup for about 20 minutes, or until the vegetables are soft. Remove the pan from the heat and allow the soup to cool slightly. Put it in the liquidiser or rub it through a sieve. Correct seasoning and chill the soup in the refrigerator for about 3 hours (or store in the freezer). Stir in the cream just before serving.

Serve the chilled soup in individual bowls. Trail a little yoghourt over the surface of each bowl and sprinkle with finely chopped parsley.

PEARS IN TARRAGON CREAM

For this simple first course, choose firm, but ripe, squat pears. They are served with a classic French tarragon cream.

PREPARATION TIME: *10 min.*
CHILLING TIME: *1 hour*

INGREDIENTS *(for 6):*
6 dessert pears
½ pint double cream
2 tablespoons tarragon vinegar
Caster sugar
Salt and black pepper

Chill the pears in the refrigerator. Beat the cream and vinegar together until thick, but not too stiff. Season to taste with sugar, salt and freshly ground pepper. Peel and halve the pears and scoop out the centre cores with a teaspoon.

Serve the pears, rounded side up, on individual small plates and with the tarragon cream spooned over them.

QUAIL EGGS IN PÂTÉ

The small cream and brown-mottled quail eggs have a flavour all their own, which is less 'gamey' than that of seagull eggs. The creamy texture blends well with pâté and jelly and makes an unusual starter.

PREPARATION TIME: *30 min.*
CHILLING TIME: *2 hours*

INGREDIENTS *(for 6):*
10 oz. tin beef consommé
2 level teaspoons powdered gelatine
6 quail eggs
6 oz. pâté de foie gras
24 stoneless black olives
GARNISH:
Parsley

Pour the consommé into a saucepan and stir in the powdered gelatine. Heat the consommé over low heat, stirring continuously until the gelatine has dissolved. Remove from the heat and leave the consommé to cool.

Put the quail eggs into a pan of boiling water and boil them gently for 4 minutes. Lift out the eggs and plunge them into cold water. Shell the eggs and put them in a bowl of cold water.

Brush six shallow ramekin dishes with oil. Divide the pâté into six equal portions and spread it over the base and up the sides of the ramekins. Nest an egg in the pâté and surround it with four olives. Spoon the jellied consommé over the eggs and olives and leave to set in the refrigerator for about 2 hours. Remove the ramekins 30 minutes before serving and decorate them with sprigs of parsley.

Serve the eggs with hot French bread and butter.

EGGS IN PROVENÇALE SAUCE

The fragrant spicy sauce in which these eggs are baked is typical of Provençale cuisine. The classic sauce takes some time to prepare and cook, but as it stores well in the home freezer, double or treble quantities can be made. Omit the garlic if the sauce is to be stored for longer than 1 month.

PREPARATION TIME: *30 min.*
COOKING TIME: *1 hour*

INGREDIENTS *(for 6):*
2 lb. ripe tomatoes
1 large onion
2 cloves garlic
2 tablespoons olive oil
¼ level teaspoon ground basil
1 bay leaf
Bouquet garni
Small piece lemon peel
1 level tablespoon tomato paste
Caster sugar
Salt and black pepper
6 eggs

Skin the tomatoes* and cut them in half, crossways. Remove the seeds with a teaspoon, and coarsely chop the pulp. Peel and finely chop the onion and garlic. Heat the oil in a heavy-based pan and cook the onion over low heat for 10 minutes. Add the garlic with the tomato pulp, basil, bay leaf, bouquet garni*, chopped lemon peel and tomato paste. Season to taste with sugar and salt. Stir the ingredients thoroughly, and simmer for 30 minutes or until the contents have reduced* to a thick purée*. Remove the bouquet garni and bay leaf.

Put 2 tablespoons of the sauce into each of six ramekin dishes.

Make a hollow in the centre of the sauce, and break an egg carefully into each. Sprinkle the eggs with salt and freshly ground pepper. Bake the eggs for about 10 minutes, or until just set, in the centre of an oven pre-heated to 375°F (mark 5).

Serve at once, with warm, crusty French bread.

BRAWN WITH SPICED PRUNES

Brawn is a traditional English dish made from pork trimmings and pig's head. It dates from the 15th century and is always served cold, usually as a first course. However, it also makes an attractive main course for lunch or supper. Preparations should begin at least 2 days in advance.

PREPARATION TIME: *1¾ hours*
COOKING TIME: *4 hours*

INGREDIENTS *(for 8):*
½ pig's head
8 oz. rock or sea salt
2 onions
4 shallots
2 carrots
2 turnips
12 whole allspice
Bouquet garni
4 cloves
2 blades mace
6 peppercorns
Juice of a lemon
Oil
Salt and black pepper
SPICED PRUNES:
1 lb. prunes
1 pint cold tea
¾ pint white wine vinegar
½ lb. brown sugar
1 level teaspoon pickling spice
GARNISH:
Cucumber and tomato slices

Make the spiced prunes first, as they have to steep in pickling liquid for 24 hours. Soak the prunes in the cold tea for 8 hours or overnight. Cook the prunes, with the cold tea, over low heat for 20 minutes or until tender.

Meanwhile, put the vinegar into a separate pan and stir in the sugar. Add the pickling spice, wrapped in muslin. Bring to the boil and simmer briskly for 5 minutes. Remove the pan from the heat and stir in half the cooking liquid from the prunes. Drain the prunes and pack them into a preserving jar, pour over the spiced vinegar and seal immediately. The prunes are ready for use 24 hours later.

Ask the butcher to cut the half pig's head in two and to remove the eye. Scrub the portions under cold running water until thoroughly clean. Leave them to soak for 12 hours in a bowl of cold water to which 8 oz. salt has been added.

Remove the pig's head, rinse it thoroughly in fresh water and place it in a large saucepan. Cover with fresh cold water. Bring to the boil, and cook the pig's head at near-boiling point for 2 hours or until the flesh leaves the bones easily. Remove the meat from the pan. Strip all the flesh, including the ear, tongue and brain, from the bones – it should yield approximately 2 lb. of meat. Return the bones to the pan with the cooking liquid and bring back to the boil.

Meanwhile, peel and roughly slice the onions, shallots, carrots and turnips. Add the vegetables to the boiling liquid, together with the allspice, bouquet garni*, cloves, mace, peppercorns and lemon juice. Continue boiling

this stock, uncovered, for about 1 hour until the liquid has reduced* to just over ½ pint. Remove from the heat, strain and set the liquid aside until cold.

Skin the tongue and dice that and all the meat finely. Put the meat in a large bowl and work it through the fingers until thoroughly mixed, discarding any pieces of gristle. Remove the solidified fat from the surface of the cold stock, and strain the liquid through two thicknesses of muslin into a clean pan. Season with salt and freshly ground pepper and bring to the boil. Remove the pan from the heat immediately and stir in the chopped meat.

Clean and thinly slice the cucumber and the tomato. Brush a 2 pint tin mould with oil and

decorate the base with thin slices of cucumber and tomato, and a few cut-up prunes. Spoon the brawn carefully into the mould, without disturbing the decorative pattern. Firm the top of the brawn and set it aside for 1 hour.

Cover the brawn with a wooden board, with a heavy weight on top, and chill in the refrigerator for at least 24 hours.

To serve, turn the brawn out of the mould. Arrange the spiced prunes around the brawn, garnished with a few tomato slices for added colour.

Fish

CRÈME VICHYSSOISE

Despite its French name, this soup was created by the chef of a New York hotel in 1910 and has since become universally famous. It is always served chilled.

PREPARATION TIME: *30 min.*
COOKING TIME: *35–40 min.*
CHILLING TIME: *3 hours*

INGREDIENTS *(for 6)* :
2 lb. leeks
1 lb. potatoes
2 oz. butter
1 stick celery
1 pint chicken stock
1 pint milk
Salt and black pepper
Freshly grated nutmeg
½ pint double cream
GARNISH:
Grated carrot

Trim the roots and coarse outer leaves from the leeks and wash them thoroughly in cold water. Slice the leeks diagonally into ¼ in. pieces. Peel and coarsely dice the potatoes. Melt the butter in a large sauté pan and add the leeks and potatoes. Cook the vegetables over moderate heat for 7 minutes, stirring continuously. Add the scrubbed and coarsely chopped celery to the pan. Pour over the stock and milk, and bring the soup to the boil. Season with salt, freshly ground pepper and nutmeg. Simmer the soup for 25 minutes or until the vegetables are tender.

Allow the soup to cool slightly before liquidising it or rubbing it through a sieve. Correct seasoning and stir in the cream.

Chill the soup in the refrigerator for 2–3 hours. Serve in individual bowls, garnished with fresh grated carrot.

MACKEREL WITH WHITE WINE SAUCE

Mackerel, one of the tastiest fish to be caught around British shores, would be more highly prized if it were less common. Here, a creamy white wine sauce lifts it a few rungs up the status ladder.

PREPARATION TIME: *20 min.*
COOKING TIME: *30 min.*

INGREDIENTS *(for 4)* :
4 small or 2 large mackerel
Seasoned flour
2 oz. unsalted butter
Juice of half lemon
SAUCE:
¼ pint fish stock
¼ pint dry white wine
¼ pint double cream
Salt and black pepper
1 egg yolk
GARNISH:
Finely chopped parsley

Clean and fillet each mackerel* into two. Rinse under cold water, dry and coat each fillet with seasoned flour*.

Make the wine sauce before frying the fillets. Bring the stock (made from the fish trimmings) and the white wine to the boil. Simmer over low heat for about 15 minutes, or until it has reduced* by half. Stir in the cream, heat the sauce through, and season to taste with salt and freshly ground pepper. Beat the egg yolk in a bowl; stir a little of the warm sauce into the egg. Add the egg yolk to the sauce and return the pan to the heat for 1 minute. Keep the sauce warm, but do not let it boil.

Melt the butter in a frying pan; put the fillets, flesh-side down, into the pan and fry over low heat for 5–6 minutes; turn the fish over and cook the other side for the same period. Remove the fillets from the pan and keep warm on a serving dish. Add the lemon juice to the butter in the pan, and pour the mixture over the fillets.

Serve the mackerel sprinkled with parsley, and pour the sauce into a warm sauce boat. Buttered spinach and sauté potatoes* can accompany the mackerel for a main course.

SCALLOP CHOWDER

Chowder is derived from the French *chaudière,* meaning kettle, in which this thick soup was traditionally cooked. A classic scallop chowder includes pork.

PREPARATION TIME: *15 min.*
COOKING TIME: *1 hour*

INGREDIENTS *(for 4–6)* :
12 scallops
Juice of a lemon
½ pint fish stock
1 large onion
6 oz. belly pork
4 potatoes
1 carrot
1 parsnip
1 green pepper
2 sticks celery
1 pint milk
Salt and black pepper
Juice of an orange
1 level tablespoon plain flour
1 oz. butter
GARNISH:
Paprika

Slide the scallops* from their shells, and discard the beards and any black threads. Wash the scallops under cold running water, sprinkle with lemon juice and allow to stand for 15 minutes.

Cut each scallop into four pieces and put them in a saucepan with the fish stock. Bring to the boil, cover the pan with a lid, and simmer for 10 minutes.

Peel and thinly slice the onion. Put the belly pork in a sauté pan and cook over low heat until the fat runs. Remove the pork and add the onion to the pan, cooking it in the pork fat until transparent. Peel and dice the potatoes, carrot and parsnip. Cut the pepper in half, remove the stem, seeds and white midribs, and slice the flesh. Add these vegetables, with the cleaned and roughly chopped celery, to the onion.

Pour the milk into the pan and bring to simmering point. Season to taste with salt and freshly ground pepper. Add the orange juice; return the belly pork to the pan, and simmer the chowder, covered, until the vegetables are tender.

Lift out the belly pork and dice it finely. Stir the scallops, the fish stock and the diced pork into the chowder.

If necessary, make a beurre manié* from the flour and butter and use it to thicken the chowder.

Serve the chowder in individual bowls, sprinkled with paprika.

Meat

TURBOT WITH SWEET CORN

The delicate flavour of turbot should not be impaired by strong sauces and garnishes. In this recipe, the baked fish is complemented by sweet corn and a Bearnaise sauce.

PREPARATION TIME: *15 min.*
COOKING TIME: *25 min.*

INGREDIENTS *(for 6)*:
6 turbot steaks or fillets (4–6 oz. each)
2 teaspoons lemon juice
Black pepper
4 oz. unsalted butter
15 oz. tin sweet corn
½ pint Bearnaise sauce

Wipe the turbot with a damp cloth. Butter two large sheets of kitchen foil and place the turbot steaks on one sheet. Sprinkle with lemon juice, grind over a little pepper and dot the fish with knobs of butter. Cover with the second piece of foil and seal tightly to form a loose parcel. Bake the turbot for 25 minutes on the centre shelf of an oven pre-heated to 350°F (mark 4).

Heat the sweet corn over moderate heat, then stir 2 oz. butter into it. Season with freshly ground pepper and spread the sweet corn over the base of a shallow serving dish. Arrange the turbot on the sweet corn, pour over the juices from the foil parcel, and coat each steak with Bearnaise sauce*.

Serve with broccoli spears au gratin (see January vegetables).

CRAB WITH MUSHROOMS

This combination of mushrooms and crabmeat, frozen or tinned, makes a good main course. The dish can also be served as a starter, and shrimps can be substituted for crab.

PREPARATION TIME: *10 min.*
CHILLING TIME: *1 hour*

INGREDIENTS *(for 4–6)*:
8 oz. crabmeat
½ lb. button mushrooms
2 cloves garlic
Juice of half lemon
Tabasco sauce
6 tablespoons olive oil
¼ level teaspoon caster sugar
Salt and black pepper
¼ pint double cream
GARNISH:
3 oz. black olives
Chopped parsley

Trim and finely slice the mushrooms* into a serving dish. Crush the garlic and add to the mushrooms, together with the strained lemon juice, a few drops of Tabasco and the olive oil. Season to taste with sugar, salt and freshly ground pepper. Blend all the ingredients thoroughly, spoon them into a shallow serving dish; leave to chill for 1 hour.

Just before serving, blend the flaked crabmeat with the cream and stir this mixture into the mushrooms.

Garnish the crab and mushrooms with olives and finely chopped parsley. Serve with warm crusty bread and butter. A salad of green peppers, endive and Florence fennel tossed in an Italian dressing (see January vegetables) would also go well with the crab.

FILET DE BOEUF EN CROÛTE

Whole fillet of beef in puff pastry is a classic, if highly extravagant, French dish. For a special occasion, however, the time and expense involved are well worth while.

PREPARATION TIME: *1 hour*
CHILLING TIME: *1 hour*
COOKING TIME: *1½ hours*

INGREDIENTS *(for 8)*:
4 lb. fillet of beef
½ clove garlic (optional)
1 oz. unsalted butter
2 oz. pâté de foie gras
½ level teaspoon ground thyme
1½ lb. prepared puff pastry
1 egg
1 dessertspoon olive oil
CUCUMBER SAUCE:
½ cucumber
2 fluid oz. double cream
4 oz. plain yoghourt
½ level teaspoon ground ginger
3 teaspoons lemon juice
Salt

MUSHROOM SAUCE:
1 small onion
8 oz. mushrooms
½ pint chicken stock
1 oz. unsalted butter
1 level dessertspoon plain flour
¼ pint milk
Salt and black pepper
2 tablespoons Madeira (optional)
1 egg yolk
GARNISH:
Watercress

Trim any fat from the fillet, roll it into a neat shape, and tie it at intervals with fine string.

Cut the garlic into slivers and insert them into the beef with the point of a sharp knife. Soften the butter under the grill and spread over the top of the fillet. Cook the meat for 10 minutes in a roasting tin on the centre shelf of an oven pre-heated to 425°F (mark 7). Remove the beef from the oven and leave to cool. When the beef is quite cold, remove the string.

Roll out the prepared puff pastry*, ⅛ in. thick, to an oblong 3½ times the width of the fillet, and its length plus 7 in. Spread the pâté over the top of the fillet, place the meat, pâté-side down, in the centre of the pastry, and sprinkle with the thyme. Fold the pastry over and under the meat, brushing the seams with water and sealing them thoroughly. Turn the pastry over so that the join is underneath; prick the top with a fork and decorate with leaves cut from the pastry trimmings. Cover the pastry with a cloth and leave it in the refrigerator for at least 1 hour.

Meanwhile, prepare the cucumber and mushroom sauces. For the cucumber sauce, coarsely grate the chilled cucumber. Just before serving, mix it with the cream, yoghourt, ginger and lemon juice. Season to taste with salt.

To make the mushroom sauce, peel and finely chop the onion and the trimmed mushrooms*. Put these ingredients in a saucepan with the stock and bring to the boil. Reduce the heat and simmer the mixture for 30 minutes. Cool slightly, then liquidise the mixture.

Melt the butter in a pan, stir in the flour and cook the roux* for 3 minutes, stirring continuously. Gradually blend in the milk, and bring the sauce to boiling point over low heat. Mix in the mushroom purée, season with salt and pepper, and stir in the Madeira. Simmer for a further 10 minutes, then remove from the heat and allow to cool slightly. Stir in the beaten egg yolk just before serving.

Beat the egg with the oil and brush it over the pastry to glaze it during cooking. Set the pastry roll on a wet baking tray, and bake in the centre of an oven pre-heated to 425°F (mark 7) for 35 minutes. The pastry should then be golden brown, and the beef rosy-pink inside.

Place the beef in its pastry on a bed of watercress and serve with broccoli spears au gratin (see January vegetables) and the cucumber and mushroom sauces in separate sauce boats.

VEAL AND HAM PIE

Veal pies first became popular in Britain during the 18th century. They were often cooked as raised pies or made into jellied moulds – the following recipe is a simpler farmhouse version.

PREPARATION TIME: $2\frac{1}{2}$ hours
COOKING TIME: 40–45 min.

INGREDIENTS (for 4–6):
2 lb. pie veal
1 shin bone
$1\frac{1}{2}$–2 pints stock
2 bay leaves
Bouquet garni
1 level tablespoon chopped parsley
6 black peppercorns
Salt and black pepper
8 oz. piece cooked gammon
3 hardboiled eggs
Rind from a lemon
8 oz. flaky pastry (standard recipe)
1 egg
1 teaspoon olive oil

Ask the butcher to saw the shin bone into pieces. Place the veal and the shin bone in a large pan, and cover with stock. Add the bay leaves, bouquet garni*, parsley and peppercorns. Bring to the boil, cover the pan with a lid and simmer gently for 2 hours. Allow to cool slightly, then remove the meat from the liquid, cut it into small pieces and remove any pieces of fat. Strain the liquid, season to taste with salt and pepper and set it aside.

Cut the gammon into narrow strips and mix with the veal. Shell the hardboiled eggs, place them in the centre of a 2 pint pie dish, and pack the veal and gammon round them. Grate the lemon rind and sprinkle it over the top. Pour the liquid over the pie filling to just cover it.

Roll out the flaky pastry* to a thickness of $\frac{1}{4}$ in. Cover the pie with the pastry and make a slit in the centre to allow the steam to escape. Beat the egg, mix it with the olive oil, and brush over the pastry. Bake the pie for 10 minutes in the centre of an oven pre-heated to 450°F (mark 8). Reduce the heat to 400°F (mark 6) and bake for a further 20 minutes or until the pastry is golden brown. Give the pie a half turn halfway through cooking. Top up, if necessary, with more stock, through the pastry slit.

Serve the pie hot with boiled potatoes and a green vegetable or, ideally, cold with a mixed salad tossed in a tarragon-flavoured dressing.

LAMB À LA GREQUE

Greek cooking is characterised by its use of spices and aubergines. Lamb is the meat most commonly used in Greece, but it is often lean and stringy and more suitable for casserole dishes than for roasting.

PREPARATION TIME: 1–$1\frac{1}{2}$ hours
COOKING TIME: $1\frac{1}{4}$ hours

INGREDIENTS (for 6):
3 lb. boned shoulder of lamb
$\frac{1}{2}$ lb. aubergines
Salt and black pepper
4 tablespoons olive oil
4 oz. caster sugar
1 lb. apricots
2 large onions
15–16 oz. tin tomatoes
6 oz. tin tomato paste
4 bay leaves
$\frac{1}{4}$ level teaspoon crushed coriander seeds
$\frac{1}{4}$ level teaspoon grated nutmeg
Juice of a lemon
3 oz. unsalted butter
2 pints chicken stock
8 oz. long grain rice
$\frac{1}{2}$ level teaspoon curry powder
GARNISH:
4 oz. stoned black olives
Orange peel

Remove the stalk ends and wipe the aubergines; cut them lengthways into $\frac{1}{4}$ in. thick slices. Place the aubergine slices in a bowl and sprinkle them with 2 teaspoons salt, to draw out the excess water. Mix thoroughly, cover with a cloth and leave for 45 minutes. Drain the aubergines and wipe them dry with a cloth.

Heat the olive oil in a heavy-based pan and fry the aubergine slices for just 1 minute until golden, then drain on absorbent kitchen paper.

Dissolve the sugar in a pan containing 8 fluid oz. cold water. Boil this syrup for 10 minutes and meanwhile, halve and stone the apricots. Add the apricots to the syrup and poach* them for 5–15 minutes or until just tender.

Trim any excess fat from the lamb, cut the meat into 1 in. cubes and fry it over low heat in a dry sauté pan, turning it frequently, until the fat runs and the meat turns a light brown colour.

Peel and finely chop the onions, add them to the lamb and continue cooking until the onions are transparent. Add the chopped tomatoes with their juice, the tomato paste, bay leaves, coriander seeds, nutmeg, parsley, salt, pepper and lemon juice. Top up the apricot syrup with water to make $\frac{1}{2}$ pint, pour it over the lamb and bring the mixture to boiling point.

Line the base of a large buttered casserole with the aubergine slices and spoon over the lamb mixture.

Cover the casserole tightly with foil and the lid. Cook for 1 hour in the centre of an oven pre-heated to 350°F (mark 4). Remove the covering from the casserole, lay the apricots over the lamb and return the casserole to the oven while preparing the rice.

Bring the stock and 6 pints of water to the boil in a large saucepan. Add 2 teaspoons salt and the rice, stirring until the water returns to the boil. Cover the pan with a lid and boil the rice for 12–14 minutes or until just tender. Drain the rice through a sieve and rinse under hot water.

Melt the remaining butter in a saucepan and stir in the rice. Mix in the curry powder. Spoon the rice in a ring on to a warm serving dish and fill the centre with the lamb and aubergines. Garnish the rice with black olives, the apricots, and narrow strips of orange peel.

Serve with a lettuce and tomato salad tossed in an oil and orange juice dressing.

ROLLATINE DE MANZO AL FORNO

The name of this Italian dish means – quite simply – beef rolls cooked in the oven. Wafer-thin slices of beef and ham are rolled round a savoury and sweet stuffing and cooked in wine.

PREPARATION TIME: *45 min.*
COOKING TIME: *1 hour*

INGREDIENTS *(for 6)*:
12 thin slices sirloin of beef (each approx. 4 in. by 3 in. by $\frac{1}{4}$ in.)
12 wafer-thin slices cooked ham
3 cloves garlic
12 thin slices salami
4 hardboiled eggs
5 oz. raisins
2 oz. grated Parmesan cheese
8 level tablespoons finely chopped parsley
$\frac{1}{2}$ level teaspoon grated nutmeg
$\frac{1}{2}$ level teaspoon oregano
Salt and black pepper
1 oz. unsalted butter
$\frac{1}{2}$ pint beef stock
$\frac{1}{2}$ pint dry white wine
4 bay leaves
6 cloves
2 tablespoons Marsala wine

Place each slice of beef between sheets of waxed or greaseproof paper and flatten it with a rolling pin. Cover the beef slices with ham, trimmed to fit, and spread with peeled and crushed garlic.

Finely chop the skinned salami, the hardboiled eggs and raisins, and put them in a bowl. Blend in the cheese, parsley, nutmeg and oregano, and season with salt and freshly ground pepper.

Divide this mixture equally over the beef and ham slices. Fold over the short sides to keep the stuffing in place and roll the slices up. Tie the parcels with fine string.

Place the rolls in a buttered ovenproof dish. Pour over the stock and wine and cook for 30 minutes in the centre of the oven, pre-heated to 375°F (mark 5). Add the bay leaves, cloves and Marsala, and cook for a further 30 minutes.

Serve the beef rolls with fettucine al burro (see January rice and pasta) and cauliflower with almonds · (see January vegetables).

PORK CHOPS WITH ALMONDS AND SHERRY

When a special main course is required at short notice, this dish may provide the solution. Choose large, thick pork chops, preferably with the kidneys still attached.

PREPARATION TIME: *10 min.*
COOKING TIME: *20 min.*

INGREDIENTS *(for 4)*:
4 pork chops
1 clove garlic
1 level teaspoon crushed dill seeds
1 tablespoon olive oil
$1\frac{1}{2}$ oz. unsalted butter
4 oz. flaked almonds
4 fluid oz. dry sherry

Trim any excess fat off the chops, leaving $\frac{1}{4}$ in. round the edge. Peel and crush the garlic and rub this and the dill seeds into both sides of each chop. Brush the chops all over with oil and put them under a hot grill, for 8 minutes to each side. Brush the chops again with oil when they are turned.

Meanwhile, melt the butter in a small pan and cook the almonds over low heat until they are straw-coloured. Pour in the sherry, boil until bubbling, and then reduce the heat to simmering point and continue cooking until the almonds turn a caramel colour.

Arrange the chops on a serving dish, with the sherry sauce and almonds poured over them. Creamed potatoes and Brussels sprouts with soured cream (see December vegetables) would be suitable vegetables.

VIENNESE VEAL STEAKS

The influence of Hungarian cooking – with its emphasis on soured cream and paprika – is evident in this Austrian recipe.

The veal steaks should be thick, not thin escalopes, and long slow cooking blends the flavours of herbs, spices, wine and cream.

PREPARATION TIME: *10 min.*
COOKING TIME: *1 hour*

INGREDIENTS *(for 4)*:
4 veal steaks (each 1 in. thick and approx. 6 oz.)
$\frac{1}{2}$ level teaspoon rosemary spikes
2 oz. unsalted butter
1 tablespoon olive oil
1 clove garlic
Seasoned flour
6 oz. mushrooms
3 fluid oz. dry white wine
8 fluid oz. soured cream
Tabasco sauce
Salt and black pepper
1 level teaspoon paprika
GARNISH:
Chopped parsley or paprika

Trim and wipe the veal steaks. Make small incisions in them with the point of a knife and insert small spikes of rosemary. Heat the butter and oil in a heavy-based pan over low heat. Peel the garlic, and fry it until brown, then discard.

Coat the veal steaks lightly with seasoned flour*, shake off any surplus, and fry the steaks in the butter and oil until brown, turning them once.

Cover the pan with a lid and cook the steaks over low heat for a further 12 minutes. Add the trimmed and sliced mushrooms* to the steaks. Turn the mushrooms until they have absorbed most of the fat. Pour the wine into the pan and mix in well. Increase the heat, then add the soured cream. Season to taste with salt, freshly ground pepper, a few shakes of Tabasco and the paprika. Turn down the heat and simmer the steaks, uncovered, for a further 30 minutes.

Lift out the steaks and, if necessary, reduce* the sauce to the desired consistency by boiling and stirring for 5 minutes.

Pour the sauce over the steaks and serve at once, sprinkled with parsley or a little paprika. Parsnips Molly Parkin (see December vegetables) would go well with the steaks.

CROWN ROAST OF LAMB

The crown is formed by joining two best ends of lamb, and the hollow between them is stuffed with a savoury filling. The cutlet bones are frequently decorated with cutlet frills, but glazed onions make an unusual, and edible, garnish for this meat dish.

PREPARATION TIME: *45 min.*
COOKING TIME: *2 hours*

INGREDIENTS *(for 6)* :

2 best ends of lamb (6 cutlets
   each)
2 oz. beef dripping
STUFFING :
½ lb. cranberries
¼ pint chicken stock
1 oz. caster sugar
1 onion
¼ lb. mushrooms
½ lb. belly pork

1 oz. butter
1 clove garlic
4 level tablespoons chopped
   parsley
1½ level teaspoons ground thyme
4 oz. fresh white breadcrumbs
1 egg
Salt and black pepper
GARNISH :
Glazed onions

Ask the butcher to trim off any excess fat and to shape the best ends of lamb into a crown*.

For the stuffing, put the cranberries, stock and sugar in a saucepan; if necessary, top up the stock with sufficient water to cover the fruit. Bring the cranberries to the boil and cook over high heat until they burst open, and the liquid has reduced* to a thick sauce.

Peel and finely chop the onion, trim and coarsely chop the mushrooms*, and mince the belly pork. Melt the butter in a pan and fry the onion until soft but not coloured. Add the peeled and crushed garlic and cook for 1 minute. Add the mushrooms, turning them in the butter until they are lightly coloured. In a bowl, combine the cranberries and the onion and mushroom mixture with the minced belly pork. Mix in the parsley, thyme and breadcrumbs. Beat the egg lightly and use to bind the stuffing. Season to taste with salt and freshly ground pepper.

Spoon the stuffing into the hollow crown. Wrap foil round the cutlet bones to protect them during roasting. Melt the dripping in a roasting pan and place the stuffed crown in it. Roast on a shelf low in a preheated oven at 375°F (mark 5), for 10 minutes. Reduce the heat to 350°F (mark 4) and continue roasting. Allow 30 minutes to the pound, and baste* frequently.

Remove the crown roast and keep it warm. Skim off as much fat as possible and boil the pan juices to make a gravy. Sweeten the gravy with redcurrant jelly or a tablespoon of cranberry sauce, and pour it into a warm sauce boat.

Serve the crown roast with garlic potatoes and a chicory and orange salad (see December vegetables). Spike a glazed onion (see December vegetables) on each cutlet bone.

Poultry & Game

TEAL À LA NORMANDE

Normandy is famed throughout France for the excellence of its cuisine. The region is chiefly agricultural, producing fine butter and cream, well-nurtured cattle and large fruit crops. Game birds, fish and shellfish abound. All these products form the basis for Normandy cooking. Teal (wild duck), partridge and quail are suitable for this recipe.

PREPARATION TIME: *20 min.*
COOKING TIME: *35 min.*

INGREDIENTS *(for 4)*:
4 teal
3 oz. unsalted butter
4 russet dessert apples
Juice of a lemon
½ pint double cream
2 tablespoons brandy
¼ level teaspoon crushed coriander seeds
Salt and black pepper
GARNISH:
Apple peel
Watercress

Wipe the trussed teal inside and out with a damp cloth. Melt the butter in a large, heavy-based pan. Fry the teal, covered, over low heat for about 10 minutes, turning them occasionally, until they are browned all over. Transfer the birds to a dish and keep them warm.

Core, but do not peel the apples, chop them coarsely and fry in the pan juices, with the lemon juice, for about 5 minutes, until they colour slightly. Put the apples in the bottom of a casserole dish just large enough to take the teal. Place the teal on top of the apples and pour over the cream and brandy. Sprinkle the crushed

coriander seeds over the birds, together with a little salt and freshly ground pepper. Cover the casserole with a lid and cook in the centre of an oven, pre-heated to 325°F (mark 3), for 35 minutes. Baste* the birds three times during cooking.

Remove the casserole from the oven, lift out the teal and spread the apple mixture over the base of a warm serving dish. Set the teal on the apples and garnish each bird with a freshly cut spiral of apple peel; decorate the vents with sprigs of watercress.

Leeks with fried rice (see January vegetables), or any green vegetable, would go well with this casserole.

CHICKEN PUDDING

This is an adaptation of a classic English pudding dating back to medieval times when tough goose or chicken was steamed with onions, in a crude flour and water paste. Chicken pudding in enriched shortcrust pastry is more digestible.

PREPARATION TIME: *30 min.*
COOKING TIME: *3 hours*

INGREDIENTS *(for 4)*:
4 chicken portions
4 oz. piece green bacon
12 oz. leeks
8 oz. shortcrust pastry (standard recipe, plus 1 egg)
Seasoned flour
3 oz. mushrooms
½ level teaspoon powdered thyme
¼ level teaspoon crushed rosemary
1 heaped tablespoon chopped parsley
½ pint chicken stock

Remove the rind and cut the bacon into small cubes. Fry them in a pan, without extra fat, over moderate heat until the fat runs. Lift out and drain the bacon.

Trim the roots and outer coarse leaves from the leeks, wash them thoroughly. Cut the leeks into thin round slices.

Set aside a third of the prepared shortcrust pastry*. Roll out the remainder, ¼ in. thick, on a floured surface, and use it to line a buttered 2 pint pudding basin. Cut each chicken portion into smaller pieces and coat thoroughly with seasoned flour*. Trim and slice the mushrooms*.

Mix together the chicken, bacon, mushrooms, leeks, thyme, rosemary and parsley, and place in the basin. Pour in the stock until the basin is half full.

Roll out the remaining pastry and cover the pudding, crimping the edges to ensure a good seal. Cover the top of the basin with buttered greaseproof paper and tie down with a pudding cloth or aluminium foil.

Bring a large pan of water to the boil and lower the pudding into it – the water should reach two-thirds up the sides of the basin. Cover the pan with a lid, bring the water back to the boil and keep at a fast simmer for 3 hours, topping up with boiling water when necessary.

Invert the cooked pudding on to a hot dish, and serve. No potatoes are needed, but Brussels sprouts with soured cream (see December vegetables) would be suitable.

BLANQUETTE OF TURKEY

After Boxing Day, cold turkey tends to lose its charms; even so, the last left-overs may be turned into a savoury main course, and an excellent stock can be made from the carcass.

PREPARATION TIME: *20 min.*
COOKING TIME: *30 min.*

INGREDIENTS *(for 4–6)*:
1½ lb. cooked turkey meat
1 large onion
3 oz. unsalted butter
2 oz. plain flour
1 pint turkey or chicken stock
1 small tin pimentoes
2 oz. button mushrooms
1 clove garlic
Pinch each of powdered mace and nutmeg
2 egg yolks
4 tablespoons double cream
1 tablespoon lemon juice
Salt and black pepper

Cut the turkey meat into small pieces and peel and thinly slice the onion. Melt the butter in a large frying pan and cook the onion over low heat until soft and transparent. Mix in the flour and cook this roux* for 3 minutes. Gradually stir in the stock, and simmer the sauce until it thickens.

Meanwhile, slice the drained pimentoes thinly, trim and slice the mushrooms* and peel and crush the garlic. Add these ingredients to the sauce, with the turkey; season to taste with salt, freshly ground pepper, mace and nutmeg. Heat the mixture through and then remove from the heat. Beat the egg yolks, cream and lemon juice until the mixture has the consistency of thin cream. Blend this slowly

into the turkey mixture and return the pan to the heat. Heat through over low heat, but do not let the mixture boil.

Spoon the blanquette of turkey into a warm serving dish, and serve with Brussels sprouts tossed in a little butter, soft brown sugar and allspice.

DUCK WITH CHERRIES

Duck cooked in this way requires little attention, and as carving is done beforehand, it presents no problems when brought to the table. The finished dish is also suitable for freezing.

PREPARATION TIME: *20 min.*
COOKING TIME: *1¼ hours*

INGREDIENTS *(for 4)*:
1 duck (approx. 5 lb.)
Salt and black pepper
1 oz. unsalted butter
4 fluid oz. Madeira or sweet sherry
15–16 oz. tin morello or black cherries
Lemon juice
5 fluid oz. port
3 level teaspoons cornflour
GARNISH:
3 heaped tablespoons chopped parsley

Joint the duck* into four equal portions and prick the skin thoroughly with a darning needle. Season with salt and freshly ground pepper. Melt the butter in a large sauté pan and fry the duck over low heat for about 20 minutes or until brown all over. Drain the fat from the pan and pour the Madeira and the juice from the cherries over the duck. Bring the contents to simmering point, cover the pan tightly with a lid and continue simmering the duck for 45–55 minutes.

Lift the duck portions from the pan, drain on crumpled absorbent paper and keep them warm.

Skim as much fat as possible from the pan juices and stir in the port. Mix the cornflour with 2 tablespoons of cold water, and stir into the pan juices until thickened. Bring to the boil and adjust seasoning; add the cherries and heat through.

Arrange the duck portions, coated with the sauce, on a dish. Sprinkle with parsley, and serve with Jerusalem artichokes in butter (see January vegetables).

WILD GOOSE IN CIDER

Some species of wild geese are protected in Britain, but others, such as Brent, grey and Canada geese, sometimes appear on the market in winter. A young wild goose weighs about 7 lb. and, unlike the domesticated variety, is completely lean. The flesh is dark and has a 'gamey' flavour.

PREPARATION TIME: *15 min.*
COOKING TIME: *3¼ hours*

INGREDIENTS *(for 4–6):*
1 wild goose
4 oz. butter
1 onion
6 cloves
Half an orange
Salt and black pepper
½ lb. belly pork
1 pint dry cider
½ pint stock
2 tablespoons Calvados (optional)
GARNISH:
Watercress and oranges
Game chips

Wipe the goose thoroughly, inside and out, with a damp cloth. Use the giblets to make stock*.

Put 3 oz. butter, the peeled onion stuck with the cloves, and half an orange inside the goose. Sew up the vent or secure it with small skewers. Rub salt, freshly ground pepper and the remaining butter over the skin. Remove any rind and gristle and cut the belly pork into thin slices. Tie these over the breast of the goose.

Place the goose, breast-side down, in a large roasting tin, pour in half the cider and all the stock and cover the pan with a tent of foil. Roast the goose in the lower half of an oven, pre-heated to 450°F (mark 8), for 15 minutes. Baste* with more cider, replace the foil and reduce the heat to 375°F (mark 5). Continue roasting for about 3 hours, allowing 20 minutes to the pound, plus 20 minutes extra. Baste every 20 minutes, topping up with more cider. For the last 30 minutes of cooking, roast the goose on its back.

Remove the roasting pan from the oven, pour the warmed Calvados over the goose and set it alight. As soon as the flames die down transfer the goose to a serving dish and keep it warm.

Pour the pan juices into a saucepan and boil them briskly until they have reduced* to a thin gravy.

Serve the goose and the crisp belly pork garnished with game chips*, sprigs of watercress and small halved oranges. Red cabbage*, cooked with apple and vinegar, is an excellent accompaniment. Serve the gravy separately.

Rice & Pasta

SPAGHETTINI WITH MUSSEL SAUCE

The fine thin strands of spaghetti, known as spaghettini, make a lighter-than-usual pasta dish. It is here served in an unusual sauce for a main course.

PREPARATION TIME: *1 hour*
COOKING TIME: *15 min.*

INGREDIENTS *(for 4–6)* :
1 lb. spaghettini
4 pints mussels
2 heaped tablespoons salt
8 tablespoons olive oil
3 cloves garlic
¼ pint fish stock
Black pepper
1 level tablespoon finely chopped parsley

Wash the mussels* under cold running water, scrubbing the shells and scraping off the beards. Leave the mussels in a pail of cold water to which has been added 2 tablespoons salt.

Set a large pan of lightly salted water to boil. Meanwhile, heat 3 tablespoons oil in a large sauté pan. Add 2 peeled and crushed cloves of garlic and fry in the oil until brown. Remove the garlic. Put the mussels in the pan, place over high heat, cover with a lid, and shake the pan for 5 minutes, or until the shells have opened. Remove the pan from the heat and discard any mussels that remain closed. Turn the contents of the pan into a bowl and ease the mussels from the shells, retaining the liquid.

Put the spaghettini into the pan of boiling salted water, stirring until the water boils again. Cook the spaghettini for 7–10 minutes, stirring occasionally until just tender. Drain thoroughly in a colander.

Heat the remaining oil in the sauté pan over low heat. Peel and crush the remaining garlic and fry until golden. Pour half the contents of the pan over the spaghettini and toss until it gleams. Return the mussels and their liquid to the sauté pan and heat through gently. Add the fish stock and continue cooking for 1–2 minutes until thoroughly heated. Pepper well, and stir in the parsley.

Spoon the mussels and liquid over the spaghettini, toss and serve at once, with slices of warm crusty bread.

RISOTTO ALLA MILANESE

There are several versions of Milanese rice, some being made with chicken broth, others with white wine or Marsala. The classic flavouring of saffron, however, is always included. The rice can be served as a course on its own, and is also the traditional accompaniment to Osso Buco (see July meat).

PREPARATION TIME: *20 min.*
COOKING TIME: *20 min.*

INGREDIENTS *(for 6)* :
1 lb. Italian or short grain rice
1 marrow bone
1 small onion
3 oz. unsalted butter
¼ pint dry white wine
2 pints beef stock
½ level teaspoon powdered saffron
3 oz. grated Parmesan cheese

Ask the butcher to chop the bone into several pieces, so that the marrow can be easily extracted with a skewer – it should yield about 2 oz. Peel and finely chop the onion.

Melt half the butter in a large, heavy-based pan, add the onion and fry over moderate heat until transparent. Pour the wine over the onion and boil briskly until reduced* by half. Add the rice and sauté, stirring continuously, until it begins to change colour.

Stir the boiling stock, a cupful at a time, into the rice, until completely absorbed. Blend in all the stock and finally stir in the saffron. The rice should be tender after 15–20 minutes. If necessary, add a little hot water to prevent the rice drying out.

Stir the remaining butter and grated Parmesan cheese into the rice and serve at once.

RICE AND CHEESE CROQUETTES

These small, crisp rice cakes go well with fish, lamb and veal dishes. They can also be served on their own, with an apricot sauce. Brown rice may be used, but this requires boiling for 45 minutes.

PREPARATION TIME: *20 min.*
STANDING TIME: *1 hour*
COOKING TIME: *20 min.*

INGREDIENTS *(for 4–6)* :
8 oz. long grain rice
2 pints chicken stock
1 level tablespoon salt
Juice of half lemon
4 oz. grated Emmenthal cheese
1 oz. softened butter
Black pepper
2 eggs
4 oz. fresh white breadcrumbs
Oil for frying

Vegetables & Salads

Bring 6 pints of water and the stock to the boil in a large pan. Add the salt, lemon juice and rice, stirring until the water returns to the boil. Cover the pan with a lid and boil the rice for about 12 minutes or until tender. Drain in a colander and rinse the rice with boiling water.

Put the drained rice in a mixing bowl, stir in the cheese and butter, a few twists of freshly ground pepper and 1 lightly beaten egg.

Shape the rice mixture into 3 in. long croquettes*, roll them in the breadcrumbs, then dip them in lightly beaten egg. Roll the croquettes in the bread-crumbs again, then leave them on a plate to set in the refrigerator for 1 hour.

Heat sufficient oil in a large pan to come no more than one-third up the sides. The oil is hot enough for deep frying (375°F) when a cube of bread rises to the surface and is golden brown in 60 seconds. Arrange the croquettes in the frying basket and lower it carefully into the hot oil; turn off the heat immediately. After 3–5 minutes the croquettes should have risen to the surface and be golden brown and crisp.

Remove them from the oil, drain on crumpled kitchen paper and serve at once.

WALDORF SALAD

This American salad was created at the Waldorf-Astoria Hotel in New York. The tart combination of apple and celery makes it an excellent counter-balance to rich meats such as duck and pork.

PREPARATION TIME: *45 min.*
STANDING TIME: *30 min.*

INGREDIENTS *(for 6)* :
1 lb. tart red dessert apples
2 tablespoons lemon juice
1 level teaspoon caster sugar
¼ pint mayonnaise
½ head celery
2 oz. shelled walnuts
1 lettuce

Wash and core the apples, slice one apple finely and dice the remainder. Dip the apple slices in a dressing of lemon juice, caster sugar and 1 tablespoon of the mayonnaise*. Set aside. Toss the diced apple in the dressing and let it stand for 30 minutes.

Scrub and chop the celery and chop the walnuts. Add the celery and walnuts to the diced apple, with the rest of the mayonnaise, and mix thoroughly. Line a serving bowl with the cleaned and chilled lettuce leaves, pile the salad into the centre and garnish with the apple slices.

GLAZED ONIONS

These small buttered onions are both tasty and decorative with elaborate joints of meat, such as fillet of beef en croûte or roast crown of lamb.

PREPARATION TIME: *15 min.*
COOKING TIME: *20 min.*

INGREDIENTS *(for 4)* :
1 lb. button onions or shallots
2 oz. unsalted butter
2 level tablespoons caster sugar

Fill a large saucepan with water, bring to the boil, and put in the washed onions. Cook over low heat for 7 minutes, then drain and peel the onions.

Melt the butter in the saucepan, add the onions and toss them over low heat for 3 minutes. Sprinkle over the sugar and continue tossing the onions for a further 4 minutes until they are evenly glazed and tender. Serve the onions with the glaze.

CHICORY AND ORANGE SALAD

A slightly sharp, refreshing salad which goes well with most kinds of game, cold meats or stuffed joints.

PREPARATION TIME: *20 min.*

INGREDIENTS *(for 6)* :
4 heads of chicory
3 oranges
French dressing

Remove any brown outer leaves and the root ends from the chicory. Wash and drain thoroughly, then cut the chicory into thin slices, crossways. Peel the oranges with a sharp knife, removing all the white pith with the peel. Slice the oranges thinly in cross-section and remove the pips. If the oranges are large, cut each slice in two.

Mix the chicory and orange slices in a serving bowl, and pour over the French dressing* (made with orange juice instead of vinegar). Toss and serve.

SWEET POTATOES WITH APPLES

Sweet potatoes are a staple vege-table in the southern United States. This particular recipe is a popular Creole dish which can be served on its own as a vegetable casserole, or with roast lamb.

PREPARATION TIME: *20 min.*
COOKING TIME: *40 min.*

INGREDIENTS *(for 6)* :
1 lb. sweet potatoes
1¼ lb. cooking apples
3 oz. butter
1 level teaspoon salt
6 oz. soft brown sugar
1 level teaspoon nutmeg
1 tablespoon lemon juice

Peel and thinly slice the sweet potatoes; peel, core and thinly slice the apples. Butter a casserole dish, and in it arrange alternate layers of sweet potatoes and apples, starting and finishing with sweet potatoes. Sprinkle each layer with salt, sugar, nutmeg and lemon juice, and dot with the remaining butter.

Set the casserole on the lowest shelf of an oven pre-heated to 400°F (mark 6) and cook for 40 minutes or until the potatoes are tender. Serve straight from the casserole.

PARSNIPS MOLLY PARKIN

This vegetable casserole is an unusual combination of parsnips, tomatoes, cheese and cream. It goes well with roast lamb and pork.

PREPARATION TIME: *40 min.*
COOKING TIME: *40 min.*

INGREDIENTS *(for 6)* :
2 lb. parsnips
1 lb. tomatoes
5 tablespoons oil
3 oz. butter
3 level tablespoons soft brown sugar
Salt and black pepper
6 oz. grated Gruyère cheese
½ pint single or double cream
4 rounded tablespoons fresh white breadcrumbs

Peel the parsnips, cut away and discard any hard central cores. Slice the parsnips thinly. Skin the tomatoes*, remove the seeds and cut the flesh into slices. Heat the oil in a pan and lightly fry the parsnips for 4 minutes.

Grease a 2 pint casserole dish with half the butter, and place a layer of parsnips over the base. Sprinkle with a little sugar, salt, freshly ground pepper and add a little cream, before covering with a layer of tomatoes. Spread a little more cream and cheese over the tomatoes and repeat these layers until all the ingredients are used up, finishing off with cream and cheese. Top with the breadcrumbs and dot with the remaining butter.

Cook the parsnip casserole for 40 minutes in the centre of an oven pre-heated to 325°F (mark 3). Serve straight from the casserole.

BAKED CAULIFLOWER CHEESE

In this dish the strong, smooth flavour of Gruyère cheese contrasts well with crisp cauliflower. It can be served with grilled or roasted meats.

PREPARATION TIME: *20 min.*
COOKING TIME: *50 min.*

INGREDIENTS *(for 6)* :
1 large cauliflower
1 onion
2 oz. unsalted butter
3 oz. fresh white breadcrumbs
½ pint milk
2 oz. grated Gruyère cheese
Salt and black pepper
Ground nutmeg
5 beaten eggs

Cut away the coarse outer leaves from the cauliflower and break off the florets. Bring a large pan of lightly salted water to the boil. Add the florets, cover the pan with a lid, and boil gently for 5–8 minutes. Drain.

Meanwhile, finely chop the onion. Melt 1 oz. of butter and fry the onion for 10 minutes. Butter the inside of a 3½ pint baking dish and line it with 1 oz. of breadcrumbs.

In a saucepan, bring the milk to the boil, add the Gruyère cheese and the remaining butter. Season to taste with salt, pepper and a little nutmeg. Stir in the remaining breadcrumbs and the fried onion. Remove from the heat and blend in the beaten eggs. Fold the cauliflower into the sauce and spoon the mixture into the baking dish.

Bake on the lower shelf of an oven pre-heated to 325°F (mark 3) for 50 minutes or until firm.

POMMES DE TERRE NOISETTE

Small golden balls of fried potatoes make an attractive garnish for steaks, chops or sautéed meat. They should be left to soak for a few hours to remove excess starch. The cooked potatoes can be tossed in dissolved meat jelly and sprinkled with parsley. They are then known as *pommes de terre à la parisienne.*

PREPARATION TIME: *20 min.*
COOKING TIME: *10 min.*

INGREDIENTS *(for 6)* :
2 lb. potatoes
3 level tablespoons salt
3 oz. unsalted butter

Peel the potatoes and leave them to soak for 2 hours in cold water in which 2 tablespoons salt have been dissolved. Drain and dry the potatoes. Using a ball scoop, take out small balls, about the size of walnuts, from the potatoes.

Bring a pan of water to the boil, add 1 tablespoon salt and cook the potato balls over low heat for 3 minutes. Drain through a colander and dry on a cloth.

Melt the butter over gentle heat in a sauté pan. Toss the potatoes in the butter for about 5 minutes until golden and cooked through.

Using a perforated spoon, lift the potato balls into a warm serving dish, sprinkle with a little salt and serve.

Sweets & Puddings

GARLIC POTATOES

Mashed or creamed potatoes are given additional flavour by garlic. The bitterness is reduced if the garlic is boiled for a few minutes first.

PREPARATION TIME: *20 min.*
COOKING TIME: *2 hours*

INGREDIENTS *(for 6)*:
3 lb. potatoes
20 cloves garlic
4 oz. unsalted butter
1 oz. plain flour
½ pint milk
1 level teaspoon salt
Black pepper
3 tablespoons double cream
3 heaped tablespoons finely chopped parsley

Wash and dry the potatoes, prick them with a fork, and bake for 1½ hours or until tender on the centre shelf of an oven pre-heated to 400°F (mark 6).

Put the garlic in a small pan, cover with water; boil for 2 minutes, then drain and peel. Melt 2 oz. butter in a heavy-based saucepan and add the garlic. Cover the pan, and cook the garlic gently for 10 minutes or until tender. Remove the garlic. Stir the flour into the butter in the pan and cook over low heat for 2 minutes. Gradually blend in the boiling milk, stirring constantly until the sauce is smooth and thick. Add the salt, a few twists of pepper and the garlic. Boil for 2 minutes.

Liquidise the sauce or rub it through a sieve, then return it to the pan and heat through. Set aside.

Scoop the flesh from the baked potatoes, rub it through a sieve and beat in the remaining butter,

a little at a time. Season to taste with salt and pepper. Stir the cream into the garlic purée, then beat the mixture into the potatoes. Stir in the parsley.

Heat the mashed potato through if necessary, pile it back into the potato skins and serve at once.

BRUSSELS SPROUTS WITH SOURED CREAM

Brussels sprouts are a popular winter vegetable, but like cabbage, they are too often overcooked to a tasteless mass. Properly cooked sprouts should be just soft to the bite. A dressing of soured cream and nutmeg gives the vegetable an unusual flavour.

PREPARATION TIME: *10 min.*
COOKING TIME: *15 min.*

INGREDIENTS *(for 6)*:
1½ lb. Brussels sprouts
1 level tablespoon salt
Juice of half lemon
½–1 level teaspoon freshly grated nutmeg
5 fluid oz. double cream

Peel and wash the sprouts. Bring a large pan of water to the boil, add the salt and the sprouts. Bring back to the boil, and cook for 5 minutes until the sprouts are just tender. Drain well. Stir the lemon juice and nutmeg into the cream.

Return the sprouts to the saucepan and toss over moderate heat for a few minutes to dry them out completely. Pour in the cream, toss the sprouts over gentle heat for 1 minute and serve.

APPLE-RUM MERINGUE

Meringue is a favourite topping for many sweets. In this recipe, it covers tart cooking apples over rum-soaked ratafia biscuits. Macaroons or sponge fingers may be used instead of ratafias.

PREPARATION TIME: *30 min.*
COOKING TIME: *15 min.*

INGREDIENTS *(for 6)*:
4 oz. ratafia biscuits
4 tablespoons white rum
1½ lb. cooking apples
1 oz. unsalted butter
½ level teaspoon cinnamon
4 oz. soft brown sugar
3 egg whites
¼ level teaspoon salt
3 oz. granulated sugar
3 oz. caster sugar

Cover the base of a china flan dish with the ratafias, and pour the rum over them. Peel, core and thinly slice the apples into a saucepan; add the butter, cinnamon, brown sugar and 2–3 tablespoons water. Simmer for 10–15 minutes or until the apples are just cooked. Leave to cool, then spoon the apples over the ratafias.

Beat the egg whites with the salt until stiff, but not dry. Stir in the granulated sugar and beat for about 2 minutes or until the meringue mixture is smooth and glossy. Fold in the caster sugar, and immediately spoon the meringue over the apples in the flan dish. Swirl the meringue into soft peaks with a spatula.

Bake the flan for 10–15 minutes, in the centre of an oven pre-heated to 350°F (mark 4) until the meringue is pale beige. Serve hot or cold with a bowl of cream.

PARIS-BREST

In the late 19th century, this sweet was created in honour of a famous bicycle race which was run on a circular route from Paris to Brest and back again. It is a concoction of choux pastry filled with Chantilly cream.

PREPARATION TIME: *30 min.*
COOKING TIME: *30 min.*

INGREDIENTS *(for 4)*:
1 oz. unsalted butter
1 level teaspoon caster sugar
¼ pint milk
4 oz. plain flour
3 eggs
1½ oz. flaked almonds
CHANTILLY CREAM:
½ pint double cream
3 level tablespoons icing sugar

For the choux pastry*, put the butter, caster sugar and milk into a saucepan over moderate heat, and bring to the boil. Stir in the sifted flour, remove the pan from the heat, and beat vigorously with a wooden spoon until the

dough leaves the sides of the pan clean. Beat 2 eggs, one by one, into the choux. Then add the yolk of the third egg, beating vigorously until the dough is smooth and shiny. If necessary, beat in the remaining egg white.

Spoon the dough into a forcing bag fitted with a large plain nozzle. Pipe a ring, about 1½ in. wide and 8 in. in diameter, on to a greased baking tray. Sprinkle the almonds over the dough and bake for 30 minutes on the middle shelf of an oven pre-heated to 425°F (mark 7) for 30 minutes, or until dark brown.

Cool the choux ring on a wire rack, then split it in half, horizontally, with a sharp knife.

For the Chantilly cream, whip together the double cream, 2 tablespoons sifted icing sugar and an egg white until light and fluffy. Spoon the cream into the hollow bottom half of the ring. Cover with the lid, and dust with the remaining icing sugar.

ORANGE CHIFFON CREAM

The taste of fresh oranges is predominant in this flan case filled with a fluffy mixture of eggs and cream. For a dinner party, cover the chilled flan with extra whipped cream.

PREPARATION TIME: *45 min.*
COOKING TIME: *30 min.*
CHILLING TIME: *1 hour*

INGREDIENTS *(for 6):*
6 oz. shortcrust pastry (standard recipe)
2 level teaspoons powdered gelatine
4 eggs
5 level tablespoons caster sugar
¼ pint fresh orange juice
1 tablespoon lemon juice
Grated rind of an orange
¼ pint double cream
GARNISH:
Plain chocolate, orange matchsticks

Roll out the prepared shortcrust pastry*, $\frac{1}{6}$ in. thick, and use to line an 8–9 in. wide flan ring. Prick the base with a fork and bake blind* for 10 minutes in the centre of the oven, pre-heated to 400°F (mark 6). Reduce the heat to 375°F (mark 5) for a further 20 minutes. Cool on a wire rack.

Sprinkle the gelatine over 5 tablespoons of cold water in a small bowl. Set aside. Separate the eggs and beat the yolks with the sugar until they are pale yellow and thick. Beat in the orange and lemon juice.

Pour the creamed egg mixture into a double saucepan or set the bowl over a pan of barely simmering water. Cook over low heat, stirring continuously, until the mixture thickens. Remove from the heat and mix in the orange rind and the dissolved gelatine. Blend thoroughly and leave to cool slightly. Beat the cream and egg whites, in separate bowls, until stiff, and carefully fold first the cream, then the egg whites, into the orange mixture.

Spoon the mixture into the flan case and chill for at least 1 hour.

Just before serving, grate plain chocolate over the cream and garnish with orange matchsticks.

CHAMPAGNE CHARLIE

George Leybourne, star of the English music hall of the 1890's, often ordered champagne for his audiences, a gesture which earned him the nickname of 'Champagne Charlie'. This ice cream, named after him, is a superb sweet for a special occasion.

PREPARATION TIME: *10 min.*
COOKING TIME: *10 min.*
FREEZING TIME: *5 hours*

INGREDIENTS *(for 6):*
6 oz. caster sugar
2 oranges and 2 lemons
1 pint chilled champagne
1 pint double cream
6 fluid oz. brandy
36 ratafia biscuits
GARNISH:
Langues de chat
Lemon peel

One hour before beginning preparations, set the refrigerator to its coldest setting.

Put the sugar in a pan with $\frac{1}{4}$ pint of water. Bring to the boil and boil rapidly for 6 minutes to make a syrup. Meanwhile, grate the rind from one orange and squeeze the juice from the oranges and lemons. Add the rind and the strained juice to the syrup and leave to cool. Stir in the chilled champagne.

Pour the mixture into a plastic container, and cover with the lid or a double layer of foil. Freeze for 1½–2 hours or until frozen round the edges. Scoop the mixture into a chilled bowl and whip until smooth. In a separate bowl, beat the cream until stiff, and blend it slowly into the champagne syrup until it is smooth and uniform in colour. Blend in 2 tablespoons of brandy. Spoon the mixture into the container, cover and freeze for about 3 hours.

About 30 minutes before serving, place six ratafia biscuits in the bottom of each champagne glass. Pour a dessertspoon of brandy over the biscuits and leave them to soak. Scoop the ice cream into the glasses. Hang a thin spiral of lemon peel from the rim of each glass and pour a teaspoon of brandy over each portion.

Serve immediately, with a separate plate of langues de chat.

MERINGUE À LA REINE

These small meringue boats, with a cream filling, were first served at the French court in the 18th century. It is said that Queen Marie Antoinette was so fond of them that she even made them with her own hands.

PREPARATION TIME: *15 min.*
COOKING TIME: *2 hours*

INGREDIENTS *(for 6):*
3 egg whites
Salt
3 oz. granulated sugar
3 oz. caster sugar
1 oz. lightly toasted nibbed almonds
½ pint double cream
3 tablespoons sweet sherry
Juice of an orange
GARNISH:
Crystallised fruit

In a warm dry bowl, whisk the egg whites, with a pinch of salt, until stiff but not dry. Add the granulated sugar and continue whisking for 2 minutes until the meringue mixture is smooth and glossy. Gently fold in the caster sugar and almonds.

Spoon the meringue into a forcing bag, fitted with a $\frac{1}{2}$ in. wide rosette nozzle. Pipe out 3 in. long oval shapes (or barquettes) on to a lightly floured baking tray. Bake the meringues in the centre of the oven, pre-heated to 275°F (mark 1), for 1½–2 hours. The meringues should then have a faint tint of beige. Leave the barquettes on a wire rack to cool.

Whip the cream and beat in the sherry and strained orange juice. Fill the hollows in the barquettes with the cream mixture and garnish with crystallised fruit.

SOURED CREAM FLAN

This flan, whose texture is reminiscent of cheesecake, makes a good weekday dessert and may be served hot or cold. For a more elaborate sweet, a chilled apricot purée could be served with it.

PREPARATION TIME: *40 min.*
COOKING TIME: *40 min.*

INGREDIENTS *(for 6):*
6 oz. shortcrust pastry (standard recipe)
3 eggs
5 oz. caster sugar
8 oz. sultanas
½ level teaspoon ground cinnamon
¼ level teaspoon ground cloves
¼ level teaspoon salt
5 oz. soured cream
Grated rind of a lemon

Roll out the prepared shortcrust pastry*, $\frac{1}{6}$ in. thick, on a floured surface. Line a 9 in. flan ring with the pastry. Prick the base with a fork and leave it to rest in the refrigerator.

Separate the eggs and beat the yolks thoroughly with the sugar until pale yellow and thick enough to leave a trail. Finely chop the sultanas and beat them into the eggs, together with the cinnamon, cloves, salt, soured cream and lemon rind. Beat the egg whites in a separate bowl until stiff, but not dry. Fold the egg whites carefully and evenly into the yolk mixture, and spoon it into the flan case. Bake for 15 minutes on a shelf low in the oven, pre-heated to 425°F (mark 7), then reduce the heat to 350°F (mark 4) for a further 25 minutes.

Leave the flan for about 10 minutes before removing the ring and serving the flan.

Savouries & Snacks

RED FLANNEL HASH

An American favourite, this colourful hash is often served with poached or fried eggs.

PREPARATION TIME: *15 min.*
COOKING TIME: *15–20 min.*

INGREDIENTS *(for 4)*:
2 oz. lean streaky bacon (finely chopped)
1 finely chopped onion
1 oz. dripping or lard
¾ lb. mashed potatoes
4–6 oz. cooked, diced beetroot
½ lb. corned beef (flaked)
2 level tablespoons finely chopped parsley
2 tablespoons double cream
Salt and black pepper

Fry the bacon and onion in the lard for 2 minutes or until the onion is transparent. Lift the bacon and onion from the pan into a mixing bowl and blend in the potatoes, beetroot, corned beef, parsley and cream. Season with salt and ground pepper.

Re-heat the fat in the pan, add the hash mixture and press it down firmly and evenly with the back of a spoon. Cook over high heat for 15 minutes or until it is well browned on the bottom. Turn the hash out, upside-down, on to a warmed serving dish.

CROQUE-MONSIEUR

This hot, fried sandwich – a speciality of France – may be served either as a snack, an hors-d'oeuvre or as a savoury.

PREPARATION TIME: *10 min.*
COOKING TIME: *10 min.*

INGREDIENTS *(for 4)*:
8 square slices white bread (⅓ in. thick)
3 oz. butter
4 slices lean ham
4 oz. grated Cheddar cheese
Fat or oil for frying

Butter the bread and cover four of the slices with the ham and cheese. Top with the remaining bread, and press the sandwiches firmly together. Trim off the crusts, and cut each sandwich into three fingers. Fry the bread fingers in hot fat until golden brown on both sides. Drain on absorbent paper before serving.

BACON PANCAKE

A simple, inexpensive family meal is the perfect answer for the busy housewife in the Christmas month. For a touch of colour, serve the pancake with grilled tomatoes.

PREPARATION TIME: *15 min.*
COOKING TIME: *30 min.*

INGREDIENTS *(for 4)*:
3 oz. plain flour
½ pint milk
2 eggs
Salt and black pepper
1½ level teaspoons mixed herbs
½ lb. streaky bacon
1 oz. lard or dripping

Sift the flour into a bowl and stir in half the milk. Add the eggs and remaining milk and whisk until the batter* is smooth and light. Season with salt and ground pepper, and mix in the herbs.

Remove the rind and cut the bacon rashers in ½ in. wide strips. Fry in the lard over medium heat for 3–4 minutes. Measure 2 tablespoons of the fat into a fireproof dish, add the drained bacon and pour over the pancake batter. Bake in the centre of a pre-heated oven, at 350°F (mark 4), for 30 minutes or until set.

TURKEY OR CHICKEN TOASTS

This quick recipe solves the problem of what to do with Christmas leftovers from turkey, and cooked vegetables such as cauliflower, carrots, beans or broccoli.

PREPARATION TIME: *15 min.*
COOKING TIME: *5 min.*

INGREDIENTS *(for 4)*:
8 thin slices turkey or chicken (skinned)
¼ pint thick white sauce
Salt and black pepper
Dried tarragon
4 slices buttered white toast
½ lb. cooked, chopped vegetables
2 oz. grated Cheddar cheese

Make the white sauce* and season with salt, ground pepper and tarragon. Toast the bread, trim off the crusts and spread with butter. Arrange the turkey on the toast, cover with the vegetables and spoon over the sauce.

Sprinkle the toasts with the cheese and brown under a hot grill until the cheese has melted and is golden brown on top. Serve at once.

CHRISTMAS PUDDING WITH DESTINY SAUCE

The Christmas pudding can look a sorry mess on Boxing Day. But served with a light creamy sauce, it becomes a mouth-watering new dessert.

PREPARATION TIME: *5–10 min.*
COOKING TIME: *5 min.*

INGREDIENTS *(for 4–6)*:
8 thin slices Christmas pudding
¼ pint double cream
1 level tablespoon sifted icing sugar
2 tablespoons port
1½ oz. unsalted butter
2 level tablespoons caster sugar

Beat the cream until thick, then blend in the icing sugar and port. Chill in the refrigerator until required.

Fry the Christmas pudding in the butter, over medium heat, for 4 minutes, turning once. Arrange the slices on a warm serving dish, dust with the caster sugar and serve the chilled cream in a separate bowl.

In the Midst of Winter

Late December has always been a time for celebration. In Northern Europe, Odin and his fellow gods were worshipped at that time in an orgy of eating and drinking. The Romans celebrated Saturnalia, and the peoples of Egypt and Persia adored their gods of plenty. The early Christian Church wisely refrained from banishing the pagan festivities and named instead December 25 as the date when Christ was born. Mid-winter, with its solstice celebrations, was an established time for feasting.

The British took to the Christian celebrations as enthusiastically as they had once enjoyed the old Celtic festival. The whirlwind of merry-making continued until abruptly halted by the Puritans in the 17th century – even plum pudding was declared food fit for heathens only, and carols were condemned as evil chants. Charles II, however, restored the merry-making at Christmas.

Two 19th-century figures, Charles Dickens and Prince Albert, created the modern Christmas – Dickens with his *Christmas Carol*, and Prince Albert by popularising the Christmas tree.

A white Christmas is more often seen on Christmas cards than in reality. This is largely due to a reform of the calendar in 1752, when 11 days were 'lost' so that Christmas day fell earlier in the year. Snow is now more common in January than in December.

Christmas dinners for six people

Dinner on Christmas Eve should be impressive, but not so grand that it will overshadow the feast on Christmas Day. Chilled crème vichyssoise* or haddock mousse* would be a good first choice. Roast sirloin of beef would make a splendid main course, but a less expensive boeuf bourguignonne is a good alternative, served with buttered noodles or rice with leeks*. Lobster Newburg is another ideal main course.

In Elizabethan days, Christmas dinner always began with fresh oysters served on a bed of cracked ice. Shrimps in soured cream (see December starters) might be preferred. For a main course, the Victorians had turkey or roast goose, a fatty bird with succulent flesh. Like duck it serves fewer people than its size would seem to indicate – a 10 lb. goose yields approximately eight servings.

Nowadays, turkey is the highlight of Christmas dinner in Britain, its popularity owing much to the classic English stuffings and the accompanying sauces. Serve the golden-brown turkey garnished with sprigs of watercress, chipolata sausages and bacon rolls. Both plain and roast potatoes are traditional; so too are Brussels sprouts, either plain or cooked with chestnuts. Bread sauce, spiced cranberries, gravy or port wine sauce are served separately.

Lastly comes the Christmas pudding, shrouded in a blue haze of brandy flames, and served with brandy butter and/or cream. Mince pies, crystallised fruits, dates, figs and nuts, and port, round off a Christmas dinner to remember.

Ten days before Christmas, prepare 2¼ lb. almond paste*. Brush the cake with apricot glaze*, and when nearly set cover the top and sides with the rolled out almond paste. Three days later, make up 2½ lb. Royal icing*, spread it over the top and sides and leave to set. The cake can be

decorated in a simple trellis pattern, with rosettes at the intersections. For a Christmas scene, as depicted on this cake, colour almond paste and roll it out thinly. Trace the design on thin cardboard and cut the paste from these shapes. Fix the decoration with Royal icing

Christmas Cake

PREPARATION TIME: 2½ hours
COOKING TIME: about 5 hours

INGREDIENTS:
12 oz. self-raising flour
½ level teaspoon salt
1 level dessertspoon mixed spice
1 level teaspoon ground nutmeg
1 level teaspoon ground cinnamon
½ level teaspoon ground cloves
¼ lb. ground almonds
1 lb. currants
1 lb. stoned raisins
1 lb. sultanas
½ lb. glacé cherries
¼ lb. blanched almonds
½ lb. whole mixed citrus peel
1 oz. angelica
1 large lemon
12 oz. unsalted butter
10 oz. soft dark brown sugar
8–9 large eggs
8 tablespoons brandy
Almond paste
Royal icing

Butter a 10 in. wide, round or square cake tin thoroughly; line it with a double layer of grease-proof paper brushed with melted butter. Tie a double layer of brown paper round the outside of the tin, allowing it to protrude well above the rim – this prevents the Christmas cake burning during baking.

Sift all the dry ingredients – flour, seasoning, spices and ground almonds – together into a large bowl. Mix in all the finely chopped fruits and the chopped almonds. Blend thoroughly.

Cream together, in a separate bowl, the sugar, butter and grated lemon rind, until fluffy. Beat in 8 eggs, one at a time. Stir them into the flour and fruit mixture, followed by the lemon juice and 4 tablespoons brandy. The mixture should be soft and moist. If necessary add the remaining egg beaten with a little milk.

Spoon the cake mixture into the prepared tin, level the top and bake the cake on the shelf below the centre of a pre-heated oven, at 300°F (mark 2), for 1½ hours. Reduce the heat to 250°F (mark ½) and bake for a further 3–3½ hours. The cake is done when it begins to shrink from the sides. Cover the cake with brown paper during the last few hours to prevent burning.

Remove the cake from the oven, leave to cool slightly before turning it out on to a wire rack to cool. When completely cold, wrap the cake in foil, seal tightly and store until six weeks before Christmas. Then, make holes with a skewer in the bottom of the cake and, using a funnel, pour in 4 tablespoons brandy. Reseal the cake and leave until needed for icing.

Christmas Pudding

PREPARATION TIME: 1¼ hours
COOKING TIME: 10 hours

INGREDIENTS *(for 2 large puddings)*:
1 lb. stoned raisins
2 oz. mixed peel
2 oz. blanched almonds
½ lb. currants
½ lb. sultanas
¼ lb. plain or self-raising flour
½ level teaspoon ground nutmeg
½ level teaspoon ground mixed spice
½ level teaspoon ground cinnamon
1 level teaspoon salt
2 oz. ground almonds
1 lb. shredded suet
½ lb. fresh white breadcrumbs
¼ lb. soft brown sugar

6 large eggs
4 tablespoons brandy
8 fluid oz. milk
1 oz. unsalted butter

Chop the raisins, mixed peel and blanched almonds. Mix together, in a large bowl, all the fruits, the sifted flour, spices, salt and ground almonds. Blend thoroughly until all the fruit is well coated (this is easiest done with the hands). Work in the suet, breadcrumbs and sugar. Beat the eggs lightly and stir them into the pudding mixture. Add the brandy and milk, stirring until the pudding has a soft dropping consistency.

Butter well two 2½ lb. pudding basins, spoon in the pudding and cover each basin with a pleated, double layer of buttered grease-proof paper. Tie down with a pudding cloth.

Set the pudding basins in one or two large pans of boiling water, reaching two-thirds up the sides of the basins. Boil steadily for 6 hours, and top up with boiling water as necessary. Remove the puddings, leave them to cool, then cover them with fresh grease-proof paper and cloths. Store in a cool place.

On Christmas Day, boil the puddings for a further 4 hours. Turn them out of the basins and garnish each pudding with a sprig of holly. Pour over warmed brandy and set alight. Serve with brandy butter.

Brandy butter
3 oz. unsalted butter
3 oz. caster sugar
Grated rind of half orange
2–3 tablespoons brandy

Cream the butter until soft and pale in colour. Beat in the sugar and orange rind. Gradually beat in the brandy until the mixture is frothy. Chill in the refrigerator for 2–3 hours or until solid.

Oat Biscuits
PREPARATION TIME: 15 min.
COOKING TIME: 20–25 min.

INGREDIENTS (for 24 biscuits):
3 oz. plain flour
½ level teaspoon bicarbonate of soda
3 oz. Demerara sugar
3 oz. rolled porridge oats (medium cut)
3 oz. unsalted butter
1 tablespoon rum
1 tablespoon golden syrup

Sift the flour and bicarbonate of soda into a bowl; add the sugar and the oats, blending thoroughly. Heat the butter with the syrup and the rum in a small pan until the butter has just melted. Pour into the flour mixture and blend thoroughly with a wooden spoon.

Shape the dough into balls, 1 in. wide, between floured hands. Set the balls well apart on greased baking trays. Bake in the centre of the oven, pre-heated to 325°F (mark 3), for 20–25 minutes or until golden brown.

Wassail Cup
PREPARATION TIME: 5 min.
COOKING TIME: 20 min.

INGREDIENTS:
6 pints brown ale
1 lb. soft brown sugar
1 large stick cinnamon
1 level teaspoon grated nutmeg
½ level teaspoon ground ginger
2 lemons, thinly sliced
1 bottle medium dry sherry

Pour 2 pints of the ale into a large pan. Add the sugar and cinnamon stick, and simmer the mixture slowly over low heat until the sugar has dissolved. Add the spices and lemon slices, the sherry and remaining ale.

Before serving the cup, remove the lemon slices.

A wassail cup, with roasted apples and fresh lemon slices floating on top

Christmas Eve Dinner

Lobster Newburg

PREPARATION TIME: *15 min.*
COOKING TIME: *30 min.*

INGREDIENTS:

1½ lb. cooked lobster
4 oz. unsalted butter
4 slices white bread
5 fluid oz. sherry or Madeira
1 tablespoon brandy (optional)
Salt and black pepper
3 egg yolks
7 fluid oz. double cream
Paprika

Carefully extract the meat from the tail and claws of the lobster* and cut it into 1½–2 in. pieces. Trim four circles from the bread and leave to soak in 3 oz. melted butter until this has been absorbed. Bake the butter-soaked bread on a baking tray in the centre of the oven for 25 minutes, at 300°F (mark 2).

Meanwhile, melt the remaining butter in a heavy-based pan, add the lobster meat and season with salt and pepper. Heat through over very low heat for 5 minutes, then pour over the sherry or Madeira and brandy. Continue cooking over very low heat until the wine has reduced* by half, after 10 minutes. While the lobster is cooking, beat the egg yolks and stir in the cream.

Remove the pan from the heat and pour the egg and cream mixture over the lobster. Shake the pan until the cream has mixed thoroughly with the wine, then move it gently to and fro over gentle heat until the sauce has the consistency of thick cream. Do not stir, or the meat will disintegrate and the sauce curdle. After about 3 minutes the lobster should be ready. Adjust seasoning and spoon the lobster and sauce on the bread rounds. Sprinkle the lobster with a little paprika and serve at once.

Boeuf Bourguignonne

PREPARATION TIME: *30 min.*
COOKING TIME: *3 hours*

INGREDIENTS:

2 lb. top rump of beef, cut into 2 in. cubes
4 oz. unsalted butter
1 tablespoon olive oil
1 finely sliced onion
1 level tablespoon plain flour
3 tablespoons brandy
2 cloves garlic
Bouquet garni
Salt and black pepper
1 bottle red wine
6 oz. streaky green bacon (diced)
20 baby onions
6 oz. mushrooms
Finely chopped parsley

Melt 3 oz. butter in a large, flame-proof casserole dish, add the oil and then the meat. Cook over high heat until the meat is browned, then add the sliced onion. Cook until transparent, sprinkle over the flour and continue cooking for a few minutes. Pour over the warmed brandy and set it alight.

Add the crushed garlic, the bouquet garni*, salt and plenty of pepper. Pour over enough wine to cover the meat. Bring to simmering point, cover the casserole with a lid and cook in the centre of a pre-heated oven, at 300°F (mark 2), for 2 hours.

Meanwhile, fry the bacon in the remaining butter until crisp, add the small onions and cook until golden. Stir the contents of the pan into the casserole and continue cooking for a further 30 minutes. Add the sliced mushrooms and cook for another 15 minutes.

Remove the bouquet garni, sprinkle the casserole generously with parsley and serve straight from the pan.

Christmas Trimmings

Stuffings and sauces

Stuffings are essentially English, and many date from medieval times. The following go with turkey, goose, duck and capon.

Chestnut stuffing for turkey: *2 oz. unsalted butter; 1 peeled and chopped onion; turkey heart and liver (chopped); 6 oz. sliced mushrooms; 8 oz. chestnut purée; 1 small tin pâté de foie gras; 1 stick of celery (chopped); 4 oz. chopped green bacon; 1 level tablespoon chopped parsley; salt and black pepper; 2 oz. breadcrumbs (optional)*

Fry the onion, turkey heart and liver and mushrooms in the butter, until this has been absorbed. Stir the chestnut purée with the pâté, and blend in the contents of the pan, with the celery, bacon and parsley. Season and, if necessary, add enough breadcrumbs to bind the stuffing. Fill the breast end of the turkey with the chestnut stuffing and fill the body cavity with sausage stuffing.

Sausage stuffing: *1½ lb. pork sausage meat; 4 oz. fresh white breadcrumbs; 2 chopped shallots; 4 oz. minced belly pork; 1 beaten egg; salt and black pepper*

Work the breadcrumbs and the shallots into the sausage meat, together with the minced pork. Bind the stuffing with the egg and season to taste.

Forcemeat stuffing for goose: *4 oz. veal; 4 oz. lean pork; 1 goose liver; 1 small onion; ½ oz. butter; 2 large slices crustless white bread; 1 heaped tablespoon chopped parsley; 1 level tablespoon chopped thyme; 4 fluid oz. red wine; 1 large egg; salt and black pepper*

Put the veal, pork, goose liver and peeled onion through the fine blade of the mincer. Fry this mixture in the butter until golden brown. Remove from the heat and stir in the bread, soaked in a little milk and squeezed dry. Add the herbs and wine, and use the beaten egg to bind the stuffing before seasoning to taste.

Apricot stuffing for goose and duck: *¾ lb. dried apricots; juice of a lemon; 1 level tablespoon soft brown sugar; 1 large green pepper, finely chopped; 1 large, peeled, cored and diced cooking apple; 4 sticks chopped celery; 4 oz. fresh white breadcrumbs; 3 oz. melted butter; grated rind of an orange; 2 beaten eggs; salt and black pepper*

Soak the apricots for 8 hours in cold water. Put them in a pan with the lemon juice and the sugar; bring to the boil and simmer for 20 minutes. Set aside to cool. Strain the apricots, chop them roughly and mix with the pepper, apple and celery. Stir in the breadcrumbs, melted butter, orange rind and the eggs. Season to taste and bind the stuffing with about 6 tablespoons of the apricot juice.

Prune and apple stuffing for goose and duck: *20 prunes; juice and rind of half lemon; 1 level tablespoon soft brown sugar; 2 oz. cooked rice; 2 large cooking apples, peeled, cored and roughly chopped; goose liver; 1 stick celery, chopped; ½ level teaspoon ground mace; 1 heaped tablespoon chopped parsley; salt and black pepper; 1 beaten egg*

Soak the prunes in cold water for 8 hours. Put them, with the water, lemon juice and sugar into a pan, bring to the boil and simmer for 20 minutes. Set aside to cool, then remove the stones and quarter the prunes. Mix the prunes with all the remaining ingredients, adding the egg last. Stir in as much of the prune juice as the stuffing will absorb and pour the remainder into the bird before stuffing it.

Spiced cranberries: *1 lb. cranberries; ¼ oz. each of root ginger, whole cinnamon and whole allspice; 6 cloves; ½ pint cider vinegar; 8 oz. Demerara sugar*

Put the cranberries in a pan with all the spices tied in muslin. Pour over the vinegar and bring to the boil. Simmer the cranberries until soft and the skins begin to pop, after about 25 minutes. Add the sugar and simmer for a further 20 minutes. Remove the spices and store the preserve in small jars. Serve cold with roast turkey.

Bacon rolls: *½ lb. streaky bacon; 1 oz. beef dripping*

Remove the rind and stretch the bacon rashers*. Cut each across into two, roll up and secure with wooden cocktail sticks. Fry the bacon in the dripping until crisp, after about 12 minutes. Remove the sticks before serving the rolls.

Port wine sauce: *¼ pint port; ¼ pint mutton gravy (made from the brown jelly beneath cold mutton dripping and made up to ¼ pint with boiling water – a beef stock cube may also be used); 1 tablespoon red currant jelly; salt and black pepper*

Add the port and red currant jelly to the strained mutton gravy. Bring to the boil; season and pour into a warm sauce boat.

A turkey with its trimmings is the highlight of Christmas dinner

Christmas in Europe

Italy

Traditional Christmas fare varies considerably between the north and the south, but stuffed roasted capon is enjoyed throughout the country. Ham, too, is popular, and is often served in a pastry case with glacé fruits (*Mostarda di Frutta*) and a mustard syrup.

Prosciutto in Crosta

PREPARATION TIME: *1 hour*
COOKING TIME: *3¾ hours*

INGREDIENTS *(for 8–10)*: *1 ham (approx. 6 lb.); 1 chopped onion; 1 large chopped carrot; 1 stick chopped celery; 1 clove; 1 bottle dry Spumanti; 1 pint stock; 1 lb. prepared puff pastry; 1 beaten egg; 1½ oz. butter; 1½ oz. plain flour; salt and black pepper; 3 level teaspoons French mustard; 14 oz. tin Mostarda di Frutta*

Soak the ham for 2 hours in cold water, then cut away the skin. Put the prepared vegetables in a large pan, add the ham, clove, wine and stock. Cook the ham, covered, over moderate heat for 3 hours, then cool in the liquid.

Remove the fat from the ham. Roll out the puff pastry*, ¼ in. thick, place the ham in the centre and wrap the pastry over it, sealing the edges firmly. Decorate with pastry leaves and brush with egg. Set the ham on a damp baking tray and cook in the centre of a pre-heated oven, at 425°F (mark 7), for 35 minutes.

Make a white sauce* from the butter, flour and 1 pint of the strained cooking liquid. Stir in the mustard, and season. Decorate the ham with the *Mostarda di Frutta*. Serve the sauce separately.

Germany

Traditional Christmas fare in Germany includes roast goose or pork with red cabbage, and game such as hare, venison and pheasant. *Christstollen*, which are fruity yeast cakes, are traditional, and in many households the main dish on Christmas Eve is still carp cooked in beer.

Karpfen in Bier

PREPARATION TIME: *35 min.*
COOKING TIME: *1¾ hours*

INGREDIENTS *(for 6)*: *1 carp (approx. 3–4 lb.); 3 tablespoons white wine vinegar; 2 chopped carrots; 1 chopped leek; 1 chopped onion; 1 bay leaf; 1 clove; salt and black pepper; 6 oz. gingerbread; 1½ pints brown ale; juice and rind of a lemon*

Clean the carp and leave it to soak for 1 hour in cold water and the vinegar. Put the chopped vegetables, bay leaf, clove, salt and pepper into a pan large enough to hold the carp. Add 1 pint of water. Simmer this stock, under the lid, for 1 hour. Break the gingerbread into cubes and soak in ½ pint of brown ale.

Put the carp into the stock, with the lemon juice and remaining ale. Cook over low heat for 20 minutes, or until the carp is tender. Lift out the fish and keep it warm. Strain the liquid, add the gingerbread and boil this mixture rapidly until it has reduced* by half.

Strain the sauce over the carp and garnish with lemon rind.

Rumania

In the countryside, where old traditions die hard, Christmas centres round folk singing and dancing, churchgoing and orgies of eating. Pork is the favourite meat and comes in a vast variety of smoked hams and sausages, and as stuffings for cabbage (*sarmale*). Sucking pig and lamb are spit-roasted over an open fire and are traditionally served with roasted aubergines. In Rumania, feasting continues until New Year and is then followed by a short period of strict fasting which continues until January 6.

Sucking pig

PREPARATION TIME: *20 min.*
COOKING TIME: *4–4½ hours*

INGREDIENTS *(for 6–8)*: *1 three-week old sucking pig (approx. 10 lb.); 10 fluid oz. rum; 10 fluid oz. olive oil; 2 level tablespoons salt*

If oven space permits, truss the prepared piglet with the legs stretched out, or fold them underneath the belly. Insert a wooden plug in the mouth, and protect the tail and ears with foil.

Mix the rum and oil and brush it all over the piglet. Rub the salt into the skin. Place the piglet on a rack in a large roasting tin and cook on the lower shelf of an oven pre-heated to 325°F (mark 3). Allow 25 minutes to each pound. Baste every 15 minutes with more rum and oil.

When cooked, remove the foil and replace the wooden plug with a rosy apple. To carve, cut off the head with the forelegs, and then the rear portion and legs. Slit along and through the backbone, remove the rib cage and carve the meat and crackling into narrow slices. Carve the shoulder and legs in wide slices.

Spain

The Christmas symbol is the crêche, a miniature representation in wood and ceramic of the manger scene. In towns, international Christmas fare is usually turkey and sucking pig, while the mountain districts favour less festive dishes, usually with lamb. This dish of lamb with pimento and tomatoes comes from Navarre. Every sweetshop displays its own version of *turron*, a sweetmeat cake based on nougat. New Year is a more festive occasion, and it is not until Epiphany, January 6, that gifts are exchanged and distributed to children by the 'Three Wise Men'.

Cordero la Chilindron

PREPARATION TIME: *20 min.*
COOKING TIME: *50 min.*

INGREDIENTS *(for 6): 2 lb. boned leg or shoulder of lamb; 1 red pimento; salt and black pepper; 2 tablespoons olive oil; 2 chopped cloves garlic; 1 finely chopped onion; 4 oz. diced Parma ham; 15–16 oz. tinned tomatoes*

Put the pimento under a hot grill. Turn it frequently until charred all over, then rub the skin off under cold water. Remove the stalk end of the charred pimento and the seeds inside, and cut the flesh into narrow strips.

Cut the lamb into 1½–2 in. cubes, removing excess fat. Season to taste with salt and freshly ground black pepper. Heat the oil in a large, heavy-based pan and fry the garlic until golden. Add the onion, lamb and ham and cook over moderate heat for about 10 minutes or until the lamb is browned. Stir the chopped pimento and tomatoes, with their juice, into the pan.

Simmer the lamb, uncovered, over low heat for about 40 minutes or until tender.

Serve with buttered rice, crusty French bread and a tossed green side salad.

France

The main Christmas meal, the *réveillon,* is served after Midnight Mass on Christmas Eve. The menu for this family occasion may include pâté de foie gras, oysters or other shellfish. Game, roast goose or turkey stuffed with chestnuts and truffles are also traditional. But whatever the glories of the Christmas spread, the *réveillon* must include a dish of black pudding. The following dish, which comes from the Normandy region, combines the traditional ingredients: goose and black pudding, garnished with small red apples.

Oie à la Normande

PREPARATION TIME: *25 min.*
COOKING TIME: *2¾ hours*

INGREDIENTS *(for 6–8): 1 goose (approx. 10 lb.); 1 lb. black pudding; 1 crushed garlic clove; 2 large dessert apples, peeled and grated; 2½ fluid oz. port; salt and black pepper*

Skin the black pudding and pound it smooth with the goose liver and garlic. Blend in the apples and bind the stuffing with the wine. Stuff the goose with this mixture. Prick the skin all over with a skewer, and rub it thoroughly with salt and pepper.

Place the goose in a roasting tin and cover with foil. Roast on the lowest shelf of an oven, pre-heated to 400°F (mark 6), and allow 15 minutes to the pound, plus 15 minutes. After 1 hour, drain the fat from the pan and pour 4 fluid oz. cold water over the goose. Remove the foil 30 minutes before cooking is complete, and baste the goose every 10 minutes with the pan juices.

Serve the goose on a thick bed of unsweetened apple purée and garnish with polished apples set on cocktail sticks.

Scandinavia

Outside Britain, it is the Scandinavians who most joyously celebrate Christmas. From December 13, St Lucia's Day, until well into the New Year, the tables are laden with traditional Christmas fare. This includes rich cakes and biscuits, vast spreads of *smörgåsbord* with numerous dishes of cold pickled fish, meats, salads and cheeses. The Christmas meal is served on Christmas Eve and may include roast goose or duck, or the popular loin of pork which has a crisp crackling.

Roast Loin of Pork

PREPARATION TIME: *15 min.*
COOKING TIME: *3¼ hours*

INGREDIENTS *(for 8): 6 lb. loin of pork; 2 oz. dripping or butter; coarse salt; 6 cloves; 12 small bay leaves*

Have the loin deeply scored into ½ in. wide strips. For a really crisp crackling place the joint, skin side down, in a roasting pan and pour in boiling water to a depth of 1 in. Set the pan just below centre of an oven, pre-heated to 450°F (mark 8). Cook for 15 minutes.

Remove the pan, pour off the liquid and set aside for basting.

Grease the pan with dripping and rub the skin of the loin with salt. Insert the cloves and bay leaves in the score marks. Roast the pork, skin side up, at 350°F (mark 4), at 30 minutes to the pound. Baste every 30 minutes.

Serve the loin of pork garnished with roasted half apples filled with red currant jelly. Traditionally, the Christmas joint is served with sugar-browned potatoes* and long-cooked red cabbage.

303

Basic Cooking

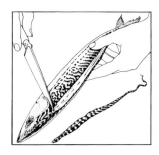
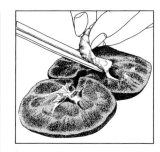

Methods

Fruit

Preserving

Pastry

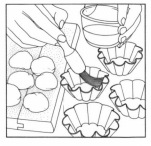

Baking with Yeast

Buns and Scones

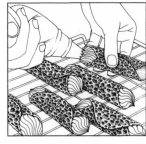

Cake-making

Biscuits

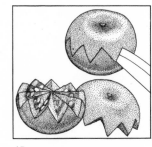

Cake Fillings and Toppings

Confectionery

Garnishes

TO AVOID CONSTANT REPETITION OF BASIC INFORMATION, SOME
TECHNICAL WORDS AND PHRASES USED IN THIS BOOK HAVE BEEN
MARKED WITH AN ASTERISK *. FULL INFORMATION ABOUT TERMS
MARKED IN THIS WAY WILL BE FOUND BY REFERRING TO THE INDEX

Stocks and Soups

The basis for all soups is good fresh stock usually made from the bones and flesh of fish, meat and poultry, with added vegetables, herbs and spices. The stock ingredients should harmonise with those of the finished soup.

There are five basic stocks: brown (or household stock), white, fish, vegetable and game stock. Brown stock can be used for most soups, although fish, vegetables and game soups all gain in flavour when prepared with their own type of stock.

Fresh bones and meat are essential ingredients for brown and white stocks. Use marrow bone and shin of beef for brown stock, and knuckle of veal for a white stock and ask the butcher to chop the bones into manageable pieces. The chopped bones release gelatine while cooking, which gives body to the stock.

Vegetables give additional flavour, but avoid potatoes which make the stock cloudy. Strong-flavoured vegetables, such as turnips, swedes and parsnips, should be used sparingly.

STOCKS

Brown Stock
PREPARATION TIME: *15 min.*
COOKING TIME: *5 hours*

INGREDIENTS *(for 6 pints)* :
1 lb. marrow bones
2–3 lb. shin of beef
1½ oz. butter or dripping
1–2 leeks
1 large onion
1–2 celery sticks
½ lb. carrots
2 bouquets garnis
Salt and black peppercorns

Blanch* the bones for 10 minutes in boiling water, then put them, with the chopped meat and butter or dripping, in a roasting tin. Brown the bones in the centre of the oven for 30–40 minutes, at a temperature of 425°F (mark 7).

Turn them over occasionally to brown them evenly. Put the roasted bones in a large pan, add the cleaned and sliced vegetables, the bouquets garnis* and peppercorns. Cover with cold water, to which ½ teaspoon of salt has been added.

Bring the contents slowly to boiling point, remove any scum from the surface and cover the pan with a tight-fitting lid. Simmer the stock over lowest possible heat for about 4 hours to extract all flavour from the bones. Top up with hot water if the level of the liquid should fall below the other ingredients.

Strain the stock through a fine sieve or muslin, into a large bowl. Leave the stock to settle for a few minutes, then remove the fat from the surface by drawing absorbent paper over it. If the stock is not required immediately, leave the fat to settle in a surface layer which can then be easily lifted off.

Once the fat has been removed from the stock, correct seasoning if necessary.

White Stock
This is made like brown stock, but the blanched veal bones are not browned. Place all the ingredients in a large pan of water and proceed as for brown stock.

Fish Stock
The basis for this stock is bones and trimmings, such as the head and the skin. White fish such as cod, haddock, halibut, whiting and plaice can all be used.

PREPARATION TIME: *5–10 min.*
COOKING TIME: *30 min.*

INGREDIENTS *(for 1 pint)* :
1 lb. fish trimmings
Salt
1 onion
Bouquet garni or 1 large leek and 1 celery stick

SKIMMING STOCK

Lifting scum from boiling stock

Removing surface fat

Wash the trimmings thoroughly in cold water and put them in a large pan, with 1 pint lightly salted water. Bring to the boil over low heat and remove any surface scum. Meanwhile, peel and finely chop the onion and add to the stock with the bouquet garni* or the cleaned and chopped leek and celery. Cover the pan with a lid and simmer over low heat for 30 minutes. Strain the stock through a sieve or muslin. Store, covered, in the refrigerator.

Fish stock does not keep well and should preferably be used on the day it is made.

Game Stock
The ingredients for this stock can be the carcass of a chicken, turkey or game bird, together with the scalded feet of the bird, and the cleaned giblets. Cook as for white stock, simmering for 2–3 hours. Strain and remove the fat.

Vegetable Stock
This inexpensive but quick and tasty stock is made from un-cooked vegetables. The ingredients may include the outer leaves of cabbage, lettuce and other greens, cauliflower stalks, and peelings from carrots, leeks and parsnips. Chop these trimmings roughly, put them in a pan and cover with lightly salted water. Put the lid on the pan, and simmer the stock over low heat. A bouquet garni* and 6–8 peppercorns may be added for extra flavour. Strain the stock through muslin.

Cooking stock in a pressure cooker
Place the stock ingredients, with lightly salted water, in the pressure cooker – it must not be more than two-thirds full. Bring to the boil and remove the scum from the surface before fixing the lid. Lower the heat and bring to 15 pounds pressure. Reduce the heat quickly and cook steadily for 1 hour. Strain the stock and remove the fat.

Storing stock
If not required for immediate use, store prepared stocks in the refrigerator. After the fat has been removed, pour the cooled stock into a container and cover with a lid. It will keep for three or four days, but to ensure absolute freshness, boil up the stock every two days. Fish and vegetable stocks spoil quickly and should be made and used on the same day. If refrigerated they will keep for two days.

Freezing stocks
Stocks can be satisfactorily stored in a home freezer, where they will keep for up to two months. Boil the prepared stock over high heat to reduce* it by half. Pour the concentrated cooled stock into ice-cube trays, freeze quickly and transfer the stock cubes to polythene bags. Alternatively, pour the stock into ½ or 1 pint freezing containers, leaving a 1 in. space at the top.

To use frozen stock, leave it to thaw at room temperature, or simply turn it into a saucepan and heat over low heat, stirring occasionally. Add 2 tablespoons water to every cube of concentrated stock.

Ready-made stocks
Many ready-made stock preparations are available, usually in the form of bouillon cubes, meat extracts, and meat-and-vegetable extracts. In an emergency, these preparations are acceptable replacements for home made stocks, but they have a sameness of flavour and lack body and jellying qualities. As they are highly seasoned, be careful about extra flavourings until the soup has been tasted.

SOUPS

There are an enormous number of classic and international soups which all fall into two distinct categories, according to their consistency: thin soups and thick soups. Thin soups are again divided into consommés and broths; and thick soups into purée and cream soups. Thick soups also include classic velouté soups which are based on a velouté sauce, but these are seldom made today.

Thin Soups
(consommé and broth)
A consommé is a clear soup made from meat, poultry, fish or vegetables and clarified stock. The basic stock must be accentuated by the main ingredient, so that a beef consommé is made from brown stock and lean beef, a chicken consommé from chicken stock and chicken flesh. Consommés are particularly suitable for party menus and may be served piping hot or chilled as a jellied soup.

Beef Consommé
PREPARATION TIME: 15 min.
COOKING TIME: 2 hours

INGREDIENTS (for 6):
½ lb. lean beef
1 small carrot
1 small onion or leek
3 pints brown stock
Bouquet garni
1 egg white

Shred the meat finely, and peel and chop the vegetables. Put all the ingredients in a large pan, adding the egg white last. Heat gently, whisking continuously with a wire whisk, until a thick froth forms on the surface. Cease whisking, reduce the heat immediately and simmer the consommé very slowly for 1½–2 hours. Do not let the liquid reach boiling point, as the foam layer will break up and cloud the consommé.

Strain the consommé into a bowl through a double layer of muslin, or a scalded jelly bag. Strain the consommé again through the egg foam in the muslin – it should now be perfectly clear and sparkling.

Reheat the consommé, correct the seasoning if necessary, and serve hot or cold.

CLEARING CONSOMMÉ

Whisking consommé to a froth

Straining cooked consommé

Broths
These semi-clear soups are easy to make and consist of uncleared brown or white stock with added meat, vegetables, rice or barley. Broths are often a by-product of the main course, pot-au-feu being a classic example.

Scotch Broth
This is a nourishing, easily prepared soup which is a complete meal in itself.

PREPARATION TIME: 30 min.
COOKING TIME: 2–3 hours

INGREDIENTS (for 8):
1 lb. flank of mutton or scrag end or middle neck of lamb
2 oz. pearl barley
2 onions
½ lb. carrots
½ lb. turnips
3 leeks
Salt and black pepper
Finely chopped parsley

Ask the butcher to chop the meat into small pieces. Put the meat with 6 pints of water in a large pot. Bring to the boil and remove any scum from the surface. Reduce the heat, add the barley and simmer for 20–30 minutes.

Meanwhile, peel and finely chop the onions, carrots and turnips. Trim and thoroughly wash the leeks, then cut them into thin rounds. Add all the vegetables to the pot, with 1 teaspoon salt and several twists of pepper. Cover the pot and simmer for 2 hours. Lift out the bones, strip off as much meat as possible and stir this back into the broth. Adjust seasoning to taste and serve the broth sprinkled with finely chopped parsley.

Pot-au-feu
PREPARATION TIME: 20 min.
COOKING TIME: 2½ hours

INGREDIENTS (for 6–8):
2 lb. topside of beef
5 pints brown stock
2 large carrots
1 turnip
2–3 leeks
1 stick of celery
2 large onions
1 small cabbage
1 set of chicken giblets

Tie the meat firmly with string to keep its shape during cooking. Put it in a large deep pan or casserole and add the cold stock. Cover the pan with a lid and bring the stock slowly to boiling point. Remove any scum.

Meanwhile, peel the carrots, turnip and onions and cut them into even chunks. Remove the roots and outer coarse leaves from the leeks and cut the white part into rounds. Clean and roughly chop the celery, wash and quarter the cabbage. Add all the vegetables, except the cabbage, to the pan and simmer gently for 1½ hours. Add the cleaned chicken giblets, continue simmering for another 30 minutes before adding the cabbage. Cook until the cabbage is tender, after 15–20 minutes.

Lift out the meat and vegetables, and keep them hot on a serving dish. Remove the string and carve the meat into slices. Serve with the vegetables and boiled potatoes and a horseradish sauce* or tomato sauce*.

Serve the soup the following day, with a garnish of rice, pasta or bread croûtons*, or with any remaining meat and vegetables stirred in.

Thick Soups
This group includes purée soups which are thickened with starchy ingredients, such as flour, cereals, pulses and potatoes. Cream soups are thickened with butter, cream and egg yolks.

The thickening agents, known as liaisons, also enrich the texture of a soup and change its colour. Liaisons must be added in correct proportions to the liquid, otherwise the soup may curdle or become too starchy.

Liaison to liquids:

¼–½ oz. flour......1 pint liquid	*(for purées rich in starch)*
½–1 oz. flour......1 pint liquid	*(for purées with little starch)*
1–2 egg yolks......1 pint liquid	
5 fl. oz. cream......1 pint liquid	

Purée Soups
For these soups, the main ingredients are rubbed through a sieve or put through a liquidiser. The soup is further thickened with a starchy liaison. Purée soups are usually made from vegetables, but can also be prepared from meat, poultry, game, fish and even fruit.

A purée made from starchy vegetables, such as dried peas, split peas, haricot and butter beans, or potatoes, will produce a thick soup that needs little or no additional starch. It can be adjusted to soup consistency by adding stock or water. A thin purée from spinach or watercress will need thickening with flour. This also prevents the purée from sinking to the bottom. Mix the correct liaison of flour with a little hot soup, then stir it back into the soup, and bring to boiling point over gentle heat.

MAKING PURÉE SOUPS

Sieving cooked vegetables

Scraping purée off the sieve

Stocks and Soups

Potato Soup

PREPARATION TIME: *15–20 min.*
COOKING TIME: *20 min.*

INGREDIENTS (*for 4–6*):
2 leeks
1 lb. potatoes
1½ oz. butter
2 pints white stock
Salt and black pepper

Wash and finely chop the leeks and peel and roughly chop the potatoes. Cook the leeks in 1 oz. of butter in a large pan until soft, but not coloured. Add the potatoes, and pour over the stock; season lightly with salt and freshly ground pepper. Bring the ingredients to the boil, cover with a lid and simmer until the potatoes are quite tender.

Remove the soup from the heat and leave it to cool slightly. Rub the soup through a sieve or put it through a liquidiser, a little at a time. Reheat the purée soup over low heat, adjust seasoning and stir in the remaining butter.

Tomato Soup

PREPARATION TIME: *25 min.*
COOKING TIME: *30 min.*

INGREDIENTS (*for 6*):
1 lb. ripe tomatoes
1 onion
1 oz. butter
Salt and black pepper
3 oz. long grain rice
2 pints white stock
Bouquet garni

Peel and finely chop the onion. Skin the tomatoes*, cut them in half and remove the seeds with a teaspoon. Chop the tomato flesh roughly. Melt the butter in a large heavy-based pan and cook the onions over low heat until transparent. Add the tomato flesh, and season with salt and pepper. Blend in the rice and stock, and add the bouquet garni*. Bring the soup to boiling point and cover the pan with a lid. Reduce the

heat and simmer the soup for 15–20 minutes, or until the rice is tender. Remove the bouquet garni.

Rub the purée through a sieve - a liquidiser will not get rid of any remaining tomato pips. Re-heat the soup over low heat and adjust seasoning.

Cream Soups

These thick soups are a combination of a purée soup and Béchamel sauce*. They are thickened and enriched with cream, egg yolks or both.

Most cream soups are based on a vegetable purée, but chicken or fish can also be used as the main ingredients. For creamed chicken soup, the meat is cooked separately in white stock. It is then minced finely, added to a Béchamel sauce and thinned down, if necessary, with stock to the required consistency.

Cream soups take little time to prepare and are excellent for storing in a home freezer.

Care is required when thickening with cream or egg yolks to prevent the soup curdling. Put the cream or yolks in a small bowl and beat in a little hot soup until the liaison has the same temperature as the soup. Blend the liaison slowly into the hot soup, stirring continuously, but do not let the soup reach boiling point. The soup can also be re-heated in the top of a double saucepan.

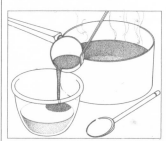
Ladle a little of the hot soup into a bowl of cream or egg yolks

Cream of Vegetable Soup

PREPARATION TIME: *20 min.*
COOKING TIME: *15–20 min.*

INGREDIENTS (*for 4*):
1 lb. mixed vegetables (carrots, celery, leeks, cabbage)
2 oz. butter
1 pint Béchamel sauce
Salt and black pepper
½–¾ pint milk
¼ pint fresh cream

Peel or scrape and wash the vegetables before chopping them finely. Blanch the vegetables for 2 minutes in boiling water, then drain thoroughly.

Melt the butter in a heavy-based pan over low heat, and cook the vegetables, covered, for 5–10 minutes, until soft. Blend in the Béchamel sauce and simmer gently for 15 minutes or until the vegetables are tender.

Rub the thick mixture through a sieve or put it through a liquidiser to make a smooth purée. Re-heat the soup without boiling, over low heat, thinning with milk to the desired consistency. Correct seasoning, and blend in the cream just prior to serving.

SOUP GARNISHES

Garnishes are added to soups either as an embellishment to improve the flavour or to provide a contrasting texture.

Consommé julienne, for example, is garnished with julienne (narrow) strips of carrot, celery, leek and turnip. These strips are boiled until soft in lightly salted water, then rinsed in cold water and added to hot consommé just before serving.

Consommé royale is a garnish of firm savoury egg custard cut into tiny fancy shapes. Beat one egg with one tablespoon of cleared stock and pour into a small bowl or dariole moulds. Bake the moulds in a pan of water

for 20 minutes or until firm, in the centre of a pre-heated oven at 350°F (mark 4).

Pasta is used to garnish many thin soups. Macaroni, tagliatelli and spaghetti can be broken into short pieces and added to purée soups for the last 20 minutes of cooking. For hot consommés, cook the pasta separately so that the starch will not cloud the soup.

Cheese makes a pleasant accompaniment to most vegetable soups. Choose a well-flavoured hard cheese, and serve it finely grated in a separate dish or sprinkled over the soup. Finely chopped fresh herbs may be mixed with the cheese.

Bread croûtons are a classic garnish with thick soups. Serve the small toasted or fried bread cubes in a separate dish or sprinkled over the soup.

Dumplings* are ideal for turning a meat or vegetable soup into a substantial family meal.

Mix 4 oz. self-raising flour with 2 oz. shredded suet and a sprinkling of salt and pepper. Bind the mixture with sufficient cold water to make a soft dough. Shape the dough into 16 balls and drop them into the simmering soup for the last 15–20 minutes of cooking.

Melba toast is made by toasting thin slices of white bread, splitting them through the middle, and toasting the uncooked surfaces under a hot grill. Alternatively, cut stale bread into very thin slices, place them on a baking tray and dry them off in the bottom of the oven until crisp and curling at the edges.

Vegetable and fruit garnishes add colour to plain cream soups. Celery leaves, watercress and parsley should be trimmed and washed before floating them on top of the soup.

Cucumber may be cut into julienne strips as a garnish for

chilled soups. For hot soups, sauté cucumber strips or thin rounds of leeks in a little butter.

Thin slices of lemon or orange make an attractive garnish for clear soups and tomato soup.

A garnish of thinly sliced mushrooms lends additional texture and flavour to cream soups. Fry the sliced mushrooms in a little butter until soft, but not coloured. Drain thoroughly before spooning them over the soup.

Thin onion rings add more flavour to soups. They can be sautéed like cucumber strips and leek rounds; alternatively, coat them in milk and flour, and deep fry them until crisp and golden.

SOUP GARNISHES

Julienne strips

Cut-outs for consommé royale

Cutting bread croûtons

Slicing Melba toast

Sauces, Gravies and Dressings

Sauces first came into widespread use in the Middle Ages, to disguise the flavour of long-stored meat that had been inadequately cured. Today, they are used to add flavour to bland food, colour to simple meals and moisture to otherwise dry foods.

There are two main groups of sauces: savoury and dessert. The first group includes white, brown and egg-based sauces; and the cold sauces and salad dressings. Horseradish, mint and the puréed fruit sauces are other savoury sauces which do not belong in any particular sub-group.

French chefs have created most of the hundreds of variations on the basic savoury sauces. Most dessert sauces, on the other hand, originated in England or America.

The main ingredient of all sauces is the basic liquid, which may be milk, wine, stock, vegetable or fruit juices. These are thickened with fat, flour, arrowroot, eggs, cream or blood, or they may be boiled down (reduced) to the desired consistency.

BASIC WHITE SAUCE

This is prepared either by the roux or the blending method:

Roux method

A roux is usually composed of equal amounts of butter and flour which are then combined with liquid (usually milk) to the required consistency. Melt the butter in a heavy-based pan, blend in the flour, and cook over low heat for 2–3 minutes, stirring constantly with a wooden spoon.

Gradually add the warm or cold liquid to the roux, which will at first thicken to a near solid mass. Beat vigorously until the mixture leaves the sides of the pan clean, then add a little more milk. Allow the mixture to thicken and boil between each addition of milk. Continuous beating is essential to obtain a smooth sauce. When all the milk has been added, bring the sauce to the boil; let it simmer for about 5 minutes and add the seasoning.

A basic white sauce can also be made by the one-stage method.

This consists of putting the basic ingredients (fat, flour and liquid) into a pan at the same time. Cook over low heat, beating until the sauce has thickened. Boil for 3 minutes and season.

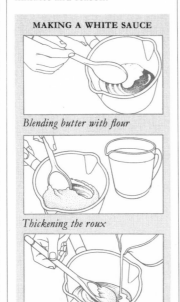

MAKING A WHITE SAUCE

Blending butter with flour

Thickening the roux

Adding the remaining milk

Blending method

For this method the thickening agent is mixed to a paste with a little cold milk. Mix 1 oz. plain flour (or ½ oz. cornflour) with a few tablespoons taken from ½ pint of cold milk. Blend to a smooth paste in a bowl, and bring the remaining milk to the boil.

Pour the hot milk over the paste and return the mixture to the pan. Bring to the boil over low heat, stirring continuously with a wooden spoon. Simmer the sauce for 2–3 minutes, until thick. Add a knob of butter and seasoning and cook for 5 minutes.

A basic white sauce can be made into other savoury sauces. Delicately flavoured rich sauces, such as Béchamel and Velouté have evolved from the basic white sauce. These sauces are, in turn, the main components for the compound white sauces.

Béchamel Sauce

PREPARATION TIME: *20 min.*
COOKING TIME: *5–10 min.*

INGREDIENTS (*approx. ½ pint*):
½ pint milk
1 small bay leaf
Sprig of thyme
½ small onion
¼ level teaspoon grated nutmeg
1 oz. butter
1 oz. plain flour
Salt and black pepper
2–3 tablespoons single or double cream (optional)

Put the milk with the bay leaf, thyme, onion and nutmeg in a pan, and bring slowly to the boil. Remove from the heat, cover with a lid and leave the milk to infuse for 15 minutes. In a clean heavy-based pan, melt the butter, stir in the flour and cook the roux for 3 minutes.

Strain the milk through a fine sieve and gradually blend it into the roux. Bring to the boil, stirring continuously, then simmer for 2–3 minutes. Adjust seasoning and stir in the cream.

SIMPLE WHITE SAUCES

	Pouring sauce	Other ingredients	Method of preparation	Serving suggestions
Butter sauce	½ pint white sauce (use lightly salted water instead of milk)	1 egg yolk 1 tablespoon water 3 oz. butter	Beat the egg yolk with water and blend into the sauce with the butter cut into knobs	*Fish or vegetables*
Caper sauce	½ pint white sauce (use half milk and half white or fish stock)	1 tablespoon caper juice or lemon juice 1 tablespoon capers	Add caper juice or lemon juice to the stock before making the sauce. Add the finely chopped capers to the sauce just before serving	*Boiled fish or mutton*
Cheese sauce	½ pint white sauce	2 oz. mature Cheddar cheese ½ level teaspoon dry mustard (optional) Pinch cayenne	Beat the grated cheese into the sauce until smooth. Season with mustard and cayenne	*Eggs, fish, pasta and vegetables*
Egg sauce	½ pint white sauce	1 hardboiled egg 2 level tablespoons chopped chives	Finely chop the egg and the chives and add to the sauce	*Poached or steamed fish*
Fish sauce	½ pint white sauce (made from half milk and half fish stock, and simmered with a bay leaf and the rind of ½ lemon. Use the strained liquid.)	2 oz. shrimps or 1 teaspoon anchovy essence	Peel and chop the shrimps. Before seasoning the sauce, add the shrimps or anchovy essence	*Poached or steamed fish*
Mushroom sauce	½ pint white sauce	2 oz. mushrooms ½ oz. butter Squeeze lemon juice	Trim and slice the mushrooms. Sauté in butter and lemon juice until tender. Drain before folding into the sauce	*Fish, meat, poultry*
Onion sauce		1 onion ¾ oz. butter ¾ oz. flour ½ pint milk	Sauté the finely chopped onion in the butter for 5 minutes, until soft. Blend in flour to make the roux, and then the milk	*Mutton and tripe*
Parsley sauce	½ pint white sauce	2 level tablespoons parsley	Finely chop the parsley and add to the sauce, just before serving	*Bacon, boiled or steamed fish, and vegetables*

SAUCE CONSISTENCIES

Consistency	Uses	Ingredients Butter, flour	milk
Thin sauce	Basis for soups	½ oz. each	½ pint
Pouring sauce *(medium)*	For accompanying sauces	¾ oz. each	½ pint
Coating sauce *(medium thick)*	For coating sauces	1 oz. each	½ pint
Panada sauce *(very thick)*	For binding croquettes and as basis for soufflés	2 oz. each	½ pint

Sauces, Gravies and Dressings

COMPOUND WHITE SAUCES

	Ingredients	Method of preparation	Serving suggestions
Allemande sauce	½ pint Velouté sauce 2 egg yolks ⅛ pint white stock 1½ oz. butter	Beat the egg yolks with the stock and blend into the sauce. Simmer gently, stirring until thick, smooth and reduced by one-third. Stir in the butter (cut into pieces) and adjust seasoning	*Chicken, eggs, fish, vegetables*
Aurora sauce	½ pint Velouté sauce 4 tablespoons tomato purée or 1 tablespoon concentrated tomato paste 1½ oz. butter	Blend the tomato purée or tomato paste into the sauce. Stir in the butter (cut into pieces), and correct the seasoning	*Eggs, poultry, sweetbreads, fish, vegetables*
Chantilly sauce	½ pint Suprême sauce ¼ pint double or whipping cream	Whip the cream until light and fluffy. Fold into the Suprême sauce	*Serve immediately with poultry or offal*
Chaudfroid sauce	½ pint Velouté sauce ½ pint jellied white stock 4 tablespoons single cream	Add the stock and cream to the sauce. Cook over gentle heat until reduced to coating consistency. Adjust the seasoning	*Cold as a coating for chicken, eggs and fish*
Hungarian sauce	½ pint Velouté sauce 1 onion 1 oz. butter Bouquet garni ¼ level teaspoon paprika Pinch salt 6 tablespoons white wine	Sauté the finely chopped onion in the butter until clear. Add the rest of the ingredients. Bring to the boil and reduce by half. Strain through a sieve before adding to the sauce	*Fish and veal*
Mornay sauce	½ pint Béchamel sauce 2 oz. grated Parmesan or Gruyère cheese	Blend the cheese into the sauce. Do not re-heat	*Chicken, eggs, veal, fish, vegetables and pasta*
Suprême sauce	½ pint Velouté sauce 2 egg yolks 2 tablespoons double cream 1 oz. butter	Beat the egg yolks and cream together. Blend into the sauce and heat without boiling. Stir in the butter (cut into pieces)	*Serve immediately with eggs, poultry and vegetables*

COMPOUND BROWN SAUCES

	Ingredients	Method of preparation	Serving suggestions
Demi-glace sauce	½ pint Espagnole sauce ¼ pint jellied brown stock	Add the jellied stock to the Espagnole sauce. Bring to the boil and cook until the sauce is shiny and thick enough to coat the back of a spoon	*Game: add 3 tablespoons Madeira to finished sauce* *Poultry: add 4 oz. mushrooms and 1 tablespoon Madeira*
Devilled sauce	½ pint Espagnole sauce 1 small onion ⅛ pint white wine 1 tablespoon wine vinegar Sprig of thyme Small bay leaf 1 tablespoon parsley Cayenne	Finely chop the onion and mix with the wine, vinegar, thyme and bay leaf. Bring to the boil and reduce by half. Strain and add to the Espagnole sauce. Boil for a few minutes, add the chopped parsley and cayenne to taste	*Grilled chicken*
Red wine sauce	½ pint Espagnole sauce ½ onion 2 oz. butter ½ pint red wine Bouquet garni	Sauté the finely chopped onion in 1 oz. butter until clear. Add the rest of the ingredients and boil to reduce by half. Strain and add to Espagnole sauce. Cook until reduced by one-third. Stir in 1 oz. butter and serve immediately	*Game*
Robert sauce	½ pint Espagnole sauce 1 onion ½ oz. butter 8 tablespoons red wine 1 teaspoon mustard	Sauté the chopped onion in butter. Add the red wine and boil until reduced by half. Strain and add to the Espagnole sauce. Heat gently and stir in 1 teaspoon mustard	*Roast pork*
Tomato sauce	½ pint Espagnole sauce (made from tomato juice instead of brown stock) 4 oz. ham	Dice the ham and add to the finished sauce	*Serve with grilled chicken, meat leftovers, chops, pasta, meat patties*

310

Velouté Sauce

PREPARATION TIME: *5–10 min.*
COOKING TIME: *1 hour*

INGREDIENTS (½ pint):
1 oz. butter
1 oz. plain flour
1 pint white stock
Salt and black pepper
1–2 tablespoons single or double cream (optional)

Make the roux with the butter and flour. Gradually stir in the hot stock until the sauce is quite smooth. Bring to boiling point, lower the heat, and let the sauce simmer for about 1 hour until reduced by half. Stir the sauce occasionally. Strain through a sieve, season to taste, and stir in the cream.

BROWN SAUCES

A basic brown sauce is made by the roux method, using the same proportions of flour, fat and liquid (brown stock) as for a basic white sauce. Melt the fat in a pan and stir in the flour. Cook the roux over low heat, stirring continuously with a wooden spoon, until the roux is light brown in colour. Gradually stir in the brown stock and proceed as for a white sauce.

Espagnole Sauce

This classic sauce, made from a brown roux, is the basis of many compound brown sauces.

PREPARATION TIME: *10 min.*
COOKING TIME: *1¼ hours*

INGREDIENTS (approx. ½ pint):
1 carrot
1 onion
2 oz. green streaky bacon
1 oz. butter
1 oz. plain flour
¾ pint brown stock
Bouquet garni
2 level tablespoons tomato paste
Salt and black pepper

Peel and dice the carrot and onion. Remove rind and gristle from the bacon and chop the rashers. Melt the butter in a heavy-based pan, and cook the vegetables and bacon over low heat for 10 minutes or until light brown.

Blend in the flour, stirring the roux until brown. Gradually blend in ½ pint stock, stirring constantly until the mixture has cooked through and has thickened. Add the bouquet garni*, cover with a lid and set the pan on an asbestos sheet. Simmer for 30 minutes. Add the remaining stock and the tomato paste. Cover the pan again, and continue cooking for 30 minutes, stirring frequently. Strain the sauce through a sieve, skim off fat, and adjust seasoning.

MAKING ESPAGNOLE SAUCE

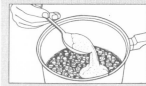

Blending in the flour

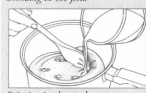

Stirring in the stock

Straining the sauce

Gravies

The most frequently used brown sauce is gravy, made from the pan residues of a roast joint, boiled up with brown stock. Gravies may be thick or thin.

Thick gravy

Pour off most of the fat from the roasting tin, leaving about 2 tablespoons of the sediment. Stir in 1 level tablespoon plain flour and blend thoroughly with the fat. Stir constantly with a wooden spoon, cooking until the gravy thickens and browns. Gradually blend in ½ pint hot brown stock or vegetable liquid. Bring the gravy to boiling point, and cook for 2–3 minutes. Season to taste, strain and serve hot with a roast.

Thin gravy

Pour all the fat from the pan, leaving only the pan residues. Add ½ pint hot vegetable liquid or brown stock (this may be made from a stock cube). Stir well and boil for 2–3 minutes to reduce* slightly. A hot thin gravy is traditional with roast beef.

Thickening agents for sauces

Basic white and brown sauces can be thickened or enriched with various other liaisons: cornflour or arrowroot with water; beurre manié (kneaded butter and flour); egg yolks and cream.

Cornflour and arrowroot

To thicken ½ pint of liquid to a sauce of coating consistency, stir 1 level tablespoon cornflour with 3 dessertspoons cold water, and mix into a smooth paste. Blend a little of the hot liquid into the liaison, then return this to the sauce. Bring the sauce to the boil, stirring constantly for 2–3 minutes to allow the starch to cook through.

Arrowroot is best used to thicken clear sauces that are to be served at once. To thicken ½ pint sauce use 2¼ level teaspoons arrowroot mixed to a paste with water. The sauce cannot be reheated and quickly loses its thickening qualities.

Beurre manié

This liaison is ideal for thickening sauces, casseroles and stews at the end of cooking. Knead an equal amount of butter and flour (1 oz. each) into a paste with a fork or the fingers. Add small pieces of the beurre manié to the hot liquid. Stir or whisk continuously to dissolve the butter and disperse the flour. Simmer the sauce until it is thick and smooth and has lost the starchy taste of raw flour. Do not let the sauce boil or the beurre manié will separate out.

Egg yolks and cream

These are used when enriching a basic white sauce. Mix 1 egg yolk with 2–3 tablespoons cream in a bowl. Blend in a little of the hot sauce until the liaison has the same temperature. Remove the sauce from the heat and stir in the liaison with a wooden spoon. Return the pan to the heat and simmer the sauce over low heat, without boiling. Over-heating causes the sauce to curdle.

EGG-BASED SAUCES

These rich sauces require care and practice to prevent them curdling. They are made from egg yolks and a high proportion of butter. Through continuous whisking, these two main ingredients are emulsified to a thick and creamy consistency.

Hollandaise Sauce

PREPARATION AND COOKING TIME: *20 min.*

INGREDIENTS (½ *pint*):
3 *tablespoons white wine vinegar*
1 *tablespoon water*
6 *black peppercorns*
1 *bay leaf*
3 *egg yolks*
6 *oz. soft butter*
Salt and black pepper

Boil the vinegar and water with the peppercorns and the bay leaf in a small pan, until reduced* to 1 tablespoon. Leave to cool. Cream the egg yolks with ½ oz. butter and a pinch of salt. Strain the vinegar into the eggs, and set the bowl over a pan of boiling water. Turn off the heat. Whisk in the remaining butter, ¼ oz. at a time, until the sauce is shiny and has the consistency of thick cream. Season with salt and pepper.

Until the technique of egg-based sauces has been mastered, a Hollandaise sauce may sometimes

Whisking in pieces of butter to thicken Hollandaise sauce

curdle during preparation. This is usually because the heat is too sudden or too high, or because the butter has been added too quickly. If the finished sauce separates, it can often be saved by removing from the heat and beating in 1 tablespoon of cold water.

Bearnaise Sauce

This sauce is similar to Hollandaise sauce, but has a sharper flavour. It is served with grilled meat and fish.

PREPARATION AND COOKING TIME: *20 min.*

INGREDIENTS (½ *pint*):
2 *tablespoons tarragon vinegar*
2 *tablespoons white wine vinegar*
½ *small onion*
2 *egg yolks*
3–4 *oz. butter*
Salt and black pepper

Put the vinegars and finely chopped onion in a small saucepan; boil steadily until reduced to 1 tablespoon. Strain and set aside to cool. Follow the method used for making Hollandaise sauce.

COLD SAUCES

Mayonnaise and its variations are the most widely used of savoury cold sauces. They are served with hors-d'oeuvre, salads, cold meat, poultry and vegetable dishes. Mayonnaise, like Hollandaise and

Bearnaise sauce, is based on eggs and fat, but oil is used instead of butter.

It is essential that all the ingredients and equipment are at room temperature. Assemble the bowl, egg and oil at least 1 hour before making a mayonnaise.

Mayonnaise

PREPARATION TIME: *20 min.*

INGREDIENTS (¼ *pint*):
1 *egg yolk*
¼ *level teaspoon salt*
½ *level teaspoon dry mustard*
Pinch caster sugar
Black pepper
¼ *pint olive or salad oil*
1 *tablespoon white wine vinegar or lemon juice*

Beat the egg yolk in a bowl until thick. Beat in the salt, mustard, sugar and a few twists of freshly ground pepper. Add the oil, drop by drop, whisking vigorously between each addition of oil so that it is absorbed completely before the next drop. As the mayonnaise thickens and becomes shiny, the oil may be added in a thin stream. Finally, blend in the vinegar.

The flavour of the mayonnaise can be varied by using a tarragon, garlic or chilli vinegar, or by substituting lemon juice for vinegar. Chopped herbs – parsley, chives or crushed garlic – may also be added when the mayonnaise is finished.

Alternatively, fold ¼ pint of whipped cream into the finished mayonnaise.

A mayonnaise may curdle if the oil was cold or was added too quickly, or if the egg yolk was stale. To save a curdled mayonnaise, whisk a fresh yolk in a clean bowl, and gradually whisk in the curdled mayonnaise. Alternatively, whisk in a teaspoon of tepid water until the mayonnaise is thick and shiny.

	Ingredients	Method of preparation	Serving suggestions
MAYONNAISE SAUCES			
Anchovy mayonnaise	¼ pint mayonnaise 2 teaspoons anchovy essence	Mix the anchovy essence thoroughly into the finished mayonnaise	*Fish and vegetable salads*
Orange mayonnaise	¼ pint mayonnaise Rind of an orange 1–2 tablespoons whipped cream	Fold the grated orange rind and lightly whipped cream into the mayonnaise	*Salads*
Remoulade sauce	¼ pint mayonnaise 1 teaspoon each chopped capers, chervil, gherkins, parsley, tarragon, onion	Mix the finely chopped herbs and vegetables and blend into the mayonnaise	*Cold shellfish and egg dishes*
Tartare sauce	¼ pint mayonnaise 2 teaspoons capers 3 cocktail gherkins 1 teaspoon chives 1 tablespoon double cream	Finely chop the gherkins and chives. Add all the ingredients to the mayonnaise	*Fried or grilled fish*

Sauces, Gravies and Dressings

SALAD DRESSINGS

A good dressing is essential to a salad, but it must be varied to accord with the salad ingredients. A sharp vinaigrette sauce is probably best for a green salad, but egg, fish, meat and vegetable salads would nearly always need additional flavours. For a mixed fruit and green salad, vinaigrette sauce might be too sharp.

There are no hard rules on the mixing of salad dressings, but olive oil, or a good salad oil, is a matter of choice.

The principle of a dressing is the temporary suspension of oil in vinegar. A dressing can be kept for several days in a lidded container (not a screw-top jar) in a refrigerator, but needs to be shaken vigorously before use.

Sauce Vinaigrette
PREPARATION TIME: *3 min.*

INGREDIENTS *($\frac{1}{4}$ pint)*:
6 tablespoons oil
2 tablespoons vinegar
1 dessertspoon finely chopped herbs
Salt and black pepper

Put the oil and vinegar in a bowl or in a screw-top jar. Whisk with a fork or shake vigorously before seasoning to taste with herbs, salt and freshly ground pepper.

French Dressing
PREPARATION TIME: *3 min.*

INGREDIENTS *($\frac{1}{3}$ pint)*:
8 tablespoons oil
4 tablespoons vinegar
2 level teaspoons French mustard
$\frac{1}{2}$ level teaspoon each salt, black pepper
Caster sugar (optional)

Whisk or shake all the dressing ingredients together, seasoning with sugar (optional). Either of the following ingredients can be added to a basic French dressing: 1–2 crushed garlic cloves; 2 tablespoons chopped tarragon or chives; 1 tablespoon tomato paste and a pinch of paprika; 2 tablespoons each finely chopped parsley and onion; 1 teaspoon anchovy essence (for cold fish or cold, cooked vegetable salads).

For a spicy French dressing, mix 1 level teaspoon curry powder to a smooth paste with 1 tablespoon of oil. Cook the paste over low heat, and in it sauté 1 small, finely chopped onion. Cool and add to French dressing for serving with cooked vegetables.

MISCELLANEOUS SAUCES

Bread Sauce
PREPARATION TIME: *20 min.*
COOKING TIME: *15 min.*

INGREDIENTS *(1 pint)*:
1 onion
1–2 cloves
1 bay leaf
1 pint milk
3 oz. fresh white breadcrumbs
1 oz. butter
Salt and black pepper

Peel the onion and stick the cloves into it. Put the onion, bay leaf and milk in a pan and bring to the boil. Remove the pan from the heat, cover with a lid and leave to infuse for 15 minutes. Add the breadcrumbs and the butter. Cook the sauce, uncovered, over lowest possible heat for 15 minutes, then remove the onion and bay leaf. Season to taste with salt and freshly ground black pepper. Serve with chicken or turkey.

Horseradish Sauce
PREPARATION TIME: *10 min.*

INGREDIENTS *(about $\frac{1}{3}$ pint)*:
3 rounded tablespoons fresh grated horseradish
$\frac{1}{4}$ pint soured cream
Salt and black pepper
Pinch dry mustard

Peel and coarsely grate the horseradish root. Fold it into the soured cream and season to taste with salt, freshly ground pepper and mustard.

Serve horseradish sauce with roast beef.

Mint Sauce
PREPARATION TIME: *10 min.*
RESTING TIME: *30 min.*

INGREDIENTS *(for 4–6)*:
Small handful mint leaves
1–2 level teaspoons caster sugar
2 tablespoons vinegar

Wash and dry the mint leaves. Put them on a board, sprinkle with the sugar, and chop them finely. Place the chopped mint in a jug and stir in 2 tablespoons boiling water. Add the vinegar and leave the sauce to stand for 30 minutes.

Alternatively, add the chopped mint to 3–4 tablespoons chopped red currant jelly. Blend in the finely grated rind of an orange and mix thoroughly.

Serve with roast lamb.

Apple Sauce
PREPARATION TIME: *10 min.*

INGREDIENTS *($\frac{1}{2}$ pint)*:
1 lb. cooking apples
1 oz. unsalted butter
Caster sugar (optional)

Peel, core and slice the apples. Put them in a pan with 2–3 tablespoons of water and cook over low heat for about 10 minutes. Rub the cooked apples through a coarse sieve or put them in the liquidiser to make a purée*. Stir in butter and season with sugar, if necessary.

Serve with roast pork, grilled sausages and bacon, roast goose and duck.

Cranberry Sauce: see Index
Gooseberry Sauce: see Index

DESSERT SAUCES

The sweet dessert sauces are mainly of British and American origin. They are most often served warm with baked and steamed puddings, stewed and poached fruit and with ice cream.

Apricot Sauce
PREPARATION TIME: *5 min.*
COOKING TIME: *6 min.*

INGREDIENTS *($\frac{1}{2}$ pint)*:
4 level tablespoons apricot jam
Juice and rind of half lemon
1$\frac{1}{2}$ level teaspoons arrowroot
1 oz. caster sugar (optional)

Pare the rind from the lemon, leaving behind the white pith. Squeeze out the juice. Blend the arrowroot with $\frac{1}{4}$ pint water in a small pan, and stir in the jam. Cook over low heat until the jam has melted, then stir in the lemon rind and juice.

Bring the sauce to the boil and cook for 2 minutes, stirring continuously. Strain the sauce through a sieve, return it to the pan and re-heat; sweeten to taste.

Serve the sauce hot with steamed or baked puddings. It may also be served cold with ice cream, in which case reduce the arrowroot to 1 level teaspoon.

Brandy Sauce
PREPARATION AND COOKING TIME: *10–12 min.*

INGREDIENTS *($\frac{1}{2}$ pint)*:
2 tablespoons brandy
1 level tablespoon cornflour
$\frac{1}{2}$ pint milk, less 2 tablespoons
1 level tablespoon caster sugar

In a bowl, blend the cornflour to a smooth paste with 1 tablespoon of the milk. Bring the remaining milk to the boil; pour it over the cornflour, stirring well. Return the sauce to the pan, add the sugar and brandy and cook over low heat for 2–3 minutes.

Serve hot with steamed fruit puddings. Brandy sauce is traditional with Christmas pudding and mince pies.

Butterscotch Sauce
PREPARATION AND COOKING TIME: *25 min.*

INGREDIENTS *($\frac{1}{2}$ pint)*:
3 oz. granulated sugar
1$\frac{1}{2}$ level teaspoons arrowroot
1 oz. unsalted butter

Heat the sugar over gentle heat in a heavy-based pan, until dissolved. Increase the heat and let the sugar bubble until it caramelises to a golden brown. Remove the pan from the heat, add (without stirring) 6 tablespoons of boiling water and return the pan to the heat. Simmer the caramel for a few minutes, stirring all the time, until dissolved.

Blend the arrowroot with 4 tablespoons water and stir into the caramel. Bring the mixture to the boil, over low heat. Add the butter, cut into small pieces, and cook the sauce until thick and clear, stirring all the time to prevent the sauce burning.

Serve warm with ice cream and sundaes, baked apples and plain steamed sponge puddings.

Chocolate Sauce I
PREPARATION AND COOKING TIME: *15 min.*

INGREDIENTS *($\frac{1}{2}$ pint)*:
2 oz. bitter chocolate
2 level teaspoons cornflour
7 fluid oz. water, less 1 tablespoon
2 oz. unsalted butter
3 oz. caster sugar
1 teaspoon vanilla essence

Break the chocolate into small pieces. Blend the cornflour with 2 tablespoons of the measured water in a small bowl or cup. Put the chocolate in a small pan, add the rest of the water, and cook over low heat until dissolved and smooth. Do not allow the chocolate mixture to boil. Stir the blended cornflour quickly into the chocolate, add the butter and sugar.

Cook the chocolate sauce for a few minutes, stirring continuously, then add vanilla essence to taste.

Serve the sauce hot with poached pears and steamed or baked puddings.

Chocolate Sauce II

PREPARATION AND COOKING TIME: *10 min.*

INGREDIENTS ($\frac{1}{3}$ *pint*):
4 oz. plain dark chocolate
$\frac{1}{2}$ oz. unsalted butter
2 tablespoons water
2 tablespoons golden syrup or
   clear honey
1 teaspoon vanilla essence
   (optional)

Break the chocolate into pieces and put them in a small pan with the butter, water and syrup. Cook over low heat until the chocolate has melted, then stir in the vanilla essence.

Serve the chocolate sauce hot with vanilla ice cream or warm with profiteroles.

Honey Sauce

PREPARATION AND COOKING TIME: *8 min.*

INGREDIENTS ($\frac{1}{4}$ *pint*):
2 oz. unsalted butter
1$\frac{1}{2}$ level teaspoons cornflour
4–6 oz. thin clear honey

Melt the butter in a small pan over low heat, without browning it; stir in the cornflour.

Gradually blend in the honey and bring the sauce to the boil, stirring all the time. Heat for 2–3 minutes to cook the cornflour.

Serve the sauce warm with, for example, vanilla ice cream and banana splits.

Sauce Sabayon

PREPARATION TIME: *7 min.*
COOKING TIME: *5 min.*

INGREDIENTS ($\frac{1}{2}$ *pint*):
2 egg yolks
2 oz. caster sugar
$\frac{1}{4}$ level teaspoon arrowroot
2$\frac{1}{2}$ fluid oz. sherry, white wine,
   fruit juice or strong black coffee

In a deep bowl, whisk the yolks and sugar until thick, creamy and pale in colour. Blend the arrowroot to a paste with a little of the liquid, then whisk it with the rest of the liquid into the eggs. Place the bowl over a pan of gently simmering water and whisk the sauce until thick and frothy.

Serve at once with fruit puddings and apple pie.

Sour Cream Sauce

PREPARATION TIME: *10 min.*
CHILLING TIME: *30 min.*

INGREDIENTS ($\frac{1}{2}$ *pint*):
$\frac{1}{4}$ pint double cream
$\frac{1}{4}$ pint soured cream
1 level teaspoon caster sugar

Whisk the cream until it just holds its shape, then fold in the soured cream and the sugar. Refrigerate for about 30 minutes.

Serve with cooked fruit, fruit pies, mince pies and fruit salads.

Syrup Sauce

PREPARATION AND COOKING TIME: *8 min.*

INGREDIENTS ($\frac{1}{3}$ *pint*):
4 level tablespoons golden syrup
2 level teaspoons arrowroot
2 tablespoons lemon juice

Blend the arrowroot to a smooth paste with $\frac{1}{4}$ pint of water in a small pan. Add the syrup and lemon juice. Bring the sauce to the boil, over low heat, stirring all the time, and cook until thick.

Serve hot with light steamed puddings, and warm with ice cream, pancakes and waffles.

Fish

Fish are sold fresh, frozen, salted from the barrel, smoked, pickled or tinned. Flat fish, such as plaice, sole, turbot and whiting, are sold whole or filleted. Whole round fish, such as cod, haddock and hake, are also sold as steaks and cutlets.

Many shellfish are sold already boiled and even prepared. The exceptions are mussels and oysters which must always be bought live.

Cook fish on the day it is bought, and for a main course allow 7–8 oz. of fish per person, or one good-sized fillet, steak or cutlet. A medium-sized mackerel or trout will serve one person. If the fish course is to be followed by several other courses, halve the suggested fish quantities for a main course. However, it is better to err on the generous side, and cold fish can easily be used up.

PREPARATION OF FISH

Fishmongers will usually clean and fillet fish ready for cooking. But if this has not been done, a few simple preparations are necessary. Unwrap the fish as soon as possible and if it has to be stored in the refrigerator for any length of time, wrap it in plastic or foil to prevent its smell spreading to other food.

Preparation of fish includes scaling, cleaning, skinning and sometimes filleting.

Scaling

Cover the wooden board with several sheets of newspaper. Lay the fish on the paper and, holding it by the tail, scrape away the scales from the tail towards the head, using the blunt edge of a knife. Rinse the scales off under cold water. Alternatively, cook the fish without removing the scales, and skin it before serving.

Scrape fish scales from tail to head, using the back of a knife

Cleaning

Once scaled, the fish must be cleaned, or gutted. This process is determined by the shape of the fish – in round fish the entrails lie in the belly, but in flat fish they are found in a cavity behind the head.

Round fish

(cod, herring, mackerel, trout, for example). Slit the fish, with a sharp knife, along the belly from behind the gills to just above the tail. Scrape out and discard the entrails. Rinse the fish under cold running water and, with a little salt, gently rub away any black skin inside the cavity.

The head and tail may be left on the fish if it is to be cooked whole, but the eyes should be taken out. Use a sharp knife or scissors to cut off the lower fins on either side of the body and the gills below the head. Alternatively, cut the head off just below the gills and slice off the tail.

Flat fish

(plaice, sole, for example). Make a semi-circular slit just behind the head, on the dark skin side. This opens up the cavity which contains the entrails. Scrape these out and wash the fish. Cut off the fins, and cook the fish whole.

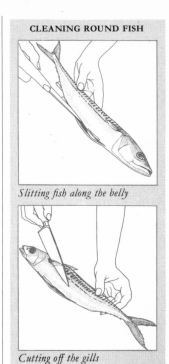

CLEANING ROUND FISH

Slitting fish along the belly

Cutting off the gills

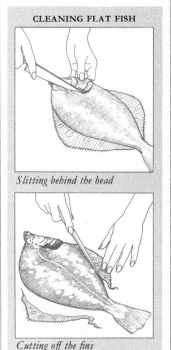

CLEANING FLAT FISH

Slitting behind the head

Cutting off the fins

Fish

Skinning
Again, the method varies according to the type of fish.

Round fish
These are usually cooked with the skin on, but it is also possible to remove the skin before cooking. Cut away a thin strip of skin along the backbone. Using a sharp knife, loosen the skin round the head, and then gently draw it down towards the tail. Cut it off. Repeat on the other side.

Flat fish
Lay the fish, dark skin uppermost, on the board. Make a slit across the skin just above the tail. Slip the thumb into the slit, and gently loosen the skin. Holding the fish firmly by the tail, pull the skin quickly towards the head (dip the fingers in a little salt to get a better grip), and cut it off. The white skin on the other side may be removed in the same way, but it is usually left on.

Filleting and boning
The fish can now be cut into serving portions. Fillets of both round and flat fish are popular as they provide a solid piece of fish without any bones.

Round fish
To fillet a large fish, such as haddock, cut the head off the cleaned fish, and then cut along the backbone, working towards the tail. Insert the knife blade at a slight angle to the bone and, keeping the sharp edge towards the tail, gently ease the flesh from the bone with slicing movements.

Continue cutting in line with the backbone, until the whole fillet is freed and can be lifted off. With the tip of the knife, ease off the backbone to reveal the other fillet, and cut off the tail. If the fish is large, the fillets can be cut into serving-size portions.

Boning large round fish
(salmon and salmon trout)
Using a sharp knife or scissors, cut the fins and gills off the cleaned fish, and cut an inverted V into the tail. Wash the fish under cold water to remove all traces of blood, then place it in a fish kettle or large flameproof dish and poach it in Court Bouillon (see Cooking methods).

Lift the poached fish on to a board, and with a sharp knife or scissors snip the skin just below the head and above the tail. Carefully peel off the skin, leaving head and tail intact. Snip the backbone below the head and above the tail, then with the blade of a sharp knife split the fish along the backbone. Ease the bone out from the back without breaking the fish.

Boning small round fish
Smaller round fish such as herrings and mackerel may be filleted as already described, but are more often boned and cooked whole or with a stuffing.

To bone a cleaned herring, cut off the head, tail and fins. Open out the split fish and spread it flat, skin side up. Press firmly along the centre back of the fish to loosen the backbone, then turn the fish over. Starting at the head, ease away the backbone with the tip of the knife, removing at the same time as many of the small bones as possible. The herring can now be folded back into its original shape or cut into two long fillets.

Steaks and cutlets
Large round fish are often sold in thick cutlets, from the middle of the fish, or as steaks, from the tail end. These should be cleaned, but not skinned before cooking. The small central bone is best removed after cooking. If it is removed before cooking, the centre should be stuffed.

Filleting flat fish
A large sole or plaice will yield four small fillets, two from each side. Lay the fish, dark skin up, on the board and with a sharp knife cut off the fins. Make the first cut along the backbone, working from the head towards the tail. Then make a semi-circular cut, just below the head, through half the thickness of the fish. Slant the knife against the backbone, and with short sharp strokes of the knife separate the left fillet from the bone. Make a thick cut just above the tail and remove the fillet. Turn the fish round and remove the right fillet in the same way. Turn the fish over and remove the fillets on the other side.

COOKING METHODS

A number of basic cooking methods are suitable for all fish whether they are whole, filleted or cut into steaks. But whatever cooking method is chosen, fish should be cooked for a short time only and at low heat. Prolonged cooking time and high heat toughens the flesh and destroys the flavour.

Baking
This method is suitable for small whole fish and for individual cuts, such as fillets and steaks.

Brush the prepared fish with melted butter and season with lemon juice, salt and freshly ground pepper. Make three or four diagonal score marks on each side of whole round fish so that they will keep their shape. Lay the fish in a well-buttered, shallow ovenproof dish. Bake in the centre of a pre-heated oven at 350°F (mark 4), allowing 25–30 minutes for whole fish and 10–20 minutes for fillets and steaks.

During baking, baste* the fish frequently – this is particularly important with white fish.

SKINNING A ROUND FISH

Cutting skin from the backbone

Drawing skin towards the tail

SKINNING A FLAT FISH

Slitting skin above the tail

Drawing skin towards the head

CUTTING A ROUND FISH INTO TWO FILLETS

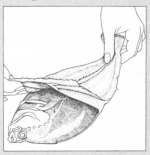

1. *Cutting along the backbone*

3. *Freeing the backbone*

2. *Easing the flesh from the bone*

4. *Cutting off the tail*

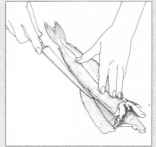

BONING A COOKED SALMON

Peeling skin towards tail

Snipping the backbone

Easing backbone from the fish

BONING A HERRING

Slitting fish along the belly

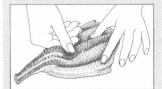
Pressing along the backbone

Easing away the backbone

REMOVING THE FOUR FILLETS FROM A FLAT FISH

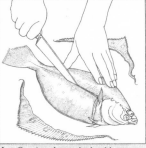
1. *Cutting down the backbone*

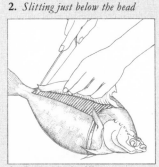
2. *Slitting just below the head*

3. *Separating fillet from the bone*

4. *Removing the fillet*

Alternatively, lay streaky bacon rashers over the fish to provide basting during cooking.

Before baking, fish may be stuffed with a filling of fine breadcrumbs seasoned with salt, pepper, herbs or parsley and bound with a little melted butter. Spoon the filling loosely into the cavity, as it tends to swell during cooking. Close the opening on round fish with cocktail sticks.

Whole flat fish have only small cavities which must be opened up to allow room for stuffing. To do this make an incision down the centre of the back as far as the fins. Ease the flesh from the backbone on either side with the knife blade to form a cavity and loosely stuff this. Leave the pocket open.

For individual stuffed fillets, spread the mixture over the fish, roll it up and secure with wooden skewers.

Baking can also be done in foil, which is excellent for sealing-in both flavour and aroma. It also cuts down on oven cleaning. Place the prepared fish on buttered foil and sprinkle with lemon juice, salt and pepper. Wrap the foil loosely over the fish, place in a baking tin, and cook in the centre of a pre-heated oven at 350°F (mark 4). Allow 20 minutes for steaks, and about 8 minutes per pound for large fish plus 10 minutes extra in all.

Braising

Large flat fish, such as brill and turbot, can be cooked by this method which adds flavour to their somewhat dry flesh. Peel and finely chop 2 carrots, 1 onion, 1 leek or parsnip. Sauté these vegetables in a little butter and spread them over the base of an ovenproof dish. Lay the prepared fish on top and sprinkle with salt and freshly ground pepper. Add a few sprigs of fresh herbs, such as parsley and thyme, or a bay leaf. Pour over enough fish stock or white wine to come just level with the fish.

Cover the dish and cook in the centre of a pre-heated oven at 350°F (mark 4) until the fish flakes when tested with a fork. Lift out the fish carefully and strain the cooking liquid. This may be used as a sauce and can be thickened with egg yolks or cream, or by fast boiling until it has reduced* to the desired consistency.

Frying

This is one of the most popular cooking methods, and is suitable for steaks and fillets of cod, haddock, hake and eel and for small whole fish such as herrings, mackerel, sprats, whitebait and trout. The fish may be shallow or deep fried.

Shallow frying

(eels, herrings, mackerel, mullet, plaice, sole, trout, whiting). Coat the prepared fish in seasoned flour* or dip them first in lightly beaten egg, then in dry breadcrumbs, shaking off any surplus. Heat an equal amount of butter and cooking oil in a frying pan over moderate heat. Put in the fish and fry until brown on one side; turn it over with a fish slice. Allow approximately 10 minutes frying depending on the thickness of the fish. Remove from the pan and drain on absorbent paper.

Deep frying

(fillets, whole sprats, sardines, whitebait). A deep pan, ideally one fitted with a wire frying basket, is essential. The frying medium is oil or cooking fat. Olive oil imparts the finest flavour, but as it is expensive a good quality vegetable oil, dripping or vegetable fat may be substituted for olive oil. The deep fryer should be no more than half-filled with oil and heated over moderate heat to 375°F. A cooking thermometer will give the accurate temperature; if this is not available, test by frying a 1 in. cube of day-old bread in the oil. If the bread browns in 60 seconds the oil has reached the correct temperature.

Because of the high temperature required for deep frying, the fish must be coated with batter or egg and breadcrumbs.

After frying fish, strain the fat or oil, using a fine mesh strainer or a sieve lined with a piece of kitchen paper. The food particles left in unstrained fat will cause the fat to decompose during storage. The strained oil should be stored in sealed bottles, and used only for frying fish. The oil can be used again and again, provided it is always strained.

Coating batter
PREPARATION TIME: *10 min.*

INGREDIENTS:
4 oz. plain flour
Salt
1 egg
¼ pint milk (approx.)

Sift the flour and a pinch of salt into a bowl. Make a hollow in the centre of the flour, and break the egg into it. Beat these ingredients with a wooden spoon and gradually mix in the milk. Beat steadily until the batter is smooth and free of lumps.

For a lighter coating batter, which gives a crisper finish to the fried fish, add 1 level tablespoon olive oil to the sifted flour and salt. Beat in the yolk of the egg, with 3–4 tablespoons milk, until the batter is smooth. Just before using the batter, beat the egg white until stiff and fold it into the batter. The prepared fish should first be dipped in seasoned flour*, then in batter.

Egg and breadcrumb coating

Roll the prepared fish in seasoned flour*, then dip it in beaten egg. Coat with dry breadcrumbs, pressing them in well and shaking off any surplus.

Before frying, check the temperature of the oil in the deep fryer. Use the frying basket only for fish coated with eggs or breadcrumbs – batter-coated fish will stick to the basket. Fry only a few pieces at a time as overcrowding the pan lowers the temperature of the oil and ruins the coating. Fry the fish for 5–10 minutes, until crisp and golden.

As soon as the fish is fried, lift it out with a perforated spoon and leave to drain on crumpled absorbent paper.

Grilling

This quick cooking method is suitable for small whole fish, round or flat, and fillets, cutlets and steaks. Whole fish should be scored with three or four diagonal cuts on each side of the body. This allows the heat to penetrate more evenly and prevents the fish splitting.

Brush white fish, such as plaice or sole, with melted butter or oil, and sprinkle them with lemon juice or a little finely chopped onion. Baste* two or three times during grilling to prevent the flesh from drying out. Oily fish need no brushing or basting.

Grill all fish under a pre-heated grill at moderate heat. Allow 4–5 minutes for fillets, and 10–15 minutes for thick steaks, cutlets and whole fish. The fish is cooked when the flesh separates into flakes when tested with a knife.

During grilling, whole fish and thick steaks should be turned over once to ensure that both sides are evenly cooked. Thin steaks and fillets need to be cooked on one side only.

Poaching

This is ideal for all types of fish, whether whole, filleted or cut into steaks. Poaching – slow simmering in liquid – can be done in a large saucepan or fish kettle on top of the stove, or in a shallow covered dish in the oven at 350°F (mark 4). For easy removal after poaching, tie a large fish loosely in muslin or place it on a buttered wire rack.

Cover the fish completely with lightly salted water (1½ level teaspoons salt to 2 pints of water). Add to the pan a few parsley or mushroom stalks, a good squeeze of lemon juice, a slice of onion and carrot, together with a bay leaf and 6 peppercorns. For fish fillets, use a poaching liquid of equal amounts of milk and water, lightly seasoned with salt, pepper and 1 bay leaf.

Bring the liquid to the boil over moderate heat, then cover the pan and lower the heat. Simmer the fish until it flakes when tested with a fork, allowing 8–10 minutes per pound. Lift out the cooked fish with a perforated spoon, and use the poaching liquid as the base for a sauce.

Whole fish, such as salmon, trout and salmon trout, are usually poached in a classic preparation or fish stock known as Court Bouillon.

Court Bouillon

PREPARATION TIME: *10 min.*
COOKING TIME: *20 min.*

INGREDIENTS:
2 carrots
1 onion
2 sticks celery
2 shallots
1 bay leaf
3 parsley stalks
2 sprigs thyme
2 tablespoons lemon juice
½ pint dry white wine
Salt and black pepper

Peel and finely chop the vegetables. Put them in a large saucepan with all the other ingredients and 1½ pints of water. Bring to the boil, cover with a lid and simmer over low heat for 15 minutes. Leave the Court Bouillon to cool slightly, then strain it and pour over the fish to be poached.

Steaming

Fillets and thin cuts of fish cooked in this manner are ideal for invalids and young children.

Roll the fillets or lay them flat in the perforated steamer compartment and sprinkle lightly with salt and freshly ground pepper. Set the steamer over a pan of boiling water and cook the fish for 10–15 minutes or until tender.

If a steamer is not available, place the fish on a buttered deep plate, cover with a piece of buttered greaseproof paper and another plate or a lid from a saucepan. Set the plate over a pan of boiling water and steam for about 15 minutes.

SHELLFISH

Small shellfish are served as hors-d'oeuvre, and in soups and sauces. Large shellfish, such as crabs, lobsters and crawfish, can be served either as a first or a main course. If they are bought ready-prepared, they must be used on the day of purchase.

All fresh shellfish must be boiled before being dressed or used in a recipe. Oysters, which are usually eaten raw, are the one exception. Shellfish require little cooking time, and over-boiling causes the flesh to become tough and fibrous.

Most shellfish have indigestible or unwholesome parts, such as the beard of the mussel, and the 'dead men's fingers', or gills, in crabs and lobsters. These parts, together with the stomach sac and the intestinal tubes, must be removed during preparation.

Shellfish are often served with lemon, or vinegar, or with a sharp sauce. The acid in the ingredients is thought to make the meat of shellfish more easily digestible.

Clams

These shellfish resemble oysters, but are smaller, and the shells may be hard or soft. Clams are served raw, like oysters, or they may be prepared and cooked like mussels. Allow 12 clams per person. Both smoked and tinned clams are also available.

Cockles

These small shellfish are usually sold already cooked. If fresh cockles are available, the tightly closed shells should be left in a bucket of lightly salted water for about 1 hour to remove the sand.

Scrub the shells with a stiff brush, and put them in a large pan with ½ in. of water in the bottom. Cover the pan with a lid and cook over low heat, shaking the pan frequently. As soon as the shells open, remove the cockles from the pan.

Serve the cockles cold, with vinegar and brown bread and butter.

Crab

This is usually bought cooked, and has often been dressed by the fishmonger. When buying a fresh crab, make certain that it has two claws and that it is heavy for its size. The edible parts of a crab are the white meat in the claws and the creamy-brown meat in the body shell. Allow 8–10 oz. dressed crab per person.

Wash the crab and put it in a large saucepan with plenty of cold water seasoned with 1 tablespoon lemon juice, a few parsley stalks, 1 bay leaf, a little salt and a few peppercorns. Cover the pan with a lid and bring the water slowly to boiling point. Cooking time is short – a 2½–3 lb. crab, about 8 in. across the body shell, should be boiled for only 15–20 minutes. Leave the crab to cool in the cooking liquid.

Dressed crab

Place the cooked crab on a board and twist off the legs and two large claws. Twist off the pincers and crack each claw open with a claw cracker, a hammer or the handle of a heavy knife.

Empty the white meat into a bowl and use a skewer or the handle of a teaspoon to scrape all the white meat from the crevices in the claws. Set the small legs aside for decoration or, if they are large, crack them open with a hammer and extract the white meat with a skewer.

Place the crab on its back and firmly pull the body (to which the legs were attached) away from the shell. Remove and discard the greyish-white stomach sac which lies behind the head in the shell, and the grey feathered gills known as 'dead men's fingers'.

Using a spoon, gently scrape the soft brown meat from the shell and put it in another bowl until required.

Cut the body part in two and pick out the white meat left in the leg sockets. Using the handle of a knife, tap and trim away the shell edge along the natural dark line round the rim. Scrub the inside of the shell thoroughly under cold water, dry, brush it with oil and set aside.

Finely chop the white meat and season it to taste with salt, black pepper, cayenne and a few drops of white wine vinegar. Mix the brown meat with 1–2 tablespoons fresh white breadcrumbs and season with salt, pepper, lemon

DRESSING A COOKED CRAB

1. *Twisting off the legs*

2. *Cracking the claws*

3. *Extracting meat from the legs*

4. *Pulling the body from the shell*

5. *Removing intestines*

6. *Scraping out brown meat*

7. *Trimming the shell*

8. *Dressed crab ready for serving*

juice and finely chopped parsley. Place the brown meat in the centre of the shell and then arrange the white meat on either side of the brown meat.

Crawfish (langouste)
This is a type of lobster, but lacking the large claws. All the meat is contained in the tail and is usually sold frozen.

Lobsters
These are usually sold ready-cooked, but ideally lobsters should be purchased alive. The shells are then grey-brown, but turn bright red during cooking. Fishmongers supply live lobsters with the fierce pincers secured with rubber bands. The average lobster will serve two people for a main course.

Rinse the lobster under cold running water. Grip it firmly round the body part and drop it into a large pan of boiling salted water. Cover with a lid and bring back to the boil. Simmer over low heat, allowing 20 minutes for a 1 lb. lobster and 30 minutes for a 1½ lb. lobster. Leave to cool.

Dressed lobster
Twist the claws and pincers off the boiled lobster. Using a hammer, or a special lobster cracker, crack open the large claws and carefully extract the meat. Remove the thin membrane from the centre of each claw. The head may be cut off or left on.

Place the lobster on a board, back upwards, and split in half along its entire length with a sharp knife. Open out the two halves and remove the gills, the dark intestinal vein which runs down the tail, and the small stomach sac which lies in the head. The green creamy liver in the head is a delicacy and should not be discarded. The spawn – or roe – in a female lobster should also be kept; it is bright coral red and contained in the tail. It is usually added to the accompanying sauce.

Extract the meat from the tail, and with a small skewer pick out the meat from the feeler claws or set them aside for decoration. Wash and polish the empty half shells and put all the meat back in them. Garnish with the claws and serve with a sauce vinaigrette* or mayonnaise*.

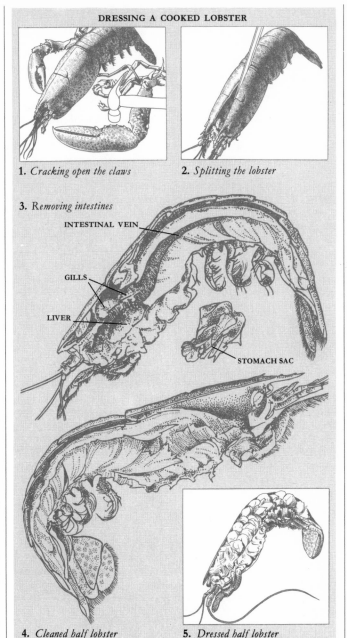

DRESSING A COOKED LOBSTER

1. *Cracking open the claws*

2. *Splitting the lobster*

3. *Removing intestines*

INTESTINAL VEIN

GILLS

LIVER

STOMACH SAC

4. *Cleaned half lobster*

5. *Dressed half lobster*

Dressed lobster may also be served hot. Brush the prepared lobster halves, in their shells, with oil or melted butter, and put them under a hot grill for about 10 minutes. Dot with more butter and sprinkle with a little salt and cayenne pepper. Serve with a butter or shrimp sauce* and a tossed green salad.

Fish

Mussels

These must always be bought alive and absolutely fresh. As soon as possible put them into a pail of cold salted water and throw away any mussels with open or broken shells. If time allows, sprinkle a little oatmeal or flour into the water. The live mussels will feed on the oatmeal and excrete their dirt. Throw away any mussels that float to the surface.

Scrub the shells with a stiff brush to remove all grit. With a sharp knife, scrape away the beard or seaweed-like strands protruding from each shell, and also scrape off the barnacles growing on the shells. Rinse the mussels in several changes of cold water to remove remaining grit.

Put the cleaned mussels in a large, heavy-based pan containing $\frac{1}{2}$ in. of water or white wine, chopped parsley and shallots or onions. Cover the pan with a lid and steam the mussels over low heat. As soon as the shells open, take the pan off the heat and remove a half shell from each. Keep the mussels warm under a dry cloth, and strain the cooking liquid through muslin. Serve with the liquid poured over them.

Oysters

Until the 19th century, oysters were everyday fare, but as the oyster beds became almost totally depleted by indiscriminate gathering, English oysters are now something of a luxury. They are considered to be among the finest in the world, and are served raw as an hors-d'oeuvre, when six oysters per person should be allowed.

Scrub the tightly closed shells with a stiff brush to remove all sand. Open the shells over a fine strainer, set in a bowl to catch the oyster juice. Hold the oyster in one hand, rounded shell up, and insert the tip of an oyster knife, or a knife with a short strong blade, into the hinge. Twist the knife to prise the hinge open and cut the two muscles which lie above and below the oyster. Run the knife blade between the shells to open them and discard the rounded shell. After opening the shell, cut away the oyster with a knife.

Serve the oysters lightly seasoned with salt and pepper in their flat shells, and on a bed of cracked ice. They are traditionally served with lemon wedges and with thin slices of brown bread and butter.

Alternatively, grill the oysters for 3–4 minutes under a hot grill and top them with a little cream and grated cheese. The oyster liquid can be used to flavour a white sauce.

Prawns and shrimps

These small shellfish are available all year round and are usually sold ready-cooked and often shelled. Live prawns and shrimps are grey-brown in colour, but turn bright red during cooking. Drop the live prawns or shrimps into a pan of boiling water, cover with a lid and boil for 5 minutes. Leave prawns and shrimps to cool in the cooking liquid.

The large Dublin Bay prawns are often sold as scampi, though correctly this name should be applied only to the large prawns from the Bay of Naples. Scampi is only available ready-cooked and frozen, but Dublin Bay prawns should be boiled for 10–15 minutes if purchased alive.

To shell cooked prawns and shrimps, hold the fish between two fingers, then gently pull off the tail shell and twist off the head. Peel away the soft body shell, with the small crawler claws.

These shellfish are served hot or cold, as hors-d'oeuvre, in sea-food cocktails, salads, curries, soups and sauces. The large prawns may be coated in batter or in beaten egg and bread-crumbs and then deep fried.

Scallops

Fresh scallops are often sold already opened and cleaned, with the beards and all intestines removed.

Wash and scrub the tightly closed shells of live scallops in cold water. Place the scallops, rounded shells uppermost, on a baking tray set on the top shelf of an oven pre-heated to 300°F (mark 2) until the shells open, after about 5 minutes.

Once the shells have opened, cut through and remove the hinge muscles, and detach the rounded shells. Clean these thoroughly and set them aside – they make excellent small hors-d'oeuvre containers. The scallop, attached to the flat shell, is surrounded by a beard-like fringe which must be scraped off. Also remove the black intestinal thread. Slide a sharp knife blade under the scallop and carefully ease off the white flesh with the coral attached.

Put the white and orange scallop flesh in a pan of cold water. Bring to the boil, remove any scum and simmer the scallops for 5–10 minutes, being careful not to overcook them.

Scallops may also be baked, deep fried or grilled, or served in a cheese or mushroom sauce.

Whelks and winkles

These fish with convoluted shells closely resemble each other, but the winkles are smaller. Both are sold ready-cooked, from stalls at the seaside and in London streets, where they are served cold, with salt, pepper and vinegar. Whelks are shelled before serving, but winkles are left in their shells and must be extracted with a long pin.

CLEANING MUSSELS

Scrubbing the shell

Scraping the shell clean

Cutting away beard

SHELLING COOKED PRAWNS

Removing the tail shell

Twisting off the head

Peeling off body shell

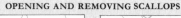

OPENING AND REMOVING SCALLOPS

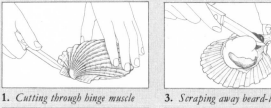

1. *Cutting through hinge muscle*

3. *Scraping away beard-like fringe*

2. *Detaching rounded shell*

4. *Easing scallop from shell*

PREPARING OYSTERS FOR SERVING

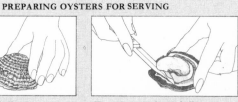

Opening oyster shell

Easing oyster from shell

SMOKED AND PRESERVED FISH

A small group of fish are preserved or cured by salting, brining and/or smoking. There are two methods of smoking, cold and hot. Cold-smoked fish require cooking, but hot-smoked fish are ready for the table, because they have been partially cooked during smoking.

Cod, smoked

Cold-smoked, cook as smoked haddock.

Cod roe, smoked

Ready to eat; serve as an hors-d'oeuvre or appetiser on lettuce leaves with lemon wedges and crisp fingers of toast.

Eel, smoked

Hot-smoked, available whole or in fillets to serve as hors-d'oeuvre.

Haddock, smoked

Cold-smoked. Poach* fillets on top of the stove in a pan of milk, or milk and water, allowing 8 minutes per pound. Alternatively, put the haddock in a buttered ovenproof dish, dot with butter and add a few tablespoons of milk. Cover the dish and bake in the centre of a pre-heated oven, at 350°F (mark 4), for 15 minutes. Smoked haddock is also suitable for grilling.

Arbroath smokies are small, whole, cold-smoked haddocks or whiting. Brush the smokies with melted butter or oil and put under a hot grill for 3 minutes each side.

Herrings, smoked

These include bloaters, bucklings and kippers. Bloaters are lightly salted before being cold-smoked without gutting. Clean the bloaters before grilling them in the same way as Arbroath smokies (see Haddock, smoked).

Bloaters should be used on the day of purchase.

Bucklings are hot-smoked and ready for eating. Serve as an hors-d'oeuvre with a sharp sauce or dressing.

Kippers can be bought with the bone in, or filleted and packed in vacuum-sealed bags ready for cooking. Grill kippers under a hot grill for 5 minutes. Cook vacuum-packed fillets according to instructions.

Herrings, salted

These include rollmops and Bismarck herrings. Both are boned herring fillets preserved in spiced vinegars. Rollmops are rolled round a stuffing of onions, gherkins and peppercorns, Bismarck herrings are flat fillets. Both are ready for serving as an appetiser.

Mackerel, smoked

Hot-smoked, ready for serving. Use for hors-d'oeuvre or as a main course with a soured cream dressing and new potatoes.

Salmon, smoked

Hot-smoked, ready for eating. Serve in very thin slices, with lemon wedges and brown bread and butter.

Sprats, smoked

Cold-smoked. Peel off the skins, brush the sprats with melted butter and put under a hot grill for 4 minutes, turning once. Serve as an appetiser.

Fillets of salted sprats are often sold as Norwegian anchovies. Soak in milk for 1–2 hours to remove excess salt.

Trout, smoked

Hot-smoked and ready for serving cold as a first or main course. Either sharp or mild horseradish sauce may be served with filleted smoked trout.

Meat

It has been said that the British had no need to invent a national cuisine since they have always had the best meat in the world. Home produce is still more highly prized, and consequently more expensive, than imported chilled and frozen meat.

Frozen meat is usually sold thawed, but if it is still chilled or frozen when purchased, it should be allowed to thaw at room temperature before cooking. Fresh meat will keep for two to three days in the refrigerator. Remove the wrapping paper as soon as possible after purchase and wipe the meat with a damp cloth to remove any blood or sawdust. Place the meat on a clean dish, wrap it loosely in plastic film and, leaving the ends open to allow the air to circulate, store in the refrigerator.

Minced meat and offal do not keep well and should preferably be used on the day of purchase. Once meat has been cooked, it should be cooled as quickly as possible before storing. For a detailed guide to joints and cuts of meat, see pp. 34–45.

COOKING METHODS

There are no set rules for cooking meat, as each cut lends itself to preparation, cooking and presentation in several different ways. In general, however, the tender cuts are roasted or grilled, while the tougher cuts are more suitable for pot-roasting, boiling, braising, frying and stewing.

Roasting

This is the traditional method for cooking large joints of meat. It can be done in several ways, oven roasting being the most common, and again there are two methods. With quick-roasting, the meat is cooked at a high temperature which quickly seals in the juices, thus preserving the full flavour. At the same time, however, the joint shrinks.

Slow-roasting is done at low temperature over a long period. This method reduces shrinkage of the meat and produces a joint that is usually more tender than a quick-roasted one.

Whichever roasting method is used, the joint must first be weighed and the cooking time calculated. Put the meat, fat side up, on a wire rack in a shallow roasting tin. Rub a lean joint with dripping or lard first.

Place the tin in the centre of the oven. During roasting the melting fat naturally bastes* the joint; otherwise spoon the pan juices over it from time to time.

Roasting times and temperatures

The size and shape of a joint, and the way in which it has been prepared, influence cooking times. Large joints require less roasting time per pound than small ones, and joints on the bone cook more quickly than boned joints because bones are a conductor of heat. A joint on the bone is considered to have a better flavour than a boned joint.

Rolled joints with a wide diameter take less cooking time than roasts with a narrow diameter although they may weigh the same. Joints which weigh less than 3 lb. should always be slow-roasted for at least 1½ hours. Smaller joints are unsatisfactory for roasting as they shrink and dry out.

Meat thermometer

A meat thermometer, which registers the internal temperature of meat, is useful for assessing roasting times. Before cooking, insert the thermometer into the thickest part of the meat, but make certain that it does not touch bone or fat. When the thermometer registers the required internal temperature, the joint will be cooked. This type of thermometer is particularly useful for cooking beef where there are wider margins of 'doneness' dictated by personal preference.

Spit-roasting

This traditional roasting method has been revived by the invention of the rôtisserie. This device is attached to a cooker and consists of a horizontal revolving shaft or spit driven by electricity or by clockwork. The spit can hold large joints of meat, whole game or poultry and kebabs.

Spit-roasting can be applied to prime joints, but for even roasting the joint must have a uniform shape. Rolled and stuffed joints must be tied firmly or skewered so as to keep their shape.

Thread the meat on the spit so that the weight is evenly distributed, place it on the rôtisserie and operate it according to the manufacturer's instructions. While the joint revolves, it is basted with its own juices and cooks evenly.

Foil roasting

Roasting in foil is becoming more and more popular, mainly because it saves the oven from being spattered with the roasting juices. Wrap the joint loosely in foil, sealing the edges firmly; basting is unnecessary, but remove the foil for the last 20–30 minutes of cooking to brown the joint. Foil wrapping is particularly recommended for slightly tough

Meat

joints as the moist heat tenderises the meat. At the same time, foil deflects heat, and the oven temperature should consequently be raised.

Clear plastic roasting bags are now available – which completely eliminate splashing of the oven, and the joint bastes and browns during roasting. There is no need to remove the bag until the joint is finished.

Pot-roasting

This is particularly suitable for smaller and slightly tougher joints, such as brisket and topside of beef. Melt enough fat to cover the base of a deep, heavy-based pan, put in the meat and brown it over high heat. Lift out the meat, put a wire rack or a bed of root vegetables in the bottom of the pan, and replace the joint.

Cover the pan with a tight-fitting lid and cook over low heat until the meat is tender; allow 45 minutes per pound. Turn the meat frequently.

Alternatively, put the browned meat in a deep baking dish, cover it tightly and cook in the centre of a pre-heated oven, at 325°F (mark 3); allow 45 minutes per pound. Lift out the cooked meat, drain the fat from the juices and use them for gravy or sauce.

Braising

A cooking method used for smaller cuts of meat, such as less tender chops and steaks, and for large offal, such as hearts. Coat the meat with seasoned flour* and brown it evenly in hot fat. Place the meat on a bed of diced, lightly fried root vegetables in a casserole or heavy-based saucepan. Pour over enough water or stock and tomato purée to cover the vegetables; add herbs and seasonings.

Cover the casserole with a tight-fitting lid and cook in the centre of a pre-heated oven, at

325°F (mark 3), or on the stove until tender after 2–3 hours. Add more liquid if necessary.

Stewing

This long, slow-cooking method is suitable for the tougher cuts of meat. Cut the meat into 1 in. cubes, coat them in seasoned flour* and brown them quickly, in a pan of very hot fat.

Lift the meat on to a plate and fry a few sliced carrots, onions and turnips in the fat until golden. Sprinkle in 1–2 tablespoons of flour, or enough to absorb all the fat; fry until the mixture is pale brown. Stir in sufficient warm stock or water to give a pouring consistency, season with salt, pepper and herbs and bring the sauce to the boil.

Put the meat in a flameproof casserole, pour over the sauce and vegetables and cover with a tight-fitting lid. Simmer the stew on top of the stove or in an oven, at 325°F (mark 3), until tender, after 1½–3 hours.

Boiling

Suitable for whole joints, tongues and salted joints. Bring a pan of water, in which the joint will fit snugly, to the boil. Add salt (2 level teaspoons to each 1 lb. meat), a bouquet garni*, a large onion studded with cloves, and the meat. Bring the contents of the pan to the boil, remove any scum from the surface, then cover the pan with a tight-fitting lid and lower the heat.

Simmer the meat over very low heat until tender. Add a selection of chopped root vegetables to the pan for the last 45 minutes of cooking, if the joint is to be served hot. For a cold, boiled joint, leave the meat to cool in the cooking liquid. Drain the meat thoroughly before serving.

Salted joints should be placed in cold water and brought quickly to the boil. Drain the meat and proceed as already described. A very salty joint should be soaked in water for several hours before being boiled.

Grilling

This quick-cooking method is suitable for small tender cuts, such as prime steaks and chops, and for sausages, liver, kidney, bacon and gammon rashers.

Brush the meat with oil or melted butter, and sprinkle with a little salt and pepper (omit salt on beef steaks as this draws out the juices, and on bacon and gammon rashers). On pork chops, snip the outer layer of fat or rind at 1 in. intervals to prevent curling and shrinkage during grilling.

Grease the grill bars of the pan with oil or butter to prevent the meat from sticking to them. Put the meat on the pan and set it under a pre-heated grill. Turn the meat once only during grilling and baste with the pan juices if the meat begins to dry out.

Frying

Another quick-cooking method for the same types of meat as suggested for grilling, and frying times are the same.

Melt just enough butter or oil to cover the base of a frying pan (dripping may be used for beef and lard for pork), and heat it quickly. Put the meat in the pan and cook it on a high heat, turning once only. For thick cuts, lower the heat after the meat has browned and continue frying until tender.

Lift out and drain the fried meat and keep it warm while making the gravy. Pour the fat from the pan, and stir a little stock or wine into the pan juices. Bring to the boil, correct seasoning and pour the gravy into a warm sauce boat.

Bacon rashers need little or no extra fat for frying. Place the rashers so that the lean parts overlap the fat in a cool pan, then fry over moderate heat, turning over, until the rashers are cooked.

Sausages are often pricked with a fork before frying to prevent the skins bursting. This is unnecessary if they are fried over low heat for 20 minutes.

COOKING TIMES

Cooking methods	Quick-roasting at 425°F (mark 7)	Slow-roasting at 350°F (mark 4)	Stuffed joints	Meat thermometer recommended internal temperatures	Boiling	Grilling and frying
Beef	On the bone 20 mins. per lb. +20 mins. extra Off the bone 25 mins. per lb. +25 mins. extra	On the bone 27 mins. per lb. +27 mins. extra Off the bone 33 mins. per lb. +33 mins. extra	+5–10 mins. per lb.	Rare: (flesh and juice are bloody) 140°F Medium: (juices are bloody) 160°F Well done: (flesh brown and dry) 170°F	20 mins. per lb. +20 mins. extra Salt beef: 25 mins. per lb. +25 mins. extra	Steaks (1 in. thick) Rare: 7 mins. Medium: 10 mins. Well done: 15 mins.
Veal	On the bone 25 mins. per lb. +25 mins. extra Off the bone 30 mins. per lb. +30 mins. extra	On the bone 35 mins. per lb. +35 mins. extra Off the bone 40 mins. per lb. +40 mins. extra	+5–10 mins. per lb.	180°F	20 mins. per lb. +20 mins. extra	Chops: 12–15 mins. Escalopes (beaten and crumbed): 2 mins. each side
Lamb	On the bone 20 mins. per lb. +20 mins. extra Off the bone 25 mins. per lb. +25 mins. extra	On the bone 25 mins. per lb. +25 mins. extra Off the bone 35 mins. per lb. +35 mins. extra	+5–10 mins. per lb.	180°F	Mutton: 20 mins. per lb. +20 mins. extra	Cutlets: 7–10 mins. Chops: 12–15 mins. Kidneys: 5–10 mins. Liver (½ in. thick slices): 4–6 mins.
Pork	On the bone 25 mins. per lb. +25 mins. extra	Off the bone at 375°F (mark 5) 35 mins. per lb. +35 mins. extra	+5–10 mins. per lb.	190°F	20 mins. per lb. +20 mins. extra	Chops: 15–20 mins. Sausages: 10–15 mins.
Bacon and Gammon				160°F	Cured bacon and ham 25 mins. per lb. +25 mins. extra. Weigh after soaking	Bacon rashers (¼ in. thick): 5–10 mins. Gammon steaks: 10–15 mins. Bacon chops: 10–15 mins.

BEEF

Allow 8–12 oz. per person from a joint on the bone, and 6–8 oz. per person from boned joints. For average portions, allow a 5–6 oz. steak per person.

Roasting

The best beef joints for roasting include sirloin, the rib joints, thick flank and whole fillet. Topside and rump, too, may be slow-roasted, but are more suitable for pot-roasting.

Sirloin and rib joints are sold on the bone or as rolled joints. Boning and rolling may also be done at home without a lot of trouble.

Boning and rolling (of sirloin)

Lay the joint, bones down, on a steady board. Using a sharp, broad knife, cut the joint across the grain at the thick bone at the top of the joint (chine bone). Insert the knife at the top where the meat has been loosened and move it downwards, following the bones carefully, in sawing movements until the meat comes away from the bones in one piece. Use the bones for stock or a soup.

Lay the boned joint on the board, skin side up, and roll it tightly from the thickest end. Tie it securely with a piece of string to hold its shape. Cut 2 in. strips of pork fat and tie them, slightly overlapping, round the joint. A wider strip of fat may be tied over the top of the rolled joint to provide extra fat during roasting. Remove this piece of fat before carving.

Larding (fillet)

A whole piece of fillet is an excellent, if expensive, joint for roasting. As it has no fat this must be added in some form to prevent the meat drying out during roasting. First trim any skin or sinews

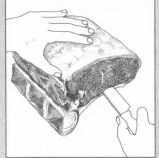
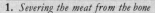

BONING AND ROLLING SIRLOIN

1. *Severing the meat from the bone*

3. *Laying pork fat round the joint*

2. *Rolling up the boned meat*

4. *Rolled joint with fat tied on top*

from the fillet, then cut fat pork or green bacon rashers into strips narrow enough to be threaded through the eye of a larding needle. Thread short lengths of the fat at intervals through the fillet, about ½ in. deep and on all four sides. A fillet encased in pastry does not need larding.

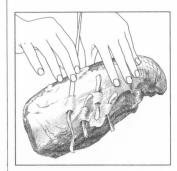

Lard beef fillet by threading short lengths of fat through the meat

Alternatively, wrap thin fat bacon rashers, slightly overlapping, round the fillet and secure with thin string. Fillet should be quick-roasted, at 12–15 minutes per pound, or roasted on a spit when 15–20 minutes per pound should be allowed.

Pot-roasting and braising

Flank, brisket, topside, rump and silverside are the best joints for pot-roasting or braising; for cooking these joints, follow the directions given under Meat.

Boiling

Silverside and brisket are ideal for slow boiling with vegetables. These joints can often be bought salted or pickled, or the pickling may be done at home. See recipe for Spiced Brisket of Beef on page 185.

Salting or pickling

(silverside, brisket)

Put 1 gallon cold water with 1½ lb. salt, 1 oz. saltpetre and 6 oz. brown sugar in a large pan. Bring to the boil and boil for 20 minutes. Strain the liquid through muslin into a large earthenware bowl and leave to cool. Put the meat in the liquid, and keep it submerged by covering it with a weighted plate. Leave the meat in the salting liquid for 5–10 days, depending on thickness. Soak in cold water for about 1 hour before boiling.

Grilling and frying

These cooking methods are suitable for all steaks – fillet, sirloin, rump, porterhouse and T-bone. Follow the general directions, but never sprinkle beef with salt as this draws out the juices. Both fillet and rump steaks are also used for the classic Russian dish, Boeuf Stroganof.

Boeuf Stroganof

PREPARATION TIME: *10 min.*
COOKING TIME: *25 min.*

INGREDIENTS *(for 4–6):*
1¼–1½ *lb. fillet or rump steak*
1 *onion*
4 *oz. mushrooms*
2 *oz. unsalted butter*
1–2 *dessertspoons tomato purée or French mustard*
2 *level dessertspoons plain flour*
2 *fluid oz. soured cream*
Salt and black pepper
Lemon juice

Wipe and trim the steak. Beat it flat between two sheets of waxed paper and cut it into narrow short strips. Peel and finely chop the onion and trim and slice the mushrooms*. Heat 1 oz. of the butter and fry the vegetables over low heat until soft and just beginning to colour. Stir in the tomato purée (or mustard) and enough flour to absorb the fat. Continue

frying over very low heat for 2–3 minutes then carefully blend in the soured cream.

Heat the remaining butter in a clean pan and fry the meat over high heat until brown all over; blend it into the sauce. Season to taste with salt, freshly ground pepper and lemon juice. Serve immediately with fluffy boiled rice and green beans, baby Brussels sprouts or peas.

Stewing

This slow-cooking method is ideal for all the tougher cuts of beef, such as flank, chuck, clod and shin. Stews are ideal for winter meals, they store well in a home freezer, and many people consider them best if cooked a day in advance. A pre-cooked stew must, however, be heated through thoroughly before being served.

The Hungarian stews – or gulyas – are internationally famous and differ from a British stew in their piquant, sweet and spicy flavour. They are ideally made from chuck steak, but lean boned shoulder of lamb or pork may also be used.

VEAL

The flavour of veal is delicate, and the flesh tends to be dry unless carefully cooked. It does not keep well and should be used on the day of purchase. Allow 8 oz. per person from veal on the bone, and about 6 oz. per person of boneless veal.

Roasting

This method is suitable for large joints such as shoulder and loin, both of which may be roasted on the bone or boned and stuffed with forcemeat*. As the meat is fairly dry, it must be basted* frequently. Boned breast is the most economical veal joint. It is ideal for stuffing – allow 1 lb. stuffing to a 6 lb. breast. Use the slow-roasting method rather than the quick-roasting one.

Pot-roasting and braising

Boned and stuffed shoulder and middle neck can be pot-roasted or braised. Stuffed breast is also recommended for braising, allowing about 3 hours for a 6 lb. stuffed joint.

Boiling and stewing

Veal sold for stews and pies usually comes from the neck and knuckle. Both of these contain a large amount of bone, and if bought on the bone, allow 1 lb. per serving.

Grilling and frying

Thick cutlets cut from best end of neck are suitable for grilling, frying and braising.

PREPARING VEAL ESCALOPES

Placing escalope between paper

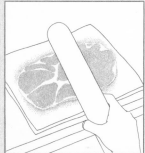

Beating escalope out thinly

For frying, the most popular veal cuts are escalopes. These are cut from the tender fillet, or frequently from the top of the leg. The latter are less tender than fillet slices, and as both are often sold ready prepared it is often difficult to see the difference.

For escalopes, purchase ideally $\frac{1}{4}$ in. thick slices from the butcher. Put them between sheets of waxed paper and beat them flat with a meat hammer or rolling pin. They should be no less than $\frac{1}{8}$ in. thick, and are then dipped in beaten egg and coated with fresh white breadcrumbs. Fry in hot butter for 5 minutes, turning once.

LAMB AND MUTTON

Lamb is a rather fatty meat, and mutton even more so, and the fat which rises to the surface from stewed, boiled or braised lamb should be skimmed off. Dust the basted skin of roast lamb with seasoned flour* to absorb excess fat and to crisp the top.

Allow $\frac{3}{4}$ lb. lamb on the bone per person, and 6–8 oz. of boned lamb per serving.

Roasting

The double or single loin, with the kidneys attached, can be roasted whole.

Whole leg and shoulder of lamb are among the most popular cuts. They are usually sold on the bone, but may also be purchased boned for stuffing and rolling. Give the butcher 1–2 days' notice.

Best end of neck is probably the most versatile joint of all meats. It is relatively inexpensive and can be used in a number of ways. It is the basis of many classic stews – Lancashire hot pot, Navarin of lamb, Scotch broth, to name but a few – but the joint is also excellent for roasting when prepared in classic joints, such as crown roast and guard of honour.

Crown roast

Many butchers will prepare a crown roast if given a few days' notice, but if this is not possible, buy two matching pieces of best end, each containing seven to eight rib portions or cutlets.

Trim as much fat as possible from the thick part of each best end, and with a sharp knife cut the top 1½–2 in. layer of meat from the thin end of the bones. Scrape off all gristle and meat to leave the bone ends clean. When the two pieces of meat have been prepared, sew them together, with a trussing needle and fine string, having the thick ends of the meat as the base of the crown.

Slit the lower half of the formed crown between each bone, about two-thirds up from the base and, if necessary, tie a piece of string round the middle. Fill the cavity of the crown with a vegetable, rice or cranberry stuffing* before or after slow-roasting the joint.

Butchers who sell prepared crowns often put the trimmings of the joint into the hollow crown. These should be removed before stuffing and roasting. (They can be used for stock.) The circle of fat used to cover the trimmings may be replaced on top of the stuffing as it bastes the joint during roasting, but it should be removed for the last 30 minutes.

A guard of honour is also prepared from two best ends of lamb, but the tops of the bones are trimmed clean to about 2½–3 in. The two pieces of meat are then joined and sewn together, skin side up, along the bottom meaty part of the joints. Fold the meat together, skin outside, so that the cleaned bones meet and criss-cross on top. Protect these with foil. Fill the cavity with a savoury stuffing, and tie the joint at intervals to keep its shape during roasting, at low temperature.

PREPARING A CROWN ROAST

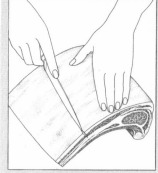

1. Trimming meat from bones

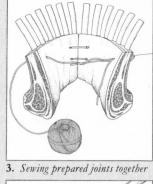

3. Sewing prepared joints together

2. Scraping bone ends clean

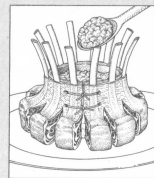

4. Filling the crown with stuffing

Pot-roasting and braising

Boned breast of lamb is the best joint for pot-roasting and braising. It is usually bought already boned, stuffed and rolled, but make sure most of the fat has been trimmed off.

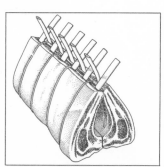

Join together two best ends of lamb to make a guard of honour

Stewing and boiling

Breast of lamb, middle and scrag are the best and most economical cuts for stews and casseroles. As they are all fatty, they should be trimmed of as much fat as possible before cooking.

Grilling and frying

Cutlets, from best end of lamb and with a high proportion of bone, may be grilled or fried. Chops from the loin are thicker and less bony than cutlets, and chump chops, cut from the leg end of the loin, have even less bone and are oval in shape. Both types of chops are excellent for grilling and frying. Noisettes are neatly trimmed, round slices taken from a best end of lamb. Cut off the thick chine bone at

BONING AND ROLLING BEST END OF LAMB

1. *Easing out rib bones*

2. *Rolling up the boned joint*

3. *Trimming off excess fat*

4. *Cutting joint into noisettes*

the thick end of the best end and trim away all excess fat from the meat. Using a sharp pointed knife, cut along either side of each rib bone and ease it out. Roll up the boned joint, lengthways, and tie it with fine string at $\frac{1}{2}$ in. intervals. Cut the rolled joint into 2 in. thick slices and fry or grill for about 6 minutes on each side.

PORK

Pork must be thoroughly cooked to be digestible, and underdone pork can be dangerous. A pork joint should have a moderate amount of fat – lean pork is generally lacking in flavour, and fatty pork is wasteful. Allow $\frac{1}{2}$–$\frac{3}{4}$ lb. of pork on the bone per person, 6 oz. of boned meat.

Roasting

All pork joints are suitable for roasting, on or off the bone. The leg and the loin, both large and expensive joints, together with the more reasonably priced blade joint, have the largest area of skin which gives good crackling.

To obtain the characteristic crackling, the skin on these joints must be evenly and deeply scored. The butcher will usually do this, but before roasting make sure that all the score marks penetrate the depth of the skin and that they follow the grain of the meat. Rub the skin with olive or vegetable oil and with coarse salt to ensure crisp crackling. This can be removed to make carving easier.

Leg and the fore-end of loin are often boned, stuffed and

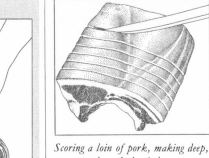

Scoring a loin of pork, making deep, even cuts through the rind

rolled before roasting; hand of pork, which is an awkward joint to carve, should also be boned and rolled.

Boiling

The most suitable joints for this cooking method are fresh or salted hand, salted leg (or the knuckle end) and salted belly pork. These cuts are sold already salted, having been immersed in brine for 7–10 days.

Boiled joints of pork may be served hot with vegetables, but are more often served cold with salads.

Grilling and frying

All types of chops are suitable for these methods. Large loin chops often have a thick strip of fat around the outer edge. This fat tends to curl during cooking, and to prevent this snip the fat with scissors at 1 in. intervals.

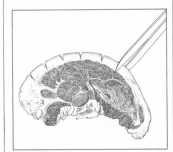

Snipping the fatty edge of a loin chop to prevent it from curling

Lean spare rib cutlets are usually grilled or braised, as are Chinese spare ribs which are cut from the lower rib section of the belly. Belly pork may be cut into $\frac{1}{2}$ in. thick slices and grilled or coated with beaten egg and breadcrumbs and then fried. Slices of lean fillet may be cooked in the same way, but pork fillet is usually stuffed and roasted or braised.

BACON, GAMMON AND HAM

These cured meats are sold as whole joints or as rashers and steaks. They are suitable for boiling and for grilling and frying.

Cooking methods

Whole joints of bacon and gammon should be soaked in cold water for at least 2–3 hours, or preferably overnight, to remove excess salt. They are then boiled or parboiled before being roasted or baked. Joints suitable for boiling and roasting include the fore hock, collar, back and ribs, and the gammon cuts.

Put the joint in a large pan, cover with cold water and bring slowly to boiling point. Cover the pan with a lid and reduce the heat so that the meat is cooked at a slow simmer. Fast boiling hardens the tissue and causes shrinkage of the meat. For a boiled joint, follow the times given in the chart on p. 320.

Lift out the boiled joint, allow it to cool and set slightly, then peel off the skin and serve the bacon hot. Alternatively, leave the bacon to cool in the cooking liquid, peel off the skin and cover the joint with toasted breadcrumbs. Serve cold.

To roast or bake a bacon joint, first simmer it for half the cooking time. Then wrap the joint in foil and cook in the centre of a preheated oven at 350°F (mark 4)

for the remaining cooking time. Half an hour before cooking is completed, remove the foil and peel off the skin.

To finish the joint, score a diamond pattern in the exposed fat, insert whole cloves in the intersections and pat brown sugar over the top of the joint to glaze it. Return the joint to the oven and roast at 425°F (mark 7) for the last 30 minutes. Honey, golden syrup or marmalade may be used for glazing instead of brown sugar. Large gammon joints may be studded with tinned half pineapple rings or apricot halves and basted with the syrups from these fruits.

Cured hams are sold with cooking instructions which vary according to the curing methods. Follow the manufacturers' instructions carefully when cooking these hams.

PREPARING GAMMON FOR SERVING

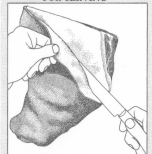

Skinning a gammon joint

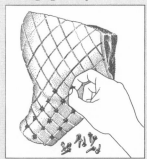

Studding the joint with cloves

Grilling and frying

All bacon rashers (streaky, long and short back, best back) and corner gammon rashers, usually cut $\frac{1}{4}$ in. thick, are suitable for both grilling and frying. Thicker rashers, such as bacon chops, $\frac{1}{2}-\frac{3}{4}$ in. thick and cut from best back, and gammon steaks, are also ideal for grilling. To prevent the fatty edges curling during cooking, snip them as for pork chops.

Before cooking bacon rashers, the rind and any gristle or small bones must be cut off. The rind is easiest removed with sharp kitchen scissors: cut out the gristle with a knife.

Streaky bacon rashers are often rolled up, grilled or baked, and used as a garnish with poultry. The rashers are also used for larding lean meat joints or tied over the breast of poultry and game birds. Before rolling or tying streaky bacon rashers, they must be stretched. Lay the rashers on a board and run the blade of a knife over each rasher. For bacon rolls, rind and gristle must be removed, but this is not necessary for larding.

Removing bacon rind

Cutting away the gristle

Stretching bacon rashers

PREPARING BACON ROLLS

OFFAL

Some of the internal organs, known as offal, of beef, veal, lamb and pork, are edible. These organs include the hearts, kidneys, livers, brains, tongues and sweetbreads. By extension, offal also includes beef and veal marrow bones, oxtail, and pigs' heads and trotters, as well as pork sausages, and black and white puddings. Offal is highly nutritious, easily digestible and generally cheap.

Brains

Calf, lamb and pork brains may all be prepared and cooked in the same manner. Soak the brains in lightly salted cold water to remove all traces of blood. Snip off any pieces of bone and all fibres. Put the brains in a pan of well-flavoured stock, bring to the boil and simmer over low heat for about 20 minutes. Drain thoroughly, then leave the brains to cool and press under a weight.

Cut the cold brains into $\frac{1}{2}$ in. slices, coat them in beaten egg and breadcrumbs and fry in butter until golden brown. Alternatively, coat the slices in batter* and deep fry them. Allow 2 sets of brains per person.

Hearts

Ox, calf and lamb hearts are used. They are usually stuffed and pot-roasted, braised or stewed. Ox heart, however, being very tough and muscular, is better chopped and used in casseroles. Calf and lamb hearts are more tender; allow one heart per person.

Rinse off all the blood under cold running water and snip out the stumps from the arteries and the tendons with scissors. Stuff the hearts with an onion or sage stuffing and sew up the opening. Pot-roast or braise the hearts for $1\frac{1}{2}-2$ hours or until tender.

Kidneys

Ox kidneys are strongly flavoured and are used, chopped, for braising, or in pies and puddings. Calf, lamb and pig kidneys are all suitable for grilling and frying, although pork kidneys are less tender than calf and lamb. Allow two to three kidneys per person.

Kidneys are sometimes sold in a thick layer of solid fat; this must be removed, and the thin transparent skin surrounding the kidneys must be peeled off. Cut the kidney in half lengthways and snip out the central core.

Brush the kidneys with melted butter, sprinkle with salt and pepper, and grill or fry them for not more than 6 minutes, turning them once only.

Fat from lamb kidneys can be rendered down for frying and roasting; fat from ox kidneys is used for suet crust and, after rendering down, is also suitable for deep-frying.

Liver

Ox liver, which is slightly coarse and tough, should be soaked for at least 1 hour in cold water to remove excess blood. It is best braised, although it can be sautéed like calf, lamb and pork liver.

Cut ox liver into $\frac{1}{4}$ in. slices, coat with seasoned flour* and brown in butter together with thinly sliced onion and a few bacon rashers. Put the liver in a casserole dish, with the onion and bacon, cover with stock or tomato sauce. Put the lid on the dish or cook in the centre of a pre-heated oven, at 350°F (mark 4), for 45 minutes.

For grilling and frying, calf and lamb liver are preferable. Cut off any gristly portions and remove, with a knife or scissors, any central cores. Wash and dry the liver thoroughly, then cut into $\frac{1}{4}$ in. thick slices. Brush with melted butter and sprinkle with salt and pepper before grilling the liver.

Alternatively, coat the slices in seasoned flour and fry in butter over gentle heat. Avoid overcooking liver as this toughens it – as soon as blood begins to run, turn over the slices and cook the other side for a shorter time.

Pork liver may be prepared and cooked as calf and lamb liver, and is also used in pâtés, stews and casseroles.

STUFFING A HEART

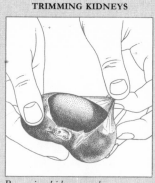

Snipping out arteries and tendons

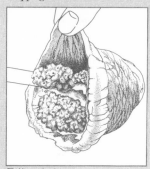

Filling the heart

TRIMMING KIDNEYS

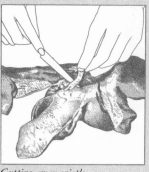

Removing kidney membranes

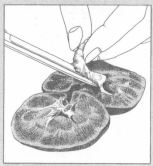

Snipping away the core

PREPARING LIVER

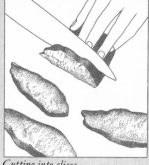

Cutting away gristle

Cutting into slices

Paunch

The stomach of a sheep is used for the traditional Scottish haggis. It is turned inside out and thoroughly cleaned and scrubbed before being stuffed. The stuffing consists of the cooked, minced heart, lungs and liver, seasoned with salt, pepper, cayenne, nutmeg and grated onion. This is mixed with 8 oz. oatmeal and 8 oz. shredded beef suet. The stuffing should only fill half the paunch as it swells during cooking. Add 2 tablespoons white stock and sew up the opening. Wrap the haggis in a clean cloth and boil over gentle heat for 3 hours.

Sweetbreads

Calf and lamb sweetbreads are prepared in the same way. One pair of sweetbreads will serve two people. Soak the sweetbreads in cold water for 1–2 hours to remove all blood. Drain and put in a pan with cold water.

Bring to the boil and drain off the liquid immediately; cover the sweetbreads with cold salted water and bring them to the boil again over low heat. As soon as boiling point is reached, lift out the sweetbreads and rinse under cold running water. Remove the black veins which run through the sweetbreads and as much as possible of the thin membranes which cover them.

Put the sweetbreads in a pan, barely cover with white stock and add a knob of butter and a squeeze of lemon juice. Bring to the boil, cover the pan with a lid and simmer gently for 15–20 minutes. Leave the sweetbreads to cool in the liquid, then drain. Coat with seasoned flour, beaten egg and breadcrumbs and fry in butter or bacon fat until golden brown. Serve with a creamy sauce and sautéed mushrooms. They can be used as a filling for vol-au-vents.

Tongues

Ox tongue is the largest, weighing 4–6 lb. It can be purchased salted or fresh, and is cooked whole and usually served cold. Soak a salted tongue overnight in cold water, drain and put in a large pan. Cover with cold water, bring to the boil, then drain thoroughly. Return the tongue to the pan, cover with fresh cold water and add 6 peppercorns, 1 bouquet garni* and a sliced onion. Bring to the boil, cover with a lid and simmer for 2–3 hours or until tender (cook a fresh tongue for 5–6 hours).

Plunge the cooked tongue into cold water, then peel off the skin, starting from the tip end. Remove bones and gristle from the root end and trim it off neatly. Arch the tongue into a round shape and press it into a deep, round cake tin, about 7 in. wide. Spoon over a little of the strained stock, cover the tongue with a weighted board and leave to set.

Lamb tongues are much smaller, weighing only about 8 oz. each. Soak them for 1–2 hours in lightly salted water. Boil the tongues, with 1 sliced onion, 1 bouquet garni, a few peppercorns and enough water to cover, for about 2 hours. Peel the tongues and serve them hot with parsley sauce made from the stock. Alternatively, press the tongues in jellied stock as described for ox tongue and serve cold.

Peel the skin away from a cooked tongue, starting at the tip

Tripe, ox

This is sold blanched and partly cooked, and additional cooking time varies according to the pre-cooking. Always check with the butcher how much longer the tripe should be cooked.

PREPARATION TIME: *10 min.*
COOKING TIME: *approx.*
2¼ hours

INGREDIENTS *(for 4)*:
1 lb. tripe
3 large onions
1 pint milk
1 oz. butter
1 oz. plain flour
Salt and black pepper
1 rounded tablespoon finely chopped parsley

Cut the tripe into ¾ in. pieces, and peel and roughly chop the onions. Place these ingredients in a heavy-based pan, pour over the milk to cover (if necessary, top up with water). Cover the pan tightly with a lid and cook over gentle heat for about 2 hours or until the tripe is tender. Strain through a coarse sieve and set aside about 1 pint of the liquid.

Make a roux* from the butter and flour and gradually blend in the liquid. Bring to the boil and season to taste with salt and ground pepper. Re-heat the tripe and onions in the sauce, add the parsley and serve.

Marrow bones

The marrow contained in the large thigh and shoulder bones of the ox is considered a delicacy. Have the bones sawn into manageable lengths, scrape and wash them before sealing the ends with a flour and water paste. Tie each bone in a piece of pudding cloth and simmer gently in a court bouillon* for 1½–2 hours. Drain, then extract the marrow with a pointed teaspoon and spread on toast.

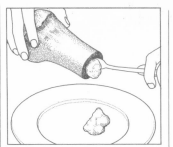

Scoop cooked marrow from the bone, using a small, pointed teaspoon

Veal bones

The bones of young calves contain a large quantity of gelatine which sets to jelly after boiling. Calf's head and feet are ideal for jellied stocks and brawns; they are, however, scarce and pigs' trotters, which also contain gelatine, may be used instead.

Oxtail

Although not strictly offal, this is often classed as such. It is sold skinned and jointed into approx. 2 in. pieces and is ideal for rich stews. As oxtail has a high proportion of fat and bone, allow one oxtail for three to four servings.

PREPARATION TIME: *25 min.*
COOKING TIME: *3–3½ hours*

INGREDIENTS *(for 4)*:
1 oxtail
1 oz. seasoned flour
2 oz. dripping or oil
2 onions
½ lb. carrots
2 sticks celery
½ pint brown stock
Bouquet garni

Trim as much fat as possible from the jointed oxtail and toss in seasoned flour*. Heat the dripping in a heavy-based pan and brown the oxtail over high heat. Lift out the oxtail and put in a casserole. Fry the sliced onions, carrots and celery in the fat until lightly brown, sprinkle in the remaining seasoned flour and cook until it has absorbed all the fat. Stir in the stock gradually, then pour this sauce over the oxtail. Add the bouquet garni*, cover the casserole tightly with a lid and cook on a shelf low in the oven, at 300°F (mark 2), for about 3 hours or until tender. Add more stock during cooking if the oxtail is drying out.

Pig's head

This is often used for making brawn*. It must be soaked for at least 24 hours in cold salted water before being boiled. Calf's head, too, makes an excellent brawn, but is now rarely obtainable except from specialist offal shops.

Sausages

Pork – and beef – sausages are rarely home-produced today. Originally, they consisted of equal amounts of lean minced meat and fat, seasoned with salt, pepper and herbs. This mixture is stuffed into the blanched intestines with the aid of a sausage funnel attached to a mincer. Twist the filled intestines every 3–4 in. Commercial sausages contain up to one-third of their weight in breadcrumbs.

Black and white puddings

Black puddings are made from seasoned pig's blood and suet, and white puddings from white minced pork meat and fat. These mixtures are stuffed into blanched pig intestines and slowly poached before being marketed. Cut black and white puddings in half lengthways or into thick slices and fry in hot butter.

Trotters

Pig's feet or trotters contain a large amount of gelatine and are used, with pig's or calf's head, to produce brawn or jellied stock.

Carving Meat

Boned and rolled joints present no carving problems as the bones have already been removed. But for many people, carving meat with the bone in can be daunting. However, knowing about the position of the bones in the joints makes carving them less difficult. When carving, it is essential to use a sharp knife and a two-pronged fork with a thumb guard. With this equipment, the carver can produce neat slices which leave the joint looking respectable enough to serve cold. Meat may be carved across the grain, because this makes it more tender. Beef should be thinly sliced; pork and veal slightly thicker than beef; and lamb fairly thickly.

WHOLE GAMMON

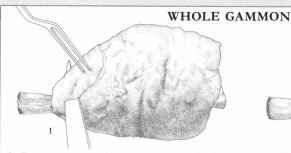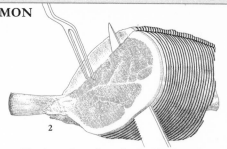

1. Remove a triangular section next to the bone at the knuckle end. Slanting the knife, carve in a 'V' formation along the bone, taking a slice first one side then the other. **2.** Gradually work so that the knife is at an oblique angle, cutting long thin slices. Continue carving to the end of the ham.

WING RIB

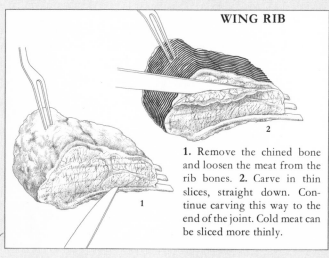

1. Remove the chined bone and loosen the meat from the rib bones. **2.** Carve in thin slices, straight down. Continue carving this way to the end of the joint. Cold meat can be sliced more thinly.

SIRLOIN

1. Loosen the meat from the bone by inserting a knife between the bone and the meat. **2.** Carve the meat down to the bone. Turn the joint, remove the meat from the bone, and slice.

MIDDLE GAMMON

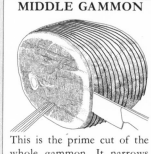

This is the prime cut of the whole gammon. It narrows towards the bone end, so the cuts made into the joint opposite the bone should be thicker at the outside, then taper towards the bone.

PORK LOIN

1. Using a small, sharp knife remove the chine bone and free the meat from the bones. **2.** The crackling on top of the joint can be removed in sections to make the carving of the meat easier. **3.** The loin is sliced at an angle so that the pieces of meat are not too small. The fillet of meat on the underside and the kidney can be cooked with the joint, or grilled or fried separately. Pork should not be sliced as thickly as lamb, nor as thinly as beef.

HAND AND SPRING

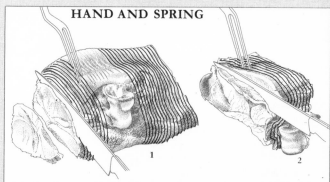

The hand is removed for boiling. Detach the rib bones from the underside and the crackling from the top. The joint is fatty on one side, lean on the other. **1.** Carve slices from each side in turn until the bone in the centre is reached. **2.** Turn the joint over and carve meat from either side of the bone.

SHOULDER OF LAMB

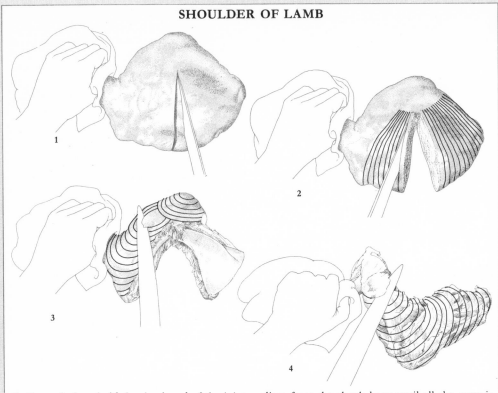

SADDLE OF LAMB

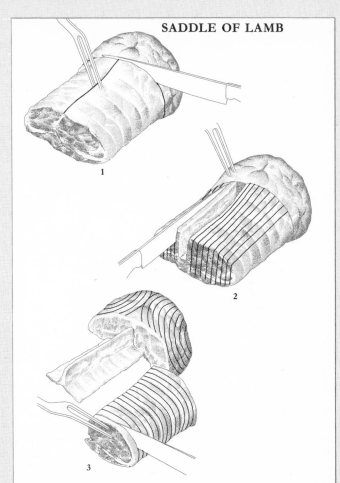

1. Use a cloth to hold the shank end of the joint in the left hand. Turn the joint so that the thickest part is uppermost. From the centre of the shoulder cut a long slice about $\frac{1}{4}$ in. thick down to the bone. **2.** Continue slicing from both sides of the first cut, taking smaller slices from each side of the ridge on the blade bone. **3.** Cut horizontal slices from the shank bone until all the meat is carved from the top of the joint. **4.** As the end of the shank bone is reached, only small slices of meat can be removed. Then turn the joint over, remove the pieces of fat from the underside of the shoulder and carve thin horizontal slices from the remaining meat.

1. Cut across the base of the chump and at a right angle down the centre of the saddle, forming a 'T' shape. **2.** To carve the French way, cut fairly thick slices down the length of the saddle. **3.** The English way is to remove the meat completely before it is carved. The chump end is carved from each side of the saddle in turn, slanting the slices towards the middle. Turn the joint over and slice the fillet lengthways.

LEG OF LAMB

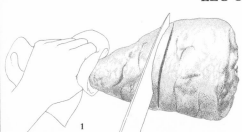 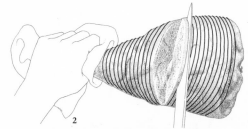

1. Use a cloth to hold the shank end of the joint in the left hand and turn the meatiest side of the joint uppermost. Take two slices about $\frac{1}{4}$ in. thick from the centre of the leg, cutting down to the bone. **2.** Continue slicing both sides of the first cut, gradually angling the knife to obtain longer slices. Then turn the joint over, remove fat and carve horizontal slices along the leg.

LAMB LOIN

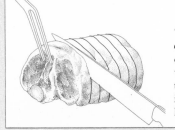

This joint follows on from best end of neck. The butcher will chop the bone at regular intervals in the natural divisions of the bone. The joint is carved into chops when roasted. Lamb loin is ideal for a barbecue.

Poultry and Game

As with many foods which were once seasonal, poultry and game are now available all the year round, because of the advent of freezing. Even so, freshly killed poultry is superior in taste to frozen birds, and game is at its best when it is in season, which lasts from late summer until early spring.

PREPARATION OF POULTRY

Most poultry is sold ready for cooking – that is hung, plucked, drawn and trussed. Oven-ready frozen poultry must be thawed slowly before cooking. It should be left in its film wrapping and placed in a refrigerator or cool larder for 24–48 hours, according to size, to thaw. It must never be thawed in hot water.

Fresh poultry which is not sold ready for cooking must be prepared in the following way:

Hanging
After killing, poultry should be hung, head downwards, in a cool airy place. The length of time each bird is hung depends on the weather and the age of the bird. Chickens should be hung for about 24 hours; geese and ducks for 1–2 days, turkeys for 3–5 days. Older birds a few days longer.

Plucking
Pluck the feathers before hanging, and just after killing, because they are most easily removed while the bird is still warm. Hold the bird firmly on a large sheet of paper and begin plucking at the top of the breast. Take out two or three feathers at a time, pulling them down towards the head.

After plucking, singe the remaining down and hairs from the bird with a lighted taper, wipe the bird with a clean cloth and remove any remaining quills with tweezers.

Drawing
Lay the bird on its back and cut off the head, leaving about 3 in. of neck. Slit the skin along the underside of the neck and loosen it; pull the skin towards the body. Cut or twist off the neck close to the body; remove the crop and windpipe, and any fat present.

Put the fingers of the right hand into the neck opening, palm downwards. Keeping the fingers high under the breastbone, dislodge the entrails, but do not attempt to remove them.

Using a knife, make a slit at the vent end and with the left hand pull out the entrails and any excess fat. Cut the bitter gall bladder away from the liver, and set the heart, liver, gizzard and neck aside for stock or gravy.

Wipe the bird thoroughly, inside and out, with a damp cloth.

Make a slit in the skin around the knee joint at the base of each drumstick to expose the four or five tendons. Using a skewer, pull out one tendon at a time, leaving them attached to the foot. Bend the shank backwards until the skin is taut, then twist the bone to dislocate it. Cut through the skin and discard the foot.

Stuffing
After drawing, poultry is trussed ready for cooking, but it is usually stuffed first. A stuffing improves the flavour and appearance of poultry, and it also makes the meat go further.

Stuffings are based on bread-crumbs – made from day-old

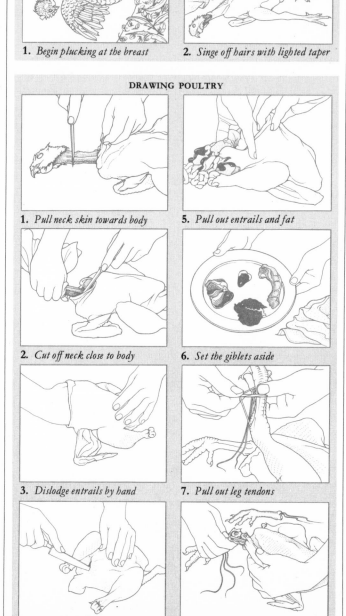

PLUCKING POULTRY AND GAME

1. *Begin plucking at the breast*

2. *Singe off hairs with lighted taper*

DRAWING POULTRY

1. *Pull neck skin towards body*

2. *Cut off neck close to body*

3. *Dislodge entrails by hand*

4. *Cut to enlarge the vent*

5. *Pull out entrails and fat*

6. *Set the giblets aside*

7. *Pull out leg tendons*

8. *Twist and break bone*

bread – meat and rice to which butter or chopped suet is added together with herbs and seasonings. As a stuffing expands during cooking it is necessary to stuff the bird loosely; a basic 4 oz. stuffing or forcemeat mixture is sufficient for a 3½ lb. chicken.

Basic Forcemeat Stuffing
PREPARATION TIME: *15 min.*

INGREDIENTS:
4 oz. white breadcrumbs
1 oz. butter (melted)
1 small onion
Salt and black pepper
1 egg
Stock or water

Put the breadcrumbs in a bowl and stir in the melted butter. Peel and finely chop the onion and blend into the breadcrumbs. Season with salt and pepper; beat the egg lightly and mix into the breadcrumbs. Add enough stock or water to give a moist but firm consistency.

Using a small spoon, fill the cavity of the bird with the stuffing. Chicken is stuffed from the neck end, duck and goose from the vent end. Turkey is usually stuffed from both neck and vent ends.

The basic stuffing can be mixed with 2 tablespoons finely chopped parsley or 1 teaspoon chopped sage.

Celery stuffing
Chop 3 sticks of celery finely and sauté them in a little butter for a few minutes. Add to the basic stuffing. This mixture may be flavoured further by adding 4 oz. dried, finely chopped apricots.

Apple stuffing
Chop 2 medium-sized cooking apples finely. Replace the butter in the basic stuffing with 1 oz. bacon fat or finely chopped streaky bacon and blend in the apples.

Mushroom stuffing

Trim and chop 4 oz. of mushrooms* and sauté them in the melted butter for the basic stuffing. Mix with the breadcrumbs, onion, egg and seasonings.

Rice stuffing

Melt 1 oz. of butter and lightly fry 1 small finely chopped onion until transparent. Add 4 oz. long grain rice and fry with the onion for 2–3 minutes. Season with salt and pepper, and pour ½ pint stock or water over the rice. Bring the mixture to the boil, then cover the pan with a lid. Cook over low heat until all the liquid has been absorbed and the rice grains are tender and separate.

Sausage stuffing

For a large bird, a meaty stuffing helps to keep the flesh moist. Make up the basic stuffing and mix it with 8 oz. sausage meat. Alternatively, melt 1–2 oz. of butter and lightly fry 1 finely chopped onion and 1 lb. of sausage meat for 2–3 minutes. Turn the mixture into a bowl and add 1 oz. white breadcrumbs, salt and pepper to taste, 1 beaten egg and water to bind. Leave the mixture to cool before stuffing the bird.

Trussing

Once stuffed, the bird should be trussed so as to keep it in shape during cooking, and to make it look attractive when it reaches the table. To tie up a bird, use a trussing needle, which has an eye large enough to take a piece of fine string. If a trussing needle is not available, use poultry skewers and string to secure the bird.

Using a trussing needle

Place the chicken, breast down, on a board. Fold the loose neck skin over the back, closing the neck opening. Fold the wing tips over the body so as to hold the

TRUSSING POULTRY WITH A NEEDLE

1. *Fold loose neck skin over back*

6. *Insert needle in first joint*

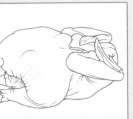

2. *Fold wing tips to hold neck skin*

7. *Tie string securely on wings*

3. *Slit the skin above the vent*

8. *Truss through right side of tail*

4. *Push parson's nose through slit*

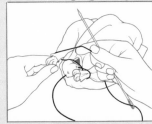

9. *Loop string around legs*

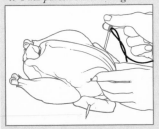

5. *Push needle through body*

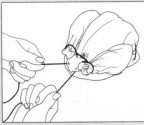

10. *Pull legs closely together*

TRUSSING WITH A SKEWER

Insert skewer below thighs

Cross string over back of bird

Loop string round drumsticks

neck skin in position. Turn the chicken, breast side up.

Make a slit in the skin above the opening at the vent of the body, and put the tail (parson's nose) through this.

Thread the trussing needle with string. Insert the needle through the second joint of the right wing, push it through the body, and out through the corresponding joint on the left side. Insert the needle through the first joint, where the wing is attached to the body, on the left side. Pass the needle through the body again and out through the corresponding joint on the right side. Tie the ends of the string securely.

To truss the legs, press them close to the body; thread the needle again and pass it through the right side of the parson's nose. Loop the string first around the right leg and then around the left

leg. Pass the needle through the left side of the parson's nose, pull the string tightly to draw the legs together and tie the ends.

Trussing with a skewer

Fold the neck skin and wing tips over the back of the bird as already explained, and pull the parson's nose through the slit above the vent.

Lay the bird on its back and, pushing the legs up towards the neck, insert a poultry skewer just below the thigh bone. Push the skewer through the body so that it comes out below the thigh bone on the other side.

Turn the bird on its breast. Pass a piece of string over the wing tips and beneath and up over the ends of the skewer. Cross the string over the back of the bird.

Turn the bird on to its back again, loop the string round the drumsticks and parson's nose, then tie the string securely.

Barding

After trussing, the bird is ready for cooking. If it is to be roasted, the lean breast flesh should be protected to prevent it from drying out. This is known as barding and consists of covering the breast with bacon rashers.

During cooking, the fat from the bacon melts and bastes the flesh, thus keeping it moist. About 20 minutes before the end of cooking time, remove the crisp bacon rashers from the breast and return the bird to the oven.

Cover the breast with bacon rashers and secure with string

329

Poultry and Game

Jointing

A chicken – or duck – can be cooked whole or cut into joints. A small bird can be halved by placing it, back down, on a board and cutting lengthways down and through the breastbone and then through the backbone.

Each half can be further divided into two. Tuck the blade of the knife underneath the leg joint and slice this away from the wing portion, holding the knife at an angle of 45 degrees.

To joint a chicken, pull the chicken leg away from the body, and slice down to where the thigh joins the carcass. Break the bone and cut the whole leg away with a knife. A large leg joint can be cut into the drumstick and thigh. Next, cut down from the breast towards the wing joint, severing the wing from the body, and fold the breast meat over the wing joints. Cut along the natural break in the rib cage to separate the top of the breast from the lower carcass. Divide the top. Divide this breast meat into two or three pieces. The remaining carcass can be used for making stock.

Boning

For a classic galantine of chicken, the bird must be boned whole. Lay the drawn bird on its breast on a board, and remove the wings at the second joint. The feet and first joint of the legs should have been removed when it was drawn.

Using a small sharp knife, make a cut down the centre of the back, starting at the neck end. Carefully cut the flesh away from the rib cage down to the wing joints. Nick the sinews where the wing joins the carcass.

Holding the exposed wing bone in one hand, scrape the flesh away along the wing bone. Cut off the sinews at the end of the bone and pull the bone from the flesh. The flesh of the wing has now been pulled inside out. Repeat with the other wing.

Cut along and down the carcass until the leg joint is reached. Nick the sinews between the ball-and-socket joint. Pulling at the end of the leg bone with one hand, scrape along the bone until the next joint in the leg is reached. Sever the sinews around this joint and pull the bone from the flesh, scraping down with the knife. The legs are also turned inside out as the bone is pulled away. Repeat with the other leg, then continue working down either side of the breastbone, being careful not to puncture the skin. Finally, work the flesh away from the tip of the breastbone and remove the carcass.

COOKING METHODS

Roasting is the most popular method of cooking whole chicken, duck, goose, guinea fowl and turkey. With the exception of duck and goose, which are fatty birds, all poultry should be barded or generously brushed with butter before roasting.

Boiling and steaming is suitable for older birds and joints. The cooked flesh is mainly used in other dishes, such as fricassées and curries. Braising and casseroling are ideal, but slow, methods of cooking older birds or joints.

Grilling or frying is reserved for whole small and young birds, and for chicken joints.

CHICKEN

Boiling

Rub the surface of a whole chicken with lemon juice to preserve the colour, and place it in a pan. Add a bouquet garni*, a peeled carrot and onion, and sufficient water to just cover the bird. For every pound of poultry add $\frac{1}{2}$ teaspoon salt. Bring the water to the boil, and remove any scum from the surface. Reduce the heat to a gentle simmer, then cover with a lid and cook until the bird is tender, after 2–3 hours; chicken joints need only 15–20 minutes. Lift the chicken from the pan and serve hot or cold with a white sauce. Use the cooking liquid to make sauce, or as the basis for a soup.

Braising and casseroling

Lightly fry a whole bird or joints in a little butter until golden. Remove the bird from the pan and fry about 1 lb. of cleaned, roughly chopped vegetables, such as carrots, onions, celery and turnips, in the butter. Replace the poultry on the bed of vegetables, and cover the pan tightly with a lid. Cook over low heat on top of the stove or in the centre of an oven, at 325°F (mark 3), until tender. Braising is a slow process, up to 3 hours, but cooking time depends on the size and age of the bird.

JOINTING A CHICKEN OR DUCK

1. *Cut off legs*

2. *Break the leg joints*

3. *Slice towards wing joint*

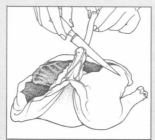

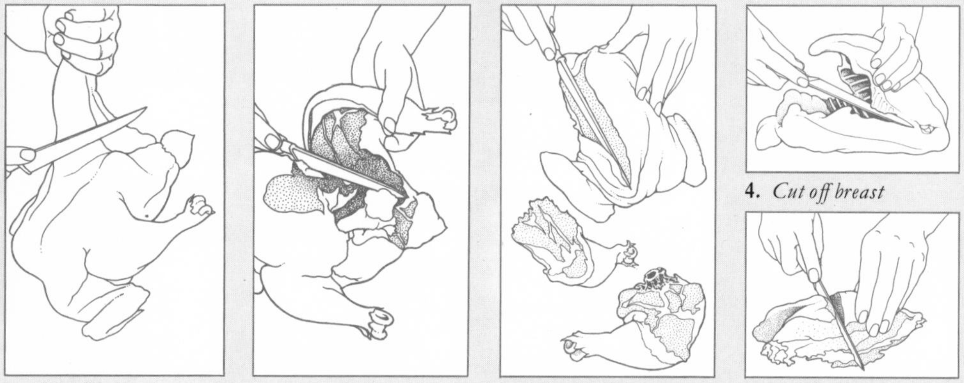

4. *Cut off breast*

5. *Cut breast in half*

BONING A CHICKEN OR SMALL GAME BIRD

1. *Remove wing tips at first joint*

2. *Nick the sinews at wing joint*

3. *Scrape flesh along wing bone*

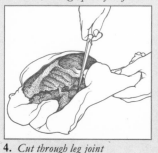
4. *Cut through leg joint*

5. *Sever sinews at leg joint*

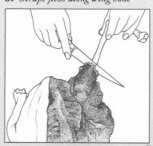
6. *Turn leg inside out*

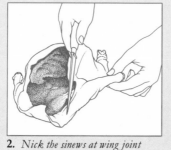

For a chicken casserole, fry the joints in butter until golden, then put them in a flameproof casserole dish. Pour stock, wine or a mixture of both over the base of the dish to a depth of 1 in. Add seasoning, chopped herbs or a bouquet garni, and cover the dish with a lid. Cook as for braising, on top of the stove or in the oven, for 1–1½ hours or until tender. A selection of lightly fried vegetables, such as button onions and mushrooms, baby carrots and small new potatoes, may be added halfway through cooking.

Grilling and frying
Spring chicken, poussins and small guinea fowl are excellent for grilling. One average bird (weight about 1½ lb.) will serve two persons. To prepare a whole bird for grilling, place it on its breast, cut through the backbone and open the bird out. Flatten the bird with a meat mallet, breaking the joints where necessary.

Brush the bird all over with melted butter, and season lightly with salt and pepper. Cook the bird on the grill pan under moderate heat for 20–30 minutes, turning it over frequently.

Before frying chicken joints, coat them with seasoned flour*, or with beaten egg and breadcrumbs. For shallow-frying, brown the joints quickly in hot fat, then lower the heat and fry gently until the meat is tender, after 15–20 minutes. For deep-frying, heat the oil to 375°F and cook the coated joints for 10–15 minutes or until tender and crisp on the outside.

Roasting
A roasting chicken weighing up to 3½ lb. will serve 3–4 persons. Place the barded chicken in a roasting tin in the centre of a preheated oven at 375°F (mark 5). Allow 20 minutes per pound, plus 20 minutes over. A chicken weighing 4–6 lb. will give 4–6 servings. It should be roasted at 325°F (mark 3), allowing 25 minutes per pound, plus 25 minutes over. A capon, with an average weight of 6–8 lb., provides 8–10 portions; it should be roasted at 325°F (mark 3).

Alternatively, loosely wrap the chicken in foil and roast at 400–425°F (mark 6–7), allowing 20 minutes per pound, plus an extra 20 minutes. Open the foil 20 minutes before cooking is completed to allow the bird to brown. Use a skewer to test that the bird is thoroughly cooked. Insert the skewer through the thickest part of the thigh; if clear juices run out, the bird is cooked.

Steaming
Place the trussed but unstuffed chicken on a wire rack or trivet over a deep pan of boiling water. Cover the chicken with foil and steam for 3–4 hours, topping up with more water when necessary. Remove the skin from the cooked chicken and use the flesh in invalid diets or in made-up dishes.

Galantine of chicken
PREPARATION TIME: 1½–2 hours
COOKING TIME: 1½ hours

INGREDIENTS (for 6):
1 chicken (approx. 4 lb.)
1 small onion
½ lb. minced veal
½ lb. minced lean pork
Salt and black pepper
Mixed herbs
Juice and rind of a lemon
¼ lb. mushrooms (optional)
1 egg
Stock
¼ lb. lean ham
8 olives (stoned)

Clean and bone the chicken as already explained. Use the carcass, bones and giblets to make a well-flavoured stock.

For the stuffing, peel and finely chop the onion and mince the chicken liver. Put the veal and pork in a bowl, mix in the onion and chicken liver and season to taste with salt, freshly ground pepper and mixed herbs. Add the lemon juice and rind, together with the finely chopped mushrooms. Beat the egg and stir into the stuffing, with enough stock to give a firm, moist consistency.

Lay the boned chicken on a board, skin side down, and spread over it half the stuffing mixture, to within ½ in. of the edges. Top with the ham, cut into ½–¾ in. wide strips, and the olives. Cover with the remaining stuffing. Draw the long sides of the chicken over the stuffing and sew it neatly together with fine string.

Wrap the stuffed chicken in a double layer of muslin and tie the ends securely. Tie one or two pieces of string round the chicken parcel to keep it in shape. Put it in a large pan and cover with stock. Cover with a lid and simmer for about 1½ hours.

When cooked, lift out the chicken parcel and press it between two plates with a heavy weight on top. Leave the galantine until nearly cold, then remove the string and muslin and return the chicken to press until cold.

Remove the sewing thread from the cold galantine, before decorating and serving it as chicken chaud-froid*.

Roast Boned Chicken
Proceed as for galantine of chicken, but do not tie the stuffed chicken in muslin. Instead, place it seam downwards in a greased roasting tin; brush the top generously with melted butter or oil and sprinkle with salt and freshly ground pepper.

Cover the chicken with buttered greaseproof paper and roast in the centre of a pre-heated oven, at 400°F (mark 6), for 1¼–1½ hours. Remove the paper after 1 hour to allow the skin to brown.

Serve the boned chicken hot or cold, cut into slices.

Coq au vin
PREPARATION TIME: 40 min. .
COOKING TIME: about 1¼ hours

INGREDIENTS (for 4):
1 chicken (approx. 3–3½ lb.)
Bouquet garni
Salt and black pepper
4 oz. pickled belly pork or
  4 oz. green streaky bacon
4 oz. button onions
1 large clove garlic
4 oz. button mushrooms
2 oz. unsalted butter
1 tablespoon olive oil
2 tablespoons brandy
1 pint Burgundy or red wine
½ pint stock
Beurre manié
GARNISH:
4 oz. glazed onions
2 oz. button mushrooms
1 level tablespoon chopped parsley

Clean and truss the bird. Use the giblets with the bouquet garni*, a little salt and freshly ground pepper to make stock. Dice the pickled pork or bacon having first removed the rind and gristle. Peel the onions and garlic and trim and slice the mushrooms*.

Heat the butter and oil in a flameproof casserole dish or pan and fry the pork or bacon until the fat runs. Remove from the casserole. Brown the bird all over in the hot fat, then spoon off any surplus fat. Warm the brandy in a spoon or small pan, set it alight and pour it flaming over the bird. As soon as the flames subside, pour in the wine and add the pork, onions, mushrooms and crushed garlic. Pour over enough stock to make the liquid come halfway up the bird. Cover with a lid and cook over low heat on top of the stove or in the oven, at 300°F (mark 2), for 1 hour or until the bird is tender, turning it from time to time.

Remove the bird and divide it into joints; keep these warm on a serving dish. Lift out the onions, bacon and mushrooms with a perforated spoon and arrange them over the chicken. Reduce* the cooking liquid by brisk boiling, then lower the heat and gradually whisk in pieces of beurre manié* until the sauce has thickened. Correct seasoning and pour the sauce over the chicken.

Serve garnished with glazed button onions*, fried or grilled button mushrooms and freshly chopped parsley.

Chicken liver pâté
Frozen chicken livers are readily available and are excellent for pâtés and terrines.

PREPARATION TIME: 15 min.
COOKING TIME: 10 min.
CHILLING TIME: 2–3 hours

INGREDIENTS (for 6):
1 lb. chicken livers
2 oz. butter
1 small onion
2 bay leaves
Dried thyme
Salt and black pepper
2 tablespoons brandy

Melt the butter and fry the peeled and finely chopped onion, the bay leaves and a good pinch of thyme for 2–3 minutes. Trim away any green bits of gall bladder, and cut the chicken livers into small pieces; add to the pan. Cook over low heat for 5 minutes or until the livers are cooked. Discard the bay leaves and put the liver mixture in a liquidiser until smooth, or mince the liver twice.

Season to taste with salt and freshly ground pepper and stir in the brandy. Pour the pâté into a jar and leave to chill in the refrigerator for several hours.

DUCK

Duck is prepared for roasting in the same way as chicken. Because duck is a fatty bird, it does not need barding or brushing with butter before cooking, but the skin should be pricked all over with a needle to allow the fat to run out of the bird during cooking. Season the duck with salt and pepper, and cook in a moderately hot oven, 400°F (mark 6), allowing 20 minutes per pound.

Duck can also be jointed and braised for about 1 hour in the oven, at 350°F (mark 4).

Because the meat is very rich, duck is best served with sharply flavoured sauces and fruit, such as oranges, peaches and cherries. When buying, allow 1 lb. of duck per person.

GOOSE

Goose is more fatty than chicken, and therefore does not need to be brushed with melted butter before cooking. Before roasting a young bird, stuff it from the vent end, sprinkle with salt, and bard the bird with any fat taken from its inside. Loosely cover the bird with a piece of foil and roast at 400°F (mark 6), allowing 15 minutes per pound, plus an extra 15 minutes. Alternatively, slow-roast the goose, near the bottom of the oven, at 350°F (mark 4), allowing 25 minutes per pound. Serve with apple sauce. When shopping, allow ¾ lb. of goose for each person.

GUINEA FOWL

All the methods of cooking chicken can be applied to guinea fowl, particularly braising. When roasting the bird, bard the lean breast meat well, otherwise the flesh will dry out. An average guinea fowl serves three to four people while a guinea chick will only serve two people.

TURKEY

A drawn turkey is usually filled with two different stuffings. The neck end can be stuffed with chestnut or veal forcemeat, and the body cavity filled with a sausage stuffing*. An average (10–12 lb.) turkey will require a sausage stuffing made from at least 2 lb. of sausage meat.

Chestnut stuffing

PREPARATION TIME: *20 min.*

INGREDIENTS:
1 portion basic forcemeat stuffing
2 level tablespoons chopped parsley
2 oz. streaky bacon
8 oz. chestnut purée
Grated rind of a lemon

Make up the basic veal forcemeat stuffing and blend in the finely chopped parsley. Remove rind and gristle and chop the bacon finely; fry it without any extra fat for 2–3 minutes or until crisp. Mix the drained bacon thoroughly into the stuffing, together with the chestnut purée and finely grated lemon rind.

Veal Forcemeat

PREPARATION TIME: *20 min.*

INGREDIENTS:
3 oz. white breadcrumbs
1 oz. butter (melted)
1 small onion
4 oz. lean veal
2 oz. lean bacon
Salt and black pepper
1 egg
Stock or water

Mix the breadcrumbs with the butter and blend in the finely chopped onion. Put the veal and bacon through the fine blade of a mincer and add to the breadcrumbs. Season to taste with salt and pepper, then add the lightly beaten egg and enough stock or water to bind the stuffing.

Roasting

Before roasting the stuffed and trussed turkey, it should be generously coated with softened butter and barded with fat bacon strips. Roasting methods depend on the size of the bird and the time available. At low oven temperature, the turkey must be frequently basted. At the higher temperature, wrap the bird loosely in foil to prevent the flesh from drying out. About ½ hour before cooking is complete, open the foil to allow the bird to brown.

When buying turkey, allow ¾ lb. oven-ready weight per person, and 1 lb. if the bird is not drawn and trussed.

GAME BIRDS

All game birds should be hung before plucking and drawing to allow the flavour to develop and the flesh to become tender. Most game birds are bought already hung, plucked and trussed (and sometimes barded). Freshly killed birds should be hung by their heads in a cool, airy place. The period of hanging depends on the age of the bird, the weather and individual taste. Young game is hung for a shorter time than old, and warm, damp weather causes the flesh to decompose quicker than cold, dry weather. On average, hang game birds for 7–10 days or until the breast feathers can be easily plucked out.

After hanging, game birds are plucked, drawn and trussed in the same way as poultry, but the feet are left on. They are best cooked quite simply, and young birds are excellent for roasting; they do not require stuffing. Older and tougher birds are better braised or casseroled.

Braising

Older birds and those of uncertain age are best cooked by this method. Before cooking, cut the bird into joints, coat with seasoned flour* and brown in hot fat in a pan. Remove the browned game from the pan and place in a casserole dish. Rinse the pan with ¼ pint dry red wine or game stock. Add the liquid to the casserole, cover tightly with a lid and cook in the centre of a pre-heated oven, at 325°F (mark 3), for 1 hour, or until the meat is tender.

Grilling

Small, tender birds, such as grouse, partridge and quail, can be grilled. Split them through lengthways along the breastbone and flatten the bird; brush generously with melted butter. Place under a hot grill and cook for 25–30 minutes, basting continuously and turning frequently.

Roasting

Before roasting, game birds must be barded with strips of fat pork or bacon. Sprinkle the inside with salt and pepper and put a large knob of butter inside the bird to keep it moist. Place the prepared game bird on a piece of toast in the roasting tin. Baste frequently during cooking and remove the fat strips for the last 10–15 minutes. Sprinkle the breast lightly with flour and continue cooking until brown.

Serving roast game

Small birds, such as grouse, partridge, quail, snipe and woodcock, are served whole on their toast, and garnished with watercress. One bird should be allowed per person. Larger birds are split through lengthways to give two portions. Chips* or matchstick potatoes* are traditional with roast game and so too are fried breadcrumbs or bread sauce*. A well-flavoured brown gravy, a tossed green salad, buttered sprouts or braised celery are served separately.

ROASTING TIMES FOR TURKEY

Weight of bird	Method 1 (325°F –mark 3)	Method 2 (450°F –mark 8)
6–8 lb.	3–3½ hours	2¼–2½ hours
8–10 lb.	3½–3¾ hours	2½–2¾ hours
10–14 lb.	3¾–4¼ hours	2¾–3 hours
14–18 lb.	4¼–4¾ hours	3–3½ hours
18–20 lb.	4¾–5¼ hours	3½–3¾ hours
20–24 lb.	5¼–6 hours	3¾–4¼ hours

ROASTING TIMES FOR GAME BIRDS

Bird	Temperature	Time
Capercaillie	400°F (mark 6)	30–45 minutes
Grouse	400°F (mark 6)	30–45 minutes
Ortolan	425°F (mark 7)	20 minutes
Partridge	400°F (mark 6)	30–45 minutes
Pheasant	425°F (mark 7)	Allow 20 minutes per pound
Pigeon	425°F (mark 7)	Allow 20 minutes per pound
Plover	425°F (mark 7)	30–45 minutes
Ptarmigan	400°F (mark 6)	30–45 minutes
Quail	425°F (mark 7)	20 minutes
Snipe	425°F (mark 7)	20 minutes
Woodcock	425°F (mark 7)	20 minutes

WILD DUCK

These game birds, which include mallard, teal and widgeon, should be hung for only 2–3 days. After hanging, the birds are plucked, drawn and trussed as other game.

Wild duck should not be overcooked. Coat the bird with softened butter, and roast at 425°F (mark 7), allowing 20 minutes for teal, and 30 minutes for mallard and widgeon. For extra flavour, baste with a little orange juice or port.

Serve with game chips*, fried breadcrumbs* and orange salad.

WILD GOOSE

This can be prepared and roasted in the same way as the domestic kind but, as the flesh is dry, it should be barded thoroughly first.

FURRED GAME

This includes hare, which is a true game animal, and rabbit which is now specially bred for the table. Hare is available in the shops between August and February. It is prepared for cooking by hanging, skinning and paunching (removing the entrails).

Rabbit is eaten when 3–3½ months old. Fresh or frozen prepared rabbits are sold paunched and skinned. If necessary, rabbit can be prepared at home in the same way as hare. However, it should never be hung, but skinned and paunched as soon as killed.

Preparing hare and rabbit

Hare is usually sold already hung, otherwise it should be hung by the feet for a week to 10 days. Place a bowl under the head of the hare to collect its blood, which may be used to thicken the gravy. One or two drops of vinegar added to the collected blood prevent it coagulating.

SKINNING A HARE OR RABBIT

1. *Cut off feet at the first joint*

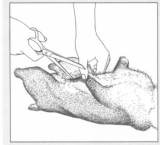

2. *Slit the skin along the belly*

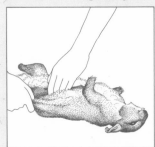

3. *Ease skin away from the flesh*

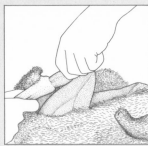

4. *Pull the skin over the hind legs*

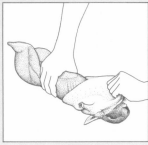

5. *Pull the skin towards the head*

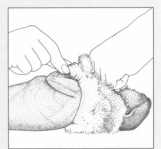

6. *Ease skin off forelegs and head*

PAUNCHING A HARE OR RABBIT

Cut open belly with scissors

Remove all internal organs

Skinning a hare

Lay the hare on several pieces of paper and begin by cutting off the feet with a sharp knife. Follow the six step-by-step instructions as illustrated opposite. On a young hare to be roasted whole, the head is left on, but the eyes removed. On an older animal, the head is cut off above the ears.

Paunching and trussing

Once skinned, the hare must be cleaned or paunched. Slit the belly from the hind legs towards the head with a pair of scissors. Draw out all the internal organs. The kidneys, liver and the heart can be kept and used for sauce. Take care not to break the gall bladder as it imparts a bitter taste. Discard all the other organs. Catch any blood in a basin. Wipe out the inside with a damp cloth.

If the hare is to be roasted whole, cut the sinews of the hind legs at the thighs so that the legs can be brought forward. Press them close to the body and secure with skewers or a trussing needle and string. Tuck the forelegs up and close to the body and truss in the same way as the hind legs.

Jointing

A hare or rabbit is more often stewed or braised rather than roasted whole. Cut the skinned and paunched animal into eight joints. First cut off, with a sharp knife, the skin flaps below the rib cage and discard them. Divide the carcass in half lengthways along the backbone, then cut off the hind legs at the top of the thigh, breaking the bone. Cut off the forelegs round the shoulder bones, then cut each half into two.

If the saddle – the section between the hind legs and forelegs – is to be roasted whole, cut off the belly flaps, hind and forelegs as already described, but do not slit the hare through the backbone.

JOINTING A HARE OR RABBIT

Remove skin flaps below rib cage

Divide carcass in half

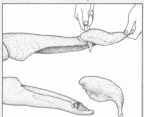

Cut off hind legs at the thighs

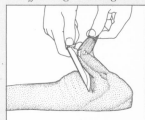

Remove the forelegs

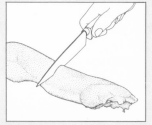

Divide remaining carcass

COOKING HARE AND RABBIT

Braising

This is a suitable cooking method for a jointed hare or rabbit. Coat the joints in seasoned flour* and brown them in hot fat in a pan. Remove the joints from the pan and place in a casserole. Rinse the pan with ½ pint red wine or game stock, scraping up the pan residues. Pour this liquid over the joints, cover tightly with a lid and cook at 325°F (mark 3) for about 2 hours, or until the meat is tender. Add a little more stock or wine, if necessary, and thicken the juices with a little of the reserved blood, soured cream or beurre manié* before serving.

Roasting

Fill the body cavity of the animal with forcemeat* and sew the flesh together. Lay slices of fat bacon over the back and add 2 oz. dripping to the pan. Roast the hare at 350°F (mark 4) for 1½–2 hours. Frequent basting is necessary. The bacon should be removed 15 minutes before cooking is completed to allow the hare to brown.

Jugged hare

PREPARATION TIME: *25 min.*
COOKING TIME: *2½–3 hours*

INGREDIENTS *(for 6)*:
1 hare
1 large onion
2 carrots
2 sticks celery
2 oz. streaky bacon
2 oz. butter
Salt and black pepper
Bouquet garni
Grated rind of half lemon
1½–2 pints stock
1 oz. plain flour
4 tablespoons port

Order the hare already jointed and ask the butcher to include the blood with the order. Alternatively, cut the skinned and paunched hare into eight joints. Peel and roughly chop the onion, carrots and celery, and remove rind and gristle from the bacon. Chop the bacon and fry it in a deep, heavy-based pan until the fat runs. Add the butter and fry the hare joints until well browned, then add the prepared vegetables, salt and freshly ground pepper, the bouquet garni* and finely grated lemon rind. Pour over enough stock to cover the meat and bring to the boil.

Cover the pan tightly with a lid and cook over very low heat for 2½–3 hours, or until tender. Mix the flour to a smooth paste with a little water and stir it into the stew; cook for a further 2–3 minutes. Mix together the port and blood, remove the pan from the heat and carefully stir in the blood mixture. Do not re-heat the stew, but serve at once, with dumplings*.

VENISON

This must be hung in a cool airy place for 2–3 weeks, or until it is slightly high. Using a clean, damp cloth, wipe away any moisture as it accumulates on the flesh during hanging.

Meat from a young deer is delicate and can be cooked without marinating, but the flesh of an older animal is tougher and is usually steeped in a marinade for 12–48 hours before cooking.

COOKING METHODS

Frying

Chops or cutlets taken from the loin of venison are suitable for frying. Trim any surplus fat and gristle from the cutlets or chops and flatten them slightly with a meat cleaver. Season lightly with salt and freshly ground pepper and fry the cutlets over high heat, in oil or butter, for about 12 minutes or until tender, turning them once only.

The fillet, cut into 2 in. thick slices, can also be fried. Flatten the slices a little, then fry over high heat, without fat, for 1 minute on each side to seal the meat. Add butter and reduce the heat; continue cooking for about 8 minutes, turning the slices once.

Roasting

Shoulder, haunch and saddle of venison are large joints which are suitable for roasting after marinating. Cover the joint with a thick paste of flour and water, to keep the meat moist, before roasting just below the centre of the oven, at 375°F (mark 5), allowing 35 minutes per pound. Remove the paste 20 minutes before cooking is completed to allow the meat to brown.

Alternatively, brush the joint generously with oil, then wrap it in foil before roasting.

Serve roast venison with a sharp red currant jelly.

Marinade

PREPARATION TIME: *10 min.*

INGREDIENTS:
1 large onion
1 carrot
1 stick celery
1–2 cloves garlic
Bouquet garni
6 black peppercorns
1½ pints red wine
½ pint olive or vegetable oil

Peel and chop the onion, carrot and celery and crush the garlic. Put these ingredients in a bowl, together with the bouquet garni*, peppercorns, wine and oil. Mix thoroughly and pour the marinade over the venison in a shallow dish. Leave the bowl, covered, in a cool place and turn the meat frequently.

Venison stew

Meat from the shoulder, neck and upper loin is slightly tough, and is best used for stews. It should be cut into 1 in. cubes and marinated.

PREPARATION TIME: *30 min.*
COOKING TIME: *1½ hours*

INGREDIENTS *(for 4)*:
2 lb. venison
½ lb. streaky bacon
2 oz. butter
2 onions
3 level tablespoons plain flour
½ pint red wine
1 clove garlic
Bouquet garni
Salt and black pepper
MARINADE:
1 finely chopped onion
Salt and black pepper
Sprig of thyme
1 bay leaf
6 tablespoons oil
2 tablespoons brandy

Mix the marinade ingredients together and steep the meat for 4 hours, then lift it out, drain thoroughly and wipe dry.

Cut off rind and gristle and chop the bacon. Fry in a heavy-based pan over moderate heat until the fat runs. Add the butter and the peeled, roughly chopped onions; cook until transparent. Sprinkle over the flour and let this roux* brown, stirring all the time; add the marinated and dried venison.

Cook until brown, stirring constantly, add the wine until the sauce just covers the meat. Mix in the crushed garlic, add the bouquet garni* and cover the pan with a lid. Cook over low heat for ¾–1 hour, then stir in the strained marinade and continue cooking until the meat is quite tender, about 45 minutes.

Remove the bouquet garni, and correct seasoning with salt and freshly ground pepper.

CARVING POULTRY AND GAME

The technique for carving poultry follows certain basic steps which consist of removing first the legs and wings and then carving the breast meat downwards in thick or thin slices. When carving turkey, serve each person with both white meat – from the breast – and brown meat – from the body or legs.

Chicken and large game birds, such as pheasant, blackcock and capercaillie, are carved in the same way as turkey. Small game birds, for example grouse, wigeon and partridge, are either served whole, one per person, or they may be cut in half in the same way as duckling.

Whole saddle of hare and venison are carved in the same way as saddle of lamb (see p. 327).

DUCKLING

Small duckling – and some larger game birds – are often jointed after cooking and half a bird is served to each person. Remove the trussing string or skewers from the roast duckling, then split the bird in half with a carving knife or with a pair of poultry shears or strong kitchen scissors. Insert the scissors in the neck end and cut along the centre of the breastbone to the vent; split the bird in half by cutting through the backbone.

DUCK

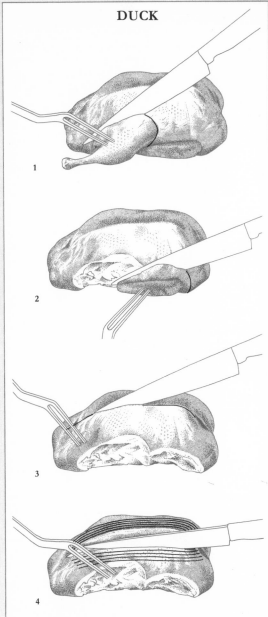

GOOSE

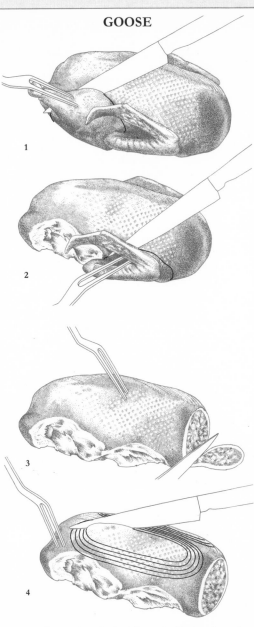

TURKEY

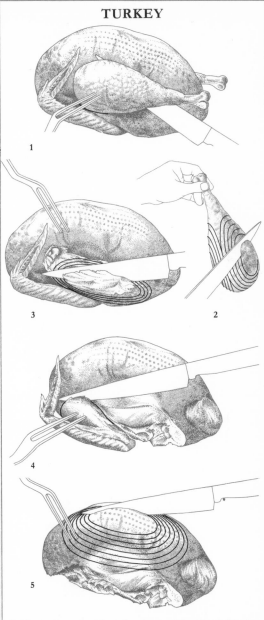

1. Cut off both legs. **2.** Remove the wings on either side of the breast, and detach the wishbone from the neck end. **3.** Slice down the centre of the breast. **4.** To carve the meat from the breast, hold the knife blade at an angle of 45 degrees to the breast, then cut fairly thick, slightly wedge-shaped slices parallel to the first cut along the breastbone

1. Begin by cutting the legs from the bird at the point where the thigh bones meet the body. **2.** Remove both wings. **3.** Cut thick slices across the neck end with the stuffing. **4.** Fairly thick and even slices are then taken from both sides of the breastbone along the whole length of the bird. To remove these slices, carve downwards with the knife blade held almost flat

1. Begin by removing the drumsticks. **2.** Hold the knuckle end of the drumstick in one hand and slice the meat downwards following the direction of the bone. Rotate the drumstick and carve until all meat is removed. **3.** Slice the meat from the thigh bones. **4.** Remove the wings. **5.** Cut the breast meat in thin downward slices from either side of the breastbone

Vegetables

Vegetables are at their best for food value and flavour when fresh. But if they have to be stored, keep them in a cool airy place, such as a larder or in the vegetable compartment of the refrigerator. However, certain fruits and vegetables should not be stored together. Carrots stored next to apples will take on a bitter taste; and potatoes will quickly spoil if they are stored with onions. Cut the leaves from root vegetables before storing, to prevent the sap rising from the roots.

Choose vegetables that are crisp and firm rather than hard. The size is sometimes an indication of age and quality. For example, very small vegetables may be flavourless because they are immature, whereas over-large vegetables may be old, and therefore coarse.

Prepare vegetables immediately before cooking by thorough washing and, if necessary, scrubbing with a brush. But do not soak vegetables at any stage during preparation because their mineral salts and vitamins are soluble in water. Because the most nutritious part of root vegetables and onions lies just under the skin, only a thin outer layer should be peeled away with a knife. If the vegetables are young, just scrape them lightly.

Vegetables can be used whole or can be cut up for quicker cooking. To cut vegetables, use a sharp kitchen knife. When slicing, do not lift the point of the knife from the chopping board but use it as a pivot. Keep the wrist flexible and raise the knife just above the vegetable before chopping down again. Guide the knife with a forefinger down the back of the blade.

Some vegetables – cabbages, for example – may be merely halved and quartered before cooking; but most can be prepared by the following methods:

Slicing
Cut the vegetables into narrow rounds or slices, and divide these into strips. Fine match-like sticks, known as Julienne strips, are used to garnish soups.

Dicing
Slice the vegetables lengthways into sticks; then cut these across into small cubes.

Shredding
Cut thin slivers from the sides of a vegetable, such as cabbage, which has been quartered. Slice evenly and rhythmically, always bringing the knife just above the vegetable before pressing down again.

Rounds
Cut the vegetable crossways to get thick, round slices.

Chopping
Cut the vegetables finely or roughly as required.

COOKING METHODS

After preparing vegetables, do not soak them. Only peeled potatoes need to be kept in water; otherwise they turn brown. Dried peas and beans are quicker to cook if soaked.

Boiling
Perhaps the most common mistake in British cooking is to over-boil vegetables.

Use only a minimum of salted water, and for each $\frac{1}{2}$ pint of water, add $\frac{1}{2}$ teaspoon of salt. Root vegetables are put into cold salted water, and all other vegetables into boiling water.

Bring the water to the boil. Add the prepared vegetables, cover the pan and quickly return to the boil. Reduce the heat and boil at moderate heat until the vegetables are tender but firm. The vegetable liquid can be used to make stock, sauce or gravy.

Steaming
Method 1 – Place the prepared vegetables in a steamer above rapidly boiling water. Sprinkle with salt, allowing 1 teaspoon to each pound of prepared vegetables. Cover the steamer with a tightly fitting lid, and steam until just tender, usually 3–5 minutes longer than the vegetables would take to boil.

Method 2 – Use a wide shallow pan. Melt 1–2 oz. butter in the pan, and add the prepared vegetables. Cover the pan with a tightly fitting lid, and heat over moderate heat until steam forms. Reduce the heat and cook until the vegetables are tender, shaking the pan occasionally.

Pressure cooking
Pressure cook older root vegetables and dried peas and beans. Follow the manufacturer's instructions, and time the cooking with care. Vegetables will quickly over-cook by this method.

Shallow frying (sauté)
This method is suitable for very tender vegetables such as aubergines, courgettes and tomatoes, or for onion slices. Cook these vegetables in butter in an uncovered pan.

Most other vegetables must be pre-cooked or par-boiled before frying. Heat butter, oil or other fat in a heavy-based pan, add the prepared and thoroughly drained pre-cooked vegetables, and fry until tender and golden brown.

Deep frying
Potatoes are often deep-fried, but this method can be used to cook other vegetables, such as onions, which are usually coated with flour or batter, or egg and breadcrumbs, before frying.

Heat the fat or oil in a deep, heavy-based pan to 375°F. To check the temperature, drop a cube of bread in the heated fat or oil; if it browns in 40–50 seconds, the correct temperature has been reached.

Before placing the vegetables in the fat, dry them on absorbent kitchen paper or a clean tea towel. Place a few pieces of vegetable at a time in the fat; cook until crisp.

Braising
This method is suitable for root vegetables and onions. After preparing the vegetables, blanch them by plunging them into a pan of boiling water for 2–3 minutes.

Lightly fry the drained vegetables in butter in a pan. Then add $\frac{1}{4}$–$\frac{1}{2}$ pint of stock to each pound of prepared vegetables. Season lightly, add a knob of butter, and cover with a tightly fitting lid. Cook until tender.

Lift the vegetables out of the pan and reduce the juices by rapid boiling, or thicken with cornflour.

Baking
Brush the prepared vegetables (cucumber, courgette, marrow) with melted butter or oil and cook in an oven set at 400°F (mark 6) until tender.

Roasting
This method is applied to roots and tubers, usually cooked around a meat joint. Place the prepared vegetables in the hot fat and cook at 425°F (mark 7) for $\frac{3}{4}$–1 hour. Alternatively, par-boil the vegetables for 10 minutes, drain, and then add to the hot fat. Roast for only 20–30 minutes.

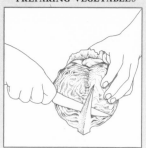

Removing stalk from cabbage

Shredding quartered cabbage

SLICING AND DICING

Slicing turnips into rounds

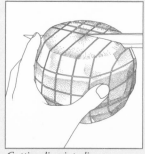

Cutting slices into dice

PREPARATION AND COOKING OF VEGETABLES

Artichokes, Globe

PREPARATION:

Cut off stalk and, using scissors, trim off point from each outer leaf; rinse and drain. Rub cut surfaces with lemon. Chokes can be removed before or after cooking. Spread top leaves apart and pull inside leaves out to reveal hairy choke. Using a teaspoon, scrape away hairs to expose the heart or fond. Remaining leaves around the base can also be stripped away leaving just the fond.

COOKING METHODS:

Boiling Whole artichokes: 40–45 min., in salted water. Without chokes: for 15–20 min. Drain upside-down.

Braising Blanch for 5 min. Refresh in cold water. Place on a bed of sautéed vegetables, moistened with wine or stock and add a bouquet garni*. Cover and cook for 1 hour.

Steaming Whole artichokes: Method 1, for 50–55 min. Without chokes: Method 1, for 20–25 min. Stuffed artichokes: Method 1, for 30–35 min.

SERVING SUGGESTIONS:

Hot: with melted butter or Hollandaise sauce*. To eat, pull out one leaf at a time and dip edible base of leaf in accompanying sauce. Scrape off fleshy base of leaf between the teeth. When leaves are removed, eat heart with knife and fork.

Cold: with mayonnaise*, French dressing* or tartare sauce*.

Artichokes, Jerusalem

PREPARATION:

Scrub and thinly peel under running water; place in acidulated water*.

COOKING METHODS:

Boiling For 25–30 min. in salted acidulated water. Drain. Artichokes can also be boiled in their skins and then peeled.

Steaming Whole artichokes: Method 1, for 35–40 min. Quartered: Method 2, for 30 min.

Deep-frying Par-boil for 20 min., dry, cut in thick slices, dip in a light batter; deep-fry 3–4 min.

SERVING SUGGESTIONS:

Boiled or steamed with melted butter, Hollandaise*, Béchamel* or cheese sauce*.

Asparagus

PREPARATION:

Cut off woody parts from base of stems. Using knife, scrape white part of stems downwards. Tie asparagus in bundles, all heads together.

COOKING METHOD:

Boiling For 11–14 min. in salted water to just below the heads.

SERVING SUGGESTIONS:

Serve 8–10 stems per portion: an average bundle gives 3–4 portions. Hot: with melted butter, Mornay* or Hollandaise sauce. Cold: with French dressing or mayonnaise.

Aubergines

PREPARATION:

Wipe, trim both ends and peel if necessary. Slice, dice or halve. Sprinkle cut surfaces with salt and leave for 30 min. Rinse and dry.

COOKING METHODS:

Frying Coat prepared slices in seasoned flour or leave plain. Fry in butter.

Grilling or baking Brush aubergine slices with melted butter or oil.

Stuffing and baking Cut aubergine in half lengthways. Scoop out the pulp, leaving ¾ in. thick shell. A savoury mixture, including the pulp and other ingredients, is piled back into the shells then baked at 325°F (mark 3) for 20–30 min.; other recipes include moussaka* and ratatouille*.

SERVING SUGGESTIONS:

Fried or grilled with meat; stuffed with Parmesan cheese topping, tomato or cheese sauce.

Avocado pears

PREPARATION:

Just before serving, slice in half lengthways, round the stone, using a stainless steel or silver knife to prevent discoloration of the flesh. Leave the skins on if avocadoes are to be served as a first course with a filling or dressing. The flesh can also be carefully scooped out and mixed with salad vegetables or sea food.

If avocado is to be left for any length of time, toss the flesh in lemon juice to prevent discoloration.

COOKING METHODS:

Baking Peel off skin from halved avocadoes, slice thinly, place in buttered ovenproof dish, sprinkle with lemon juice and seasoning; cover with slices of chicken breast, white sauce, crumbs and butter. Bake at 375°F (mark 4) for 45 min.

SERVING SUGGESTIONS:

Usually served fresh with sauce vinaigrette*, as a dip or a mousse.

Beans, Broad

PREPARATION:

Young and tender beans: wash, top and tail, and cook in their pods. Mature beans: remove from pods. Large beans: remove from their skin after cooking and make into a purée.

COOKING METHODS:

Boiling For 15–20 min., both in and out of their pods. Mature beans, up to 30 min.

Steaming Method 1, for 10–15 min.

SERVING SUGGESTIONS:

Serve small beans shelled or in their pods, tossed in butter, and sprinkled with finely chopped parsley or savory. Serve more mature beans with a white, parsley or cream sauce.

Beans, French

PREPARATION:

Young beans: wash, top and tail; leave whole or cut into 1½–2 in. lengths. Mature beans: top, tail and string before slicing.

COOKING METHODS:

Boiling For 5–10 min. in salted water. Refresh with cold water. Drain well, then re-heat with butter and herbs.

Steaming Method 1, for 10–15 min.

SERVING SUGGESTIONS:

Dress with garlic, anchovy or herb butters*.

Beans, Runner

PREPARATION:

Wash, top, tail and string. Cut into oblique slices 1½–2 in. long.

COOKING METHODS:

Boiling For 5–10 min. in salted water.

Braising Par-boil mature runner beans in salted water for 5 min., then drain. Finish cooking in a tightly covered casserole with butter, savory and sliced onion, with enough stock to cover. Cook for 1 hour at 350–375°F (mark 4–5).

Steaming Method 1, for 20 min.

SERVING SUGGESTIONS:

As for French beans.

Beetroots

PREPARATION:

Cut off leaf stalks 1–2 in. above the root, but do not trim off tapering root. Wash carefully to prevent the beetroot 'bleeding'.

COOKING METHODS:

Boiling Depending on the size, for 1–2 hours, in salted water. Slide off the skin when cooked.

Steaming Method 1, for about 2 hours.

Baking Wrap beetroots in buttered paper. Bake at 325°F (mark 3) for ½–1 hour.

SERVING SUGGESTIONS:

Cooked beetroot can be sliced or diced, and served cold in salads.

Broccoli

PREPARATION:

Wash thoroughly in cold water; drain well. Remove any coarse outer leaves and tough part of the stalk.

COOKING METHODS:

Boiling For 15–20 min. in salted water.

Steaming Method 1, for 20–25 min.

SERVING SUGGESTIONS:

With Bearnaise sauce*.

Brussels sprouts

PREPARATION:

Wash, trim off damaged outer leaves. Make an 'X' cut in base of stems.

COOKING METHODS:

Boiling For about 10 min. in minimum of salted water.

Braising Par-boil in salted water for 5 min. Drain and keep warm. Sauté thinly sliced onion rings. Add a little stock and seasoning. Simmer 5 min. Add sprouts; simmer for further 5 min., and baste occasionally.

Steaming Method 1, for about 15 min.

SERVING SUGGESTIONS:

Tossed with butter, soured cream and seasoning.

Cabbages

PREPARATION:

Remove the coarse outer leaves; cut cabbage into quarters and remove hard centre core. Wash thoroughly, drain and cook either in wedges or finely shredded.

COOKING METHODS:

Boiling Shredded cabbage: cook in salted water for 5–8 min. Cabbage wedges: for 10–15 min.

Braising Par-boil cabbage wedges in salted water for 10 min. Refresh in cold water. Place on a bed of sautéed vegetables. Add bouquet garni* and enough stock to cover. Bake for 1 hour at 350–375°F (mark 4–5). Red cabbage: braise shredded cabbage in butter, add chopped apples, vinegar and sugar to taste. Simmer covered for 1 hour.

Steaming Shredded cabbage: Method 1, for 10 min. Cabbage wedges: Method 1, for 20 min.

SERVING SUGGESTIONS:

Toss boiled white and green cabbage with butter and seasoning.

Carrots

PREPARATION:

Top and tail; scrub in cold water. Scrape young carrots; peel old ones with a potato peeler. Small carrots can be left whole; large ones can be cut into quarters, rings, sticks or cubes.

COOKING METHODS:

Boiling For 10–30 min. in salted water or stock.

Steaming Method 1, for 15–40 min., depending on age and size.

SERVING SUGGESTIONS:

Toss boiled carrots with butter, chopped parsley or mint, or serve with a Béchamel sauce.

Cauliflowers

PREPARATION:

Cut off damaged outer leaves. If cauliflower is to be cooked whole, cut an 'X' in base of stalk. Alternatively, separate cauliflower into individual florets. Wash well in cold water.

COOKING METHODS:

Boiling For 12–15 min., in salted, acidulated water, partially covered with saucepan lid.

Steaming Method 1, for 15–25 min.

Frying Par-boil florets for 10 min. Drain and cool; dip in egg and breadcrumbs, and deep-fry for 3 min.

SERVING SUGGESTIONS:

With white, cheese or parsley sauce. Serve deep-fried florets with tartare sauce.

Vegetables

PREPARATION AND COOKING OF VEGETABLES

Celeriac

PREPARATION:
Wash, slice, then peel, dice or cut into matchstick strips.

COOKING METHODS:
Boiling For 25–30 min. in salted, acidulated water with lid on. Drain.
Steaming Method 1, for 35 min.
Frying Sauté matchstick celeriac strips in butter for 30 min.

SERVING SUGGESTIONS:
Boiled celeriac with Béchamel or Hollandaise sauce. Celeriac can also be puréed, or grated fresh as a salad vegetable.

Celery

PREPARATION:
Trim away root end and remove damaged outer stalks and green tops. Separate stalks and scrub clean in cold water. Remove any coarse fibres and cut stalks into even lengths: 2–2½ in. for boiling; 3–4 in. for braising or steaming.

COOKING METHODS:
Boiling For 15–20 min. in salted water, covered with a lid.
Braising Blanch halved or whole heads of celery for 10 min. Sauté diced bacon, sliced onions and carrots in buttered casserole. Add celery and enough stock to cover. Bring to boil, cover and simmer 1½–1¾ hours.
Steaming Method 1, for 20–30 min.
Au-gratin Sprinkle with grated cheese or breadcrumbs, and bake or grill.

SERVING SUGGESTIONS:
Boiled and steamed with cheese or parsley sauce, made from half the cooking liquid and the same quantity of milk. Fresh as a salad vegetable.

Chicory

PREPARATION:
Trim away outside damaged or wilted leaves. Separate into spears or slice across. If chicory is green, it should be blanched before cooking to reduce its bitterness.

COOKING METHODS:
Boiling For 15–20 min. in salted, acidulated water.
Braising Scoop out the hard core at the base and leave chicory whole. Blanch, if necessary, and drain. Butter casserole, arrange chicory in base and dot with more butter. Add 2–3 tablespoons water and a little lemon juice and salt. Cover and bake for 1–1¼ hours at 350°F (mark 4).

SERVING SUGGESTIONS:
Serve boiled chicory with cheese, Béchamel or tomato sauce.

Corn

PREPARATION:
Strip the husks off the cobs and remove the silky threads.

COOKING METHODS:
Boiling Cook whole corn cobs in water for 5–10 min. Add salt halfway through cooking time.
Steaming Method 1, for 10–15 min.

SERVING SUGGESTIONS:
With butter, salt and pepper.

Courgettes

PREPARATION:
Wash, trim both ends; cook without peeling, either whole, sliced in rounds, or halved with the centres scooped out before filling with a savoury mixture.

COOKING METHODS:
Boiling For 10–15 min. in salted water.
Steaming Whole courgettes: Method 1, for 15–20 min. Sliced: Method 2, for about 10 min.
Baking Par-boil hollowed-out courgettes for 5 min. Drain, brush with butter and season. Bake at 375°F (mark 5) for 25 min.

SERVING SUGGESTIONS:
Sprinkled with tarragon or chopped parsley.

Cucumbers

PREPARATION:
Peel cucumber, cut into strips, slice or dice. If cucumber is to be stuffed, cut in half lengthways and scoop out seeds.

COOKING METHODS:
Boiling For about 10 min. in salted water.
Steaming Method 1, for 20 min. Method 2, for 10–20 min.
Baking Peel, slice thickly, dot with butter and freshly chopped herbs. Bake at 375°F (mark 5) for 30 min.

SERVING SUGGESTIONS:
Boiled cucumber with a white or cream sauce flavoured with dill, tarragon or celery seeds. Cucumber is also used as a raw salad vegetable or garnish.

Endive

PREPARATION:
Discard damaged outer leaves. For salads, separate remaining leaves and wash thoroughly in cold water. Leave vegetable whole for braising.

COOKING METHOD:
Braising As for lettuce.

SERVING SUGGESTIONS:
Fresh as a salad vegetable.

Fennel

PREPARATION:
Trim off top stems and slice off base. Scrub well in cold water.

COOKING METHOD:
Braising As for celery.

SERVING SUGGESTIONS:
Thinly sliced as a salad vegetable or as a garnish. Also used to flavour sauces and fish dishes.

Kale

PREPARATION:
Separate leaves from stems, remove mid-rib from leaves. Wash thoroughly in cold water. Cut leaves in pieces.

COOKING METHODS:
Boiling For 8–10 min. in salted water.
Steaming Method 1, for about 15 min.

SERVING SUGGESTIONS:
Toss with butter and seasoning.

Kohl rabi

PREPARATION:
Cut off leaves around bulb and trim off tapering roots. Scrub in cold water, then peel thickly. Small globes can be left whole. Slice or dice large ones.

COOKING METHODS:
Boiling Depending on size, for ½–1 hour in salted water. Drain.
Braising Par-boil in salted water for 5 min. Braise with a little chopped onion and bacon; moisten with white wine or stock. Cook for 1 hour or until tender, depending on size.
Steaming Method 1, for about 1 hour.

SERVING SUGGESTIONS:
Kohl rabi can be mashed, puréed, baked au gratin and used for fritters. Toss boiled kohl rabi in melted butter, seasoned with finely chopped herbs, or serve with a white sauce.

Leeks

PREPARATION:
Cut off roots and green tops; remove coarse outer leaves if necessary. Cut down through the white part and wash carefully to remove dirt from leaves. Leeks can be left whole or halved, sliced into thick rings or 2 in. lengths.

COOKING METHODS:
Boiling Boil 2 in. pieces of leeks in salted water for 15 min. Sliced into rings, for 10 min. Whole, for 20 min.
Braising Blanch leeks in boiling salted water for 5 min. Drain, sauté in butter for 5 min. Add stock or water to cover and a bouquet garni. Cover and cook for 1 hour.
Steaming Method 1, for about 25 min. depending on the size of leeks. Leeks cut in rings: Method 2, for about 10–15 min.
Frying Prepared leeks may be blanched for 5 min., drained and marinated in lemon juice. Dip in a light batter before deep-frying.

SERVING SUGGESTIONS:
Boiled with a Béchamel or Mornay sauce. Use young leeks as a salad vegetable.

Lettuce

PREPARATION:
Trim off base and remove any damaged outer leaves. Separate the leaves and wash in cold water; drain well if used for a salad. Leave whole if lettuce is to be braised.

COOKING METHODS:
Boiling For 10 min. in salted water. Drain thoroughly and chop finely. Heat butter in a pan and add a little chopped onion, garlic and cream. Stir in chopped lettuce and season.
Braising Blanch 5–6 min. Refresh under cold running water, and drain thoroughly. In a casserole, melt butter and fry a little chopped bacon, carrot and onion. Fold in tops of lettuce to make a neat shape and lay on fried vegetables. Add stock to a depth of ½ in., cover, bake 40–45 min. at 325–350°F (mark 3–4). Pour over reduced* pan juices.

SERVING SUGGESTIONS:
Boiled with Mornay or Hollandaise sauce. Fresh, shredded in green salads, tossed in dressings. Also used for garnish.

Marrows

PREPARATION:
Marrow may be peeled, seeded and cubed for boiling, or cut into thick rings for stuffing. It may also be halved lengthways and deseeded before filling.

COOKING METHODS:
Boiling For about 10 min. in salted water.
Steaming Method 1, for 20–40 min., depending on the age and size of the marrows.
Frying Marrow can be sautéed in butter and herbs for 7–10 min. Shake the pan occasionally.
Baking Whole or halved stuffed marrow can be baked for ¾–1 hour. Serve with a tomato sauce. Marrow rings can be stuffed with a savoury filling and baked in a well-buttered dish covered with foil for 20–30 min.

SERVING SUGGESTIONS:
Toss in butter, or serve with a white or cheese sauce.

Mushrooms

PREPARATION:
Cultivated mushrooms: trim the base of the stalks, rinse mushrooms in cold water; dry well. Field mushrooms: peel, and trim stems. Leave whole, quarter or slice thinly.

COOKING METHODS:
Steaming Cover and cook in the top of a double saucepan with a little butter and salt for 20 min., or until tender.
Frying and grilling Field mushrooms and flat cultivated mushrooms are suitable for frying and grilling. Button mushrooms can be dipped in fritter batter and fried. Fry sliced mushrooms in butter for 3–5 minutes, serve with juices. Brush whole mushrooms with butter or oil, grill under moderate heat for 6–8 minutes, turning once.

SERVING SUGGESTIONS:
Fried, with pan juices, cream and thyme. Button mushrooms as garnish or fresh in salads.

PREPARATION AND COOKING OF VEGETABLES

Mustard and cress

PREPARATION:
Snip the cress from its bed into a colander or sieve; rinse thoroughly in cold water and dry well.

SERVING SUGGESTIONS:
Use in salads, sandwiches or as a garnish for savoury dishes.

Okra

PREPARATION:
Wash thoroughly but do not remove the stems.

COOKING METHODS:
Boiling For 7–15 min. in salted water. Alternatively, par-boil for 5 min., then finish cooking in butter.
Braising Par-boil okra in boiling salted water for 5 min.; braise for a further 30–45 min.

SERVING SUGGESTIONS:
Toss in melted butter or serve with Hollandaise sauce.

Onions

PREPARATION:
Trim roots and peel away papery skins. Onions can be left whole or chopped, sliced or diced. Spring onions need the root removed and the green tops trimmed.

COOKING METHODS:
Boiling Cook in salted water for 20–30 min., depending on size.
Braising Par-boil large onions for 15–20 min. Remove the centres of the onions and fill the cavities with a savoury mixture. Bake for 45–60 min., at 350–375°F (mark 4–5).
Shallow-frying Cut onions in thin slices and fry gently in hot fat.
Deep-frying Slice onions thinly, dip in milk and seasoned flour* before deep-frying for about 3 min.

SERVING SUGGESTIONS:
Boiled with a white or cheese sauce.

Parsnips

PREPARATION:
Cut off roots and tops, peel. If young, cut in thick slices; if mature, cut in quarters and remove the hard core.

COOKING METHODS:
Boiling For 30–40 min. in salted water.
Roasting Par-boil for 5 min. Drain and roast with a joint of meat, or

braise in butter with a little stock.
Steaming Method 1, for about 35 min.; this should be applied only to young parsnips.
Purée Parsnips can be boiled with carrots and pumpkin, then puréed with a little butter and nutmeg.
Deep-frying Cut parsnips into thin slivers and deep-fry like crisps.

SERVING SUGGESTIONS:
Tossed with butter and parsley.

Peas

PREPARATION:
Shell fresh peas. (Mange-tout or sugar peas are cooked, pods and all, in the same way as French beans.)

COOKING METHODS:
Boiling Gently for 15–20 min. in salted water with a sprig of mint and 1 teaspoon of sugar. A little lemon juice helps to preserve the colour.
Steaming Method 1, for about 25 min.

SERVING SUGGESTIONS:
Tossed with butter and chopped mint.

Peppers

PREPARATION:
Wash, cut in half lengthways and remove the stalk, seeds and whitish membrane around the sides. Slice or dice as required. If peppers are to be filled with a savoury mixture, cut around the stalk and lift away the core. Scoop out membrane and seeds.

COOKING METHODS:
Baking Par-boil in salted water for 10 min. Drain, fill with a savoury meat or vegetable filling. Add a little stock and bake at 350°F (mark 4) for 25–30 min.

SERVING SUGGESTIONS:
Hot: with cheese or tomato sauce.
Cold: with French dressing.
Diced or sliced fresh pepper is used in salads or as garnish.

Pulses (dried peas, beans, lentils)

PREPARATION:
Pick over and wash the pulses under running water. Place in a large bowl and cover with boiling water; soak for 2 hours.

COOKING METHODS:
Boiling Put in a saucepan and add salt—1 teaspoon for ½ lb. pulses. Bring to

the boil, cover and simmer as follows: butter beans: 2½–3 hours, haricot beans: 2–2½ hours, lentils: ½–¾ hour, peas: 1–1½ hours, split peas: ¾–1 hour. Pulses can also be soaked overnight in cold water, drained, placed in a saucepan with fresh water and salt. Bring to the boil and simmer: butter beans 1 hour, haricot beans ¾ hour, peas ½ hour, split peas ½ hour.

SERVING SUGGESTIONS:
Hot: puréed with butter and seasoning. Cold: tossed in garlic-flavoured French dressing. Also used in soups and stews.

Pumpkin

PREPARATION:
Wash and cut pumpkin into bite-size pieces. Peel off skin, and remove pith and seeds.

COOKING METHODS:
Boiling For 20–30 min. in salted water.
Steaming Method 1, for 35–40 min.
Roasting For 45–50 min. around a joint of meat.

SERVING SUGGESTIONS:
With a cheese sauce.

Radishes

PREPARATION:
If eaten whole cut off the tops, leaving ½ in. of stalk, and remove the tapering root; wash well in cold water.

COOKING METHOD:
Boiling Cook large radishes whole in salted water for about 10 min.

SERVING SUGGESTIONS:
As a raw salad vegetable or as a garnish for savoury dishes. Serve boiled radishes with a well-seasoned parsley sauce.

Salsify

PREPARATION:
Scrub well in cold water, cut off top and tapering root end. Scrape off skin, cut into 1–2 in. lengths. Plunge immediately into cold, acidulated water.

COOKING METHOD:
Boiling For 45 min. in salted water.

SERVING SUGGESTIONS:
With a butter, white or Bearnaise sauce. Use leaves in salads or cooked as a green vegetable.

Seakale

PREPARATION:
Trim roots; wash under cold running water. Tie the stalks in bundles.

COOKING METHODS:
Boiling For 25 min. in salted acidulated water. Drain.
Steaming Method 1, for 30 min.

SERVING SUGGESTIONS:
Boiled or steamed with Béchamel, cheese or Bearnaise sauce. Cold with French dressing. The leaf ends can be used in salads.

Seakale beet, chard

PREPARATION:
Prepare and cook white leaf stalks as for seakale; the green leaves as spinach.

Shallots

PREPARATION:
Prepare and cook as for onion.

SERVING SUGGESTIONS:
Used to flavour stocks and soups.

Silver beet

PREPARATION:
Trim ribs free of green leaves; wash thoroughly. Tie ribs in bundles.

COOKING METHODS:
Leaves and ribs can be cooked as separate vegetables. Cook the leaves as for spinach, ribs as for celery.

Spinach

PREPARATION:
Wash spinach several times in cold water to remove dirt and grit. Do not dry, but place in a saucepan with no extra water.

COOKING METHOD:
Boiling Sprinkle leaves with a little salt; cover and cook gently, shaking the pan occasionally for about 10 min. Drain thoroughly.

SERVING SUGGESTIONS:
Re-heat with cream and seasoning, chop finely or make into a purée.

Swedes

PREPARATION:
Trim stalk and root ends, peel thickly and cut in ½–1 in. cubes.

COOKING METHODS:
Boiling For 30–40 min. in salted water. Drain and dry out over gentle heat.

SERVING SUGGESTIONS:
Toss with melted butter and seasoning; or mash with butter, nutmeg and salt. Use in stews and casseroles.

Sweet potatoes

PREPARATION:
Scrub well and peel, if necessary.

COOKING METHODS:
Boiling Cook in jackets in salted water, covered, for about 25 min. If peeled, cook uncovered for 15 min.

SERVING SUGGESTIONS:
As potatoes.

Tomatoes

PREPARATION:
Remove stalk if necessary. To skin: see illustrations.

COOKING METHODS:
Grilling Cut tomato in half, top with a small knob of butter and season. Grill under moderate heat for 5–10 min.
Baking Prepare tomatoes as above or leave whole. Arrange in a shallow greased baking dish. Bake at 350°F (mark 4) for 15 min. Whole tomatoes should be placed stalk end down, cut crossways on top and brushed with oil, before baking.

SERVING SUGGESTIONS:
Hot: as first course or accompaniment to savoury dishes. Cold: sliced or quartered in salads and as garnish.

Turnips

PREPARATION:
Wash, trim stalk ends and tapering roots. Peel thickly. Small young turnips can be left whole; large ones should be quartered.

COOKING METHODS:
Boiling For 25–30 min. in salted water.
Steaming Method 1, for 30–40 min.

SERVING SUGGESTIONS:
Toss in parsley and butter, or serve with a white sauce.

Watercress

PREPARATION:
Wash thoroughly in cold water and drain well.

SERVING SUGGESTIONS:
Watercress is used in salads or as a garnish for savoury dishes. Chopped watercress can be mixed with salad vegetables or mixed into sauces and mayonnaise.

Vegetables

PREPARING GLOBE ARTICHOKES FOR COOKING

1. *Cutting stalk off artichoke*

2. *Slicing off top leaves*

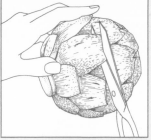

3. *Trimming points off leaves*

4. *Removing choke from fond*

CHICORY

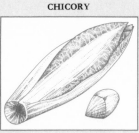

Cutting out the white bitter root at the base of blanched chicory

CORN ON THE COB

Stripping the green husks and silky threads from corn on the cob

TWO WAYS OF SKINNING FRESH TOMATOES

1. *Put in hot water for 1 min.*

2. *Peel soft skin from wet tomato*

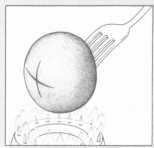

1. *Hold tomato over open gas flame*

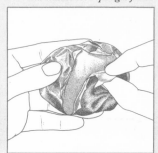

2. *Peel away charred tomato skin*

ASPARAGUS

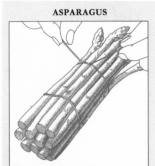

Tying bundles with fine string

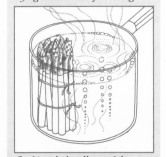

Cooking the bundles upright

MARROW

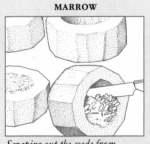

Scraping out the seeds from peeled marrow slices

MUSHROOMS

Trim by removing stalks, and peeling ragged skin

PEPPERS

Slicing peppers from which stalk and seeds have been removed

CAULIFLOWER

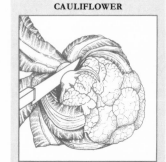

Removing tough stalk and leaves

Breaking away small florets

PEELING, SLICING AND CHOPPING ONION

Peel off skin and trim root. Cut onion in half, through the root, then cut downwards in slices. To chop, turn the onion and slice across the first cuts. To dice, chop again across these cuts

POTATOES

Potatoes fall into two main categories: early and maincrop.

Early potatoes are best boiled, chipped, roasted or used in salads. When buying early potatoes, check that any soil on them is damp and that the skin rubs off; these are signs of freshness.

Maincrop potatoes can be jacket-baked, roasted, chipped and used in potato salads.

PREPARATION OF POTATOES

New potatoes need only be washed, scraped lightly, and washed again. They may also be boiled in their skins and peeled before serving, to save scraping time. Old potatoes should be washed well, peeled thinly, and then cut into even-sized pieces, and cooked as soon as possible.

A pound of old potatoes gives about 3 portions; a pound of new ones about 4 portions.

COOKING METHODS

Boiled

Cut the potatoes into even-sized pieces and put into cold salted water; bring to the boil and simmer under lid about 15–20 minutes for new potatoes and about 20 minutes for old potatoes.

Mashed

Boil old potatoes. Drain well, and dry the potatoes in the pan over low heat. Using a potato masher or a fork, mash the potatoes in the pan until free of lumps. Alternatively, rub the potatoes through a sieve on to a dish.

Creamed

Put mashed potatoes in a clean pan. To each pound of potatoes add 1 oz. of butter, a little milk and seasoning, and put the pan over gentle heat; beat the mixture until light and fluffy. For a smoother mixture beat in 1 egg.

Duchesse potatoes

Prepare a portion of creamed potatoes with an egg and put the mixture in a piping bag. Pipe into mounds, about 2 in. high, on a lightly greased baking tray, or into a border round a shallow ovenproof dish. Bake near the top of the oven at 400°F (mark 6) for about 25 minutes, or until golden.

Potato croquettes

Prepare creamed potatoes. Roll the mixture into small balls, and coat thickly with egg and breadcrumbs. In a frying pan heat the fat to 375°F – at this temperature a cube of bread dropped into the fat should brown in 40–50 seconds. Fry the croquettes for 2–3 minutes, drain thoroughly and fry again, at the same temperature, for 2–3 minutes.

Fried (or sautéed)

Boil potatoes until they are almost cooked, and cut them into slices about $\frac{1}{4}$ in. thick. Fry in hot fat, turning them until crisp and golden brown on both sides.

Chips

Peel old potatoes and cut them into $\frac{1}{4}$–$\frac{1}{2}$ in. slices. Cut these slices into strips $\frac{1}{4}$–$\frac{1}{2}$ in. wide. Soak in cold water. Drain well and dry thoroughly before using. Put some fat into a fryer (or a deep saucepan) and heat to 385°F. When a chip dropped in the fat rises to the surface, surrounded by bubbles, the fat is hot enough for frying. Place a layer of chips in a wire basket and lower into the fryer; cook for 4–6 minutes, or until golden. Drain well on absorbent paper. Just before serving, fry all the chips again for 1–2 minutes. Drain, sprinkle with a little salt, and serve.

Matchstick chips

Peel old potatoes and cut them into very small chips, about the size of matchsticks. Cook in the same way as chips, allowing a shorter cooking time – about 3 minutes for the first frying.

Crisps (game chips)

Peel and wash the potatoes. Cut into thin rounds. Soak in cold water, dry, and fry in hot fat in the same way as chipped potatoes. For the first frying, allow only 3 minutes.

Jacket-baked

Select good-sized old potatoes, allowing one per person. Scrub, wash, dry and prick all over with a fork. Cut a small cross through the skin on the upper side of the potato. Bake near the top of an oven set at 400°F (mark 6). Cut through the cross and open up the potato. Top with a knob of butter.

Anna potatoes

Peel old or new potatoes and slice them thinly. Arrange the slices in layers in a well-greased ovenproof dish. Sprinkle each layer with salt, pepper and melted butter. Cover the dish lightly with buttered greaseproof paper or foil and bake for 1 hour in the centre of the oven, at 375°F (mark 5). Serve at once.

Roasted

Select old potatoes. Peel and cut them into even-sized pieces. Parboil for 5 minutes, then drain well. Place in a roasting tin with melted lard or dripping, and roast near the top of the oven at 425°F (mark 7) for 40 minutes, turning once. When golden brown, drain on absorbent paper.

Alternatively, put the cut potatoes around a meat joint to roast for the last 50–60 minutes of cooking time.

FRESH HERBS AND THEIR USE

Fresh – or dried – herbs are much used in cooking to impart additional flavour to a dish. The choice of herb is entirely personal, but certain herbs go particularly well with certain foods.

Basil Use with oily fish, roast lamb, chicken, duck and goose. Also with tomato dishes.

Bay Use in bouquet garni*; with oily fish, pork, veal, goose and in pâtés and terrines.

Chervil As garnish to soups, with delicate fish and shellfish. Also in salads and herb butters.

Dill Use to flavour sauces, salad dressings and mayonnaise. As garnish to fish soups, and to flavour lamb and mutton stews.

Fennel Use with roast lamb and mutton, oily fish and to flavour sauces. Fennel seeds are ideal with roast pork and chicken.

Garlic The traditional French flavouring, particularly with tomato and shellfish dishes. Much used in stews, dressings and herb butters.

Marjoram Ideal with strongly flavoured oily fish, also with roast lamb, pork and veal, chicken, duck and partridge. A favourite herb with tomato dishes. Marjoram may be used as substitute for the Italian herb origano.

Mint Fresh mint sauce is traditional with roast lamb and mutton. Use to flavour peas, new potatoes and carrots. Fresh leaves are used as a garnish with fresh fruit salads and iced tea.

Parsley The traditional garnish with fish and many soups. Used to flavour sauces and vegetable dishes. A necessary ingredient of bouquet garni and maître-d'hôtel butter.

Rosemary A favourite herb with oily grilled fish, and much used to flavour roast lamb, pork, duck and goose. May also be added to casseroled potatoes.

Sage Mainly used in stuffings for pork, chicken and duck. Also used to flavour oily fish, especially eel.

Savory Summer savory has a more delicate mint flavour than winter savory. Both are used to flavour salads and soups, grilled fish and egg dishes. Especially good with runner beans.

Tarragon Use to flavour white wine vinegar for pickling and in salad dressings and mayonnaise. Excellent with oily fish, in omelettes and for herb butters.

Thyme The traditional ingredient of a bouquet garni. Use to flavour oily fish, and roast pork, veal and poultry.

Eggs

Eggs are probably the most useful of all foods. There is no waste on them apart from the shell. They are rich in vitamin B2, fairly rich in protein and low in calories: a 2 oz. egg contains only 90 calories – fewer than 1 oz. of cheese. They can be boiled, fried, baked, poached or scrambled and used for meringues. Added to other foods, eggs act as a raising agent in soufflés, cakes and pastry, and as an emulsifying agent in mayonnaise and salad dressings. They are used to thicken soups and sauces, to bind stuffings and croquette mixtures, and as a crisp coating for fried food.

Freshness
Test an egg for freshness by lowering it into a bowl of water. If it lies on its side it is quite fresh; if it stands on end it is less fresh; and if it floats to the top it is stale and possibly bad. When broken, a fresh egg smells pleasant, the yolk is round and firm and the white evenly distributed. A stale egg usually has a slight smell, and spreads out thinly when broken.

Storing eggs
Eggs kept at normal room temperature, about 18°C (65°F), will stay fresh for about 10 days, but they are better stored in a cool larder. In the refrigerator they will keep for as long as 2 months. Remove the eggs from the refrigerator at least 45 minutes before using.

Separated eggs should be stored in the refrigerator, in separate covered containers. Pour a thin layer of milk or water over the yolks to prevent them hardening. Yolks can be stored for 4 days, but whites should not be kept for more than 2–3 days.

Separating eggs
Knock the egg sharply against the rim of a bowl or cup to break the shell in half. Slip the yolk from one half-shell to the other until all the white has drained into the bowl, then slide the yolk into another bowl.

Beating eggs
Whole eggs should be beaten vigorously, turning them over with upward movements, using a fork, spoon, whisk or electric mixer. Beating draws in air and so increases the volume of the eggs; the biggest volume is obtained from eggs beaten in a warm room – at a temperature of 24°C (75°F). Beaten eggs must be used immediately before they lose air.

SEPARATING FRESH EGGS

Break the shell in half

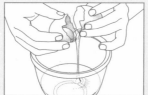
Drain egg white from shells

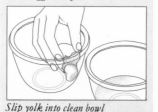
Slip yolk into clean bowl

When mixing egg yolks and sugar, beat the yolks first, then add the sugar and continue beating until the mixture drops in broad ribbons.

Egg whites, beaten to a stiff but not dry foam, are used for soufflés or meringues. Use a spotlessly clean and dry bowl, of a shape which keeps the whisk in constant contact with the egg whites.

Folding in egg whites
Pile the beaten egg whites on top of the mixture, and with a metal spoon draw part of the mixture from the bottom of the bowl over the whites. Incorporate all the whites carefully so that they do not lose their air content.

Baked eggs (eggs en cocotte)
Melt ½ oz. of butter in a small, fireproof dish, break an egg into a cup and slide it into the dish. Season lightly with salt and freshly ground pepper. Bake in the centre of a pre-heated oven at 350°F (mark 4) for 8–10 minutes or until the white is just set. Serve immediately.

Alternatively, spoon 2 tablespoons of cream over the seasoned egg and set the dishes in a pan of hot water. Bake as before.

Boiled eggs
Eggs may be soft-boiled (softly set white, with a runny yolk), medium-boiled (firm white, with a just-soft yolk), or hardboiled (firm white, dry, solid yolk).

COOKING TIMES	
Soft-boiled	
Large eggs	4½ min.
Standard eggs	4 min.
Medium eggs	3–3½ min.
Medium-boiled	
Large eggs	6½ min.
Standard eggs	6 min.
Medium eggs	4–5 min.
Hardboiled	
Large eggs	12 min.
Standard eggs	11 min.
Medium eggs	10 min.

Soft-boiled eggs
Bring a pan of cold water to boiling point over gentle heat and, with a spoon, carefully lower each egg into the water. To boil a large number of eggs, put them in a wire basket or egg holder so that all the eggs can be immersed in the water at the same time.

Medium-boiled eggs
Put the eggs in a saucepan and cover them with cold water; bring to the boil over low heat. As soon as it boils, remove the pan from the heat, cover it with a lid and leave the eggs to stand for the necessary time.

Hardboiled eggs
Cook the eggs in boiling water for 10–12 minutes. Plunge them immediately in cold water to prevent further cooking and to make shelling easier. Tap the eggs round the middle with the back of a knife, and pull away the two half-shells. Shelled eggs should not be exposed for long to air as they become tough; put eggs to be served cold in iced water.

Fried eggs
Melt a knob of butter (1–2 oz. is sufficient for four eggs), or equal amounts of oil and butter, in a frying pan over low heat. Break the eggs, one by one, on to a saucer and slide them into the fat. Reduce the heat immediately and baste* the eggs with the butter to ensure even cooking. Fry the eggs for 3–5 minutes, or until the whites are firm.

Poached eggs
Fill a heavy-based frying pan with cold water to a depth of 1 in., add a pinch of salt and bring to the boil. Reduce the heat and keep the water just simmering. Break the eggs, one by one, on to a saucer and slide them carefully into the gently simmering water. Using two spoons quickly gather the whites over and round the yolks. Cover the pan with a lid and cook the eggs for 4–5 minutes, or until the yolk is set and the white firm.

For more regularly shaped poached eggs, round pastry cutters may be set in the pan and the eggs slid inside them. Alternatively, an egg poacher can be used: half fill the pan of the poacher with water, bring to the boil, then reduce the heat and keep the water simmering. Melt a knob of butter or margarine in each egg container and break an egg into them. Season lightly with salt and freshly ground pepper. Cover the pan with the lid and cook the eggs for 2 minutes or until they just set.

For poached eggs, gather the egg whites round the yolks

Scrambled eggs
Use 2 large or standard eggs per person, and for each egg allow ½ oz. butter and 1 tablespoon cream or top of the milk. Beat the eggs with a little salt and freshly ground pepper in a bowl. Melt the butter in a heavy-based pan or in the top of a double boiler, pour in the egg mixture and cook over low heat. As the egg mixture begins to thicken, stir it continuously until it is soft.

Remove the pan from the heat and stir in the cream or milk.

Omelettes
There are two types of omelettes – plain and fluffy (soufflé). Plain

omelettes are always served as a savoury course, while fluffy omelettes may be savoury or sweet. Cook omelettes in a special omelette or small frying pan.

Plain omelette

PREPARATION TIME: *3 min.*
COOKING TIME: *1½–2 min.*

INGREDIENTS *(for 1):*
2 eggs
1 tablespoon milk or water
¼ level teaspoon salt
Freshly ground pepper
Knob of butter

Break the eggs into a bowl, add the milk (or water), salt and pepper; beat until blended, but not foamy. Heat the butter in the pan without letting it brown, and pour in the egg mixture. Cook the omelette over moderate heat and lift it up round the edges with a spatula so that the liquid egg runs underneath. When the omelette is almost set, but still slightly runny on top, allow the underside to become golden. Fold the omelette in half with the spatula and quickly turn it upside-down on to a warm plate. Serve at once.

Savoury omelettes

Many ingredients can be added to the omelette mixture before cooking, or they can be cooked separately and spooned over the omelette before folding it over.

Cheese: add 1 oz. finely grated cheese to the beaten egg mixture before cooking.

Ham: sprinkle 1 tablespoon of finely chopped ham over the omelette before folding.

Fluffy omelettes

These can be filled like plain omelettes with savoury ingredients, or they can be served as a sweet course.
PREPARATION TIME: *15 min.*
COOKING TIME: *3–5 min.*

INGREDIENTS *(for 2):*
2 eggs
¼ level teaspoon salt
Black pepper
½ oz. butter

Separate the eggs and whisk the whites until stiff, then beat in the salt and a few twists of pepper. Beat the egg yolks with 2 tablespoons of water until thick, and fold them into the whites.

Melt the butter in an omelette pan and spoon in the egg mixture. Cook over moderate heat until the underside is golden. Place the omelette, in the pan, under a hot grill to brown the top lightly. Add any savoury filling, and fold the omelette in half.

For a sweet omelette, omit salt and pepper and whisk the egg whites with 1 oz. caster sugar. Add a few drops of vanilla essence to the creamed egg yolks, then cook the omelette as already described. Spread the omelette with a thin layer of warm jam or fruit purée, before folding it in half. Sprinkle with caster sugar before serving.

MAKING AN OMELETTE

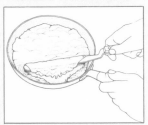

Lifting omelette round the edge

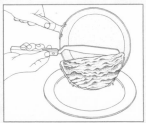

Turning omelette on to a plate

Soufflés

These light airy egg dishes may be sweet or savoury and are served hot or cold. Hot soufflés are based on a thick white sauce to which egg yolks are added before the beaten whites are folded in. To allow even rising during baking, always use a straight-sided buttered soufflé dish and let the soufflé mixture come no more than three-quarters up the sides. It is not necessary to prepare a hot soufflé with a paper collar (see Cold soufflés), but it is vitally important to serve the soufflé the moment it is taken from the oven.

Ham soufflé

PREPARATION TIME: *20 min.*
COOKING TIME: *45 min.*

INGREDIENTS *(for 4–6):*
3 eggs
½ pint thick white sauce
Salt and black pepper
3 oz. cooked chopped ham

Butter a 7 in., 2 pint soufflé dish and tie a paper collar round it. Separate the eggs, and prepare the white sauce*. Cool it slightly, then stir in the chopped ham. Beat the egg yolks, one at a time, into the basic sauce, and whisk the whites in a bowl until stiff. Fold the whites carefully into the soufflé mixture and spoon it into the dish.

Set the prepared soufflé dish in a pan of hot water and bake in the centre, or just above, of a pre-heated oven at 350°F (mark 4) for 40–45 minutes or until well risen and golden brown.

Hot soufflé variations

Caramel: omit salt and pepper from the white sauce. Heat 3 tablespoons of caster sugar until melted and brown, and stir into the sauce, before adding the eggs.

Cheese: blend 4 oz. finely grated mature Cheddar cheese into the sauce.

Chocolate: omit salt and pepper from the sauce and blend in 2 oz. plain melted chocolate.

Corn: blend 2 oz. sweet corn kernels and 2 oz. grilled, chopped bacon into the sauce.

Fish: add 3 oz. cooked, finely flaked haddock to the sauce.

Cold soufflés

These sweet soufflés are made with whipped cream and gelatine. As they are not baked but left to set in the refrigerator they cannot rise. To achieve the characteristic risen look of a soufflé, the dish is prepared with a paper collar extending above the rim. Cut a band, 3 in. deeper than the dish, from a double layer of greaseproof paper, and fold up 1 in. along one of the long edges. Wrap the band round the dish, the folded edge level with the base, and the upper edge extending beyond the rim by 2 in. Tie the band securely in place with string. Spoon the prepared soufflé mixture into the dish until it reaches almost to the top of the collar.

When the soufflé has set, remove the paper collar. This is easiest done by running a warmed knife blade between the set soufflé and the paper.

Lemon soufflé

PREPARATION TIME: *25 min.*
CHILLING TIME: *1–2 hours*

INGREDIENTS *(for 4):*
2 lemons
3 eggs
3 oz. caster sugar
2 level teaspoons gelatine
¼ pint double cream

Grate the rind from the lemons and squeeze out the juice. Separate the eggs, and beat the egg yolks, sugar, lemon rind and juice in a bowl until thick.

In a small bowl, mix the gelatine with 2 tablespoons of cold water and set the bowl in a pan of hot water until the gelatine has dissolved and is clear. Allow the gelatine to cool slightly, then pour it into the lemon mixture. Beat the cream, until it just holds its shape, then fold it into the lemon mixture. Whisk the egg whites until stiff and fold them carefully into the mixture when nearly set. Spoon the lemon soufflé into a prepared 6 in. or 1½ pint soufflé dish and chill until set.

Cold sweet soufflé variations

Chocolate: melt 2–3 oz. dark chocolate and stir into the yolk mixture, with 1 tablespoon brandy or rum.

Coffee: add 4–5 tablespoons strong black coffee and 1 tablespoon Tia Maria or Curaçao liqueur to the yolks.

Orange: add the grated rind of a large orange and 4 tablespoons orange juice.

MAKING A SOUFFLÉ COLLAR

Wrapping paper band round dish

Securing band with string

Rice and Pasta

These foodstuffs are cereals which form the basic diet in many countries. Pasta comes from Italy, and rice is imported from America, the Far East and the Mediterranean countries. Because these cereals are rather bland in themselves they combine well with many other types of food. Both can replace vegetables with a main course.

RICE

There are several varieties of rice – white polished rice, brown unpolished rice and wild rice. In addition, par-boiled rice and instant rice are widely available.

White and brown rice

White and brown rice both come in three grain sizes – long, medium and short grain – and are named after the areas in which they are grown.

Long grain rice is suitable for savoury dishes, such as curries, risottos, salads and paellas. Medium grain rice is most suitable for stuffings, croquettes and rice moulds.

Short grain rice is best used for sweet puddings and for moulds.

Par-boiled rice

Because it is steamed by a special process before milling, par-boiled rice retains much of its food value and flavour.

Instant rice

This has been fully cooked, then dehydrated before packaging. It is prepared by soaking it in hot water for 5 minutes, and then cooked according to the manufacturer's directions. Instant rice may be used for snacks and quick sweet or savoury rice dishes.

Wild rice

This is not a cereal, but long green seeds from a grass growing wild in the northern United States. Its unique flavour makes it an ideal accompaniment for game, but it is expensive and not widely available.

Cooking white rice

Wash rice before cooking it by putting it in a strainer and rinsing it under cold running water. Allow 2 oz. uncooked rice per person. During cooking, rice almost trebles in bulk.

After cooking, rice should be dry and slightly fluffy, separated into individual grains. To obtain this result, cook rice by boiling or by absorption methods.

Boiling white rice

Use 1 pint of water and 1 teaspoon salt to each 2 oz. of rice. Measure the water into a large pan and bring to the boil; add the salt and rice. Boil the rice rapidly for 12–15 minutes, or until soft, but not mushy. To test the rice, squeeze a grain between thumb and forefinger – when cooked, the centre will be just soft.

Drain the rice in a sieve and rinse it under hot water. Return it to the pan, with a knob of butter, and toss the rice to coat it evenly with butter.

Cover the pan with a lid and set it for 10 minutes to dry the rice. Shake the pan occasionally to prevent the grains from sticking together.

Alternatively, put the drained rice in a shallow, buttered baking dish, cover it tightly and dry in the centre of an oven pre-heated to 325°F (mark 3) for 10 minutes.

Absorption method 1

This is an easy cooking method which ensures tender separate grains. For each cup of rice (enough for three servings), use 2 cups of water or clear stock and ½ level teaspoon salt. Bring the water to the boil in a large pan, then add the salt and rice, stirring for a few minutes.

As soon as the water boils again, cover with a folded tea cloth and the upturned lid. To prevent the steam from escaping, place a weight, such as a kettle filled with water, on the lid. Cook the rice over low heat for 15 minutes, and do not at any time uncover the pan.

At the end of 15 minutes, all the water should be absorbed and the rice dry and tender. Remove the pan from the heat and separate the grains with a fork. Serve immediately.

Alternatively, cook the tightly covered rice over low heat for 10 minutes, remove from the heat and leave the rice for 10 minutes before uncovering it.

Absorption method 2

Rice can also be cooked by absorption in the oven. Use the same measurements as in the first method, and put the rice in a casserole dish. Pour over boiling salted water, stir thoroughly and cover the dish tightly with foil and a lid. Cook the rice in the centre of a pre-heated oven at 350°F (mark 4) for 30–45 minutes, or until all the liquid is absorbed and the grains are soft.

Cooking brown rice

Brown rice can be cooked in the same way as white rice, but needs a longer time. For boiled rice allow about 25 minutes, and with the absorption method simmer the rice for 45 minutes. Brown rice cooked in the oven needs about 1 hour.

Cooking wild rice

This can be cooked in salted boiling water for about 25–30 minutes, then drained and dried in the same way as boiled white rice. However, if time permits, a better flavour and improved texture can be obtained by covering the rice with boiling water. Leave it to stand for 20 minutes, then drain. Repeat this four times, adding 1 level tablespoon of salt to the water the last time.

Fried rice

This can be prepared from uncooked or cooked rice.

PREPARATION TIME: *5 min.*
COOKING TIME: *30 min.*

INGREDIENTS *(for 4)*:
4 oz. long grain rice
2 rashers streaky bacon
1 onion
1 oz. butter or oil
½–¾ pint chicken stock
Salt and black pepper

Remove rind and gristle from the bacon and chop the rashers roughly. Peel and finely chop the onion. Fry the bacon over low heat, without any butter, until the fat runs. Add the butter, rice and onion, and continue frying until the onion is transparent and the rice faintly coloured. Pour ½ pint of stock over the rice and cook over moderate heat until all the liquid is absorbed. Stir occasionally, and add more stock as required until the rice is just tender, after about 20 minutes. Season to taste.

Rice mould

Cold cooked rice can be made into an attractive hot or cold main course. Heat a garlic-flavoured sauce vinaigrette* and toss the rice in this – cooked peas may also be added. Pack the dressed rice and peas loosely into a ring mould and smooth the top.

If the rice is to be served warm, set the ring mould in a roasting tin of boiling water. Cover the mould with foil and simmer on top of the stove for 10–15 minutes. Place a serving dish on top of the mould and turn it upside-down. The centre of the mould can be filled with chopped chicken, flaked fish, prawns or shrimps in a creamed or curry sauce.

If the rice is to be served cold, put the mould in the refrigerator for about 1 hour or until firm. Turn the mould upside-down on to a serving dish and fill the centre with a seafood bound with a sharp mayonnaise*.

Rice salads

Cold left-over rice makes a good basis for a variety of salads. Toss the rice in a well-flavoured sauce vinaigrette* or a thinned-down mayonnaise*, and serve with cold meat, fish or poultry. For a more substantial course, mix the dressed rice with chopped ham or chicken, flaked fish and chopped pimentoes, cooked peas and sweet corn kernels. Fresh herbs, such as finely chopped parsley, chives and tarragon may also be mixed with a rice salad.

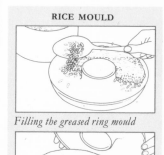

RICE MOULD

Filling the greased ring mould

Turning out the set rice

PASTA

Pasta dishes include macaroni, spaghetti, tagliatelle, lasagne, ravioli, cannelloni, vermicelli and many others. The basis of pasta is flour from a hard durum wheat, which grows particularly well in Italy. The flour is mixed with oil and water, and sometimes spinach purée and egg, to a paste. This is moulded into long threads, tubes, strips and other different shapes, sometimes enclosing a stuffing or filling. Pasta is dried before being sold.

Pasta can be served as a main savoury dish, as a side dish (instead of potatoes, for example), as an hors-d'oeuvre or as a garnish with soups. As a first or main course, pasta is usually served with a savoury sauce or filling, and with grated Parmesan cheese.

Cooking and serving pasta
All pasta is boiled, but cooking times vary according to the shape, size and freshness of the different kinds. Pasta should be cooked until it is just firm to the bite (*al dente*). Too long cooking turns pasta into a soft and soggy mass. Allow 3–4 oz. of pasta for each person.

COOKING TIMES	
Cannelloni	20 min.
Lasagne	10–15 min.
Macaroni	15 min.
Ravioli	15–20 min.
Spaghetti	10–12 min.
Tagliatelle	10 min.
Vermicelli	5 min.

For every 2 oz. of pasta, use 1 pint of water, and 1 level teaspoon salt. Bring the salted water to the boil and add the pasta. The long strands of spaghetti should not be broken up. Hold the spaghetti at one end and lower the other into the boiling water; as the spaghetti softens and curls round in the water, push the rest of the spaghetti down.

Keep the pasta at a steady boil, uncovered, until just tender. Stir occasionally to prevent the pasta from sticking to the pan. To test, try a piece between the teeth; it should be just soft. Drain thoroughly in a colander, return the pasta to the pan with a good knob of butter or a tablespoon of olive oil. Toss thoroughly, season with salt and pepper.

Types of pasta
There are more than 30 different types of pasta on sale in specialist shops throughout Britain. The more easily available are shown in the illustration opposite. Reading from top to bottom are five types of straight spaghetti, from the threadlike capellini, followed by fedelini, spaghettini, spaghetti, and the thicker mezzani. Below is fusilli, a spindle-shaped spaghetti, followed by a ribbon pasta, mafalde and the large tubular cannelloni, suitable for filling with savoury mixtures. Tagliatelle, a flat and narrow ribbon noodle, is available as yellow and green (*verde*) pasta. Below tagliatelle are two tubes of the familiar macaroni.

Pasta in fancy shapes, all of which are served with a savoury sauce or butter and Parmesan cheese, includes elbow macaroni, butterfly farfalle, wheel-shaped ruote, shell pasta known as conchiglie, corkscrew tortiglioni and the small hat-shaped cappelletti.

Pasta used for soup garnishes comes in many small and decorative forms, such as nocchette, followed by conchigliette, the tiny rings known as anellini and the grain-like semini. Last is the smallest of all, acini di pepe.

Do not break spaghetti, but curl the strands gradually into boiling water

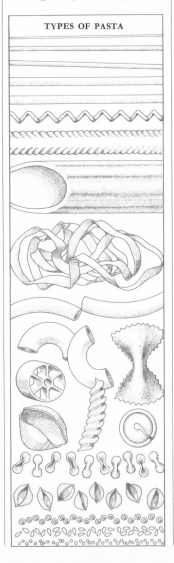

TYPES OF PASTA

Fats and Oils

Fats and oils play an important part in cooking, as they contribute to or sometimes alter the flavour of food, more so when frying.

FATS

These are derived from animal foods, such as meat and dairy products, from oily fish and from nuts or vegetables. Cooking fats include butter, blended fats, dripping, lard, margarine and suet.

Butter
This is made from the fatty substances skimmed from full cream milk. It is churned and then pressed to squeeze out water, and sometimes salt is added. It is used as the cooking medium for egg dishes, for sautéed vegetables, for shallow frying and in the baking of cakes and biscuits.

Clarified butter
This is sometimes used in recipes for frying and grilling. It is an expensive cooking medium, as 8 oz. of butter produces only about 5 oz. of clarified butter. Melt 8 oz. of unsalted butter in a small pan over gentle heat and cook, without stirring, until the butter begins to foam. Continue to cook the butter without browning until the foaming stops. Remove the pan from the heat and let it stand until the milky deposits have sunk to the bottom, leaving a clear yellow liquid. Pour this liquid carefully, through muslin, into a bowl. Clarified butter can be used in liquid or solid form.

Melted butter
Usually served as a sauce with poached fish and boiled vegetables. Heat the butter over low heat and season lightly with salt, freshly ground pepper and a few drops of lemon juice.

Beurre noisette
Melted butter allowed to brown lightly before being seasoned. It is served with eggs, brains, poached skate, fish roe and boiled vegetables.

Beurre noir
Melted butter heated until it becomes nut-brown, but not black. Add 2 tablespoons of finely chopped parsley, 1 tablespoon of wine vinegar and 1 tablespoon of chopped capers to every 4 oz. of butter. Serve with the same types of food as beurre noisette.

Meunière butter
This sauce is made from the butter in which fish has been shallow-fried. Add a little extra butter to the pan juices and cook until lightly brown. Blend in a squeeze of lemon juice and a little chopped parsley.

Savoury butters
These are used to garnish meat, fish and vegetable dishes, or they may be added to sauces. Softened butter is flavoured with varying ingredients according to the dish it is meant to garnish. On average, allow 1 oz. of butter per person.

Soften the butter in a bowl, before blending in the flavouring ingredient. Herbs and vegetables must be finely chopped, pounded or thoroughly crushed. A mortar and pestle are ideal for this purpose. When all the ingredients are combined, roll the butter flat between two sheets of damp greaseproof paper. Chill thoroughly in the refrigerator before cutting the butter into small fancy shapes.

Fats and Oils

SAVOURY BUTTERS

Butter (4 oz.)	Flavouring	Preparation	Serving suggestions
FISH BUTTERS:			
Anchovy butter	6 anchovy fillets	Rinse the anchovies in cold water to remove salt and oil. Dry. Rub through a sieve and blend with the butter	*Grilled meat or fish. As a garnish for cold hors-d'oeuvre, or added to a white sauce*
Crab or shrimp butter	4 oz. crabmeat or 4 oz. cooked peeled shrimps	Rub the crabmeat or shrimps through a sieve and blend with the butter	*As a garnish for cold hors-d'oeuvre or cold fish, or add to fish sauces*
FRUIT BUTTERS:			
Lemon butter	Grated rind of half lemon Salt and black pepper	Blend the grated lemon rind with the butter. Season to taste with salt and pepper	*As garnish for cold hors-d'oeuvre*
Tomato butter	2 level tablespoons concentrated tomato paste	Blend the tomato paste with the butter	*Grilled meat or fish, as garnish for cold hors-d'oeuvre, or added to sauces and thick soups*
HERB BUTTERS:			
Chive butter	8 tablespoons (2 oz.) chopped chives	Blanch and drain the chives. Chop finely and pound to a paste. Blend into the butter	*Grilled meat or fish*
Chivry (ravigote) butter	1 teaspoon each chervil, chives, parsley and tarragon 1 tablespoon chopped shallot	Wrap the herbs in muslin and blanch in scalding hot water for 3 minutes. Drain, dip the bag in cold water, drain again, and wring dry. Blanch the shallots and pound, with the herbs, to a paste. Blend with the butter	*As a garnish for cold hors-d'oeuvre, or added to white sauces*
Maitre d'hôtel butter	1 tablespoon finely chopped parsley Salt and black pepper Lemon juice	Blend the parsley with the butter and season to taste with salt, ground pepper and a few drops of lemon juice	*Grilled meat or fish, boiled vegetables and coated fried fish*
Tarragon butter	2 oz. fresh tarragon leaves	Blanch the tarragon in scalding-hot water, drain and dry. Pound to a paste and blend with the butter	*As garnish for cold hors-d'oeuvre*
Nut butter	2 oz. blanched almonds, walnuts or pistachio nuts	Crush the almonds or nuts to a fine paste; add a few drops of water to prevent the paste from becoming oily. Blend the paste with the butter	*As garnish for cold hors-d'oeuvre, or added to sauces and soups*
VEGETABLE BUTTERS:			
Garlic butter	4 cloves garlic	Peel and crush the garlic and blend with the butter	*As garnish for cold hors-d'oeuvre, or added to white sauces*
Green butter	4 oz. spinach	Blanch the spinach, drain and wring out as much moisture as possible. Pound until smooth, then blend with the butter	*Add to white sauces or use as garnish for cold fish*
Horseradish butter	4 tablespoons grated horseradish	Pound the horseradish smooth in a mortar, with the butter	*As garnish for cold hors-d'oeuvre, or added to white sauces*
Mushroom butter	4 oz. button mushrooms 1 oz. butter Salt and black pepper	Chop the mushrooms finely, cook them lightly in butter and season to taste. Pound until smooth, then blend with the butter	*As garnish for cold hors-d'oeuvre, or added to white sauces*
Shallot butter	4 oz. shallots	Blanch the shallots in scalding-hot water and drain thoroughly. Peel and chop them finely. Pound to a paste, then blend into the butter	*Grilled meat or fish*
MISCELLANEOUS BUTTERS:			
Mustard butter	1 tablespoon dry mustard	Blend the mustard thoroughly with the softened butter	*Grilled meat or fish*
Snail butter	1 tablespoon chopped shallot 1 teaspoon chopped parsley 1 clove garlic Salt and black pepper	Chop the shallot and parsley finely. Peel and crush the garlic. Blend into the butter and season with salt and pepper	*Stuffed into snail shells*

Dripping

This is the rendered fat from beef or mutton. It is sold already rendered down.

Dripping may be used for deep-frying but, as it has a fairly high water content, it tends to spatter and is better used for roasting and shallow-frying.

Lard

This is processed from pure pork fat and is excellent for both shallow and deep-frying. It can be used in flaky pastries and in some cakes.

Margarine

Made from vegetable oils blended with milk and vitamins, and sometimes with butter, margarine is interchangeable with butter for baking purposes. It is not suitable for deep-frying, due to its high water content, but excellent for sautéed food.

Suet

The fat deposits from the loins and round the kidneys of beef or sheep. It is sold fresh for grating or already shredded and packed. Suet is used in some pastries, in mincemeat, Christmas puddings and stuffings.

OILS

Edible oils are liquid forms of fat, derived from fish, vegetables, cereals, fruit, nuts and seeds. Oils vary in colour and flavour, and choice is a matter of individual taste. Most oils are suitable for frying, and sometimes for baking, but for mayonnaise and salad dressing olive, corn or sunflower oils must be used.

Cooking with oil

Vegetable oils (and lard) or oil in combination with butter can be used for shallow-frying. They are, however, more frequently used for deep-frying. Good-quality oils or lard can be heated to the high temperatures that are necessary to seal and crisp food on the outside without being absorbed into the food.

Deep-frying

For deep-frying, use a deep, heavy-based saucepan or a special deep-fryer fitted with a wire basket. Fill the pan no more than one-third with oil or melted lard, and heat over moderate heat. The general temperature of 375°F is suitable for most deep-frying. The temperature can be accurately assessed from a cooking thermometer, but if this is not available, drop a cube of day-old bread into the hot oil. It should sink to the bottom, then rise to the surface and brown in 60 seconds.

Fritters and croquettes are fried at 375°F, while potato chips and crisps can be fried at 385°F. At this heat a bread cube should brown in 40 seconds. The higher heat is necessary because the water content of potatoes lowers the temperature of the oil. However, for best results, deep-fry potatoes twice, at 375°F. Fry them for 2–3 minutes to extract the water, drain thoroughly and re-heat the oil before frying the second time to crisp the outside.

Frying times vary according to the size and type of food. For foods comprising previously cooked ingredients, such as croquettes, allow only 2–3 minutes. Fritters need 3–5 minutes; potato chips, 4–6 minutes; and coated chicken joints should be fried for 15 minutes.

Oil and lard can be used several times for deep-frying. After cooking, leave the oil to cool, then strain it into a bowl or jar. Store the oil or lard, covered, in a cool larder or the refrigerator, for up to three months.

Sweets and Puddings

In Britain, desserts are served before cheese, although gourmets maintain that desserts should follow the cheese. Family favourites include sweet pies, tarts and flans (see pastry), as well as steamed puddings and custards. For party occasions, jellies, mousses and home-made ice creams are ideal desserts.

STEAMED, BOILED AND BAKED PUDDINGS

Puddings can be steamed in a special decker steamer or in a large saucepan. Stand the pudding on a trivet or on skewers so as to raise it. Pour water into the pan until it reaches halfway up the basin. Keep at least a 1 in. space around the basin.

Whichever steaming method is used, the water in the steamer or pan must be kept gently boiling throughout cooking. Top up with boiling water at intervals.

Preparing a pudding basin

Butter the basin lightly and cut and butter a disc of greaseproof paper to fit the base; this prevents the pudding from sticking when it is turned out. Fill the basin no more than two-thirds with pudding mixture. Butter a piece of greaseproof paper thoroughly and make a 1 in. pleat in the centre to allow for the pudding to rise. Lay the paper over the top of the basin and cover it with a piece of pleated foil. Tie the paper and foil covering securely with string below the lip of the basin. Make a string handle to lift the pudding out.

Many traditional and regional suet puddings are boiled rather than steamed. The pudding basin is covered tightly with a pudding cloth and immersed completely in a pan of boiling water. More usually, however, the pudding mixture is placed inside a scalded and flour-dusted pudding cloth. This is easiest done by laying the cloth over a colander, spooning in the pudding mixture and tying the corners tightly to shape the pudding. The two knots help to lift the pudding.

STEAMED PUDDINGS

Place pudding cloth over colander

Spoon in mixture and tie up cloth

The pudding, ready for steaming

Turning out a pudding

Lift the pudding from the steamer or pan and remove the covering. Leave to cool and shrink slightly, then loosen the pudding at one side of the basin to let in the air. Place a dish over the basin, and turn it upside-down.

Baked puddings

Apart from steaming and boiling, puddings can also be baked in the oven. The pudding mixture should be a little softer than for steamed puddings to give a crisp surface. To prevent jam-based puddings from caramelising, set the dish in a shallow tin of water. Bake in a pre-heated oven, at 350–375°F (mark 4–5).

Delaware Pudding

PREPARATION TIME: *35 min.*
COOKING TIME: *2¼ hours*

INGREDIENTS *(for 6)*:
½ oz. butter
2 tablespoons golden syrup
4 oz. margarine
4 oz. caster sugar
2 eggs, beaten
6 oz. self-raising flour
2 tablespoons milk
2 small cooking apples (½ lb.)
2 oz. currants
2 oz. Demerara sugar
1 level teaspoon cinnamon

Butter a 2 pint pudding basin and spoon the syrup over the base. Beat the margarine with the sugar until light and fluffy. Gradually beat in the eggs, and then the flour and milk alternately.

Mix the peeled and sliced apples with the remaining ingredients. Put a thin layer of the pudding mixture over the syrup, top with half the spicy apples, another thin layer of pudding mixture and then the remaining apples. Spoon over the remaining pudding mixture. Cover the basin and steam the pudding for about 2¼ hours.

Viennoise Pudding

PREPARATION TIME: *45 min.*
COOKING TIME: *2 hours*

INGREDIENTS *(for 6)*:
6 individual sponge cakes
2 tablespoons sherry
3 oz. sultanas
3 oz. chopped mixed peel
3 oz. caster sugar
Grated rind of a lemon
1 oz. lump sugar
½ pint milk
3 eggs

Golden Layer Pudding

PREPARATION TIME: *45 min.*
COOKING TIME: *2 hours*

INGREDIENTS *(for 6)*:
½–¾ lb. golden syrup
1 lemon
6 oz. self-raising flour
Pinch salt
1 level teaspoon baking powder
4 oz. shredded suet
4 oz. fresh white breadcrumbs

Butter a 1½ pint pudding basin and put 3 tablespoons of syrup over the base. Grate the rind from the lemon, remove the pith and cut the lemon into thin slices. Lay these over the syrup.

Sift together the flour, salt and baking powder, then stir in the suet, half the breadcrumbs and the lemon rind. Add enough water to give a light but manageable dough. Turn this out on to a floured surface and knead lightly. Divide the dough into four unequal pieces and roll out the smallest piece to a round that fits the bottom of the basin. Cover the dough with a layer of syrup and sprinkle with breadcrumbs. Roll out another piece of dough, slightly larger, put it in the basin and repeat the layers of syrup and breadcrumbs. Dust the top with flour and cover the basin with buttered greaseproof paper and foil. Steam the pudding for about 2 hours.

Butter a 1½ pint ovenproof glass dish thoroughly. Cut the sponge cakes into small cubes, put them in a bowl and sprinkle over the sherry. Leave to soak for 30 minutes. Stir the sultanas, peel, caster sugar and lemon rind into the soaked sponge, then turn the mixture into the dish.

Put the lump sugar, with 1 tablespoon of water, in a small, heavy-based pan and dissolve it over gentle heat without stirring; cook until the sugar has a toffee-like consistency and is coffee-coloured. Add the milk and cook gently until the toffee has dissolved. Beat the eggs in a bowl, pour the milk mixture over them and mix thoroughly. Strain this custard mixture over the sponge, cover the dish with buttered greaseproof paper and foil, and steam for about 2 hours.

Apple Crumble

PREPARATION TIME: *25 min.*
COOKING TIME: *45 min.*

INGREDIENTS *(for 4–6)*:
1½ lb. cooking apples
1 oz. caster sugar
Grated rind of half lemon
TOPPING:
6 oz. plain flour
3 oz. margarine
2 oz. caster sugar
½ oz. Demerara sugar

Peel, core and slice the apples thinly. Put them, sprinkled with caster sugar, into a 3 pint pie dish; top with lemon rind.

For the topping, sift the flour into a mixing bowl, cut up the margarine and rub it lightly into the flour with the tips of the fingers. Mix in the caster sugar. Spoon the crumble mixture over the apples and press it down lightly. Sprinkle the Demerara sugar on top. Place the dish on a baking tray and bake in the centre of the oven at 400°F (mark 6) for 45 minutes.

Sweets and Puddings

JELLIES, MOULDS AND MOUSSES

These cold desserts are all made with gelatine, an extract from animal bones, tendons and skin. Gelatine is available in powder and leaf form, and while powdered gelatine is easier to use, some cooks consider that leaf gelatine gives a more sparkling finish to a fruit jelly.

Some fresh fruit – pineapple, for example – contains enzymes which prevent the gelling action taking place. However, these enzymes are destroyed if either tinned or cooked fruit is used in jellies.

Setting gelatine

Jellied mixtures left to set in a refrigerator need less gelatine than those set at normal room temperature. In hot weather, and without refrigeration, increase the amount of gelatine by one-third, or reduce the amount of liquid. Desserts made in individual glasses need less gelatine than a dessert made in a mould for turning out later. Jellied mixtures tend to toughen if kept too long, especially in a refrigerator. They are best eaten on the day of making.

Directions for making powdered gelatine are given on the packets. In general, one packet (3 level teaspoons) will set one pint of liquid for moulding in a refrigerator, and 2 level teaspoons will set the same amount of liquid spooned into serving glasses. Fruit purées and ingredients of a similar consistency, such as moulds and mousses, need 1 level teaspoon gelatine to gell $\frac{1}{2}$ pint for setting in glasses.

For coating and glazing with jelly, for whisked jellies and for setting fruit decorations, use the jelly when it has set to the consistency of unbeaten egg white.

Leaf gelatine

Thin leaf gelatine must be washed in cold water and then soaked in a basin of cold water until soft, after 15–20 minutes. Squeeze the softened gelatine lightly to extract surplus water, and place it in a bowl with the measured amount of liquid used in the recipe. Place the bowl in a pan of hot water and heat, without boiling, over low heat until dissolved. Six sheets of leaf gelatine equal 1 oz. of powdered gelatine.

Grape Jelly

PREPARATION TIME: *40 min.*
SETTING TIME: *about 3 hours*

INGREDIENTS *(for 4):*
1$\frac{1}{4}$ lb. large white grapes
Juice of 2 oranges
Juice of a lemon
2 level tablespoons caster sugar
4 tablespoons water
1$\frac{1}{2}$ level teaspoons powdered gelatine
$\frac{1}{4}$ pint single cream

Dissolve the sugar with 2 tablespoons of water in a small pan over low heat, and dissolve the gelatine in a cup with the remaining water. Stir the hot sugar liquid into the gelatine, blend thoroughly and stir it all into the fruit juices. The liquid should now measure $\frac{1}{2}$ pint; make up with cold water if necessary. Leave to cool until it has gelled to the consistency of unbeaten egg white.

Peel and pip the grapes*; this is easiest done by dipping the whole bunch in boiling water for 30 seconds, then stripping off the skin and extracting the pips from the stalk ends. Strain the fruit juices into a measuring jug.

Divide the grapes equally between four sundae glasses, and spoon the jelly over them. Leave in the refrigerator until set, and just before serving float a thin layer of cream on top of each.

Honeycomb Mould

PREPARATION TIME: *45 min.*
SETTING TIME: *3 hours*

INGREDIENTS *(for 6):*
Rind of a lemon
1 pint milk
2 eggs
2 oz. caster sugar
3 level teaspoons gelatine
2 tablespoons water

Peel the rind from the lemon as thinly as possible. Put the milk in a saucepan with the lemon rind and heat over very low heat for about 10 minutes.

Meanwhile, separate the eggs and beat the yolks with the sugar until thick and creamy. Strain the hot, not boiling, milk into the egg mixture, and stir thoroughly. Return this custard to the pan and cook over low heat until it begins to thicken. Remove the pan from the heat.

Dissolve the gelatine in the water, leave it to cool slightly, then stir it into the custard. Put aside until it begins to set. Whisk the egg whites until stiff; then fold them into the custard.

Rinse a 1$\frac{1}{2}$–2 pint jelly mould with cold water, and spoon the mixture into the mould. Leave in the refrigerator until set. To turn out, dip the mould in hot water for 5 seconds, place a serving dish over the mould and turn upside-down.

Raspberry Mousse

PREPARATION TIME: *45 min.*
SETTING TIME: *2 hours*

INGREDIENTS *(for 6):*
1 lb. raspberries
3 whole eggs
2 egg yolks
4 oz. caster sugar
3 level teaspoons powdered gelatine
3 tablespoons water
$\frac{1}{2}$ pint double cream
Grated chocolate

Set eight raspberries aside for garnish and put the remainder (hulled* and washed) in a pan and simmer for about 5 minutes until soft. Rub the raspberries through a sieve – the purée should measure about $\frac{1}{2}$ pint.

Put the whole eggs and the egg yolks in a bowl, together with the sugar. Place the bowl over a pan of hot water and whisk the eggs until thick and fluffy. Take the bowl from the pan and set in a basin of chilled water or ice cubes. Whisk the egg mixture until cool.

Dissolve the gelatine in the water, stir it quickly into the raspberry purée, and then whisk this into the egg mixture. Whip the cream lightly and fold it into the raspberries when beginning to set. Spoon the mousse into a serving dish and leave in the refrigerator until set.

Just before serving, sprinkle coarsely grated chocolate over the mousse and decorate with the whole raspberries.

The texture of this mousse is light and creamy; for a firmer set increase the gelatine to 4 level teaspoons.

SYLLABUBS AND TRIFLES

Syllabubs, which date back to Elizabethan times, were originally a drink, consisting of a bubbling wine, Sill or Sille, mixed with frothing cream. They later developed into a rich sweet with the addition of brandy and sherry, cream and sugar. The trifle, developed from the syllabub in the 18th century, became a little more substantial by the addition of sponge cake and jam.

Both syllabubs and trifles are ideal for dinner parties, as they can be made well in advance. The basis is still wine or liqueur or both, with eggs and cream.

Syllabub

PREPARATION TIME: *30 min.*
RESTING TIME: *8 hours*

INGREDIENTS *(for 4):*
1 lemon
6 tablespoons white wine or sherry
2 tablespoons brandy
3 oz. caster sugar
$\frac{1}{2}$ pint double cream

Peel the lemon thinly, leaving all the white pith behind, and squeeze out the juice. Put the rind and 4 tablespoons of lemon juice in a bowl, add the wine (or sherry) and brandy and leave the mixture to stand, covered, for several hours or overnight.

Strain the liquid into a clean bowl, add the sugar and stir until dissolved. Pour the cream slowly into the liquid, stirring all the time. Whisk the syllabub until it stands in soft peaks, then spoon it into small individual glasses or custard cups. Keep the syllabub in a cool place, but not in a refrigerator, until serving. Serve with soft sponge fingers or ratafia biscuits.

Separated Syllabub

PREPARATION TIME: *20 min.*
RESTING TIME: *8 hours*

INGREDIENTS *(for 4):*
2 egg whites
4 oz. caster sugar
Juice of half lemon
$\frac{1}{4}$ pint sweet white wine
$\frac{1}{2}$ pint double cream

Whisk the egg whites in a deep bowl until they form stiff peaks. Fold in the caster sugar, lemon juice and wine with a metal spoon. In another bowl, whisk the cream until it just holds its shape, then fold it into the egg whites.

Spoon the syllabub into tall, slim glasses and leave overnight or for several hours in a cool place. Serve with small macaroons or ratafia biscuits.

Sherry Trifle

PREPARATION TIME: *30 min.*
CHILLING TIME: *30 min.*

INGREDIENTS *(for 6–8):*
6–8 trifle sponge cakes
¼ lb. strawberry or other red jam
29 oz. tin sliced peaches
4 tablespoons sherry
4 tablespoons peach juice
2 tablespoons nibbed almonds
1 pint pouring custard
½ pint double cream
2 oz. small macaroons

Split the sponge cakes in half, lengthways, spread them with a thin layer of jam and sandwich them together. Cut the sponge cakes into ½ in. slices and arrange them over the base of a shallow glass dish. Drain the peach slices, set a dozen aside for decoration and arrange the remainder, two slices together, upright around and between the sponge cake, so that the peaches stand above the sponge. Sprinkle the sherry and peach juice over the sponge. Prepare the custard*.

Scatter the almonds over the sponge cakes and peaches, and spoon the warm custard over them. Cover the dish with foil and leave until cold. Whisk the cream until it just holds its shape and spoon it over the custard. Swirl the cream with a knife and decorate with peach slices and macaroons. Chill.

Syllabub Trifle

PREPARATION TIME: *30 min.*
RESTING TIME: *4 hours*

INGREDIENTS *(for 6–8):*
1 lb. strawberries
½ lb. green grapes
6 oz. small macaroons
3 egg whites
6 oz. caster sugar
¼ pint dry white wine
Juice of half lemon
2 tablespoons brandy
½ pint double cream

Hull*, wash and drain the strawberries, and remove the pips from the grapes*. Set 6–8 strawberries aside, and arrange half the remainder together with half the grapes over the base of a glass dish. Set 8 macaroons aside, and lay half of the remainder over the fruit. Cover the macaroons with the rest of the strawberries and grapes and lay the last macaroons over them.

Whisk the egg whites with half the sugar until stiff, but not dry, then fold in the remaining sugar with a metal spoon. Mix the wine, lemon juice and brandy, and blend it carefully into the egg whites. Whisk the cream until it just holds its shape, set a little aside for decoration, and fold the egg-white mixture into the remaining cream.

Spoon the cream over the macaroons, smoothing it neatly on top, and leave the trifle in a cool place, not the refrigerator, for several hours.

Decorate the trifle with the reserved strawberries and macaroons sandwiched with cream.

EGG CUSTARDS

There are two types of custard: baked or steamed, and the softer pouring custard which is used as a sauce.

Egg whites set a baked custard, and the yolks give it the creamy consistency. However, as the yolks thicken at a higher temperature (149°F) than the egg whites (144°F), it is important to cook custards at the correct heat. Too much heat, especially direct heat, will cause an egg custard to curdle. Use a double saucepan for making a pouring custard and stand a set custard in a shallow container with a little cold water. If a double saucepan is not available, use an ordinary saucepan over very gentle heat.

For baked custards, 2 whole eggs plus 2 egg yolks will set 1 pint of milk. For a pouring custard use 4 egg yolks – the whites cause curdling – to every pint of milk.

Custard Sauce

PREPARATION AND COOKING TIME: *20 min.*

INGREDIENTS *(for 1 pint):*
1 pint milk
2 level tablespoons sugar
½ vanilla pod
4 egg yolks

Put the milk in a saucepan with the vanilla pod and heat over very gentle heat without boiling. Remove the pan from the heat, cover and leave to infuse for 10 minutes. Remove the vanilla pod.

Whisk the yolks in a bowl, and gradually stir in the hot milk. Strain the custard back into the pan or into a double saucepan with hot, not boiling, water in the base. Stir the custard continuously over very low heat until it is creamy and thick enough to coat the back of a wooden spoon. If the custard is to be used cold, pour it into a bowl and sprinkle with sugar to stop a skin forming.

A curdled custard can often be rescued by turning the custard into a cold bowl and whisking.

Baked Custard Pudding

PREPARATION TIME: *15 min.*
COOKING TIME: *35 min.*

INGREDIENTS *(for 4):*
1 pint milk
½–1 oz. butter
Strip of lemon rind
2 whole eggs
2 egg yolks
1½ level tablespoons caster sugar
Grated nutmeg

Butter the inside of a 1½ pint pie dish. In a saucepan, bring the milk and lemon rind (free of all pith) to just below boiling point,

then remove from the heat. Beat the eggs and yolks in a bowl, using a fork, until well mixed but not frothy. Beat in the sugar. Pour the milk over the eggs, then stir and strain the custard into the pie dish. Dot the custard with tiny flakes of butter, and sprinkle the surface with grated nutmeg.

Set the pie dish in a shallow baking or roasting tin, with about 1 in. of cold water. Bake the custard in the centre of a pre-heated oven, at 350°F (mark 4), for about 35 minutes or until the custard is set and the top golden brown. Serve warm or cold.

MERINGUES

Meringue, with its crisp outer texture and aerated inside, forms the basis for many desserts: shells and baskets can be filled with cream or fresh fruit. Meringue is also a favourite topping for sweet pies and flans.

Meringue is quite easy to make provided a few points are observed – the whisk and bowl must be absolutely clean and dry, and the eggs quite free from yolk. Ideally, use 2–3 day old eggs. The shapes of whisk and bowl also influence a good meringue; a balloon whisk gives the greater volume but takes longer to whisk the whites than a rotary whisk. An electric mixer is the quickest, but gives the least volume. Choose a wide bowl when using a balloon whisk, and a narrow deep bowl for a rotary hand whisk.

The sugar for a meringue must be fine. Caster sugar is generally used, but equal quantities of caster and icing sugar produce a meringue of pure white colour and crisp melting texture. Do not use granulated sugar, as the coarse crystals break down the egg albumen, thus reducing the volume.

Basic Meringue

INGREDIENTS:
2 egg whites
4 oz. caster sugar

Put the egg whites in a bowl and whisk them until they are fairly stiff and have the appearance of cottonwool. Tip in half the sugar and continue whisking the stiff whites until the texture is smooth and close, and stands in stiff peaks when the whisk is lifted. Lightly but evenly fold in the remaining sugar with a metal spoon.

Meringue Shells

Line a baking tray with non-stick paper or kitchen foil. Using two dessertspoons, set the meringue in six to eight small mounds on the tray, and shape them into ovals with the spoons.

Alternatively, spoon the meringue mixture into a fabric forcing bag fitted with ½ in. wide plain or rose nozzle: turn the top of the bag down over the hand to form a cuff, then fill the bag using a metal spoon. Ease the meringue down towards the nozzle by twisting the top of the bag. Pipe six to eight meringue whirls on to the baking tray.

Sprinkle the meringues lightly with caster sugar and set the tray in the coolest part of the oven – this is usually the lowest shelf. Dry the meringues, in a pre-heated oven, at the lowest possible heat for 2–3 hours.

Halfway through drying, the meringues may be taken out and the base of the shells pressed in lightly to make more space for cream filling. Return the shells, placed on their sides, to the oven until completely dry.

Cool the meringues on a wire rack. Unfilled, they will keep for about a week in an airtight container. To serve, fill the hollows of the meringues with sweetened cream.

Meringue Cuite

This is made with icing sugar and has a firmer texture than basic meringue; it is ideal for making hollow basket shapes, to be filled with cream or fruit.

INGREDIENTS *(for 6 baskets)*:
8–9 oz. icing sugar
4 egg whites
Vanilla essence

Sift the icing sugar on to a sheet of greaseproof paper. Whisk the egg whites until frothy with a hand rotary or electric beater. Whisk in the sugar, a little at a time, and last of all flavour with a few drops of vanilla essence.

Set the bowl over a pan half-filled with simmering water, and whisk the meringue until it holds its shape and leaves a thick trail when the whisk is lifted out.

Meringue Baskets

Line one or two baking trays with non-stick kitchen paper. Pencil six circles, 3 in. wide and a little apart on the paper. Spread about half the prepared meringue cuite evenly over the pencilled circles to form the bases for the baskets, and spoon the remaining meringue into a fabric forcing bag fitted with a six to eight point rose nozzle. Pipe two layers, one on top of each other, round the edge of each basket base. Dry the meringues in the bottom of a cool oven, set at 275–300°F (mark 1–2) for about 45 minutes or until the baskets come easily away. Cool on a wire rack.

Serve the basket filled with Chantilly cream* or vanilla ice cream, and with fresh or tinned and drained fruit.

ICE CREAM AND SORBETS

Home-made cream ices and water ices (or sorbets) are quite different in both texture and flavour to the commercial varieties. It is as easy to make these at home as it is to make an egg custard or sugar syrup. Indeed, a basic ice cream is more often than not based on a custard enriched with double cream. The basis of a water ice is a sugar syrup flavoured with fruit juice or purée.

Pointers to success

1. The amount of sugar in the mixture is important – if too much, the ice cream will not freeze, and if too little it will be hard and tasteless. Freezing does, however, take the edge off the sweetness and this must be borne in mind when tasting. In sorbets or water ices it is even more important to have the correct amount of sugar, as the soft yet firm consistency depends on the sugar content.
2. Some recipes recommend milk instead of cream, especially for strong-flavoured ice cream. The milk must be evaporated, not fresh dairy milk.
3. Use maximum freezing power. Whichever method is used for freezing the cream, it has a better texture if frozen quickly. Chill the equipment as well as the ingredients before starting.
4. Once the ice cream is frozen, it should be transferred to a shelf in the refrigerator for a little while before serving. Rock-hard ices are never pleasant and lose much of their flavour.
5. Ice cream may be stored in the freezing compartment of the refrigerator for the length of time indicated by the star rating.

Making ice cream in a refrigerator

Set the dial of the refrigerator at the coldest setting about 1 hour before the ice cream mixture is ready to freeze.

Make up the mixture according to the recipe. Remove the dividers and pour the mixture into ice trays or any other suitable freezing container, such as refrigerator boxes, loaf tins and stainless-steel dishes. Cover the trays or containers with foil or lids and place in the freezing compartment.

To obtain a smooth texture, the ice crystals must be broken down as they form and the ice cream mixture whisked at intervals until part frozen and slushy. Remove the tray from the freezing compartment and scrape the ice crystals, which have formed on the sides and base, towards the centre. Whisk the mixture with a fork until smooth, and return the tray, covered, to the freezing compartment. Thereafter, leave the ice cream undisturbed until it is firm, after 2–3 hours.

Freezing time varies with different refrigerators, but several hours are necessary in every case. When freezing and maturing of the ice cream is completed, return the dial to its normal temperature setting or other food in the refrigerator may be spoilt by exposure to low temperatures.

Making ice cream in a home freezer

Set the dial to 'quick-freeze' about 1 hour before the ice cream is ready to be frozen.

Prepare the ice cream mixture according to the recipe, place it in a mixing bowl in the freezer and leave it until mushy.

Remove the bowl from the freezer and whisk the mixture thoroughly with a rotary beater. Pour the ice cream into empty ice-cube trays or rigid polythene containers, and freeze until firm. Set the dial of the freezer to its normal temperature. If the ice cream is to be stored for any length of time the container should be sealed or over-wrapped and labelled.

Vanilla Ice Cream

PREPARATION TIME: *25 min.*
FREEZING TIME: *about 3 hours*

INGREDIENTS *(for 6)*:
½ pint milk
Vanilla pod
1 whole egg
2 egg yolks
3 oz. caster sugar
½ pint double cream

Bring the milk almost to the boil with the vanilla pod, then leave to infuse off the heat for about 15 minutes. Remove the vanilla pod. Cream the whole egg, yolks and sugar until pale. Stir in the vanilla-flavoured milk and strain this mixture through a sieve into a clean pan. Heat the custard mixture slowly over gentle heat, stirring all the time, until the mixture thickens enough to just coat the back of a wooden spoon. Pour into a bowl and leave to cool.

Whip the cream lightly and fold it carefully and thoroughly into the cooled custard. Spoon into ice cube trays or a suitable freezing container, cover and set in the freezing compartment until half-frozen. Whisk the ice cream thoroughly, then freeze until firm.

MAKING ICE CREAM

Whisking the egg yolks

Breaking up ice crystals

For a praline ice cream, add 2 oz. crushed praline, nut brittle or toasted hazel nuts to the beaten, half-frozen ice cream before returning it to the freezing compartment.

For coffee ice cream, add 1 tablespoon coffee essence to the cooled custard mixture.

Tinned, drained pineapple, thoroughly crushed, may be added to the ice cream at half-frozen stage.

Rich Chocolate Ice Cream

PREPARATION TIME: *20 min.*
FREEZING TIME: *4 hours*

INGREDIENTS *(for 6)*:
3 oz. caster sugar
4 egg yolks
1 pint single cream
Vanilla pod
7 oz. plain chocolate

Put the sugar with 6 tablespoons of water in a small pan and heat gently until the sugar is dissolved. Bring to the boil and continue boiling until the sugar has reached the thread stage* – about 220°F. Beat the egg yolks in a mixing bowl, then pour in the syrup in a thin stream, whisking all the time.

Put the cream, vanilla pod and chocolate, broken into small pieces, in a pan and cook over low heat until just below boiling point. Remove the vanilla pod and pour the chocolate cream into the egg mixture, whisking until it is thoroughly mixed. Cool and freeze.

Black Currant Sorbet

PREPARATION TIME: *30 min.*
FREEZING TIME: *3–4 hours*

INGREDIENTS *(for 6)*:
½ pint water
4 oz. caster sugar
½ lb. fresh or frozen black currants
1 teaspoon lemon juice
2 egg whites

Put the water in a saucepan together with the sugar. Heat over low heat until the sugar has dissolved, then bring to the boil and boil gently for 10 minutes. Set aside to cool.

Meanwhile, strip and wash the fresh black currants. Put the fresh or frozen currants, with 2–3 tablespoons of water, in a pan and cook over low heat for 10 minutes. Rub the currants through a sieve and make up the purée with the sugar syrup and extra water to make a total of 1 pint. Leave until quite cool. Stir in the lemon juice and pour the mixture into ice cube trays or a shallow freezing container. Place in the freezing compartment or the freezer until nearly firm.

Whisk the egg whites until stiff, but not dry. Turn the frozen mixture into a chilled bowl, break it down thoroughly with a fork, and carefully fold in the egg whites. Return the sorbet mixture to its container and freeze until firm.

Granita

A true Italian granita is a fruit (or coffee) flavoured, coarse-textured water ice.

PREPARATION TIME: *15 min.*
FREEZING TIME: *3–4 hours*

INGREDIENTS (*for 4*):
4 oz. caster sugar
8 fluid oz. fresh lemon juice
Finely grated rind of 2 lemons

Put the sugar in a pan with ½ pint of cold water. Bring to the boil over gentle heat until the sugar has dissolved, then continue boiling, without stirring, for 5 minutes. Remove the syrup from the heat and leave it to cool.

Stir the fruit juice and rind into the cooled syrup and pour the mixture into ice cube trays, with the dividers left in. Set the trays in the freezer compartment

and freeze until mushy. Remove the trays and scrape the ice crystals with a fork from the sides towards the centre. Repeat twice at 30 minute intervals, then return the trays to the freezing compartment and leave to freeze solid.

Remove the frozen cubes from the trays – this is easiest done by rubbing a cloth wrung out in hot water over the base and sides of the trays. Crush the cubes coarsely with a pestle, and spoon them into glasses. Serve at once.

BATTERS

Batters provide the basis for a large number of dishes from simple lemon pancakes to Russian blini, French crêpes suzettes and American waffles.

Batter is a mixture of flour, salt, egg, milk or other liquid. The proportions vary, depending on the consistency required. Pancakes, for instance, need a thin, cream-like batter, while fritters need a thick coating batter. For crisp coating batters, 1 tablespoon of oil may be used with ¼ pint of water, or the liquid may be half milk and half water.

Batters do not, as some people think, need to stand for a while before being cooked, although this may be done for practical reasons. Batter may be left, covered, at room temperature for any time up to 4 hours, or up to 24 hours in a refrigerator. It may be necessary to add a little more liquid to restore the batter to its original consistency.

Basic pancake batter

PREPARATION TIME: *10 min.*

INGREDIENTS (*for 8–10 pancakes*):
4 oz. plain or self-raising flour
Pinch of salt
1 egg
½ pint milk

Sift the flour and salt into a large bowl. Using a wooden spoon make a hollow in the centre of the flour and drop in the lightly beaten egg. Slowly pour half the milk into the flour, gradually working the flour into the milk. When all the flour is incorporated, beat the mixture with a wooden spoon, whisk, or rotary beater, until it becomes smooth and free of lumps. Allow it to stand for a few minutes. Then add the remainder of the milk, beating continuously until the batter is bubbly and has the consistency of single cream.

Basic coating batter

PREPARATION TIME: *10 min.*

INGREDIENTS:
4 oz. plain flour
Pinch of salt
1 egg, beaten
¼ pint milk

Follow the method given for basic pancake batter.

Pancakes with Lemon

PREPARATION TIME: *10 min.*
COOKING TIME: *25 min.*

INGREDIENTS (*for 8 pancakes*).
½ pint pancake batter
2 lemons
2 oz. caster sugar
Lard (for frying)

Finely grate the rind from 1 lemon and mix with the sugar. Squeeze the juice from both lemons. To make 8 pancakes, use a 7 in. heavy-based shallow frying pan with sloping sides. Add just enough lard to gloss the pan to prevent the batter sticking. Fierce heat is necessary, and the pan should be really hot before the batter is poured in.

Pour in just enough batter to flow in a thin film over the base – tilting the pan to spread it. Use a jug or ladle for pouring in the batter. The heat is right if the

underside of the pancake becomes golden in 1 minute; adjust the heat to achieve this. Flip the pancake over with a palette knife or spatula, or toss by flicking the wrist and lifting the pan away from the body. The other side of the pancake should also be done in about 1 minute.

Turn the pancake out on to sugared paper, sprinkle with lemon and sugar, roll up and keep warm until all the pancakes are fried. Serve immediately, sprinkled with the rest of the sugar and lemon juice.

To store pancakes: if they are to be kept for a short time, stack them in a pile and cover with a clean tea cloth. If they are to be stored for one or two days, put oiled greaseproof paper between each pancake, stack them and wrap the whole pile in kitchen foil and store in the refrigerator.

To re-heat pancakes: if pancakes are to be served with lemon and sugar, wrap three or four pancakes in foil and heat through in the oven at 300°F (mark 2). Remove foil, sprinkle each pancake with sugar and squeezed lemon, then roll up, place on a hot dish and dust with sugar. Alternatively, brush a flat tin with melted butter, arrange overlapping pancakes on it, brush with butter and put into a hot oven for 4–5 minutes. Alternatively, heat the pancakes in a frying pan in, for example, an orange sauce as for crêpes suzettes*.

For savoury, stuffed pancakes, fill them with a freshly made filling, top with a sauce or grated cheese, and heat the pancakes through under a moderate grill. Alternatively, stuff the pancakes, place them in a flat baking dish or tin, cover with foil and heat in a pre-heated oven at 375°F (mark 5) for about 30 minutes.

COOKING PANCAKES

Pour batter into greased pan

Flip over the half-cooked pancake

Straighten pancake with knife

Roll up on sugar-dredged paper

351

Sweets and Puddings

Toad-in-the-hole

A traditional British dish, which consists of sausage baked in batter, toad-in-the-hole is economical and easy to prepare.

PREPARATION TIME: *20 min.*
COOKING TIME: *45 min.*

INGREDIENTS *(for 4)*:
1 lb. pork sausages
½ pint pancake batter made with milk

Grease a roasting tin (about 10 × 12 in.) and place the sausages in it. Put the tin in a pre-heated oven, at 425°F (mark 7), for 10 minutes until the fat runs from the sausages and is sizzling. Remove the tin from the oven, pour the batter over the sausages, and return to the oven. Cook for about 35–45 minutes, until the batter is well-risen and golden brown. Serve at once.

Yorkshire pudding and Popovers

PREPARATION TIME: *20 min.*
COOKING TIME:
Popovers: 20 min.
Pudding: 35–40 min.

INGREDIENTS *(for 4)*:
½ pint pancake batter made with milk
1 oz. dripping or lard

To make a Yorkshire pudding, heat the dripping in a small baking tin towards the top of a pre-heated oven at 425°F (mark 7) until smoking hot. Pour in the prepared batter and bake for 35–40 minutes.

To make popovers, grease 12 individual patty pans with a knob of fat in each. When the fat is hot, pour in the batter so that the tins are about two-thirds full. Return the pans to the top of a pre-heated oven at 425°F (mark 7) for about 20 minutes or until well risen and crisp. Serve the popovers or pudding at once.

A Yorkshire pudding can also be cooked underneath a joint of beef: place the meat on a grid so that the fat and meat juices drip down into the pudding.

Fritter batter

PREPARATION TIME: *5 min.*
RESTING TIME: *1 hour*
INGREDIENTS:
4 oz. plain flour
Pinch of salt
1 tablespoon corn oil
¼ pint water
1 egg white

Sift the flour and salt together into a bowl. Make a well in the centre, add the oil and water, beating until smooth. Allow the batter to rest for 1 hour.

Whisk the egg white until stiff, but not dry, then fold it evenly into the batter with a metal spoon.

Fruit Fritters

PREPARATION TIME: *15 min.*
COOKING TIME: *12 min.*

INGREDIENTS:
¼ pint fritter batter
1¼ lb. tinned peach halves, pineapple rings or
1½ lb. bananas or
3 cooking apples
Caster sugar

Prepare the basic fritter batter. Fill a deep fryer halfway up with corn oil and heat to 375°F. While the oil is heating, prepare the fruit: drain the syrup from the tinned fruit and dry it thoroughly on absorbent kitchen paper.

If using bananas, remove the skin and cut the bananas into chunks. Peel, core and cut the apples in thick slices.

Whisk the egg white until stiff, but not dry, and fold it evenly into the prepared batter with a metal spoon.

Dip the chosen fruit into the batter. Allow any excess to drain

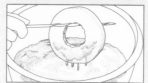

Draining batter from fritter

Draining fried fritters

off, and fry the fruit in the hot oil for 2–3 minutes, turning the fruit halfway through cooking. Fry only a few pieces at a time. Drain on absorbent kitchen paper. Keep the fried fritters warm in the oven at 300°F (mark 2) until they are all cooked. Serve dredged with caster sugar.

Waffles

PREPARATION TIME: *12 min.*
COOKING TIME: *20 min.*

INGREDIENTS *(for 20 waffles)*:
6 oz. plain flour
Pinch of salt
3 level teaspoons baking powder
1 oz. caster sugar
2 eggs, separated
½ pint milk
2 oz. butter
Vanilla essence

Sift the flour, salt and baking powder into a bowl and stir in the sugar. Make a well in the centre and drop in the egg yolks; mix thoroughly with a wooden spoon, then gradually beat in the milk and butter alternately. Stir in a few drops of vanilla essence. Whisk the egg whites until stiff, but not dry, and fold them evenly into the batter with a metal spoon or spatula.

Heat the well-greased waffle

iron until it is hot. Using a bristle brush cover the waffle iron with melted butter, pour in a little batter and cook for about 30 seconds until golden brown on each side. Serve the waffles hot, with butter and honey or syrup or jam.

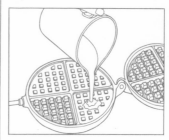

Waffles: pouring batter into the well-greased sections of a hot iron

Kromeski

PREPARATION TIME: *30 min.*
RESTING TIME: *1½ hours*
COOKING TIME: *15 min.*

INGREDIENTS *(for 12 kromeski)*:
¼ pint fritter batter
1 oz. butter
1 oz. plain flour
¼ pint milk
1 small egg yolk
Salt and black pepper
8 oz. cooked chicken
1 small green pepper
12 thin back bacon rashers

Prepare the batter and leave to stand for 1 hour. Meanwhile, melt the butter in a small pan. Remove the pan from the heat and with a wooden spoon stir in the flour. Return the pan to the heat and cook the roux* for a few minutes without colouring. Then gradually stir in the milk and simmer gently. Cook the sauce, stirring all the time, for 3–5 minutes until it is thick and smooth. Remove from the heat and beat in the egg yolk. Season to taste with salt and freshly ground pepper.

Finely chop the cooked chicken. Cut the stalk from the pepper, remove the seeds and the midrib and dice the flesh finely. Blanch* the diced pepper in boiling water for 1 minute. Drain and cool quickly in cold water, then drain again. Blend the chicken and pepper into the white sauce and set aside to cool.

Divide the cooled mixture into 12 equal portions, on a floured board. Mould each portion into a cork shape, using a knife and the fingers. Cut the rind from the bacon and wrap each chicken shape in a bacon rasher, securing it with a wooden cocktail stick. Leave in a cool place to set for about 30 minutes.

Dip the kromeski in the batter. In a large pan, fry a few kromeski at a time in deep fat heated to 375°F for about 5 minutes. Lift the kromeski out with a perforated spoon, and drain on absorbent kitchen paper. Remove the sticks and serve the kromeski hot.

Mould mixture into cork shapes

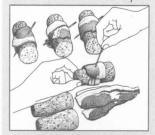

Kromeski wrapped in bacon

Fruit

Fresh fruit makes delicious eating on its own, in fruit salads and with cheese. In this section will be found recipes and suggestions on how to stew, poach and bake fruit, on how to prepare fresh fruit salads and fruit purées to be used in ice creams and sorbets or as filling for pies and puddings. Fruit is also used for jams and jellies, pickles and chutneys. For detailed buying guide see pp. 10–17.

With crop-spraying so widespread in modern fruit farming, it is essential that all fruit should be washed in running water before serving, expecially if it is to be eaten fresh. Apart from soft fruits such as blackberries, most fruit will keep in good condition for up to a week if stored in a refrigerator.

Apples
Both cooking and dessert apples are used for sweets and puddings. They can be baked, stewed, made into purées (1 lb. makes $\frac{1}{2}$ pint purée) or used as fillings for pastry, baked and steamed puddings, cream-based foods and mousses. Both types are also used for making jams, jellies, pickles and chutneys. Sliced apples for decoration should be dipped in lemon juice to prevent discoloration.

Apricots
Perfect ripe fruit are excellent served as a dessert fruit. They can also be poached in sugar syrup or used in pie fillings, sweetened with vanilla sugar. Stone apricots by cutting them in half with a sharp knife, following the slight indentation line. Twist the two halves in opposite directions to separate them and remove the stone with the point of a knife.

Bananas
These are usually served raw or used fresh in fruit salads. They may also be sautéed in butter.

Slice bananas as close to serving time as possible, or leave them in fresh or tinned grapefruit, lemon, lime or orange juice to prevent discoloration.

Blackberries
These berries go well with apples, and are used as pie fillings, in apple snow, fruit puddings, jams and jellies. Hull* the berries before use.

Cape Gooseberries
These are sometimes served as a sweetmeat dipped in fondant*. Peel the calyx back to form petals round the berry and dip in liquid fondant; leave to set and serve in tiny paper cases.

Cherries
Both white and black heart cherries are served as a dessert fruit. For cooking in pies, puddings, compôtes and jams, choose Morello cherries. Strip them of the stalks and ideally push out the stones with the special tool known as a cherry stoner.

Chinese Gooseberries
Serve these as a dessert fruit. Cut them in half crossways and scoop out the juicy flesh with a teaspoon. They can also be used for jams and jellies.

Currants
Black currants are always served cooked, in pies, suet and sponge puddings and in ice creams and sorbets. They are also used for jams, jellies and fruit syrups.

Split the fruit lengthways

Separate the two halves

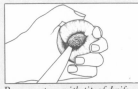

Remove stone with tip of knife

CAPE GOOSEBERRIES

Peel away dry petals

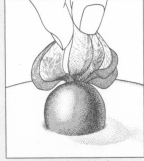

Dip fruit into liquid fondant

Red currants may be eaten fresh, or in a sugar frosting (see Garnishes, pp. 403–4). Red currants are also suitable for compôtes, fruit salads, pastries, jams and jellies. White currants can be eaten fresh. Before cooking, strip all currants off the stalks by running a fork down the length of the stalk.

Custard Apples
Serve this dessert fruit on its own, or with sugar and cream.

Damsons
These are used, stoned, in pies and puddings and for the traditional preserve, damson cheese*.

Dates, fresh
Serve these as a dessert fruit or use in fresh fruit salads. Squeeze the stem end to remove the date from its slightly tough skin.

Figs, fresh
These dessert fruits are served fresh; cut them open with a knife and fork and eat only the soft red flesh inside. Cream may be served with them.

Gooseberries
Dessert varieties are served on their own, but acid gooseberries are usually cooked. They may be served as a sauce with meat and fish, and they are used for favourite desserts such as gooseberry fool and in pies, puddings,

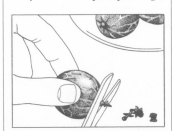

Top and tail gooseberries by snipping off stalk and flower ends

jams, jellies and chutneys. Top and tail with a knife or with scissors.

Grapes
These delicious fruits are served for dessert, plain or in a sugar frosting (see Garnishes pp. 403–4). They also make a good addition to fresh fruit salads. They are not cooked, except for the classic garnish known as à la Véronique. Most grapes are easily peeled, away from the stem end using the fingernails. If the skins are difficult to remove dip a few grapes at a time in boiling water for 30 seconds, then plunge them immediately into cold water.

Remove the pips from whole grapes by digging the rounded end of a clean new hair grip into

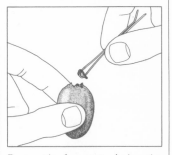

Remove pips from grapes by inserting a hair grip from the stalk end

the stem end of the grape; scoop out the pips. Alternatively, make a small cut down the length of the grape, being careful not to cut right through, and ease out the pips with the tip of the knife.

Grapefruit
This popular citrus fruit is usually served fresh as a breakfast dish or a first course. To prepare a grapefruit, cut the fruit in half 'crossways' and use ideally a curved saw-edged grapefruit knife to cut round inside the skin to loosen the flesh. Make deep cuts between the grapefruit

Fruit

Cut grapefruit in half crossways

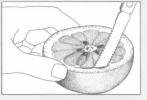

Loosen flesh from skin

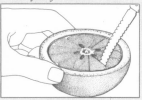

Cut between individual segments

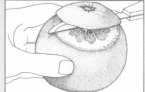

Cut off slice from stalk end

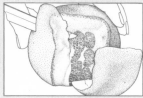

Remove strips of pith and peel

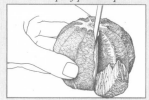

Cut out the segments

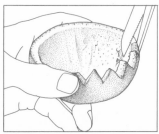

To make vandyke grapefruit, snip small V-shapes from empty half shells

pieces close to the membranes dividing them. Flip out any pips with the point of the knife. The central core may be cut away, but this is not essential. Serve with or without sugar.

For hot grapefruit, sprinkle the halves with a little sherry and Demerara or soft brown sugar, and put under a hot grill for a few minutes to glaze.

Empty half grapefruit shells look attractive as serving 'dishes'. Use kitchen scissors to cut out a series of small V's round the edge of the half shells (known as vandyking). Florida cocktail – half orange and half grapefruit segments with a mint-leaf garnish – is usually served in this way.

To peel and segment a whole grapefruit, hold the fruit firmly with the tips of the fingers and cut a thin slice from the stem end of the fruit until the flesh just

shows. Place the grapefruit, cut side down, on a plate and with a sawing action cut the peel and pith off in strips to reveal the flesh. Trim off any remaining pith. Carefully cut out each segment of fruit by placing the knife close to the membrane and cutting through to the centre: work the knife under the segment and up against the next membrane to release the segment.

Greengages
Ripe fruits are served fresh and are also delicious halved and stoned as pie fillings.

Kumquats
These fruits are eaten whole, including the skin, and are also used fresh as a garnish for duck. They may be preserved whole in syrup and served with cream.

Lemons
Lemon is one of the most useful fruits in the kitchen and both the rind and juice are used in a large number of dishes. It makes an attractive garnish for food and long drinks. Rub sugar lumps over the skin of a lemon until they are well coloured and use the lumps whole or crushed in iced drinks.

Lemon juice can be substituted for vinegar in any recipe, except pickling, and can be used to sour fresh or evaporated milk or fresh cream: add 1 tablespoon juice to $\frac{1}{4}$ pint. Store lemons in the refrigerator and, if cut, wrap in plastic film.

Limes
These are used in a similar way to lemons, and lime juice is particularly good squeezed over melon wedges. It also gives a fresh tangy flavour to salad dressings.

Lychees (litchis)
Lychees are served as a dessert fruit on their own or added to fruit salad. Pinch the parchment-like outer skin to crack it and peel it off.

Mangoes
These tropical fruits should not be cut until just before serving. Cut the fruit lengthways, into three slices, above and below the stone. However, in this way the aroma escapes and ideally

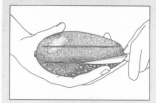

Cut three horizontal slices

Serve the slices unpeeled

fresh mango should be served whole with only the skin cut. Peel the skin back with a knife and scoop out the pulp with a spoon. Mango is also made into chutney and served as a side dish with curries.

Melons
Cool ripe melon is served as a first or last course, with sugar, finely chopped stem ginger or a squeeze of fresh lemon or lime juice. Refrigerate melon only long enough to chill it, or the delicate flavour will be lost.

To prepare a large melon, such as honeydew, cut it in half length-

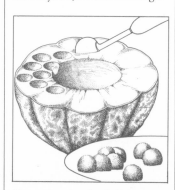

To scoop out melon balls, use a small semi-circular scoop

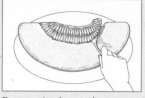

Cut melon in half lengthways

Remove pips from melon segments

Cut skin from melon

ways with a sharp knife. Cut each half lengthways into segments and scoop out the pips with a spoon or fork. A fully ripe melon segment may be served with the skin attached or the skin may be loosened by running the knife blade between flesh and skin. Leave the skin underneath the melon segment.

A small melon, such as Charantais or Ogen, usually only serves two persons. Cut it in half, crossways, and scoop out the pips with a teaspoon.

To shape a large melon into a basket, first cut a thin slice from the base so that the melon will stand upright. From the top, make one vertical cut $\frac{1}{2}$ in. from the centre to halfway down the melon; make a similar cut $\frac{1}{2}$ in. to the other side. Cut the melon horizontally, stopping at the downward cuts and lift out the two sections, leaving a 1 in. wide handle. Remove the pips from the melon, and take out the flesh with a small ball scoop.

Nectarines

These tender dessert fruits need no peeling. Serve with dessert knives and forks, cut the fruits in half and slip out the stones.

Oranges

The most widely available citrus fruits, oranges are served fresh on their own and in fruit salad. They are much used in cooking, especially in sauces and stuffings and provide the essential ingredient for all British breakfasts – marmalades.

Peel and cut oranges as described under grapefruit. Alternatively, peel oranges in round strips, remove all pith and cut the orange into slices across the grain. If oranges do not peel easily, chill them in the refrigerator for 1 hour or cover them with boiling water and leave for a few minutes.

Passion Fruit

The sharp tangy juice of this tropical fruit is used to flavour cocktails, punches or fresh fruit cups, as well as fruit pies. It may also be served as a dessert fruit and the flesh scooped out with a teaspoon and eaten with a little sugar.

Peaches

These fruits are usually served whole as a dessert, but are also excellent in fruit salads, flans and pies. Peach purée can be used as base for ice creams, soufflés and other sweet recipes. To peel fresh peaches, dip them in a bowl of boiling water, count up to ten, then drain and put the peaches at once in a bowl of cold water. Peel off the skin in downward strips with a small knife.

Pears

Really ripe dessert pears can be eaten on their own or served in fruit salads. They may also be poached* and served chilled with a raspberry or hot chocolate sauce*. To prepare pears for poaching, cut them in half lengthways with a sharp knife. Fresh pears discolour quickly and stainless steel or silver tools should be used in the preparation. Scoop out the core and pips with a pointed spoon. Poach the pears at once before they turn brown.

Persimmons

For serving fresh, wash and lightly chill the fruits and serve with a pointed spoon, to dig the juicy flesh out of the skin. A squeeze of lemon or lime may be added, and the skin can be marked in quarters and peeled back for an attractive presentation. The pulp may be used as a basis for ice creams, milk drinks, jellies and sauces.

Pineapple

A ripe pineapple is best served as a dessert fruit. Slice off the leaf and the stem ends, and cut the pineapple across into ½ in. thick slices. Using a sharp knife cut off the skin and the woody 'eyes' in the flesh of each slice. Remove the tough centre core with a small plain pastry cutter or an apple corer. Arrange the slices on a flat dish, sprinkle with caster sugar and 2 tablespoons of liqueur. Leave to marinate* for about 2 hours before serving.

For a spectacular party sweet, slice off the leaf end only and, without splitting the skin, cut round the edge of the pineapple between the flesh and skin, loosening it at the base as well. Extract the pineapple flesh, remove the core and cut the flesh into wedge-shaped pieces. Set the pineapple shell on a serving

PREPARING PINEAPPLE

Slice off leaf top

Remove skin from pineapple slices

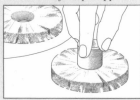
Stamp out centre woody cores

dish, replace the wedges and cover with the pineapple top. Pineapple shells also make attractive containers for fruit salads, pineapple sorbet or ice creams.

Plums

A few varieties are excellent as dessert fruits. All types are also suitable for pies, fruit salads, flans, baked and steamed puddings, jams, chutneys and pickles.

Pomegranates

These fruits are served fresh as a dessert. Serve them with the top sliced off and dislodge the large seeds with a nut pick or spoon; suck the flesh from the seeds.

Quinces

These are only served cooked, usually in the form of jam or jelly, or in small amounts, combined with apple, as pie filling.

Raspberries

Like other soft fruit, ripe raspberries should be used as soon as possible after picking. If it is necessary to wash them, put them in a colander and let water flow gently through them. Drain and use at once.

To make raspberry purée, rub the fruit through a nylon sieve, pressing it with a wooden spoon, or use an electric liquidiser and sieve the purée to remove the seeds – 1 lb. fresh raspberries will give ½ pint purée.

Rhubarb

Particularly suited for pie fillings, in baked puddings, fools and jams, rhubarb blends well with many other flavours, such as grated orange rind, ginger and cinnamon. Forced tender rhubarb needs little preparation apart from cutting off the root ends and the leaves. Older rhubarb is somewhat coarser, and tough strings of skin must be peeled off. Wash and drain thoroughly before use.

Poached rhubarb makes a quick and tasty dessert served with a jug of cream. Cut the trimmed rhubarb into 1 in. pieces and layer them with 3–4 oz. caster sugar in an ovenproof dish. Sprinkle with the juice and grated rind of an orange. Cover and cook in the centre of a preheated oven, at 350°F (mark 4), for about 35 minutes.

To hull strawberries, remove the green leaves and soft centre stalk

Strawberries

Like raspberries, these soft fruits must be eaten soon after picking. The calyxes at the stalk ends are sometimes left on the berries for decoration, but strawberries are usually hulled*. Serve whole or sliced (use a stainless-steel knife to prevent discoloration). Strawberry purée is made in the same way as raspberry purée and yields the same amount.

Ugli Fruits

These may be prepared and served as grapefruit halves; as they are sweet, they do not need any sugar.

Fresh Fruit Salad

PREPARATION TIME: *30 min.*
STANDING TIME: *1–2 hours*

INGREDIENTS *(for 6)*:
4 oz. granulated sugar
2 tablespoons lemon juice
1 tablespoon orange liqueur or Kirsch
½ lb. white or black grapes
2 dessert apples
2 ripe dessert pears
2 oranges
2 bananas

Put the sugar, with ¼ pint of water, in a small pan, heat gently to dissolve the sugar, then bring to the boil for 2–3 minutes. Set aside until cold, then add the lemon juice and liqueur and pour into a large serving bowl.

Peel the grapes* and remove the pips. Add the grapes to the sugar syrup in the bowl. Wipe the apples, quarter them, discard the cores and thinly slice the apple quarters into the bowl. Halve and peel the pears, remove the cores and cut the pears into chunks. Add to the bowl. Peel and cut oranges into segments, and squeeze the orange membranes into the bowl. Peel and slice the bananas and add, with the oranges, to the bowl. Turn the

Fruit

fruit in the syrup. Cover and leave in a cool place, preferably not the refrigerator, for 1–2 hours to develop the flavours.

When fresh strawberries are available, use 1 apple and 1 pear and include ½ lb. hulled* and halved small strawberries. Stoned cherries, plums and greengages, halved apricots, sliced peaches and red currants are also good for fresh fruit salads, as are pineapple, grapefruit and melon.

Pineapple in Kirsch

PREPARATION TIME: *20 min.*
CHILLING TIME: *1 hour*

INGREDIENTS *(for 8)*:
1 small pineapple
2 large oranges
8 maraschino cherries
2 level tablespoons caster sugar
2 tablespoons Kirsch

Cut all the skin from the pineapple*; slice the flesh into eight rounds and remove the cores. Slice the peel and white pith from the oranges and cut each orange into eight slices, crossways. Arrange one slice of pineapple and two of orange on individual dessert plates and top with a cherry. Dissolve the sugar in 2 tablespoons of water in a small pan over gentle heat, add the Kirsch and spoon the syrup over the pineapple.

Chill and serve with a jug of chilled cream.

Banana Flambé

PREPARATION TIME: *5 min.*
COOKING TIME: *5 min.*

INGREDIENTS *(for 6)*:
6 firm bananas
2–3 oz. unsalted butter
3 tablespoons Demerara sugar
3 tablespoons orange liqueur,
* brandy or rum*

Peel the bananas and cut them in half lengthways. Fry in hot butter until just beginning to colour.

Sprinkle the bananas in the pan with sugar, add the liqueur and set it alight. Let the flames burn for a few seconds, then serve the bananas at once, with the pan juices spooned over them.

Black Currant Brulée

PREPARATION TIME: *12 min.*
COOKING TIME: *8–10 min.*

INGREDIENTS *(for 4)*:
½ lb. stripped black currants
3 oz. Demerara sugar
1½ level teaspoons arrowroot
¼ pint soured cream
Light soft brown sugar
Ground cinnamon

Simmer the stripped black currants in 4 tablespoons of water until tender; add the Demerara sugar, bring to the boil and simmer for a few more minutes. Blend the arrowroot with 1 tablespoon of water, stir it into the currants and boil gently, stirring all the time, for 1–2 minutes.

Cool the black currant mixture before spooning it into four small flameproof dishes. Top the fruit with soured cream and cover with a thin layer of brown sugar mixed with a pinch of ground cinnamon. Set the dishes under a hot grill for a few seconds until the sugar bubbles and caramelises.

Compôte of Red Currants

PREPARATION TIME: *30 min.*
CHILLING TIME: *2–3 hours*

INGREDIENTS *(for 4–6)*:
1 lb. red currants
7 oz. caster sugar

Strip the currants from the stems, rinse and drain. Put the currants in a pan, together with the sugar and 2 tablespoons of water. Shake the pan over low heat until the sugar has dissolved, then set aside until lukewarm. Spoon the compôte into a serving dish and chill for several hours. Serve with crème chantilly*.

Pears in Red Wine

PREPARATION TIME: *10 min.*
COOKING TIME: *about 1 hour*

INGREDIENTS *(for 4)*:
4 firm dessert pears
2 oz. Demerara sugar
½ pint red wine

Halve the pears lengthways, scoop out the cores and peel the pears. Lay them in a single layer in an ovenproof dish and sprinkle with the sugar. Mix the wine with ½ pint of water and pour it over the pears. Cover the dish with foil and cook in the centre of a pre-heated oven, at 350°F (mark 4), for about 50 minutes, or until the pears are tender.

Lift the pears out with a perforated spoon and set them in a serving dish. Boil the cooking liquid briskly until it has reduced by half, then spoon it over the pears. Serve the pears hot or cold, with a bowl of cream or crème chantilly*.

Peaches in Wine

PREPARATION TIME: *20 min.*
CHILLING TIME: *20 min.*

INGREDIENTS *(for 4)*:
4 ripe yellow peaches
4 level teaspoons caster sugar
6–8 tablespoons sweet white wine

Peel the peaches, cut them in half and remove the stones. Slice the peaches into individual serving glasses, sprinkle with sugar and spoon the wine over them. Chill for about 20 minutes.

Poached Apricots

PREPARATION TIME: *10 min.*
COOKING TIME: *10 min.*

INGREDIENTS *(for 4)*:
1 lb. fresh apricots
3–4 oz. granulated sugar
Lemon rind or cinnamon stick

Wash and dry the apricots. Put the sugar with ½ pint of water and thinly pared lemon rind or

cinnamon in a saucepan and place over low heat until the sugar has dissolved. Bring to the boil and cook for 2 minutes. Strain this syrup through a sieve.

Cut the apricots in half with a small sharp knife. Twist the two halves to separate. Discard the stones. Return the syrup to the pan, place the apricot halves, rounded side down, in the syrup and bring slowly to the boil. Reduce the heat, cover and simmer gently until the fruit is tender, about 10 minutes. Leave to cool.

Cook plums in a similar way; they should be poached for 10 minutes only.

Baked Fruit Flambé

PREPARATION TIME: *30 min.*
COOKING TIME: *20 min.*

INGREDIENTS *(for 6)*:
1 medium pineapple
1 lb. plums
4 tablespoons marmalade
Grated rind and juice of a lemon
½ level teaspoon ground cinnamon
¼ oz. soft brown sugar
2 oz. unsalted butter
4 tablespoons white rum

Peel, core and slice the pineapple. Cut the slices in half. Cut the plums in half, and remove the stones. Place the pineapple and plums in a wide shallow casserole. In a small pan, heat together the marmalade, lemon rind and juice, cinnamon, sugar and butter. Stir well and pour the mixture over the fruit. Cover and cook in a pre-heated oven at 400°F (mark 6) for about 20 minutes. Just before serving, place the rum in a warm ladle, ignite with a match and pour it flaming over the fruit. Serve with a jug of cream.

Brown Sugar Apples

PREPARATION TIME: *15 min.*
COOKING TIME: *30 min.*

INGREDIENTS *(for 4)*:
1½ lb. cooking apples
1 oz. butter
Grated rind and juice of a lemon
5–6 oz. Demerara sugar

Peel and core the apples and cut them into even thin slices. Butter a deep pie dish and arrange the apples in layers, sprinkling each layer with the lemon rind and juice, and sugar. Dot the top with flakes of butter.

Bake the apples in the centre of a pre-heated oven at 375°F (mark 5) for about 30 minutes. Serve with cream.

Baked Apples

PREPARATION TIME: *10 min.*
COOKING TIME: *30–45 min.*

INGREDIENTS *(for 4)*:
4 large cooking apples
2½ oz. soft brown sugar
2½ oz. butter
Grated rind and juice of a lemon
4 oz. glacé cherries
1 tablespoon brandy

Wipe the apples and remove the cores, using a sharp knife or apple corer. Make a cut in the skin around the middle of each apple. Place the apples in an ovenproof dish. Fill the cavity of each apple with a little sugar and a small knob of butter. Bake in the centre of a pre-heated oven at 350°F (mark 4) for about 30 minutes, basting occasionally with the apple juices.

Meanwhile, grate the lemon rind and squeeze out the juice. Melt the remaining butter and sugar in a small saucepan. When the sugar has dissolved, boil gently to a rich caramel colour. Add the lemon rind and juice, cherries and brandy to the pan, and blend thoroughly, using a wooden spoon to loosen the caramel. Simmer for 1–2 minutes. Spoon over the baked apples and serve hot.

Preserving

Fruit can be made into jams, jellies and cheeses. It may also be made into pickles and chutneys, or it may be bottled. The most suitable methods of preserving depend on the type of fruit and its quality and ripeness. Only the finest-quality fruit should be used for bottling and freezing, while bruised and under-ripe fruit can be used to make jams and jellies. Over-ripe fruit is ideal for syrups and chutneys.

Marmalades, see pp. 94–95.

JAMS AND JELLIES

Both these types of preserves are a combination of fresh fruit, sugar and water, which are boiled together until setting point is reached. A good set depends on the presence of pectin, acid and sugar in correct proportions. Pectin, which is found in the fruit cells, reacts with sugar to give a gel, and acid speeds the release of pectin.

Fruits have natural pectin and acid in varying quantities. Apples, black currants, damsons, gooseberries and red currants are rich in pectin and acid, and are therefore excellent for jams and jellies. Fruits such as apricots, greengages, loganberries, plums and raspberries are less rich in pectin and acid. They make good jams, but set less firmly than pectin-rich fruit.

Fruits lacking in pectin and acid include cherries, melons, rhubarb and strawberries. These do not give a good set on their own and pectin and acid must be supplemented.

Testing for pectin

Put 1 teaspoon of the cooked, but unsweetened, fruit pulp in a glass and leave to cool. Add 3 teaspoons of methylated spirit and shake gently. If a large clot forms, the fruit has sufficient pectin for the jam to set; if there are numerous small clots the pectin content is too low.

Missing pectin can be supplemented by adding lemon juice, which is rich both in pectin and acid content. Allow 2 tablespoons lemon juice to each 4 lb. of fruit. Alternatively, add $\frac{1}{2}$ teaspoon of citric or tartaric acid to the fruit before cooking.

Commercial pectin may also be used in the proportions of 2–4 oz. liquid pectin or $\frac{1}{4}$ oz. powdered pectin to 1 lb. of fruit. The more pectin present, the more sugar it will set, but too much pectin flavour spoils the fruit.

Sugar

Use preserving or granulated sugar, as these dissolve quickly. The sugar should be warmed in the oven before being used.

Sugar has a hardening effect on fruit; it should therefore only be added to thoroughly softened fruit. Strawberries, which quickly lose their shape during cooking, are best sprinkled with sugar and left overnight before cooking.

Preserving pans

Choose a large, heavy-based pan made from aluminium or stainless steel. Copper or brass preserving pans can be used to make jams, jellies and marmalades, but should not be used for pickles and chutneys, because the vinegar in these preserves reacts adversely with the metal. The pan should be wide in relation to its depth to allow for rapid evaporation before the sugar is added, and for quick boiling afterwards.

Preparing the fruit

Select fresh, slightly under-ripe fruit and cut out any bruised or damaged parts. Berries should be hulled*, currants stripped from their stems and gooseberries topped and tailed.

Wash and drain the fruit carefully. Soft fruit is easiest cleaned by placing it in a sieve or colander, and immersing this in cold water several times. Large fruit such as apples should be chopped, and stone fruits should be halved and quartered and the stones removed.

Cooking the fruit

Put the prepared fruit in the preserving pan, and add water if specified. Bring the fruit and water to simmering point over very gentle heat. Simmering softens the skin and breaks down the flesh while releasing the pectin. When the fruit has been reduced* to a pulp and the volume has decreased by one-third, remove the pan from the heat and add the warmed sugar. Stir thoroughly until the sugar has dissolved. One tablespoon of glycerine added after the sugar has dissolved prevents scum forming.

Return the pan to the heat and boil rapidly until setting point is reached. This varies from 3 minutes to 20 minutes, according to the type and quantity of the fruit. If fruit is over-boiled, the jam becomes sticky and flavourless, and its colour darkens; if boiled too little, it fails to set.

Setting point

The most accurate method of testing for setting is with a cooking thermometer. Jams and jellies have generally reached setting point when the thermometer registers 22°F.

Alternatively, use the saucer test. Put a teaspoonful of jam on a cold saucer. As the jam cools, a skin forms. If the skin crinkles when pushed with a finger, setting point has been reached.

Yet another method is the flake test. Stir the jam with a wooden spoon and hold it flat so that the jam in the bowl of the spoon can cool. Turn the spoon on its side and allow the jam to drop. If the jam sets partly on the spoon and falls away in large flakes rather than drops, setting point is reached.

Potting and covering

As soon as setting point is reached remove the pan from the heat. Leave it to stand for 15 minutes before removing any scum with a slotted spoon. Pour the jam into thoroughly cleaned and dried warm jars.

Put a waxed disc (wax side down) on top of the jam, and press gently to release any air bubbles. Wipe the rim of the jar with a clean damp cloth before covering with cellophane. Wet the cellophane covers before putting them over the jars; as the cellophane dries it contracts to an airtight fit. Greaseproof paper dipped in egg white, tissue paper dipped in milk, or Porasan preserving skin may also be used as coverings.

Leave the jam-filled jars to cool completely before labelling them. Store in a cool, dark place.

MAKING JAMS AND JELLIES

1. *Cook fruit in a heavy-based pan*

2. *Add warmed preserving sugar*

3. *Flake-test for setting point*

4. *Saucer test for setting point*

5. *Remove scum from finished jam*

6. *Pour jam into warmed jars*

Preserving

JAMS

Apple (yield 10 lb.):
6 lb. cooking apples
2 pints water
Rind and juice of 4 lemons
1½ oz. ground ginger (optional)
6 lb. sugar

Peel, core and chop the apples. Tie peel and core in muslin and put with the apple and water into the preserving pan. Add the finely grated lemon rind and the juice, together with the ginger if used. Cook until pulpy, then squeeze out and discard muslin bag. Stir in the sugar and boil until setting point is reached.

Apricot (yield 5 lb.):
3 lb. apricots
Juice of a lemon
¾ pint water
3 lb. sugar

Cut the washed and drained apricots in half, and remove the stones. Quarter the apricots and put them, with the lemon juice and water, in the pan. Crack about 12 of the stones, remove the kernels and blanch* in boiling water for 5 minutes before splitting them in half. Add to the pan. Simmer until the fruit is pulpy, stir in the sugar and boil rapidly until setting point is reached.

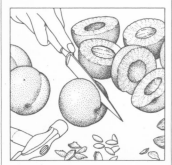

To prepare apricots for jam, cut them in half, and remove stones and kernels

Blackberry (yield 10 lb.):
6 lb. blackberries
¼ pint water
Rind and juice of 2 lemons
6 lb. sugar

Put the cleaned fruit, the water and lemon rind and juice in the pan. Simmer until the fruit is soft. Stir in the sugar and boil rapidly until setting point is reached.

Black Currant (yield 10 lb.):
4 lb. black currants
3 pints water
6 lb. sugar

Put the cleaned fruit in the pan with the water. Bring to the boil and simmer until soft. Stir in the sugar and boil rapidly until setting point is reached.

Cherry (yield 7 lb.):
6½ lb. dark (Morello) cherries
Juice of 3 lemons
3½ lb. sugar

Stone the cherries, and tie the stones in muslin. Put them in the pan, with the cherries and lemon juice. Simmer over low heat until the juices begin to run and the fruit is tender. Remove the muslin bag, stir in the sugar, and proceed in the usual way.

Gooseberry (yield 6 lb.):
3 lb. gooseberries
1 pint water
4 lb. sugar

Bring the cleaned gooseberries and water to the boil and simmer until tender. Stir in the sugar and proceed in the usual way.

Plum (yield 10 lb.):
6 lb. plums
1 pint water
6 lb. sugar

Follow the instructions given for apricot jam.

Raspberry (yield 10 lb.):
6 lb. raspberries
6 lb. sugar

Put the cleaned fruit in the pan without any water, and heat gently until the fruit begins to break up and the juices run. Simmer until reduced by a third, stir in the sugar; and proceed as usual.

Rhubarb (yield 5 lb.):
4½ lb. rhubarb
Juice of 3 lemons
3 lb. sugar

Wipe and trim the rhubarb, and cut the stems into 1 in. pieces. (Prepared weight should be 3 lb.) Layer with sugar in a large bowl, and add the lemon juice. Leave overnight. Put the contents of the bowl into the pan, bring to the boil, and boil rapidly until setting point is reached.

For additional flavour, wrap a bruised ginger root in muslin and add to the rhubarb before boiling.

Strawberry (yield 6½ lb.):
4 lb. strawberries
4 lb. sugar

Hull*, wash and drain the strawberries. Layer with the sugar in a large bowl. Cover with a cloth and leave in a cool place for 24 hours. Bring the contents of the bowl to the boil in a pan, and boil for 5 minutes. Leave the strawberries in the bowl for 48 hours, then boil for 20 minutes or until setting point is reached.

Marrow (yield 10 lb.):
8 lb. marrow
Rind and juice of 4 lemons
6 lb. sugar

Peel the marrow and remove pith and seeds. Dice the marrow – it should weigh 6 lb. Put in a steamer and cook until just tender. Leave the cooked marrow in a bowl, and add the lemon rind and juice, together with the sugar. Cover and leave for 24 hours. Boil the marrow over gentle heat until the sugar has dissolved. Continue cooking until the marrow is transparent and the syrup thick.

JELLIES

Fruit jellies should be bright and clear, with a good flavour and not too firmly set. Jellies, like jams, are best made from fruit rich in pectin and acid.

Prepare the fruit as for jams, then simmer it in water – the amount depends on the hardness of the fruit. Cook the fruit slowly for ¾–1 hour or until quite tender, then strain it through a scalded jelly bag and leave to drip for at least 1 hour. Do not squeeze the bag as this makes the jelly cloudy.

Measure the quantity of strained juice and add sugar. Bring the juice and sugar to boiling point and boil rapidly for

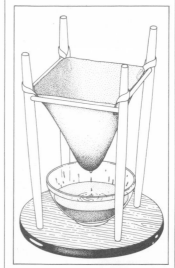

Up-end a stool to strain fruit juice through a scalded jelly bag

about 10 minutes or until setting point is reached. Take the pan off the heat and remove any scum.

The amount of sugar used depends on the pectin content of the fruit. Test as for jam and allow 1–1¼ lb. of sugar to each pint of juice rich in pectin. For juice of lesser pectin quality, allow ¾ lb. of sugar to each pint. Correct yield cannot be given, as this depends on the ripeness of the fruit and the number of extracts taken.

Fruit particularly rich in pectin can be boiled a second time to yield another extract: allow the cooked fruit to drip for only 15 minutes, then return the fruit pulp to the pan with half the quantity of water used initially; simmer for 30 minutes. Strain and leave to drip for 1 hour. Mix the two extracts together, add sugar and finish cooking.

Pour the juice into warm jars and cover as for jams.

Blackberry
4 lb. blackberries
1 pint water
Juice of 2 lemons
Sugar

Simmer the fruit with the water and lemon juice until quite tender. Strain once through a jelly bag and measure the juice. Allow 1 lb. of sugar to each pint of juice, then follow general instructions.

Black Currant
4 lb. black currants
2–3 pints water
Sugar

Simmer the fruit with 2 pints of water for the first extract. Return the strained pulp with 1 pint of water for the second extract. If only one extract is taken, use 3 pints of water. Allow 1–1¼ lb. of sugar to each pint of juice.

Crab Apple

4 lb. crab apples
3 pints water
Sugar

Simmer the washed and chopped fruit with the water until the apples have cooked to a pulp, and the liquid has reduced by one-third. Strain and allow 1 lb. of sugar to each pint of juice.

Damson

6 lb. damsons
3 pints water
Sugar

Simmer the fruits with all the water to take one extract. Each pint of juice will require 1 lb. of sugar to set.

Gooseberry

4 lb. gooseberries
2–3 pints water
Sugar

For jelly, there is no need to top and tail gooseberries. Proceed as for black currant jelly and follow general instructions.

Quince

2 lb. quinces
3 pints water
¼ oz. citric acid
Sugar

Chop or mince the fruit. Take two extracts, following the general instructions. Use 2 pints of water and the citric acid for the first extract, 1 pint of water for the second. Allow ¾–1 lb. of sugar to each pint of juice.

Red Currant

6 lb. red currants
2–3 pints water
Sugar

Take two extracts, following general instructions and the recipe for black currant jelly.

CHEESES AND CURDS

Fruit cheeses are only practicable when there is a glut of fruit, as a large quantity is needed to give a small amount of preserve.

Fruit cheeses are made from stone fruits, such as damsons, plums or quinces, or fruits with strong flavours. The finished preserve has a firm solid consistency and should be left to mature for at least 2 months.

Curds are made with eggs which diminish their keeping qualities. They are of soft spreading consistency and should be made only in small quantities. Use within 1 month.

Damson Cheese (approx. yield 5–6 lb.) :

6 lb. damsons
½ pint water
Sugar

Remove any stalks and leaves from the fruit; wash thoroughly. Put the damsons and water in a heavy-based pan and cover with a lid. Simmer over gentle heat until quite soft, then rub through a sieve.

Weigh the fruit pulp and return it to a clean, dry pan. Boil rapidly until the pulp is thick and has reduced by about one-third. Add the sugar, allowing 1 lb. sugar to 1 lb. of pulp. Continue cooking, stirring all the time, until a spoon drawn across the base of the pan leaves a firm line.

Pour the cheese into small, straight-sided pots brushed with glycerine. Cover as for jam.

Lemon Curd (approx. yield 1 lb.) :

Grated rind and juice of two large lemons
3 eggs
4 oz. butter
8 oz. sugar

Beat the eggs lightly and mix in the lemon rind and juice, butter and sugar. Place in the top of a double boiler or in a bowl over hot water. Heat gently, stirring occasionally until the sugar has dissolved and the curd thickens. Pour into small, clean, dry jars and cover immediately.

Mincemeat (approx. yield 4½–5 lb.) :

This is a short-time preserve. It is steeped in brandy or rum, and left to mature for about 1 month.

½ lb. cooking apples
½ lb. currants
½ lb. stoned raisins
½ lb. sultanas
4 oz. glacé cherries
4 oz. chopped mixed peel
4 oz. shelled walnuts
8 oz. shredded suet
1 lb. Demerara sugar
2 level teaspoons mixed spice
3–4 fl. oz. brandy or rum

Peel, core and chop the apples. Clean and mince the dried fruits; mix in a large bowl with the nuts and apples. Blend in the suet, sugar and spice. Add enough brandy or rum to give a moist mixture. Cover the bowl with a cloth and leave for 48 hours to allow the fruit to swell.

Stir well and put the mincemeat into clean jars. Seal and cover as for jam.

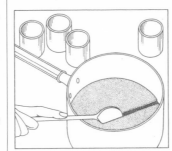

Fruit cheese is ready for potting when a spoon leaves a clear line

FRUIT SYRUPS AND WINES

Syrups are made from the sweetened juices of berry fruits, such as blackberries, currants and strawberries. Syrup is a useful way of preserving ripe fruit.

Wash and drain the fruit thoroughly. Put in a pan and cook over gentle heat until the juices run freely. Most fruits require no additional water, but black currants need ½ pint of water to each 1 lb. of fruit, and blackberries ½ pint of water to each 6 lb. of fruit. Use a wooden spoon to crush whole fruit. Bring the fruit rapidly to the boil, then boil for 1 minute and remove the pan from the heat.

Strain through a scalded jelly bag and leave to drain overnight. Press the pulp in the bag to squeeze out any remaining juices.

Measure the quantity of extracted juice, and allow ¾ lb. sugar to each pint of juice. Cook over very gentle heat until the sugar has dissolved, stir and strain the mixture through muslin. Pour into sterilised bottles to within 1½ in. of the top, and seal with scalded screw caps or corks.

Corks and stoppers should be boiled for 15 minutes before using. Secure the corks with insulation tape to prevent them from blowing off during processing.

Place the filled bottles on a trivet in a deep pan. Fill the pan with water to within 1 in. of the top of the bottles. Heat the water to 170°F and hold at this temperature for 30 minutes. Alternatively, bring the water to simmering point and hold; simmer for 20 minutes.

Lift out the bottles, tighten the screw caps or press in the corks, and leave to cool. When the corks are dry, brush the top of each bottle with melted paraffin wax, covering the corks and ½ in. of the neck.

To serve, dilute one part syrup with five parts water.

Fermented syrups

These are made from the same types of berries as fruit syrups, but no heat is applied, and a fuller fruit flavour is thus obtained.

Place the fruit, without any water, in a large earthenware bowl or jar and crush it well. Cover the bowl with a cloth and leave the fruit to ferment. When bubbles appear on the surface of the crushed fruit, fermentation is complete. Most fruits ferment within 24 hours if kept in a warm place, but black currants take about 4 days.

Strain the fermented fruit through a jelly bag and leave to drip overnight; then squeeze the bag to obtain any remaining juice. Add 1 lb. of sugar to each pint of juice, stir until dissolved, then strain the syrup through muslin. Pour into clean bottles, and seal with sterilised caps or corks.

MAKING FRUIT SYRUPS

Strain the fermented syrup

Seal caps on bottled syrup

Preserving

Fermented syrups can be processed by heating the sealed bottles as for fruit syrups. Alternatively, a chemical preservative, such as sulphur dioxide, can be added to the syrups. Allow one fruit-preserving tablet (dissolved in 1 tablespoon of water) to each pint of juice. Stir into the strained syrup before bottling and sealing.

Fermented strawberry syrup is low in acid, and requires citric acid in the proportions of $\frac{3}{4}$ oz. to each 4 pints of juice. Add this with the sugar.

HOME-MADE WINES

These are made on the same principle as fermented syrups, but require careful control to produce a good wine. Boiling water is added to the fruit, and this mixture, known as 'must', is left to ferment for a specified time. The strained juice is mixed with fresh yeast or wine yeast tablets before the sugar is added.

Wine-making equipment, obtainable from most chemists, is necessary for the successful making of wines, and the manufacturers' instructions should be carefully followed.

Home-made wine should be left to mature for 6–9 months; it is then syphoned into clean bottles, corked tightly and left for up to 1 year before using.

BOTTLING

This preserving method involves sterilisation of fruit. It must be of the finest quality, fresh and ripe, but not mushy.

All types of fruit are suitable for bottling. Berries should be carefully cleaned, stalks, stems and leaves being removed; gooseberries should be topped and tailed, and rhubarb cut into even lengths. Apples, pears and quinces should be peeled, cored, quartered or sliced, while peeled apricots and peaches can be bottled whole or in halves and the stones removed. Plums are usually bottled whole.

Syrup and jars for bottling

Fruit may be preserved in water, but the flavour and colour is improved when fruit is bottled in syrup made from 8 oz. of sugar to 1 pint of water.

Pack the prepared fruit into sterilised bottling jars. Do not dry the insides of the jars; the fruit slips more easily into place when jars are wet. Allow 10–12 oz. fruit to each 1 lb. jar. Pack the fruit as closely as possible without squashing it, and pour the syrup over it. Release any air bubbles by inserting a sterilised knife blade down the side of the jar or by jerking the filled jar. Add a little more syrup if necessary.

Seal the jars with glass or metal discs and with clips or screw bands. If using screw bands, screw down and then give a quarter turn to loosen. This allows steam to escape from the jars during processing, and prevents them from bursting. Bottling jars and clips and screw bands can be used again, but new sealing discs must be bought every time.

Methods of bottling

Processing of the fruit can be done in a water bath or pressure cooker.

For the water-bath method an accurate thermometer is necessary. Place the filled jars on a trivet in a large pan, making sure that the jars do not touch each other. Pour in enough water to reach the level of the syrup in the jars. Heat the water gently, gradually raising the temperature until it reaches 130°F in 1 hour

BOTTLING FRUIT

Pack fruit firmly into jars

Pour sugar syrup over fruit

Release air bubbles from filled jars

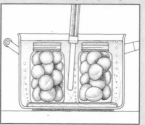

Bottle fruit at 165–190°F

Maintain 5 lb. pressure

and the required temperature in $1\frac{1}{2}$ hours. Soft berry fruits and apple slices must be held at 165°F for 10 minutes; all other fruit should be held at 180°F for 15 minutes, with the exception of figs and pears which should be held at 190°F for 30 minutes.

When the fruit has been processed, remove the jars from the pan on to a dry warm surface. Tighten the screw bands immediately and leave the jars undisturbed overnight.

When using a pressure cooker, make sure that it is deep enough to take the preserving jars and that there is a reliable control to maintain a steady 5 lb. pressure. Cover the bottom of the pan with water to a depth of 1 in., put in the trivet and set the prepared jars on top. Cover the cooker but leave the vent open, and heat until the steam flows – this should take between 5 and 10 minutes.

Close the vent and raise the pressure to 5 lb. Hold this pressure for 1 minute or, if the fruit is tightly packed, hold for 3 minutes. Pears and figs need 5 minutes. Remove the pan from the heat. Leave to cool for 10 minutes before releasing the pressure. Open the pressure cooker, remove the jars and tighten the screw bands.

Bottling tomatoes

Tomatoes can be bottled on their own or in brine. Use small to medium-sized, peeled tomatoes, and pack them tightly so that no liquid is needed. Sprinkle over them 1 level teaspoon salt and $\frac{1}{2}$ level teaspoon sugar to each 1 lb. of tomatoes. Process the jars in a water bath, holding the temperature of 190°F for 40 minutes.

Alternatively, pack the tomatoes in jars and cover with brine made from $\frac{1}{2}$ oz. salt to 1 quart of water. Process in a water bath, at 190°F for 30 minutes or in a pressure cooker for 5 minutes at 5 lb. pressure.

Tomato Purée
6 lb. ripe tomatoes

Wash and quarter the tomatoes. Cook them over low heat in an aluminium or stainless steel pan until the juices run and the tomatoes have reduced to a pulp. Rub through a nylon sieve; return the purée to the boil, then pour it into hot jars. Seal the jars as for bottling and process in a water bath, holding the temperature at 165°F for 10 minutes.

PICKLING

Pickles are fresh vegetables or fruit preserved in vinegar. Good-quality vinegar, with an acetic acid content of at least 5 per cent, is essential for pickling. White vinegar shows off the colour and texture of pickles, but malt vinegar gives a better flavour. Whichever vinegar is chosen it is usually flavoured with spices.

See illustration on p. 384.

Preparing spiced vinegar

To make spiced vinegar, add $\frac{1}{2}$ oz. each of whole allspice, whole cinnamon, cloves, whole bruised ginger and white peppercorns to 1 quart of vinegar. Steep the spices in the vinegar for 1–2 months and shake the bottle occasionally. Strain before use.

For immediate use, spiced vinegar can be prepared by a quicker method. Put the spices and vinegar into a bowl, cover and stand it in a pan of cold water. Bring the water to the boil, remove the pan from the heat, and leave the spices in the warm vinegar for about 2 hours. Keep the bowl covered so that no flavour is lost. Strain the vinegar before use.

Methods of pickling

Wash and prepare the vegetables or fruit according to the recipe. Vegetables must be liberally sprinkled with coarse salt to draw out excess water which would otherwise dilute the vinegar. Put the vegetables in layers with the salt or immerse them completely in a brine solution of 1 lb. coarse salt to 1 gallon of water.

Leave the vegetables to steep in the salt for 24–48 hours, then rinse in cold water and drain thoroughly. Do not use metal sieves or colanders.

Pack the vegetables into clean, dry jars to within 1 in. of the top. Pour over enough spiced vinegar to come $\frac{1}{2}$ in. above the vegetables. Seal the jars tightly with vinegar-proof metal caps, greaseproof paper and muslin dipped in melted paraffin wax, or with preserving skins. It is essential that the jars are sealed airtight, otherwise the vinegar will evaporate and the pickle dry out.

The number of jars needed depends on the size of the pickled vegetable and how tightly they are packed. In general, 1 lb. solid ingredients will fill a 1 lb. jar.

Label and date the jars. Store in a cool, dry place for at least 1 month before using.

Sweet pickles

For sweet pickles, omit the peppercorns when preparing the spiced vinegar, and use this as a base for a syrup, allowing 2 lb. of sugar to each pint of spiced vinegar. Simmer the fruit in the syrup until just tender. Pack the fruit or vegetables in jars, pour over the syrup and seal.

When sweet-pickling whole fruit, prick them lightly to prevent shrinkage.

Pickled Beetroot

3 lb. uncooked beetroot
1 pint spiced vinegar (approx.)

Wash the beetroot carefully without damaging the skins. Cook in lightly salted water until tender, after about 2 hours. Peel and cut the beetroot into small dice or slices. Pack into jars and cover with cold spiced vinegar.

Pickled Cucumber

3 large cucumbers
4 large onions
4 level tablespoons coarse salt
1 pint distilled vinegar
6 oz. granulated or preserving sugar
1 level teaspoon celery seeds
1 level teaspoon mustard seeds

Wash, dry and thinly slice the cucumbers. Peel and slice the onions. Mix the two ingredients together in a bowl and sprinkle with the salt. Leave for 2 hours, then rinse and drain.

Bring the vinegar, sugar and spices to the boil and simmer for 3 minutes. Pack the drained cucumber and onion loosely in warm jars. Cover with the spiced vinegar and seal immediately.

Pickled Peaches

4 lb. peaches
1 pint spiced vinegar syrup

Peel the peaches*. Cut away any discoloured parts, then halve and quarter the peaches, removing the stones. Poach* in the hot spiced vinegar syrup for 10 minutes or until tender.

Pack the fruit tightly into warm jars. Boil the syrup rapidly for 2–3 minutes to reduce it, remove any scum, and pour the syrup over the fruit. Seal at once.

Pickled Onions

6 lb. small onions
2 pints spiced vinegar

Select small, even-sized onions and put them, unpeeled, in brine. Leave for 12 hours, then peel the onions and immerse them in fresh brine for a further 24–36 hours. Remove from the brine, rinse and drain thoroughly. Pack into clean jars and cover with cold spiced vinegar. Seal. Leave for 2–3 months before using.

Pickled Red Cabbage

1 large red cabbage
3 pints spiced vinegar (approx.)

Select a firm, brightly coloured cabbage. Remove outer leaves and centre stalk. Shred the cabbage finely, and layer it with salt in a large bowl. Leave for 24 hours, then drain and rinse thoroughly. Pack the cabbage loosely into jars; cover with cold spiced vinegar and seal. Use within 3 months.

Piccalilli

6 lb. prepared vegetables (cucumber, marrow, small onions, cauliflower, beans)
3 pints white vinegar
6 level teaspoons dry mustard
2 level teaspoons ground ginger
9 oz. granulated sugar
1½ oz. plain flour
4 level teaspoons turmeric

Clean and prepare the vegetables. Cut the cucumber and marrow into 1 in. cubes; peel the onions, break the cauliflower into florets; and cut the beans into 1 in. lengths. Immerse the vegetables in brine and leave overnight.

Spice the vinegar with mustard and ginger, and add the sugar.

Rinse and drain the vegetables thoroughly. Put them in a pan, pour over the hot vinegar syrup, and simmer for 20 minutes. Lift the vegetables out with a slotted spoon and pack into warm jars.

Mix the flour and turmeric to a smooth paste with a little vinegar. Stir this into the hot syrup. Boil for 2 minutes, then pour over the vegetables and seal.

Tomato Sauce

6 lb. ripe tomatoes
½ lb. granulated sugar
½ pint spiced vinegar
1 level teaspoon paprika
2 level teaspoons salt
Cayenne pepper

Wash and quarter the tomatoes. Cook them over gentle heat until the juices run, then increase the heat and boil rapidly until reduced to a pulp. Rub through a nylon sieve and return the purée to a clean pan. Stir in the sugar, vinegar, paprika, salt and a pinch of cayenne. Bring to the boil and cook until the mixture has a sauce consistency.

Pour the tomato sauce into warm bottles and seal. Process the bottles for 30 minutes (see fruit syrups).

CHUTNEYS

These are usually made from fruit such as apples, gooseberries plums and tomatoes. Flavourings are added in the form of spices, onions, garlic and salt, and the preserve is sweetened with sugar, or sugar and dried fruits. Chutneys require long, slow cooking in an aluminium or stainless steel pan. The preserve should be smooth and pulpy with a mellow flavour. Pour the chutney into warm, clean jars, and cover with vinegar-proof tops or preserving skins. Leave for 2–3 months before using.

See illustration on p. 384.

Apple Chutney

4 lb. cooking apples
1 pint vinegar
2–3 cloves garlic
1½ lb. soft brown sugar
4 oz. crystallised ginger or 2 level teaspoons ground ginger
½ level teaspoon mixed spice
Cayenne pepper
½ level teaspoon salt

Peel, core and chop the apples. Cook with $\frac{1}{2}$ pint of vinegar and the crushed garlic until thick and pulpy. Add the remaining vinegar, the sugar, ginger, mixed spice, a good pinch of cayenne, and salt; continue cooking for a further 20 minutes or until thick. Pot and cover.

Apple Mint Chutney

4 lb. cooking apples
1 lb. ripe tomatoes
1 pint vinegar
1 lb. soft brown sugar
4 oz. crystallised ginger or 2 level teaspoons ground ginger
½ level teaspoon mixed spice
Pinch cayenne pepper
½ level teaspoon salt
1 lb. seedless raisins
2 oz. finely chopped mint

Peel, core and chop the apples, and skin and chop the tomatoes*. Cook the apples with $\frac{1}{2}$ pint of vinegar until thick and pulpy, then stir in the remaining vinegar, the sugar, ginger, mixed spice, cayenne pepper and raisins.

Cook for a further 15 minutes, then stir in the mint and cook for 5 more minutes or until thick. Pot and cover.

Tomato Chutney

6 lb. ripe tomatoes
½ lb. onions
4 level teaspoons whole allspice
1 level teaspoon cayenne pepper
1 tablespoon salt
½ pint vinegar
¾ lb. soft brown sugar

Skin and quarter the tomatoes* and put them in a large pan, together with the peeled and thinly sliced onions. Add the allspice, tied in muslin, and the cayenne and salt. Cook over gentle heat until the mixture is pulpy, then stir in the remaining ingredients. Simmer until thick. Pot and cover.

Pastry

The many different kinds of pastry which are made in Britain today have evolved over the centuries from a crude flour and water dough mixture invented by the Romans. The paste was wrapped round meat and game before roasting and was not intended to be eaten. It served only to retain the meat juices and aroma.

As time passed, the paste was enriched with fat and milk and began vaguely to resemble today's shortcrust pastry. By medieval times, pastry-making was well-established and rich-crust pastry coverings, known as coffers, became as important as the contents of the huge fruit, fish, meat and game pies they coveted.

As different areas and localities developed their own puddings and pies, many pastry variations emerged from the basic fat, flour and water recipe. Perhaps the most famous of all is the 14th-century raised hot-water crust. This was indigenous to Britain and was used with meat and game pies. It was moulded from the inside with a clenched fist, in the same way as a clay pot, and then filled and baked until crisp and brown. The method is perpetuated in the Melton Mowbray pork pies.

By the 17th century both flaky and puff pastries were being used for elaborate pies, and the decorations and intricate patterns on the finished pies were works of art. Later still, continental pastry-making was added to the ever-growing number of recipes, and yet today the basic art of pastry-making is much as it has been for centuries.

Pastry is no longer used principally to retain the juices of the filling it covers. Its chief purpose is to complement the flavour of the filling and at the same time to provide a convenient casing in which anything from a steak and kidney pudding to a lemon meringue pie may be cooked. It also helps to eke out a limited amount of meat, fish, game or fruit.

Although much mystique surrounds pastry-making, there are no great secrets to guarantee instant success, for pastry-making is an art which is mastered by care, patience and practice. There are, however, a few essentials which must be observed before good results can be achieved. The kitchen, working surface and utensils should be cool, and the recipe must always be strictly adhered to, especially in regard to measurements. Pastry should be made as quickly as possible, and handling kept to a minimum. Many pastries are best rested in a cool place before they are cooked.

Shortcrust, with its variations, is probably the best known and most commonly used pastry. Next in popularity are the more robust pastries, such as suet and hot-water crust. Choux, and the flaky and rough puff pastry are slightly more difficult, while puff pastry is considered to be the hardest of all. But even with these, patience and practice can achieve splendid results.

SHORTCRUST PASTRY

This popular and versatile pastry is used for savoury and sweet pies, tarts, flans and tartlets. It is usually made by the 'rubbing-in' method, but there are several other ways of making shortcrust. Plain flour is recommended; self-raising flour may be used, but the pastry will be more crumbly. The fat should be lard or a white vegetable fat; ideally, use equal amounts of lard and firm margarine. Margarine alone produces a yellow, firm pastry.

The standard recipe is for 8 oz. shortcrust which always means 8 oz. flour to 4 oz. fat. The amount of flour may be doubled or halved, but proportions should remain the same: half the fat to the amount of flour.

The standard recipe yields enough pastry to cover a 2 pint dish, or a 9 in. flan ring, or to line and cover a 7 in. pie plate.

The following basic shortcrust pastries may be used for both savoury and sweet pies. Enriched shortcrust pastry, however, is mainly used for flans. Shortcrust pastries are usually baked in the centre of a pre-heated oven, at 400°F (mark 6).

Traditional Shortcrust
PREPARATION TIME: *15 min.*

INGREDIENTS:
8 oz. plain flour
½ level teaspoon salt
2 oz. lard
2 oz. margarine or butter
2–3 tablespoons cold water

Sift the flour and salt into a wide bowl. Cut up the firm fats and rub them into the flour, using the tips of the fingers, until the mixture resembles fine breadcrumbs. Lift the dry mixture well out of the bowl and let it trickle back through the fingers to keep the pastry cool and light. Add the water, sprinkling it evenly over the surface (uneven addition of the water may cause blistering when the pastry is cooked). Mix the dough lightly with a round-bladed knife until it forms large lumps.

Gather the dough together with the fingers until it leaves the sides of the bowl clean. Form it into one piece and knead it lightly on a floured surface until firm and free from cracks. Chill for 30 minutes before use.

Roll the pastry out as required, using short, light strokes and rotate the pastry regularly to keep it an even shape.

One-stage (Fork) Pastry

A shortcrust pastry using soft table margarine to give a yellow-tinted pastry with a smooth appearance and soft crumb.

PREPARATION TIME: *10 min.*

INGREDIENTS:
5 oz. soft table margarine
8 oz. plain flour
2 tablespoons water

Put the soft margarine with 2 tablespoons of flour and the water in a deep mixing bowl. Cream these ingredients with a fork until well mixed. Still using the fork, work in the remaining flour to form a manageable dough. Turn this on to a floured surface and knead lightly until smooth. Chill for 30 minutes.

PREPARING TRADITIONAL SHORTCRUST PASTRY

1. *Rubbing fat into flour*

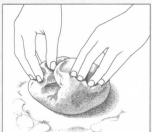

3. *Kneading dough lightly*

2. *Mixing water into dough*

4. *Rolling out the pastry*

To make one-stage pastry, cream margarine with flour and water

Shortcrust Pastry with Oil

This pastry produces a tender, flaky crumb. It must be mixed quickly and used at once – if left for any length of time, or chilled, it dries out and cannot be rolled.

PREPARATION TIME: *15 min.*

INGREDIENTS:
5 tablespoons corn oil
2½ fluid oz. cold water
8 oz. plain flour
¼ level teaspoon salt

Whisk the oil and water together in a large bowl, using a fork. Continue whisking until they are evenly blended. Sift the flour and salt together and gradually add it to the oil. Use two knives to incorporate the flour to a dough, then turn it on to a floured surface. Knead the pastry lightly and quickly until smooth and shiny. Roll out and bake as traditional shortcrust.

For shortcrust pastry with oil, use two knives to mix the flour and oil

Enriched Shortcrust Pastry

PREPARATION TIME: *10 min.*

INGREDIENTS:
5 oz. plain flour
Pinch salt
3 oz. unsalted butter or margarine
1 egg yolk
1½ level teaspoons caster sugar
3–4 teaspoons water

Sift the flour and salt into a wide bowl. Cut up the fat and rub it into the flour with the fingertips until the mixture resembles breadcrumbs. Beat the egg yolk, sugar and 2 teaspoons of water in a separate bowl and pour it into the flour mixture. Stir with a round-bladed knife, adding more water as necessary until the mixture begins to form a dough. Gather this into a ball and turn it on to a floured surface. Knead lightly.

American (Stir 'n' Stir) Crust

This rather sticky shortcrust pastry is particularly suited to double crust fruit pies. The texture of the baked pie is more like shortbread than shortcrust.

PREPARATION TIME: *10–15 min.*

INGREDIENTS:
5 oz. table margarine
1½ oz. butter
8 oz. self-raising flour
½ level teaspoon salt
3 tablespoons cold water

Beat the margarine and butter in a bowl until soft and well blended. Gradually add the sifted flour and salt, working it in with a wooden spoon. Finally add the water, blending thoroughly. The mixture will be sticky and difficult to work. Chill for at least 30 minutes.

Roll out the pastry on a well-floured surface or between sheets of waxed or non-stick paper, dredged with flour.

Cheese Pastry

A shortcrust pastry ideal for cheese straws, as a crust for vegetable pies, and for flan cases.

PREPARATION TIME: *10 min.*

INGREDIENTS:
4 oz. plain flour
Salt and cayenne pepper
2 oz. butter or margarine
2 oz. Cheddar, Lancashire or Cheshire cheese
1 egg yolk
2–3 teaspoons cold water

Sift the flour, a pinch of salt and a shake of cayenne into a wide bowl. Cut up the fat and rub it into the flour with the fingertips until the mixture resembles fine breadcrumbs. Blend in the grated cheese and stir in the egg yolk mixed with 1 tablespoon of water to ensure even distribution. Add more water to give a stiff dough.

Knead the dough lightly on a floured surface, and chill.

Covering a Pie Dish

Roll out the pastry to the required thickness (no more than ¼ in. thick) and 2 in. wider than the pie dish, using the inverted dish as a guide. Cut a 1 in. wide strip from the outer edge of the pastry and place it on the moistened rim of the pie dish. Seal the strip with water where it joins and brush the whole strip with water.

Fill the pie dish and set a pie funnel in the centre; lift the remaining pastry on the rolling pin and lay it over the pie dish. Press the pastry strip and lid firmly together with the fingers. Trim any excess pastry with a knife blade held at a slight angle to the dish.

To seal the pastry edges firmly so that they do not come apart during baking, hold the knife blade horizontally towards the pie dish and make a series of shallow cuts in the pastry edges – this is known as 'knocking up'. Use the pastry trimmings to cut decorative shapes for the top of the pie. Cut a slit into the centre of the pastry for the steam to escape, and decorate the edges.

Preparing a Double Crust Pie

Divide the pastry into two portions, one slightly larger than the other. Shape the larger portion into a ball and roll it out on a lightly floured surface, to a thickness of a 10p coin. Rotate the pastry between rolls to keep the edge round; if the edge begins to break pinch it together with the fingers. Roll out the pastry about 1 in. wider than the inverted pie plate.

Fold the pastry in half and lift it on to the pie plate; unfold and loosely ease the pastry into position, being careful not to stretch the pastry. Put the cold filling over the pastry base, keeping it slightly domed in the centre. Roll out the remaining pastry for the lid, allowing about ½ in. beyond the rim. Brush the edge of the pastry lining with water, then lift the lid on the rolling pin and place in position over the filling.

Seal the edges by either folding the surplus edge of the lid firmly over the rim of the lining, or by trimming the edges almost level with the plate and knocking them up with a knife. Cut a slit in the centre of the pastry lid for the steam to escape.

Lining a Pie Plate

For an open pie, roll out the pastry ⅛ in. thick and about 1 in. wider than the pie plate. Lift the pastry into the plate and ease it loosely over the base and sides. Trim the pastry with scissors to ½ in. from the plate edge, then fold the pastry under the rim of the plate. Flute the edge (see Finishing and Decorations) so that the points protrude over the plate rim and thus prevent shrinking during baking.

COVERING A PIE DISH

Trim the pastry to fit the dish

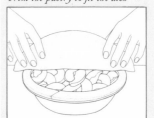

Cover the filled pie dish

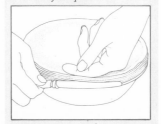

'Knock up' pastry edges

MAKING A DOUBLE CRUST PIE

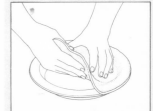

Lift pastry into pie plate

Place pastry lid in position

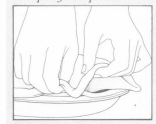

Fold surplus pastry under

Pastry

Lining a Flan Case

Flans are baked in plain or fluted rings set on baking trays or in a French fluted flan tin with a loose base. Roll the pastry out as thinly as possible, $\frac{1}{8}$ in. or less, to a circle 2 in. wider than the ring. With the rolling pin, lift the pastry and lower it into the flan ring. Lift the edges carefully and press the pastry gently into shape with the fingers, taking care that no air pockets are left between the ring and the pastry. Trim the pastry in a plain ring with a knife or scissors, just above the rim, and knock up the edges. On a fluted flan ring, press the pastry against the inner fluted ring edges then use the rolling pin to cut the pastry level with the rim.

LINING A FLAN RING

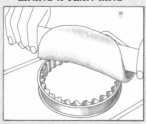

Lay pastry over flan

Press pastry into fluted ridges

Roll off surplus pastry

Lining Tartlet Moulds

Set the small moulds closely together on a baking tray. Roll out the pastry, $\frac{1}{8}$ in. thick, to a rectangle or square large enough to cover the whole area of moulds. Lay the pastry loosely over the moulds, press it into the moulds with a small ball of pastry. Run the rolling pin over the moulds, first in one direction, then in the other, and trim off any surplus. Press the pastry into shape with the fingers and prick the bases (see Baking Blind).

To line a sheet of patty pans, use a plain or fluted cutter, $\frac{1}{2}$–$\frac{3}{4}$ in. wider than the patty, to cut out rounds from the pastry. Ease the pastry rounds into the patties and prick them with a fork.

LINING TARTLET MOULDS

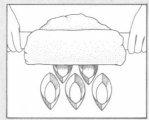

Lay pastry over the moulds

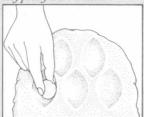

Shape moulds with pastry ball

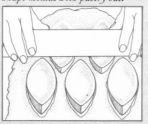

Trim off surplus pastry

Baking Blind

Sometimes pastry, especially flan cases and individual tartlets, has to be baked before the filling is put in. This is known as baking blind. Line the pastry case with foil or greaseproof paper cut to shape and weigh it down with dried beans (if kept specially for this purpose, the beans can be used again and again). Bake the pastry case in the centre of a pre-heated oven at 400°F (mark 6) for 15 minutes. Remove the beans and foil and bake for a further 5–10 minutes or until the pastry is dry and lightly browned.

Alternatively, and especially for tartlets, prick the base and sides of the pastry with a fork before lining it with foil. Dried beans are not necessary if the pastry is pricked.

Flan cases and tartlet moulds should be left on a wire rack to cool and shrink slightly before being eased out of their moulds.

To bake blind, cover pastry with paper and weigh down with beans

Finishing and Decorations

The knocked up edges of a covered pie can be finished in a number of decorative ways. To make a fluted pattern, press the outer edge between thumb and index finger, at intervals of $\frac{1}{2}$–$\frac{3}{4}$ in. Draw the back of a knife between the indentations towards the centre of the pie for about $\frac{1}{2}$ in.

Alternatively, press the edges together with the back of a fork, or use the thumb to make a scalloped pattern.

DECORATING PIE EDGES

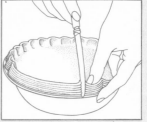

Making a fluted pattern

Making scalloped edges

The top of a covered pie may be decorated with the pastry trimmings. Roll the pastry out thinly and cut it into small plain or fluted circles, stars and diamonds. Arrange these in a pattern over the glazed top.

To make leaves, cut the pastry into 1–$1\frac{1}{2}$ in. wide strips and cut these into diamond shapes. With the back of a knife, trace first the midribs, then the internal veins in each leaf shape.

For a tassel, cut a 1 in. wide pastry slice about 6 in. long. Make cuts, $\frac{3}{4}$ in. long, at intervals of $\frac{1}{4}$ in., then roll up the strip, place it on the pie and open out the cut edges.

Finish the edges of open flans and tarts by fluting or crimping. A simple method, using a pair of scissors, is to make cuts just over $\frac{1}{4}$ in. deep and a little over $\frac{1}{4}$ in. apart around the pastry edge. Fold alternate pieces of pastry inwards and bend the remaining pieces outwards. Or the edges can be decorated with thin pastry strips that have been twisted or braided. Moisten the pastry edge with water before putting on a twisted or braided border.

PASTRY DECORATIONS

Pastry leaf shapes

Pastry tassel

Cut edges on a flan

Twisted pastry strips

A lattice pattern is a traditional decoration for many open flans. Cut the rolled out pastry trimmings into $\frac{1}{2}$ in. wide strips (a pastry wheel gives an attractive edge) and long enough to cover the flan. Moisten the flan edges, then lay half the strips over the filling, 1 in. apart, and lay the remaining strips criss-crossing the first. Trim the strips to shape at the outer edge, or fold the pastry lining down over them for a neater finish. For a really professional touch, the pastry strips should be interwoven by laying them over the filling 1 in. apart, and a strip of pastry at a right angle across the centre. Lift alternate lengths of the first strips of pastry on one half of the tart and place a strip at right angles. Replace the top strips and repeat with the other side of the tart to complete the interwoven effect. The strips may also be twisted before being arranged in the lattice pattern.

Lattice pattern: lay pastry strips over flan top; interleave crossing strips

Pies can be decorated with pastry flowers. Simple flowers are made by rolling a small piece of pastry to the size and shape of an acorn. Cut out two diamond shapes and pinch the edges to round them to a petal shape. Dampen the base of the petals and wrap around the wide base of the acorn shape. Pinch the pastry to seal the pieces together, then bend the tip of each petal slightly outwards.

More ornate flowers can be made by making a cross with a knife on a small, flattened round of pastry. Set the round on a square of dampened pastry; set this in turn on another square of dampened pastry, similar in size,

DECORATIVE PASTRY FLOWERS

Simple flower shapes

Ornate pastry flowers

to form a star pattern. Shape the corners of the squares to resemble petals. Pinch and shape each point of the central round of pastry into a petal to complete the flower.

Glazing

Brush the decorated pie or flan before baking to give a shiny golden look. Brush savoury pies with beaten whole egg or with egg yolk diluted with a little water or milk, and a pinch of salt. Glaze sweet pies with milk or egg white and dust with caster sugar.

Apple Pie

PREPARATION TIME: *20 min.*
COOKING TIME: *35 min.*

INGREDIENTS *(for 4–6):*
6–8 oz. shortcrust pastry
1½ lb. cooking apples
2–3 oz. caster or Demerara sugar
Milk

Peel and core the apples and cut them into chunky slices. Place a pie funnel in the centre of a 1½ pint pie dish, arrange half the apple slices in the dish, sprinkle over the sugar and add the remaining fruit with 3 tablespoons of water.

Cover the pie with the rolled-out pastry, decorate it and brush the top with milk. Dust with caster sugar. Make a slit in the centre of the pastry lid for the steam to escape. Set the pie on a baking tray and bake in the centre of the oven pre-heated to 400°F (mark 6) for 35–40 minutes. If the pastry browns too quickly, cover it with a double layer of moistened greaseproof paper.

For variation, the water may be replaced with orange juice and the grated rind of half an orange mixed with the sugar.

Alternatively, use 1 lb. apples and ½ lb. blackberries for the filling. Other fruits, such as halved and stoned apricots, damsons, plums and greengages, topped

and tailed gooseberries and 1 in. pieces of trimmed rhubarb also make good fruit pies. For gooseberry and rhubarb pie, increase the amount of sugar to 4 oz.

Cheese and Onion Pie

PREPARATION TIME: *30 min.*
COOKING TIME: *35 min.*

INGREDIENTS *(for 4–6):*
8 oz. shortcrust pastry
4 large onions (approx. 1 lb.)
6–8 oz. coarsely grated mature cheese
½ level teaspoon grated nutmeg
1 level teaspoon salt
Black pepper
2 teaspoons Worcestershire sauce
Milk

Peel and quarter the onions, cook them in boiling water for about 15 minutes, or until they are just tender. Drain thoroughly in a colander, then cool slightly before chopping them roughly.

Divide the prepared pastry in two and roll out each half to fit an 8–9 in. pie plate. Line the plate with half the pastry and cover with half the cheese and the onions. Season with nutmeg, salt, pepper and Worcestershire sauce. Top with the remaining cheese, and cover the pie with pastry. Seal and knock up the edges. Brush with milk and make a small slit in the pastry lid. Bake in pre-heated oven, at 400°F (mark 6), for 30–35 minutes.

See illustration on p. 377.

Lemon Meringue Pie

PREPARATION TIME: *30 min.*
COOKING TIME: *40 min.*

INGREDIENTS *(for 4–6):*
4 oz. shortcrust pastry
1 large thin-skinned lemon
2–3 level tablespoons granulated sugar
2 level tablespoons cornflour
2 eggs
½ oz. unsalted butter
4 oz. caster sugar

Roll out the pastry and line an 8½ in. pie plate or a 7 in. flan ring. Bake the pastry case blind in the centre of a pre-heated oven, at 400°F (mark 6) for about 15 minutes or until the pastry is crisp and golden. When cold, remove the pastry from the pie plate or ease away the flan ring.

Meanwhile, peel the rind from the lemon in thin slivers, carefully omitting all white pith. Squeeze the juice from the lemon and set it aside. Put the lemon peel, granulated sugar and ½ pint of water in a pan; cook over low heat until the sugar has dissolved, then bring this syrup to the boil. Remove the pan from the heat. Blend the cornflour in a bowl with 3 tablespoons lemon juice, then pour in the syrup through a strainer, stirring thoroughly. Separate the eggs, and beat in the egg yolks, one at a time, together with the butter. The mixture should be thick enough to coat the back of a wooden spoon; otherwise return it to the pan and cook for a few minutes without boiling. Spoon the lemon mixture into the cooked pastry case, set on a baking tray.

Whisk the egg whites until stiff, then add half the caster sugar and continue whisking until the meringue holds its shape and stands in soft peaks. Fold in all but 1 teaspoon of the remaining sugar, using a metal spoon.

Pile the meringue over the lemon filling; spread it from the edge towards the centre, making sure that the meringue joins the pastry edge to prevent the meringue 'weeping'. Sprinkle the meringue with the remaining sugar. Reduce the heat to 300°F (mark 2) and bake the pie in the centre of the oven for 20–30 minutes, or until the meringue is crisp. Serve the pie warm, rather than hot or cold.

See illustration on p. 377.

Duke of Cambridge Tart

PREPARATION TIME: *15 min.*
COOKING TIME: *35 min.*

INGREDIENTS *(for 4):*
4 oz. shortcrust pastry
2 oz. glacé cherries
1 oz. angelica
1 oz. chopped mixed peel
3 oz. butter
3 oz. caster sugar
2 egg yolks

Roll out the pastry and use to line a 7 in. fluted flan ring. Chop the cherries and angelica, or snip them with scissors, mix them with the peel and cover the base of the flan case evenly with the fruit.

Put the butter, sugar and egg yolks in a small pan over low heat, and beat steadily with a wooden spoon. Bring the mixture to the boil and pour it over the fruit. Bake the tart in the centre of the pre-heated oven, at 375°F (mark 5), for about 40 minutes.

Cheese and Bacon Quiche

PREPARATION TIME: *30 min.*
COOKING TIME: *40 min.*

INGREDIENTS *(for 4–6):*
6 oz. shortcrust pastry
2 oz. onion
½ oz. butter or margarine
4 oz. lean streaky bacon
4 oz. grated Cheddar cheese
2 large eggs
¼ pint milk
2 tablespoons single cream or top of the milk
Salt and black pepper
1 tablespoon freshly chopped parsley (optional)

Roll out the pastry and use it to line an 8–8½ in. flan ring. Peel and finely chop the onion, fry it in the butter over low heat for 5 minutes until soft and transparent. Set aside. Remove the rind and gristle from the rashers and cut the bacon into small pieces. Fry until the fat runs and the bacon begins to crisp. Drain off the fat.

Pastry

Mix the onion and bacon and arrange it in the flan case; cover with the cheese.

Lightly whisk the eggs with the milk and cream; add the chopped parsley and season to taste. Spoon this mixture over the flan filling and bake in the centre of a pre-heated oven, at 400°F (mark 6), for 30 minutes. Reduce the heat to 350°F (mark 4) and bake for a further 10 minutes, until the filling is set and the pastry crisp and golden brown. Serve the quiche warm or cold.

Plum and Cinnamon Pie

PREPARATION TIME: *5 min.*
COOKING TIME: *40 min.*
STANDING TIME: *1 hour*

INGREDIENTS *(for 6):*
8 oz. American stir'n' stir pastry
2 16 oz. tins golden plums
1 level tablespoon fine tapioca
¼ level teaspoon powdered
  cinnamon
1 oz. butter
1 egg white
Granulated sugar

Drain the plums, reserving the syrup, and remove the stones. Blend the tapioca and cinnamon in a bowl with 6 tablespoons of the plum syrup and leave it to stand for 30 minutes.

Roll out half the prepared pastry and use it to line a 10 in. pie plate. Mix the plums with the tapioca mixture and spoon it over the pastry base; dot with butter. Roll out the remaining pastry for the lid and cover the pie. Seal the edges, knock them up and make a slit in the lid. Brush the top with beaten egg white and dust generously with sugar. Chill for 30 minutes.

Set the pie on a heated baking tray and bake in the centre of a pre-heated oven at 400°F (mark 6) for about 40 minutes. Serve the pie warm, with whipped cream.

See illustration on p. 377.

Rum and Butter Tarts

PREPARATION TIME: *15 min.*
COOKING TIME: *15–20 min.*

INGREDIENTS: *(for 12–14 tarts):*
4 oz. shortcrust pastry
3 oz. currants
1 oz. butter
3½ oz. light soft brown sugar
1 tablespoon single cream or top of the milk
Rum or rum essence
½ egg or 1 egg yolk

Cover the currants with boiling water and leave them to stand until they are plump – about 10 minutes; drain thoroughly. Roll out the pastry and use to line 12–14 patty tins about 2½ in. long. Use a plain or fluted pastry cutter.

Melt the butter in a small pan, remove from the heat and stir in the sugar, cream and rum to taste. Add the currants and stir in the thoroughly beaten egg.

Using a teaspoon, divide the currant mixture evenly between the small tarts. Do not let the filling come more than three-quarters up the pastry. Bake just above the centre of an oven pre-heated to 375°F (mark 5) for 15–20 minutes or until the pastry is crisp and the filling golden.

Cheese Straws

PREPARATION TIME: *10 min.*
COOKING TIME: *35 min.*

INGREDIENTS:
4 oz. cheese pastry

Roll out the prepared pastry as thinly as possible to a rectangle. Trim the edges evenly, then cut the pastry into strips, ¼ in. wide and 2 in. long, using a floured knife blade. Set the straws on greased baking trays and bake just above the centre of a pre-heated oven, at 400°F (mark 6), for 12 minutes, or until golden.

Leave the cheese straws to cool on a wire rack.

BISCUIT CRUST

This uncooked crust is ideal for flan cases with fluffy chiffon-type fillings.

PREPARATION TIME: *15 min.*
CHILLING TIME: *2 hours*

INGREDIENTS:
8 oz. digestive, wheatmeal, rich tea or gingernut biscuits
5 oz. butter
1–2 oz. sugar (optional)

Crush the biscuits, a few at a time, with a rolling pin between two sheets of greaseproof paper or in a plastic bag. For a fine crumb, break up the biscuits roughly and put them in a liquidiser. Turn the crumbs into a deep bowl. Melt the butter in a small saucepan over low heat. Add the sugar, if used, to the crumbs and mix with the melted butter, stirring until evenly combined.

Spread the crumbly mixture into a 7–8 in. wide shallow pie plate or flan dish; alternatively, use a flan ring placed on a flat serving dish or a loose-bottomed flan tin. With the back of a spoon, press the crumbs over the base and up the sides to form a shell.

Chill the flan case in the refrigerator for 2 hours before filling it.

Chocolate Cream Pie

PREPARATION TIME: *20 min.*
CHILLING TIME: *1 hour*

INGREDIENTS *(for 6):*
1 portion biscuit crust
FILLING:
½ pint milk
1 oz. caster sugar
1 oz. plain flour
1½ level teaspoons cornflour
2 eggs
1 oz. unsalted butter
3–3½ oz. dark plain chocolate, grated
2 teaspoons brandy or rum
Icing sugar

TOPPING:
¼ pint double cream
1 tablespoon milk
Grated chocolate (optional)

Make up the biscuit crust according to the basic recipe and line an 8½ in. French fluted flan case.

Heat the milk. Blend the sugar, flour, cornflour and beaten egg together in a bowl, then stir in the milk. Return this mixture to the pan and cook over low heat, stirring continuously, until the mixture thickens and just comes to the boil. Remove the pan from the heat and stir in the butter, cut into small pieces, the chocolate and brandy. Stir until smooth, then leave to cool slightly. Spoon the filling into the biscuit crust, and dust it with icing sugar to prevent a skin forming. Chill.

Just before serving, whip the cream with the milk until thick enough to hold its shape. Spoon this in an even layer over the chocolate filling. Dust with coarsely grated chocolate.

See illustration on p. 377.

Quick Lemon Cheesecake

PREPARATION TIME: *20 min.*
CHILLING TIME: *2–3 hours*

INGREDIENTS *(for 4–6):*
Biscuit crust
6 oz. rich tea biscuits
3½ oz. butter or margarine
2 oz. caster sugar
FILLING:
Half 1-pint lemon jelly tablet
8 oz. soft cream cheese
2 oz. caster sugar
Grated rind of a large lemon
TOPPING:
3 tablespoons lemon juice
1½ level teaspoons arrowroot
1 oz. caster sugar
Butter

Make up the biscuit crust from the given ingredients and follow the basic recipe. Shape the crust in an 8 in. flan ring set on a flat plate, or use a fluted loose-bottomed flan case.

Put the jelly tablet in a measuring jug and make up to ¼ pint with hot water; stir until the jelly has dissolved, then chill in the refrigerator until it has the consistency of unbeaten egg white. Beat the cream cheese with the sugar and the lemon rind, and gradually beat in the jelly. Spoon the smooth filling into the biscuit crust and chill until the filling has set.

Make the lemon juice up to ¼ pint with water. In a small pan, blend the arrowroot to a smooth paste with a little of this liquid, add the rest of the liquid and the sugar. Bring to the boil, stirring, and keep boiling until the mixture is clear. Remove the pan from the heat and add a knob of butter. Cool the mixture until lukewarm, then spoon it evenly over the filling. Chill until required.

PREPARING A BISCUIT CRUST

Crush biscuits in a polythene bag

Stir in the melted butter

Press the mixture into flan case

SUET CRUST PASTRY

This traditional British pastry is used for steamed or boiled savoury and sweet puddings, and for roly-poly puddings and dumplings. Suet is available already shredded and pre-packed, but for the best results use fresh beef suet. Correct mixing and handling achieve a pastry of a light spongy texture. For an even lighter texture replace 2 oz. of the measured flour with 2 oz. fresh white breadcrumbs.

PREPARATION TIME: *15 min.*
RESTING TIME: *15 min.*

INGREDIENTS *(for 2 pint pudding)*:
8 oz. self-raising flour or 8 oz. plain flour and 3 level teaspoons baking powder
$\frac{1}{2}$ *level teaspoon salt*
4 oz. shredded suet
$\frac{1}{4}$ *pint cold water (approx.)*

Sift the flour and salt into a bowl (together with baking powder if plain flour is used). Add the suet – remove the skin from fresh suet, then grate or chop it finely with a little of the flour to prevent sticking – and mix thoroughly. Using a round-bladed knife, stir in the water to form a light, elastic dough. Turn the dough on to a lightly floured surface, and sprinkle it with a little flour. Knead the dough lightly with the fingertips and shape it into a ball. Put the dough on a plate and cover with an inverted bowl; leave to rest for 10–15 minutes while the filling is prepared.

Lining a Pudding Basin

Grease a 2 pint pudding basin. Cut one quarter from the prepared suet pastry and set it aside for the lid. Roll out the remaining pastry, on a floured surface, to a circle, 2 in. wider than the top of the basin and about $\frac{1}{4}$ in. thick.

Sprinkle the pastry with flour, fold it in half and then in half again to form a triangle. Roll the pastry lightly towards the point.

Place the pastry triangle inside the basin, point downwards, and unfold it, moulding it to shape. Spoon in the prepared filling. Turn the pastry overhanging the rim of the basin in over the filling and brush with water.

Roll out the remaining pastry to a circle that fits the top of the basin. Lift the pastry lid on the rolling pin and lay it over the filling. Press the edges firmly together to seal them.

Fold a pleat in a square of kitchen foil or buttered grease-proof paper – the pleat allows the pudding to rise during cooking. Place the paper over the pudding and twist it under the rim of the basin. Cover the top of the pudding with a clean napkin or cloth, tie it securely with string below the rim and tie the ends into a knot on top of the pudding.

Beef and Carrot Pudding

PREPARATION TIME: *20 min.*
COOKING TIME: *2 hours*

INGREDIENTS *(for 4)*:
8 oz. suet pastry
$\frac{1}{2}$ *lb. onions*
2 oz. dripping
1 lb. lean minced beef
$\frac{1}{2}$ *lb. carrots*
2 tablespoons ready-made brown sauce
1 level teaspoon mixed herbs
2 level tablespoons flour
$\frac{1}{2}$ *pint beef stock*
Salt and black pepper

Peel and finely chop the onions. Melt the dripping in a pan over moderate heat and fry the onions until they begin to colour. Stir in the minced beef and coarsely grate the peeled carrots straight into the pan. Cook for a further 5 minutes, stirring occasionally. Stir in the brown sauce, herbs,

flour and the stock. Season to taste with salt and black pepper, and remove the pan from the heat. Leave the beef mixture to cool.

Line a 2 pint pudding basin with the prepared suet crust and spoon the mince mixture into the basin. Cover with the pastry lid, and seal the edges. Cover the pudding with paper and a napkin, and set the basin in a large saucepan. Pour boiling water into the pan until the water reaches half-way up the sides of the basin. Cover the saucepan with a lid and simmer for 2 hours. Top up the pan with boiling water when necessary. Serve the pudding straight from the basin, with boiled floury potatoes.

Apple and Ginger Roll

PREPARATION TIME: *30 min.*
COOKING TIME: *1½ hours*

INGREDIENTS *(for 8)*:
8 oz. suet crust
1 lb. cooking apples
$\frac{1}{2}$*–1 level teaspoon ground ginger*
2 oz. Demerara sugar
2 oz. sultanas
Caster sugar

Put a large saucepan, half full of water, on to boil. Peel and core the apples, then cut them into even, not too thin slices and put them in a bowl. Mix the ginger and the Demerara sugar together and mix them with the apples.

Roll the prepared suet crust pastry into a rectangle about $\frac{1}{4}$ in. thick. The width of the rectangle must be at least 2 in. smaller than the diameter of the saucepan. Spread the apple filling over the pastry to within $\frac{1}{2}$ in. of the edges, and sprinkle with the sultanas. Turn the edges in over the filling and brush them with water. Roll up the pastry from the longest side and wrap it in kitchen foil, making a pleat in it to allow for expansion during

cooking. Leave a short space at each end and twist the foil tightly to seal.

Place a heat-proof inverted plate in the pan. Lower the roll into the water and bring it back to the boil. Reduce the heat, cover the pan with a lid and boil gently for 1½ hours. Add more boiling water, if necessary, to keep the roll covered. Lift the roll carefully from the saucepan with a fish slice. Leave it to stand for a few minutes, then remove the foil. Put the apple roll on a hot serving dish and dredge with caster sugar. Serve at once with a custard or butter-scotch sauce*.

Dumplings

PREPARATION TIME: *5 min.*
COOKING TIME: *15 min.*

INGREDIENTS *(8 dumplings)*:
4 oz. suet crust pastry
Salt and black pepper
Mixed herbs or chopped parsley or 1 oz. grated cheese

Half fill a large saucepan with water and put it to boil. Make the pastry as described in the basic recipe, adding the herbs or cheese to the dry mix. Divide the pastry into eight equal pieces, and shape these into balls.

Put the dumplings into the boiling water, bring it back to the boil, then reduce heat and cover the pan. Simmer gently for 15 minutes – the dumplings will break up if the water is allowed to boil rapidly. The dumplings can be used as garnish for soups or they may be added to casserole dishes for the last 15 minutes.

LINING AND COVERING A PUDDING BASIN

1. *Fold the pastry into a triangle*

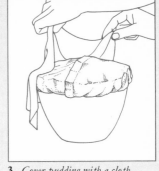

3. *Cover pudding with a cloth*

2. *Set pastry, point down, in basin*

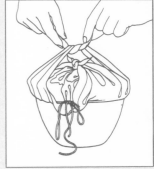

4. *Knot the ends over pudding*

HOT-WATER CRUST PASTRY

This crisp pastry has evolved from the original coffer paste. It is used for raised savoury meat and game pies and is usually served cold. The pastry is moulded by hand while still warm or fitted into a loose-bottomed cake tin or pie mould.

PREPARATION TIME: *15 min.*
RESTING TIME: *20 min.*

INGREDIENTS:
12 oz. plain flour
½ level teaspoon salt
4 oz. lard or soft table margarine
1 egg yolk

Sift the flour and salt into a warmed bowl. Put the fat with ¼ pint water into a small sauce-pan over low heat until the fat has melted, then bring to the boil. Make a well in the flour and drop in the egg yolk. Cover the egg with a little of the flour, then quickly add the hot fat mixture, stirring with a wooden spoon until the mixture is cool enough to handle.

Turn the dough on to a lightly floured surface and knead it quickly until soft and pliable. Shape the dough into a ball, put it on a warm plate and cover with an inverted bowl. Leave in a warm place for 20 minutes.

To mould the pastry, cut off one-third of the dough and set aside for the lid; keep it warm. Roll out the pastry thickly and use to line a hinged tin pie mould or a loose-bottomed cake tin set on a baking tray, both thoroughly greased. Alternatively, flour an empty 2 lb. jam jar, place the ball of warm dough on its base and carefully mould the dough evenly over the base and two-thirds down the sides of the jar. Set the jar aside while the dough cools and settles, then carefully ease out the jar. Spoon the filling into the pastry mould, roll out the remaining pastry for the lid, moisten the edges with water or egg glaze and cover the filling with the pastry lid. Seal the edges firmly. Cut a slit in the pastry lid and decorate the top.

Pastry moulded round a jar should have a protective band of foil tied round it to prevent the pie collapsing during baking.

Raised Veal and Bacon Pie
A raised hot-water crust pie takes time and is therefore better made in a large quantity. Cook the pie the day before to give the jellied stock time to set.

PREPARATION TIME: *1 hour*
COOKING TIME: *about 6 hours*

INGREDIENTS *(for 8)*:
PASTRY:
1 lb. plain flour
1 level teaspoon salt
1 egg yolk
6 oz. lard
Jellied veal stock
2 lb. veal bones, chopped
1 carrot
1 onion
2 bay leaves
6 peppercorns
FILLING:
1 lb. lean pork
¾ lb. pie veal
½ lb. lean streaky bacon
1 onion
½ level teaspoon salt
¼ level teaspoon black pepper
½ level teaspoon dried sage
Grated rind of half lemon
1 tablespoon chopped parsley
½ lb. pork sausage meat
Egg for glazing

Prepare the stock first: put the chopped veal bones with the cleaned carrot and peeled onion in a large saucepan. Add the bay leaves and peppercorns and enough water to cover. Bring to the boil, remove the scum from the surface, then cover the pan with a lid. Reduce the heat and simmer the stock for 2½ hours. Strain the stock through muslin, pour it into a clean pan and reduce* to about ½ pint by fast boiling. Leave to cool.

For the filling, put the pork, veal, half the bacon (with the rind removed) and the peeled onion through the coarse blade of a mincer. Mix it thoroughly in a large bowl, then add the salt, pepper, sage, lemon rind and parsley. Moisten the mixture with 3 tablespoons of the stock.

Make the pastry as in the basic method and leave it to rest. For the pie use a greased hinged pie frame, 5¾ in. wide by 7½ in. long and 3¼ in. deep, or a 7 in. loose-bottomed cake tin lined with foil. Roll out two-thirds of the pastry into a circle large enough to line the chosen mould. Fold the pastry in half and lower it into the mould, then unfold the pastry and ease it smoothly and evenly into the base and up the sides. Press the dough well into any indentations in the pie frame.

Line the base of the pastry case with sausage meat. Spoon the minced meat mixture over the top, pressing it down lightly and keeping it slightly domed. Beat the egg with salt and brush over the pastry edge. Roll out the remaining pastry to form a lid, lift it on the rolling pin over the filling. Press the lid on to the pie edge and pinch the edges firmly together to seal. Trim the pastry.

Glaze the top of the pie by brushing with egg; roll out the pastry trimmings and cut them into leaf shapes. Arrange these in a pattern on the lid and brush with more egg. Make a wide hole in the centre of the pie lid.

Set the pie on a baking tray and bake in the centre of a pre-heated oven, at 450°F (mark 8) for 20 minutes. Reduce the heat to 325°F (mark 3), cover the pie with kitchen foil and continue baking for a further 3 hours. Leave the pie to cool in the mould until quite firm. Remove the mould or tin, and when the pie is nearly cold pour the cool liquid stock slowly through a small funnel into the pie.

Leave the pie to set completely, generally for several hours, when the stock will have set to jelly round the meat. Serve the pie cold, cut into slices or wedges.

See illustration on p. 377.

MOULDING AND FILLING A RAISED HOT-WATER CRUST PIE

1. *Flour a 2 lb. jam jar*

2. *Mould dough over base*

3. *Leave to cool on jar*

4. *Ease out the jar*

5. *Cover the filled pie*

6. *Cut hole in lid*

7. *Protect with paper*

8. *Pour in liquid stock*

CHOUX PASTRY

This pastry is a French speciality and is used for cream buns, chocolate eclairs and profiteroles. During cooking, the pastry should treble itself in size through the natural lift of air. The feather-light pastry surrounds a large cavity which is filled with cream.

PREPARATION TIME: *20 min.*

INGREDIENTS:
2½ oz. plain flour
2 oz. butter
Pinch of salt
¼ pint milk and water mixed (half of each)
2 beaten eggs

Sift the flour and salt on to a sheet of greaseproof paper. Put the butter and the liquid in a heavy-based pan and cook over low heat until the butter melts, then raise the heat and rapidly bring the mixture to the boil. Draw the pan off the heat and pour in all the flour. Stir quickly with a wooden spoon until the flour has been absorbed by the liquid, then beat until the dough is smooth and comes away from the sides of the pan. Do not overbeat or the fat may leak out.

Cool pastry slightly, then beat in the beaten eggs, a little at a time. The pastry should be shiny and be thick enough to hold its shape, but not stiff. If the pastry is not going to be used immediately, cover the saucepan closely with a moist sheet of greaseproof paper and with the lid to keep the dough pliable.

Cream Buns

PREPARATION TIME: *20 min.*
COOKING TIME: *50 min.*

INGREDIENTS *(for 10)*:
1 portion choux pastry
½ pint double cream
Icing sugar

The characteristic light, crisp texture and crazy-paving tops of these cream buns are achieved by baking the pastry in its own steam. A large, shallow tin with a tight-fitting lid is necessary, or use a heavy baking tray and invert a deep roasting tin over it. Seal the join with a flour and water paste after the choux buns have been placed inside.

Spoon the warm choux pastry into a forcing bag fitted with a ½ in. plain meringue nozzle. Pipe small rounds of the pastry on to the greased tray, setting the buns well apart. Cover the tray with the tin and bake just above the centre of an oven pre-heated to 400°F (mark 6) for 40–50 minutes.

Leave the buns undisturbed during cooking, or the steam will escape and cause the buns to collapse. The end of the cooking time can be estimated by giving the tin a gentle shake – if the buns are baked they will rattle.

Cool the buns on a wire rack, then make a slit through the base and fill them with whipped cream; dust with icing sugar.

Cheese Aigrettes

PREPARATION TIME: *20 min.*
COOKING TIME: *15–20 min.*

INGREDIENTS *(for 24)*:
1 portion choux pastry
3 oz. finely grated Cheddar cheese
Pinch of cayenne pepper
Oil or fat for deep frying

Make the pastry, following the basic recipe, and beat in the finely grated cheese and cayenne pepper after the eggs. Heat about 2½ in. of corn oil or fat in a deep fryer, without a basket, to 375°F or until a cube of bread turns golden in 30 seconds. Drop teaspoons of the pastry into the hot fat, about six at a time, and fry for 4–6 minutes until puffed and golden brown. Lift the cheese puffs out with a perforated spoon and leave to drain on absorbent kitchen paper.

Pile the cheese aigrettes on to a hot serving dish and dust with more grated cheese.

Chocolate Eclairs

PREPARATION TIME: *20 min.*
COOKING TIME: *25–30 min.*

INGREDIENTS *(for 12–16)*:
1 portion choux pastry
½ pint double cream
1 level tablespoon caster sugar
Chocolate glacé icing from ½ lb. icing sugar

Make up the choux pastry and spoon it into a forcing bag fitted with a ½ in. plain meringue nozzle. Pipe out 3 in. lengths on to a greased baking tray, starting with the end of the nozzle touching the tray and lifting it while pressing the mixture out. Cut off the required lengths with a wet knife.

Bake the eclairs just above the centre of an oven pre-heated to 425°F (mark 7) for about 20 minutes. If the eclairs are not thoroughly dry, reduce the heat to 350°F (mark 4) and continue baking for a further 10 minutes. Remove the eclairs from the oven, slit them down one side to let the steam escape and leave on a wire rack to cool. Whisk the cream and sweeten it with sugar.

When the eclairs are cold, fill them with whipped cream, using a forcing bag and plain nozzle; cover the tops with chocolate glacé icing*.

Profiteroles

PREPARATION TIME: *1 hour*
COOKING TIME: *15 min.*

INGREDIENTS *(for 20–25)*:
1 portion choux pastry
½ pint double or whipping cream
Icing sugar
¼ lb. plain dark chocolate
1 small tin evaporated milk

MAKING CHOUX PASTRY

1. *Heat butter and liquid*

3. *Beat dough until smooth*

2. *Pour flour into melted butter*

4. *Gradually add beaten egg*

PIPING OUT CHOCOLATE ECLAIRS

Spoon choux into a forcing bag

Pipe out 3 in. lengths of dough

Make up the choux pastry and spoon it into a forcing bag fitted with a plain ½ in. vegetable nozzle. Pipe 20–25 small bun shapes, well apart, on to greased baking trays, and bake in a pre-heated oven, in the centre or just above, at 425°F (mark 7) for about 15 minutes until well risen, puffed and crisp. If the profiteroles are not thoroughly dry after 15 minutes, reduce the heat to 350°F (mark 4) and continue baking for a further 10 minutes. Cool on a wire rack.

Split the buns not quite in half, lengthways. Fill the hollow centres with whipped cream and dust the tops with sifted icing sugar. To serve, carefully pile the profiteroles into a pyramid on a serving dish and pour a little chocolate sauce over them; serve the remainder separately.

To make the sauce, melt the chocolate, broken into pieces, in a bowl over a pan of hot water. Stir in the evaporated milk and beat thoroughly.

See illustration on p. 377.

Pastry

FLAKED PASTRIES

These include flaky pastry, rough puff pastry and puff pastry, all of which are characterised by fat and air being trapped between thin layers of dough. During baking the trapped air expands and lifts the pastry into several flimsy and crisp layers.

Certain procedures are common to all three pastries to ensure crisp flakes: 1. Handle the pastry lightly and as little as possible; 2. The fat and the dough should have the same consistency and temperature – the fat is therefore made pliable on a plate before use; 3. To prevent the fat from melting out during baking, and thus spoiling the texture, the pastry must be chilled during and after making, and before baking; 4. Roll out the pastry evenly; do not let the rolling pin go over the edges as this will force out the air, and never stretch the pastry; 5. Before baking brush the top of the shaped pastry with beaten egg glaze, but do not let it drip down.

For lining pie dishes and flan cases, see Shortcrust pastry.

FLAKY PASTRY

This pastry is used as crusts for savoury pies, for Eccles cakes, sausage rolls, jam puffs and cream horns. It should be made in a cool atmosphere, and it is not advisable to make flaky pastry in hot weather.

PREPARATION TIME: *30 min.*
RESTING TIME: *about 2 hours*

INGREDIENTS *(for 1¼ lb.)*
8 oz. plain flour
½ level teaspoon salt
3 oz. lard
3 oz. butter or margarine
7 tablespoons iced water (approx.)
1 teaspoon lemon juice

Sift the flour and salt into a wide bowl. Work the lard and butter on a plate until evenly blended, and divide it into four equal portions. Rub one portion of the fat into the flour with the fingertips until the mixture resembles breadcrumbs. Add the water and lemon juice and mix the ingredients with a round-bladed knife to a soft, manageable dough. Turn it out on to a lightly floured surface and knead until all cracks have disappeared. Cover the dough with a clean polythene bag and leave it to rest in a cool place for 20 minutes. Keep the fat cool as well.

On a lightly floured surface roll out the dough, about 24 in. long, 8 in. wide and ¼ in. thick. Brush off all surplus flour. Cut another quarter of the fat into small flakes and dot them evenly over two-thirds of the pastry and to within ½ in. of the edges. Fold the unbuttered third of the pastry over the fat and fold the buttered top third down. Turn the dough so that the folded edge points to the left and seal all the edges firmly with the side of the little finger.

Cover the pastry with a polythene bag and leave it to rest again in a cool place for about 20 minutes.

Turn the pastry so that the fold points to the right-hand side. Roll the pastry out as before, cover two-thirds with another quarter of fat, and repeat the folding, sealing and resting as before. Continue with the remaining fat, giving the pastry a half-turn between each rolling. Finally, roll out the pastry to the original rectangle, brush off any surplus flour, fold it up and wrap it loosely in polythene. Leave it to rest in a cool place for at least 30 minutes before shaping. Bake in the centre of a pre-heated oven, at 425°F (mark 7).

PREPARING FLAKY PASTRY

Roll out the cooled dough

Dot fat over two-thirds of pastry

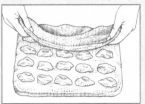
Fold unbuttered dough up

Fold buttered dough over

Seal pastry edges

Eccles Cakes

PREPARATION TIME: *30 min.*
COOKING TIME: *15 min.*

INGREDIENTS *(for 10–12 cakes)*:
Half portion flaky pastry
1 oz. unsalted butter
1 oz. soft brown sugar
1 oz. chopped mixed peel
2 oz. currants
1 egg white
Caster sugar

Make the filling for these little cakes first: beat the butter and sugar until pale and fluffy. Chop the peel finely and add to the creamed butter, together with the currants. Roll out the prepared pastry, ¼ in. thick. Cut it into rounds with a 3 in. plain cutter.

Put a teaspoon of the filling in the centre of each pastry round and draw the edges together to cover the filling completely. Reshape each cake into a round. Turn the cakes over and roll them lightly into flat rounds until the currants just show through the pastry. Score the top of the cakes into a lattice pattern.

Leave the cakes to rest on greased baking trays for 10 minutes in a cool place. Then brush them with lightly beaten egg white and sprinkle generously with caster sugar. Bake the cakes towards the top of the oven, pre-heated to 425°F (mark 7), for about 15 minutes or until golden and puffed.

See illustration on p. 377.

Cream Horns

PREPARATION TIME: *30 min.*
COOKING TIME: *10 min.*

INGREDIENTS *(for 8 horns)*:
Half portion flaky pastry
1 egg
Raspberry or black currant jam
5 fluid oz. double cream
4 tablespoons single cream
Icing sugar

Roll the prepared pastry out to a strip 24 in. long and 4 in. wide. Beat the egg and brush it over the pastry. Cut the pastry into eight ribbons, 24 in. long and ½ in. wide, using a sharp knife. Wind each pastry strip round a cream horn tin, starting at the tip and with the glazed side of the pastry outside; overlap each turn by about ⅛ in. As it rises during baking, the pastry should come just short of the metal rim of the horn. Set the moist horns on a baking tray, join downwards.

Bake towards the top of a pre-heated oven at 425°F (mark 7) for 8–10 minutes, until the horns are light golden. Leave to cool for a few minutes, then with one hand grip the rim of each tin with a clean cloth and carefully twist the tin. Hold the pastry lightly in the other hand and ease it off the tin. Leave the horns to cool completely, then put a teaspoon of jam into the base of each horn. Just before serving, whip the two creams and spoon them into the horns. Dust with icing sugar.

MAKING CREAM HORNS

Cut pastry into ribbons

Shape pastry round tins

ROUGH PUFF PASTRY

A cross between flaky and puff pastry, rough puff pastry is easier to make than puff pastry, and is as light in texture as flaky pastry, but becomes heavy when cold. It is an excellent pastry for savoury pie crusts, sausage rolls and tarts.

PREPARATION TIME (Including resting): *1 hour*

INGREDIENTS *(for 1¼ lb.)*
6 oz. butter
8 oz. plain flour
1 level teaspoon salt
1 teaspoon lemon juice
¼ pint iced water

Cut the firm but not hard butter into walnut-sized pieces. Sift the flour and salt together into a wide bowl and add the butter, with the lemon juice and water. Mix the ingredients lightly with a round-bladed knife to form a soft elastic dough.

Turn the dough on to a floured surface and knead it lightly – as the dough is soft it needs careful handling. Shape it into a rectangle, then roll it into a strip about ¾ in. thick, 12 in. long and 4 in. wide, keeping the edges straight. The butter will be seen clearly as yellow streaks in the pastry. Fold the bottom third of the pastry up, and the upper third down. Turn the pastry so that the fold points towards the left-hand side, and seal the edges lightly with the edge of the little finger. Roll out the pastry again, keeping it ½ in. thick and to a rectangle of 18 in. by 6 in. Repeat the folding and rolling four times, giving the pastry a half-turn each time.

Place the pastry in a polythene bag and leave it in a cool place for 20 minutes before every two rollings. Rest the finished pastry for 10 minutes before shaping.

Bake in the centre of a pre-heated oven, at 425°F (mark 7).

Add butter to sifted flour

Mix in iced water

First rolling-out

Fold the dough in three

Sausage Rolls

PREPARATION TIME: *20 min.*
COOKING TIME: *30 min.*

INGREDIENTS *(for 18 rolls)*:
1 portion rough puff pastry
1 lb. sausage meat
Flour
1 egg

Cut the prepared rough puff pastry, 18 in. by 6 in., into two strips each 3 in. wide. Divide the sausage meat in half, shape it into two long rolls to fit the pastry strips, and coat the meat lightly with flour. Lay the sausage meat in the centre of the pastry strips, brush the edges with beaten egg and fold the pastry over. Seal the two long edges firmly.

Brush the two pastry lengths with beaten egg and cut them into 2 in. long pieces. Score the top of the pastry lightly with the point of a knife. Set the sausage rolls on greased baking trays and bake just above the centre of a pre-heated oven at 425°F (mark 7), for 25–30 minutes or until golden brown and puffed.

SAUSAGE ROLLS

Cover sausage meat with pastry

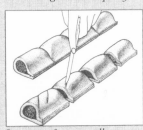

Score tops of sausage rolls

PUFF PASTRY

This is regarded as the finest and most professional pastry. It is time-consuming but well worth making if a large quantity is required. Uncooked puff pastry may also be stored in the home freezer for up to 3–4 months. When only small amounts of pastry are needed, commercially frozen and chilled puff pastry are particularly useful. Puff pastry, which is used for savoury pie crusts, as wrappings for meat and poultry, for vol-au-vents, cream horns, mille feuilles and palmiers, must be rolled out six times.

Vol-au-vents, patties and pastry crusts, which need the greatest rise and flakiness, should always be shaped from the first rolling of the finished dough. Second rolling, including trimmings from the first rolling, can be used for small items such as palmiers and cream horns.

Prepared uncooked puff pastry can be stored for two to three days in the refrigerator.

PREPARATION TIME: *30–45 min.*
RESTING TIME: *2½ hours*

INGREDIENTS:
1 lb. plain flour
2 level teaspoons salt
1 lb. butter
½ pint iced water
1 teaspoon lemon juice

Sift the flour and salt into a large bowl. Cut 4 oz. of the butter into small pieces and rub it into the flour with the fingertips. Add the water and lemon juice and, using a round-bladed knife, mix the ingredients to a firm but pliable dough. Turn the dough on to a lightly floured surface and lightly knead it until smooth. Shape the pastry into a thick round and cut through half its depth in the form of a cross.

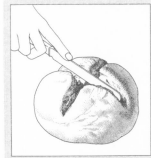

Cut a cross in rounded dough

Fold out the four flaps

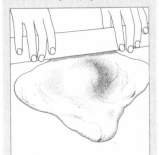

Roll out the flaps

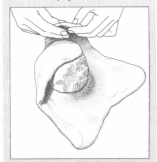

Place remaining butter in centre

Pastry

Open out the four flaps and roll them out until the centre is four times as thick as the flaps. Shape the remaining firm butter to fit the centre of the dough, leaving a clear ½ in. all round. Fold the flaps over the butter, envelope style, and press the edges gently together with a rolling pin. Roll the dough into a rectangle 16 in. × 8 in., using quick short strokes. Roll lightly but firmly, back and forth, so as not to squeeze out the butter. Brush off any surplus flour between rollings. Fold the dough into three and press the edges with the edge of the little finger. Wrap the pastry in a cloth or greaseproof paper, cover with polythene and leave in a cool place for 20 minutes.

Roll out the pastry, raw edge pointed to the left, to a rectangle as before. Fold and leave to rest for 20 minutes. Repeat rolling, folding and resting four times, giving the dough a half-turn every time. Leave the dough to rest for 30 minutes in the refrigerator before shaping it. Puff pastry, properly made, should rise about six times in height and should generally be baked in the centre, or just above, of a pre-heated oven, at 450°F (mark 8).

Steak and Wine Pie

PREPARATION TIME: *45 min.*
COOKING TIME: *3 hours*

INGREDIENTS *(for 6):*
12–16 oz. prepared puff pastry
2¼ lb. lean chuck steak
½ lb. kidney
1 large onion
6 oz. mushrooms
2 cloves garlic (optional)
3 oz. seasoned flour
3 tablespoons corn oil
3½ oz. butter
1 pint beef stock
½ pint dry red wine
Salt and pepper
1 egg

Trim the meat and cut it into 1 in. pieces. Skin, core and chop the kidneys*. Peel and thinly slice the onion and mushrooms and peel and crush the garlic if used. Toss the meat and kidneys in seasoned flour*. Heat the oil with 2 oz. of the butter in a frying pan, and fry the meat over high heat until evenly browned. Blend in the remaining seasoned flour and spoon the contents of the pan into a large casserole. Melt the remaining butter in a clean pan and fry the onion for 5 minutes; add the mushrooms and garlic and fry for 2–3 minutes. Pour in the stock and wine, bring to the boil and pour over the meat.

Cover the casserole with a lid and cook in the centre of a pre-heated oven, at 325°F (mark 3), for 1½–2 hours or until the meat is tender. Lift the meat out with a perforated spoon and put it in a 3½ pint pie dish with a pie funnel in the centre. Reduce* the casserole juices by fast boiling and pour over meat. Leave to cool completely.

Roll out the pastry, ¼ in. thick, to fit the pie dish. Moisten the rim and lift the pastry over the meat. Seal the edges and brush the pastry with beaten egg. Bake in the centre of a pre-heated oven, at 450°F (mark 8), for 20 minutes until golden.

Vol-au-vent

The following quantity makes one large 7 in. wide vol-au-vent case, eight 3 in. cases for individual servings, or 12–14 small bouchée cases for cocktail snacks.

PREPARATION TIME: *20 min.*
COOKING TIME: *30 min.*

INGREDIENTS:
1 lb. prepared puff pastry
1 egg
6–8 oz. diced, cooked chicken,
flaked salmon or 4 oz. prawns
½ pint Béchamel sauce

For a large case, roll out the pastry to a 7½ in. square. Using a 7 in. plate or lid as a guide, cut round it with a sharp knife, held at a slightly oblique angle so as to give a bevelled edge. Place the pastry upside-down on a moist baking tray.

Brush the top of the pastry with beaten egg and mark a 6 in. wide circle on the pastry with a knife. Cut through half the depth of the pastry, following the mark of the inner circle. Draw a lattice pattern with the knife on the rim of the pastry and leave to rest in a cool place for 15 minutes.

Bake the vol-au-vent case in the centre of a pre-heated oven at 450°F (mark 8) for about 20 minutes or until risen and brown, then reduce the heat to 350°F (mark 4) for about a further 20 minutes. Cover with moist greaseproof paper if the case browns too quickly.

When cooked, carefully ease out the pastry lid and discard any soft pastry from the centre. Fill the case with chicken, salmon or prawns blended with the Béchamel sauce. Serve the case hot with the filling hot, or cold with a cold filling.

Baked vol-au-vent case: scoop out the centre half-cooked pastry

Small vol-au-vent cases are made in a similar way. The pastry should be rolled out ½ in. thick and cut into 3 in. rounds for the cases and 1½ in. rounds for the lids. Bake in a pre-heated

oven at 450°F (mark 8) for 20 minutes. For bouchée cases, roll the pastry out, ¼ in. thick, and use 2 in. and 1 in. cutters for cases and lids respectively. Bake at 450°F (mark 8) for about 15 minutes.

Mille Feuilles

PREPARATION TIME: *40 min.*
COOKING TIME: *20 min.*

INGREDIENTS *(for 6):*
½ lb. prepared puff pastry
¼ lb. raspberry jam
½ pint pastry cream
6 oz. icing sugar
Cochineal

On a lightly floured surface, roll out the pastry thinly into a rectangle 10 in. by 9 in. Prick it all over with a fork. Lift the pastry on to a moist baking tray and bake just above centre of a pre-heated oven at 450°F (mark 8) for 20 minutes or until well risen and golden brown. Cool the pastry on a wire rack, then cut it in half lengthways. Spread the top of one piece with two-thirds of the raspberry jam; cover with pastry cream*.

Blend the sifted icing sugar in a bowl with just enough cold water to give a coating consistency. Mix 1 tablespoon of the icing in a cup with a few drops of cochineal colouring and spoon it into a piping bag.

Spread the remaining raspberry jam over the second piece of pastry and turn it upside-down on to the pastry cream. Press the pastries together, then cover the top of the pastry with white icing. Pipe thin lines of pink icing at ½ in. intervals, lengthways, over the white icing. Draw the tip of a knife quickly across the width of the pastry, at ½ in. intervals, to give the icing a feathered effect. Leave the mille feuille to set, then cut it into six equal slices.

Palmiers

PREPARATION TIME: *15 min.*
COOKING TIME: *14 min.*

INGREDIENTS *(for 12):*
½ lb. prepared puff pastry
1 oz. caster sugar
5 fluid oz. double cream
4 tablespoons single cream
Vanilla sugar

On a lightly floured surface, roll out the pastry to a rectangle 12 in. by 10 in. Sprinkle the pastry with caster sugar. Fold the long sides so that they meet in the centre. Sprinkle with the remaining sugar, and fold the pastry in half, lengthways, hiding the first folds. Press lightly and evenly with the fingertips along the pastry. Cut the pastry across into 12 slices.

Place the palmiers on a moist baking tray, cut side down and well apart to give them room to spread. Open out the top of each palmier slightly and flatten the whole slice lightly with a round-bladed knife. Bake the palmiers towards the top of a pre-heated oven at 425°F (mark 7) for 10 minutes, then turn them over and bake for about a further 4 minutes.

Serve the palmiers plain. Alternatively, whip together the two creams, flavoured with vanilla sugar*. Sandwich in pairs with the cream.

See illustration on p. 377.

PALMIERS

Cut folded pastry into slices

Open and flatten palmier slices

PÂTÉ SUCRÉE

This pastry is the French equivalent of British enriched shortcrust pastry. It is thin and crisp, yet melting in texture, and neither shrinks nor spreads during baking. Pâté sucrée is usually baked blind, but flan cases and moulds need not be weighed down.

PREPARATION TIME: *15 min.*
RESTING TIME: *1 hour*

INGREDIENTS:
4 oz. plain flour
Pinch salt
2 oz. caster sugar
2 oz. butter
2 egg yolks

Sift together the flour and salt on to a cool working surface or, preferably, a marble slab. Make a well in the centre of the flour and put in the sugar, soft butter and the egg yolks. Using the finger-tips of one hand, pinch and work the sugar, butter and egg yolks together until well blended. Gradually work in all the flour from the sides and knead the pastry lightly until smooth. Leave the pastry in a cool place for at least 1 hour to rest before rolling it out. Bake in the centre of a pre-heated oven, at 350–400°F (mark 4–6).

Bateaux de Miel

PREPARATION TIME: *15 min.*
COOKING TIME: *7 min.*
CHILLING TIME: *30 min.*

INGREDIENTS *(for 6)*:
One-third portion pâté sucrée
4 oz. unsalted butter
4 oz. caster sugar
4 oz. ground almonds
3 teaspoons thick honey
2 teaspoons coffee essence
Coffee glacé icing

Roll out the prepared pastry on a lightly floured surface and use to line six boat-shaped moulds,

about $4\frac{1}{2}$ in. long (see lining moulds under Shortcrust pastry). Press the pastry lightly into shape. Set the moulds on a baking tray, prick the pastry with a fork and bake blind in the centre of a pre-heated oven, at 375°F (mark 5), for 5–7 minutes or until tinged light brown. Remove from the oven, ease the pastries out of the moulds and cool on a wire rack.

Beat the butter until soft, then add the sugar and beat until light and fluffy. Beat in the almonds, honey and coffee essence. Divide the mixture evenly between the cooled pastry boats, piling the mixture up to a peak along the length, and smooth the surface. Chill in the refrigerator for about 30 minutes.

When the filling has set, coat the pastries with glacé icing* based on 4 oz. icing sugar. Leave to set before serving.

Bateaux Saint André

PREPARATION TIME: *20 min.*
COOKING TIME: *20 min.*

INGREDIENTS *(for 6)*:
One-third portion pâté sucrée
$\frac{1}{2}$ lb. cooking apples
1 oz. caster sugar
$\frac{1}{2}$ egg white
4 oz. icing sugar

Peel, core and dice the apples and cook them with the sugar and 1 tablespoon water until they have reduced to a thick purée. Set aside to cool.

Roll out the pâté sucrée thinly and use to line six boat-shaped moulds, $4\frac{1}{2}$ in. long. Proceed as described for Bateaux de Miel. Divide the apple purée equally between the pastry-lined moulds.

Whisk the egg white lightly in a small bowl, then gradually beat in the sifted icing sugar, using a wooden spoon. Spread a thin layer of this meringue mixture over each boat. Roll out the pastry trimmings thinly, cut them

into short narrow strips and lay two strips across each boat.

Bake the pastry boats in the centre of a pre-heated oven, at 375°F (mark 5), for about 10 minutes, until the pastry has set and the meringue is pale beige. Leave the pastries to cool slightly, then ease the mould away.

Bateaux aux Fruits

PREPARATION TIME: *20 min.*
COOKING TIME: *5–7 min.*

INGREDIENTS *(for 6)*:
One-third portion pâté sucrée
14 oz. tinned fruit (apricot halves, pineapple pieces, cherries)
3 tablespoons apricot glaze
$\frac{1}{2}$ oz. pistachio nuts

Roll out the pastry and line six boat-shaped moulds as for Bateaux de Miel. Set the lined moulds on a baking tray and bake them blind in the centre of a pre-heated oven at 375°F (mark 5) for 5–7 minutes or until tinged brown. Cool slightly, then ease the pastries out of the moulds and cool on a wire rack.

Brush the inside of the pastry boats with hot apricot glaze*. Drain the tinned fruit thoroughly, cut the apricot halves in two and, if cherries are used, remove the stones. Arrange the fruit in the pastry boats, brush with more apricot glaze and garnish with blanched pistachio nuts.

See illustration on p. 377.

Glazed Almond Flan

PREPARATION TIME: *30 min.*
COOKING TIME: *50 min.*

INGREDIENTS *(for 6–8)*:
1 portion pâté sucrée
3 rounded tablespoons apricot or raspberry jam
3 oz. unsalted butter
3 oz. caster sugar
2 eggs
3 oz. ground almonds
2 oz. icing sugar

Roll out the pâté sucrée thinly and line an 8 in. wide, loose-bottomed fluted flan tin. Trim the edges and set the trimmings aside. Spread the jam over the pastry.

Beat the butter and sugar until light and fluffy. Beat in the eggs a little at a time, then stir in the almonds. Spoon this mixture over the jam and level the surface.

Roll out the trimmings, and cut them into $\frac{1}{4}$ in. wide strips. Lay these in a lattice pattern on top of the filling. Set the flan on a baking tray and bake just above the centre of the oven pre-heated to 350°F (mark 4) for 45–50 minutes or until golden brown.

Brush the baked flan, while still hot, with glacé icing* made from the sifted icing sugar and enough water to give a coating consistency. Return the flan to the oven for 5 minutes, leave to cool.

COMMON FAULTS IN PASTRY MAKING

Shortcrust
Hard and/or tough pastry: due to too much liquid, too little fat, over-handling or insufficient rubbing in.
Soft and crumbly pastry: too little water: too much fat, or self-raising flour used instead of plain.
Shrunk pastry: excess stretching during rolling out.
Soggy pastry: filling too moist or sugar in a sweet pie in contact with pastry. For a double crust pie, use ideally a metal pie plate and either brush pastry base with egg white or butter the pie plate before lining with pastry.

Toss the prepared fruit filling with a mixture of 1 tablespoon flour and 4 oz. caster sugar before covering with a pastry lid.
Sunken pie: oven temperature too low; cold pastry put over hot filling; too much liquid in filling, or too little filling.

Speckled pastry: undissolved sugar grains in enriched pastry crust.

Hot-water Crust
Cracked pastry: insufficient liquid; too little kneading; liquid not boiling when added to flour.
Dry, difficult-to-mould pastry: liquid not boiling when added to flour; too much liquid; dough not cooled enough to set to required shape.
Hard pastry: insufficient fat or liquid.

Suet Pastry
Heavy pastry: insufficient baking powder; water not kept on the boil during cooking.
Tough pastry: dough handled too much and rolled out excessively.
Soggy pastry: paper and cloth covering over filled pie too loose, and water not kept boiling during cooking.

Choux Pastry
Mixture too soft: insufficient cooling of the flour before adding eggs; eggs added too quickly.
Pastry did not rise: self-raising flour used; oven too cold; too short baking time.
Sinking after removal from oven: insufficient baking; further period of baking sometimes remedies this defect.

Flaky, Rough Puff and Puff Pastries
Too few layers: insufficient resting and chilling; heavy rolling causing fat to break through and intermingle with the pastry; fat too soft.
Fat running out during baking: oven too cool.
Hard and tough pastry: too much water; over-kneading.
Shrinking pastry: insufficient resting; over-stretching during rolling.

Baking with Yeast

Home-baked bread has a strikingly different taste and texture from commercially baked loaves. Our daily bread is composed of such basic ingredients as flour, yeast, salt and liquid; enriched dough mixtures for buns and tea breads – such as babas and Sally Lunns – also include butter and spices, dried fruits and nuts.

In the North of England and in Scotland, where home-baking is much more popular than in the south, there are more types of flour to choose from. Flour is the most important factor in bread-making, and the so-called 'strong' flours are essential for well-made loaves. A 'strong' flour has a high gluten content (from which protein is formed) of 10–15 per cent and aids rising in combination with yeast; it absorbs liquids easily and produces bread of light and open texture.

In the south, most health shops stock strong flours, specially recommended for bread-making.

Flour

Brown flour produces a yeast dough of closer texture and with less rise than a white dough. It does not store well and should be bought as required. Wholemeal flour contains 100 per cent wheat, and wheatmeal flour has 80–90 per cent wheat including all the germ and some bran. Both these types of flour give the characteristic mealy taste to bread.

Yeast

Fresh or dried yeast may be used in bread-making. Many small private bakers will supply fresh yeast, and some supermarkets and health stores also stock it. Dried yeast is more concentrated than fresh yeast: $\frac{1}{2}$ oz. or 4 level teaspoons of dried yeast is the equivalent of 1 oz. of fresh yeast.

Fresh yeast should have a creamy-beige colour, and a firm consistency which crumbles easily when broken up. It can be stored in a loosely tied polythene bag in a cool place for up to 5 days, in a refrigerator for up to a month, or in the home freezer for up to a year.

Fresh yeast is added to flour in three different ways: it is rubbed in, blended with liquid or added as a batter. Rubbing in is suitable for soft doughs, quick-breads and sweet doughs. Blending with liquid is the basic way and is suitable for all bread recipes. The batter method is best suited for rich yeast doughs, and works equally well with fresh and dried yeast. It is not advisable to cream fresh yeast with sugar, as this results in the breakdown of some of the living yeast cells.

Rubbing-in method Crumble the yeast into the sifted flour and salt with the tips of the fingers. Add the specified amount of liquid to the flour and yeast mixture to make a soft dough. Work the dough with the finger-tips to distribute the yeast evenly.

Blending with liquid Blend the yeast with part of the measured liquid; add this mixture to the flour and salt, together with the remaining liquid.

Batter method Mix one-third of the measured flour with the yeast, blended with all the liquid and 1 level teaspoon of sugar. Leave in a warm place until frothy, about 20 minutes, then add the rest of the flour, the salt and any other ingredients specified.

Dried yeast This can be stored in a tightly lidded container for up to 6 months. Dried yeast is reconstituted in some warm water (110°F). (This water should be taken from the amount to be used in the recipe, first dissolved in the proportion of 1 level teaspoon sugar to $\frac{1}{2}$ pint water.) Sprinkle the yeast over the water and leave in a warm place until frothy – after about 15 minutes.

Salt

Apart from improving the flavour of bread, salt also affects the gluten in the flour. If salt is omitted, the dough rises too quickly. If there is too much salt, this kills the yeast and gives the bread a heavy or uneven texture. Measure the salt carefully.

Liquid

This may be milk, water or a mixture of both. The amount varies from recipe to recipe, depending on the absorbency of the flour. Milk adds food value and strengthens doughs, improves the keeping quality and the colour of the crust. For plain bread, however, water alone gives a better texture.

Fat

This is used in enriched yeast doughs for buns, croissants and tea breads which have a soft outer crust. Fat makes a dough soft and also slows down yeast action so that the dough rises less than plain bread dough.

Sugar

Too much sugar added to a dough mixture delays fermentation of the yeast cells; always follow the given quantities.

Making the dough

Sift the flour and the salt into a mixing bowl, make a well in the centre and add all the liquid at once. Mix it in with one hand until thoroughly incorporated.

Add more flour if necessary, and beat the dough against the sides of the bowl until it comes away cleanly. Knead the dough on a lightly floured surface.

Kneading is most important, as it strengthens and develops the dough and enables it to rise. Gather the dough into a ball with the tips of the fingers, then fold the dough towards the body. Press down on the dough and away from the body with the palm of the hand. Give the dough a quarter-turn and repeat the kneading.

Knead the dough for about 10 minutes until it feels firm and elastic and no longer sticks to the fingers – it is better to knead the dough too much rather than too little. Bread dough may be kneaded in an electric mixer.

MAKING BREAD DOUGH

Pour the liquid into the flour

Knead until the dough is elastic

Rise dough in polythene bag

Rising

After kneading, the dough must be set aside for rising and proving (second rising) until it has doubled in size. A large polythene bag is useful for the rising process. Pour a few drops of corn oil into the bag and swirl it round to distribute it evenly in a thin film. Put the dough in the bag, tie it loosely and leave the dough until it has doubled in size and springs back when lightly pressed with a finger. The time the dough takes to rise depends on the temperature and the surroundings, but ideally the dough should be allowed to rise slowly, at a low temperature over a long period. Allow 12 hours in a cool room or larder, and about 2 hours at normal room temperature, away from draughts. Dough left to rise in a refrigerator will need 24 hours.

If time is short, the dough can be made to rise in 45–60 minutes in a warm place, for example over a pan of warm water. Too much heat, however, may kill the yeast.

Knocking back and proving

After the initial rising the dough has to be kneaded again, to knock out the air bubbles and to ensure a good rise and even texture. Shape the kneaded dough as required and put it into tins or on to baking trays. Slip the tins or trays into oiled polythene bags and leave the loaves to rise at room temperature until double their size. This second rising is also known as proving.

Baking

Remove the tins or baking trays from the polythene bags and bake at 400–450°F (mark 6–8), according to the individual recipes. A bowl of hot water placed in the bottom of the oven creates steam, which improves the bread texture.

PREPARING LOAVES FOR BAKING

Shape or roll up risen and proven dough to fit greased loaf tins

TRADITIONAL BREAD SHAPES

Score the top of a tin loaf with a knife — *Cob loaf is a slightly flattened ball of dough* — *Arrange dough in a round tin for a crown loaf*

Storing

Place the baked and cooled loaves in clean polythene bags, leaving the end open. To refresh a crusty loaf, wrap it in kitchen foil and put in the oven at 450°F (mark 8) for about 10 minutes. Leave it to cool in the foil.

White Bread

PREPARATION TIME: *25 min. (plus rising and proving)*
COOKING TIME: *30–40 min.*

INGREDIENTS *(for 4 loaves)*:
3 lb. strong plain flour
2 level tablespoons salt
1 oz. lard
1 oz. fresh yeast
1½ pints water less 3 tablespoons

Sift the flour and salt together into a large bowl and rub in the lard with the fingertips. In a small bowl, blend the yeast with ½ pint of the measured water. Make a well in the centre of the flour and pour in the yeast liquid and the remaining water. Work the dough mixture with one hand until it leaves the sides of the bowl clean. If necessary add a little extra flour.

Turn the dough on to a lightly floured surface and knead it for about 10 minutes until smooth and elastic. Shape it into a round, then set it aside to rise until it has doubled its size.

Divide the risen dough into four equal portions on a lightly floured board. Flatten each piece firmly with the knuckles to knock out any air bubbles, then knead for 2–3 minutes. Stretch each piece of dough into an oblong the same length as the tin, ease it into the greased tin and score the dough lightly along the top. Alternatively, fold the dough into three along the long edges or roll it up like a Swiss roll. Tuck the ends under so that the dough, seam downwards, fits a 1 lb. tin.

Brush the top of the dough with lightly salted water. Place the tins in lightly oiled polythene bags and leave in a warm place to rise (prove), until the dough reaches the top of the tins. Remove the polythene, brush the top of the dough with salted water again and set the tins on baking trays.

Bake the loaves in the centre of a pre-heated oven at 450°F (mark 8) for about 30 minutes, or until the loaves shrink slightly from the sides of the tins and the upper crust is a deep golden brown. For really crusty bread, turn the loaves out of the tins on to a baking tray and return them to the oven for a further 5–10 minutes. When done, baked loaves sound hollow when tapped on the base. Leave the bread to cool on a wire rack.

Cob Loaf Roll each piece of dough into a ball, flatten it and place on a floured baking tray.
See illustration on p. 379.

Crown Loaf Divide a quarter of the risen dough into five or six balls. Set these in a greased, 5 in. wide cake tin or a deep sandwich tin.
See illustration on p. 378.

Lardy Cake

PREPARATION TIME: *30 min. (plus rising and proving)*
COOKING TIME: *30 min.*

INGREDIENTS:
One-third portion white bread dough
4 oz. lard or margarine
4 oz. caster sugar
1 level teaspoon mixed spice
3 oz. sultanas
Cooking oil

Roll out the risen dough with a rolling pin, on a lightly floured surface, to a strip ¼ in. thick. Cut the lard into flakes and put one-third of these over the dough to within ½ in. of the edges. Mix the sugar with the spice and sultanas and sprinkle one-third over the fat. Fold the dough up loosely from one of the short sides.

Roll the dough out again into a strip and cover with another third of lard and sugar, together with half the sultanas. Roll up again, then roll out into a strip for the third time. Cover the dough with the remaining lard, sugar and sultanas.

Roll up the dough, then roll out and shape it to fit a greased roasting tin, 10 in. long by 8 in. wide. Lift the dough into the tin and press it down well, particularly in the corners. Put the tin in an oiled polythene bag and leave to rise (or prove) until doubled in size. Remove the polythene, brush the top of the dough lightly with oil and sprinkle with a little extra sugar. Score a criss-cross pattern across the surface of the dough with the point of a knife.

Bake the lardy cake in the centre, or just above, of a pre-heated oven at 425°F (mark 7) for 30 minutes. Turn the cake out of the tin and leave to cool on a wire rack. Serve lardy cake sliced, plain or buttered.
See illustration on p. 378.

Wholemeal Bread

PREPARATION TIME: *20 min. (plus rising and proving)*
COOKING TIME: *30–40 min.*

INGREDIENTS *(for two 2 lb. or four 1 lb. loaves)*:
3 lb. plain wholemeal flour
2 level tablespoons caster sugar
2 level tablespoons salt
1 oz. lard
2 oz. fresh yeast
1½ pints warm water

PREPARING A LARDY CAKE

1. *Sprinkle spiced sultanas over dough*

2. *Fold the dough loosely*

3. *Press dough into corners of tin*

4. *Score surface with a knife*

Sift the flour, sugar and salt into a large bowl. Cut up the lard and rub it into the flour with the fingertips until the mixture resembles fine breadcrumbs. Blend the yeast, in a small bowl, with $\frac{1}{2}$ pint of the measured water and pour it into a well in the centre of the flour; add the remaining water. Using one hand, work the mixture together and beat it until the dough leaves the bowl clean. Knead the dough on a lightly floured surface for 10 minutes.

Shape the dough into a large ball and leave it to rise in a lightly oiled polythene bag until it has doubled in size. Turn the dough on to a lightly floured surface and knead again until firm. Divide the dough into two or four equal pieces and flatten each piece firmly with the knuckles to knock out any air bubbles. Stretch and roll each piece of dough into an oblong the same length as the tin; fold it into three or roll it up like a Swiss roll. Lift the dough into the greased tins, brush the top with lightly salted water and place each tin inside an oiled polythene bag. Tie the bag loosely and leave to rise until the dough reaches the top of the tins.

Remove the tins from the bags, set them on baking trays and bake in the centre of a pre-heated oven at 450°F (mark 8) for about 30 minutes or until the loaves shrink from the sides of the tins. Cool the loaves on a wire rack and test by tapping them.

For a fancy wholemeal loaf divide a quarter of the dough into four equal pieces; shape them into rolls the width of a greased 1 lb. loaf tin and fit them, side by side, into the tin. Finish as before. For a cob loaf, shape each quarter portion of dough into a round, flatten them slightly then dust with flour and place on a floured baking tray.

Quick Wheatmeal Loaves

PREPARATION TIME: *20 min. (plus rising)*
COOKING TIME: *30–40 min.*

INGREDIENTS *(for one 1 lb. loaf and 8 rolls, or two 1 lb. loaves)*:
$\frac{1}{2}$ *lb. plain brown flour*
$\frac{1}{2}$ *lb. strong plain white flour*
2 level teaspoons salt
2 level teaspoons caster sugar
1$\frac{1}{4}$ oz. lard
$\frac{1}{2}$ oz. fresh yeast
1$\frac{1}{2}$ pint warm water
2–3 tablespoons cracked wheat or crushed cornflakes

Sift the two flours, the salt and sugar into a bowl. Cut up the lard and rub it into the flour with the fingertips. Blend the yeast with all the warm water until the yeast has dissolved. Make a well in the centre of the flour and pour in the yeast liquid. Mix to a soft, scone-like dough, beating until it leaves the side of the bowl clean (if necessary, add a little more flour).

Divide the dough into two equal portions. Shape each piece to half fill a greased 1 lb. loaf tin and brush the top of the dough with lightly salted water; sprinkle with cracked wheat or crushed cornflakes. Place the tins on a baking tray in a lightly oiled polythene bag, tie loosely and leave in a warm place until the dough has doubled in size. Remove the polythene and bake the loaves in the centre of a pre-heated oven at 450°F (mark 8) for about 40 minutes. Test by tapping the loaves; if they sound hollow, they are baked. Cool on a wire rack.

Rolls Divide the whole, risen dough after re-kneading into 8 equal pieces. Roll each into a round on an unfloured surface, using the palm of one hand. Shake a little flour on to the palm of the hand, and press the dough down, hard at first, easing up until

the rounds have the shape of a roll. Set the rolls well apart on floured baking trays, put them into oiled polythene bags and leave in a warm place until doubled.

Remove the polythene and bake the rolls just above the centre of the oven, pre-heated to 450°F (mark 8), for about 40 minutes. Cool on a wire rack.

For soft rolls, set the shaped rolls $\frac{3}{4}$ in. apart on the baking trays and sprinkle generously with flour. The rolls will bake into contact with each other along the sides and the flour on top will give a soft surface.

Flowerpot Loaves Wheatmeal bread may also be baked in flowerpots. Use clay pots – never plastic – grease them thoroughly inside and bake them empty in a hot oven several times to seal the inner surface and prevent the dough sticking. A clay flowerpot 4–5 in. wide will hold half a portion of wheatmeal dough. Finish and bake the loaf as already described.

See illustration on p. 379.

Apricot and Walnut Loaf

PREPARATION TIME: *30 min. (plus rising)*
COOKING TIME: *40–45 min.*

INGREDIENTS *(for one 1 lb. loaf)*:
Half portion quick wheatmeal dough
4 oz. dried apricots
1 oz. caster sugar
2 oz. chopped walnuts
TOPPING:
1 oz. butter or firm margarine
1 oz. caster sugar
1$\frac{1}{2}$ oz. plain flour

Cut the dried apricots roughly with scissors and put them in a bowl or on a floured board, with the risen dough, the sugar and walnuts. Work the mixture together until no streaks can be

seen. Line the bottom of a 1 lb. loaf tin with buttered greaseproof paper and grease the sides of the tin. Put the dough in the tin and set in a lightly oiled polythene bag; leave in a warm place for about 1 hour or until the dough has risen to within $\frac{1}{2}$ in. of the rim of the tin.

Meanwhile, make the topping. Rub together the butter, sugar and flour in a small bowl until the mixture resembles coarse breadcrumbs. Cover the risen dough evenly with the crumb mixture, and set the tin on a baking tray. Bake in the centre of a pre-heated oven at 400°F (mark 6) for 40–45 minutes. Leave the baked loaf in the tin for 10 minutes, then turn it out to cool on a wire rack.

See illustration on p. 379.

Enriched White Bread

PREPARATION TIME: *35 min. (plus rising and proving)*
COOKING TIME: *35–45 min.*

INGREDIENTS:
1 lb. strong plain flour
1 level teaspoon caster sugar
2 level teaspoons dried yeast
8 fluid oz. warm milk
1 level teaspoon salt
2 oz. margarine
1 egg
GLAZE:
1 egg
1 level teaspoon caster sugar
1 tablespoon water
Poppy seeds (optional)

Mix 5 oz. flour, the sugar, yeast and all the milk in a large bowl: set it aside in a warm place for about 20 minutes or until frothy. Sift the remaining flour and the salt into another bowl and rub in the margarine. Make a well in the centre, add the beaten egg and the frothy yeast mixture. Mix with one hand to make a fairly soft dough that leaves the side of the bowl clean.

Turn the dough out on to a lightly floured surface, knead it for about 10 minutes until smooth, then place it in an oiled polythene bag and leave to rise and double in size. Knead the risen dough lightly on a floured surface before shaping it.

Poppy-seed Plaits Divide the dough into three, and roll each into a 12 in. long strand. Set the three strands side by side on a flat surface, and pass the left strand over the centre strand, then the right strand over the centre strand. Continue like this until the whole length is plaited. Finally join the short ends neatly together and tuck them under.

Place the plaits on a lightly greased baking tray. Beat the egg with the sugar and water to make the glaze. Brush the plaits evenly and sprinkle with poppy seeds. Put the plaits on the tray inside a lightly oiled polythene bag and set aside to rise (prove) again until the dough has doubled in size. Remove the polythene bag and bake the loaves in the centre of a pre-heated oven at 375°F (mark 5) for 35–40 minutes. Tap the bottom of the loaves with the knuckles – if they sound hollow they are done. Cool on a wire rack.

See illustration on p. 379.

CONTINUED ON P. 385.

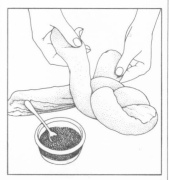

Plaited loaf: for a three-strand plait, begin crossing the dough near the top

Pastry

**VEAL AND
BACON PIE**
(page 368)

ECCLES CAKES
(page 370)

PROFITEROLES
(page 369)

CHEESE AND ONION PIE
(page 365)

BATEAUX AUX FRUITS
(page 373)

**PLUM AND
CINNAMON PIE**
(page 366)

LEMON MERINGUE PIE
(page 365)

PALMIERS
(page 372)

CHOCOLATE CREAM PIE
(page 366)

377

Bread, Buns and Scones

SALLY LUNN
(page 387)

CROWN LOAF
(page 375)

LARDY CAKE
(page 375)

BRIOCHES
(page 386)

OVEN SCONES
(page 388)

SODA BREAD
(page 389)

CHELSEA BUNS
(page 385)

GIRDLE SCONES
(page 388)

SINGIN' HINNY
(page 389)

FLOWER-
POT LOAF
(page 376)

CRESCENT
(page 386)

COB LOAF
(page 375)

BATH BUNS
(page 385)

PINWHEEL
(page 386)

POPPY SEED PLAIT
(page 376)

APRICOT AND WALNUT LOAF
(page 376)

379

Cakes

RASPBERRY BUNS
(page 392)

SWISS ROLL
(page 395)

VICTORIA SANDWICH
(page 393)

ROCK BUNS
(page 392)

CHOCOLATE LAYER CAKE
(page 393)

SWISS TARTS
(page 394)

PINEAPPLE AND CHERRY LOAF
(page 393)

GENOESE SPONGE
(page 395)

GINGERBREAD
(page 396)

DUNDEE CAKE
(page 394)

MADEIRA CAKE
(page 393)

COCONUT CASTLES
(page 394)

Biscuits

Confectionery

1 STUFFED DATES
2 CHOCOLATE-COVERED PINEAPPLE
3 GINGER MARZIPAN
4 COCONUT ICE
5 COLLETTES
6 PEPPERMINT CREAMS
7 CHOCOLATE FUDGE
8 ALMOND PETITS FOURS
9 RUM TRUFFLES
10 PEANUT BRITTLE
11 CHOCOLATE-COVERED DATES
12 MARZIPAN CONFECTIONERY

(pages 402-403)

Pickles and Chutneys

(pages 360–361)

Piccalilli

Tomato Chutney

Pickled Cucumber

Pickled Red Cabbage

Pickled Onions

Apple Mint Chutney

Pickled Beetroot

Crown Loaf Divide all the risen dough into 12 equal pieces – about 2 oz. each. Shape these with the palm of the hand, and put them in a greased, 9 in. wide sandwich tin and place the balls in a circle around the inner edge of the tin, with three or four balls in the centre. Brush with glaze, leave to rise (prove) and bake as already described, for 45–60 minutes.

Fancy Rolls Enriched white dough is ideal for light, dinner-type rolls which can be shaped in a variety of ways. Use about 2 oz. of risen dough for each roll. Roll a piece of dough out, about 4 in. long, cut it in half lengthways and, holding each strip at both ends, twist it three times. Alternatively, roll each strip into a strand and tie it into a knot in the centre.

Shape 2 oz. pieces of dough into oblong miniature loaves and score the surface with five or six marks, at even intervals. With a scissor-point, make triangular

FANCY ROLLS

Twisting strips of dough

Snipping small cuts in rolls

Shaping triangular rolls

cuts between the score marks, through the dough, so that the points are slightly raised.

Divide a 2 oz. piece of dough into three, shape into balls and set them on a baking tray in such a way that all three balls touch each other.

Alternatively, roll a 2 in. piece of dough into a thick strand and shape into a snail or 'S' form.

Brush the rolls with egg glaze and set them aside to rise (prove) until doubled in size. Bake the rolls just above the centre of a pre-heated oven, at 375°F (mark 5), for 10–15 minutes or until golden.

Babas

PREPARATION TIME: *40 min. (plus rising)*
COOKING TIME: *15–20 min.*

INGREDIENTS *(for 16 babas):*
8 oz. strong plain flour
1 oz. fresh yeast
6 tablespoons warm (110°F) milk
½ level teaspoon salt
1 oz. caster sugar
4 eggs
4 oz. butter
4 oz. currants
Lard
SYRUP:
4 tablespoons clear honey
4 tablespoons water
3 tablespoons rum (approx.)
GARNISH:
½ pint whipped cream

Blend the yeast, milk and 2 oz. of the measured flour together in a large bowl and beat with a wooden spoon until smooth. Leave the yeast in a warm place for about 20 minutes or until frothy. Sift the remaining flour and the salt into the yeast and blend in the sugar, the lightly beaten eggs, softened butter and the currants. Beat the mixture, which should be fairly soft, with a wooden spoon for 4 minutes.

Grease 16 small ring moulds with lard and, using a teaspoon, spoon in the dough until the moulds are half full. Set the ring moulds on baking trays and cover them with sheets of lightly oiled polythene.

Leave the babas to rise in a warm place until the dough has risen about two-thirds up the sides of the moulds.

Bake the babas just above the centre of an oven pre-heated to 400°F (mark 6) for 15–20 minutes or until golden brown.

Meanwhile, prepare the syrup: heat the honey and water in a small pan over low heat; stir in rum to taste. Leave the baked babas to cool for a few minutes in the moulds before turning them out on to a plate. While the babas are still hot, spoon the warm syrup over them until it has soaked in. Leave to cool, then transfer the rum-soaked babas to a serving dish and fill the centres with spooned or piped whipped cream.

Serve at once.

MAKING BABAS

Spoon dough into ring moulds

Pour warm syrup over babas

Decorate with piped cream

Bath Buns

PREPARATION TIME: *20 min. (plus rising and proving)*
COOKING TIME: *15 min.*

INGREDIENTS *(for 12 buns):*
1 lb. strong plain flour
1 oz. fresh yeast or 1 level tablespoon dried yeast
3 oz. plus 1 level teaspoon caster sugar
¼ pint warm milk
¼ pint warm water less 4 tablespoons
1 level teaspoon salt
2 oz. butter or margarine
2 eggs
6 oz. sultanas
1–2 oz. chopped mixed peel
Crushed lump sugar

Sift 4 oz. of the measured flour into a large mixing bowl. Add the yeast, crumbling it if fresh, and 1 level teaspoon of sugar. Make a well in the centre of the flour, add the warm milk and water and stir thoroughly with a wooden spoon to incorporate all the ingredients. Set the bowl aside in a warm place until frothy, about 20–30 minutes.

Meanwhile sift the remaining flour and the salt into a bowl, and add the remaining sugar. Melt the butter in a small pan, but do not let it boil. Beat the eggs. Stir the butter and the eggs into the yeast mixture with a wooden spoon, then gradually mix in the sifted flour, the sultanas and peel. Beat the dough, with one hand, against the sides of the bowl, then turn it on to a lightly floured surface. Knead the soft dough until smooth and no longer sticky, about 5 minutes.

Put the dough in a large bowl inside a lightly oiled polythene bag and leave it in a warm place until it has doubled in size. Remove the polythene bag and beat the dough in the bowl with a wooden spoon or the hand. Place 12 tablespoons of the dough on

greased baking trays, cover them with polythene and leave to rise (prove) again until doubled in size. Remove the polythene, brush the buns with beaten egg and sprinkle the tops with coarsely crushed lump sugar. Bake just above the centre of a pre-heated oven at 375°F (mark 5) for 15–20 minutes.

See illustration on p. 379.

Chelsea Buns

PREPARATION TIME: *20 min. (plus rising and proving)*
COOKING TIME: *30–35 min.*

INGREDIENTS *(for 9 buns):*
8 oz. strong plain flour
½ level teaspoon caster sugar
½ oz. fresh yeast
4 fluid oz. warm (110°F) milk
½ level teaspoon salt
½ oz. margarine or lard
1 egg
3 oz. dried fruit (sultanas, currants or seedless raisins)
1 oz. chopped mixed peel
2 oz. light soft brown sugar
½–1 oz. melted butter
Clear honey

Sift 2 oz. of the measured flour into a bowl and add the caster sugar. Crumble in the yeast and beat in the milk with a wooden spoon. Leave this yeast mixture in a warm place for about 20 minutes or until frothy. Sift together the remaining flour and the salt and rub in the margarine. Make a well in the centre, add the beaten egg and pour in the yeast mixture. Using one hand, gradually work in the flour.

Beat the dough in the bowl until it leaves the sides clean; it should be fairly soft and pliable. Turn the dough on to a lightly floured surface and knead it for 10 minutes, until smooth. Put it in a lightly oiled polythene bag and leave it to rise at room temperature for 1–1½ hours or until it has doubled in size.

Baking with Yeast

Knead the risen dough on a lightly floured surface until smooth, then roll it out with a well-floured rolling pin, to a rectangle 12 in. by 9 in. Mix the dried fruit, peel and soft brown sugar together, brush the dough with melted butter and spread the fruit mixture on top to within ½ in. along the longer edges. Roll up the dough from the long sides and press the join to seal it.

Cut the roll into nine equal slices and lay them flat, in rows of three, in a greased, 7 in. square cake tin. Leave to rise in a polythene bag, in a warm place, for about 30 minutes.

Remove the polythene bag and bake the buns in the centre of a pre-heated oven at 375°F (mark 5) for 30–35 minutes. Turn the buns on to a wire rack and, while still hot, brush them with honey.

See illustration on p. 378.

CHELSEA BUNS

Roll dough like Swiss Roll

Cut roll into slices

Danish Pastries

PREPARATION TIME: *45 min.*
(plus rising)
RESTING TIME: *50 min.*
COOKING TIME: *10 min.*

INGREDIENTS:
8 oz. plain flour
Pinch salt
1 oz. lard
1 level tablespoon caster sugar
½ oz. fresh yeast
5 tablespoons cold water
2 eggs
5 oz. unsalted butter
PINWHEEL FILLING:
Almond paste
1 oz. butter
1 oz. caster sugar
1 level teaspoon powdered cinnamon
Currants and chopped mixed peel
GARNISH:
Glacé icing
Crushed lump sugar

Sift the flour and salt into a large bowl. Cut up the lard and rub it into the flour with the fingertips; add the sugar and make a well in the centre of the flour. Blend the yeast with the water in a small bowl until creamy and smooth, then add it to the flour together with 1 lightly beaten egg. Gradually work in the flour, then beat the soft dough until it leaves the sides of the bowl clean.

Turn the dough out on to a lightly floured surface and knead it until smooth. Put it inside a lightly oiled polythene bag and leave it in the refrigerator for 10 minutes.

Beat the butter with a wooden spoon until soft but not oily, then shape it into a rectangle about 5 in. by 9½ in. On a floured board, roll out the dough to a 10–11 in. square and place the butter in the centre. Fold the two unbuttered sides over so that they just overlap the butter. Seal the open sides with the rolling pin, then roll the dough into an oblong strip, about three times as long as it is wide, and fold it in three.

Place the dough in a lightly oiled polythene bag and leave in the refrigerator for 10 minutes. Remove the polythene and roll out the dough, in the opposite direction, to an oblong strip and fold in three. Repeat the resting, rolling and folding twice more. Finally, rest the dough for 10 minutes in the refrigerator before rolling it out to any of the following shapes:

Almond Squares Roll out half the dough to a 10 in. square, then cut it into four equal pieces. Fold two corners of each square to meet in the centre, envelope style, and repeat with the other two corners. Press down firmly to seal. Place a small round of almond paste in the centre.

Crescents Roll out the dough as for almond squares, and cut each square diagonally in half. Place a small piece of almond paste at the base of each triangle, then roll it up from the base and curve into a crescent shape.

See illustration on p. 379.

Cockscombs Roll out half the dough and cut it into 2 in. wide strips. Cut the strips into 4 in. pieces and make a series of V-shaped indentations through two-thirds of the width.

Open out the pastry piece along the cuts and shape the uncut edge into a slight arch. Brush the pastries with beaten egg and sprinkle with crushed cube sugar.

Pinwheels Roll out half a portion of pastry dough to a rectangle 12 in. by 8 in. Cream the butter with the sugar and cinnamon and spread over the dough to within ¼ in. of the edges. Scatter a few currants and a little mixed peel over the butter. Cut the dough in half, length-

ALMOND SQUARES

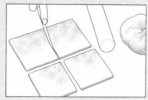

Cut dough into squares

Shape square to envelope style

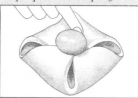

Place almond paste in centre

COCKSCOMBS AND PINWHEELS

Cutting cockscomb pastries

Cutting pinwheels nearly through

Overlapping pinwheels

ways, and roll each piece, from the shorter end, into a thick roll. Cut this into 1 in. thick slices.

See illustration on p. 379.

Alternatively, make cuts, 1 in. apart, through three-quarters of the depth of the rolls. Ease the near-cut pinwheels apart so that they overlap each other slightly; bake for about 30 minutes.

Set the pastry shapes well apart on greased baking trays and cover with sheets of oiled polythene. Leave the pastries to rise in a warm place for 20 minutes. Remove the polythene and brush the pastries with lightly beaten egg. Bake near the top of a pre-heated oven, at 425°F (mark 7), for about 10 minutes or until golden. Leave on a wire rack and, while still warm, brush almond squares, crescents and pinwheels with glacé icing*.

Brioches

PREPARATION TIME: *25 min.*
(plus rising and proving)
COOKING TIME: *10 min.*

INGREDIENTS *(for 12 brioches):*
8 oz. strong plain flour
½ level teaspoon salt
1 level tablespoon caster sugar
½ oz. fresh yeast
1½ tablespoons warm water
2 eggs
2 oz. butter, melted

Sift the flour and salt into a bowl and add the sugar. Cream the yeast with the water in a small bowl, and stir it, together with the beaten eggs and the melted butter, into the flour with a wooden spoon. Beat the dough until it leaves the sides of the bowl clean, then turn it out on to a lightly floured surface and knead for 5 minutes.

Put the dough in an oiled polythene bag and leave it to rise at room temperature for 1–1½ hours or until it has doubled in size. Turn the risen dough on to a lightly floured surface and knead it until smooth. Shape the dough into a sausage and divide it into 12 equal pieces.

Brush 3 in. fluted patty pans with oil and shape three-quarters of each piece of dough into a ball; place it in a patty pan. Using a floured finger, press a hole in the centre of the dough as far as the base of the tin. Shape the remaining piece of dough into a knob and insert it in the hole. Press lightly with the fingertip to unite the two pieces of dough. When all 12 brioches have been shaped, set the patty pans on a baking tray and cover them with oiled polythene. Leave to rise (prove) until the dough is puffy and just below the tops of the tins.

Remove the polythene and bake the brioches in the centre of a pre-heated oven at 450°F (mark 8) for 10 minutes or until golden brown.

See illustration on p. 378.

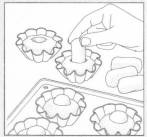

BRIOCHES

Brush fluted tins with oil

Insert dough knob in centre

Croissants

PREPARATION TIME: *1–1½ hours (plus rising and proving)*
RESTING TIME: *1 hour*
COOKING TIME: *15–20 min.*

INGREDIENTS *(for 12 croissants)*:
1 lb. strong plain flour
2 level teaspoons salt
1 oz. lard
1 oz. fresh yeast
½ pint warm water, less 4 tablespoons
1 egg
4–6 oz. hard margarine or butter
½ level teaspoon caster sugar

Sift the flour and salt into a bowl. Cut up the lard and rub this into the flour with the fingertips until blended to a coarse breadcrumb consistency. Cream the yeast with the water in a small bowl and pour it into a well in the centre of the flour; together with the lightly beaten egg. Gradually incorporate the flour with one hand and beat the dough until it leaves the sides of the bowl clean.

Transfer the dough to a lightly floured surface and knead it for about 10 minutes, until smooth. Roll out the dough to a strip, about 20 in. by 8 in. and ¼ in. thick. If necessary, trim the edges with a knife. Soften the margarine with a knife until pliable but not creamy, and divide it into three portions. Flake one portion of the margarine and dot it over the upper two-thirds of the dough, leaving a ½ in. border round the edges.

Fold the dough into three, bringing up first the unbuttered part of the dough, then folding the opposite part over. Give the dough a half turn, and seal the edges by pressing with the rolling pin. Shape into a long strip again by gently pressing the dough at intervals with the roll-

ing pin, and roll out to a rectangle. Dot as before with the second portion of flaked margarine, then fold, turn the pastry and roll again before adding the last of the margarine. Fold in three again. Work as quickly as possible to avoid the dough becoming warm and soft, thus melting the margarine. Keep the edges straight and the corners square.

Put the folded dough in an oiled polythene bag and leave in the refrigerator for 30 minutes. Remove the polythene, roll out the dough and repeat the rolling and folding three times more, but without adding any fat. Return to the oiled polythene bag and the refrigerator for another 30 minutes.

To shape the croissants, roll the dough out, on a lightly floured surface, to a rectangle about 22 in. by 13 in. Cover with oiled polythene and leave on the table for 10 minutes. Trim the edges with a sharp knife, to a rectangle 21 in. by 12 in.; divide the dough in half lengthways. Cut each strip into six triangles, 6 in. wide at the base.

Beat the egg with a few drops of water and the sugar, and brush over the triangles. Roll up each triangle loosely, finishing with the tip underneath, then carefully curve the pastry into a crescent shape. Place the croissants, well spaced, on ungreased baking trays.

Brush the tops with a little more egg glaze, cover them with oiled polythene and leave at room temperature to rise (prove) for about 30 minutes or until light and puffy. Brush again with egg glaze before baking the croissants in the centre of a pre-heated oven at 425°F (mark 7) for 15–20 minutes. Use a palette knife to ease the croissants off the baking tray, and serve them while still warm.

MAKING CROISSANTS

Flake fat over two-thirds of dough

Fold the dough into three

Seal with a rolling pin

Roll up dough triangles

Curve triangle to a crescent

Sally Lunn

PREPARATION TIME: *25 min. (plus rising)*
COOKING TIME: *15–20 min.*

INGREDIENTS *(for 2 loaves)*:
1 lb. strong plain flour
2 oz. butter
¼ pint milk plus 4 tablespoons
1 level teaspoon caster sugar
½ oz. fresh yeast
2 eggs
1 level teaspoon salt
SUGAR TOPPING:
1 level tablespoon caster sugar
1 tablespoon water

Melt the butter in a small pan, then add the milk and sugar. Put the yeast in a bowl, beat the eggs and add them, with the warm milk mixture, to the yeast: blend thoroughly until the yeast has dissolved. Sift the flour and salt into a large bowl, make a well in the centre and pour in the milk mixture. Gradually incorporate the flour with the fingers of one hand and beat the dough against the bowl until it leaves the sides clean. Knead on a lightly floured surface until smooth.

Divide the dough into two equal portions, knead each piece into a ball and place it in a greased 5 in. round cake tin. Slide each tin into an oiled polythene bag and leave in a warm place for about 1 hour or until the dough has risen almost to the top of the tins.

Remove the polythene and set the tins on baking trays and bake just above the centre of a pre-heated oven at 450°F (mark 8) for 15–20 minutes. Meanwhile, make the sugar topping by heating the sugar and water in a small pan over low heat until the sugar has dissolved: boil rapidly for 1–2 minutes.

Turn the Sally Lunns out on to a wire rack and, while still warm, brush the tops with the sugar.

See illustration on p. 378.

Yorkshire Tea Cakes

PREPARATION TIME: *20 min.*
(plus rising and proving)
COOKING TIME: *20 min.*

INGREDIENTS *(for 5 cakes)*:
1 lb. strong plain flour
1 level teaspoon salt
1 oz. caster sugar
1 oz. lard
2 oz. currants
½ oz. fresh yeast
½ pint warm (110°F) milk

Sift the flour and salt together into a large bowl, add the sugar and rub in the lard until evenly blended. Stir in the currants, then make a well in the centre. In a small bowl, blend the yeast with the milk until smooth and creamy. Pour this liquid into the well, mix the ingredients together, beating the dough against the bowl until it leaves the sides clean (add a little extra flour if necessary).

Turn the dough out on to a lightly floured surface and knead for about 10 minutes. Put the dough in a lightly oiled polythene bag and set aside to rise at room temperature for about 1½ hours or until it has doubled in size. Remove the polythene, place the risen dough on a lightly floured surface and knead well. Divide the dough into five equal portions and shape each portion into a round; roll each of these into a 6½–7 in. wide, flat cake.

Set the cakes well apart on lightly greased baking trays and brush the tops with milk. Cover the trays with sheets of oiled polythene. Leave the cakes to rise (prove) in a warm place for 45 minutes or until doubled in size.

Bake the cakes at or just above the centre of the oven, pre-heated to 400°F (mark 6), for about 20 minutes. Cool on a wire rack and serve the cakes split in half, either cold or toasted, and with plenty of butter.

Buns and Scones

Scones are quick and easy to make. They should be soft and light as a sponge, and oven-fresh, so there should be no delay between making and baking. They are ideal for tea, served toasted and hot, or fresh with butter or thick cream and home-made preserves.

Many traditional scones are baked on a griddle or girdle. This is a thick, round iron plate, usually with a half-hoop handle. It is heated on top of the cooker, and the correct heat is important – if too hot, the outside crust of the scones becomes too brown, leaving the centre uncooked. To test for correct heat, sprinkle a little flour on the surface; it should turn light brown in 3 minutes.

Teabreads, halfway between a bread and a cake, are also popular for tea, as they keep well and can be made in advance. Soda bread is a good substitute for yeast bread in an emergency, and can be made shortly before it is required.

Drop Scones

PREPARATION TIME: *5 min.*
COOKING TIME: *3–5 min. per batch*

INGREDIENTS *(for 15–18 scones)*:
4 oz. self-raising flour
Pinch of salt
1 level tablespoon caster sugar
1 egg
About ¼ pint milk
Lard for cooking

Set a griddle, heavy-based frying pan or hot-plate over heat. While it is warming, sift the flour and salt into a bowl and stir in the sugar. Make a well in the centre and drop in the egg; gradually add the milk, working in the flour with a spoon until a smooth batter is formed.

Grease the heated surface lightly with a little lard. When a slight haze appears, pour on small rounds of batter, well apart, either from a jug or with a spoon to give perfect rounds. As soon as the scones are puffed, bubbling on the surface and golden on the undersides, turn them over with a palette knife to brown on the other side. Serve at once, or place the scones between folds in a clean tea towel until serving time.

COOKING DROP SCONES

Pour batter on to greased griddle

Turn over half-cooked scones

Cheese Scones

PREPARATION TIME: *10 min.*
COOKING TIME: *15 min.*

INGREDIENTS *(for 16 scones)*:
8 oz. plain flour
½ level teaspoon salt
2½ level teaspoons baking powder
2 oz. butter or firm margarine
4 oz. grated Cheddar cheese
About ¼ pint milk

Sift together the flour, salt and baking powder. Mix the butter into the flour until it resembles fine breadcrumbs. Blend in the cheese. Gradually add the milk, mixing it with a round-bladed knife until the dough is soft and manageable.

Turn the dough on to a lightly floured surface, divide into two equal portions and knead them lightly with the fingertips. Shape each portion into a round, ¾ in. thick. Cut each round into six triangular portions and set them on a greased baking tray; prick the top with a fork.

Bake the scones in the centre of a pre-heated oven at 425°F (mark 7) for 12–15 minutes. Cool slightly before serving.

Oven Scones

PREPARATION TIME: *15 min.*
COOKING TIME: *10 min.*

INGREDIENTS *(for 10–12 scones)*:
8 oz. plain flour
Pinch of salt
½ level teaspoon bicarbonate of soda
1 level teaspoon cream of tartar
1½ oz. firm margarine
About 4 tablespoons each milk and water mixed
Milk for glazing

Sift together the flour, salt, bi-carbonate of soda and cream of tartar into a wide bowl. Cut up the margarine and rub it into the flour. Gradually add the milk and water and mix with a round-

bladed knife to give a soft but manageable dough.

Knead the dough quickly on a lightly floured surface, to remove all cracks. Roll the dough out ½ in. thick, and cut out 2 in. rounds with a plain or fluted pastry cutter. Knead the trimmings together, roll them out and cut out as many scones as possible. Set the scones on a heated, un-greased baking tray, brush them with milk and bake them near the top of a pre-heated oven at 450°F (mark 8) for about 10 minutes, until well risen and light golden brown.

See illustration on p. 378.

Girdle Scones

PREPARATION TIME: *5 min.*
COOKING TIME: *10 min.*

INGREDIENTS *(for 12 scones)*:
8 oz. plain flour
1 level teaspoon bicarbonate of soda
2 level teaspoons cream of tartar
½ level teaspoon salt
1 oz. lard or firm margarine
1 oz. caster sugar
About ¼ pint milk

Heat a griddle, hot-plate or a heavy-based frying pan. Sift the flour, bicarbonate of soda, cream of tartar and salt into a bowl; cut up the lard and rub it into the flour with the fingertips until the mixture resembles fine bread-crumbs. Stir in the sugar, and gradually add the milk, mixing the dough with a round-bladed knife until soft but manageable.

Divide the dough in half. Knead each piece lightly and roll into two flat rounds, ¼–½ in. thick. Cut each round into six even triangles and cook on the greased griddle until evenly brown on one side, then turn and cook on the second side; allow about 5 minutes for each side. Cool on a wire rack.

See illustration on p. 379.

Sweet Sultana Scones

PREPARATION TIME: *15 min.*
COOKING TIME: *10 min.*

INGREDIENTS *(for 12 scones)*:
8 oz. plain flour
$\frac{1}{2}$ level teaspoon bicarbonate of soda
$\frac{1}{2}$ level teaspoon cream of tartar
Pinch of salt
$1\frac{1}{2}$ oz. firm margarine
1 oz. caster sugar
2 oz. sultanas
About $\frac{1}{4}$ pint soured milk or buttermilk
Milk for glazing

Sift together the flour, bicarbonate of soda, cream of tartar and salt. Cut up the margarine and rub it into the flour with the fingertips until the mixture resembles fine breadcrumbs. Add the sugar and sultanas. Gradually add the soured milk (prepare this by mixing $\frac{1}{2}$ tablespoon fresh lemon juice into $\frac{1}{4}$ pint milk). Mix to a light, manageable dough, using a round-bladed knife.

Turn the dough on to a lightly floured surface and knead lightly until smooth. Roll out $\frac{1}{2}$ in. thick and cut out the scones with a 2 in. plain or fluted pastry cutter. Re-knead the trimmings lightly to cut more scones. Set on an ungreased heated baking tray, brush the tops with milk and bake near the top of a pre-heated oven at 450°F (mark 8) for about 10 minutes.

Cool on a wire rack.

GIRDLE SCONES

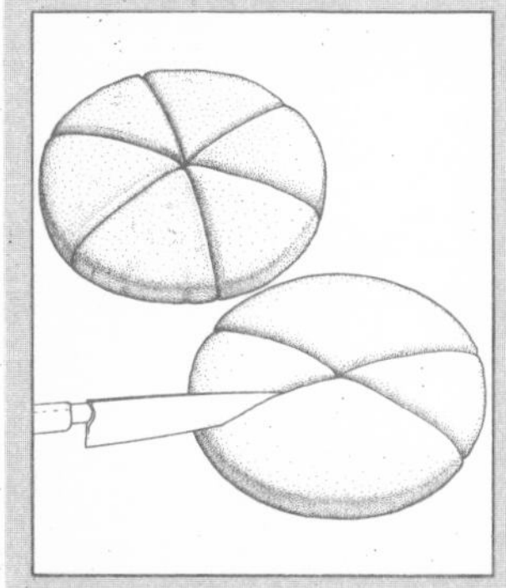

Cut dough round into triangles

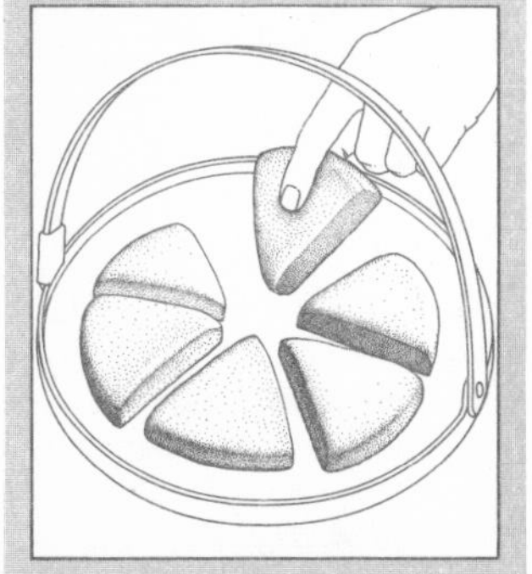

Cook scones on greased griddle

Wholemeal Scone Round

PREPARATION TIME: *10 min.*
COOKING TIME: *15 min.*

INGREDIENTS:
2 oz. plain flour
3 level teaspoons baking powder
Pinch of salt
6 oz. plain wholemeal flour
2 oz. firm margarine
2 oz. caster sugar
About $\frac{1}{4}$ pint milk

Sift the flour, baking powder and salt into a mixing bowl. Blend in the wholemeal flour and cut the margarine into knobs; rub this into the flour with the fingertips, until the mixture resembles fine breadcrumbs. Mix in the sugar. Add sufficient milk to give a light, soft dough, using a round-bladed knife for mixing.

Turn the dough on to a lightly floured surface. Knead it lightly until smooth, then shape it into a flat round, 6 in. wide. Mark it into six equal triangles with the back of a floured knife blade.

Set the scone round on a heated, lightly floured baking tray and bake near the top of the oven, pre-heated to 450°F (mark 8), for about 15 minutes.

Serve the scones warm, split and liberally buttered.

Welsh Cakes

PREPARATION TIME: *15 min.*
COOKING TIME: *25 min.*

INGREDIENTS *(for 16 cakes)*:
8 oz. plain flour
1 level teaspoon baking powder
Pinch of salt
$1\frac{1}{2}$–2 oz. butter or firm margarine
$1\frac{1}{2}$–2 oz. lard
3 oz. caster sugar
2–3 oz. currants
1 egg
About 2 tablespoons milk

Heat a griddle, heavy-based frying pan or hot-plate. Sift the flour, baking powder and salt into a bowl; cut up the butter and lard and rub into the flour with the fingertips until the mixture resembles fine breadcrumbs. Stir in the sugar and currants. Beat the egg lightly and add it to the flour mixture, with just enough milk to give a firm paste similar to short-crust pastry.

Roll the dough $\frac{1}{4}$ in. thick, on a floured surface, and cut out rounds using a 3 in. plain or fluted pastry cutter. Bake the cakes on the greased griddle, over low heat for about 3 minutes on each side, until golden brown. Cool on a wire rack, and serve with a dusting of caster sugar.

Singin' Hinny

This Northumberland girdle cake hisses or sings when it is cooking, hence the name.

PREPARATION TIME: *10 min.*
COOKING TIME: *10 min.*

INGREDIENTS:
12 oz. plain flour
1 level teaspoon salt
2 level teaspoons baking powder
2 oz. ground rice
2 oz. caster sugar
2 oz. lard
3 oz. currants
$\frac{1}{4}$ pint milk
$\frac{1}{4}$ pint single cream

Heat a griddle, heavy-based frying pan or hot-plate. Sift the flour, salt and baking powder into a bowl, then stir in the ground rice and sugar. Cut up the lard and rub it into the dry ingredients with the fingertips until the mixture resembles fine breadcrumbs. Stir in the currants and gradually work in the milk and cream mixed together, using a round-bladed knife. Beat the dough lightly until soft and manageable.

Turn the dough on to a floured surface and pat or roll it out into a large round, $\frac{1}{4}$ in. thick, or into 3 small rounds. Prick the top with a fork and put the cakes on the greased griddle.

Cook over low heat for about 5 minutes, then turn the cakes carefully with a palette knife and cook until golden.

Slice the singin' hinny into halves and butter liberally, then sandwich together and serve while still warm.

See illustration on p. 379

Soda Bread

PREPARATION TIME: *15 min.*
COOKING TIME: *30 min.*

INGREDIENTS:
1 lb. plain flour
2 level teaspoons bicarbonate of soda
2 level teaspoons cream of tartar
1 level teaspoon salt
1 oz. lard
1–2 level teaspoons caster sugar (optional)
$\frac{1}{2}$ pint soured milk, or 9 fluid oz. buttermilk made up to $\frac{1}{2}$ pint with milk

Sift the flour, bicarbonate of soda, cream of tartar and salt into a bowl. Cut up the lard and rub it into the flour with the fingertips until the mixture resembles fine breadcrumbs. Mix in the sugar if used. Make a well in the centre of the flour, add the milk (soured with 1 tablespoon of lemon juice) or the buttermilk, and mix to a soft but manageable dough, working the ingredients with a round-bladed knife.

Turn the dough on to a floured surface, knead it lightly and shape it into a 7 in. round; flatten it slightly. Mark the round into four with the back of a knife, set it on a floured baking tray and bake in the centre of a pre-heated oven at 400°F (mark 6) for about 30 minutes.

Cool on a wire rack and serve fresh, as a teabread or as a substitute for yeast-baked bread.

See illustration on p. 378.

Bran Teabread

PREPARATION TIME: *10 min.*
RESTING TIME: *8 hours*
COOKING TIME: *$1\frac{1}{4}$–$1\frac{1}{2}$ hours*

INGREDIENTS:
3 oz. All Bran
8 oz. sultanas
8 oz. light soft brown sugar
$\frac{1}{2}$ pint milk
6 oz. self-raising flour
1 level teaspoon baking powder

Mix the All Bran, sultanas, sugar and milk in a bowl and leave to stand overnight, covered with a cloth.

Grease and line a loaf tin (9 in. by 5 in. top measurements). Sift the flour and baking powder into the soaked ingredients, blend thoroughly and spoon into the prepared tin. Level the top of the mixture and bake in the centre of a pre-heated oven, at 375°F (mark 5), for about $1\frac{1}{4}$ hours until the bread is well risen and just firm to the touch. If the loaf browns too quickly, cover it with a double sheet of greaseproof paper.

Turn out the loaf, remove the paper and cool on a wire rack. Serve the loaf sliced and buttered. It is best left for a day or two to mature before serving, and will keep for 1 week in a tin.

Cake-making

The key to successful cake-making lies in following the recipe in detail, and in understanding the reaction of the various ingredients to each other. The basic ingredients are fat, flour, raising agents, eggs, sugar and often fruit. Using the right size tins, correct oven position and temperature are also important factors.

Basically cakes fall into two categories: those made with fat, and the sponge types made without fat. The exception to sponge mixtures is the Genoese sponge which combines the two methods.

In fat-type cakes, the fat is either rubbed in, creamed or melted. Rubbed-in mixtures are generally used for plain, everyday cakes, such as Tyrol cake, while creamed cakes are rich and soft with a fairly close even grain and soft crumb as in a Victoria sandwich.

In melted cakes, e.g. gingerbread, the fat, often with liquid, sugar, syrup or treacle added, is poured into the dry ingredients to give a batter-like consistency. Mix cakes by hand or use an electric mixer after incorporating the flour with fat and eggs.

Before starting to mix, make sure to have the right size tin. Bigger, smaller or shallower tins than those called for can cause a cake to fail. If the tin is of incorrect size, fill to only half its depth so that the cake will rise to, but not above, the top. Test frequently to see if the cakes are cooked. Prepare the tin either by lining or by greasing with butter and sprinkling with flour. Set the oven to the correct temperature if the cake is to be baked at once after mixing, and assemble the necessary ingredients – eggs, butter and firm margarine should be at room temperature.

Fats

Butter, margarine, whipped-up white fat, lard and corn oil are all used in cakes. However, they are not always interchangeable.

Butter gives the best flavour and improves the keeping quality of cakes, but firm margarine can be used in place of butter in most recipes, with only a slight difference in flavour. Soft table margarine, sold in tubs, is composed of blended oils; it is particularly suitable for cakes where all the ingredients are mixed in one operation.

Whipped-up white fat is light and easy to blend with other ingredients. Like lard, this fat contains little or no salt and is almost 100 per cent fat; both can be used interchangeably in recipes.

Corn oil is suitable for most recipes using melted fat, but it is advisable to follow the manufacturer's instructions, as the characteristics of oils vary. It is easy to mix in and gives a soft texture, but the cakes do not keep quite so well.

Flour

Plain or self-raising flour or a mixture of both are used for cakes. Whichever type of flour is used, it should always be sifted with a pinch of salt. Salt is added not only for flavour, but because of its chemical effect in toughening up the soft mixture of fat and sugar.

Self-raising flour is popular, as it eliminates errors in calculating the exact amount of raising agents, which are already evenly blended throughout the flour.

A mixture of plain and self-raising flour is ideal for rich cakes which would rise too much if self-raising flour only were used. Other cakes, and in particular whisked cakes such as sponges, should be made only with plain flour, as they have their own natural raising agent – air.

In some melted cakes plain flour is mixed with bicarbonate of soda. These cakes contain treacle, which on its own is slightly acid and must be offset by an alkali to act as a raising agent.

Raising agents

Baking powder is a ready-made blend of soda and cream of tartar, and these together form carbon dioxide. The rubbery substance in flour – known as gluten – is capable, when wet, of suspending carbon dioxide in the form of tiny bubbles.

Since all gases expand when heated, these bubbles become larger during baking, and thus cause a cake to rise.

However, cake mixtures can hold only a certain amount of gas, and if too much raising agent is used the cake will rise well at first, but later collapse, and this results in a heavy, close texture. A combination of cream of tartar and bicarbonate of soda is sometimes used as an alternative to baking powder, in the proportion of 2:1.

Eggs

These give lightness to cake mixtures, as they expand on heating and trap the air beaten into the mixture. When whisked egg is used in a cake mixture, air instead of carbon dioxide causes it to rise.

Cakes with a high proportion of egg, such as sponge cakes, need little if any raising agent.

In creamed mixtures, the eggs are beaten in, not whisked, and a little additional raising agent is required. In plain cakes, where beaten egg is added with the liquid, the egg helps to bind the mixture but does not act as the main raising agent.

Sugar

Granulated sugar is the least expensive white sugar; it can be used in rubbed-in cakes, but as it is coarse it may give a spotted appearance to the cake crust. Caster sugar, being finer, creams more easily with fats and gives a finer, softer cake.

Demerara sugar should only be used in recipes for melted cakes, where sugar is dissolved, unless otherwise recommended.

Soft brown sugar, medium or light brown in colour, is good for rubbed-in, melted and fruit cakes. The colour and flavour add richness and the soft, moist quality helps to keep certain cakes in good condition longer.

Barbados sugar, very dark brown, full-flavoured and moist, is used in rich fruit mixtures for wedding and birthday cakes. Syrup, honey and treacle, often combined with sugar, are used to sweeten, colour and flavour cakes such as gingerbread. They give a close, moist texture.

Fruit and peel

Always choose good-quality dried fruit. Stored sultanas sometimes become hard, but they can be plumped up in hot water, and thoroughly drained and dried.

Sultanas can be bought ready-washed or unwashed. Unwashed are cheaper, but the fruit should be washed well, drained and left to dry thoroughly before use. Alternatively, clean sultanas by rubbing in a sieve with a little flour to remove the stalks.

Seedless raisins are similar in size to sultanas, but ready-prepared seeded or stoned raisins are large and juicy. To remove the stones from a raisin, work it between the finger-tips to ease out the stones, occasionally dipping the fingers in water. Wash any syrup from glacé cherries and dry them thoroughly.

Peel can be bought ready-chopped, but make sure that it looks soft and moist. Coarsely chopped, thin cut peel sometimes needs more chopping to make it finer. 'Caps' of candied orange, lemon, grapefruit and citron peel should be stripped of sugar before being shredded, grated, minced or chopped.

Preparing cake tins

All cakes should be baked in tins that have been greased, greased and floured, sugared or lined with paper. The appearance of a finished cake depends largely on the expert preparation of the cake tin.

Sandwich tins and cake tins for rubbed-in mixtures are often greased only by brushing melted white fat evenly over the inside. But as an extra precaution against sticking and for ease of turning out, a paper liner of greased greaseproof fitted into the base is a good idea. The paper does not necessarily have to reach the edge of the tin but the centre must be covered.

For fatless sponges, flour the greased tin to give an extra crisp crust, or dust it with flour, blended with an equal amount of sugar. Shake the dusting mixture round the tin until evenly coated, and remove any excess by gently tapping the inverted tin.

For baking small cakes or buns, fluted paper cups set in patty tins are by far the easiest to use; otherwise grease the patty pans thoroughly.

Non-stick paper can be used instead of greaseproof paper to line both round and rectangular tins. Tins with a non-stick surface need no greasing or lining, but a paper lining helps to protect against a solid crust, especially during long baking. For cakes baked in non-stick tins, the baking time should be reduced by a few minutes as these tins brown the contents more quickly.

Lining a round cake tin

Cut a strip of greaseproof paper as long as the circumference of the tin and 2 in. wider than the depth of the tin. Make a fold about 1 in. deep along one of the long edges, and cut this at $\frac{1}{2}$ in. intervals up to the fold, at a slight angle. Curve the strip round and slip it around the sides of the greased tin, nicked fold downwards so that this lies flat against the base of the tin.

Cut a circle of paper slightly smaller than the bottom of the tin and drop it in over the nicked paper. Brush with melted fat. For rich cakes with long cooking times, double-line the tin.

Lining a rectangular tin

Measure the length and width of the tin and add twice the tin's depth to each of these measurements. Cut a rectangle of greaseproof paper to this size and place the tin squarely in the centre. At each corner, make a cut from the angle of the paper as far as the corner of the tin.

Grease the inside of the tin and put in the paper so that it fits, closely overlapping at the corners. Brush again with melted fat.

Oven positions

In gas cookers, the hottest shelf is at the top, but in electric cookers the heat is more evenly distributed. A cake is generally baked in the centre of the oven.

When baking two cakes, place them side by side but do not let them touch the sides of the oven

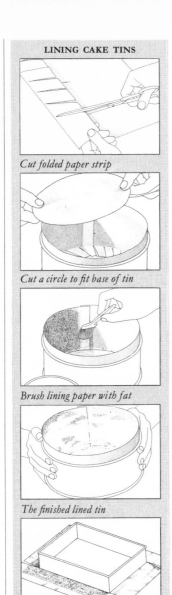

LINING CAKE TINS

Cut folded paper strip

Cut a circle to fit base of tin

Brush lining paper with fat

The finished lined tin

Centre a square tin over paper

Cut and fold paper to fit tin

or each other. If the tins are too large, bake the cakes on two oven shelves but avoid placing the tins directly over each other, and switch the tins over when the cake mixture has set.

Small cakes are usually baked above the centre, but not at the top of the oven. Place the tins or patty pans on baking trays before putting them in the oven.

Cooling cakes

With only a few exceptions, all cakes should be thoroughly cooled before being cut, frosted or stored. After baking, most cakes are best left to settle in their tins for 5–10 minutes before being turned out. Large cakes and rich fruit cakes are often left to get lukewarm before turning them out.

Run a spatula, small palette knife or round-bladed knife around the edge of the cake (do not use metal tools on non-stick tins). Place a wire rack over the cake and invert both the cake and rack, then lift the tin carefully. The lining paper may be peeled off or left on. Turn the cake with the aid of a second rack or the hand so that the top is uppermost. Leave the cake to cool completely on the wire rack. To prevent the wire mesh marking the surface of a soft-textured cake place a tea towel over the rack before turning the cake out.

Storing cakes

Storage time depends on the type of cake. Generally, iced cakes stay fresh longer than un-iced cakes, and the more fat in the cake mixture the longer it keeps. Fatless sponges should preferably be eaten on the day of baking as they go stale quickly.

Store both plain and iced cakes in airtight cake tins or similar containers. Cream-filled cakes are best kept in the refrigerator.

TURNING OUT CAKES

Run knife along inner edge of tin

Invert cake on to covered rack

Wrap fruit cakes with the lining paper left on in kitchen foil before storing. If slightly warm when wrapped they retain the moisture better.

Most cakes also store well in the home freezer.

RUBBED-IN CAKES

These plain cakes are the easiest of all to make. As the proportion of fat to flour is half or less, rubbed-in mixtures are best eaten when fresh or within 2–3 days of baking. Rubbing in consists of blending flour and fat to a crumb-like mixture, using the tips of the fingers.

To keep the mixture cool, raise the hands high when letting the crumbs drop back into the bowl. Shake the bowl occasionally to bring bigger crumbs to the surface. Make sure the texture is even, but do not handle more

than necessary, or the crumbs will toughen and the fat becomes soft and oily.

The amount of liquid added can be critical: too much results in a doughy texture, whereas too little gives a crumbly cake which quickly dries out. For a large cake, the mixture should only just drop off the spoon when gently tapped.

Tyrol cake

PREPARATION TIME: *25 min.*
COOKING TIME: *1¾ hours*

INGREDIENTS:
8 oz. plain flour
Pinch of salt
1 level teaspoon ground cinnamon
3½ oz. margarine
2 oz. caster sugar
2 oz. currants
2 oz. sultanas
1 level teaspoon bicarbonate of soda
¼ pint milk
3 level tablespoons clear honey

Grease a 6 in. round cake tin. Sift the flour, salt and cinnamon into a bowl, cut up the margarine and rub into the flour until the mixture resembles fine breadcrumbs. Stir in the sugar, currants and sultanas and make a well in the centre. Dissolve the bicarbonate of soda in the milk, stir in the honey and pour this mixture into the well in the flour. Using a wooden spoon, gradually work in the dry ingredients, adding more milk if necessary to give a firm dropping consistency.

Spoon the cake mixture into the prepared tin and level the top. Bake in the centre of the oven, pre-heated to 325°F (mark 3), for 1¾–2 hours or until well risen.

Test with a fine skewer – if it comes away clean, the cake is cooked. Cool on a wire rack.

Cake-making

Strawberry shortcake

PREPARATION TIME: *25 min.*
COOKING TIME: *20 min.*

INGREDIENTS:
8 oz. plain flour
1 level teaspoon cream of tartar
½ level teaspoon bicarbonate of soda
Pinch of salt
2 oz. butter or margarine
1½ oz. caster sugar
1 egg
3–4 tablespoons milk
FILLING:
½ lb. hulled strawberries
½ pint double cream
1 tablespoon milk
Caster sugar
Butter

Sift together the flour, cream of tartar, bicarbonate of soda and salt into a bowl. Cut the butter into small pieces and rub into the flour until the mixture resembles fine breadcrumbs. Blend in the sugar. Make a well in the centre, stir in the beaten egg and enough milk to give a soft but manageable dough. Knead lightly on a floured

STRAWBERRY SHORTCAKE

Spread with cream and fruit

Decorate top with piped cream

surface, then roll the dough out into a 7 in. circle.

Place on a greased baking tray, dust lightly with flour and bake towards the top of an oven preheated to 425°F (mark 7) for about 20 minutes. Cool slightly on a wire rack.

For the filling, slice the strawberries thickly. Whisk together the cream and the milk, sweetened with caster sugar to taste, until it holds its shape. Cut the warm shortcake into three layers, horizontally, with a serrated knife, and lightly butter each. Spread the cream over all three circles, then top with the sliced strawberries and sandwich the cake together. Decorate the top with piped cream.

Cherry and coconut cake

PREPARATION TIME: *30 min.*
COOKING TIME: *1¼ hours*

INGREDIENTS:
12 oz. self-raising flour
Pinch of salt
6 oz. margarine
8 oz. glacé cherries
2 oz. desiccated coconut
6 oz. caster sugar
2 large eggs
¼ pint milk
Granulated sugar

Grease a 7½–8 in. round cake tin. Sift the flour and salt into a bowl, and rub in the cut-up margarine. Quarter the cherries, toss them in the coconut and add, with the sugar, to the flour, stirring lightly to combine. Beat the eggs and stir into the mixture, together with sufficient milk to give a stiff but dropping consistency.

Turn the mixture into the prepared tin, level the surface, dust with granulated sugar and bake in the centre of the oven pre-heated to 350°F (mark 4) for about 1¼ hours or until well risen and golden brown. Cool on a wire rack.

Rock buns

PREPARATION TIME: *15 min.*
COOKING TIME: *15 min.*

INGREDIENTS *(for 12 buns):*
8 oz. plain flour
Pinch of salt
2 level teaspoons baking powder
2 oz. butter or margarine
2 oz. lard or whipped-up fat
4 oz. mixed dried fruit
4 oz. Demerara sugar
Grated rind of half lemon
1 large egg
1–2 tablespoons milk

Grease two baking trays. Sift together the flour, salt and baking powder into a bowl. Rub the fat into the flour until the mixture resembles fine breadcrumbs. Stir in the fruit, sugar and lemon rind. Beat the egg with 1 tablespoon of milk. Using a fork, stir the egg mixture into the dry ingredients, adding a little more milk if necessary to give a stiff dough – the mixture should just knit together.

Using two forks, place the mixture in 12 small heaps on the greased baking trays. Keep the mixture rough to give a rocky appearance which will remain after baking. Bake just above the centre of the oven, pre-heated to 400°F (mark 6), for 15–20 minutes, or until golden brown. Cool on a wire rack and serve the rock buns fresh.

See illustration on p. 380.

Raspberry buns

PREPARATION TIME: *25 min.*
COOKING TIME: *10–15 min.*

INGREDIENTS *(for 10 buns):*
7 oz. self-raising flour
Pinch of salt
1 oz. ground rice
3 oz. caster sugar
3 oz. butter or margarine
1 egg
1 tablespoon milk
Raspberry jam
Beaten egg

Grease two baking trays. In a bowl, sift together the flour, salt, ground rice and sugar. Add the fat, cut in small pieces, and rub into the flour with the fingertips until the mixture resembles fine breadcrumbs. Beat the egg lightly with the milk and mix this in with a round-bladed knife, until the mixture forms a light and manageable dough.

Shape the dough between the palms of the hands into 10 even-sized balls. Make a hole with a floured finger in the centre of each ball and drop in a little raspberry jam. Close up the opening, pinching the edges together.

Place the buns well apart on the baking trays, as they double in size when baked. Brush with beaten egg and bake just above the centre of the oven pre-heated to 425°F (mark 7) for 10–15 minutes. Cool on a wire rack.

See illustration on p. 380.

Apple cakes

PREPARATION TIME: *30 min.*
COOKING TIME: *15 min.*

INGREDIENTS *(for 16 cakes):*
1 lb. cooking apples
Brown sugar
8 oz. plain flour
2 level teaspoons cream of tartar
1 level teaspoon bicarbonate of soda
Pinch of salt
4 oz. margarine
4 oz. caster sugar
1 egg
Caster sugar for dusting

Grease 16 patty tins thoroughly. Peel and core the apples and cook them, with brown sugar to taste, over low heat until they form a thick purée.

Meanwhile, sift together the flour, cream of tartar, bicarbonate of soda and salt. Cut the margarine into small pieces and rub this into the flour until the mixture

resembles fine breadcrumbs. Stir in sugar and mix in the beaten egg to form a soft but manageable dough. Knead lightly on a floured surface and roll out, ⅛ in. thick. Handle the dough carefully, as it crumbles easily. Cut out 16 bases and 16 lids with a plain 2½ in. wide pastry cutter. If necessary, knead the trimmings and roll out more shapes.

Lift the cake bases into the tins with a palette knife. Cover with a teaspoonful of the apple purée and top with a lid – this seals itself during cooking. Sprinkle the tops with caster sugar. Bake just above the centre of the oven, pre-heated to 400°F (mark 6), for about 15 minutes. Leave to cool slightly in the tins, then ease the cakes out with a palette knife and cool completely on a wire rack. Serve while still fresh.

APPLE CAKES

Roll dough between waxed paper

Stamp out rounds with cutter

Put lids over apple filling

CREAMED CAKES

These are all made from the basic method of blending fat with sugar. Put the cut up butter or margarine into a bowl large enough to allow the fat – and sugar – to be beaten vigorously without overflowing. With a wooden spoon, beat the fat against the sides of the bowl until soft; add the sugar and beat or cream the mixture until fluffy and pale yellow. After 7–10 minutes the volume should have increased greatly and the mixture should drop easily from the spoon. Eggs may be added whole or beaten.

If an electric mixer is used, set the dial at the speed suggested in the manufacturer's instructions, and allow 3–4 minutes for beating. Switch off the mixer from time to time and scrape the cake mixture down into the bowl.

Victoria sandwich

PREPARATION TIME: *15 min.*
COOKING TIME: *25 min.*

INGREDIENTS:
4 oz. butter or margarine
4 oz. caster sugar
2 large eggs
Vanilla essence
  or grated lemon or orange rind
4 oz. self-raising flour

Grease two 7 in. straight-sided sandwich tins and line the bases with buttered greaseproof paper. In a bowl, beat the butter until soft, then add the sugar and cream until light and fluffy. Beat in the eggs, one at a time, then add a few drops of vanilla essence or finely grated lemon or orange rind. Beat in the sifted flour.

Divide this mixture equally between the two tins, and level off the surface. Bake the cakes side by side, if possible, in the centre of the oven pre-heated to 350°F (mark 4) for about 25 minutes. Cool on a wire rack.

CREAMED CAKE MIXTURE

Stand bowl on damp cloth

Beat butter and sugar until fluffy

Break egg into mixture and stir

Alternatively, add beaten egg

Fold in sifted flour

Layer the two cakes with jam or a butter cream filling* and dust the top with caster or sifted icing sugar. Alternatively, cover with a soft icing*.

See illustration on p. 380.

Chocolate layer cake

PREPARATION TIME: *25 min.*
COOKING TIME: *30 min.*

INGREDIENTS:
4 oz. butter or margarine
4 oz. caster sugar
2 large eggs
2 level tablespoons cocoa
4 oz. self-raising flour
Pinch of salt
FILLING:
1½ oz. butter or margarine
3 oz. icing sugar
2 teaspoons coffee essence
1 tablespoon top of the milk

Grease a straight-sided 8 in. wide sandwich tin and line with paper, cutting the band of paper to come ½ in. above the rim. Grease the paper lining.

Beat the butter until soft, then add the sugar and cream the mixture until light and fluffy. Beat the eggs before beating them into the mixture, a little at a time. In a small bowl or cup, blend the cocoa with enough cold water to make a paste. Lightly beat this into the creamed mixture, alternately with the sifted flour and salt. Turn the cake mixture into the prepared tin, level the surface and bake in the centre of a pre-heated oven at 350°F (mark 4) for about 30 minutes or until well risen and spongy to the touch.

Meanwhile, make the filling. Beat the butter until soft and creamy, sift the icing sugar and add a little at a time. Stir in the coffee essence and milk.

Turn the cake on to a wire rack, and remove the lining paper. Cut the cold cake in half horizontally, and spread the bottom half with the filling; place the top in position and lightly press the two halves together. Dust the top with sifted icing sugar. Using the back of a knife blade, draw a lattice pattern across the sugar.

See illustration on p. 380.

Madeira cake

PREPARATION TIME: *20 min.*
COOKING TIME: *1–1¼ hours*

INGREDIENTS:
6 oz. butter or margarine
6 oz. caster sugar
3 large eggs
5 oz. self-raising flour
4 oz. plain flour
Pinch of salt
Grated rind and juice of half lemon
Citron peel

Grease a 7 in. round cake tin and line with greaseproof paper. Beat the butter until soft, then add the sugar and cream until light and fluffy. Add the eggs, one at a time, beating well between each addition. Fold in the sifted flours and salt, alternately with the strained lemon juice and

CHOCOLATE LAYER CAKE

Sift icing sugar over layered cake

Draw lattice pattern across sugar

rind. Turn the mixture into the prepared tin and level the surface. Arrange slices of thinly cut citron peel over the top.

Bake in the centre of an oven pre-heated to 325°F (mark 3) for 1–1¼ hours. Leave to cool in the tin for 10 minutes, then turn out on to a wire rack.

See illustration on p. 381.

Pineapple and cherry loaf

PREPARATION TIME: *35 min.*
COOKING TIME: *1½ hours*

INGREDIENTS:
6 oz. glacé cherries
1½ oz. glacé pineapple
3 oz. ground almonds
Grated rind of half lemon
6 oz. butter or margarine
6 oz. caster sugar
3 eggs
3 oz. self-raising flour
3 oz. plain flour
Pinch of salt

Grease a loaf tin, 4½ in. by 9 in. (top measurement); line with buttered greaseproof paper. Wash and dry the cherries, cut them in half and set 10 aside. Chop the pineapple and mix with the cherries, ground almonds and lemon rind.

Beat the butter until soft, then add the sugar, and cream the mixture until light and fluffy. Beat the eggs before adding them to the mixture a little at a time. Sift and fold the flours and salt, a third at a time, into the creamed mixture. Lastly fold in the fruit.

Spoon into the prepared tin, level the surface and arrange the reserved cherries on top. Cover the tin loosely with kitchen foil, taking care that it does not touch the cake mixture. Bake in the centre of an oven pre-heated to 350°F (mark 4) for about 1½ hours or until well-risen and firm to the touch. Cool on a wire rack and remove the lining paper.

See illustration on p. 381.

Cake-making

Dundee cake

PREPARATION TIME: *20 min.*
COOKING TIME: *3½ hours*

INGREDIENTS:
8 oz. plain flour
Pinch of salt
8 oz. butter or margarine
8 oz. caster sugar
4 large eggs
12 oz. sultanas
12 oz. currants
6 oz. chopped mixed peel
4 oz. small glacé cherries
Grated rind of half lemon
2–3 oz. whole almonds

Grease an 8 in. round cake tin and line with double paper. Tie a band of brown paper round the outside of the tin and let it extend about 2 in. above the rim. Set the tin on a double piece of brown paper on a baking tray.

Sift together the flour and salt. Beat the butter until soft, add the sugar and cream until light and fluffy. Beat the eggs into the mixture, a little at a time. Fold in the flour and, when evenly combined, fold in the sultanas, currants, peel, cherries and lemon rind. Blanch* the almonds, slip off the skins and chop 1 oz.; add to the cake mixture. Spoon into the tin.

BLANCHING WHOLE ALMONDS

Slide off softened skins

Split almonds in half

Split the rest of the almonds lengthways, and arrange them, rounded side up, over the levelled cake surface. Bake just below the centre of an oven, pre-heated to 300°F (mark 2), for about 3½ hours. If the cake shows signs of browning too quickly, cover the top with a sheet of damp grease-proof paper, and reduce the heat to 275°F (mark 1) for the last hour. Remove the cake from the oven when a skewer comes away clean from the cake.

Cool in the tin for 30 minutes, then turn out and cool on a wire rack. Wrap the cake in foil, with the lining paper in position. The cake is best kept for at least 1 week and up to 1 month to bring out the full flavour.

See illustration on p. 381.

Orange butterflies

PREPARATION TIME: *15 min.*
COOKING TIME: *10 min.*

INGREDIENTS *(for 12 cakes):*
3 oz. butter or margarine
3 oz. caster sugar
1 large egg
1 level teaspoon grated orange rind
5 oz. self-raising flour
Pinch of salt
1 tablespoon orange juice
Orange-flavoured butter cream
Icing sugar

Grease 12 patty tins. Beat the butter until soft, then add the sugar, and cream until light and fluffy. Add the beaten egg. Sift the flour and salt, add the orange rind and fold this into the creamed mixture alternately with the orange juice. Using a teaspoon, fill the patty pans to half their depths. Bake just above the centre of a pre-heated oven at 400°F (mark 6) for 10–15 minutes or until well-risen and golden. Cool the cakes on a wire rack.

Cut a slice from the top of each cake and pipe or spoon in a little butter cream*. Cut each top slice in half and insert these in the butter cream to resemble the wings of butterflies. Dust with sifted icing sugar and serve.

Coconut castles

PREPARATION TIME: *20 min.*
COOKING TIME: *20 min.*

INGREDIENTS *(for 6–8 cakes):*
4 oz. butter or margarine
4 oz. caster sugar
2 eggs
4 oz. self-raising flour
Pinch of salt
4 tablespoons red jam
1 tablespoon water
2 oz. desiccated coconut
6 glacé cherries
Angelica

Grease six dariole moulds*. Beat the butter until soft, add the sugar, and cream until light and fluffy. Beat in the beaten eggs. Gradually fold in the sifted flour and salt. Divide the mixture evenly between the moulds, filling them no more than two-thirds full. Set on a baking tray and bake in the centre of an oven, pre-heated to 350°F (mark 4) for 20 minutes or until golden. Cool on a wire rack.

When the castles are cold, bring the jam and water to the boil and cook for 1 minute. Level the wide base of the castles if necessary, brush them all over with the jam and roll in coconut. Garnish with a cherry and angelica leaves.

See illustration on p. 381.

Swiss tarts

PREPARATION TIME: *25 min.*
COOKING TIME: *20 min.*

INGREDIENTS *(for 6 cakes):*
4 oz. butter
1 oz. caster sugar
Vanilla essence
4 oz. plain flour
Icing sugar
Red currant jelly

Place 6 paper baking cases in a sheet of patty tins and set on a baking tray. Beat the butter until soft, add the sugar, and cream until light and fluffy. Beat in a few drops of vanilla essence and gradually add the flour, beating well between each addition.

Put the mixture in a fabric piping bag fitted with a large star vegetable nozzle. Pipe the mixture into the paper cases, starting at the centre, and piping with a spiral motion round the sides, leaving a shallow depression in the centre. Bake in the centre of an oven, pre-heated to 350°F (mark 4) for about 20 minutes or until set and tinged with colour.

Leave the cakes in their paper cases to cool on a wire rack. Dredge with icing sugar and top each tart with a little red currant jelly.

See illustration on p. 380.

Farmhouse fruit cake

PREPARATION TIME: *10 min.*
COOKING TIME: *about 1½ hours*

INGREDIENTS:
6 oz. soft tub margarine
6 oz. caster sugar
3 oz. sultanas
3 oz. seedless raisins
3 oz. glacé cherries, chopped
12 oz. self-raising flour
Pinch of salt
1 level teaspoon mixed spice
3 tablespoons milk
3 eggs

Grease an 8 in. round cake tin and line with buttered grease-proof paper. Mix the margarine and all the dry ingredients in a bowl, then add the milk and eggs and beat with a wooden spoon until well mixed, for 2–3 minutes. Turn into the prepared tin and level the top.

Bake in the centre of the oven pre-heated to 350°F (mark 4) for about 1½ hours. When a warm skewer comes away clean, the cake is cooked. Leave the cake in the tin for 15 minutes before turning out on to a wire rack to cool.

Coffee walnut cake

PREPARATION TIME: *20 min.*
COOKING TIME: *35–40 min.*

INGREDIENTS:
4 oz. soft tub margarine
4 oz. caster sugar
2 large eggs
2 oz. chopped walnuts
1 tablespoon coffee essence
4 oz. self-raising flour
Pinch of salt
1 level tablespoon baking powder
FILLING:
3 oz. soft tub margarine
8 oz. icing sugar
2 teaspoons milk
2 teaspoons coffee essence
Walnut halves

Grease two 7 in. straight-sided sandwich tins, and line the bases with buttered greaseproof paper. Put the margarine and sugar, eggs, chopped walnuts and coffee essence in a bowl. Sift in the flour with the salt and baking powder. Beat these ingredients with a wooden spoon for 2–3 minutes or until well combined. Divide the mixture between the prepared tins, level the surface and bake in the centre of an oven, pre-heated to 325°F (mark 3), for 35–40 minutes, or until well-risen and spongy to the touch.

When baked, turn the cakes out on a wire rack to cool before removing the lining paper.

Meanwhile make the filling: beat the margarine, sifted icing sugar, milk and coffee essence in a bowl until smooth. Sandwich the cakes together with two-thirds of the filling, top with the remaining filling and mark the surface with the prongs of a fork in a decorative pattern. Place walnut halves on top of the cake.

WHISKED CAKES

These are the lightest of all cake mixtures, their texture depending entirely on the incorporated eggs. The fatless cake mixture is used for sponges, which should be baked as soon as they are mixed.

Use a hand-operated, rotary or balloon whisk and to stabilise the mixture, place the deep bowl of eggs and sugar over hot, not boiling, water. Do not let the mixture become too hot or the sponge will have a tough texture. For a maximum rise, the mixture should be thick enough to leave a trail when the whisk is lifted. If an electric mixer is used, it is unnecessary to heat the bowl.

Blending in the flour is another important step. Sift the flour two or three times, the last time over the whisked egg mixture, then fold it carefully into the mixture without flattening the bulk. Use a metal spoon or plastic spatula in a figure-of-eight movement.

Strawberry cream sponge
PREPARATION TIME: *20 min.*
COOKING TIME: *15 min.*

INGREDIENTS:
3 oz. plain flour
Pinch of salt
3 eggs
3 oz. caster sugar
Strawberry jam
¼ pint double or whipping cream
Caster or icing sugar for dusting

Butter and dust with flour and sugar two 7 in. straight-sided sandwich tins. Sift the flour with the salt twice into a bowl or on to a sheet of greaseproof paper. Place a deep mixing bowl over a pan of hot water, break the eggs into the bowl and gradually whisk in the sugar. Continue whisking until the mixture is pale, and thick enough to leave a trail. Carefully fold in the sifted flour and salt. Divide the mixture equally between the two tins, putting any scrapings from the bowl at the side of the tins, not in the middle. Bake just above the centre of an oven, pre-heated to 375°F (mark 5), for about 15 minutes or until pale brown and springy to the touch.

Carefully ease away the edges of the baked cakes with a palette knife, and cool on a wire rack.

When cold, spread the bases of both sponges with a thin layer of jam, cover one sponge with whipped cream and place the other cake, jam downwards, on top. Press lightly together and dust with caster or sifted icing sugar. Chill until serving.

Swiss roll
PREPARATION TIME: *15 min.*
COOKING TIME: *10 min.*

INGREDIENTS:
3 oz. plain flour
Pinch of salt
3 large eggs
3 oz. caster sugar
1 tablespoon hot water
Jam or cream filling

Sift the flour and salt twice into a bowl or on to greaseproof paper. Butter a Swiss-roll tin measuring 12 in. by 8 in., and line with buttered greaseproof or non-stick paper.

Put the eggs and caster sugar in a large bowl over a pan of hot water, and whisk until the mixture is pale and leaves a thick trail. Remove from the heat, sift half the flour and salt over the egg mixture, and fold it in carefully, using a large metal spoon. Repeat with the remaining flour, and add the hot water. Turn the mixture quickly into the prepared tin, tilting it until evenly covered with the mixture. Bake at once just above the centre of an oven, pre-heated to 425°F (mark 7), for about 10 minutes or until well-risen, light golden and springy.

MAKING A SWISS ROLL

Tilt tin to spread mixture evenly

Remove lining paper from cake

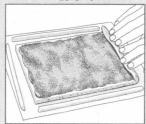
Spread warm jam over cake

Roll up sponge on sugared paper

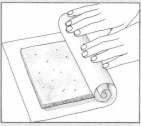
Rolling sponge for cream filling

Have ready a sheet of sugar-dredged greaseproof or non-stick paper. Turn the soft cake out on to the paper at once, remove the lining paper and quickly trim off the crisp edges from the sponge with a sharp knife. Spread with 4–5 tablespoons warm jam, to within ½ in. of the edges. Roll up the sponge at once from the short side, making the first turn firm, then rolling it lightly. Cool on a wire rack covered with a clean tea towel, and with the join of the sponge underneath.

The Swiss roll may also be spread with a butter-cream filling, just before serving. In this case, do not remove the lining paper, but roll the sponge round it while still warm. When cold, carefully unroll the sponge, then spread with whipped cream, butter cream*, or pastry cream* and roll up again.

Before serving, dust with caster or sifted icing sugar.

See illustration on p. 380.

ENRICHED BUTTER SPONGE CAKES

When butter is added to a whisked sponge mixture, it is known as Genoese sponge, a richer variety than fatless sponges and one which needs slightly longer baking, but keeps better. Genoese sponge mixtures are used for gâteaux, layered with cream and fruit, or baked and cut into small individual cakes before being iced and decorated.

Genoese sponge
PREPARATION TIME: *15 min.*
COOKING TIME: *30 min.*

INGREDIENTS:
1½ oz. unsalted butter
2½ oz. plain flour
1 level tablespoon cornflour
3 large eggs
3 oz. caster sugar

Grease a 9 in. straight-sided sandwich tin, a deep, 8 in. cake tin, or a 7 in. square tin, and line with buttered greaseproof paper. Heat the butter in a pan over low heat until melted but not hot; remove from the heat and leave to stand for a few minutes. Sift together the flour and cornflour three times. Put the eggs in a large deep bowl over a pan of hot water, whisk for a few seconds, then add the sugar and continue whisking until the mixture is quite pale in colour and leaves a thick trail when the whisk is lifted out.

Remove the bowl from the heat and whisk for a few minutes longer, until the mixture is cool. Using a metal spoon, carefully fold in half the sifted flour, then pour in the melted butter in a thin stream at the side of the bowl. Fold in the remaining sifted flour. Turn this mixture into the prepared tin and bake near the top of an oven, pre-heated to 375°F (mark 5), for about 30 minutes or until well-risen and spongy to the touch. Invert on to a wire rack and leave to cool; remove lining paper.

The sponge, if baked in a deep tin, can be split horizontally into three equal layers and sandwiched together with a cream and fruit or butter cream* filling, and the top decorated with cream. A shallower sponge should be split into two layers only and sandwiched together as already described.

A sponge baked in a large shallow tin can be cut into fancy individual shapes. Brush these with warm apricot glaze* and cover with plain or coloured glacé or fondant icing*. Decorate with glacé cherries, crystallised violets and roses, mimosa balls, silver dragees or blanched pistachio nuts.

See illustration on p. 381.

Cake-making

Iced petits fours

PREPARATION TIME: $1\frac{1}{4}$ hours
COOKING TIME: 30 min.

INGREDIENTS (for 24–30 cakes):
3 large eggs
3 oz. caster sugar
$2\frac{1}{2}$ oz. plain flour
1 level tablespoon cornflour
$1\frac{1}{2}$ oz. unsalted butter
Apricot glaze
1 lb. almond paste
Glacé icing (from 1 lb. icing sugar)
Food colourings
Flavourings (optional)
Decorations

Grease and base-line a rectangular tin, 1 in. deep by 10 in. by 6 in. Make up the eggs, sugar, flours and butter as described for Genoese sponge. Turn the mixture into the tin, levelling the top evenly, and bake just above the centre of a pre-heated oven, at 375°F (mark 5), for about 30 minutes. Turn out to cool on a covered wire rack and remove the lining paper.

Cut the sponge, on a flat surface, into 24–30 small shapes, such as squares, diamonds, rounds and crescents. Brush the petits fours with warm apricot glaze*, and roll out the almond paste* thinly. Cut the paste into the same type of shapes as the petits fours and lay them over the brushed cakes.

Make up the glacé icing* into a coating consistency, divide it into four portions and colour three of these green, pink or lemon. Flavouring may be added to match each colour. Set the petits fours on a wire tray over a plate and carefully spoon the icing over the cakes, using a teaspoon and letting the icing run down the sides. When the icing is nearly set, decorate the cakes with, for example, glacé cherries, angelica, mimosa balls, silver

ICED PETITS FOURS

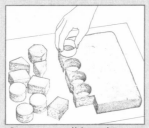
Stamp out small fancy shapes

Brush with apricot glaze

Top with thin almond paste

Cover with glacé icing and decorate

dragees, nuts, or crystallised violets and rose petals.

When dry and set, put the petits fours in small paper cases and serve.

Almond petits fours

PREPARATION TIME: 20 min.
COOKING TIME: 20 min.

INGREDIENTS (for 24–30 cakes):
2 egg whites
4 oz. ground almonds
2 oz. caster sugar
Almond essence
Rice paper
Glacé cherries
Angelica

Line two or three baking trays with rice paper. Whisk the egg whites in a deep bowl until stiff; lightly fold in the almonds and sugar and add a few drops of almond essence.

Spoon the mixture into a forcing bag fitted with a large rose vegetable nozzle and pipe it

ALMOND PETITS FOURS

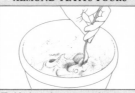
Fold almonds into egg whites

Pipe out rosettes and 'S' shapes

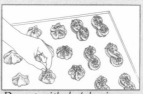
Decorate with glacé cherries

on to the baking trays in small rosettes and 'S' shapes. Decorate the petits fours with glacé cherries or strips of angelica.

Bake in the centre of a pre-heated oven, at 350°F (mark 4), for about 20 minutes or until golden brown.

See illustration on p. 383.

MELTED CAKES

These have a dense, slightly tacky texture and a consistency similar to a thick batter. Treacle or syrup is a major ingredient, with baking powder as the main raising agent together with bicarbonate of soda.

Gingerbread

PREPARATION TIME: 15 min.
COOKING TIME: $1\frac{1}{2}$ hours

INGREDIENTS:
1 lb. plain flour
3 level teaspoons ground ginger
3 level teaspoons baking powder
1 level teaspoon bicarbonate of soda
1 level teaspoon salt
8 oz. Demerara sugar
6 oz. butter
6 oz. black treacle
6 oz. golden syrup
$\frac{1}{2}$ pint milk
1 large egg

Grease a 9 in. square cake tin, about 2 in. deep, and line with buttered greaseproof paper. Sift all the dry ingredients, except the sugar, into a large bowl. Warm the sugar, butter, treacle and syrup in a pan over low heat until the butter has just melted. Stir the melted ingredients into the centre of the dry mix, together with the milk and beaten egg. Beat thoroughly with a wooden spoon. Pour the mixture into the prepared tin and bake in the centre of an oven, pre-heated to 350°F (mark 4), for about $1\frac{1}{2}$ hours, or until well-risen and just firm to the touch.

Leave to cool in the tin for 15 minutes, then turn out to cool on a wire rack. When cold, wrap in foil, without removing the lining paper.

Store gingerbread for 4–7 days before cutting into chunks, to give the flavour time to mellow.

See illustration on p. 381.

Parkin

PREPARATION TIME: 20 min.
COOKING TIME: 45 min.

INGREDIENTS:
8 oz. plain flour
Pinch of salt
2 level teaspoons baking powder
2 level teaspoons ground ginger
2 oz. margarine or butter
2 oz. lard
8 oz. medium oatmeal
4 oz. caster sugar
6 oz. golden syrup
6 oz. black treacle
4 tablespoons milk

Grease a tin, 10 in. by 8 in. by $1\frac{1}{2}$ in. deep and line with buttered greaseproof paper. Sift together the flour, salt, baking powder and ginger into a bowl. Cut the margarine and lard into small pieces and rub into the flour until the mixture resembles fine breadcrumbs. Stir in the oatmeal and sugar. Warm the syrup and treacle, pour it into the centre of the dry ingredients, together with the milk, and beat lightly with a wooden spoon until thoroughly blended.

Turn the mixture into the prepared tin, and bake in the centre of a pre-heated oven at 350°F (mark 4) for about 45 minutes or until the mixture has begun to shrink away from the sides of the tin. It often sinks slightly. Cool on a wire rack. Leave the lining paper in place, wrap the cake in foil and store for at least a week.

Serve parkin cut into thick slices.

Biscuits

The word 'biscuit' comes from the French *bis cuit*, 'twice cooked', and this is a literal description of what happened in the early days of biscuit-making. At the start of a long sea voyage, small, hard cakes were taken aboard, to form part of the crew's daily diet. These cakes had to be cooked before loading, otherwise they would have gone mouldy, and before eating their 'hard tack', the sailors would have the cakes cooked again. Biscuits today are only once cooked, and although usually at their best when freshly baked, some can be stored in airtight containers for about 1 week.

Bake biscuits at or just above the centre of the oven; if two baking trays are used place them above each other in the oven, and halfway through baking switch them over so that all the biscuits brown evenly. Cool the baked biscuits on a wire rack, lifting them from the baking trays as soon as cooked. Some biscuits, however, especially those made with syrup or honey, are soft when baking is completed – leave these on the trays to settle for a few minutes.

Generally, biscuits fall into one of half a dozen main groups: bar types, drop cookies, shaped cookies, piped cookies, prepared biscuits and rolled biscuits.

SHAPED COOKIES

The dough for shaped cookies is fairly soft and needs quick and light handling. Alternatively, it can be chilled in the refrigerator until stiff, and moulded in the palms of the hands.

Ginger nuts

PREPARATION TIME: *15 min.*
COOKING TIME: *15 min.*

INGREDIENTS *(for 24 biscuits)*:
4 oz. self-raising flour
½ level teaspoon bicarbonate of soda
1 level teaspoon ground ginger
½ level teaspoon ground cinnamon
2 level teaspoons caster sugar
2 oz. butter
3 oz. golden syrup

Grease two or three baking trays. Sift the flour, bicarbonate of soda, ginger and cinnamon into a bowl; add the sugar. In a small pan, melt the butter, without boiling, and stir in the syrup. Mix this into the dry ingredients, using a wooden spoon. Shape the dough between the hands into a thick sausage shape before cutting it into 24 even pieces. Roll each piece into a small ball, set them well apart on the baking trays and flatten slightly.

Bake just above the centre of an oven pre-heated to 375°F (mark 5) for about 15 minutes, or until the tops have cracked and are golden brown. Cool for a few minutes on the baking tray before lifting on to a wire rack. As soon as quite cold, store the ginger nuts in an airtight tin, as they quickly go soft.

Jumbles

PREPARATION TIME: *40 min.*
COOKING TIME: *12–15 min.*

INGREDIENTS *(for 10–15 biscuits)*:
2½ oz. butter
2½ oz. caster sugar
Half a beaten egg
5 oz. self-raising flour
1 teaspoon finely grated lemon rind
1 oz. ground almonds

Grease two baking trays. Cream the butter with a wooden spoon until soft, but not oily, then add the sugar and continue beating until light and fluffy. Beat in the egg and add the sifted flour, lemon rind and almonds. Form the mixture into three rolls, ½–¾ in. wide; cut these into 4 in. long pieces and form them into 'S' shapes.

Place on the baking trays, and bake in the centre of a pre-heated oven at 400°F (mark 6) for about 12 minutes, or until risen and pale brown. Cool for a few minutes, then transfer to a wire rack.

See illustration on p. 382.

Orange creams

PREPARATION TIME: *30 min.*
COOKING TIME: *20 min.*

INGREDIENTS *(for 18 biscuits)*:
4 oz. butter
3–4 oz. caster sugar
2 level teaspoons golden syrup
1 egg yolk
Finely grated rind of an orange
7 oz. plain flour
½ level teaspoon cream of tartar
1 level teaspoon baking powder
FILLING:
2 oz. butter
3 oz. icing sugar
Orange juice

Grease two or three baking trays. Cream the butter and sugar, using a wooden spoon, until light and fluffy. Beat in the syrup, egg yolk and orange rind. Sift the flour, cream of tartar and baking powder over the creamed ingredients and fold in with a metal spoon to give a soft dough.

Shape the dough into 36 balls about the size of large marbles and set them well apart on the baking sheets. Bake just above the centre of a pre-heated oven at 375°F (mark 5) for about 20 minutes, or until lightly coloured and risen. Cool on a wire rack.

For the filling, beat the butter until soft, then gradually beat in the sifted icing sugar with as much orange juice as the filling will take without becoming too soft. Colour it pale orange.

Spread the filling over half the biscuits, and sandwich together.

See illustration on p. 382.

DROP COOKIES

Baked drop cookies can be soft with a cake-like texture, or crisp and even brittle, often irregular in shape. The soft dough is dropped in mounds on to a baking tray.

Brandy snaps

PREPARATION TIME: *15 min.*
COOKING TIME: *20–30 min.*

INGREDIENTS *(for 16 biscuits)*:
2 oz. butter
2 oz. caster sugar
2 level tablespoons golden syrup
2 oz. plain flour
½ level teaspoon ground ginger
1 teaspoon brandy
Finely grated rind of half lemon
FILLING:
6 fluid oz. double cream
1 tablespoon milk

Grease or line two baking trays with non-stick kitchen paper, and butter the handles of a few wooden spoons thoroughly. Melt the butter, with the sugar and syrup over low heat. Stir until smooth, then remove.

Sift the flour and ginger, and stir it into the melted ingredients, together with the brandy and lemon rind. Mix thoroughly with a wooden spoon, and leave to cool for 1–2 minutes.

Drop the mixture in teaspoons, at 4 in. intervals, on to the baking trays. Bake towards the top of a pre-heated oven, at 350°F (mark 4), for 7–10 minutes or until the biscuits are bubbly, lacy in texture and golden brown. Rotate the baking so that not too many will be ready for rolling at the same time.

Remove the biscuits from the oven and quickly roll each snap loosely round a buttered spoon handle, easing them round with a palette knife. Leave the snaps on the handles until set, then twist them gently off and cool on a wire rack. If the biscuits set before they have all been shaped into snaps, return them to the oven for a few minutes until soft and pliable again.

Just before serving, whisk together the cream and milk until light and fluffy. Pipe or spoon the cream into both ends of each snap. Unfilled brandy snaps will keep in an airtight container for up to 1 week.

See illustration on p. 382.

BRANDY SNAPS

Roll snap round spoon handle

Remove shaped brandy snap

Pipe cream into brandy snaps

Biscuits

Coconut wafers

PREPARATION TIME: *20 min.*
COOKING TIME: *12 min.*

INGREDIENTS *(for 18 biscuits)*:
2 oz. butter
2 oz. caster sugar
1 level tablespoon golden syrup
2 teaspoons lemon juice
2 oz. plain flour
1 oz. fine desiccated coconut

Grease two or three baking trays. Cream the butter and sugar until light and fluffy, then beat in the syrup. Add the lemon juice, sifted flour and the coconut. Drop the dough in teaspoons on to the baking trays, setting them well apart as the wafers spread.

Bake just below the centre of an oven pre-heated to 350°F (mark 4) for about 12 minutes, when the edges of the wafers should be golden brown and the centres lightly coloured. Cool slightly before lifting carefully from the baking trays on to a wire rack.

See illustration on p. 382.

Ginger drops

PREPARATION TIME: *10 min.*
COOKING TIME: *15–20 min.*

INGREDIENTS *(for 18 biscuits)*:
4 oz. plain flour
½ level teaspoon bicarbonate of soda
1 level tablespoon ground ginger
1 oz. golden syrup
1 oz. stem ginger, chopped
2 oz. butter or margarine
2 oz. Demerara sugar
2 tablespoons milk

Grease two baking trays. Sift together the flour and bicarbonate of soda. In a small pan, warm the syrup. Cream the butter and sugar until light and fluffy, then stir in the syrup and stem ginger, half the sifted flour and 1 tablespoon of milk. Add the remaining flour and milk and mix to a soft dough. Drop the mixture in tea-spoons, easing it off with the little finger, on to the baking trays, setting them well apart.

Bake just above the centre of an oven pre-heated to 350°F (mark 4) for about 15 minutes. Cool on a wire rack.

See illustration on p. 382.

PIPED COOKIES

The dough for piped cookies is fairly soft and should be piped through a medium-sized fabric forcing bag often fitted with a star-shaped vegetable nozzle.

Lemon meltaways

PREPARATION TIME: *20 min.*
RESTING TIME: *30 min.*
COOKING TIME: *30 min.*

INGREDIENTS *(for about 20 biscuits)*:
4 oz. butter or block margarine
1 oz. icing sugar
Finely grated rind of half lemon
4 oz. plain flour
Sieved apricot jam
GLAZE:
2 level tablespoons icing sugar
2 teaspoons lemon juice, approx.

Grease two baking trays. In a deep bowl, beat the butter with a wooden spoon until creamy, add the sifted icing sugar and continue beating until the mixture is pale and fluffy. Stir in the lemon rind and flour to give a soft dough. Spoon the mixture into a forcing bag, fitted with a medium star vegetable nozzle, and pipe out about 20 shell shapes, a little apart from each other. Chill for 30 minutes in the refrigerator.

Bake in the centre of a pre-heated oven at 325°F (mark 3) for about 25 minutes or until lightly browned. For the glaze, blend the sifted icing sugar with enough lemon juice to give a coating consistency.

Leave the baked biscuits on the baking trays, brush them with soft sieved jam and then with the lemon glaze. Return the biscuits to the oven for a further 5 minutes, then set them on a wire rack to cool and crisp.

See illustration on p. 382.

Short fingers

PREPARATION TIME: *45 min.*
COOKING TIME: *10–15 min.*

INGREDIENTS *(for 12 biscuits)*:
4½ oz. butter
1 oz. icing sugar
5 oz. plain flour
3 oz. plain cooking chocolate
BUTTER CREAM:
1 oz. butter
2 oz. icing sugar
Vanilla essence

Grease two baking trays. Cream the butter with a wooden spoon until soft, but not oily, then beat in the sifted icing sugar. Stir in the sifted flour. Put the mixture

SHORT FINGERS

Pipe out 2 in. long fingers

Sandwich with butter cream

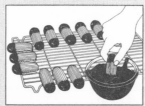

Coat tips of biscuits in chocolate

in a forcing bag, fitted with a medium star vegetable nozzle, and pipe it in 2 in. long fingers, on to the baking trays. Bake just above or in the centre of a pre-heated oven, at 375°F (mark 5) for 10–15 minutes or until pale golden brown.

Meanwhile, break the chocolate into small pieces and place them in a bowl over hot water until melted. To make the butter cream, cream the butter until soft, then beat in the sifted icing sugar and a few drops of vanilla.

Leave the baked biscuits to cool completely on a wire rack. When cold, sandwich them in pairs with the butter cream. Dip one end of each biscuit in the melted chocolate and place them on a rack with the chocolate end protruding over the edge. When the chocolate has set, repeat the procedure with the other ends. Leave the biscuits for about 1½ hours before serving.

See illustration on p. 382.

Macaroons

PREPARATION TIME: *10 min.*
COOKING TIME: *15 min.*

INGREDIENTS *(for 24 biscuits)*:
Rice paper
4 oz. ground almonds
6 oz. caster sugar
2 egg whites
1 level tablespoon cornflour
¼ teaspoon vanilla essence
12 blanched almonds

Line two or three baking trays with rice paper. Mix the ground almonds with the sugar and add the unbeaten egg whites, setting 1 tablespoon aside. Using a wooden spoon, work the mixture until the ingredients are evenly blended. Stir in the cornflour, vanilla essence and 2 teaspoons of water. Spoon the mixture into a forcing bag fitted with a ½ in. plain nozzle. Pipe the biscuits on to the rice paper in large round buttons; top each with half an almond. Brush lightly with the remaining egg white.

Bake the macaroons just above or in the centre of a pre-heated oven, at 375°F (mark 5), for about 15 minutes or until lightly browned, risen and slightly cracked. Cut the rice paper to fit round each macaroon and leave to cool on a wire rack. Serve preferably on the day of baking.

See illustration on p. 382.

BAR-TYPE BISCUITS

These have a cake-like texture, with the exception of shortbread, and are baked in one complete piece before being cut up.

Boston brownies

PREPARATION TIME: *15 min.*
COOKING TIME: *35 min.*

INGREDIENTS *(for 16–20 biscuits)*:
2½ oz. butter or block margarine
2 oz. cooking chocolate
6 oz. caster sugar
2½ oz. self-raising flour
Pinch of salt
2 eggs
½ teaspoon vanilla essence
2 oz. shelled walnuts

Grease and flour a shallow 8 in. square tin. Melt the butter and chocolate in a bowl over hot water, and add the sugar. Sift the flour and salt into a bowl, and stir in the chocolate mixture, beaten eggs, vanilla essence and chopped walnuts. Beat the mixture until smooth, then spoon into the prepared tin.

Bake in the centre of an oven pre-heated to 350°F (mark 4) for about 35 minutes or until the mixture is risen and beginning to leave the sides of the tin. Leave in the tin to cool slightly before cutting the cake into 1½–2 in. squares.

See illustration on p. 382.

Shortbread

PREPARATION TIME: *20 min.*
RESTING TIME: *1 hour*
COOKING TIME: *1 hour*

INGREDIENTS *(for 8 biscuits)*:
5 oz. plain flour
Pinch of salt
1 oz. rice flour or ground rice
2 oz. caster sugar
4 oz. butter or block margarine

Sift the flour, salt and rice flour into a bowl. Add the sugar and grate the butter, taken straight from the refrigerator, into the dry ingredients. Work the mixture with the fingertips until it resembles breadcrumbs. Press the mixture into a 7 in. straight-sided sandwich tin and level the top. Prick the top all over with a fork and mark the mixture into eight equal portions, cutting through to the base of the tin.

Chill the shortbread in the refrigerator for 1 hour, then bake in the centre of a pre-heated oven, at 300°F (mark 2), for about 1 hour or until pale-straw coloured. Cool the shortbread in the tin before cooling it on a wire rack. Break into wedges.

See illustration on p. 382.

Spiced black currant bars

PREPARATION TIME: *25 min.*
RESTING TIME: *1 hour*
COOKING TIME: *30 min.*

INGREDIENTS *(for 16 biscuits)*:
8 oz. plain flour
Pinch of salt
2 level teaspoons baking powder
2 level teaspoons mixed spice
4 oz. butter or block margarine
5 oz. caster sugar
1 level tablespoon golden syrup
1 large egg, beaten
½ lb. black currant jam
3 oz. shelled walnuts

Sift together the flour, salt, baking powder and spice. Cream the butter with the sugar until light and fluffy, then beat in the

SHORTBREAD
Grate butter into flour and rice

Mark mixture into portions

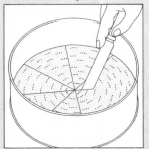
SPICED BLACK CURRANT BARS

Spread jam over grated dough

Grate remaining dough over jam

syrup and beaten egg. Fold in the flour and mix the ingredients thoroughly to a manageable dough. Wrap this loosely in kitchen foil and chill until firm, about 1 hour.

Grease and line two shallow 12 in. by 4 in. cake tins. Coarsely grate or flake half the chilled dough into the tins, and press the top down lightly. Spread the jam over the dough, then grate the remaining dough over the jam and top with the chopped walnuts. Bake just above the centre of an oven pre-heated to 350°F (mark 4) for about 30 minutes. Leave to cool in the tins. Cut into bars, about 1½ in. wide.

ROLLED BISCUITS

For rolled biscuits the dough must be stiff enough to be rolled to a thickness of ⅛–¼ in. before cutting out a variety of shapes. Dough that is difficult to handle, is best rolled between sheets of non-stick paper.

Butter shorts

PREPARATION TIME: *30 min.*
COOKING TIME: *25 min.*

INGREDIENTS *(for 16 biscuits)*:
4 oz. butter
2 oz. caster sugar
6 oz. plain flour
Caster sugar for dredging

Grease two baking trays. Cream the butter with a wooden spoon until soft, but not oily, add the sugar and beat until pale and fluffy. Work in the sifted flour and knead lightly together with the fingertips to form a ball. Roll this out ⅛ in. thick, on a lightly floured surface or between sheets of non-stick paper.

Using a 2½–2¾ in. fluted pastry cutter, stamp out rounds and lift them on to the baking trays with a small palette knife. Prick each biscuit with a fork twice, and

bake just above or in the centre of a pre-heated oven, at 300°F (mark 2), for about 25 minutes or until faintly tinged with brown. Cool on a wire rack and serve the biscuits dredged with caster sugar. Butter shorts will keep in a container for about 10 days.

Easter biscuits

PREPARATION TIME: *35 min.*
COOKING TIME: *15–20 min.*

INGREDIENTS *(for 24 biscuits)*:
4 oz. butter or block margarine
5 oz. caster sugar
1 egg
1 egg yolk
2 oz. currants
6 oz. plain flour
2 oz. rice flour
1 level teaspoon mixed spice
1–2 tablespoons milk

Line two or three baking trays with non-stick or buttered greaseproof paper. Cream the butter with a wooden spoon until soft, add 4 oz. of the sugar and beat thoroughly until pale and fluffy. Separate the egg and beat in the two egg yolks, and then stir in the currants. Sift the flours, together with the spice, into the creamed ingredients, a little at a time. Stir to combine, adding a little milk if necessary to bind the mixture to a soft but manageable dough.

Knead the dough lightly on a floured board, then roll it out ¼ in. thick. Cut into rounds with a 2½ in. fluted cutter, and set the biscuits on the baking trays. Mark lines, about ¼ in. apart, with the back of a knife. Bake just above or in the centre of a pre-heated oven at 350°F (mark 4) for 15–20 minutes. After 10 minutes, brush the biscuits with the unbeaten egg white and dredge with the remaining sugar. Leave the biscuits to cool slightly, then lift on to a wire rack.

Serve while quite fresh.

PREPARED BISCUITS

These are usually round and thin, with a crisp texture. The soft dough is shaped into a long roll, wrapped in waxed, non-stick paper or kitchen foil and chilled for at least 2 hours. The roll is then cut into thin slices with a sharp knife and baked on greased baking trays. As the dough will keep for about 1 week in the refrigerator, the biscuits can be sliced and baked as required.

Refrigerator cookies

PREPARATION TIME: *20 min.*
CHILLING TIME: *2 hours*
COOKING TIME: *10 min.*

INGREDIENTS *(for 48 biscuits)*:
8 oz. plain flour
1 level teaspoon baking powder
5 oz. butter
6 oz. caster sugar or light, soft brown sugar
1 teaspoon vanilla essence
1 egg
2 oz. plain chocolate
2 oz. ground hazelnuts
Caster sugar for dusting

Sift together the flour and baking powder. Beat the butter with a wooden spoon until soft, add the sugar and continue beating until light and fluffy. Beat in the vanilla essence and the beaten egg. Add the flour, and grate the chocolate finely into the mixture; lastly add the nuts. Stir just enough to combine the ingredients. Shape the dough, on a lightly floured surface, into a sausage about 2 in. wide. Wrap in foil or paper, secure the ends and chill.

To bake the biscuits, slice off as many thin biscuits as required from the roll. Set them, well spaced out, on a greased baking tray. Sprinkle with sugar and bake in the centre of a pre-heated oven, at 375°F (mark 5), for about 10 minutes. Cool on a wire rack.

See illustration on p. 382.

Cake Fillings and Toppings

Fillings and toppings serve not only to make a cake more attractive, they also have a practical use. Cakes which have been filled and iced stay moist longer. There are four basic types of fillings: butter cream, cooked fudge frosting, fluffy cooked frosting and soft sugar icing. For some of these, a sugar thermometer is essential.

Butter cream

This is perhaps the most frequently used filling and topping. The sugar, which may be caster or icing sugar or a mixture of both, is added in small amounts to creamed butter, then beaten to a light spreading consistency. Whole eggs, egg whites or yolks may also be added.

Cooked fudge frosting

This needs careful attention, as the soft fudge sets quickly and makes spreading difficult. It is used as a topping rather than a filling. A sugar mixture is cooked to a given temperature, cooled, then beaten until creamy. If the frosting sets too quickly, the bowl can be placed over hot water and a teaspoon or two of warm water or milk beaten in.

Fluffy cooked frosting

For this type of frosting, sugar, egg whites, water and flavourings are beaten over boiling water until the mixture stands in stiff peaks. A similar frosting can be made by cooking a syrup from sugar and water, then beating it slowly into whisked egg whites. Both types of frosting spread and swirl easily, but they develop a thin sugar crust after a few days.

Soft sugar icing

This is an uncooked icing comprised of icing sugar and a liquid, together with flavouring and colouring. All soft icings are easy to use and go well with soft-textured cakes such as sponges. The icing coats the surface smoothly; it is poured over the cake and left to find its own level. A Royal icing used for wedding and birthday cakes is a cross between a fluffy cooked frosting and a soft sugar icing.

Using fillings and toppings

Numerous variations are possible with a little flair and imagination, but the basic procedure should always be followed:

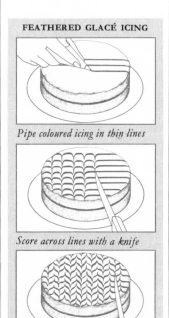

FEATHERED GLACÉ ICING

Pipe coloured icing in thin lines

Score across lines with a knife

Turn cake and score again

Always cool a cake thoroughly before filling and icing, and brush off any loose crumbs which would stick to the icing.

Cut surfaces, such as those produced when a slab cake is cut up into smaller cakes, are often covered with a thin layer of almond glacé or fondant icing.

Do not put a firm-textured frosting or filling on a soft crumbly surface. For crumbly sponge cakes, use a light cream filling which spreads easily.

Make sure that the top of the cake is completely flat if it is to be iced. The cake can be turned upside down and the underside iced if this is more level.

To sandwich two layers of cake, place one layer, top side down, on a plate or flat surface and spread the filling to the edge. Allow the filling to set for a few minutes, then place the second layer, top side up, on the filling and lightly press the two together.

Before coating a cake with soft icing, put the cake on a wire rack over a plate. Pour the icing over the centre of the plain or filled cake, and gradually work the icing over the top and down the sides with a palette knife.

For a professional touch, spread the icing evenly round the sides of the cake before rolling it in chopped nuts or chocolate vermicelli. Spread the icing evenly over the top of the cake, then pipe on coloured icing in thin lines, $\frac{1}{2}-\frac{3}{4}$ in. apart, using a plain writing tube. Before the icing has set, draw lines, at right angles, over the coloured icing with the blunt edge of a knife blade. Turn the cake 180 degrees and draw the knife between the intersections.

To coat a cake with butter cream, place it on a board and decorate the sides first. Spread the coating evenly round the sides, using a round-bladed knife, then pile more butter cream on top of the cake. Smooth the cream evenly to the edges with a small palette knife, then finish the top with a swirled, latticed or roughed-up pattern, using a fork, knife or confectioner's comb.

The sides may also be covered with butter cream and then decorated. Cover the sides before the top, spreading the cream evenly with a palette knife. Roll the sides carefully in chocolate vermicelli or chopped nuts, then spread butter cream or fondant icing over the top.

Piped decorations should be applied after the covering icing has set, but shaped decorations, such as rose buds, should be applied while the icing is still soft.

To make rose buds from coloured Royal icing, fix a small square of waxed paper to an icing nail with a little of the soft icing. Using a plain or star-shaped small nozzle on the icing bag, pipe a centre cone on to the paper, and then pipe on small petal shapes. Work from right to left and overlap the petal slightly until a rose of the required size is formed. Remove the waxed paper, and when the rose bud has set place it on the still soft icing.

ROYAL ICING ROSES

Pipe cone on to waxed paper

Pipe on overlapping petals

Butter cream

PREPARATION TIME: *10 min.*

INGREDIENTS:
4 oz. butter or margarine
6–8 oz. icing sugar
Vanilla essence (optional)
1–2 tablespoons milk

Beat the softened butter with a wooden spoon or in an electric mixer, until creamy. Gradually beat in the sifted icing sugar a spoonful at a time, adding a few drops of vanilla essence (if used) and the milk for a more liquid consistency. This amount is sufficient to coat the sides and top of a 7 in. cake.

To this basic butter cream, a number of different flavours may be added:

Almond: add 2 level tablespoons finely chopped, toasted almonds. Substitute almond essence for vanilla essence.

Chocolate: add 1–1½ oz. melted chocolate and omit 1 tablespoon milk; alternatively, blend 1 level tablespoon cocoa with 1 tablespoon hot water, cool and add, omitting the milk.

Coffee: omit vanilla essence and milk; flavour with 2 level teaspoons instant coffee blended with 1 teaspoon water, or use 2–3 teaspoons coffee essence.

Ginger: omit vanilla essence; add 2 oz. finely chopped stem ginger.

Liqueur: omit milk and vanilla essence; add 2–3 teaspoons liqueur.

Mocca: omit vanilla essence, mix 2 level teaspoons cocoa with 2 level teaspoons instant coffee powder to a smooth paste with hot water, cool before adding and omit milk.

Orange: omit vanilla essence and milk; beat in 2 tablespoons fresh orange juice, the finely grated rind of 1 small orange and, if wanted, 1 teaspoon orange bitters.

Rich butter cream (Crème au beurre)

PREPARATION TIME: *20 min.*

INGREDIENTS:
3 oz. caster sugar
4 tablespoons water
2 egg yolks
4–6 oz. unsalted butter

Put the sugar and water in a heavy-based pan and dissolve over low heat without boiling. When dissolved, bring the syrup to the boil and boil steadily for 2–3 minutes until 225°F is reached. Beat the egg yolks in a deep bowl and pour over the syrup in a thin steady stream, whisking all the time. Continue to whisk until the mixture is thick and cool (the bowl may be stood in iced water). Cream the butter with a wooden spoon. Gradually beat the egg syrup into the butter, a little at a time.

For additional flavour, add 2 oz. plain chocolate, melted and cool but still liquid, 1–2 tablespoons coffee essence, or grated orange or lemon rind.

Honey butter frosting

PREPARATION TIME: *15 min.*

INGREDIENTS:
3 oz. butter
6 oz. icing sugar
1 level tablespoon clear honey
1 tablespoon lemon juice

Beat the butter, which should be at room temperature, until soft but not oily. Gradually sift in the icing sugar, beating well. Halfway through, beat in the honey and lemon juice.

Caramel icing

PREPARATION TIME: *20 min.*

INGREDIENTS:
5 tablespoons top of the milk
3 oz. butter
2 level tablespoons caster sugar
12 oz. icing sugar

Warm the milk and butter in a small saucepan. In another pan, heat the caster sugar over a medium heat until it turns to a golden caramel. Remove both pans from the heat, pour the milk mixture over the caramel, and return to low heat. Continue heating until the caramel has dissolved, stirring occasionally. Gradually stir in the sifted icing sugar, and beat until the icing is smooth and of a spreading consistency. Use fairly quickly.

Chocolate fudge frosting

PREPARATION TIME: *30 min.*

INGREDIENTS:
1 lb. caster sugar
½ pint water
2 level tablespoons golden syrup
2 oz. unsalted butter
2 oz. cocoa

Place all the ingredients in a saucepan and cook, without boiling, until the sugar has dissolved. Bring to the boil and continue boiling over low heat until the sugar thermometer registers 238°F.

To prevent sticking, move the thermometer occasionally and draw a wooden spoon across the base of the pan, but do not beat. Remove the pan from the heat and leave the mixture until cool, then beat with a wooden spoon until thick. Coat the cake quickly.

American frosting

PREPARATION TIME: *30 min.*

INGREDIENTS:
1 lb. caster or lump sugar
Pinch cream of tartar
2 egg whites
Vanilla essence (optional)

A sugar-boiling thermometer is necessary for this frosting; if this is not available, make the slightly softer Seven-Minute Frosting. Put the sugar and 8 tablespoons of water in a heavy-based pan over low heat and dissolve the sugar without stirring. Blend the cream of tartar with 1 teaspoon of water and add this paste to the syrup. Bring to the boil and continue boiling, without stirring, until the thermometer registers 240°F (read the thermometer at eye level). Just before this temperature is reached, whisk the egg whites in a large bowl until stiff. Remove the syrup from the heat and when the bubbles subside, pour the hot syrup in a long, thin stream on to the egg whites, whisking all the time. Continue whisking until the frosting is thick and opaque. Add a few drops of vanilla essence and spread the frosting quickly over an 8 in. cake.

Seven-minute frosting

PREPARATION TIME: *10 min.*

INGREDIENTS:
1 egg white
6 oz. caster sugar
Pinch of salt
2 tablespoons water
Pinch of cream of tartar

Put all the ingredients in a deep bowl and using a rotary or electric mixer whisk for a few minutes. Place the bowl over a pan of hot water and continue to whisk until the mixture is thick enough to stand in 'peaks', after 7 minutes. Use at once in the same way as American frosting.

Glacé icing

PREPARATION TIME: *10 min.*

INGREDIENTS:
4–6 oz. icing sugar
1–2 tablespoons warm water
Food colouring (optional)

Sift the icing sugar into a deep bowl. Add the water, a little at a time, until the mixture is thick enough to coat the back of a wooden spoon. Add a few drops of colouring if required.

A more glossy icing can be obtained by dissolving 1 oz. caster sugar in 4 tablespoons of water in a small pan over low heat. Bring to the boil and bubble gently for 5–7 minutes or until the liquid has reduced* by about half. Remove the pan from the heat and cool the pan in cold water until the base is lukewarm. Beat in the sifted icing sugar, a little at a time. Use the icing at once, to cover the top of a 7 in. cake or 12–18 buns.

The basic glacé icing may be flavoured with, for example, 1 tablespoon of lemon juice to replace 1 tablespoon water, 1–1½ teaspoons coffee essence as part of the amount of water. Strained orange juice may replace all the water and a few drops of orange colouring may also be added. Alternatively, blend 2 level teaspoons of cocoa with 1 tablespoon of the water, or replace 1 tablespoon water with 1 tablespoon liqueur.

Fondant icing

This traditional icing for petits fours is less brittle than glacé icing. It is only worthwhile making in large amounts.

PREPARATION TIME: *30 min.*

INGREDIENTS:
¼ pint water
1 lb. caster or lump sugar
Pinch of cream of tartar or 1 oz. glucose

Put the water in a large heavy-based pan, add the sugar and dissolve to a syrup, without boiling, over low heat. Using a brush dipped in cold water, wipe round the pan at the level of the syrup to prevent crystals from forming. Add the cream of tartar or glucose dissolved in a little water. Bring the syrup to the boil and continue boiling steadily until the syrup registers 240°F

(read the thermometer at eye level). Pour the syrup very slowly into a heat-resistant bowl; leave until a skin forms on top.

Using a wooden spatula work the icing in a figure-of-eight movement until it becomes opaque and firm. Knead the icing until smooth and store in an airtight tin until required. Before using, heat the fondant icing in a bowl over hot water, adding a little sugar syrup until the icing has the consistency of double cream. Add flavouring and colouring as for glacé icing and use to cover about 24 petits fours or a 7–8 in. cake.

Royal icing

PREPARATION TIME: *15 min.*

INGREDIENTS:
4 egg whites
1¾–2 lb. icing sugar
1 tablespoon lemon juice
2 teaspoons glycerine

Whisk the egg whites in a large bowl until frothy. Stir in the sifted icing sugar, a little at a time, beating thoroughly with a wooden spoon. When half the sugar has been added, beat in the lemon juice. Continue adding more sugar, beating well after each addition until the icing forms soft peaks when pulled up with a wooden spoon. For piping purposes the icing should be slightly firmer. Stir in the glycerine, which keeps the icing soft.

Ideally, leave the icing to rest for 24 hours, covered with polythene, and work it through before using. The above amount is sufficient to coat the top and sides of a 10 in. wide and 2 in. deep cake. Leave the coating to set before piping on the decorations.

An electric mixer may be used, but care must be taken not to overbeat the icing – a fluffy Royal icing results in a rough surface and will also break when piped.

Apricot glaze

PREPARATION TIME: *15 min.*

INGREDIENTS:
1 lb. apricot jam
1 tablespoon lemon juice
4 tablespoons water

Bring all the ingredients slowly to the boil, reduce the heat and simmer for 5 minutes. Put the mixture through a sieve, return it to the pan and boil gently for another 5 minutes. Cool the apricot glaze before storing it in a screw-top jar. Use as required to glaze fruit tarts or to hold almond paste on cakes.

Uncooked almond paste

PREPARATION TIME: *10 min.*

INGREDIENTS:
4 oz. icing sugar
4 oz. caster sugar
8 oz. ground almonds
1 teaspoon lemon juice
Almond essence
1 egg

Sift the icing sugar into a bowl and mix in the caster sugar and almonds. Add the lemon juice and a few drops of almond essence. Gradually stir in the beaten egg using a wooden spoon or the fingers until the mixture is a firm but manageable dough. Knead lightly, and roll out.

This quantity makes enough paste to cover a 7 in. cake.

Cooked almond paste

This paste resembles marzipan in texture and can be used for confectionery as well as for coating.

PREPARATION TIME: *40 min.*

INGREDIENTS:
1 lb. lump sugar
¼ pint water
¼ level teaspoon cream of tartar
12 oz. ground almonds
2 egg whites
2 oz. icing sugar
Almond essence (optional)

Dissolve the lump sugar in the water over low heat. Increase the heat and bring the syrup to the boil; stir in the cream of tartar dissolved in a teaspoon of water. Boil until the syrup reaches 240°F (read the thermometer at eye level). Remove the pan from the heat and stir rapidly with a wooden spoon until the syrup becomes cloudy. Stir in the ground almonds and the un-beaten egg whites at once; return the pan to the heat for a few minutes, stirring continuously.

Turn the almond mixture on to a working surface and gradually work in the sifted icing sugar with a palette knife. As soon as the paste is cool enough, knead it with the fingers until it has a malleable consistency; add more sifted sugar if needed. Roll out the paste and use to cover a 9 in. wide cake.

Pastry cream (Crème pâtissière)

PREPARATION TIME: *10 min.*

INGREDIENTS:
1 pint milk
4 oz. caster sugar
2 oz. plain flour
1 level tablespoon cornflour
2 large eggs
2 oz. unsalted butter

Heat the milk in a pan over low heat. In a bowl blend together the sugar, flour, cornflour and beaten eggs; gradually stir in the warm milk. Return the mixture to the pan over low heat and stir continuously until it thickens and just comes to the boil. Remove from the heat and stir in the butter. Cool the cream in the pan, covered closely with greaseproof paper and the lid to prevent a skin forming.

Use the cooled, thick cream on its own or with chopped fruits or nuts as a filling between layers of sponge cake.

Confectionery

Sweet-making is an absorbing hobby, and with practice and imagination the finished result looks temptingly professional. Home-made sweets, packed in decorative boxes, make ideal presents for Christmas and birthdays. Set the individual sweets in paper cases and put waxed paper between the layers.

Many traditional sweets, such as fudge and toffee, are based on concentrated sugar syrup, boiled to high temperatures. A cooking thermometer and a large, heavy-based pan are essential. Use a wooden spoon when needed, to move the mixture backwards and forwards while the syrup is reducing. The thermometer should be moved occasionally, as fudge and toffee tend to settle round the bulb and give inaccurate readings.

For chocolate-covered sweets, use good-quality plain chocolate. Put it, broken into small pieces, in a bowl and set this over a pan of hot water. Stir the chocolate continuously with a fork until melted – it should be just warm and must never be allowed to boil. Dip the sweets, one at a time, into the chocolate, holding each between two forks, and brush off any excess on the side of the bowl. Leave the sweets to set on non-stick or waxed paper.

See illustrations on p. 383.

Chocolate fudge

PREPARATION TIME: *about 1 hour*

INGREDIENTS *(for 1½ lb.)*:
1 lb. caster sugar
½ pint water
1 large tin condensed milk
4½ oz. chocolate dots or plain cooking chocolate (grated)
2 oz. seedless raisins (optional)

Put the sugar and water in a heavy-based 6 pint pan and dissolve the sugar over low heat. Bring to the boil, add the condensed milk and boil gently until the thermometer registers 240°F. Stir occasionally to prevent sticking. Remove the pan from the heat and add the chocolate, and raisins if used.

Beat the mixture until thick and creamy, using a wooden spoon; pour it into a buttered tin, about 5½ in. by 8 in. by 1 in.

Leave to cool for several hours, then cut the fudge into 1 in. squares with a sharp knife. Wrap in waxed paper.

Collettes

PREPARATION TIME: *1 hour*

INGREDIENTS *(for 18)*:
9 oz. chocolate dots
4 tablespoons strong black coffee
2 oz. butter
2 egg yolks
Rum
Blanched hazel nuts

Melt 4 oz. of the chocolate dots. Cool slightly, then put a tea-spoon of the melted chocolate into a small paper sweet case; press another case over the chocolate to squeeze it up the sides. Repeat with the remaining chocolate. Leave overnight.

The next day, peel off the paper cases. Melt the remaining chocolate dots as before, and stir in the coffee. When cool, beat in the softened, but not oily, butter and the egg yolks; add rum to taste. Spoon this mixture into a forcing bag fitted with a large star nozzle and pipe into the chocolate cases. Top each collette with a hazelnut and leave to set.

Coconut ice

PREPARATION TIME: *30 min.*

INGREDIENTS *(for 24–30)*:
1 lb. caster sugar
¼ pint milk
5 oz. desiccated coconut
Cochineal

Oil or butter a shallow tin, 8 in. by 6 in. Dissolve the sugar in the milk over low heat, then bring to the boil and boil gently for about 10 minutes or until the temperature reaches 240°F (read the thermometer at eye level). Remove the pan from the heat and stir in the coconut.

Pour half the mixture quickly into the tin, spreading it evenly. Colour the remainder pale pink with a few drops of cochineal and pour quickly over the first layer. Leave until half-set, then mark the coconut into 1 in. squares with a knife. Cut up when quite cold.

Chocolate-covered dates

PREPARATION TIME: *20 min.*

INGREDIENTS:
1 box dates
Almond paste
4 oz. plain chocolate
Cocktail cherries
Shelled walnuts

Using a small, pointed knife, make a small slit in each date and remove the stone. Fill the cavities with plain almond paste* and close the dates again. Melt the chocolate in a bowl over a pan of hot water and, with the aid of two forks, dip the dates in the chocolate. Coat evenly and brush off any surplus on the edge of the bowl.

Dry the chocolate-covered dates on sheets of waxed or non-stick paper. Just before set, decorate the dates with well-drained cocktail cherries cut in half or with pieces of shelled walnuts.

Chocolate-covered pineapple

PREPARATION TIME: *20 min.*

INGREDIENTS:
Small tin pineapple rings
6–7 oz. plain chocolate
Decorations

Drain the pineapple rings thoroughly and cut them into halves or quarters. Break up the chocolate and melt in a bowl over a pan of hot water. Using two forks, carefully dip the pineapple chunks in the chocolate, coating them evenly.

Dry on waxed or non-stick paper, and before the chocolate sets, decorate with crystallised violets, yellow mimosa balls or silver dragees.

Honey fruit nut caramels

PREPARATION TIME: *30 min.*

INGREDIENTS:
3 oz. butter
5 oz. golden syrup
6 oz. clear honey
4 oz. walnut halves
4 oz. stoned dates

Grease and line with non-stick paper a shallow tin measuring 8 in. by 5 in. Melt the butter in a large, heavy-based pan set over low heat; add the syrup and honey. Bring the mixture to the boil and continue boiling over gentle heat until the thermometer registers 270°F. Meanwhile, chop the walnuts and dates finely.

Remove the pan from the heat and add the nuts and dates. Beat the mixture vigorously with a wooden spoon until opaque in colour. Pour it into the tin and leave to cool. When almost set, cut through the caramel with a buttered knife, into ¾–1 in. squares. Leave to set for about 24 hours, then break the squares apart; wrap them in waxed paper and store.

Marzipan confectionery

INGREDIENTS:
Almond paste or marzipan
Food colouring
Almonds
Granulated sugar
Dates
Plain chocolate for melting
Stem ginger

Cooked almond paste* or bought marzipan is popular for many sweets. The almond paste may be coloured pink, green or yellow with a little food colouring, and used as a base or filling for sweets.

Stuffed dates: make a slit in the top of the dates and remove the stones. Fill the cavities with a small piece of plain or coloured almond paste; roll the stuffed dates in granulated sugar or decorate them with blanched almonds.

Ginger marzipan: shape pieces of almond paste into marble-sized balls, dip the bases in melted chocolate and top with well-drained pieces of stem ginger.

Peanut brittle

PREPARATION TIME: *1 hour*

INGREDIENTS:
12 oz. loaf or cube sugar
¼ pint water
½ lb. golden syrup
2 level teaspoons powdered glucose
1 oz. butter
3 oz. browned peanuts
½ teaspoon lemon essence
2 level teaspoons bicarbonate of soda

Dissolve the sugar in the water, together with the syrup and glucose, in a large, heavy-based pan set over low heat. Bring to the boil and boil gently until the thermometer registers 300°F (read at eye level).

Add the butter, warmed nuts (rub the skins off first) and lemon essence; heat until the butter is just melted. Stir in the bicarbonate of soda (the mixture will froth rapidly for a few minutes), and pour it quickly on to an oiled marble slab or large clean baking tray.

When cold, break the brittle into pieces; store in single layers between waxed or non-stick paper.

Peppermint creams

PREPARATION TIME: *30 min.*

INGREDIENTS (*for 25*):
8 oz. icing sugar
1 egg white
Peppermint essence

Sift the icing sugar into a bowl and blend with enough beaten egg white to form a stiff paste. Add a few drops of peppermint essence to taste.

Knead the paste lightly in the bowl, using the fingertips. Roll the paste out ¼ in. thick, between sheets of non-stick or waxed paper. Stamp out 1 in. rounds with a plain cutter, and leave the mints to dry for about 24 hours.

Rum truffles

PREPARATION TIME: *35 min.*
CHILLING TIME: *1 hour*

INGREDIENTS (*for 12*):
3 oz. plain chocolate
1 egg yolk
½ oz. butter
1 teaspoon rum
1 teaspoon top of the milk or single cream
2 oz. chocolate vermicelli or drinking chocolate

Melt the chocolate in a small bowl over a pan of hot water. Add the egg yolk, butter, rum and milk. Beat the mixture until thick, then chill in the refrigerator until firm enough to handle.

Shape the mixture into 12 balls and toss at once in vermicelli or drinking chocolate.

Garnishes

A well-chosen garnish adds texture, colour and flavour to a dish. It should be fresh and simple rather than cluttered, and if the dish is hidden by a sauce, the garnish should give a clue to what is in the sauce. For instance, a dish served *à la véronique* – that is, with a sauce containing white grapes – is always garnished with small bunches of grapes. Many garnishes are classic – lemon and parsley, for example, are traditional with fried fish. Breadcrumbs are another classic garnish; the term *au gratin* means that a dish has been sprinkled with crumbs and placed under a hot grill.

Angelica

Used alone or with cherries to decorate sweets and puddings. Buy angelica in strips of a good green colour without too much sugar. Excess sugar can be removed by placing angelica for a short time in hot water; drain and dry well. Use chopped, cut into strips, diamond or leaf shapes.

Aspic jelly

This is used for coating, for holding a garnish in position and is also used chopped to garnish a cold dish. The jelly can be made from reduced cleared stock or from crystals to which a little sherry is added. For coating purposes, allow the jelly to set to the consistency of unbeaten egg white, then place the item to be coated on a wire rack over a plate or tray. Spoon over the jelly until an even layer adheres. Leave until set, and repeat if necessary. Decorate by dipping pieces of garnish – tarragon, carrot, olives or truffle slices – in a little cool but liquid aspic before setting it in position with the point of a skewer. When set, glaze with more aspic. For chopped aspic turn the jelly on to a piece of wet greaseproof paper and chop it roughly or into cubes.

Bacon rolls

A popular garnish, often an integral part of a recipe or used with dishes *au gratin*, scrambled egg or cheese flans. Cut off the rind and gristle from thin streaky bacon rashers, place on a board and, using a round-bladed knife, stretch the bacon lengthways by stroking it with the knife. Cut each rasher into two, roll up and grill until lightly browned and cooked. Drain on kitchen paper.

Bread croûtons:

See Soup Garnishes, p. 308.

Breadcrumbs

Fried crumbs are a traditional garnish for game and *au gratin* dishes. Melt 1 oz. butter or margarine in a frying pan, stir in 4 oz. fresh white breadcrumbs and fry over moderate heat until the crumbs are evenly browned and golden. Turn frequently.

Celery tassels

Edible garnish used with dips. Scrub the celery stalks, cut them in 2 in. lengths, then cut down the lengths at narrow intervals almost to the base. Leave the stalks in a bowl of water to curl.

Garnishes

Carrot curls

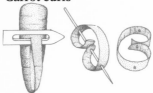

Sandwiches may be decorated with these. Clean the carrots, and with a potato peeler pare down the length of each carrot to remove a wafer-thin slice. Twist the slices, fasten with wooden cocktail sticks and put in iced water to curl.

Chantilly cream

Used as a piped or spooned decoration for sweets. Whisk $\frac{1}{2}$ pint of chilled double or whipping cream in a deep cold basin, using a hand whisk. When the cream becomes opaque, add 3–4 level teaspoons caster sugar and a few drops of vanilla essence and continue to whisk slowly until the cream just holds its shape. Whipped cream thickens by the pressure needed to force it through a nozzle, so it should be light and fluffy to begin with. Pipe the cream through a fabric forcing bag and use a vegetable nozzle.

Chocolate

This takes on many forms as a decorative finish to cold desserts, classic gâteaux and simple cakes. Kept in a cool airtight tin, chocolate shapes will store for about 1 week.

Squares: break cooking chocolate into a small bowl, place over a pan of hot water and allow the chocolate to melt slowly. Line a baking tray with non-stick or waxed paper. Pour the melted chocolate in a thin stream over the paper, and with a small palette knife spread the chocolate to a thin smooth layer. Leave to cool until firm, then cut the chocolate into squares with a warm sharp

knife. Peel the paper carefully away from the squares.

Leaves: melt the chocolate as for squares and meanwhile clean and dry small rose leaves. Hold the leaves with some tweezers and dip the underside of the leaf in the melted chocolate. Leave to dry chocolate side up. When the chocolate has set, carefully ease the leaves away.

Cucumber

Sliced cucumber is a traditional garnish to a cold mousse or terrine. Deckled or ridged cucumber makes a more unusual decoration: wipe but do not peel a piece of cucumber; score it along the length with a fork or canelling knife, so that it has a serrated edge when cut into slices.

Gherkin fans

Drain cocktail gherkins thoroughly, then slice each three or four times lengthways almost to the stalk end. Ease the slices apart to open out like a fan.

Glacé cherries

These should be washed, in warm water, to remove the sticky syrup, and dried before being used whole, halved or chopped. Crystallised cherries or maraschino cherries also make an attractive decoration; the latter must be well dried to prevent the bright red colour bleeding.

Grapes and red currants

These are used frosted, either singly or in small clusters, to garnish sweet mousses, fruit soufflés and ice creams, or as a dessert fruit on their own. Brush single or small clusters of black or white grapes or strips of red currants with lightly beaten egg white; dredge heavily with granulated or caster sugar. Leave on a wire rack to dry.

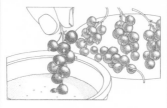

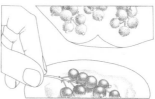

Lemon and orange spirals

Used to decorate long drinks and the plain surface of desserts, such as cheese cake. Using a potato peeler, pare off lemon or orange peel, free of white pith, in a continuous spiral. Hang the twisting peel from the rim of the glass.

Mint leaves

Sugared, these are seasonal delicacies with summer fruits. Select firm small sprigs of leaves, or individual leaves, brush them lightly with egg white and dredge thoroughly with caster sugar. Dry and use on the same day.

Mushrooms

'Turned', these are a traditional garnish with grilled meat. Choose large button mushrooms, wipe with a damp cloth and trim the stem level with the cap. With a sharp knife make a series of curv-

ing cuts, $\frac{1}{4}$ in. apart, following the natural shape of the cap and from the top of the cap to the base. Take out a narrow strip along each indentation. Sauté the mushrooms in a little butter.

Nuts

Almonds are bought whole, halved or finely chopped (nibbed almonds), or flaked. Plain or roasted, all make quick finishes for trifles, gâteaux and sweet soufflés. Whole almonds, bought with or without their skins, can be used whole, split in two along their natural seam, cut into slivers or chopped. For slivered almonds blanch whole unskinned almonds in boiling water for 2–3 minutes; rub off the skins and, while still soft, cut the almonds into strips. For toasted almonds, spread the nuts, cut to the required shape, in a shallow pan and brown under a grill until golden.

Pistachio nuts should always be blanched to remove the skin. Put the nuts in boiling water and soak for about 5 minutes – a pinch of bicarbonate of soda brightens the green of the nuts. Pour off the water and add some cold. Ease off the skins by pinching each nut between thumb and forefinger, and dry the nuts before using them for garnish.

Hazel nuts need to be toasted before the skins can be removed. Place the shelled nuts in a single layer on a shallow pan and toast under a medium grill until the skins are dry and the nuts begin to colour. Cool slightly, then rub the nuts against each other in a bag to loosen the skins.

Parsley

This is the most versatile and useful of all garnishes, in sprigs or chopped. Wash freshly picked parsley as soon as possible, shake well and remove long stems. Place the parsley in a jar of water reaching to the base of the leaves, or put the parsley stems in a polythene bag, tied at the neck. Parsley will then stay crisp and green for several days. Change the water in the container daily.

Chopped parsley can be used as a garnish arranged in neat lines or at random; scissors can be used for chopping, but the result is coarser than when chopped with a knife. Gather the parsley into a tight bunch and with scissors snip off as much as is required straight on to the dish to be garnished.

To chop large quantities of parsley, place the stripped leaves on a chopping board. Using a sharp straight-bladed knife, hold the handle firmly with one hand and the tip of the knife blade with the other; lift the handle in a see-saw action, gradually chopping the parsley finely or coarsely as required. Alternatively, bunch the parsley leaves in one hand on the chopping board and, using the knife, gradually shred the parsley, moving the fingers back to reveal more parsley. Small wooden chopping bowls equipped with curved-bladed knives are available for chopping parsley, herbs, shallots and garlic. To preserve the vivid green, put chopped parsley in a piece of muslin, tie loosely and hold the bag under cold water for a few minutes to rinse thoroughly. Squeeze dry, then shake the parsley out into a bowl. Chopped parsley will keep for a day or two in a lidded container in the refrigerator.

Fried parsley makes an attractive garnish for fried fish. Allow four sprigs of parsley per person, and remove the long stems from the perfectly dry parsley. Heat lard or oil to about 375°F, put the parsley in the frying basket and immerse it in the hot fat. As soon as the hissing ceases lift out the parsley.

Radish roses

Used to garnish cold entrées, open sandwiches, hors-d'oeuvre and salads. Make 6–8 cuts lengthways through a radish from the base towards the stalk; put the radishes in a bowl of iced water until they open like flowers. Long radishes look attractive when cut at intervals along the length to open out concertina-fashion.

Spun sugar

Used as a decoration for Austrian tortes. Bring 1 lb. sugar and ½ pint water to the boil. Boil until the syrup reaches 312°F. Remove from heat, stir in a pinch of cream of tartar. As the syrup cools it forms fine threads when dropped from a wooden spoon. Holding an oiled spoon horizontally, pass syrup over the handle, twirling the fine threads.

Tomatoes

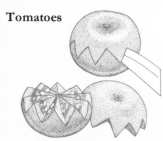

Serrated or vandyked tomatoes can be stuffed or used as tomato halves as a garnish for salads, flans, fried or grilled fish and meat.

Choose firm tomatoes of even size. Using a small sharp knife, make a series of small V-shaped indentations round the circumference of the tomato. Carefully pull the two tomato halves apart. Oranges, grapefruit and melons may also be separated in this way.

Twists and butterflies

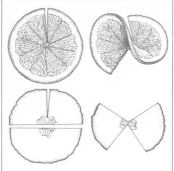

Tomatoes, cucumbers, beetroot, lemons and oranges make attractive garnishes to any number of dishes, both savoury and sweet. Slice the vegetable or fruit thinly, though not wafer-thin. For twists, cut each slice through to the centre, then twist the two halves in opposite directions and place in position. For butterflies, cut two deep V-shaped incisions to meet near the centre of each round lemon slice. Remove the two wedges to leave a butterfly shape.

Watercress

Another favourite garnish for meat, poultry and fish dishes. Trim off the stems, and wash the watercress leaves in plenty of salted water. Lift out, rinse and shake well. Discard any ragged and yellow leaves, and arrange the watercress in small bunches to be added as garnish just before the dish is served. Washed watercress, with part of the stem left on, will keep for 1 day in the refrigerator if stored in a polythene bag.

Wine with Food

The rules about storing, serving and drinking wine have grown out of the experience of connoisseurs, who discovered how to treat wine and when to serve it to best advantage. However, these rules are not rigid and they can be changed to suit individual tastes.

Wine is made by crushing grapes to extract the juice, which is allowed to ferment. During fermentation the grape sugar turns into alcohol and the juice becomes wine.

There are two main categories of wine: table wines and fortified wines. Table wines are drunk with a meal. Fortified wines, to which a spirit, usually brandy, has been added, include aperitifs, which are served before a meal, and dessert wines, such as port.

Table wines may be red, white or pink (rosé) in colour; the variations in colour are the result of different methods of fermentation. In the making of red wine, the grape juice is fermented with skin; rosé is made in the same way, but the juice is drawn off after a short time and allowed to ferment without the skins. In the making of white wine, only the juice is fermented so that it never acquires a colour.

The extremes of wine flavour are dry or sweet; a dry wine is one in which the sugar has been fermented out.

The label on the wine bottle gives the name of the wine and indicates whether it is dry or sweet. The country of origin will also be given; in the case of expensive wines, the district and the vineyard may be listed. The year of production may also be given.

Buying wine

Britain has traditionally taken its wines from France, Germany and Italy. And since joining the Common Market, it has imported even more wines from Italy and Sicily, and the less well-known wine-producing regions of France. Wines are also imported from Spain, Portugal, Hungary, Austria, Yugoslavia, Greece, North Africa and Chile.

The choice of wine available can be confusing, and the best adviser is a reliable wine merchant.

The price of wine varies according to quality. Other factors also influence prices. For example, wines which are bottled at the vineyards where they are produced are at the top end of the price range, because it is more expensive to ship wine in bottles than it is in casks. However, at the lower end of the price scale, there are many palatable wines.

These cheaper wines are imported in bulk, and then bottled and labelled in Great Britain.

Anyone wishing to learn more about wines should sample as many as possible. For those who can afford substantial wine purchases, buying by the case can be a sound investment.

Storing and serving wine

Wine should be placed in a dry, dark place, such as a cellar, which has a temperature of 50–60°F. Table wines should be stored lying down; this keeps the corks moist. A dry cork can allow the entry into the wine of organisms which spoil the wine. Most fortified wines are not affected by the air in the same way as table wines, so they can be stored in an upright position.

Before serving a red wine, stand it upright and leave it to reach room temperature gradually.

Only a young Beaujolais may be served slightly chilled.

A red wine should be opened in order to allow it to breathe; this helps to develop and release the bouquet, or smell, and taste of the wine. Most young strong wines should be opened a few hours before serving. When an older red wine is served, the cork can be drawn from the bottle about an hour or so before the wine is drunk.

A red wine throws a harmless deposit, or sediment, to the bottom of the bottle so it is best decanted. This involves carefully pouring off the wine through a filter leaving the sediment behind. White wine seldom needs decanting because its sediment is colourless, tasteless and, like the deposit in red wine, harmless.

A white wine should always be served well chilled, although fine old white wine needs only a minimum of chilling. Leave the wine to stand in the refrigerator for an hour or so before serving. If it has been kept in a cool place, such as a cellar, it may not need further chilling.

Drinking wine

The best kind of glass from which to drink table wine has a large bowl and a stem. With this kind of glass, it is possible to admire the colour and the clarity of the wine. The glass should be half to two-thirds filled with wine. There should be a space at the top of the glass so that the bouquet of the wine, particularly a red one, can be delicately sniffed. Swirl the wine round in the glass to release the bouquet. When tasting white wine, hold the glass by its stem, rather than under the bowl, to avoid unnecessarily warming the contents. After sipping the first mouthful, allow it to remain for a few seconds on the palate before swallowing.

Wine with the meal

Many meals are improved by wine. If the meal is an informal one, one wine only is usually served. However, it should be chosen with care to complement all the dishes of the meal.

On a special or formal occasion, when a different wine is drunk with each course, there is a definite order of serving. A white wine should precede a red one, except in the case of sweet dessert wines; a dry wine should be served before a sweet one; and a young wine should come before an old one.

Sherry and port or Madeira, can be served with the soup course. Fish should be accompanied by medium dry or dry white wines, such as Muscadel or Alsace Riesling from France, or Moselle from Germany. Other French wines – white burgundies such as Meursault and Chassagne-Montrachet, Vouvray, Graves, Chablis, Pouilly-fuissé – are also appropriate with fish.

Poultry should be served with a medium light red wine, but a white wine is also acceptable. For example, a chicken salad is best with a white Portuguese *vinho verde,* a Riesling or a light Graves.

Serve red Bordeaux wine (claret) or Beaujolais (a red burgundy) with lamb; and a Rioja Reserva from Spain, a Valpolicella Classico from Italy or a fine claret, with veal. Claret or burgundy, is excellent with duck and pork. Substantial dishes, such as braised beef or steak and kidney pudding, can be accompanied by robust French wines, such as Beaune, Pommard or a Gevrey-Chambertin.

Spicy dishes tend to overpower wine, but they can be matched by a good dry sherry, a Madeira or an Alsatian wine like a Gewürztaminer, which has a sweet taste and a pungent aroma. In the case of an Indian curry, beer should be served instead of wine, and tea is the best accompaniment to Chinese food.

At the dessert course, serve the heavier, sweeter wines: a good Barsac (from Bordeaux), such as Château Climens or Château Coutet, or a sweet sparkling wine from France or Italy. If cheese precedes the dessert course, it can be accompanied with any remaining red wine. But a strong cheese, such as Stilton, demands a fortified wine: port, for first choice, or Madeira, or sherry.

Cooking with wine

It is the flavour of wine and not its alcoholic content that improves the taste of food. When wine is added to a dish or a sauce, the cooking drives off the alcohol.

Never drown a dish in wine; practise restraint. When cooking fish, veal, chicken, sweetbreads, and similar delicate foods, use a medium dry white wine, such as an Entre-deux-mers. Red meats, such as lamb, beef and game, are prepared with red wines. However, certain classic fish and poultry dishes, such as *Filet de sole, mâtelotes* and *Coq au vin,* should be prepared with red rather than white wine.

Apart from adding flavour to food, wine can be used to make it moist and tender. Fish marinated in white wine, or meat steeped in red wine, are enhanced in both texture and taste. Fish need not be marinated for more than an hour; but dry meats, such as hare, venison or beef, may be left for up to four days. A useful marinade consists of 1 part olive oil to 3 parts dry red or white wine (depending on the use), to which a bouquet garni* grated onion and garlic are added.

Wine left over after a meal can be kept for use in cooking or as a marinade. Pour the wine into a small bottle and cork it to keep out the air; white wine can be kept in the same way in the refrigerator. If there is no wine left over, cook with some of the wine to be drunk at the meal.

Fortified and dessert wines, such as Madeira, Marsala, port, sherry and vermouth can be used to enhance simple dishes. Marsala is an ingredient of the Italian dessert *zabaglione,* and sherry is added to trifles.

Wine is not the only alcoholic drink that improves a dish. Beer and cider can also be used in cooking, although they do not have as many uses as wine. Beer is an essential ingredient of classic dishes, such as Welsh rarebit and *Carbonade à la Flamande*; also it makes an excellent marinade.

Spirits, such as brandy, whisky, or gin, can be used to flame kebabs, shellfish, steaks, veal escalopes, and other dishes which do not require long cooking.

Before flaming a dish, warm the spirit slightly in a ladle. Then set it alight with a match and pour it over the hot food.

Spirits can be used to flavour dishes. For example, apricot brandy can be used to flame pancakes; Calvados, an apple-based brandy from France, can be added to baked apples. Framboise, a French *eau-de-vie* or clear spirit, can be poured over raspberries. And Kirsch is an excellent marinade for pineapple.

Drinks before and after a meal

An aperitif served before a meal should stimulate the appetite without numbing the palate.

A light dry sherry, such as fino or manzanillo, is a popular aperitif. Serve it slightly chilled, but not so cold that the bouquet is killed.

Another aperitif is vermouth, a drink based on white wine and sharpened with wormwood and various herbs. There are both dry and sweet variations.

Champagne can be served at the beginning of a meal. However, if this famous drink is too costly, a dry sparkling wine or a well-chilled white or *rosé* wine can be served in its place. *Vin blanc cassis,* which is dry white wine flavoured with black currant juice, is also a suitable aperitif.

One of the best ways to end a meal which has been accompanied by fine wines is to serve a refreshing glass of mineral water. However, there is a wide choice of after-dinner wines and spirits available: brandies, liqueurs, and *eaux-de-vie.*

Party drinks

A punch is an ideal party refreshment because it can be made in large quantities. It can be prepared by mixing various alcoholic or non-alcoholic drinks to be served hot or cold. The Digest and Negus punches are suitable for festive winter occasions; Sangria and the Fruit Cup are more suitable for hot summer weather.

Digest Punch

INGREDIENTS:
2 lemons
Cinnamon
Nutmeg
Cloves
Mace
6 tablespoons sugar
1 bottle brandy or rum

Pare the rind from the lemons. Add the rind, cinnamon, nutmeg, cloves and mace to taste along with the sugar, to ½ pint of water. Bring to the boil and simmer. Strain the mixture into a warmed punch bowl. Add the strained lemon juice and the brandy or rum. Serve at once.

Negus

This punch is named after a famous figure of Queen Anne's day, Colonel Negus, who had a penchant for sweetening wines.

INGREDIENTS:
1 pint port
12 sugar cubes
1 lemon
Pinch of nutmeg

Pour the port into a bowl. Rub the sugar lumps on the rind of the lemon and float them in the port. Then add the lemon juice, nutmeg, and pour in a quart of boiling water. Serve.

Sangria

This famous Spanish punch has a rich red colour and a fruit garnish. After adding the ice cubes to the bowl, the Sangria can be left in the sun to cool and dilute itself. Chill the bowl first.

INGREDIENTS:
1 litre red wine
1 glass brandy
1 glass port
1 small bottle lemonade
Fresh fruit

Mix the ingredients in a bowl and cool with ice cubes. Serve.

Fruit Cup

Any kind of fruit, such as cherries, peaches, plums, raspberries or strawberries, can be used in the making of this summer drink.

INGREDIENTS:
Fresh fruit
3 oz. caster sugar
6 fluid oz. brandy
1 bottle white wine
Soda water

Wash and slice the fruit. Put the fruit in a bowl and add sugar and brandy. Allow to stand for 1 day. Then add the chilled white wine, which may be diluted with soda water. Serve.

The Cook's Workshop

A woman spends a great part of her life in the kitchen. Therefore, it should be planned carefully so that the housewife can work with efficiency and comfort. Every detail which is to be changed in an existing kitchen or included in a new kitchen must be noted down before the work is begun. Once the work is in progress it can be costly to make changes. If the work can be done by one firm, costs can be kept to a minimum. To employ different workmen to do the plumbing and electrical work, and to fit the kitchen units, can add to the expense.

PLANNING A KITCHEN

For the greatest efficiency, a kitchen should be laid out so that the storing, preparing, cooking and serving of food flows smoothly in a logical sequence. If this is not possible, make sure that the food storage, the working areas, the cooker and sink are all close together. This saves time and effort.

Most working surfaces are about 3 ft high, but some manufacturers make other sizes. For a woman of about 5 ft 3 in. tall, 2 ft 9 in. is usually a convenient height. Taller women need the 3 ft size.

If there are young children in the home, their safety should be considered. Child gates should be fitted to stop them entering the kitchen when no one is there. Safety guards should be fitted around cookers. Crayleigh Safeguard Products, 92 Portland Place, London W1, or Fisher, Segal, Bilton Way, Brimsdown, Enfield, Middlesex, will provide a list of suppliers. If detergents and disinfectant are to be kept in a cupboard under the sink, make sure it has a lock. Power points should be placed out of the reach of children. Cookers with drop front ovens should be anchored. A child can tip one over by standing on the door.

When redesigning an old kitchen, although the dimensions of the room cannot be easily altered, space might be saved by, for example, replacing a door to the dining room by a serving hatch.

In planning a kitchen the following basic requirements should be taken into account:

1. There must be a clear space in the kitchen wide enough for the installation of the cooker. If there is a solid-fuel cooker in the kitchen, some means of disposing of the ashes must be provided. Cookers should not be placed under a window.

2. Allow two clear spaces for storage or installation of other appliances, one space not less than 2 ft wide, and the other not less than 2 ft 8 in. wide. These spaces may be under work surfaces.

3. A sink unit should be not less than 3 ft 3½ in. wide, with at least one drainer.

4. There should be a work surface on each side of the sink, and on each side of the cooker.

When drawing up the plans for do-it-yourself alterations in the kitchen, it is essential to take accurate metric measurements of the room. Wood and many other building materials are sold mainly in metric sizes and it can be confusing to convert these into feet and inches. Draw a plan of the kitchen on squared paper with a metric grid. Cut out paper models to scale of the kitchen units and slide them round on the plan to get an idea of lay-out. Use a metal or wood metric rule to take the following measurements:

1. The kitchen wall from the top of the skirting board to the ceiling.

2. The position and widths of the doors and frames and the side on which the doors are hinged.

3. The position and dimensions of the windows, including the height from the floor to the sill.

4. The dimensions and position of any wall recesses or protrusions, pipes, meter boxes, switches or points.

5. The position of service points – water, drainage, power, gas.

6. The central-heating boiler, if any. Note the size and position of the boiler service door. The appliances to be included in the plan should be listed on a separate piece of paper as in the following suggested plan:

KITCHEN STORAGE UNITS

Storage units should be within easy reach of the working area, and those items which are used most frequently should be the most easily accessible. One of the commonest mistakes in the kitchen is to place drawers and cupboards so high that they cannot be reached with ease, or so low that there has to be constant stooping.

Cooking utensils, cutlery, crockery, glass, table and kitchen linen, and bowls should be kept on shelves or in drawers. Perishable food should never be stored in closed space, but on shelves where air can circulate. Store buckets and cleaning materials – including brooms, floor mops, and vacuum cleaners – in a cupboard.

Shelves To allow for the economical storage of different articles, shelving should be of various widths, and should be adjustable vertically. Shelves for general storage may be open or enclosed.

Drawers These should be of differing depth to allow for the various gadgets they are to hold. Keep one drawer for cutlery.

Cupboards Shallow cupboards no deeper than 9½ in. are useful for storing bulky kitchen gadgets, in infrequent use, but mixers or mincers should be readily available on a working surface. It is an advantage to have everything in the cupboard on show as soon as the doors are opened. Often such cupboards can be built into what would otherwise be wasted space. Sliding doors save space but collect more dust than hinged doors.

The store cupboard Pantries have been largely discarded in favour of refrigerators and home freezers. But a pantry or ventilated food cupboard can still be used to keep semi-perishable foods, such as fresh vegetables and fruit. To fulfil planning requirements, a new kitchen must have one cupboard with outside ventilation.

Infill units Some manufacturers make excellent small infill units to utilise the space between top and base units. Infill units with sliding glazed doors to exclude steam can provide suitable storage for small cream jugs, egg cups and mustard pots.

Wall-mounting There is now a large range of wall-mounted items, such as tin openers, spice racks and coffee grinders. Wall-mounted equipment saves both time and storage space, and helps to ensure that work surfaces are kept clear.

High-level storage The space at the top of a wall-cupboard which reaches to the ceiling can be used for non-perishable items, such as tinned foods, soaps and kitchen paper. Little-used saucepans can also be transferred to high-level storage. Use a stool with steps to reach them.

CHECK LIST FOR KITCHEN EQUIPMENT

	EXISTING APPLIANCE			TO BE PURCHASED		
	Height	Width	Depth	Height	Width	Depth
Cooker						
Refrigerator						
Washing machine						
Dishwasher						
Tumbler dryer						
Food mixer						
Freezer						
Ironing equipment						
Microwave cooker						
Water-softening unit						

Small electrical appliances, such as toaster, coffee percolator, electric grinders and sharpeners, etc.: fill in each one if kept in the kitchen

The Cook's Workshop

KITCHEN DECORATION

Flooring The kitchen floor should be hard-wearing, resistant to staining, easy to clean, non-slip and preferably heat-proof. The flooring which most meets all the requirements is modern ceramic tiling, usually coated with liquid polish to give a glossy, dirt-resistant finish.

Cork tiling is an attractive flooring which provides warmth under foot. It should be sealed with clear polyurethane varnish to resist knocks, stains and grease. Heavy-duty vinyl is both decorative, practical and reasonably priced.

Wall finishes Kitchen walls should be washable and resistant to steam and grease. Tiles, plasticised wallpaper, and gloss or vinyl silk paints are all suitable for use either individually or in a combination.

KITCHEN EQUIPMENT

Cookers

There are three common means of providing heat for cooking.
1. Fuel-storage cookers for solid fuel, oil or gas.
2. Gas.
3. Electricity.

Microwave cookers, although now too expensive for the average home, are growing in importance.

Solid-fuel cookers

A major advantage of the solid-fuel cooker is the cheap running cost. Two hods of coke, loaded twice a day, can provide the cooking and domestic hot water for the average family.

Solid-fuel cookers take up more than twice as much space as a standard gas or electric cooker and are therefore used most successfully in large houses or farmhouses. However, this type of cooker does create more dirt in the kitchen.

Gas cookers

Gas cooking offers advantages not shared by other means of cooking: instant heat, fine adjustment and, with the advent of natural gas, a minimal degree of pollution.

Many gas cookers have inner glass doors for visible oven cooking. Some also have self-cleaning oven liners which keep themselves clean by oxidising splashes which touch the top and sides of the oven. Although spilt foods on the bottom tray of the cooker must still be wiped, cleaning is greatly simplified. Other special features on some gas cookers include:
1. Thermostatic controls, which give accurate time control and ensure greater safety. These are now available on hot-plate burners on top of the cooker.
2. Spark ignition which ignites the gas automatically.
3. Flame-failure device which cuts off the gas flow if the flame is extinguished.
4. New gas tap and burner designs to restore the sensitive control which was lost with the introduction of natural gas.
5. Automatic timing which switches on and off at pre-set times. Usually with a fail-safe device in case of faulty ignition.
6. Left or right hand door hinging which allows for easier kitchen planning.
7. Control panel on the top surface of the hob which is out of reach of small children.

Electric cookers

The following features are well worth looking out for but are not necessarily shared by all makes of electric cookers:

Self-cleaning interiors There are two versions of self-cleaning oven interiors. In the automatic self-cleaner type of interior, the door is closed, the cleaning cycle switched on, automatically locking the oven door to avoid accidents, and the oven temperature is greatly increased. Food splashes are carbonised into a fine dust which can be wiped away with a damp cloth once the oven has cooled.

The stay-clean oven interior is covered with a special coating which also works by oxidisation. However, the cleaning process is continuous.

Oven doors Most makes feature inner glass doors for visible oven cooking.

Ceramic cooking surfaces Glass ceramic hobs are available in floor-standing cookers and in split-level cookers where the glass ceramic hob forms a cooking counter. The flat smooth surface with its concealed electric heating elements is easy to clean with a damp cloth.

Automatic timing controls Automatic timers on electric cookers offer great advantages. Dishes are placed in their cooking utensils in the oven or on the hot plate, and the timing device is set to switch itself on and off at predetermined times.

Fan-assisted cookers Used originally in catering ovens, the principle of fan-assisted oven cooking has now been applied to domestic cookers. A 2 kW electric element fitted round a small fan is placed behind the back panel of the oven. Heated air is blown gently around, heating the oven more quickly and keeping it at an even temperature, irrespective of internal oven position of the shelves.

Cookers with fan-assisted ovens have all the other features of the modern electric cooker.

Microwave cookers

Microwave cookers work on an entirely different principle from normal cooking. Very high frequency microwaves are produced and beamed into the food, where they are converted into heat. The food cooks from the inside, and the interior of the oven and the plate on which the food stands remain cool. The special advantage of a microwave oven is the speed with which it can cook food, but as it cannot brown foods on its own, meat tends to have a boiled look when cooked.

Although microwave cookers are now more readily available, they are still outside the scope of most family budgets.

Cooker hoods

These remove cooking odours and steam from the kitchen and absorb grease from the air. The Xpelair hood is fitted with a duct which takes fumes to the outside air. For light cooking smells, it can purify and recirculate the internal air.

One disadvantage of the external duct system is the expense involved in fitting the duct which should never terminate below a bedroom window. Moreover, the removal of heated indoor air and substitution of cool outside air adds to the cost of heating.

Cooker hoods are also manufactured for installation without ducts. This type of hood draws fumes and grease into a charcoal filter which acts like a sponge, removing impurities from the air. The filter must be replaced periodically.

Refrigerators

The ideal temperature for short-term storage of perishable foods is just above freezing point. A refrigerator provides this, with a temperature range of between 34°F and 44°F (1°C and 7°C).

Freezer compartments Most refrigerators have a very-low-temperature frozen-food storage compartment. In many current models half the storage space is given over to frozen foods, and the other half is for normal refrigerator storage. There is a star rating for freezer compartments, and star ratings one to three are suitable for storing already frozen food, while the four-star compartment will freeze unfrozen food.

One star: Temperature approx. 21°F (−6°C). Frozen foods may be kept up to 1 week.

Two stars: Temperature approx. 10°F (−12°C). Frozen foods may be kept for up to four weeks.

Three stars: Temperature 0°F (−18°C). Frozen foods may be kept for up to three months.

Four stars: The compartment has a freezing capacity to a recognised standard. Frozen foods may be kept for up to three months.

The top of the refrigerator cabinet next to the frozen-food compartment and immediately below it are the coldest areas. The door storage area is the least cold part of the refrigerator. Highly perishable foods may be stored in the coldest parts, and the foods which need only to be chilled can be put lower down in the refrigerator or in the door.

All refrigerators should be defrosted, washed and tidied out regularly. Defrosting may be entirely manual, semi-automatic or fully automatic. The interior of the refrigerator should be washed with plain warm water containing a little dissolved bicarbonate of soda.

Never attempt to dislodge ice from the freezing compartment with a knife nor place an electric fire in front of the open refrigerator. A bowl of hot water placed on the freezing shelf speeds up defrosting.

STORING FOODS IN THE REFRIGERATOR

Food	Storage time	Comments
Bacon, smoked	7 to 10 days	Keep wrapped
Bacon, green	Slightly shorter than smoked bacon	Keep wrapped
Butter and fats	2 to 3 weeks	Keep wrapped or covered
Cheese, soft (except Brie, Camembert)	4 to 5 days	Keep in covered carton Remove 1 hour before serving
Fish	1 to 2 days	Keep tightly covered or wrapped in foil
Fruit, soft and green vegetables	1 to 5 days	Keep covered but allow some air to reach the fruit
Leftovers (containing meat, sauces or potatoes)	1 day	Keep meat tightly covered
Meat and poultry	1 to 3 days	Store in the chiller tray, or immediately below it; keep meat and poultry loosely wrapped in foil. Remove poultry giblets
Meat joints, large	4 days	Drain off meat juices; cover loosely
Milk and cream	3 to 5 days	Keep covered

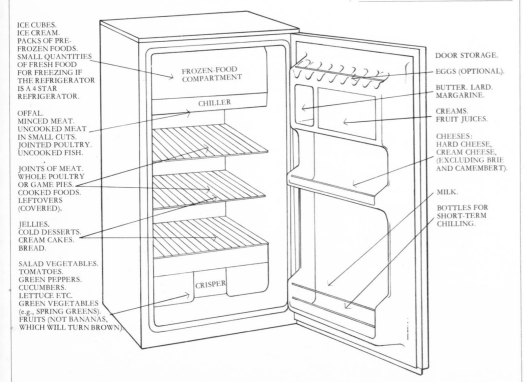

ICE CUBES. ICE CREAM. PACKS OF PRE-FROZEN FOODS. SMALL QUANTITIES OF FRESH FOOD FOR FREEZING IF THE REFRIGERATOR IS A 4 STAR REFRIGERATOR.

OFFAL. MINCED MEAT. UNCOOKED MEAT IN SMALL CUTS. JOINTED POULTRY. UNCOOKED FISH.

JOINTS OF MEAT. WHOLE POULTRY OR GAME PIES. COOKED FOODS. LEFTOVERS (COVERED).

JELLIES. COLD DESSERTS. CREAM CAKES. BREAD.

SALAD VEGETABLES. TOMATOES. GREEN PEPPERS. CUCUMBERS. LETTUCE ETC. GREEN VEGETABLES (e.g., SPRING GREENS). FRUITS (NOT BANANAS, WHICH WILL TURN BROWN).

FROZEN-FOOD COMPARTMENT

CHILLER

CRISPER

DOOR STORAGE.

EGGS (OPTIONAL).

BUTTER. LARD. MARGARINE.

CREAMS. FRUIT JUICES.

CHEESES: HARD CHEESE, CREAM CHEESE, (EXCLUDING BRIE AND CAMEMBERT).

MILK.

BOTTLES FOR SHORT-TERM CHILLING.

Dishwashers

An automatic dishwasher will wash, rinse and dry a full load of dishes in 15–90 minutes, depending on the make. Dishwasher capacity is usually measured by the number of place settings a machine will hold and wash at once.

Dishwashers are made to fit in beneath an existing work surface, or as a dishwasher and sink unit combined. It can also be installed at other convenient levels.

Space is needed for plumbing at the back of the machine and for opening the door at the front. If the machine stands on the floor, the level should be sufficiently high above the outside drain to allow the water to drain away properly. Sink, dishwasher and waste disposal unit should be close together.

During the washing cycle, small food particles from the dirty dishes are dispersed and trapped by fine mesh filters, which may or may not be self-cleaning. In some models these bits are disposed of automatically. Some of the more expensive dishwashers have acoustic insulation which helps to reduce the noise made by the machine.

Automatic laundry machines

Ideally, the washing machine and tumbler dryer should be in a utility room or separate laundry. But sometimes this is not possible, and they have to go in the kitchen.

There is a choice between machines which have the controls at the front and fit under a work top, and those which stand level with the work top and have controls on the top rear of the machine.

Most of the new automatic machines are of the front-opening tumble-action type. The capacity of tumble machines varies from 6½ lb. to 12 lb. dry weight of clothes. Machines are usually designed to take in hot and cold water.

On the programme switch or selector guide of most washing machines are the numbers corresponding to the 'wash care' labels which are attached to most ready-made garments.

Food mixers

There are two basic types of food mixer: the hand-held, light-duty whisk, and the heavier, stand-mounted machine with a large range of optional attachments, such as whisks, beaters and dough hooks.

The hand-held mixer is useful when preparing dishes with several ingredients which require whisking in separate bowls. It can also be used for making sauces and puddings which must be whisked while they are cooking. Most mixers have a choice of speeds to deal with different types of mixing, such as whisking an egg or mixing a fruit cake. The beaters can be removed for easy cleaning.

The more versatile hand-held mixers can also be mounted on a stand. Some come complete with liquidiser and have a slicer or shredder and coffee mill as optional extras. Others, which come complete with a stand, two beaters, two whisks and a wall bracket, may have a slicer and shredder, and a potato peeler, as optional attachments.

Stand-mounted mixers are heavy-duty machines which can cope with all types of mixing and whisking from whipping cream to kneading bread.

Liquidisers These can be bought either as attachments for most stand-mounted mixers or as independent units. They are useful for making puréed foods, mayonnaise and soups, for chopping dry ingredients such as breadcrumbs, and for liquidising fruit and vegetables.

Tin openers

Hand-held, wall-mounted or electric tin openers come in a large range of styles. Electric tin openers can be used on a work surface or fixed to the wall, out of the reach of children.

Coffee grinders

There are some non-electric coffee grinders, such as imitations of the wall-mounted Victorian coffee grinder. The electrical coffee-grinding devices are optional extras on many food mixers. To keep the maximum flavour of the coffee, only a small quantity of coffee beans should be ground at one time.

KITCHEN TOOLS

The needs of the family will indicate which kitchen tools will be essential and which are unnecessary. There is a large range of electrical tools, such as toasters, coffee percolators, kettles, knife-sharpeners, potato peelers and carving knives.

The following list of kitchen equipment includes all the basic requirements, apart from cutlery, tableware and glassware.

BAKING AND ROASTING EQUIPMENT
BAKING TRAYS
BAKING TIN, LARGE
BAKING TIN, SMALL
BARQUETTES (BOAT SHAPES)
BASTING SYRINGE
BUN TINS (1 SET)
CAKE TINS (3 SIZES)
CASSEROLES WITH LIDS (OVEN AND/OR FLAMEPROOF)
FLAN RINGS (PLAIN AND FLUTED)
GRATIN DISHES (OVEN AND/OR FLAME-PROOF)
GRIDDLE
HORN TINS
LOAF TINS (1 LB. AND 2 LB.)
PATTY PANS
PIE DISHES (DEEP AND SHALLOW)
PIE FUNNEL
PIE PLATES (2 SIZES)
RAMEKINS (1 SET)
SANDWICH TINS
SOUFFLÉ DISHES
SWISS ROLL TINS
TARTLET TINS
TERRINE

BOWLS AND JUGS
COFFEE POT
MILK JUGS
MIXING BOWLS (LARGE AND SMALL)
PUDDING BOWLS (3 SIZES)

CUTTING TOOLS
APPLE CORER
BALL SCOOP
CHEESE SLICER
CHERRY STONER
CLEAVER, MEAT
EGG SLICER
KITCHEN SCISSORS
KNIFE SHARPENER
KNIVES
  BREAD KNIFE
  CARVING SET
  FILLETING KNIFE
  GRAPEFRUIT KNIFE
  CHEF'S KNIVES (2 SIZES)
  SERRATED KNIFE
  VEGETABLE KNIFE
MANDOLIN SLICER
MEAT SAW
PASTRY CUTTERS (PLAIN AND FLUTED)
PASTRY WHEEL
POTATO CHIPPER (FLUTED)
POTATO PEELER
POULTRY SHEARS
VEGETABLE PEELER

GRINDERS AND GRATERS
COFFEE MILL
FOOD MILL
GARLIC PRESS
GRATER, STAINLESS STEEL
MINCER
MOULI FOOD MILL
NUTMEG GRATER
PEPPER MILL
PESTLE AND MORTAR
ZESTER

HOLLOW WARE (POTS AND PANS)
DEEP FRYER
DOUBLE SAUCEPAN
EGG POACHER
FISH KETTLE
FRYING PANS
KETTLE
MILK PAN
PRESERVING PAN
PRESSURE COOKER
SAUCEPANS (3 SIZES MINIMUM)
STEAMER

MOULDS
CHARLOTTE MOULD
JELLY MOULDS
PIE MOULDS
RING MOULD
TIMBALE MOULDS

OPENERS
TIN OPENERS
CORKSCREW
BOTTLE OPENERS
SCREW-TOP JAR OPENER

SPOONS AND FORKS
COOK'S FORK
COOK'S SPOON
PERFORATED DRAINING SPOON
FISH SLICE
KITCHEN CUTLERY, STAINLESS STEEL
SKIMMING LADLE
SOUP LADLE
WOODEN SPOON (3 SIZES)

STRAINERS
COLANDER
SALAD SHAKER
SIEVE, NYLON
SIEVE, WIRE
TEA OR COFFEE STRAINER

WEIGHING AND MEASURING EQUIPMENT
COOKING THERMOMETER

KITCHEN TIMER
MEASURING CUP
MEASURING JUGS
MEASURING SPOONS
SCALES

CONTAINERS
BREAD BIN
FLOUR BINS
PLASTIC STORAGE CONTAINERS
STORAGE JARS AND TINS

GENERAL EQUIPMENT
ASPIC CUTTERS
BALLOON WHISK
BISCUIT CUTTERS, ASSORTED
CAKE DECORATING EQUIPMENT
CAKE RACKS
CHOPPING BOARD
FLOUR SIFTER
FORCING BAG AND NOZZLES
FUNNEL
JELLY BAG
MUSLIN
NEEDLES, LARDING AND TRUSSING
NUTCRACKERS
PALETTE KNIVES (2 SIZES)
PASTRY BOARD
PASTRY BRUSH
ROLLING PIN
ROTARY WHISK
SKEWERS
SPATULA
SQUEEZER
SUGAR SIFTER
TONGS FOR GRILLING AND FRYING
TRIVET, ADJUSTABLE
WAFFLE IRON
WOODEN COCKTAIL STICKS

CLEANING UTENSILS
BOTTLE BRUSHES
DISH MOPS AND BRUSHES
SCOURERS
TEA CLOTHS

KITCHEN STATIONERY
ALUMINIUM FOIL
CUTLET FRILLS
GREASEPROOF PAPER
KITCHEN PAPER, ABSORBENT
NON-STICK AND WAXED PAPER
PAPER CASES FOR CAKES AND SWEETS
PLASTIC FOOD BAGS
RICE PAPER
SELF-CLINGING PLASTIC FOIL
STRING

Non-stick coating is becoming popular for use with aluminium, steel and copper pans. Take care not to over-heat this type of coating, otherwise the surface will gradually break down, and never use steel tools which will scratch these surfaces.

Care of pans

Before using an aluminium pan for the first time, wash it with hot water and detergent, then rinse and dry. After use, avoid abrasives, but use scouring pads if necessary. To remove discoloration, boil a solution of lemon peel and water in the pan.

Wash stainless-steel pans with hot water and detergent. Remove stains with a stainless-steel powder. The copper-lined pans coated with tin or nickel should be washed with hot water and detergent. Clean the outside with vinegar and salt.

Wash non-stick pans in warm soapy water, using a sponge. If necessary soak the pan, but do not use abrasive powders or scourers.

Casseroles

Flameproof glass can be used over low heat on top of the stove as well as in the oven. China, earthenware and porcelain are generally intended for use only in the oven, unless marked flame-proof. Cast-iron or steel-coated vitreous enamel can be used either on the hob or in the oven. Cleaning with soapy water is usually effective, and scourers should never be used.

Measuring spoons, measures, jugs and scales

With the changeover to metric measure, there will be a new range of standard scales, measures, spoons and jugs, which will carry the new system. Eventually, ingredients will be measured not in teaspoons, table-spoons, pints and fluid ounces, pounds and ounces, but in litres, decilitres and millilitres, kilogrammes and grammes.

Cup measures

The standard measure will, when full and levelled, contain 3 decilitres, which is three-tenths of a litre, or 300 millilitres or just over half a pint. A set of measures will consist of:

1 measure $= 3$ decilitres
$= 10\frac{1}{2}$ fluid oz.
$\frac{1}{2}$ measure $= 1.5$ decilitres
$= 5\frac{1}{4}$ fluid oz.
$\frac{1}{3}$ measure $= 1$ decilitre
$= 3\frac{1}{2}$ fluid oz.
$\frac{1}{4}$ measure $= 0.75$ decilitre
$= 2\frac{1}{2}$ fluid oz.
$\frac{1}{6}$ measure $= 0.5$ decilitre
$= 1\frac{3}{4}$ fluid oz. (opt.)

Standard measuring spoons

The levelled metric capacity of a spoon (British Imperial Standard) is approximately as follows:
20 ml. $= 4$ teaspoons (opt.)
15 ml. $= 1$ tablespoon
10 ml. $= 2$ teaspoons
5 ml. $= 1$ teaspoon
2.5 ml. $= \frac{1}{2}$ teaspoon
1.25 ml. $= \frac{1}{4}$ teaspoon (opt.)

Measuring jugs

Jugs may be purchased in either 1 litre or 5 decilitre ($\frac{1}{2}$ litre) sizes graduated as follows:
1 litre jug ($= 35$ fluid oz.) is marked at 7.5 dl. (26 oz.), 5 dl. ($17\frac{1}{2}$ oz.), 1.5 dl. ($5\frac{1}{4}$ oz.), 1 dl. ($3\frac{1}{2}$ fluid oz.)

Scales

The metric unit for solid weights is the kilo (Kg), which contains 1000 grammes. The British Imperial ounce is roughly the equivalent of 28 grammes. On spring balance scales, each kilo will be marked in 500 grammes, 250 grammes and 125 grammes. Each of these is further marked into 25 grammes.

Pots and pans

For the average family, the following pans are necessary: one 3 pint pan, two 5 pint pans, one 2 pint milk pan and one 9–10 in. frying pan.

Aluminium pans conduct heat well and evenly. This type of pan is inexpensive and can be used on any type of cooker.

Enamel-coated pans Enamel-coated pans are heavy-based and conduct heat evenly. They should never be subjected to too fierce heat, and metal scourers should never be used on them. Before using a new pan follow the manufacturers' instructions.

Stainless steel pans with bases made of aluminium or copper, which conduct heat evenly, are durable and easy to clean. Copper-lined pans with tin, nickel or non-stick coating, although expensive, are popular with professional cooks because they are hard-wearing and conduct heat well. But they are heavy and tarnish quickly. Abrasive cleaners should never be used.

COOKING AND BAKING EQUIPMENT

Reading from left to right:

A. *Clockwise: jelly bag, hair sieve, cooking timer, polythene storage containers, measuring jug, colander, aspic cutters, metal sieves (or strainers); in the centre, tea strainer, bulb baster, rolling pin*

B. *Above, fluted pie mould, flanked by plain and fluted pastry cutters. In the centre fluted flan rings. On the left, cream horn tins, boat-shaped mould and fluted tartlet tin*

C. *Set of glass mixing bowls, set of pudding basins, pestle and mortar*

D. *Fancy biscuit cutters in front of dariole mould. At the back, Swiss roll tins, round sandwich tins. Griddle iron, sheets of patty pans*

E. *Brioche tins placed on loaf tins, and in front a savarin mould*

F. *Charlotte mould, baking tray with roasting tins and jelly moulds, fluted ring mould and, in front, ring mould*

G. *Enamelled flameproof casserole dishes*

H. *Vegetable mouli, square grater, rotary grater, hand-operated mincer, chopping board and fruit squeezer*

I. *Set of soufflé dishes, small ramekin dishes, pie dishes with pie funnel, set of gratin dishes*

J. *Clockwise: aluminium preserving pan, double boiler, deep fryer, steamer,* asbestos mat, omelette pan, fish kettle with detachable grid. In the centre, egg poacher

K. *Wire rack, square loose-bottomed cake tins, round loose-bottomed cake tins, non-stick solid cake tins, waffle iron*

L. *Large fabric forcing bag, plain and star vegetable nozzles, plain and star-shaped piping or icing nozzles, small plastic icing bag with set of screw-on nozzles*

The Cook's Workshop

Reading left to right, first row:

1–3. *Set of cook's knives.*

4. *Carving steel.*

5. *All-purpose knife.*

6. *Carving knife.*

7. *Ham slicer.*

8. *Bread knife.*

9. *Grapefruit knife.*

10. *Meat tenderiser.*

11. *Meat bat.*

12. *Meat cleaver.*

13. *Herb chopper.*

14. *Kitchen scissors.*

15. *Poultry shears.*

16. *Nutcrackers.*

17. *Cherry stoner.*

Second row:

18. *Wooden kitchen fork.*

19. *Carving fork.*

20. *Serving tongs.*

21 & 22. *Ladles.*

23. *Three types of palette knives.*

24. *Rubber spatula.*

25. *Wooden spatula.*

26. *Fish slice.*

27. *Basting spoon.*

28. *Perforated spoon.*

29. *Five types of wooden spoons.*

Third row:

30. *Potato peeler.*

31. *Pastry wheel.*

32. *Pastry brush.*

33. *Ball scoop.*

34. *Canelling knife.*

35. *Apple corer.*

36. *Bottle opener.*

37. *Corkscrew.*

38. *Mandolin slicer.*

39. *Larding needle.*

40. *Trussing needle.*

41. *Garlic crusher.*

42. *Potato masher.*

43. *Rotary whisk.*

44. *Balloon whisk.*

45. *Skewers.*

46. *Universal cooking thermometer.*

47. *Manual tin opener.*

48. *Spiked tin opener.*

49. *Bottle brush.*

SAFETY IN THE KITCHEN

General safety procedures

1. Appliances approved by the British Electrotechnical Approvals Board and the British Gas Corporation are safe.
2. For rewiring and extension wiring, use an approved firm on the roll of the National Inspection Council for Electrical Installation Contracting.
3. Before cleaning or examining appliances, plugs must be removed from the wall socket.
4. Damaged switch covers or socket outlets should be replaced immediately.
5. If an iron is dropped, it should be examined by a qualified electrician before further use.
6. The kitchen should be provided with enough socket outlets to avoid trailing flexes and overloaded circuits.
7. Flex, which must be kept in good condition, should never be joined together with insulating tape.
8. Never touch plugs or switches with wet hands.

Cookers These should not be positioned near the door, for obvious safety reasons. Gas cookers should not have extractor fans fitted directly above them. Both electric and gas cookers can be equipped with safety guards to prevent children reaching and knocking over pans.

New gas cookers are fitted with an automatic device which cuts off the gas supply when the pilot light is not igniting. If the pilot light fails on older models, and a smell of gas is noticeable, open the windows to create a draught; contact the gas maintenance engineers. On no account attempt to trace a gas leak with a naked flame.

Gas cookers must be adequately ventilated, and kitchens equipped with extractor fans should also have an inlet for fresh air. Simmering devices, such as asbestos sheets, are not recommended for gas cookers.

Deep fryers Never fill more than a third full with hot oil or fat. If the oil should catch fire *never* douse the flames with water, but cover the pan with its lid or a baking tray. Turn off the heat.

Fire extinguishers Ideally every kitchen should be equipped with some form of fire extinguisher, not an aerosol spray. Alternatively, keep an asbestos blanket handy.

Kettles These should be disconnected from the socket outlet before filling or pouring out.

Knives Keep these out of reach of children, preferably on a wall-mounted magnetic knife rack, or in wooden cases, apart from other kitchen tools.

Laundry equipment All washing machines must be earthed by a properly connected three-pin plug. Never leave children alone when the machine is being used. Irons should be connected to a wall socket and never to a ceiling lighting point or to any lamp holder.

Electric mincers Nothing should be used for pushing down the food which is being minced except the plunger provided for the purpose.

Waste disposal units For clearing blockages, follow the manufacturer's instructions.

To wire a plug

All domestic electrical appliances sold in the UK are wired according to the international colour coding:

Live (L)   Brown
Neutral (N)   Blue
Earth (E)   Green/Yellow

Older equipment must continue to have plugs connected as follows:

Live (L)   Red
Neutral (N)   Black
Earth (E)   Green

To rewire a plug, remove the cover of the plug by unscrewing the central screw; remove screw nuts and washers. With some plugs it may also be necessary to remove the cartridge fuse.

Strip the covering off the end of each wire, exposing about $\frac{1}{2}$ in. (13 mm) of bare wire. Twist the ends of the wire and attach each to the approximate pin. (Neutral – left; Live – right; Earth – middle.)

In some plugs, the wire strands are turned round the terminals of the pins; in others they are passed through a hole in the pins. If necessary, strip more of the insulating covering off to pass the wire strands through the holes. Replace washers and screws firmly, leaving no exposed wires. Replace cartridge fuse in a fused plug. Tighten screws which hold flexible cord firmly.

Replace the cover of the plug, screwing securely.

Replacing a cartridge fuse in a 13 amp plug

Disconnect plug and remove cover by unscrewing central screw. Remove cartridge. Replace with a new cartridge fuse of the correct loading:

For an appliance with maximum loading of 750 watts such as a television, blanket, lamp, food mixer, radio, use a *blue 3 amp fuse*.

For an appliance with a loading of 750 watts and over, such as a kettle, iron, convector heater, radiant fire, heated washing machine, and also refrigerator, freezer or vacuum cleaner, use a *brown 13 amp fuse*.

Home Freezing

The freezer is a time and money saver for anyone who cooks for a family. It enables a cook to plan well ahead, both in bulk-buying and in cooking. And, if the rules for the preparation, packaging and thawing of the raw materials are carefully followed, frozen food loses nothing in freshness and quality. A freezer can also be housed in a garage or cellar, which means a saving of valuable kitchen space.

Buying a freezer

A freezer is an expensive piece of equipment, and it is worth buying a reliable one, fitted with a battery alarm in case of power failure, and a 'super-freeze' switch for quick freezing of new stocks. There are two basic types of freezer, the upright cupboard variety and the chest-shaped, top-opening cabinet.

The cupboard variety is slightly more expensive to run; it takes up less floor space, and filling and stock-taking is easy.

The chest variety necessitates a list of contents and the use of wire racks and baskets so that the housewife will know where everything is and by what date it must be used. But this type is less expensive to buy and can serve as an additional work surface in the kitchen if the chest is not opened too often.

Size of freezer

One cubic foot of storage space will contain 20–25 lb. of food. A minimum of 2 cu. ft of freezer space should be allowed for each member of the family – more if the family entertains frequently.

Running costs

A freezer uses less electricity than a refrigerator – on average about two units of electricity per cu. ft per week. The fuller the freezer is packed, the cheaper it is to run. To keep costs down, the top or door should be opened as infrequently as possible.

Care and maintenance of the freezer

The freezer should have a yearly service, carried out by the firm that sold the machine. The contents of the freezer should be insured against power failure or breakdowns. Where possible, an arrangement should be made with a deep-freezing firm with emergency generators to store food at short notice.

The freezer must be cleaned out at least once every six months, using the following methods:
1. Remove packages and wrap them in newspaper to prevent thawing.
2. Turn off the electricity and place bowls of boiling water in the cabinet to speed up thawing.
3. Scrape the ice from the sides and scoop it up from the bottom.
4. When the freezer is empty, wipe it with a clean cloth dipped in a solution of bicarbonate of soda or vinegar and water to remove stale smells.
5. As soon as the freezer is defrosted, turn the electricity to maximum, check and return the packages.

If a bag or package breaks in the freezer, the contents should be cleared at once to prevent any odour contaminating other food.

Food should be labelled with the name, weight and date on which it was frozen, and the date by which it should be used. Foods should be stored and used in rotation, and the storage life carefully adhered to.

In an emergency

The deep freeze should not be opened until at least six hours after the power has been restored, after a breakdown of electricity. If no warm air enters the cabinet the contents will remain frozen for up to 48 hours.

Bulk buying for the freezer

The prices for all fresh foods fluctuate according to season. Buy eggs, meat and poultry, fruit and vegetables in peak condition at their lowest prices, and in quantities which can easily be frozen on the day of purchase. Fish should only be frozen when absolutely fresh and must be bought from a reputable fishmonger.

Bulk suppliers of deep-frozen products can be found in most parts of the country.

Equipment for the freezer

Wire racks, shelves and baskets are necessary to store food in the freezer. Good-quality heavy-duty polythene bags, plastic containers and stockinet can be re-used if washed after use.

Strong, fireproof casseroles and baking dishes save time if they can be used to cook, freeze and serve a meal. Square or oblong shapes are easier to store than round ones.

Suitable packaging materials

Wrapping: Stockinet for over-wrapping meat and poultry which is first packed in polythene bags, aluminium foil and waxed freezer paper.

Bags: Heavy duty polythene bags in a wide range of sizes, and tin-foil bags.

Cartons and containers: Square and rectangular cartons are easier to store than round. Plastic and polythene containers with snap-on lids, waxed cardboard cartons and containers, aluminium trays and basins. Washed yoghurt, margarine or soured cream cartons.

Sealing materials: Sealing iron for sealing polythene bags. Rubber bands.

Labelling materials: Self-sticking, moisture-proof labels. Waterproof felt pen or chinagraph to mark packages.

Successful packaging

If food is improperly wrapped, it will develop 'freezer burn' – white spots on the surface. If this occurs the food must be used immediately. The flavour and texture may be damaged, and food may require a sauce to make it palatable.

Squeeze as much air as possible from the packages before sealing them properly. Solid goods should be packed as closely as possible; liquids should have at least $\frac{1}{2}$ in. headspace to allow for expansion during freezing. Separate items, such as hamburgers or croquettes packaged in the same container, should be separated with a layer of waxed paper to prevent sticking.

GUIDE TO FREEZING OF PRE-COOKED FOOD

Being able to freeze pre-cooked dishes for later use has numerous advantages. Leftovers can be stored for later use. Time can be spent in the kitchen when it is convenient. Quantities of recipes can be doubled to save time, energy and cooking expense, with one dish eaten at once and the other frozen. People who entertain frequently can do most of the cooking well in advance. And those with large families can stock up for the holidays.

For successful freezing follow these pointers:

1. Working surroundings must be scrupulously clean, as freezing does not destroy germs in food.
2. Use top-quality ingredients and season lightly; more seasoning can always be added later.
3. Always slightly undercook dishes which are to be frozen, allowing for the time the food will be in the oven to heat through.
4. When recipes for soups, sauces and casseroles call for the addition of cream or egg yolks, omit these before freezing and add them when the dishes are being re-heated. Do not freeze dishes with custard or mayonnaise.
5. Omit garlic before freezing (it can be added later) unless the food is going to remain in the freezer for only a short time.
6. Be generous with sauces, so that meat, chicken, fish and game will not dehydrate when frozen.
7. Cool all cooked and baked dishes thoroughly before packing and freezing.
8. Garnish re-heated food before serving, not before freezing.
9. Pack and label all pre-cooked foods carefully and note the number of portions. Soups can be frozen in square containers, removed when solid and then packed in polythene bags; casseroles can be frozen in their cooking dishes, turned out and packed in polythene bags to be returned to their dishes for thawing and re-heating.
10. Do not freeze the following, as the results are disappointing: whole roast joints or poultry; cold meat without a sauce; jellies; sandwiches with mayonnaise, hardboiled egg, tomato, cucumber or banana fillings.

FREEZING PREPARED AN

Food (storage time in brackets)	Method	Thawing and serving
Biscuits *unbaked* (6 months)	Shape dough into cylinders about 2 in. wide and wrap in foil or polythene. Shape soft mixtures on to a paper-lined tray, freeze, then pack carefully in rigid containers, separating layers with paper	Slightly thaw rolls of uncooked dough, slice and bake. Shaped biscuits can be cooked from frozen state but will need 7–10 minutes more cooking time
baked	Pack as for shaped soft biscuits before freezing	Cooked biscuits may be crisped in a warm oven after thawing
Bread (4 weeks)	Wrap in polythene bags	Thaw in wrapper at room temperature (3 hours for 1½ lb.) or overnight in refrigerator. May be thawed in oven at 300°F (mark 2) for about 30 min., but this causes it to go stale quickly. Sliced bread may be toasted or fried from frozen state
bought part-baked bread and rolls (4 months)	Freeze immediately after buying; leave loaves in own wrapper, pack rolls in polythene bags or foil	To cook, place frozen unwrapped loaf in oven at 425°F (mark 7) for about 40 min. Cool before cutting. Bake unwrapped rolls at 400°F (mark 6) for 15 min.
Cakes (6 months – iced cakes lose quality after 2 months)	Use less essence and spice than usual. Fill cakes with cream, but not jam before freezing. Wrap unfilled layer cakes separately or separate with waxed paper or cellophane; pack in foil or polythene. Freeze iced cakes unwrapped until icing has set, then wrap in foil or cellophane and pack in boxes to protect icing	Cream-filled cakes are best sliced while frozen. Unwrap iced cakes before thawing so that paper does not stick to icing. Leave plain cakes in wrapping and thaw at room temperature: allow 1–2 hours for plain layer cakes and small cakes, 4 hours for iced cakes
Croissants and Danish pastries, *unbaked* (6 weeks)	Prepare dough to the stage when all fat has been absorbed, but do not give final rolling. Wrap tightly in polythene bag	Leave in polythene bags but unseal it and re-tie loosely to allow dough to rise. Thaw overnight in refrigerator or for 5 hours at room temperature. Complete rolling and shaping before baking
baked (Croissants 2 months, Danish pastries 1 month)	Wrap in polythene bags or foil, or in rigid foil containers	Thaw in wrapping at room temperature for about 1 hour. If wished, heat in oven, unwrapped at 350°F (mark 4) for 5 min.
Ice cream (home-made 3 months, commercial 1 month)	Wrap bought ice cream in moisture-proof bags; freeze home-made ice cream in moulds or waxed paper, and overwrap with polythene	Place in refrigerator for 1–1½ hours to soften
Meat dishes (2 months)	Cook for a slightly shorter time than usual to allow for re-heating. Do not season heavily. Make sure meat is completely immersed in gravy or sauce. It is better to add potatoes, rice, noodles, garlic and celery at time of serving. Pack in rigid foil containers; or freeze in foil-lined casserole, remove and pack in polythene bags	Turn frozen food out of container into saucepan to re-heat. Pre-formed foil-lined dishes may be re-heated in original casserole for 1 hour at 400°F (mark 6), reducing heat if necessary to 350°F (mark 4) for last 40 min.
Meat loaves, pâtés, terrines (1 month)	Make in usual way, taking care not to season or spice heavily. When cold, remove from tins or moulds and wrap in polythene to freeze	Thaw in wrapping for 6–8 hours, or overnight in refrigerator

RE-COOKED DISHES

Food (storage time in brackets)	Method	Thawing and serving
Mousses, cold soufflés (2 months)	Freeze in special toughened glassware, or line dishes or moulds with foil, freeze, then remove from container and wrap in polythene bags to store	Thaw in refrigerator for 6–8 hours, or at room temperature for 2–3 hours
Pancakes *unfilled* (2 months)	Stack pancakes between layers of greaseproof paper or cellophane, wrap conveniently sized stacks in foil or polythene	Thaw in wrapping at room temperature for 2–3 hours, or overnight in refrigerator. To thaw quickly, unwrap, spread out pancakes and thaw at room temperature for about 20 minutes. Heat individual pancakes in a lightly greased frying pan for 30 seconds each side. Or heat stack of pancakes wrapped in foil in oven at 375°F (mark 5) for 20–30 min.
filled (1–2 months)	Choose fillings which are suitable for freezing. Do not season heavily. Pack filled pancakes in foil containers, seal and overwrap	Remove overwrapping, place frozen pancakes in foil container, unopened, in oven at 400°F (mark 6) for about 30 min.
Pastry, *uncooked* (3 months)	Make as usual and roll out to size required. Line foil plates or pie dishes, freeze unwrapped, remove from pie dishes, and wrap in polythene. Roll out pastry lids and separate with waxed paper before wrapping in polythene. Stack, separating the layers with two sheets of waxed paper, place on cardboard and wrap. Single or double crust fruit pies may be frozen uncooked with the filling in place, ready for baking. Do not make slits in the top crust before freezing. Wrap in foil or polythene bags when frozen solid	Return pie shells to original dishes. Thaw pastry lids at room temperature before fitting on filled pies. Pie cases can be baked frozen (ovenproof glassware should be left to stand at room temperature for 10 min. before baking). Add 5 min. to baking time. Place unwrapped fruit pies in oven at 425°F (mark 7) for 40–60 min. Slit tops of crusts when beginning to thaw
cooked (pastry cases and fruit pies 6 months; meat pies 3 months)	Bake pies in foil containers and cool quickly. Wrap in foil or polythene. Tops may be protected with an inverted foil dish before wrapping	Thaw at room temperature; pies for 2–4 hours. Re-heat in oven
Pizzas, *unbaked* (3 months)	Prepare to baking stage. Wrap in foil or polythene. Freeze, overwrap	Remove wrapping and place frozen pizza in cold oven set at 450°F (mark 8); bake for 30–35 min.
baked (2 months)	Wrap in foil or polythene and freeze as for unbaked pizza	Remove wrapping and heat in oven at 350°F (mark 4) for about 15 min.
Sauces, soups, stocks (2–3 months)	Cool thoroughly, pour into rigid containers or wrap in polythene when frozen solid	Heat from frozen state until boiling point, or thaw for 1–2 hours at room temperature
Scones and teabreads (6 months)	Wrap in polythene bags in convenient quantities	Thaw scones for 30–60 min. at room temperature; warm in oven if wished. Thaw teabreads in wrapping for 2–3 hours, at room temperature, or place frozen in oven at 400°F (mark 6) for 10 min.

GUIDE TO FREEZING FRESH FOOD

Vegetables

Freeze only young, unblemished, freshly picked vegetables.

Most vegetables must be blanched before being frozen. Blanch* the prepared vegetables, 1 lb. at a time in 6 pints of boiling water. The water should be brought back to the boil within 1 minute of adding the vegetables. Blanching time varies for different vegetables (see chart). Immediately after blanching, the vegetables should be plunged into iced water to cool and to prevent further cooking. Drain the cooled vegetables thoroughly and pack in rigid containers or polythene bags.

Vegetables will store for 1 year unless otherwise stated.

Meat

Only good-quality fresh meat should be frozen, and the best results are obtained when the meat has been fully hung before freezing. Cut the meat into convenient sizes, such as joints and chops. Remove as much bone as possible so that the meat will take up less space in the freezer. The bones can be used to make stock.

Meat to be used in stews and casseroles can be cut into cubes and packed in rigid containers.

Remove excess fat, as it can become rancid if exposed to oxygen. For the same reason, pack meat carefully in airtight wrappings. Pad sharp corners or bones with foil or thin self-adhesive plastic wrap, to prevent them from perforating the packaging. Pack the meat, first in foil, then overwrap with heavy-duty polythene, excluding as much air as possible.

Weigh the meat before freezing, and label it with weight, description and date. Cutlets, chops, steaks and hamburgers should be interleaved with waxed paper or thin polythene, so that they can be easily separated.

Allow meat to thaw slowly in its wrapping in a cool place or in the refrigerator. If it is needed in a hurry, the thawing can be speeded up by placing the meat, in its wrapping, in cold water; part of the flavour is, however, lost. Small cuts of meat such as chops and steaks can be cooked from the frozen state, but it is advisable to cook them over lower heat than usual.

Poultry and game

Only young plump birds should be frozen fresh, whole or jointed. Older birds, whether poultry or game, are best cooked as casseroles before freezing.

Remove giblets, clean and freeze separately as they have a shorter storage life. Clean the birds thoroughly, do not stuff them, but truss ready for cooking. Pad the legs with foil, before wrapping the whole bird in heavy-duty polythene. Label with weight, description and date. Pack jointed birds interspersed with waxed paper, in portions.

Stuffings should be frozen separately, as they store only for one month. Pack livers in polythene bags and freeze for use in pâtés and risottos.

Poultry and game birds should be thawed slowly, in their wrappings in the refrigerator. In an emergency a frozen bird can be thawed, wrapped, in cold water.

Young game birds, well-hung, are frozen as poultry. Hare must be hung, skinned and cleaned; it is best frozen in joints ready for cooking. Rabbit is frozen like hare, but is not hung first. Venison should be well-hung before jointing and freezing.

Fish

Fish should be frozen fresh and within 12 hours of being caught. It is not advisable to freeze even fresh shellfish at home, but some bulk suppliers offer de-frozen crab and lobster meat, as well as containers of prawns and shrimps. These may be stored in the home freezer for about one month.

Small round fish may be frozen whole after scaling and gutting. Larger round fish should have heads and tails removed. Flat fish is best frozen in fillets, interleaved with waxed paper. To preserve moisture in the prepared fish rub with a little olive oil. Wrap in heavy-duty polythene, or pack in rigid containers; label as usual.

The delicate flavour of whole salmon and trout can be maintained by freezing these fish in a sheet of ice. Dip the fish in cold salted water several times (placing it on a tray in the freezer between immersions) so that a layer of ice forms round the fish and seals it from the air. Then pack in heavy-duty polythene.

Thaw whole fish slowly, preferably in the refrigerator, and cook immediately it is thawed. Cutlets, steaks and fillets may be cooked from the frozen state.

Fruit

Top-quality fruit in peak condition is suitable for freezing whole; slightly over-ripe fruit is better made into purées.

To prepare fruit for freezing, wash it in chilled water, drain and dry thoroughly. Soft berries, such as strawberries and raspberries should be washed only if absolutely necessary.

415

Home Freezing

Keep fruit in a cool place or in the refrigerator until it is prepared for freezing. Stoned fruit may be frozen whole, halved or sliced. There are three ways of freezing: dry-freezing, sugar-freezing and syrup-freezing.

Dry-freezing is particularly suitable for small whole berry fruits. Spread the cleaned and dry fruit in a single layer on paper-lined trays. Place in the freezer until firm, pack in rigid containers or heavy-duty bags.

Sugar-freezing is recommended for soft fruits such as blackberries, raspberries, and strawberries. Pick over the fruit, but do not wash. Layer the fruit with caster sugar in rigid containers or mix the two together, allowing 4 oz. sugar to 1 lb. prepared fruit.

Syrup-freezing is the best method for non-juicy fruits, and those which discolour during preparation and storage. The strength of the syrup varies according to the fruit (see chart). Pack the fruit in rigid containers, leaving a $\frac{1}{2}$ in. headspace.

Label all packages with the name of the fruit, the weight, the amount of sugar added and the date of freezing.

Whole and sliced frozen fruit will store for up to one year, fruit purées for 6–8 months, and fruit juices for 4–6 months.

All frozen fruit should be thawed slowly in their unopened containers. To serve fruits as a dessert thaw in the refrigerator for 6 hours or at room temperature for 2–3 hours. Serve chilled.

Dessert fruits frozen in syrups should have the lid removed from the container and a piece of waxed paper pressed over the fruit to keep them immersed.

Frozen fruit to be stewed can be cooked without thawing, but fruit for pies and puddings should first be thawed.

FREEZING VEGETABLES

Vegetables	Preparation and Packing	Cooking
Artichokes, globe	Remove coarse outer leaves and stalks; trim tops and stems, removing 'chokes'. Wash in cold water, blanch in acidulated water* for 7 min. Cool and drain. Pack in rigid containers	Cook frozen in boiling salted water for 8 min. or until leaves are tender and easily removed
Asparagus	Remove woody parts, cut into even lengths, and wash well. Grade into thick and thin stems. Blanch thin stems for 2 min., thick ones for 4 min. Cool and drain. Pack tips to stalks in rigid containers or wrap small bundles in waxed paper or foil	Cook frozen in boiling salted water for 5–8 min.
Beans (French, runner, broad)	Wash well. Trim French, slice runner and shell broad beans. Blanch for 3 min., cool and pack in polythene bags	Cook frozen in boiling salted water: whole beans and broad beans 7–8 min.; sliced beans for 5 min.
Broccoli	Trim off woody parts and outer leaves. Wash in salted water; divide into small sprigs and grade in sizes. Blanch for 3–5 min., cool and drain. Pack in rigid containers, stalks to tips	Cook frozen in boiling salted water for 5–8 min.
Brussels sprouts	Choose small, compact sprouts. Remove outer leaves and wash thoroughly. Grade into sizes. Blanch for 3 min., cool and drain. Pack in polythene bags	Cook frozen in boiling salted water for 8 min.
Cabbages (green and red)	Choose young crisp cabbages. Wash thoroughly, shred finely, blanch for 2 min., cool and drain. Pack in polythene bags	Cook frozen in boiling salted water for 8 min.
Carrots	Choose young carrots. Remove tops, wash and scrape, leave whole. Blanch for 5 min., cool and drain; pack in polythene bags	Cook frozen in boiling salted water for 8 min.
Cauliflower (storage time: 6 months)	Choose firm, compact, white cauliflower. Wash and break into florets. Blanch for 3 min. in acidulated water, cool and drain. Pack in polythene bags	Cook frozen in boiling salted water for 8–10 min.
Celery	Use crisp, young stalks; remove stem bases and leaves. Cut into 1 in. lengths. Blanch for 3 min., cool and drain. Pack in polythene bags. Alternatively, pack in rigid containers and cover with some of the blanching liquid; leave $\frac{1}{2}$ in. headspace	Thaw at room temperature for 1 hour and add to casseroles and stews. Cook in blanching liquid for about 10 min., to serve as accompanying vegetable
Corn on the cob	Freeze fresh, young corn only. Remove husks and threads. Blanch for 4 min., cool and dry. Pack individually in waxed paper or foil	Cook frozen corn in boiling salted water for 4–5 min.

Vegetables
Courgettes
Mushrooms (storage time: 3 months)
Parsnips
Peas
Potatoes
Spinach
Tomatoes
Turnips

FREEZING MEAT

Meat (storage time in brackets)	Preparation and packaging	Thawing
Joints (beef 8 months; lamb, pork and veal 6 months)	Wrap in heavy-duty polythene bags, seal well and label. May be overwrapped with stockinet	Thaw thoroughly before cooking, preferably in a refrigerator. Allow 5 hours per lb. in a refrigerator, 2 hours per lb. at room temperature
Cutlets, chops, hamburgers, steaks and cubed meat (3 months)	Pack in suitable quantities. Separate cutlets, chops, hamburgers and steaks with waxed paper. Pack in polythene bags or rigid containers	These small cuts can be cooked frozen over gentle heat
Minced meat and sausage meat (3 months)	Pack in small quantities in bags or rigid containers	Thaw in a cool place for $1\frac{1}{2}$ hours or refrigerator for 3 hours
Offal and sausages (1–3 months)	Clean and trim offal. Pack in small quantities in polythene bags	Thaw in a cool place for $1\frac{1}{2}$ hours or a refrigerator for 3 hours

Game
Birds (6–8 months)
Hare, rabbit (6 months)
Venison (up to 12 months)

FREEZING POULTRY

Poultry	Preparation and packaging	Thawing
(Chicken 12 months; duck 4–6 months; goose 4–6 months; turkey 6 months; giblets 3 months; livers 3 months)	Wrap whole birds in heavy-duty polythene. Trim bones from joints and wrap individually before packing in heavy-duty polythene. Pieces for pies and casseroles may be packed in rigid containers. Pack giblets and livers separately in polythene bags	Thaw in wrapping in the refrigerator, a whole bird for 8 hours, joints and pieces for 2–3 hours. Thaw livers and giblets in wrapping in the refrigerator for 2 hours

Fish (storage time in brackets)
Whole fish (6 months)
Fillets, steaks (6 months)

Preparation and Packing	Cooking
Select young courgettes. Wash, trim off ends and cut into ½ in. slices. Blanch for 1 min., cool and drain. Alternatively, sauté in a little butter, cool quickly. Pack in rigid containers, leaving ½ in. headspace	Cook frozen in butter
Wipe clean, but do not peel. Mushrooms more than 1 in. wide should be sliced. Sauté in butter, cool quickly and pack in rigid containers, leaving ½ in. headspace	Cook frozen mushrooms in butter, or add to stews and casseroles
Trim, peel and cut into quarters, or slice and dice. Blanch for 2 min., cool and drain. Pack in polythene bags or rigid containers	Cook frozen in boiling salted water for 5–10 min.
Shell young peas. Blanch for 1 min., shaking basket to distribute heat evenly. Cool, drain and pack in polythene bags	Cook frozen in boiling salted water for 7 min.
Freeze only small new potatoes whole. Blanch for 4 min., cool, drain and pack in polythene bags. *Chips:* peel, wash and dry, cut into even-sized chips. Fry in deep fat for 3 min. Drain on absorbent paper and cool quickly. Pack in polythene bags	Cook frozen in boiling salted water for 15 min. Thaw chips partially at room temperature for 30–60 min. Deep-fry for 3 min.
Select young leaves, trim off stalks. Wash thoroughly, drain. Blanch in small quantities for 2 min. Cool and press out excess moisture. Pack in rigid containers, leaving ½ in. headspace	Cook frozen spinach in melted butter for 7 min.
Best frozen as purée or juice. *Purée:* skin, core and simmer in their own juice for 5 min., or until soft. Pass through a nylon sieve or liquidiser; cool and pack in rigid containers in quantities suitable for use. *Juice:* wash, quarter and core tomatoes. Simmer for 5–10 min. Press through a nylon sieve and add 1 level teaspoon salt to every 2 pints of juice. Cool and pack in rigid containers	Use frozen purée in sauces, soups and stews Thaw juice in container in the refrigerator and serve chilled
Trim, peel and dice young turnips. Blanch for 2½ min., cool and drain; pack in polythene bags. *Mashed:* cook until tender, drain and mash; freeze in rigid containers, leaving ½ in. headspace	Cook frozen diced turnips in boiling salted water for 5–10 min. Heat mashed turnips in a double boiler with butter and seasoning

FREEZING GAME

Preparation and packaging	Thawing
as poultry	as poultry
Wrap each joint in plastic film and pack several portions in heavy-duty polythene	Thaw in wrapping in the refrigerator for 2–3 hours
Freeze well-hung meat in joints or cutlets. Wrap joints in plastic film and polythene bags; overwrap with stockinet. Pack cutlets individually	Thaw in wrapping in the refrigerator for 5 hours

FREEZING FISH

Packaging	Thawing
Pack tightly in heavy-duty polythene	Thaw large fish in wrapping in a refrigerator for about 6 hours. Small whole fish may be cooked frozen over low heat
Wrap each piece in waxed paper, then pack in suitable portions in heavy-duty polythene	Thaw in wrapping in a refrigerator for about 3 hours

FREEZING FRUIT

Fruit	Preparation and packing
Apples	Peel, core and slice, dropping slices into cold acidulated water. Blanch for 1–2 min., cool in iced water. Drain well. Dry or sugar freeze. Pack in polythene bags or rigid containers, leaving ½ in. headspace *Purée:* Prepare as for slices. Stew in the minimum of water, add sugar to taste. Cook until soft and beat to a smooth pulp. Cool before packing in rigid containers, leaving ½ in. headspace
Apricots	Plunge into boiling water for 30 seconds and peel. Remove stones and halve or slice. Freeze in syrup made from 1 lb. sugar to 2 pints water and add 500 mg. ascorbic acid to each pint of syrup. Pack in rigid containers, leaving ½ in. headspace
Blackberries, loganberries, raspberries and strawberries	Dry or sugar freeze, then pack in bags or rigid containers. *Purée:* press through a nylon sieve and sweeten to taste with caster sugar. Pack in rigid containers. Use for fools and mousses
Black currants and red currants	Wash, dry and remove from stalks unless wanted for decoration. Dry or sugar freeze until firm, then pack in rigid containers. Black currants may be puréed. Cook with the minimum of water, and sugar to taste. Cool and pack in rigid containers. Use for drinks, ices and puddings
Cherries	Remove stalks, wash and dry cherries and dry freeze. Alternatively, remove stones, and sugar freeze until firm. Pack in rigid containers, leaving ½ in. headspace. Stoned cherries may also be frozen in syrup made with 8 oz. sugar to 1 pint water; add ¼ teaspoon ascorbic acid to every 2 pints syrup. Pack in rigid containers, leaving ½ in. headspace
Damsons	Best frozen as purées. Wash, cook gently in the minimum of water, sweetening to taste; pass through a nylon sieve. Cool and pack in rigid containers
Gooseberries	Wash, dry, top and tail. Dry freeze or pack in syrup (made with 1 lb. sugar to 1 pint water); store in rigid containers, leaving ½ in. headspace. *Purée:* stew in the minimum of water, pass through a nylon sieve and sweeten to taste. Cool and pack in rigid containers. Use for sauces and fools
Grapefruit	Peel, removing all pith. Divide into segments and sugar freeze using 8 oz. caster sugar to 1 lb. prepared fruit; when juice starts to run, pack segments in rigid containers. Alternatively, freeze in syrup made with equal quantities of sugar and water; pack in rigid containers, leaving ½ in. headspace
Greengages	Wash in cold water, halve and remove stones. Pack as for apricots
Lemons	Squeeze out juice, strain and freeze in ice cube trays; pack frozen cubes in polythene. Remove all pith from the peel, cut into fine strips, blanch for 1 min., cool and pack in small quantities in polythene bags. Or freeze grated peel
Melons	Cut in half and remove seeds. Cut flesh into cubes or balls. Freeze in syrup made with 8 oz. sugar to 1 pint water. Pack in rigid containers, leaving ½ in. headspace
Oranges	Freeze and pack segments as for grapefruit; freeze juice and rind as for lemon. Seville oranges can be frozen whole in polythene bags. Use thawed for marmalade, allowing extra fruit to counterbalance loss of pectin during freezing
Peaches	Peel and stone peaches, cut in half or slice; brush immediately with lemon juice to prevent discoloration. Freeze and pack in syrup as for apricots. Alternatively, purée peeled and stoned peaches, add 1 tablespoon lemon juice and 4 oz. sugar to each 1 lb. prepared fruit. Pack in rigid containers
Pineapple	Peel and cut into slices or chunks. Pack them in rigid containers, separating with non-stick paper or double thickness of cellophane. Or freeze in syrup made with 8 oz. sugar to 1 pint water, including any pineapple juice from the preparation. Pack in rigid containers, leaving ½ in. headspace. Mix crushed pineapple with sugar, allowing 4 oz. caster sugar to ¾ lb. prepared fruit; pack in rigid containers
Plums	Wash, halve and remove stones. Freeze as for apricots
Rhubarb	Wash, trim and cut into 1 in. lengths. Blanch for 1 min., drain, cool. Do not use aluminium containers for packing. Sugar freeze and pack in polythene bags. Alternatively, freeze in syrup made with equal quantities of sugar and water; pack in rigid containers and leave ½ in. headspace. *Purée:* stew in a little water, sweeten to taste and press through a nylon sieve; cool and pack in rigid containers, leaving ½ in. headspace

A to Z of Cookery Terms

The terms described in this glossary occur throughout the book, and are also seen on many restaurant menus. Letters in brackets indicate the country of origin. A stands for Austria; F for France; G for Germany; Gr for Greece; H for Hungary; Hol for Holland; I for Italy; In for India; R for Russia; S for Spain; Sw for Switzerland; T for Turkey; and US for the United States.

A

acidulated water The addition of lemon juice or vinegar to cold water – which prevents discoloration of some fruits and vegetables. To every ½ pint of water, add 1 teaspoon of lemon juice or vinegar

à la (F) In the style of, e.g. à la Russe, meaning 'in the Russian style'

à la carte (F) 1. Bill of fare from which the diner selects individual dishes. 2. Dishes cooked to order

à l'anglaise (F) In the English style, e.g. boiled and served without a sauce

à la crème (F) Served with cream or a cream-based sauce

al dente (I) Of pasta; cooked – but firm to the bite

alla (I) In the style of, e.g. alla parmigiano, meaning 'in Parmesan style'

allumettes (F) Vegetable strips of matchstick length

amandine (F) Cooking or coating with almonds

antipasti (I) Cold or hot Italian hors-d'oeuvre

à point (F) Of meat, medium cooked

arrowroot Starch made by grinding the root of an American plant of the same name. Used for thickening sauces

aspic Clear jelly made from the cooked juices of meat, chicken or fish

au bleu (F) Blue; fish cooked immediately after being caught will turn blue

au gratin (F) Cooked food, covered with a sauce, sprinkled with crumbs or grated cheese, dotted with butter and browned under the grill

B

bain marie (F) 1. A large pan of hot water, or 'bath', in which a smaller pan is placed for cooking contents or to keep foods warm. 2. A double saucepan with water in the lower half

barding Covering lean meat, game and poultry with thin slices of pork fat or bacon to prevent the flesh drying out during roasting

basting Moistening meat or poultry with pan juices during roasting by using a spoon or bulb baster

beating Mixing food to introduce air, to make it lighter and fluffier, using a wooden spoon, hand whisk or electric mixer

binding Adding eggs, cream, melted fat or roux panada to a dry mixture to hold it together

bitok (R) Small meat patty made from raw minced beef and bread, and bound together with egg

blanching Boiling briefly 1. To loosen the skin from nuts, fruit and vegetables. 2. To set the colour of food and to kill enzymes prior to freezing. 3. To remove strong or bitter flavours

blanquette (F) Veal, chicken or rabbit stew in a creamy sauce

blender Electric liquidiser with a goblet. A set of rotary blades is attached to the base of the goblet and rapidly reduces most ingredients to a smooth consistency

blending Combining ingredients with a spoon, beater or liquidiser to achieve a uniform mixture

blini, bliny (R) Pancake made of buckwheat and yeast, and traditionally served with caviar and sour cream

boiling Cooking in liquid at a temperature of 100°C (212°F)

boning Removing bones of meat, poultry, game or fish

bouchée (F) Small puff-pastry case, baked blind and filled with a savoury or sweet mixture

bouquet garni (F) A bunch of herbs, including parsley, thyme, marjoram, bay, etc., tied with string; or a ready-made mixture of herbs in a muslin bag. Used for flavouring soups and stews

bourguignonne (F) In the style of Burgundy, e.g. cooked with red wine

braising Browning in hot fat and then cooking slowly, in a covered pot, with vegetables and a little liquid

brine Salt and water solution used for pickling and preserving

brioche (F) Soft bread made of rich yeast dough, slightly sweetened

brochette (F) Skewer used for grilling chunks of meat, fish and vegetables over charcoal or under a grill

broiling (US) Grilling

browning Searing the outer surface of meat to seal in the juices

brulé (F) Applied to dishes such as cream custards finished with caramelised sugar glaze

C

canapé (F) Appetiser consisting of small pieces of fresh or fried bread, toast or biscuits, topped with savoury mixtures

cannelloni (I) Large macaroni tubes, stuffed with savoury fillings

capers Pickled flower buds of the Mediterranean caper bush. Used in sauces and garnishes

caponata (I) Sicilian dish of fish, aubergines, tomatoes, onions, capers and black olives

carbonnade (F) Beef stew made with beer

casserole (F) 1. Cooking pot, complete with lid, made of ovenproof or flameproof earthenware, glass or metal. 2. Also, a slow-cooked stew of meat, fish or vegetables

cassoulet (F) Stew of haricot beans, pork, lamb, goose or duck, sausage, vegetables and herbs

champignon (F) Mushroom; champignon de Paris, cultivated button mushroom

Chantilly (F) Whipped cream, slightly sweetened and sometimes flavoured with vanilla

Charlotte 1. Hot, moulded fruit pudding made of buttered slices of bread and filled with fruit cooked with apricot jam. 2. Cold, moulded dessert consisting of sponge fingers and filled with cream and fruit, or a cream custard set with gelatine

Charlotte mould A plain mould for charlottes and other desserts, sometimes used for moulded salads

chasseur (F) Cooked with mushrooms, shallots and white wine

chaud-froid (F) Elaborate dish of meat, poultry, game or fish, masked with a creamy sauce, decorated and glazed with aspic. Served cold

chiffonade (F) A garnish made of shredded lettuce, sorrel and spinach. Used for decorating soups or cold dishes

chilling Cooling food, without freezing it, in the refrigerator

chine Of pork; a pair of loins left undivided

chining Separating the backbone from the ribs in a joint of meat to make carving easier

chinois (F) 1. In the Chinese style. 2. Applied to a conical-shaped sieve with a fine mesh

chorizo (S) Smoked pork sausage

chowder (US) Fish dish, half-way between a soup and stew

civet (F) Brown game stew

clarified butter Butter cleared of water and impurities by slow melting and filtering

clarifying 1. Clearing fats by heating and filtering. 2. Clearing consommés and jellies with beaten egg white

cocotte (F) Small ovenproof, earthenware, porcelain or metal dish, used for baking individual egg dishes, mousses or soufflés

coddling Cooking slowly in simmering water. Applied to eggs

colander Perforated metal or plastic basket used for draining away liquids

compôte (F) Dessert of fresh or dried fruit, cooked in syrup and served cold

concassé (F) Roughly chopped. Applied to vegetables, such as tomatoes

condé (F) 1. Dessert made with rice, e.g. pear condé. 2. Pastry biscuits topped with icing and glazed in the oven

conserve Whole fruit preserved by boiling with sugar and used like jam

coquille (F) 1. Scallop. 2. Shell-shaped ovenproof dish used to serve fish, shellfish or poultry

cordon bleu (F) Highly qualified cook. According to legend, King Louis XV of France once awarded a blue ribbon to a female chef who had prepared an outstanding meal

corn starch Finely ground flour from maize, which is used for thickening sauces, puddings, etc.

corn syrup (US) Syrup obtained from maize, which is used for baking, confectionery, etc.

coupe (F) Goblet used for serving ice cream, fruit and shellfish cocktails

crème (F) Applied to fresh cream, butter and custard creams, and thick creamy soups

crème brulée (F) Cream custard with caramelised topping

crème caramel (F) Cold moulded egg custard with caramel topping

crème fraiche (F) Cream that has been allowed to mature but not to go sour

creole Of Caribbean cookery; prepared with pimentoes, tomatoes, okra, rice and spicy sauces

crêpe (F) Thin pancake

crêpes suzette (F) Pancakes cooked in orange sauce and flamed in liqueur

crimping 1. Making a decorative border to pie crusts. 2. Gashing fresh skate, then soaking it in cold water

and vinegar before cooking, so that the flesh firms

croquettes (F) Cooked foods moulded in small shapes, dipped in egg and crumbs, and deep-fried

croûstade (F) Small crispy fried or baked bread or pastry shape which is filled with a savoury mixture

croûtes (F) 1. Pastry covering meat, fish and vegetables. 2. Slices of bread or brioche, spread with butter or sauce, and baked until crisp

curd Semi-solid part of milk, produced by souring

curdle 1. To cause fresh milk or a sauce to separate into solids and liquids by overheating or by adding acid. 2. To cause creamed butter and sugar in a cake recipe to separate by adding the eggs too rapidly

cure To preserve fish or meat by drying, salting or smoking

D

dariole Small, cup-shaped mould used for making puddings, sweet and savoury jellies, and creams

darne (F) Thick slice cut from round fish

daube (F) Stew of braised meat and vegetables

deep fat Hot fat or oil which is deep enough to cover food during frying

deep-frying Frying food by immersing it in hot fat or oil

déglacer (F) Diluting pan juices by adding wine, stock or cream to make gravy

devilling Preparing meat, poultry or fish with highly seasoned ingredients, for grilling or roasting

dice Cut into small cubes

dough Mixture of flour, water, milk and/or egg, sometimes enriched with fat, which is firm enough to knead, roll and shape

dredging Sprinkling food with flour or sugar

dress 1. To pluck, draw and truss poultry or game. 2. To arrange or garnish a cooked dish. 3. To prepare cooked shellfish in their shells, e.g. crab and lobster

dressing 1. Sauce for a salad. 2. Stuffing for meat or poultry

dripping Fat which drips from meat, poultry or game during roasting

dumpling 1. Small balls made of dough, forcemeat or potato mixture, which are steamed or poached. Used to garnish soups and stews. 2. Fruit encased in dough and baked

dusting Sprinkling lightly with flour, sugar, spice or seasoning

E

éclair (F) Light, oblong choux pastry split and filled with cream, usually topped with chocolate icing

en croûte (F) Food encased in pastry

en papillote (F) Food wrapped, cooked and served in oiled or buttered paper or foil

entrée (F) 1. Third course in a formal meal, following the fish course. 2. Main dish, sauced and garnished

entremêt (F) Sweet or pudding

escalope Thin slice of meat which is beaten flat and shallow-fried

F

faggot 1. Small savoury cake made of pork offal, onion and bread, which is usually baked. 2. A small bunch, e.g. of herbs which are tied with string

farina (I) Fine flour made from wheat, nuts and potatoes

farle Round, flat oatmeal cake baked on a griddle

fines herbes (F) Mixture of finely chopped fresh parsley, chervil, tarragon and chives

flake 1. Separating cooked fish into individual flaky slivers. 2. Grating chocolate or cheese into small slivers

flambé Flamed; e.g. food tossed in a pan to which burning brandy or other alcohol has been added

florentine 1. Of fish and eggs; served on a bed of buttered spinach and coated with cheese sauce. 2. Thin petit-four biscuit made of nuts, glacé fruit and chocolate

foie gras (F) The preserved liver of specially fattened goose or duck

folding in Enveloping one ingredient or mixture in another, using a large metal spoon or spatula

fondue (Sw) Melted cheese and white wine dish into which diners dunk cubes of bread

fool Cold dessert consisting of fruit purée and whipped cream

freezing Solidifying or preserving food by chilling and storing it at 0°C (32°F)

fricadelles (F) Meat balls, made with minced pork and veal, spices, white breadcrumbs, cream and egg; poached in stock or shallow-fried

fricassée (F) White stew of chicken, rabbit, veal and vegetables which are first fried in butter, then cooked in stock and finished with cream and egg yolks

frost 1. To coat a cake with an icing of confectioners' sugar. 2. To dip the rim of a glass in egg white and caster sugar and then chill in a refrigerator until set

fumet (F) Concentrated broth or stock obtained from fish, meat or vegetables

G

galantine (F) Dish of boned and stuffed poultry, game or meat glazed with aspic and served cold

galette (F) 1. A flat pastry cake traditionally baked for Twelfth Night. 2. A flat cake of sliced or mashed potato

garnishing Enhancing a dish with edible decorations

gelatine Transparent protein, made from animal bones and tissue, which melts in hot liquid and forms a jelly when cold. Used for sweet and savoury dishes

genoise (F) A rich sponge cake consisting of eggs, sugar, flour and melted butter; baked in a flat tin

ghee (In) Clarified butter made from the milk of the water buffalo

giblets Edible internal organs and trimmings of poultry and game, which include the liver, heart, gizzard, neck, pinions and sometimes feet and cockscomb

gill Liquid measure equal to $\frac{1}{4}$ pint or 5 fluid oz.

glacé (F) Glazed, frozen or iced

glace de viande (F) Meat glaze or residue in the bottom of a pan after roasting or frying meat. Or concentrated meat stock

glaze A glossy finish given to food by brushing with beaten egg, milk, sugar syrup or jelly after cooking

gnocchi (I) Small dumplings made from semolina, potatoes or choux pastry

goujon (F) Gudgeons – small fish fried and served as a garnish

goulash (H) Beef and onion stew flavoured with paprika and tomato

granita (I) Water ice

granité (F) Sorbet

gratiné (F) See au gratin

gravy 1. Juices exuded by roasted meat and poultry. 2. A sauce made from these juices by boiling with stock or wine, and sometimes thickened with flour

grèque, à la (F) 1. In the Greek style, e.g. cooked in stock with olive oil. 2. Dishes garnished with savoury rice and dressed with oil and vinegar

griddle Flat metal plate used to bake breads and cakes on the top of the stove

grissini (I) Breadsticks

groats De-husked grain, especially oats, sometimes milled

Gugelhupf (G) Sweetened yeast cake with dried fruit, baked in a fluted ring mould

guiche (F) Alsatian open tart with savoury filling based on cream and eggs. Equivalent to quiche

H

haggis Savoury Scottish pudding, consisting of chopped offal, suet, onions and oatmeal, which is boiled in the stomach lining of a sheep

hamburger (US) Minced, meat patty which is fried or grilled and served in a soft round bun

hanging Suspending meat or game in a cool, dry place until it is tender

hard sauce Sweet butter sauce flavoured with brandy, rum or whisky, which is chilled until hard, and melts when served on hot puddings

haricot (F) Dried seeds of the haricot bean plant

haricot vert (F) Green bean

hash Dish of leftover chopped meat, potatoes or other vegetables, which are fried together

haslet Dish of pig entrails and herbs, which is made into cakes and baked

herbs Plants without a woody stem. Culinary herbs, which are available in fresh or dried form, include basil, bay leaf, chervil, marjoram, mint, oregano, parsley, rosemary, sage, savory, tarragon and thyme. Used for their aromatic properties

hors-d'oeuvre (F) Hot or cold appetisers served at the start of a meal

hulling Removing green calyx from strawberries, raspberries and loganberries

I

icing Sweet coating for cakes

infusing Steeping herbs, tea leaves or coffee in water or other liquid to extract the flavour

Irish coffee Coffee flavoured with Irish whiskey and topped with thick cream

J

joint 1. Prime cut of meat for roasting. 2. To divide meat, game or poultry into individual joints

jugged Meat dishes, such as jugged hare; stewed in a covered pot

jus (F) Juices from roasting meat used as gravy

K

kebab (T) Meat cubes marinated and grilled on a skewer

kedgeree (In) Breakfast or lunch dish of cooked fish or meat, rice and eggs

kosher Food prepared according to Orthodox Jewish law

L

langouste (F) Crawfish

langue du chat (F) Flat, finger-shaped crisp biscuit served with cold desserts

lard Natural or refined pork fat

larding Threading strips of fat through lean meat, using a special needle. This prevents the meat becoming dry during roasting

lasagne (I) Wide ribbon noodles, sometimes coloured green

leaven Substance, such as yeast, which causes dough or batter to rise

legumes (F) 1. Vegetables. 2. Plants with seed pods, such as peas and beans

lentils Seeds of a legume, soaked and used in soups, stews and purées

lyonnaise (F) In the Lyons style; usually with onions

M

macaroni (I). Tubular-shaped pasta of varying lengths and shapes

macedoine (F) Mixture of fruit or vegetables

macerate To soften food by soaking it in liquid

marinade Blend of oil, wine or vinegar, herbs and spices. Used to tenderise and flavour meat, game or fish

marinate To steep in marinade

marinière (F) 1. Of mussels; cooked in white wine and mussels, and served in half shells. 2. Of fish; cooked in white wine and garnished with mussels

marmite (F) Earthenware stock pot

mâtelote (F) In the sailor's style; e.g. fish stew made with wine or cider

medallions (F) Small circular cuts of meat, fish or pâté

meringue (F) Whisked egg white blended with sugar, which is spooned or piped on top of sweet pies or into small shapes and baked crisp at very low temperature

meunière (F) In the style of a miller's wife; e.g. fish cooked in butter, seasoned, and sprinkled with parsley and lemon juice

milanese (F) In the Milan style; of escalopes coated in egg, breadcrumbs, seasoned with grated Parmesan cheese, and fried in butter

mirabelle (F) 1. Small yellow plum, used as tart filling. 2. A liqueur made from this fruit

mirepoix (F) Mixture of finely diced vegetables and ham which, when fried in butter, is used as a base for brown sauces and stews

mocca 1. High quality coffee served after dinner. 2. A blend of coffee and chocolate flavours

mouler (F) To grind soft food into a purée, or dry food into a powder

moules (F) Mussels

moussaka Near-Eastern dish of minced meat, aubergines and tomatoes, which is topped with cheese sauce or savoury custard

mousse Light sweet or savoury cold dish made with cream, whipped egg white and gelatine

muesli (Sw) Dish of raw rolled oats, coarsely grated apple, nuts and dried fruit served with cream

N

navarin (F) Stew of lamb and vegetables

neapolitan (I) Ice creams and sweet cakes in layers of different colours and flavours

niçoise (F) In the Nice style, e.g. cooked with tomatoes, onion, garlic and black olives

noodles Flat ribbon pasta made from flour, water and egg

normande, à la (F) In the Normandy style, e.g. cooked with cider and cream

nouilles (F) Noodles

O

offal Edible internal organs of meat, poultry and game

osso buco (I) Dish of braised marrow bones prepared with tomato and wine

P

paella (S) Dish of saffron rice, chicken and shellfish, which is named after the large shallow pan in which it is traditionally cooked

panada Thick sauce made of flour or bread and used to bind ingredients

panetone (I) Cake-like bread with raisins, which is served at Christmas

paprika (H) Ground, sweet red pepper

par-boiling Boiling for a short time to cook food partially

parfait (F) Frozen dessert made of whipped cream and fruit purée

Parmentier (F) Applied to dishes containing potatoes; the term is derived from Antoine Parmentier who introduced the potato to France

pasta (I) Paste made with flour and water, sometimes enriched with egg and oil. Used to make macaroni and spaghetti, etc.

pasteurising Method of sterilising milk by heating it to 60–82°C (140–180°F) to destroy the bacteria. The term is derived from Louis Pasteur, who developed the method

pastry Dough made with flour, butter and water and baked or deep-fried until crisp

pastry wheel Small, serrated wooden or metal wheel for cutting and fluting pastry

pasty Small pastry pie with a savoury filling

pâté (F) 1. Savoury mixture which is baked in a casserole or terrine, and served cold. 2. Savoury mixture baked in a pastry case and served hot or cold. 3. Pastry or dough

pâté à choux (F) Choux pastry

patty 1. Small, flat, round or oval-shaped cake of food, such as potato cake or fish cake, which is served hot or cold. 2. Small, flat, individual pie, such as a chicken patty, which is served hot or cold

paupiette (F) Thin slice of meat rolled round a savoury filling

pavé (F) 1. Cold savoury mousse mixture set in a square mould coated with aspic jelly. 2. Square sponge cake, filled with butter cream and coated with icing

peanut Groundnut, eaten plain or roasted. Used to make peanut butter and oil

pearl barley De-husked barley grains, used in soup

pease pudding Purée of cooked, dried peas which is made into puddings, boiled and served with pork

pectin Substance extracted from fruit and vegetables. Used to set jellies and jams

percolator Two-part coffee pot which forces boiling water from lower half up through coffee grains contained in upper half, and then filtered through

perdrix (F) Partridge

petits fours (F) 1. Tiny sponge cakes, iced and decorated. 2. Small fruits, e.g. grapes and cherries, coated in sugar glaze. 3. Marzipan coloured and shaped to resemble miniature fruits

petit pois (F) Tiny young green peas

pickle To preserve meat or vegetables in brine or vinegar solution

pilaf, pilau (T) Near-eastern dish of cooked rice mixed with spiced, cooked meat, chicken or fish

pimento Green or red pepper

pintade (F) Guinea fowl

pipe To force meringue icing, savoury butter, potato purée, etc., through a forcing bag fitted with a nozzle, to decorate various dishes

piquante (F) Pleasantly sharp and appetising

pith In citrus fruit, the white cellular lining to the rind covering the flesh

pizza (I) Open-faced pie consisting of a rich yeast dough, topped with tomatoes, cheese, anchovies and olives

pizzaiola (I) Meat or chicken, cooked in red wine, tomato sauce and flavoured with garlic

plat du jour (F) Dish of the day

pluck 1. Offal. 2. To remove the feathers from a domesticated or game bird

poaching Cooking food in simmering liquid, just below boiling point

polenta (I) Corn meal, made from maize, which is dried and ground

potage (F) Thick soup

praline (F) Sweet consisting of unblanched almonds caramelised in boiling sugar

preserving Keeping food in good condition by treating with chemicals, heat, refrigeration, pickling in salt or boiling in sugar

printanier (F) Garnish of spring vegetables

prosciutto (I) Raw smoked ham, served finely sliced

provençale (F) In the Provence style, e.g. cooked with garlic and tomatoes

pudding 1. Baked or boiled sweet dessert. 2. Boiled suet crust which is filled with meat or poultry

pulp 1. Soft, fleshy tissue of fruit or vegetables. 2. To reduce food to a soft mass by crushing or boiling

purée (F) 1. Sieved raw or cooked food. 2. Thick vegetable soup which is passed through a sieve or an electric liquidiser

Q

quenelles (F) Light savoury dumplings made of meat or fish and used as a garnish or in a delicate sauce

quiche (F) Open-faced pastry case filled with a savoury mixture. See also guiche

R

ragoût (F) Stew of meat and vegetables

ramekins 1. Individual ovenware dishes. 2. Small pastry cases with cream-cheese filling

ratafia 1. Flavouring made from bitter almonds. 2. Liqueur made from fruit kernels. 3. Tiny macaroon

ratatouille (F) Stew made of aubergines, onions, peppers and tomatoes cooked in olive oil

ravioli (I) Small savoury-filled pasta envelopes which are boiled and served with a sauce and grated cheese

reducing Concentrating a liquid by boiling and evaporation

relish Sharp or spicy sauce made with fruit or vegetables which adds a piquant flavour to other foods

rendering 1. Slowly cooking meat tissues and trimmings to obtain fat. 2. Clearing frying fat by heating it

rennet Substance extracted from the stomach lining of calves. Used to coagulate milk for junket and for making cheese curd

rice paper Edible, glossy white paper made from the pith of a tree grown in China. Used for macaroon base

rigatoni (I) Ribbed macaroni

risotto (I) Savoury rice, fried and then cooked in stock or tomato juice and finished with cheese

rissole Small roll or patty made of cooked minced meat

roasting Cooking in the oven with radiant heat, or on a spit over or under an open flame

roe 1. Milt of the male fish, called soft roe. 2. Eggs of the female fish, called hard roe. 3. Shellfish roe, called coral because of its colour

romano (I) In the style of Rome

rôtisserie (F) Rotating spit used for roasting or grilling meat or poultry

roulade (F) Roll of meat, vegetables, chocolate cake, etc.

roux (F) Mixture of fat and flour which, when cooked, is used as a base for savoury sauces

S

saignant (F) Of meat; underdone

salami (I) Spiced pork sausage, which is sold fresh or smoked

salmi (I) Stew made by first roasting game and then cooking it in wine sauce

samovar (R) Metal tea urn heated from an inner tube, in which charcoal is burnt

sauté (F) To fry food rapidly in shallow, hot fat, tossing and turning it until evenly browned

savarin (F) Rich yeast cake, which is baked in a ring mould and soaked in liqueur-flavoured syrup. Served cold with cream

scald 1. To heat milk or cream to just below boiling point. 2. To plunge fruit or vegetables in boiling water to remove the skins

scallion Young onion with an undeveloped bulb. Used for salads and as a garnish

scallop Edible mollusc with white flesh and orange coral or roe. The deep, fluted shell is used for serving the scallops and other foods

scaloppine (I) Small escalopes of veal, weighing 1–1½ oz. and about 3 in. square

Schnitzel (G) Veal slice; see escalope

scoring 1. Cutting gashes or narrow grooves in the surface of food, e.g. in pork rind to produce crackling. 2. Making a pattern of squares or diamonds on pastry crust

searing Browning meat rapidly with fierce heat to seal in the juices

seasoned flour Flour flavoured with salt and pepper

seasoning Salt, pepper, spices or herbs, which are added to food to improve flavour

sifting Passing flour or sugar through a sieve to remove lumps

simmering Cooking in liquid which is heated to just below boiling point

skewer Metal or wooden pin used to hold meat, poultry or fish in shape during cooking

skimming Removing cream from the surface of milk, or fat or scum from broth or jam

smoking Curing food, such as bacon or fish, by exposing it to wood smoke for a considerable period of time

sorbet (F) Water ice made with fruit juice or purée

soufflé (F) Baked dish consisting of a sauce or purée, which is thickened

with egg yolks into which stiffly beaten egg whites are folded

soufflé dish Straight-sided circular dish used for cooking and serving soufflés

sousing Pickling food in brine or vinegar, e.g. soused herrings

spaghetti (I) Solid strands of pasta of various thicknesses

spit Revolving skewer or metal rod on which meat, poultry or game is roasted over a fire or under a grill

spring-form mould Baking tin with hinged sides, held together by a metal clamp or pin, which is opened to release the cake or pie

starch Carbohydrate obtained from cereal and potatoes

steaming Cooking food in the steam rising from boiling water

steeping 1. Soaking in liquid until saturated with a soluble ingredient. 2. Soaking to remove an ingredient, e.g. salt from smoked ham or salt cod

sterilising Destroying germs by exposing food to heat

stewing To simmer food slowly in a covered pan or casserole

stirring Mixing with a circular movement, using a spoon or fork

straining Separating liquids from solids by passing them through a metal or nylon sieve or through muslin

Strudel (A) Thin leaves of pastry dough, filled with fruit, nuts or savoury mixtures, which are rolled and baked

stuffing Savoury mixture of bread or rice, herbs, fruit or minced meat, used to fill poultry, fish, meat and vegetables

suet Fat around beef or lamb kidneys

syllabub Cold dessert of sweetened thick cream, white wine, sherry or fruit juice

syrup A thick sweet liquid made by boiling sugar with water and/or fruit juice

T

table d'hôte (F) Meal of three or more courses at a fixed price

tagliatelle (I) Thin flat egg noodles

terrine (F) 1. Earthenware pot used for cooking and serving pâté. 2. Food cooked in a terrine

timbale (F) 1. Cup-shaped earthenware or metal mould. 2. Dish prepared in such a mould

truffles Rare mushroom-like fungus, black or white in colour, with a firm texture and delicate taste. Expensive delicacies, truffles are mainly used for garnishing

trussing Tying a bird or joint of meat in a neat shape with skewers and/or string before cooking

tube-pan Ring-shaped tin for baking cakes

turnover Sweet or savoury pasty made by folding a circle or square of pastry in half to form a semicircle or triangle

tutti frutti (I) Dried or candied mixed fruits, added to ice cream

U

unleavened bread Bread made without a raising agent which, when baked, is thin, flat and round

V

vanilla sugar Sugar flavoured with vanilla by enclosing it with a vanilla pod in a closed jar

velouté (F) 1. Basic white sauce made with chicken, veal or fish stock. 2. Soup of creamy consistency

vermicelli (I) Very fine strands of pasta

vinaigrette (F) Mixture of oil, vinegar, salt and pepper, which is sometimes flavoured with herbs

vinegar A clear liquid, consisting of chiefly acetic acid, obtained by the fermentation of wine, cider or malt beer

vol-au-vent (F) Light flaky case of puff pastry

W

wafer Thin biscuit made with rice flour; served with ice cream

waffle Batter cooked on a hot greased waffle iron to a crisp biscuit

whey Liquid which separates from the curd when milk curdles. Used in cheese-making

whipping Beating eggs until frothy and cream until thick

whisk Looped wire utensil used to beat air into eggs, cream or batters

Wiener Schnitzel (A) Veal slice cooked in the Viennese style, e.g. coated in egg and breadcrumbs, fried in butter and garnished with anchovies and capers

Y

yeast Fungus cells used to produce alcoholic fermentation, or to cause dough to rise

yoghourt Curdled milk which has been treated with harmless bacteria. In the Middle East it is served as a sauce with meat, fish and vegetables; in Europe mainly with or in desserts

Z

zabaglione (I) Dessert consisting of egg yolks, white wine or marsala and sugar, which are whisked together in the top of a double boiler over boiling water until thick and foamy

zest (F) Coloured oily outer skin of citrus fruit which, when grated or peeled, is used to flavour foods and liquids

zester Small tool for scraping off zest

Index

This index includes references to Buying for Quality, Twelve Months of Recipes, Basic Cooking, Wine with Food, Cook's Workshop, Freezing and A-Z of Cookery. Figures in italics refer to illustrations.

TYPESETTING BY TYPESETTING SERVICES LTD, GLASGOW,
AND FRED. A. CHURCHILL & PARTNERS LTD, SOUTHAMPTON.
SEPARATIONS BY ADROIT PHOTOLITHO LTD, BIRMINGHAM,
AND REPROCOLOR LLOVET, BARCELONA.
PRINTING BY SIR JOSEPH CAUSTON & SONS LTD, EASTLEIGH.
PAPER AND BOOKBINDING MATERIAL BY KONINKLIJKE NEDERLANDSCHE
PAPIERFABRIEK NV, MAASTRICHT; BOWATER UK PAPER CO.,
GRAVESEND, AND RED BRIDGE BOOK CLOTH CO. LTD, BOLTON.
BOOKBINDING BY HAZELL, WATSON & VINEY LTD, AYLESBURY.